# Handbook of

# North American Indians

# Handbook of North American Indians

WILLIAM C. STURTEVANT

*General Editor*

VOLUME 2

# Indians In Contemporary Society

GARRICK A. BAILEY
*Volume Editor*

SMITHSONIAN INSTITUTION

WASHINGTON

2008

For sale by the Superintendent of Documents,
U.S. Government Printing Office, Washington, D.C. 20402.

**Library of Congress Cataloging in Publication Data**

Handbook of North American Indians.

   Bibliography.
   Includes index.
   CONTENTS:

      v. 2. Indians in Contemporary Society.

   1. Indians of North America.
I. Sturtevant, William C.

E77.H25   970'.004'97                    77-17162

For sale by the Superintendent of Documents, U.S. Government Printing Office
Internet: bookstore.gpo.gov   Phone: toll free (866) 512-1800;   DC area (202) 512-1800
Fax: (202) 512-2104 Mail: Stop IDCC, Washington, DC 20402-0001

ISBN 978-0-16-080388-8

ISBN 978-0-16-080388-8

9 780160 803888

# Contents

This map is a diagrammatic guide to the 10 culture areas of Native North America referred to in this volume and throughout the *Handbook*. These culture areas are used in organizing and referring to information about contiguous groups that are or were similar in culture and history. They do not imply that there are only a few sharply distinct ways of life in the continent. In reality, each group exhibits a unique combination of particular cultural features, while all neighboring peoples are always similar in some ways and dissimilar in others. The lines separating the culture areas represent a compromise among many factors and sometimes reflect arbitrary decisions. For more specific information, see the chapter "Introduction" in volumes 5–15 of the *Handbook*.

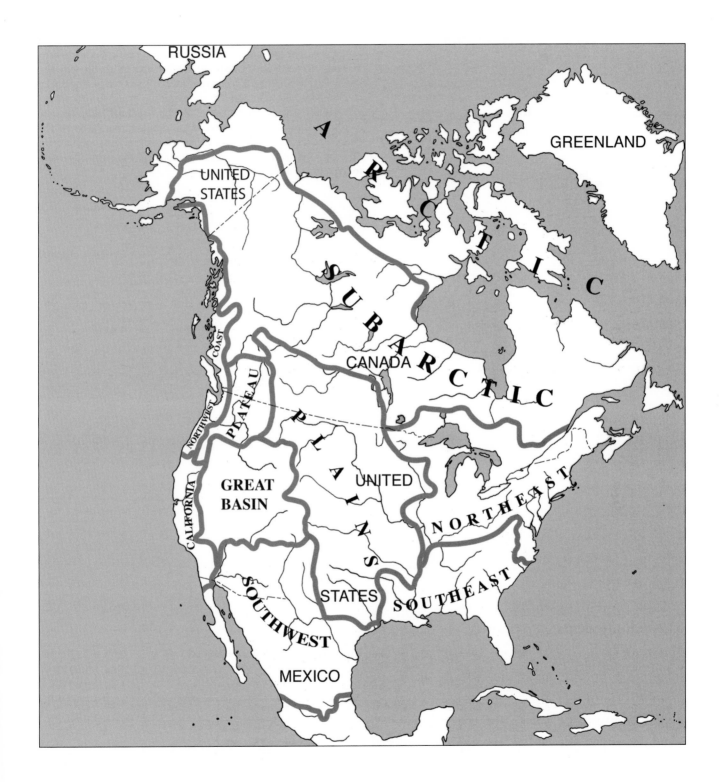

# Conventions for Illustrations

- ● Native settlement
- ■ Non-native or mixed settlement
- Seattle    Settlement
- *Missouri R.*    Geographic feature
-     Drainage
- ——————— Reservation border
- – – – – – – – National border
- – — – — – — State border
- Indian reservations and reserves
- Water

## Credits and Captions

Credit lines give the source of the illustrations or the collection where the artifacts shown are located. The numbers that follow are the catalog or negative numbers of the repository. When the photographer mentioned in the caption is the source of the print reproduced, no credit line appears. "After" means that the Handbook illustrator has redrawn, rearranged, or abstracted the illustration from the one in the cited source. Measurements in captions are to the nearest centimeter if available; "about" indicates an estimate or a measurement converted from inches to centimeters.

| | | | |
|---|---|---|---|
| Amer. | American | Inst. | Institute |
| Anthr. | Anthropology, Anthropological | Lab. | Laboratory, Laboratories |
| Arch. | Archives | Lib. | Library |
| Arch(a)eol. | Arch(a)eology, Arch(a)eological | ms. | manuscript |
| b. | born | Mt. | Mount |
| Bur. | Bureau | Mus. | Museum |
| ca. | about | NAA | National Anthropological Archives |
| cat. | catalog | Nat. | Natural |
| Coll. | Collection(s) | Natl. | National |
| © | copyright | neg. | negative |
| d. | died | no. | number |
| Dept. | Department | opp. | opposite |
| Div. | Division | pl. | plate |
| Ethnol. | Ethnology, Ethnological | Prov. | Provincial |
| fig. | figure | Res. | Reservation, Reserve |
| Ft. | Fort | Soc. | Society |
| Hist. | History | St. | Saint |
| Histl. | Historical | Terr. | Territory |
| I. | Island | U. | University |
| Inc. | Incorporated | vol. | volume |
| Ind. | Indian(s) | | |

## Metric Equivalents

| | | | | |
|---|---|---|---|---|
| 100 cm = 1m | 10 cm = 3.937 in. | 1 km = .62 mi. | 1 in. = 2.54 mi. | 25 ft. = 7.62 m |
| 10 mm = 1cm | 1 m = 39.37 in. | 5 km = 3.1 mi | 1 ft. = 30.48 cm | 1 mi. = 1.60 km |
| 1,000 m = 1km | 10 m = 32.81 ft. | 10 km = 6.2 mi | 1 yd. = 91.44 cm | 5 mi. = 8.02 km |

meters 0 1 2 3 4 5 6 7 8 9 10 11 12 13 14 15 16 17 18 19 20
feet 0 5 10 15 20 25 30 35 40 45 50 55 60 65
meters 0 10 20 30 40 50 60 70 80 90 100 110 120 130 140 150 160 170 180 190 200
feet 0 50 100 150 200 250 300 350 400 450 500 550 600 650
centimeters 0 1 2 3 4 5 6 7 8 9 10 11 12 13 14 15 16
inches 0 1 2 3 4 5 6

(actual size)

# Preface

This is the fifteenth volume to be published of a 20-volume set planned to give an encyclopedic summary of what is known about the prehistory, history, and cultures of the aboriginal peoples of North America north of the urban civilizations of central Mexico.

The aim of this volume is to provide a basic reference work on Indians and Arctic peoples as a continuing element in a changing and sometimes difficult environment responding to the social forces around them, making such accommodations as circumstances require, but remaining identifiably Indian in a contemporary society.

Volumes 5–15 of the *Handbook* cover aboriginal cultures and their histories in each of the culture areas of North America (mapped in those volumes). Other volumes in the *Handbook* are, like this one, continental in scope. Thus, volume 1 contains general descriptions of anthropological and historical methods and sources and summaries for the whole continent of certain topics regarding social and political organization, religion, and the performing arts. Volume 3 gives the environmental and biological backgrounds within which the Native American societies developed, summarizing the early and late human biology or physical anthropology of Indians and Arctic peoples, and surveys the earliest prehistoric cultures. Volume 4 contains details on the history of the relations between Whites and Native American societies. Volume 16 is a continent-wide survey of technology and the visual arts—of material cultures broadly defined. Volume 17 surveys the Native languages of North America, their characteristics, and historical relationships. Volumes 18 and 19 are a biographical dictionary. Volume 20 contains an index to the whole series and includes a list of errata found in all preceding volumes.

The first handbook covering these topics was issued by the Smithsonian Institution in two volumes in 1907–1910, entitled *Handbook of American Indians North of Mexico* (Hodge 1907–1910). Subsequent handbooks covered South America in seven volumes (Steward 1946–1959) and Middle America in 16 volumes (Wauchope 1964–1976). By 1965 it was evident that the earlier handbook on North America was badly out of date. An entirely new up-to-date reference encyclopedia on North American Indians was clearly needed.

Preliminary discussions on the feasibility of a new *Handbook* and alternatives for producing it began in 1965 in what was then the Smithsonian's Office of Anthropology. In the early years, the content and production of all volumes of this *Handbook* were planned, as indicated in the detailed history of the development of the whole *Handbook* given in volume 1 (with a listing of the entire editorial staff). By 1971 funds were available and plans had advanced to the point where the details of the *Indians in Contemporary Society* volume could be worked out. In 1970 D'Arcy McNickle agreed to serve as editor for the volume, and he met with a planning committee (Roger Buffalohead, Vine Deloria, Jr., Bernard L. Fontana, Walter M. Hlady, Nancy Oestreich Lurie, Robert W. Rietz, Sam Stanley, and Robert K. Thomas) to organize the contents and choose the authors to be invited. In the summer of 1971 the Volume Editor began inviting contributors. During the mid-1970s work on this volume proceeded very slowly. In 1978 Vine Deloria, Jr., was named the editor after McNickle's death in 1977. Under the editorships of McNickle and Deloria many draft manuscripts were received and edited. However, work on the proposed 20-volume series proved to be monumental. In 1980 active work on this volume came to a halt while editorial attention was devoted to other volumes in the series, which advanced more rapidly. In early 2005, Deloria was contacted about finishing this volume. However, over the intervening 25 years his interest in the project had waned and his health was declining. He died in November of that year.

In June 2005 Garrick A. Bailey accepted the position of Volume Editor. Accordingly, a specially selected Planning Committee (listed on p. [v]) assisted the Volume Editor to revise the outline of chapters and select a new list of authors. Between October and December 2005 the Volume Editor sent each new contributor a tentative outline and a brief description of the topics to be covered. One author remaining from Deloria's editorship was sent new suggestions for revising and updating his chapter with the assistance of a newly invited coauthor. Each author was provided a "Guide for Contributors" prepared by the General Editor, which described the general aims and methods of the *Handbook* and the editorial conventions. One convention has been to avoid the present tense, where possible, in historical and cultural descriptions. Thus a statement in the past tense, with a recent date or approximate date, may also hold true for the time of writing. With the exception of Vine Deloria's originally proposed chapter "Activism, 1950–1980," the contents of this volume reflect the state of knowledge since 2000, rather than in the early 1970s when planning first began.

As they were received, the chapter manuscripts were reviewed by the Volume Editor, the General Editor's staff, and sometimes one or more referees, who included a member of the Planning Committee and often authors of other chapters. Suggestions for changes and additions often resulted. The published versions frequently reflect more editorial intervention than is customary for academic writings, since the encyclopedic aims and format of the *Handbook* made it necessary to attempt to eliminate duplication, avoid gaps in coverage, prevent contradictions, impose some standardization of organization and terminology, and keep within strict constraints on length. Where the evidence seemed so scanty or obscure as to allow different authorities to come to differing conclusions, authors have been encouraged to elaborate their own views, although the editors have endeavored to draw attention to alternative interpretations published elsewhere.

The first editorial acceptance of an author's manuscript was on June 7, 2006, and the last on July 31, 2007. Edited manuscripts were sent from the Washington office to authors for their final approval between January 8, 2007, and September 20, 2007. These dates for all chapters are given in the list of Contributors. Late dates may reflect late invitations as well as late submissions.

## Volume Editor's Notes

In June 2005 I was contacted by William C. Sturtevant and asked to assume the position of Volume Editor for the *Indians in Contemporary Society*. This request came at an unusual time in that I had just finished several long-term projects and had no major commitments. Thus, I agreed to come to Washington to discuss the volume. At the time, I was informed that after three decades the Smithsonian administration was going to close the Handbook office and abolish the positions of the editorial staff at the end of September 2007. Thus, all work on the volume, except for the actual printing, would have to be completed in slightly less than two years. Although I thought at the time that many of the existing chapter drafts could be used, two years seemed an extremely short period for such an undertaking. Only after conversations with Daniel Rogers, Chair of the Department of Anthropology, National Museum of Natural History, and Hans-Dieter Sues, Associate Director of Research and Collections, National Museum of Natural History, about the importance of this volume being published, did I agree.

With his usual enthusiasm, Bill Sturtevant wanted to get started immediately with organizing a new planning committee (listed on p. [v]). A core committee consisting of Ives Goddard (Smithsonian Institution), JoAllyn Archambault (Smithsonian Institution), and Sally McLendon (City University of New York, Hunter College) was quickly assembled to meet with Bill and me. The main focus of this meeting was to discuss names of potential individuals to serve on an expanded planning committee, to participate as Native consultants, and to be authors. Three things were obvious. We had to have one or more people from Canada on the committee, as much input from Native American scholars as possible, and finally, chapter authors and committee members from a range of other disciplines as well as from anthropology and history.

During the summer I had time to review the existing chapter drafts as well as time to discuss the volume with Vine Deloria. Although I realized that production of this volume would be a rushed job, I did not fully realize the magnitude of the task. After reviewing the drafts and making a critical assessment, I quickly understood that it was going to require a great deal more work than I had anticipated. The Native American world had changed dramatically since the 1970s when these chapters were drafted. Many chapter topics were no longer so relevant as they had been. Basically, the committee was going to have to start over. In the end only two of the original chapters were retained and one of these had to be rewritten.

Since academics are notoriously difficult to locate during the summer months, contacting potential members for the committee progressed slowly. It took me until early September to recruit the remaining members of the committee: David Miller (Native Studies, First Nations University of Canada), David Wilkins (American Indian Studies, Political Science, Law and American Studies, Minnesota), Eva Garroutte (Sociology, Boston College), and Robert Warrior (Native American Studies and English, University of Oklahoma). Ideally, like planning committees for other *Handbook* volumes, the full committee should have been invited to meet in Washington with several days to discuss the planning and organization of the volume. Unfortunately, we did not have the luxury of time. Chapter topics had to be defined and authors identified as quickly as possible. Thus, we were forced to resort to using lengthy teleconference calls on September 27 and October 11, 2005, follow-up e-mails, and telephone calls.

Our work on refining the proposed list of chapters and identifying and contacting individuals to write began immediately. We had to find individuals capable not only of writing on the particular topic but also of doing such within a very short time. At first we requested that authors submit their chapter drafts by April 2006. Many indicated that while they were willing to write they could not meet the deadline. Others indicated a willingness if they could have a coauthor. A great deal of negotiation was involved in finalizing chapter authors and in many cases we had to extend deadlines. The *Handbook* staff was still working on volume 3, *Environment, Origins, and Population*, and was unable to start work on these chapters until the late spring of 2006.

It was not until December 2005 that the committee and I finalized the list of chapters and authors. We dropped many potential chapters because an author could not be found. Our selection of authors was a highly mixed group of professionals. The academics were drawn from law, English, sociology, political science, psychology, economics, theater, journalism, art history, education, and Native studies programs as well as from anthropology and history or some combination of these disciplines. Other authors included both active and retired American, Canadian, and Native government officials and employees as well as individuals in business. While 32 of 46 chapters were written by Americans, 14 chapters were written by Canadians. In attempting to have a strong Native voice, over half of the chapters were either authored or coauthored by Native scholars.

The receipt of chapter drafts started in January 2006, and continued until June 2007. The first edited chapter was approved in June 2006.

## Linguistic Editing

As far as possible all cited words in Indian languages were rewritten in the appropriate orthography by the Linguistic Editor. Words in the names of institutions and organizations appear in the spelling in use locally.

## Binomials

The scientific names of animal and plant genera and species, printed in italics, have been checked to ensure that they reflect modern usage by biological taxonomists. The plant and animal names submitted have been brought into agreement with those in previously published culture area volumes of the *Handbook*, unless those names have been superseded by more current usage in consultation with curators in appropriate departments of the National Museum of Natural History.

## Bibliography

All references cited by contributors have been unified in a single list at the end of the volume. Citations within the text, by author, date, and often page, identify the works in this unified list. Cesare Marino, the *Handbook* Researcher, served as bibliographer. Wherever possible, he resolved conflicts between citations of different editions, corrected inaccuracies and omissions, and checked direct quotations against the originals. The bibliographic information has been verified by examination of the original work or from standard reliable library catalogs (especially the National Union Catalog, the published catalog of the Harvard Peabody Museum Library, and the OCLC/PRISM on-line catalog). The unified bibliography lists all the sources cited in the text of the volume; it also includes works submitted by contributors or consulted by the *Handbook* research staff

but not cited in the chapters. Not listed in the bibliography are personal communications, either to the authors or to editors, and legal citations that appear in the chapters. The sections headed Sources at the ends of some chapters provide general guidance to the most important sources of information on the topics covered.

## Illustrations

In late 2006, authors were requested to submit appropriate illustrations for their chapters. To varying degrees they complied with this request. Yet considerations of time, space, balance, reproducibility, and availability often required modifications in what was submitted. Much original material was provided by editorial staff members from research they conducted in museums and other repositories, in the published literature, and from correspondence and telephone interviews. Locating and selecting suitable photographs, drawings, and paintings for the following chapters was the responsibility of Elizabeth M. Hartjens of Imagefinders, Inc.: Indians in the Military; Activism, 1950–1980; Activism Since 1980; Health and Health Issues in the United States; Gaming; Department of Indian Affairs and Northern Development; Nunavut; James Bay Cree; Nisga'a; The Freedmen; Métis; The Native American Church; Powwows; Native Museums and Cultural Centers; Theater; Film; Literature; and Repatriation. All other research and photographic selections were provided by the Production Manager, Diane Della-Loggia. Many individuals, including professional photographers, have generously provided free photographs and the documentation on them. Images credited to AP are from AP/Wide World Photos, New York. All uncredited drawings are by the Scientific Illustrator, Roger Thor Roop.

All digital sketch maps were produced by Daniel G. Cole of the National Museum of Natural History Information Technology Office, who redrew those submitted by authors and created many new ones using information from the chapter manuscripts, from their authors, and from other sources.

Layout and design of the illustrations were the responsibility of the Scientific Illustrator, Roger Thor Roop. Captions for most illustrations were composed by Hartjens and Della-Loggia while some were supplied by authors. Map captions were written by Cole. Native place-names in map captions were supplied by authors and edited by the Linguistic Editor. All illustrations, including maps and drawings, and all captions, have been approved by the Technical Editor, Volume Editor, and the authors of the chapters in which they appear.

## Acknowledgments

During the first few years of this project, the *Handbook* editorial staff in Washington worked on materials for all volumes of the series. Since intensive preparation of this volume began in 2006, especially important contributions were provided by: the Editorial Liaison and Staff Coordinator, Paula Cardwell (1984–2007); the Production Manager and Manuscript Editor, Diane Della-Loggia (1972–2007); the Researcher and Bibliographer, Cesare Marino (1983–2007); the Scientific Illustrator, Roger Thor Roop (1999–2007); the Illustrations Researcher, Elizabeth M. Hartjens (November 2006 through September 2007); and the Rights and Reproduction Coordinator, Erica Paige Choucroun (May 2006 until April 2007). Throughout, Malinda Rhone served as bibliographic assistant while Mary Ecker served as the volunteer assistant during the summer of 2007. The index was compiled by Coughlin Indexing Services, Inc.

Valuable administrative supervision was provided by J. Daniel Rogers, Chair, and Laurie Burgess, Deputy Chair, of the Department of Anthropology, National Museum of Natural History.

William C. Sturtevant was officially named the General Editor of the *Handbook of North American Indian* series in 1966. In January 2007 he retired but continued to play an active role as the General Editor. On March 2, 2007, William "Bill" Sturtevant passed away at the age of 80. Throughout the 41 years of his editorship he remained tirelessly dedicated to upholding the high standards of excellence that brought much acclaim to the series. During the intensive planning and organization of this volume the Planning Committee was fortunate to have received his invaluable counsel.

In February 2007 Ives Goddard became an emeritus member of the Department of Anthropology, National Museum of Natural History. He was of particular assistance on matters of historical and geographical accuracy and continued to serve as Technical Editor as well as the *Handbook* Linguistic Editor and until March 2007 advisor to the General Editor.

Beyond the members of the Planning Committee and those individuals acknowledged in appropriate sections of the text, the Volume Editor would especially like to thank Gerald Taiaiake Alfred (British Columbia) and J.R. Miller (Saskatchewan) for their suggestions concerning the chapters on Canada and potential authors for these chapters. Contributor Margaret Seguin Anderson wishes to thank Deanna Nyce, Wilp Wilxo'oskwhl Nisga'a, who provided assistance in reviewing and comments on the Nisga'a chapter.

Acknowledgment is due to the Department of Anthropology, National Museum of Natural History, Smithsonian Institution (and to its other curatorial staff), for releasing Sturtevant and Goddard from part of their curatorial and research responsibilities so that they could devote time to editing the *Indians in Contemporary Society* volume of the *Handbook*. The Department is also owed thanks for supporting the participation of Chair J. Daniel Rogers and Deputy Chair Laurie Burgess. Bailey acknowledges the financial support of the University of Tulsa, Oklahoma, and released time from teaching, which enabled him to edit this volume. Special acknowledgement is made to Roger Blais, Provost, and Thomas Benediktson, Dean, of Henry Kendall College of Arts and Sciences for their support and encouragement.

October 2007                                              Garrick A. Bailey

# Introduction

GARRICK A. BAILEY

The chapters in this volume read very differently from those in other volumes. In part this is due to the wide range of academic disciplines represented by the authors. In greater part, the difference is that many, if not most, chapter authors, both Native and non-Native, have been involved in initiating the very changes that they discuss. Thus, in many chapters, particularly those written by Native authors, there is a strong personal component. It is also important to realize that Native scholars frequently evaluate certain events and occurrences differently from their non-Native colleagues. Thus, the differing emphasis in importance given certain topics within chapters may be a reflection of cultural viewpoints. Finally, what this volume is attempting to describe is an extraordinarily dynamic and volatile period in Native American history. Significant changes were occurring in the Native American world literally as these chapters were being written.

## Terminology

The term Indian as used in both the title of this volume and the title of the encyclopedia is and has been an abused term. Not all Native peoples of North American are or were "Indians." The Arctic peoples of Alaska and northern Canada—Inuit, Inupiat, Yup'ik, and Aleut (vol. 5)—are socially, culturally, linguistically, and physically distinct from the "Indians" who lived to the south. The term Indian has been objected to because it was originally proper to the people of India. After 500 years of misuse, the term Indian has become deeply imbedded in everyday language, institutional names, and even laws. Since the 1980s both Native and non-Natives attempted to correctly identify the Native populations by the introduction of new terms; the former names of tribal groups are often given in parentheses for readers to make the connection with previous literature.

In Canada the term First Nations is frequently used, but only for "Indians." Inuit and Métis are distinguished. In official reference to all Native people of Canada—First Nations, Inuit, and Métis—the term aborigine is used, but the term Native also appears. In addition, when speaking collectively of themselves the First Nations of Canada use the term Native Americans. In the United States, "native" or "Native American" or "American Indian" are commonly used for Indians. Sometimes the term tribe is used as a synonym for Indian. In Alaska the term Native Alaskan is the collective term for Indians and Arctic peoples. In the United States, in reference to all the Native people of the 49 mainland states, the term American Indians and Alaskan Native is government usage. However, both groups receive services from the Bureau of Indian Affairs and the Indian Health Service, and Native Alaska communities have the legal status of "recognized tribes."

There is no agreement, even among Native peoples themselves, on which term is most appropriate. To see this lack of agreement one needs only to look at the names of Native organizations in the United States and Canada. Attempts to standardize terminology only seem to add to the confusion. Here only the terms in chapter titles were standardized. The terms Indian or Tribal in chapter titles refer to the Native Americans and Alaska Natives in the United States. The term aboriginal in a chapter title refers collectively to all Native peoples of Canada. Finally, the term Native American, when used in a chapter title, refers collectively to the native peoples of the United States and Canada. Within the chapters term usage is not standardized.

## Mexico

In the *Handbook of North American Indians* volumes, North America is defined not in its geographic sense but in terms of Native cultures. Thus, North America as used in the *Handbook* includes those Native cultures north of Mesoamerica. The difficulty is in defining the cultural boundary separating the peoples of the southernmost part of North America, what anthropologists term the Southwest culture area, from those of Mesoamerica. In volumes 9 and 10, *Southwest*, the Southwest culture area is defined as including a large portion of northern Mexico—Seri, Mayo, Yaqui, Tarahumara, and Northern Tepehuan, to name only some of the peoples (vol. 10:*ix*). However, the cultures of the Native peoples of North America have changed dramatically since the 1500s in response to contact and domination by Europeans.

The Southwest was one of the earliest regions to experience contact with Europeans and the last to be militarily conquered. Within less than a decade following the conquest of the Aztecs, Spanish military expeditions were penetrating the region in search of more cities to plunder. This region of deserts, grasslands, and often rugged mountains occupied by relatively small horticultural communities and scattered hunting and gathering groups initially had little to offer the conquistadors. As a result the Spanish frontier expanded slowly northward during the sixteenth century into present-day Sinaloa and Chihuahua, affecting only the southernmost peoples of the Southwest. In the 1590s the government of New Spain established missions and settlements among the Pueblo peoples of present-day New Mexico and Arizona. These missions and settlements were well north of the other areas of New Spain and remained geographically isolated throughout the Spanish and Mexican periods. By the end of the seventeenth century the northern limit of Spanish missions, farms, ranches, and mines had reached approximately what is today the border between the United States and Mexico. Facing armed resistance from the Indians, mainly the Navajo and Apache, Spanish expansion was brought to a halt. A defensive line of presidios was constructed from Altar, Sonora, to San Antonio, Texas. The Southwest Indians had become divided between those who were under varying degrees of Spanish control and cultural influence, the Eastern Pueblos and the southernmost groups, and the northern peoples who remained politically autonomous. This division remained throughout the eighteenth century and even after Mexican independence in 1821. The Treaty of Guadalupe Hidalgo in 1848, which ended the Mexican-American War, and the Gadsden Purchase of 1853 added a new dimension to this division. The new boundary between the United States and Mexico, with the exception of the Pueblos, approximated the existing boundary between the Spanish-Mexican controlled portion of the Southwest and that of the independent tribes. Thus, the Southwest culture area today is best seen as being divided into two subareas. In the northern portion, the Native peoples since the 1850s have been strongly influenced by Anglo-American social, cultural, political, and economic institutions. In the southern portion, the Indians have in most cases been influenced since the 1600s by Spanish and Mexican social, cultural, political, and economic institutions (Spicer 1962). Thus, today there is an Anglo-Native Southwest, with stronger cultural and social ties to the other Native groups of the United States and Canada, and a Hispanic-Native Southwest with stronger ties to the other Native peoples of Mexico (T.B. Hinton 1983; Griffen 1983).

It is important to note that several Native groups have communities on both sides of the border. In 1848, a group of Kickapoo (vol. 15:656–667) and Seminole (vol. 14:452–453, 466, 469–473) moved to Mexico and negotiated an agreement with Mexican authorities in which they received land in exchange for their assistance in fighting Apache, Comanche, and Kiowa raiders. Eventually most of the Seminole returned to the United States, but a Kickapoo community remained, while retaining close social ties to kinsmen in the United States. In 1900 many Mexican Kickapoo were allotted land on the Kickapoo Reservation in Oklahoma. In

1977 the Texas legislature recognized them as the Kickapoo Traditional Tribe of Texas, a subgroup of the Kickapoo tribe of Oklahoma. In 1989, in addition to their land near Nacimiento, Coahuila, they received a 125-acre reservation at Eagle Pass, Texas. With dual Mexican and American citizenship they freely move across the border and operate a casino at Eagle Pass.

Due to conflicts with Mexican authorities, in the 1880s many Yaquis from Sonora took refuge in Arizona. During the Mexican Revolution of 1910–1921, others joined them. Yaquis from Arizona and Sonora, like the Kickapoo, regularly visit one another, maintaining a strong common identity and culture. In 1964 they were granted land by the federal government at Pascua, near Tucson, Arizona, and in 1978 they received federal recognition as the Pascua Yaqui Tribe of Arizona (vol. 9:250–263). A membership roll was created in 1980. In 1994, any Yaqui by blood who was an American citizen was given a three-year opportunity to apply for tribal enrollment. The members of the Pascua Yaqui Tribe of Arizona have the same legal rights as any other federally recognized tribe. In 2007 numbering almost 15,000, the tribe is a member of the Intertribal Council of Arizona, operates a casino in the Tucson area, and participates in local intertribal powwows.

The Gadsden Purchase of 1853 split the Tohono O'odham (Papago) homeland between the United States and Mexico. While the vast majority in 2007 live in the United States and are United States citizens, 1,000–2,000 live adjacent to the border in Sonora (vol. 9:139–142). Although those living in Sonora are not American citizens, they are enrolled members of the Tohono O'odham tribe, and as such receive services from the United States Indian Health Service. Until the 1990s Sonoran Tohono O'odham passed freely over the border to visit the hospital at Sells, Arizona, using only their tribal membership cards. However, tightened border controls have made this difficult, and there are attempts to make the Sonoran members of the tribe American citizens.

The Pima, Cocopa (vol. 9:99–112), and possibly other border tribes maintain limited cultural and social contacts with Native communities in Mexico. However, with few exceptions, the surviving Native communities in northern Mexico, because of their geographical isolations, linguistic differences, and economic and political status have not participated in nor been affected by the pan-Native political, social, and cultural movements that have so dramatically transformed the lives of the Native peoples of the United States and Canada since the mid-twentieth century. Therefore, this volume will describe only the Native peoples in the United States and Canada.

## Native North America Today

In 1967, speaking before a hearing of the President's National Advisory Commission on Rural Poverty, Clyde Warrior, a

Ponca Indian from Oklahoma and the President of the National Indian Youth Council, stated that:

> if there is one thing that characterizes Indian life today it is poverty of the spirit. We still have human passions and depth of feeling . . ., but we are poor in spirit because we are not free—free in the most basic sense of the word. We are not allowed to make those basic human choices and decisions about our personal life and about the destiny of our communities which is the mark of free mature people . . . the world and our lives in it pass us by without our desires or aspirations having any effect.
>
> . . . Our choices are made for us. . . . On reservations these choices and decisions are made by federal administrators, bureaucrats, and their "yes men" euphemistically called tribal governments. Those of us who live in non-reservation areas have our lives controlled by local white power elites. . . . They are called social workers, "cops", school teachers, churches, etc, . . . . They . . . tell us what is good for us and how they've programmed us (Josephy 1971:84–85).

Legally American Indians and Alaska Natives were wards of the federal government, and as such were treated as children not only by federal officials, but often by state and local officials as well. In the following months and years copies of Warrior's statement were circulated among government officials. This statement, later entitled "We are not free," is included on the list of the 73 Basic Readings in United States Democracy by the United States Information Agency of the State Department.

Although Warrior was speaking only about the situation in the United States, his remarks could have been applied to the situation confronting all of the Native peoples of North America at that time. What Warrior so eloquently described was the legacy of European conquest—the increasing despair and powerlessness of the conquered. Many, perhaps the majority, of Native Americans themselves had come to question the value of their cultural traditions, languages, and even their own continued existence as distinct peoples.

In 2007, the Native American world is far different from the world in which Warrior lived. The repressive policies of assimilation and acculturation that had for more than 100 years degraded their cultural traditions, social institutions, and languages are gone. Native Americans today, as a group, have far greater autonomy and control over their political, economic, and personal lives that at any time since the early nineteenth century. For many native communities these changes have resulted in significant improvements in the economic well being of their people. For all there has been an increased pride and awareness of who they are, which has resulted in a revitalization of traditional cultural institutions and the emergence of what some call a Native American renaissance.

This volume is concerned with events that precipitated the Native activist movements of the 1960s and 1970s and the resulting changes. The chapters in the first two sections of this volume examine the political and legal changes that have redefined the relationship between Native peoples and the dominant society in the United States and Canada. Chapters in the third section are concerned with demographic changes, while in the fourth section some of the broad social and cultural developments among Native peoples are discussed.

## Changes in Political and Legal Status

After World War II two broad trends emerged that were going to play a significant role in the lives of the Native peoples of North America. First, with the industries of Europe and Japan damaged or destroyed, North America emerged as the dominant industrial region of the world. The expanding economies of the United States and Canada were going to make increasing demands for natural resources. Within the United States, sources of additional natural resources were on Indian trust lands, or in the case of Alaska, on lands where the aboriginal title had yet to be extinguished. Outside the United States the closest and most important potential source of resources was Canada. In Canada, many of these undeveloped resources were in Native-occupied areas. Whether they liked it or not, many Native Americans were living in areas in which resources were going to be developed. Gas and oil wells were going to be drilled. Uranium and coal were going to be mined. Timber was going to be cut, and rivers were going to be dammed and land flooded for hydroelectric power and to supply water to distant cities and farms. The only question was how this was to be accomplished. Were Native peoples going to have a voice in these developments? and how much, if any, would they benefit? Government agencies could force contractual agreements on Native groups. If not, in both countries there were influential groups who supported either the abolishing of Native rights or the ignoring of them.

World War II signaled the beginning of the end of the colonial world, as one after another of the former European colonial possessions gained independence. The second trend—the rise of nationalism—did not stop at the borders of the old colonial world. Although they differed greatly in their particular aspirations, in North America minority ethnic groups—African-Americans, Hispanics, and Québecois—as well as Native Americans would began to increasingly demand changes in the political status quo.

It is important to note that there are fundamental differences in the basic legal status of the Native peoples in the United States and Canada. The basis for legal status of Native peoples in both countries is derived from their constitutions, legislative acts, and judicial interpretations of their rights. The United States Constitution gives Congress the right "to regulate commerce with foreign nations, and among the several states and with the Indian tribes." Unlike the United States Constitution, the Canadian Constitution is not a single document, but rather an amalgamation of various written texts, acts, charters, statutes, and proclamations together with unwritten "established practices." The two earliest and most basic documents relative to Native rights are the Royal Proclamation of 1763 and the Constitution Act of 1867, earlier called the British North America Act. The Proclamation of 1763 recognized the existence of an aboriginal land title that only the Crown could alienate. The Constitution Act of 1867, which joined three separate British colonies and created the Dominion of Canada, gave the national government legislative authority over matters pertaining to "Indians and lands reserved to Indians," while public lands (Crown lands) and resources were placed under the authority of the separate provinces. Later, other British colonies entered the federation as provinces and introduced other constitutional documents relevant to Indian rights. Long ignored, it was not until 1939 that the Supreme Courts of Canada in *Re: Eskimo* ruled that Section 91–24 of the Constitution Act, the provisions concerning Indians, also applied to the Inuit. Whether these provisions apply to Métis has yet to be determined.

Except for the provision that Native peoples are to be treated collectively as "tribes," the United States Congress has wide ranging authority relative to Native rights. Although at times critical, the role of the federal courts is limited to the interpretation of congressional acts. In contrast, in Canada, since Native rights are embedded in its Constitution, the most basic questions concerning Native rights are constitutional questions that the federal courts decide.

During the colonial period the British Crown recognized that Native peoples had what became termed "aboriginal title" to their lands. The Royal Proclamation of 1763, which applied to certain North American colonies that become the United States and Canada, stated that only the Crown could alienate the aboriginal title. However, what constituted aboriginal title was not defined in the Proclamation. After American independence, the Congress and the courts began defining "aboriginal title" and thus Native rights somewhat differently from their counterparts in British Canada. Canada adhered to the British concept that all of the land in a region, upon discovery, became Crown land and all resident people subjects of the Crown. It was not until 1888 that Canadian courts ruled that the aboriginal land title "consisted of only a personal and usufructuary right, dependent upon the good will of the Sovereign" (J.R. Miller 2000:343). Between 1790 and 1834 the United States Congress passed a series of Trade and Intercourse Acts, which gave the federal government exclusive authority over all matters pertaining to Indian tribes, including the extinguishing of aboriginal title. Based on these acts, in the early decades of the nineteenth century, the courts came to define aboriginal title and rights somewhat differently. In 1823 Justice John Marshall noted that discovery entitled the discovering European power to title good relative only to other European governments. "As for the Indians: 'They were admitted to be the rightful occupants of the soil, with a legal as well as just claim to retain possession of it, and use it according to their own discretion; but their rights to complete sovereignty, as independent nations, were necessarily diminished' . . ." (Canby 2004: 368–369). Native land interests, aboriginal title, were initially termed as "right of occupancy" and later "original Indian title." This original Indian title belonged collectively to a "tribe" and not to any individual. Only the federal government had the right to extinguish this title and could do so by either purchase or conquest. In cases of conquest, which could take the form of unilateral appropriation, no compensation was required. However, when tribal land holdings or reservations were once defined by federal treaty or statute, title to these lands became "recognized title" and as such "property" as defined and protected under the constitution (Canby 2004:376–377). Unless specifically excluded by treaty or statue, tribal property rights included full rights to all natural resources. In contrast, the status of "reserve" land in Canada can be either Crown land on which the aboriginal title has been extinguished and that is reserved for the use and benefit of native peoples or a land area defined by treaty on which the aboriginal title has not been extinguished. In both cases actual Native rights to nature resources that were not used in a "traditional" manner were unclear.

The United States and Canada also differ in the basis for according individuals "native rights." The United States recognizes specific tribes as having rights and recognizes individuals as having Native rights only by virtue of membership in one or another of these tribes. In 1924 the federal government conferred citizenship on all Indians and Alaska natives, meaning that they were both citizens as well as tribal members. In Canada, the federal government recognizes individuals and First Nations as having "native rights" and maintains a registry, or list, of Status Indians. Until 1960, when the right to vote in national elections was granted to Status Indians, the difference between Status and non-Status Indians was that the non-Status Indians were enfranchised and as such had no legal rights as Indians. A register of Status Inuit was never created, and until the 1982 Constitution, the native status of Métis was generally ignored.

These basic differences noted, Native policies in the United States and Canada have followed and continue to follow the same broad trends. Based on the assumption that Native peoples would eventually become fully integrated and thus "vanish" into the dominant society, during the nineteenth century both governments formally adopted policies of forced assimilation. While according special rights to Natives that these governments protected, at the same time these same policies gave government officials the authority to tightly regulate and control the political, economic, social, and cultural lives of Native peoples. By the mid-twentieth century many political leaders in both countries thought that the time had come to abolish Native rights and lead all Native peoples to fully integrate, politically and economically, into the dominant society.

Starting in 1946 the United States Congress began passing a series of laws designed to end the special legal status of Indians and Native Alaskans. The first was the Indian Claims Commission Act, the purpose of which was to award monetary compensation for all unresolved tribal claims, land and otherwise, against the United States. The unresolved Alaska Native aboriginal land title question was to be handled later. In 1951 the Bureau of Indian Affairs began a relocation program, providing assistance in moving Indian families and individuals from impoverished reservations and rural areas to cities. Finally, in 1953 two acts were passed. The first, House Concurrent Resolution 108, more commonly called the Termination Act, called for the ending of all government trust responsibilities and Indian programs for tribes and their members. This was to be accomplished on a tribe by tribe basis over time. However, the act specified particular tribes and groups of tribes to be terminated at the "earliest possible time." The second, Public Law 280, extended state civil and criminal jurisdiction over Indian Country in five states and provided the opportunity for other states to do likewise. Up to this time, state courts had not had jurisdiction on Indian lands under federal control.

In 1946 a Special Joint Committee of the Senate and House of Commons of Canada was appointed to "examine and consider the Indian Act . . . and suggest amendments they may deem advisable." In 1948 it reported that the policies of assimilation were not working and recommended less coercion and intervention. In 1951 a revised Indian Act was proclaimed, which adopted the basic recommendations proposed by the joint committee. In essence the change was from forced or coerced assimilation to a more passive form of assimilation termed integration. Regardless, the intent was the same, the eventual assimilation of Native people. The recommendations of the Special Joint Commission concerning Indian land claims were ignored. In 1960 Status Indians received the right to vote without losing their native rights, later becoming what many termed Citizens Plus. In the late 1960s revisions of the Indian Act became a priority. In 1969, after a year of meetings and discussions between Native leaders and officials, Prime Minister Pierre Trudeau presented the White Paper on Indian Policy. The White Paper called for ending the separate legal status of Indians, abolishing the Department of Indian Affairs and Northern Development, transferring of Indian land to individuals, and recognizing the existence of aboriginal claims. It rejected the creation of a formal Indian Claims Commission.

In 1944 the National Congress of American Indians (NCAI) was organized with the encouragement and support of the Bureau of Indian Affairs. This was the first national organization of Indian leaders in the United States. However, the failure of NCAI to stop the passage of the termination acts and other detrimental legislation led many Native people to soon doubt its effectiveness. In 1961, a group of younger educated Indians formed the National Indian Youth Council. These young activists, modeling their actions after those of the Black civil rights movement, began publicly to protest government policies. During the mid-1960s even more militant Indian organizations emerged, and in 1968 the American Indian Movement was founded in Minneapolis. In 1961 the National Indian Council, the first national Indian organization in Canada, was established and quickly assumed an activist role. When the National Indian Council split, the National Indian Brotherhood and the Canadian Métis Society were formed. Collectively, these national organizations, and other smaller local organizations, effected major changes in the policies of both the United States and Canada.

The late 1960s was a period of well-publicized Native protests. The first major shift in United States policy occurred in 1968 in President Lyndon Johnson's message to Congress in which he called for an end to the termination program and for self-determination for Native Americans. In that year the Indian Civil Rights Act was passed, which required tribal approval before states could extend civil and criminal jurisdiction as provided under Public Law 280. Faced with mounting criticism, in the spring of 1970 Prime Minister Trudeau announced that "if the White people and the Indian people in Canada don't want the proposed policy, we're not going to force it down their throats" (J.R. Miller 2000:337). The following year the White Paper was withdrawn. In July 1970 President Richard Nixon presented his Message to Congress on Indian Affairs. In his message, he repeated and greatly elaborated on Johnson's message of 1968, calling for an end to the termination and assimilation policies and proposing a policy of self-determination for Native peoples. The nadir had been passed.

The 1970s witnessed beginnings of what would eventually become an almost complete reversal in Native policy in the United States and Canada. The policies of assimilation vanished together with the idea that Native peoples would eventually and necessarily become fully absorbed into the dominant society. A doctrine of self-determination emerged together with the recognition that many of the basic legal rights of Native peoples had been ignored or abrogated. The decades since 1970 have been characterized by legislation, constitutional changes, and court decisions that defined Native rights.

For over a century the issue of aboriginal land title in Alaska had been ignored. In 1971 the Alaska Native Claims Settlement Act was passed, creating a unique framework for managing Native affairs and properties. A two-tier system was created, consisting of for-profit regional corporations to manage land and resources, and nonprofit tribal and community governments concerned with providing governmental services. The Indian Self-Determination and Education Assistance Act of 1975 provided for the contracting of services of the Bureau of Indian Affairs and the Indian Health Service to tribal governments. In 1978 both the Tribally Controlled Community College Act and the American Indian Religious Freedom Act were passed. In 1982 The Indian Tribal Government Tax Status Act, which gave tribes tax advantages similar to those of the states, was passed. Through these and other acts, passed in the 1980s and 1990s, Congress redefined the federal-tribe relationship, expanded the authority of tribal governments, and provided additional funding for tribally controlled programs.

Simultaneously, litigation in federal courts was redefining the authority of tribal governments relative to both the federal and state governments. In 1974 the Supreme Court ruled that the Trade and Intercourse Acts applied within the boundaries of the 13 original states. The following year in *Passamaquoddy* v. *Morton* the federal court ruled that the federal trust responsibility applied to all tribes, regardless of whether or not the tribe had been formally recognized by the government. As a result in 1978 the Department of Interior established regulations for extending formal federal recognition to previously "unrecognized" tribes. However, the case that would have by far the greatest impact on Native Americans was *California* v. *Cabazon Band of Mission Indians*. In this 1987 case the Supreme Court, noting a distinction between criminal/prohibitory law and civil/regulatory law, ruled that a tribe had sovereign immunity from state civil/regulatory laws. This ruling provided the legal basis for the development of tribal casinos, and the following year Congress passed the Indian Gaming Regulatory Act of 1988. Prior to the development of casinos, tribal governments had been primarily dependent upon federal grants and contracts for funding. Casinos changed this. In 2006 the total funding for the Bureau of Indian Affairs and Indian Health Service amounted to about $8 billion. That same year tribal casinos realized over $22 billion in revenue.

The protests of Native groups concerning aboriginal land titles and treaty rights had been ignored by the national and provincial governments and courts of Canada for over a century. In the early 1970s this began to change when the federal government made funding available to native groups to pursue claims. In 1973 the Nisga'a succeeded in bringing their aboriginal land claim case against British Columbia before the Supreme Court. Although the court did not reach a decision in the case, splitting 3-3-1, it did recognize that aboriginal title still existed in Canada and implied that it was more than a use right. Responding to the court's findings, in 1974 the Office of Native Claims was created within the Department of Indian Affairs and Northern Development to research and evaluate aboriginal land claims. In 1975 the James Bay and Northern Quebec Agreement was signed between the province of Quebec and the East Cree and Quebec Inuit. During this same period the federal government began transferring the responsibility for some programs, such as education, to Native communities and organizations.

In 1982 a new Constitution was drafted and adopted. Relative to Native peoples the two most important provisions were the recognition of existing Aboriginal and treaty rights and the definition of Aboriginal peoples of Canada as the Indian, Inuit, and Métis. In 1985, the Indian Act was amended, providing for the reclaiming of Indian status for some, but not all, Indians who had lost Indian status.

While Native groups were unsuccessful in having a statement on Native self-government included in the 1982 Constitution, a Parliamentary Task Force on Indian Self-Government was created. The report of this task force the following year recommended that the recognition of Indian self-government should be part of the constitution. While this recommendation was rejected, there has been an increasing acceptance of the right of self-government for Native groups. However, the nature of Aboriginal land title and Native control over resources, together with the rights of Native peoples to self-government, continue to be constitutional issues in Canada. Aboriginal land claims agreements, such as the Nisga'a Agreement in 1998 and the Nunavut Agreement in 1999, have provided particular Native groups with a far greater degree of self-government and control over resources.

## Demographic Changes

In United States and Canadian census data collected during the last decades of the twentieth century two trends are apparent. The first is that the Native population is growing at a far more rapid rate than that of the general population. Between 1950–1951 and 2000–2001 the combined Native populations, as enumerated in the national censuses of the United States and Canada, increased from slightly more than 500,000 to over five million. The second is that Native residence is rapidly shifting from rural to urban areas. In 1950 almost 90 percent of the Native population in both countries was rural. By 2000–2001 over 50 percent were living in cities.

The difficulty with comparing these figures over time and between the two countries and even within the two countries is that they are not quite comparable. The term Native American covers a wide range of individuals who vary greatly in biological ancestry, social identities, and legal statuses.

Between the 1950–1951 and the 2000–2001 censuses both countries changed from the ethnic identity of the individual being determined by the enumerator, to one of self-identification by the individual or head of the household. During this period, identification as Native became more socially acceptable, and even at times advantageous. As a result, increasing numbers of individuals have chosen to identify as Native or of Native ancestry. Thus re-identification, as well as higher birth rates, have contributed greatly to the population growth. In the United States census the Native population is divided into two main groupings, American Indian and Alaskan Natives and individuals of mixed-race. In reality, this is a social and not biological division, since the majority of individuals who identify only as American Indian and Alaskan Native are also of mixed ancestry. In Canada there is a similar division between individuals who identify as "Aboriginal" and individuals who identify as of "Aboriginal ancestry." "Aboriginal" individuals are further enumerated as being Indian, Inuit, or Métis.

In the 2000–2001 census, the two countries showed a combined total of approximately 3.5 million individuals who identified solely as Native and almost 2 million others who identified as being of some degree of Native ancestry.

The United States and Canada accord special legal privileges to some, but not all, Native peoples. In the United States only members of the 564 federally recognized tribes or communities have special status as Indian or Native Alaskan. In 2000 the Bureau of Indian Affairs estimated that there were 1.7 million members of recognized tribes or communities, a number less than half of those who identified as Indian or Alaska Native or mixed race on the census. There are many reasons for this difference. Many historic Native groups were never formally recognized by the federal government and their descendants, while counted as Indian or Native Alaskan in the census, are not counted by the Bureau of Indian Affairs. In addition, each tribe or community determines its own membership. In most cases tribes require members to be lineal descendents of individuals listed on tribal rolls created around 1900. For a variety of reasons many individuals and families were not included on these rolls. Further, qualifications for membership are usually based on degree of Native ancestry; however, the degree of required native ancestry varies greatly. Most tribes require a one-quarter degree or more tribal ancestry for membership. Because of mixed tribal ancestries, many individuals who are one-quarter degree or more Native do not meet the minimum requirement for membership in any one tribe. A few tribes require only descent from an individual on an earlier tribal roll regardless of degree of ancestry. Thus, there are full-blood or near full-blood native individuals in the United States who do not have legal status as Native, and individuals who are as little as 1/1024th Native in ancestry who do have legal status as Native. Since the 1970s the number of "recognized tribes and communities" has increased and many other Native groups have applied for recognition. However, the tribal membership status and thus the "Indian" status of one specific group, the Freedmen among the Cherokee, Creek, Choctaw, Chickasaw, and Seminole, has changed over time. Finally, it is important to realize that many individuals who could become tribal members and thus receive federal Native services have not done so. It is also the case that many individuals who are enrolled members of recognized groups do not "self-identify" as Native or even racially mixed for the Census.

In Canada legal status as Indian is determined by the federal government and not by Native groups. To this end the Department of Indian Affairs and Northern Development keeps an official register of Status Indians. Historically, Canada attempted to assimilate the Indian population by enfranchising individuals. Once given the right to vote the individual lost his status as Indian and his name was removed from the list. This changed in 1960 when the right to vote was granted to all Status Indians. However, Indians who had already lost Indian Status were not reinstated as "Status Indians." A 1985 amendment to the Indian Act changed this

policy relative to certain categories of non-Status Indians, creating what some term C-31 Indians. In the census Statistics Canada enumerates not just individuals who identify as Indian, but whether these individuals are Status or non-Status Indians. In 2001 Census Canada reported 558,000 Status Indians and 104,000 non-Status Indians. However, the register of Status Indians showed a total of 690,000. So, in contrast to the United States where there are many fewer legally recognized Natives than are counted by the census, in Canada there are actually more. Although the Métis are today recognized as a separate aboriginal group, many Métis are legally registered as Status Indians. Also, many of the individuals who are listed as of "aboriginal ancestry" are registered as Status Indians. Finally, there are some individuals with Indian Status who identified neither "Indian" or of "aboriginal ancestry" for the census.

The Métis were officially recognized as an aboriginal people by the 1982 Constitution without any clear definition of who was to be considered a Métis. As a result several new populations of mixed Indian-European ancestry have identified themselves as Métis.

Thus, in Canada, like the United States, the Native population is a diverse grouping of peoples. Urbanization in both countries and the resultant intermarriages of individuals from different native peoples as well as with non-Natives add to the complexity of identities and legal status.

## Pan-Nativism and the Native American Renaissance

The policies to assimilate native peoples into the general populations of the United States and Canada failed. While they certainly effected major changes in the cultural traditions and lifeways of Native communities, they did not succeed in destroying their social cohesiveness or the cultural distinctiveness of these communities.

Increased political autonomy and economic control over their resources were not ends in themselves. Far more importantly these changes provided Native peoples with the means by which they could regain control over their own past and future. Government policies and native activism resulted not just in increased political self-determination and economic prosperity, but social and cultural changes as well. The Native peoples of the United States and Canada have entered the most socially and culturally dynamic period in their collective history. Thousands of traditional and nontraditional, formal and informal, local, regional, national, and international Native social and cultural institutions, associations, events, and activities have come into existence. A new level of social identity, a generic identity, as Native has emerged. Collectively these changes are resulting in what many are calling a Native American cultural renaissance.

One of the unintended consequences of the policies of assimilation was the creation of a pan-Indian or pan-Native identity. The boarding schools, the college and university scholarship programs, and urbanization created mixed communities of Native peoples. It was in these settings that Native peoples, as individuals, realized that there was a commonality of experience and interests that transcended their particular cultural, linguistic, and historical differences, and collectively distinguished them from the dominant society. Even in the nineteenth century and earlier, there had been intertribal (inter-nation) social gatherings and political alliances, but these had been regional. It was not until the early 1960s that significant organized national groups began to emerge. These first organizations were political activist groups, primarily consisting of urban and college-educated Native peoples. However, by the late 1960s pan-Native activism had assumed new important social and cultural dimensions involving not just students and urban individuals and families, but also Native peoples drawn from the rural areas and a full spectrum of educational and cultural backgrounds. A pan-Native American social identity, together with shared cultural traditions, has emerged.

Political self-determination did not bring with it control over what was said, written, or taught about Native Americans. Many Native Americans realized that before they could be truly liberated from the constraints of colonialism they had take control, not only of their present, but also their past. Anthony Pico, Chairman of the Viejas Band of Kumeyaay of California, summarized this problem when he wrote:

> The . . . portrayal of American Indians and this country's history needs to be debunked and exposed because the self-serving rationalizations of the past are still robbing generations of American Indians of our lives and future. The task of breaking American Indian stereotypes, dispelling myths and putting tribal issues into context falls on the media. . . . If the press doesn't understand us, the public will never get past the stereotypical ignorance that has plagued Indians from the day the first Europeans arrived. . . . They [the press] also can help free America's original people from the lethal grip of despair and generational cycle of dysfunction that result from being viewed as disposable icons, defined to fit the designs of others. . . . The victors not only get the spoils of war, they get to write the history (Pico 2005).

The realities of Native American life stand in sharp contrast to nineteenth-century stereotypes of "red devils" or "noble savages." Beyond those images, Native Americans have been viewed as anachronisms, with no place "as Natives" in the modern world. These images, direct or implied, of the Native American are seen in the movies and television as well as in museums in displays of ethnographic items and art; they are read in newspapers, novels, histories, and other academic and popular writings; they are taught in the primary and secondary schools, as well as in colleges and universities. Native Americans struggle with finding their own identity and their own past, against images of an "imaginary Native" who never existed.

The problem with these images of the Native American is not just that they are incorrect and demeaning, but that Native Americans, particularly younger people, were and are influenced by these images, thus threatening the social and cultural integrity and continuity of Native peoples. Increased political autonomy and economic resources have provided the Native peoples the means, for the first time, to directly and indirectly confront the Western stereotypic images of the Native American. The cultural renaissance that emerged in the 1970s can be seen as both a necessary response to these stereotypic images as well as a reflection of the increased pride Native peoples have in their own past and traditions.

The Native cultural renaissance is occurring at two distinct but integrated levels. At the local level almost all communities, tribes, and nations have experienced a renewed interest in their unique history, language, and culture. Most have seen increased participation, sometimes dramatic, in traditional religious and cultural events. Native communities have established a wide array of traditional and non-traditional cultural educational programs. Many have assumed control over local schools, introducing courses on native history, culture, and language to the curriculum. A few have established Native-controlled colleges and universities. However, the Native renaissance has found its most conspicuous growth in the proliferation of pan-Native organizations, institutions, events, and activities—religious, social, cultural, and educational.

While most native communities have witnessed revitalization and increased interest in their traditional religious practices and ceremonies, there has been a dramatic growth in Native American Church membership. After a long period of conflict with Christian missionaries and government officials, as well as traditional religious leaders, the church emerged as not just intertribal, but as international, with chapters in the United States, and Canada. In most communities conflict between the members of the Native American Church and traditionalists has disappeared. In some regions, where the Church had declined during the mid-twentieth century, it has been revitalized as younger, particularly more formally educated members of the communities, have been drawn to the Church.

The activities and events that by far bring together the greatest number of Native participants are the public social and cultural events. In both diversity of activities and the numbers of participants these events have dramatically increased since the 1980s. However, the most important of these events fall into two broad and frequently overlapping categories—athletic events and powwows. There are many all-Native basketball, softball, baseball, and golf tournaments as well as rodeos and other athletic events. Many are national or international. Others, like the annual Intertribal Canoe Journey, involving communities in Alaska, British Columbia, Washington, and Oregon, are regional. In 1990, the first of the North American Indigenous Games was held in Edmonton. This multisport event, modeled after the

Olympics, is held about every two years in a different city in the United States or Canada. The 2006 games, held in Colorado, attracted nearly 10,000 native athletes from North America (*Indian Country Today*, July 14, 2006).

As large and as important as all-Native athletic events have become, powwows are by far the most important of Native social activities. Most Indian communities of any size in the United States and Canada, rural or urban, host at least one and frequently several powwows during the year. Most are small, involving only the members of the host community and a few neighboring communities; however, since the 1980s mega-powwows have developed. These powwows, usually held in urban centers, attract several thousand dancers and singers, together with their families. Collectively these powwows bring together Native peoples regardless of tribe or nation, religious beliefs and practices, educational levels, and economic status. The overlapping participation in these powwows has created a broad social network that encompassed the majority of Indian peoples in both Canada and the United States.

There have always been intellectuals and scholars in traditional native society, whether or not members of the dominant society have recognized them. Starting in the 1960s and 1970s there began emerging more, usually academically trained, Native intellectuals and scholars—school teachers, college professors, writers, journalists, and other professionals. Adopting Western institutional models, these individuals have been in the forefront of reclaiming control over the Native American cultural past and future. Building on polit-

ical and legal changes that have resulted in increased economic power, an increasing number of Native-controlled and directed museums, cultural programs, language programs, primary and secondary schools, colleges and universities, newspapers, radio stations, and internet web sites have been created. Today, Native American studies programs, some with departmental status, and most faculty being Native Americans, exist in many universities. Native law has become a specialty in a number of law schools. For the first time there is a Native theater and Native film industry. In fine art, Native American artists have broken way from the restraints of "tourist" arts. While there were native writers and scholars as early as the nineteenth century, their numbers were few. A true Native American literature, with novelists, poets, and playwrights, has emerged. A Native American academic literature and tradition, with Native American scholars and researchers in history, anthropology, sociology, political science, education, and other disciplines, introduced a new Native American theoretical perspective and direction to academic studies. One of the most important contributors to the reclaiming of control over the Native American past was the passage of the Native American Graves Protection and Repatriation Act in 1990. This act provided for the reclaiming of Native human remains, funerary objects, items of cultural patrimony, and certain religious items housed in federally funded museum and institutional collections. In Canada similar agreements have been negotiated. Native people are in the process of reasserting control over their past, present, and future.

*9*

# Indians in the Military

PAMELA BENNETT AND TOM HOLM

Of the transitions Native Americans have experienced since White contact, one of the most important is the result of their participation in World War II. Since the arrival of the Spaniards in North America, Natives have been pressed into serving the allies and auxiliaries for European armed forces in the battle for control of the New World. During the American Revolution the Continental Congress authorized the recruitment of 2,000 Native auxiliaries and, indeed, the first treaties signed between Native nations and the United States were actually military alliances. Native Americans served in every one of America's wars since then and, in 1866, the Indian Scouting Service was formed as a special branch of the United States Army. Natives served in their own infantry and cavalry units in the 1890s and were heavily recruited and even drafted without the benefits of American citizenship during World War I (Dunlay 1987:11–24; Enloe 1980: 192–193).

During the World War I era, 1914–1917, most government polices toward American Indians were built on the idea that Indians were wards of the government. To the average White American, wardship and citizenship (semi-bondage and freedom), were not compatible. Government, it was felt, could not regulate citizens without infringing upon the individual liberties of the nation's citizenry. Most Americans in the early part of the twentieth century were steadfastly opposed to many forms of government interference in the private lives of voting Americans. According to this line of thought, Indians would have to remain wards, and therefore, noncitizens, in order to carry out the policies of acculturation, allotment of reservation lands, and education. Therefore, prior to 1917 many Indians living in the country were not United States citizens. While some had obtained citizenship by taking allotments under the Dawes Severalty Act of 1887, many others during this time had been denied citizens' rights by judges who ruled them to be legally incompetent, a judgment often linked to a desire to control Indian land. Furthermore, a few Native people refused to request citizenship because they feared it would deny tribal sovereignty and destroy the basis from which treaties had been established.

According to federal law, persons not holding citizenship were exempted from military service, yet when the United States plunged into war in 1917 thousands of American Indians entered the armed service, regardless of their individual legal positions at the time. For example, Choctaw volunteers formed a squad of code talkers to encrypt communication (vol. 14:529). Refusing to take advantage of their draft-exempt status, Native peoples took a military oath to defend the Constitution of the United States without possessing any rights under it. The Indian policy reform newsletter, *The Indian's Friend*, reported that a year later there were over 10,000 American Indians in the Army, Navy, and Marine Corps. The periodical stated that "Indians, men and women alike, are doing their bit to help make the world safe for democracy" (*The Indian's Friend* 1918; ARCIA 1920:8–10). Ultimately, more than 12,000 Native people served in World War I (U.S. Department of Defense 2006).

American involvement in World War I created a tremendous outburst of patriotism—the kind of patriotism that called for unswerving loyalty to the government. As a result, the war created a rationale under which the government could become increasingly more regulatory of individuals without facing significant opposition. Congress, for example, with the sedition, espionage, and subversion acts, could essentially remove the guarantees of the Bill of Rights. Regulation, and with it a kind of wardship, became less incompatible with freedom in the American mind. Given this notion, it was not difficult for many Whites to overcome their qualms about conferring citizenship on those Indian people who had fought so bravely in France.

It was not until the country's lawmakers became fully imbued with the idea that individual liberty could be subordinate to the public welfare or to national security, and thus able to place controls on the White population, that American Indian citizenship became justifiable to most Whites. Conferring citizenship, however, did not release Native peoples from wardship status; there was, apparently, no constitutional conflict. Subsequently, Indian soldiers and sailors received citizenship in 1919, and in 1924 the United States offered certificates of citizenship to all American Indians not already holding them (U.S. Statutes At Large 1941:350, 1943:253). However, the result of these wartime ideologies meant that Indians received very few of the actual freedoms of citizenship, yet were expected to accept any and all of the responsibilities that went with it. For example, many American Indians were denied the right to vote, wear tribal clothing, or conduct traditional religious ceremonies, yet they were not excluded from certain duties. Therefore when World War II broke out, for the first time American Indian males between the ages of 21 and 44 became eligible for military conscription. Ironically, their eligibility for conscription came out of their voluntary patriotic participation during World War I. In order to fully appreciate the gravity of post-World War II federal Indian policies, it is important to understand the role of American Indians during the war years (Holm 2005:194–198).

## Indian Patriotism

In 1942 the *Saturday Evening Post* published an article by Richard L. Neuberger, a White political liberal who, like others of his time, saw Native peoples as conquered, disenfranchised, and impoverished. The *Post* article informed its readership that a Nazi propaganda broadcast, purportedly by Josef Goebbels, had predicted an "Indian uprising in the United States should American Indians be asked to fight against the Axis" (Neuberger 1942:79; U.S. Department of Defense 2006). If quoted correctly, these German statements were not without a certain degree of elementary logic. In the name of American progress, Indians had been slaughtered, dispossessed of lands, forcibly stripped of many aspects of their tribal cultures, and left the poorest of the nation's poor. Radio Berlin posed a legitimate question; reportedly they asked, "How could the American Indians think of bearing arms for their exploiters?" (Neuberger 1942a:628). However, contrary to German propaganda, the *Post* reported that American Indians were wholeheartedly embracing the war effort (Neuberger 1942a:628–630). Defying the logic assumed by the Axis powers, American Indians joined the armed forces in record numbers; indeed, Indian participation in World War II was so great that it later became part of American folklore and popular culture.

With the onslaught of World War II, American Indians readily accepted military responsibility. There was little protest against the draft or attempts to avoid service on the grounds of its being a "White man's war"; American Indians behaved as they had during the World War I: they volunteered in record numbers. They signed with their selective service centers in the cities and at their agencies. In fact, many Indians refused to wait the prescribed time to enter the military and either requested early conscription or contacted a recruiter and volunteered (Dale 1949:230; Dinnerstein, Nichols, and Reimers 1970:266; G.D. Nash 1979:152; Bernstein 1991:35; Franco 1997:61–64; Townsend 2000:61–62). According to Commissioner of Indian Affairs John Collier, less than six months after the attack on Pearl Harbor there were over 7,500 American Indians in the armed forces (Collier 1942:29). By October the number of American Indians in the military had swollen to well over 10,000 (Sergeant 1942:708). By 1944 almost 22,000 American Indians, without counting those who had become officers, were part of

the United States armed forces (ARCIA 1944:235). According to the Department of Defense, more than 24,000 reservation Indians and another 20,000 off-reservation Indians served in the Armed Forces (U.S. Department of Defense 2006). At the time, this combined figure represented more than 10 percent of the entire Native American population, and in some tribes, military participation reached as high as 70 percent (U.S. Department of Defense 2006). As Commissioner Collier (1942:29) explained, "While this seems a relatively small number, it represents a larger proportion than any other element of our population."

Native peoples drew some of the deadliest of wartime tasks (Neuberger 1942:629). This experience not only mirrored the Indian experience in World War I but also remained the status quo for Indians in military service up to at least the Vietnam War. For an entire realm of American wartime experience from World War I to Vietnam, American Indians volunteered, served in greater numbers based on their population, and often served in the most hazardous of wartime assignments. Because Native people in the military were not organized into separate units as were Blacks and Japanese Americans, they were exposed to American culture in a way not possible from the reservation. Nonetheless, they were spoken of as being different from Whites. Secretary of the Interior Harold Ickes wrote about the "inherited talents" of American Indians that made them "uniquely valuable" to the war effort. According to Ickes, the Native American fighting man had "endurance, rhythm, a feeling for timing, co-ordination, sense perception, an uncanny ability to get over any sort of terrain at night, and, better than all else, an enthusiasm for fighting. He takes a rough job and makes a game of it. Rigors of combat hold no terrors for him; severe discipline and hard duties do not deter him" (Ickes 1944:58).

An authority on the Plains tribes added to the "natural warrior" image of the American Indian, noting that "the Indian, whose wars never ended, was a realistic soldier. He never gave quarter or expected it." Moreover, "his warfare was always offensive warfare" (Vestal 1942:9). For the most part, American Indians accepted these attitudes toward them and often did their best to conform to such views. In 1942, a month after America entered the war, the *New York Times* reported that Chief Kiutus Tecumseh, a Shawnee of Cashmere, Washington, was attempting to organize an Indian "scouting force" (January 1942). One Sioux man, Kenneth Scission of South Dakota, volunteered for a British-trained American commando unit and quickly managed to become the group's leading killer of the enemy. On a single patrol, Scission was reported to have added, "ten notches on his Gerand rifle" (Ickes 1944:58). Robert Stabler, a member of the Omaha nation, landed alone and under heavy fire to mark the beaches for the infantry in advance of the assault at Licata, Sicily, in 1943. During the Normandy invasion of 1944, 13 American Indians were in the first wave of paratroops dropped with demolitions in advance of the Allied landings in France.

Total Indian casualties in World War II were about 1,250, of which 550 were deaths, 100 of those Sioux (Holm 1996:105; Bernstein 1991:61).

## Sacrifice and Courage: Native Heroes

Nearly 45,000 Native men and women served in World War II and distinguished themselves with courage and sacrifice (U.S. Department of Defense 2006). The Office of Indian Affairs reported in November 1945 that 71 Indian soldiers in the Army had received the Air Medal (vol. 4: 271), 51 had received the Silver Star, 47 received the Bronze Star, and 34 had received the Distinguished Flying Cross (U.S. Department of Defense 2006). Moreover, numerous Purple Hearts were awarded to Native servicemen; this award preserved the outward signs that one had not only engaged the enemy but had shed his own blood for the United States (U.S. Department of the Interior 1944:235–236). Three Indian soldiers received the nation's highest decoration for bravery in battle, the Medal of Honor.

In 1944 Lt. Ernest Childers (fig. 1), a Creek tribal member from Broken Arrow, Oklahoma, was awarded the Medal

Natl. Arch., U.S. Army Signal Corps: 208-N-24772.

Fig. 1. Lt. Ernest Childers, Creek, receiving congratulations from Gen. Jacob L. Devers, July 13, 1944, after being awarded the Congressional Medal of Honor in Italy for destroying 2 enemy machine gun nests.

12

of Honor for his distinguished actions in the fighting in Sicily with the 45th Thunderbird Division. Indeed, it was in Sicily that Childers received a battlefield commission. In September 1943, near Oliveto, Italy, and under machine gun fire, Childers and eight men charged the enemy. In spite of a broken foot in the assault, Childers ordered covering fire and advanced up the kill, singlehandedly killing two snipers and destroying two machine-gun emplacements (U.S. Department of Defense 2006). In doing so, he facilitated the advance of his battalion, which had been in danger of annihilation. Childers's exploits implanted the "warrior" image in the collective American mind. American Indians, in spite of their treatment, were, "brave and loyal fighters for democracy" (U.S. Department of Defense 2006; *New York Times* April 1944). The second recipient of the Medal of Honor was Jack C. Montgomery, an Oklahoma Cherokee and first lieutenant. Montgomery also served with the 45th Infantry Division Thunderbirds. On February 22, 1944, in Italy, Montgomery's rifle platoon was pinned down under heavy fire by three echelons of enemy forces. He singlehandedly attacked all three positions, taking prisoners in the process (U.S. Department of Defense 2006). The third recipient of the Medal of Honor was Van Barfoot, a Choctaw from Mississippi and a second lieutenant in the same infantry division as Childers and Montgomery. In May 1944 on the march from Anzio to Rome, Barfoot wiped out two machine gun embankments, repelled a German tank assault, destroyed a German fieldpiece, carried two wounded commanders to safety, and captured 17 German soldiers—all on the same day (U.S. Department of Defense 2006)!

Perhaps the first American Indian to gain fame in World War II was Maj. Gen. Clarence L. Tinker (fig. 2). Tinker, an Osage tribal member, had become the first person of Native descent since the Civil War to become a general officer in the United States Army. After the attack on Pearl Harbor, Tinker was made commander of the Air Forces in charge of the all-but-destroyed air force in Hawaii. One of America's pioneer bomber pilots, Tinker reorganized the remaining forces and by the Battle of Midway in June 1942, Tinker had turned them into a well-trained, highly disciplined unit. When the Japanese began their assault of Midway Island in early June 1942, Tinker elected to lead a force of the early model B-24 bombers against the retreating Japanese naval forces (U.S. Department of Defense 2006). Refusing to assign anyone else the task, Tinker ignored the danger. Witnesses saw his plane spiral out of control and plunge into the sea near Midway Island; in all, Tinker and eight other crewmen lost their lives (U.S. Department of Defense 2006). Cited for bravery, he was posthumously awarded the Distinguished Service Medal. In the words of John Collier, the Osage general "exemplified the modern Indian soldier" (Collier 1942:30; Vogel 1974:334; Ickes 1944:58). Tinker was not the only high-ranking officer in the military of Indian descent. Listed on the Dawes Commission Rolls as one-eighth Cherokee, Joseph J. "Jocko" Clark was the first American Indian to have received an appointment to

Natl. Arch.:342FC-3A-146277AC.

Fig. 2. Clarence Tinker, Osage. An accomplished flyer who started his flight training in 1920, Tinker held a number of commands in the Army Air corps prior to World War II. Photographed when Tinker was a colonel, 1939.

Annapolis. Clark became a rear admiral and was active in many parts of the Pacific during World War II (Vogel 1974: 335; *New York Times* Jan. 1944).

Less known but no less important are the contributions made by Native women in the armed forces. The Women In Military Service For America Memorial Foundation is actively attempting to fill in the historical gap on Native women veterans. The contributions of these women are significant. As early as the 1898 Spanish-American War, Native women officially served. During the war four Lakota Roman Catholic sisters, of the Congregations of American Sisters, from South Dakota served as nurses. One, Sister Anthony, died as a result of disease and was buried with military honors (Bellafaire 2006). Fourteen Native women served in World War I and nearly 800 Native women served in World War II. Elva (Tapedo) Wale, a Kiowa, joined the Women's Army Corps and became an Air WAC. Another Women's Army Corps volunteer was Bernice (Firstshoot) Bailey from Lodge Pole, Montana. Joining in 1945, she gained the rank of corporal and served until 1948 as part of the army of occupation in Germany (Bellafaire 2006). Many Indian women used military service as a career choice and gained officer rank. Still others joined for the duration of the war.

Private Minnie Spotted Wolf from Butte, Montana (fig. 3), was the first female Native American to join the Marine Corps Women's Reserve. Enlisting in 1943, she had worked her entire life breaking horses, cutting fence posts, driving a two-ton truck and doing typical ranch chores. She commented that Marine boot camp was, "Hard, but not too hard" (Bellafaire 2006). Ola Mildred Rexroat, an Oglala Sioux from the Pine Ridge Reservation, joined the Women's Airforce Service Pilots and towed targets for aerial gunnery students at Eagle Pass Army Air Base in Texas. After the war she joined the Air Force and served another 10 years (Bellafaire 2006).

Native women continued to serve in the armed forces in a variety of capacities following World War II, including service in Korea, Vietnam, and both Gulf wars. The combat death of Pvt. Lori Piestewa during the Second Gulf War (fig. 4) marked the first time a Native woman had died in combat service on foreign soil. This event highlighted the past and present willingness of Native women to fight and, if necessary, to pay the ultimate sacrifice. While Indian women have long served their communities in times of need, they have also served their country as interpreters, spies, and even warriors in individual capacities. World War II saw some of the largest enlistment numbers of Native women in ratio to their population numbers.

The distinctive images of American Indian participation in World War II were the Navajo and Comanche code talkers and a Pima man, Ira Hamilton Hayes (b. 1923, d. 1955) (fig. 5). Hayes became a national hero in 1945 when he and his fellow Marines were photographed raising the American flag on Mount Suribachi during the battle for the island of Iwo Jima. The photograph captured and exemplified the courage, strength, and tenacity of America's struggle against the enemy. Hayes was returned to the United States to help promote the sale of war bonds in 32 cities and, in general, to bolster morale.

Even though Hayes survived the war, he lived in poverty and alcoholism. In 1961, a motion picture of his life, *The Outsider*, helped solidify this image of Indian people after the war. Hayes became, along with hundreds of other Indian veterans, an "outsider," a microcosm that reflected the relative status of Indian people in America (Vogel 1944:329; Friar 1972:216–218; Washburn 1971:80).

If Ira Hayes's life came to symbolize for Whites what had happened to Indian veterans after the war, the Navajo code talkers became the symbol of the great contribution Indians made during the war (fig. 6). Early in 1942 the Marine Corps recruited an all-Navajo platoon at the Navajos' request (Sergeant 1942:709). When basic training ended in July of that year the men were assigned to units overseas. In battle the Navajos acquitted themselves with much glory, attracting coverage in the national press (*New York Times* July 1942). During the war their mission had been kept secret. Trained in communications, they had employed the Navajo language as a code, which helped in large measure to foil the Japanese attempts to break the advance of American

13

top, Women in the Military Service For America Memorial Foundation, Inc., Washington, D.C.; bottom, Natl. Arch., USMC photo:208-NS-4350-2.

Fig. 3. Women in the military during World War II. top, Elva (Tapedo) Wale, Kiowa, who joined the Women's Army Corps and became an Air WAC, working on bases around the U.S. bottom, Minnie Spotted Wolf (left), Crow, in the Marine Corps, Celia Mix, Potawatomi (center), and Viola Eastman, Chippewa (right) were photographed at Camp Lejeune, N.C., in 1943.

marines in the Pacific. In 1945, when it was revealed that the Navajo language had helped the United States win the war against Japan, the code talkers became national heroes and part of the American folklore (*New York Times* Sept. 1942). Not so well known but equally important, the Army Signal Corps recruited Comanche code talkers for service in the European theater 12 months before the war began (Bernstein 1991:46; Meadows 2002; Stabler 2005). In the postwar years nearly every motion picture that depicted the fighting in the Pacific contained scenes of (usually anonymous) Indians speaking their Native language into field radios and leaving the enemy hopelessly confused and ready to be soundly defeated (Paul 1973).

Women in Military Service For America Memorial Foundation, Inc., Washington, D.C.

Fig. 4. Pfc Lori Piestewa from Tuba City, Ariz. Her Hopi father was a Vietnam veteran; her grandfather was a World War I veteran. Piestewa was a member of the Army's 507th Army Maintenance Company that lost its way and was ambushed in Nasiriyah, Iraq, March 23, 2003. She was taken prisoner and died soon after of her injuries. Photographed at Ft. Bliss, Tex., 2003.

Natl. Arch.: 75-N-PIM-33.

Fig. 5. Ira Hamilton Hayes, Pima, who joined the Marine Corps after the outbreak of World War II and trained at the Marine Corps Parachutist School in San Diego, Calif., one of 3 Native American Marines to do so. In 1945 he participated in the American invasion of Iwo Jima. Hayes, 4 other Marines, and a Navy hospital corpsman raised the second U.S. flag on Mt. Suribachi in the iconic photograph by Associated Press photographer Joe Rosenthal. Photographed in 1943.

**Contributions on the Home Front**

American Indians gave the United States more than heroes. Indian people also contributed food and money to the war effort. The Crows of Montana offered their reservation's resources and tribal funds to the government for the duration of the war (*New York Times* Jan. 1942). The Navajo, Wind River Shoshone (Franco 1997:100), and several other tribal governments authorized the secretary of the Interior to purchase war bonds from tribal funds (*New York Times* Jan. and April 1945). In this manner alone the tribes contributed millions of dollars to the war effort. In 1944 Secretary Harold Ickes reported that at least two million dollars worth of bonds had been purchased by Indians in one year (Ickes 1944:58). In that same year Indian Commissioner John Collier estimated that the total American Indian commitment to the war effort in monetary terms amounted to approximately 50 million dollars (U.S. Department of the Interior 1944:238).

Throughout the war Indian men and women not already in the armed forces left the reservations to find work in the cities. The war had, of course, expanded industry and the war economy was booming; jobs were easy to obtain and easy to keep. It was estimated that between 1941 and 1945, approximately 40,000 American Indians left their home areas to work in the factories of a wartime nation. John Collier called this movement ". . . the greatest exodus of Indians" that had ever taken place. More importantly, it was looked upon as an inspiring commitment to the United States, made especially poignant by the fact that prior to the war, Native peoples had not been welcomed outside their homelands (U.S. Department of the Interior 1944:237; Dale 1949:230).

Native women participated in the armed forces as WACS, WAVES, and the Army Nurse Corps, and they also participated in the war effort on the home front. By 1944, the reservations were critically short of a male workforce so Indian women accounted for most of the food production. They drove heavy equipment, repaired tractors, and herded cattle. Principally because of Native women, the production of Indian livestock doubled between 1933 and 1943. Agricultural output greatly increased as well, accounting for a significant rise in the standard of living on many reservations compared to the terrible conditions of the Depression years. Whether on the home front or war front, Native women served the United States with the same fervor and commitment as the men. By 1945 it was estimated that nearly 150,000 American Indians directly participated in the industrial, agricultural, and military aspects of the American war effort (U.S. Department of the Interior 1944:237; Ickes 1944:58; Ritzenthaler 1943:325–326).

Tribal councils seldom needed prodding to support the war effort. Native Nations formed civil defense units and served as airplane spotters and air-raid wardens on rotating shifts. Home guard units were detailed to protect strategically important sites. The Kashia Indian Reservation near Stewart's Point, California, organized 17 tribal members to patrol the countryside for saboteurs (Townsend 2000:172). The Klamath of Oregon passed a resolution to allow the building of an airstrip for training pilots. The United Pueblos offered all their automobiles and trucks to the New Mexico Carrier Association for transportation of war-related material (Bernstein 1991:68). Other tribes purchased hundreds of thousands of dollars of war bonds. Others, such as the Red River band of Chippewas, the Montana Crow, and the Columbia River and Quileute pledged the resources from herding, trapping, or fishing on reservation land. The Cheyenne River Sioux leased 288,746 acres of tribal land and 43,546 acres of trust allotments for an aerial gunnery range. The areas, relatively free from bad weather and large production activities, were attractive to the defense effort for use as airports, aerial gunnery ranges, and bombing ranges. While some tribes benefited from the leases, others, such as the Pine Ridge Reservation in South Dakota, did not. The 1942 leases and land purchases forced some Indians from

15

their homes, and only 10 percent managed to return to livestock industry at the end of the war (Franco 1999:102–103).

Two reservations were even called upon to participate in the government's internment of Japanese Americans. In 1942 the War Relocation Authority gave the Indian Bureau the care of 20,000 Japanese Americans. Forced from their homes on the Pacific coast, these American citizens of Japanese descent were sent to the Colorado River and Gila River Indian reservations, in the Arizona desert, home to the Mohave and the Pima, respectively (Sergeant 1942:709; U.S. Department of the Interior 1945:238).

There were a great number of other Indian contributions. In the press American Indians were used to boost morale. Newspapers and magazines projected images of Indians as being loyal, brave, trustworthy fighters dedicated to the American cause. To most Americans the war was a duel to the death between democracy and fascism. It was a war to free the people of the world from the clutches of Nazi totalitarianism. American Indians, in throwing themselves wholeheartedly into the war effort, seemed to validate the American sense of mission. Indians, they reasoned, had been treated miserably yet even they were totally committed to the American crusade against the Nazis. One young Columbia River tribal member noted that although his people had been badly treated by the United States, Hitler, he reasoned would be much worse. "We know that under Nazism we should have no rights at all," he said, "we would be treated as slaves" (Neuberger 1942:628).

The media outlook on American Indians during the war years was decidedly ambiguous. The press generally viewed the Indian war effort as a great boost to the nation's morale. During the first years of the war, groups of American Indians adopted and made "chiefs" of Franklin D. Roosevelt, Gen. Douglas MacArthur, Wendell Willkie, and even Joseph Stalin (*New York Times* Feb. and June 1942, Feb. 1944). In an effort to show autonomy, tribes individually declared war on the Axis. The League of the Iroquois in New York had never ceased hostilities with Germany. The Grand Council of the League simply renewed their declaration of war made in 1917 and included Italy and Japan. Many tribal dancers and singers aided war bond rallies and elders posed in their war bonnets for pictures with young men in their new uniforms. The entire press coverage of American Indians during the war was geared to give the impression that Indian people were not only aiding other Americans in the war effort but also hoping to share in the victory over fascism and become part of the American democratic way of life.

## The Choice to Fight

Reasons for responding to the nation's call to arms were as varied as the individuals and Indian Nations who served, but there were some commonalities. While some Indian people had a strong urge to become accepted by the general population on the basis of their war efforts, still others chose to serve in order to stand by treaties their nation had made with the United States government. This is an important consideration, since treaties were guaranteed and carried the weight of supreme law. Even though the United States government had often abrogated treaties at will and had eroded Indian sovereignty to wardship status, internal tribal sovereignty remained generally intact. Bound by treaties and cases of law, the United States had a fiduciary and federal trust responsibility to tribal nations. Should the United States lose the war, these federal trust responsibilities and sovereignty of Indian Nations would no longer be upheld.

Some called on the warrior spirit of Native people, especially among those Indian nations with just such a heritage (vol. 13:822). Additionally, there were benefits in active service, such as the opportunity to learn a trade and contribute to the home reservation economy. For those who hoped to be welcomed into the non-Indian society after victory, they saw their efforts as working favorably toward this end. "We want to win the war," an Indian rancher reportedly said, "because victory will mean new hope for men and women who have no hope" (Neuberger 1942:630). Perhaps a more common reason and in many ways more important, a great many Indian peoples viewed their participation in the war effort as opportunity for strengthening their own communities as Indian people, allowing for a move into the greater society without giving up their Indian identity and culture.

top, The White House; bottom left, Natl. Arch.:127USMC #69889-B; bottom, Natl. Arch.:137, Hist. of Mus. and Records Relating to Public Affairs, USMC Reserve and Histl. Studies, 1942–1948, Box 5, folder 6, part 1.

Fig. 6. Navajo code talkers. top, Pres. George W. Bush awarding Congressional Gold Medals in a ceremony in the rotunda of the U.S. Capitol, July 26, 2001, to 4 of the 5 surviving original code talkers (left to right): Allen June, Lloyd Oliver, Chester Nez (hidden), and John Brown, Jr. Brown addressed the assembly, expressing thankfulness in being honored, pride in his service, and the importance of remembering the servicemen who gave their lives during the war. The Congressional Gold Medal was awarded to each of the original 29 Navajo code talkers as well as a silver medal to each man who later qualified as a code talker. It is estimated that 375–420 Navajos served as code talkers. The program remained classified until 1968 (Jevec 2001). bottom left, Corp. Henry Bake, Jr., and Pfc. George H. Kirk, Navajos serving with the Marine Signal Unit, operating a portable radio set in the jungle close behind the front lines, at Bougainville, Solomon Is., Dec. 1943. The code talkers served as communicators only in the Asian theater. bottom right, Navajo code, consisting of 211 works, most of which were Navajo terms that had been given an additional military meaning, for example, 'fighter plane' for the Navajo word for 'hummingbird' and 'squad' for 'black sheep.' In addition, they devised Navajo names for the 26 letters of the English alphabet. Words not included in the 211 terms were spelled out using the alphabet.

In its renewed declaration of war against Germany, Japan, and Italy, the Six Nations of the Iroquois not only demonstrated that Indian and White Americans shared a common belief in democracy but also made a pronounced statement against the racist policies of Nazi Germany without mentioning the racism at home. One council member wrote, "It is the unanimous sentiment among the Indian people that the atrocities of the Axis nations are violently repulsive to all sense of righteousness of our people" (Neuberger 1942:629–630). Other Indian people saw the Axis powers as a threat to liberty. The Cheyennes condemned the German, Japanese, and Italian alliance as, "an unholy triangle whose purpose is to conquer and enslave the bodies, minds and souls of all free people"(Neuberger 1942:629). A number of California Indians representing 30 reservations simply thought of themselves as loyal American citizens ready to aid the country. This same group was, at the time, engaged in several lawsuits and claims against the United States government. When war came they telegraphed President Roosevelt indicating their readiness to serve "our great Nation" (Collier 1944:30; Franco 1997). In the same vein, the Navajo tribal council declared that "any un-American movement among our people will be resented and dealt with severely" (Ickes 1944:58).

Among some tribes a strong warrior tradition still existed. The ideologies of most tribal groups and nearly all the tribes with the strongest war traditions were based on ideals of continuity and order. In traditional societies there was a common belief that the Creator had placed the group on earth for a specific reason. Tradition and religion were so integrated as to be inseparable. Tribal social, economic, and ecological order must be maintained or the entire system would be thrown out of balance and the "good life" destroyed. Tribal societies were not static. There were adaptations and changes as in every other social group; however, certain obligations to tradition still had to be maintained. Much of Native American ceremonialism came out of the effort to preserve the social continuity of the tribe and to observe certain obligations to the retention of the traditional view of world order.

Within tribes with a strong warrior tradition, such as the Sioux and Kiowa of the Plains, the keepers of social philosophy and tribal ceremony were most often males who had counted coup on an enemy of the tribe and therefore, on an enemy of the continuity of tribal conceptions of order. After the Indian wars and the end of battling traditional enemies, the number of these prestigious people began to dwindle. The soldier societies to which many of these men belonged were rapidly becoming devoid of members. Because there were no wars, the younger men were not able to count coup and become part of the warrior society. The ceremonies of the warrior societies also began to die out. The world wars offered many Indian people the opportunity of becoming, not just American servicemen, but soldiers in the tribal meaning of the term.

Because World War II lasted longer and therefore offered more opportunity to become involved, it gave some Indian servicemen and women the chance to gain prestige among the Whites, and more importantly, obtain status within their own tribes. Kiowa veterans of World War II, for instance, were able to revive the Gourd Dance, a ceremony from the warrior society (vol. 13:919–920, 1018–1019), where previously only a handful of men had status as a result of war to participate in the ceremonies. The revival of the society, which has since become splintered, meant that a ceremonial obligation to the cultural viability of the tribe could be retained and with it, the Kiowa ideals of order and social continuity. Victory dances were held after the war by several tribes. One Hunkpapa Sioux ceremony held at Little Eagle, South Dakota, gave a great deal of prestige to the returning veterans because they were able to take part in the dance with Takes-His-Gun, an elder and veteran of the tribal wars who symbolized the continuity of Hunkpapa society (J.H. Howard 1951:36).

The warrior tradition within tribal societies became an explanation for all Indian participants in the war. John Collier reported that many Indian men, young and old alike, came to the agencies with rifles in hand, ready to sign up for the army and "proceed immediately to the scene of the fighting" (Collier 1942:29; Neuberger 1942:79). A Blackfeet, contemptuous of the selective service system, was said to have stated, "Since when has it been necessary for Blackfeet to draw lots to fight?" (Neuberger 1942:630).

These commitments made by Indian men and women to the war effort, through active military service, economic and resource contributions, and supportive home-front activities, were not without adverse consequences. Many Americans viewed Indian heroism as evidence of equality as citizens. Therefore, the "special status" of Indian tribes should be dismantled. This philosophy was one argument for the termination policy of the 1950s and 1960s ("Termination and Relocation," this vol.).

# Termination and Relocation

LARRY W. BURT

Termination and relocation represented the last attempts in longstanding federal Indian policies to assimilate Indians. More specifically the goal was to dissolve traditional cultures, to end the special status of Indians based on the acceptance of some degree of separate tribal sovereignty as distinct political entities, and to withdraw the government from Indian affairs and delivery of services to Native Americans. Relocation became one of the central components of the termination movement. Its purpose was to move Indians as individuals or as families off reservations and into urban areas. It was sometimes referred to as "individual termination" because Indians lost access to federal Indian assistance programs that existed on reservations.

## Background and Origins

In the 1930s under the presidency of Franklin Roosevelt, Secretary of the Interior Harold Ickes and Commissioner of Indian Affairs John Collier and the Indian Reorganization Act of 1934 had made major strides toward halting the forced assimilation policies that had dominated federal Indian policy since the late 1800s. They led a generation of Indian policy reformers who looked less to religion, less to the ideology of universal stages of human development of anthropologist Lewis Henry Morgan, and less to the social Darwinism of British intellectual Herbert Spencer than the assimilationists of the past. Instead, they turned increasingly to anthropologists like Franz Boas, Ruth Benedict, and Alfred Kroeber, whose theories of cultural pluralism contributed to a greater understanding and toleration of the traditions of native people. In what became known as the Indian New Deal they attempted to turn federal Indian policy toward accepting native cultures and returning to the bilateral, tribe-to-government, relations of the past (Ragsdale 1989:422–423; Kelly 1983:291–299; vol. 4:72–74, 265–268).

The Indian Reorganization Act made permanent the trust status of allotments and banned any further allotment under the 1887 Dawes Severalty Act. It initiated conservation measures to protect the remaining Indian land base, and it created a revolving fund credit program to help finance both tribal and individual business enterprise to improve the dismal economies on most reservations. Perhaps most important in the long term the Act encouraged self-government by encouraging Native Americans to organize politically. They could draw up constitutions and elect their own political leadership, giving them a greater voice in the decision-making process (Washburn 1973, 3:2209–2017).

With the waning of Franklin Roosevelt's New Deal liberalism during and after World War II, conservative opponents of the Indian New Deal had enough political strength to launch a drive to pull federal policy back in their direction. Most of John Collier's opponents—Sens. Elmer Thomas of Oklahoma, Lynn Frazier of North Dakota, and Burton Wheeler of Montana—were also some of the most outspoken critics of the New Deal. Most of them shared much the same motivation as the assimilationists of the late nineteenth and early twentieth centuries. They believed that Indian sovereignty could not coexist with American sovereignty and that individual rights based on United States citizenship should displace tribal rights based on membership in any Indian group. They looked at Native American cultures as "museum pieces" and criticized Collier and the Reorganization Act for taking Indians "back to the blanket" (Armstrong 1945:47–52; Watkins 1954:457; Myer 1953:193).

What emerged was a "liberation" view of federal Indian policy. Paternalistic government programs of sending bureaucrats to go on reservations and teach and enforce assimilation had failed. Only a sink-or-swim approach to integrating Indians as individuals rather than as tribes would succeed. "Terminationist" later became the label for this position. Advocates called for an end to the reservation system and a withdrawal of the government's role in Indian affairs by eliminating the Indian Reorganization Act, the Bureau of Indian Affairs, and separate tribal sovereignty. Native Americans should be dealt with the same as other Americans. They saw the Bureau as another unnecessary and stifling government bureaucracy. Native Americans needed to be freed from government paternalism and from the restrictions of separate Indian culture and status. Indian trust land status and tribal economic development violated the free marketplace based on individual property rights and private enterprise. They only prevented Indians from integrating into American life and competing as individuals in an open economy and society (Burt 1982:4–5, 19–20).

Assimilationists of the mid-twentieth century added another rationale to support their position. Some merged the anticommunism of the post-World War I period with their hatred of New Deal programs and bureaucracies and saw reservations as little better than concentration camps with Indian traditions of communal land ownership too closely resembling the ways of communist totalitarianism. By the mid-1940s critics of the Indian New Deal in Congress had blunted Collier's efforts by cutting funding levels and blocking any further legislation they opposed (*Congressional Record* 1951:13402, 1952:2493, 1953:10294).

In the post-World War II period, other forces outside of Native American communities came to support termination. During the war the government had invested heavily in the development of infrastructure in the American West that would contribute to a vibrant economic boom. Farmers, ranchers, miners, manufacturers, and the lumber industry sought out as much undeveloped land as possible. Indian lands in trust held some of the best remaining untapped resources, and termination held the promise of opening new areas to economic expansion. Local governments in this rapidly growing West looked for new sources of revenue to pay for increasing administrative and operating expenses, and subjecting Indian land to taxation seemed a promising way to help solve the problem. Conservatives in Congress also searched for ways to cut federal expenditures, and Indian programs became one of many targets for those who worked to lower the federal budget. In addition, the postwar economic boom nationally, technological innovations, and the explosion in the consumer culture all seemed to lend credibility to the assimilation that terminations promoted by encouraging a common assumption that everyone wanted to live like modern White Americans (G. Nash 1977:197–212; Burt 1982:4–5; Davies 1966:132).

Factors originating within reservations and Indian communities contributed to the momentum toward termination. Indian opinion was mixed on the issue. Some Indians favored termination, especially those who had left their reservations and become assimilated into non-Indian communities or who had lived on or near reservations that had not maintained traditions as much as others. A number of Native American World War II veterans had grown accustomed to the more equal treatment and status they had experienced in the military and lobbied for the removal of barriers to full individual rights, such as laws against liquor sales to Indians in some states. Such efforts did not always mean support for the kind of termination envisioned by non-Indians. Few at the time realized the complexities of Indian status and rights. Only decades later did many come to understand that civil rights sometimes meant different things to different people. For many Indians, tribal rights based on separate sovereignty were just as important as individual rights (Bernstein 1991:24–44, 58, 87, 110, 114).

For a large, industrial society mobilizing to battle against fascism, it quickly became obvious that the social complications of racism impeded the smooth prosecution of the war. Moreover, racism seemed outdated and simply wrong in the broader context of a nation of diverse people unified in a common cause. A segregated American military fighting a crusade against fascism and its beliefs in racial inequality invited comparison to the embarrassing contradiction in America's historical treatment of its own racial minorities. The war also provided rich opportunity to link war goals of defending democracy internationally to movements for expanding democracy and civil rights at home. African-Americans fought for "Double V," victory both abroad and at home. Minority veterans came out of the war with the conviction that they should not have to return to a status of anything less than full inclusion and equality (McCullough 1992:588; Hamby 1973:188–189, 214, 232–233, 243, 291).

At first, those congressmen leading the terminationist campaign against the Indian Reorganization Act were not otherwise supporters of the emerging civil rights movement. Opponents came from both parties, but they were all critics of the New Deal from western states. Some from both parties had ties to non-Indian economic interests that saw individualistic assimilation as the best means to gain access to resources on Indian lands unavailable to them under restricted trust status. In the late 1930s and 1940s, critics introduced bills to repeal the Indian Reorganization Act, to strip the Bureau of authority to manage tribal funds, to remove trust restrictions on allotments, and to allow states to extend their penal laws over reservations. They did not yet have the votes for any dramatic policy reversal, but they eventually succeeded in stalling the Indian New Deal by cutting its funding levels, blocking any further legislation, and insisting that the Bureau plan for federal withdrawal from Indian affairs (Stefon 1978:4–5; Burt 1982:4–5; Painter 1981:3, 10–15).

In response, Collier came up with a long-term plan to get the government out of Indian affairs. But his version of assimilation included assimilating Indians as tribes more than as individuals in order to protect tribal autonomy and self-government. His plan called for rehabilitating reservations at federal expense and gradually transferring the government's role to tribal councils. The Bureau generated specific rehabilitation plans for several reservations, but they collected dust. Congress was unwilling to spend the necessary money and the plans languished without support. Commissioner Collier resigned in 1945, but he remained confident that what he had left behind would survive the difficult political climate and represent a lasting legacy (Tyler 1964:27, 29–30; Hasse 1974:42–54; Collier 1963).

The departure of the small group of committed cultural pluralists within the Department of the Interior signaled a fundamental shift in the administration of Indian affairs. Harold Ickes left in early 1946, and Felix Cohen, assistant solicitor of the Bureau and one of the authors of the Reorganization Act, did the same in late 1947. Collier, Ickes, and Cohen fought on in the press to defend the Indian New Deal, but they were outsiders now. The next three commissioners—William Brophy, John Nichols, and William Zimmerman (acting)—faced the same kind of opposition from congressional assimilationists as Collier did. While they favored Collier's plan for federal withdrawal, they were less forceful in promoting the cultural preservation and separate tribal sovereignty dimensions of the Indian New Deal. Ickes's replacement as secretary of the interior was Julius Krug, most recently head of the War Production Board and a professional bureaucrat. Liberals saw him as too favorable to big business, but he could be sensitive to minority issues. He often accepted recommendations from his commissioners in opposing assimilationist legislation, but he lacked Ickes's drive as an Indian policy reformer and his interest and experience in Indian affairs (Collier 1949:276–278, 1949a:22–26; Cohen 1948:161–167, 1948a:1–8; Philp 1999:69–71, 76, 80–83).

## Termination Legislation

The 1946 off-term elections swept Republicans into control of Congress for the first time since 1930 and put terminationists into their strongest position since the Indian New Deal. Conservatives in this Eightieth Congress sought to reverse as many of Roosevelt's liberal policies as possible. Assimilationists advocating termination still took little interest in larger civil rights issues and came to include Republican Sens. Arthur Watkins of Utah, Hugh Butler of Nebraska, and Karl Mundt of South Dakota; Republican Reps. Wesley D'Ewart of Montana and E.Y. Berry and Francis Case of South Dakota; Democratic Sens. Clinton Anderson and Dennis Chavez both of New Mexico; and Democratic Rep. Reva Beck Basone of Utah.

The actions of congressional terminationists were piecemeal and not coordinated into a coherent movement. Watkins and Butler introduced a bill for the termination of California Indians. Separate bills in the House called for ending Indian trust land status, eliminating bans on liquor sales, and providing an avenue for voluntary termination through a vote by tribal members. The Department of the Interior and some congressional Democrats opposed most individual tribal termination bills in committee actions, arguing that tribes under consideration were not ready. With only one exception, bills getting beyond committee action in the Eightieth Congress were minor, local matters that did little to affect overall policy (*Congressional Quarterly Almanac* 1948:325–26, 493, 688–89; U.S. Congress. House. Subcommittee on Indian Affairs 1947).

The only major piece of legislation affecting Indian policy in 1946 was one that all sides agreed upon. The Indian Claims Commission Act created a special court to hear cases by tribes against the government for inadequate compensation in land settlements or failure to properly administer responsibilities over trust lands. Previously, each group first had to go through the cumbersome process of obtaining special enabling legislation from Congress to sue the government. Some supported the Indian Claims Commission Act for reasons of justice, efficiency, or the many worthwhile things that settlement money could do on reservations desperately in need economic development. Terminationists, however, saw it as a final settlement between antagonists so that no controversies over past dealings with Indians would linger after tribes were terminated. President Harry Truman worried about the cost of Indian claims settlements. The inflationary economy of the postwar years created strong pressure to reduce federal expenditures. The Eightieth Congress twice came close to overriding presidential vetoes of tax reduction bills and would not accept any spending increases. But when Wyoming Democratic Rep. Joseph O'Mahoney, Chair of the House Committee on Interior and Insular Affairs, convinced Truman that the claims bill would reduce Bureau expenditures over the long term, Truman backed the measure and ensured its passage (Lurie 1978:97–110; Vance 1969:325–336; Truman 1946:414; Watkins 1957:50; Tyler 1964:27, 29–30; Hasse 1974:42–54).

The easing of budgetary concerns allowed President Truman to support the Indian Claims Commission bill based on his growing sense of justice and advancing civil rights. In fact, Truman proved a bit more assertive than Roosevelt in promoting civil rights for racial minorities overall. By the time he entered politics in the 1920s, he had developed a strong belief in the Constitution as a solid anchor, a source and protector of liberties and freedoms. In a 1940 campaign speech that was surprisingly bold for the time and place he expressed belief in "the brotherhood of all men before the law," arguing that "if any class or race can be permanently set apart from, or pushed down below the rest in political and civil rights, so may any other class or race." The federal government, according to Truman, had the responsibility to guarantee equal treatment before the law, equality of opportunity, and civil rights for all Americans (D.R. McCoy and R.T. Ruetten 1973:61, 65; M.R. Gardner 2002:6).

The divide in the Democratic Party muted the civil rights issue even after the Democrats regained control of Congress in the 1948 election. In Indian affairs, Democrats promoted no alternative to termination, but their leadership of key congressional committees kept tribal termination bills from getting beyond committee action. The only major Indian policy bill in the Eighty-first Congress was the Navajo-Hopi Rehabilitation Act of 1950, a response to the national press coverage of the poverty and lack of economic development on the Southwest reservations. Inevitable comparisons with the dollars recently approved in the Marshall Plan for the rehabilitation of war-torn western Europe generated widespread congressional support for assistance to people in need at home (J.L. Freeman 1950; R.W. Young 1961:1).

The legislation roughly conformed to the rehabilitation portion of the plans for federal withdrawal that Collier had devised before leaving office. It therefore drew the ire of terminationists on the Senate Public Lands Committee, who eliminated money from the bill for "futile" rehabilitation projects because a "short-sighted" Bureau would administer it. In the rare and fleeting limelight of national public attention, Arizona Democrat Richard F. Harless's amendment to restore the appropriation prevailed. Terminationists tried one more time to put their own stamp on the bill by supporting an amendment by Rep. Antonio M. Fernandez of New Mexico to put both the Hopi and Navajo reservations under state jurisdiction, but Truman vetoed the bill because of Indian opposition to the amendment. Congress removed the state take-over provision, and the president signed the bill the next year (*Congressional Quarterly Almanac* 1948:565).

Within the White House there was one staunch opponent of termination. Anthropologist Philleo Nash, whose uncle had served as special assistant to commissioner John Collier, worked in the Office of War Information from 1942 to 1946. After that, he became special assistant to David K. Niles, Truman's special assistant on racial relations. Nash understood the implications of the policy choices the administration faced and recognized that Indian policy was dangerously adrift. In a 1949 memo to Niles he referred sarcastically to a "semblance of an Indian policy we now have," and noted that recent handling of the Navajo-Hopi situation highlighted the "floundering" of the Bureau of Indian Affairs. Nash urged the administration to "find and state our goals and set some standards of performance against which bills and programs can be measured." Almost prophetically, he predicted "a number of bad bills freeing the Indians are going to be thrown at us unless we get some orientation on this problem into the Interior Department and out to the country" (Nash 1949:35, 54–55, 84–85, 1949a:1–3, 5).

Truman paid no attention to Nash's warnings, and instead his actions were guided by the need to compromise with a fiscally conservative Congress and by his overall understanding of civil rights for minorities. Congress passed Public Law 162, setting up a Commission on Organization of the Executive Branch of Government to recommend how federal services might be made more efficient and costs reduced. The recommendations of this bipartisan commission became known as the Hoover Report, because former President Herbert Hoover served as chair. The report offered ways of cutting costs in the executive branch. In Indian affairs, it criticized the cultural pluralism promoted by the Indian Reorganization Act and embraced assimilation as the primary federal goal (Leuchtenburg 1983:12–15; U.S. Commission on Organization of the Executive Branch of the Government 1949).

Dillon Myer became the first commissioner after passage of the Reorganization Act to advocate termination. He had little inclination as a social reformer and had no experience with Indian matters. He tried to dismantle reservations as he had Japanese-American internment camps after World War II. Nash lobbied to have Myer forced out, but his influence proved no greater than in his earlier advice for the administration to develop a coherent Indian policy. Myer also clashed with Indians and with tribes, an early indication that most Indians did not want termination at the expense of their native identity or tribal sovereignty (Myer 1951:346–353).

President Truman did not live long enough to see the outcome of Nash's predictions about bad bills coming from Congress if the administration did not develop a credible Indian policy. Truman had not sided with terminationists in Congress, largely because of opposition from Indians or the Department of the Interior. Neither was he aware of the policy void caused by inattention and confusion that would allow much more aggressive and organized terminationists to shape Indian policy. He had acted on behalf of both individual civil rights for Indians and on behalf of the rights of particular tribes, and like many Americans, he saw no distinction between the two (Philp 1999:79–80).

In the deliberations of Truman's Committee on Civil Rights, the history of Indian self-government and the issue of tribal rights were recognized. However, in its final report, *To Secure These Rights* (S.F. Lawson 2004), the only mention of particular Indian rights involved violations of state citizenship rights, such as Arizona and New Mexico's denying Indians the right to vote. And even those examples were included within a long list of violations experienced by many minority groups (D.B. McCoy and R.T. Ruetten 1973:84–89, 204; Bernstein 1991:164; Carr 1947).

Terminationists used some of the same rhetoric as the civil rights movement—terms like emancipation, freedom, and liberation. To further confuse matters, Truman shared much of the terminationists' disdain for the Bureau of Indian Affairs. He wrote "The Government created Indian bureaus for the alleged protection of Indian rights. Every one of our Indian bureaus in Washington was saddled with crooks and cheats." But the reasons for his anti-Bureau sentiments were different from those of terminationists. Instead of seeing the Bureau as an obstacle to Indians mixing and competing with the mainstream, he saw it as a big part of the violation of Indian rights throughout history (Truman 1989:285).

In *Where the Buck Stops* Truman devoted a seven-page chapter to Indians. All but the last two paragraphs decried the historic mistreatment of Indians. He read history, he likely knew more about Indian history than most presidents, and he even showed sympathy for wrongs committed against tribes as well as individual Indians. But he did not address his own policies, except that he "tried to look after Indian rights all the time I was president." For evidence he offered a couple of the cases where he vetoed bills that he felt exploited Indians. While he was willing to aggressively use the power of the federal government to champion civil rights, he never understood Indian status sufficiently to perceive that his own policies needed to go beyond just defending certain tribes when Congress tried to perpetrate an injustice (Truman 1989:281–288).

When Dwight D. Eisenhower won the presidential election and Republicans took control of the Congress in 1953, terminationists forged ahead with their agenda. Eisenhower selected as commissioner of Indian affairs a terminationist banker from New Mexico, Glenn Emmons. The first significant legislative measure involved the transfer of law-and-order jurisdiction on reservations. For over a century tribes had shared responsibility with federal and state governments in a tangle of jurisdictional authority. In the late 1940s congress had passed several bills giving jurisdiction over specific groups to certain states. These were generally noncontroversial, usually because tribes did not have their own courts or effective police (Wilkinson and Biggs 1977: 148–151).

In the 1953 session the House Subcommittee on Indian Affairs introduced separate legislation that would transfer Indian jurisdiction in California, Minnesota, Nebraska, Oregon, and Wisconsin. The subcommittee combined the bills and promoted it as part of the broader effort to withdraw the federal government from Indian affairs. The Red Lake Chippewa of Minnesota, the Warm Springs Band of Oregon, and the Menominee of Wisconsin voiced objection, so the proposal was amended to exempt them. But then Rep. Hugh Butler of Nebraska added provisions that would allow any state to assume jurisdiction by legislation or by changes in state constitutions. Congress passed Public Law 280 on August 15, 1953 (Burt 1982:24–25).

Opposition followed almost immediately. Many Indian-advocacy groups and tribes voiced strong objection. Indians feared the loss of treaty rights, such as hunting and fishing, if they had to conform to state recreation regulation, and they anticipated discrimination with Indians having to appear before state officials and courts dominated by non-Indians. President Eisenhower criticized the measure because it included no provision for Indian consent before state takeover, and he suggested an amendment providing for tribal approval. But he signed it anyway, and Congress made no such change for prior consent. Over subsequent years Public Law 280 became one of the most hated of termination policies, but fears never became reality because any state that considered taking over law-and-order jurisdiction insisted that the federal government reimburse states for the added costs, and Congress provided no such funding (Burt 1982:25).

The next important congressional action came when Rep. William Henry Harrison of Wyoming introduced House Concurrent Resolution 108 in 1953. It expressed goals of phasing out the Bureau of Indian Affairs and subjecting Indians to the same rights and responsibilities as other American citizens. It called for the termination of the Flathead, Klamath, Menominee, Potawatomi, and Turtle Mountain Chippewa tribes and all groups within California, Florida, New York, and Texas. Individual bills for terminating some of these groups had been introduced in Congress in the previous few years. Resolution 108 passed August 1, 1954, without debate on the consent calendar with few congressmen aware of it (Fixico 1986:93–94).

With the opening of the 1954 congressional session Congress moved to implement Resolution 108. To expedite the process Sen. Arthur V. Watkins scheduled joint hearings of members of both House and Senate subcommittees on In-dian affairs to consider bills to terminate particular tribes. Each tribal member would be entitled to an interest in group assets. Tribes could choose to sell all group assets and distribute the proceeds, organize into corporations under state law, or choose a private trustee to replace the Bureau. If they did not take action, the secretary of the interior would appoint a trustee, sell all tribal assets, and dispense the returns. Trust status on individual Indian allotments would end on a specified date, and thereafter all tribal members would become subject to the same laws as non-Indians. Indian Reorganization Act charters and all tribal sovereignty and governing authority would be revoked (Fixico 1986:103–104; Burt 1982:30).

Watkins started with six bands of Southern Paiute and Western Shoshone in Utah, even though they had not been specified in Resolution 108. Hearings were also held on the Alabama-Coushatta of Texas, the Potawatomi of Oklahoma, about 60 small bands in western Oregon, the Klamath of Oregon, the Confederated Salish and Kootenai of the Flathead Reservation in Montana, the Seminole of Florida, the Chippewa on the Turtle Mountain Reservation in North Dakota, over 100 small groups in California, the Menominee of Wisconsin, and seven bands of Shoshones and Paiutes in Nevada. Strong opposition voiced in the hearings clearly limited legislative success. Congress quickly passed bills terminating the Menominee, then the western Oregon bands, the Klamath, and four bands of Southern Paiutes. Over the next eight years, Congress also terminated the Peoria, Wyandot, and Ottawa of Oklahoma, and 38 small groups in California (Fixico 1986:99–106).

As individual termination bills were implemented, it became clear that while a few terminated tribes made it through the change relatively well, the transition in most cases was difficult and the impact devastating. Many groups sank deeper into poverty, and the problems created usually far outweighed any benefits or improvements. In the end 106 groups and 10,922 individual Indians were terminated (table 1) by 14 bills, but most of the groups were small and with little land or had enough largely assimilated members who were favorable to give the appearance of tribal acceptance. The exceptions were the Menominee (Peroff 1982) and the Klamath (Stern 1965). Terminationists worked especially hard on these groups in the hope that they might become models for future action (Burt 1982:47). The terminated tribes represented only about 3 percent of the total number of individuals and 3.2 percent of trust land. These numbers diminished over the next decades because Congress restored the status of many of the affected groups (Ragsdale 1989:432).

## Reducing the Government's Role in Indian Affairs

Commissioner of Indian Affairs Emmons did everything within his authority to withdraw federal functions and gov-

**Table 1. Tribes Terminated**

| Group | Number | Acres | Effective date |
|---|---|---|---|
| Menominee, Wis. | 2,221 | 233,881 | 1961 |
| Klamath, Oreg. | 2,133 | 617,000 | 1961 |
| 61 Western Oreg. bands | 2,903 | 253 | 1956 |
| Alabama-Coushatta, Texas | 385 | 3,200 | 1955 |
| Mixed-Blood Utes, Utah | 269 | 21,143 | 1961 |
| Southern Paiute, Utah | 130 | 42,893 | 1957 |
| Lower Lake Rancheria, Calif. | 8 | 99.5 | 1956 |
| Peoria, Okla. | 230 | 0 | 1959 |
| Ottawa, Okla. | 244 | 0 | 1959 |
| Coyote Valley Ranch, Calif. | 30 | 0 | 1957 |
| 31 Calif. rancherias | 814 | 0 | 1958–1964 |
| Catawba, S.C. | 631 | 834 | 1962 |
| Ponca, Nebr. | 442 | 834 | 1966 |
| Wyandotte, Okla. | 423 | 94 | 1959 |
| Modoc, Okla. | 29 | 0 | |

SOURCES: Wilkinson and Biggs 1977; U. S. Congress. House of Representatives 1964; *Congressional Record* 1957.

ernmental expenditures from Indians and reservations. While reservation economies were among the worst in the country, Emmons wanted to limit the federal role in economic development, so his program attempted to attract private businessmen to set up operations on reservations that would employ Indians. He began by setting up the American Indian Research Fund to solicit money from private foundations to perform resource surveys to inform businessmen of the potential of economic development on reservations. In 1955 he used the Bureau as a liaison, bringing industrialists, Indians, and local community officials together to negotiate plans to entice businessmen into the program (D.T. Beals 1954; U.S. Congress. House 1955:214).

Realizing that this would compete with local and state governments, he encouraged tribes to offer incentives such as rent-free buildings or land on which industries could build. The Bureau stressed the skills that Indians allegedly had in working with their hands and the advantages of opening new sources of labor and opening up new sources of labor and sales markets. Because of the lack of transportation and infrastructure on most reservations, the Bureau especially looked to labor-intensive industries like electronics, textiles, woodworking, and metal fabrication. The arrangements Emmons was promoting would, of course, give businessmen considerable control over reservations and their economies, and although never openly stated, reservations would become sources of cheap labor and consumers of manufactured products (Burt 1977:320–323).

In matters of education, Emmons altered the Indian New Deal emphasis on promoting as much as possible John Dewey's ideas of creating Indian community schools that went beyond just the education of children to serve as centers of overall reservation life. The new Bureau educational director, Hildegard Thompson, promoted goals that served to further termination and encourage assimilation by putting Indian children in local public schools and preparing them for jobs in urban America. While this succeeded in increasing the pitifully low percentage of Native American children receiving any education at all, it also sometimes resulted in Indian students going through difficult experiences where not only were they by far the least affluent in their classes, but also they felt the embarrassment of not fitting in socially and not having clothes and amenities more often enjoyed by their White classmates (Szasz 1977:65–66, 123–124).

The Bureau negotiated with state and county governments to convince them to take over the construction and maintenance of roads on reservations. Reservation roads were woefully inferior to those in surrounding areas, so Emmons first had to convince Congress to increase funding for reservation transportation infrastructure. Emmons had more than tripled the dollars spent on reservations roads after only one year as commissioner. Congressional passage of the Federal Highway Act in 1954 helped considerably because much of the additional costs could be authorized under government agencies other than the Bureau and still appear to be reducing the bureau's budget and responsibilities. This road transfer program continued throughout the 1950s and succeeded far beyond most other projects of the time (U.S. Department of the Interior 1954:50–51).

Another Bureau responsibility taken out of the agency's hands involved health care. Native American death rates stood at the very bottom of national averages in nearly every category in the 1950s—20 times worse for measles, four times for pneumonia and influenza, and nine times for tuberculosis. Congress underfunded Indian health care, and the Bureau faced many other problems. Bureau physicians earned far less money than those in private practice or in other government agencies, and few doctors proved willing to work on isolated reservations without modern facilities, teaching programs, or living quarters. Congressional terminationists tried to transfer Indian health care to the Public Health Service within the Department of Health, Education, and Welfare in 1952 but failed to win sufficient congressional support (U.S. Congress. Senate 1954:6–11; *New York Times*:76).

Opinion on the change was split in ways not typical of most Native American issues. Some Indians and Indian organizations, such as the National Congress of American Indians, approved of the transfer, believing that it would lead to improved congressional funding and better health in general. The Department of Health, Education, and Welfare did not welcome taking over such a monumental task, and many Indians objected to closing local reservation clinics and hospitals and traveling to more distant facilities. Congress approved the change in late summer, 1954. The Public Health Service did receive a higher level of funding than the Bureau, and Indian health statistics did improve gradually. But the change also resulted in the closing of some small reservation hospitals in remote areas, making it more difficult for many Indians to travel to the nearest clinics and hospitals (Sorkin 1971:51–54; Pratt 1971).

Another tactic in withdrawing the federal government from Indian affairs reverted to an old assimilationist policy of making it easier to remove restrictions on Indian trust land by issuing fee patents so it could be sold—usually to non-Indians who could purchase Indian land allotments dating back to the Dawes Severalty Act of 1887. In the 1930s Commissioner Collier had ended the practice entirely in an attempt to halt the erosion of the Indian land base and put tribal interests above personal interests (Parman 1994:93).

In 1947, the Bureau opened the process again, allowing fee patents if an allotment was not a part of a grazing or timber area that benefited an entire tribe, but tribes or other Indians still had the first opportunity to buy advertised plots. Early in Emmons's term as commissioner Congress failed in an attempt to pass a bill that would have ended trust status when an Indian reached age 21. Emmons then did everything he could administratively to accelerate fee patenting and return the priority to individuals rather than tribes. In 1954, he issued an "All or None" policy, requiring an Indian to include all of his land, not just a portion of it, when he applied for a change in his land title. He also made it harder for Native Americans to sell allotments to other tribal members by requiring Indians to fee patent their allotments before selling it to fellow tribesmen and thus allow non-Indians who usually could better afford a purchase to acquire the plot. When some tribes argued that this hampered tribal economic development, Emmons responded by insisting that his responsibility was to facilitate individual Indians' in receiving the highest price possible.

## Relocation

Another program to improve the dismal economic conditions among Indians involved moving them off reservations. For many years some Indians had moved into non-Indian communities in search of job opportunities. World War II accelerated this trend because of the availability of employment in war industries. After the war, some Indians returned to their reservations and others stayed and to some extent integrated into cities and mainstream American lifestyles. The Bureau sought to continue the process by negotiating arrangements with the United States Employment Service in the Department of Labor. But the numbers represented only a small percentage of Indians, and most of those had become largely assimilated. That a very large portion came from Oklahoma revealed the high rate of assimilation among Indians in that state (Neils 1971:1; Burt 1986:85–86; Philp 1985:181).

The impetus for enlarging the program and turning it toward termination goals began in the winter of 1947–1948 when massive blizzards struck the Navajo and Hopi reservations. A large-scale airlift of relief provisions was required to prevent starvation and disaster. This became an embarrassment for the government at the same time that Congress was working on the massive Marshall Plan for Europe. Many pointed out the obvious contrast in the government's willingness to spend money to help people in distress. Indian issues and problems rarely received national attention, but in this case Congress proved willing to fund a 10-year, 90-million dollar effort known as the Navajo-Hopi Rehabilitation Act. In many ways it violated terminationist goals and more closely resembled the Indian New Deal or the federal withdrawal plans designed by Commissioner Collier (Carroll 1950:6–7; J.L. Freeman 1950:25–27; R.W. Young 1961:1).

The Department of the Interior conducted a study and investigation into the situation and concluded that chronic poverty among the Navajo and Hopi resulted from too many people and too little economic development potential. Outdated resource surveys provided most of the data for the final report (uranium mining potential was not given much consideration, for example), but out of this experience a "surplus population" theory grew, and thereafter terminationists turned relocation into a program that fit well within their goals. The Navajo-Hopi Rehabilitation Act included Indian job placement into Denver, Salt Lake City, and Los Angeles. In 1951, Commissioner Myer expanded the program beyond the Navajo and Hopi. He sent staff to encourage relocation and administer the program in places of high Indian population, such as New Mexico, Arizona, California, Utah, and Colorado. He opened field offices in Chicago, Los Angeles, Salt Lake City, and Denver. Myer publicly introduced his program in early 1952, referring to it as Operation Relocation. By the time he left office about 2,600 Indians were leaving reservations annually (Burt 1986:85–89; Philp 1985:177–178).

Commissioner Emmons gave relocation an even higher priority, but he had to do it with already meager existing resources. The Bureau in the early 1950s gave a bare minimum of help from an overworked and undermanned staff about life in an American urban environment. Officials helped find a first job, counseled relocatees minimally on matters such as how to use a city map, make a telephone call, use a checking account, make and live within a budget, and purchase at a large grocery or department store. The Bureau also gave the roughly 25 percent who were least affluent a small amount of money to transport family and household goods and to live on until a job could be found (Carroll 1950:31; Madigan 1956:10–12; U.S. Department of the Interior 1954:24).

Emmons expanded the Bureau's recruitment efforts. Indians usually learned about relocation from officers specifically assigned this effort and placed on reservations or from literature distributed in places frequented by Native Americans. The promotionals directed their appeal toward the hope of a material prosperity that few Indians enjoyed. Brochures with pictures of contented Indian men working at good jobs or of women standing beside modern appliances like televisions or refrigerators naturally appealed to those unaccustomed to such amenities (vol. 4:76–77) (Madigan 1956:10–11; *New York Times* December 16, 1956:75; Carroll 1950:29).

Bureau officials denied the existence of quotas, but they encouraged and pressured relocation officers to enlist as many people as possible. The Bureau contended that it carefully screened applicants to exclude those unlikely to make a successful adjustment to life in the city, but the process was often haphazard and sometimes less than selective (Carroll 1950:28; Herbert Hoover interview with Gordon Jones, June 2, 1971, tape 684, 17–19; S. Ward 1972). Officers simply drove around the reservation and asked Indians they encountered, "Do you want to go to California or somewhere to get a job?" (Herbert Hoover interview with Alfred DuBray, July 28, 1970, tape 0533, 26, SDOHC, USD).

For some Native Americans the decision to relocate was deliberate, well thought out, and in fact what the person wanted. But for many it was not a selection between various life alternatives but rather a desperate last resort. Many moved because they saw no other escape from the many personal, family, and financial problems that were all too typical of reservation poverty. The case of a niece of Choctaw leader Harry Belvin is an example. When her husband lost his job and could not get a loan, the couple and their children applied for relocation. In the end many Indians found themselves ill-prepared to make the transition. Many had little education, poor eyesight with no glasses to improve their vision, drinking problems, criminal records, limited ability to speak English, health problems, or a lack of job experience or skills (General Session 1956:48; Carroll 1950:28; M. Harris 1971:24–25).

After arriving in a city, relocatees had help from the Bureau in locating a first residence, but the rent had to fit within the bureau's aid package. Most ended up in lower-class neighborhoods, often in burgeoning Indian enclaves. Often the Bureau placed Indians in large, high-rise apartment complexes, and many could not adjust to the crowded, confined settings after lives on sparsely populated reservations (Patrick 1973:55; J.R. Wagner and R. Corrigan 1970:

1496; Anonymous 1967:39; Pine Ridge Meeting 1956:20; Kelsey 1968).

The Bureau also helped in finding a first job. Some found satisfying, permanent employment, but many landed in positions far from what they expected. Most Native Americans lacked job skills and experience, so they had to take work at the bottom of wage and status scales. To make matters worse, available jobs were often insecure, and if a relocatee lost his or her first position, finding another could be difficult, as Bureau assistance ended after Indians found housing and a job. Two national recessions, one in the mid-1950s and another in the late 1950s, made the search even harder (Carroll 1950:44).

Cultural dislocation worsened the adjustment. The fast-paced lifestyles in cities sometimes proved a difficult change, especially for those from tribes that had most retained traditional, communal ways. A former relocation officer noted the situation well by describing the cultural shock for an Indian who "has never been permanently employed, has never looked at a clock, and is expected with a week's counseling or three weeks' counseling to go out and face the world" (Hoover 1971). The Bureau sometimes would not reveal the names or addresses of relocatees living close to one another since association with other Indians might hinder rather than encourage the desired assimilation.

When problems became overwhelming, Indians moved back home. The Bureau claimed that only 30 percent of relocatees ever returned, but critics of the program contended that the real number was at least twice that figure.

As criticism escalated Commissioner Emmons stepped up the relocation program. He convinced Congress to more than triple funding. In late 1956, the Bureau opened offices in Saint Louis, San Francisco, and San Jose and expanded the aid to relocatees. It offered small grants for purchasing household goods, furniture, clothing, and one year of medical insurance and authorized up to three weeks of emergency subsistence for those who had lost their jobs and were ineligible for unemployment compensation. Congress helped further by creating a Vocational Training Act to fund trade school education, on-the-job training, or experience through apprenticeship. The national economic recession beginning in 1957 slowed relocation because of the greater difficulty in finding jobs. But by the end of the 1950s, at least 30,000 Indians had relocated. Relocation became one of the few significant components of termination that survived after the later discrediting and dismantling of that policy. In fact, the number who relocated in the two decades after the 1950s almost tripled as assistance increased even more (Metzler 1963:143).

When viewed as a component of a termination policy, relocation had some success. Many Indians adjusted well in the way intended. Some even became quite successful and affluent in America's cities. Most Native Americans who stayed in cities were only slightly more prosperous than those on reservations after factoring the higher cost of living in urban areas. Many others became a part of the country's urban underclass, shifting many of the problems and costs of poverty and alienation from reservations to city and local governments (Gundlach and Roberts 1978:122–126; Brinker and Taylor 1974:145; Clinton, Chadwick, and Bahr 1975: 130–131).

## The Demise of Termination

By the late 1950s termination came under heavy criticism and support faded. Tribes, led by the National Congress of American Indians and influenced by the civil rights activists of other ethnic minorities, mounted an effective opposition. Church groups protested what they saw as a social injustice. State and local governments' interest in termination declined as it became clear that the costs of taking over the financial burden of social services in reservations outweighed the benefits of taxing Indian land. Conservationists and environmentalists feared that breaking up reservations would result in the harmful development of ecologically important regions. Republicans lost their congressional majorities and key subcommittee positions. Many of the Democrats who replaced them became vocal critics, coming to view termination as a violation of native tribal and sovereign rights rather than as an extension of United States citizenship rights. More and more the specter of abandoning indigent people and unwanted responsibilities replaced the prospect of "liberation." In 1958, Secretary of the Interior Fred Seaton became the first administrative official to acknowledge the controversy and back away from a faltering policy by announcing that no more tribes would be terminated unless they fully supported any change (Burt 1982:74–80, 107, 113).

As Indians around the country united and developed the means to make their voices heard, liberals, some moderates, and a few conservatives in Congress came to support a more Indian-defined type of self-determination on reservations. Some congressmen, like Democratic Sen. Frank Church of Idaho, continued to promote termination into the mid-1960s. But most came to see that civil rights for Indians should include consideration of tribal rights as well as individual United States citizenship rights.

The uprising against termination among many Indians contributed to major changes in federal Indian policy. Tribes and reservation Indians had created organizational structures and practical experience in the political battles against termination. Relocation created enclaves of Indians from many different groups together in cities around the country at a time of broader civil rights movements among other minorities. This facilitated and encouraged an urban pan-Indian identity and an activism that when influenced by a resurgence of Indian culture and sense of tribal sovereignty contributed to the Red Power movement and the self-determination policies of the 1960s and beyond (Burt 1986:95).

27

# Indian Land Claims

JUDITH ROYSTER

Under American law, the Indian tribes that had long occupied the United States did not have full ownership of their lands. Instead, they held aboriginal or original title, sometimes called Indian title—a right to occupy and use the land subject to the right of the federal government to acquire it. In 1823, the United States Supreme Court adopted this rule, taken from the international doctrine of discovery (*Johnson v. M'Intosh*, 21 U.S. 543). The United States, and only the United States, had the legal right to acquire lands from the Indian tribes.

The Supreme Court stated that the United States had two options for acquiring Indian title: conquest or purchase. Although Chief Justice John Marshall recognized that conquest was an "extravagant . . . pretension," the Supreme Court nonetheless used conquest to bolster its decision that Indian tribes did not possess full title to their lands (*Johnson v. M'Intosh*, 21 U.S. 543 [1823]). In reality, very few Indian tribes had been militarily conquered. Instead, the United States routinely used purchase to acquire Indian lands, even in situations where the tribes had suffered a military defeat (Newton 1980:1215, 1228). Treaties and agreements between Indian tribes and the federal government were the primary means of transferring lands to the United States throughout the period of tribal land acquisition; the "overriding goal" of treaty-making was the acquisition of tribal lands (Newton 2005:§1.03[1]). Even after treaty-making was ended by Congress in 1871, the United States continued to acquire Indian lands through agreements and statutes.

The circumstances under which treaties and agreements for land were negotiated varied significantly. In the early years of the Republic, treaties were often instruments of peace and friendship, typically fixing boundaries between the tribes and the United States. As the United States grew larger and stronger, becoming the dominant presence, the relative positions of the parties changed. Indian tribes were increasingly in weaker bargaining positions, forced to cede their lands and either remove to entirely new lands or settle on relatively small parcels of reservations within their aboriginal territories. In some instances, federal negotiators told Indian tribes in no uncertain terms that the tribes could either sell their lands or starve (Newton 2005:§1.03[1], 1992:822).

The result of the treaty and agreement process, particularly in the nineteenth century, was often the confiscation of tribal lands. Tribes were forced to cede lands, often under implicit or explicit threats from the government if they did not. Land cessions may have been by instruments called agreements, but the tribal parties did not have equal bargaining power with the United States. Most tribes were paid for the land they ceded, but payment was often grossly inadequate for the value of the ceded territories (Wishart 1990).

Many tribes protested vigorously from the time their lands were appropriated by the government. The Sioux Nation, for example, challenged the 1877 statute that took their sacred Black Hills from the time of the government's action, lobbying Congress and bringing lawsuits as soon as claims were authorized (vol. 13:836–838) (*United States* v. *Sioux Nation of Indians*, 448 U.S. 371 [1980]) (Lazarus 1991). But for a considerable period of time after the takings of their land, there was little many tribes could do. For an Indian tribe to bring a land claim was a long, slow, and frustrating process, if it was possible at all. This chapter traces the history of Indian land claims, from the mid-nineteenth century through the Indian Claims Commission to modern claims in the federal courts.

## Claims Prior to 1946

In 1855, Congress established the federal Court of Claims to hear claims against the United States (10 U.S. Stat. 612). A few tribes took advantage of the new court, and filed lawsuits to redress their grievances against the federal government. Congress responded quickly, apparently in reaction to some tribes' support of the Confederacy during the Civil War, and in 1863 expressly prohibited the Court of Claims from hearing any claims based on treaties with foreign nations or Indian tribes (12 U.S. Stat. 765). Although the limitation on the Court of Claims's jurisdiction technically covered only treaty-based claims, it was interpreted to bar any claims by Indians or Indian tribes (Newton 2005:§5.06[2]; Rosenthal 1990:9–10).

Without access to the Court of Claims, Indian tribes were left with only one option: a special jurisdictional statute. Indian tribes could petition Congress for such a special statute granting jurisdiction to the Court of Claims, but the route to a special statute was long and slow. The first congressional authorization after 1863 did not occur until 1881, and Congress enacted just 39 special jurisdictional statutes before 1923. Less than half these claims, just 17, resulted in awards to the Indian plaintiffs. From the onset of the First World War in 1914 until 1923, only eight special jurisdictional statutes were enacted, and only three of these resulted in awards to the Indians (Newton 2005:§5.06[2]; Rosenthal 1990:17).

The pace picked up significantly in 1924, when Congress accorded United States citizenship to all native-born Indians (43 U.S. Stat. 253). Prior to that 1924 act, citizenship in an Indian tribe was considered incompatible with citizenship in the United States, but Indians' participation in the United States military during World War I spurred congressional action (Newton 2005:§14.01[a]; Rosenthal 1990:17–18). Once Indians were recognized as United States citizens, denying them the access that all other citizens had to redress grievances against the United States became problematical. Throughout the 1920s, tribes filed greater numbers of petitions, and Congress enacted more special jurisdictional acts each year (Rosenthal 1990:18–19). By 1946, Congress had enacted 142 special jurisdictional statutes for Indian claims (Newton 2005:§5.06[2]).

Despite the increase in special jurisdictional statutes after Indian citizenship, few of the tribal claims were successful. Only a small number resulted in awards, and most of the rest were dismissed on technical grounds. There was no uniformity in the jurisdictional statutes to support a consistent approach by the court (Cohen 1942:374–376). The Court of Claims would exclude any claim not specifically authorized by the special jurisdictional statute and would interpret the statutes narrowly against the tribes. In one case, the Supreme Court ruled that a special jurisdictional statute allowing Cherokee Indians to sue to determine the validity of a federal statute affecting them did not create a controversy that the federal courts could hear (*Muskrat* v. *United States*, 219 U.S. 346 [1911]). Delay in court rulings was a further frustration for Indian plaintiffs. Five to 10 years often elapsed between passage of the special jurisdictional act and trial or dismissal of the claim (Rosenthal 1990:19–20).

Those tribes that did prevail on the merits of their claims in the Court of Claims often faced the obstacle of offsets. Claims were referred to the General Accounting Office for a search for any government expenditures that were not required by treaty or agreement. These government "gratuities" included items such as the expense of educating Indian children at government boarding schools, despite strong tribal opposition to the boarding schools. Between 1929 and 1935, of the Indian claimants suing under special jurisdictional acts that permitted offsets, all except two had their cases dismissed because the offsets exceeded the damages award. Despite this impact on tribal compensation for government wrongdoing, Congress in 1935 required the use of offsets in all cases (49 U.S. Stat. 571; Rosenthal 1990:29–32; Newton 2005:§1.04).

The move toward reform of the claims process for Indian claims traces to the influential Meriam Report of 1928. Pre-pared at the behest of the secretary of the interior, the Meriam Report detailed the deplorable conditions in Indian country after nearly half a century of the federal policy of assimilation and allotment of tribal lands, and helped inaugurate a new federal policy of tribal reorganization and revitalization (Newton 2005:§1.05). The Report criticized the claims process as "burdensome and unjust," bringing greater attention to the problems faced by Indian parties attempting to redress claims against the government (Meriam 1928: 805–811).

Legislation was introduced in Congress in 1930 to establish an Indian claims court, conceptualized as a judicial body. Bills for a specialized court were again introduced in 1934 and 1935; all failed. In 1935, the first bill to create an Indian Claims Commission was presented to Congress. That bill, as well as subsequent Commission bills in 1937, 1940, 1941, 1944, and 1945, failed to pass (Vance 1969:327–328).

## Indian Claims Commission

Congress finally established a specialized tribunal to address Indian claims in 1946. The Indian Claims Commission was enacted into law on August 13, 1946 (60 U.S. Stat. 1049). In his signing statement, President Harry Truman succinctly identified the policies behind the new Commission: "I hope that this bill will mark the beginning of a new era for our Indian citizens. They have valiantly served on every battlefront. They have proved by their loyalty the wisdom of a national policy built on fair dealing. With the final settlement of all outstanding claims which this insures, Indians can take their place without special handicap or special advantage in the economic life of our nation and share fully in its progress" (Vance 1969:325). The Commission was thus the product of several strands of federal policy. It was in part a recognition of and reward for Indian' military service in World War II. In was in part an attempt to make up for past wrongs done to the Indian people, following closely on a war that had starkly demonstrated the evils of oppression. And it was in part a way to clear a path for a new federal policy of termination. Although termination would not become official federal policy until the early 1950s, Senate and House reports in 1943 and 1944 strongly criticized the reorganization policy and encouraged a return to assimilation of Indians (Newton 2005:§1.06) ("Termination and Relocation," this vol.). Resolving any existing claims of Indian tribes was a necessary precursor to initiation of the new policy.

The Indian Claims Commission was established to resolve the so-called "ancient claims," those claims arising before the date the Indian Claims Commission Act was signed into law. Congress established five classes of claims that the Commission could hear:

(1) claims in law or equity arising under the Constitution, laws, treaties of the United States, and Executive orders of the President; (2) all other claims in law or equity, including

those sounding in tort, with respect to which the claimant would have been entitled to sue in a court of the United States if the United States was subject to suit; (3) claims which would result if the treaties, contracts, and agreements between the claimant and the United States were revised on the ground of fraud, duress, unconscionable consideration, mutual or unilateral mistake, whether of law or fact, or any other ground cognizable by a court of equity; (4) claims arising from the taking by the United States, whether as a result of a treaty of cession or otherwise, of lands owned or occupied by the claimant without the payment for such lands of compensation agreed to by the claimant; and (5) claims based upon fair and honorable dealings that are not recognized by any existing rule of law or equity (60 U.S. Stat. 1049).

The claims could be brought no matter how old they were, but the tribes were required to file any claims they had within five years of the date the statute was enacted. Virtually every tribe filed at least one claim. Many of those were land claims concerned with the undervaluation of Indian lands acquired by the United States, primarily in the West (Rosenthal 1990:116).

Indian Claims Commission decisions were appealable to the Court of Claims. Decisions of the Court of Claims could be reviewed by the United States Supreme Court on a discretionary writ of certiorari (60 U.S. Stat. 1049).

The Commission was initially constituted for 10 years: five years to allow the claims to be filed, and an additional five years for the Commission to resolve them. That original 10-year term proved entirely inadequate, in part because of the sheer number of claims filed and in part because of the procedures the Commission adopted to resolve the claims. The initial three appointed Commissioners were sworn into office on April 10, 1947. By the end of that year, 17 claims had been filed. By early 1951, 263 cases had been filed. But the last six weeks of the filing period saw a huge influx of cases. The time and expense of preparing a petition, as well as an interest in seeing how the Commission handled the early cases, led many tribes to wait until the last days to file. By the time the filing period ended on August 13, 1951, 370 petitions were received, eventually separated into over 600 dockets. By the end of 1954, only 55 dockets had been adjudicated (Rosenthal 1990:114–116; U.S. Indian Claims Commission 1980:7–8).

The pace at which the claims moved through the process remained slow throughout the life of the Commission. It was not uncommon for a claim to take six to 12 years to resolve (Rosenthal 1990:122). Congress extended the Commission for an additional five years (70 U.S. Stat. 624 [1956]). Because the Commission's work remained incomplete, with only 125 cases dismissed or adjudicated by 1960, Congress extended the Commission for another five years in 1961 (75 U.S. Stat. 92). Progress remained slow, and the Commission received five-year extensions in 1967 and 1972, with the extension act of 1967 changing the number of Commissioners from three to five in an effort to resolve more claims more expeditiously (81 U.S. Stat. 11 [1967];

86 U.S. Stat. 114 [1972]). Nonetheless, 176 dockets remained unresolved by March 1975. Although the pace of the Commission's work had increased, Congress's impatience and desire to have the claims finalized prevailed. In 1976, Congress enacted the final extension of the Commission to September 30, 1978 (90 U.S. Stat. 1990). The final act provided that the Indian Claims Commission would, no later than December 31, 1978, transfer all remaining claims to the Court of Claims. The Commission certified 20 cases to the Court of Claims before it expired, leaving an additional 68 dockets unresolved on the date of its expiration (U.S. Indian Claims Commission 1980:7–20).

By the time it ended its run, the Indian Claims Commission had dismissed Indian claims in 204 dockets, and had made awards of over $818 million. Its final report states that it completed 342 dockets by awards, but that the number of awards was 274. The discrepancy appears to be the result of awards that were on appeal at the time the final report was issued (U.S. Indian Claims Commission 1980:125). Figure 1 shows the judicially established Indian lands.

*As a Court*

As originally constituted, the Indian Claims Commission was intended to function as a claims tribunal rather than a court. In fact, Congress specifically rejected bills in the 1930s to establish a special court for Indian claims. The Indian Claims Commission was directed to "establish an Investigation Division to investigate all claims referred to it by the Commission for the purpose of discovering the facts relating thereto." This investigative arm was to "make a complete and thorough search for all evidence affecting claims" held by government agencies, and submit that evidence to the Commission (60 U.S. Stat. 1049 [1946]). The Investigative Division did no more than send out inquiries to tribes, and it never fulfilled its intended functions. Instead, the Indian Claims Commission functioned as a court throughout its life. John T. Vance, the last Chairman of the Commission, blamed much of the Commission's failure to meet its congressional mandates on the fact that it acted as a judicial body rather than a claims tribunal (Vance 1969: 333–335).

Because the Commission functioned as a court, Indian claimants needed to be represented by lawyers. Nonetheless, legal representation for land claims was problematical for many tribes. The Indian Claims Commission Act provides that Indians "may retain" attorneys to represent them, and tribal plaintiffs preferred to retain attorneys in lawsuits where the government was represented by the United States Department of Justice. Contracts with tribal lawyers had to be approved by the secretary of the interior, just as they had for attorneys representing tribal claims under special jurisdictional statutes. Under the Indian Claims Commission Act, tribes organized under the Indian Reorganization Act of 1934 could choose attorneys as provided for in their constitutions and bylaws, but in practice these contracts were generally subject to secretarial approval as well. Delays in approvals, and rejections of tribal choices, helped frustrate the resolution of Indian claims (Rosenthal 1990:117–118).

The Commission was given jurisdiction to hear five types of Indian claims against the United States. The first four of these were legal claims: claims arising under federal law; other claims in law and equity; claims based on fraud, duress, or the like; and claims for takings under the Fifth Amendment of the Constitution. The fifth type was an entirely new type of claim, grounded not in law but morality. Indians could bring "claims based upon fair and honorable dealings that are not recognized by any existing rule of law or equity" (60 U.S. Stat. 1049 [1946]). Despite the promise of clause 5, the Court of Claims, on appeal from a Commission ruling in favor of the government, held that clause 5 claims could only extend to the types of claims brought in the Court of Claims prior to establishment of the Commission. The effect was to read clause 5 out of the Indian Claims Commission Act and eliminate tribes' ability to bring claims based on moral rather than legal grounds (Newton 1992:776–778, 783).

In addition to limiting its jurisdiction to legal claims, the Indian Claims Commission also limited the remedy it could award. "Once the Commission became a court, it became a claims court. In other words, it viewed its remedial arsenal as restricted to money damages, a view that seems consistent with the legislative intent" (Newton 1992:773). Moreover, federal courts held that the jurisdiction of the Commission to hear claims was exclusive, meaning that Indian tribes had to bring their historic claims before the Commission, and could not use the federal courts to seek other remedies. Thus, when the Oglala Sioux Tribe sued for ownership of the Black Hills on the ground that the land had been taken unconstitutionally, the federal court dismissed the claim, holding that the tribe's only avenue of redress for its historic claim was the Indian Claims Commission. The result for tribes that wanted their land returned was devastating. Their only avenue of redress was the Indian Claims Commission, but the Commission could only award money damages; it could not order the return of the land (*Oglala Sioux Tribe* v. *United States*, 650 F.2d 140 (8th Cir. 1981); Barsh 1982:73–74).

*Procedures and Awards*

Once it decided to operate as a court, the Indian Claims Commission adopted and used judicial procedures very similar to those followed by the federal Court of Claims. In particular, the Commission established a three-part approach to Indian land claims. In phase one, the title phase, the tribal claimants established their rights to the land. If the tribal right to the land was upheld by the Commission, phase two, the valuation-liability phase, began. Phase three was the offset phase, which occurred if government liability was established at phase two (Rosenthal 1990:120, 138).

If a tribe had a treaty, agreement, statute, or executive order delimiting tribal lands, the title phase of a Commission trial was relatively straightforward. Absent a documentary source of title, a tribe was required to prove that it had exclusive occupation of a definable territory for a sufficiently long time—that is, aboriginal title to the lands. In this phase of the trial, as well as in phase two, the Commission depended heavily on expert witnesses in anthropology, ethnography, and history, not only for the "facts" but also for their theories, interpretations, and conclusions. Both the government and the tribal claimants hired these experts, who often presented conflicting interpretations for the Commission to resolve (Rosenthal 1990:121–125; Newton 1992:818).

The valuation-liability phase was generally the longest phase of a trial before the Commission, establishing the value of the land and the government's liability for taking or undervaluing the land. Indian land was valued as of the time of the government's action extinguishing the Indians' title. Although the Commission considered multiple factors in assigning a fair market value to the land—location, natural resources, climate, and so forth—the value of the land at the time of the federal appropriation might be only pennies an acre (Kaplan 1985:81–82). Once the value of the land was established, it was compared with the federal compensation, if any, to arrive at the amount of the award (Rosenthal 1990:138).

Valuing Indian land at the time of title extinguishment would not have been as much of a hardship for tribes if the Commission had awarded interest, but the Commission's practice was a no-interest rule. Except for claims for takings of property under the Fifth Amendment of the United States Constitution, which carry interest on the award, the Indian Claims Commission adhered to its no-interest approach (*Fort Berthold Reservation* v. *United States*, 390 F.2d 686, 690 (Ct. Cl. 1968)). The Commission's exact reasoning is unknown, but it was likely intended to protect the federal treasury from large awards. The interest on awards, even at the government rate of five percent a year, would often have outstripped the amount of the actual award several times over (Newton 1992:820–821; Carlson 1985:97–99). Nonetheless, the no-interest rule "implicitly puts members of the tribe today in the position that they would have been had their ancestors simply placed the money under a mattress (or some equivalent) and waited for the present" (Carlson 1985:99). An award of nineteenth-century value without accompanying interest thus did little to make tribes whole for the government's wrongdoing.

Because the Commission did follow the general rule for Fifth Amendment takings and awarded interest on those claims, it needed a method to determine when a compensable taking had occurred. In large part, such a method was necessary because of two apparently conflicting Supreme Court decisions on federal liability for appropriation of Indian lands. The *Lone Wolf* case in 1903 held that Congress had plenary power to alter Indian land rights as it saw

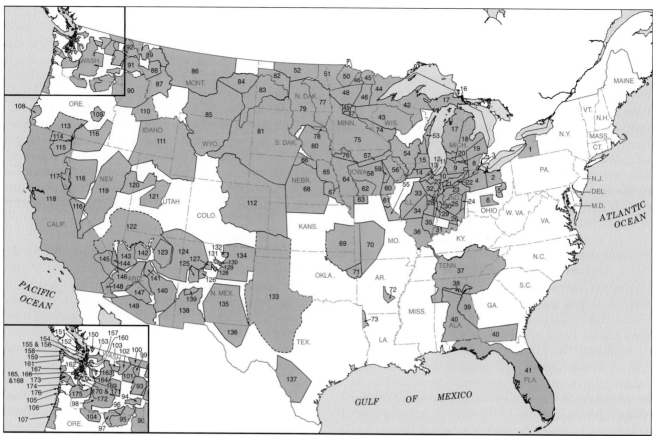

Fig. 1. Judicially established Indian land areas. This map portrays the results of cases before the U.S. Indian Claims Commission or the U.S. Court of Claims in which a tribe proved its original tribal occupancy. Each tract so established is enclosed with a solid black line; a dashed line indicates that the case was settled before an exact area was defined (U.S.G.S. 1978; BIA Geographic Data Service Center 1998). 1, Seneca, 4,105,733 acres; 2, Delaware, Wyandot, Potawatomi, Ottawa, Chippewa, 2,747,040 acres; 3, Ottawa, 709,112 acres; 4, Delaware, Ottawa, Shawnee, Wyandot, 4,491,153 acres; 5, Delaware, 1,163,291 acres; 6, Shawnee, 1,865,020 acres; 7, Potawatomi, Ottawa, Chippewa, 591,088 acres; 8, Potawatomi, 1,948, 248 acres; 9, Potawatomi, 3,040,056 acres; 10, Potawatomi, 3,011,057 acres; 11, Potawatomi, 522,086 acres; 12, Potawatomi, 751,249 acres; 13, Potawatomi, 15,982 acres; 14, Potawatomi, 2,016,814 acres; 15, Potawatomi, 3,825,122 acres; 16, Sault Ste. Marie band of Chippewa, 153,327 acres; 17, Ottawa and Chippewa, 13,648,993 acres; 18, Saginaw Chippewa, 7,462,264 acres; 19, Saginaw Chippewa, 3,300992 acres; 20, Grand River band of Ottawa, 1,192,372 acres; 21, Miami Potawatomi, 1,458,480 acres; 22, Miami Potawatomi, 782,240 acres; 23, Miami, 3,027,970 acres; 24, Miami of Eel River, 754,483 acres; Miami and Delaware, 3,954,616 acres; Miami and Wea, 3,062,488 acres; 27, Potawatomi and Wea, 626,937 acres; 28, Potawatomi, Wea, and Kickapoo, 480,509 acres; 29, Wea and Kickapoo, 561,066 acres; 30, Wea, 1,388,223 acres; 31, Delaware and Piankashaw, 2,086,626 acres; 32, Potawatomi and Kickapoo, 1,873,666 acres; 33, Kickapoo, 7,512,818 acres; 34, Kaskaskia and Kickapoo, 3,501,058 acres; 35, Piankashaw, 2,547,363 acres; 36, Kaskaskia, 6,388,729 acres; 37, Cherokee, 32,319,178 acres; 38, Creek, 1,317,662 acres; 39, Creek, 5,216,015 acres; 40, Creek, 21,086,793 acres; 41, Seminole, 31,337,339 acres; 42, Chippewa bands of Lake Superior and the Mississippi, 10,311, 704 acres; 43, Chippewa bands of Lake Superior and the Mississippi, 13,518,869 acres; 44, Lake Superior band of Chippewa, 5,995,545 acres; 45, Bois Forte band of Chippewa, 2,092,998 acres; 46, Mississippi bands of Chippewa, 4,787,742 acres; 47, Chippewa bands of lake Superior and the Mississippi, 1,117,146 acres; 48, Pillager and Lake Winnibigoshish bands of Chippewa, 5,864,476 acres; 49, Pillager band of Chippewa, 739,948 acres; 50, Red Lake band of Chippewa, 3,792,183 acres; 51, Red Lake and Pembina bands of Chippewa, 6,750,779 acres; 52, Pembina band of Chippewa, 7,961,081 acres; 53, Potawatomi, 1,396,981 acres; 54, Winnebago, 7,966,739 acres; 55, Sac and Fox, 3,775,317 acres; 56, Sac and Fox, 3,672,138 acres, 57, Sac and Fox, 2,244,824 acres; 58, Sac and Fox, 8,853,573 acres; 59, Sac and Fox, 1,047,189 acres; 60, Iowa Sac and Fox, 1,139,816 acres; 62, Iowa, 3,253,921 acres; 63, Iowa, 1,456,728 acres; 64, Otoe and Missouria, Iowa, Omaha, Sac and Fox, 10,145,180 acres; 65, Omaha, 5,064,236 acres; 66, Ponca, 2,511,045 acres; 67, Otoe and Missouria, 3,058,491 acres; 68, Pawnee, 22,511,288 acres; 69, Osage, 17,772,035 acres; 70, Osage, 11,971,616 acres; 72, Quapaw, 1,031,438 acres; 73, Caddo, 732,892 acres; 74, Mdewakanton band of Santee Sioux, 3,996,735 acres; 75, Eastern or Mississippi Sioux, 27,480,227 acres; 76, Yankton Sioux, 1,775,242 acres; 77, Sisseton and Wahpeton Santee Sioux, 9,864,311 acres; 78, Sisseton Santee Sioux, 555,834 acres; 79, Teton and Yanktonai Sioux, 14,084,930 acres; 80, Yanktonai?, 11,346,542 acres; 81, Teton Sioux, 59,124,725 acres; 82, Three Affiliated Tribes of Ft. Berthold, 4,413,348 acres; 83, Arikara, Mandan, Hidatsa, 12,410,550 acres; 84, Assiniboine, 6,396,643 acres; 85, Crow, 37,249,088 acres; 86, Blackfeet and Gros Ventre, 30,528,124 acres; 87, Flathead, 6,340,063 acres; 88, Upper Pend d'Oreille, 3,020,687 acres; 89, Kootenai, 5,294,818 acres; 90, Nez Perce, 13,191,293 acres; 91, Coeur d'Alene, 3,084,509 acres; 92, Kalispel, 2,420,830 acres; 93, Spokane, 2,235,197 acres; 94, Palouse, 697,999 acres;

95, Cayuse, 2,435,330 acres; Walla Walla, 370,892 acres; 97, Umatilla, 1,001,321 acres; 98, Yakima, 8,690,303 acres; 99, Colville, 464,475 acres; 100, Lakes, 1,121,349 acres; 101, Sanpoil and Nespelem, 1,433,878 acres; 102, Okanagan, 1,016,006 acres; 103, Methow, 402,768 acres; 104, Warm Springs Sahaptins, 1,499,497 acres; 105, Clatsop, 31,189 acres; 106, Tillamook, 239,890 acres; 107, Alsea, 1,152,956 acres; 108, Coquille, Chetco, and Tututni, 1,678,134 acres; 109, "Snake," 1,709,804 acres; 110, Lemhi Northern Shoshone, 5,117,140 acres; 111, "Shoshone," 38,3555,050 acres; 112, Northern Cheyenne and Northern Arapaho, 50,917, 918 acres; Klamath, 6,358,532 acres; 114, Modoc, 1,811,259 acres; 115, Achumawi, 3,100,269 acres; 116, Northern Paiute, 26,135,301 acres; 117, Washoe, 1,703,649 acres; 118, California Indians, 82,851,671 acres; 119, Western Shoshone, 24,614,438 acres; 120, Gosiute, 6,005,636 acres; 121, Uintah Ute, 6,139,435 acres; 122, Southern Paiute, 24,098,363 acres; 123, Hopi, 4,716,295 acres; 124, Navajo, 20,915,963 acres; 125, Acoma Pueblo, 1,748,453 acres; 126, Laguna Pueblo, 707,303 acres; 127, Zia, Jemez, and Santa Ana Pueblos, 553,591 acres; 128, Santo Domingo Pueblo, 215,064 acres; 129, San Ildefonso Pueblo, 117,717 acres; 130, Nambe Pueblo, 66,501 acres; 131, Santa Clara Pueblo, 82,128 acres; 132, Taos Pueblo, 360,297 acres; 133, Kiowa, Comanche, and Apache, 64,523,170 acres; 134, Jicarilla Apache, 14,223,269 acres; 135, Mescalero Apache, 19,178,399 acres; 136, Mescalero Apache, 6,2442,732 acres; 137, Lipan Apache, 12,587,702 acres; 138, Chiricahua Apache, 14,634,476 acres; 139, Chiricahua Apache, 893,445 acres; 140, Western Apache, 9,664,689 acres; 141, Tonto Apache, 1,220,663 acres; 142, Havasupai, 2,443,392 acres; 143, Walapai, 5,183,048 acres; 144, Mohave, 1,052,118 acres; 145, Chemehuevi, 3,799,018 acres; 146, Yavapai, 9,246,951 acres; 147, Pima and Maricopa, 3,814,191 acres; 148, Quechan, 2,185,185 acres; 149, Papago, 9,113,041 acres; 150, Nooksack Salish, 80,128 acres; 151, Lummi Salish, 90,194 acres; 152, Samish Salish, 7,959 acres; 153, Upper Skagit, 445,959 acres; 154, Swinomish Salish, 26,554 acres; 155, Lower Skagit, 57,357 acres; 156, Kikiallus Salish, 8,448 acres; 157, Stillaguamish Salish, 58,334 acres; 158, Makah, 120,254 acres; 159, S'Klallam (Clallam Salish), 454,261 acres; 160, Snohomish Salish, 152,712 acres; 161, Quileute, 110,699 acres; 162, Skokomish Salish, 358,916 acres; 163, Skykomish Salish, 125,573 acres; 164, Snoqualmie Salish, 223,313 acres; 165, Suquamish Salish, 89,348 acres; 166, Duwamish Salish, 50,486 acres; 167, Quinault, 271,279 acres; 168, Squaxin Salish, 19,512 acres; 169, Muckleshoot Salish, 104,298 acres; 170, Puyallup Salish, 56,874 acres; 171, Steilacoom Salish, 10,969 acres; 172, Nisqually Salish, 156,096 acres; 173, Lower Chehalis, 509,416 acres; 174, Upper Chehalis, 321,576 acres; 175, Cowlitz, 1,696,980 acres; 176, Chinook, 46,456 acres.

fit, allotting tribal lands and selling the "surplus" (*Lone Wolf* v. *Hitchcock*, 187 U.S. 553) (B. Clark 1994). But the *Shoshone Tribe* case in 1937 held that if Congress grants tribal lands to others or takes them for its own purposes, just compensation is due for the takings (*Shoshone Tribe* v. *United States*, 299 U.S. 476). The Court of Claims, on review of an Indian Claims Commission decision, formulated an approach to reconciling these cases (*Fort Berthold Reservation* v. *United States*, 390 F.2d 686, 691 (Ct. Cl. 1968)). The "*Fort Berthold* test" for whether a taking has occurred provides:

> It is obvious that Congress cannot simultaneously (1) act as trustee for the benefit of the Indians, exercising its plenary powers over the Indians and their property, as it thinks is in their best interests, and (2) exercise its sovereign power of eminent domain, taking the Indians' property within the meaning of the Fifth Amendment to the Constitution. In any given situation in which Congress has acted with regard to Indian people, it must have acted either in one capacity or the other. Congress can own two hats, but it cannot wear them both at the same time.
>
> Some guideline must be established so that a court can identify in which capacity Congress is acting. The following guideline would best give recognition to the basic distinction between the two types of congressional action: Where Congress makes a good faith effort to give the Indians the full value of the land and thus merely transmutes the property from land to money, there is no taking. This is a mere substitution of assets or change of form and is a traditional function of a trustee.

In 1981, the United States Supreme Court adopted and affirmed this approach to determining whether a taking of Indian lands had occurred in *United States* v. *Sioux Nation of Indians* (448 U.S. 371). The Sioux Nation's road to a court decision was long and complicated, starting with a special jurisdictional statute in 1920, a claim before the Indian Claims Commission in 1950, and finally a special statute in 1978 authorizing the Court of Claims to review the merits of the Commission's 1974 decision that there had been a taking of Sioux land in 1877, including the sacred Black Hills (*United States* v. *Sioux Nation of Indians*, 448 U.S. 371, 384–390; Newton 1992:830–835). Applying the *Fort Berthold* test to the federal appropriation of the Black Hills and other Sioux lands, the Supreme Court determined that a taking had occurred. The United States had not made a "good faith effort" to compensate the Sioux Nation for the lands taken in 1877 by federal statute. The Supreme Court thus affirmed a judgment, including interest, of $122 million. With interest accruing, the judgment fund had grown to over $315 million by the end of 1991, and to $570 million by mid-2001. The tribes of the Sioux Nation have consistently refused to accept the money, insisting instead upon the return of the land (Lazarus 1991).

The offset phase of a Commission trial on a land claim took place if the tribal claimants established government liability at phase two. The use of offsets to reduce tribal awards, a feature of claims under special jurisdictional statutes, was specifically addressed by the Indian Claims Commission Act. The Act itself did not require offsets, but allowed them if the Commission "finds that the nature of the claim and the entire course of dealings and accounts between the United States and claimant in good conscience warrants such action." In addition, Congress limited what "funds expended

33

gratuitously" could be considered offsets, eliminating some of the government's expenditures that tribes found most offensive. These included monies spent on removal of tribes, Indian administration, or for health or educational purposes (60 U.S. Stat. 1049 [1946]).

There appears to be no clear pattern concerning the Commission's approach to offsets, although the Commission was less inclined than the Court of Claims to allow them. Over time, the defense of offsets seems to have become increasingly discredited. In addition, the Commission developed a rule to help mitigate some of the effects of offsets. If a tribe signed a peace treaty after resisting the federal government militarily, offsets were not necessarily allowed. The theory was that such treaties were not akin to arms-length contracts between equal parties, and that the offsets could not be considered compensation. But if a treaty was merely a land cession agreement, offsets could be considered a part of the tribe's compensation. This "treaty of peace (no offsets allowed)/treaty of cession (offsets allowed)" approach was upheld by the Court of Claims. Ultimately the Commission made findings of offsets in 37 dockets and approved settlements including offsets in 149 dockets. The total offsets amounted to $9.6 million, less than two percent of all awards (Newton 1992:819–820; Rosenthal 1990:122, 125–126; Barsh 1982:19–20).

## Claims After 1946

Section 24 of the Indian Claims Commission Act provided that any claim accruing after the date the Act was signed into law could be brought in the Court of Claims (60 U.S. Stat. 1049 [1946]). As amended, the "Indian Tucker Act," which gave tribes access to the Court of Claims, provided:

> The United States Court of Federal Claims shall have jurisdiction of any claim against the United States accruing after August 13, 1946, in favor of any tribe, band, or other identifiable group of American Indians residing within the territorial limits of the United States or Alaska whenever such claim is one arising under the Constitution, laws or treaties of the United States, or Executive orders of the President, or is one which otherwise would be cognizable in the Court of Federal Claims if the claimant were not an Indian tribe, band or group (28 U.S.C. § 1505).

Claims that are "otherwise . . . cognizable" in the claims court are set forth in a statute known as the Tucker Act (28 U.S.C. § 1491(a)(1).): "The United States Court of Federal Claims shall have jurisdiction to render judgment upon any claim against the United States founded either upon the Constitution, or any Act of Congress or any regulation of an executive department, or upon any express or implied contract with the United States, or for liquidated or unliquidated damages in cases not sounding in tort." Section 24 of the Indian Claims Commission Act provided specifically that Indian claimants in the claims court would be "entitled to

recover in the same manner, to the same extent, and subject to the same conditions and limitations" as non-Indian claimants before the same court.

In 1946, the court given jurisdiction over new Indian claims was called the Court of Claims. That court has subsequently undergone two name changes. The Claims Court was created in 1982, and vested with the full jurisdiction of the Court of Claims, including post-1946 Indian claims as well as unresolved cases from the Indian Claims Commission (96 U.S. Stat. 25). In 1990, there were still 12 cases from the Commission that were pending before the Claims Court (Newton 1992:774). At the same time, Congress created the Federal Circuit and vested it with jurisdiction over appeals from the Claims Court (96 U.S. Stat. 25). In 1992, Congress changed the name of the Claims Court to the Court of Federal Claims (106 U.S. Stat. 4506). Cases from the Court of Federal Claims are also appealed to the Federal Circuit, and may then be reviewed by the United States Supreme Court on a discretionary writ of certiorari.

Although Indian claims for takings of their property under the Fifth Amendment of the Constitution included an award of interest from the date of the taking, the Supreme Court created limitations on Indians' Fifth Amendment claims. In the 1955 decision in *Tee-Hit-Ton Indians* v. *United States*, the Supreme Court distinguished between types of Indian title to land (348 U.S. 272). The Tee-Hit-Ton Band of Tlingit held aboriginal title to land in Alaska, including part of the Tongass National Forest. When the federal government permitted logging in the forest in 1951, the Band sued in the Court of Claims for a partial taking of its property. The Supreme Court agreed that the Band held aboriginal title to the land, and that the aboriginal title had never been extinguished. Nonetheless, the Court held that aboriginal title was not "property" within the meaning of the Fifth Amendment. Therefore, because the Constitution requires "just compensation" only for a taking of property, no compensation was due to the Tee-Hit-Ton Band. The Band had not been deprived of any property.

In so holding, the Supreme Court differentiated between aboriginal title and "recognized" title. If Congress had "recognized" tribal title through a treaty, agreement, or statute, the Court ruled, then the tribal title became a property interest and its taking would be subject to compensation under the Constitution. Absent congressional action according legal rights in the land, the Indians had only "permissive occupation" rather than rights in the land. In a now-infamous passage, the Court stated:

> The line of cases adjudicating Indian rights on American soil leads to the conclusion that Indian occupancy, not specifically recognized as ownership by action authorized by Congress, may be extinguished by the Government without compensation. Every American schoolboy knows that the savage tribes of this continent were deprived of their ancestral ranges by force and that, even when the Indians ceded millions of acres by treaty in return for blankets, food and trinkets, it was not a sale but the conquerors' will that deprived them of their land

(*Tee-Hit-Ton Indians* v. *United States*, 348 U.S. 272, 289–290 [1955]).

Despite the Court's statement, the distinction between aboriginal title and recognized title was a new rule, motivated by fiscal and political considerations. Alaska Native peoples held aboriginal title to most of Alaska, title that had not been extinguished by the purchase of Alaska from Russia in 1867. The financial consequences to the United States Treasury of compensation for Alaska Natives would have been severe. Moreover, the *Tee-Hit-Ton* case was decided in the middle of the termination era of federal Indian policy, when American policy was aimed at depriving Indian tribes of sovereignty and extending state sovereign authority over Indians as over other citizens (Newton 1980:1246–1253).

The effect of *Tee-Hit-Ton* on aboriginal land claims before the Court of Claims was immediate: no compensation was due for takings of aboriginal property. The United States government argued that the same rule should apply to cases before the Indian Claims Commission, which had begun its work less than a decade before *Tee-Hit-Ton* was decided. The Commission, however, rejected the distinction. The result was that claims for the taking of aboriginal land that accrued after August 13, 1946, were not compensable because the claim would be brought (as was the Tee-Hit-Ton Band's) directly in the Court of Claims. But a claim for a confiscation of aboriginal title that arose prior to that date would have been brought before the Indian Claims Commission, which could and did award damages for the loss of aboriginal title (Newton 1980:1256–1257).

The distinction that the United States Supreme Court drew between recognized title and other Indian title was not confined to aboriginal ownership. In cases in the 1940s, the Court determined that no compensation was required by the Constitution when Indian lands set aside by executive order were subsequently restored to the public domain. Like the rule mandating no compensation for aboriginal title lands, however, the no-compensation approach for executive order lands applied to claims brought before the Court of Claims, but not those brought before the Indian Claims Commission. On appeal from a Commission ruling, the Court of Claims determined that claims for confiscation of executive order lands were covered by clause 4 of the Commission's grant of jurisdiction (*Fort Berthold Reservation* v. *United States*, 390 F.2d 686, 696–697 (Ct. Cl. 1968)). Thus the no-compensation rule for executive order lands, like the no-compensation rule for aboriginal title, applied only to claims that arose after August 13, 1946 (Newton 1980:1257–1259).

## Distribution of Judgments

Once a tribal claimant received an award from the Indian Claims Commission, or later from the Court of Claims,

Congress needed to appropriate money to pay the award. In the early days of the Indian Claims Commission, monies appropriated by Congress were transferred to the tribe's trust account and available for use as determined by the tribe and the Bureau of Indian Affairs. In 1960, Congress required that it approve, by legislation, a distribution plan for the tribal judgment funds. Unhappy with the resulting workload, Congress in 1973 enacted the Distribution of Judgment Funds Act to avoid the need for individual statutes (25 U.S.C. §§ 1401–1407; Newton 2005:§5.06[7]; Barsh 1982:23–24).

The 1973 statute requires the secretary of the interior to develop a distribution plan and submit it to Congress. If Congress does not disapprove the plan within 60 days by joint resolution, it becomes effective. Funds to satisfy judgments must still be appropriated, but the appropriation occurs automatically (Newton 2005:§5.06[7]).

In developing a distribution plan, the secretary of the interior is directed to serve the interests of those entitled to a share of the judgment, giving due consideration to the statements of tribal members. Per capita distributions were a nearly universal feature of distribution plans. Congress limited per capita distribution to no more than 80 percent of the judgment, unless special circumstances dictated otherwise. Nonetheless, almost half the distributions by act of Congress were entirely per capita, with no monies reserved for tribal programs. Funds that were set aside for tribal uses were often not available for programs at the discretion of the tribes; rather, most of the plans provided for Interior Department approval of actual disbursements. In addition, judgment funds have been used to pay for programs for which other federal funds were available, raising the suspicion that judgment funds have been substituted for federal monies that otherwise would have gone to the tribes (Barsh 1982: 31–34, 81; Newton 2005:§5.06[7]).

## Trade and Intercourse Act Claims

Since the first Congress met in 1790, federal statutes have prohibited any sale of Indian lands without the consent of the federal government. The final version of the Trade and Intercourse Act, enacted in 1834, provides: "No purchase, grant, lease, or other conveyance of lands, or of any title or claim thereto, from any Indian nation or tribe of Indians, shall be of any validity in law or equity, unless the same be made by treaty or convention entered into pursuant to the Constitution" (25 U.S.C. § 177). The original 13 states had been accustomed to dealing directly with tribes prior to the ratification of the Constitution, and they continued to negotiate treaties with tribes and to authorize private land purchases from Indians after 1790. Some states maintained that the Act did not apply to them. However, these agreements and purchases did violate the Act, and the resulting land transactions were void as a matter of federal law (Clinton and

Hotopp 1979:18, 42–43). Thus, the affected tribes claimed, their title to the land had never been extinguished and was still intact.

Indian tribes began to pursue Intercourse Act claims in the 1960s and 1970s, in part because of a 1966 federal statute that expressly recognized tribes' rights to bring suit in federal court to litigate questions of federal law (28 U.S.C. § 1362). The Supreme Court subsequently held that a tribal claim under the Trade and Intercourse Act was a question of federal law that tribes could assert in federal district court (Clinton and Hotopp 1979:49–50; Singer 2006:619–622). Claims for appropriation of Indian lands under the Intercourse Act are not brought under the federal claims process because the claims are not against the United States. Instead, the claim is against the party—usually a state or its subdivisions—that violated the federal statute.

In general, an Intercourse Act claim arises in one of two ways. In some cases, the claim is based on aboriginal title. Tribes assert that treaties with the states ceding Indian lands were void, and that the tribes' aboriginal title to the land has thus never been extinguished. In other cases, primarily in New York, the claim is based on recognized title. The tribes entered into valid treaties with the United States that recognized tribal reservations, but subsequent state actions acquired tracts of reservation land in violation of the Intercourse Act (Vollman 1979:11–12). An Intercourse Act claim generally requires proof of four elements. A tribe is required to show that it was an Indian "tribe" within the meaning of the Intercourse Act; that the land in question is or was held by the tribe under aboriginal title, recognized title, or executive order; that the tribal title had been extinguished without the consent of the federal government; and that the trust relationship between the United States and the tribe had not been extinguished or abandoned (Clinton and Hotopp 1979:57).

The best-known of the eastern land claims cases is that brought by the Oneida Nation in 1970 against two New York counties for two years' back rent on county-owned property that the Oneida claimed had been taken in violation of the Intercourse Act. The property at issue was part of land acquired by the state of New York in 1795 by a treaty with the Oneida Nation that had not been consented to by the United States. The United States Supreme Court ruled in 1985 that the 1795 transfer of land to New York was not valid, and that the Oneida's claim was not barred by any statute of limitations (*County of Oneida* v. *Oneida Indian Nation*, 470 U.S. 226 [1985]; Vollman 1979:6–8; Singer 2006:606–607, 622–623).

Subsequently, the Oneida Nation challenged municipal property taxes on lands to which the tribe retained aboriginal title and which the tribe had purchased in fee. The tribe argued that, under principles of federal law, states and their subdivisions have no authority to tax Indian lands without the express consent of Congress. In 2005, however, the United States Supreme Court held that the tribe's claim against the city was barred, because the Oneida had waited too long to bring suit challenging the taxes. The taking of Oneida land occurred in the state treaty of 1795, and the tribe waited until 1970 to first file suit on the claim. Consequently, the Supreme Court ruled, the legal doctrine of laches prevented the Oneida's case from being heard (*City of Sherrill* v. *Oneida Indian Nation*, 544 U.S. 197 [2005]; Singer 2006:607–608). The Supreme Court, in its ruling against the Oneida, did not take account of the substantial barriers that existed to the tribe's bringing suit before the late 1960s (Singer 2006:615–627). As a result, the odd outcome of the case is that while the Oneida Nation holds aboriginal title to the lands taken illegally in the 1795 treaty, and full title to the lands at issue in the 2005 case, it does not possess the property rights that other tribes enjoy on their lands (Singer 2006:611).

## Congressional Claims Resolutions

Congress may always choose to settle a land claim by legislation. In some instances, Congress has restored land that was wrongfully taken to tribal ownership. The best known example is the Blue Lake of the Taos Pueblo. After the Indian Claims Commission ruled in 1965 that the lake and the surrounding area were taken unjustly, the Taos Pueblo pursued a return of their sacred land. In 1970, after urging by President Richard Nixon, Congress enacted legislation restoring the taken area to the tribe (84 U.S. Stat. 1437; Barsh 1982:73–75). Nonetheless, land restoration is not a policy that Congress has adopted or a practice that it has often pursued.

A number of the eastern tribes' land claims were settled by federal statute. Congress enacted settlement acts for tribes in Rhode Island, Maine, Connecticut, Massachusetts, and the Seneca Nation in New York. In general, these settlement acts resolved ongoing litigation over land claims by the tribes. Most of the land claims acts extinguished the tribes' aboriginal title, gave congressional approval to the historic transfers that otherwise violated the Intercourse Act, and provided for lands and appropriations. In addition to statutes for the eastern tribes, Congress also enacted land settlements for the Miccosukee and Seminole tribes in Florida, the Puyallup in Washington State, the Crow in Montana, the Santo Domingo Pueblo in New Mexico, the Torres-Martinez Desert Cahuilla Tribe in California, and the Cherokee, Choctaw, and Chickasaw in Oklahoma (25 U.S.C. ch. 19).

The largest land claim settled by Congress was that of the Alaska Natives (R.D. Arnold 1978). Although the Supreme Court ruled in 1955 in *Tee-Hit-Ton* that aboriginal title was not a property right for which the Indians were entitled to compensation, the 1958 Alaska Statehood Act recognized the existence of Native claims. In order to resolve those claims, Congress enacted the Alaska Native Claims Settlement Act (ANCSA) in 1971 (43 U.S.C. §§ 1601–1642). ANCSA extinguished all aboriginal title in Alaska—amounting to more than 360 million acres—and revoked all reservations in the state other than the Annette Island Reserve of the Metlakatla Indian Community (M.E. Thomas 1986, 1988). In return, Congress appropriated $462.5 million and reconveyed 38 million acres of land to Alaska Natives (Newton 2005:§§4.07[3][b][i]–[ii][B]).

ANCSA, enacted during the termination era of federal Indian policy, imposed a corporate model on the Alaska Natives in order to speed their assimilation. The statute established a complex web of village and regional corporations, accorded the corporations the right to select lands from among the 38 million acres designated, and issued stock in the corporations to any Alaska Native alive on December 18, 1971. The lands could be sold freely, but the corporate stock was restricted against alienation for 20 years (Newton 2005:§§4.07[3][b][ii][B]–[C]). By 1988, it was apparent that once the shares became alienable, Alaska natives would likely lose control over their own corporations and likely lose title to their lands as well. In that year, Congress amended ANCSA to provide that the restriction on alienation of the corporation' stock was extended indefinitely. In addition, the amendments made provisions for stock ownership for Alaska natives born after December 18, 1971 (Newton 2005:§4.07[3][b][ii][C]). See "Alaska Native Corporations," this volume.

# Activism, 1950–1980

VINE DELORIA, JR.*

Indian leaders during the twentieth century established a strong tradition of activism on behalf of their tribes. From the intense activities of spokesmen like Carlos Montezuma and Charles A. Eastman before World War II (vol. 4:306–307) to the hopeful work in the Bureau of Indian Affairs under Commissioner John Collier by leaders D'Arcy McNickle and Robert Bennett, Indian leadership provided a demonstrable tradition of service. The founding of the National Congress of American Indians (NCAI) in 1944 (vol. 4:312) and its initial work on the Indian Claims Commission provided an impetus for Indians eager to seek reforms in the treatment of reservation peoples by the federal government.

## 1950s

The NCAI can be best understood as the first intertribal effort to affect policy and programs on a national basis. Previous efforts were sporadic and depended as much upon the occasion for concern as upon the ability of the tribes to understand the need for national action. In 1954 a determined group of congressmen, in an effort to hasten the assimilation of Indians into the American economic mainstream, devised the termination policy ("Termination and Relocation," this vol.). Under the leadership of Sen. Arthur Watkins of Utah and Congressman E.Y. Berry of South Dakota, they passed several acts terminating the rights to federal status of specific tribes. When word of the haste with which the policy was being put into effect reached Indians, an immediate response was generated by the National Congress of American Indians.

During the winter of 1954 the NCAI sponsored an emergency conference to oppose this legislation. For nearly six weeks the nation's capitol witnessed a stream of tribal delegations arriving to lobby their state congressional delegations against the termination policy. Most tribes were able to get themselves exempted from the new policy by reminding their senators and congressmen of their many unresolved problems that could not be resolved by walking away from them. While many tribal delegations had visited the District of Columbia in the past to lobby for individual pieces of legislation favorable to their reservations, there had never been a sustained drive by a coalition of tribes for a common purpose of affecting national policy.

The 1954 emergency conference can rightly be characterized as the first unified effort in the postwar years by Indians to change national Indian policy. It was, also, the last significant effort by Indians to maintain the dignity and aloofness that had characterized Indian negotiations with federal officials. Thereafter the Indian delegations that arrived at the nation's capitol became increasingly dissatisfied with the attitudes and promises given by federal officials with respect to the solution of Indian problems. Whether the 1954 conference still contained a majority of traditional Indians who naively believed that federal officials would not promise what they could not deliver, or whether the rapidly changing times made peaceful and dignified conferences outdated, the fact remains that the conference made a deep and lasting impression on the people who attended. Departing delegates returned home convinced that they must quickly become a political force if they were to survive.

The middle and late 1950s saw Indians devote an increasing amount of time and energy to voter registration and political activities on the state level. Tribes began visiting congressional offices and participating in fundraising dinners of candidates. Several individuals made efforts to get into Congress themselves. Benjamin Reifel, a Teton Sioux and former Bureau of Indian Affairs career employee, won a seat in the House of Representatives from South Dakota, serving 1961–1971. Activism during these years was founded on the belief that given the right set of circumstances and the proper forum for discussion, the legislative and executive branches of the federal government would respond to Indian needs. This attitude was later severely criticized by younger Indians who refused to credit any politician with good will, but during the late 1950s it represented a sensible and responsible posture for the Indian community.

*This chapter was written in 1980 when Vine Deloria (b. 1933, d. 2005) was serving as editor of this volume. As executive director of the National Congress of American Indians from 1964 to 1967, and then as a college professor and prolific writer, he was the best known American Indian activist of the 1960s and 1970s. Through countless public appearances and publishing more than 20 books, he became the voice of the Native American political movement during this period.

The 1960s shattered all previous conceptions of social reform and reality; Indians, like other groups caught in the backwaters of American life, were puzzled at the developments. The progress toward achieving integration of schools and public facilities, which looked so promising a few years earlier, was slowing to a barely perceptible crawl, and young Blacks were impatient with the reluctance shown by White America to fulfill their constitutional responsibilities. Freedom rides, sit-ins, and marches began, and soon the South was struggling with an irresistible wave of activists who demanded immediate integration. When the intensity of the conflict filled television screens and the seriousness of the movement could be seen by the public, attitudes changed rapidly.

Young Indians, attending the American Indian Chicago Conference in 1961 (vol. 4:315), saw their elders content with passing wordy resolutions begging the federal government to help them and they recoiled at the submissive attitude shown by the older Indians. The contrast between Indian leadership and the courageous efforts of the young Blacks who, against the cautious counsel of their elders, were in the process of integrating lunch counters and bus stations, was all too evident and indicated the need for a greater effort by Indians to bring their needs to the attention of federal policy makers. The result of poetic resolutions sent to the White House from the Chicago conference was a few token gestures and a great deal of rhetoric and the disappointment among Indians at the response of the John F. Kennedy administration, followed shortly thereafter by the authorization of the Kinzua Dam (vol. 15:513, 515) to flood much of the Allegany Seneca reservation in New York (fig. 1). Some form of Indian activism similar to that employed by the civil rights movement was made a certainty.

AP Images.

Fig. 1. George D. Herron (Seneca), left, and Sidney Carney (Choctaw), special Bureau of Indian Affairs liaison representative for the Senecas (Josephy 1968), at the deepest part of the dam for the Kinzua power project near Salamanca, N.Y. Despite strong Indian opposition the federal government constructed the dam, granting the Senecas $15 million as compensation for the land taken for the power project in western N.Y. and Pa. (Bilharz 1998; W.N. Hoover 2005). Photographed Oct. 16, 1964.

In 1964, while the Seneca question was still in the air, the National Indian Youth Council organized a "fish-in" in Washington State to protest the treatment of Indian fisherman by state fish and game officials (vol. 4:316–317). First Marlon Brando and then Dick Gregory made their appearances on behalf of the Indian fishermen. Dignified tribal officials railed against the apparent interference into Indian matters by celebrities. Frantic efforts by Indian leaders to turn aside the obvious attractiveness of protests did little except create a sense of alienation in the mind of young Indians, who refused to sit on the sidelines while the rest of the country moved forward. Rapidly the Youth Council became the popular Indian organization and the NCAI became less attractive as a means of presenting Indian concerns. Still dominated by the same people who had organized the group in the 1940s, the NCAI gradually became the bastion of conservatism with its only hope the prayer that Indians would remain dignified and not take to the streets and rivers. That kind of behavior, NCAI officials never tired in admonishing the young, was not "the Indian way."

By 1968 the split between the two groups was nearly complete. The Youth Council adopted increasingly more radical rhetoric and slogans while the NCAI moved toward embracing the stance advocated by the Bureau of Indian Affairs. A delegation of Indians joined the Poor People's March during the summer of 1968 and there made contacts with young people of other backgrounds who also saw a need for radical action. Dissatisfied with the posture of the national Indian community toward activist tactics and unhappy with the political stance of many tribal leaders who refused to criticize the Vietnam war for fear they would lose funding for the poverty programs then being conducted on the reservations, the younger generation hungered for more action.

By a strange coincidence not uncommon in history, 1968 saw the organization in Minneapolis of the Indian Patrol, which arose out of a concern for police brutality against Indians in the slum sections of the city. On weekends there was a disproportionate percentage of Indians arrested with a corresponding rise in incidents involving beatings and maltreatment of Indians who were arrested. The Indian Patrol followed police cars when they entered areas with a heavy concentration of Indians. Police brutality quickly declined when the police understood that witnesses to their tactics were readily available. Wherever possible the Indian Patrol assisted Indians in reaching their homes without incident and soon a whole host of social services was being performed by the Indian Patrol, which made it one of the premier organizations in the urban areas of the nation. As its popularity soared and its fame grew the Indian Patrol became a sponsor of federally funded programs and changed its name to the American Indian Movement.

By mid-1969 tempers were short in Indian country. The administration of President Richard Nixon, after rejecting termination as a policy, appeared to be without a policy. Indians sought a means of dramatizing the conditions on the reservations and in the cities that would be uniquely Indian, 39 competitive with the Blacks who dominated the media, and yet would be of such a nature that a substantial percentage of the Indian community would support it. Indian students in the San Francisco Bay area colleges, remembering a previous humorous effort by Dick McKenzie and others to claim Alcatraz Island in San Francisco Bay under the Treaty of Fort Laramie of 1868, decided that such an effort, in a period characterized by symbolic media events, would give them immediate access to the public. A national meeting of urban Indian centers was held at the San Francisco Indian center and several days later the center was destroyed in an unfortunate fire leaving the Bay area Indians without a meeting place. Two days later a contingent of 19 Indian students invaded Alcatraz and issued a proclamation comparing the desolate island to their home reservations and demanding title to the former prison (fig. 2).

AP Images.

Fig. 2. Indians, who are part of the Indians of All Tribes, Inc., occupying the former prison at Alcatraz, standing on the dock of Alcatraz I. in San Francisco Bay. Indian activists had attempted an occupation before. When the island was closed and declared surplus federal property in 1964, 5 Sioux Indians under the leadership of Richard McKenzie claimed the land under the 1868 treaty that entitled them to take possession of surplus federal property. The 1969 occupation was supported by many tribes and was led by Richard Oakes (Mohawk). His initial group consisted of 80 Indian students from the University of California at Los Angeles and 20 other Native Americans, among them Jim Vaughn (Cherokee), Joe Bill (Eskimo), and Ross Harden (Winnebago). Photographed Nov. 25, 1969.

Media response to the Alcatraz invasion was immediate and positive. Movie stars made pilgrimages to the rock to offer advice and encouragement. A rock band donated a launch to carry people and supplies to the island. Indians of every persuasion arrived at Alcatraz declaring their willingness to fight for the place. The resulting confusion and explosion of energies meant that the leaders of the occupation had to find an immediate way to relieve the escalating tensions. One large group left the island and occupied lands in northern California claimed by one of the tribes but leased to a large corporation. Another group marched to the state capitol and watched as the California legislature passed a resolution petitioning Congress for transfer of the title to Alcatraz to a nonprofit corporation to be established by the Indians.

The occupation lasted nearly 19 months. During its course the nature of the Indian protest changed radically. Where it had initially been inspired by college-aged students with a desire for a new national policy, it evolved into a strange community without goals or energies that simply clung to a precarious existence on the island, without hopes and lacking plans for consummating the elaborate programs that had motivated the original protestors. The invasion became a symbolic event whose meaning transcended the immediate political gains, but as the occupation dragged on and the Indians failed to bring about a successful conclusion, the protest became the source of ironic and sometimes bitter jokes. One cartoon showed Army generals peering at a map of the San Francisco Bay area with an arrow at Alcatraz and the caption, "First Alcatraz, then Sausalito, then Richmond, and finally the whole country," an obvious parody of the Vietnam domino theory. Stand-up comedians loved to declare that unless the Indians got out of that prison they would all be thrown in jail, a twist of words appropriate to the occasion.

## 1970s

Alcatraz sparked a mode of protest that seemed uniquely Indian. American guilt feelings were high with the story of the My Lai massacre in Vietnam, and the obvious parallels with Indian sufferings a century before produced a tolerance in the public mind for occupations of important federal properties on the justification that these lands should be immediately yielded to the tribes. That no piece of occupied property was adjacent to a reservation did not escape a watchful public, and the sheer fantasy of this wish fulfilled a number of emotional needs that might otherwise have manifested themselves in violence. Had Indians sought land adjoining one of the important reservations it might have produced a wholly different public response. Thus, Fort Lawton, a partially used Army installation in the Seattle area, was invaded by a group of Indians (vol. 4:319) led by Jane Fonda who spent most of her time declaring that she guessed this protest would work to deprive her of the Academy Award, a protesting-too-much device that focused attention on her nomination and helped her secure the award.

In 1971 a group of Sioux and Chippewa moved into the Mount Rushmore Memorial, South Dakota, and protested the treatment of Indians and the desecration of the sacred Black Hills. The protest was deliberately symbolic, although the message behind it was generally lost on the public since media coverage, away from the national networks and major newspapers, was sporadic. In Milwaukee, Indians occupied an abandoned Coast Guard station, and rumors were rife that they would continue a platform of conquest with the yacht club as their eventual goal. In Chicago, Indian protestors established an "Indian village" when some Indian mothers were evicted from their apartments, and this protest saw the first violent response by police forces indicating that there was a limit to the public patience and that Indian protests were becoming tiresome to many television viewers.

In June 1972 a middle-aged Oglala Sioux named Raymond Yellow Thunder was brutally abused and killed in Gordon, Nebraska. When local authorities appeared to be covering up the incident, the American Indian Movement announced a march on the small Nebraska town to seek redress, and nearly 1,000 Indians streamed in to demand justice. *Life* magazine featured a cover picture and story emphasizing the nature of the Indian protest, and the public began to look more seriously at the Indian activism that was spreading across the country. Gordon was the turning point in the activist movement. Confrontation with rural White police was an entirely different matter from dealing with sophisticated urban human-relations personnel from the mayor's office or the liberal federal officials detailed to keep track of Alcatraz. The media image of Indians experienced a radical transformation with the Gordon incident. No longer were Indians seen as a contemporary group using sophisticated symbolic gestures to make a particular point. From that protest forward Indian demonstrations were phrased in the archaic language of the frontier. "Uprisings" and "battles" and "skirmishes" became the words to describe protests and demonstrations. The world view of the nineteenth century emerged to interpret the Indian movement.

The fall of 1972 was a presidential election season wherein Richard Nixon buried the Democrat George McGovern. Part of the Indian strategy for embarrassing the administration and gaining additional concessions was to march on the nation's capitol with a list of 20 points that summarized the major reforms Indians wanted during Nixon's second term. Correctly figuring that people were exhausted with campaign rhetoric and would welcome a diversion, the caravan, aptly called The Trail of Broken Treaties, entered the District of Columbia the weekend preceding the presidential election.

Planning for this massive demonstration had left something to be desired. Indians assigned to secure housing and appointments with important officials, and to provide for the feeding of caravan participants during their stay in Wash-

ington, had failed to do even the preliminary work. With the national media focused on the caravan the leadership had all become chiefs abandoning any role of administrative responsibility that had been assigned to them. The result was chaos the first day. As evening approached and recalcitrant Bureau of Indian Affairs officials refused to negotiate some of the demands of the protestors, the Indians occupied the headquarters of the Bureau of Indian Affairs and settled in for a well-publicized siege (vol. 4:197).

The weekend was spent in a series of misdirected confrontations and negotiations with each side unable to determine who had the executive power to speak for the other side; agreements made one hour were voided by counterdirectives issued by others in the next hour. Some time during the weekend the Indians were able to smuggle a substantial amount of documents from the Bureau offices and whisk them away to distant parts of the country. As the nation went to the polls and several ominous deadlines passed without incident a general agreement was made that called for the government to provide $66,000 for travel money back to the reservations and for a general amnesty to be declared that would enable the Indians to escape prosecution for their activities. As the Indian negotiators were returning to the building after consummating this agreement, rumor spread that federal security forces were then planning a military assault on the occupants of the building. Before calmer voices could prevail some of the more energetic protestors began destroying parts of the building. Finally peace was restored and the Indians left the building. Tribal officials were taken on a tour through the building the next week and expressed horror at the destruction of the building.

Outcry at the sacking of a federal building rose as the first damage reports were made public. Estimates ran as high as $2 million but these included overtime pay for security officers and a number of other items that could also have been charged to ordinary security operations in the nation's capital. Still, there was no doubt that Indians had caused more damage to federal buildings than any other group in American history including the British sack of Washington during the War of 1812. The public, strangely, did not feel the Indians unjustifed in their attack. Several congressmen, testifying at hearings held months after the events, pointed out that their mail was still running heavily in favor of the Indians.

The caravan participants straggled home during the next several months, while some, being accustomed to life in Washington, remained in the hotels for weeks afterward living on handouts and trying to readjust themselves to a calmer, less spectacular life. Federal agents scoured the country seeking stolen records and office machines that had been taken by the departing protestors. Months passed before any significant number of records were returned. The American Indian Movement dominated the caravan but did not really control it. Charismatic personalities directed group energies as the occasion allowed and at times no single personality was able to control the emotions of the demonstrators. Yet when the occupation was over the

*41*

personalities prominent in the American Indian Movement—Dennis Banks, Russell Means, Clyde Bellecourt, and Carter Camp—had clearly assumed national leadership roles that had far more influence than that of any elected tribal or organizational figure.

Fear of the unpredictability of the Indian activists became centered in the actions and antics of these personalities. While this aura of leadership had benefits, it also closed off many opportunities for constructive leadership, which these people might have given. The mass of Indians clearly wanted more action, and the major American Indian Movement leaders were trapped between the need to perform and the necessity to chart a constructive goal for the movement. Western law enforcement officials and a significant number of federal officials saw that control of charismatic leadership was the first step in bringing the movement under control, and violent conflict became inevitable. Russell Means and a contingent of Oglala Sioux announced that they would return to the Pine Ridge Reservation in South Dakota to celebrate their victory over the federal government. Richard Wilson announced that he would fulfill his responsibilities as chairman of the tribe and oppose the arrival of American Indian Movement people to the reservation. The stage was set for armed confrontation.

In January 1972 Wesley Bad Heart Bull, an Oglala Sioux from the Pine Ridge Reservation, was killed in a fracas in an off-reservation bar, and minor charges were filed against his killer. The facts of the situation were clouded at best, but the Indian protestors were already committed to reforms and needed an incident such as this one to cite as an example of the treatment of Indians in South Dakota. A march was planned for Custer, South Dakota, to protest the cavalier treatment accorded the slayer of Bad Heart Bull. South Dakota police officials, determined to put an end to Indian activism in the state, met the demonstration with force and a minor building was set afire in the course of the ensuing confusion. Charges were filed against Indians involved in the protest, and within the week Dennis Banks, hoping to alleviate some of the pressure that was building in the state, addressed the South Dakota legislature on the conditions of Indians and promised to cooperate with state officials in seeking solutions to problems.

Richard Wilson had his problems with the American Indian Movement mystique then pervading the reservation. The tribe had its elections every two years, and discontent was spreading over the reservation with his administration. Tribal police forces were vastly expanded to protect tribal property against any occupation, and political opponents of Wilson began accusing the tribal police of brutality. Several sporadic protests occurred at the agency headquarters that did little to resolve the problems and much to irritate both parties in the conflict. As tribal police became more oppressive, tribal members became more vocal in their criticisms and the police retreated into a siege mentality. When Wilson presided over his own impeachment proceedings and made a farce out of tribal constitutional procedures, tempers ex-

ploded and Indians of many political persuasions sent word to Means and Banks demanding that American Indian Movement take an active leadership role in ousting Wilson from office.

On the morning of February 28 a small force of Indians in a caravan moved into the hamlet of Wounded Knee, site of a brutal massacre of Indians in 1890 and popularized by a best-selling book of the previous season by Dee Brown (1971), *Bury My Heart at Wounded Knee*. Announcing that they would hold the village until prominent politicians arrived to negotiate the conditions on the reservation and the violation of the 1868 Treaty of Fort Laramie with the Sioux, the protestors drew worldwide media coverage (vol. 13: 836). Sens. George McGovern and James Abourezk of South Dakota made trips to the occupied village to determine that the inhabitants, originally described as hostages, were in good health. For the most part the local people described their treatment as proper; some expressed sympathy for the activists, thus nullifying any excuse for the government or the tribe to attempt to regain the village by force.

The occupation lasted until early May and seemed to encapsulate all the memorable events and personalities of the 1960s (fig. 3). National personalities famed for activities in other causes made their pilgrimage to Wounded Knee to express sympathy with the Indians. In a spasm of irony Ralph Abernathy offered to use his influence with the Nixon administration to secure favorable terms for surrendering the village—an influence that was probably less than that already possessed by the American Indian Movement. Issues were impossible to separate, and this confusion led to fruitless negotiations on several occasions. A strange coalition of forces had invited the American Indian Movement to occupy Wounded Knee, and no consensus could be reached by representatives of the occupants on the terms for surrender.

Although there were different versions of the surrender terms, it was generally agreed that they included submission to criminal charges for activities occurring during the occupation, that the Indians would give up any arms they might possess, and that the White House would initiate an investigation of the tribal government and begin a series of open meetings on the reservation to probe into the violations of the 1868 treaty and recommend reforms in line with treaty promises. A first meeting was held in June on the reservation but no further meetings were held because of an inability of the Indians and the administration to come to an agreement on future subjects for discussion. Most of the prominent personalities involved in Wounded Knee were charged with the commission of federal crimes and tried. But blatant misconduct by federal security agencies, most notably the Federal Bureau of Investigation, led to mistrials or acquittals. Of 198 defendants charged with over 600 counts based on activities occurring during the occupation, only six were convicted and of these two were pleas of *nolo contendere*, which meant that no defense was offered during the trial.

Wounded Knee ended the escalation toward violence that characterized the middle period of Indian activism. Reper-

AP Images.

Fig. 3. Occupation of Wounded Knee, S. Dak. left, Members of the Oglala Sioux tribe marching to the cemetery where nearly 200, mostly Minneconjou, victims were buried after the 1890 massacre at the site. Third in line is Carter Camp (Oglala), a leader of the American Indian Movement. Photographed March 10, 1973. right, Kent Frizzel (right), assistant U.S. attorney general, being offered a peace pipe by a member of the American Indian Movement during a ceremony ending the standoff. Next to Wallace Black Elk (Oglala), kneeling, are American Indian Movement leaders: Russell Means (Oglala), Dennis Banks (Ojibwa) wearing a headband, and Carter Camp, wearing a vest. Photograph by Jim Mone, April 5, 1973.

cussions of Wounded Knee manifested themselves primarily in a virtual blackout of stories on Indians. Television networks and major newspapers cried out that they had been victimized and exploited by the Indians at Wounded Knee and in the aftermath Indian stories disappeared from the media. But there was equal evidence that the networks and newspapers had used Indians as much as they had been used. The excitement of reporting on a real Indian war, as many of them described it, was an old tradition of yellow journalism and modern reporters did little to add credit to their profession. Stories were written in a style that would have made William Randolph Hearst and Gordon Bennett green with envy. The media seemed to focus on the more spectacular personalities in the Indian community to the exclusion of more responsible spokesmen elected by the tribes to represent their interests. Inflammatory language used to describe interracial conflicts was highlighted by the media in reporting the activities of the Indian activists, and moderate, reasonable proposals rarely received the attention that they deserved.

In 1978, after the trials deriving from Wounded Knee had been concluded, a threat based in part on the bad image that Indians received following Wounded Knee, called forth another protest. Congressmen Lloyd Meeds and Jack Cunningham of Washington State offered bills in the House of Representatives that, if passed, would have effectively eliminated Indian treaty rights and federal services. Although there was little sentiment in Congress for such legislation, Indians around the country, fearful of the revival of termination as a policy, organized a march on Washington popularly called The Longest Walk. Although there were substantial misgivings among Indians about the walk, a significant number of Indians participated in it. The demonstration accomplished very little in the way of concrete changes but it

was surprisingly peaceful. Traditional Indians, primarily older people, joined the march in its final days before it entered the nation's capital and assumed control of the activities, taking leadership away from the militant leaders who had planned it. This intervention and the consequent religious emphasis given to the activities of the marchers gave clear evidence that traditional religious leaders had become the dominant force in Indian country supplanting the personalities and styles of the late 1960s and early 1970s.

The Indian activist movement was clearly a phenomenon that depended upon the style of a particular period in American history. Relying largely upon the eagerness of the communications media, primarily television, to communicate easily understood symbols and to look sympathetically upon conditions of poverty without asking deeper questions of causes and solutions, the movement in its most exciting days was largely a creation of the press. When the feeling of exhilaration finally entrenched itself in the national Indian psyche and manifested itself in events that could not be controlled, such as the occupation of the Bureau of Indian Affairs and the village of Wounded Knee, the media recoiled in horror and acted as if the Indians had been planning destructive events from the beginning. The outmoded image of Indians as marauding hostiles of the frontier was basically reinforced in the minds of the public.

Although the activists attempted to relate to other movements in American society, the responsibility to maintain their roots in the Indian community presented them with immense difficulties. A partial solution to this problem was to emphasize the religious nature of the protests and demonstrations. Raising the religious issue enabled them to blunt criticism from traditional members of the tribes. It also placed them in a slightly superior intellectual bargaining

Fig. 4. Vine Deloria, Jr. (Lakota), at age 69, scholar, influential advocate of Indian rights, and author of *Custer Died for Your Sins: An Indian Manifesto* (1969). Photograph by Cyrus McCrimmon, Golden, Colo., 2002.

position when articulating moral claims against society and the federal government, since Indians were believed to have a primacy in complaining against pollution and corruption by other activist groups. Land restoration issues could be raised via the religious tradition that, in another context, would have been seen and understood as simple land confiscation. Because the Indians were able to reach out and establish sympathetic relations with ecologists, Blacks, and Chicanos, and colonized peoples around the world, they were able to keep their movement alive much longer than anyone expected.

The religious issue reversed itself once it was disconnected from the political goals of the younger generation. Many older Indians reluctantly concurred with activist interpretations of Indian religious beliefs while the major personalities were able to maintain sufficient national following to be formidable in conferences. After Wounded Knee tribal elders exerted an increasingly important influence and by the time of The Longest Walk were able to take charge of the protesting energies and direct them in the direction they thought most constructive. This phenomenon was in direct contrast to the developments in the civil rights movement where initial activities had been inspired by Black Christian ministers who were later preempted by vocal activists. Insofar as the activist movement was able to create a supratribal national identity, which had been lacking for four centuries,

the Indian movement was an outstanding success. Judged on the basis of political achievements and structural changes wrought in the federal relationship it was sporadic with both successes and failures to its credit.

As the movement developed and activists had to pay attention to the traditional elements on the reservations a cry of "tribal sovereignty" was raised. This phrase had an entirely different meaning from its traditional use by legal minds when argued in an activist context. Far from affirming the primacy of tribal governments organized under the Indian Reorganization Act and beholden to the secretary of the Interior for governing powers, the tribal sovereignty of which the activists spoke referred primarily to a goal of dissolving existing tribal governments and returning to the old government of general councils and chiefs and headmen that once was common among Plains tribal groups.

Tribal sovereignty in the activist context required a larger stage to be considered as a sensible restoration of things Indian. Early in the movement the Iroquois chiefs proved to have considerable influence as they articulated a theory of restoration of the international status of Indian tribes as it might have been conceived prior to the American Revolution. This idea matured slowly in the minds of Western Indians but eventually was accepted as a reasonable way to bring international pressures to bear on the United States. Additionally the theory had a certain attractiveness for a people who had never been viewed as having this lofty status. One constructive result of this belief was the concentration of a number of skillful young Indians on the larger issues of preparing documents and arguments to be used in raising world consciousness concerning Indians. In September 1977 a large delegation went to Geneva, Switzerland, where they made a presentation to the Decolonization Subcommittee of the United Nations.

During the course of the activist phase of modern Indian life horizons were raised considerably above the abstract concepts that were discussed in workshops in the late 1950s and early 1960s. Where the workshops had basically concentrated on a narrow analysis of the conditions of rural people, the movement had moved far beyond to conceive of a much broader sweep of history and raised issues of the international status of Indians, which had not been within the scope of any earlier discussions. This growth to maturity was unprecedented in the Indian experience and indicated a new view of Indian identity that greatly surpassed any conceptions held by other minority groups during the same time. The maturity shown by the tribal elders in assuming command at the later stages of the movement reassured many people that Indians had arrived at a position of strength as a national community fulfilling the dreams and visions of earlier leaders and prophets such as Tecumseh and Pontiac.

# Activism Since 1980

ROBERT WARRIOR

Activism has taken a number of forms in the American Indian world since 1980, which is true even when activism is defined rather tightly as political action done through protest or with direct participation of people on reservations, in cities, on college campuses, and in other places. This sort of activism has not resulted in a single narrative thread that might help give shape to the activism that has occurred since 1980. As such, then, activism after the 1970s makes more sense in terms of a set of dynamics than it does a progression of events that move toward a specific end. These dynamics are, in many ways, a primary legacy of the preceding era, when a much more cogent sense of historical movement obtained.

The 1970s was a crucial decade because of the emergence into Indian politics of a viable presence of individuals and groups who defined themselves primarily by their willingness to break with established political methods and channels and by their links to local, grassroots people in bringing about changes in the treatment of Indian people on reservations and in cities (P. Smith and R. Warrior 1996). While it is certainly true that anyone—a national spokesperson, someone working in Washington to change federal policy, or a tribal councilmember seeking to get better results for his or her community—could be seen in the earlier period as being an activist, those who dominated the world of Indian politics in the 1970s redefined the basic shape of Native activism. By 1980, a focus on the importance of local, direct action had taken hold and the meaning and role of activism in American Indian communities had shifted considerably from what it had been two decades before.

Activism of this sort, of course, had been present in Native communities throughout the twentieth century, perhaps most importantly by members of the Native American Church in their ongoing struggles to institutionalize their religious movement and protect its adherents from repressive laws through which the ceremonial use of peyote was criminalized and otherwise discouraged. In spite of their successes, stalwarts of the Native American Church remained, for the most part, on the margins of the Indian world. In the 1970s, radical forms of protest, community organizing, and critique of tribal officials and national organizations had moved from the margins of the Indian world to the center. A feature of the time since is the persistence in Native communities of the idea that people formerly on the margins of the

Indian world, including spiritual leaders, have as much a stake in the future as anyone else and can be and often are heard in political life.

The most obvious place to start looking at the prospects for activism since 1980 is the American Indian Movement (AIM), the organization that came to the fore of public consciousness in the era of protest politics. The leaders of AIM and its commitment to radical action and community organizing continued to affect the political dynamics of the Indian world even as the organization itself became less and less a cohesive national group. The importance of American Indian activism comes not so much from an analysis of specific organizations and the actions they have undertaken since the 1980s as it does from a style of politics that remains crucial to understanding in the sweep of historical and cultural change in Native North America.

## Changes in the American Indian Movement

In the summer of 1980, activist leader Russell Means (fig. 1), Oglala Sioux, spoke to the largest audience of his career when he delivered a speech to the Black Hills International Survival Gathering in South Dakota. The event drew more than 10,000 people to the Black Hills in an effort to draw attention to what organizers saw as the dire economic prospects of the region. Sioux and other Native people whose focus was on the ongoing land claims to the Black Hills based on the 1868 Fort Laramie Treaty were in attendance, but the gathering appealed primarily to White environmental groups and ranching interests in an effort to create a coalition against the federal government and mining interests that were seeking to exploit the uranium and other mineral resources in the hills.

The Survival Gathering is a bit of a red herring in the history of Native activism insofar as the large numbers of people involved is not consonant with its significance or impact. Means's speech, in fact, might be the most important aspect of what transpired. Published in the politically left-leaning magazine *Mother Jones* and anthologized widely and analyzed academically in various ways ever since, "For America to Live, Europe Must Die" (Means [1980] 1995) is perhaps the fullest published statement by a radical Native

AP Images.

Fig. 1. Russell Means (Oglala Sioux), actor and activist, testifying before a Senate select committee. Means, a founder of the American Indian Movement, embodies Native American activism to such an extent that he became the subject of one of Andy Warhol's iconic pop portraits from his American Indian series, painted in 1976. The painting hangs in the Dayton Art Institute, Ohio. Photograph by Marcy Nighswander, 1989.

leader in the era. As such, it provides unique perspective on the state of American Indian activism a decade after Means and others from the American Indian Movement had taken the Indian world by storm with high-profile protests, radical rhetoric, and unprecedented success at organizing grassroots Native people.

Means, by that point in history, was reinventing himself as the repercussions of the AIM heyday after the 1972 occupation of the Bureau of Indian Affairs building in Washington, D.C., and the 1973 takeover of Wounded Knee were ending. Over the previous seven years, Means had lost his bid for the presidency of the Oglala Sioux Tribe in a disputed election, traveled the world in helping establish an international presence for radical indigenous politics, and served a year in prison for his involvement in one of the riots that had broken out during an AIM protest (a prosecution that arose from one of many indictments Means faced). All the while, he was the most visible leader of AIM, an organization that struggled to maintain itself in the midst of constant threats of criminal indictments, federal infiltration, and ideological conflict.

The Survival Gathering was among a set of developments in the ongoing struggle of the Sioux to regain control of the Black Hills, the most spiritually significant portion of their homelands, and Means used his speech there as a platform to announce the new direction of his activism. The address went on for over two hours, but the upshot of what Means said there was a rejection of "the European materialist tradition of despiritualizing the universe," a tradition that for

Means included capitalism, Christianity, and Marxism. Means argued instead in favor of "the traditional Lakota way and the ways of the other American Indian peoples, . . . the way that knows that . . . humans must be in harmony with *all* relations" of the natural world (Means [1980] 1995:547). This was a cultural way of peoples whom Means describes, by turn, as "natural" and "correct."

During the speech, Means referenced what he saw as the foundational ideas of Isaac Newton and Rene Descartes as he argued against human acquisitiveness and domination over natural resources. He advocated resistance against anyone of any race who continued the materialist assault on natural resources. His enemies, thus, were not those who are genetically European, but those who advocated ideas and participated in the culture that derives from the intellectual heritage of European philosophies. Marxism, while in Means's view pretending to represent a break with its predecessors, was really just another version of "the same old song" of unbridled acquisitiveness.

In contrast to much of the struggle he had helped lead over the previous decade, surviving in the face of continuing assaults on the natural order, according to Means, is the revolution that Sioux philosophy calls for. "We don't want power over white institutions," Means said, "we want white institutions to disappear . . . We learn from the elders, from nature, from the powers. And when the catastrophe is over, we American Indian people will still be here to inhabit the hemisphere. I don't care if it's only a handful living high in the Andes. American Indian people will survive; harmony will be reestablished. *That's* revolution" (Means [1980] 1995:548). This revolution, Means, stated, happens through local work among traditional American Indian people.

Means focused specifically on his rejection of Marxism even as he also rejected, at least in part, his own past as an activist leader. "I should state clearly," he says, "that leading anyone toward Marxism is the last thing on my mind. . . . In fact, I can say I don't think I'm trying to lead anyone toward anything. To some extent I tried to be a 'leader,' in the sense that the white media like to use that term, when the American Indian Movement was a young organization. This was a result of a confusion I no longer have. You cannot be everything to everyone. I do not propose to be used in such a fashion by my enemies. I am not a leader. I *am* an Oglala Lakota patriot. That is all I want and all I need to be. And I am very comfortable with who I am" (Means [1980] 1995:550).

This speech is, in many ways, a study in contradictions. This most famous and widely read speech of Means's career is one of the only examples of something he delivered from a written text, but he went out of his way to say at the beginning that the act of writing itself is something he detested as part of the lifelessness of Eurocentric thinking. Also, it was a pointed critique of Marxism and the American left in an era in which American Marxism and other forms of the radical left were in a shambles hardly befitting such an impassioned response. It is also, of course, a speech about the importance of working primarily with Indians using Indian philosophies that Means delivered to a group that was primarily White people.

AIM had undergone major changes in its ideology over the previous two years, and many inside and outside were already talking about the organization strictly in the past tense.

## American Indian Movement in 1980

Informality is central to understanding the American Indian Movement. While AIM had a specific leadership structure, could boast of chapters in various cities and on reservations, and maintained offices and records, most of its problems at the outset of the 1980s could be read as coming directly from its lack of clear lines of communication and decision-making. All the major leaders gained titles (field director, national chairman, or executive director, for instance) that made it sound like any of them might be in charge.

The loose structure led to some of the worst and most embarrassing missteps of the movement years, including the case of Douglass Durham, a non-Native federal agent and former police officer who, pretending to be Native, managed to infiltrate AIM so successfully that he had the title of director of security when he was exposed in 1975 (Dewing 1986; Churchill and VanderWall 1988). Anna Mae Pictou Aquash's murder in 1976 can also be seen as having AIM's informality as a proximate cause, and the murder is easily the ugliest case of internal brutality of the movement years (Lame Woman 2002).

Aquash was in the inner circles of power and leadership in AIM before being killed because of unfairly coming under suspicion of being an agent of the federal government (Brand 1978; Mihesuah 1993). Her killers were young movement "dog soldiers" at the time of her murder. Fueled by their own sense of extreme loyalty and heavy doses of drugs and alcohol, they kidnapped, tortured, and killed Aquash. Whether AIM leaders ordered her killing is not clear (Giago 2002).

These cases of what can transpire from organizational chaos are as serious as another is bewilderingly funny. In the mid-1970s, one of AIM's national leaders absentmindedly left a briefcase full of original organizational notes at an airport pay telephone booth in spite of knowing full well that he was being tailed by federal agents. With barely any effort the agent was able to gain access to the sorts of sensitive information that even years of infiltration might not uncover. AIM's fast and loose style lent itself to mistakes, a lack of organizational discipline, and a notion of leadership accountability that was like a shell game.

By 1980 AIM had not so much imploded as it had lost momentum. Means's speech, in fact, reflected a concerted effort on the part of many within the organization to address this lack of momentum. At a meeting in the spring of 1979, AIM leaders attempted to address problems of a lack of effective organization and lines of communication. These were addressed through a new central committee structure through which AIM could continue its commitment to being "a strong advocate organization for the grass-roots Native people" (American Indian Movement 1979). Perhaps most importantly, though, those seeking to reverse AIM's fortunes laid claim to a version of history in which the group had at its core a "self-identification as a spiritual movement." "Elders" were central to this new version of AIM and to activism. Such elders, in this formulation, had recognized the early movement, had from the beginning prompted a primary concern for treaty rights, and would now resolve disputes, approve plans, and authorize movement activities through counsel and ceremonies. This, then, was the organizational effect of the shift toward religious and spiritually defined activism that was occurring by the late 1970s and that has continued since.

## Another Perspective

The evolution of activist politics toward religiously defined leadership and action was hardly a matter of consensus, nor was it a simple matter of wiser and older heads taking command of the activist movement. While the internal dynamics of AIM and other activist elements from the 1970s can seem unimportant when seen through a veneer of personalities and a culture of informality, significant ideological changes were part and parcel of the shifts of the early 1980s. One document that provides an alternative perspective on the status of Native activism at the advent of the Reagan years is an open letter that International Indian Treaty Council chairman Jimmie Durham (1980), Arkansas Cherokee, made public in the wake of his resignation from the Treaty Council and AIM in that period. Though he was never in the media spotlight in the way Means and other leaders were, Durham played a significant role in the intellectual and ideological development of Native politics in the late 1970s.

Durham's letter came out in December 1980. In it, he writes that "one of the main failures of AIM was our inability from the top leadership on down, to squarely face our weaknesses and our failures." The leading proponent and strategist of efforts to internationalize the American Indian struggle, Durham led the Treaty Council's efforts to bring North American indigenous issues to the attention of the United Nations and other organizations between 1974 and 1979. The Treaty Council was an offshoot of AIM, but it featured a much stronger organizational structure, offices in New York and San Francisco, and a newsletter that was published regularly. Perhaps most importantly, Durham saw the Treaty Council as having clear political ideals and a promising agenda for Indians to be part of an international decolonization movement.

Those ideals and that agenda, for Durham, became moot with the emergence of AIM's defining itself as a spiritual movement in the late 1970s and early 1980s. To him,

AIM's great achievement had been its development into an international people's movement committed to the liberation of Indian people. That achievement had come about through efforts to make AIM responsive to reservation people along with its initial constituencies in cities. Unfortunately, as Durham wrote, "AIM has always been plagued by fakes, crooks, opportunists, and alienated individuals" (Durham 1980).

Far from starting as a spiritual movement, Durham reminded his readers that AIM had begun in 1968 as an effort to end police harassment of Minneapolis Indian bar patrons. Later developments made the movement national, and the 1973 Wounded Knee takeover had opened new vistas for understanding the Indian struggle as one involving both reservation and urban people against colonialism based in a struggle to protect economic resources through political means. His vision was of a peoples movement that could mobilize the mass of Indian people to confront and change the political and economic structures that oppressed them.

Though obviously slanted toward his own position, Durham in his open letter provided clear documentation of an important split between the wing of AIM centered in Minneapolis, and South Dakota AIM, the loosely organized set of stalwarts that emerged in the aftermath of Wounded Knee, when "Russell Means and the Sioux of South Dakota," Durham wrote, "became the most important part of the new AIM. . . . The old Minneapolis AIM leadership did not want to give up its control over the organization" (Durham 1980).

Out of this conflict, Durham saw a healthy move toward more clearly defined political principles in which local work would provide the foundation for an international case. This had been true as long ago as 1971, when Durham argued that "a national organization could only be legitimized by the people if it had a direct and democratic relationship to the grassroots people on the reservation and making their demands and concerns the first priority of AIM" (Durham 1980). Durham argued pointedly against seeing local programs in Minneapolis for the benefit of Indians in the cities as national.

While Durham's remarks reflect his own disappointment in being on the losing side of a battle to define AIM, his comments remain important since he is one of the few people from that era who provided analysis of what was lost in the move toward what Means advocated in his Survival Gathering speech. Most important to Durham, the activist movement lost a standpoint from which to critique the colonial system in which Indian affairs takes place. Overcoming the structures of federal intervention in Native life, especially tribal councils elected under the auspices of the Bureau of Indian Affairs, was no longer the focus of activism. Instead, Durham detected a de facto capitulation to an older model in which community organizers were at the mercy of the personal integrity of leaders working within a corrupt system. Also, lacking a drive toward more clearly articulated principles, activists were all the more susceptible to cults of personality and anti-intellectualism.

Durham raised concerns regarding the centrality of political ideas originating from relatively small groups, especially the Iroquois and the Hopi. While expressing respect for the tradition of resistance that existed among those groups, Durham argued that they had also been "subject to a very thorough romanticism" in which strategies that were successful for people without a viable land base seduced others into thinking they could proceed in a likewise fashion without close attention to economic structures.

The Survival Gathering was evidence for Durham of "just how confused and empty the politics of AIM had become, and how removed AIM was from the people on the reservations." Reaching out to ranchers against corporate interests, Durham said, "means forgetting about any sort of alliance between Indians, Blacks and Chicanos to fight repression and build organizations for our mutual benefit. . . . Unbelievably, the Survival Gathering believes that the Indian struggle must unite with ranchers against corporations. These are the very same ranchers who most directly and immediately oppress Indian people." Without much hope, Durham called for AIM to engage to regroup in a more democratic and political way.

In 1990, Paul Smith (Comanche Tribe of Oklahoma), one of Durham's allies from those years, summarized what had happened like this: "Political contradictions increased during this time as well, as some leaders adopted a spiritualist approach and denounced alliances with progressives, and others moderated their views and worked within tribal governments." As such, according to Smith, AIM would go on to exist "only through the rhetoric of national leaders who pretended AIM was still viable" (P. Smith 1990:23).

This has been a rather long way to go to get only to the end of 1980, but these are important issues for several reasons. Primarily, the shifting ground of Native activism deserves to be seen as participating in the same sorts of ideological wrangling as other social movements from the period. Absent a critical history of AIM and other radical groups in the years after Wounded Knee, Means's speech and Durham's open letter provide evidence that there were intellectual currents among people working in Native activism that helped shape the sorts of actions and projects that activists participated in. Internal forms of political analysis, in other words, were part and parcel of activism. Though evidence of that sort of analysis can be next to impossible to find, it is crucial to note that such analysis can be assumed to be present throughout Native political history, even in the midst of events that seem to outstrip the ability of those involved to keep pace.

Though Durham, Smith, and other commentators are certainly correct in seeing AIM as in decline by 1980, the organization, the name, and most of all the ethos of the American Indian Movement survived in various ways. The Minneapolis group continued to see itself as the legitimate heir of AIM's legacy and continued to support the survival schools and some other efforts that it began in the 1970s. It participated in national efforts to protest the use of Native

American sports mascots. Perhaps its most vocal activities have been its periodic condemnations of others who have laid claim to the AIM name.

In spite of these efforts to police its name, Minneapolis AIM has not been able to stop its use in various places, usually in cities and usually in situations when radical political option becomes attractive. The Indian world has not lacked for a steady stream of new dog soldiers who find nothing so emboldening as wearing a windbreaker imprinted with "AIM Security" or radicals who feel empowered by hanging an "AIM Office" sign scribbled on cardboard with magic marker in an urban ghetto storefront window.

## After 1990

Even when it was enjoying its most high-profile successes, AIM had never been the only game in town. The movement years of the 1970s mobilized and emboldened not only recurring generations of young men and women in search of symbolic action but also created new awareness of avenues available for creating change in the Native world. Much of this activism remains as hard to find as it was in the 1950s and 1960s, as small groups have organized themselves to address issues and conditions on reservations, in cities, on campuses, and elsewhere. Some of these efforts have become national and international in scope. What follows is a discussion of a combination of some of the most significant

of these efforts and some of those that are not as well known but which typify the sorts of political action American Indian people have engaged in since 1980.

The instance of Native activism most akin to the sorts of protests and takeovers of the 1970s did not happen until 1990 and took place in Canada. The impact of the Oka Crisis of 1990 (fig. 2) was felt across international boundaries and drew participants and significant support from Natives based within the United States (York and Pindera 1991).

In the spring of 1990, members of the Mohawk community on Oka Reserve, Quebec, erected a barricade to block traffic leading into territory that they claimed as theirs but on which its titular owners from the Quebec city of Oka had decided to expand a private golf course. As with other protests of this era, Oka had a religious dimension insofar as the proposed golf course expansion was slated for land the Mohawks claimed as an ancestral burial site (Alfred 1995). The protest turned into an armed confrontation, then a protracted standoff with both Quebec police and the Royal Canadian Mounted Police (MacLaine and Baxendale 1990). As the crisis heightened, Mohawks at nearby Kahnawake (Caughnawaga) blockaded a bridge running through their reserve that linked the city of Montreal with its southern suburbs.

The Oka crisis lasted 78 days, polarizing many in Canada while inconveniencing residents of the Montreal suburbs. One of the Quebec police officers died in the conflict. Plans for expanding the golf course that had triggered the protests were abandoned (Ciaccia 2000). Subsequent actions involving violent confrontations with police have occurred in

AP Images.

Fig. 2. Oka crisis. left, Mohawk men using golf carts for transportation, after a police assault to remove Mohawk barricades at the Kahnesatake Res., Oka, Que. A policemean was killed in the assault. The barriers were erected by the Mohawks in a land dispute between the Town of Oka and the Mohawk. The town council voted to build a golf course on land claimed by the Indians. right, Mohawk man raising his weapon as he stands on an overturned police vehicle blocking the highway. Photographs by Tom Hanson, July 11, 1990.

Canada, including the land dispute in Caledonia, Ontario, where members of the Six Nations Reserve claim land as theirs that is being developed.

Periodic instances of violence and militancy in the United States have not been on the scale of Oka or Wounded Knee. In 1987, Native activists Eddie Hatcher and Timothy Jacobs staged an armed takeover of newspaper offices in Robeson County, North Carolina, in hopes of drawing attention to worsening conditions of the Lumbees and other people of color there (Asheville Global Report 2005).

Protests do not have to threaten violence, of course, to draw public attention to the causes of their organizers. One successful and high-profile political action has been the broad-based campaign to end the use of American Indian mascots for scholastic, collegiate, and professional sports teams. This campaign has enjoyed wide support from Native and non-Native organizations, including the Washington,

D.C.-based Morningstar Foundation and the National Congress of American Indians. The federal Commission on Civil Rights and the National Collegiate Athletic Association (NCAA) have come out strongly against the use of Native American mascots, as well. At its base, though, the anti-mascot movement has involved local individuals and groups that lead the charge against specific mascots (fig. 3).

The University of Illinois at Champaign-Urbana has been a center of protest, though the University of Oklahoma, Norman; Stanford University, Palo Alto, California; and some others had resolved similar situations by getting rid of their Native mascots since the early 1970s. The nickname of the University of Illinois is the Fighting Illini, and one of its mascots was Chief Illiniwek, a fictional character portrayed each year by a student who performs caricatured dances while wearing a buckskin outfit, feathered Plains-style headdress, and painted red stripes on his face.

AP Images.

Fig. 3. Protesting the use of mascots and names relating to Native Americans in sports. left, Chief Illiniwek, symbol of the University of Illinois, as portrayed by student Kyle Cline dancing at a football game in Sept. 2005. The university ended the 81-year tradition of the appearance of the chief after pressure from Native American and other activists and the National Collegiate Athletic Association. The last appearance was in Feb. 2007. Photograph by Darrell Hoemann, Sept. 2, 2005. right, Michael Haney (Seminole, d. 2005), center, with the National Coalition on Racism in Sports and the Media and Ken Rhyne (Tuscrora), of the American Indian Movement, speaking to the media before an Atlanta Braves and Cleveland Indians game during the 1995 World Series. Photograph by John Basemore, Oct. 20, 1995.

Students who found the actions of the chief character offensive mounted protests at sporting events and eventually initiated a complaint against the university, claiming that the antics of this character created a hostile learning environment for them as Native Americans. As the flagship state university, Champaign-Urbana has many prominent and powerful supporters in the ranks of its boosters and fans, so these efforts have prompted considerable reaction in favor or keeping the nickname and mascot. In spite of various rulings against it and ongoing actions by students, faculty, and others in protest, the university maintained its commitment to the chief until the governing board declared the caricature ended in 2007 (fig. 3). A documentary film about the controversy, Jay Rosenstein's *In Whose Honor?*, was widely shown on campuses and in classrooms around the United States (Sturm 2000).

Less well-known are dozens of cases of smaller schools, including many junior highs and high schools, that have changed their nicknames and mascots since the 1970s. These changes have come about primarily through the work of Native students and their parents organizing to bring attention to what they see as the deleterious effects of stereotypical images of Native Americans on the psychology and learning environment of young people. A consistent complaint in these protests has been that mascots and nicknames are often the basis of ridiculing or trivializing American Indian spiritual and cultural practices. Elders have often been enlisted to lend credibility to such contentions.

The Grand Council of AIM, the name currently used by the AIM group centered in Minneapolis, has played an important role in maintaining the momentum of such actions. Other Native groups have also been important to these efforts, including the Native American Journalists Association, which advocates that newspapers and other media outlets avoid using Native nicknames in its coverage of sports teams.

The most significant development in the anti-mascot campaign has been the NCAA's 2005 decision to ban what it calls hostile and abusive images and mascots from championships and other events that it directly sponsors. To participate in NCAA tournament games, teams cannot feature such images on the uniforms or paraphernalia of their athletes, cheerleaders, or band members. Further, schools not in compliance with the NCAA's guidelines are no longer eligible to host the association's tournament games without removing all evidence of such images from their facilities.

The NCAA's decision was the most prominent victory of antimascot activists, though actions continue against professional sports franchises like the Cleveland Indians of Major League Baseball and the Washington Redskins of the National Football League. While plenty of vituperative sports fans have found this campaign to be part and parcel of overly sensitive elements of American society gaining too much power over issues that promascot fans deem harmless fun, nearly every group of people who have studied this issue has agreed that the promotion of stereotyped images of

Native Americans is, indeed, damaging and offensive. At the same time, plenty of Native American people, including a lot of activists, have wondered why so much effort has gone into fighting against something that is by and large removed from the day to day lives of the American Indian people with the highest needs.

Something similar was true of efforts to counter plans across the Americas and in Europe to celebrate the 500th anniversary in 1992 of the arrival of Christopher Columbus in the New World. Many indigenous groups throughout the Americas made plans to counter large-scale celebrations of the Quincentenary, including many who worked in concert with progressives of various sorts. One meeting brought indigenous delegates from hundreds of nations together in Ecuador to articulate a Native response to the past five centuries (Wearne 1996).

In the end, neither the celebrations nor counter-celebrations ended up as more than a blip on the radar screen of the early 1990s. Thousands of vigils and plenty of protests took place, but the Quincentenary never became as big an event in reality as it was in the minds of some progressives who thought it might spark a renewed sense of political activism in an era that most would agree was fairly moribund for their causes.

Much more significant than these externally driven efforts to the history of how activism has developed in Native North America has been the increased sophistication of low-profile, community-based efforts to address Native needs. Such actions, almost by definition, are difficult to find, but they have been undertaken since the beginning of the 1980s.

One of the best chronicles of this sort of community organizing is Winona LaDuke's (1999) *All Our Relations: Native Struggles for Land and Life*. It focuses on case studies of indigenous groups in the United States and Canada that are succeeding on their own terms at creating social, cultural, and economic programs to benefit their communities. La Duke, a running mate of Green Party presidential candidate Ralph Nader in 1996 and 2000, is a community organizer with extensive experience in creating local programs and helping link other organizers in an informal network of similarly minded political activists (fig. 4).

As she says of those like her, "We live off the beaten track, out of the mainstream in small villages, on a vast expanse of prairie, on dry desert islands, or in the forests. We often drive old cars, live in old houses and mobile homes. There are usually small children and relatives around, kids careening underfoot. We seldom carry briefcases, and we rarely wear suits. You are more likely to find us meeting at a local community center, outside camping, or in someone's house than at a convention center or at a $1,000-per-plate fundraiser" (LaDuke 1999:3).

This, as neatly as a thousand examples, sums up the nature of what became of at least one wing of activism after the tumult of the 1970s. Put simply, organizers like LaDuke went home. There, they have worked against mining and nuclear waste companies, ranchers, and the chronic poverty of

AP Images.

Fig. 4. Winona LaDuke (White Earth Ojibwa), an activist in land and environmental issues and Green Party vice-presidential candidate in 1996 and 2000, after receiving the Reebok Human Rights Award. Photograph by Charles Wenzelberg, New York, 1988.

Native communities. Often, their enemies are elected tribal councils. Spirituality and reliance on the guidance of elders and religious leaders have been central to nearly all actions like the ones La Duke chronicles.

Though she does not lay overt claim to a feminist perspective, LaDuke focuses throughout her written work on the efforts of Native women to bring their talents and perspectives to the table of activism. The first of her case studies in *All Our Relations* involves the work of Katsi Cook and other Mohawk women to address the effects of industrial pollution on the health of local communities, especially its alarming presence in breast milk. For Cook, a mother represents the "first environment" for a baby, and the primary issue facing those who do environmental justice is making women healthy. Cook's perspective, then, typifies what for LaDuke is the most important aspect of contemporary activism—its focus on work from the bottom up rather than the top down. Children, women, and old people, in LaDuke's book, are often at the bottom and are often the primary source of change in indigenous communities.

This is not, it bears repeating, an offshoot of the sort of cultural feminist organizing that occurred among other women of color in the early 1980s. Plenty of LaDuke's cases, in fact, involve significant male leadership and almost all of them involve both men and women working together to create new conditions for their communities. Most of these cases feature situations so dire and so far off the radar screen of national and even sometimes tribal politics that it's hard to conceive of anyone interested in helping being turned away.

LaDuke's chapter on the Independent Seminoles provides an ideal example. Living on a small parcel of nonreservation land in the Florida Everglades, this 300-member nation attempts to live out its understanding of its culture without benefit of relationships with the federal government, the state government of Florida, or even the tribal government of the Seminole Tribe of Florida a few miles down the road.

The Seminole Tribe has helicopters, state of the art medical care, and plenty of jobs for any tribal member who wants one. Their wealth comes from accepting a settlement of longstanding land claims, but more importantly from the development of an extensive gaming economy. The Seminoles, in fact, were the progenitors of modern Indian gaming, having won a 1981 Supreme Court case, *Seminole Tribe v. Butterworth,* from which all subsequent gaming law for Indians everywhere derives. The tribe runs numerous casinos on several reservations in Florida, including two that are affiliated with the internationally celebrated Hard Rock chain of restaurants, purchased by the Seminole Tribe in 2006 ("Gaming," fig. 4, this vol.).

LaDuke presents the choice between the lifeway of the Seminole Tribe and that of the Independent Seminoles as a stark one, but she also argues that the Independent Seminoles gladly accept a life of fewer things in favor of a way of life that is consonant with that of their ancestors. As she writes, "At each intersection on the path of life, there is a choice to be made, and it is weighted against the values, the history, and the present circumstances, and the futures of generations of people. These decisions are not taken lightly in most indigenous societies, but are carefully deliberated, in the best of circumstances" (LaDuke 1999:32). This is the sort of decision-making that the Independent Seminoles and others who remain close to land and tradition engage in, according to LaDuke.

The Seminole Tribe, and other tribes like it that have moved closer to more modern notions of what indigenous life is, view things differently. "In the worst of circumstances," she argues, "these decisions are made behind closed doors by a select few—all too often, those few selected in some fashion by the federal government or some other vested interest. These decisions, however, in the case of most peoples, will affect the entire social and political fabric as well as the next set of decisions" (LaDuke 1999:32).

LaDuke presents people like the Independent Seminoles as being heroic, joyful, resolute, and hopeful in the face of incredible odds. These descriptions recall Durham's warning against the ease with which some romanticize small groups of indigenous people following ancient traditions. At the same time, the cases La Duke highlights provide evidence that there can be and are alternatives to the dominant ways of life that most people in the world follow.

LaDuke counters the potential for romanticism by showing how small groups of Native activists have taken on different sorts of tasks across the continent, from fighting off mining interests on the Northern Cheyenne Reservation, Montana, to the ongoing efforts of the Dann family in Nevada and other Western Shoshones to end the federal government practice of testing nuclear weapons on their lands. What binds these activists together is their insistence on being connected to grassroots people and communities. Though LaDuke says there are over 200 organizations through which groups like these work together, this is primarily an acephalous network of people and communities operating primarily on its own energies.

In many ways, the development of this network hearkens back to the activism of the late 1950s and early 1960s, when small, isolated groups of activists were more likely to feel connected to each other through mimeographed newsletters exchanged informally than to national organizations that purport to represent Native communities. Certainly mobile phones, electronic mail, and wireless internet connections make it easier for such people to find each other and stay in touch. Further, some tactics reflect a much more sophisticated knowledge of legal systems, and a more robust infrastructure of not-for-profit groups exists to support the work of community organizers. Still, the fundamental ethos of Native people seeking to address their own problems without the interference of outsiders remains remarkably similar to that earlier time.

While the persistence of this sort of activism is perhaps not a surprise, political activism within the larger frame of North American and global life has undergone tremendous changes during that same period. Native activists have taken part in actions that reflect these changes, including global forums that address women's issues, economics, and social justice. Native groups have also been involved in many of the mass protests that have broken out to protest the impact of globalization on local community needs ("The Global Indigenous Movement," this vol.).

The best example of American Indians using new methods for activism is the Cobell lawsuit, which was filed in 1996. Elouise Cobell (fig. 5), Blackfeet, acting as a holder of one of the Bureau of Indian Affairs Individual Indian Money accounts in a case that has come to include virtually every individual Indian person whose has moneys held in trust by the United States, holds that the secretary of the Interior and other government officials have mishandled her account. Federal agencies have had to admit that they cannot adequately account for moneys entrusted to them for over a century, and the sense from early on has been that Cobell and her codefendants have a strong case that the Department of the Interior was negligent in its treatment of Indians. Most observers expect that the suit will result in a significant settlement from the federal government. Following Cobell's success, tribes have also sued the government for mismanagement of their trust assets.

Cobell has been represented by the Native American Rights Fund, a legal advocacy group that started during the 1970s that has gone on to become one of the strongest not-for-profits serving the Indian world. The Fund, based in Boulder, Colorado, works with tribes and individuals on a number of issues ("Lawyers and Law Programs," this vol.). The trust issues that are at the center of Cobell's litigation represent a real innovation in activist engagement. Like the anti-mascot campaign, the trust effort has been based in the work

AP Images.

Fig. 5. Acting to secure justice in Indian finances held by the federal government. left, Elouise Cobell (Blackfeet), in front of an oil well on the Blackfeet Indian Res. near Browning, Mont. Cobell is the lead plaintiff in a class action lawsuit filed in 1996 against the Bureau of Indian Affairs to overhaul its accounting system regarding royalties and 300,000 Indian trust accounts. Photograph by Ray Ozman, 1999. right, Cobell, center, with Tex G. Hall (Three Affiliated Tribes of Ft. Berthold), left, president of the National Congress of American Indians, and Jimmy Goddard (Blackfeet) on Capitol Hill, prior to a House Resources Committee hearing on Native American trust funds. Photograph by Terry Ashe, Washington, 2002.

of individuals in local settings and has grown to include national organizations. While the final settlement appears to end up being a small fraction of the $176 billion estimates some close to the case discussed early on, Elouise Cobell and others who started this case have demonstrated that there are numerous ways to go about seeking justice.

**Conclusion**

Both Russell Means and Jimmie Durham seem to have been prescient in their 1980 remarks. Means correctly predicted the dominance of small groups focused on local issues using cultural resources in the search for survival in the face of the continuing erosion of Native rights. Durham, though, posed questions that remain in spite of the successes and persistence of Native activism into the twenty-first century. Durham's concern for the lack of a people's movement in the decline of AIM continues to haunt the Native world of community organizing. It seems fair to say that activism in the United States has arrived at a point where a default style of activism focused on culture, spirituality, and small groups of people struggling for justice with only loose connections to larger networks of other Native and non-Native activists is the dynamic in play.

# The Federal-Tribe Relationship

ALEX TALLCHIEF SKIBINE

Upon its formation, the United States continued a practice initiated by England in the seventeenth century and entered into a treaty relationship with many Indian tribes. A treaty being an agreement between two or more sovereign nations, the very existence of such treaties is evidence that the United States considered tribal nations to be sovereign nations. In the next two centuries, the nature of the relationship evolved. Even though the treaty relationship with Indian tribes was ended by an act of Congress in 1871, this did not mean that the United States stopped recognizing Indian tribes as sovereign entities. The 1871 Act provided that "no obligation of any treaty, lawfully made and ratified . . . prior to March 3, 1871, shall be hereby invalidated or impaired" (102 Stat. 3641, 25 U.S.C. 71).

In 1831, Justice John Marshall wrote that "the relation of the Indians to the United States is marked by peculiar and cardinal distinctions which exist no where else" (*Cherokee Nation* v. *Georgia*, 30 U.S. 1, 16 [1831]). This statement is still true today. One reason is that the relationship between the tribes and the United States is not defined in the United States Constitution, although some scholars have argued that the Constitution recognizes the existence of Indian tribes as sovereign political entities since the commerce clause provides that Congress shall have the power "to regulate Commerce with foreign nations, and among the several states, and with Indian Tribes" (Article I, section 8, clause 3) (Singer 2003).

In 2006, most Indian tribes are said to have a government-to-government relationship with the United States. There are over 330 federally recognized Indian tribes in the lower 48 states and 230 recognized Native village groups in Alaska. There are 322 federally recognized Indian reservations, comprising over 55 million acres of land in the lower 48 states. In order to be recognized as an "Indian" by the federal government, a person usually must have some Indian blood and be recognized as an Indian by his or her federally recognized tribal community. For many purposes, however, a person also has to be officially enrolled as a tribal member with a federally recognized Indian tribe.

The United States is said to have adopted since the early 1960s a policy of encouraging self-determination and self-government for Indian tribes. Under this policy, the United States recognizes Indian tribes as political entities with a certain degree of sovereignty over both their lands and the people who live there. To best understand the nature of this government-to-government relationship, it is important to understand three cardinal principles or doctrines that delineate the contour of this relationship. These three doctrines are to a great extent interrelated.

The first one is the tribal sovereignty doctrine. Under this doctrine, Indian tribes are said to possess inherent powers of self-government that are derived from their original sovereignty that preexisted the formation of the United States. Under the second one, the congressional plenary power doctrine, control over Indian affairs is vested exclusively in the United States Congress, which is said to have "plenary" power in this area. A corollary of this doctrine is that the various states where the Indian tribes are located have only the degree of authority over Indians within Indian reservations as the Congress has chosen to give them. Even the limited authority states have over non-Indians within the reservations can be completely pre-empted by the federal government. The third one is the trust doctrine. Under this doctrine, the United States is said to have a trust relationship with Indian tribes, the federal government being the trustee and the Indian tribes being the beneficiaries of the trust. The trust doctrine is related to the first two doctrines in that it is derived principally from the treaties that the Indian tribes, as sovereign nations, signed with the United States. In those treaties, the tribes generally ceded huge amount of lands to the United States, which in return agreed to take the Indian tribes under its protection. It is also derived from the various acts of Congress enacted pursuant to the plenary power doctrine. Finally, it is derived from opinions of the Supreme Court that have interpreted these treaties and statutes, as well as principles of international law.

## History

### Congressional Policies

Scholars have identified five distinct periods in tribal-federal relations (Cohen 2005:26–113).
• TREATY PERIOD, 1778–1871 The first treaty between the United States and a tribe was signed in 1778 with the Delaware Nation (17 Stat. 13). The treaty period can be

subdivided into three periods. Treaties signed between the United States and the Indian nations started out as treaties of peace and friendship, the object of which was to secure peace on the frontier and obtain the allegiance of the Indian nations should any war break out with other European or Indian nations. In the second period, the United States signed treaties of removal. The purpose of these treaties was to make more land available for non-Indian settlement by obtaining the consent of the tribes to be removed away from their ancestral lands, usually to somewhere west of the Mississippi. In the third period, the United States used the treaty mechanism to obtain the consent of tribes to reduce the size of their original reservations. These treaties were mostly treaties of land cessions confining tribes to smaller and smaller reservations.

Except for the Trade and Intercourse Acts, and certain acts allowing for federal jurisdiction in limited circumstances over certain crimes committed within Indian reservations, the Congress enacted no comprehensive legislation affecting Indian tribes. The purpose of the Trade and Intercourse Acts, the first one of which was enacted in 1790, was to make sure control over Indian affairs remained with the Congress. These acts delineated the boundaries of the Indian country, provided that only the United States could acquire lands from Indian tribes, and instituted a license requirement for anyone intending to trade with the tribes.

• ALLOTMENT ERA, 1871–1928   During the allotment era, Congress adopted a policy attempting to assimilate Indians into the mainstream of the American population. The main tool of this policy was the allotment process, under which Congress took tribal land and allotted such lands to the individual tribal members. Usually each head of family received a 160-acre allotment, and each family member an 80-acre parcel. The idea was to break up the communal ownership of the tribal land base and transform individual Indians into farmers.

The allotment policy was deemed a failure as early as 1928 and officially abandoned in 1934; however, it had lasting effects. Tribal lands not allotted to individual Indians were declared surplus land and made available for sale to non-Indians. As a result it is estimated that tribes collectively lost over 90 million acres. In addition, the acquisition of reservation land by non-Indians created a checkerboard pattern of Indian and non-Indian land within Indian reservations that has resulted in many jurisdictional conflicts between tribal and state governments. Such influx of non-Indians also meant that on many reservations, these non-Indians became a substantial part, and in some cases the majority, of the total population.

• INDIAN REORGANIZATION, 1928–1942   The Indian Reorganization Act of 1934 (48 Stat. 984, 25 U.S.C. 461 et seq.) not only repealed the policies of assimilation of the allotment era but also provided a mechanism for formalizing the government-to-government relationship between the tribes and the United States. Section 16 of the Act provided for the adoption of tribal constitutions, which would have to be ap-

proved by the secretary of the interior (25 U.S.C. 476). This section provided that the powers vested in the tribal governments under such constitutions shall be "in addition to all powers vested in any Indian tribe or tribal council by existing law." Section 16 was amended to provide that "each Indian tribe shall retain inherent sovereign power to adopt governing documents under procedures other than those specified in this section" (25 U.S.C. 476(h)(1).

• TERMINATION ERA, 1943–1961   Under the policy of termination, the trust relationship between a designated tribe and the United States was said to be terminated. This did not mean that the tribe ceased to exist, but it did mean that the federal government stopped officially recognizing such tribe as a quasi-sovereign domestic dependent nation having a government-to-government relationship with the United States. Although many tribes suffered specifically by being earmarked for termination, perhaps the defining and landmark piece of legislation enacted by the United States Congress during this era was Public Law 280, which allowed states to assume a certain amount of criminal jurisdiction in Indian country. It opened the doors of the state courts to adjudicate civil disputes arising in Indian country. Although it provided for the assumption of state jurisdiction, P.L. 280 was not an abrogation of Indian sovereignty as such since it did not prevent tribes from exercising concurrent jurisdiction with the states. Although the termination policy was eventually repealed when Congress adopted the policy of self-determination, P.L. 280 was never repealed.

• SELF DETERMINATION ERA, 1961–PRESENT   The first speech announcing the repudiation of the termination policies was delivered by President Lyndon Johnson on March 6, 1968, when he proposed "a new goal for our Indian programs: a goal that ends the old debate about termination of Indian programs and stresses self-determination as a goal that erases old attitudes of paternalism and promotes partnership and self-help" (L.B. Johnson 1968:336).

*The Supreme Court during the Marshall Era, 1801–1835*

Indian tribes used to possess the full attributes of national sovereignty, exercising complete and exclusive governmental authority over both their territories and the people living within it. The previously full sovereignty of the Indian nations was first qualified by the United States Supreme Court in the 1823 decision, *Johnson v. M'Intosh* (21 U.S. 543 [1823]). In this case, Justice Marshall applied the doctrine of discovery to Indian tribes. Under this doctrine, upon "discovery" of new lands, the European discoverer obtained ultimate title to all the discovered lands even if such lands were already occupied by aboriginal people. The tribes' right to property, therefore, was reduced to a right of occupancy, which right could be acquired only by the discoverer, through either purchase or conquest. As a result, Indian tribes were deprived of the right to transfer their lands to anyone but the United States. The application of the doctrine of discovery to American Indian tribes was not an invention of Justice Marshall. These principles had been applied for over 200 years before 1823 by England and the colonies (R.J. Miller 2005). Concerning the effect of the doctrine on tribal sovereignty, the Court in *Johnson* v. *M'Intosh* stated

> Those relations which were to exist between the discoverer and the natives, were to be regulated by themselves. The Rights thus acquired being exclusive, no other power could interpose between them. In the establishment of these relations . . . the [natives'] rights to complete sovereignty, as independent nations, were necessarily diminished, and their power to dispose of the soil, at their own will, to whomsoever they please, was denied by the original fundamental principle that discovery gave title to those who made it. While the different nations of Europe respected the right of the natives, as occupants, they asserted the ultimate dominion to be in themselves.

Under the doctrine of discovery as interpreted in *Johnson*, the Indian tribes lost three attributes of sovereignty. First, their national territories became geographically incorporated within the exterior limits of the United States. Second, the complete ownership of their lands was reduced to a right of occupancy and they lost the right to transfer their lands to anyone other than the United States. Finally, they became subject to the "ultimate dominion" of the United States, which Justice Marshall qualified by saying that the doctrine of discovery gave the United States "a right to such a degree of sovereignty as the circumstances of the people [the Indians] would allow them to exercise" (at 587).

In *Cherokee Nation* v. *Georgia*, the state of Georgia was attempting to impose its sovereignty on the Cherokee Nation, and the issue was whether the Cherokee Nation could file a suit challenging the actions of Georgia directly in the United States Supreme Court. In order for the Court to have such original jurisdiction, the Cherokee Nation had to be either one of the states comprising the Union or a foreign nation. The Court held that it was neither. Instead, the Cherokee Nation was a "domestic dependent nation." It is in this decision that Justice Marshall first laid the foundation for what would eventually become known as the trust relationship when he stated that the Indian tribes "were in a state of pupilage. Their relation with the United States resembles that of a ward to his guardian" (30 U.S. (5 Pet) 1, 11–12 [1831]). Marshall also made clear that under the doctrine of discovery, the Indian tribes had lost their status as true international sovereigns, stating that the tribes "were so completely under the sovereignty and dominion of the United states, that any attempt to acquire their lands, or to form a political connection with them, would be considered by all an invasion of our territory, and an act of hostility" (at 17–18). Thus under *Cherokee Nation*, the tribes lost a fourth attribute of sovereignty—the right to enter into treaties or other political relationships with any nation other than the United States.

Nevertheless, being subjected to the doctrine of discovery did not mean that Indian nations had lost all attributes of sovereignty. Justice Marshall, in a third case, *Worcester* v.

*Georgia* (31 U.S. 515 [1832]), further clarified the status of Indian nations within the United States. At issue in *Worcester* was whether the state of Georgia could extend the application of its laws inside the territory of the Cherokee Nation. The Court held that Georgia had no such jurisdiction because the Cherokee Nation was still a sovereign Indian nation, and exclusive control over the relations with the Indian tribes had been vested by the Constitution to the United States Congress. After rejecting the proposition that the Cherokee Nation had lost its right to self-government because in its treaty with the United States it acknowledged itself to be under the protection of the United States, Marshall stated that the Cherokee Indians' relation with the United States was "that of a nation claiming and receiving the protection of one more powerful; not that of individuals abandoning their national character, and submitting as subjects, to the laws of a master . . . the settled doctrine of the law of nations is, that a weaker power does not surrender its independence—its right of self-government, by associating with a stronger" (31 U.S. at 555, 560–561). Perhaps the best statement summarizing the relations existing between the United States and the Indian tribes is the following:

> From the commencement of our government congress has passed acts to regulate trade and intercourse with the Indians, which treat them as nations, respect their rights and manifest a firm purpose to afford that protection which treaties stipulate. All these acts . . . manifestly consider the several Indian nations as distinct political communities, having territorial boundaries, within which their authority is exclusive, and having a right to all the lands within those boundaries, which is not only acknowledged but guaranteed by the United States (31 U.S. at 37).

The main purpose of the doctrine of discovery was to avoid conflicts between European nations when such nations were involved in the conquest and colonization of non-Western countries. Under Chief Justice Marshall's interpretation of the doctrine, it also gave ultimate title and political dominion to the discovering nation. Nevertheless, even under Marshall's conception of the doctrine, although subject to the ultimate dominion of the United States, Indian tribes retained most of their original sovereignty.

## Congressional Plenary Power Over Indian Affairs

In the Marshall era, the Court did not have to decide precisely what was the source and extent of Congress's power over Indian tribes. Although the treaty power was used by the United States to obtain the land it wanted from the tribes, it was never used by the United States to grant Congress plenary power, in the sense of absolute power, over the tribes. Besides, not all tribes signed treaties with the United States. Until the allotment era, Congress did not attempt to exercise plenary power over the tribes. This changed in 1885 when

Congress enacted the Major Crimes Act (18 U.S.C. 1153), giving federal authorities jurisdiction to prosecute in federal courts Indians committing certain major crimes within Indian reservations. The power of Congress to enact such legislation without the consent of the tribes or in violation of previous treaties was quickly challenged in the Supreme Court. In a historic decision, the Supreme Court in *United States* v. *Kagama* (118 U.S. 375 [1886]) upheld the power of Congress to enact such legislation. After finding that the constitutional power of Congress to regulate commerce with the Indian tribes could not be the source of such power since in many cases crimes by one tribal member could not possibly affect commerce, the Court first stated

> These Indians are within the geographical limits of the United States. The soil and the people within these limits are under the political control of the Government of the United States. . . . This power of Congress to organize the territorial governments, and make laws for their inhabitants, arises not so much from the clause in the Constitution . . . as from ownership of the Country in which the territories are, and the right of exclusive sovereignty which must exist in the National Government, and can be found nowhere else (118 U.S. at 379–380).

In order to counter the argument that that the tribal territory was no longer within a federal territory but within a state of the Union, California, the Court relied on another source of congressional power, stating "These Indian tribes are the ward of the nation. They are communities dependent on the United States. . . . They owe no allegiance to the States, and receive from them no protection. Because of the local ill feeling, the people of the States where they are found are often their deadliest enemies. From their weakness and helplessness, so largely due to the course of dealing with the federal government with them, and the treaties in which it has been promised, there arises the duty of protection, and with it the power" (118 U.S. at 383). In other words, the Court relied on the fact that because the tribes had become dependent and weak, the Congress had a duty to protect them, and the existence of this duty vested Congress with complete power over tribes.

The reliance on what would eventually become known as the trust doctrine to justify plenary power in the Congress is problematic since it would seem that under the trust, the United States can only use the power for the benefit of the tribes, not to their detriment. To get around this conundrum, the Court in *Lone Wolf* v. *Hitchcock* (187 U.S. 553 [1903]) relied on the political question doctrine. Under this doctrine, some issues are said to have been constitutionally delegated solely to the political branches of the government. Courts, therefore, cannot question the legitimacy of decisions affecting such issues. The issue in *Lone Wolf* was whether Congress could allot the reservations of the Kiowa tribe without the consent of the tribe and in violation of a previous treaty signed between the tribe and the United States. After first stating that Congress had "paramount power over the prop-

erty of the Indian, by reason of its exercise of guardianship over their interests," the Court held that "plenary authority over the tribal relations of the Indians has been exercised by Congress from the beginning, and the power has always been deemed a political one, not subject to be controlled by the judicial department of the government" (187 U.S. at 565). The Court then held that the actions of Congress affecting tribal property interests would be presumed to have been enacted for the benefit of the Indians pursuant to the trust relationship.

After all Indians became citizens of the United States through a 1924 act of Congress (8 U.S.C. 1401) and Indian tribes became more incorporated into the American polity pursuant to the Indian Reorganization Act of 1934, the use of the political question and the trust doctrines to allow Congress to violate the constitutional rights of Indians became questionable. Reliance of the trust relationship as an extra-constitutional source of a plenary authority for the Congress was first questioned in 1974 when the Court in *Morton* v. *Mancari* declared "the plenary power of Congress to deal with the special problems of Indians is drawn both explicitly and implicitly from the Constitution. Article I. Section 8, Clause 3 provides Congress with the power to regulate Commerce . . . with the Indian tribes . . . Article II section 2, clause 2 gives the president the power, by and with the advice and consent of the Senate, the make treaties. This has often been the source of the government's power to deal with the tribes" (417 U.S. 535, at 551–552 [1974]).

Finally, the use of the political question doctrine was set aside in *Delaware Tribal Business Committee* v. *Weeks* (530 U.S. 73 [1977]), when the Court stated that although "the power of Congress has always been deemed a political one, [this] has not deterred this Court, particularly in this day, from scrutinizing Indian legislation to determine if it violates the equal protection component of the Fifth Amendment" (530, U.S. at 84). In *United States* v. *Sioux Nation* (448 U.S. 371 [1980]) the Court extended the holding of *Weeks* to constitutional rights other than equal protection. In that case, the Court recognized that under the trust doctrine, the Congress has the power to control and manage tribal affairs but "this power to control and manage is not absolute, while extending to all appropriate measures for protecting and advancing the tribe, it is subject to limitations inhering in . . . a guardianship and to pertinent constitutional restrictions" (448 U.S. 371, at 415).

These cases indicate that although Congress is said to have plenary authority over Indian tribes, unless the power is truly exercised for their benefit, other provisions of the Constitution restrict the exercise of that power. The problem from a tribal perspective is that unlike vested property rights or rights to equal protection, the right of tribal self-government is not a constitutionally protected right. The Supreme Court has so far refused to use the trust doctrine as a limit on congressional power to interfere with tribal self-government (Skibine 2003a). Unlike with its cases concerning the Interstate Commerce clause, the Court has also so far refused to limit the power of Congress derived from the Indian commerce clause to commerce-related actions (Clinton 2002). Thus the Court has continued to assert without any credible historical evidence that "the central function of the Indian Commerce Clause is to provide Congress with plenary power to legislate in the field of Indian affairs" (*Cotton Petroleum Corp.* v. *New Mexico*, 490 U.S. 163, 192 [1989]).

In a 2004 opinion, *United States* v. *Lara* (124 S. Ct. 1628), the Supreme Court seemed to acknowledge that the plenary power of Congress to govern Indian tribes may not be solely derived from the commerce and treaty powers. Thus, after agreeing that "during the first century of America's national existence . . . Indian affairs were more an aspect of military and foreign policy than a subject of domestic or municipal law," the Court stated that "insofar as that is so, Congress's legislative authority would rest in part, not upon "affirmative grant of the Constitution" but upon the Constitution's adoption of preconstitutional powers that are "necessary concomitants of nationality" (124 S. Ct. 1628, at 1634).

In adopting this position, the Court may have been influenced by scholars who had put forth the argument that in the 1886 case of *United States* v. *Kagama,* the Court had really relied more on the concept of "inherent" congressional power than on the trust relationship to justify congressional plenary power over Indian tribes (Cleveland 2002; Frickey 1996). It seems that the only preconstitutional understanding about Indian tribes is that they were subject to the doctrine of discovery under which European countries could assume "ultimate dominion" over them. There are questions whether a plenary-type power of Congress over Indian tribes can be morally justified if, ultimately, its foundation stems from on an understanding of the doctrine of discovery in preconstitutional times. Some scholars view this doctrine as having been mostly based on racist theories about Indians and religious discrimination against non-Christians (Newcomb 1993; R.A. Williams 1983, 1990, 2005:51–58).

## Inherent Tribal Sovereignty

The concept of inherent tribal sovereignty as delineated by Chief Justice Marshall did not change for 146 years after the 1832 case of *Worcester* v. *Georgia*. The 1942 *Handbook of Federal Indian Law* stated

> The whole course of judicial decisions on the nature of Indian tribal powers is marked by adherence to three fundamental principles: (1) An Indian tribe possesses . . . all the powers of any sovereign state. (2) Conquest renders the tribe subject to the legislative power of the United States and, in substance, terminates the external powers of sovereignty of the tribe . . . but does not by itself affect the internal sovereignty of the tribe, i.e., Its powers of local self-government. (3) these powers are subject to qualifications by treaties and by express legislation of Congress (Cohen 1942:123).

Under Marshall's view of the doctrine of discovery, the limit on the tribes' external powers of sovereignty consisted of preventing tribes from selling their lands to anyone other than the United States or entering into treaties or having relations with nations other than the United States. Starting in 1978, under the guidance of Justice William H. Rehnquist, the Court extended the concept of "external relations" to include all tribal relations with nontribal members in order to discover many additional restrictions on the tribes' sovereign power to control nonmembers of the tribe.

### Limitations on Tribal Sovereignty during the Rehnquist Era, 1986–2006

From 1978 until 2003, the Supreme Court severely restricted the ability of a tribe to assert jurisdiction over persons who are not members of that tribe. These cases are important because they reflect the Court's attempt to transform the tribes from governments having a territorially based sovereignty to entities whose jurisdiction is more membership based (Dussias 1993). Such a view impedes the ability of tribes to manage and govern their reservations. The Court's attack on tribal sovereignty also challenged the primacy of the United States Congress, which is considered to be vested with the primary role of regulating the relations with the tribes. This has resulted in some incongruity between the announced policies of the Congress encouraging and protecting tribal self-government and the decisions of the Supreme Court.

• BASED ON CONFLICT WITH AN OVERRIDING SOVEREIGN FEDERAL INTEREST   In *Oliphant* v. *Suquamish Indian Tribe* (435 U.S. 191[1978]), the issue was whether the Indian tribe could assume criminal jurisdiction over a non-Indian who had committed a crime while on the tribe's reservation. After first finding that for the last 200 years, the three branches of the federal government had shared a presumption that tribes did not possess such inherent sovereign authority, the Court stated that even if one ignored congressional policies, tribes do not have criminal jurisdiction over non-Indians because such authority would be "inconsistent with their status." Citing legal precedents that had relied on the doctrine of discovery, the Court concluded that "upon incorporation into the territory of the United States the Indian tribes thereby come under the territorial sovereignty of the United States and their exercise of separate power is constrained so as not to conflict with the interests of this overriding sovereignty" (435 U.S. at 1021–1022). Finding that from the formation of the Union and the adoption of the Bill of Rights, the United States has had an overriding sovereign interest in protecting its citizens from unwarranted intrusion into their personal liberty, the *Oliphant* Court concluded that because the power to criminally punish is an important manifestation of the power to restrict personal liberty, "by submitting to the overriding sovereignty of the United States, Indian tribes therefore necessarily give up their power to try non-Indian citizens of the

United States except in a manner acceptable to Congress" (435 U.S. at 1021).

• BECAUSE JURISDICTION OVER NON-MEMBERS IS AN EXERCISE OF "EXTERNAL" RELATIONS  Shortly after *Oliphant* was decided, the Court substantially reformulated the *Oliphant* doctrine in *United States* v. *Wheeler* (98 S. Ct. 1079 [1978]). At first, *Wheeler* seemed like a reaffirmation of tribal sovereignty since the Court held that when a tribe prosecutes one of its own members, it acts pursuant to its retained inherent sovereign power and not pursuant to delegated federal authority. However, in his opinion for the Court, Justice Potter Stewart also made the following comment:

> The areas in which such implicit divestiture of sovereignty has been held to have occurred are those involving the relations between an Indian tribe and nonmembers of the tribe . . . These limitations rest on the fact that the dependent status of Indian tribes within our territorial jurisdiction is necessarily inconsistent with their freedom independently to determine their external relations. But the powers of self-government . . . are of a different type. They involve only the relations among members of a tribe (98 S. Ct. 1079, at 1087–1088).

The importance of this language is that it equated "external relations" with any relations involving nonmembers, and then reduced the concept of tribal self-government to merely involve the relations among members of the same tribe. Justice Stewart cited no authorities lending support for such a broad concept of "external relations" and such a narrow concept of self-government. Yet these two findings would play a major role in subsequent cases further limiting tribal sovereign authority over nonmembers.

• UNNECESSARY TO TRIBAL SELF-GOVERNMENT  Justice Stewart had a chance to use the statement contained in his *Wheeler* opinion in his 1981 opinion for the Court in *Montana* v. *United States* (101 S. Ct. 1245 [1981]), the case which would eventually become the leading opinion in this area of the law. The issue in the case was whether the Crow Indian tribe had the inherent power to control nonmembers fishing on what the Court had held was non-Indian fee land within the Crow Indian reservation. After quoting the language from *Wheeler*, Justice Stewart stated that "exercise of tribal power beyond what is necessary to tribal self-government or to control internal relations is inconsistent with the dependent status of the tribes" (101 S. Ct. 1245 at 1258). Justice Stewart then announced what would become known as the *Montana* general rule and stated that "the inherent powers of an Indian tribe do not extend to the activities of nonmembers of the tribe" (101 S. Ct. at 1258). However, the Court came up with two exceptions to this general rule and stated:

> To be sure, Indian tribes retain inherent sovereign power to exercise some forms of civil jurisdiction over non-Indians on their reservation, even on non-Indian fee lands. A tribe may regulate, through taxation, licensing, or other means, the activities of nonmembers who enter consensual relationships with the tribes or its members, through commercial dealing, contracts, leases or other arrangements. A tribe may also retain inherent power to exercise civil authority over the conduct of non-Indians on fee lands within its reservation when that conduct threatens or has some direct effect on the political integrity, economic security or the health and welfare of the tribe (at 1258).

Although the *Montana* court summarily dismissed the argument that any of the two exceptions applied to the current case, these two exceptions could have potentially allowed a substantial amount of tribal regulation over nonmembers. The next Supreme Court case on this issue foreclosed any such possibility.

The issue in *Strate A-1 Contractors* (117 S. Ct. 1404 [1997]) was whether the tribal court had jurisdiction over a law suit filed by one nonmember against another over an accident that occurred on a highway running through the reservation but over which the state owned a right of way. After finding that for jurisdictional purposes, the state right of way was equivalent to the fee land owned by nonmembers in the *Montana* case, the Supreme Court held that because the adjudicatory jurisdiction of the tribal court could never exceed the legislative jurisdiction of the tribal legislature, the issue was whether the tribal government had the jurisdiction to regulate nonmembers driving on the state highway running through the reservation. After first dismissing the *Montana* consensual relationship exception out of hand, the Court concluded that regulation of nonmembers driving on the state highway was not necessary to tribal self-government because "neither regulatory nor adjudicatory authority over the state highway accident at issue is needed to preserve the right of reservation Indians to make their own law and be ruled by them" (at 1416). Although *Strate* involved a nontribal member plaintiff, lower courts have extended this ruling to cases where the plaintiff is a tribal member (*Wilson* v. *Marchington*, 127 F.3d 805, 9th Cir. 1997). The Court did not explain why nonmembers driving through the reservation could never have a direct impact on the health of the tribal members. Therefore, it seems that after *Strate*, nonmember activities that might fit into the second Montana exception might be few if any.

• BECAUSE OF CONFLICT WITH STATE INTERESTS  In *Nevada* v. *Hicks* (121 S. Ct. 2304 [2001]), the Court seemed to take a different approach in limiting tribal inherent powers. The issue was whether the tribal court had jurisdiction over a law suit filed by a tribal member against state game wardens who had committed various torts while investigating hunting violations alleged to have been committed by this tribal member while off the reservation. The important difference from previous cases was that in this case, the torts alleged to have been committed by the nonmembers occurred while on land owned by a tribal member. All the justices agreed that this difference was not important and that the *Montana* general principle of no tribal jurisdiction over nonmembers applied on Indian-owned land. Although all the justices agreed that the tribal court was without jurisdiction, the Court was divided on the reasons for such conclusion.

Justice Antonin Scalia wrote the opinion for the Court. After observing that the right of Indians to make their own laws and be ruled by them requires "an accommodation between the interest of the tribes and the federal government, on the one hand, and those of the state, on the other" (121 S. Ct. at 2309–2311) Justice Scalia concluded that the state's interest in having its agents free of tribal jurisdiction while investigating crimes was superior to the tribal interest in regulating such state officers. Justice Souter filed a concurring opinion stating that rather than balancing the tribal against the state interest, he would go directly to the second *Montana* exception and hold that the tribal court had no jurisdiction. Justice Sandra Day O'Connor filed another concurring opinion in which she criticized the other six Justices for not considering the fact that the incidents occurred on land owned by a tribal member as an important factor in deciding whether the tribal court had jurisdiction. The ultimate result of *Hicks* was that the *Montana* rule was extended to Indian-owned lands within Indian reservations. Beyond that, the justices were not in agreement on how to evaluate the reach of tribal jurisdiction over nonmembers on reservation lands owned by tribal members or the tribe.

• THROUGH "ACTIONS OF THE POLITICAL BRANCHES" OF THE FEDERAL GOVERNMENT   In all previous cases, it seemed that the Court relied on the doctrine of discovery since it took the position that the tribes' divestiture of inherent sovereign powers over nonmembers occurred upon the tribes' incorporation into the United States. In these decisions, the Court gave to itself the primary role in deciding what was external relations, what conflicted with an overriding federal interest, or what was necessary to tribal self-government. In other words, the actions of Congress and the executive branch seemed to play no role in such determinations. A later Supreme Court case on this issue may indicate the beginning of a reversal in this trend. The issue in *United States* v. *Lara* was whether the Congress could enact legislation recognizing and reaffirming the inherent sovereign power of tribes to prosecute nonmember Indians even though the Supreme Court had held in a previous case, *Duro* v. *Reina* (495 U.S. 676 [1990]), that such tribal power had been implicitly divested upon the tribes' incorporation into the United States. The argument against such congressional reaffirmation of tribal power was that the Court's previous decisions on this issue reflected, as stated by Justice Souter, "a previous understanding of the jurisdictional implications of dependent sovereignty [which] was constitutional in nature" (541 U.S. 193, at 228). Congress could not overturn the decision by reaffirming the existence of a tribal power once the Court had held this power lost upon incorporation.

The majority of the Court held that decisions such as *Oliphant* and *Duro* were not constitutional decisions but were based on federal common law. As such, Congress could reaffirm the existence of the tribal sovereign power to prosecute nonmember Indians. More importantly, the Court stated that the statute enacted by Congress reaffirm-

ing such tribal prosecutorial power merely "relaxes the restrictions, recognized in *Duro*, that the political branches [of the government] had imposed on the tribes' exercise of inherent prosecutorial power" (541 U.S. at 200). In other words, these "restrictions" did not naturally flow from the fact that Indian tribes were incorporated into the United States through the doctrine of discovery. Instead, these restrictions flowed from actions taken by the Congress and the executive. Although the Court did not say that this was the "only" way that a tribe could have its sovereignty divested, the *Lara* decision can be seen as reinstating the primacy of Congress in determining the sovereign status of Indian tribes. It remains to be seen how this language in *Lara* will be reconciled with seemingly inconsistent language in other Supreme Court decisions. For sure, a position relying on congressional action to find divestiture of tribal sovereignty is more consistent with democratic norms than using the antiquated doctrine of discovery, especially now that tribal members are United States citizens and tribes have been somewhat incorporated into the American political system.

*Legislation, 1961–Present*

• THE INDIAN CIVIL RIGHTS ACT OF 1968   Although the federal government started abandoning the policies of termination in the early 1960s, Congress did not officially adopt a policy of tribal self-determination until 1975. During this transition period, Congress enacted an important statute, the Indian Civil Rights Act of 1968 (25 U.S.C. 1301 et seq.) In 1896, the Supreme Court in *Talton* v. *Mayes* (163 U.S. 376 [1896]) held that because tribal governments were exercising governmental power pursuant to their own inherent sovereignty when prosecuting their own members, they were not subject to those provisions of the United States Constitution applicable to the exercise of federal or state power. In the Indian Civil Rights Act, Congress made applicable to tribal governments most of the provisions contained in the Bill of Rights. This act does not "fit" well in either the termination or the self-determination era. On one hand, it is perhaps one of the most invasive assertions of congressional plenary power over the internal affairs of Indian tribes. On the other hand, it amended P.L. 280, a 1953 law that allowed states to acquire a certain amount of jurisdiction inside Indian reservations, to provide that from now on, Indian tribes would have to consent before any additional assumption of state jurisdiction pursuant to P.L. 280 could be made. The act also amended P.L. 280 by providing that states could, with the approval of the secretary of the interior, retrocede any jurisdiction previously assumed pursuant to P.L. 280.

In 1978 the Supreme Court in *Santa Clara Pueblo* v. *Martinez* (436 U.S. 49 [1978]) greatly reduced the potential interference in internal tribal affairs by federal courts when it interpreted the Indian Civil Rights Act as not abrogating the tribes' historical sovereign immunity from suit in federal courts. This meant that except for cases involving deprivation of personal liberty, plaintiffs asserting deprivation of civil rights at the hands of tribal governments can file such claims only in tribal courts. In cases involving imprisonment or other types of serious restrictions on personal liberty, plaintiffs can have access to federal courts through a writ of habeas corpus (25 U.S.C. 1303).

• THE INDIAN SELF-DETERMINATION AND EDUCATION ASSISTANCE ACT OF 1975  In this act "Congress took a major step in reordering federal-tribal relations" (Cohen 2005:412). Although the act (88 Stat. 2003, 25 U.S.C. 450 et. seq.) did not directly reduce or expand the sovereign powers of Indian tribes, it had a tremendous impact on the ability of tribes to exercise these powers. As first enacted, the Self-Determination Act only allowed Indian tribes to enter into procurement-type contracts with the Bureau of Indian Affairs and the Indian Health Service to take over implementation of programs previously managed by these two agencies for the benefit of Indians. Assuming the management and implementation of these contracts allowed tribes to strengthen their governmental infrastructure and further develop expertise in executive management of governmental programs (J. Hamilton and T.M. Johnson 1995).

A 1988 amendment to the Act (102 Stat. 2296) created a demonstration self-governance program allowing some tribes to replace these contracts by entering into funding compacts with the Bureau of Indian Affairs. The funding compacts allowed tribes to implement their own budget priorities and policies. In 1994, the Act was further amended to make permanent the 1988 demonstration project and extend its availability to all tribes (108 Stat. 4272 [1994]). Under this amendment, tribes can enter into a single "tribal self-governance Compact" that represents a single annual funding agreement covering all funds the Department of the Interior would have spent on that tribe had it not entered into the compact. Legislation enacted in 2000 allows tribes to enter into similar kinds of compacts for programs administered by the Indian Health Service.

• THE INDIAN CHILD WELFARE ACT OF 1978  The purpose of the Indian Child Welfare Act of 1978 (92 Stat. 3069, 25 U.S.C. 1901 et seq.) was to stop the unwarranted removal of Indian children from their families and their subsequent adoption by non-Indian families. Studies had found that 25–35 percent of all Indian children had been removed from their families by state welfare agencies (H.R. Rep. No. 96-1386, 95th Cong. 2nd sess. 9, 1978). The Act achieved this goal by providing that for Indian children residing on Indian reservations, tribal courts would have exclusive jurisdiction over Indian child custody proceedings involving termination of parental rights, adoptions, and placements in foster care. For Indian children not residing on reservations, the Act provided that, unless vetoed by either of the parents, such proceedings shall be removed from state courts to tribal courts upon the petition of the child's custodian, parent, or tribe, unless there was good cause not to remove such proceedings. For cases not re-

moved to tribal courts, the Act provided that in placing such Indian children, state courts should give preference first to members of the child's extended family, second, to families from the same tribe as that of the child, and third to any other Indian family. Finally the Act provided that the judgments of tribal courts in child custody proceedings should be given full faith and credit by state and federal courts (T. Johnson 1991, 1993).

• TRIBAL AMENDMENTS TO ENVIRONMENTAL LAWS  Application of federal environmental laws to Indian reservations has both positive and negative implications for tribal sovereignty. On one hand, general federal environmental laws have been applied on Indian reservations without the consent of the tribes. On the other, the Congress has enacted amendments to these laws that in many instances treat the tribes as states for the purpose of allowing tribes to assume primacy (primary regulatory authority) over the implementation of these federal mandates. Since these federal environmental laws have been called an exercise in cooperative federalism between the states and the federal government, the very fact that the Congress has recognized tribes as virtual states in some of these statutes signifies that Congress is considering tribes to be an integral part of this cooperative federalism. "Treatment of tribes as states" is provided for in the Clean Water Act (33 U.S.C. 1251 et seq.), the Safe Drinking Water Act (42 U.S.C. 300j-11(a) and (b)(1)), and the Clean Air Act (42 U.S.C.7601(d)). The only major federal environmental statute not containing such a section is the Resource Conservation and Recovery Act, which regulated disposal of solid and hazardous waste (42 U.S.C. 6901, 6903 (13)). Lower federal courts have held that this law treats tribes as municipalities (*Backcountry Against Dump v. EPA*, 100 F.3d 147 (D.C. Cir. 1996)).

• TRIBAL RESTORATION ACTS  Starting with the 1973 Menominee Restoration Act, Congress enacted at least 16 tribal-specific restoration acts. In these acts, Congress "restored" to federal recognition tribes that had had their relationship with the federal government terminated during the termination era. It is somewhat of a paradox that while these restoration acts represent the clearest example that the termination policies have been repudiated, many of these restoration acts extend application of P.L. 280 to the territories of such tribes. Inasmuch as P.L. 280 allowed a certain amount of state jurisdiction inside Indian reservations, it was perhaps the single most detrimental legislation enacted during the termination era (Goldberg-Ambrose 1997).

• THE INDIAN GAMING REGULATORY ACT OF 1988  The Indian Gaming Regulatory Act of 1988 (25 U.S.C. 2701 et seq., 102 Stat. 2467) is perhaps the most important legislation defining the status of Indian tribes within the United States structure of federalism in that it attempts to accommodate the interests of the federal government, the tribes, and the states. Congress divided gaming on Indian lands into three classes. Class I are games played for no meaningful wager; these games were left to tribal regulation. Class II consists of bingo, bingolike games, and nonbanking card games. These games are regulated by the tribes and a newly created federal agency, the National Indian Gaming Commission. Class III games consist of all other games, which includes most casino-type games. These games are regulated pursuant to a tribal-state compact approved by the secretary of the Interior ("Gaming," this vol.).

Under the Indian Gaming Regulatory Act as first enacted, Congress was careful to balance the sovereign interests of the tribes and the states. The states' interests were recognized by providing for state approval of the compacts, and the tribal interests were protected by providing that tribes could sue states in federal courts if the states failed to negotiate these compacts in good faith. The Supreme Court upset this delicate congressional balancing by holding in a 1996 decision, *Seminole Tribe* v. *Florida* (517 U.S. 44), that the Indian commerce clause did not give Congress the power to abrogate the states' eleventh-amendment sovereign immunity from suit and thereby allow tribes to sue states in federal courts. After that decision, the secretary of the interior issued regulations taking the position that if a state invoked its sovereign immunity after being sued by a tribe for lack of good faith negotiation, the secretary could take the matter in hand and issue gaming regulations for that particular tribe. These regulations have been challenged by the states, and the outcome of such litigation is uncertain.

• THE *DURO* FIX OF 1990 (104 STAT. 1892)  This legislation is the only time that Congress has, after disagreeing with a Supreme Court decision divesting Indian tribes of an original inherent sovereign power, decided to overturn such decision by "reaffirming" the existence of such tribal power, here the power to criminally prosecute nonmember Indians. The Court in *Lara* only decided that Congress could "reaffirm" such tribal power. Left unanswered was whether this "*Duro*-fix" legislation is unconstitutional on due process and equal protection grounds. By 2006, two lower federal courts had upheld the constitutionality of the act against such attacks (*Means* v. *Navajo Nation*, 432 F.3d 924 [9th Cir. 2005] and *Morris* v. *Tanner*, 288 F. Supp. 2d 1133 [2003]).

**The Trust Relationship**

Flowing from the doctrine of discovery, the treaties, congressional statutes, and court decisions, the trust relationship has been at times beneficial for Indian tribes and at other times damaging to them. First used in 1886 to justify congressional plenary power over Indian tribes (*United States* v. *Kagama*) the doctrine has never been used by the Supreme Court to impose limits on the power of Congress to interfere with tribal self-governments. The doctrine has been used by the Court to control the actions of the executive branch.

Scholars have identified two strands to the trust doctrine (M.C. Wood 1995). The first one is called the sovereign trust; the second one is the guardian ward strand. The first one is initially derived from the treaties signed between the United States and the tribes. In those treaties, in exchange for receiving from the tribes a huge amount of lands, the United States agreed to guarantee the tribes' right to self-government and the integrity of the tribes' reservation borders. The United States also agreed to provide the tribes economic assistance, since such land cessions meant that the tribes' no longer had access to lands necessary for their economic self-sufficiency. This strand of the doctrine is referred to as the sovereign trust doctrine because the purpose of the doctrine is the protection of the tribes' existence as sovereign nations.

The other strand of the doctrine, the guardian-ward trust, was developed during the allotment era. Under that strand, the trust doctrine was used to legitimize federal power over Indians, and the reason for its existence was the weakness of the tribes and the perceived incompetence and racial inferiority of the Indians. Its purpose was to provide a period of guardianship, which was thought to be needed because Indians were considered incompetent to manage their affairs or assimilate immediately into the mainstream of American society. Starting in the 1930s, Congress focused on using the trust doctrine to help tribes achieve self-government and economic self-sufficiency.

*Congressional Action*

The main conclusion that can be drawn from analyzing legislation enacted since the 1970s pursuant to the trust doctrine is that such legislation decisively follows the sovereign trust strand of the doctrine. Such legislation can be divided into four categories. First are statutes that, although not impacting the concept of inherent tribal sovereignty, make possible the exercise of such sovereignty by providing financial assistance to Indian tribes. A second group of statutes consists of legislation that has been protective of tribal cultural rights, which some scholars have termed "cultural sovereignty" (Coffey and Tsosie 2001). A third group of statutes promotes economic development within Indian reservations. Finally, many federal statutes were enacted to protect and promote the health, education, and welfare of tribal members. Not discussed here are all the federal statutes making resources available to states and local governments that also allow tribes to participate as governmental entities. Such legislation is excluded because the inclusion of tribes in such programs is not so much the result of the trust doctrine as it is the implicit recognition that tribes have become an integral part of American federalism under a third sphere of sovereignty (Skibine 2003).

• SUPPORT FOR TRIBAL GOVERNMENTS  The Indian Self-Determination Act of 1975 is the leading statute providing a source of federal funds to permit tribal governments to administer governmental programs. It "is the law most responsible for changes in [federal] services to Indians in the modern era. . . . These laws, and others building on their approach, have resulted in a revolution in Indian services" (Cohen 2005:1346). In 1970, only about 2 percent of Bureau of Indian Affairs and Indian Health Services programs were administered by tribes; in 2006 the number is over 50 percent. Another statute providing support and funding to tribal governments is the Indian Tribal Justice Support Act of 1993 (25 U.S.C. 2801 et seq.), in which Congress declared its purpose to "further the development, operation, and enhancement of tribal justice systems."

• PROTECTION OF TRIBAL CULTURAL RIGHTS AND RESOURCES   The major federal legislation protecting tribal cultural rights is the Native American Graves Protection and Repatriation Act of 1990 (8 U.S.C. 1170, 25 U.S.C. 3001–3013.) The act has three main purposes. First is the repatriation to the Indian tribes of culturally affiliated Native American remains, funerary objects, sacred objects, and objects of cultural patrimony located in museums that are either owned by the federal government or receive federal funding. The second purpose is to prevent the unauthorized excavation of Indian graves or artifacts located on federal or Indian land. Finally, the act provides criminal penalties for trafficking in Native American remains and for the sale of cultural items prohibited under the act. A somewhat related act is the Archeological Resources Protection Act of 1979 (16 U.S.C. 470 et seq.), which prohibits the excavation or removal of archeological resources from Indian land without a permit. Such permits can only be issued with the consent of the tribe or the Indian landowner.

Other legislation protective of Indian cultures includes the Native American Language Act of 1990, which adopts the preservation of Native languages as a federal policy (25 U.S.C. 2901–2906). As amended, the Act created a grant program "to ensure the survival and continuing vitality of Native American Languages" (42 U.S.C. 2991b-3, 2992d (e)). Also enacted in 1990 was the Indian Arts and Crafts Act (25 U.S.C. 305–305e, 18 U.S.C. 1159), whose purpose was to prevent the sale of items fraudulently represented as having been made by Native Americans.

Although Congress enacted the American Indian Religious Freedom Act in 1978, this Act only amounted to a declaration that "it shall be the policy of the United States to protect and preserve for American Indians their inherent rights of freedom to believe, express, and exercise, the traditional religions of the Indians" (42 U.S.C. 1996). The Act did not prevent the Supreme Court from allowing the federal government to build roads through sacred Indian religious areas in *Lying* v. *Northwest Indian Cemetery Protective Association* (485 U.S. 439 [1988]) or from allowing states to punish Indians for performing religious ceremonies involving the use of Peyote in *Oregon* v. *Smith* (494 U.S. 872 [1990]). To remedy some of these shortcomings, Congress amended the American Indian Religious Freedom Act in 1994 to protect Indians using peyote in traditional Indian religious ceremonies (42 U.S.C. 1996a).

• PROMOTING TRIBAL ECONOMIC DEVELOPMENT   Although Congress has enacted relatively few tribe-specific statutes in this area, funds have been set aside for tribes by Congress and the executive branch from funds appropriated as part of general programs available to states, municipalities, and other entities (Cohen 2005:1306–1334). Among the most important pieces of legislation were the Indian Financing Act of 1974 (25 U.S.C. 1451 et seq.), the Indian Mineral Development Act of 1982, and the Indian Tribal Governmental Tax Status Act of 1982 (26 U.S.C. 7871), allowing tribes to issue tax-free bonds. Finally, in the Indian Gaming Regulatory Act of 1988, Congress stated that "the purpose of this Act is to provide a basis for the operation of gaming by Indian tribes as a means of promoting tribal economic development, self-sufficiency, and strong tribal governments" (25 U.S.C. 2702 1). There is no question that the act greatly contributed to the growth of tribal gaming as a means to generate economic development since tribal yearly revenues grew from $212 million in 1988, the year the legislation was enacted, to over $14.8 billion in 2002 (Cohen 2005:858).

• PROTECTING TRIBAL HEALTH, EDUCATION, AND WELFARE   Legislation enacted pursuant to the trust relationship includes the Indian Health Care Improvement Act of 1976 (25 U.S.C. 1601 et seq.), the Tribally Controlled Community College Act of 1978 (25 U.S.C. 1801 et seq.), the Indian Education Act (20 U.S.C. 7401, et seq.), the Tribally Controlled Schools Act of 1988 (25 U.S.C. 2501 et seq.), the 1996 Native American Housing Assistance and Self-Determination Act (25 U.S.C. 4101 et seq.), and the Native American Education Improvement Act of 2001 (Pub. L. 107-110 Title X).

*Support in the Courts*

Even though courts have not been receptive to striking down acts of Congress on the ground that they are in violation of the United States trust responsibilities toward the tribes, the courts have been willing to support the trust relationship against the actions of the executive branch (M.C. Wood 1995). The use of the trust doctrine in this area has taken two forms. First are actions for injunctive and declaratory relief. In these law suits, the plaintiffs are using the courts to force the federal agencies to do something or stop them from doing something. A class action suit brought by Elouise Cobell on behalf of thousands of Indians, demanding an account of funds held for them by the Bureau of Indian Affairs, even resulted in the enactment of legislation addressing some of the problems, the Trust Fund Reform Management Act of 1994 (108 Stat. 4239, codified at 25 U.S.C. 4001 et seq., and 25 U.S.C. 151–162a).

In the second type of lawsuit, tribes or individual Indians sue the United States for money damages because the United States through its agencies has allegedly mismanaged tribal trust assets. The Supreme Court has held that in order to be successful, the Indian plaintiffs have to show that the federal statutes or regulations alleged to have been violated by he United States "can fairly be interpreted as mandating compensation by the federal government for damages sustained" (*United States* v. *Mitchell*, 463 U.S. 206 [1983]). In order to make such showing, the plaintiffs have to show more than just the existence of a "bare" trust. Instead, they have to show that the statutes or regulations have vested the federal agency with supervision or control over the tribal asset at issue and that the agency has breached specific trust duties in managing such property. These trust duties can either be found in the statutes and regulations, or implied from the fact that the agency has assumed complete control over the trust asset (*United States* v. *White Mountain Apache Tribe*, 537 U.S. 465 [2003]).

65

# The State-Tribe Relationship

CAROLE GOLDBERG

From the earliest years of colonial settlement in North America, relations between tribes and local non-Indian communities have been troubled, in part because the settlers wanted to displace the Indians from their lands and assume governing power over their territories. British colonial authorities, interested in preventing such discord, often stepped in to protect Indians against loss of their land and sovereignty, through treaties and proclamations (vol. 4:5–12). In the American period, this pattern persisted, with states seeking Indian resources and governing authority, and the federal government mostly claiming to be trustee and protector of the Indians, first through treaties and later through federal legislation and Supreme Court decisions (vol. 4:29–80).

The major difference between the British colonial and American eras is that the United States government is far more accountable to the states and their non-Indian citizens than the British ever were to the colonies. The United States Constitution establishes that accountability through representation of states in the Senate, as well as through the greater voting strength of non-Indians under a one-person, one-vote election system for president and for members of the House of Representatives. Native nations have no representation as such within the American system. Thus, although the extent of federal government support for state versus tribal interests has varied over time, there are numerous examples of federal statutes, regulations, and court decisions that have advanced states' desires for tribal land and sovereignty at the expense of the Indians.

Since the 1960s, as Indian nations have asserted their sovereignty and the federal government has proclaimed a policy of tribal self-determination, clashes have continued between tribes and states over taxation, water rights, environmental control, gaming, child welfare, hunting and fishing, and myriad other subjects. Tribes and states are both federally recognized sovereigns, sharing geography as well as some common citizens. Yet "the state is often seen by the tribes as relentlessly expansionary in seeking to extend its authority over the reservation and, in the process, to limit the tribe's authority and demean its very existence" (Pommersheim 1991:249). In the absence of clear congressional resolution, many of these conflicts have resulted in litigation; however, beginning in the last quarter of the twentieth century, some have been resolved through tribal-state negotiation and cooperative agreements. Although the Supreme Court in 1886 described the states as the "deadliest enemies" of the tribes (*U.S.* v. *Kagama*, 118 U.S. 375), and certain hostilities persist, increasingly states and tribes are becoming partners in law enforcement, administration of federal benefit programs, and protection of natural resources, among other endeavors.

## Colonial and Early Federal Period

Under British colonial rule of North America, the individual colonies had considerable leeway to manage day-to-day Indian affairs, subject to ultimate control in the London-based Board of Trade. Responding to the demands of land speculators and land-hungry settlers, some of these colonies, such as Massachusetts Bay, Virginia, and Connecticut, tolerated or permitted fraudulent and violent practices by colonists bent on expropriating Indian resources. When the tribes took up arms in protest, as in the Pequot War of 1637 in Connecticut and Bacon's Rebellion of 1675 in Virginia, the colonists treated the Indians' resistance as justification for decimating and subjugating them (Jennings 1975). Colonies entered into diplomatic relations only with the most powerful tribes, such as the Mohawk Nation, which made a treaty with New York in 1679 (Richter 2001).

Eventually, the British realized that policies carried out in many of the colonies were undermining London's geopolitical objectives, by driving the Indians into alliance with the French and by fomenting Indian wars that rendered the entire colonial enterprise less profitable for the mother country. So, beginning in the 1750s, the British government assumed firmer control over relations between the colonists and the tribes, prohibiting colonial governors from issuing speculative "preemption rights" for Indian-occupied lands and banning other practices that inflamed relations with the tribes (Banner 2005). In 1763, after the British victory in the French and Indian Wars, the Crown delivered the Royal Proclamation of 1763, intended to prohibit non-Indian settlement west of the Appalachian Mountains. This Proclamation also acknowledged colonists' frauds and abuses which caused the Indians "great Dissatisfaction," and affirmed the sanctity of existing treaties, including their promises of protection against non-Indian settlement on tribal lands (Calloway 2006).

This colonial experience established a pattern of intergovernmental relations that continued beyond 1776. Local settlers' and speculators' desire for land and other resources had fueled resentment against the British and the quest for independence. Yet the new nation was weak and needed the tribes as allies or at least as neutrals. For example, evidence of centralized control of Indian relations can be found in the early appointment of treaty negotiators for northern, southern, and middle departments of Indian affairs and in the negotiation of a United States treaty with the Delaware in 1778. Indeed, to cement an alliance with the Delaware, the United States offered the possibility of tribes forming a state to be represented in Congress, with the Delaware serving at its head (Treaty of Fort Pitt, 7 Stat. 13; Kappler 1904–1941, 2:3–5).

When the Articles of Confederation were ratified in 1781, the relative roles of states and the federal government were left ambiguous. Article IX of the Articles granted the Continental Congress "the sole and exclusive right and power of . . . regulating the trade and managing all affairs with the Indians, not members of any of the States, provided, that the legislative right of any State within its own limits be not infringed or violated" (Continental Congress 1777:Art. IX [1904–1937, 9:919]). This language failed to clarify which Indians were "members" of the states and what "legislative rights" attached to the states. So when New York officials disrupted treaty negotiations between national representatives and the League of the Iroquois, claiming that the state possessed the exclusive right to treat with those Indians, the Articles of Confederation could offer no definitive resolution to the conflict. Dissatisfaction with this state of affairs was one of the motivations for establishing the United States Constitution in 1787. As one committee of the Continental Congress proclaimed on the eve of the Constitutional Convention,

> An avaricious disposition in some of our people to acquire large tracts of land and often by unfair means, appears to be the principal source of difficulties with the Indians. . . . [It] cannot be supposed, the state has the powers [to make war with Indians or buy land from them] without making [the Indian affairs clause of Article IX] useless. [N]o particular state can have an exclusive interest in the management of Affairs with any of the tribes, except in some uncommon cases (Continental Congress 1787 [1904–1937, 33:457–459]).

The Constitution deleted all the phrases from the Articles that had fueled state claims to power over Indian affairs. In Article I, section 8, it stated simply that Congress shall have the power "to regulate Commerce with foreign Nations, and among the several States, and with the Indian Tribes." This provision simultaneously recognized the governmental status of tribes by linking them with foreign nations and states, and asserted the federal government's authority over Indian relations. Based on the records of the Constitutional Convention, the debates over ratification, and the overall historical context, it appears that the Framers intended the Indian commerce clause to preclude or preempt all state involvement in Indian affairs (R.N. Clinton 1995); however, the United States Supreme Court has not consistently interpreted the provision to bar all state power in Indian country. Compare *Moe* v. *Salish and Kootenai Tribes* (425 U.S. 463, 481 n.17 [1976]), denying preemptive effect, with *Montana* v. *Blackfeet Tribe* (471 U.S. 759, 764 [1985]), acknowledging that "the Constitution vests the Federal Government with exclusive authority over relations with Indian tribes." It is clear that when the federal government acts to conduct Indian relations, states are broadly precluded from making any laws that would impair federal policies or the achievement of federal objectives, including protection of tribal self-government.

In the early decades of the Republic, the federal government in fact made many treaties that acknowledged the political autonomy of tribes and promised to insulate them from state authority, for example, the Treaty of New Echota with the Cherokee in 1835 (7 Stat. 478; Kappler 1904–1941, 2:439–449) and the Treaty of Washington with the Creek and Seminole in 1856 (11 Stat. 699; Kappler 1904–1941, 2:756–763). But local citizens continued to press for tribal lands and to resist tribes' claims of control over their territories. Thus New York made its own treaties to acquire land from the Iroquois tribes (*Oneida Indian Nation* v. *County of Oneida*, 414 U.S. 661 [1974]), and Georgia attempted to extend its laws into lands the federal government had guaranteed to the Cherokee (*Worcester* v. *Georgia*, 31 U.S. 515 [1832]). The stage was set for a showdown between state and federal power when Samuel Worcester, a Protestant missionary expending federal "civilization" funds, entered Cherokee territory in 1830 without a license from the Georgia governor, as required by state law. After Georgia authorities arrested him and the Georgia courts sentenced Worcester to four years in prison, the case made its way to the United States Supreme Court, which held that the Indian commerce clause, the treaty with the Cherokees, and the federal statute authorizing Worcester's presence among the Cherokees fully precluded any exercise of state jurisdiction within Cherokee territory. As the Court stated,

> The Cherokee nation, then, is a distinct community, occupying its own territory, with boundaries accurately described, in which the laws of Georgia can have no force, and which the citizens of Georgia have no right to enter, but with the assent of the Cherokees themselves, or in conformity with treaties, and with the acts of Congress. The whole intercourse between the United States and this nation, is, by our Constitution and laws, vested in the government of the United States (*Worcester*, 31 U.S. at 520; Washburn 1973, 4:2622).

This decision afforded the Cherokees scant protection, as citizens of Georgia and other states elected a new president and members of Congress who were willing to force the  *67*

Cherokees to leave the state. Likewise, it failed to protect the California Indians two decades later when armed state militias began hunting down Indian men, women, and children, and the state passed laws effectively enslaving them (Hurtado 1988). Nonetheless, the Supreme Court's 1832 decision in *Worcester* v. *Georgia* established a strong legal principle against state involvement in Indian affairs that remains largely intact in the twenty-first century. According to that principle, states may extend their authority into Indian country only if Congress specifically allows them to do so (*Williams* v. *Lee*, 358 U.S. 217 [1959]; Washburn 1973, 4:2785–2787).

In the late nineteenth century, Congress began implementing policies of forced assimilation that invited non-Indians into Indian country, prompting some erosion of the general rule. Often framed in paternalistic terms, these policies were also responsive to local citizens demanding greater access to Indian lands. Through the Dawes Severalty Act of 1887, Congress allocated parcels of tribal land to individual Indians in trust, selling off the remaining "surplus" lands to non-Indians (vol. 4:61–70). The individual Indians would normally receive full ownership to their allotments (fee title) after 25 years, although Congress accelerated the process in some instances. Not only did more than 50 million acres of "surplus" tribal lands pass into non-Indian hands, but also nearly 30 million additional acres of allotted lands passed by sale or involuntary transfer from the Indian fee owner into non-Indian ownership once the federal trust period expired (Newton 2005:77–78, 1042). As non-Indians became a greater presence in Indian country, states began claiming authority to tax, regulate, and criminalize their conduct. Despite the language of federal treaties and the Indian commerce clause, the United States Supreme Court ultimately upheld state power where no Indian interests were considered affected, for example where the state prosecuted one non-Indian for committing a crime against another (*U.S.* v. *McBratney*, 104 U.S. 621 [1881]), or the state taxed the cattle of a non-Indian who was grazing them on land leased from a tribe (*Thomas* v. *Gay*, 169 U.S. 264 [1898]).

Where Indian interests were present, the general principle barring state authority within Indian country remained untouched. Thus, when the states of Kansas and New York tried to tax lands of individual Indians, the Supreme Court replied in 1867 that so long as the tribes maintained their federally recognized governmental status, they were "separated from the jurisdiction of [the states], and to be governed exclusively by the government of the Union" (*In re Kansas Indians*, 72 U.S. 737, 755 [1866]). And nearly 100 years later, the Supreme Court denied the Arizona state courts power to hear a breach of contract action brought by a non-Indian against a tribal member involving an on-reservation purchase. According to the Court, "the basic policy of *Worcester* has remained," meaning that "absent governing Acts of Congress, the question has always been whether the state action infringed on the right of reservation Indians to make their own laws and be ruled by them" (*Williams* v. *Lee,* 358 U.S. at 219–220).

Early property disputes over land and other natural resources clarified that federal law, not state, was to govern Indian rights. As early as the 1790s, Congress had asserted its authority over Indian lands, passing statutes, known as Trade and Intercourse Acts, that prohibited the transfer of such lands without Congress's consent (now codified at 25 U.S.C. § 177). As the United States expanded westward in the nineteenth century, controversies arose between state citizens and tribes over water rights and rights to hunt and fish. In the arid West, for example, states wanted to subject waters flowing through Indian reservations to state legal regimes, known as prior appropriation. Under those legal rules, water rights belong to the first to divert water for beneficial use such as irrigation. Because non-Indian citizens of the states had greater access than the tribes to financing for agriculture and other purposes, the prior appropriation regime worked to the non-Indians' advantage. The United States Supreme Court intervened, holding that tribal water rights were to be governed by federal law, which meant that treaties, statutes, and federal executive orders setting aside reservations would be read as reserving adequate water for tribal use, regardless whether or when the tribes actually appropriated the water (*Winters* v. *U.S.*, 207 U.S. 564 [1908]). Likewise, states wanted to subject Indians' rights to hunt and fish to state licensing laws and limitations, in order to make fish and game available for non-Indians' commercial and recreational pursuits. The issue came to a head when the state of Washington authorized non-Indians to place fish wheels on the Columbia River, sharply diminishing the supply of salmon available to the downstream Yakima Nation. The United States Supreme Court stepped in again, affirming that the Yakima had property rights to fish that were guaranteed under federal treaties, and the state of Washington could not limit the enjoyment of those rights (*U.S.* v. *Winans*, 198 U.S. 371 [1905]).

## Federal Laws Allowing State Involvement in Indian Affairs

Until the middle of the twentieth century, Congress had rarely acted to authorize state involvement in Indian affairs, the prominent exception being the Dawes Severalty Act. The Supreme Court later interpreted this language to authorize state property taxes on the former trust allotments, even though they might still be owned by Indians within reservations (*County of Yakima* v. *Confederated Tribes and Bands of the Yakima Indian Nation*, 502 U.S. 251 [1992]). In the 1920s Congress allowed some state taxation of mineral production from tribal lands (25 U.S.C. §§ 398, 398c) and permitted state officers to enter Indian lands to inspect health and education conditions and to enforce sanitation and quarantine regulations (25 U.S.C. § 231).

After World War II Congress enacted a series of laws granting states broad civil and criminal jurisdiction over Indians engaged in activities in Indian country. These laws departed dramatically from prior federal practice because they did not rest upon tribal consent; indeed, in some instances they violated treaty provisions that promised tribes protection against state jurisdiction. Congress established a policy known as "termination," which promoted an end to federal recognition of tribes as governments, an end to the specially protected trust status of tribal lands, and an end to federal health, education, and other benefits to Indians (vol. 4:76–78). Justified on the basis of extending "equal rights" to Indians, this policy envisioned the complete assimilation of Indians into the American polity. It was also a means of reducing federal government expenditures, an important postwar priority. For the tribes not yet ready for termination, Congress saw state civil and criminal jurisdiction as an intermediate stage, promoting assimilation by familiarizing Indians with non-Indian legal norms and shifting federal law enforcement and criminal justice expenses to the states. Combating "lawlessness" on reservations was the main rationale Congress offered for state jurisdiction, although relying on the states was the cost-saving way for the federal government to pursue that end.

At first, Congress introduced state jurisdiction on a state-by-state or reservation-by-reservation basis. The earliest laws targeted all the tribes in New York State (25 U.S.C. §§ 232, 233), as well as certain individual tribes in Iowa, North Dakota, and Kansas (Newton 2005:583). Congress addressed specific subject areas, conferring state jurisdiction to adjudicate Indian water rights (43 U.S.C. § 666) and state jurisdiction to regulate liquor sales on reservations (18 U.S.C. § 1161; *Rice* v. *Rehner*, 463 U.S. 713 [1983]). In 1953, Congress decided to take a more comprehensive approach to the extension of state jurisdiction on reservations. It adopted a law known as Public Law 280, which mandated state criminal and civil jurisdiction on the reservations in California, Minnesota, Nebraska, Oregon, and Wisconsin, with Alaska added once it became a state in 1958. For these "mandatory" Public Law 280 states, Congress eliminated most of the federal criminal jurisdiction designed for offenses committed by or against Indians on reservations. Only a few specific reservations in these states were excluded from the new jurisdictional arrangement. Public Law 280 allowed all other states to opt for civil and criminal jurisdiction, an offer that some states accepted in full or for certain subject areas only. Some of these "optional" Public Law 280 states failed to take proper measures to accept jurisdiction under the law, and others took it, only to return it later because they objected to new responsibilities for law enforcement and criminal justice without the benefit of additional federal funding. Thus, by the beginning of the twenty-first century, only three "optional" states exercised substantial jurisdiction under the statute—Florida, Idaho (only over certain subjects), and Washington (a complex scheme involving certain subjects and certain reservation lands) (Newton 2005:537–588).

The absence of tribal consent to the original terms of Public Law 280 engendered immediate controversy; President Dwight Eisenhower expressed misgivings about the law even as he signed it (Goldberg-Ambrose 1997:98). In 1968, Congress amended the Act to require tribal consent if a state wanted to opt into Public Law 280's state jurisdiction regime (25 U.S.C. §§ 1321–1322). No tribe has given its consent since then. At the same time, Congress did not allow tribes to undo state jurisdiction in the six mandatory states or in the states that had already opted for jurisdiction. There was only a provision that states were allowed to return, or retrocede, their jurisdiction back to the federal government (25 U.S.C. § 1323), putting tribes in the position of having to persuade state authorities. From 1968 to 2006, more than two dozen retrocessions occurred, including all the reservations in Nevada (an optional state) as well as selected reservations in Minnesota, Montana, Nebraska, Oregon, Washington, and Wisconsin (Goldberg and Champagne 2006).

Public Law 280 contains certain exceptions to state jurisdiction, largely to protect the federal government against claims for compensation if Indian property rights were affected. Thus, the law bars state jurisdiction over tribal trust property and over federally protected hunting and fishing rights. And because Public Law 280 diverges so significantly from the basic principle of federal Indian law denying state authority over Indians, courts have tried to interpret its provisions strictly, resolving all ambiguities and doubts against state jurisdiction. This judicial tendency accelerated in the 1970s, when Congress abandoned termination as federal policy and instead embraced a policy of tribal self-determination. Among other things, courts have construed Public Law 280 as not allowing state regulation in Indian country (as opposed to criminal jurisdiction or state adjudication); as not allowing application of local (as opposed to statewide) laws; and as not allowing state jurisdiction over the tribes themselves (as opposed to individual Indians). Furthermore, Public Law 280 has not stripped the tribes themselves of civil or criminal jurisdiction, leaving tribal jurisdiction to operate concurrently with state. As a result of all these court decisions, Public Law 280 has not diminished tribal sovereignty as much as it might have, a result probably consistent with the fact that Congress abandoned termination as its objective.

Perhaps the most far-reaching effects of Public Law 280 have been practical rather than legal–significant gaps and vacuums in law enforcement, regulation, and criminal justice on the affected reservations. While federal authority has largely been withdrawn, tribal and state jurisdiction are either uncertain or inadequately developed. For example, although Public Law 280 did not remove tribal jurisdiction or sever the federal government's trust relationship to affected tribes, the Department of the Interior invoked the Act as reason to deny federal funding for tribal law enforcement and courts. As a consequence, these tribal institutions developed much more slowly in Public Law 280 jurisdictions than elsewhere in Indian country, leaving affected tribes with no way to address problems such as domestic violence or illegal dumping. At the same time, the absence of federal funding for Public Law 280 states, combined with the exemption of tribal trust lands from state property taxes and longstanding friction between many tribal and nontribal communities, has generated tribal complaints that county police patrols and responses are insufficient to meet community needs. Furthermore, uncertainties about the reach of states' Public Law 280 jurisdiction, such as the line between criminal jurisdiction (allowed) and regulatory jurisdiction (not allowed) have inhibited county law enforcement's initiative and left some areas of tribal community concern completely unattended. In some Public Law 280 states, for instance, it is extremely difficult to find any court that has authority to hear an eviction action when a tribe wishes to remove a non-Indian from tribal lands (Goldberg-Ambrose 1997).

Despite the difficulties that Public Law 280 engendered, Congress established the same state jurisdiction regime in a variety of statutes enacted in the last quarter of the twentieth century to resolve tribal land claims and to restore certain terminated tribes to federally recognized status. For example, when Congress recognized the Mashantucket Pequot Tribe in Connecticut and settled its land claim by placing certain lands in trust for their reservation, it also said that state jurisdiction should prevail on that reservation "as if" the state had opted into Public Law 280 (25 U.S.C. § 1755). In other instances, Congress simply passed settlement or tribal recognition acts that announce the existence of state civil and criminal jurisdiction, without alluding to Public Law 280. The Rhode Island Indian Claims Settlement Act of 1978, recognizing the Narragansett Tribe, is one such law (25 U.S.C. § 1708(a)). Some of these tribally specific laws include provisions that do not appear in Public Law 280, such as language addressing the application of state gaming law to tribes (25 U.S.C. § 737(a), Alabama and Coushatta Tribes) or barring state jurisdiction over internal tribal matters (Maine Indian Claims Settlement Act). Much confusion has ensued over whether these laws should be interpreted to accord with Public Law 280 (e.g., *Alabama-Coushatta Tribes of Texas* v. *Texas*, 208 F. Supp. 2d 670 [E.D. Tex. 2002]).

The 1990s brought new sources of funding for tribal police and courts on reservations subject to state jurisdiction, under Public Law 280 or otherwise. These resources came from tribal economic development, such as gaming, and from grants extended by the United States Department of Justice (Newton 2005:1410–1412). With such resources in hand, some tribes, such as the Tulalip tribes (Duhlelap) of Washington State, have succeeded in achieving retrocession of the state's Public Law 280 jurisdiction. Tulalip had been dissatisfied with the level of law enforcement service it had received from its local county, and many members viewed the adversarial and punitive state criminal justice system as incompatible with the tribe's values and culture, which emphasize helping tribal members become healthy, contributing members of the community who take their communal responsibilities seriously. Since retrocession the tribe has instituted a tribal police department and court that operate according to tribal notions of justice, thereby enhancing the legitimacy of the entire criminal justice system. Other tribes have used newly available resources to establish cooperative agreements with state and county police agencies and courts. These include cross-deputization agreements, allowing officers from the state side and the tribal side to make arrests under the authority of the other. Some states, such as Wisconsin, have provided state funding to encourage such arrangements (Wis. Stat. § 165.90).

## Areas of Conflict

In the third quarter of the twentieth century, most Indian nations embarked on programs to build institutions and economies that would enable them to exercise effective governmental powers over their territories and people (Wilkinson 2005). These tribal initiatives included land claims litigation to restore tribal land bases; lawsuits to quantify reserved tribal water rights and to affirm treaty-based hunting and fishing rights, some of which include off-reservation fisheries; creation of tribal administrative agencies to regulate zoning and environmental pollution on reservations and to provide services to tribal communities; establishment of tribal business enterprises, such as smoke shops and gaming; systems of taxation aimed at non-Indians doing business or buying goods on reservations; and development of court systems capable of managing civil lawsuits involving nonmembers, child welfare matters, and a host of other disputes. States have often resisted such tribal projects. Moreover, they have attempted to exclude Indians living on reservations from political and economic benefits available under state law. Contributing to the contentious relations has been the fact that tribal Indians do not pay state property taxes on trust land and are exempt from state income and sales taxes for on-reservation activities. (They do, however, pay other state taxes, including sales taxes on off-reservation purchases.) Furthermore, Indians on reservations are typically not subject to state law, absent federal law to the contrary.

With tribal natural resource claims for land, water, fish, and game, the source of rivalry between states and tribes was not so different from centuries past–local non-Indians unwilling to accept tribal rights based on prior occupation and federal treaties. Many of these tribal claims had lain dormant for decades, often because federal officials had bowed to state pressures and declined to protect the Indians' rights. In the meantime, non-Indians had made use of these resources, developing expectations that they believed deserved protection as well. Furthermore, many of these resources had come under increasing pressure from growing non-Indian populations, causing severe shortages.

These resource-related struggles have produced some of the most intense hostility from states and their non-Indian citizens, directed at tribes and their members. In the Pacific Northwest, where tribes sued to confirm their treaty-based rights to one-half the fish from certain off-reservation waters, and in the upper Midwest, where tribes claimed substantial on- and off-reservation hunting and fishing rights, the non-Indian reaction was fierce (vol. 7:177–178). Commenting on one of the many appeals that the state of Washington brought to challenge the Indians' fishing rights, the Ninth Circuit Court of Appeals wrote, "Except for some desegregation cases, the district court has faced the most concerted official and private efforts to frustrate a decree of a federal court witnessed in this century" (quoted in *Washington* v. *Washington State Commercial Passenger Fishing Vessel Association*, 443 U.S. 658, n.36 [1979]). Federal courts ultimately ruled for the tribes, allowing only limited state regulation of the fisheries for conservation purposes (Id.; *Minnesota* v. *Mille Lacs Band of Chippewa Indians*, 526 U.S. 172 [1999]). Opponents of the tribal fishing rights emphasized that their objection was to race-based treaty rights, not individual Indians.

A comparably angry non-Indian reaction greeted court decisions supporting land claims by Eastern Indians. These claims were brought under the centuries-old Intercourse Act, which requires federal permission for any transfer of Indian lands. In the case of New York tribes, the state had negotiated its own treaties in the late 1700s, bypassing the federal approval process. Although the tribes later protested and tried to get the United States to sue the state on their behalf, they gained permission to bring lawsuits on their own only in 1966. Within less than 20 years, they had decisions from the United States Supreme Court indicating that their claims were still valid (*Oneida Indian Nation* v. *County of Oneida*; *County of Oneida* v. *Oneida Indian Nation*, 470 U.S. 226 [1985]). Other Eastern tribes, including the Mashantucket Pequot in Connecticut and the Passamaquoddy and Penobscot in Maine, were able to settle similar claims, through federal statutes that granted federal recognition, established reservations, and sometimes also provided compensation, for example, the Maine Indian Claims Settlement Act (25 U.S.C. §§ 1721–1735). Even though the Indians insisted that they were focusing their land recovery efforts on publicly owned lands, and not seeking to evict individual homeowners, non-Indian groups mounted campaigns against the tribal land claims. As in the fishing disputes, opponents argued that the Indians wanted to vindicate race-based treaty rights (Upstate Citizens for Equality 2006). Later, the federal courts showed less enthusiasm for carrying through on these land claims (*City of Sherrill* v. *Oneida Indian Nation*, 544 U.S. 197 [2005]); *Cayuga Indian Nation* v. *Pataki*, 413 F. 3d 266 [2d Cir. 2005]).

When tribes began exercising regulatory powers, especially over non-Indian activities on reservations, states often opposed them because they wanted to impose their own regulations in the interests of their non-Indian citizens. These concerns sometimes reflected the fact that activities located in one jurisdiction, state or tribal, may have spillover effects across the border. For example, in Wisconsin, the Mole Lake Band of Lake Superior Chippewa Indians wanted to control the quality of water in Rice Lake, their primary source of wild rice, from pollution caused by a proposed off-reservation zinc-copper sulfide mine. The state viewed the Mole Lake Band's attempted regulation as an affront to its sovereignty, as well as a restriction on industrial activity that could benefit the state's economy. The tribe, in turn, viewed the state's willingness to allow the mine as an infringement of its right to carry on its commercial rice-gathering activities and an impairment of its ceremonial practices that depended on clean water (*Wisconsin* v. *EPA*, 266 F.3d 741 [7th Cir. 2001]).

Regulatory conflicts of this type often result in litigation. Departing from its earliest principles denying all state authority on reservations, the Supreme Court has taken the position that tribes can control the activities of non-Indians only where federal and tribal interests are stronger than the countervailing state interests. Thus, for example, the Court upheld the exclusive right of the Mescalero Apache to license non-Indian hunting and fishing on its tribal lands, noting that the federal government had supported the tribe in its efforts to manage reservation wildlife, and the state was not contributing to the maintenance of the resource or experiencing any ill effects outside the reservation (*New Mexico* v. *Mescalero Apache Tribe*, 462 U.S. 324 [1983]).

In the particular case of environmental regulation, Congress has asserted its preeminent role in Indian affairs, and legislated an accommodation of state and tribal interests. In statutes such as the Clean Air Act and the Clean Water Act (42 U.S.C. § 7601(d)(2)(B); 33 U.S.C. § 1377(e)), Congress has affirmed that tribes have primary authority over reservation environments, much as states do over their non-reservation territory, as long as they comply with minimum standards set by federal law. Federal environmental laws put the federal Environmental Protection Agency in the position of mediating and resolving cross-boundary disputes, such as the one involving the Mole Lake Band and the state of Wisconsin.

Tribal regulation has provoked state resistance when the objects of regulation are non-Indians, especially those located on non-Indian private property within the reservation, typically as a long-term consequence of allotment. These non-Indian individuals have argued that only the states should have authority to regulate their activities, even though their lands are still within reservation boundaries. Tribes, in contrast, have contended that if they are to be free to promote their cultures and ways of life, they must have control over all individuals within their territories, regardless of tribal membership status. One such conflict erupted into litigation when a non-Indian landowner within the Hoopa Valley Reservation in California wanted to cut down trees on her property. Because the trees were located along the path of one of the tribe's most ancient and sacred ceremonies, the tribe had passed a zoning law prohibiting logging in that area. The landowner's position was that only the state or county should be able to zone her property (*Bugenig* v. *Hoopa Valley Tribe*, 266 F.3d 1201 [9th Cir. 2001]). The United States Supreme Court has established a presumption favoring state rather than tribal authority to regulate what non-Indians do on their fee lands (private property); but even there, the Court has allowed for tribal control under exceptional circumstances, notably where the non-Indians have voluntarily connected themselves to the tribe in some way, or where the non-Indians' conduct is deeply threatening to the well-being of the tribal community (*Montana* v. *U.S.*, 450 U.S. 544 [1981]). This complex legal doctrine departs from the older principle barring state jurisdiction from Indian country altogether. It also creates uncertainty and unpredictability about who has jurisdiction on reservations—the tribes or the states—thereby exacerbating conflict.

States complain when tribes seek to restrain non-Indian activities, and they often oppose tribal efforts to develop their own enterprises that may have off-reservation impacts or that would be unlawful if conducted outside the reservation. Among the types of tribal development that have attracted such state opposition are solid waste landfills (McGovern 1995), nuclear waste sites (Skibine 2001), and gaming facilities. The tribes' position is normally that they have sovereign authority over their own territory and are not subject to state control. The states tend to focus on the non-Indian involvement in such operations, that is, as patrons, and the spillover effects on their territory to justify their claims.

Basic principles of federal Indian law rarely aid the states in their efforts to seize control. In the case of high stakes bingo, for example, the United States Supreme Court held that states have no authority to limit or ban tribal games, at least if the state is allowing other forms of gambling (*Cabazon Band of Mission Indians* v. *Wilson*, 124 F. 3d 1050 [9th Cir. 1997]). However, even when the states lose in the courts, they may be able to persuade Congress to deploy its Indian affairs power to adjust relations. Thus, for example, after the Supreme Court rendered its decision on high stakes bingo, Congress passed the Indian Regulatory Gaming Act of 1988, which allows tribes to mount casino gaming ventures, but only where the state allows such games under at least some circumstances, and only where the tribe has negotiated a compact with the surrounding state (25 U.S.C. § 2701 et seq.). The Act also requires states to negotiate these compacts in good faith and sets up an elaborate mechanism for resolving conflicts over whether the states have done so. Although the Act prohibits state taxation of tribal gaming revenues, states and tribes may negotiate for tribal payments to the states in exchange for state guarantees of a tribal monopoly on the games in question. The state of Connecticut, for example, has negotiated for a sizeable percentage of the tribal gaming revenues from the two federally recognized tribes in that state. States

and tribes have also negotiated over labor organizing rights at tribal casinos, off-reservation environmental impacts, and tribal obligations to provide remedies for customers injured on casino premises. Where local non-Indian populations dislike gaming as a form of commercial activity or the scale of a particular casino development, the Act has given rise to tribal-state conflict.

Competition for tax revenue has often been a source of contention between Indian nations and states. One recurring issue has been whether states have authority to tax non-Indians making purchases at reservation-based tribal enterprises, such as smoke shops and gas stations. States have been concerned that if they are unable to impose their state taxes on such purchases, tribes will be able to attract customers away from near-reservation non-Indian businesses by undercutting them on the price. Tribes, in turn, have complained that if states can tax such transactions, the tribes are effectively precluded from imposing their own taxes–taxes that may be crucial to maintaining their tribal governments. The Supreme Court has addressed many such cases (*Washington* v. *Confederated Tribes of the Colville Indian Reservation*, 447 U.S. 134 [1980]); *Department of Taxation and Finance of New York* v. *Milhelm Attea & Bros., Inc.*, 512 U.S. 61 [1994]), finding that states are entitled to tax tribal dealings with non-Indians where the tax falls on the non-Indian, and the tribes are merely seeking to market a tax exemption. At the same time, courts have rejected state taxes where the tax falls on the tribe, or where the tribe is contributing value to the transaction. The courts' underlying concern seems to be that taxing power should roughly go along with a government's services to and responsibility for the individuals or businesses being taxed.

The Supreme Court's apparent support for state taxing authority over non-Indians on reservations has been tempered by the Court's recognition that tribes enjoy sovereign immunity, meaning that they cannot be sued without their consent. This tribal immunity from suit has made a special difference in sales tax disputes, because states typically require sellers to add sales taxes to the purchase price of goods and then to remit the tax money to the states. So where the seller is a tribe and the buyer is a non-Indian, the state has a right to tax the purchase, but no power to compel the tribe to turn over the amount of the tax (*Oklahoma Tax Commission* v. *Citizen Band Potawatomi Indian Tribe of Oklahoma*, 498 U.S. 505 [1991]). In effect, this combination of legal rulings has left the states with rights but no legal remedies, creating the conditions for tribal-state disagreements.

As Native nations have developed their court systems, conflicts with states have ensued over which government's court system can hear civil lawsuits against non-Indians involving reservation-based claims. While tribal jurisdiction is normally upheld when the dispute involves a contract between the non-Indian and the tribe or a tribal member, the situation is not so clear for other kinds of claims, such as personal injury (tort) actions or civil rights suits. Where injuries have occurred on lands owned by non-Indians or on state-maintained roads, the Supreme Court has said that tort actions against non-Indians must normally be brought into state rather than tribal court (*Strate* v. *A-1 Contractors*, 520 U.S. 438 [1997]). And in one distinctive circumstance, the Court has extended this ruling to civil lawsuits arising on Indian-owned land (*Nevada* v. *Hicks*, 533 U.S. 353 [2001]). This particular lawsuit was brought by a tribal member against a state officer who had entered the tribal member's on-reservation home to search for evidence of an off-reservation offense. The Supreme Court emphasized in this case that the tribe involved had no authority to prevent state officers from entering for purposes of enforcing off-reservation law.

Tribes and states have also encountered difficulties over which government's court system can hear child welfare matters involving Indian children, especially those living outside reservations. When they are involuntary, these child welfare matters entail allegations of child abuse or neglect leading to foster care placement or, most drastically, termination of parental rights. There are also voluntary child welfare proceedings, where parents wish to place their children in foster care or adoption. General principles of federal Indian law dictate that unless Congress directs otherwise, child welfare proceedings should be handled by the Native nations' own tribunals, at least where on-reservation children are involved. Whether Public Law 280 allows state courts to entertain such proceedings has been the subject of some controversy (compare the Wisconsin attorney general's opinion discussed in *Doe* v. *Mann*, 285 F. Supp. 2d 1229 (N.D. Cal. 2003) and *Doe* v. *Mann*, 415 F. 3d 1038 (9th Cir. 2005). For off-reservation children, the situation was more complex, both states and tribes claiming jurisdiction until Congress addressed the problem in the Indian Child Welfare Act of 1978, which was passed in response to studies and testimony showing that state courts were divesting large numbers of Indian parents of their children and placing those children in non-Indian homes. These studies demonstrated that state agencies' misunderstanding of tribal cultures and unwarranted preference for non-Indian families were driving such placements. Tribes were becoming concerned that they were losing their most precious resource, their future generations. Accordingly, the Act affirmed the exclusive authority of tribal courts over proceedings involving on-reservation children (absent federal law to the contrary) and required state courts to transfer many cases involving off-reservation Indian children to tribal court. State child welfare agencies have generally been reluctant to comply with these provisions, invoking and creating exceptions designed to keep the cases in state court (Graham 1998).

There is a long history of states denying political participation as well as services, such as education, to tribal members on reservations (Newton 2005:894–961). Although all Indians became citizens of the United States in 1924 and are entitled to equal treatment and benefits from the states, states have often justified their discriminatory policies by noting that Indians do not pay property taxes on trust lands and are eligible for special federal benefits. Through lawsuits that began in the 1970s, federal courts have established that states must afford equal political rights and services to Indians (Newton 2005:905–915). The Voting Rights Act of 1965 has been helpful to tribal members seeking to achieve greater participation in state politics and programs. Particularly helpful have been rulings requiring states and counties to substitute geographic districts for at-large elections, allowing substantial Indian minority populations to achieve representation for the first time (*United States* v. *Blaine County, Mont.*, 363 F.3d 897 [9th Cir. 2004]).

Since the early twentieth century, the federal government has assumed some of the financial burden of education, health, welfare, and other services to tribal Indians. It has also compensated states and counties that provide public education to reservation-based populations (Newton 2005: 1337–1413). Beginning in the 1990s reductions in federal funding for a variety of Indian programs forced tribes to rely more heavily on state and local services. Some of the states, beset by tight budgets, have resisted these demands, even though tribal members living on reservations are state citizens, entitled to the same services as all others (Goodman, McCool, and Herbert 2005:15–33). Furthermore, the federal government began decentralizing and devolving many federal authorities to state and local governments, sometimes expressly including tribes, and sometimes forcing tribal communities to rely on pass-throughs from the states (Masten 2001; Cornell and Taylor 2006). An illustration of a program that has directed states to set aside funds for tribal administration and distribution of benefits to eligible Indians is Temporary Aid to Needy Families (42 U.S.C. § 612; Newton 2005:1406). Where states are merely authorized to make agreements with tribes to administer portions of their programs, as with foster care and adoption assistance, tribes have sometimes had difficulty negotiating satisfactory arrangements (Cross 2006).

## Twenty-first Century

By the end of the twentieth century, unremitting conflict between states and tribes was giving way to more complex, cooperative relations. Clashes did continue, as when the Narragansett Tribe of Rhode Island established a smoke shop on their reservation in June 2003 and refused to pay a state tax, believing it inapplicable to the tribe under a settlement act that Congress had passed in 1978 (25 USC § 1701 et seq.). Rather than negotiate a solution with the tribe, state authorities secured a search warrant from the state courts and raided the smoke shop. In a confrontation between state troopers and tribal police and office holders, eight people were injured and several Narragansetts were arrested, including their chief sachem, three tribal councilmen, and a federally deputized tribal law enforcement officer. The state police confiscated not only the tribe's cigarettes but also money from the cash register and various tribal documents (*Narragansett Indian Tribe* v. *Rhode Island*, 449 F. 3d 16 [1st Cir. 2006]). In 1990, the attorney general of South Dakota made the statement that "Indian reservations are a 'divisive system' of government that have outlived their usefulness" (Pommersheim 1991:271).

Nonetheless, in many parts of the country, an era of more cooperative relations between tribes and states is evident. Partly this development reflects the cost and uncertainty of litigation as a means of resolving differences. The United States Supreme Court's doctrines addressing tribal and state jurisdiction have created so many gray areas that both sides have become interested in less risky alternatives (Pommersheim 1991:268). In addition, tribal economic development, through gaming and other enterprises, has opened up the possibility of tribal campaign contributions to state candidates and tribal members running for state office. This increased tribal influence over state political processes, while sometimes controversial, has contributed to the willingness of state governments to work more respectfully with tribal governments. Finally, both states and tribes have come to appreciate that there are mutual gains to be achieved through negotiated relations, including improved services to their respective citizens and more robust economic growth benefiting on- and off-reservation communities. Supporting this development has been a joint project of the National Conference of State Legislators and the National Congress of American Indians, which has provided educational forums, publications and training materials, and models of cooperation to the benefit of both sets of governments (S. Davis and A. Kanegis 2006).

States and tribes have employed a variety of mechanisms to establish more respectful relations. One such instrument has been sovereignty accords or policy statements that expressly acknowledge Indian nations as governments and prescribe consultation and negotiation with tribes wherever possible. For example, in 1989, the 26 tribes in the state of Washington and the state, through its governor, promulgated a "Centennial Accord," announcing government-to-government relations designed to afford respect for the sovereignty of each government, enhance communication between the state and tribes, and facilitate resolution of issues (Clinton, Goldberg, and Tsosie 2005:986–988). Each party's claims to treaty rights, sovereign immunity, and jurisdiction were expressly preserved.

Officials of tribes and states have also come together in various settings to exchange concerns, reduce possibilities for conflict, and establish the basis for more collaborative operations. Some states, for example, have established commissions or committees on Indian affairs, with representatives from both state and tribal governments, designed to promote state policies and legislation that improve intergovernmental relations. For example, the Arizona Commission on Indian Affairs consists of tribal and non-Indian board members appointed by the governor, as well as state officials who serve ex officio. Among its other activities, it

helps create an awareness of the needs of Indians in the state by bringing hundreds of tribal leaders to meet with state legislators at an annual Indian Nations and Tribes Legislative Day (Rhoades 1997). State court and tribal court judges, with encouragement from the United States Department of Justice, have established their own forums for mutual education and exchange of ideas for greater cooperation. These gatherings have attempted to achieve greater common ground in understanding the boundaries of jurisdiction and the unique characteristics of each other's systems of justice (Bureau of Justice Assistance 2006).

In this environment of greater communication and interaction, one result has been state legislation and executive branch policies that expressly respect tribal interests, both on and off reservations. California, for example, has enacted laws providing for the repatriation of Native American human remains and cultural objects, offering protection that extends beyond the terms of the federal statute on that subject (California Public Resources Code § 5097.991; California Health and Safety Code §§ 8010–8011). Several states have adopted laws providing for the recognition and enforcement of judgments and orders of tribal courts (Wis. Stat. § 806.245(1)(e); Wyo. Stat. Ann. § 5-1-111(a)(iv)). At the executive branch level, the Arizona Department of Environmental Quality has established its own policy "regarding intergovernmental relations with the Sovereign Tribal Nations within Arizona boundaries," which includes commitments to providing technical assistance, data sharing, and development of intergovernmental memoranda of understanding, all in the interest of "advancing the environmental challenges of Arizona through State/Tribal cooperation and coordination" (Arizona Department of Environmental Quality 2006).

The most telling indications of improving tribal-state relations are the hundreds of negotiated agreements addressing taxation, environmental protection, law enforcement, child welfare services, and the allocation of rights to natural resources such as water, among other subjects (Ashley and Hubbard 2004; Clinton, Goldberg, and Tsosie 2005:999–1000). Through these agreements, Indian nations and states may agree to disagree about jurisdiction or property rights issues and then cooperate through such means as sharing tax revenues or other resources, cross-deputizing officers, recognizing one another's judgments, or jointly producing land use plans. Montana and Nebraska have enacted statutes encouraging such cooperation between states and tribes and specifically authorizing negotiation of agreements (Mont. Code Ann. § 18-11-101; Nebr. Rev. Stat. § 13-1501).

As of 1998, for example, more than 200 tribes in 18 states had resolved taxation disputes by forming intergovernmental agreements (Clinton, Goldberg, Tsosie 2005:786). These agreements may include terms addressing tax compliance problems, revenue sharing, reimbursement for tribal or state services, and off-reservation business's concerns with reservations as low-tax competitors. For example, Nevada and Louisiana have agreed that tribes may keep all revenues from on-reservation sales to nonmembers, as long as the tribes impose taxes at the same rate as the state (Zelio 2006). Likewise, in 1999 the Navajo Nation established its own motor vehicle fuel excise tax, which raises approximately $12 million a year for building and maintaining tribal roads. New Mexico, in turn, amended its fuel tax to allow stations owned by the Nation or its members to deduct tribal fuel taxes from the respective state taxes, thereby eliminating most multiple taxation (U.S. Department of Transportation, Federal Highway Administration 2003).

Another instance of productive intergovernmental agreement involves the Cooperative Land Use Program established by Swinomish Tribe of Washington State and the local government of Skagit County. This program, launched with a memorandum of understanding in 1987, provides a framework for conducting permitting activities within the boundaries of the "checkerboarded" reservation, consisting of Indian-owned and non-Indian owned land in almost equal measure. Setting aside jurisdictional conflicts, the two governments created a common Comprehensive Land Use Plan as well as similar implementing ordinances and administrative procedures and a forum for resolving any conflicts that may arise (Solomon 1995; Zaferatos 2004.) Before the Cooperative Land Use program went into effect, frequent litigation over jurisdictional issues had poisoned relations in the area, burdened the tribe and non-Indian residents alike, and discouraged private investment on the reservation. One of the many benefits of this cooperative relationship has been a more attractive environment for economic development.

Negotiated agreements have been useful in resolving conflicts between tribes and states over natural resources. For example, after the Leech Lake Band of Chippewa Indians won a court victory affirming its hunting, fishing, and wild rice-gathering rights on the reservation, it made an agreement with the state of Minnesota, which acknowledged the tribe's freedom from state regulation of such activities on the reservation. The tribe agreed to prohibit commercial taking of game, fish, and rice and to enact a conservation code. As to non-Indians, the parties established a system where the state licensed non-Indians seeking to hunt on the reservation but charged them an additional fee imposed by the tribal council and rebated to the tribe for resource management purposes (Getches 1993:151). Water rights have been a frequent subject of negotiated agreements, addressing topics such as application of state versus tribal water law, leasing of reserved tribal waters off reservation, whose personnel (state or tribal) will administer headgates, provision of technical information, and dispute resolution among individual water users (Getches 1993:159–60).

# Tribal Government in the United States

SHARON O'BRIEN

The United States Constitution established a federal system comprised of a national and state governments. According to the 1789 constitution, the federal government is a government of enumerated powers, that is, allowed to exercise only those powers declared in the document, such as regulating commerce among the states, coining money, and providing for foreign relations. The Tenth Amendment reserves all other powers not granted to the federal government to state governments. These powers include the supervision of education, collection of state taxes, and the establishment of local governments for counties, cities, and townships.

Not mentioned in the Constitution and usually overlooked in discussions of the political system of government are tribal governments—governments that exist within the United States physical territory, but not totally incorporated within its political structure. At the time the framers drafted the Constitution tribal governments were considered legally outside of United States political jurisdiction. The United States, as had the European powers, recognized the Indian nations as inherent sovereigns, governments that exercised exclusive authority over all peoples and activities that occurred within their territories. American traders not only had to obtain permission of tribes to enter and trade within their lands but also had to acquire a document, similar to a passport or license, from the federal government to engage in trade with the tribes.

Tribal governments in the early twenty-first century exercised only a small portion of the powers they enjoyed prior to and for a few decades following the establishment of the United States. To understand the current legal status and authority of tribal governments, it is necessary to understand the history of tribal-federal relations and in particular the federal policies, laws, and court decisions that have impacted tribal governments. See "The Federal-Tribe Relationship," this volume.

In 2007, the federal government recognized 564 tribes and bands and their governments. States have acknowledged and established relations with another 45 tribal governments. Approximately 225 more groups have claimed indigenous identity. Of these, the tribal governments of approximately 100 have petitioned for federal recognition ("Recognition," this vol.). The following examination of tribal governing structures and powers pertains only to the federally recognized tribes.

To accurately assess the powers individual tribal governments retain requires knowledge of a tribe's specific historical relationship with the federal government, the states, and possibly neighboring tribes; general and specific congressional statutes, and judicial decisions extinguishing tribal rights; and its internal governing documents and laws. This required specificity of knowledge is due to the fact that each tribe possesses a separate and distinct relationship with the federal government. This individual relationship is based partly on treaties, if any, the tribe concluded with the national government, and on federal legislation and court decisions particular to that tribe. A tribe may have concluded one treaty, none, or more than a dozen treaties with the federal government. Treaties may contain provisions extinguishing a specific tribal power or may reserve specific rights. For example, the Chickasaw Nation in their 1786 treaty extinguished their criminal jurisdiction over non-Indians within their lands by ceding that authority to the United States, whereas several Washington State tribes and bands in their 1854 treaty with the United States reserved their right to fish at their accustomed places on lands ceded to the United States.

Congressional legislation, such as the Major Crimes Act of 1885, the Indian Civil Rights Act of 1968, and the Indian Child Welfare Act of 1978, among others, has impacted the governing authority of all tribes. Some instances, such as passage of termination legislation, may affect certain identified states and tribes. When assessing tribal, federal, or state authority in a state affected by the termination acts, it is necessary to determine if the state has assumed or retroceded a particular regulatory authority. On the other hand and rather illogically, a Supreme Court ruling concerning a specific tribe and a particular treaty provision applies to all tribes, even if they have never signed a treaty with the United States.

The last determinative factor in assessing tribal authority is to examine if a tribal government has assumed jurisdiction within a particular venue. A particular tribe, for example, may not have established a tribal court system for reasons associated with the tribe's territorial and population size, the number of non-Indian inhabitants, funding, leadership, or political and cultural divisions. This decision does not preclude the tribe from exercising its authority in the future.

## Tribal Governing Structures and Citizenship

The Indian Reorganization Act of 1934 was designed to revitalize tribal governments. The Act required tribes to vote for or against accepting the Act, which included provisions protecting tribal land holdings, making economic loans available, and accepting constitutions to reestablish tribal governments. The constitutional documents drafted pursuant to the Reorganization Act, and the similar Oklahoma Welfare Act, provided tribes with constitutions generally reflecting Euro-American political values and structures. The Bureau of Indian Affairs held 258 elections. One hundred and eighty-one tribes voted to accept political organization under the Act; 77, including the largest, the Navajo, voted against acceptance (Haas 1947). The Navajo have never adopted a written constitution, but they have created a sophisticated governing and administrative system that combines traditional law with procedures able to meet the challenges of a modern and complex society (vol. 10:624–635). Of the 40 to 50 percent without constitutions, many are small Alaska communities who operate without constitutions according to traditional practices.

Eventually, 45 to 60 percent of the federally recognized tribes constituted their governments under the Reorganization Act or a similar law. A few tribes, such as the Warm Springs Indians of Oregon, incorporated the role of traditional leaders into their present government. The Rio Grande Pueblos of New Mexico preserved their traditional theocracies, which in some Pueblos operate in tandem with a constitutionally elected government.

The Reorganization Act did provide tribes whose traditional governments had virtually disappeared with an avenue to regain some control from the Indian agent or Bureau administrator. These constitutions did possess a number of deficiencies that became increasingly apparent. They were not written by tribal leaders or based on traditional cultural beliefs and institutions and thus did not reflect tribal values. Rather than providing tribes with governmental structures that promoted communal values, responsibility, mediation, and consensus building, these constitutions created governmental frameworks that reflected American values of individualism, competition, private property, and capitalism by providing for majority rule, an adversarial legal system, and the protection of individual rights.

The constitutions included a provision granting the Secretary of the Interior approval power over constitutional amendments and other decisions. Equally, if not more, problematic was the failure of these constitutions to establish separate branches of government. Most constitutions established a unified government, consisting of an elected tribal council that performs the executive, legislative, and judicial functions. The council elects the tribe's executive officials from among their own members and the council hears and settles all disputes. In small homogenous tribal communities, this system can work fairly well. But in tribes with larger and more diverse populations, the lack of checks and balances through independent governing branches or some other means has sometimes allowed one tribal group or faction to gain control of the tribal decision-making structure, providing no representation of minority interests or accountability to the membership for its decisions. Tribal members unhappy with council decisions have no recourse but to wait until the next election, a structural defect in the governing system that has led to instability and the election of a new council every few years. A further shortcoming is the absence of carefully defined powers held by the tribal council or executive branch. This omission has created situations in which tribal officials, often under Bureau pressure, have made decisions such as leasing and development agreements unsupported by the majority of tribal members. After a tribal election, often many employees, not those in political positions, lose their jobs.

Tribal constitutions differ in the number of councilors and tribal executives elected, the length of their term in office, and the requirements for elections (fig. 1) (vol. 14:763). The Nez Perce of Idaho, for example, require candidates to be 25 years of age, possess one-quarter tribal ancestry, and have resided on the reservation for a year prior to election. Most tribes address their head leader as chief, but other terms exist. The Seneca of New York have a president and vice-president, and the Pueblos of New Mexico address their leaders as governor and vice-governor.

Mohegan Tribal Publications, Uncasville, Conn.

Fig. 1. The Mohegan Tribal Council, elected for 4-year staggered terms, has all executive and legislative responsibilities not granted to the Council of Elders, which according to the tribal constitution oversees judicial and cultural matters. The Tribal Council chair is the executive officer of the tribe. back row, left to right, William Quidgeon, Jr., treasurer; Mark W. Hamilton; Mark F. Brown; Ralph James Gessner, Jr.; and Cheryl A. Todd; front row, Allison D. Johnson, recording secretary; Bruce "Two Dogs" Bozsum, chairman; Marilynn Malerba, vice-chair; and Roberta Harris-Payne, corresponding secretary. The office of tribal chief is separate, a lifetime position. The tribe achieved federal recognition in 1994. Photograph by Bill Gucfa, Uncasville, Conn., 2005.

Since the 1980s, tribes, aware of their government's inadequacies, have expended considerably creative energies and resources to create, expand, and restructure their governments, especially the judicial branch. Fashioning an effective government that reflects and reinforces a community's chosen values is complicated, multifaceted, and involves complex social, cultural, and legal concerns. Tribal communities may be more internally homogenous yet exhibit a greater diversity in values and belief systems than their surrounding non-Indian neighbors. To varying degrees, tribal communities in the twenty-first century are societies in transition, comprised of members comfortable with American political and social values, individuals that profess and live by traditional beliefs and practices, and many people possessing strands of both perspectives. For example, the principal chief of the Cherokee Nation delivered a State of the Union address (vol. 14:370). Tribal members that have assimilated western political ideals may regard the creation of a tribal judiciary that replicates the outside state's system—an adversarial system incorporating strict due process, and punishment—as the most responsible and efficient framework. Other members may see the creation of a new judicial branch as an opportunity to reinstill important cultural values of community responsibility, respect, and honor by implementing mediation and rehabilitation programs.

Tribes have effected changes in their governing structures by passing constitutional amendments and enacting laws and regulations to improve governmental accountability, responsibility, and efficiency (fig. 2). A few tribes, including the Cherokee and Osage Nations of Oklahoma, and the Crow Nation of Montana, have, or are in the process of drafting completely new constitutions through constitutional conventions. The Chitimacha constitution was established in 2000 (vol. 14:651). Tribes have responded to demands to reintegrate traditional values into the government by restoring traditional tribal names, integrating cultural interpretations into tribal codes, and most visibly, by establishing traditional judicial systems.

The Dine (Navajo), Muscogee Creek, and Seneca, among others, have instituted Peacemaker courts along side their regular tribal courts. The Ho-Chunk (Winnebago) of Wisconsin have created an advisory board of elders to counsel their courts. These traditional courts offer the opportunity to have individuals, usually elders well versed in cultural beliefs, to hear and settle disputes according to traditional law. Penalties are generally of a rehabilitative nature and may include the involvement of family members and friends.

Tribal governments have established specialized courts, such as the Conservation Court of the Chippewa-Ottawa, the Juvenile Court of the San Carlos Apache, and the Healing to Wellness Courts of the Yakama Nation, Picuris Pueblo, and Cherokee Nation of Oklahoma to handle drug abuse cases. Small and with few resources, several California rancherias have formed the Qual-a-wa-loo Intertribal Court. The Navajo operate the largest tribal court system, handling more than 90,000 cases a year. Administered by the Navajo

Fig. 2. Osage government. Charles Lohah, second from left, judge of the Supreme Court of the Osage Nation; Archie Mason, third from left, speaker of the Osage Nation Congress; and Douglas Revard, member of the Osage Nation Congress, in the congressional chambers of the Osage Nation Congress. The mural depicts images of contemporary Osage—ceremonial dance, ballerinas, Roman Catholicism, and the previous tribal government. It was painted by Robin Polhamus, about 1980. The officials are listening to a presentation from Joseph Kubes, a representative from Thompson West, a legal publishing firm, concerning the codification and publication of Osage tribal laws. The Osage already use the firm's online service called Westlaw, to research laws of the federal government and other tribes. Photograph (cropped) by James Elsberry, Pawhuska, Okla., 2007.

attorney general, the three-tiered system includes a Supreme Court, 12 trial courts, and 250 Peacemakers in the tribe's 110 districts.

By 2002, 175 tribes had formal court systems, employing an estimated 200 judges, 153 prosecutors, and 20 peacemakers. Among these 175 tribal court systems, several tribes, including the Colville of Oregon, the Cherokee (vol. 14:362) and Chickasaw Nations of Oklahoma, the Ho-Chunk, the Kickapoo of Kansas, and the Pawnee Nation of Oklahoma, have created appellate courts to review lower tribal court decisions. Tribes in the Northwest, Southwest, and Northern Plains have formed three separate Intertribal Courts of Appeals that function as the final appellate court for member tribes. Tribal courts are free to establish their own judicial rules. Thus, the constitution, laws and rules of a particular tribe must be examined to determine if the tribal court possesses the right of judicial review, if judges are elected or appointed, required to be Indian, or have a law degree, or if lawyers appearing in tribal court are required to pass a tribal bar.

Tribal governments since the 1970s have contended with a variety of complex issues, the thorniest of which concerns the determination of membership. International law recognizes that sovereign governments possess the right to determine their own citizenship requirements. Nations primarily follow the rule of *jus soli* or *jus sanguinis* or some combination of the two. According to the rule of *jus soli*, individuals born within the territorial limits of a nation's territory are, or have, an opportunity to become citizens of that territory. The rule of *jus sanguinis,* the law of the blood, provides for the inheritance of citizenship through the parents. The United States, adopting the common law system, emphasizes *jus soli*, or the territorial location of birth.

Indian nations historically employed a variety of methods to determine citizenship depending upon their cultural structures and practices. Children born into matrilineal tribes followed their mother's clan rules and vice versa. Tribes also naturalized or adopted outsiders into their communities, symbolizing the process with a variety of ceremonies. Sauk and Fox families, for example, adopted individuals to fulfill or replace those recently deceased. In many communities, the individual's clan membership had far greater impact than one's racial heritage on a family, clan, or tribal decision to adopt and grant citizenship to an individual.

The importance tribes attach to racial heritage in most membership decisions is a by-product of the Dawes Severalty Act of 1887, which required the federal government to establish tribal rolls of members eligible to receive individual allotments of reservation lands. The Dawes rolls, as well as other rolls that the government compiled, were notoriously flawed. Traditionalists who recognized the Act's cultural and economic destruction in some cases refused to participate and went unlisted, while intermarried non-Indians with little tribal involvement were entered on the rolls. Each name listed included family information and noted the person's degree of Indian blood that clerks expressed as a fraction, often based on appearance.

Tribes used these rolls to determine citizenship eligibility, and by extension, tribal benefits, such as payments for land purchases, judicial awards, and federally funded programs. Many tribes adopted either descendancy, blood quantum, or some combination of the two, for tribal enrollment and voting privileges. Enrollment based on descendancy requires verification that the individual is the descendant of a family member listed on one of the defined rolls. Many Oklahoma tribes have adopted a descendancy requirement for enrollment. As the degree of Indian blood has decreased, some tribes have adopted a two-tiered membership system: descendancy for enrollment, but proof of the tribally defined blood quantum for election to office.

The majority of tribes in 2007 possess a blood quantum requirement for enrollment. The degree of tribal, or in some cases, Indian blood, ranges from the White Mountain Apache demand of 50 percent to the Tunicas-Biloxi's requirement of one sixty-fourth. The Lakota (Teton Sioux) combine blood quantum and domicile, requiring children to possess one-quarter and to be born on the reservation for enrollment. The Tohono O'odham (Papago) grant automatic citizenship to children if both parents reside on the reservation. A few tribes, such as the Onondaga and Seneca of New York follow traditional clan rules, extending tribal citizenship only to those children born to enrolled mothers. The Santa Clara Pueblo enrolls only those children born to enrolled fathers.

Tribal enrollment issues have become important as tribes wrestle with questions such as what constitutes Indian identity and what are the rights and responsibilities of tribal members? These questions are significant given the dilution of Indian blood through intermarriage, the numbers of tribal members living off-reservation, and the wealth that some tribes have acquired through gaming and other enterprises.

Scholars estimate that half of all Indians in 1900 were full bloods; in 1990, only 20 percent could claim full blood status. The Pawnee Nation of Oklahoma initially established a one-quarter Pawnee Indian blood requirement for those born after 1938 but amended their constitution in 2003 to lower the requirement to one-eighth.

Intermarriage, jobs, and education have led many tribal members to live off-reservation for at least a portion of their lives. According to the 2000 census, more than 60 percent of tribal members reside off-reservation. The term off-reservation is problematic, for it can include tribal members who live a few miles outside reservation boundaries; those who live several hundred miles, but return several times a year to see family and attend tribal functions; or those who have severed their ties with their reservation and culture. During the termination era, off-reservation members generally voted to dissolve the tribal government, sell the reservation lands, and split the proceeds among the membership.

Tribes have reacted to these situations in a variety of ways. The Tigua Pueblo of Ysleta del Sur, El Paso, Texas, concerned with the decrease in tribal membership due to intermarriage, lowered their blood quantum requirements from one-quarter to one-sixteenth. The Salish-Kootenai Tribe of Montana chose to emphasize the importance of Indian blood by *increasing* their requirement from one-sixteenth to one-quarter. The Pequot of Connecticut and the Eastern Cherokee of North Carolina both increased their blood quantum requirements to one-sixteenth in response to requests for enrollment from individuals eager to partake of gaming profits. Opening up membership rolls by lowering blood quantum requirements ensures tribal survival. Raising enrollment standards emphasizes the importance of Indian racial heritage and provides existing members with a greater share of the tribal resources.

## Administration of Justice

The maintenance of peace and security is one of the most essential responsibilities performed by governments. To adequately discharge this function, governments must have the ability to enforce the law and to administer justice as well as provide for public safety (fig. 3). Larger tribes, such as the Lakota, had specialized societies to enforce tribal rules at specific times or events, hunting, moving, and warfare. The Cherokee, Creek, Seminole, Choctaw, and Chickasaw had, and have, companies referred to as the Lighthorsemen.

In the late 1880s, the federal government, in an assimilationist effort, established Indian police on reservations to enforce the Code of Federal Regulations, a series of laws that, in addition to maintaining the peace, prohibited tribal members from practicing banned religious ceremonies. Although the Bureau continues to operate 37 law enforcement agencies on reservations, many tribal governments have established their own police forces responsible for enforcing tribal law. According to the 2000 census, tribes operated

Fig. 3. Johnathan Springer, Saginaw Chippewa tribal member, tightening a hose attachment to a fire hydrant on the Isabella Res., Mich. He is participating in the summer youth work program, which involves tribal youth in the workforce. The Saginaw Chippewa tribe allocates the profits from its business enterprises to build infrastructure, such as the tribal fire department. Photograph by Martin Curry, 2007.

171 law enforcement agencies, employing approximately 2,303 full-time and 88 part-time sworn trained officers with general arrest powers. By 2003, tribal governments, in conjunction with the Bureau, were operating 70 jails with an inmate capacity of 2,226. Following the 1978 Supreme Court decision of *Oliphant* v. *Suquamish Tribe of Indians*, which caused a jurisdictional vacuum by denying tribal police the authority to arrest non-Indians, some states and tribes entered into cross-deputization agreements. Such agreements allowed tribal police, acting as state officials, to arrest non-Indians on tribal lands, and the state police, deputized as tribal officials, to arrest tribal members.

Maintaining security requires more than a government's ability to arrest and detain individuals. Tribal governments must also possess the ability to administer justice including assessing the guilt or innocent of those who have broken the community's laws; adjudicating disputes between and among individuals; and determining if individuals, agencies, or businesses have failed to maintain the government's standards as expressed in established laws and regulations.

Tribes have invested considerable time and resources in expanding the efficiency of their legal systems, at the same time that federal legislation and court decisions have significantly reduced the individuals, territory, and subject matter over which tribal courts may exercise their jurisdiction. The 1885 Major Crimes Act granted the federal government criminal jurisdiction over any individual committing one of originally seven, now more than 20, major crimes. Tribal courts may retain concurrent jurisdiction over serious crimes, but the 1968 Indian Civil Rights Act limited tribal courts to imposing fines smaller than $5,000 and terms less than one year in jail. Therefore, most tribes have found exercising this jurisdiction impractical.

In 1990, the Supreme Court extended the *Oliphant* ruling in the *Duro* decision. Tribal police were prohibited from arresting a burglar, rapist, or murderer if he was not a tribal member, a situation that limited the ability of tribal governments to police and protect their communities. Cognizant of the jurisdictional vacuum the Court had created, Congress enacted legislation to return criminal jurisdictional authority over Indians to tribes, and in 2004 the *United States* v. *Lara* decision confirmed this.

Resolving civil disputes and ensuring regulatory compliance are additional aspects of maintaining a peaceful and safe environment. As in the case with criminal jurisdiction, the Supreme Court has limited the jurisdictional reach of tribal governments in civil and regulatory areas. Tribal courts may regulate and adjudicate disputes concerning marriages, divorces, adoptions, inheritance, and other domestic matters between and among tribal members. The extent to which tribal courts can exercise civil jurisdiction when one party is a tribal member and the other a non-Indian, such as in a divorce, remains somewhat unclear given the Supreme Court's recent limitations on tribal authority over non-Indians. Case law indicates that tribal courts possess jurisdiction if both parties agree. Whether state courts take precedence over tribal courts when one party sues in state court and the other in tribal court, is ambiguous.

Prior to 1978, state courts handled the vast majority of Indian adoptions and foster care decisions, resulting in many Indian children being raised off-reservation by non-Indian families. To correct this situation, Congress passed the Indian Child Welfare Act in 1978. The Act basically provides that tribal courts, not state courts, have jurisdiction over the adoption process and the Act mandates states to follow the tribe's preference in placement.

## Development and Regulation of Land, Resources, and Businesses

Tribal courts may hear cases involving an agency's violation of tribal regulations. The authority to establish standards and regulate agencies and businesses is a vital responsibility through which tribal governments protect the health and security of the community and environment, control growth and development, and preserve valuable material and immaterial community goods. The authority of tribal governments to manage reservation property, establish environmental and conservation standards, license and tax businesses, and protect cultural resources and sacred sites is crucial.

Any true discussion of tribal sovereignty begins with the land, for land provides and nurtures all of life. Traditional native values did not regard land as a wilderness to be subdued and dominated, or as a commodity to be developed and despoiled of its resources. Humans occupy a small part of the environment, yet being wholly dependent upon it for survival, are responsible for protecting the earth and the creatures that share it. These traditional views continue to inform tribal governments' management of their land base, regulation of wildlife, and environmental protection of water and air.

Tribal land bases range in size from the Navajo Reservation, which is larger than 10 of the 50 states in America, to small rancherias of only a few acres. Approximately 135 tribal entities had their lands allotted. By 1934 when Congress ended the sale of individual allotments, two-thirds of Indian allotments has passed to White ownership, often by sale. Total Indian landholdings had dwindled from 138 million acres in 1887 to only 48 million acres, a loss of 90 million acres, or two-thirds of the land base. Serious jurisdiction and management problems resulted from the effect of the "checkerboard" pattern created from ownership of Indian land by tribes, individual Indians, and non-Indians. On a few reservations, non-Indians owned more than or nearly half the land within the reservation boundaries. For example, on two reservations located in Washington, non-Indians own 63 percent of the Suquamish reservation and 46 percent of the Swinomish reservation. Some Indian land, such as the Navajo reservation, escaped allotment. Following *Atkinson Trading Company* v. *Shirley* in 2001, the existence and extent of a reservation's checkerboarding is now

the most important factor in assessing tribal regulatory authority within reservation boundaries.

Tribal governments possess the authority to purchase, develop, lease, and assign tribal lands and to enact environmental, conservation, and zoning codes necessary to protect the tribal land base, environment, and wildlife resources. Problems caused by the allotment process, such as checkerboarding and fractionated heirship, land parcels owned by so many heirs that putting the land to productive use is unmanageable, seriously complicate tribal management of reservation lands. Many tribes have established land consolidation programs that assist when funds are available, in purchasing and transferring to tribal trust lands non-Indian owned or fractionated parcels. From a practical standpoint, having a consolidated land base allows tribal governments more effectively to administer tribal environmental, conservation, and zoning standards.

Tribal governments have established environmental agencies responsible for enforcing tribally adopted water and air quality codes. Tribal agencies and codes may be independently established or created pursuant to laws such as the Clean Water Act and Environmental Protection Agency programs. Beginning in the 1980s, Congress amended a number of environmental laws that recognized tribes as governmental entities, like the states, as capable of implementing federal environmental programs. Federal law mandates a minimum environmental standard but allows states, and now tribes, to establish their own air and water quality standards at any point above the minimum. The Supreme Court recognized the right of tribal governments to establish their own water quality standards in *Albuquerque* v. *Browner*. Isleta Pueblo, located on the Rio Grande River in New Mexico, established a higher water quality standard than that of the city of Albuquerque, upstream. The Environmental Protection Agency had approved the higher standards, accepting Isleta's argument that the river's water had to meet a certain level of cleanliness for use in sacred ceremonies. Arguing that acceptance of such standards would force the city to spend millions on their treatment plant to ensure that the river's water met the Isleta standards, Albuquerque filed suit. In finding that Isleta Pueblo had met the Clear Water Act's requirements, the court recognized the inherent sovereign authority of tribes to impose standards more stringent than those of the federal government. Tribal authority to enact environmental standards and their authority over the Indian children pursuant to the Indian Child Welfare Act remain two areas in which the courts have recognized that tribal governments retained the authority to impose their will on state governments, as in *Montana* v. *United States* (450 U.S. 544 [1981]).

The responsible management and conservation of wildlife is another regulatory area complicated by the existence of multiple jurisdictions. It is also an area of considerable importance to many tribes. Tribal leaders vigilantly preserved their people's right to hunt and fish in many treaties. Hunting and fishing remain traditionally significant and important *81* food sources for many tribal members. During the 1970s and 1980s, tribal members from the Northwest Coast to the Great Lakes engaged in protests, "fish-ins," and legal battles, and endured physical violence to preserve their hunting and fishing rights from competing sports and commercial fishing interests. Given the cultural importance associated with hunting and fishing, the courts have held that these rights are implicitly reserved in all treaties, unless explicitly extinguished.

An important corollary to a tribe's right to hunt and fish is the power to regulate hunting and fishing to ensure the survival of fish stock and wildlife. The migratory nature of wildlife makes conservation an extremely complex endeavor when multiple jurisdictions exist. Following four decades of legal disputes over hunting and fishing rights and regulation, the courts have settled on the following rules. Tribal governments possess the authority to regulate tribal members' hunting and fishing within the reservation, and on off-reservation treaty lands. Tribal governments can also regulate seasons, bag limits, species, methods, and other provisions on their lands to control and preserve wildlife.

States possess the authority to regulate non-Indian hunting and fishing rights on non-Indian lands within reservation boundaries. States also possess the authority to intervene in off-reservation tribal hunting and fishing rights, if mandated by conservation needs. The federal government, under the plenary doctrine, can regulate Indian hunting and fishing but has rarely exercised its authority. Less clear is whether the state or the tribe possesses the authority to regulate nonmembers hunting or fishing on tribal lands. Current law suggests that if a tribe has implemented a comprehensive game and fisheries program, the tribe's regulatory scheme prevails.

Several tribes have established sophisticated fisheries and wildlife programs designed not only to conserve but also to expand existing stocks. Many tribes in Washington and Oregon have established fish hatcheries that have added significant numbers of hatchlings to dwindling salmon and steelhead stocks. Twenty western Washington tribes co-manage the natural resources in partnership with the state. The tribes are involved in protecting and restoring salmon, shellfish, and wildlife populations and their habitats (fig. 4). The Nez Perce of Idaho are at the forefront of the recovery and reintroduction program of the gray wolf into the Northern Rockies of Idaho. In an effort to develop tourism on the reservation, tribes such as the Mescalero Apache of New Mexico have opened their reservation by selling licenses to non-Indian hunters and fishers to hunt and fish for certain species during assigned seasons.

Taxation, like licensing, is another mechanism governments use to generate money and regulate businesses as well as social behavior. Although tribal governments have rarely levied taxes on tribal members or member-owned businesses, tribes have taxed non-Indians and non-Indian owned businesses operating within reservation boundaries. The

Northwest Ind. Fisheries Commission, Kingston, Wash.

Fig. 4. Taking samples of steelhead salmon eggs from the South Fork Skokomish River, Wash., near the Skokomish Res. left to right, Jim Huinker, Skokomish Tribal fisheries finfish biologist; Dan Minton, Wash. Dept. of Fish and Wildlife fish hatchery specialist; Rick Bush, Natl. Oceanic and Atmospheric Administration research fish biologist; and Alex Gouley, Skokomish, steelhead salmon recovery biologist. The egg samples are being collected as part of a 16-year study to gauge the effectiveness of supplementing wild steelhead (*Oncorhynchus mykiss*) populations. Puget Sound steelhead were considered "threatened" in May 2007 under the federal Endangered Species Act; miles of spawning and rearing habitat have been degraded by increased human population. The eggs are reared in state hatcheries and released into the rivers of origin at various stages in their life cycle. Photograph by Tiffany Royal, 2007.

Creeks, for example, in 1857, imposed a tax on non-Indian traders operating in the Nation. Until 2004 tribal governments assumed this authority extended to all non-Indian-owned businesses located within reservation boundaries. The *Atkinson Trading Company* ruling limited this authority to businesses located on tribal owned or trust lands.

Tribes assume that they can regulate, through taxation and other means, individually owned businesses on tribal lands. A tribal government's authority to attract, regulate, and establish businesses and industries on reservations is imperative to the future survival of Indian society. Tribal governments operate a diverse array of businesses, ranging from timber and energy companies, manufacturing plants, resorts, and casinos. The Mississippi Choctaw, among the most successful tribal entrepreneurs, are the largest employers in east-central Mississippi. Since the 1970s, they have attracted light industries to their reservation, including factories that manufacture greeting cards and wire harnesses for Ford Motor Company. When Ford informed the Choctaw that they were moving the harness factory to Mexico, the Choctaw in 1999 opened their own automotive wiring harness facility in Empalme, Sonora, Mexico, employing approximately 1,400 people, none Choctaw. The first tribe to take advantage of the North American Free Trade Act, the Choctaw opened electronics and plastic plants in Mexico.

In the late 1970s, tribes began opening bingo halls and more extensive gaming operations as revenue producing businesses. Among these tribes were the Cabazon and Morongo bands in California. In the mid-1980s, California attempted to close their facility, arguing that California law did not allow high stakes bingo. In 1987, the Supreme Court sided with the Cabazon (*California* v. *Cabazon Band of Mission Indians*, 480 U.S. Stat. 202), by finding California's law ineffective in overruling "the pre-emptive force of federal and tribal interests." The following year, Congress enacted the Indian Gaming Regulatory Act to provide a statutory basis for Indian gaming operations designed to promote "tribal economic development, self-sufficiency, and strong tribal governments." To quiet state protests, the Act contained a clause that tribes wanting to open Class III gaming operations, which included the more profitable games, such as slot machines, had to negotiate a compact with the state. In these agreements, the two governmental entities worked out issues relating to the allocation of criminal and civil jurisdiction and payments from casino profits to the state. Aware that forcing tribes to obtain permission from the state for Class III gaming undercut the tribes' inherent authority as recognized in *Cabazon*, the Act encouraged states to negotiate and redress to the federal government if they refused. In *Seminole Tribe* v. *Florida* (517 U.S. Stat. 44 1996), the Court ruled that portion of the Gaming Act unconstitutional. States were free to decline, leaving tribes with no recourse ("Gaming," this vol.).

Casinos have brought employment and offered tribes the opportunity to improve tribal social services. The Minnesota Prairie Island Indian Community has used its casino profits to construct housing, a community center, an administrative office, and a waste water treatment plant. The Arizona Tohono O'odham's profits have translated into educational scholarships, a community college, nursing facility, and 11 youth centers. Casino profits have provided some tribes with the opportunity to devote increasing time and resources to the preservation and management of their cultural resources. Even among tribes with few economic resources, this area is of vital concern.

For decades, tribal people lobbied for the return of their ancestors' remains, stored in boxes and on shelves in museums across the country. In 1990, Congress passed the Native American Graves Protection and Repatriation Act. All federally funded museums and institutions must remit Indian remains and certain cultural objects to the tribes. The act has presented tribal governments with an overwhelming task, as tribal members are called upon to travel to scores of museums to verify their possessions and provide for their receipt ("Repatriation," this vol.). Tribal members must determine proper reburial practices and provide for the safekeeping of objects that outside museums have often been preserved with toxic chemicals. Tribal governments are establishing cultural resources departments, whose responsibilities may include overseeing the return and proper reburial of tribal remains, protecting sacred sites, and administering one of the more than 140 tribal museums and archives operated by tribes ("Native Museums and Cultural Centers," this vol.). Tribal governments may also request such departments to develop tribal laws and regulation regarding the protection of sacred knowledge and the control and dissemination of tribal stories, songs, dances, and information. In 1983 Santo Domingo Pueblo sued the *Santa Fe New Mexican* for publishing pictures of tribal dances in violation of tribal law.

## Provision of Social Services

Providing educational services, health care, and housing are among the most significant responsibilities that tribal governments perform. Each tribal government administers social programs and services differently, depending upon their economic, leadership, and administrative resources. While the block grants provided to tribes under the Tribal Self-Governance Act of 1994 have improved tribal opportunities to administer their own programs according to their own needs and priorities, the continuing decline in the availability of federal funding has undercut tribal services, especially in health care.

Indian life expectancy and health care dramatically improved in the late twentieth century but remains lower than other population groups in the United States. Diabetes, heart disease, and alcoholism rates bring early deaths and a lowered quality of life to many Indian people, making health care a top tribal priority ("Health and Health Issues in the United States," this vol.). By negotiating for compacts with the Indian Health Service, tribal governments control and allocate the expenditure of their health care dollars. Tribal health departments administer facilities ranging from full-service hospitals to small medical and dental clinics (fig. 5). Diabetes programs and alcohol and drug abuse treatment programs based on traditional values and beliefs are other major concerns of tribal health departments.

Reflecting traditional values, tribal governments place a high priority on developing programs to care for elders. The Cheyenne River Sioux tribe, South Dakota, illustrated these values by naming their agency responsible for overseeing the needs of tribal elders, the Wisdom Keeper's Department. Tribal governments commonly provide meeting facilities and serve hot meals to their older members. Among the first community expenditures from casino profits are specially constructed housing (fig. 6) and nursing facilities. Often, tribes locate these buildings near the Head Start programs or schools, thereby allowing for greater interaction among the generations and the opportunity for tribal elders, recognized as the repositories of cultural knowledge, to share that information with the younger generations.

Tribal Education Departments, often the oldest and largest governmental agencies, may operate educational programs ranging from kindergartens to tribal community

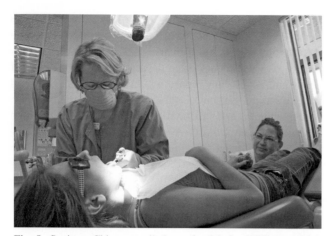

Fig. 5. Saginaw Chippewa tribal member Marion Williams (right) holds on to her daughter Morgan Mena as dental assistant Monica Richer conducts a checkup at the Nimkee Dental Center on the Isabella Res., Mich. The Saginaw Chippewa tribe directed revenues from its business enterprises to build a health clinic that houses medical and pharmacy departments as well as a dental clinic. The care is free to all tribal members. Photograph by Martin Curry, 2007.

colleges. Most reservation students attend local public schools, but for those tribal governments with sufficient populations and resources, the establishment of tribally controlled schools is a goal. The Mississippi Band of Choctaw Indians operated the largest tribally controlled school system with 1,800 students in three counties in 2007. Tribally controlled educational facilities allow tribal governments to incorporate tribal history, cultural practices and values, and the native language into the standard educational curriculum ("Languages and Language Programs," this vol.).

Tribal governments, with assistance from the 1990 Native Language Preservation Act (P.L. 101-477) provide adult language classes and create internet sites with language materials and instruction. Several tribes, including the Blackfeet Nation in Montana, nations of the Iroquois Confederacy in New York, and the Cherokees located in both Oklahoma and North Carolina, sponsor native language immersion programs in their Head Start programs with some programs extending beyond. Tribal communities have greatly improved the educational level of their members since the 1980s. More than 30 tribal governments have established tribal community colleges ("Tribal Colleges and Universities," this vol.).

## Conclusion

Tribal governments have expanded and improved the efficiency and accountability of their governing structures since the 1970s. Many tribes have established independent judicial branches and staffed new administrative departments to preserve their culture, protect the environment, and provide better health and educational services. Many, though not all, have improved their financial resources through the establishment of tribally owned businesses, especially gaming.

Mohegan Tribal Publications, Uncasville, Conn.

Fig. 6. Fort Hill Community, housing for the elderly built in 2002 by the Mohegan tribe in a craftsman style without destroying any of the tribe's history or prehistory on reservation lands. left, The 3-story building containing 35 apartments where Mohegan residents pay well below market rate. right, Turtle, an important figure in Northeast creation narratives, embedded in the building wall. Photographs by Bill Gucfa, Uncasville, Conn., 2002.

Congress has supported the expansion of tribal services through the self-governance acts and amendments to environmental, welfare, and other laws, thereby providing tribes with increased freedom to establish and fund tribal programs according to tribal, not federal priorities. Tribal autonomy in the operation of these programs is not unlimited, raising the concern that tribal governments, through their administration of federal programs, are becoming replicas of state governments, at the expense of operating more culturally reflective programs.

# The Bureau of Indian Affairs and Reservations

ANGELIQUE EAGLEWOMAN (WAMBDI A. WASTEWIN)

The Bureau of Indian Affairs (BIA) has primary responsibility for administration and oversight of federal programs serving the 564 federally recognized tribes and their members, as well as managing the federal trust responsibility for tribally owned properties and trust properties of individual tribal members. One major exception is health services. In 1955 the administration of the Indian Health Service was transferred from the BIA and Department of the Interior to the then Department of Health Education and Welfare. In addition there are also state-recognized tribes and reservations whose properties are not the responsibility of the BIA and whose members are not entitled to services provided by the BIA. Finally there are several hundred organized and unorganized Native American groups that are recognized by neither the federal government nor their state government.

The purpose and the nature of the programs of the BIA are frequently misunderstood. Since 1924 all American Indians have been citizens of the United States and as such they are, as individuals, entitled to full participation in all governmental programs—federal, state, and local. However, there are certain legal and jurisdictional limitations on state and local governments in delivering services in federally recognized Indian communities. Trust lands, both tribal and individual, are not subject to taxation, while on most reservations, state and local courts do not have jurisdiction ("The Federal-Tribe Relationship," this vol.). In addition, treaties and agreements require that the federal government provide certain other services to these tribes and their members. Thus the federal government, primarily through the BIA, has to provide for primary and secondary education, a judiciary and policing, and a range of other social and economic programs.

## Structure and Function of the Bureau of Indian Affairs

The Bureau of Indian Affairs was created in 1824 "in a time of war on Indian people" (Gover 2000–2001:163; for a summary history see vol. 4:255–263). As federal policy shifted from military strategy to assimilation of tribal peoples, the BIA was transferred in 1849 from the Department of War to its present location as an agency of the Department of the Interior (Taylor 1984:34). The Department of the Interior has primary responsibility in the areas of land and resource management, wildlife conservation, territorial affairs, and Native American affairs. Residing within the executive branch of the federal government, the BIA is overseen at its highest level by the presidential appointee serving as the secretary of the interior. The secretary appoints the assistant secretary for Indian affairs, a position created in 1977 replacing the former lower-ranking commissioner of Indian affairs, to administer the BIA on a day-to-day basis.

The Bureau of Indian Affairs is headquartered in Washington, D.C. There are 12 regional offices (vol. 4:274), nearly 100 agencies, and an estimated 10,000 employees (McCarthy 2004:16). The 12 BIA service regions are: Alaska Region (Alaska except for a part in the Northwest Region), Eastern Region (Alabama, Florida, Connecticut, Louisiana, Maine, Massachusetts, Mississippi, New York and North Carolina), Eastern Oklahoma Region, Great Plains Region (Nebraska, North Dakota and South Dakota), Midwest Region (Iowa, Michigan, Minnesota, and Wisconsin), Navajo Region (part of Arizona and part of New Mexico), Northwest Region (part of Alaska, part of Montana, Idaho, Oregon, and Washington), Pacific Region (California), Rocky Mountain Region (part of Montana and Wyoming), Southern Plains Region (Kansas, Texas and Western Oklahoma), Southwest Region (Colorado and part of New Mexico), and Western Region (Nevada, Utah, and part of Arizona). Each region has a central office with a regional director providing oversight of the BIA responsibilities to the tribal governments and enrolled tribal members within the area. Under each of the area offices are varying numbers of local agency offices located on specific reservations and managed by an agency superintendent.

### Tribal Membership Prerequisite and Indian Preference

Federal recognition of a tribe or Indian group is a prerequisite for receipt of BIA services. For individual Indians, the BIA has historically required documentation of the lineage of the individual to determine whether the individual possessed a threshold blood quantum of federally recognized Indian blood, often set at a minimum of one-fourth degree. For example, receipt of BIA higher education loans and grants is conditioned on proof of one-fourth degree or more Indian blood (25 C.F.R. § 40.1). As tribal governments have asserted self-determination, the tribes have for the most part set enrollment standards incorporating a blood quantum standard with several requiring only a showing of lineal descendant to the original tribal rolls. The BIA delivers services to tribal members of federally recognized tribes verified through tribal enrollment officials. As an example, receipt of financial and social services requires enrollment in a federally recognized Indian tribe, except for Alaska Natives, where the standard includes one-fourth degree or more Native blood and United States citizenship (25 C.F.R. § 20.100).

As part of the Indian Reorganization Act of 1934, Congress passed into law Indian preference for all positions within the Bureau of Indian Affairs (25 U.S.C. § 472). To qualify for Indian preference, a federal employee candidate must provide proof of Indian descent in one of the following ways: membership in any recognized Indian tribe now under federal jurisdiction; descendants of such members who were, on June 1, 1934, residing within the present boundaries of any Indian reservation; all others of one-half or more Indian blood of tribes indigenous to the United States; or Eskimos or other aboriginal people of Alaska (25 C.F.R. § 5.1(a)–(d)). The preference extends to "initial hiring, reinstatement, transfer, reassignment or promotion" (25 C.F.R. § 5.2(a)).

In the 1974 United States Supreme Court case, *Morton* v. *Mancari* (417 U.S. Stat. 535), a group of non-Indian BIA employees brought a class action suit challenging Indian preference as a violation of the 1972 Equal Employment Opportunities Act and racial discrimination. The opinion of the Court was unanimous in finding that the Indian preference statute did not constitute a racial qualification; rather the preference was a legitimate rational method of furthering Indian self-government by employing Indians in the BIA (417 U.S. Stat. at 554–555).

### Self-Determination and Self-Governance Contracts

With the policy shift to self-determination in the 1970s, the role of the BIA was reduced significantly from a federal agency responsible for the quality of life in Indian country to a conduit for federal funds, management of lands held in trust for tribes and tribal members, and administration of inherently federal functions (U.S. Department of the Interior 2001–2004:27). In 1975 with the passage of the Indian Self-Determination and Education Assistance Act, tribal governments and organizations were permitted to operate federal programs through contracts and grants (Taylor 1984:42). These contract and grant programs, commonly referred to as "638 contracts" derived from Public Law 93-638, led to greater federal regulations and reporting requirements for tribes (25 U.S.C. § 450 et seq.).

Within the Self-Determination Act, Title III, a self-governance demonstration project was authorized as a tribally driven initiative to contract administrative and management costs of contracted programs simplifying federal reporting requirements and creating greater local program flexibility. The success of the demonstration project led to amendment of the Act in 1994 to include Title IV, the Tribal Self-Governance program. By entering into a self-governance compact, tribes may "efficiently plan, conduct, consolidate, and administer programs, services, functions, and activities for tribal citizens according to priorities established by their tribal governments, and as a consequence, can reprioritize funding and redesign programs" (U.S. Department of the Interior 2001–2004:27).

In 2004, BIA services and federal funding were provided to 1.5 million tribal members in 31 states through three means: directly, through self-determination grants and contracts, and through self-governance compact agreements with participating tribes (U.S. Department of the Interior 2001–2004:27). Of the 562 then federally recognized tribes, the BIA reported in the same year that "over 450 federally recognized tribes have self-determination contracts or self-governance compacts with the BIA and receive annually over $650 million in funding to provide services" to tribal members (U.S. Department of the Interior 2001–2004:27).

### Education, Economic Development, and Law Enforcement

The policies of self-determination and self-governance have circumscribed BIA involvement in many areas of tribal programming and funding; however, the BIA continues to have a major role in Indian affairs. The BIA provides support for an Indian education system on 63 Indian reservations comprised of 184 elementary, middle, and high schools; 26 tribal colleges and universities, and two BIA-operated postsecondary institutions. Through grant and contract programs, 98 percent of the federal Indian education dollars are passed directly to tribal authorities managing tribal educational institutions. The funding supports salaries for educators and administrators, instructional materials, student boarding and transportation, and the maintenance of school facilities (U.S. Department of the Interior 2001–2004:4).

Cognizant of the findings of early education studies, the BIA offers educational support programs targeted for children from birth to third grade. As a component of these programs, adult literacy education and support activities are available to address the needs of parents. Reading grants have been administered by the BIA to improve reading achievement for kindergarten through third grade (U.S. Department of the Interior 2001–2004:5).

At the postsecondary level, the BIA offers a Forestry Cooperative Education in a nationwide program, Water Resources Technical Training program at New Mexico State University, Las Crucas, and a Records Management program at Haskell Indian Nations University, Lawrence, Kansas. The BIA maintains scholarship grants to any tribal member seeking a postsecondary degree. Through the Tribal Priority Allocation funding system of self-governance compacts, BIA funds directly to tribal education programs assisting tribal members in improving literacy skills and obtaining GED certificates. The BIA also provides funds for tribal members attending the Summer Law Institute for American Indians in preparation for entering the field of law (U.S. Department of the Interior 2001–2004:7).

In the area of tribal economic development, the BIA has promoted advances in energy, minerals, forestry, agriculture, wildlife and recreation, water, and range and grazing. The BIA's Guaranteed Loan Program is available to tribes, Alaska Natives, and individual tribal member owned businesses to fund Indian economic enterprises and provide employment for tribal members. The BIA has provided assistance in the development of over two million acres of tribally owned energy resources, such as oil, gas, and coal. Projections for continued development include 15 million tribally owned acres. BIA funding is available for a variety of economic development feasibility studies, including wind energy, biomass development, solar energy, and geothermal potential from tribal lands (U.S. Department of the Interior 2001–2004:17–22).

BIA has been involved in tribal projects to mine rock with the Metlakatla Tribe in Alaska (vol. 7:294–297); the Indian forestry program generating economic benefits to tribes, tribal employees, and local businesses; settlement of water development rights for the Zuni Heaven Reservation, Arizona; and regulating of grazing capacity on Indian-owned trust acres. It provides assistance through the Wildlife and Parks program to conserve and develop wildlife, fish, outdoor recreation, and ecotourism resources (U.S. Department of the Interior 2001–2004:22–27).

The BIA's Office of Law Enforcement and Security oversees public safety and property protection in Indian country through tribal contracts and has direct responsibility for uniformed patrol, detention services, and criminal investigations. The Office operates 19 detention/corrections centers, the Indian Police Academy, and 50 tribally contracted detention centers. Six BIA law enforcement district offices oversaw 206 law enforcement programs in 2004. Community safety and education programs are provided to Indian Country schools by BIA and tribal officers. Drug and crime prevention are key goals for BIA-funded law enforcement (U.S. Department of the Interior 2001–2004:29–31).

*Fiduciary Trust Programs*

In 1994, Congress created the Office of the Special Trustee for American Indians charged with the task of providing a plan to improve the trust asset management and other trust responsibilities of the Bureau of Indian Affairs (Cohen 2005:405). One of the core legal responsibilities of the secretary of the interior exercised through the BIA is as the trustee for tribal land (Taylor 1984:66). In the area of land oversight, the BIA as a whole has administrative responsibility and management of 56 million acres of land held in trust for tribal governments and tribal individuals across the United States. During 2001–2004, the BIA managed over 100,000 leases for both individual tribal members owning over 10 million

acres and tribes owning approximately 45 million acres (U.S. Department of the Interior 2001–2004:10).

Some of the services offered by the BIA as trustee over Indian lands held in trust include operating the Land Titles and Records Office recording and preserving documents related to tribal land, creating an Indian land inventory through official land boundary surveying, conducting historical accounting of trust funds from leases on Indian owned lands, and overseeing the consolidation of Indian land (U.S. Department of the Interior 2001–2004:14–16).

### Federal Indian Trust Responsibility over Tribal Lands

One of the primary functions of the BIA, to oversee the federal-Indian trust responsibility, has its roots in the United States Supreme Court decision, *Cherokee Nation* v. *Georgia*, 30 U.S. (5 Pet.) 1, 17 (1831), where tribal governments were described as "domestic dependent nations" under the protection of the United States. In terms of tribal lands, the Supreme Court held in *Johnson* v. *M'Intosh* (21 U.S. Wheat 543, 574 [1823]) that based upon international law principles tribes held only the right of occupancy and were limited in their ability to alienate their lands. The United States was described as holding a superior title to the Indian occupants and was the sole authorized buyer of tribal lands according to the opinion (21 U.S. Wheat at 588).

Prior to these court decisions, the United States Congress had enacted various Indian Trade and Intercourse Acts (25 U.S.C. § 177) in the 1790s, with permanent status in 1802 and 1834 (Prucha 1962:261–269). One of the purposes of these Acts was to deny legitimacy to any tribal land transaction that lacked federal approval granted through "treaty or convention entered into pursuant to the Constitution" (25 U.S.C. § 177). After 1871 when the policy of treaty-making with tribes was abandoned, Congress passed specific statutes to authorize tribal land divestment.

In the late 1800s, the goals of federal Indian policy had shifted from treaty-making with tribal governments to a primary goal of individualization of the Indian people as citizen farmers owing allegiance to the federal government rather than to tribes (McDonnell 1991:6). To further this goal, a national policy of allotment of tribal landholdings was heralded in with the passage of the Dawes Severalty Act or General Allotment Act of 1887 (25 U.S.C. § 331–333). The purpose of the Act was to divide tribal lands into 160-acre or smaller parcels for each Indian head of household to pursue an agrarian lifeway and then to declare the majority of remaining lands "surplus" to be sold to the United States (L.S. Parker 1989:47–48). The Indian allotments were restricted for a period of 25 years from alienation and held in trust status by the United States (25 U.S.C. § 348). However, the trust period was viewed by many as an obstacle to the assimilation policy of allotment,; in response, Congress passed the Burke Act in 1906 allowing for an individual to be declared "competent" to receive a fee patent for their allotment. Upon the receipt of the patent, the land was available for sale, encumbrance, taxation and application of state civil and criminal laws (Royster 1995:10–11).

The tribal land base diminished from 138 million acres in 1887 to 48 million acres in 1934 as a result of the Dawes Severalty Act (Kickingbird and Ducheneaux 1973). With the implementation of the allotment policy, "the thrust of the federal-Indian relationship to that of property management, and with the need for supervision over the use of property came the expansion of the administrative structure of the Bureau of Indian Affairs" (Deloria and Lytle 1984:5). Federal officials recognized after the critical Meriam Report in 1928 the total failure of the allotment policy to effectuate any beneficial purpose to Indians and the resulting dire consequences for the many left landless and homeless. In 1934 with the passage of the Indian Reorganization Act, the trust status of Indian allotments was extended until further act of Congress, and the allotment policy was officially ended (Cohen 2005:1043).

The tribal and individual allotment landholdings in trust status continue within the administration and management of the Bureau of Indian Affairs, which "supervises and approves or disapproves land and resource development and uses on Indian lands" as the trustee agency of the United States (Fitzpatrick 2003–2004:191). The scope of the federal government's fiduciary duties over tribal lands was considered in the 1980s by the United States Supreme Court.

In two landmark cases, *United States* v. *Mitchell* (445 U.S. Stat. 535 [1980] Mitchell I) and *United States* v. *Mitchell* (463 U.S. Stat. 206 [1983] Mitchell II), the Supreme Court set forth the requirements Indian tribes must meet to pursue an action against the federal government over a breach of the trustee responsibilities. In *Mitchell I*, the Supreme Court reversed the United States Claims Court holding that the Dawes Act provided a cognizable legal claim for damages in a breach of trust suit under the Tucker Act for the mismanagement of tribal timber resources on allotted lands (455 U.S. Stat. at 542). The Court held that the Dawes Act "created only a limited trust relationship between the United States and the allottee" and did not provide "that the United States has undertaken full fiduciary responsibilities as to the management of allotted lands" (455 U.S. Stat. at 542).

In *Mitchell II*, the breach of trust action was based upon specific federal forestry statutes and regulations that "clearly establish fiduciary obligations of the Government in the management and operation of Indian lands and resources, they can be fairly interpreted as mandating compensation by the Federal Government for damages sustained" (463 U.S. Stat. at 226). Taken together, *Mitchell I* and *Mitchell II* stand for the proposition that an action by Indians or tribes for breach of fiduciary duties against the United States will proceed only where specific federal statutes or regulations govern those duties unlike the general provisions of the Dawes Act.

This principle was applied by the Supreme Court in 2003 in two breach of trust actions brought by tribes against the United States. In the first, *United States* v. *White Mountain Apache* (537 U.S. Stat. 465 [2003]), the tribe relied upon a 1960 statute allowing the BIA to use and occupy specific buildings on tribal lands for its claim that damages were owed to rehabilitate and restore the property. The Supreme Court upheld the tribe's assertion that the 1960 statute supported "a fair inference that an obligation to preserve the property improvements was incumbent on the United States as trustee" due to the use made of the trust property by the Department of the Interior (537 U.S. at 475). In the second, *United States* v. *Navajo Nation* (537 U.S. 488 [2003]), the Court rejected the tribe's assertion that a federal statute requiring federal approval of a coal mining lease translated into a fiduciary duty to obtain the highest royalty rate available for the tribe. The Court likened the lease approval statute to the general provisions of the Dawes Act where no actionable fiduciary duty arose (537 U.S. Stat. at 508). Thus, this series of cases illustrates that the Court does not regard the trust relationship arising out of the general provisions of the Dawes Act as a basis for damages in any claim concerning tribal allotted lands.

## Federally Recognized Indian Lands

The holding in *Johnson v. M'Intosh* restrained tribes from the selling of tribal interest in lands to any buyer except the United States government as holder of superior title. The initial strategy employed by United States officials to gain ownership of large areas of land was the treaty-making process (St. Germain 2001:83–87). Tribal territories encompassed vast expanses of land and the land itself was honored as the sustenance of all life. The tribal view of land stewardship and the Anglo-American view of land ownership were fundamentally opposed during the era of initial contact (Fixico 1996:41).

Often at the conclusion of extended warfare or pressure by local non-Indian settlers, treaties were entered into for the transfer of millions of acres to the United States in exchange for reservation of specific lands, peaceful relations, goods, and services (Frantz 1999:15). After reservation lands were allotted, the policy allowed for the disposing of remaining lands identified as surplus in direct "violation of the treaty terms related to the size of the reservation that those tribes had negotiated for with the United States" (Rosser 2005:262). Tribal land holdings were estimated at 2.3 percent of the original tribal land base (Frantz 1999:39). Nearly one-half the lands retained after the allotment era were desert or semiarid and as a consequence "virtually useless for agricultural, pastoral, and other subsistence purposes" (McCoy 2002–2003:422).

Federal Indian lands are recognized under a variety of names: as reservations, rancherias, pueblos, and Indian communities within the United States (fig. 1). There are six ways that tribal lands have been obtained: treaty reservations, federal statutes, executive action, action of a foreign nation, purchase, and aboriginal possession (Pevar 1992: 87). Federally recognized Indian lands are characterized as generally nonalienable, within the borders of the United States, and within the jurisdiction of one or more federally recognized tribes (vol. 4:217).

As part of the policy of the 1800s, Congress passed into law the Removal Act providing that any unorganized territory west of the Mississippi River would be divided into districts for Indians removed from the East who would have permanent title to the new lands (Satz 1975:130). Due to this policy, the Cherokee, Chickasaw, Seminole, Creek, and Choctaw were removed to Oklahoma from their eastern homelands (Foreman 1934:17). A majority of the 40 tribes in Oklahoma were removed from other homelands to new lands that were subsequently opened up to settlement and lost to non-Indians.

The policy of removal further resulted in splitting tribes into separate groups on different reserved lands in different regions of the United States. "The Seminole, for example, are in Florida and Oklahoma, the Cheyenne in Montana and Oklahoma, the Ho-Chunk Nation (Winnebago) in Wisconsin and Nebraska, the Oneida in New York and Wisconsin, and the Sioux are located on many reservations in North and South Dakota, Minnesota, . . . Nebraska" and Montana (McCoy 2002–2003:430). Another federal policy was to remove separate tribal peoples and assign them to share one reservation area. Examples include the Kiowa, Comanche, and Apache in western Oklahoma, the Mandan, Hidatsa, and Arikara composing the Three Affiliated Tribes of the Fort Berthold Reservation, the Eastern Shoshone and Northern Arapahoe of the Wind River Reservation in Wyoming, and the Cheyenne and southern Arapaho of western Oklahoma (McCoy 2002–2003:430).

Tribal government jurisdiction is closely tied to the status of land. Tribal government authority extends over all reservation lands (Frantz 1999:66–67). Closed reservations are those that successfully resisted the allotment policy and continue the policy of holding all land within the reservation boundaries as tribal land. The largest unallotted reservation is the 16-million acre Navajo Reservation (Hightower-Langston 2003:412). Open reservations are those that were subjected to the allotment policy leading to "checkerboard" ownership of the lands by the tribal government, individual tribal members, and non-Indians.

A survey in 1984 found that 80 percent of lands within reservation boundaries were under tribal control with individual tribal member allotments comprising 19 percent of those lands. On three of the largest Indian reservations, Pine Ridge in South Dakota, Crow Reservation in Montana, and Fort Berthold Reservation in North Dakota, allotments accounted for 60–80 percent of the total tribal land base. In Oklahoma, the Osage Reservation is almost entirely comprised of allotted lands (Frantz 1999:51–54). Ninety-three percent of Indian reservation lands are geographically distributed in 11 western states and South Dakota with only three percent east of the Mississippi River (Frantz 1999:41).

Federally recognized lands comprise the legal landscape known as "Indian country" (ARCIA 1882:xxi). This term was legally defined in a 1948 statute whereby Congress delineated the extent of federal criminal jurisdiction within tribal lands. The categories of tribal lands encompassed within the definition of Indian country are: Indian reservations, all dependent Indian communities, and all Indian allotments including rights-of-way through such lands (18 U.S.C. § 1151).

In 2003, there were approximately 310 federally recognized Indian reservations in 33 states (Hightower-Langston 2003:412). Indian reservations are primarily those lands reserved by a tribe through entering into a treaty with the United States. Treaties were often the means employed to divest a tribe of large areas of land and reserve a particular tract for the tribal members to continue to live upon (Pevar 1992:87). Reservations have also been created by executive order and by the setting aside of former Indian lands for tribes through act of Congress. In 1927, Congress passed a statute prohibiting the creation of any further presidential executive-order reservations (25 U.S.C. § 398d). After passage of the Alaska Native Claims Settlement Act in 1971, all tribal lands in Alaska set aside by executive order, legislation, or secretarial order were revoked with the exception of the Annette Island Reserve established in 1891 (U.S. Department of Commerce 1974:5–6) (vol. 7:294–297).

In California, the Indian population is the largest in the United States and tribal lands are composed of both reservations and rancherias. Although 18 treaties were negotiated between 1851 and 1852 setting aside over 8.5 million acres for reservations with over 100 Indian groups in California, the U.S. Senate failed to ratify any of the treaties (Tiller 2005:360; Heizer 1972) (vol. 8:701–704). Executive order and federal statute authorized military reservations providing shelter and protection for Indians from the surrounding settlers were established ad hoc until 1855 (Kawahara and LaPena 2006:28).

From 1906 to 1934, 54 rancherias and one Indian village were reserved to California tribal members in addition to the eight recognized Indian reservations within the state (Tiller 2005:360). Rancherias, federally recognized land holdings for certain tribes in California, share the characteristics of other federally recognized Indian lands in being nonalienable, having tribal jurisdiction, and a location within the United States. Of the 104 federally recognized tribes in California, 52 hold less than a combined 200 acres of trust land and 12 are entirely without trust land (Kawahara and LaPena 2006:29).

Pueblos, the land holdings of the 18 Pueblo tribes of the Southwest, were recognized under distinct titles in the Treaty of Guadalupe-Hidalgo with the Republic of Mexico in 1848 (9 Stat. 922). In the 1876 U.S. Supreme Court case, *United States* v. *Joseph* (94 U.S. Stat. 614 [1876]), the Court described the Pueblo lands as follows: "[t]he pueblo Indians . . . hold their lands by a right superior to the United States. Their title dates back to grants made by the government of Spain before the Mexican Revolution,—a title which was fully recognized by the Mexican government, and protected by it in the treaty of Guadaloupe [sic] Hidalgo, by which this country and the allegiance of its inhabitants were transferred to the United States" (94 U.S. Stat. at 618). Between 1838 and 1931, the titles of the Pueblos were confirmed by congressional acts extending federal superintendence and restrictions on alienation over the Pueblo lands (Cohen 2005:323).

Dependent Indian communities are another category of federally recognized Indian land forming contemporary Indian country. The category of dependent Indian community was informed by the decisions in *United States* v. *Sandoval* (231 U.S. Stat. 28 [1913]), and *United States* v. *McGowan* (302 U.S. Stat. 535 [1938]), where the Supreme Court held that lands of the Santa Clara Pueblo and the Reno Indian Colony of Nevada, respectively, comprised Indian country as these lands were intended for Indian use and under federal supervision (Cohen 2005:192). In the 1998 *Alaska* v. *Native Village of Venetie* (522 U.S. Stat. 520), case, the Supreme Court considered whether the lands of the Native Village of Venetie continued as Indian country following the Alaska Native Claims Settlement Act and concluded that the lands were no longer set aside for tribal members and the federal superintendence of those lands had been revoked as well by the Act (522 U.S. Stat. at 533). Therefore, to be within the definition of dependent Indian community under the federal statute, lands must be set aside for the use of Indians and under federal superintendence, such as placed in trust status or held as restricted allotments.

*Individual Tribal Member Allotments*

The Dawes Severalty Act of 1887 opened reservation lands by dividing land holdings into specific acreage allotments for individual Indian ownership (Royster 1995:10). A prior policy of including allotment clauses in treaties was followed between 1854 and 1882 by the commissioner of Indian affairs to divide up the tribal land base. With the 1887 Act, Congress authorized the policy without regard to tribal consent and passed authorizing legislation to carry out the parceling of tribal lands (Cohen 2005:1041).

The allotment policy goal of assimilating Indian people into citizen farmers ultimately failed and "the only goal that allotment achieved was that it transferred millions of acres of Indian lands to non-Indians" (Cross 2000:912). The end of the allotment era was officially signaled with the passage of the Indian Reorganization Act of 1934 (25 U.S.C.

§ 461–465, ch. 1, § 1.05). The vast majority of lands that passed into fee simple ownership during the allotment years remain so (Royster 1995:17–18).

Indian-owned allotments retain the trust status in the United States government and are managed by the Bureau of Indian Affairs. Indian allotments are held by the United States as trustee and may not be sold, leased, or burdened without the approval of the Bureau of Indian Affairs (Cohen 2005:1046). The advantage of the trust status to the Indian owners lies in the exemption from federal, state, or local taxation securing the parcel to the owner within tribal jurisdiction (Frantz 1999:52) Allotments not used as homesteads have often been leased out to non-Indians with the approval of the Bureau of Indian Affairs to provide productive use for the land and to generate lease income for the Indian allottee (25 C.F.R. § 162). For example, the regulations for agricultural leases allow the BIA to "assist prospective tenants in contacting the Indian landowners or their representatives for the purpose of negotiating a lease" and the BIA will "assist the landowners in those negotiations upon request" (25 C.F.R. § 162.206).

The BIA standard for approving a lease of Indian lands is whether "the lease is in the best interest of the Indian landowner" (25 C.F.R. § 162.214). The BIA responsibilities for leasing Indian lands (25 C.F.R. § 162.108) include both the responsibility to "ensure that tenants meet their payment obligations to Indian landowners, through the collection of rent on behalf of the landowners and the prompt initiation of appropriate collection and enforcement actions" and the responsibility to "ensure that tenants comply with the operating requirements in their leases, through appropriate inspections and enforcement actions as needed to protect the interests of the Indian landowners." In 2000, Congress sought to increase economic development opportunities for tribes by exempting leases of tribal lands for a period of seven years or less from the requirement of secretarial approval unlike leases by individual Indian allottees (25 U.S.C. § 81(b)).

*Cobell Litigation: Trust Accounts and Trust Reform*

The proceeds from the leasing of Indian allotments are collected by the BIA and deposited into Individual Indian Money accounts administered by the Department of the Treasury (25 U.S.C. § 161). On June 10, 1996, the *Cobell* v. *Babbitt* (30 F.Supp.2d 24 (D.D.C. 1998) Cobell I) class action lawsuit on behalf of over 300,000 beneficiaries was filed against the United States seeking an accounting of trust funds and reform of the trust accounting system.

On November 5, 1998, the trial court bifurcated the lawsuit into two phases with phase one proceeding with a "trial to determine the extent to which the defendants have violated their trust duties" and phase two reserved the "trial on the extent to which the defendants have remedied those breaches" (*Cobell* v. *Norton*, 226 F.R.D. 67, 73 (D.D.C. 2005)). In 1999, the trial court held the interior secretary,

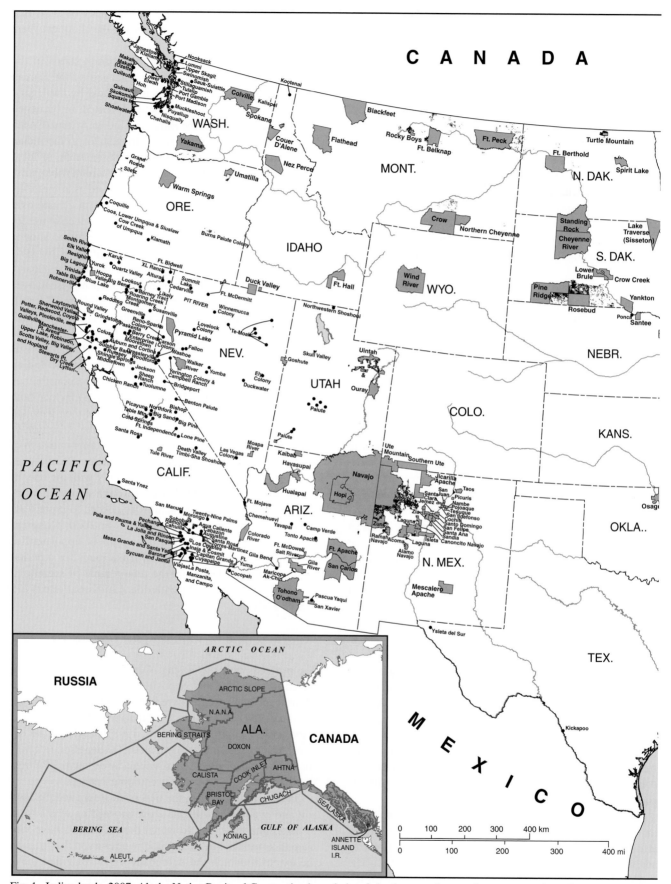

Fig. 1. Indian lands, 2007: Alaska Native Regional Corporation boundaries, federal reservations, and state reservations. Speckling on the map indicates either the reservation itself (e.g., Siletz, Ore.) or off-reservation tribal trust land (e.g., Red Lake, Minn.). For some reserva-

CANADA

Red Lake

Bois Forte (Nett Lake)
Bois Forte (Vermillion Lake)
Bois Forte (Deer Creek)
Grand Portage

Leech Lake

White Earth

Fond du Lac

Red Cliff

*Lake Superior*

MINN.

Mille Lacs

St. Croix

Lac Courte Oreille

Bad River

L'Anse (Ontonagon)  L'Anse

Lac Vieux Desert

Hannahville

Bay Mills
Sault Ste. Marie

Lac du Flambeau

Mole Lake

Upper Sioux  Shakopee

Lower Sioux

Prairie Island

Flandreau

Potawatomi

Menominee

Stockbridge-Munsee

Oneida

Ho-Chunk

*Lake Michigan*

WIS.

MICH.

Little Traverse Bay

Grand Traverse

Little River Ottawa

Isabella

*Lake Huron*

St. Regis

MAINE

Passamaquoddy
Passamaquoddy (Indian Township)

Penobscot

Passamaquoddy (Pleasant Point)

VT.  N.H.

N.Y.

*Lake Ontario*

Oneida

MASS.  R.I.

Hassanamisco

Tuscarora  Tonawanda

Onondaga

Winnebago
Omaha

IOWA

Sac & Fox

ILL.

Huron Potawatomi

Pokagon Potawatomi

IND.

*Lake Erie*

Cattaraugus

Allegany  Oil Springs

OHIO

PA.

Eastern Pequot
Mohegan
Schaghticoke
CT.  Narragansett  Wampanoag
Golden Hill  Mashantucket Pequot
Shinnecock
Poospatuck

Rankokus

N.J.

DEL.

M.D.

Sac & Fox  Iowa

Kickapoo

Potawatomi

KANS.

MO.

W. VA.

VA.

Pamunkey
Mattaponi

KY.

Tallige
Cherokee

PA.

Osage

AR.

OKLA..

TENN.

Cherokee

Catawba

N.C.

S.C.

ATLANTIC

OCEAN

MISS.

ALA.

GA.

Mississippi Choctaw

Poarch Creek

Tama

LA.

Mowa Choctaw

TEX.

Alabama-Coushatta

Tunica-Biloxi

Coushatta

Chitimacha

FLA.

Tampa

Ft. Pierce

Brighton

Immokalee  Big Cypress

Coconut Creek

Miccosukee  Hollywood (Dania)

*GULF OF MEXICO*

• ▪  federal reservations

▲  state reservations

——  Alaska Native Regional Corporation boundaries

0   100   200   300   400 km

0   100   200   300   400 mi

tions, especially in the Plains, only the external boundaries are shown (e.g., Lake Traverse, S. Dak.) without indications of the "checker-boarding" resulting from the alienation of lands since 1887. When multiple small reservations are grouped, the word "and" is used, whereas when a reservation has the word "and" in its title, an ampersand is used.

93

treasury secretary, and assistant interior secretary in contempt of court for failing to produce necessary documents and imposed monetary sanctions (*Cobell* v. *Babbitt*, 37 F.Supp.2d 6 (D.D.C. 1999) *Cobell II*).

In phase one of the serial litigation, testimony revealed that the Department of Treasury pooled all deposits for beneficiaries in one account rather than maintaining separate accounts (*Cobell* v. *Norton*, 240 F.3d 1081, 1089 (D.C. Cir. 2001) *Cobell VI*). As a result of the failure to adequately maintain accounting of trust funds, the exact number of accounts is unknown and the federal government is unable to state the amount of money that is or should be held in the trust accounts (*Cobell VI*, 240 F.3d at 1089). Furthermore, the District of Columbia Circuit Court reported that the Interior Department admitted in testimony that the trust fund breach includes those duties imposed by the 1994 American Indian Trust Fund Management Reform Act (25 U.S.C. § 4001–4061), intended to prevent further mismanagement of trust accounts (*Cobell VI*, 240 F.3d at 1090).

Congress held hearings on the likelihood of settling the litigation begun by Elouise Cobell with officials from the Department of the Interior and the attorneys for the Indian beneficiaries (House Resources Oversight Hrg. Feb. 16, 2005). The plaintiffs in the *Cobell* litigation have estimated the amount owed to Indian beneficiaries since 1887 to "total nearly 137.5 billion" (Panoff 2004:522). Any solution to this historic and contemporary trust fund mismanagement will necessarily need to include settling the expectations of tribal members who are the beneficiaries of tribal lands held in trust with the United States and have had that trust relationship severely breached.

*Tribal Land Acquisition*

In the aftermath of the allotment policy, Indian tribes have prioritized the acquisition and addition of lands to their tribal land holdings. Upon the passage of the Indian Reorganization Act, the secretary of the interior was instructed to restore any remaining identified surplus tribal lands to tribal ownership (25 U.S.C. § 463). The Act explicitly provided authority for the secretary "in his discretion, to acquire through purchase, relinquishment, gift, exchange, or assignment, any interest in lands, water rights, or surface rights to lands, within or without existing reservations . . . for the purpose of providing land for Indians" (25 U.S.C. § 465). Appropriations for the purchase of lands for Indians were supported by the statute with a limit of two million dollars in any one fiscal year. This land acquisition authorization further provided that any lands acquired "shall be taken in the name of the United States in trust for the Indian tribe or individual Indian for which the land is acquired, and such lands or rights shall be exempt from State and local taxation" (25 U.S.C. § 465). Finally, the Act permitted the secretary "to proclaim new Indian reservations on lands acquired pursuant to any authority conferred by this Act, or to add such lands to existing reservations" (25 U.S.C. § 467).

As tribes have secured funding through economic development or federal land acquisition programs, they have purchased fee lands to add to their land holdings and increase the tribal jurisdiction area. In the 1998, *Cass County, Minnesota* v. *Leech Lake Band of Indians* (524 U.S. Stat. 103) case, the Supreme Court held that former allotment fee lands reacquired by a tribe remain subject to state taxation unless placed into trust status with the federal government. The process for placing land into trust status is governed by federal regulations.

*Fee-to-Trust Regulations*

In 1980, the first federal regulations were adopted governing the process of placing lands acquired by tribes into trust status with the United States (25 C.F.R. § 151). The regulations revised in 1995 distinguish between taking lands into trust that are on-reservation and those that are off-reservation. For on-reservation acquisitions, the regulations provide that upon written request to have lands taken into trust "the Secretary of the Interior will notify state and local governments having regulatory jurisdiction over the land to be acquired." This notice allows the governments 30 days to register comments regarding the impact on regulatory jurisdiction, real property taxes, and other assessments should the land be placed into trust (25 C.F.R. § 151.10).

Criteria are set out that allow the secretary of the interior to evaluate fee-to-trust requests. The eight criteria for on-reservation acquisitions are: statutory authority for the acquisition; need for additional land by the tribe or individual Indian; purpose for which the land will be used; for individual Indians, the amount of land owned in trust and the level of assistance required to handle his affairs; impact on the state and local subdivision from the removal of the land from tax rolls; jurisdictional problems and conflicts of land use which may arise; whether the BIA is able to discharge the additional responsibilities resulting from the acquisition of the land in trust status; and compliance with the National Environmental Policy Act (25 C.F.R. § 151.10). For off-reservation acquisitions, the seven criteria for tribal on-reservation acquisitions apply with the addition of the following two criteria: location of the land with greater scrutiny given when the land is a distance from the tribe's reservation and a tribal business plan specifying the anticipated economic benefits when the acquisition is for business purposes (25 C.F.R. § 151.11).

Approval of the trust application is followed by publication of the decision in the *Federal Register* for 30 days, an examination of the land title, and execution of an instrument of conveyance to the secretary of the interior and then the land is officially taken into trust (25 C.F.R. § 151.12–151.14). Denial of a trust application for both on-reservation and off-reservation lands gives rise to appeal rights of the secretarial decision by filing a petition in the Interior Board of Indian Appeals (25 C.F.R. § 151.12).

There exists a tension between tribal governments seeking to reacquire lands within their reservation boundaries or territories and the nontribal governments interested in keeping those same lands on state and county tax rolls subject to state regulation (Sheppard 1998–1999:682). The only exclusion from the comment period for state and local officials is for trust acquisitions that are categorized as mandatory. The text of 25 C.F.R. 151.10 provides that on-reservation trust acquisitions be evaluated on the basis of eight separate criteria "unless the acquisition is mandated by legislation." The text of 25 C.F.R. 151.11 for off-reservation trust acquisitions contains 10 criteria to evaluate the acquisition where the "acquisition is not mandated." Within the *Code of Federal Regulations*, the only trust acquisitions that are contemplated as mandatory have been those that are specifically legislatively mandated, rather than all acquisitions based on the Indian Reorganization Act.

Two Interior Board of Indian Appeals decisions address when trust acquisitions are legislatively mandated. In the first, *Todd County, South Dakota* v. *Aberdeen Area Director, Bureau of Indian Affairs* (33 IBIA 110 (January 19, 1999)), the Board held that the federal law under consideration, "Isolated Tracts Act" mandated that when isolated tracts on the Rosebud Reservation were mortgaged, leased, or sold, the proceeds would be used to acquire lands within approved land consolidation areas and such acquired lands were mandatory trust acquisitions. The Board strictly construed the plain meaning of the federal law, Public Law 88-196 (1963), intended to provide the Rosebud Sioux Tribe with the ability to finance land acquisitions within approved land consolidation areas by mortgaging, leasing, or selling isolated tracts of little or no economic benefit to the tribe. The acquired land in the land consolidation areas was intended to be placed into trust status when the tribe followed the provisions of federal law.

In the second case, *Confederated Salish and Kootenai Tribes of the Flathead Nation* v. *Northwest Regional Director, Bureau of Indian Affairs* (35 IBIA 226 (November 9, 2000)), the tribes argued that their specific federal legislation was applicable to a parcel of donated land and was a mandatory trust acquisition. The Board parsed the federal law, Public Law 90-402 (1968) and found that the procedure for mandatory trust acquisition was only operative when the Tribes disposed of certain tracts described in the law and then used those monies to purchase additional lands. In the instant case where the lands were donated to the tribes, the Board found that the acquisition was not a mandatory trust acquisition under the terms of the law.

These cases demonstrate that mandatory trust acquisitions have been narrowly defined as directed only when a specific federal law provides the procedure under which such an acquisition is made. In both these cases, the federal laws were intended specifically for each tribe and directed that certain tracts be utilized to secure funds to purchase the mandatory trust acquisitions.

Tribes face a lengthy and challenging process for placing lands into trust under the fee-to-trust BIA regulations. With the exceptions of the state and local government notice and the publication in the *Federal Register*, there are no time limits set forth in the trust process regulations.

State and local governments are provided the opportunity to comment on tribal trust applications and oppose the removal of tribally purchased lands from state and local tax rolls. State governments have been successful in arguing that lands under state jurisdiction for a length of time may not be reclaimed by tribes. In *City of Sherrill, New York* v. *Oneida* (544 U.S. Stat. 197 (2005)), the Supreme Court denied tax exempt status and tribal jurisdiction to lands that were repurchased by the Oneida within their original tribal territory in the state of New York. The Court opined that because the lands had been under state jurisdiction for two centuries, the legitimate reliance by the state on the land being subject to state jurisdiction and the inaction of the Oneida for a long period of time barred the tribe's claim that the lands regain reservation status. This case illustrates another hurdle for tribes in reclaiming their territory where the only option is to build revenue to repurchase the lands under state jurisdiction as a result of the allotment policy, treaty cessions, and other land transfers.

### Indian Lands Acquired for Gaming

Lands purchased by a tribe for the purpose of conducting a gaming enterprise are subject to additional requirements under the Indian Gaming Regulatory Act (25 U.S.C. § 2719). Under this federal statute, the secretary of the interior must first determine that taking lands into trust for a tribal gaming enterprise "would not be detrimental to the surrounding community" (25 U.S.C. § 2719(b)(1)(A). Upon this determination, the governor of the state where the land is located and where gaming will be conducted must concur with the secretarial determination for the trust application to proceed. The three exceptions to this process are when the lands are part of a settlement land claim, the Indian reservation has been newly recognized pursuant to the federal acknowledgment process, or the lands are part of a restored reservation for a tribe that has regained federal recognition (25 U.S.C. § 2719(b)(1)(B)). As a result of the Indian Gaming Regulatory Act, lands acquired by a tribe for the purpose of conducting gaming are subject to a higher degree of difficulty to complete the fee-to-trust process.

### Heirship, Fractionation, and Land Consolidation

Few original owners of allotments drew up wills to devise their allotments. As the allotments passed to multiple heirs through the generations, a situation has occurred where multiple owners own fractions of interests in the original allotment. With the allotment remaining in trust status through the generational devise to heirs, the BIA inherited the administration of the fractionated interests, the income to each owner of an interest, and the determination of productive use to offset the costs of such administration (Cohen 2005: 1068).

In 1983, Congress attempted to address the cumbersome and costly problem of fractionation in Indian lands by passing the Indian Land Consolidation Act (25 U.S.C. § 2201 et seq). The Act provided funds for tribes to purchase at fair market value interests in allotted lands with the consent of a majority of owners in an allotment (25 U.S.C. § 2204). An escheat provision of the Act allowed small interests to escheat to the tribe; however, the original and revised versions of this provision were stricken by the Supreme Court in *Hodel* v. *Irving* (481 U.S. Stat. 704 [1987]) and in *Babbitt* v. *Youpee* (519 U.S. Stat. 234 [1997]), as unconstitutional takings without just compensation in violation of the Fifth Amendment of the Constitution.

In 2004, Congress amended the Indian Land Consolidation Act with passage of the American Indian Probate Reform Act intending to govern the descent of trust or restricted land (25 U.S.C. § 2206). The Probate Act provides that trust and restricted land may only be devised to: the decedent's Indian spouse, any other Indian person, or the Indian tribe with jurisdiction over the land (25 U.S.C. §2206(a)(1)). Further, the Act states that should the owner of trust or restricted land devise the land to a non-Indian, a life estate will be created for the non-Indian's life with the descent to follow the Act upon expiration of that interest (25 U.S.C. § 2206(a)(2)). Indian co-owners in a tract of land may pay the fair market value of the decedent's interest into the probate estate to prevent the interest from transferring to the Indian tribe having jurisdiction (25 U.S.C. § 2206(a)(4)). If there is no surviving spouse, the interests pass according to the "single heir rule." When the oldest heirs are unavailable the land may pass to the tribe. By executing a will, Indian landowners override the descent provision of the Act. Thus, the descent laws for Indian lands should allow for the consolidation of interests in allotted lands by either Indian co-owners purchasing available interests in probate or by descent to tribes. With consolidation of the interests in allotments, the administrative burden on the BIA should be less and the productive use for such lands be more easily ascertainable by Indian owners or tribal government owners.

## State-Recognized Indian Lands

Tribes that were officially terminated or never officially recognized by the federal government may still establish themselves under state law. There are a number of state-recognized tribes that engage in a relationship with state governments rather than the federal government. Ten eastern states have legislated recognition processes for tribal groups: Alabama, Connecticut, Delaware, Georgia, Louisiana, Massachusetts, North Carolina, New York, Tennessee, and Virginia (Brownell 2000–2001:303). The rights of such tribes are defined in state legislation.

For example, under Connecticut law state-recognized tribes "have certain special rights to tribal lands as may have been set forth by treaty or other agreement" (Conn. Gen. Stat. § 47.59a). Connecticut law provides protections to the three state-recognized tribes as self-governing with the power to: determine residency and tribal membership on reservation land; determine the form of tribal government; regulate commerce and trade on the reservation, enter into contracts, and determine tribal leadership according to tribal custom (Conn. Gen. Stat. § 47.59b).

State-recognized tribes often seek federal acknowledgment through the federal process. However, "applying for federal recognition through the Bureau of Indian Affairs is wrought with red tape, leaving several tribes waiting an indefinite amount of time for recognition" (Katz 2003:19). State-recognized tribes may still receive the benefit of many federal Indian laws. For example, the Native American Housing Assistance and Self-Determination Act includes state recognized tribes within the definition of "Indian tribe" with benefits under the Act (25 U.S.C. § 4103(12)(C)). The Indian Arts and Crafts Act of 1990 provides that "any Indian group that has been formally recognized as an Indian tribe by a State legislature or by a State commission or similar organization legislatively vested with State tribal recognition authority" is included in the term "Indian tribe" for the purposes of the Act (25 U.S.C. § 305d).

Of the 43 state-recognized tribes, only 10 have recognized tribal lands under state law. The state-recognized tribes identified as having tribal lands are: the Golden Hill in Connecticut, the Schaghticoke Bands in Connecticut, the Tama Tribal Town in Georgia, the Delaware Muncie in Kansas, the Hassanamisco in Massachusetts, the Rankokus in New Jersey, the Shinnecock and Poospatuck in New York, the Tallige Cherokee Nation in Scioto County, Ohio, the Pamunkey and the Mattaponi in Virginia (Cohen 2005: 170). Without federal recognition, these lands are not characterized as "Indian country" with tribal jurisdiction and the application of federal law attached to federally acknowledged tribal lands.

# Health and Health Issues in the United States

JENNIE R. JOE

As citizens of the United States, Indians and Alaska Natives are eligible to participate in all public, state, and other health programs. Thus, many Natives receive Medicare, Medicaid, veterans, and other public health benefits and services. Others are covered by private health insurance through employment. Some tribes who have profitable gaming enterprises provide health insurance for their members. In addition, enrolled members of the 564 federally recognized tribes are eligible to receive health care from the Indian Health Service in the Department of Health and Health Services. Several treaties in which Indians ceded lands called for benefits, including health care, to be provided in return. However, the annual appropriations by Congress for the Indian Health Service are discretionary. They are not an entitlement, as is Medicare.

Reports of the United States Commission on Civil Rights (2003, 2004) conclude that American Indians and Alaska Natives have lower life expectancy than any other racial or ethnic group and that this population suffers disproportionately from preventable diseases such as diabetes, tuberculosis, cancer, and alcoholism (vol. 3:789–798) (U.S. Commission on Civil Rights 2004). Most federal studies are not known to lead to immediate solutions but serve as an important source toward improvement. Federal studies also are meaningful because the federal government has a key role in the delivery and funding of health care resources for tribal and urban based Indian communities. The federal government not only provides direct care in some communities but also contracts or awards grants to tribes and urban Indian organizations to provide health care services.

This chapter describes the history and policies that govern health care for American Indians and Alaska Natives. It reviews the contemporary health problems and challenges faced by health care delivery resources, including the changing picture of health research and the efforts to address the health disparities experienced by this population. American Indians and Alaska Natives experience common as well as unique health disparities, including limited access to health care and uncertain funding of health care.

## Traditional Indigenous Health Resources

Prior to European contact, most tribal communities had well-established indigenous health care delivery resources.

At the core of most was the belief that all aspects of an individual's life—mental, physical, and spiritual—were interrelated. Emphasis was placed on promotion of good health or the prevention of ill health or misfortune. The beliefs and practices that promoted healthy lifeways were codified in various tribal taboos, customs, and practices taught and learned from early childhood. Social and cultural disruptions after contact changed these norms and subsequently had considerable impact on the health and lifeways of most tribal communities.

European contact on all the shores of the Americas brought epidemics of unfamiliar and devastating communicable diseases to a population that had no immunity or experience with them (Crosby 1972; Cook 1973). The indigenous healers and their array of treatment modalities were ineffective against these new diseases, and as the epidemics recurred, they led to drastic depopulation ("United States Native Population," this vol.). The rippling effects of the epidemics continued after certain communicable diseases waned. For example, smallpox epidemics often left survivors with unsightly facial and other disfigurement, which drove unknown numbers to commit suicide (E.W. Stearn and A.E. Stearn 1945; Fortuine 1984; Duffy 1951).

Understandably, the consequences of communicable diseases crippled tribes in other ways, especially since these diseases affected the most fragile, namely, the young and the elderly. Infant and childhood mortality slowed population growth while mortality among the aged destroyed a valuable resource for the survivors. In most tribes, elders are the repository of tribal history, language, and cultural knowledge. Because most experienced and knowledgeable healers are elders, the high mortality rates for this group drastically decreased the tribes' number of skilled healers.

The arrival and settlement of the Europeans altered indigenous environments through the introduction of imported crops and animals. The importation of some of these unfamiliar domesticated animals and crops added to the health problems of the indigenous populations, some directly by the introduction of animal-borne diseases through food sources and others indirectly by destroying and replacing indigenous vegetation used as herbal medicine (Head 2001; Boserup 1966; Viola and Margolis 1991).

Most tribes made use of indigenous plants to treat health problems and injuries. The plants were ritually harvested during certain seasons and prepared in a number of different ways. Some were used to treat minor ailments while others were saved for more elaborate healing ceremonies. Skilled herbalists were found in most tribal groups, and they not only treated patients directly but also supplied herbs to the community as well as to other practitioners. As Western allopathic medicine evolved, significant numbers of the herbs used by the tribes were eventually integrated into the pharmacopeia of the United States (Vogel 1970; Shemluck 1982; M. Martin 1981).

Other common practitioners found in tribal communities included bonesetters (those who set fractures) and wound specialists (those who removed arrowheads or spear points and treated wounds). Because these practitioners were highly skilled, some of the early European settlers utilized them when they had no access to their own physicians or other practitioners. The utilization of indigenous healers or practitioners by the colonists declined as the number of European newcomers increased and each immigrant group imported their own health-care resources.

For native peoples, much of the natural world was viewed as sacred and spirituality was an integral part of one's daily living. To maintain health, individuals were taught to maintain a balance of the key strands of those elements that made up this state of health: the physical, the mental, the sociocultural, and the spiritual. Native healers were therefore expected to tend to their patient's needs, which encompassed all these strands. Dealing with the spiritual aspects of life required healers to be knowledgeable about the use of supernatural sources so that they could call upon these forces to aid them in assisting patients. This special knowledge and access to supernatural resources placed most healers in a unique powerful position within their communities. To diminish this powerful position of healers and the importance of their ceremonies, government officials outlawed some of the more important healing practices, such as the Sun Dance in the northern Plains and the ceremonial potlatches among tribes on the Northwest Coast (L.B. Boyer, R.M. Boyer, and A.E. Hippler 1974).

Each Sun Dance participant was fulfilling a personal vow by sacrificing or enduring the fast and the piercing. Organized church leaders misinterpreted the act as unnecessary body mutilation. The practice of potlatches was also seen by the colonists as occasions that kept tribes in poverty, whereas to the native participants, the celebrations helped express thanksgiving and the gift exchanges acknowledged cooperation and support offered by kin or other members of one's community.

Some physicians refused to provide medical service to native patients if these patients had any visible evidence of having utilized a tribal healer (Joe 2003; Primeaux 1977). The attacks on tribal healers and tribal healing ceremonies

added to the distrust native peoples developed for Western medicine. This distrust has lessened over time, but initially many Indian patients did not come to hospitals or to clinics until there were no other alternatives, thus delaying seeking health care until it was too late for successful treatment or cure. This situation fueled the idea that hospitals were places of death, not places for restoration of health. Slowly the acceptance of allopathic medicine became more common, helped by the introduction and use of antibiotics and other scientific medical advances. Today, allopathic medicine is used in all tribal communities, but the use of traditional tribal healing resources (where available) also continues, either alongside allopathic medicine or in combination with other forms of healing, including what is now called integrative or alternative medicine. The increased utilization of allopathic medicine has been aided by the fact that traditional healing ceremonies are no longer practiced in a number of tribes, primarily because there are no healers to conduct them.

## Federal Role in Health Care

During the late eighteenth and early nineteenth century Indian Affairs were under the Secretary of War. In 1824 the Office Of Indian Affairs was created within the War Department. The initial health resources from the federal government were offered on a limited basis. Some treaties called for the services of a physician while others might include allocation of specific medical supplies. Some of the services negotiated were difficult to fulfill. For example, if the government could not find a willing physician who wanted a contract to serve a tribe, the government could easily forego its treaty obligations, and in most of these situations, the tribes did not have the resources to enforce treaty obligations. In 1832, smallpox vaccinations were given to tribes considered "friendly" to the United States (Cohen 1982; J.D. Pearson 2004). The vaccinations were also administered to Indians living near military outposts to protect the populations there.

In 1836 the Office of Indian Affairs initiated the provision of health services to two tribes, the Ottawa and Chippewa (Sorkin 1971). Treaties began to call for the services of a physician or the allocation of specific medical supplies.

In 1849, the Indian office was transferred to the newly established Department of Interior, where it was eventually renamed the Bureau of Indian Affairs (BIA). In 1873, the BIA established a medical and education division within its agency to develop and improve health and education programs for American Indians. In 1877, the BIA abolished the medical and education division although it subsequently maintained responsibility for health care and education for most reservations. For example, by 1880, the

AP Images.

Fig. 1. Indian Health Service hospitals. left, Serving the Cheyenne River Sioux in Eagle Butte, S. Dak. Photograph by Jim Holland, 2001. right, Alaska Native Medical Center in Anchorage, opened in 1997, the largest hospital serving Alaska Natives. Photograph by *Anchorage Daily News*/Anne Raup, 1997.

government was managing four hospitals and had contracts with approximately 77 physicians (Bennett 1958). The health care services delivered during this time were focused primarily on Indian children enrolled in federal boarding schools. Finally in 1911, funding for provision of general but limited health care services for tribes was allocated by Congress.

The role of the federal government in the provision of health care services to American Indians and Alaska Natives is based on four legislative actions: the Snyder Act of 1921, the Transfer Act of 1954, the Indian Self-Determination and Education Assistance Act of 1975, and the Indian Health Care Improvement Act in 1976. The Snyder Act directed the Indian Affairs Office to "direct, supervise, and expend such moneys as Congress may from time to time appropriate for the benefit, care, and assistance of the Indians throughout the United States." The Act included provision for "relief of distress and conservation of health." Under the Snyder Act, the BIA received additional funding to build health facilities or to improve existing ones. The Bureau also sought permission to utilize physicians from the Public Health Service to supplement the few civilian physicians they had under contract. For the next few years, the BIA targeted some of the major health problems experienced by this population, for example, tuberculosis, trachoma (fig. 2), infant mortality, and maternal mortality. The advent of World War II resulted in the reallocation of much of the federal resources to the war effort, resulting in a drastic reduction in federal health resources for health care for tribes. With diminished resources, the health status among American Indians continued to deteriorate and mortality rates remained essentially unchanged (Shelton 2004; Sorkin 1971).

The Transfer Act, as part of the termination policy, allowed for the move of the health care service responsibility from the Bureau of Indian Affairs to the Public Health Ser-

vice within the Department of Health, Education, and Welfare. In 1955, 2,900 employees and the facilities were transferred. At the time of the transfer, some of the leading health problems were still various forms of infectious diseases and malnutrition; infant and maternal mortality were the leading causes of death. Public health improvements became a major challenge for the Indian Health Service (IHS). Significant progress was made by IHS in improving the health of American Indians, some of it helped by advances in modern medicine. There was also a substantial investment by IHS in improving the availability of safe water and sanitation facilities (fig. 3), which contributed to reducing some of the infectious diseases, especially infant and

U.S. Dept. of Health and Human Services, Ind. Health Service, Washington: 1025.

Fig. 2. Nurse with children in a waiting room at the Navajo Medical Center in Ariz. that treats tuberculosis and trachoma. Photographed in 1966.

99

Fig. 3. Indoor toilet being installed for a Sioux family, S. Dak., 1965.

childhood gastrointestinal infections. Concerted efforts instituted to encourage prenatal care and increased hospital delivery also helped decrease maternal and infant mortality (Brenneman 2000).

Even with the expanded services, many health needs of the Native populations were unmet. In 1975 The American Indian Policy Review Committee was established to study all government programs relating to Native Americans. The Commission found that while health care had improved, health conditions were still far below that of the general population. In fact, some Natives had less access to IHS services than before the Transfer Act.

In the 1950s the BIA initated a program to relocate Indians from reservations and rural areas to cities ("Termination and Relocation," this vol.), in order to give Indians access to better economic opportunity, while ending their dependence on BIA and IHS services. By the 1970s the urban population numbered more than 200,000, many of whom were not prepared by their education or job skills to take advantage of the urban situation. Health issues became a problem for much of this population, and there were no IHS services in the cities. In the early 1960s local and private organizations established store-front clinics to meet the needs. Advocates lobbied Congress for an addition to the appropriation to include urban Indian clinics as part of the IHS funds, and in 1966 Congress funded a pilot clinic in Rapid City, South Dakota. Clinics in Seattle, San Francisco, Tulsa, and Dallas followed.

The Indian Self-Determination and Education Assistance Act authorized the IHS to enter into contracts with tribes to take over management of their health care facilities and resources if they wished. An amendment allowed tribes another choice, to reprioritize funds to target health problems they deemed urgent. In the 1990s, a presidential executive order instructed federal agencies to consult with tribes on policies that affect them prior to implementation of new federal programs.

The goal of the Indian Health Care Improvement Act is to improve the health status of American Indians and Alaska Natives to be comparable to that of the general national population (U.S. Congress. Office of Technology Assessment 1986). The act provided funding for urban Indians, recruiting and retaining health care professionals serving Native Americans, and construction of health care facilities.

## Indian Health Care System

The health care system for American Indians and Alaska Natives is by far the most complex of any health care system in the United States. Not all individuals of Native American ancestry qualify for benefits and services. The most basic eligibility criteria used by IHS requires Indian patients to be enrolled members of a federally recognized tribe and to live on or near a reservation or an Alaska Native village. According to the 2007 data, IHS serves approximately 1.9 million Natives directly through their own or tribal facilities. Of this number about 600,000 live in cities served by 34 urban clinics (Indian Health Service 2007).

Indian Health Service programs operate in five ways: directly through medical facilities; through contracts with tribes in their own facilities; through urban organizations that manage clinics; through private providers for emergency and specialized treatments not available in IHS or tribal facilities; and in regional epidemiology centers of the federal Centers for Disease Control.

Funding is equally complex. The IHS, like all federal agencies, receives a varying annual appropriation from Congress. For fiscal year 2006 it was $3.1 billion. Of this, 54 percent was allocated to tribes to administer services through contracts. Tribal health care receives funding from the IHS, other government agencies, third-party insurance, and tribal revenue.

In 2007, there were approximately 15,000 employees of IHS, 88 percent Native Americans in the administrative positions, 94 percent in technical and clerical positions, and 50 percent in the professions. The Indian Health Care Improvement Act of 1976 included scholarships for Natives pursuing careers in health care, and in the succeeding 30 years, 8,000 Natives became physicians, nurses, and other health specialists. Tribal health employees include another several thousand people.

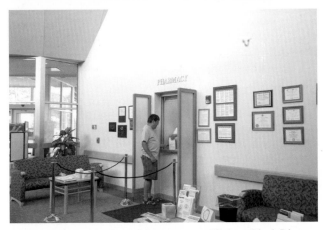

Fig. 4. Ho-Chunk Nation health care. top, Clinic at Black River Falls, Wis. center, Optical department, staffed by Cathy Shegonee. bottom, Pharmacy. Photographs by Paul Arentz, 2007.

*Direct IHS Services*

Programs of IHS are administered through 12 regional offices (fig. 5). In 2006, the IHS managed 37 hospitals, 64 health centers, 50 health stations, and five school health units. In comparison, tribes managed 12 hospitals, 116 health centers, 97 health stations, and 3 school-based health units. In addition, Alaska Native villages through their nonprofit corporations managed 176 village clinics. Initiatives of IHS

or tribes include injury prevention, alcohol abuse, diabetes, and mental health.

*Tribally Operated Services*

Under the Indian Self-Determination and Education Assistance Act, tribal governments assumed management of existing health programs, including hospitals, clinics, heath centers, and school health centers. In 2006, there were 72 compacts, representing 322 tribes, with 93 funding agreements totaling over one billion dollars. In addition, contracts totaled over $500 million (Indian Health Service 2007). Some tribally operated health programs have expanded, with resources from gaming. A few have incorporated tribal healing resources, following the lead of IHS (Roubideaux 2004).

Although more tribes are electing to manage their own health care services, there are some cautionary notes. Some tribal members indicate that the quality of health care has improved (National Indian Health Board 1998; Joe 2003). Tribes that have the population base or other resources to build or improve the health programs inherited have been more successful in sustaining their programs, but small tribes may not have a stable or adequate financial base to take over management of their health program.

**Urban Health Care**

By the early 1960s, a number of urban-based Indian organizations with the help of advocates began to establish small free clinics to serve Indian families without health resources. Over time, many advocated for the continuation of these clinics by lobbying Congress for a special "add-on" of the federal appropriation for urban Indian clinics as a part of the annual Indian Health Service funding. Fortunately, the passage of the Indian Care Health Improvement Act in 1976 gave the IHS authorization to fund or to support existing urban-based Indian health programs. Initially the "add-on" funded approximately 43 urban-based Indian health programs. In 2006 there were 34, most in western states, but others in Chicago, Detroit, Boston, and New York. Urban clinics are managed by nonprofit organizations. All receive some funding through the IHS, and most receive other funds in the form of grants from other federal agencies, their state of local government, or private sources. Some urban clinics serve all Indians, whether they are enrolled members of a recognized tribe or not. While facilities serving Native Americans are eligible to bill Medicare and Medicaid for expenses, many users of IHS are not enrolled in these programs (M. Dixon and Y. Roubideaux 2001; General Accounting Office 2005; Zuckerman et al. 2004).

The types of health care services offered by the urban-based programs vary, depending on the size of their user populations, their proximity to existing Indian Health Service facilities, and their ability to attract and make use of other funding resources. The smaller operations focus on

*101*

Fig. 5. Indian Health Service regions with the regional office locations, as well as the headquarters in Rockville, Md. While most regions are contained within neighboring states, exceptions are: the Nashville region is discontinuous from eastern Texas to Maine; the Albuquerque region includes El Paso; the Navajo region solely encompasses Navajo lands; the Tucson region serves the Tohono O'odham, San Xavier, and Pascua Yaqui reservations; the Phoenix region includes all lands in Ariz., Nev., and Utah exclusive of the Navajo and Tucson regions; and the Calif. region serves native Hawaiians.

making referrals, on delivering health promotion programs, and on providing various forms of health education. The larger facilities offer direct outpatient medical care services, including dental, mental health, and other specialty services. For example, 20 urban-based Indian health programs offer more direct medical services (Forquera 2001). These clinics face challenges. As the number of uninsured increases, the clinics find that the demand for services rapidly outpaces their ability to provide quality health care. Some of this demand is also due to the increasing number of patients with multiple health problems that require costly care.

Since the urban programs provide service to only a portion of the urban Indian population, the general health status of the larger segment of the urban Indian population is not readily available. An Urban Indian Health Institute was established by the Seattle Indian Health Board to address this problem. The goal of the Institute is to improve the collection of health data and to advocate for more research into the health needs and health outcomes of American Indians and Alaska Natives living in the cities.

**Health Disparities**

Since the 1970s, health and life expectancy for Natives have improved. In 1972–1973 life expectancy at birth was

63.6 years; in 1999–2001 is was 74.5 years. Table 1 shows that from 1993 to 1997 mortality rates increased among American Indians and Alaska Natives for alcoholism and diabetes but remained constant for accidents, suicides, and pneumonia and influenza. Mortality rates from malignant neoplasms, while less than the mortality rates for the total population, increased significantly at the same time that mortality rates from cancer in the national population decreased slightly. It is worth noting that cancer incidences are low for this population, but cancer mortality rates are high due to late diagnosis and limited access to treatment. Mortality rates for heart disease continued to increase among American Indians and were slightly higher than the mortality rates for heart disease in the general population. The majority of the health conditions are preventable.

Data available on health behaviors of American Indians and Alaska Natives indicate that they are more likely to smoke, abuse alcohol, be overweight, and are less likely to engage in leisure time recreational physical activity. Significant numbers of American Indians and Alaska Natives, especially females, also report experiencing psychological distress (Barnes, Adams, and Powell-Griner 2005). Eighteen percent of Native adults reported that they had no health insurance (Schneider and Martinez 1997:6).

One of the most disturbing changes in Native health is the increase in diabetes, which ranks fourth in causes of Native mortality (Gold Book 2005:20; Tanner 2006; Joe and Frishkopf 2006). The increase in chronic health problems in children is undoing gains made in improving health through immunization, prenatal care, and childhood nutrition.

## Indian Health Advocates

Over the years various coalitions have formed to help advocate for improvement of health care services for American Indians and Alaska Natives. Significant among these coalitions are the National Congress of American Indians and the National Indian Health Board. The urban Indian health programs formed the advocacy coalition, the National Council

**Table 1. Mortality Rates of the Indian Population Compared to the U.S. Population All Races**

| Cause of mortality | 1993 | 1997 |
|---|---|---|
| alcoholism | +579% | +638 |
| tuberculosis | +475% | +400 |
| diabetes | +231 | +291 |
| accidents | +212% | +215 |
| suicide | +70 | +67 |
| pneumonia and influenza | +61 | +67 |
| heart disease | +8% | +20% |
| malignant neoplasms | −15% | −2% |

SOURCE: Trends in Indian Health 1997, 2004.

of Urban Indian Health, with board representatives from 34 programs. Some groups developed around professional organizations such as the Association of American Indian Physicians, the national Network of Native Researchers (a group of health-related researchers), and Friends of Indian Health Service, a new IHS advocacy organization.

Political lobbying experiences with the federal government launched other endeavors. California tribes lobbied their state legislature to establish a state Indian health office and to support a network of clinics serving both rural and urban Indians. The state of New York supports health programs for Indians, also.

## Research and Ethics

Much of the early research conducted among tribes did not call for community partnerships, and strict protocols for protection of human subjects also did not exist. The consequences of these research activities have been both positive and negative. Some early recordings and observations are utilized by tribal members, while others are not acknowledged because they are found to be degrading or replete with misinformation. Other abuses include the lack of respect accorded tribal members who not only were key informants but also were not credited for their contributions. Moreover, researchers have not always been motivated to explore questions or problems viewed as important by the tribal communities they studied.

In many American Indian and Eskimo communities, there is a strong resistance to any type of health-related research, and as a result, tribes have established various means to exercise greater control over research projects being proposed or conducted in their communities. Most tribal organizations have established research committees, and the Navajo Nation has a federally recognized Institutional Review Board. The community members serving on these committees or boards are asked by their respective tribes not only to help oversee studies once underway but also initially to review the proposed studies to determine if they will benefit the tribe. Understandably, not all applications are approved. Funding agencies have endorsed this practice by requiring investigators to provide documents indicating approval of their project by the tribes as a part of its proposal review process. Tribal research committees also require investigators to get approval from the tribe before publishing or presenting study results. This role ensures that publications of study results do not perpetuate negative stereotypes or other misinformation as well as inform the tribe about the results of the studies.

In many instances, the active role of tribes in research has also increased the demand for certain research methodologies over others. The community-based participatory research model is among those strongly encouraged. It includes tribes not only in determining research priorities but also in designing the studies as well as assisting with the data collection and analysis. Where tribes have the resources, they have established their own research units to carry out studies requested by the tribe or by governing Indian organizations.

Genetic research proposals are routinely subjected to extra scrutiny by tribes because of their strong resistance to this type of research. In particular, the Human Genome Diversity Project, which sought to understand the genetic variation of human species by sampling DNA of populations worldwide and preserving these cell lines to be studied by future geneticists, was the subject of some concern. Some Indian health advocates and Native researchers believed that future research using these cell lines would be conducted without their permission or patents claimed by researchers who collected the initial samples. Genetic research poses certain difficulties for indigenous peoples: "for people whose life ways and whose very existence are jeopardized by insensitive exploitation, the preservation of their cells bespeaks an almost cynical hereditarianism. The geneticist seemed to expect to look people in the eye and tell them that their DNA means more than their customs, their land, their traditions, and their lives. And then they professed surprise when those people failed to share their priorities" (Marks 1995:72). Native communities are attractive for genetic research, especially those considered isolated and less changed by genetic admixture. One tribe in Arizona, for example, filed a suit against a genetics researcher and her employers (Arizona State University where the researcher was employed at the time when the research was conducted and the University of Arizona, where the researcher is currently employed) for misuse of DNA samples and failing to obtain new consent for conducting a study that went far beyond the original intent of the study (Rubin 2004). To avoid breech of research ethics and foster research partnerships with tribes, some academic institutions have drawn up and implemented memoranda of agreement.

The National Institutes of Health, which has been present since the 1960s at the Phoenix Indian Medical Center in Phoenix, Arizona, conducts diabetes research. Each research project proposed is negotiated with the tribe. Although the scientific knowledge gained from these studies is welcomed internationally, the relationship between the tribe and NIH has had its share of frustrations, mainly because the tribe does not see medical results, that is, a cure (Sevilla 2000). As its partnership continues to develop with the tribe, the National Institutes of Health has now included more research activities that explore diabetes prevention and culturally appropriate interventions.

Not all health-related research being conducted with tribes was harmful. The participation of the Navajos in one clinical trial in the 1950s that tested the use of Isoniazid for treatment of tuberculosis was a significant contribution (Jones 2002). Another clinical trial conducted with the help of the White Mountain Apache Tribe in the 1980s helped prove that Hemophilus Influenza B vaccine can be useful for children (Dr. J. Justice, personal communication 1999). The Strong Heart Study among tribes from four regions of the United States, a longitudinal study on cardiovascular disease, and the Genetics of Coronary Artery Disease in Alaska Natives have contributed significantly to what is known about regional differences and what impact these regional differences have on the progress of heart disease, the impact of diabetes on heart disease, and the impact of familial or genetic factors on heart disease.

The increased burden of chronic diseases that are easily cured by allopathic medicine and by traditional healing practices offered by tribal healers has encouraged some tribal communities to look to the advances in biomedicine and genetic research. For example, one tribe in Arizona (Salt River Pima) awarded one million dollars a year for five years to a biotech firm to focus on diabetes research. Education institutions are implementing programs to increase the

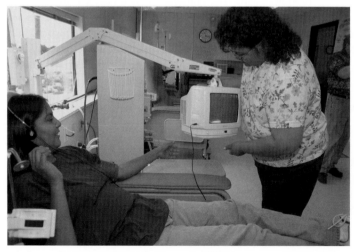
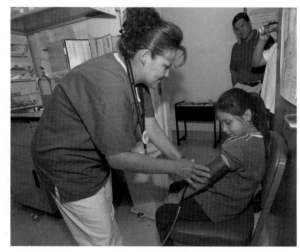

U.S. Dept. of Health and Human Services, Ind. Health Service, Washington: left, 0202; right, 0250.

Fig. 6. Indian Health Service care in the Southwest. left, Nurse preparing a patient for dialysis, N. Mex., 2000. right, Checking blood pressure in a Navajo clinic, N. Mex., 2000.

number of future Indian scientists. A number of tribal community colleges are improving and developing science curricula to encourage students to consider a career in health research. In 2006, the National Cancer Institute and other branches of the National Institutes of Health were funding tribal community colleges to expand their science curricula.

## Conclusion

The 2000 census figures indicate that Indians and Eskimos comprise a young population, but they are more likely to be unemployed or disabled due to chronic health problems. Many are eligible for federal health care provided by Indian Health Service or tribal health programs. Many do not have health insurance or live in cities where access to federal health services is not easy. Where health data are collected, researchers find that significant numbers die from diabetes, heart disease, cancer, accidents, homicide, and suicide, some of which is preventable. Retrospective epidemiological data indicate that major causes of morbidity and mortality for this population have shifted since the second half of the twentieth century from infectious diseases to chronic diseases.

Because the burden of many diseases is disproportionate for Indians and Eskimos, intervention and health promotion programs call for community participation and for tribes to have a management role in their health care delivery systems. Increasing numbers now operate some or all of the health programs once managed by the federal government. In addition, tribes and urban groups are active in research, not only in supporting regional epidemiology centers, but also in charting their own health-related research priorities. Health researchers are partnering with tribal groups or are hired by them to conduct research that benefits the local communities. Today, health promotion and disease prevention undertaken by tribes utilizes models that emphasize culture and language as an important element in decreasing avoidable deaths and illnesses.

# Restoration of Terminated Tribes

GEORGE ROTH

House Concurrent Resolution 108, called the Termination Act, was passed in 1953. Termination meant ending the special federal relationship with the tribes, including recognition of tribal governments and their sovereign powers, protected federal trust status for tribal and individual lands, and housing, health, education and economic programs that were limited to members of federally recognized tribes ("Termination and Relocation," this vol.) In the late 1960s termination was replaced with the policy of self-determination, but the terminated groups had to be restored on a case-by-case basis.

The path to restoration took many years and differing routes, consonant with the varied character of the tribes that had been terminated. The first restoration, of the Menominee in 1973, was followed in the 1977 by Siletz, but it took until the early 1990s for most of the termination acts to be reversed. Most restorations were done legislatively, and their terms reflected the political negotiations that went into the specific restoration. The exception was in California, where most restorations came through court rulings that the legal requirements for termination had not been fulfilled; hence, the terminations were not effective.

In a few instances, terminated tribes petitioned for federal recognition under the Interior Department recognition process but were subsequently legislatively restored (Graton Rancheria and Coos, Lower Umpqua, and Siuslaw). The Interior Department recognition regulations do not allow a tribe terminated by legislation to be administratively restored. One of the mandatory criteria requires that neither the petitioning group nor its members be the subject of congressional legislation that has either expressly terminated or has forbidden the federal relationship (25 USC 83.7(g)). The Department does not have the authority to reverse termination that resulted from an act of Congress nor to recognize a group Congress has legally barred from recognition.

Studies of termination indicated that members of terminated tribes had lost ground economically and educationally, so that that rationale for any further termination was already gone in the 1960s; within this, the groundwork was laid for restoration of terminated tribes. Restoration was aided by increased Indian militancy and the generally increased public support for tribal rights in the 1970s.

The restoration movement was greatly aided by the shift in federal Indian policy away from further termination and toward self-determination that began in 1958. During the administration of President John F. Kennedy, Commissioner of Indian Affairs Philleo Nash resisted congressional pressure to push termination, promoting a policy of developing tribal governments and economies. President Lyndon Johnson in 1968 proposed "ending the debate about termination of Indian programs and substituting self-determination as a goal" (L.B. Johnson 1968). This was followed by President Richard Nixon's self-determination policy. Congress, the original driver of termination, remained termination's strongest proponent, and an opponent of restoration, until the early 1970s. The last termination act was passed in 1964, although termination bills continued to be introduced for some years afterward. In 1971, the Senate officially repudiated the termination policy.

A 1977 policy declaration by the commissioner of Indian affairs advised "in terms of equity, there is little basis for leaving those terminated tribes without Federal recognition (if they want it restored) while the large majority of tribes still enjoy their special status as Indians" (R.V. Butler 1977:8). In practice, the Interior Department supported all restoration legislation, though not necessarily the specific terms of the restorations.

## Restoration of Tribes

Menominee restoration broke the ice, establishing the viability of restoration and addressing some of the questions involved in reversing termination and as well as some of the irreversible changes. The irreversible ones included the status of the former reservation land, which often had changed radically and could not be completely restored to its previous status. In some cases, issues of defining membership in the restored tribe became paramount. Who would govern the restored tribe and how was often critical, as was the extent of jurisdiction the state government would have. Often, the state and local authorities gained more jurisdiction than they had before termination, as part of the price of supporting restoration. Restorations after the rise of Indian gaming have resulted in restrictions or prohibitions on possible gaming by the restored tribe.

The success of the Menominee of Wisconsin in being restored in 1973 paved the way for the eventual restoration of almost all of the terminated tribes. The process by which the tribe developed non-Indian support to reverse termination, the internal conflicts over whether and how to restore, and the issues with non-Indians that had to be resolved illustrate the restoration process throughout the country. There were also some important differences among restorations because of differences in the circumstances of the particular tribe and in the political negotiations leading to restoration.

Menominee, terminated by a 1954 act, with termination effective in 1961, had been chosen for termination in part because the government concluded that its members were relatively acculturated and successful in non-Indian society and because of the successful lumbering operation conducted by the tribe on the extensive woodlands of the reservation. With termination, the Menominee reservation became a new county within Wisconsin. The land and the lumber operation were transferred to Menominee Enterprises, a corporation established with individual Menominee as stockholders.

It quickly became clear that the expectations that the lumbering enterprise would provide sufficient taxes to make the new county government viable economically were wrong (Peroff 2006). Further, Menominee Enterprises was not economically viable because of the tax load and changes in the lumber market. As a result, the enterprise reluctantly began to sell some of the former tribal lands to non-Indian resort developers.

Bureau of Indian Affairs reports as early as 1965 concluded that termination was not producing the economic success and assimilation of Indians that had been the aim of termination (Peroff 2006:220). By 1972, there was strong support for restoration from the Wisconsin legislature and governor and a majority of the state's congressional delegation (Peroff 2006:213). The state supported restoration as it became clear that the new county would require financial support from the state and other authorities. The termination act did not provide federal funding to support the new county or the logging enterprise.

Menominee movements for restoration began as early as 1964, but an effective movement began with the formation of DRUMS (Determination of Rights and Unity for Menominee Stockholders) in the early 1970s. This group, partly based off-reservation, displaced the governing elite which had run the tribe, and, after termination, ran Menominee Enterprises. DRUMS's success lay in part in its ability to sufficiently unify what was a factionally divided tribe and to convince key non-Indian supporters that the tribe really wanted restoration (Peroff 2006:180). Opinion within the tribe was by no means unanimous for restoration, with opposition from the old elite, especially those who had had some economic success after termination. Also, many members did not want to return to the former status as wards of the government and sought a restoration that provided for more self-governance than before termination. On the other hand, the sale of reservation lands to non-Indians helped to create tribal support for the restoration effort.

DRUMS was successful in mobilizing support from non-Indians for restoration, including the League of Women Voters, Common Cause, and the Democratic and Republican party platforms for the election of 1972, as well as national Indian organizations, and some recognized tribes. Linking the issue of Native American rights with civil rights in general appealed to various non-Indian constituencies.

The 1973 restoration act transferred the lands and assets of the Menominee Enterprises corporation back into federal trust. It defined the membership of the tribe, which had been strongly debated within the tribe, established an interim governing body, and detailed who could vote on a new constitution and bylaws. The resolution of these critical issues reflected considerable negotiation by the tribe with the federal government. Finally, the act specified restoration of federal Indian services and defined the powers of the tribal government. The restoration act preserved some rights of the 1,900 non-Indian landowners who had acquired property within Menominee County, including protection of hunting and fishing rights.

The Siletz of Oregon were the second tribe restored, but their restoration came with limitations. The 1977 restoration act deferred reestablishment of a reservation, requiring an extensive study and negotiation with federal agencies and other interests (Siletz Restoration Act, Public Law 95-195). In 1980, additional legislation granted the Siletz a 36-acre site in the town of Siletz and more extensive federal land elsewhere to provide income from timber (Siletz Reservation Act, Public Law 96-340). The most difficult issue for restoration and reestablishing a reservation was hunting and fishing rights. The restoration act specified that it did not restore those rights, reflecting non-Indian opposition and legal cases that had found that the Klamath and Menominee had retained such rights notwithstanding their termination. Finally, the restoration act specified that the state of Oregon would continue to have civil and criminal jurisdiction on the reservation, a key demand of local non-Indians in return for support of restoration (U.S. Congress. Senate 1980, 1980a).

The restoration of Grand Ronde in Oregon in 1983 took a path similar to that of Siletz, requiring a separate, later act to establish a reservation and not restoring tribal hunting and fishing rights (Grand Ronde Restoration Act, Public Law 98-165) (vol. 12:494). As at Menominee, Klamath, and elsewhere, a significant minority opinion within the tribe opposed or did not support restoration. The tribe after termination had continued to meet annually and for other important matters (U.S. Congress. House of Representatives 1983). In 1975, it reorganized under a revised constitution and bylaws and incorporated a nonprofit association to seek restoration.

Unlike some termination acts, the 1954 Klamath termination act effectively envisioned the continued existence of a tribe, specifically protecting the tribe's hunting and fishing rights, and to some degree the water rights of the tribe. The termination act included language indicating the continued existence of at least a limited form of tribal government.

The Klamath had a reservation of originally 880,000 acres, which, like the Menominee's, had large stands of commercial timber. However, they did not have the community lumbering operation of the Menominee and, unlike the Menominee, the Klamath termination act did not make any satisfactory provision for retention of land by the tribe. Although the act's land provisions were complex, they effectively provided for the sale of all of the tribe's valuable land base with the members to receive payment from the proceeds. As implemented, the termination act left no practical means for individual members to retain or purchase substantial forest land, almost all of which eventually became a National Forest or a National Wildlife Refuge.

In 1975 the Klamath Tribe re-established its 1953 constitution and tribal government (U.S. House of Representatives 1986) (vol. 12:462). The tribe began restoration efforts in 1980 and in 1982 adopted a new constitution and by-laws with a 10-member executive committee. By 1986, when they were restored, the Klamath had gained the unanimous support of the Oregon congressional delegation. Well before restoration, with the help of the Native American Rights Fund, the Klamath successfully litigated to protect critical water and hunting and fishing rights, prevailing against the state of Oregon and farmers and other users of the Klamath Basin waters (Haynal 1994; Native American Rights Fund 2001).

Klamath restoration, in 1986, was one of the last, perhaps because of the conflicts over these water, hunting and fishing, or land rights issues. The restoration act did not address these questions except in very general terms, calling for consultation with local and state authorities and consideration of their interests in any land acquisitions or other economic development. Like most other restoration acts, the act defined an area equivalent to a reservation for eligibility for federal Indian services and gave the state civil and criminal jurisdiction over any reservation (Klamath Indian Tribe Restoration Act, Public Law 99-398).

The restoration act did not provide for the immediate restoration of a reservation. A Klamath reservation of 556 acres was established in 1996 (Tiller 2005:898). The Klamath Tribe's comprehensive Economic Self Sufficiency Plan, called for by the restoration act, was submitted to the secretary of the Interior in 2000. The plan emphasized, as the economic foundation, the eventual restoration of most of their former lands as a reservation, as well as provision of health and education services and development of the tribal government.

Tribal structures were sometimes substantially altered by restoration. In Utah, where four small Paiute bands had been terminated, the restoration act restored them as a single tribe, the Paiute Tribe of Utah (Public Law 96-227). The act included a fifth band, the Cedar City Paiute, that had not been terminated but did not have a reservation and whose recognized status at the time of the termination act and later was uncertain. The terminated Klamath Tribe of Oregon had included all the Modocs including those who had been re-

moved to Oklahoma in the nineteenth century. However, Congress restored the Modoc in Oklahoma as a separate tribe in 1978, which remained separate after Klamath restoration.

The last restoration outside California was of the Catawba of South Carolina in 1993. Catawba restoration was delayed because it was simultaneously pursuing land claims against the state and others. The Catawba began efforts in 1976 to negotiate a land claims settlement, with lengthy litigation between 1980 and 1992 (Native American Rights Fund 1984). The threat of further litigation in 1993 helped lead to successful negotiations with the state and legislation that both restored the Catawba and settled the land claim. A complex settlement agreement with South Carolina limited the addition of new reservation lands, the tribe's jurisdiction over its reservation lands, and the forms of gaming allowed (Catawba Indian Tribe of South Carolina Land Claims Settlement Act of 1993, Public Law 103-116; D.B. Miller 1993).

A 1954 act partitioned the ownership of the assets of the Ute Indian Tribe of Utah between the "mixed blood and full blood" members of that tribe and terminated the former. They remained terminated in 2006 (68 U.S. Stat. 868). This unusual approach to termination developed out of conflicts within the reservation community over how to utilize a substantial claims award as well as funds from mineral resources. Those categorized as "mixed bloods" generally sought higher individual payments while the "full bloods" were generally more in favor of using the funds for development of the reservation and also feared the fund would be used by the mixed bloods to gain control of the tribe. The mixed bloods, about 25 percent of the membership then, primarily came from one of the three component bands of the tribe, the Uintah. Under the termination act, they retained a share, as individuals, in the mineral resources of the reservation and in hunting and fishing rights. The Ute Tribe has refused to accept the mixed bloods back into membership. In 2006, a federal judge dismissed a mixed-blood lawsuit seeking either restoration as part of the Ute Tribe or separate tribal recognition.

## California

The 1958 California Rancheria Act (72 U.S. Stat. 619) provided for the termination of the trust relationship for 41 rancherias, which were named in the act. All the rancherias to be terminated were relatively small bands or groups that had been placed on a series of quite small reservations dating from the period between 1907 and 1932 (Office of Federal Acknowledgment 1996).

An August 11, 1964, amendment of the Rancheria Act allowed for any rancheria to be terminated and allowed the lands of rancherias that were unoccupied to be taken out of trust and sold (78 Stat. 390). Termination actions under the 1964 amendment were primarily directed at rancherias that the Bureau of Indian Affairs concluded were uninhabited and for which there was no identifiable band. Some rancherias were unoccupied because they were difficult to live on. Consequently, members of the band for which it was purchased either did not settle there at all or subsequently moved away, sometimes joining another rancheria (Office of Federal Acknowledgment 1996).

Under section 3 of the Rancheria Act, as amended, a series of actions was required before termination could be accomplished. These actions included a land survey, construction or improvement of Indian Bureau roads, and completion of adequate sewage and water supplies. A "distribution plan" set forth how the rancheria land was to be distributed to individual members and in some cases sold or transferred to a community association of the members. Actual termination required a notice in the *Federal Register*, proclaiming the termination and listing the members and their dependents, if any, who were declared terminated.

As of May 2007, 23 of the 41 rancherias listed in the 1958 act had been restored by court decision that declared the termination to have been invalid and three had been restored by legislation (table 1). The Department of the Interior never issued a final termination proclamation for seven other rancherias for which all the actions required under the 1958 act had not been completed. Court rulings and administrative action, such as canceling distribution plans, resulted in recognized status being affirmed or clarified for six of the seven. The seventh became part of another, already recognized tribe. As of July 2006, eight rancherias listed in the 1958 act and terminated had not been restored (table 2).

Two occupied rancherias were terminated under the 1964 amendment, and neither of these has been restored. Actions to terminate four other rancherias under the 1964 amendment were never completed and were abandoned in the 1970s. The land of five unoccupied rancherias was taken out of trust status and sold, there being no defined group to vote on termination, although these are also considered terminated.

Restoration in California, unlike elsewhere, was almost entirely accomplished through litigation that overturned the terminations. Numerous lawsuits had been filed by 1975, mostly with the aid of California Legal Services or other public assistance. Key litigation was *Duncan* v. *Andrus*, which determined in 1977 that the Robinson rancheria had not been legally terminated because the section 3 requirements had not been completed, a fact to which the federal government had stipulated (U.S.D.C., N.D. Calif 1977, 517 F. Suppl. 1). The decision restored both the terminated individuals and the rancheria itself to federal status and set the direction for future litigation settlements. The most far-reaching decision came in the 1983 *Tillie Hardwick* decision, which restored 17 rancherias, again with the concurrence of the Department as far as lack of completion of section 3 requirements (*Tillie Hardwick* v. *U.S.* [U.S.D.C., N.D. Calif.], order 12/22/1983). Other lawsuits resulted in restoration of additional rancherias (table 2). Three tribes unable to be restored through litigation because section 3 requirements were completed were restored through legislation: Paskenta and United Auburn in 1994 and Graton Rancheria in 2000.

**Table 1.   Legislative Restoration of Terminated Tribes**

| Name | Terminated[a] | Restored[b] | Restoration Act |
|---|---|---|---|
| Menominee, Wis. (60 Stat. 250) | 6/17/1954 | 12/22/1973 | 88 U.S. Stat. 770 |
| Confederated Tribes of Siletz Res., Oreg. (68 Stat. 724) | 8/13/1954 | 11/18/1977 | 91 U.S. Stat. 1415 |
| Wyandotte Tribe of Okla. (70 Stat. 893) | 8/1/1956 | 5/15/1978 | 92 U.S. Stat. 247 |
| Ottawa Tribe of Okla. (70 Stat. 963) | 8/3/1956 | 5/15/1978 | 92 U.S. Stat. 247 |
| Peoria Tribe of Okla. (70 Stat. 937) | 8/2/1956 | 5/15/1978 | 92 U.S. Stat. 247 |
| Modoc[c] Okla. (68 Stat. 718) | 8/13/1954 | 5/15/1978 | 92 U.S. Stat. 247 |
| Paiute Indian Tribe of Utah[d] (68 Stat. 1099) | 8/2/1956 | 4/3/1980 | 94 U.S. Stat. 317 |
| Confederated Tribes of Grand Ronde Community, Oreg. (68 Stat. 724) | 8/13/1954 | 11/22/1983 | 97 U.S. Stat. 1064 |
| Confederated Tribes of Coos, Lower Umpqua and Siuslaw, Oreg. (68 Stat. 724) | 8/13/1954 | 10/17/1984 | 98 U.S. Stat. 2250 |
| Klamath Indian Tribe of Oregon (68 Stat. 718) | 8/13/1954 | 8/27/1986 | 100 U.S. Stat. 849, 2095 |
| Alabama-Coushatta Tribes of Texas (68 Stat. 768) | 8/23/1954 | 8/31/1987 | 101 U.S. Stat. 666 |
| Coquille Tribe, Oreg. (68 Stat. 724)[e] | 8/13/1954 | 6/28/1989 | 102 U.S. Stat. 91 |
| Ponca Tribe of Nebr. | 9/15/1962 | 10/31/1990 | 104 U.S. Stat. 1167–70 |
| Catawba Indian Nation, S.C. (73 Stat. 592) | 9/21/1958 | 10/27/1993 | 107 Stat. 1118 |
| United Auburn Indian Community, Calif. (72 Stat. 619) | 8/18/1958 | 10/31/1994 | 103 Stat. 324 |
| Paskenta Band of Nomlaki Indians, Calif. (72 Stat. 619) | 8/18/1958 | 11/2/1994 | 108 U.S. Stat. 4793 |
| Graton Rancheria, Calif. (72 Stat. 619) | 2/18/1966 | 12/27/2000 | 114 U.S. Stat. 2939 |
| Mixed Blood Ute of the Ute Reservation, Utah (68 Stat. 868) | 8/27/1954 | Not restored | |

[a]Actual termination may have occurred later, based on the terms of the act.
[b]Actual restoration may have occurred later, based on the terms of the act.
[c]Was terminated as part of the Klamath Tribe of Oregon.
[d]Restores, as a single tribe, 4 terminated tribes—Shivwitz, Kanosh, Koosharem, and Indian Peaks—and confirms the status of Cedar City Paiute Band.
[e]At the time of termination, this tribe was a faction of the Coos, Lower Umpqua, and Siuslaw. They were not included in the Coos as restored.

**Table 2. Status of Terminated California Rancherias**

| Tribe (Rancheria) | Termination Date | Restoration Date | Authority for Restoration |
|---|---|---|---|
| | *Listed in 1958 Act—Terminated and Restored* | | |
| Auburn (United Auburn) | 1967/08/18 | 1994/10/31 | Act of 10/31/1994 (108 Stat. 4533) |
| Big Valley | 1965/11/11 | 1984/06/11 | *Hardwick* v. *U.S.* (1983) |
| Blue Lake | 1966/09/22 | 1984/06/11 | *Hardwick* v. *U.S.* (1983) |
| Buena Vista | 1961/04/11 | 1984/06/11 | *Hardwick* v. *U.S.* (1983) |
| Chicken Ranch (Jamestown) | 1961/08/01 | 1984/06/11 | *Hardwick* v. *U.S.* (1983) |
| Chico (Mechoopda) | 1967/06/02 | 1992/04/17 | *Scotts Valley* v. *U.S.* (1992) |
| Cloverdale | 1965/12/30 | 1984/06/11 | *Hardwick* v. *U.S.* (1983) |
| Elk Valley | 1966/07/16 | 1984/06/11 | *Hardwick* v. *U.S.* (1983) |
| Graton (Sebastopol) | 1966/02/18 | 2000/12/27 | Act of 12/27/2000 (114 Stat. 2939) |
| Greenville | 1966/12/08 | 1984/06/11 | *Hardwick* v. *U.S.* (1983) |
| Guidiville | 1965/09/03 | 1991/09/06 | *Scotts Valley* v. *U.S.* (1991) |
| Lytton | 1961/08/01 | 1991/09/06 | *Scotts Valley* v. *U.S.* (1991) |
| Mooretown | 1961/08/01 | 1984/06/11 | *Hardwick* v. *U.S.* (1983) |
| Paskenta | 1961/04/11 | 1994/10/31 | Act of 11/2/1994 (108 Stat. 4793) |
| Picayune | 1966/02/18 | 1984/06/11 | *Hardwick* v. *U.S.* (1983) |
| Pinoleville (Ukiah) | 1966/02/18 | 1984/06/11 | *Hardwick* v. *U.S.* (1983) |
| Potter Valley | 1961/08/01 | 1984/06/11 | *Hardwick* v. *U.S.* (1983) |
| Quartz Valley | 1967/01/20 | 1984/06/11 | *Hardwick* v. *U.S.* (1983) |
| Redding (Clear Creek) | 1962/06/20 | 1984/06/11 | *Hardwick* v. *U.S.* (1983) |
| Redwood Valley | 1961/08/01 | 1984/06/11 | *Hardwick* v. *U.S.* (1983) |
| Robinson (East Lake) | 1965/09/03 | 1977/06/29 | *Duncan* v. *Andrus* (1977) |
| Rohnerville (Bear River) | 1966/07/16 | 1984/06/11 | *Hardwick* v. *U.S.* (1983) |
| Scotts Valley (Sugar Bowl) | 1965/09/03 | 1991/09/06 | *Scotts Valley* v. *U.S.* (1991) |
| Smith River | 1967/07/29 | 1984/06/11 | *Hardwick* v. *U.S.* (1983) |
| Table Bluff | 1961/04/11 | 1981/09/21 | *Table Bluff* v. *Watt* (1981) |
| | *Listed in 1958 Act—Terminated and Not Restored* | | |
| Alexander Valley | 1961/08/01 | | |
| Cache Creek[a] | 1961/04/11 | | |
| Indian Ranch Colony | 1964/09/22 | | |
| Mark West | 1961/04/11 | | |
| Nevada City | 1964/09/22 | | |
| Ruffeys (Etna) | 1961/04/11 | | |
| Strawberry Valley | 1961/04/11 | | |
| Wilton | 1964/09/22 | | |
| | *Terminated Under 1964 Act and Not Restored* | | |
| Mission Creek | 1970/07/14 | | |
| Shingle Springs/El Dorado[b] | 1966/07/16 | | |

| | *Listed in 1958 Act—Final Termination Action (Proclamation) Not Taken* | |
|---|---|---|
| *Rancheria for Affirmation of Status* | *Date of Affirmation* | *Authority* |
| Big Sandy (Auberry) | 1984/01/09 | *Big Sandy* v. *Watt* (1983) |
| Cold Springs | 1977/05/31 | Land distribution plan revoked by request. |
| Hopland | 1983/06/22 | *Smith* v. *U.S.* (1982) |
| Middletown | | No termination actions taken. |
| Montgomery Creek | | No termination actions taken. Now part of the Pit River Tribe |
| Table Mountain | 1984/01/09 | *Table Mountain* v. *Watt* (1983) |
| Upper Lake | 1981/07/06 | *Upper Lake* v. *Andrus* (1981) |

| | *1964 Act—Lands Sold as Uninhabited Rancherias* |
|---|---|
| | *Date of Sale of Lands* |
| Colfax | 1965/12/22 |
| Likely[c] | 1965? |
| Lookout (West Parcel)[d] | 1965/11/23 |
| Strathmore | 1967/09/29 |
| Taylorsville | 1966/11/04 |

SOURCE: Office of Federal Acknowledgment, Department of the Interior.
[a]May now be part of Scott's Valley tribe.
[b]Other Shingle Springs is recognized.
[c]Some lands unsold.
[d]East Parcel is part of Pit River Tribe.

Lawsuits concerning termination had begun in the late 1960s, at first only seeking damages or other relief from claimed failure to complete implementation of the Rancheria Act requirements. A 1972 Bureau task force on terminated rancherias concluded that the social condition of the terminated rancherias had in most cases deteriorated (Commissioner of Indian Affairs 1977). The commissioner of Indian affairs in 1975, after a study of the status of the terminated rancherias, concluded that where section 3 requirements had not been fulfilled, termination was not complete (Commissioner of Indian Affairs 1975). The Department changed this position in 1977, concluding that the Department could not reverse a termination where notice had been published without a court ruling on the specific rancheria, such as was issued that year in the Robinson rancheria case.

The extent to which the original rancheria land could be restored varied greatly, and the specific terms by which this could be done were complicated. In some cases, some communal land remained in the hands of an organization of band members, and in some cases at least some members retained as land distributed to them as individuals. In cases where no land remained in Indian hands, after restoration, other lands have been sought and put into trust (e.g., at Chico, where the original rancherias became the site of a college). Lands have been added for rancherias where some of the original land was restored to federal status. Most restored rancherias in 2007 had at least some trust land, with continuing efforts to add more.

Unsuccessful proposals have been made for legislative restoration of additional terminated rancherias. In its 1997 report to Congress, the Advisory Council on California Indian Policy recommended that three terminated rancherias—the Wilton Miwok Indian Community, Federated Indians of the Graton Rancheria, and the Mishewal Wappo Tribe of Alexander Valley—should be immediately restored by Congress and that the others should receive "special consideration when they are ready to seek restoration" (Advisory Council on California Indian Policy 1977; Gover 2000). As of May 2007, only Graton had been restored. In 1999, the Pacific Region of the Bureau of Indian Affairs, working with California Indian Legal Services and the Advisory Council, conducted research and meetings and identified seven rancherias for the Department to support for restoration, two of them unoccupied in 1964 (Risling 1999). Restoration of six other rancherias was not recommended, the study concluding they were unoccupied and in some cases the former residents could not be located or "were not ready for restoration."

Rancheria membership as defined at termination by the specific published lists was limited to the actual adult residents of the rancheria at the time of termination and their dependents. Consequently, the termination rolls were much smaller than the membership of the band when the rancheria was created. The court decisions restoring the rancherias and the settlement agreements implementing them did not address the determination of membership, even though in some cases many or all of the members at the time of termination

had died. Determination of tribal membership of some of the restored rancherias has remained a contentious issue. In some instances, recognition petitions were filed by groups that were part of, or were affiliated with, a terminated rancheria. In a few cases petitioners from the original band, beyond the termination list, have been included in the rancheria as restored and have withdrawn their petition. The Chukchansi Yokotch (Yokuts) petition was withdrawn after its members were included in the restored Picayune Rancheria.

In 1956, legislation anticipating the 1958 California Rancheria Act granted a fee patent of a portion of the Lower Lake rancheria to the one occupant and the sale of the rest of the land (70 U.S. Stat. 58). The rancheria was purchased for the Lower Lake Band in 1917 but was not occupied until two individuals moved there in 1947. There was little record that the United States had a relationship with a Lower Lake band after the 1930s. The assistant secretary for Indian affairs in 2000 concluded on the basis of a limited historical study that there was a Lower Lake Band extant (now the Koi Nation), that its relationship with the United States had not been terminated by the 1947 act, and that the facts warranted his "reaffirmation" of its relationship with the United States (Gover 2000).

## Nonreservation Western Oregon Populations

The Western Oregon Termination Act of 1954, in addition to terminating the federal relationship with the Grand Ronde and Siletz tribes, forbade the federal relationship for other Indians in western Oregon. The act included the names of 58 tribes and bands as well as a general clause terminating any other Indians west of the Cascade Mountains. These two clauses were included because of some uncertainty about what federal obligations and Indian rights existed in western Oregon beyond the two named reservations. Agency censuses at the time of termination and before had included a substantial number of nonreservation Indians, some of whom had received individual allotments outside the reservations. In the late nineteenth and early twentieth centuries, at least some members of the numerous small bands that originally made up the Indian population of the area had not removed to the multitribal Siletz and Grand Ronde reservations, or had left again. The list of 58 bands was, however, a list of the bands extant in the 1850s rather than bands that existed in 1954 (Bureau of Indian Affairs 1988).

The Indian agency in general did not have much of a relationship with the nonreservation Indians but some received services such as education and relocation during the termination era and were considered terminated. With one exception, at Coos Bay, the agency did not deal with or identify groups within this population at the time of termination (Bureau of Indian Affairs 1988).

In 1984, the Congress restored the federal relationship to the Coos, Lower Umpqua, and Siuslaw Tribe, centered at

Coos Bay, Oregon. A parcel of trust land had been acquired for this group in 1940, although the land was not declared a reservation. The group split in the late 1950s, with families who also had descent from the Coquille tribe breaking away as a result of seeking a separate claims payment (Bureau of Indian Affairs 1988). The Coquille group was not included in the Coos tribe that was restored, but it was recognized by Congress in 1989 as a separate tribe.

Another group drawn at least in part from this nonreservation population, which had not been recognized as a tribe in 1954, subsequently sought federal status as the Cow Creek Umpqua Tribe. The Interior Department originally opposed this legislation, raising questions about the group's historical connection with the historical Cow Creek Umpqua listed in the 1954 act, though it subsequently agreed not to oppose recognition (Sampsel 1982, 1982a; Tallmadge 2002). Legislation recognized them in 1982 as the descendants of that band and also settled their land claims. A group petitioning as the Tchinouk Indians, who were drawn from the non-reservation population, were declined recognition administratively because they could not demonstrate tribal existence, as well as being ineligible because of the termination act's ban on a federal relationship (Assistant Secretary of Indian Affairs 1985).

### Recognition of Formerly Recognized Tribes without Reservations

The termination laws and policies of the 1950s were primarily concerned with reservation tribes whose federal relationship would be terminated through legislation. However, the termination polices also changed the federal government's view of its responsibility to recognized tribes without reservations. A changed interpretation of federal responsibility toward such tribes led to the loss of federal recognition of several nonreservation recognized tribes. The change in policy was explained by the Bureau's director for its Northwest region in 1955, when he recommended that federal responsibility be viewed from the perspective of obligations connected with ownership of trust land, that is, a reservation, and not on the basis of "tribes, treaty tribal groupings, etc. not connected with the land" (D.C. Foster 1955).

In western Washington, five nonreservation tribes lost recognition (vol. 7:177–179). Although the Nooksack and Skagit-Suiattle had both voted in 1935 to come under the provision of the Indian Reorganization Act, an indication of recognition (Haas 1947:10), the Nooksack were told by the Department in 1947 that they were not under the Act (Gershuny 1971). Neither they nor the Skagit-Suiattle remained recognized by 1961. The Nooksack were administratively recognized again in the early 1970s, as were the Skagit-Suiattle, who were then organized as two separate tribes, the Upper Skagit and the Sauk-Suiattle ("Recognition," this vol.). However, the Jamestown S'Klallam and Snoqualmie, also in western Washington, who had been recognized before 1952, did not regain recognition until later, through the Interior Department's recognition process established in 1978.

The Death Valley Timbi-Sha (Western) Shoshone of California were similarly recognized as a non-reservation tribe until the early 1950s and became recognized again in 1983 through the recognition process. The Louisiana Coushatta had been extended federal services in the 1930s, but they had no reservation. In 1953 the Interior Department determined them to be outside the scope of Indian Service responsibilities, although failing to get their agreement for a termination resolution. In 1973, the Bureau reviewed their recognition request and concluded that they were eligible for the services of a recognized tribe (vol. 14:409).

### Iroquois

Although never officially terminated, the New York Iroquois by the end of the 1950s had only limited federal services and supervision, in part due to termination era policies (Taylor 1972:188; U.S. Congress. House of Representatives 1953:16, 36). The Iroquois reservations were considered to be state as well as federal reservations, an unusual dual status whose history facilitated efforts, characteristic of termination, to transfer responsibility for tribes to the states (Taylor 1972:79, 141). A 1950 act transferred court jurisdiction to state courts. The underlying treaty obligations and federal trust status of the land were never terminated, and in the 1960s the Bureau under Commissioner Nash administratively reaffirmed the federal relationship and eligibility for federal services.

# Recognition

GEORGE ROTH

Beginning in the 1960s, there were increased efforts by groups without federal status to seek recognition as Indian tribes. Supporting this was the growth of federal Indian self-determination policies, the civil rights movement, and increased resources, from new federal programs for minorities and poor people to develop their organizations. Significant roles were played by Indian movements seeking land claims and restoration of treaty rights, which became increasingly active in the 1960s, accelerating in the 1970s.

## Recognition and Tribal Political Existence

Federal recognition is not about whether a group is Indian, or has a traditional culture, or can demonstrate Indian ancestry. While these may be the basis of eligibility for various private, state, and even some federal programs, recognition by the federal government means recognition of status as a semisovereign entity, entitled to a government-to-government relationship with the United States and, at least in part, distinct from the state within which the tribe is located.

Many of the groups seeking federal recognition are not "tribes" by any definition, let alone groups which could be legally sustained as a distinct political community and thus entitled to federal recognition. Some may be "tribes" in an ethnological sense, without being able to demonstrate the necessary historical continuity as a political community. Groups seeking recognition come from all areas of the country and from widely varying Indian cultures. These groups are as small as 150 members and as large as 55,000. Some are centered around distinct settlements occupied only by the group's members, while others are widely scattered. They range from relatively traditional bands to distinct communities with over 300 years of close contact with non-Indians who have not maintained traditional culture. And they include not only groups of a common tribal ancestry but also voluntary organizations of socially unaffiliated individuals with no history and no Indian ancestry.

The definitions of tribe used by federal courts and the Department of the Interior derive from earlier executive branch actions, including treaties and other dealings with Indian tribes, and from a long series of legal cases that have dealt with the rights and status of tribes and, consequently, what the definition was of an Indian tribe.

The definition of Indian tribe in the 1901 *Montoya* v. *United States* decision (180 U.S. 261, 268, 1901) has been influential. *Montoya* described a tribe as composed of Indians of common ancestry, united in a community with a single leadership or government, and presently inhabiting or having historically inhabited a particular territory. The law at issue, on Indian "depredations," required distinguishing between tribes, as relatively permanent political bodies, and fluid and temporary groups that may have been responsible for attacks on non-Indians.

Another line of cases established the fundamental legal view that the unique status of Indian tribes rested on the fact that Indian tribes maintained separate political and social existences (Roth 2001). This view was first established in the 1832 Supreme Court decision in *Worcester* v. *Georgia* (31 U.S. (6 Pet.) 515). The court stated that Indian tribes were "domestic dependent nations," within the borders of the United States and under its control, but not part of it. Later court decisions, following *Worcester*, referred to Indian tribes as "distinct political communities" (Department of the Interior 1894). Some cases concerned whether a tribe had dissolved as a political community and become assimilated (*Kansas Indians,* 72 U.S. (5 Wallace) 737 [1866]).

A tribe existed as long as its members as a whole kept up a political relationship with each other, that is, "maintained tribal relations." The legal interpretation was that the federal government had no responsibility for groups whose members had assimilated into non-Indian society, were no longer a distinct community, and no longer followed a tribal leadership, because they were considered to have "given up tribal relations" (L.B. Smith 1906:725). This held even if there had been federal recognition of the tribe in the past (*Elk* v. *Wilkins*, 112 U.S. 94 [1884] 104).

In order for a group of Indians to be a federally recognized as an Indian tribe between the 1830s and the 1970s, it was necessary that the federal government considered that the tribe existed as a distinct political community and also that the federal government had taken a specific action that acknowledged that it had a political relationship with a particular tribe and a responsibility for it.

Some tribes in the 13 original states had come under colonial control before the United States became independent and had never established a relationship with the federal government. The federal government from the 1830s or earlier held that it had never accepted jurisdiction or responsibility for them, that their members had become citizens of the states (W.A. Jones 1899), and that, having substantially lost their powers of self-government, "the laws of the state have been extended over them for the protection of their persons and property" (*Worcester* v. *Georgia* concurring opinion of Justice McLean, 31 U.S. [6 Pet.] 1832 at 582–3).

In 1975, a federal court decision in *Passamaquoddy* v. *Morton* (528 F.2d 370 (1st Cir. 1975)), a land claims suit, held that the 1834 and earlier Non-Intercourse Acts had established a federal trust responsibility for all tribes. Contrary to the government's past policy and past court decisions, there was no requirement to show a specific act recognizing a tribe in order for the Non-Intercourse Act to apply. (The Non-Intercourse Acts required federal approval of the sale of the land of Indian tribes to non-Indians.) This left the need to determine which of the many unrecognized claimants were historical tribes, that is, political communities that had existed historically and continued to exist. Based on this principle, the Department of the Interior (*Federal Register* 1978) established by federal regulations the administrative process for tribal recognition. The regulations established a particular definition of tribal existence based on the core ideas of social community, political influence, and historical continuity of tribal existence from past legal and policy precedents.

## Decisions in the Late 1960s and Early 1970s

A number of groups made efforts in the 1960s to become recognized, and more did so in the early 1970s. Motivations, besides land claims and treaty rights, included economic development and affirmation of identity as Indian. One important motivation for a substantial number of groups in the South to seek recognition was to support a clearly distinct third status in the two-part racial classification. These groups' efforts to maintain a distinct status as Indian long predated the 1960s, focusing mostly, but not exclusively, on the local and state level (Lerch 1992; Paredes 1992).

In 1967, the Burns Paiute of Oregon were recognized (table 1), reversing a 1946 Interior Department legal opinion that they did not form a tribe that could be organized as a tribal government under the Indian Reorganization Act of 1934 (Department of the Interior 1967). The 1967 decision found substantial evidence of federal treatment as a band under federal jurisdiction within the preceding several decades.

Five additional groups were recognized as tribes by the Department of the Interior between 1971 and 1973, after fairly limited reviews by the Department. All were groups for which there was good evidence of prior federal recognition, most of it within the previous 30 years, and evidence in the record that the group had continued to exist as a distinct

**Table 1. Tribes Recognized 1961–2006 by Administrative Recognition Other than the Code of Federal Regulations**

Burns Paiute Indian Colony of Oregon
    Solicitor's opinion M-36799, 12/16/67
Nooksack Tribe of Washington
    Solicitor's opinion M-36833, 8/13/71
Upper Skagit Indian Tribe of Washington
    Deputy commissioner's letter of 6/9/72
Sauk-Suiattle Indian Tribe of Washington
    Deputy commissioner's letter of 6/972
Coushatta Tribe of Louisiana
    Assistant secretary letters, 6/27/73 and 6/13/73; memo from acting director of Indian services
Original Band of Sault Ste. Marie Chippewa Indians of Michigan
    Commissioner of Indian affairs letter, 9/7/72; solicitor opinion of 2/27/74
Passmaquoddy Tribe of Maine
    Based on federal court order of 12/23/75 in *Passamaquoddy* v. *Morton* (528 F. 2d 370 [1st Cir. 1975])
Penobscot Tribe of Maine
    Based on federal court order of 12/23/75 in *Passamaquoddy* v. *Morton* (528 F. 2d 370 [1st Cir. 1975])
Stillaguamish Tribe of Washington
    Acting secretary of the Interior letter 10/27/1976; regional solicitor opinion 4/4/79
Karuk Tribe of California
    Assistant secretary of Indian affairs letter of 1/2/79
Jamul Indian Village of California
    Designation by secretary as half-blood Indian community, 7/8/81
Ione Band of Miwok Indians of California
    Assistant secretary of Indian affairs letter of 3/22/94
Lower Lake Band of California
    Assistant secretary of Indian affairs action, 12/29/2000
Shoonaq on Kodial I., Alaska
    Assistant secretary of Indian affairs action 12/29/2000
King Salmon on the Naknek R., Alaska
    Assistant secretary of Indian affairs action 12/29/2000

and identifiable community. Four of these tribes, the Nooksack (Gershuny 1971), Upper Skagit, and Sauk-Suiattle of Washington and the Coushatta of Louisiana were nonreservation tribes that had lost recognition during the termination era of the 1950s (see "Restoration of Terminated Tribes," this vol.).

The Sault Sainte Marie Chippewa of Michigan were recognized in 1972 by administrative action that provided for land to be taken into trust and the group to be organized under the Indian Reorganization Act (Commissioner of Indian Affairs 1972). This group was closely related to the Ojibwa resident on the Bay Mills Reservation, who were organized as a tribe in the 1930s exclusive of related band members resident off-reservation. The 1972 decision was based in part on their continuous historical functioning as a band, residence on land held in trust for Bay Mills, and ancestry tracing to a 1910 federal claims payment roll (the Durant roll). The recognition was upheld after a court chal-

114

ROTH

lenge, which noted that the 1979 decision in the *United States* v. *Michigan* treaty fishing case had identified them as a successor to the Chippewa signatories to the 1855 Michigan Ottawa-Chippewa treaty (*City of Sault Ste. Marie* v. *Andrus*, 532 F. Supp. 157 [DDC 1980], aff'd, 672 F.2d 893 [D.C. Cir. 1981]).

The Louisiana Coushatta had been extended federal services in the 1930s and between 1941 and 1951 were provided medical and other services (U.S. Congress. House of Representatives 1952:1248). In 1953, the Interior Department determined the Coushatta to be outside the scope of Indian Service responsibilities, in part because no reservation had been established (R.V. Butler 1973). In 1973, the Bureau of Indian Affairs conducted research in response to a Coushatta request for services and concluded that they were eligible for the services of a recognized tribe. The decision cited the maintenance of self-government and traditional language and the past federal relationship as the basis for being restored. Other requests before the mid-1970s were denied or rejected without a detailed review. Some of these groups have gained recognition.

### Effects of Litigation

#### Land Claims

Beginning in the 1970s, unrecognized groups increasingly sought through litigation to win claims for land losses as well as to regain rights under treaties. Successful claims required demonstrating continuous historical tribal existence, but, at this point, did not also require federal recognition. There were different ideas about the appropriate definition of tribe and what was evidence sufficient to demonstrate tribal existence. The *Passamaquoddy* court ruling and a subsequent one concerning Mashpee strengthened an emphasis on historical continuity in determining tribal existence, requiring that the group making land claims be a tribe not just now but at the time of the Non-Intercourse Act, and in between. A 1974 Supreme Court decision concerning the Oneida, a recognized tribe, had held that, contrary to past federal policies and court decisions, the Non-Intercourse Acts applied within the 13 original states (Brodeur 1985:86).

The 1975 *Passamaquoddy* decision, which was extended to the Penobscot of Maine, resulted in their recognition. The legal effort was spearheaded by Thomas Tureen, who was affiliated with the nonprofit legal aid organization, Pine Tree Legal Assistance. Subsequent lengthy negotiations with the federal government and Maine resulted in the 1980 federal Maine Indian Claims Act, which provided for a final land settlement agreement with the state (Brodeur 1985:109, 115–117).

The *Oneida* and *Passamaquoddy* decisions soon resulted in other land claims suits by unrecognized East coast groups. However, in the Maine case the federal government had

stipulated that the Passamaquoddy and Penobscot were Indian tribes for purposes of the Non-Intercourse act, based on a review by the Department of their history, influenced in part by their historically continuous state recognition and state reservation dating to colonial times. Subsequent land claims suits by unrecognized groups proceeded without this stipulation and without federal participation, requiring a determination of tribal existence.

In 1976, the Mashpee of Cape Cod, Massachusetts, filed suit for the loss of tribal lands. The judge ruled that the Mashpee had to first establish that they had continued to exist as a tribe before the merits of the claim of lost lands could be considered. The case was tried before a jury, with 40 days of expert testimony.

The Mashpee court took into account the difficulty of an unrecognized group maintaining the kinds of political powers that an Indian tribe still independent of the United States might have. The judge's instructions to the jury effectively required only some significant degree of political influence be retained. At the same time, the case as tried focused substantially on the Mashpee's adoption of non-Indian cultural forms and marriage with non-Indians, effectively linking cultural assimilation with abandonment of tribal relations (Brodeur 1985:43–46; Campisi 1991:39–46). The jury was asked to determine if the Mashpee existed as a tribe at certain specific historical dates. It concluded that it was a tribe at some points but not at others and thus had not met the requirement to have existed continuously as a tribe. In 2007 the Department of the Interior recognized the Mashpee, concluding that the tribe had existed continuously since contact.

The outcome of the Mashpee trial discouraged unrecognized groups from further pursuing their claims in court, encouraging them and the states to negotiate settlements (Brodeur 1985:5). After initiating litigation, the Narragansett (filed in 1976), Gayhead Wampanoag (1974), and Mohegan (1980) chose to seek recognition administratively, eventually negotiating agreements with the respective states and localities concerning land claims. Federal legislation implementing settlement agreements for Gayhead and Mohegan took effect after they became recognized administratively. In 1983, the Western Pequot (Mashantucket), over initially strong executive branch opposition, were able to gain legislation that both recognized them federally and implemented a claims settlement.

#### Treaty Rights

In the 1970s, recognized status and the definition of tribal existence were also at issue in Washington as a result of the 1974 treaty fishing rights decision in *United States* v. *State of Washington* (384 F. Suppl. 312). The court concluded that the Treaty of Point Elliott and related treaties gave the signatory Indian tribes rights to harvest half of the fish in the Puget Sound area (vol. 7:176–178).

Several unrecognized groups were allowed to intervene and one, the Stillaguamish, remained unrecognized after the decision. The Stillaguamish in April 1974 petitioned the Department for recognition, based on the decision and on the materials filed in *United States* v. *State of Washington*. In 1976, the Department concluded that the Stillaguamish should be dealt with as a tribe because the 1974 decision had ruled they had treaty rights and thus the Department had a trust obligation to protect these rights (Frizzell 1976a).

In 1975, the Interior Department established a moratorium on federal recognition to consider the nature and extent of the Interior secretary's authority to extend recognition to Indian tribes, and, if there was such authority, what the appropriate criteria should be (Frizzell 1976). The moratorium was in response to other unrecognized claimants seeking inclusion under *United States* v. *State of Washington* as well as requests for recognition from elsewhere in the country. Congress and some recognized tribes expressed concern about extension of treaty rights to more groups and the bases for extending federal recognition.

Five unrecognized groups in 1974 sought to intervene in *United States* v. *State of Washington*, based on claims to be the social and political continuation of various treaty tribes, and in 1975 they petitioned the Department to recognize them. The United States and the recognized Tulalip Tribes opposed the intervention request. A federal judge ruled in 1979 that none was a political successor-in-interest to the treaty signers and had not lived as continuous, separate, distinct and cohesive Indian cultural or political communities (*United States* v. *State of Washington*, 476 F. Supp. 1101, 1105–1110) (W.D. Wash. 1979).

Federal recognition was held to be a requirement to exercise treaty rights (*United States* v. *State of Washington*, 641 F.2d at 1371). The Ninth Circuit Court of Appeals in 1981 rejected this particular conclusion, but, reviewing the evidence concerning tribal existence, found that none of the five had continued to exist as tribes and thus were not entitled to treaty rights. The court rejected the argument that simply "because their ancestors belonged to treaty tribes, the appellants benefited from a presumption of continuing existence." The court further defined as a single, necessary, and sufficient condition for the exercise of treaty rights, that Indian tribes must have functioned since treaty times as "continuous separate, distinct Indian cultural or political communities" (*United States* v. *State of Washington*, 641 F.2d 1368. 1372–1374 (9th Circuit 1981)). The five were subsequently reviewed under the recognition regulations (table 2). Two were recognized (Samish in 1996 and Snoqualmie in 1999), two were denied (Duwamish in 2002 and Snohomish in 2004), and one has a proposed finding to deny recognition (Steilacoom in 2000). Although the five groups had been active for many years and tended to be viewed as equivalent, the recognition review found that they varied greatly. The Department's decisions were based on a much more extensive body of evidence than the courts'.

After the Maine cases and when extending recognition to the Stillaguamish the Department further reviewed the federal relationship with these previously unrecognized tribes.

The Department concluded that federal legal obligations from these recognitions, initially for purposes arising from the Non-Intercourse Act and treaty fishing rights, provided the basis under existing federal laws for the full status and federal services of any recognized tribe (Frizzell 1976a).

## The Recognition Process

In late 1973, Sen. Henry Jackson of Washington and others in Congress began inquiries into the bases for tribal recognition as a result of the increasing litigation and requests for recognition (Butler 1974; H. Jackson 1973). In 1975, Congress established the American Indian Policy Review Commission (AIPRC) to review federal Indian laws and policies of all kinds. Their final report opposed the Interior Department view that Indian services were only for the recognized tribes, citing certain statutes such the 1921 Snyder Act, and recommended a congressional resolution affirming "Congress' intention to recognize all Indian tribes as eligible for the benefits and protections of general Indian legislation and directing the executive branch to serve all Indian tribes" (AIPRC 1977:480). The report recommended establishment of an office independent of the Bureau of Indian Affairs to review petitions for federal recognition (AIPRC 1977:482). The recommended criteria for recognition set a substantially lower standard than the regulations being developed by the Interior Department at the same time.

Congress did not adopt the Commission recommendations but in 1977 and 1978 considered legislation to establish a recognition process. Ultimately, the congressional committees agreed the Department would establish its administrative process through regulations, without the enactment of legislation specifying procedures and requirements (Bee 1982:114–116).

### Administrative Process

The Department of the Interior established the current administrative process for tribal recognition in October 1978 (Title 25 *Code of Federal Regulations*, Part 83). The Department issued the regulations after extensive comment from and consultation with Congress, recognized tribes, unrecognized groups, Indian organizations, states, and attorneys representing Indian interests. The 1978 regulations required the Department of the Interior to publish in the *Federal Register* a list of those tribes recognized by the United States. This annual publication provides a legal notice of which tribes are recognized and, by exclusion, which groups are not (Department of the Interior 2005).

The recognition process is housed in the Interior Department because it is the lead federal agency for Indian affairs. The process is carried out under the secretary of the Interior's general authority to administer Indian affairs and to promulgate regulations to facilitate that administration

**Table 2. Groups Recognized and Denied Through the Recognition Regulations**

| Name | Effective Date | Membership |
|---|---|---|
| *Recognized* | | |
| Grand Traverse Band of Ottawa and Chippewa, Mich. | 5/27/80 | 297 |
| Jamestown S'Klallam Tribe, Wash. | 2/10/81 | 175 |
| Tunica-Biloxi Indian Tribe, La. | 9/25/81 | 200 |
| Death Valley Timbi-Sha Shoshone Band, Calif. | 1/3/83 | 199 |
| Narragansett Indian Tribe, R.I. | 4/11/83 | 1,170 |
| Poarch Band of Creeks, Ala. | 8/10/84 | 1,470 |
| Wampanoag Aguinnah, Mass. | 4/11/87 | 521 |
| San Juan Southern Paiute Tribe, Ariz. | 3/28/90 | 188 |
| Mohegan Indian Tribe, Conn. | 5/14/94 | 972 |
| Jena Band of Choctaw, La. | 8/29/95 | 189 |
| Huron Potawatomi Inc., Mich. | 3/17/96 | 602 |
| Samish Indian Tribe, Wash. | 4/26/96 | 590 |
| Match-E-Be-Nash-She-Wish Band of Potawatomi Indians, Mich. | 8/23/99 | 143 |
| Snoqualmie Indian Tribe, Wash. | 10/6/99 | 313 |
| Cowlitz Tribe of Indians, Wash. | 1/4/02 | 1,517 |
| Mashpee Wampanoag, Mass. | 5/23/07 | 1,453 |
| *Denied* | | |
| Lower Muskogee Creek Tribe-East of the Mississippi, Ga. | 12/21/81 | 1,041 |
| Creeks East of the Mississippi, Fla. | 12/21/81 | 2,696 |
| Munsee-Thames River Delaware, Colo. | 1/3/83 | 34 |
| Principal Creek Indian Nation, Ala. | 6/10/85 | 324 |
| Kaweah Indian Nation, Calif. | 6/10/85 | 1,530 |
| United Lumbee Nation of NC and America, Calif. | 7/2/85 | 1,321 |
| Southeastern Cherokee Confederacy, Ga. | 11/25/85 | 823 |
| Northwest Cherokee Wolf Band, Oreg. | 11/25/85 | 609 |
| Red Clay Inter-tribal Indian Band, Tenn. | 11/25/85 | 87 |
| Tchinouk Indians, Oreg. | 3/17/86 | 304 |
| MaChis Lower Alabama Creek Indian Tribe, Ala. | 8/22/88 | 275 |
| Miami Nation of Indians of Ind. Inc., | 8/17/92 | 4,381 |
| Ramapough Mountain Indians, Inc., N.J. | 1/7/98 | 2,500 |
| Mowa Band of Choctaw, Ala. | 11/26/99 | 4,000 |
| Yuchi Tribal Organization, Okla. | 3/21/2000 | 327 |
| Duwamish Indian Tribe, Wash. | 5/8/2002 | 356 |
| Chinook Indian Tribe/Chinook Nation, Wash. | 7/5/2002 | 1,566 |
| Muwekma Ohlone Tribe of San Francisco Bay, Calif. | 12/16/2002 | 419 |
| Nipmuc Nation, Mass. | decision: 6/25/04[a] | 526 |
| Webster/Dudley Band of Chaubunagungamaug Nipmuck Indians, Mass. | decision 6/25/04[a] | 357 |
| Snohomish Tribe of Indians, Wash. | 3/5/04 | 1,113 |
| Golden Hill Paugussett Tribe, Conn. | 3/18/05 | 108 |
| Eastern Pequot Indians of Conn. | 10/14/05 | 1,004 |
| Paucatuck Eastern Pequot Indians, Conn. | 10/14/05 | 144 |
| Schaghticoke Tribal Nation, Conn. | 10/14/05 | 271 |
| Burt Lake Band of Ottawa and Chippewa, Mich. | 1/3/07 | 320 |

NOTE: Pending cases and cases with only proposed findings have not been listed.

SOURCE: Office of Federal Acknowledgment (2007a)

[a]Decision not final; pending as of 8/1/2006.

(25 U.S.C. 9, 25 U.S.C. 2, and 43 U.S.C. 1457). There is no specific legislation authorizing the recognition process or providing definitions and procedures. The federal courts have upheld the recognition process and the Department's authority to issue the recognition regulations (*Miami Nation of Indiana* v. *Babbitt*, 887 F. Supp. 1158 (N.D. Ind. 1995));

*James* v. *United States Department of Health and Human Services* (824 F.2d 1132 (D.C. Cir. 1987)).

The regulations require that a group seeking federal recognition demonstrate that it has existed as a distinct political community continuously from first sustained contact with Europeans until the present and thus maintained a degree of political sovereignty, without a break. It may not be a group that came into existence after the beginning of European settlement.

The regulations break this requirement into seven criteria, all of which must be demonstrated in order for a petitioner to be recognized (25 C.F.R. 83.7). The two central criteria require that the petitioner demonstrate that it has exercised political influence or authority within the group throughout its history (83.7(c)) and that it has remained a distinct social community throughout history (83.7(b)). Both criteria may be demonstrated by a wide variety of evidence, through both formal and informal institutions and social relationships. A petitioner may have evolved from several tribes or bands that combined historically or be a portion of a tribe that divided historically. The regulations require that external observers, such as a state, scholar, or other tribe have identified the petitioner as an Indian entity from 1900 until the present (83.7(a)).

Another important criterion requires that the petitioner submit a list of all its members and demonstrate that the members are the descendants of a specific tribe that existed historically or tribes that historically combined (83.7(e)). Miscellaneous tribal ancestry would not qualify. The petitioning group must supply a copy of its governing document, if any, or otherwise describe how it governs itself and its criteria for membership (83.7(d)). The membership definition and lists and evidence used to trace tribal ancestry serve as tools to track and evaluate social organization and social relations, including a group's definition of itself and who has affiliated with or become not affiliated with it. They are not used as a biological measure of Indianness or even Indian ancestry. Although petitioners must demonstrate ancestry from the historical tribe, they are not required to demonstrate a particular degree of Indian ancestry. Tribes have been recognized that have substantial historical and present intermarriage with Caucasians as well as with Blacks.

To be recognized under the regulations, a petitioner must be a tribe whose territory at the time of first sustained contact with Europeans was at least partly within the present boundaries of the continental United States (83.1). Hawaii, Puerto Rico, and territories are not included under the regulations.

Other important concerns are addressed by the remaining two criteria. One criterion requires that the membership of the group be composed principally of persons who are not members of any federally recognized Indian tribe (83.7(f)). This requirement seeks to avoid recognition of groups that in the present day want to separate from recognized tribes. It does not preclude recognition of groups that may be included on a recognized tribe's roll but clearly have maintained a separate existence. The last criterion requires that neither the group nor its members be the subject of congressional legislation that has expressly terminated or forbidden the federal relationship. The Department does not have the authority to reverse termination that resulted from an act of

Congress nor to recognize a group Congress has legally barred from recognition (83.7(g)).

The Department's process refers to "acknowledgment" as a tribe rather than "recognition," stating that the government acknowledges that a particular petitioner "exists as a tribe within the meaning of Federal law." This reflects the Department's view of its authority to recognize Indian tribes, based in part on the 1975 *Passamaquoddy* decision, that it is acknowledging a pre-existing but unrecognized relationship with any American Indian group that qualifies as an Indian tribe, rather than establishing a relationship for the first time.

The regulations did not adopt the assimilation concept, which was part of the examination of tribal existence in the Mashpee trial. The regulations treat the existence of distinct cultural traditions as evidence a distinct community has been maintained but do not require it. Recognition decisions have noted that a group may adopt non-Indian customs as a way to preserve the group's integrity. For example, the March 2007 Mashpee recognition concluded that a distinct community with political processes continued to exist, although a distinct culture had not been maintained (ASIA 2006a). The Mashpee adopted and utilized non-Indian governmental forms, starting with a seventeenth-century "praying town," an English-style community instigated by a missionary and between 1870 and the early 1970s controlled the governmental institutions of the town of Mashpee, which formally was like any other Massachusetts town.

The recognition regulations were revised in 1994, based on the Department's experience since 1978 and criticisms and comments from unrecognized groups, recognized tribes, Indian legal rights organizations, state governments, individual attorneys, and anthropologists and other scholars (Department of the Interior 1994). Substantial changes were made to streamline both the development of evidence by petitioners and its evaluation by the Department.

The revisions maintained the same standards for demonstrating tribal existence, and the same criteria, while clarifying requirements and definitions. The revised regulations provided detailed examples of evidence for the critical community and political influence criteria and defined the standard of proof as a "reasonable likelihood" of the validity of facts concerning that criterion (83.6(d)). An enhanced and more independent appeal process was added as well as a formal meeting to explain proposed findings. The revisions also adjusted timelines to more realistically reflect how the process was operating.

A major change allowed petitioners who could show that they had evolved from a tribe that was federally recognized at a previous point in history to demonstrate tribal existence only from the point of last unambiguous federal recognition until the present (83.8) rather than from first sustained European contact. In one such case, the Snoqualmie only had to demonstrate tribal existence from 1953 to the present.

A change was made to reduce the amount of work to review petitioners that had little or no evidence that they met certain of the criteria (83.10(e)). The revised regulations provide that if a preliminary review showed clearly either that a petitioner could not meet criteria 83.7(e) re ancestry, 83.7(f) re portion of a recognized tribe or 83.7(g) re legislative termination, then the petition need only be reviewed on that single criterion. The Mowa Choctaw of Alabama were found not to have ancestry from the historical Choctaw tribe nor from other tribes (83.7(e) (ASIA 1997). The Yuchi petitioner was rejected in part because its members were enrolled in and participating politically in the recognized Muscogee Creek Nation, even though ethnically distinct from the Creek (83.7(f)) (ASIA 1999a).

*Review Process*

Recognition decisions are made by the assistant secretary of the Interior for Indian affairs. Until July 2003 recognition decisions were prepared by the Branch of Acknowledgment and Research, within the Bureau of Indian Affairs. In 2003, that office was moved out of the Bureau and placed in the Office of the Assistant Secretary of the Department of the Interior. The recognition office, now called the Office of Federal Acknowledgment, reviews petitions using professional researchers from three disciplines: history, anthropology, and genealogy. In April 2006, the office had 12 permanent professional staff, four from each discipline. The Department's position has been that the recognition evaluation process is necessarily deliberate, detailed, fact-based, and thorough because recognition establishes a perpetual government-to-government relationship with the United States and to protect the rights of Indian tribes by only extending recognition to tribes existing continually as political bodies.

Development of the necessary documentation for a petition requires substantial time and resources, usually requiring several years of work. The documentary record of petitions is not infrequently in excess of 7,000 documents comprising 40,000 pages, including documents submitted by interested parties and developed by staff; however, much of the material provided may not be useful evidence.

The multidisciplinary approach of the Office of Federal Acknowledgment provides reviews of the petition materials from different perspectives. The Department's review is an independent evaluation of the total body of evidence rather than simply testing the propositions put forward either by a petitioner or by its opponents. Although under the regulations the burden of proof is on the petitioner to provide the necessary evidence, and the assistant secretary is not required to conduct research on a petitioner's behalf, the professional staff normally conducts some of its own research to verify and evaluate the materials and arguments submitted, and they may conduct limited additional research. This research and analysis may make a case where the petitioner or third party could not or did not.

The regulations establish a three-stage evaluation process (83.10 and 83.11). The first step is a proposed finding, about which the petitioner and any interested parties may comment either for or against. The second step is a final determination, which is issued after a review of all the comments. The petitioner and certain interested parties, such as a state, local government, other unrecognized group, or a recognized tribe, may request that an independent adjudicatory body within the Department review a final determination. That body, the Interior Board of Indian Appeals, may affirm a decision or may vacate it and return it for reconsideration, based on certain grounds, such as the interpretation of the regulations or the presentation of substantial new evidence (83.11). The regulations provide for extensive technical assistance and the multiple stages provide opportunities for petitioners and third parties to conduct focused additional research.

The Interior Department has several times reversed negative proposed findings, based on additional evidence submitted by a petitioner, for example, Gayhead Wampanoag (ASIA 1987) and Mohegan (ASIA 1994). At the same time, some petitioners, such as Miami, were unable to supply additional evidence to change the proposed finding (ASIA 1992). No positive proposed finding has been reversed by additional information, but three positive final determinations were reversed after reconsideration was ordered by the Interior Board of Indian Appeals (IBIA 2005, 2005a, IBIA re Chinook, Eastern Pequot RFD, Schaghticoke Tribal Nation RFD, Chinook RFD).

Several recognized tribes have opposed recognition of particular petitioners. These include the Navajo Tribe, which opposed recognition of the San Juan Southern Paiute, which was recognized in 1990 (ASIA 1990). The Tulalip Tribes vigorously opposed the petitions of the Snoqualmie and Snohomish petitioners, submitting extensive materials. The Snoqualmie were recognized in 1999, while the Snohomish were denied recognition in 2004 (ASIA 1999, 2004b). The Eastern Band of Cherokee and the Quinault Tribe have opposed recognition of the Lumbee and the Chinook, respectively. Other recognized tribes have submitted letters of support for recognition of particular petitioners, for example, the Turtle Mountain Chippewa have supported the Little Shell Band of Montana, who are related to them.

Connecticut has been the state most active in opposing petitions, while Vermont, Louisiana, and New Jersey among others have at times opposed petitions with substantial comments. In addition to effects of large casinos, possible land claims were of concern. Connecticut opposed the Mohegan Tribe, which was recognized in 1994, with substantial documentation and argument. It also vigorously opposed other petitioners, which have been rejected.

The quality of petitions and progress toward submitting them may be negatively affected for several reasons. Petitioners sometimes disagree with the results of their researcher's work, where this conflicts with how the group sees itself. Some petitioners are paralyzed as a result of internal conflicts. Some petitioners have received inaccurate advice from their researchers and their legal representatives, and they fail to provide appropriate information. Petitioners sometimes hide internal conflicts, although these may be the best evidence that there is a political process within the group. A group may also not continue because it concludes that it cannot meet the requirements of the regulations or believes that it will not receive a fair evaluation. For some petitioners, an adequate petition cannot be developed because it has no history as a continuously existing community and sometimes no Indian ancestry. Nonetheless, some of these petitioners have submitted large, elaborate petitions based on years of intensive historical research, for instance, the Golden Hill Paugussett (ASIA 2004a).

Professional researchers for petitioners have been predominantly anthropologists, though in some instances historians and genealogists have also been involved. Materials presented by petitioners and third parties are often significantly influenced by legal counsel for petitioners and third parties and sometimes therefore reflect different approaches to evaluation of evidence and analysis than the academic disciplines utilized in the evaluation process (Roth 1989).

Oral history based on interviews concerning events and matters contemporary with the speaker is given a substantial role as evidence in petition evaluations, in conjunction with documentation (e.g., Eastern Pequot Final Determination, ASIA 2002:81–86). However, oral history that claims to describe events and origins beyond the lifespan of the interviewee is of limited value under these circumstances, where claims about petitioner history that have no historical basis are common (Paredes 1997:38–40). Such oral history is often influenced by the recent construction or reconstruction of a group's history and identity (Haley and Wilcoxon 2005; ASIA 2005b, 1987a; M.E. Miller 2004:57–58).

*Standards, Consistency, and Complexity of Decisions*

The recognition criteria are deliberately general to allow flexibility to evaluate the enormous social, historical, and cultural diversity of petitioning groups. Decisions in different cases by necessity differ significantly, given this diversity as well as substantial differences in the kinds of evidence available (Bureau of Indian Affairs 1988). For example, factionalism, group size, economic circumstances, presence or absence of a land base, and other differences affect the form political processes may take. Political processes may in part be expressed through formal organizations, or solely through informal leaders or decision-making processes.

Some critics of decisions assert that petition evaluations are inconsistent with each other and involve subjective interpretations that do not have a clear basis and that there ought to be a more standardized approach (M.E. Miller 200463-67). Claimed inconsistencies between decisions, which are necessarily diverse, sometimes reflect superficial similarities of isolated facts in greatly differing cases. For example, that a petitioning group organized to seek redress for land or treaty claims may be the result of clearly demonstrable political processes within a distinct community, or it may be the

efforts of otherwise unaffiliated individuals whose leadership has no function or influence except with regard to this one, limited issue, for a limited time (ASIA 1992). Some claimed inconsistencies misstate the actual findings (ASIA 2002; Roth 1988). A report by the General Accounting Office in 2000 did not find inconsistency but stated that "the Department needs to make clearer the basis for its decisions" and provide better guidelines concerning how some important aspects of the regulations were to be interpreted (GAO 2000:10–11, 14).

The stated standard of proof in the regulations is that a criterion is met if there is a "reasonable likelihood" (83.6) of the validity of the facts relating to it. The regulations require there be sufficient evidence to show the criteria are met, even if there is no evidence that contradicts the facts asserted by the petitioner or a third party (59 FR 9280). The regulations explicitly require that the inherent limitations of historical research on community and political influence be taken into account. However, this does not mean "that a group can be acknowledged where continuous existence cannot be reasonably demonstrated, nor where an extant historical record does not record its presence" (59 FR 9281).

A criticism of the process has asserted that the standards, as actually applied, are unreasonably high in the light of the available historical record, especially since groups that were not recognized are not likely to have left a substantial written record. Parties opposing positive recognition decisions have argued that, rather than requiring too much evidence, these decisions' were not adequately supported by the evidence, misconstrued the evidence, or set an easier standard than stated in the regulations (Connecticut 2003).

The Office of Federal Acknowledgment's experience is that claimed "gaps" in the historical record often represent deficiencies in the petitioner's research even in easily accessible records. Alternatively, a lack of records may reflect the lack of an actual history of the group. In some cases the available evidence may in fact be too fragmentary or limited to reach a conclusion one way or another. It is possible that in some instances groups whose leadership and community in the more distant past were relatively informal and diffuse will be unable to provide oral or documentary evidence to demonstrate this.

One concern raised by critics is whether the recognition requirements are biased toward groups with a former federal or state tie or a land base (M.E. Miller 2004). Though not true of all successful petitioners, such groups are more likely to have retained enough community and polity to be now recognized. Unrecognized tribes often face limitations, such as lack of resources, difficulty maintaining a separate land base, and absence of federal support for political institutions. The effect of these factors must be balanced with the underlying legal foundations of the regulations' requirements that petitioners have maintained a significant level of community and political influence or authority to be entitled to a government-to-government relationship with the United States.

The petitioning process became complex and detailed, beyond what was anticipated when the process was established. One reason is that determining the character of a petitioner is sometimes far more complicated and difficult than appears on the surface. In addition, as the recognition process developed and more findings were issued, precedents and challenges to findings accumulated. Arguments and challenges to arguments have become more complex and sophisticated (L. Fleming 2001). Greater resources on the part of petitioners with financial backers, and on the part of their opponents, have resulted in increasingly larger bodies of documentary materials, with a concomittent increase in the amount of review required of the Department.

One of the consequences of this growth is that the Department's recognition process takes a long time to complete. Of the nine ready and waiting petitions in February 2007, two had been waiting for 10 years for their reviews to begin (Office of Federal Acknowledgment 2007a). The review itself requires several years from start to end to complete all steps, though much of this time is for petitioners and third parties preparing responses to proposed findings rather than actual departmental review. Claims of delays made by petitioners and critics may reflect that a group did not commence work until many years after its initial petition, for reasons such as internal conflict, lack of resources, or advice by legal advisors and researchers.

Increases in Department staff and resources historically have not kept pace with the growth of demands on the process. Increased efficiencies from the revised 1994 regulations and various other measures have been more than offset by growth in number and size of petitions, increased contention over decisions, and workload generated by appeals of and litigation concerning completed decisions.

## Indian Gaming

Critics of recognition sometimes claim that groups seek recognition primarily to be able establish a casino and become rich (Shays 2002). However, the present recognition process predates the major growth of Indian casinos and gaming did not become a recognition issue until the early 1990s. Forty groups had petitioned by 1978, with some requests dating back decades before. Land claims and treaty rights were early motivations for recognition, which also included preservation of the tribe and confirmation of Indian status. Nonetheless, the economic gains from gaming are such that almost all the tribes legislatively or administratively recognized since the 1970s have opened or sought to open casinos.

Beginning in the 1970s, petition development was supported by private foundations and organizations, legal assistance organizations, including the Native American Rights Fund, and, after 1978, by the Administration for Native Americans, part of the Department of Health and Human Services. Many petitioning groups have substantial financial backing from entrepreneurs who fund their petitions in return for involvement in operating a casino if the group is recognized.

As a result of increased funding, petitions prepared by groups with backers have become substantially larger and more elaborate. Such petitioners also have stronger legal representation, which is often involved in petition preparation as well as in seeking legal avenues to have their clients given a higher priority for consideration or to gain recognition through the courts. State and local opposition to recognition of additional tribes in Connecticut and some other states has been stimulated by concern over potential impact of casinos (R. Simmons 2002). Congress in 2006 had in large part ceased to legislatively recognize tribes, in part the result of local opposition to casinos.

## Status of Petitioning Groups

The Department of the Interior's administrative process remained the primary focus of recognition efforts in 2007, although a number of groups were also seeking recognition through the courts or Congress. A total of 324 groups had submitted at least a letter of intent to submit a documented petition (Office of Federal Acknowledgment 2007a). By far the largest number, 74, were from California. Other states with large numbers included Michigan and North Carolina with 21 each, Connecticut with 17, Louisiana with 14, and Virginia and Alabama with 12. Petitions or letters of intent had been received from 43 of the 49 continental states (Office of Federal Acknowledgment 2007).

As of March 2007 (Office of Federal Acknowledgment 2007a), 16 petitioners had been recognized through the administrative process, while 26 had been denied (table 2). Ten others had been recognized legislatively, two of these being restorations of terminated tribes.

Another 12 petitioners have withdrawn, merged with other petitioners, had legislation to clarify their status, dissolved their organization, were recognized by other means, or were removed from the list for other reasons. The Texas Kickapoo were found to be part of the recognized Oklahoma Kickapoo and withdrew after legislation was passed, with the support of the Department, to provide a reservation and services in Texas and the authority to organize as a tribe separately from the Oklahoma Kickapoo.

As of March 2007, eight petitioners were under consideration, while nine were ready for review. Another 79 had submitted documentation for their petition and had received the technical assistance review letter, based on a preliminary review, called for under the regulations. In some instances, no response had been received after as long as 25 years. Almost half the 324 petitioners on the Department's list in February 2006 had only submitted a letter indicating their intent to submit a documented petition. Some of these had not been heard from for more than 20 years. Despite the length of time the recognition process has been in place, and the extensive efforts made at the beginning to contact all possible groups, new petitions have continued to be submitted. Another 10 petitioners were added in 2006 alone.

One petitioner, the Ione Band of California, was recognized by the assistant secretary for Indian affairs outside the regulatory process in 1994 (as a confirmation of early 1970s recognition actions). In 1979 Karuk recognition was confirmed based on actions in the 1970s. Also outside the regulatory process, the assistant secretary recognized three nonpetitioners in 2002—the Lower Lake of California and two groups in Alaska—describing these as "reaffirmations" of a claimed existing federal relationship (table 1).

In 1981, the Jamul Indian Village of California, a nonpetitioner, was given recognized status as a community of Indians of one-half degree Indian ancestry or more. Although this approach was utilized a number of times in the 1930s, it had not been used since then. For such recognition, the Department purchased land and put it in trust as a reservation for a community of such Indians from the same tribe. The Department then organized a tribal government, based on language in the Indian Reorganization Act that says that recognized Indians include, in addition to members of recognized tribes, other Indians "of one-half degree Indian blood or more."

*Character of Groups*

The tribes recognized through the administrative process have varied enormously. Two tribes, the Death Valley (Western) Shoshone and San Juan Southern Paiute, are relatively traditional bands who maintain a significant degree of traditional language and culture. The San Juan Southern Paiute are located within the boundaries of the Navajo Reservation, in an area where the Navajo westward expansion in the nineteenth century encompassed all but a small portion of the Paiute lands (ASIA 1990). The San Juan Southern Paiute band continued to exist and was culturally and socially distinct from the surrounding Navajos, and the Paiutes did not extensively participate politically in the Navajo Nation. The Department's recognition finding concluded that although a majority of the Paiutes' names appeared on the 1930s Navajo reservation census, which the Navajo Nation used as its base membership roll, there was no evidence the Paiutes consented to be members or that the Navajo Nation had enrolled them. A Navajo Nation suit to overturn the decision, claiming the Paiutes were Navajo Nation members, was denied (*Masayesva* v. *Zah* v. *James* (D. Ariz). F. Supp. 1178, 1188. 3/13/1992).

Four tribes recognized under the regulations in the Northeast are survivors from earliest colonial contact with European settlers: the Mohegan in Connecticut, Narragansett in Rhode Island, Gayhead Wampanoag of Massachusetts, and the Mashpee Wampanoag. Each had been a colonially and then state-recognized tribe until the mid- to late nineteenth century and had maintained a distinct community but not tra-

ditional culture up until the present. A fifth state-recognized tribe, the Mashantucket (Western) Pequot of Connecticut, was legislatively recognized in 1983. In 2005, a federal court ruled directly that the Shinnecock, who have been recognized by New York from colonial times to the present, were a tribe. The Shinnecock petition as of September 2007 had not been reviewed by the Interior Department.

The Eastern Pequot and the Schaghticoke, whose state recognition by Connecticut and state reservations date to colonial times, and who are still recognized by the state, were ultimately denied federal recognition. The Interior Board of Indian Appeals vacated final determinations to recognize them, agreeing with challenges by Connecticut that the state relationship did not provide substantial evidence to demonstrate political influence as the decisions had concluded (IBIA 2005, 2005a). The reconsidered findings denied recognition, in part because, after reexamining that state relationship, it did not provide evidence to demonstrate political influence within the groups and there was insufficient other evidence of political influence for substantial historical periods (ASIA 2005, 2005a). Another Connecticut petitioner, the state-recognized Golden Hill Paugussett, was denied recognition because it could not demonstrate ancestry or other substantial connection with that historical tribe (ASIA 2004a).

Three tribes have been recognized administratively in Michigan, the Grand Traverse Band (Ottawa and Chippewa), Huron Potawatomi, and Match-E-Be-Nash-She-Wish Band of Potawatomi. Each had a past treaty with the federal government. Each had retained a land base for a community and retained some traditional culture, until the present in the first two cases and until recent decades in the last. Each had avoided removal. Two other Michigan tribes, the Pokagon Potawatomi and Little Traverse Bay bands, which have a similar character and history, were legislatively recognized in 1994, along with the Little River Band of Ottawa. The Burt Lake band of Michigan was denied in part because most of the group had joined the Little Traverse Bay band.

Four groups in western Washington have been recognized: the Samish, Snoqualmie, Jamestown S'Klallam, and the Cowlitz. Each had substantial federal contact and was descended from treaty-signing tribes, except the Cowlitz, who had declined a treaty. Although most of the historical Snoqualmie had become part of the multitribal community on the Tulalip Reservation, an off-reservation band under Chief Jerry Kanim had continued to exist. That band was separately federally recognized from reservation Snoqualmie from the 1930s or earlier until 1952. The Snoqualmie and the Jamestown S'Klallam were recognized, nonreservation tribes until approximately 1952, when, under the termination policies, the government concluded there was no trust obligation to them because they did not have a reservation. Few of the historical Cowlitz tribe or the Jamestown S'Klallam had removed to any reservations. Part of the Samish membership (about 31 percent) was enrolled in recognized Salish tribes, the Lummi and Swinomish, where they were well integrated into those tribal communities. The balance were descendants of historical Indian-White marriages who were not affiliated with the reservation tribes (ASIA 1995).

Other petitioners in western Washington, the Chinook, Duwamish, and Snohomish, did not qualify for recognition. The ancestors of their members had separated from tribal society in the late nineteenth and early twentieth century. The groups were found to be essentially voluntary organizations of descendants from the claimed tribes. Their ancestors had not maintained a distinct community from non-Indians, while other descendants of these tribes continued to be part of reservation tribes. A proposed finding that the Steilacoom were not entitled to recognition concluded that almost all of the group was not descended from the treaty-signing Steilacoom tribe (ASIA 2000).

Three tribes have been recognized administratively in the South. The Tunica-Biloxi of Lousiana, an amalgamation of the Ofo, Avoyel, and Tunica tribes and part of the Biloxi tribe, survived in part because local authorities in the mid-nineteenth century had recognized their title to a small area of land. The land was derived from a Spanish land grant. The Jena Choctaw, also in Lousiana, were a portion of the diaspora of Choctaw from Mississippi, who remained behind after Removal. The Poarch Creek of Alabama evolved from a portion of the Creek Nation that had remained behind after Removal in the 1830s. This group was centered on land set aside as individual federal trust land for one of their ancestors and was a poor, tightly clustered, and intermarried community.

Only one group who were culturally California Indians has been reviewed, the Muwekma Ohlone (ASIA 2002a). (One other California petitioner reviewed, the Timbi-Sha Shoshone, is a Great Basin tribe and two others, the United Lumbee Nation and the Kaweah Indian Nation, were recently formed organizations with no Indian ancestry.) The Muwekma were derived from a mission settlement at San Jose mission (ASIA 2002a). The group was federally recognized between 1914 and 1927. The petitioner, formed in 1984, was only derived from part of this band, whose settlement went out of existence by 1914. There was not enough information to show the present-day group maintained significant social ties as a community nor to show political influence within a community since the 1920s.

The Department has declined to recognize several petitioning groups that were recently formed organizations whose members had no previous substantial contact with each other and had no Indian ancestry and no connection with any claimed historical tribe. These include the United Lumbee Nation, Munsee-Thames Delaware and Kaweah Indian Nation. A final determination in 2006 concluded that a Vermont group claiming to be Abenaki had no connection with the historical Abenaki, nor good evidence the group existed before the 1970s (ASIA 2007). Three petitioners claiming to be Cherokee, from Tennessee, Oregon, and Alabama, were rejected as recently formed organizations of individuals with no known Cherokee ancestry (Southeastern

Cherokee Confederacy, Northwest Cherokee Wolf Band, and Red Clay Intertribal Band).

Some unrecognized groups that have existed as cohesive and distinct communities for generations, usually in rural areas, appear to have Indian identities that are relatively recently created or have been revised in recent decades. A claimed connection by ancestry or otherwise with a historical tribe either may not have been demonstrated or may not be known to the group, or a connection may not exist (Lerch 1992:54–59) (vol. 14:328, 336).

Two such distinct communities dating into the nineteenth century were reviewed by the recognition process, the Mowa Choctaw of Alabama and the Ramapough Mountain Indians of New Jersey and New York (ASIA 1996, 1997; Paredes 1992a:132–133). Neither had any Indian ancestry. The Ramapough formed as a community around 1870 and had not evolved from a historical tribe, though claiming connection with the Delaware. Other distinct communities may have evolved from historical tribes, while others may have been formed by Indians separating from one or several tribes and coalescing into a new group. Such groups are sometimes termed "nonhistorical tribes" because they have Indian ancestry and substantial histories as distinct ethnic groups but they do not have or cannot show historical continuity as distinct communities to a tribe that existed at the beginning of European settlement.

The most well-known group that has existed as a distinct community since at least the mid-nineteenth century, if not earlier, but whose tribal connection has been the subject of controversy, is the Indians of Robeson County, North Carolina, most commonly referred to since the 1950s as the Lumbee. Tribal identities claimed in the twentieth century have included Croatan, Cherokee, Tuscarora, Siouan, and Cheraw (Blu 1980, 2004; Campisi 1988). North Carolina has recognized the Indians in Robeson County as an Indian group since the 1880s and provided separate Indian schools and a college until the time of desegregation. The Lumbee have sought federal recognition since the beginning of the twentieth century, both administratively and legislatively, without success. The Indians of Robeson County are represented by multiple petitioners, reflecting divisions within the Lumbee. The largest, the Lumbee Regional Development Association, is by far the largest unrecognized group, with approximately 55,000 members.

Legislation in 1956 designated the Indians of Robeson County as the "Lumbee Indians" and recounted some conclusions concerning their history including descent from "certain coastal tribes of Indians" (70 Stat. 254–55). Though sometimes characterized as a "recognition act," the act contains specific language that it could not be the basis for extending the status reserved to recognized tribes. The Department of the Interior in 1989 concluded that this language constituted a bar to administrative recognition. The Interior Department and the Eastern Cherokee have supported legislation to allow an administrative determination and opposed recognition by legislation.

Many unrecognized groups have or claim to have a relationship to a historical tribe that had a treaty or other form of federal recognition in the past. Some take the position that once a federal relationship is established, only Congress can terminate it, not the executive branch (Peregoy 1991; ASIA 2002b). They propose that a previously recognized petitioner would be entitled to recognition unless the Interior Department could disprove their tribal character. Absent a showing of congressional action to terminate, the government would have to show that the previously recognized tribe had "voluntarily abandoned tribal relations."

One interpretation of "voluntary abandonment of tribal relations" is that there must be proof of a specific decision by the tribe to dissolve. In a decision on the Indiana Miami, a federal appeals court rejected this view, holding that the key and only issue was the continued or noncontinued existence of the tribe (*Miami Nation* v. *United States,* 255 F.3d 342, 350 (7th Cir. 2001)). It held further that the recognition regulations, by including the requirement of continuous existence, effectively embodied the voluntary abandonment standard and that there was not a requirement to show a specific tribal decision to dissolve, as opposed to demonstration that the tribe went out of existence as a result of historical processes.

The Interior Department has consistently held that having some past connection with a treaty signer or otherwise previously recognized tribe is not sufficient evidence to presume continued existence as a tribe or to be entitled to the legal status as a recognized tribe (59 FR 9282). It cites the 1981 appeals court decision in *United States* v. *Washington* and the *Miami* decision (see also *United Tribe of Shawnee Indians* v. *United States* June 13, 2001. No. 00-3140. 10th Circuit).

Petitioners claiming a treaty relationship have included the Mowa Choctaw, who were found to have no connection by ancestry or otherwise with the Choctaw tribe, and thus its treaties (ASIA 1997). The Principal Creek Nation's members were mostly descendants of the Creek Nation but were a recently formed organization with no connection with the historical Creeks other than ancestry (ASIA 1984). Another petitioner claiming Creek identity, the MaChis Creek, had no connection by ancestry or otherwise with the historical Creek tribe (ASIA 1987a). Some western Washington petitioners tracing to treaty tribes have been recognized administratively because they continued to exist as tribes (Snoqualmie), while other groups, also made up almost entirely of individuals descended from treaty tribes, had not continued to exist as distinct political communities and were denied recognition (Chinook, Duwamish).

The federal relationship ended for some groups through the operation of treaties, laws, and policies. These groups were not incorrectly "terminated" by administrative action as some have claimed, even though they may, under present-day laws and policies, be eligible to be recognized. Not all treaties established a perpetual federal relationship. The 1855 Michigan Ottawa treaty called for a 20-year period of federal services, trust protection of land and annuity payments, after which there was no further federal relationship (ASIA 1979, 2004). In some cases, tribes, or parts of them, either resisted removal to reservations designated for them or subsequently left the reservation because it was unsuitable, was occupied by enemies, or for other reasons. Under the laws and policies of earlier times, the federal government sometimes concluded it no longer had a responsibility for these groups. Portions of tribes that remained behind after Removal (e.g., Eastern Cherokee) were sometimes regarded as having separated from their tribe and thereby from a federal relationship (Roth 2001:62).

## Litigation Concerning the Recognition Process After 1978

Once decided administratively, recognition decisions are difficult to challenge in court because, under the Administrative Procedure Act of 1946, the court will not overrule a decision that is reasonable and follows the agency's rules, even if the court might have decided the facts differently. Nonetheless, recognition decisions, both for and against recognition, have been challenged in federal court by petitioners and third parties. Decisions including the San Juan Southern Paiute, Indiana Miami, and Ramapough Mountain Indians have been upheld, while the Samish decision was vacated. As of 2007, court challenges to the Schaghticoke and Muwekma decisions were in progress.

A federal court vacated the 1987 decision against Samish recognition. The decision accepted a Samish argument that they had lost former federal government benefits through having lost previous federal recognition. The court ruled the Samish were therefore entitled to a formal hearing, which the recognition regulations do not include (*Greene* v. *Babbitt* 2/25/1992 U.S.D.C. Western District of Washington). The Department recognized the Samish in 1995, based on an administrative law judge's recommended positive decision. The Department's decision was based on his factual findings about the Samish but did not accept some of the judge's interpretations of recognition regulations, which were not well supported by precedents from previous recognition decisions (ASIA 1995). A Samish argument that it had been inadvertently left off a list of federally recognized tribes in the 1960s was not supported by the evidence at the hearing, and it was not a basis of the recommended decision.

Federal district and appeals courts' decisions upholding the 1992 Interior Department decision against recognition of the Indiana Miami concluded the decisions were consistent with recognition policies and court decisions predating the regulations. The court also held that the recognition process did not require that a formal hearing be held, absent special circumstances (*Miami Nation* v. *Babbit*, 887 F. Supp. 1158, 1168–69 [N.D. Ind. 1995]).

A portion of the Miami tribe remained in Indiana after Removal or moved back soon thereafter. The Indiana Miami were all descendants of the treaty-signing Miami, but their community had gradually diminished over time. After the 1940s, they no longer were a distinct community, though a limited organization persisted to the present (ASIA 1992). The United States had treated the Indiana Miami as part of the recognized Miami tribe until 1892, albeit taking little notice of them after the 1880s. In 1892, the Department concluded that the Indiana Miami were citizens, hence by the laws of the time had ended tribal relations and were no longer entitled to a federal relationship. The court dismissed the argument that because of their previous recognition the Indiana Miami retained that status, absent congressional termination or voluntary abandonment of tribal relations.

Once the recognition under the 1978 regulations was established, the courts almost always deferred to the Interior Department recognition process as the forum for recognition and for demonstration of tribal existence for claims and treaty rights purposes. The federal courts have deferred to the executive branch because it had an established process and accumulated expertise in making decisions concerning tribal status (e.g., *Golden Hill Paugussett Tribe of Indians, et al.* v. *Lowell P. Weicker, Jr., et al.* U.S. Dist. Conn., D. 2:92CV00738(PCD)). The court in the *Mashpee* decision had declined to defer to the Department because at that time its proposed recognition process had not been finalized. The courts have long considered tribal status to be a "political question," one reserved to the executive and legislative branches.

With delays in issuing decisions on petitions, petitioning groups have frequently sought through the courts to require a speedier decision and priority in consideration. The courts in response have become involved in the recognition process, in questions of administrative procedure such as shortened review schedules and changing priority of consideration, or indicated they might become involved if delays continued.

In some instances, groups, rather than going through the administrative process, have sought a direct court ruling that the group was already recognized or was entitled to be recognized, on a variety of grounds such as a treaty connection (*United Tribe of Shawnee Indians* v. *U.S.*, 2001). The courts since 1978 rejected requests to make recognition decisions, in favor of administrative consideration. However, in part because of the projected delays in getting a decision, a federal court in 2005 ruled directly on the tribal character of the Shinnecock, a New York State-recognized tribe with a reservation on Long Island, which was seeking to establish gaming on land near its reservation. It concluded that the Shinnecock had existed continuously as a tribe (*New York et al.* v. *Shinnecock Indian Nation et al.*, 03 Civ. 3243 (TCP)(E.D. N.Y. 2005) (decision pp. 10–11)). The court's review focused on the political relationship of the Shinnecock with the state and evidence demonstrating ancestry from the tribe. The court did not determine whether the Shinnecock were entitled to federal recognition. The federal government had refused to be a party to this litigation. It refused to recognize the Shinnecock on the basis of the court's analysis concerning tribal existence, which was based on a process different from the Department's.

In 1994, an appeals court in the Golden Hill Paugussett land claims case warned that, although it preferred the administrative process, it might make the decision on tribal existence itself if a decision by the Department was delayed (*Golden Hill Paugussett Tribe of Indians, et al.* v. *Lowell P. Weicker, Jr.,* 39 F.d. 51 2nd Cir. 1994). It emphasized that judicial deference was not a denial of judicial authority to make a determination itself should circumstances warrant it.

## Legislation

Every Congress since 1989 has seen one or more bills to revise the Department's recognition process, and numerous hearings have been held, but no bill has come close to passage. Many of the bills would have moved the recognition process out of the Bureau of Indian Affairs to an independent commission. The majority of bills have sought to lower the requirements for recognition. One method was to shorten the historical period to demonstrate tribal existence, such as from 1871, the end of the treaty era, to the present, or from 1900, or from 1932, the era of the Indian New Deal. Some legislation would have established a presumption of tribal existence for a group descended from a treaty signer. By contrast, a few bills, introduced by opponents of recognition, have sought to raise the standards for recognition. Legislation has been proposed to establish a separate recognition process for California (Quesenberry 1995) because of asserted unique factors in California, particularly the extremely harsh treatment of the native peoples during and after the gold rush.

The Department of the Interior has sought to retain jurisdiction over the recognition process and almost always opposed any reduction in standards. However, in 2000, the assistant secretary for Indian affairs, who was critical of the Department's recognition process, supported legislation that would have substantially reduced the recognition requirements (Gover 2000:54–55).

## Congressional Recognition

Congress has recognized a variety of groups as tribes since 1960. While the Interior Department supported or did not oppose some recognition legislation, where there were unusual or complicated circumstances, it has opposed most congressional recognition. In some cases it expressed the view that the group did not meet the requirements of the recognition regulations or, more frequently, that this had not been demonstrated by a careful study. Some critics of the Department's recognition process have expressed the view that Congress's authority to recognize is broader than the authority the Department of the Interior presently views itself as having and that therefore the Department should not oppose most congressional recognition, even if the group might not meet the Department's criteria (Locklear 1983). The Department of the Interior (1995:67) stated that Congress may recognize "nonhistorical tribes."

The extent of congressional authority to recognize where historical continuity may not be well established has not been well tested in court. In one decision, the Supreme Court, after holding that Congress, not the court, had the right to determine when the federal status of a tribe might end, went on to declare that "it is not meant by this that Congress may bring a community or body of people within the range of this power by arbitrarily calling them an Indian tribe" (*U.S.* v. *Sandoval*, 231 U.S. 46. 2/13/1913). This language was repeated in several subsequent decisions but was not greatly elaborated upon. However, in *Morton* v. *Mancari* in 1974, the court implied a limit when it held legislation limited to federally recognized tribes was constitutional because it was based on their special status as distinct political bodies rather than being an impermissible racial classification.

The level of scrutiny by Congress of recognition requests is necessarily much less detailed than the Department's administrative process, a primary reason the Department has usually given for opposing recognition bills. A Senate Indian Affairs Committee member in 2006 stated his concern that Congress had no criteria for recognition (Shaffrey 2006; M.E. Miller 2004:122). Congressmen opposed 1994 legislation recognizing two tribes in Michigan. Congressmen argued that recognition is inherently political because it requires the support of the non-Indian majority in the state of the group to be recognized, and these may oppose recognition for reasons other than the group's qualifications (M.E. Miller 2004:53; U.S. House of Representatives 1994:17–24).

Only two tribes were legislatively recognized between 1960 and 1978, the Prescott Yavapai in 1972 and the Pascua Yaqui in 1978, both in Arizona. Almost all the Yaqui in Arizona had migrated from their homeland in Mexico early in the twentieth century, after the Mexican revolution, and established several settlements in Tucson and elsewhere in Arizona. Efforts to gain federal services and protection had begun as early as the 1930s. With the aid of positive local opinion and the then-powerful Arizona congressional delegation, they were recognized in 1978 (M.E. Miller 2004:79–122). Recognized tribes in Arizona had opposed Yaqui recognition. The testimony supporting the legislation emphasized earlier migrations of small numbers of Yaquis into Arizona, rather than major twentieth-century migration (Spicer 1977).

Between 1979 and 1994, after the administrative process began, Congress recognized 10 Indian tribes for a variety of reasons. With the increased prominence of Indian gaming, partly because of local opposition to casinos, Congress stopped enacting recognition legislation, although bills continued to be introduced. The chairman of the Senate Indian Affairs Committee, a critic of both the Interior recognition process and congressional recognition, stated in 2006 that process and congressional recognition, stated in 2006 that

congressional recognition should be reserved for special circumstances (McCain 2006).

In 1979, as negotiations were concluding for federal legislation to settle the Maine Indian land claims, an additional group, the Houlton Band of Maliseet, came forward. It presented new claims that threatened to upset the carefully crafted settlement. The Maliseets' historical territory had extended into one corner of Maine, although most of the Maliseet were within Canada. The Department conducted a limited historical and field review and concluded the group might meet the requirements of the recognition regulations. With the Department's support, Houlton Maliseet recognition was included in the 1980 Maine Indian Claims Act.

Subsequently, an additional group came forward in Maine, seeking recognition and also presenting claims. These were Micmacs, a Canadian tribe, many of whose members had migrated into Maine after 1900. In contrast to the Maliseet, there had not been historical Micmac territory within the present boundaries of the United States. Congress in recognizing the Aroostook Micmac in 1991 accepted the claim that the Micmacs had been part of a Wabanaki confederacy of tribes that extended into the United States. As with Pascua Yaqui, Congress recognized an Indian tribe that was not historically a United States tribe, which the Department opposed.

Congress responded to the land claim of a group called Cow Creek Umpqua, of Oregon, by recognizing them in 1982 in the same legislation that settled their land claim. Although the legislation referred to this as a restoration, the Interior Department concluded that there had not been such a group recognized in 1954, at the time of the Western Oregon Termination Act, hence the act was effectively a new recognition. The Department initially opposed the legislation on these grounds as well as raising questions about the group's historical connection with the Cow Creek Umpqua listed in the 1954 act (Tallmadge 2006) but subsequently agreed not to oppose the legislation.

In 1983, the Western Pequot of Connecticut (Mashantucket), a petitioner, were recognized in legislation that settled their land claim. The Eastern Pequot were unable to proceed with legislation because of a factional dispute that had divided them.

In 1968, to provide services to the unrecognized Ysleta del Sur Pueblo of El Paso (Texas Tigua) Congress enacted legislation to transfer "Federal responsibility, if any" for the Tigua to the state of Texas. The federal act included language declaring that "nothing in the act would make the tribe or its members eligible for Federal Indian services or status" (82 U.S. Stat. 93). As a result of this act, the Tigua could not obtain recognition under the recognition regulations. Despite the 1968 act, in the 1980s the Texas attorney general challenged the legality of the tribe's relationship with the state, leading to support for federal recognition legislation, which was enacted in 1987.

The Lac Vieux Desert Chippewa of Michigan, which had been rejected for administrative recognition in the early

1970s, had extensive federal contact in the 1930s. A preliminary review by the Department of their petition indicated a cohesive, fairly traditional band. However, its members were enrolled in and receiving federal services through the recognized Mole Lake Band, though resident elsewhere. Because the tribe was qualified, except for the Mole Lake enrollment, being geographically and politically distinct, the Department supported legislative recognition as a separate tribe in 1988.

Between 1973 and 2003, unsuccessful bills were introduced for 25 different groups, some of them petitioners, including four that had been denied recognition administratively (Walke 2003)—the Lower Muscogee-Creek, the Mowa Choctaw, the Duwamish, and the Indiana Miami. The land claims and apparent plans for gaming helped diminish initial public support for the Miami legislation. The Lumbee had recognition legislation introduced eight times between 1988 and 2005 but were unable to generate sufficient local support from non-Indians. Their efforts have also been opposed by several recognized tribes, especially the Eastern Cherokee.

### Division of Recognized Tribes

Historically, tribes were sometimes combined under treaty or other federal action. More than one tribe was often placed on a single reservation. Especially in the 1930s under the Indian Reorganization Act and in some instances earlier, the tribes on a reservation were treated by the federal government as a single "tribe" in a legal sense and usually, although not always, organized under a single tribal government (Cohen 1942:268–272).

Since the 1970s, ethnically distinct portions of some recognized tribes have sought to be recognized separately through legislation, court action, the recognition regulations, or through other administrative action. A group in which most members are presently part of a recognized tribe cannot be separately recognized through the administrative process (83.7(f)). This does not, however, prevent separate recognition in some special instances where a group has been nominally included on the membership list of a recognized tribe but has not become politically part of it (such as San Juan Southern Paiute). However, where two otherwise distinct tribes on a single reservation are participating in a single tribal government, they would not meet the requirements of the regulations for a petitioner to be politically autonomous of other Indian governments (83.7(c)).

An illustration of the centrifugal forces affecting recognized tribes concerns the Oklahoma Cherokee, where two constituent tribes, the Shawnee Tribe (Loyal Shawnee) and the Delaware Tribe (Delaware Cherokee) sought separate recognition. Both became affiliated with the Cherokee Nation in the 1860s as a result of federal agreements with the Cherokee under which they became citizens of the Cherokee Nation. Neither group assimilated into the Cherokee, and both maintained some form of separate governance. Al-

though eligible to enroll in the Cherokee Nation, only one-quarter of the 10,000 Delaware were members in 2006. The degree to which the Delaware and Shawnee had maintained separate tribal political structures from the Cherokee, and the meaning and interpretation of the language of the agreements, were the subject of litigation and controversy at several points in the twentieth century.

Beginning in the 1970s, the Cherokee government exercised a wider range of governmental functions, at the same time that the Delaware Tribe became more assertive and established some of its own programs. This led to a controversial 1979 Interior Department ruling that the Delaware Tribe was part of the Cherokee Nation and that federal funding and services for them were to flow through the Cherokee Nation. This was reversed in 1996, with a ruling that they were entitled to be dealt with as a separate tribe (61 Fed. Reg. 50,862). Litigation by the Cherokee Nation resulted in a court ruling in 2005 that the 1996 decision was invalid (*Cherokee Nation* v. *Norton,* 241 F. Supp. 2d 1368 (D.C. No. 98-CV-903-H)). As a result, the Delaware Tribe lost federal funding, laid off employees, and sold their tribal headquarters (Bartlesville *Examiner-Enterprise* 2006). In July 2006, the Cherokee and the Delaware negotiated a compromise to support legislation making the Delaware a separate tribe, but giving the Cherokee Nation primary jurisdiction over all lands within its defined boundaries. The Shawnee Tribe had accepted similar legislation in 2000.

The Texas (Mexican) Kickapoo are one of two bands of the Kickapoo tribe. In the 1980s they were largely enrolled with the other band, the Oklahoma Kickapoo. They reside in part on land in Mexico granted by that government in the nineteenth century, and at other times on the international border or with the Oklahoma Kickapoo. Legislation in 1983, supported by the Department, which provided them with a reservation on the border in Texas, made possible their subsequent organization and recognition as a separate tribe in 1989 (96 U.S. Stat. 2270).

The Hoopa Valley Reservation consisted of a square of land, occupied primarily by Hupa Indians, originally established in 1864 and a strip of land, added in 1891, occupied by Yurok Indians (known as the "extension"). The Yurok were not included in the Hoopa Valley Tribe when it organized in 1933. After commercial logging on the "square" began in the 1950s, the Yurok did not share in the revenue, which went to the Hoopa Valley Tribe. The Yurok and other Indians won a court judgment in 1973 that all the Indians resident anywhere on the reservation were entitled to share equally in the timber revenues (*Jesse Short et al.* v. *U.S.,* 202 Ct. Cl 870, 486 F.2d 561 [Ct. Cl. 1973]). The suit, which reflected conflict between the two tribes since the 1930s, led to the Hoopa-Yurok Settlement Act of 1988 (102 U.S. Stat. 2924). This act divided the reservation into the extension (for the Yurok) and the square (for the Hupa), along with a settlement fund. Although the Yurok were resident on the reservation and had received federal services,

*127*

they reportedly had refused to organize separately, seeking since the 1930s a single tribal government for the entire reservation (R.N. Clinton 1988). The Settlement Act provided for formation of a separate government and their recognition as a separate tribe.

The Florida Seminole were dealt with as a single recognized tribe until 1957. When part of the Seminoles organized a tribal government in 1957, as the Seminole Tribe, based on the several Seminole reservations, a more culturally conservative group known as the Miccosukee refused to join them (Kersey 1996; Sturtevant 1971). However, the Miccosukee decided in 1962 to organize formally, becoming a separately recognized tribe and eventually gaining their own reservation. A number of Seminoles, known as the Traditional Seminole, joined neither tribal organization and in 2006 were not recognized (Kersey 1996:143–144).

# Tribal Sovereignty and Economic Development

TAYLOR KEEN AND ANGELIQUE EAGLEWOMAN (WAMBI A. WASTEWIN)

The dramatic economic developments among the Indian nations of the United States since 1975 are the direct result of the increase in tribal sovereignty. For the first time since the 1800s, Native political leadership has had control over tribal natural resources as well as increased flexibility over the economic use of trust properties. Both legislation and litigation have redefined the relationships between the Indian nations and both the federal and state governments and for the first time given certain competitive advantages to Native governments.

As the British colonies were transformed into sovereign states, the United States soon adopted laws regulating trade with tribes. In the United States Constitution, the Congress was empowered in Article I, Section 8, to "regulate Commerce with foreign Nations, and among the several States, and with the Indian Tribes." The first Congress in 1790 passed a statute regulating the licensing of traders in Indian country (25 U.S.C. § 261). A set of comprehensive federal regulations developed to regulate individual licensed traders in their dealings with tribes (25 C.F.R. § 140). The federal government early on intended to control the influx of non-Indians into the Indian territory beyond the established boundaries of state governments with the Trade and Intercourse Acts.

## Tribal Government Reorganization and Corporate Charters, 1930–1960

As federal policies evolved from removal to reservation settlement to allotment, many tribal governing bodies were left in disarray or purposely ignored by federal agents administering federal policy. A significant change began with the passage in 1934 of the Indian Reorganization Act ("The Federal-Tribe Relationship" and "Tribal Government in the United States," this vol.). The provisions of the Act allowed for tribes to organize politically by adopting constitutions; once properly organized pursuant to the statute, the governing body would have the power "to negotiate with the Federal, State and local governments" (25 U.S.C. § 476[e]). Furthermore, the statute provided under section 17 that a tribe had the opportunity to petition the secretary of the Interior to hold a vote to adopt a federal charter of incorporation

as a business entity (25 U.S.C. § 477). Tribes in Oklahoma were exempted from certain provisions of the Act. A separate statute, the Oklahoma Indian Welfare Act of 1936, remedied this situation by extending all features of the Reorganization Act to those tribes. The majority of tribes presented with the choice voted to organize under those laws. Some notable exceptions included the Navajo, Cherokee Nation, Nez Perce, Coeur d'Alene, Crow, Fort Peck Sioux, Fort Totten Sioux, Crow Creek Sioux, Sisseton-Wahpeton Sioux, Turtle Mountain Chippewa, Colville, and Yakima (Haas 1947:13–20). Many of these tribes followed the spirit of the federal law by adopting their own constitutions and bylaws (Haas 1947:33–34).

The charter of incorporation under the Reorganization Act allowed the adopting tribe to create a federally chartered corporation with the power "to purchase, take by gift, or bequest, or otherwise, own, hold, manage, operate, and dispose of property of every description, real and personal, including the power to purchase restricted Indian lands and to issue in exchange for therefore interests in corporate property, and such further powers as may be incidental to the conduct of corporate business" (25 U.S.C. § 477). Once granted, a section 17 federal tribal charter may be revoked only by an act of Congress. Charters adopted along with the tribal government took time to integrate into tribal society.

From the mid-1930s to the 1960s, tribal leaders and peoples became motivated to incorporate the United States model of economic self-sufficiency to alleviate the poverty experienced on Indian lands. Blending the ability to adapt non-Indian corporate models within a tribal cultural framework became an important foundation for the successes to come.

## Tribal Self-Determination and Self-Governance

As the American civil rights movement of the 1960s and 1970s made national headlines, Native Americans sought to change the federal domination of reservation life. This struggle, popularized by the American Indian Movement, led to federal legal reform centering on tribal decision-making and a recognition and revitalization of traditional tribal ways. The first step in pruning the federal bureaucracy controlling reservation life was to master that bureaucracy and reshape federal programs to better serve tribal peoples (vol. 4:78–80, 272–275).

An essential component for the development of tribal economic systems within the United States was familiarity with federal funding sources, reporting practices, and management policies. This component became integrated into tribal governance through the implementation of the Indian Self-Determination and Education Assistance Act of 1975. In the Act's preamble, the congressional findings giving rise to the Act are set forth: "(1) the prolonged Federal domination of Indian service programs has served to retard rather than enhance the progress of Indian people and their communities by depriving Indians of the full opportunity to develop leadership skills crucial to the realization of self-government, and has denied to the Indian people an effective voice in the planning and implementation of programs for the benefit of Indians which are responsive to the true needs of Indian communities; and (2) the Indian people will never surrender their desire to control their relationships both among themselves and with non-Indian governments, organizations, and persons" (25 U.S.C. § 450[a]).

The Indian Self-Determination Act transferred federally funded social service, infrastructure, and governmental function programs from the Bureau of Indian Affairs directly to Indian nations to administer according to federal regulations (25 U.S.C. § 450f). These contracted programs are commonly referred to as "638 contracts" from the original numbering of the Indian Self-Determination Act as Public Law 93-638. Within the Indian Self-Determination Act, an authorization for the complete transfer of federal funds for the full range of administrative services to Indian nations was set forth as the self-governance demonstration project. In 1994, Congress authorized the Tribal Self-Governance Program to provide annual funding agreements between tribes and the Department of the Interior for contracted programs to be administered at the tribal level by tribal personnel with tribal discretion as to budget modification and efficiency in administration of contracted programs (25 U.S.C. § 458cc).

Through the Indian Self-Determination Act and the Tribal Self-Governance Act, tribes have the ability to transfer from the Bureau of Indian Affairs the whole gamut of programs federally funded for the benefit of tribal members. This process has indirectly led to greater management training in the tribal workforce and the development of greater efficiency by tribes in the administration of federally developed programs. These human resource development tools have contributed to the economic development of tribes by opening the door to professionally trained and educated tribal personnel to administer contracted federal programs.

## Development of Tribal Natural Resources

During the period of federal superintendence of reservation life, the Department of the Interior through the Bureau of Indian Affairs determined all aspects of development on tribal lands. The Bureau determined how natural resources would be exploited and approved the leases to oil and mining companies for reservation lands, acting as an agent for the leasing of tribally owned grazing lands (Cohen 2005:1074–1075). Economic activity until the 1960s largely centered on the federal policies of utilization of tribally owned resources such as commercial forestry, rangeland for grazing, agricultural cropland, fishing in the Pacific Northwest, and oil, gas, coal and uranium reserves in western states as well as Alaska (vol. 10:641–658).

Within Indian Territory, the Osage were the wealthiest population in the world in the 1920s from their oil royalties (Hagan 1998:24). By 1938 the market had collapsed and the Osage faced the Depression (Wilson 1985:150–151).

After World War II, the exploitation of Indian lands for energy resources accelerated. The energy needs of the United States led to exploration for uranium reserves, which were found in abundance on the Navajo and Laguna Pueblo (vol. 10:448) lands. The Bureau of Indian Affairs approved uranium leases to begin mining operations on these two reservations in the 1940s and 1950s (vol. 10:650). When the uranium leases ended, the tribes found themselves without adequate provisions for the clean up and rehabilitation of lands contaminated with uranium tailings and mining residue (Rosier 2003:149).

Coal mining leases were approved by the Bureau of Indian Affairs on the reservations of the Hopi (vol. 10:536–537), Navajo (vol. 10:649), and Northern Cheyenne (vol. 13:877) in the mid-1960s (Rosier 2003:145). Often the leases approved by the Bureau were at far lower than market value for tribal natural resources. In the negotiation of energy resource leases, the tribes received sparse geological data from the Bureau to promote fair pricing and the agency "failed to recommend certain kinds of leases that would produce bonuses if prices rose" (Rosier 2003:147). In the early 1970s with energy development companies focused on profit maximization and the Bureau failing to protect tribal interests, 26 Plains tribes formed the Native American Natural Resources Development Federation to establish tribal control over the extraction of natural resources, primarily coal, from Indian lands (Ambler 1990:70, 92).

In 1975, 25 tribes formed the Council of Energy Resource Tribes (CERT) to protect tribal interests in oil, gas, and mineral production. Federal funding of CERT created concerns about its accountability. The entanglement among CERT, tribes, and government energy policy has both benefited and plagued the organization (Ambler 1990:96–109). In the 1980s and 1990s, CERT shifted policy from rapid development to more long-range resource planning, recruiting technical assistance for tribal resources (LaDuke 1983:67). Due to the work of these organizations, legal reform was pushed forward in Congress with the adoption of the 1982 Indian Mineral Development Act and the 1983 Federal Oil and Gas Royalty Management Act. Both federal laws increased the power of tribes to control their natural resources development. Nearly $5.8 billion was reported not received by Native Americans due to inadequate government accounting procedures and lax enforcement of lease terms according to federal reports (Rosier 2003:148–149).

Tribal resources necessarily include human resources of the tribal members themselves. From the 1950s and 1960s, tribal members emerged as professionals in the social work and education fields. The 1970s provided the first generation of lawyers to represent the Indian nations. The 1980s and 1990s brought tribal members with greater "formal training in the business and managerial professions" (Barreiro and Johnson 2005:39).

## Cultural Considerations in Development

Culture and tradition inform economic decision-making for Indian nations, and this has become acknowledged as the regulation of the federal government has been removed from exploitation of tribal resources. There are a variety of approaches to economic development that have been employed by the over 500 Indian nations across North America.

Four values have been identified as enveloping the concept of Indian-centered economic values: community, connectedness, the seventh generation, and humility. Community encompasses the tribal idea of balance in the world and the idea that reciprocity must exist in all exchanges. Connectedness describes the interrelationship of all actions that must be accounted for to maintain balance. The third value, the seventh generation, involves a concept of stewardship to provide resources for the children yet to be born. The value of humility embraces the natural place of humans in the world as subject to the consequences of the development undertaken (Trosper 1999:140). Not all tribes adhere to these four values as driving their philosophy of economic development.

## Tribal Gaming Industry

In the 1980s, many tribes, following a long history of gambling and recreational activities commercialized the game of bingo introduced by Christian churches into tribal communities (EagleWoman 2006:525–526). As tribes in California developed bingo halls, state officials became more aggressive in asserting state criminal jurisdiction to halt the tribal games not in conformity with state laws. This conflict led to the Supreme Court decision in *California* v. *Cabazon Band of Mission Indians* (480 U.S. Stat. 202 [1987]), where the Court first considered the extent of California's criminal jurisdiction on tribal lands.

After surveying the relevant state laws on gambling, the Court concluded that since "California permits a substantial amount of gambling activity, including bingo, and actually promotes gambling through its state lottery, we must conclude that California regulates rather than prohibits gambling in general and bingo in particular" (*Cabazon*, 480 U.S. Stat. at 211). The Court also rejected the state's assertion that the tribal bingo enterprises violated the Organized Crime Control Act pursuant to federal law. The Court stated that the relevant test was whether the tribal activity violated the state's public policy and found that federal officials had not sought enforcement against the tribal enterprises (*Cabazon*, 480 U.S. Stat. at 213–214). In essence, the *Cabazon* decision affirmed the inherent sovereignty of tribes to regulate industry and economic ventures within the tribal jurisdiction.

In the aftermath of the *Cabazon* decision, federal legislation to regulate tribal gaming was finalized incorporating the Court's distinction between criminal/prohibitory and civil/regulatory activities for state jurisdiction. The Indian Gaming Regulatory Act of 1988 provides that a tribe may operate gaming when the tribe is located in a state "which does not, as a matter of criminal law or public policy, prohibit such gaming activity" (25 U.S.C. § 2701[5]).

The success of the few tribes able to reap substantial revenue has overshadowed the modest revenue or limited benefit of "job and income" generation experienced by a majority of the tribes entering the gaming industry (A. Meister 2005–2006:30). In 2004, Indian gaming facilities grossing the highest revenues were located in California, Connecticut, Arizona, Minnesota, Wisconsin, Oklahoma, Washington, Michigan, Florida, and New York. Facilities experiencing a downturn in profits in 2004 were located in Louisiana, Maine, Mississippi, and South Carolina (A. Meister 2005–2006:2) ("Gaming," this vol.).

Tribal gaming data for 2004 indicated significant growth of gaming revenue reaching over $19 billion, nongaming revenue at $1.9 billion, wages of $9 billion and the number of jobs estimated to be 279,000 (A. Meister 2005–2006:30). This influx of capital into tribal coffers has provided an economic base allowing for strategic planning by tribes to diversify tribal economies. A fundamental building block of such strategies is the development of tribal corporate entities.

## Tribal Development Corporations

Tribal governments have assumed a dual role under the Reorganization Act's provisions as both the governing body of the tribe and the corporate developer of tribal resources. To take advantage of the federal recognition of tribal jurisdiction and immunity, tribes have found it necessary to operate their businesses under the auspices of the tribal government to insure adherence to federal law recognition of the unique political status attached to tribal ventures (L.M. Graham 2004:612–613).

This dual role of tribal government has presented a challenge to tribal leadership to find effective ways to insulate business decision-makers from the political decision-makers. For example, the Confederated Tribes of Warm Springs, Oregon (vol. 12:171–173), voted by referendum in 1966 to finance a tribal forest-products complex and set up a separate board and business manager that "put the enterprise at arm's length from tribal government" (R.H. White 1990:204).

The primary business model in the United States is the corporation, the fictional entity in the law able to conduct business when properly organized under articles of incorporation and bylaws. Indian nations have implemented this business structure since the authorization under section 17 of the Reorganization Act provided for federal charters of incorporation. The number, extent, and purposes of tribal corporations remain within the authority of each tribe to determine.

In a ruling of the United States Internal Revenue Service, the agency stated that Indian tribes conducting commercial activities and corporations organized by Indian tribes are exempt from federal taxation (Rev. Ruling 94-16). Furthermore, tribal corporations are not required to be chartered under the specific terms of section 17 or organized under the Indian Reorganization Act at all to claim tax exemption. This exemption from federal tax structures has afforded immediate and profound advantages to tribal corporations. In contrast, if a tribe were to charter a corporation under state law, the corporation would no longer have the advantage of federal tax immunity and would be subject to state and local regulation and taxation (Rev. Ruling 94-16).

Building on the revenues generated from gaming operations, many Indian nations have created business complexes with multiple industries in order to diversify economic development and minimize risk across ventures. Examples include the Mississippi Band of Choctaw operating retail enterprises, tourism (vol. 14:160), and manufacturing enterprises, such as making auto parts for auto manufacturers and the operation of an American Greetings card company (L.M. Graham 2004:601). As of 2003, the Choctaw provided over 8,000 full-time permanent jobs with 65 percent of those in its workforce being non-Indian. In Mississippi, the Choctaw are one of the largest employers with an estimated annual payroll of $123.7 million. With the profits generated, the Choctaw have reinvested over $210 million into Mississippi economic development projects (Lyons 2005:20). The Oklahoma Choctaw also have diverse businesses (fig. 1).

Another example of casino owners ("Gaming," fig. 3, this vol.) is the Morongo Band of Mission Indians in California, who have diversified by acquiring an A&W restaurant franchise, an expanded Shell gasoline station, the three retail stores and the mail order operations of Hadley Fruit Orchards, and an Arrowhead Mountain Spring Water bottling plant valued at $26 million. All operated on the Morongo reservation (Lyons 2005:19).

The Cherokee Nation owns businesses in the gaming, hospitality, personnel services, distribution, manufacturing, telecommunications, and environmental services industries. The Nation seeks to create more jobs for Cherokee citizens and to build industries in Cherokee communities so Cherokees can be employed near their homes. In 1999 Cherokee Nation's business operations employed 700 people; in 2007 that number is nearly 4,000, and revenues are about $500 million a year (fig. 2). In 2004, the Cherokee Nation enacted the Jobs Growth Act, which requires Cherokee-owned businesses to dedicate 70 percent of their profits to a fund used to invest in new or existing businesses (*Cherokee Phoenix* 2006:17).

The Chickasaw Nation is diversifying outside of gaming, going into entertainment and hospitality. To compliment the 12 gaming centers and casinos, the Chickasaw Nation developed two hotels, seven restaurants, and a movie theater. Fur-

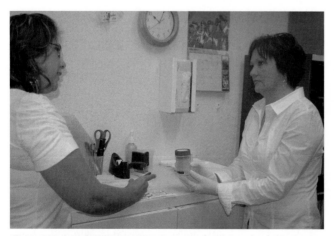

Choctaw Nation of Okla., Durant.

Fig. 1. Oklahoma Choctaw businesses. left, Rapid Results, a lab for DNA and illegal drug testing for area businesses operated by the tribe since 2001. Robin Yearby, left, is shown a drug-screening kit by Vonnie Houser. Both women are Choctaw Nation of Okla. tribal members. right, Choctaw Nation Day Care, operating since 1990. Krissy Schmitz, teacher and tribal member, leads a group of toddlers in a song. Children are Charley Hampton, Derek Downs, Holten John, and Kaydon Mimms. The tribe owns 6 day care locations in southeast Okla. Photographs by Vonna Shults, Durant, Okla., 2007.

Cherokee Nation, Tahlequah, Okla.

Fig. 2. Cherokee Nation Industries, which does aerospace and defense contracting. John Berry and Charles Foster, both Cherokee, are assembling wires for wire harnesses at the facility at Stilwell, Okla., 2007.

ther, the Chickasaw Nation operates a chocolate factory and a commercial bank. The planned Chickasaw Cultural Center and Artesian Hotel will support cultural and educational tourism (*Oklahoma Indian Gaming and Tourism Magazine* 2006:5).

Many tribes operate resorts (fig. 3), campgrounds, and golf courses.

## Legal and Judicial Support for Development

With the expansion of corporate entities, Indian nations have necessarily engaged lawyers to develop corporate and commercial legal codes, represent their interests in contract negotiations, and defend tribal positions in dispute situations. In the business world, predictability in application of law, business customs, and dispute resolution are expected. These expectations have been met by tribal governments legislating corporate and commercial codes addressing the business landscape within the tribal jurisdiction.

For example, the Business Code of the White Mountain Apache, Arizona, requires every person that shall "commence, practice, transact, or carry on any business" within the tribal jurisdiction to apply and receive a business license (§ 1.2 [2000]). The Sisseton-Wahpeton Sioux Commercial Code has the stated purpose of "enhancing the Tribe's ability to contract, resolve disputes with vendors, enter into third party financing and provide an orderly system of commercial law to the community and Tribal members" (§ 69-01-01 [1996]). Within the Absentee Shawnee Corporation Act of 1986, the provisions for establishing a corporation under tribal law are set forth including the legal requirements and consequences of the corporate entity. Tribal corporate, business, and commercial codes are a necessary outgrowth of the revitalization of tribal economic development in recent decades.

Another key component to tribal economic development is a strong and legitimate judiciary available to resolve business disputes, patron disputes, and bring determinations to bear in all manner of civil actions (see "Tribal Government in the United States," this vol.). An overview of the tribal court systems across the country results in the conclusion that "[t]he vast majority of tribal court decisions are rendered after fair procedures and deliberations by a court or jury, using standard rules and practices, and after granting all parties equal protection and due process" (Haddock and Miller 2004:209).

The civil jurisdiction of tribal courts extends to nonmembers when those nonmembers are engaged in business activities with the tribe and tribal members. In *Montana* v. *United States* (450 U.S. Stat. 544 [1981]), the Supreme Court explained that "[a] Tribe may regulate, through taxation, licensing, or other means, the activities of nonmembers who enter consensual relationships with the Tribe or its members, through commercial dealing, contracts, leases or other arrangements" (450 U.S. Stat. at 565–566). This affirmation of tribal regulatory authority over commercial relationships within the tribal jurisdiction underscores the importance of a strong independent judiciary to apply and interpret tribal business law and settle civil disputes.

## Competitive Advantages

Macroeconomics is one avenue for assessing modern tribal sovereignty. Economic advantages that are more cost efficient or profitable are considered competitive advantages over other industry players. By examining the competitive advantages of tribal enterprises, tribes can continue to establish foundational strategies that support the economic self-reliance of Indian nations (K.E. Johnson 2005:79–84).

### Tribal Immunity and Tax Exemption

In this context, "fixed" competitive advantages affect organizational entities, such as tribal corporations or Indian nations versus states and state-regulated corporations. In terms of "fixed" competitive advantages, those inherent rights retained by tribal entities are: exemption from federal income tax, immunity from state and local property and income taxes, immunity from state and local regulations, immunity from state and local labor regulations, and ultimately, tribal sovereign immunity.

Indian nations are not taxable entities under federal law, regardless of whether tribal sponsored activities occur on or off reservations or within tribal historical jurisdictional boundaries. With federal corporate tax rates above 30 percent, this puts tribal corporate entities at a tremendous cost efficient competitive advantage on cost (C. Edwards 2006:2).

*133*

Similarly, Indian nations have retained immunity from state and local property and income taxes. In some cases, this tribal tax immunity from state and local income and property taxes narrowly applies to economic activity within the borders of the tribal reservation or within a tribe's historical boundaries. United States Supreme Court cases have defined the tax immunity status of Indian nations and the contours of when and where that immunity attaches preempting state taxation.

When a tribe engages in economic activity beyond tribal borders, the Supreme Court held in *Mescalero Apache Tribe* v. *Jones* (411 U.S. Stat. 145 [1973]) that tribes are subject to nondiscriminatory state taxes for off-reservation activities upholding the imposition of state sales taxes on the gross receipts of the tribe's ski resort services (411 U.S. Stat. at 149). This decision sets forth the rule that the locus of a tribal economic activity is relevant to whether state and local taxes are preempted under federal law.

In the 1995 Supreme Court decision, *Oklahoma Tax Commission* v. *Chickasaw Nation* (515 U.S. Stat. 450), the Court held that: Oklahoma may not apply a state motor fuels tax on fuel sold by a tribe within Indian country and that state income tax does apply to both Indians and non-Indians who reside outside of Indian country within the state's borders (515 U.S. Stat. at 453). However, the Supreme Court decision in *Wagnon* v. *Prairie Band of Potawatomi* (126 S.Ct. 676 [2005]) allowed the state of Kansas to apply its motor fuel tax on the non-Indian distributor supplying fuel to a tribally owned gas station within Indian country where the legal incidence of the tax was found to be on the non-Indian distributor rather than the Indian retailer.

As this line of cases illustrates, states have been very aggressive in asserting state taxation in Indian country. The Supreme Court has proved to be a staunch vanguard for Indian nations when state taxation attempts to reach Indians residing or doing business within Indian country. However, state taxation may still reach non-Indians within Indian Country and Indians that reside outside of Indian Country.

Ho-Chunk Tribe, Black River Falls, Wisc.

Fig. 3. Ho-Chunk resort hotel of 315 rooms, Baraboo, Wisc. top left and top right, Hotel lobby. bottom, Exterior of hotel. The resort includes a casino and convention center and employs over 1,000 people, about 25% of whom are tribal members. The tribe, which employs 4,500 in all its ventures, operates 4 other casino resorts, with more in development. It is the 25th largest employer in the state. Photographs by Paul Arentz, 2007.

### Tribal Legislation on Labor Relations

Indian nations can enact legislation either prohibiting or promoting union provisions in collective bargaining agreements based in Indian Country. The Tenth Circuit Court of Appeals in *National Labor Relations Board* v. *the Pueblo of San Juan* (276 F.3d 1186 [2002]) held that tribes retain their sovereign authority to enact labor legislation within the tribal jurisdiction where tribes are not specifically mentioned in the provisions of the National Labor Relations Act (276 F.3d at 1195). In states without "right to work" legislation, tribes can enact such legislation, effectively diminishing the negotiating power of labor, which provides the perception of a more favorable business environment than the surrounding state. Conversely, in states that have enacted "right to work" legislation, tribes might enact pro-union legislation in their jurisdictional boundaries and reservations. As an indispensable factor of production, labor in Indian country is growing, and pro-union legislation would expand further tribal labor polices, such as Tribal Employment Rights Offices.

Indian nations have often legislated employment preferences similar to the federal Indian preference for qualified applicants to the Bureau of Indian Affairs (25 U.S.C. § 472). The federal Indian preference statute was upheld by the Supreme Court after challenge was brought by non-Indian civil service employees. The Court in *Morton* v. *Mancari* (417 U.S. Stat. 535, 554–555 [1974]) stated that the federal government had a legitimate reason for the Indian preference in furthering tribal self-government.

Private businesses located near Indian communities may enforce contractual tribal preference provisions. Such provisions have been subject to challenge in federal courts as discrimination based on national origin prohibited in Title VII of the federal Civil Rights Act. The Ninth Circuit Court held that the Hopi tribal member's challenge to a private employer operating under a lease with the Navajo Nation including tribal preference for Navajo tribal members constituted a suit where the Navajo Nation was an indispensable party and thus, the suit was dismissed due to tribal sovereign immunity (*Dawavendewa* v. *Salt River Project Agricultural Improvement and Power District,* 276 F.3d 1150 [2002]). In the main, Indian nations and entities may apply tribal member preferences for all tribal positions.

### Tribal Sovereign Immunity

A major tenet of sustainable tribal sovereignty is the protection of the Indian tribe trust from limitless and uncontested lawsuits, whether or not the tribal business or governmental activities occurred within the tribe's jurisdictional boundaries (L.M. Graham 2004:632). In *Kiowa Tribe of Oklahoma* v. *Manufacturing Technologies, Inc.* (523 U.S. Stat. 751 [1998]), the Supreme Court held that where there has neither been a tribal waiver of sovereign immunity or a federal law waiving tribal sovereignty immunity a suit may not

be maintained against the tribe by a private entity. In *Oklahoma Tax Commission* v. *Citizen Band Potawatomi Indian Tribe of Oklahoma* (498 U.S. Stat. 505 [1991]), the Supreme Court held that the state may not bring suit directly or by counterclaim against a tribe absent "appropriate legislation from Congress" (498 U.S. at 514). This immunity from lawsuits is a protection against hostile litigation that would drain tribal coffers.

This protection may be viewed by outside investors as an impediment to doing business in Indian country and requires tribal entities to educate others on the contours of tribal sovereign immunity. To alleviate outside investor anxiety regarding tribal sovereign immunity, Indian nations have a range of options to provide security in business transactions. For example, within business contracts, Indian nations may agree that any disputes arising out of the contract will be settled by an agreed third-party arbitrator or arbitration association. Tribes may choose to include a limited waiver of sovereign immunity in a business contract to provide judicial review in the event of a contract breach. By directly tying a breach of contract term to the relinquishment of tribal collateral, the addition of this contract term may provide greater security for those doing business within Indian lands. Finally, Indian nations may agree to hold in escrow an agreed monetary amount to offset any contract damages that may arise.

The Supreme Court has upheld the enforcement in state court of an arbitration award against a tribe where the arbitration had been agreed upon as the dispute resolution mechanism under a commercial contract. In *C & L Enterprises, Inc.* v. *Citizen Band of Potawatomi Indian Tribe of Oklahoma* (532 U.S. Stat. 411 [2001]), the Court strictly construed the contract terms and found that the tribe had agreed to "arbitrate disputes with C & L relating to the contract, to the governance of Oklahoma law, and to the enforcement in any court having jurisdiction" (532 U.S. Stat. at 414). This decision has alerted Indian nations that commercial contract language may operate as an express waiver of sovereign immunity.

### Tribal Manufactured Products and Services

As Indian nations have entered into the production of goods through manufacturing and adding value to stock goods, legal challenges from states have centered on whether such products are exempted from state taxation. A series of United States Supreme Court decisions has defined the area and engineered a test to determine when state taxes are preempted.

One of the first cases in this series is *White Mountain Apache Tribe* v. *Bracker* (448 U.S. Stat. 136 [1980]), which considered the imposition of state taxes on a non-Indian enterprise doing business exclusively on the White Mountain Apache reservation in the federally regulated timber industry (448 U.S. 137–138). The Court stated that the status of Indian nations has "given rise to two independent but related barriers to the assertion of state regulatory authority over tribal reservations and members" (448 U.S. Stat. at 142). The first barrier is when state regulatory authority is preempted by federal law and the second is based upon the rights of tribes "to make their own laws and be ruled by them" (448 U.S. Stat. at 142, quoting *Williams* v. *Lee*, 358 U.S. Stat. 217, 220 [1959]). Either barrier may stand alone effectively prohibiting state regulation.

Applying this analysis, the Court engaged in "a particularized inquiry into the nature of the state, federal, and tribal interests at stake, an inquiry designed to determine whether, in the specific context, the exercise of state authority would violate federal law" (448 U.S. Stat. at 145). The Court rejected the state's assertion that the taxes were permitted simply based upon a state interest in raising revenue (448 U.S. Stat. at 150). Because the federal regulatory scheme was "so pervasive as to preclude the additional burdens sought to be imposed" by the state, "[t]he imposition of the taxes at issue would undermine that policy in a context in which the Federal Government has undertaken to regulate the most minute details of timber production and expressed a firm desire that the Tribe should retain the benefits derived from the harvesting and sale of reservation timber" (448 U.S. Stat. at 148–149). Thus, the *Bracker* decision stands for the proposition that when a state seeks to impose its regulatory and taxation authority on Indian economic activity the proper test to be applied is whether the state regulation is preempted by federal and tribal interests. Additionally, when the economic activity is on-reservation conduct involving only Indians, the federal interest in fostering tribal self-government is at its strongest rendering state law inapplicable (448 U.S. Stat. at 144).

In *Washington* v. *Confederated Tribes of the Colville Indian Reservation* (447 U.S. Stat. 134 [1980]), the Supreme Court described the tribal interest in revenue generation as at its "strongest when the revenues are derived from value generated on the reservation by activities involving the Tribes" (447 U.S. Stat. at 156–157). The *Colville* case coupled with the *Bracker* decision upholds tribal products as a result of value generated on the reservation as exempt from the reach of state regulatory and taxing authority.

The Omaha tribe manufactured cigarettes sold on the reservation from 1997 to 2002. Four states sued over the tribe's not cooperating with the tobacco industry settlement, although state taxes were preempted for the cigarettes sold on the reservation. The Arapaho operated a smoke shop (vol. 13:853). The Squaxin of Washington State, a tribe of 936 enrolled members, has successfully manufactured tobacco products (fig. 4).

A third important case in this series is *New Mexico* v. *Mescalero Apache Tribe* (462 U.S. 324 [1983]). In this case, the Mescalero Apache tribe had devoted considerable tribal and federal resources to developing a resort complex to promote hunting and fishing activities within the tribal jurisdiction governed by tribal laws (462 U.S. Stat. at 327–329). New Mexico attempted to impose state laws and regulations by arresting nonmembers engaging in on-reserva-

tion hunting and fishing (462 U.S. Stat. at 329). The Court asserted that "[s]tate jurisdiction is preempted by the operation of federal law if it interferes or is incompatible with federal and tribal interests reflected in federal law, unless the State interests at stake are sufficient to justify the assertion of State authority" (462 U.S. Stat. at 334). Finding that the imposition of concurrent regulation by New Mexico would disrupt the tribal and federal regulatory scheme and threaten the economic development and self-government of the Mescalero Apache, the Court concluded that the state's hunting and fishing laws on the reservation were preempted. This line of cases lead to the conclusion that when tribes generate value in goods and services within the tribal jurisdiction, the result is that state regulation and taxation is preempted.

*Federal Programs and Incentives*

Congress has passed a specific law to encourage federal contractors to subcontract with Indian organizations or tribally owned economic enterprises by providing "an additional amount of compensation" equal to 5 percent of the total subcontract amount to the federal contractor (25 U.S.C. 1544). This is an incentive for federal contractors to utilize Indian-owned contractors, thereby increasing the experience of the subcontractors and their marketability.

The Bureau of Indian Affairs, recognizing the need for greater tribal self-sufficiency, has a number of programs intended to enhance tribal economic development. The Indian Revolving Loan Fund allows tribes to acquire loans for the purposes of: housing development, educational endeavors, to finance economic enterprises, and to generally promote economic development (25 C.F.R. § 101.2). Another loan option from the Bureau is the Indian Loan Guaranty and Insurance Fund, guaranteeing up to 90 percent of a loan acquired by tribal members, Indian-owned companies, and tribal enterprises (25 C.F.R. § 103.2). At the application stage, the Bureau of Indian Affairs is authorized to provide technical assistance, assistance for competent management, and assistance for financial administration to Indian loan applicants (25 U.S.C. § 1541). In addition, the Bureau has available an interest subsidy program that reimburses part of the interest due on behalf of Indian borrowers (25 C.F.R. § 103.20). Seeking to bridge access to capital issues by providing grants, the Indian Business Development Program provides equity capital through grants to Indians, Indian nations, and Indian-owned businesses (25 U.S.C. § 1521).

The purposes of the Native American Business Development, Trade Promotion, and Tourism Act of 2000 support a wide policy goal of promoting tribal economic development. The Act sets forth stated goals of: acknowledging that Indian tribes "retain the right to enter into contracts and agreements to trade freely, and seek enforcement of treaty and trade rights"; encouraging "intertribal, regional and international trade and business development" to raise the productivity and standard of living for tribal members; and promoting

Squaxin Island Tribe, Kamilche, Wash.

Fig. 4. Squaxin businesses. top left, Justin Johns, tribal member, cleaning and grading shucked oysters at Salish Seafoods, Harstine I., south Puget Sound, which employs 14 people. The oysters are harvested by hand to protect wetlands. The tribe bought an oyster company in 1975 and has expanded to sell mussels and salmon. top right, Nicholas Cooper, tribal member, operating the packaging machine at Skookum Creek Tobacco, the factory that manufactures Complete brand cigarettes. Opened in 2000, the tribally owned company distributes the cigarettes through regional as well as local outlets. bottom, Kamilche Trading Post, the gas station and retail business. It employs 54 people and is open 20 hours a day. Note the traditional cedar posts. Photographs by Theresa Henderson, 2007.

TRIBAL SOVEREIGNTY AND ECONOMIC DEVELOPMENT

"economic self-sufficiency and political self-determination" for Indian nations among other goals (25 U.S.C. § 4301 a–b).

The Act established the Office of Native American Business Development to serve as a coordination point among Department of Interior, Small Business Administration, Department of Labor, and other pertinent agencies (25 U.S.C. § 4303b). The office serves as an assistance center for Indian-owned businesses for a broad range of development needs such as marketing, technical assistance, and financial planning. Through this Act, tribes may choose among regulatory environments across national lines to manufacture goods or services piecemeal based upon which regulatory environment is most suited for the particular economic activity.

The Native American Export and Trade Promotion Program received its authorization under this Act. The goal of the program is to stimulate demand for Indian goods and services (25 U.S.C. § 4304b). The program is an avenue to encourage tribal activities such as marketing, financing of trade missions, and insuring the participation of pertinent federal agencies in international trade fairs (25 U.S.C. § 4304c). Any Indian-owned business engaged in importing or exporting activities is eligible for business development technical assistance including identification of foreign markets, any compliance with foreign or domestic laws relating to importing and exporting of tribal goods and services, and other technical assistance for entering into financial agreements with foreign partners (25 U.S.C. § 4304d).

The Act promotes tourism development demonstration projects in four areas: Oklahoma, the Pacific Northwest, the Plains, and the Four Corners region of the Southwest (25 U.S.C. § 4305). The demonstration projects are centered on facilitating the development and financing of tourism infrastructure, such as feasibility studies, market reports, and assistance for the creation of roads as part of the physical infrastructure (25 U.S.C. § 4305).

Tribal entities, like state entities, qualify for establishing Community Development Entities, which are community development financial institutions within their reservations or historical boundaries. Federally certified entities are entitled to administer federal incentives such as New Market Tax Credits to companies who provide services and meet the applicable criteria (26 U.S.C. § 45D).

Under the federal Small Business Administration, tribal corporations of Indian nations are eligible to obtain federal contracts. To be eligible, a tribal entity must initially establish economic disadvantage (13 C.F.R. § 124.109). Tribes that qualify under this program may be awarded a sole-source contract without limitations on the federal contract value (13 C.F.R. § 124.506b). Any direct award to a tribe under this program is safeguarded from challenge by any other business entity due to the regulations "no contest" provision (13 C.F.R. § 124.517). Tribal enterprises are not subject to size limitations regarding the entire range of tribal corporate affiliations (13 C.F.R. § 124.109). Due to the success of tribes qualifying in this way, there have been legislative proposals to place limits on the contract values and size of enterprises.

*Advantages for Tribal Entrepreneurs*

Indian-owned private businesses located within tribal jurisdictions are eligible for many of the federal programs and incentives described above. Additionally, Indian-owned businesses on the reservation are exempt from state and local regulation as entities regulated under tribal law. State sales taxes applicable to non-Indian transactions are permissible under federal law within tribal jurisdictions. Any corporation within a tribe's jurisdictional boundaries has the advantage of accelerated depreciation of their asset base (26 U.S.C. § 168j). Tribally located corporations receive tax credits based on wages and health insurance for tribal employees who live on or near the tribal boundaries (26 U.S.C. § 45A).

*Tribal Civil Regulatory Authority*

As recognized in the regulation of tribal gaming, Indian nations may regulate markets and industries on tribal lands similar to those that are presently regulated by states, such as health care, insurance, and commerce. This opportunity for tribes to continue expanding their civil regulatory jurisdictions may prove to be the most compelling economic opportunities as a natural outgrowth the affirmation of tribal civil regulatory authority in the 1988 *Cabazon* decision. Tribes may provide alternatives to state regulated industries. Examples of tribes regulating industry concurrently with states would be fuel and tobacco sales and distribution. Larger, and therefore, potentially more lucrative regulatory markets Indian nations may expand into include health care, insurance, and commerce.

*Labor Advantages*

With the United States developing more into a service-based economy, countries like China and India have capitalized on their low labor costs and have embraced the manufacturing industry and some service sectors like call centers. Competitively speaking, these countries can produce manufacturing goods more efficiently than service-based economies like the United States. This has enabled many of these countries not only to compete on a global basis but also to be industry leaders. Similarly, the most tangible comparative advantage of tribes is the low labor wage rate. Real per capita income for Indians residing on reservations was barely one-third of the national average for the year 2000, despite the fact that gaming multiplier effects are stronger than in nongaming reservation economies. The growth rate of reservation labor in the 1990s was 11 percent (J. Taylor 2005:27–29).

*Tribal Finance*

Tribal financing is necessary for two reasons. The first is that most Indian nations lack access to major sources of capital. The second is that financing provides capital for tribal nation building and the building of economic infrastructure. Tribal financing allows for issuing bonds and funding tribally owned business ventures, such as building a new gaming facility or any other economic activity a tribe undertakes. Indian nations, like municipalities, may issue debt that is tax exempt through bond offerings (Cohen 2005: 1306–1312).

## Theories of Tribal Economic Development and Nation Building

The Harvard Project on American Indian Economic Development in the 1990s published several pieces of research focused on economic development in Indian Country. One argued that successful governments are driven by cultural principles, spoken and unspoken, defining how persons interact as individuals within society. Pre-existing tribal norms may or may not mesh with those rules proscribed by the federal government, and in many cases where a "cultural match" is lacking, the result is ineffective tribal government (Cornell and Kalt 1991:15, 19).

Several conditions are necessary to the economic development of tribes, including the policy development relating to commerce, especially those that promote free trade and stability in tribal governments, the ability for fair and effective dispute resolution (typically a government with a sound judicial system will economically outperform one that does not), some degree of separation of business and politics and finally a competent bureaucracy that supports the economic goals of the tribe (Cornell and Kalt 1998:12–20). For example, a tribal enterprise having a separate board of directors insulating business decisions from politics increases the chances of being profitable by seven to one (Cornell and Kalt 1992:31).

Two separate and distinct approaches of economic development can be seen in modern native economic development; one, the "jobs and income approach" is short-term in nature. In many cases, if the desired outcome is merely jobs or income, the result will surely not be a long-term sustainable economy, but rather a reactive environment that pushes planners to start *any* kind of business (Cornell and Kalt 1998:5–7). The "nation building" approach is first proactive, rooted in strategic planning, involves multiple stakeholders (whether it be investor, tribal community leader, or prospective employee), and takes a wholistic approach to creating an environment where businesses can thrive in the long run, which incorporates the foundational stability of governments. In terms of process for development, especially wholistic nation building, four major milestones must be interconnected: tribes must embrace their own sovereignty, develop effective institutions, plan strategic direction, and then provide accountability and action on that strategy (Cornell and Kalt 1992:53–54).

Tribal economic development is unique in the global environment in that Indian nations seek to do more than simply maximize profit and issue shareholder dividends. Indian nations engage in economic development to achieve various goals, such as to build economic infrastructure, provide jobs and income, maintain tribal social programs, reinvest funds into community development, and sustain cultural lifeways. An example of tribal values in action is the funneling of gaming revenue into creation of cultural centers, health clinics, tribal schools, and businesses in tribal territory (Anderson 2005:40–43). Underlying these actions are the fundamental values of sharing, generosity, and the belief that the whole community benefits from wealth creation.

One key for tribal self-reliance is for tribal insiders with tribal expertise to develop economic strategic plans (D.H. Smith 2000:94). Indian nations in the twenty-first century had more economic options than they have ever had. Many tribal cultures subscribe to the concepts of interdependence and resource planning for future generations. These concepts may translate into the economic development strategies of contemporary Indian nations. The melding of culture and economic development for Indian nations will lead to stronger, more enduring, wholistic economic institutions.

# Alaska Native Corporations

ROSITA WORL

Alaska Natives, including the Aleut, Inupiat and Yup'ik Eskimos, and the Athapaskan, Tlingit, and Haida Indians, share many cultural similarities with other Native Americans. However, in 2007 they are characterized by very different institutional forms and arrangements than those of other federally recognized tribes. These differences can be attributed to a unique history. In 1971 their aboriginal land claims with the United States were resolved by congressional legislation (vol. 15:657–61).

Alaska was the last portion of mainland North America acquired by the United States, being purchased from Russia in 1867. Lacking in land suitable for agriculture, Alaska's attractions were limited to fishing, timber, gold, and later oil. As a result during the late nineteenth and early twentieth centuries migration to the new territory was meager. Contact between these settlers and the Native Alaskans was relatively limited, and the question of "aboriginal title" to land was basically ignored until the 1960s when the development of the North Slope oil fields made a settlement necessary.

Alaska Natives pursued a legislative resolution to their land claims in Congress that allowed them to form profit-making corporations. These corporations hold fee simple title to Native land. Unlike trust lands, which is the common method under which federally recognized tribes hold reservation lands and which are subject to oversight by the federal government, Alaska Natives have full control and ownership of their lands. Alaska Natives also differ from Indians in the rest of the United States in that in addition to their profit-making corporations, they have nonprofit organizations that administer governmental services at both the regional and statewide levels.

Congress did not extinguish the tribal rights and status of Alaska Natives or alter the government-to-government relationship with tribal governments when it enacted the land claims legislation. Over 200 tribes exist in Alaska, but the conveyance of lands to corporations meant that tribes in Alaska were to be governments without a land base. Ironically, the only remaining trust lands in Alaska include the Annette Island Reservation, which was created in 1891 for the Canadian Tsimshian Indians who migrated to Alaska, and the allotment lands that were conveyed to individual Natives under the Alaska Native Allotment Act of 1906 (ch. 2469, 34 U.S. Stat.197).

In 1971 Congress enacted the Alaska Native Claims Settlement Act (ANCSA), Public Law 92-203. Under ANCSA, 13 regional corporations and 200 village corporations were organized to hold 44 million acres of land (fig. 1). The corporations received nearly $1 billion for the extinguishment of their remaining aboriginal claims in Alaska. ANCSA was viewed by Congress with its major features of land, money, and corporations as a means to assimilate Alaska Natives into the larger society. Congress wanted to avoid creating any reservations or "racially defined" organizations and instead supported corporations as the vehicle to implement ANCSA.

Natives, on the other hand, viewed ANCSA and corporations as vehicles to ensure control and ownership of their land and as means to achieve self-determination (Marrs 2003:28). That Native people embraced the corporate model was evident by the 1971 Alaska Federation of Natives convention theme, "In the White Man's Society, We Need White Man's Tools" (Arnold 1978:153).

## History

The path to the congressional settlement began with the 1867 Treaty of Cession (15 U.S. Stat. 539) under which the United States purchased the occupation rights from Russia. Although Russia claimed jurisdiction of Alaska, in actuality, its control of Alaska's land was largely limited to the trading posts it operated at Sitka and Kodiak and a few other temporary settlements. The Tlingit Indians of southeast Alaska objected to the sale, arguing that the United States should have paid the $7.2 million to the rightful owners (Bancroft 1886: 609). A special agent of the Treasury Department reported in 1869 that some of the more warlike Tlingit chiefs were in favor of driving out the Americans, but they were dissuaded by a Chilkat chief who convinced them of the vulnerability of the coastal villages against the attacks of United States war vessels—a threat that was to became a reality years later with the naval bombardment of Angoon and Kake villages (*Tlingit and Haida Indians of Alaska* v. *United States,* 1959:397).

In the 100 years after America assumed jurisdiction of Alaska, Natives pursued legal and political resolutions to their aboriginal land claims. Their efforts to protect their land

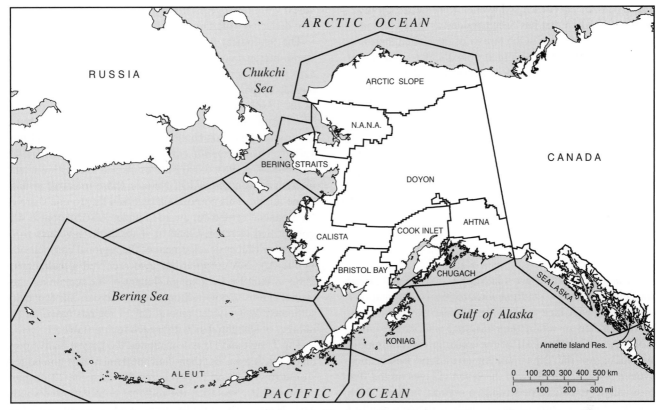

Fig. 1. The 12 Alaska Native regional corporations. A "13th region" includes Alaska Natives residing outside the state.

ownership were deterred by laws that failed to define the terms under which Alaska Natives were to settle their land claims. The 1867 Treaty of Cession provided that the "uncivilized tribes" were to be subject to the same laws as other American Indians, but it contained no provisions directing how Natives were to secure their land ownership. Subsequent congressional action, including both the Organic Act of 1884 (23 U.S. Stat. 24) and the Alaska Statehood Act of 1958 (72 U.S. Stat. 339), recognized the use and occupancy land rights of Alaska Natives, but again it failed to outline the terms by which Natives could settle their aboriginal claims.

The Alaska Statehood Act allowed the newly created state government to select 103 million acres of land. Although the act stipulated that Native lands were exempt from selection, the state ignored this provision and began to select lands used and occupied by Native villages. Additionally, the state moved to claim royalties from federal oil and gas leases on Native lands (R.S. Jones 1981:12). Political conflicts between the Natives and the State of Alaska mounted as the state moved to select land under its entitlement.

### Regional and Statewide Unification

In the face of increasing land loss and ongoing threats to their hunting and fishing economy, the independent and autonomous Native groups organized regional associations.

The geographic boundaries among the regional entities generally followed the ancient cultural and territorial divisions. In 1966, the 12 regional nonprofit organizations, which had been formed throughout the state, united under a central organization, the Alaska Federation of Natives. Land was central to the way of life of Alaska Native people and formed the core and basis of their identity. This common value became the unifying objective in seeking a settlement of their land claims, and the Federation became the voice of Native people to Congress. They vigorously protested the state's effort to select lands until their claims had been resolved. Ultimately Secretary of the Interior Stewart Udall ordered a "land freeze" on the disposition of all federal lands in Alaska and suspended federal oil and gas lease sales. The freeze prohibited the State of Alaska from selecting further lands and blocked the construction of an 800-mile Trans Alaska oil pipeline that was to bring the oil resources in the homeland of North Slope Inupiat in the Arctic to Prince William Sound.

With political pressure mounting from the State of Alaska, which was unable to select land, and from the oil industry, which was unable to develop Alaska's oil resources, the Alaska Federation of Natives seized the opportunity to lobby Congress for a land claims settlement. The Natives leading this effort were drawn from the ranks of the traditional political leaders, including hunters, fishers, and whalers. They were joined by a small cadre of western-educated Natives, a few of whom had college degrees. *141*

These Alaska Native men and women were successful in securing legislation that has been heralded as the largest aboriginal land settlement in the history of the United States.

The land settlement diverged dramatically from earlier treaty settlements with Indian tribes. It lead Alaska Natives on a different economic and political journey. While Natives celebrated in their victorious effort, they soon learned that in their haste to secure an acceptable settlement and in focusing solely on the size and allocation of the land base, they had neglected to analyze the structural issues and the potential cultural consequences of the legislative land settlement.

## Land

Of the total 375 million acres in Alaska, ANCSA authorized the conveyance of 40 million acres to Native corporations. The total acreage increased to 44 million acres when five reserves elected to retain their original reservation lands. ANCSA extinguished all of the existing reservations in Alaska except the Tsimshian Annette Island Reservation (vol. 7:294–297). It allowed the seven villages on the five reservations to choose between two options, both of which required forming corporations: to fully participate in all of the ANCSA provisions or to receive title to both the surface and subsurface estates of their revoked reservations. As a result of earlier legislative action, one village corporation, Klukwan, conveyed its reserve land to the village tribal government and also received title to 23,070 acres under a 1976 amendment to ANCSA (Public Law No. 94-456, October 4, 1976; 90 U.S. Stat. 1934, 43 U.S.C.A. § 16125d).

## Corporations

Twelve regional and 203 village corporations were incorporated to receive fee simple title to the 40 million acres of land awarded under ANCSA. Village corporations were entitled to receive 22 million acres of surface land, which were divided on a population basis. The regional corporations received full title to 16 million acres of land, which were divided on the basis of the total acreages in each region rather than on a population basis. Additionally, the regional corporations received title to the subsurface estate in the 22 million acres patented to the village corporations.

The remaining two million acres were allocated for other purposes including cemeteries and historical sites and four "urban" corporations, which had formerly been historic Native communities but were predominantly non-Native cities in the 1970s. Nine Native communities with populations less than 25 residents were also authorized to receive land under this entitlement. The total acreage for allotments, which had been filed prior to the passage of the act and con-

veyed within two years after the enactment of ANCSA, was also deducted from this two-million-acre allocation.

The Settlement Act allowed for the formation of a thirteenth regional corporation for those Natives whose permanent homes were outside Alaska. The decision to form an outside corporation was to be based on an affirmative vote of the 18,000 Natives who were residing outside of Alaska. The initial vote to establish the corporation failed, but a group of individuals challenged the vote in court and prevailed. The thirteenth corporation was formed in 1975 (Arnold 1978:196), 6,000 Natives elected to enroll in it, and the remaining non-resident Natives chose to enroll in their home region. This corporation received its pro rata share of the financial settlement awarded under ANCSA, but it was not entitled to receive land or share in the revenues from mineral or timber development of the regional corporations.

The ANCSA corporations also received a payment of $962 million for the extinguishment of the remaining aboriginal claims to 330 million acres in Alaska. The monetary settlement was divided among the 13 regions based on the number of shareholders within each region (table 1).

The Tlingit and Haida constituted the largest Native population in Alaska, but their land entitlement was limited to a single township or 23,040 acres for each the 12 eligible communities. Sealaska, the regional corporation in southeast Alaska, was initially authorized to receive 267,000 acres plus the subsurface estate of 576,000 acres, which included the subsurface lands of the village and urban corporations. The size of their land base was reduced because of an earlier land claims award. The Central Council of Tlingit and Haida Indian Tribes of Alaska was paid $7.5 million in 1968 as a result of the Court of Claims decision for the federal withdrawals of 20 million acres to create the Tongass National Forest, the Glacier Bay National Park, and the reservation for the Canadian Tsimshian. The Central Council is a federally recognized tribe and administers the funds awarded by the Court as well as a range of governmental services under the Indian Self-Determination and Education Assistance Act of 1975 (Public Law 93-638).

Congress created four urban corporations, two of which were in southeast Alaska, but failed to authorize land entitle-

**Table 1. Alaska Native Corporations, 2007**

| Corporation and Offices | Land |
| --- | --- |
| Aleut Corporation, Anchorage | 1.5 million subsurface and 66,000 surface acres |
| Arctic Slope Regional, Anchorage and Barrow | 5 million acres |
| Bering Straits, Anchorage and Nome | 2.2 million acres |
| Bristol Bay, Anchorage | 3 million acres |
| Calista, Anchorage | 6.5 million acres |
| Chugach, Anchorage | 928,000 acres |
| NANA, Kotzebue | 2.2 million acres |
| Koniag, Kodiak and Anchorage | 1 million acres in 1984 |

ments for five other southeast Alaska communities, on the basis that their populations were predominantly non-Native. These communities, which include Haines, Wrangell, Petersburg, Ketchikan, and Tenakee, are identified as the "landless villages," and they continued in 2007 to seek their land entitlements in Congress.

## Resource Revenue Sharing

One unusual provision of ANCSA is antithetical to the general expectations and motives of profit-making corporations and can be more correctly characteristic of corporate socialism. Under section 7(i), regional corporations are required to distribute 70 percent of their net profits from mineral and timber development among all regional corporations on a per capita basis. The regional corporation is then required to distribute a minimum of 50 percent of the 7(i) revenues it receives to village corporations and to a category of shareholders who are identified as "at-large" shareholders.

The mineral and timber resources vary significantly among the 12 regions in the state, and Congress imposed the 7(i) revenue-sharing provision as a means of equalizing the anticipated resource revenues between those regions that were resource rich and those regions that were resource poor. The premise of this congressional policy was that each Native group would share equally in the settlement without regard to the size of its land base.

By 2004, the resource-rich corporations had distributed more than $675 million among the regions and village corporations. Illustrative of the extent of revenue sharing is the record of the largest contributor. Sealaska Corporation, located in the forest-rich region of southeast Alaska, constitutes less than one percent of the entire ANCSA lands. Through 2005, Sealaska contributed $306.4 million in resource revenue-sharing funds and received $158.8 million from other regions (Sealaska Corporation 2005:58–59).

An unanticipated effect of the revenue-sharing provision has been its impact on timber harvests. The regional corporations with forest lands have generally doubled their annual harvest levels to meet their own corporate needs and to fund the projected revenue-sharing requirements. This has led to the criticism of "clear-cutting." The revenue-sharing funds have proven to be vital to the survival of many struggling corporations and particularly to village corporations that have limited business opportunities. One regional corporation, which was facing bankruptcy, was able to leverage a loan of $9.5 million based on the anticipated 7(i) revenues of future years (Sealaska Corporation Resolution 91-01).

## Shareholders

Another dramatic departure from treaty settlements with federally recognized tribes was the policy under which membership was recognized. Under ANCSA, Natives became shareholders and owners of stock as individuals in the Native corporations. The corporations hold title to land that was formerly owned by communal groups. Congress wanted to avoid creating any "racially defined institutions" and thus limited the restrictions on the transferability of ANCSA stock for 20 years and rejected any possibility of keeping the enrollment open for those children born after 1971. Additionally, shareholders would be able to sell their stock in 1991.

The Secretary of the Interior was authorized to prepare a roll of all Natives who were of one-fourth degree or more Alaska Native, who were born on or before the date of enactment of ANCSA, and who were living on or before December 18, 1971. The secretary's roll was to include the village and region of each enrollee. Both regional and village corporations issued 100 shares of stock to each Native enrolled in their region and village. The number of Alaska Natives enrolled in Native corporations totaled more than 78,000 shareholders. The number of shareholders in each region ranged between 1,000 shareholders enrolled in Ahtna, Inc., the smallest corporation, to over 16,500 shareholders enrolled to Sealaska, the largest regional corporation.

ANCSA also created a separate class of Natives, who have been identified as "at large" shareholders. Approximately 27,000 Natives, whose permanent homes were away from their village, were enrolled by the secretary into a regional corporation, but not a village corporation. At-large shareholders received larger payments from the initial settlement award to the regional corporations and continued to receive larger amounts resulting from the 7(i) revenue-sharing provisions of ANCSA. They are precluded from village corporation benefits including the possible receipt of land.

Individuals who were not permanent residents of one of the 12 regions and who did not enroll in the thirteenth region were enrolled to a region giving priority in the following order:

(1) the region where a Native resided on the census date of 1970 if he or she had resided in this region for two or more years;
(2) the region where a Native had previously resided for an aggregate of 10 years or more;
(3) the region where a Native was born;
(4) the region from which an ancestor of the Native came.

The ability of Natives to enroll into regional corporations based on residency criteria rather than cultural affiliation resulted in Natives enrolling into regions to which they had no cultural ties. This newly created legal identity or cross-cultural enrollment was further reinforced in those instances in which tribes adopted the ANCSA rolls as the basis of their tribal rolls. Unlike tribes in other states, whose membership has a common legal and cultural background, the ANCSA enrollment process resulted in individuals having a legal identity in one region, but a cultural identity associated with another region. Dual identities became problematic *143* when individuals, who have a legal identity in one region and a cultural identity from another region, fail to support or oppose cultural activities and expenditures of their tribe or corporation. Conversely, the cultural heritage of individuals who are culturally affiliated with another region tends to be ignored by their resident regional corporation and tribe. This cross-cultural enrollment has resulted in instances in which individuals have become prominent corporate leaders in their adopted regional homeland. The cross-cultural enrollment situation facilitated by ANCSA has been viewed by some observers as an obstacle to strengthening cultural identity and unity.

ANCSA's enrollment was based on a classification of Alaska's entire indigenous population as "Alaska Natives" rather than an individual's cultural identity as an Aleut, Athapaskan, Haida, Inupiat, Tlingit, or Yup'ik and a blood quantum of one-fourth Alaska Native. This new legal identity, Alaska Native, has served to deter a situation found among tribes that require a one-fourth blood quantum to be eligible as a member of that tribe. In some instances an individual whose ancestry was exclusively Indian could find himself denied citizenship to a tribe simply because he lacked a one-fourth blood quantum of a federally recognized tribe (Garroutte 2003:20). Under ANCSA, Alaska Natives could combine their biological identities to meet the one-fourth blood quantum.

## Subsistence Hunting and Fishing

Subsistence hunting and fishing was fundamental to Native culture and was the primary economy in rural Alaska communities. Native leaders as well as Congress sought to protect subsistence within the land claims legislation. The first Alaska Federation of Natives draft bill and the Senate version both included provisions to protect subsistence, but the final bill extinguished "any aboriginal hunting or fishing rights that may exist." The conference committee report accompanying the claims bill made it clear that Congress intended for the Secretary of the Interior and the State of Alaska "to take any action necessary to protect the subsistence needs of the Natives" (Case and Voluck 2002:284).

In the decade following the enactment of ANCSA, the Secretary of the Interior failed to initiate any action and the state's legal regime precluded protection of Native subsistence. The state did not have the same political or legal relationship with Alaska Natives as did the federal government, and the state constitution's equal access to natural resources clause prohibited the state from implementing racially based subsistence protections. Thus, it was left to Congress to adopt legislation to protect Native subsistence, which it did in 1980 with the enactment of the Alaska National Interest Land Conservation Act (Public Law No. 96-487).

While the Land Conservation Act was intended to comply with the congressional intent of ANCSA to protect Native subsistence, it instead established subsistence protections for rural Alaskans including both Native and non-Native. The Act further required the state to manage fish and wildlife on federal lands consistent with its provisions to protect subsistence uses by rural residents. Should the state fail to meet this requirement, the federal government would assume management of fish and wildlife on federal lands. The state regulations, which were developed in compliance with the federal act, were legally challenged in a lawsuit filed by sportsmen. The Alaska Supreme Court decision (*McDowell* v. *State of Alaska*, 785 P. 2d 1 Alaska 1989) invalidating the state's subsistence regulations resulted in the federal government assuming management of subsistence uses on federal lands in 1990 and created a dual management system for subsistence, which continued in 2007. Although the Land Conservation Act did not ensure the full protection of Native subsistence rights, Natives continue to resist any amendments to it that might erode their existing protections.

## Restructuring ANCSA Corporations

After the passage of ANCSA, the nonprofit regional organizations, which pursued the land claims effort through Congress, began to focus solely on providing governmental services. The regional corporations moved quickly to implement ANCSA.

The corporations spent the initial years organizing themselves, establishing their corporate offices, selecting their land entitlements, and entering a variety of business enterprises. By the early 1980s, Alaska Natives were becoming disenchanted with ANCSA. They were beginning to realize that ANCSA would not bring the riches that some had thought it would nor would ANCSA resolve the myriad of social problems facing Alaska Natives. Additionally, Native people were realizing that the expiration of the restrictions on the sale of stock in 1991 and the looming taxability of their lands 20 years after their conveyance to the corporations could lead to the loss of Native lands. At the 1982 Alaska Federation of Natives convention, delegates voted to make the "1991" issue its highest priority and to seek amendments to ANCSA to protect Native land (Alaska Federation of Natives 1991:i).

In 1983 the Inuit Circumpolar Conference, an international organization of Inuit and Yup'ik Eskimos from Alaska, Canada, and Greenland, along with the World Council of Indigenous Peoples, formed the Alaska Native Review Commission. They invited Thomas R. Berger, a former member of the British Columbia Supreme Court and a recognized advocate of Native rights, to head the Commission. His task was to review the impact of ANCSA.

Berger visited 60 villages and heard from nearly 1,500 witnesses who testified about their concerns with ANCSA. From the northern to southern regions, Alaska Natives expressed their fears that they could lose their land. Berger (1985) highlighted the conflicts between the objectives of ANCSA to assimilate Native people into the capital economy and the desire of Native people to maintain their traditional subsistence economy and cultures. Native people maintained that ANCSA corporations could not develop capital economies that could replace the subsistence economies and cultures. Perhaps the most notable result of his work was that it galvanized the tribal sovereignty movement. The cry to transfer corporate lands to the tribal governments as a means of protecting Native land became one of the proposed resolutions to the lifting of restrictions on the sale of ANCSA stock and to the threats of taxation and land alienation.

Tribal leaders, uniting under the newly formed organization, Alaska Native Coalition, argued for the "retribalization" or the return of ANCSA lands to tribes as a means of protecting Native land from alienation and taxation. They advanced a proposal to transfer ANCSA lands to "qualified transferee entities" or "QTES," which were assumed to be the traditional councils or tribal governments created under the Indian Reorganization Act of 1934 as amended in 1936 to extend to Alaska. The discussion, instead, raised the controversial question of the existence of tribes and Indian Country or territory in Alaska over which Alaska Native sovereign tribes may exercise jurisdiction.

Congress had signaled its intent to achieve the assimilation of Native people into the larger economy through the corporate structure it mandated to implement ANCSA. Congress expressly stated its opposition to the creation of any permanent racially defined institutions, and several ANCSA provisions appeared to be designed to achieve this objective. Congress chose to limit corporate stock to only those Natives who were alive in 1971, which precluded the issuance of stock to Natives born after 1971. It further permitted the sale of stock in 1991 and the taxation of Native land within 20 years after conveyance to corporations. Thus, it was not surprising that Alaska's congressional delegation and the Department of Interior opposed any amendments that would allow the transfer of ANCSA lands to tribal governments.

The congressional delegation advised the Alaska Federation of Natives that it would oppose the retribalization of ANCSA lands to tribal government without a strongly worded disclaimer that was interpreted as weakening tribal political rights and precluding the recognition of Indian Country in Alaska (Morehouse 1988–1989:37–41). The Native community agreed that the ultimate objective of the proposed 1991 amendments, as the legislation was dubbed, was to ensure the perpetual ownership of Native land. In the face of Congress's opposition and threats of the disclaimer clause, the Federation agreed to support the amendments without the QTE to ensure the passage of legislation that extended the restrictions on stock alienation and the taxation exemption on undeveloped lands. Two regional nonprofit organizations, Association of Village Council Presidents

and Tanana Chiefs Conference, withdrew from the Federation because they disagreed with this position (Morehouse 1988:16).

The Native community came to the Federation meetings to discuss the 1991 amendments with a much broader understanding of what they hoped to secure from the ANCSA amendments than in the earlier years when they had pursued the enactment of ANCSA. The Native community unanimously agreed to pursue legislation that would protect their land holdings. They were equally certain that ANCSA corporations were Native institutions, and they advanced the notion that Native corporations must accommodate the values of Native cultures. The Native leaders supported the integration of ANCSA corporate activities into the larger economy, but their proposed amendments ran counter to the wholesale assimilation of Native people into the larger society.

Although the Federation was forced to compromise in Congress, the Native community was successful in acquiring multiple protections that were fairly far reaching (ANCSA Amendments of 1987 Public Law 100-241; 101 U.S. Stat. 1788). One of the major provisions provided for enhanced land protections. Previously, Native corporations had to apply to the federal government to place their lands in a "land bank" to secure land protections, which had proven to be onerous. The 1991 law authorized the major land protections that automatically applied to all undeveloped lands owned by village and regional corporations. The following protections were adopted by the 1991 legislation: free of taxation, protection against adverse possession commonly known as squatters' rights, protection against creditors for debt owned by the corporations, protection against loss if the corporation filed for bankruptcy, and protection against loss if the corporation was involuntarily dissolved. Even if the land were developed, the protections automatically resume when the development ends. The 1991 amendments did not include provisions to allow corporations to transfer their lands to tribal governments. However, a few corporations transferred their land to tribes, but concern that the lands would not be treated as trust lands and protected by the federal government deterred the movement.

Another victory for the Natives extended automatic restrictions on the alienation of stock indefinitely unless the tribal shareholders vote to remove the restrictions. ANCSA stock cannot be sold, or pledged as collateral for a loan, or taken by a court to pay a debt. It can, however, be taken by court order to pay child support or alimony; transferred to someone else if stock ownership conflicts with the shareholder's profession; or given as a gift to a child, grandchild, niece, or nephew. The amendments did not change the inheritance provisions, which allowed tribal shareholders to will their stock to their beneficiaries upon their death. However, non-Natives who acquired stock did not receive voting rights.

Based on their cultural values and traditions and despite the potential of diluting the value of existing stock, the Native community sought an amendment that would allow for *145* the enrollment of "New Natives" or those Natives born after December 18, 1971. The 1991 amendment authorized the inclusion of New Natives and those who were eligible for enrollment in 1971 but had been excluded for unknown reasons if approved by the existing shareholders of a corporation. Additionally, the amendments allowed the issuance of stock to elders or Natives who were 65 years or older if approved by the shareholders.

The 1991 amendments allowed Native corporations to transfer some or all of its assets, such as surface land, stock, and property, to a Settlement Trust created to benefit its tribal shareholders. The purposes of the Settlement Trust are to promote the health, education, and welfare of Native shareholders.

ANCSA pitted individual rights against communal rights, and Alaska Natives went to Congress to seek the protection of their cultural values to protect the ownership of their land; to include their children as members of ANCSA corporations; and to give special benefits to their elders. In enacting the legislation, Congress acknowledged in its Findings and Declaration of Policy that Congress was "not expressing an opinion on the manner in which such shareholders choose to balance individual rights and communal rights." Also important in recognizing the unique status of ANCSA corporations, Congress explicitly stated that ANCSA and the 1991 amendments are Indian legislation and that Congress enacted ANCSA and the subsequent amendments pursuant to its authority under the Constitution of the United States to regulate Indian affairs.

The Native corporations have been successful in obtaining other benefits for their tribal shareholders through other legislative action. They were successful in securing an exemption from the Civil Rights Act under an ANCSA amendment that allowed the corporations to implement a shareholder employment preference. Native corporations were recognized as having the same status as Indian tribes in order to maintain the Native shareholder hiring preference. They were also able to obtain legislation to allow them to sell their Net Operating Losses, under which they were able to bring $426 million into the ANCSA corporate coffers. This plan rescued at least two corporations from financial insolvency and greatly improved the status of others (Colt 1991:13–14). In 1988 Congress authorized ANCSA corporations as eligible for no-bid government contracts, which in 2004 brought in more than $2.4 billion in revenues from government contracting to 13 regional and two village corporations (Native American Contractors Association 2005). These government contracts have been a great benefit and particularly to Native corporations that lack a resource base to become profitable and provide distributions and benefits to their shareholders.

Congress took legislative action requiring federal agencies to consult with Alaska Native corporations (Public Law 108-199 of 2004 and Public Law 108-447 of 2005) on the same basis as Indian tribes under Executive Order Number 13175 (November 6, 2001). President William

Clinton signed Executive Order 13175, entitled "Consultation and Coordination with Indian Tribal Governments," which required federal agencies to establish consultation with federally recognized tribes in the development of federal policies that have tribal implications. The Executive Order did not require federal consultation with Alaska Native corporations. Consultation with Native corporations was viewed as necessary to provide greater assurance that federal action, which might impact the 44 million acres of Native lands, would take into consideration the view of the Alaska Native owners. Congress had continuously classified ANCSA corporations as "tribes" for specific purposes in previous legislative actions, and again enacted legislation to require federal agencies to consult with ANCSA corporations.

ANCSA corporations, unlike other profit-making corporations, devote a significant portion of their corporate budget to nonbusiness activities or to social and political advocacy. For example, Sealaska Corporation expends approximately 20 percent of its nearly $10 million annual budget on social and political advocacy (Worl 1994:9). Perhaps the most important effort of the Native corporations has been its financial and political support to protect subsistence hunting and fishing. Most of the funds for such efforts are channeled through the Alaska Federation of Natives, which is also largely supported by the annual dues of the regional corporations.

Many of the regional Native corporations have established and support nonprofit organizations dedicated to cultural preservation and enhancement and to educational development of their shareholders and children. Some corporations allocate annual scholarship funds derived from their corporate earnings or endowments established for this specific purpose. These ANCSA affiliates are engaged in activities including restoring Native languages, protecting historical and sacred sites, recording and publishing oral traditions and song, promoting Native arts and crafts and supporting cultural and educational enrichment programs. Cook Inlet Region, Incorporated, contributed stock worth more than $30 million to its CIRI Foundation, which is expected to help the Foundation reach its goal of an endowment of $50 million (Marrs 2001:1). That corporation spearheaded, with the support of other ANCSA corporations, the establishment of statewide organizations benefiting the Native community, including the Alaska Native Heritage Center, the Alaska Native Justice Center, and Koahnic Broadcasting.

The financial performance of the Native corporations has been varied. Some have tottered on the brink of bankruptcy while a few have had extraordinary success. Two regional corporations have been named to the Forbes 500 list. The Association of ANCSA Regional Corporation Presidents/ CEOs surveyed 13 regional and 29 village corporations and found that in 2004 the 42 corporations had revenues of $4.47 billion. They paid $117.5 million in dividends to their shareholders. Their statewide employment totaled

12,536 of which 3,116 were identified as Alaska Native. The corporations donated $8.5 million to charitable organizations and distributed $5.4 million in scholarships to 3,040 recipients (Association of ANCSA Regional Corporation Presidents 2006).

Some corporations have paid substantial dividends from their corporate earnings, some as high as $65,000 in a single distribution to each tribal shareholder with 100 shares, but most have distributed negligible dividends. The executives themselves will readily concede that the corporations cannot by themselves address the myriad of problems and poverty faced by many Alaska Natives. However, the corporations have demonstrated a capacity to utilize their economic stature in the political arena to successfully advocate for beneficial legislation on behalf of the Native community. For example, Congress appropriated $45 million to the Alaska Federation of Natives over three years to support social programs within the Native communities. The political advocacy by Native corporations, particularly in the protection of subsistence hunting and fishing rights, has been one of the greatest values of ANCSA corporations, but their overall contribution to the state's economy should not be overlooked. The Native corporations represent new activity in the state's economy. They can attract capital from outside the state, which can accrue additional benefits to the state (Presidents/CEO Report 2001:4).

Despite the economic and political contributions of ANCSA corporations, they are not uniformly supported in the Native community although an extremely high percentage of shareholders participate in corporate elections and activities. Most conflicts surround money paid out as dividends or salaries. Some shareholders are distressed about the environmental impacts associated with the development activities of ANCSA corporations.

One of the conflicts within the Native community surrounding ANCSA corporations can be attributed to the emerging differences in the socioeconomic status among Alaska Natives. During the 1990 census, almost one-quarter of Alaska Natives had incomes below the poverty level. By contrast, corporate managers earn six-figure incomes. An often heard complaint is that the Native corporate managers, directors, and employees are the only ones benefiting from the corporations. The contrast between corporate salaries and many shareholders' standard of living is what bothers dissidents, said Emil Notti, a former CIRI board member, who is a critic of high corporate salaries (*Juneau Empire*

1999:55). In some villages, corporation employees and governmental workers are the only individuals who have jobs.

## Conclusion

In 1971, Alaska Natives supported legislative action to place the 11 percent of their aboriginal lands remaining in their ownership into profit-making corporations. They had, perhaps unknowingly or without understanding the full consequence of this decision, separated their aboriginal lands from their traditional and tribal governments that are characteristic of other American Indian groups.

While Congress viewed corporations as a means to assimilate Native people into the larger society, Alaska Natives initially saw corporations as a vehicle to maintain control and ownership of their land. Less than 10 years after the passage of ANCSA, they discovered the dangers that the corporate structure posed to their cultural survival. They embarked on a course of reconstructing Alaska Native corporations through a series of ANCSA amendments to protect their lands and their cultural heritage. Of equal importance, they came to realize the necessity of integrating into the capital economy as a path to economic and cultural self-determination.

ANCSA corporations are different from other profit-making corporations. They pursue both business and non-business goals, seeking to be profitable while at the same time protecting their Native way of life, including their subsistence hunting and fishing traditions. They have been variously successful with some corporations expanding into the national and international markets while other Native corporations languish on the brink of bankruptcy. They are also unique in that Congress recognizes Native corporations as federally recognized tribes for special statutory purposes in over 100 federal legislative statutes that offer special benefits and protections to Alaska Natives.

In addition to their corporations, Alaska Natives maintain a multitude of institutions including tribal governments, nonprofit regional organizations, cultural foundations, and in two instances, borough governments organized under state municipal laws. Alaska Natives are utilizing these institutions, which they once viewed as alien structures, to pursue economic self-determination and to support their collective cultural survival.

# Gaming

JESSICA R. CATTELINO

American Indian tribally operated casinos exploded in the late twentieth century. Gaming transformed reservation economies and public opinions across the United States, augmenting American Indians' political and economic power even as it exposed them to new scrutiny in American law, politics, and public culture. Gaming became "the" issue in American Indian politics not only because unprecedented amounts of money flowed onto Indian lands, but also because gaming raised fundamental questions about the role of American Indians in United States politics and culture, the scope and meanings of sovereignty, and the ways that economy structures identity and equality in Indian Country and America.

## Scale and Growth

Tribal gaming, or gaming operated by American Indian tribal governments on Indian lands, became big business in the 1990s and 2000s (vol. 14:160, 651). According to the National Indian Gaming Association, 223 of 341 federally recognized tribes in the continental United States operated gaming facilities in 2004 (National Indian Gaming Association 2004:6). In that year Indian gaming grossed $19.4 billion in revenues, as reported by the National Indian Gaming Commission. Tribal gaming revenues had grown rapidly, from $5.4 billion in 1995 to over $22 billion in 2005 (fig. 1). The top 15 (4.1% of 367) tribal gaming operations earned 37.1% of revenues in 2004, while the bottom 94 casinos (26%) grossed 0.4% of revenues (National Indian Gaming Commission 2006). The scale and economic impact of tribal casinos varied dramatically, from some of the world's largest casinos located near population centers to modest one-room operations on scattered rural Indian reservations. Not all American Indian people benefited directly from tribal gaming, and numerous casino operations were not successful, closing or downsizing soon after opening. Meanwhile, advocates for Indian social services and other programs continued to emphasize the poverty and urgent needs of most Indian people, who in the early 2000s remained among the poorest groups in the United States.

The birth and growth of Indian gaming was part of a nationwide expansion of gambling in the United States. Gross revenues from all gaming grew from $39.8 billion in 1994 to $78.6 billion in 2004, nearly doubling in a decade. Of that $78.6 billion, Indian gaming accounted for approximately 25 percent, while lotteries totaled $21.4 billion and commercial casinos grossed $30.6 billion (American Gaming Association 2006).

The origins of tribal gaming were modest. On December 14, 1979, The Seminole Tribe of Florida opened the first tribally operated high-stakes bingo hall in Native North America on the corner of State Road 7 and Stirling Road in Hollywood, Florida. Broward County sheriff Robert Butterworth promptly sought to close the bingo hall, arguing that it violated state gambling laws. The Seminole Tribe successfully defended gaming in the courts, winning a federal appellate court ruling that the relevant Florida state gaming regulations were civil, not criminal, and as such that the tribe, not the state, had jurisdiction over tribal gaming (658 F.2d 310 [5th Cir. 1981]). In 1987, the United States Supreme Court ruled similarly in *California* v. *Cabazon Band of Mission Indians* (480 U.S. 202 [1987]) that the tribal government could operate high-stakes card rooms. This ruling drew a distinction between state gaming laws that were criminal/prohibitory and those that were civil/regulatory, affirming tribal governments' protection from the civil laws. Subsequently, tribal governments across the continent began to launch gaming operations. Ensuing pressures from states and other interests led Congress to enact the Indian Gaming Regulatory Act in 1988 (Public Law 100-497).

Federal gaming laws have shaped the history and status of tribal casinos, but the top-down perspective of federal law can blind observers to the origins and meanings of Indian gaming. The origin of tribal gaming in its current form, after all, was not with federal law but with tribal action. Tribes such as Florida Seminoles (fig. 2) and Cabazons opened casinos as an assertion of their sovereignty-based right to operate and regulate on-reservation activities, but even more as a mechanism for reversing sustained and endemic reservation poverty. Decisions about whether and how to pursue gaming prompted Native communities to debate their pasts, futures, and values. Some tribal nations, including the Navajo, Onondaga, and Hopi Nations, rejected gaming, at least during the initial years, for diverse reasons that included fear of gambling's social consequences and philosophical, religious, and moral opposition to gambling.

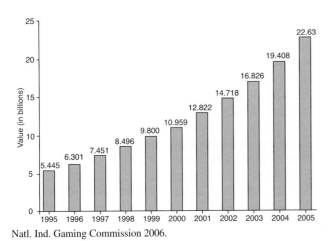

Natl. Ind. Gaming Commission 2006.

Fig. 1. Increase in tribal gaming revenues, 1995–2005.

The history of tribal gaming took shape in relation to other forms of twentieth-century tribal economic development. Historical and anthropological scholarship shows that American Indian tribes pursued myriad economic development projects throughout the twentieth century, with only rare success. On most reservations gaming was the first economic activity to overcome the structural barriers—such as federal veto power, impaired title to land and resources, limited access to capital, distance from markets, and systematic poverty and educational disadvantage—that hindered economic development (Jorgensen 1998). Yet tribal gaming did not simply drop from the sky unto Indian reservations, like a "new buffalo," nor was it a federal grant to alleviate American Indian poverty. Instead, tribal gaming emerged from the actions of Indian people and from a complex history in which American Indian economic development had been

entangled with deeply political questions about indigenous cultural distinctiveness and tribal sovereignty. From Menominee sawmills (Hosmer 1999) to Navajo wage labor and weaving (O'Neill 2005), American Indians long were engaged in diverse forms of economic action that became significant in political and cultural debates about indigeneity (Hosmer and O'Neill 2004). Native people linked some of these forms to tradition, while others were viewed as economic vehicles rather than expressions of indigeneity. Tribal gaming is among the newest and most controversial of these contingent economic forms.

## Legal Framework

The Indian Gaming Regulatory Act of 1988 stated its purposes as threefold: first, to provide a statutory basis for tribal gaming in order to promote tribal economic development and governance; second, to authorize regulation of tribal gaming; and third, to establish the National Indian Gaming Commission as the federal regulatory authority over tribal gaming (25 U.S.C. §§ 2701–2721). As gaming law scholar William Eadington argued, this act "triggered the most significant economic and social change to affect American Indian tribes since the founding of the Nation" (Eadington 1998:vi). Passage of the Act resulted from several political and economic processes: the economic success of tribal gaming; the efforts of states to regulate tribal gaming and control organized crime; the desire of tribes to assert sovereignty and avoid local and state regulation; the Reagan administration's effort to promote tribal economic self-sufficiency and reduce federal spending; and the attempt of Las Vegas and Atlantic City gambling interests to

AP Images.

Fig. 2. Casinos. left, Seminole Indian Casino in Immokalee, Fla., built in 1994, featuring a bingo hall. This is a mall operation. Photograph by Luis M. Alvarez, 1998. right, Aerial view of the Pechanga Resort and Casino on the Pechanga Indian Reservation (Luiseño) near Temecula, Calif. Photograph by Ric Francis, 2002.

limit competition (Anders 1998; Eadington 1998; Light and Rand 2005; Mullis and Kamper 2000; Rand and Light 2006; Wilmer 1997).

The Act outlined three classes of tribal gaming, which became important as the bases for differing levels of regulation and the focal points of legal and political maneuvering. First, "class I gaming" refers to social games with prizes of minimal value or traditional forms of Indian gaming (for examples, see Gabriel 1996). "Class II gaming" includes bingo (paper and electronic) played for money and card games (excluding banking games like blackjack) not prohibited by the laws of the state, so long as they are played in conformity with state regulations. The most controversial is "class III gaming," which includes all forms of gaming, such as slot machines (fig. 3), that do not fall under class I or class II. Class I gaming is within the exclusive jurisdiction of Indian tribes, and class II gaming is also within tribal jurisdiction, but subject to provisions of the Indian Gaming Regulatory Act. The Act limited the use of class II and III tribal gaming revenues to: funding for tribal government operations; provisions for the general welfare of the tribe and its members; promotion of tribal economic development; donations to charity; and funding of local government agencies. A tribe pursuing class III gaming must enter into negotiations with the state for the purpose of entering into a tribal-state compact governing gaming activities, and this provision has been the focus of litigation, political battles, and debate about sovereignty and federalism. States are to negotiate in good faith, but this has not always occurred. The Act originally specified that federal courts had jurisdiction over state failures to enter into good-faith negotiations, but in the important federalism case *Seminole Tribe* v. *Florida*

(517 U.S. 44 [1996]) the Supreme Court ruled that under the Eleventh Amendment states were immune from suit by tribes in federal court unless a state had waived its sovereign immunity. Efforts to find a remedy remained underway in 2006, with some tribes pursuing class III agreements directly with the secretary of the interior; this "fix" would place gaming negotiations at a nation-to-nation level between tribal governments and the federal government.

The National Indian Gaming Commission, established by the Indian Gaming Regulatory Act, is the independent federal agency that regulates tribal gaming. It conducts background investigations, limits the terms of tribal contracts with casino management companies, reviews tribal ordinances to ensure compliance with federal law, and enacted and enforces a set of regulations entitled the "Minimum Internal Control Standards." The Commission has the authority to fine and close tribal gaming operations (K. Washburn 2001).

At the core of tribal gaming are questions of tribal sovereignty. Gaming "represents a stand for political independence as tribes assert their sovereign right to determine for themselves what they can control on tribal lands" (W.D. Mason 2000:4). Across the United States, gaming has led to new disputes over the relative power of tribal and state sovereignty. Yet gaming also has afforded tribes financial resources for defending their sovereignty in the courts, the press, and the halls of legislatures. Gaming-funded tribal attorneys and lobbyists have built unprecedented power in Washington, D.C., and state capitals. Gaming-related defenses of tribal sovereignty through the American political and legal systems perpetuate processes whereby American Indians have built sovereignty through political, economic, and other forms of incorporation (Harvey 2000). Perhaps most importantly, gaming has strengthened tribal sovereignty by enabling some indigenous groups to regain control over key aspects of day-to-day self-governance and by allowing Native peoples to make decisions about how to live in the present and toward the future.

Gaming also poses significant risks to tribal sovereignty. Tribes had wagered their sovereignty on casinos, and Chippewa author Gerald Vizenor (1990, 1993) cautioned that only strong leadership could protect tribal sovereignty and the moral traditions of tribal cultures. Lakota journalist and publisher Tim Giago (2006) generally shared this concern. Gaming could be seen as an example of how sovereignty became demarcated by differential spatial criminalization, with the result that Indian tribes risked joining offshore corporations in a race to the ethical bottom (Perry 2006). Light and Rand (2005) proposed that such concerns could be alleviated if gaming law were guided by indigenous conceptions of sovereignty, and that it therefore could be undertaken through respectful compromise among all sovereigns. Gaming both points to the structural limitations on tribal sovereignty and affords the tools whereby tribes can reinforce their sovereignty. This illustrates the deeply material and contingent nature of sovereignty itself. By re-

AP Images.

Fig. 3. Mary Ann Andreas, chairman of the Morongo Band of Mission Indians (Cahuilla, Serrano), standing in front of some of the more than 1,000 gaming machines in the Casino Morongo outside Cabazon, Calif. By 2007 the Morongo Casino Resort and Spa offered over 2,600 slot machines, bingo, and 12 kinds of table games, with a sequestered area for high rollers, as well as 11 restaurants and bars. Photograph by Damian Dovarganes, 1998.

organizing the sovereignty of tribal nations, states, and the United States nation-state alike, gaming offers insights into the relational aspects of sovereignty and the complexity of interdependent sovereigns in a federalist system.

## The Impact of Tribal Gaming

Numerous scholars have examined the social and economic impact of tribal gaming for reservation and surrounding communities (Gardner, Kalt, and Spilde 2005; Grant, Spilde, and Taylor 2004; E. Henderson 1997; Light and Rand 2005; Stein 1997; Wilmer 1997). Published monographs on tribal gaming offer journalistic (Benedict 2001; Eisler 2001; Fromson 2003; Lane 1995); political science and legal (Light and Rand 2005; Mason 2000; Rand and Light 2006); legal anthropological (Darian-Smith 2003); or literary (Pasquaretta 2003) analyses.

According to economists at the Harvard Project on American Indian Economic Development, real per capita and family incomes from 1990 (when Indian gaming was not widespread) to 2000 increased disproportionately for American Indians, when compared to the United States population as a whole. For tribes with gaming operations, gains were significantly higher. For example, the median United States household income grew by 4 percent during the 1990s, but for nongaming tribes the increase was 14 percent, and for gaming tribes the change was 35+ percent. Nonetheless, the median household income in Indian Country remained little more than half the national level (J.B. Taylor and J.P. Kalt 2005: xi–xii).

The annual budget of The Seminole Tribe of Florida, which launched Indian Country's gaming revolution in 1979, experienced dramatic growth in the subsequent 25 years: according to the tribe's general counsel, the 1979 budget was less than $2 million, with most monies coming from the federal government. In 2006, net class II gaming revenues were approximately $600 million, and the tribal budget was over 95 percent funded by gaming (vol. 14:445) (Seminole Tribe of Florida 2006). The tribal government operated a vast array of social service programs (e.g., health clinics and universal healthcare, life-long educational benefits, elder care, housing), economic initiatives (e.g., gaming, cattle, cigarette sales, citrus and sugarcane, tourism, and investments in real estate ventures—fig. 4), and cultural programs (e.g., a museum, cultural education classes, fairs and festivals, media outlets). Household incomes grew with per capita dividend distributions to each of the 3,000 tribal citizens, and Seminoles increasingly controlled their own governance and economic activity (Cattelino 2004, 2008). Seminoles' gaming operations enjoy unusual success as a result of their location near Florida's urban centers, but Seminoles' commitment to allocating gaming revenues toward self-governance is shared by many tribes. Indeed, from housing programs to education curricula, Seminole casino-

AP Images.

Fig. 4. Members of the Seminole Tribe of Florida, including Bobby Henry, celebrating atop the Hard Rock Café marquee in Times Square, New York, after the tribe announced that it had acquired Hard Rock International, Dec. 7, 2006. The business includes 124 Hard Rock Cafés, 4 Hard Rock hotels, 2 Hard Rock casino hotels, 2 concert venues, and stakes in 3 other hotels. Photograph by Kathy Willens, 2006.

era control over tribal programs that previously had been run by the federal government represents the significance for tribal sovereignty of the day-to-day acts of tribal social service administration (Cattelino 2006).

Other tribal gaming operations are much more modest, and their measures of success differ. For example, in North Dakota most tribes considered their casinos successful because they created jobs for tribal members. The Three Affiliated Tribes' casino contributed to a reduction in reservation unemployment from 70 percent to approximately 30 percent (Light and Rand 2005:115). Casinos funded economic diversification, such as data entry and manufacturing businesses. As of 2005, no North Dakota tribe distributed per capita dividends.

Undesirable effects of Indian gaming have, in some cases, included problem gambling among Native and non-Native consumers (Cozzetto and LaRoque 1996), increased tensions with non-Indian communities, factionalism, corruption, and citizenship disputes within Indian nations. The most dramatic intratribal conflict was among Mohawks at Akwesasne, where two Mohawks were killed, the casino damaged, and political factionalism intensified by casino disputes (Hornung 1991). Tribal government secrecy fueled political turmoil when the Eastern Band of Cherokee Indians pursued their first gaming operations in the early 1990s (vol. 14:44). The tribal council's gaming plans faced opposition from Christians (Southern Baptists), some of whom rejected gaming payouts as money derived from sinful activity, as well as from some Cherokees, who founded the Eastern Cherokee Defense League in an effort to preserve the traditional culture they thought casinos threatened (Oakley 2001). Gaming has produced new forms of indigenous displacements along with successes, as illustrated by the casino-linked involuntary disenrolment of tribal members among Saginaw Chippewas, Tigua Indians of Isleta del Sur, and Oklahoma Seminoles (A. Gonzales 2003). Research is inconclusive on the causal relationship between gaming and membership disputes, though it is clear that publicity surrounding gaming proceeds has spurred many more Americans to contact tribes about establishing membership.

A notable consequence of tribal gaming has been the geographic redistribution of power, money, and media visibility in Indian Country. The locations of casino operations (fig. 5), with concentrations on the coasts and near urban centers, contrast with the location of Indian Country, which consists of large land holdings and populations in the rural West and Midwest. The contrast would be starker were the casino map to indicate profitability, since the most econom-

Fig. 5. Locations of Indian gaming operations and revenues per gaming operation by region in 2005. Regions, as defined by the National Indian Gaming Commission (2006), cross Bureau of Indian Affairs region/area office and cultural boundaries and are discontinuous in the East.

ically successful casinos are located near metropolitan centers and resorts.

Large casino profits, and concomitant visibility and political power, by recently federally recognized tribes and by low-membership coastal tribes have called attention to the existence of Native groups in areas of the country where Indians previously lacked visibility. Because coastal tribes generally do not share the symbolic repertoire of Plains peoples, who long served in American imagery as iconic of Indian people, popular ideas did not correspond to this geographic reordering of power in Indian Country. For Native people, this geographic reorientation reverberated in political organization (e.g., shaping the board membership and donor roster of groups like the Native American Rights Fund and the National Congress of American Indians), in cultural institutions (e.g., the donors and exhibits of the Smithsonian National Museum of the American Indian), and on the powwow circuit. New powwows with large prize monies extended the powwow highway eastward and to diverse reservations of gaming tribes across the United States. During the 1990s and early 2000s, geography was at the center of hard-fought disputes over off-reservation gaming, or the efforts of tribes to establish trust lands with casinos that were discontinuous with reservation lands. A cultural geography of gaming could illuminate broader political, social, and economic processes, as some geographers have suggested but not developed (Raento and Berry 1999; see also Lew and Van Otten 1998).

The uneven geographic and economic distribution of Indian gaming fueled criticism that gaming fails to serve all Native people, for example in a *Time Magazine* exposé (Barlett and Steele 2002, 2002a). This unevenness prompted some lawmakers to support "means-testing" for federal benefits to Indian tribes. It should be pointed out that such critiques homogenize Indian Country, treat gaming more as a social program than a sovereign act, and hold Native people more accountable than the general public for ongoing poverty among indigenous peoples.

## New Institutions, New Politics

Tribal gaming generated new institutions in Washington, D.C., and Indian Country. In addition to the National Indian Gaming Commission, intertribal gaming interest groups formed. The National Indian Gaming Association was founded in 1985 as a nonprofit organization of member Indian tribal nations and nonvoting associate members. The Association promotes tribal gaming interests and, according to its website, "operates as a clearinghouse and educational, legislative and public policy resource for tribes, policymakers and the public on Indian gaming issues and tribal community development" (National Indian Gaming Association 2006). Regional organizations emerged, such as the California Nations Indian Gaming Association, founded in

1988; the Great Plains Indian Gaming Association, founded in 1997; the Minnesota Indian Gaming Association, founded in 1987; and the Arizona Indian Gaming Association, founded in 1994. Regional associations act in accordance with member tribes' priorities, generally advocating for gaming interests within state governance, pooling resources and expertise, maintaining a media presence, and in some cases holding regional trade shows and policy summits. Gaming revenues and interests have shaped multi-issue Native organizations. For example, the United South and Eastern Tribes, Inc., established in 1969 as a regional coalition group, began to hold its meetings at tribal casino-hotel convention centers and grew in power and size as a result of gaming success among member tribes.

Media outlets for Indian gaming news include: *Indian Gaming Magazine*, launched in 1990, and its associated website, indiangaming.com; and the influential website (Pechanga.net) and daily e-news digest maintained by Victor Rocha, a citizen of the Pechanga Band of Luiseño Indians.

Tribal gaming opponents have organized politically, but as of 2006 antigaming local groups had not coalesced at the national level. There was at least one related national antitribal sovereignty group, Citizens Equal Rights Alliance. Among the more prominent groups of the late 1990s and early 2000s were the Connecticut Alliance Against Casino Expansion (J. Benedict 2001). In upstate New York, the organization Upstate Citizens for Equality, founded in opposition to an Oneida land claim, worked with the Coalition Against Gambling in New York to oppose Indian gaming. Similar groups emerged in California (Stand Up for California!, Concerned Citizens of Santa Ynez) and other states. They often sponsored petition drives and supported ballot initiatives opposing tribal gaming creation and expansion.

Academic institutions for the study of Indian gaming were established more slowly than trade, advocacy, and opposition groups. The Institute for the Study of Tribal Gaming Law and Policy at the University of North Dakota School of Law, Grand Forks, was founded by Kathryn Rand and Steven Light. The Harvard Project on American Indian Economic Development produced important gaming studies, and several law schools devoted resources to the study of Indian gaming law. In 2005, the Sycuan Band of the Kumeyaay Nation donated $5.5 million to San Diego State University, California, to establish an academic curriculum and research institute focused on tribal gaming.

The emergence of tribal gaming-focused political and academic institutions—both for and against tribal gaming—points to the late-twentieth-century power of gaming as an organizing force in American politics (another example was the rapid growth of state lotteries). With gaming tribes growing vocal and powerful in economic development, employment, traffic and zoning, and jurisdictional debates, they began to reassert a place in the American federalist system and political process.

Gaming catapulted many tribes into the center of local and state politics. In California, for example, tribal political power grew with casino wealth, and the 1998 Proposition 5 campaign (a statewide proposition to secure a compact authorizing class III tribal gaming) witnessed the emergence of tribes as major political players and contributors: the tribes invested over $66 million in the campaign, with Nevada interests investing $25 million (Goldberg and Champagne 2002). In 2000, several California tribes collaborated to sponsor Proposition 1A, a constitutional amendment that stipulated the terms of a gaming compact with the state. During this period, American Indians became major contributors to California electoral campaigns, their influence grew in state government, and they claimed "a place within the state's political and social landscape" (Goldberg and Champagne 2002:60; see also Rosenthal 2004). Some have claimed that such initiatives buttressed aspects of colonial hegemony by reinforcing exclusive legal forms (Darian-Smith 2002), though it is also the case that gaming-based indigenous engagements with state and federal laws complicate and potentially shift American federalism. Tribes acted less like sovereigns than like interest groups, as they developed political strategies for influencing state political processes (Skopek, Engstrom, and Hansom 2005). This approach maintained a division between sovereign and interest group activities, a distinction that may be inappropriate for American Indian tribes and for nations more generally (which often act as interest groups). Tribal gaming relied on state law, and another view is that tribes acted less as cross-border agents than as internal state political players (K. Washburn 2003–2004).

Gaming compacts between tribal nations and states reordered their relative economic power, especially in states where failing budgets were supplemented substantially by tribal revenue-sharing. These negotiated contributions are not taxes, since state governments lack power to tax tribal governments. The forms they take are diverse, from fixed percentages of revenues in Connecticut to sliding percentage scales in California (fig. 6), New Mexico, and New York (Rand and Light 2006:152). Some revenue-sharing agreements, as in California, stipulate that tribes will contribute gaming revenues to nongaming tribes in the state (Darian-Smith 2003:64). Tribes provided $750 million to state and local governments in 2003, a nearly one-third increase over 2002 (Light, Rand, and Meister 2004: 668).

While many critics have viewed these tribal-state compacts as erosions of tribal sovereignty and as potentially destructive of tribal unity (W.D. Mason 2000:219), others have considered them to be acts of sovereignty (W.D. Mason 2000:188); in any case, gaming created unexpected realignments in American federalism (McCulloch 1994; Rand and Light 2006). Despite the prolific scholarship on federal Indian law and policy, little attention has been played to the role and processes of negotiation as an expression of sovereignty in the modern era. Tribal gaming compacts reflect the limits of tribal sovereignty under a federal law that compels tribes to negotiate with states and, simultaneously, act as a vehicle for the negotiation among sovereigns over resources, jurisdiction, and the distribution of wealth.

AP Images.

Fig. 6. Anthony Pico, chairman of the Viejas band of Kumeyaay (Ipai-Tipai), watching Gov. Arnold Schwarzenegger signing an Indian gambling compact with the tribe in Sacramento, Calif., June 21, 2004. The agreement, reached with 5 California tribes, allowed their tribal casinos to increase the number of slot machines beyond 2,000 per tribe. In return the tribes agreed to pay the state a licensing fee for each additional slot machine up to $25,000 per machine. The tribes agreed to issue bonds to supply the state with $1 billion of revenue. Photograph by Rich Pedroncelli.

Some tribes have entered into revenue-sharing agreements with local governments. In California and other states, controversies arose when states failed to redistribute gaming revenues to county and municipal governments, as required under compacts. Often, tribes have relied on their non-Indian employees and other local advocates for support during conflicts with state governments (W.D. Mason 2000), and many municipalities, such as Coconut Creek, Florida, have reversed their initial suspicion of tribal casinos to become supporters (Cattelino 2007).

Gaming-based philanthropic giving opened channels of economic and social connection between American Indian tribes and their neighbors. Across the continent, tribes contributed gaming monies to local social service organizations, other Indian tribes and programs, and national causes such as disaster relief. Local charitable investments of gaming revenues provided "a model for philanthropy as a conduit to political power" (Spilde 2004:72). Nonetheless, tribal charitable giving often was ignored by local residents hostile to casino expansion or was interpreted as a "purely political gesture" (Darian-Smith 2003:86). Tribal charitable giving in the casino context, while clearly a political and moral claim in relation to casino controversies, must be understood against the historical backdrop of charitable giving *to* American Indians. For Florida Seminoles, gaming-era charitable giving reversed relationships of generosity, power, and dependency that long had structured charity from non-Indians *to* Seminoles (Cattelino 2007).

Casino job creation and gaming-funded tribal philanthropy have strengthened local relationships. However, gaming has also fueled backlashes, sometimes against casino expansion but often more generally against Indian tribes and individuals. A 2002 survey showed that non-Indians in close proximity to the Chumash casino held stronger negative views toward Chumash casino expansion than did respondents living in Santa Barbara and other more distant California locales (Darian-Smith 2003). The Meskwaki casino both strained and strengthened relations with local Whites in Iowa (Foley 2005).

## Cultural Reckoning, Emergent Stereotypes, and Federal Recognition

The 1999 final report of the National Gambling Impact Study Commission, a body established by Congress to conduct a study of gambling, noted: "a common theme among many opposed to Indian gambling is a concern that gambling may undermine the 'cultural integrity' of Indian communities" (The National Gambling Impact Study Commission 1999:6–3). Will the domination of the American gambling industry by Indian tribes advance self-determination without destroying the indigenous communities? "Or, will the high-stakes gambling trade contribute to the erasure of tribal identities and the complete assimilation of the people they distinguish?" (Pasquaretta 2003:137). The potential of gaming to revitalize indigenous community, illustrated by the Mashantucket case, contrasts with the corrosive effects of gaming upon internal divisions and traditionalism/modernization conflicts, as seen in Mohawk communities (Pasquaretta 1994:696; see also Fenelon 2000). If gambling controversies are structured by concerns about cultural loss and about whether gaming represents legitimate "Indianness" (Carpenter and Halbritter 2001), scholars have found it difficult to establish criteria by which "cultural loss" can be evaluated, and this in turn suggests the need to reconsider the analytical limits of the very notion of culture at stake in casino-related cultural loss narratives.

Tribal gaming has raised questions of indigenous authenticity that take two primary forms: concerns that gaming tribes are "losing their culture" and doubts about the legitimacy of groups' claims to Indianness in the casino context, especially accusations that groups seeking federal recognition as Indian tribes do so primarily for monetary reasons. These two ways of thinking about indigenous authenticity overlap, as illustrated by the controversies surrounding Mashantucket Pequots' gaming presence in the northeastern United States. Debates over Pequot federal recognition focus on the relationship between their casino ambitions and their authenticity as an Indian group (J. Benedict 2001;

Cramer 2005; Eisler 2001; Fromson 2003). The Mashantucket Pequot Museum and Research Center and the Foxwoods Resort Casino, Connecticut, each have undertaken representational strategies to reinforce legitimate indigenous identity in the face of widespread popular and legal critique. Faced with journalistic and legal challenges to their legitimacy as a people and a tribe, Pequots built institutions and engaged in representational practices (e.g., museum exhibits, casino design) that contributed to a project of nation-building based on historical continuity (Bodinger de Uriarte 2003). Like other Native people, Mashantucket Pequots "compartmentalized" their casino, describing it as a financial vehicle but not an expression of culture (Lawlor 2005:168). At the core of gaming controversies are identity and the politics of representation, and in the Pequot case, "the tribe's success is a victory of self-representation" (Pasquaretta 2003:90).

Casino-linked debates over indigenous authenticity have erected even greater barriers to groups seeking federal recognition as American Indian tribes. Late-twentieth-century casino controversies influenced tribal acknowledgement, which is the processes whereby the federal government examines and grants or denies recognition to groups claiming tribal status. Only federally recognized tribes can operate Indian casinos, and gaining recognition is an expensive and time-consuming process, costing nearly one million dollars per petition between 1995 and 2005 (Cramer 2005:54). As a result, many petitioning groups turned to casino financiers to fund research and legal fees associated with the acknowledgement process. This, and the specters of race and money that long have haunted politics about Indians in the United States, led to a public backlash against groups seeking recognition. Petitioners sometimes were asked to forgo casino plans in exchange for recognition backing by local, state, and federal officials. Federal recognition controversies show that casinos go to the heart of indigenous authenticity and have material effects upon American political processes of recognizing indigenous identity and community.

"Rich-Indian racism" was named as one of the most potent American cultural phenomena linked to tribal gaming. It relies upon images of Indian people as poor, such that any wealth is "surplus" and thus available for expropriation. Along with fueling arguments about authenticity, the "rich Indian" image undermined tribal sovereignty (Spilde 1998, 2004). "Rich Indian" stereotypes permeated California gaming debates (Darian-Smith 2003). "In precasino days, some Whites looked down on Mesquakis [Meskwakis] for their poverty. Now some seem to dislike them for their wealth" (Foley 2005:301).

## The Future

In the early twenty-first century public debates over gaming remained unsettled (Kallen 2006). It remained to be seen whether Congress would limit tribal gaming rights, and whether market saturation or state expansion of commercial gaming would reduce tribal casinos' profitability. At tribal leadership conferences and economic summits the topic was diversification, but tribes struggle to diversify economic development beyond gaming and related industries such as hotels and resorts. In some cases, tensions remained high between intratribal groups that support and oppose gaming, and across Indian Country tribes continued to experiment with how to restructure governance and responsibly manage new income streams in the context of gaming expansion.

State-tribal relations were ill-defined, with negotiations over casino revenue-sharing agreements reshaping the sovereignty not only of Indian tribes but also of states.

Beyond these policy considerations, gaming raises important moral and scholarly issues with regard to money, sovereignty, and indigeneity. Native peoples face tough questions about the meanings of casino wealth and the moral obligations of sovereignty within and across political boundaries. At stake are the lived experiences and future of indigeneity, the scope of tribal sovereignty, and the negotiation of citizenship and difference in the United States.

# Native Rights and the Constitution in Canada

JOHN J. BORROWS

Canada's constitution has not generally protected Aboriginal peoples as individuals or groups. Aboriginal governments have been suppressed (*Logan* v. *Styres* [1959], 20 D.L.R. [2d] 416 [Ont. H.C.]) and denied (British Columbia 1875), children forcibly taken (Milloy 1999), and traditional economic pursuits criminalized (*R.* v. *Marshall* [1999] 2 S.C.R. [S.C.C.]). There has been a negation of rights of religious freedom (*Thomas* v. *Norris* [1992] 2 C.N.L.R. 139 [B.C.S.C.]), association, due process (*Blueberry River Indian Band* v. *Canada* [1995] 130 D.L.R. [4th]193 [S.C.C.]), and equality (*Canada (A.G.)* v. *Lavell* [1974] S.C.R. 1349). The failure of Canada's constitution to limit federal and provincial interference with Aboriginal rights has harmed Aboriginal communities. Despite these injustices Aboriginal peoples are not mere victims in their relationship with the Canadian state. They have consistently resisted significant impositions and exercised their agency when relating to other governments. Aboriginal peoples have vigorously fought against laws, policies, and practices that limit their choices. Since Aboriginal peoples do not consider Canada's constitution as a universal good, they have regarded its development and application with ambiguity. At different times they have variously sought to manipulate, reform, or eliminate the country's constitutional structure relative to their interests.

Aboriginal people have mined the formal and informal sources of the Constitution to extract small pieces of jurisdictional space for greater community autonomy. The rocky road to reform has caused Aboriginal peoples to be suspicious of the constitutionalization of their rights. Thus, while Aboriginal people have participated in constitutional discussions, they have not done so enthusiastically or with one voice. Some want to be ushered into Canada's constitutional structure, while others are ambivalent. On the opposite end of the spectrum a significant number of Aboriginal groups just want to be left out of the country entirely. Furthermore, during this struggle Aboriginal issues have sometimes been overshadowed by the constitutional politics of Quebec separatism and federal policies of Aboriginal assimilation. Nevertheless, in 1982 Aboriginal and treaty rights were entrenched in Canada's constitution. Their inclusion strongly compelled national Aboriginal leaders and organizations to negotiate with the Canadian government about the meaning underlying the recognition and affirmation of their rights.

While these negotiations ultimately failed to have much of a substantive impact, they did educate a section of the public about broader Aboriginal aspirations regarding further autonomy and self-government. The higher profile Aboriginal peoples obtained in this period prepared the ground for further engagement with the Canadian state. Thus, while the entrenchment of Aboriginal rights has drawn Aboriginal people into internal Canadian debates, one should not ignore the great ambivalence with which Aboriginal peoples have participated.

## Constitutional Sources

Canada was formed by the union of three British colonies in 1867: Canada, Nova Scotia, and New Brunswick. Its architects chose not to itemize all constitutional powers in one document, as occurred in the United States. Canada's constitution is comprised of various written texts, an assortment of established practices, and a diverse array of oral traditions. Thus, constitutional reform in Canada can occur in many different ways—through formal textual amendment, changing political practice, and shifting legal interpretation. The composite nature of Canada's constitution can make working with it difficult. Governmental structures, individual rights, and state obligations must often be pieced together from different documents, conventions, customs, and cases. While reform has often been difficult, Aboriginal people have perceived this structure's subtleties and worked around its many fractures to promote their own interests, though these actions are less visible outside Aboriginal communities (Borrows 2001b:9).

The open nature of Canada's constitution is mandated by the preamble to the British North America Act of 1867 (now the Constitution Act of 1867), which established it as "a Constitution similar in Principle to that of the United Kingdom." The United Kingdom's Constitution is largely unwritten and draws upon customs, conventions, and deeply embedded principles to structure government. Canada's constitution also contains many unwritten terms. The Supreme Court of Canada has recognized numerous fundamental unwritten constitutional principles and powers in the Constitution Act (*Reference Re Secession of Quebec* [1998]

2 S.C.R. 217 at 239). In *Reference re Remuneration of Judges of the Provincial Court of Prince Edward Island (the Provincial Court Judges Reference)* ([1997] 3 S.C.R. 3 at 75) the Court found that "the preamble is not only a key to construing the express provisions of the Constitution Act, 1867 but also invites the use of those organizing principles to fill out gaps in the express terms of the constitutional scheme" ([1997] 3 S.C.R. 3 at 75). Aboriginal rights are one organizing feature of Canada's unwritten constitution. A British Columbia judgment found that the unique relationship between Aboriginal peoples and the Crown is an "underlying constitutional value" that can be given the force of law (*Campbell* v. *A.G. (B.C.)* [2000], 189 D.L.R. [4th] 333 at para. 81). The same court found that Aboriginal self-government is another underlying constitutional value, though the Supreme Court of Canada has not been explicit in this regard (*R.* v. *Pamejewon* [1996] 2 S.C.R. 821). While Canada's highest court has been slow to recognize Aboriginal governance, this fact has not stopped Aboriginal peoples from acting together to influence and manage their relationships relative to Canada's constitution. Aboriginal peoples exercise a de facto measure of governance to advance their causes relative to the Canadian state.

Despite Canada's unwritten constitutional traditions, the conventional view of early constitution making in Canada concentrated on British imperial instruments, where there is less evidence of Aboriginal agency. However, even within these documents Aboriginal rights are perceptible and can be read as providing protection and room for these groups to act. For example, the Royal Proclamation of 1763 made it illegal to occupy Aboriginal lands without Aboriginal consent (Slattery 1979:191–349). The Proclamation also mandated that treaties with Aboriginal peoples had to be made with imperial authorities. Furthermore, local colonies were forbidden from entering into land transactions with Indian nations under its terms. In 1867, when confederation occurred, section 91(24) of the British North America Act gave the federal government exclusive legislative authority relative to "Indians and lands reserved for Indians." Manitoba's entry into confederation in 1870 contained provisions related to Métis land rights (Manitoba Act, 1870 [U.K.], 32 & 33 Vict., c. 3., ss. 30–32). In 1871 British Columbia's constitutional entry contained federal obligations to liberally manage Indian lands. It also contained provincial obligations to transfer lands to the Dominion for the Indians' benefit (Tough 2003). When Alberta, Saskatchewan, and Manitoba were given responsibility over natural resources in their territories in 1930, they were constitutionally mandated to assume legal responsibilities for Indian hunting and fishing rights (Natural Resources Transfer Agreement, 1930, S.C. 1930, c. 3). Thus, Aboriginal rights can be found in written Canadian constitutional documents, though their presence only weakly reflects Aboriginal aspirations.

A more active story concerning Aboriginal constitutional relationships can be told when Canada's unwritten constitutional customs are brought alongside more conventional narratives. Canada's other constitutional sources clearly reveal Aboriginal peoples' rights and freedoms in relation to the Crown. For example, Canada's constitutional order recognizes the continuity of Aboriginal rights after the assertion of non-Aboriginal sovereignty. In the first year of Canada's confederation the case of *Connolly* v. *Woolrich* (17 R.J.R.Q. 75 at 79 [Quebec Superior Court]) affirmed the existence of Cree law on the Prairies and recognized it as part of Canadian law. The legal doctrine applied in *Connolly* is known as the doctrine of continuity and demonstrates Canada's constitutional law stems from a "great variety of sources," including Aboriginal law (Royal Commission on Aboriginal Peoples 1993). The British Court of Appeal recognized this in *R.* v. *Secretary of State for Foreign and Commonwealth Affairs, ex parte Indian Association of Alberta and others* ([1982] 2 All E.R. 118 at 123) when it held:

> These customary laws are not written down. They are handed down by tradition from one generation to another. Yet beyond doubt they are well established and have the force of law within the community ([1982] 2 All E.R. 118 at 123).

The continuing force of indigenous law has given Aboriginal peoples jurisdictional space from which to work out their constitutional relationship with the Crown, despite the often negative treatment of Aboriginal legal orders (Borrows 2006).

Treaties and agreements between Aboriginal peoples and the Crown also have constitutional significance. Many treaties helped create the country and define foundational legal relationships (J. Henderson 1994). Other treaties attempted to hold Aboriginal Nations at arms length from Canada, trying to preserve space outside Canada's constitutional order. There have been hundreds of negotiated arrangements throughout Canadian history, and they have drawn from both Aboriginal and non-Aboriginal political legal practices to frame their terms (Canada 1905–1912). For some, treaties are perhaps the most significant feature of Aboriginal peoples' relationship with the Crown because they produced promises that the pre-existing population would live together in peace and order with those who followed (Borrows 2006). They demonstrate the active attempt by Aboriginal peoples to create a relationship with the Crown partially based on their own goals.

For example, when Manitoba entered confederation, negotiation played a prominent role in constitutional development. A dispute between the Métis and the Crown arose when the Dominion Parliament attempted to unilaterally survey the old northwest territories around the Red River in 1869 (Siggins 1995). The Métis blocked surveyors from their work because they did not want to be forced into the Dominion without their participation and consent. These actions delayed Canada's expansion into this region and compelled the first government of Sir John A. Macdonald to secure the consent of the region's prior inhabitants. In particular, the Red River Métis vested a provisional government with authority to negotiate terms of union with Ottawa and bring the area into Confederation. Representatives of this government traveled to Ottawa as delegates of the Métis people to negotiate conditions for this portion of western Canada's entry. They brought with them a locally developed Bill of Rights that expressed their demands. The negotiations were challenging but an agreement was reached, and its terms were embodied in the Manitoba Act of 1870. The democratic legitimacy of this process was sealed through the Métis provisional government's acceptance of the agreement before the Dominion and the British Parliament's statutory endorsement that made it part of Canada's constitution. The people of the Métis Nation regard the Manitoba Act as embodying a treaty that recognizes and affirms their nation-to-nation relationship with Canada, even though its provisions concerning land and resources have not been appropriately fulfilled (*R.* v. *Dumont* [1988] 52 D.L.R. [4th] 25 [Man.C.A.]). Métis agency was thus important to the development of the country in Manitoba.

Aboriginal law and treaties, other constitutional conventions, and customs can be found in many places throughout Canada demonstrating the active nature of Aboriginal peoples' participation in Canada's constitutional order behind and beyond the written documents (*Campbell* v. *A.G. (B.C.)* [2000] 189 D.L.R. [4th] 333 [BCSC]). This historic example is one among many that demonstrates it has been possible for Aboriginal peoples in Canada to resist, shape, and reform Canadian constitutional practice because of the Constitution's flexible contours.

## Constitutional Suspicions

Constitutional reform was a topic of great interest in Canada through the late 1960s to the early 1990s. In that period there were numerous debates and formal proposals regarding the country's structure. Aboriginal peoples were very active advancing their aspirations in relation to the Canadian state. Some groups, like the Haudenosaunee (Iroquois), consistently resisted forcible inclusion within Canada. The confederacy generally regards itself as an autonomous entity that has an alliance with the Crown, rather than a relationship of subjugation. While Canadian courts have not accepted this view (*Logan* v. *Styres*), some Haudenosaunee act as if they are outside Canada's constitutional framework (Alfred 2006). Other First Nations have been more willing to consider themselves a part of Canada, particularly those groups such as the Nisga'a who have signed treaties with the state and regard themselves as having negotiated their way into Canada. Other groups have adopted positions somewhere between the Haudenosaunee and Nisga'a. They seek to strategically use their power to simultaneously secure a stronger place within the Canadian state even as they seek greater autonomy.

These different positions made it very difficult for Aboriginal groups to form a unified front on constitutional reform at the end of the twentieth century. There is a great diversity among Aboriginal nations in Canada with a variety of languages, geographies, cultures, spiritual traditions, and economic practices. Aboriginal diversity, coupled with a deep distrust of the Canadian state, made it very challenging for Aboriginal leaders to present constitutional reform to their people in a positive light. Many were suspicious because of the Canadian government's repeated attempts to forcibly eliminate Aboriginal languages, laws, land, government, and culture. They wondered why they should desire greater incorporation into a state that had undermined Aboriginal lifeways and community structures. Thus, many had concerns that the constitutionalization of Aboriginal rights could lead to a further erosion of indigenous languages, cultures and governments. In fact, some saw constitutional entrenchment as an attack on their inherent rights as peoples and felt their distinct legal personality would be undermined through such provisions. Many had signed treaties with the British Crown, a nation separate from Canada. They regarded potential incorporation within Canada's constitution as a breach of these international obligations. At the same time, Aboriginal peoples who had not signed treaties regarded themselves as being outside of the Canadian legal framework. They resented being forcibly included within its structures. Thus, constitutional reform was not regarded as a universal good, even if the goal was formalized entrenchment of Aboriginal rights in Canada's highest written laws.

## Constitutional Discussions

The process of constitutional reform was not difficult for just Aboriginal peoples. Canadians more generally struggled with its implications (Russell 1992). Canada's constitution has evolved over time, through the mixing of written provisions with unwritten customs, conventions, and judicial interpretation. Many wanted to allow the constitution to continue to evolve along those lines. This was not an insupportable stance; some of Canada's strongest constitutional protections are unwritten. For example, one of the most significant aspects of Canada's unwritten constitution prior to confederation was the development of responsible government, which made the executive subject to the legislative branch of government. This unwritten constitutional doctrine was carried over into confederation though not in written form. Responsible government has served many Canadians very well. Some non-Aboriginal Canadians felt that formal constitutional entrenchment might unnecessarily restrict the flexibility and strength found in Canada's unwritten constitutional traditions. For these people responsible government and other associated democratic rights and freedoms were secure without explicit entrenchment.

Of course, Aboriginal peoples did not have the same perspective on responsible government. Parliamentary sovereignty has not served Aboriginal peoples very well due to assimilative legislative forces. For example, most Aboriginal people did not get the right to vote in various political jurisdictions in Canada until between 1946 and 1969. Others never wanted this right. Thus, Aboriginal peoples have not generally participated in mainstream political institutions or organizations. This is one reason why Aboriginal advocacy has usually occurred outside the system, using unwritten constitutional provisions to assert an autonomous, semi-autonomous, or unique relationship to the Canadian state. However, during the heightened period of constitutional debate some Aboriginal people regarded written guarantees as a better way to gain greater protection against Canadian intrusions. They viewed formal amendments related to Aboriginal rights as a way to exert pressure from inside the system. Thus, despite distrust among many Aboriginal peoples concerning constitutional reform, some saw constitutional entrenchment as an opportunity to constrain the government's ability to act contrary to their rights and interests.

The process to achieve this goal was not easy. Canadian written constitutional law was dependent on the United Kingdom's legislative process. Canada's written constitution could not be amended without legislative action by the British Parliament (where Canada's constitutional statutes resided). These statutes included the Constitution Act, numerous amendments, various statutes admitting different colonies into confederation, and the Statute of Westminster, which gave Canada equality and a broader degree of legislative independence from Great Britain. While the 1931 Statute of Westminster gave Canada some independence, it did not allow for the amendment of Canada's written constitution without British Parliamentary agreement. Thus, written constitutional reform focused on Britain, and Aboriginal peoples were a part of this advocacy. However, Aboriginal peoples and Canadians often went to England for different reasons. Non-Aboriginal peoples generally wanted to sever formal links with the United Kingdom; Aboriginals were much more resistant to breaking these ties.

For most Canadians, the lack of a domestic amending formula led them to seek constitutional reform in 1927, 1931, 1935–1936, 1950, 1960–1961, and 1964. Aboriginal peoples were not part of these efforts because they were not invited. Others would have had problems participating even if invited because they regarded the Queen as their ally, and the Canadian state as their oppressor. They would not have seen the substitution of the Canadian state for the British Crown as a positive development. The fact that some Aboriginal peoples possessed or desired to have a constitutional relationship with Britain led to stronger assertions of a nation-to-nation relationship with the British Crown. Most non-Aboriginal peoples saw the British Crown's continuing control over Canadian affairs in a more negative light. However, most of the Canadian state's early efforts at reform led to failure, though they had the advantage of being tightly focused on procedural questions related to achieving a domestically controlled constitutional amendment formula.

In 1968 the Liberal government of the day (under Prime Minister Pierre Elliott Trudeau) sought to introduce broader substantive issues into the constitutional debate, such as changes to governmental institutions, distribution of powers, and the entrenchment of a Bill of Rights. There was no discussion of constitutional Aboriginal rights during this period. In fact, the Liberal government seemed to have planned the exact opposite for Aboriginal peoples. The White Paper of 1969 explicitly proposed the assimilation of Aboriginal peoples and the elimination of treaty rights and any other special or separate status (Cumming and Mickenberg 1972:331). This initiative was regarded by most Aboriginal peoples in the worst possible light (Cardinal 1969). It was deemed a great offense and has been described as "the single most powerful catalyst of the Indian nationalist movement" (Weaver 1981:171). It facilitated the development of many Aboriginal political organizations to resist the White Paper and generated coordination among them to strengthen their advocacy (Frideres 1993:286). The National Indian Brotherhood (later Assembly of First Nations) came to life and prominence in this period. The Union of British Columbia Indian Chiefs was formed through a fusion of the Indian Homemakers Association of British Columbia, the North American Indian Brotherhood, and the Southern Vancouver Island Tribal Federation (Frideres 1993:286). The Indian Association of Alberta provided leadership through this crisis, and the Manitoba Indian Brotherhood and Association of Iroquois and Allied Indians also made their views widely known (Weaver 1981:188).

In 1971 the provinces and federal government obtained a tentative agreement on broader constitutional principles in a document called the Victoria Charter. Once again, there was no mention of Aboriginal issues. Consensus over the Victoria Charter broke down because of changes in political leadership and concerns about Quebec's reaction to specific income security provisions. Other attempts to patriate the constitution in the mid-1970s also ended in failure. Aboriginal peoples were largely shut out of these constitutional discussions and were not very supportive of the entire enterprise to that point.

## Constitutional Amendment

In 1978 constitutional reform again came to the forefront of Canadian political life. At the time it seemed unlikely that Aboriginal peoples would find a place in the discussions. The most contentious issue was who possessed the authority to request an amendment to the constitution. This seemed more of a federal-provincial issue to most people. The written constitution did not provide for amendment procedures and there was uncertainty in Canada's unwritten constitutional powers about this question. Some assumed that Quebec would need to assent to any constitutional amendment because of its distinct legal and linguistic status (McRoberts 1988). Others believed that only a substantial number of the provinces representing a majority of the population needed to consent to constitutional change. At the same time Prime Minister Trudeau believed that the federal government alone could request Britain to patriate the constitution, as the domestication of its amending formula was often called. Thus, since the debate was focused along federal-provincial lines, most did not expect Aboriginal peoples to have much of a role in this debate.

Despite this perception, Aboriginal peoples played an increasingly important role in constitutional debates between 1978 and 1982. The reasons for this are complex. The federal government wanted to secure more than a domestic amending formula in patriating the constitution. As was the case a decade earlier, constitutional reform provided an opportunity to address a variety of other outstanding issues aside from the amending formula. One of these issues was the relationship of Aboriginal peoples to Canada, a factor obviously drawing some Aboriginal groups into the debate. Once again the parties had wide-ranging discussions about a Charter of Rights, institutional reform, and separation of powers. Aboriginal issues became more prominent as time passed because some Aboriginal leaders regarded constitutional incorporation in a positive light. They saw it as a way to resist policies like the White Paper and thereby provide firmer protection against legislative extinguishment of their treaties and distinct status (Frideres 1993:317).

In 1978 the National Indian Brotherhood formally identified constitutional reform as a priority for Indian bands across Canada (Sanders 1983:303). Their two main concerns were the entrenchment of Aboriginal and treaty rights in the Constitution and participation in the constitutional reform process (Sanders 1983:304). The federal government responded to this initiative by inviting the Brotherhood, along with the Native Council of Canada and the Inuit Committee on National Issues to attend constitutional negotiations with observer status. Aboriginal peoples wanted to be more than observers. Regrettably, the government's invitation did not amount to participation as Aboriginal peoples envisioned it, thereby placing them in a more antagonistic role in the process. This unfortunate development brought to the fore those within the Brotherhood and other Aboriginal groups who saw constitutionalization in a less favorable light. As a result, a strategy was developed to block constitutionalization to express opposition to reform by petitioning the Queen. While the Queen possessed no real political authority to respond to Aboriginal advocacy (because it was expected that the British Parliament would approve Canada's recommendations regarding the Constitution), Aboriginal opposition threatened to unravel fragile consensus within Canada. The threat to constitutional patriation posed by Aboriginal peoples was considerable. Thus it was a significant event when over 200 First Nations people visited England in 1979 to raise their concerns before Parliament and the British public (Sanders 1983:306).

Following these protests the federal government recognized that further antagonizing Aboriginal people could gravely threaten its constitutional objectives. Therefore, it promised formal Aboriginal involvement in the constitutional process but then proceeded to act without Aboriginal organizations in developing priorities for constitutional inclusion (Sanders 1983:309). Thus, when a meeting was held between provincial premiers and the prime minister in the fall of 1980, Aboriginal organizations once more boycotted official events. They held parallel meetings where they decided to further their advocacy in the United Kingdom. The National Indian Brotherhood chose to press the British Queen, Parliament and other Commonwealth partners to reject Canada's overtures. The Union of British Columbia Indians resolved to organize a "Constitutional Express" that would travel from Vancouver to Ottawa, raising awareness of their position. This event attracted 500 participants. When the Express arrived in Ottawa it generated a great deal of press coverage. The arrival also corresponded with a meeting of 2,000 other Indians hosted by the Assembly of First Nations, which generated further media attention. The group drafted a *Declaration of the First Nations* and presented it to the Governor General of Canada as a statement of their inherent rights. It was also decided that some members of the Express would continue to New York, London, and Rotterdam to create international pressure against constitutionalization without their consent. Finally, the Assembly of First Nations also resolved it would not participate in a Special Joint Committee meeting on the Constitution that same week because governmental recognition of its position was lacking. However, the Special Joint Committee meeting was attended by the Native Council of Canada, the Inuit Committee on National Issues, the Council of Yukon Indians, and the Nisga'a Nation. This provided a measure of input into formal constitutional decision-making.

Subsequent to these meetings the National Indian Brotherhood, Native Council of Canada, and the Inuit Committee on National Issues developed "a common position on constitutional provisions which would entrench treaty and aboriginal rights, recognize aboriginal self-government and require consent to constitutional amendments affecting their rights" (Sanders 1983:313–314). Unfortunately, cooperation between these groups was tenuous because certain treaty groups within the National Indian Brotherhood opposed working with the Métis who were a part of the Native Council of Canada. Furthermore, the Union of British Columbia Indians completely rejected constitutional entrenchment as inconsistent with their view of themselves as Nations possessing international status. One Union participant subsequently put the issue in this way, "We were fighting for nationhood, not section 35" (Poplar 2003:23).

As Aboriginal positions splintered, the same was happening between the provinces and the federal government. This led to an increasingly strong position being taken by Prime Minister Trudeau's ruling government. On October 6, 1981, the federal government insisted it had unilateral authority to request a constitutional amendment from the British Parliament to domesticate the country's amending formula. The provinces rejected this position and asserted that they had to consent to such a request. Quebec further assumed it had a veto over the entire process because of its distinct language, culture, and political history. These divisions placed the federal government under additional pressure to seek other strategic alliances. As a result during January 28–30, 1981, it struck a deal with the three national Aboriginal organizations to recognize Aboriginal and treaty rights in the Constitution. There was further agreement to insert a section in the proposed Charter of Rights and Freedoms to insulate Aboriginal collective rights from abrogation or derogation that might result from individual rights interpretations. Finally, the parties agreed to constitutionalize future conferences to deal with Aboriginal issues. While these provisions looked promising for both the federal government and Aboriginal organizations, the short-lived trust between the groups eroded. The federal government subsequently appeared to present these clauses as capable of amendment without Aboriginal consent. Many Aboriginal people felt betrayed. This led to a further fracturing within the Brotherhood. Some regional organizations quit the organization or threatened to, forcing the Brotherhood to reverse its support for the federal proposal.

Aboriginal peoples intensified their activities in England and Europe in 1981. They did not participate in litigation before the Supreme Court of Canada concerning the constitutionality of the federal government's attempted unilateral patriation (Sanders 1983:322). Instead, litigation was launched before the English courts, with various regional Aboriginal organizations participating at different points in the suit's development, including the Union of British Columbia Indians, the Indian Association of Alberta, the Federation of Saskatchewan Indian Nations, the Union of Nova Scotia Indians, the Union of New Brunswick Indians, the Four Nations Confederacy of Manitoba, and the Grand Council of Treaty Nine from Ontario. The main case eventually carried the name of the Indian Association of Alberta (*R*. v. *Secretary of State for Foreign and Commonwealth Affairs, ex parte Indian Association of Alberta and others*, [1982] 2 All England Law Reports 118). Their core argument was that while treaties were domestic, not international agreements, the British Crown had never explicitly transferred responsibility for Indians to Canada, making treaty implementation Britain's continuing responsibility. In the end, First Nations organizations from Saskatchewan and British Columbia did not participate in this case because of differences in opinion on legal strategy. The Federation of Saskatchewan Indian Nations did not agree their treaties were domestic agreements, and the Union of British Columbia Indians argued they were a part of Canada's constitutional order but their consent was needed to patriate the constitution (Sanders 1983:322).

The English Court of Appeal rejected the Alberta Indians' arguments on January 28, 1982, finding that:

> . . . the Crown was no longer single and indivisible. It was separate and divisible for each self-governing dominion or province or territory.

. . . Thus, the obligations to which the Crown bound itself in the Royal Proclamation of 1763 are now to be confined to the territories to which they related and binding on the Crown only in respect of those territories. None of them is any longer binding on the Crown in respect of the United Kingdom ([1982] 2 All England Law Reports 118 at 916).

The failure to win support from the British Parliament or the Court followed the failure of the provinces before the Supreme Court of Canada to persuade that institution that their consent was needed for patriation. On September 28, 1981, the Supreme Court of Canada had written that a "unilateral" patriation of the Constitution was legal. However, it also noted that a "substantial degree" of provincial consent was required by constitutional convention before the federal-provincial relationship could be fundamentally altered by a request to Britain for constitutional amendment. The Court's politically astute judgment, coupled with the pressure created by Aboriginal peoples in Britain, sent the federal government back to the bargaining table with the provinces, with an additional promise to include Aboriginal and treaty rights in the final document.

Unfortunately, when the provinces and federal government began to negotiate on November 5, 1981, Aboriginal rights were dropped from the accord. Aboriginal groups were shocked by this development. Provincial pressure and federal timidity were the cause of this troubling setback. This turn of events placed the Brotherhood in a tenuous position with its membership. Since the organization was uncertain about whether it could support the reinstatement of Aboriginal provisions without full First Nations backing, the political initiative was taken by other Aboriginal groups. It was led by the Native Council of Canada, the Inuit Committee on National Issues, the Native Women's Association of Canada, the Dene Nation, and the Council of Yukon Indians under the banner of the Aboriginal Rights Coalition (Sanders 1983:320). The federal government responded positively to the Coalition's submissions but insisted it could not act without provincial consent. This response resulted in a series of large Indian demonstrations in nine cities across Canada to protest the provincial position. The provinces reacted to this pressure and reconsidered their position on Aboriginal rights, eventually agreeing to their reintroduction in the accord.

## Constitutional Entrenchment

On April 17, 1982, Aboriginal and treaty rights officially became a part of Canada's written constitution. Section 35 in Part II of the Constitution Act of 1982 came into force and read:

(1) The existing Aboriginal and Treaty Rights of the Aboriginal Peoples of Canada are hereby recognized and affirmed.

(2) In this Act, "aboriginal peoples of Canada" includes the Indian, Inuit and Metis peoples of Canada.

Furthermore, section 25 in Part I of the Constitution Act read:

The guarantee in this Charter of certain rights and freedoms shall not be construed so as to abrogate or derogate from any aboriginal, treaty or other rights or freedoms that pertain to the aboriginal peoples of Canada including
    (a) any rights or freedoms that have been recognized by the Royal Proclamation of October 7, 1763;

Finally, section 37 of the Constitution read:

(1) A constitutional conference composed of the Prime Minister of Canada and the first ministers of the provinces shall be convened by the Prime Minister of Canada within one year after this Part comes into force.
(2) The conference convened under subsection (1) shall have included in its agenda an item respecting constitutional matters that directly affect the aboriginal peoples of Canada, including the identification and definition of the rights of those peoples to be included in the Constitution of Canada, and the Prime Minister of Canada shall invite representatives of those peoples to participate in the discussions on that item.
(3) The Prime Minister of Canada shall invite elected representatives of the governments of the Yukon Territory and the Northwest Territories to participate in the discussions on any item on the agenda of the conference convened under subsection (1) that, in the opinion of the Prime Minister, directly affects the Yukon Territory and the Northwest Territories.

The first constitutional conference in 1983, mandated under section 37, produced amendments to sections 35 and 25 of the Constitution Act of 1982. As a result of negotiations and agreement during this conference, subsections 35(3) and (4), 25(b) and 37.1(1) were added to the Constitution Act by the Constitution Amendment Proclamation in 1983. Thereafter Section 35 contained additional amendments which read:

(3) For greater certainty, in subsection (1) "treaty rights" includes rights that now exist by way of land claims agreements or may be so acquired.
(4) Notwithstanding any other provision of this Act, the aboriginal and treaty rights referred to in subsection (1) are guaranteed equally to male and female persons.

Furthermore, section 25 was amended by inserting an additional qualification that Charter rights were not to be construed as abrogating or derogating from:

(b) any rights or freedoms that may be acquired by the aboriginal peoples of Canada by way of land claims settlement.

Finally, section 37 was amended to provide for two more provincial ministers conferences with Aboriginal organizations. These provisions—sections 25, 35, and 37 of the Constitution Act of 1982— became the primary sections identifying Aboriginal and treaty rights in Canada's written constitution, along with section 91(24) of the Constitution Act of 1867.

## Constitutional Interpretation: Conferences and Accords

The constitution is interpreted by many people in civil society, including the courts, Parliament, legislatures, Aboriginal governments, academics, and the media. Each plays an important role in giving it meaning. There were many issues left unresolved and requiring interpretation after the proclamation of the Constitution Act of 1982. The most prominent national issue was that Quebec did not give its assent to the new constitutional package, rejecting it through its National Assembly on December 1, 1981, because it did not recognize Quebec's distinct position in Canadian society. However, Aboriginal peoples also had problems with the Act. Many regretted that they can no longer rely on the British Crown to honor historic agreements, since the constitution is wholly under the authority of the Canadian parliament. Others were wary about section 35 being seen as forcing their de facto inclusion into Canadian society without their consent. Some felt the section 37 constitutional conference would fail to produce agreement about the meaning of Aboriginal and treaty rights in section 35. Those who were more optimistic about the constitutional package were concerned about the potential for future limitations of their rights by Canadian courts. Most Aboriginal peoples thought that the major flaw in section 35 was its failure to recognize and affirm their pre-existing, inherent rights to self-government.

In the decade following the Constitution's patriation there were many opportunities to address these concerns. Provincial ministers conferences were held in Ottawa in 1983, 1984, 1985, and 1987 as directed under section 37(1), to identify, define, and discuss aboriginal and treaty rights (B. Schwartz 1986). Four major Aboriginal organizations participated in these conferences: the Assembly of First Nations, purportedly representing over 600 Indian Bands in Canada; the Native Council of Canada, representing non-Status and Métis people; the Métis National Council, representing Métis people generally; and the Inuit Committee on National Issues, representing northern territorial Inuit communities. These organizations found it difficult to achieve solidarity on many issues, though an even greater gulf separated them from the provinces and federal government. In particular, Saskatchewan, British Columbia, and Newfoundland were unwilling to accept the concept of "inherent" aboriginal rights, and most governments had difficulty recognizing undefined Aboriginal rights to self-government. There was a concern that self-government would threaten the territorial integrity of the Canadian community, even though the four organizations at the constitutional table argued they had an inherent right to self-government within the boundaries of the Canadian political community (Canada 1987:25, 39, 42-43, 329-240). While the provincial ministers' conferences produced only limited success in a substantive sense, they did perform an important educational function as the events received extensive media coverage (Brock 1991).

When the dust had settled from the last First Ministers Conference in 1987, the federal government initiated a process to secure Quebec's agreement to the constitution. Quebec had signaled its willingness to sign the constitution if its demands were accepted, including recognition of its distinct society status. Thus, negotiations between the provinces and federal government to satisfy Quebec's demands produced the Meech Lake Accord, which was signed on June 3, 1987. The Accord required a higher standard for constitutional amendment than set forth in the 1982 Constitution. Ordinarily a measure would become constitutional if it had the agreement of seven provinces representing 50 percent of the population. However, the Meech Lake Accord required the agreement of all provinces within three years to become constitutional. The heightened standard for amendment gave greater maneuvering room for those opposed to its endorsement. Aboriginal peoples lobbied both nationally and provincially for the Accord's rejection.

Aboriginal peoples were opposed to the Meech Lake Accord's ratification because they were not consulted in its development and it did not reference their distinct status and rights to self-government (Hawkes and Morse 1991:166–168). Aboriginal peoples saw the Accord as a troubling return to the situation that existed before 1982, where decisions were made that affected their future without their participation or consent (Chamberlain 1998:11). As a result of this opposition and through their alliance with other like-minded groups, the Meech Lake Accord was defeated. Aboriginal opposition was important to the Accord's defeat because Elijah Harper, a Northern Ojibwa (Oji-Cree speaker) from Red Sucker Lake Reserve who sat in the Manitoba legislature, became the public symbol of its demise. Harper consulted widely with Aboriginal groups in making his decision to resist the Accord. When the time for voting came he signaled his opposition by holding an eagle feather high in his hand. His refusal to endorse the Accord in the Manitoba Assembly prevented it from securing unanimous consent required for its passage throughout the country.

After the defeat of the Meech Lake Accord, constitutional discussions receded from the national stage. However, in 1991 Canada was once again caught up in wide-ranging constitutional debate. Unlike the Meech Lake Accord, this time there was much greater participation by Aboriginal peoples in its development. Aboriginal leaders worked with provincial premiers and the prime minister in laying out the scope of the debate. Aboriginal peoples also had a more prominent role in working on its details. Issues dealt with during these discussions were related to Canadian identity, Quebec's distinctiveness, the reform of national institutions, economic union, and clarifying of distribution of powers, including the spending power and the streamlining of government. Most importantly for Aboriginal peoples, there was a

significant package of powers related to Aboriginal and treaty rights. In particular, the Charlottetown Accord recognized First Nations' inherent right of self-government within Canada. However, the agreement was not ratified when it was taken to the Canadian public for a nation-wide referendum on October 28, 1992.

Perhaps the most lasting aspect of the failed 1992 Accord was the rise in greater prominence of the Native Women's Association of Canada. In the months leading up to the Charlottetown Accord a parallel process of consultation took place within Aboriginal communities concerning constitutional options. The Native Women's Association objected to the Canadian government only providing funding to the other four national Aboriginal organizations: the Assembly of First Nations, Native Council of Canada, Métis National Council, and the Inuit Tapirisat of Canada (replacing the Inuit Committee on National Issues). The Native Women's Association claimed it should have been separately represented in constitutional consultations, thereby bringing the distinct views of Aboriginal women to the process. They also claimed the other Aboriginal organizations were male dominated and thus incapable of presenting their views (Borrows 1994). While the government, courts, and other Aboriginal organizations ultimately rejected this view (*Native Women's Association* v. *Canada* [1994] 3 S.C.R. 627), over time the Native Women's Association has established that its views are an essential part of Aboriginal constitutional development in the country. Its voice sounds along with others seeking to manipulate, reform, or eliminate Canada's constitutional structure relative to Aboriginal peoples rights and interests. Despite the gains experienced by Aboriginal organizations through their constitutional advocacy, Canada's constitutional provisions relative to Aboriginal rights remain very much a work in progress, saturated with enormous ambiguity (Walkem 2003:223).

## Conclusion

Notwithstanding the persistence and strength of Aboriginal voices relative to their rights, Canadians and Aboriginal peoples have developed constitutional fatigue. There seems to be little appetite for reopening discussions that might lead to formal written amendments to Canada's constitution due to the failures of the Aboriginal constitutional conferences and the Meech Lake and Charlottetown accords. A five-year Royal Commission on Aboriginal Peoples also failed to lead to wide-ranging substantive constitutional change (Borrows 2001a, 2001b, 2001c). The 2006 Kelowna Accord, negotiated with provincial ministers to improve Aboriginal socioeconomic conditions, broke down. As a result of these developments Aboriginal advocacy became more prominent before the courts and through negotiated local agreements or regional treaties. More importantly, Aboriginal peoples have simultaneously continued their focus on unwritten, less formalized means of asserting and protecting their rights. This stance may prove to be most effective in sustaining Aboriginal societies because its strength is drawn from within each community. In these instances Aboriginal peoples do not have to wait for others to recognize and affirm their priorities and aspirations. Through the exercise of their own agency Aboriginal peoples keep alive their most cherished ideas and possessions.

Although Aboriginal and treaty rights were constitutionalized in 1982, it is still too early to tell whether, on balance, the entrenchment of Aboriginal rights was a development that will benefit Native people. On the positive side, section 35(1) seems to prevent Canada from unilaterally extinguishing Aboriginal and treaty rights. On the negative side, the Crown's broad power to infringe Aboriginal and treaty seems to undermine much of the autonomy and powers of governance many were seeking prior to the entrenchment of section 35. Furthermore, constitutionalization seems to have led some Canadians to believe that Aboriginal peoples' rights are best protected through Canadian constitutional instruments. Many Aboriginal people do not hold this opinion.

# Native Rights Case Law

KENT McNEIL

Most of the case law involving the rights of the Aboriginal peoples of Canada is the product of judicial decisions handed down since 1970. Moreover, unlike in the United States where the Supreme Court began grappling with issues of tribal sovereignty and land rights in the 1820s and 1830s (Cohen 2005; vol. 4:230–237), in Canada there are still significant gaps in the legal landscape. However, there has been an acceleration of judicial attention to these matters since the Aboriginal and treaty rights of the Aboriginal peoples were recognized and affirmed by section 35(1) of the Constitution Act, 1982 (Schedule B to the Canada Act 1982, U.K., c. 11; "Native Rights and the Constitution in Canada," this vol.). Since that time, the Supreme Court of Canada has decided numerous cases dealing with Aboriginal title to land, resource use rights, treaty rights, fiduciary obligations, and other matters.

Before examining the case law in relation to these matters, one needs to be aware that Canadian law has acknowledged the existence of three distinct groupings of Aboriginal peoples: the Indian, Inuit, and Métis peoples. The existence of these three groupings was explicitly recognized by section 35(2) of the Constitution Act, 1982. However, for historical, political, demographic, and other reasons, most of the case law has involved Indian or First Nation people. There is a dearth of judicial decisions on the rights of the Inuit and Métis, in part because until the 1970s they generally did not enter into treaties and did not receive recognition through federal statutes such as the Indian Act, first enacted in 1876 (S.C. 1876, c. 18, now R.S.C. 1985, c. I-5). Although many of the general legal principles from the case law relating to Indians can be applied to the Inuit, this is not necessarily so for the Métis, given that their existence postdated the arrival of Europeans in North America ("Métis," this vol.).

## European Colonization of Canada

In his seminal decision in *Johnson* v. *M'Intosh* (8 Wheat. 543, 573 [1823]), Chief Justice John Marshall of the United States Supreme Court expressed the opinion that the American colonies had been acquired by the European powers by discovery. At the same time, he seems to have acknowl-edged that the Indian nations were sovereign and independent prior to the arrival of the Europeans, for a consequence of discovery was that "their rights to complete sovereignty, as independent nations, were necessarily diminished, and their power to dispose of the soil at their own will, to whomsoever they pleased, was denied by the original fundamental principle, that discovery gave exclusive title to those who made it" (p. 574). Apparently realizing the contradiction inherent in the proposition that Europeans could acquire territories subject to Indian sovereignty by an original mode of acquisition like discovery, Marshall implicitly revised his opinion in *Worcester* v. *Georgia* (6 Pet. 515 [1832]), where he acknowledged that discovery "regulated the right given by discovery among the European discoverers, but could not affect the rights of those already in possession, either as aboriginal occupants, or as occupants by virtue of a discovery made before the memory of man" (p. 544). For European sovereignty over Indian territories to be acquired, apparently something more than "discovery" was required: the Indian nations had to be conquered by the European powers (or later the United States), or cede their territories to them by treaty (McNeil 2000:12–14). This revised position is more in keeping with standard explanations of territorial acquisition, which generally has to be derivative where territories occupied by sovereign peoples are concerned (Lindley 1926; Morin 1997).

Ignoring the alteration in Marshall's position on this in *Worcester*, the Supreme Court of Canada in *R* v. *Sparrow* ([1990] 1 S.C.R. 1075, 1103) cited his decision in *Johnson* v. *M'Intosh* as authority for their conclusion that "there was from the outset never any doubt that sovereignty and legislative power, and indeed the underlying title, to [Aboriginal title] lands vested in the Crown" (the Crown is the legal entity on whose behalf the governments of Canada and the provinces act). This statement was made in reference to British Columbia, a part of Canada that has generally been regarded as having been acquired by the British Crown by "settlement," that is, the taking of possession of a supposedly "vacant" territory by British subjects on behalf of the Crown (McNeil 1989:268). Settlement, like discovery, is an original mode of territorial acquisition that disregards the sovereignty of the Indian nations who were there at the time. It should not be applied to territories occupied by peoples with a social and political organization (*Advisory Opinion on Western Sahara*, 1975 I.C.J. Rep. 12), as was British Columbia when the settlers arrived (Asch and Macklem 1991; Monture-Angus 1999:95; Macklem 1997:113–119).

Other parts of Canada not first colonized by Britain subjects were acquired by the British Crown derivatively by conquest and cession from France, specifically Acadia (mainland Nova Scotia and part of New Brunswick) by the Treaty of Utrecht in 1713, and New France, Cape Breton Island, and Île St. Jean (Prince Edward Island) by the Treaty of Paris in 1763 (McNeil 1989:268). In its decision in *R* v. *Marshall; R* v. *Bernard* ([2005] 2 S.C.R. 220), the Supreme Court apparently accepted without question the derivative territorial title Britain had acquired from France, without inquiring into the origins of France's territorial rights. The Court has nonetheless held that the nature and content of Aboriginal rights in Canada do not depend on whether the territory in question was first colonized by France or Britain; in either case, the applicable law is the common law of Canada as articulated by the courts (*R* v. *Adams*, [1996] 3 S.C.R. 101; *R* v. *Côté* [1996] 3 S.C.R. 139).

The Supreme Court of Canada therefore appears to have accepted colonization of Canada by France and Great Britain as a given, without questioning the legality of the process by which it occurred. This apparent reluctance to examine the matter too closely is also revealed in *Delgamuukw* v. *British Columbia* ([1997] 3 S.C.R. 1010), where Chief Justice Antonio Lamer accepted without question the decision of the trial court that British sovereignty over British Columbia had been conclusively acquired when Britain and the United States signed the Oregon Boundary Treaty in 1846, designating 49° north latitude as the boundary between their territories from the Rocky Mountains to the Strait of Georgia. As in *R* v. *Sparrow*, the Court does not seem to have considered the presence of the Indian nations as relevant to this issue of sovereignty (Borrows 1999). And yet, in *Haida Nation* v. *British Columbia (Minister of Forests)* ([2004] 3 S.C.R. 511, 524), Chief Justice Beverley McLachlin said that "[t]reaties serve to reconcile pre-existing aboriginal sovereignty with assumed Crown sovereignty." How, one might ask, could the Crown have acquired British Columbia by an original mode like settlement if the Indian nations were sovereign when the British arrived? The contradiction inherent in such a position, mirroring the contradiction in Marshall's decision in *Johnson* v. *M'Intosh*, has yet to be resolved by Canada's highest court (Walters 2006).

## Canada's Constitutional Structure

Canada was created in 1867 by Confederation of three British colonies, namely Nova Scotia, New Brunswick, and the Province of Canada (consisting of Canada East, formerly Lower Canada, and Canada West, formerly Upper Canada, which became the provinces of Quebec and Ontario). This was accomplished by an imperial statute, the British North America Act of 1867 (30 & 31 Vict., c. 3), renamed the Constitution Act of 1867 in 1982 (Constitution Act, 1982, s. 53[2]). This statute was the result of negotiations by representatives from these colonies in Charlottetown, Prince Edward Island, in 1864, and Quebec City in 1866 (Creighton 1964). No representatives of the Aboriginal peoples attended these conferences.

The Constitution Act, 1867, divided public lands and resources and legislative and executive jurisdiction between the provinces and the new federal government in Ottawa. By section 109, the provinces retained public lands and resources, subject to certain exceptions such as post offices, custom houses, public harbors, and military installations that were assigned to the government of Canada by section 108. Legislative jurisdiction was divided mainly by sections 91 and 92. Without recorded discussion or debate, exclusive jurisdiction over "Indians, and Lands reserved for the Indians," was assigned to the Parliament of Canada by section 91(24) (Sanders 1988:152–152; McMillan and Yellowhorn 2004:318). When the other six provinces joined the Confederation (British Columbia, 1871; Prince Edward Island, 1873; Newfoundland, 1949) or were created out of additional territory transferred to Canada by Britain in 1870 (Manitoba, 1870; Saskatchewan and Alberta, 1905), they became subject to the same division of powers, and so exclusive federal jurisdiction over "Indians, and Lands reserved for the Indians," applies throughout Canada. However, unlike the other provinces, Manitoba, Saskatchewan, and Alberta had to wait until 1930 to get ownership of public lands and resources within their boundaries (Natural Resources Transfer Agreements, constitutionalized by the Constitution Act, 1930, 20 & 21 Geo. V, c. 26).

The term "Indians" in section 91(24) has been interpreted by the Supreme Court to include Inuit (*Reference Re Term "Indians"* [1939] S.C.R. 104). However, it is uncertain whether the Métis are included therein, as the Court has not yet decided this issue. In *R* v. *Blais* ([2003] 2 S.C.R. 236), the Court held that the Métis are not "Indians" for the purposes of a provision in the Natural Resources Transfer Agreements that provides some protection against provincial laws to Indian hunting, trapping and fishing, but the Court expressly left open the question of whether they are "Indians" for the purposes of section 91(24) (Tough 2004; Bell and Leonard 2004). Persuasive arguments have nonetheless been made that the Métis do come within the section's scope (Chartier 1978–1979; Stevenson 2002, 2004).

The words "Lands reserved for the Indians" in section 91(24) have been judicially interpreted as encompassing all collectively held Indian (and thus Inuit) lands. Included are officially created Indian reserves and lands reserved by the Royal Proclamation of 1763 (*St. Catherine's Milling and Lumber Company* v. *The Queen* [1888], 14 App. Cas. 46; Slattery 1979), as are Aboriginal title lands (*Delgamuukw* v. *British Columbia* [1997] 3 S.C.R. 1010, 1116–1118; Bankes 1998; Wilkins 1999, 2002; McNeil 2001:249–280).

One consequence of this exclusive federal jurisdiction is that the provincial legislatures cannot enact laws in relation to "Indians, and Lands reserved for the Indians" (*Dick* v. *The Queen* [1985] 2 S.C.R. 309; *Derrickson* v. *Derrickson* [1986] 1 S.C.R. 285; *Delgamuukw* v. *British Columbia*, [1997] 3 S.C.R. 1010, 1119). Provincial laws of general application (laws applying generally throughout the province that do not single out Indians or their lands for special treatment) can apply nonetheless to Indians and on Indian lands as long as they do not impair the status or capacity of Indians (*Four B Manufacturing Ltd.* v. *United Garment Workers of America* [1980] 1 S.C.R. 1031; *Dick* v. *The Queen* [1985] 2 S.C.R. 309; *R* v. *Francis* [1988] 1 S.C.R. 1025), or relate to possession or use of land (*Derrickson* v. *Derrickson* [1986] 1 S.C.R. 285; *Corporation of Surrey* v. *Peace Arch Enterprises* [1970], 74 W.W.R. 380; *R* v. *Isaac* [1975], 13 N.S.R. [2d] 460). Provincial laws of general application that do impair Indian status or capacity cannot apply to Indians of their own force but have with certain exceptions been referentially incorporated into federal law by section 88 of the Indian Act (*Dick* v. *The Queen* [1985] 2 S.C.R. 309). The major exceptions are that section 88 shields treaty rights from provincial laws and excludes the application of those laws in situations where the matter in question has been dealt with by or under the Indian Act (*Simon* v. *The Queen* [1985] 2 S.C.R. 387; *Derrickson* v. *Derrickson* [1986] 1 S.C.R. 285; *R* v. *Sioui*, [1990] 1 S.C.R. 1025; *R* v. *Sundown* [1999] 1 S.C.R. 393; *R* v. *Morris* [2006] S.C.J. No. 59; Sanders 1988; Wilkins 2000; McNeil 2000a).

Another consequence of federal jurisdiction over "Indians, and Lands reserved for the Indians" is that authority to enter into treaties and extinguish Aboriginal rights, including Aboriginal title to land, is vested exclusively in the federal government. Ever since Confederation, the provinces have lacked the authority to *extinguish* these rights (*Delgamuukw* v. *British Columbia* [1997] 3 S.C.R. 1010, 1115–1123). Somewhat contradictorily, however, the Supreme Court has said that provincial laws of general application can *infringe* these rights, though this would have to be justified after those rights were recognized and affirmed by section 35(1) of the Constitution Act, 1982 (*R* v. *Badger* [1996] 1 S.C.R. 771, 815; *R* v. *Côté*, [1996] 3 S.C.R. 139, 185; *Delgamuukw* v. *British Columbia* [1997] 3 S.C.R. 1010, 1107; McNeil 2005). Provincial governments can be parties to treaties entered into by Aboriginal peoples and the federal government ("Nisga'a," this vol.; Molloy 2000).

## Aboriginal Title to Land

Several interrelated legal issues arise in connection with Aboriginal title to land, principally involving its source, nature and content, how it can be proven, and how it can be extinguished. Unfortunately, judicial decisions have revealed considerable confusion in relation to some of these matters.

In 1888, the Judicial Committee of the Privy Council in London, effectively the highest court of appeal in civil cases for Canada until 1949, apparently accepted that the Saulteaux Nation in the Lake of the Woods region of northwestern Ontario had Aboriginal title to their lands before surrendering them to the Crown by Treaty 3 in 1873 (*St. Catherine's Milling and Lumber Company* v. *The Queen*, 14 App. Cas. 46). The Royal Proclamation of 1763 was considered the source of their title, which was not defined precisely but described vaguely as "a personal and usufructuary right, dependent upon the good will of the Sovereign" (p. 54). The Privy Council subsequently clarified that "personal" means inalienable, other than by surrender to the Crown (*Attorney-General for Quebec* v. *Attorney-General for Canada* [1921] 1 A.C. 401, 408). Consequently, the Supreme Court of Canada has ruled that Aboriginal title is proprietary in nature, and so can "compete on an equal footing with other proprietary interests" (*Canadian Pacific Ltd.* v. *Paul* [1988] 2 S.C.R. 654, 677).

In *Calder* v. *Attorney-General of British Columbia* ([1973] S.C.R. 313), the first Aboriginal title case to reach the Supreme Court after *St. Catherine's Milling*, the judge dismissed the Royal Proclamation of 1763 as the title's source and found the "usufructuary" description of it to be unhelpful. Instead, in a frequently quoted passage, he said "the fact is that when the settlers came, the Indians were there, organized in societies and occupying the land as their forefathers had done for centuries. This is what Indian title means" [p. 328]. In *Guerin* v. *The Queen* ([1984] 2 S.C.R. 335, 382), the judge described Aboriginal title as a *sui generis* or unique interest, characterized by its general inalienability and the fact that the Crown has a fiduciary obligation to deal with the land on behalf of Aboriginal peoples when it accepts a surrender of their title.

The leading Canadian case on Aboriginal title is *Delgamuukw* v. *British Columbia* ([1997] 3 S.C.R. 1010), involving a claim to approximately 58,000 square kilometers in British Columbia by the Gitksan and Wet'suwet'en (Carrier) nations (fig. 1). While not reaching any decision on the merits of the claim, the Supreme Court did clarify a number of important matters in relation to Aboriginal title. Affirming that it is both proprietary and *sui generis*, Justice Lamer went on to enumerate its unique features, starting with its source. Rejecting the view in *St. Catherine's Milling*, he found that the Royal Proclamation of 1763, instead of being the source, recognized the pre-existing Aboriginal title that arose at common law from "the prior occupation of Canada by aboriginal peoples" (p. 1082). Secondly, Aboriginal title is communal. Unlike common law proprietary interests, it cannot be held by individuals: "it is a collective right to land held by all members of an aboriginal nation" (p. 1082). Because Aboriginal title is communal, Lamer said that decision-making authority over it is vested in the community as a whole. Third, the chief justice affirmed that Aboriginal title, unlike common law interests, is inalienable other than by surrender to the Crown (McNeil 2002). Finally, it is sub-

Fig. 1. Territories claimed by the Gitksan and the Wet'suwet'en in B.C. (*Delgamuukw* v. *British Columbia*, Reasons for Judgment of Chief Justice Allen McEachren, March 8, 1991, pp. 6, 8).

ject to an inherent limit: "Lands held pursuant to aboriginal title cannot be used in a manner that is irreconcilable with the nature of the attachment to the land which forms the basis of the group's claim to aboriginal title" (p. 1088, italics and capitalization removed). So, to use one of Lamer's examples, if Aboriginal title is established by proving the land was occupied as a hunting ground, it cannot be stripmined because that would destroy its value for hunting. This inherent limit, which first appeared in *Delgamuukw*, was explicitly aimed at protecting the interests of future generations but has been criticized because it is paternalistic and imposes inappropriate restraints on economic development (Monture-Angus 1999:126–128; McNeil 2001:116–122).

In addition to dealing with the source, nature, and content of Aboriginal title, the *Delgamuukw* decision explained how it can be proven. The onus is on the Aboriginal claimants to show that the land was exclusively occupied by their people (or jointly with other Aboriginal people) at the time of British assertion of sovereignty (McNeil 2001:136–160). Occupation can be shown by physical occupation and use in accordance with Aboriginal ways of life, and by Aboriginal law (Borrows 2002). Lamer stated: "As a result, if, at the time of sovereignty, an aboriginal society had laws in relation to land, those laws would be relevant to establishing the occupation of lands which are the subject of a claim for aboriginal title. Relevant laws might include, but are not limited to, a land tenure system or laws governing land use" (p. 1100). However, the existence of Aboriginal land laws does not appear to be a requirement for title, nor do those laws, where proven, determine the nature of the title. Instead, it is a generic interest that does not vary from one Aboriginal people to another (Slattery 2000:211–215). Nonetheless, it has been suggested that Aboriginal laws in relation to land continue to be relevant internally to determine rights, interests, and obligations among the members of the Aboriginal community (Slattery 1987:742, 744–748, 2007; McNeil 2001:92–95, 2006:689–691).

Acknowledging the difficulty of proving exclusive occupation of land at the time of Crown sovereignty, Lamer said courts have to show flexibility and adapt rules of evidence such as the hearsay rule in order to allow the oral histories of Aboriginal peoples to "be accommodated and placed on an equal footing with the types of historical evidence that courts are familiar with, which largely consists of historical documents" (p. 1069). The Supreme Court has taken the same kind of approach with respect to proof of other Aboriginal rights such as fishing and trading, admitting evidence of oral histories and traditions, provided they are useful and reasonably reliable (*R* v. *Van der Peet* [1996] 2 S.C.R. 507, 559; *Mitchell* v. *M.N.R.* [2001] 1 S.C.R. 911; Roness and McNeil 2000; Borrows 2001; D.G. Newman 2005:442–443).

The Supreme Court revisited the issue of proof of Aboriginal title in 2005 in two cases that were argued together before the Court and combined in one judgment, *R.* v. *Marshall; R.* v. *Bernard* ([2005] 2 S.C.R. 220). The cases involved charges laid under provincial legislation against Mi'kmaq Indians (Micmac) in Nova Scotia and New Brunswick for unlawful cutting and possession of logs harvested on lands the provinces claimed as their own. In defense, the accused claimed the Mi'kmaq have Aboriginal title to the lands where the cutting took place, as well as a right to harvest logs based on treaty, Belcher's Proclamation of 1762, and the Royal Proclamation of 1763.

The Aboriginal title claim depended on proof of exclusive occupation of the land at the time of Crown sovereignty, taken to be 1713 for mainland Nova Scotia, 1759 for the relevant area of New Brunswick, and 1763 for Cape Breton Island (p. 252). Writing the leading judgment, Chief Justice Beverley McLachlin said the "Court's task in evaluating a claim for an aboriginal right is to examine the pre-sovereignty aboriginal practice and translate that practice, as faithfully and objectively as it can, into a modern legal right" (p. 243). Where the right claimed is Aboriginal title, "[i]t is established by aboriginal practices that indicate possession similar to that associated with title at common law" (p. 245). This requires proof of physical occupation, which "may be established in a variety of ways, ranging from the construction of dwellings through cultivation and enclosure of fields to regular use of definite tracts *of* land for hunting, fishing or otherwise exploiting its resources" (p. 246, quoting from *Delgamuukw* v. *British Columbia*). The exclusivity of the occupation can be demonstrated by proof of "effective control of the land by the group, from which a reasonable inference can be drawn that it could have excluded others had it chosen to do so" (p. 249).

On the basis of the evidence presented at trial in *Marshall* and *Bernard*, McLachlin decided that the requisite exclusive occupation had not been proven in either case. Approving the approach taken by the trial judges, she required "proof of sufficiently regular and exclusive use of the cutting sites by Mi'kmaq people at the time of assertion of sovereignty" (p. 252). In so doing, she appears to have rejected the view of the Courts of Appeal that proof of exclusive occupation of a reasonably defined territory encompassing the cutting sites would suffice. Unlike Lamer in *Delgamuukw*, she excluded any reference to Aboriginal law as a source of title or a means of proving exclusive occupation (McNeil 2006).

Justice Louis LeBel delivered a separate judgment in *Marshall* and *Bernard*, agreeing with the result McLachlin had reached but disagreeing with her approach. In his view, she relied too much on the common law, without taking sufficient account of Aboriginal law or the *sui generis* aspects of Aboriginal title described in *Delgamuukw*. He also feared that her approach would make it virtually impossible for nomadic or seminomadic peoples to prove Aboriginal title (Burke 2000). In a passage echoing the territorial approach of the Courts of Appeal, he expressed the view that "aboriginal conceptions of territoriality, land-use and property should be used to modify and adapt the traditional common law concepts of property in order to develop an occupancy standard that incorporates both the aboriginal and common law approaches" (pp. 271–272).

Regarding extinguishment of Aboriginal title, Chief Justice Lamer decided in *Delgamuukw* that only the federal government could accomplish this after Confederation, given that "Lands reserved for the Indians" are under exclusive federal jurisdiction. Prior to recognition of Aboriginal rights by section 35(1) of the Constitution Act, 1982, this could occur with or without the consent of the Aboriginal titleholders, either by treaty or by or pursuant to federal legislation (McNeil 2001–2002). However, legislative extinguishment required a "clear and plain" intention to extinguish (*R* v. *Sparrow* [1990] 1 S.C.R. 1075, 1099; *Delgamuukw* v. *British Columbia*).

Aboriginal land rights are not limited to Aboriginal title. Other more limited rights to use or take resources from the land, such as hunting, fishing, and wood harvesting rights, have been acknowledged by Canadian courts. However, the test for establishing these rights, and indeed all other Aboriginal rights, differs significantly from the test for establishing title.

## Other Aboriginal Rights

### Resource Use Rights

Although the Supreme Court acknowledged an Aboriginal right to fish for food, societal, and ceremonial purposes in *R* v. *Sparrow* ([1990] 1 S.C.R. 1075), the Court first delin-

eated a test for identifying Aboriginal rights in *R.* v. *Van der Peet* ([1996] 2 S.C.R. 507). Dorothy Van der Peet, a member of the Sto:lo Nation (Halkomelem Salish) in British Columbia, was charged with unlawfully selling 10 salmon caught under the authority of an Indian food fish license. In defense, she claimed a constitutionally protected Aboriginal right to sell or exchange fish. The Court held that, in order to establish this right, she would have to prove that selling or exchanging fish was a practice, custom, or tradition integral to the distinctive culture of the Sto:lo people when they came into contact with Europeans. She failed to do so because a majority of the Court held that, although the Sto:lo had exchanged fish with other Aboriginal peoples prior to contact, this activity "was not a central, significant or defining feature of Sto:lo society" (para. 91). In explaining the test, Chief Justice Lamer said:

> To satisfy the integral to a distinctive culture test the aboriginal claimant must do more than demonstrate that a practice, custom or tradition was an aspect of, or took place in, the aboriginal society of which he or she is a part. The claimant must demonstrate that the practice, custom or tradition was a central and significant part of the society's distinctive culture. He or she must demonstrate, in other words, that the practice, custom or tradition was one of the things which made the culture of the society distinctive—that it was one of the things that truly *made the society what it was* (p. 553).

The *Van der Peet* "integral to the distinctive culture" test has been severely criticized (Borrows 1997a; Barsh and Henderson 1997; Cheng 1997; C.E.Bell 1998; Macklem 2001:59–61; McNeil 2007a). A major problem with it, as pointed out in a dissent, is that it freezes Aboriginal rights at an arbitrary point in the past, namely European contact. Significant changes and adaptations made since then, especially if in response to European colonization, do not qualify as Aboriginal rights. Aboriginal cultures are treated as static relics of the past, rather than as dynamic and complex systems of adaptive values, norms, customs, practices, and so on, by which the people in a society live their collective lives in an ever-changing world.

A second criticism is that the integral test requires judges to distinguish between the integral aspects of a culture that "*made the society what it was*" and merely incidental aspects that were less important. On what basis are Canadian judges, the vast majority of whom have scant knowledge and no direct experience of even contemporary Aboriginal cultures, to make such a distinction? The practical difficulties are compounded by the lack of any principled basis for this distinction. In the British imperial law governing the acquisition of colonies, any pre-existing rights that did not offend fundamental conceptions of British justice should have continued after colonization (Slattery 1979:50–59; McNeil 1989:171–179; Walters 1999; Barsh 2004). So why distinguish integral aspects of pre-existing Aboriginal cultures from incidental or less important aspects where Aboriginal rights are concerned?

The *Van der Peet* test has nonetheless been applied in other cases, some of them involving resource use rights. In *R* v. *Adams* ([1997] 3 S.C.R. 101), the Supreme Court decided that the Mohawk Nation has an Aboriginal right to fish for food in Lake Saint Francis in Quebec because such fishing was integral to their distinctive culture at the time of Samuel de Champlain's visit in 1603. In *Adams*, the Court distinguished site-specific Aboriginal rights, such as a right to fish in a particular lake, from Aboriginal title, holding that the former does not depend on the existence of the latter. This was affirmed in *R* v. *Côté* ([1997] 3 S.C.R. 139), where the River Desert Band of Algonquin Indians was found to have an Aboriginal right to fish for food in the rivers and lakes of a specific geographic area in Quebec.

In *R* v. *Sappier; R* v. *Gray* ([2006] S.C.J. No. 54), involving a claim to harvest wood on public lands for personal domestic uses, such as building houses and making furniture, the Court relaxed the integral requirement somewhat by discarding "the notion that the pre-contact practice upon which the right is based must go to the core of the society's identity, i.e. its single most important defining character" (para. 40). The Court acknowledged that requiring the precontact practice to "be a 'defining feature' of the aboriginal society, such that the culture would be 'fundamentally altered' without it, has also served in some cases to create artificial barriers to the recognition and affirmation of aboriginal rights" (para. 41). The Court decided that proof that the practice "was undertaken for survival purposes is sufficient . . . to meet the integral to a distinctive culture threshold" (para. 46). Given that harvesting wood for personal domestic use had been a precontact practice essential to the survival of the Maliseet and Mi'kmaq peoples in New Brunswick, the Court found that an Aboriginal right to engage in such harvesting had been established.

The *Van der Peet* test has also been applied to the Métis, with a significant modification to take account of the fact that, given their mixed heritage, they were not present at the time of contact with Europeans. In *R* v. *Powley* ([2003] 2 S.C.R. 207), the Supreme Court held that, as members of the Métis community in the Sault Sainte Marie region of Ontario, Steve and Roddy Powley had an Aboriginal right to hunt for food (P.L. Chartrand 2003; L.N. Chartrand 2004; C.E. Bell and C. Leonard 2004). In reaching this decision, the Court held that Métis people can establish their Aboriginal rights by proving they are part of a contemporary Métis community connected to a historic Métis community that was in existence at the time of effective European control over the region (for Sault Ste. Marie, taken to be around 1850). Following *Van der Peet*, these Aboriginal rights arise from practices, customs, or traditions integral to the distinctive culture of the Métis community at that time.

*Trading and Commercial Rights*

In general, Aboriginal claimants have had more difficulty establishing Aboriginal rights with a commercial dimension than

they have had establishing subsistence rights that involve personal or community resource use. One reason for this appears to be that the Supreme Court has made a somewhat artificial distinction between Aboriginal interests that enjoy special protection and Aboriginal participation in the "commercial mainstream" (*Mitchell* v. *Peguis Indian Band* [1990] 2 S.C.R. 85, 131, 138, 144–146; *McDiarmid Lumber Ltd.* v. *God's Lake First Nation* [2006] S.C.J. No. 58, paras. 27, 107, 113, 142). The *Van der Peet* case itself is an example of the Court's rejection of a commercial right, as is *R.* v. *N.T.C. Smokehouse Ltd.* ([1996] 2 S.C.R. 672). Similarly, in *Mitchell* v. *M.N.R.* ([2001] 1 S.C.R. 911), the Court found that the Mohawk Nation had failed to establish an Aboriginal right to bring goods duty-free across the Saint Lawrence River from the United States into Canada for the purpose of trade.

Although Aboriginal commercial rights appear difficult to prove, they can be established by means of the *Van der Peet* test if the evidence is strong enough to support them. In *R* v. *Gladstone* ([1996] 2 S.C.R. 723), the Supreme Court held that the Heiltsuk Nation in British Columbia has an Aboriginal right to harvest and sell herring spawn on kelp in commercial quantities (Harris 2000). Fortuitously for the Heiltsuk, in addition to other historical and anthropological evidence, they were able to rely on a 1793 journal entry by Alexander MacKenzie, noting that they were "traders in various articles, such as cedar-bark, prepared to be wove [*sic*] into mats, *fishspawn*, copper, iron, and beads" (p. 746). Other evidence revealed that the fish-spawn trade had been in large quantities, leading the Court to distinguish *Van der Peet* and *N.T.C. Smokehouse Ltd.* because, for the Heiltsuk, "trading in herring spawn on kelp was not an activity taking place as an incident to the social and ceremonial activities of the community; rather, trading in herring spawn on kelp was, *in itself*, a central and significant feature of Heiltsuk society" (p. 748).

The different time-frames for proof of Aboriginal rights—European contact for the Indians and Inuit, and effective European control for the Métis—may create some unforeseen anomalies. For example, if the fur trade arose mainly as a result of European contact without having a sufficient foundation in precontact Aboriginal cultures, Indian and Inuit participation in it probably would not support an Aboriginal right to trade furs. The Métis, on the other hand, were actively engaged in the fur trade as a significant part of their culture, in many instances before effective European control (this was probably so around Sault Ste. Marie, where *Powley* arose). As a result, the Métis might have an Aboriginal right to trade furs where the Indians and Inuit might not, despite their role (Ray 1998). This would seem to be an unfair and historically absurd result, pointing once more to the problematic nature of the contact time-frame in the *Van der Peet* test (Slattery 2000:217–218, 2007).

*Cultural Rights*

There is not yet a significant body of case law, especially at the Supreme Court level, involving cultural rights in relation to matters such as language, physical objects, intellectual property, and access to sacred sites (C.E. Bell 2001:259; M.L. Ross 2005; Halewood 2005). However, given the emphasis on culture in the *Van der Peet* test, the Court will probably look favorably on claims relating to these kinds of matters, as long as the "integral to the distinctive culture" hurdle is met. The same can be said of claims involving family relations. In *Casimel* v. *Insurance Corporation of British Columbia* ([1994] 2 C.N.L.R. 22, 32), decided before the Supreme Court's judgment in *Van der Peet*, the British Columbia Court of Appeal held that adoption of a child in accordance with the customary law of the Stellaquo Band of the Carrier Nation "was an integral part of [their] distinctive culture," and so had the legal effect of conferring parental status on the adoptive mother and father.

In *Kitkatla Band* v. *British Columbia (Minister of Small Business, Tourism and Culture)* (2002 2 S.C.R. 146), the Supreme Court upheld the constitutional validity of provisions in a provincial statute that conferred limited protection to, and executive authority over, Aboriginal cultural property, including culturally modified trees (C.E. Bell 2001; McNeil 2003). Although no attempt was made in the case to prove an Aboriginal right to the trees, the Court apparently envisaged the possibility of such a right being established in accordance with the *Van der Peet* test.

### Self-Government

Unlike in the United States, where the Supreme Court has clearly acknowledged the inherent sovereignty of the Indian nations since at least 1832 (*Worcester* v. *Georgia*, 6 Pet. 515), in Canada the Supreme Court has yet to decide whether Aboriginal peoples have what is usually called an inherent right of self-government (Royal Commission on Aboriginal Peoples 1993). The issue came before the Court in *R* v. *Pamajewon* ([1996] 2 S.C.R. 821), involving a claim by two Ojibwa (Anishnabe) First Nations in Ontario to a right of self-government in relation to on-reserve gaming. The Court was willing to assume (without deciding) that section 35(1) of the Constitution Act, 1982, includes self-government claims, but held that any such claims would have to be proven in the same way as other Aboriginal rights by application of the *Van der Peet* test. The Court dismissed the claims because it had not been proven that high-stakes gambling and its regulation had been integral to Ojibwa culture prior to contact with Europeans (B.W. Morse 1997).

*Delgamuukw* v. *British Columbia* involved a claim to a right of self-government as well as to Aboriginal title, but the Court sent the self-government matter back to trial without commenting directly on it. However, the Court held that Aboriginal title is communal and the community has decision-making authority over it. In *Campbell* v. *British Columbia (Attorney General)* ([2000] 4 C.N.L.R. 1), a case involving the constitutional validity of self-government provisions in the Nisga'a Treaty, Justice Paul Williamson of the British Columbia Supreme Court held that this authority is governmental in nature, and so Aboriginal titleholders must have an inherent right of self-government in relation to their Aboriginal title lands. The same reasoning would seem to apply to other Aboriginal rights, as well as to treaty rights, as they are also communal and entail decision-making authority (*R* v. *Marshall* [No. 2], [1999] 3 S.C.R. 533, 547). It therefore appears that Judge Williamson's approach in *Campbell* may offer an alternative to *Pamajewon*, enabling Aboriginal groups to claim a right of self-government as a necessary incident of other rights, without having to meet the *Van der Peet* test in relation to the self-government claim itself (McNeil 2007).

A willingness to reconsider the issue of self-government may be indicated by Justice Ian Binnie's judgment, concurring in result with the majority in *Mitchell* v. *M.N.R.* ([2001] 1 S.C.R. 911). While opining that an Aboriginal right to bring goods into Canada duty-free would be inconsistent with Canadian sovereignty and the need to control Canada's borders, Binnie explained that this does not mean that claims to a right of internal self-government would necessarily fail by reason of sovereign inconsistency (Moodie 2003–2004:27–39; McNeil 2007; cp. Christie 2002). In doing so, he referred to American case law "to alleviate any concern that addressing aspects of the sovereignty issue in the context of a claim to an international trading and mobility right would prejudice one way or the other a resolution of the much larger and more complex claim of First Nations in Canada to *internal* self-governing institutions" (p. 994).

## Treaty Rights

The French and British entered into numerous treaties with the Indian nations during the colonial period (vol. 4:20–28,185–194). The early treaties relating to what is now Canada generally involved peace, alliance, and trade, rather than lands and resources. After the French and Indian (or Seven Years) War and the cession of New France to Britain by the Treaty of Paris, George III issued the Royal Proclamation of 1763, establishing a process for acquisition of Indian lands by treaty (Slattery 1979; Stagg 1981). This process was followed in what is now southern Ontario and extended north and west as European settlement proceeded (vol. 4:202–210) (Cumming and Mickenberg 1972:107–124; Royal Commission on Aboriginal Peoples 1996, 1:111–130, 155–173; J.R. Miller 2000:161–169). However, large areas of Canada, especially in the Atlantic Provinces, Quebec, British Columbia, and the North, were not covered by historic treaties. They have become the subject of modern-day negotiations and land claims agreements ("Nisga'a," "James Bay Cree," and "Nunavut," this vol.).

Unlike Aboriginal rights, treaty rights arise from specific agreements between Aboriginal peoples and colonial governments or, since Confederation in 1867, the Canadian government. Therefore, it is essential to identify the terms included in any particular treaty, and determine how they are to be interpreted. These tasks have been undertaken by Canadian courts.

The Supreme Court has said that "what characterizes a treaty is the intention to create obligations, the presence of mutually binding obligations and a certain measure of solemnity" (*R* v. *Sioui*, [1990] 1 S.C.R. 1025, 1044). It has also emphasized taking account of the historical context and looking beyond the written words, because "the treaties, as written documents, recorded an agreement that had already been reached orally and they did not always record the full extent of the oral agreement" (*R* v. *Badger*, [1996] 1 S.C.R. 771, 798). In *R* v. *Marshall* ([1999] 3 S.C.R. 456), the Court held that a 1760–1761 treaty entered into by the Mi'kmaq and the British included a right to trade fish and other items in order to gain a moderate livelihood, even though the written treaty did not explicitly provide for such a right. The Court reasoned that, given the history of relations with Europeans, discussions that took place at the time of the treaty and inclusion of a British promise to establish "truck houses" (trading posts), it was understood the Mi'kmaq would have a right to obtain the resources necessary to participate in trade (Coates 2000; Rotman 2000; Isaac 2001; Wicken 2002). In *R* v. *Marshall; R* v. *Bernard* ([2005] 2 S.C.R. 220), the Court held that this right is limited to traditional Mi'kmaq trading activity and its logical evolution; it found that trade in logs had not been engaged in by the Mi'kmaq in 1760–1761 nor was this trade a logical evolution from their trading activities at that time.

Regarding the legal status of the treaties, the Supreme Court has held they are not international agreements, nor are they mere contracts (*Simon* v. *The Queen* [1985] 2 S.C.R. 387, 404). Like Aboriginal title and the unique fiduciary relationship between the Crown and Aboriginal peoples, they are *sui generis*. Reflecting the Aboriginal understanding of the treaties, the Court has also said they are sacred (*R* v. *Badger*, [1996] 1 S.C.R. 771, 793). Since 1982, treaty rights have enjoyed the same protection as Aboriginal rights by virtue of section 35(1) of the Constitution Act, 1982 (*R* v. *Badger*; *R* v. *Côté*, [1997] 3 S.C.R. 139; *R* v. *Marshall*, [1999] 3 S.C.R. 456; *R* v. *Marshall [No. 2]*, [1999] 3 S.C.R. 533).

The Supreme Court has laid down rules for interpreting treaties (Rotman 1997; Christie 2000). Given cultural differences and the difficulty of translating terms written in a European language into oral Aboriginal languages, the words in treaties "must not be interpreted in their strict technical sense nor subjected to rigid modern rules of construction"; instead, "they must be interpreted in the sense that they would naturally have been understood by the Indians at the time of the signing" (*R* v. *Badger* [1996] 1 S.C.R. 771, 799). Since the honor of the Crown is involved, treaties should also be interpreted in a way that upholds the integrity of the Crown and avoids any appearance of "sharp dealing" (*R* v. *Badger*, 794). They must be generously and liberally construed, and any ambiguities in the written terms have to be resolved in favor of the Aboriginal parties

(*Simon* v. *The Queen*, [1985] 2 S.C.R. 386, 402; *R* v. *Badger*, 798; *R* v. *Morris*, [2006] S.C.J. No. 59, para. 29). However, in *R* v. *Marshall* ([1999] 3 S.C.R. 456, 474), Judge Binnie cautioned: "'Generous' rules of interpretation should not be confused with a vague sense of after-the-fact largess. The special rules are dictated by the special difficulties of ascertaining what in fact was agreed to. . . . The bottom line is the Court's obligation is to 'choose from among the various possible interpretations of the *common* intention [at the time the treaty was made] the one which best reconciles' the [Aboriginal] interests and those of the British Crown" (quoting from *R* v. *Sioui* [1990] 1 S.C.R. 1025, 1069, Binnie's emphasis).

A concrete example of how the honor of the Crown figures in treaty interpretation can be seen in *Mikisew Cree First Nation* v. *Canada (Minister of Canadian Heritage)* ([2005] 3 S.C.R. 388), involving a term in Treaty 8 (1899) whereby the Crown agreed the Indian parties would have hunting, trapping, and fishing rights throughout the treaty area, "saving and excepting such tracts as may be required or taken up from time to time for settlement, mining, lumbering, trading or other purposes" (Canada 1966:12). The Canadian government had authorized construction of a winter road through the traditional hunting and trapping territory of the Mikisew Cree (Rocky Cree about 170 km north of Ft. McMurray, Alta.), and argued this was a taking up of lands in accordance with this provision. Applying the concept of honor of the Crown, the Supreme Court interpreted the provision as requiring the government to consult with the Mikisew Cree and attempt to accommodate their interests before making a decision to authorize the road. Speaking for the Court, Judge Binnie said:

> . . . . the honour of the Crown infuses every treaty and the performance of every treaty obligation. Treaty 8 therefore gives rise to Mikisew procedural rights (e.g., consultation) as well as substantive rights (e.g., hunting, fishing and trapping rights). Were the Crown to have barrelled ahead with implementation of the winter road without adequate consultation, it would have been in violation of its *procedural* obligations, quite apart from whether or not the Mikisew could have established that the winter road breached the Crown's *substantive* treaty obligations as well (pp. 417–418, Binnie's emphasis).

There is often significant disagreement between the Aboriginal parties and the Crown when it comes to the interpretation of specific treaty terms (Macklem 1997; Venne 1997; Ray, Miller, and Tough 2000). For example, the 11 numbered treaties (1871–1921) covering northern Ontario, the Prairie Provinces, northeastern British Columbia, and part of the Yukon and Northwest Territories (map in vol. 4:205), all contain a written term whereby the Aboriginal parties surrendered all their lands to the Crown, in exchange for tiny reserves, annuity payments, and a few other benefits (A. Morris 1880:313–377). While the Canadian and provincial governments interpret this as an absolute surrender of Aboriginal title, Aboriginal people generally say their inten-

*173*

tion was to share the land, not give it up completely (Treaty 7 Elders and Tribal Council 1996; Cardinal and Hildebrandt 2000). In some instances, it appears that this provision was not even mentioned to the Aboriginal parties (*Re Paulette* [1973], 42 D.L.R. [3d] 8). Many issues relating to the content and interpretation of treaties are thus outstanding, and some are the subject of ongoing litigation (*Ermineskin Indian Band and Nations* v. *Canada; Samson Indian Nation and Band* v. *Canada* [2006] F.C.J. No. 1961).

## The Crown's Fiduciary Obligations

Prior to the Supreme Court's decision in *Guerin* v. *The Queen* ([1984] 2 S.C.R. 335), it was unclear whether the Crown owed legally enforceable fiduciary obligations to the Aboriginal peoples (Rotman 1996:73–87). In *Guerin*, the Canadian government argued that the relationship is political in nature, giving rise to moral, not legal, obligations. The Court disagreed, holding that the relationship is fiduciary, and so the Crown has enforceable obligations when it exercises discretionary authority over Aboriginal interests. In that case, the federal government had accepted a surrender of Musqueam reserve lands in Vancouver and leased them to a golf club on terms substantially less beneficial to the Musqueam than the terms they had approved. Damages of $10,000,000 were assessed against the Crown (Reynolds 2005:25–82). Similarly, in *Blueberry River Indian Band* v. *Canada (Department of Indian Affairs and Northern Development)* ([1995] 4 S.C.R. 344), the Supreme Court found the federal government liable for failing to retain the mineral rights on Indian reserve land that had been surrendered to it in the 1940s and granted to veterans of World War II. In *Blueberry River*, however, the Court struck a balance between the Crown's duty to respect the decision-making authority of First Nations and its obligation to protect them from exploitative contracts (McNeil 2001:313–315).

The Crown is also under fiduciary obligations when it expropriates reserve lands. In *Osoyoos Indian Band* v. *Oliver (Town)* ([2001] 3 S.C.R. 746), the Supreme Court held that, in taking reserve lands for a public purpose, the Crown has an obligation not to expropriate an interest greater than that required to meet the purpose (Rotman 2003:375). In *Semiahmoo Indian Band* v. *Canada* ([1997] 148 D.L.R. [4th] 523), the Federal Court of Appeal similarly held that, where a First Nation surrenders reserve land under threat of expropriation for a public purpose (expanding a customs facility), the Crown has an obligation to return any land not used for that purpose. In addition to ordering compensation, the Court imposed a constructive trust on the unused land.

Although the relationship between the Crown and the Aboriginal peoples is generally fiduciary, this does not mean that every aspect of the relationship gives rise to fiduciary obligations (*Quebec Attorney General* v. *Canada (Na-*

*tional Energy Board)* [1994] 1 S.C.R. 159, 183-184). In *Wewaykum Indian Band* v. *Canada* ([2002] 4 S.C.R. 245), the Supreme Court said that fiduciary obligations arise in situations where there is a cognizable Aboriginal interest in relation to which the Crown has taken discretionary control (p. 289). In that case, the Court held that the Crown can have fiduciary obligations in the context of Indian reserve creation (see also *Ross River Dena Council Band* v. *Canada* [2002] 2 S.C.R. 816) but decided that these obligations had been met on the facts (Elliott 2003).

While almost all the Supreme Court decisions involving fiduciary obligations have related to Indian reserve lands, it seems clear that the Crown can owe obligations in other contexts where it exercises control over Indian interests. For example, the Federal Court of Appeal has held that the federal government is a trustee with fiduciary obligations in situations where it manages Indian monies (*Ermineskin Indian Band and Nations* v. *Canada; Samson Indian Nation and Band* v. *Canada*). It has also been argued that the Canadian government breached its fiduciary obligations to Indian communities, families, and children by removing children from their homes and placing them in residential schools, where many of them suffered emotional, physical, and sexual abuse (J.R. Miller 1996; Milloy 1999). In *Blackwater* v. *Plint* ([2005] 3 S.C.R. 3, 25–26), the Supreme Court acknowledged these arguments but declined to rule on them because they had been raised only on appeal and had not been supported by evidence submitted at trial.

## Constitutional Protection and Infringement of Aboriginal and Treaty Rights

Section 35(1) of the Constitution Act, 1982, recognized and affirmed the "existing aboriginal and treaty rights of the Aboriginal peoples of Canada." Most of the case law examined above in relation to Aboriginal title, other Aboriginal rights, and treaty rights has involved identification and definition of the rights protected by this section.

The effect of section 35(1) is to confer constitutional protection on rights that already existed and were enforceable as common law rights, so that they can no longer be *extinguished* unilaterally by legislation (*R* v. *Van der Peet* [1996] 2 S.C.R. 507, 538; *R* v. *Marshall; R* v. *Bernard* ([2005] 2 S.C.R. 220, 241). They can, however, still be *infringed* by or pursuant to legislation that is otherwise valid, as long as the infringement can be justified by a test laid down by the Supreme Court in *R* v. *Sparrow* ([1990] 1 S.C.R. 1075). After Aboriginal people have met the initial onus of proving a right and its infringement, the Crown can then lead evidence to show that legislative infringement of that right is justified. To successfully do so, the Crown has to establish two things: that the legislation has a valid objective and that the Crown's fiduciary obligations to the Aboriginal people in question have been respected.

Regarding the first part of the justification test, the Court in *Sparrow* said that conservation and management of a natural resource (in that case, a fishery) would be a valid legislative objective, as would other "compelling and substantial" objectives, including public safety (p. 1113). But the Court specifically rejected "the public interest" as a valid reason for placing limitations on Aboriginal peoples' constitutional rights (p. 1113). However, when the Court returned to this issue of justifiable infringement in *R* v. *Gladstone* ([1996] 2 S.C.R. 723), Justice Lamer included, as potentially valid objectives, "the pursuit of economic and regional fairness, and the recognition of the historical reliance upon, and participation in, the fishery by non-aboriginal groups" (p. 775). As Judge McLachlin pointed out in her dissent in *R* v. *Van der Peet* ([1996] 2 S.C.R. 507, 664), this appears "to require a judicially authorized transfer of the aboriginal right to non-aboriginals without the consent of the aboriginal people, without treaty, and without compensation," which she refused to sanction (McNeil 2001:285–291).

Applying the *Gladstone* approach to Aboriginal title in *Delgamuukw* v. *British Columbia,* Chief Justice Lamer expanded his list of potentially valid legislative objectives to include "the development of agriculture, forestry, mining, and hydroelectric power, the general economic development of the interior of British Columbia, protection of the environment or endangered species, the building of infrastructure and the settlement of foreign populations to support those aims." In light of this, one has to wonder what value can be assigned to constitutional recognition and affirmation of Aboriginal and treaty rights (McNeil 2004; Christie 2000–2001; Dufraimont 2000).

The answer probably lies in the second part of the *Sparrow* test for justifiable infringement, namely respect for the Crown's fiduciary obligations. Elaborating, the Court said relevant questions to address would be "whether there has been as little infringement as possible in order to effect the desired result; whether, in a situation of expropriation, fair compensation is available; and whether the aboriginal group in question has been consulted with respect to the . . . measures being implemented" ([1990] 1 S.C.R. 1075, 1119). While the requirements of minimum impairment and the compensation might be impediments to infringement (McNeil 1998: 22–23; Mainville 2001), developing case law has focused on consultation as the primary protection afforded by section 35(1). The *Delgamuukw* opinion said:

> There is always a duty of consultation. . . . The nature and scope of the duty of consultation will vary with the circumstances. In occasional cases, when the breach is less serious or relatively minor, it will be no more than a duty to discuss important decisions that will be taken with respect to lands held pursuant to aboriginal title. Of course, even in these rare cases when the minimum acceptable standard is consultation, this consultation must be in good faith, and with the intention of substantially addressing the concerns of the aboriginal peoples whose lands are at issue. In most cases, it will be significantly deeper than mere consultation. Some cases may

even require the full consent of an aboriginal nation, particularly when provinces enact hunting and fishing regulations in relation to aboriginal lands ([1997] 3 S.C.R. 1010, 1113).

While these observations were made in the hypothetical context of proven Aboriginal title, subsequent case law has applied the requirement of consultation to situations where Aboriginal title or other rights have been claimed but not yet established (Lawrence and Macklem 2000; Isaac and Knox 2003).

The leading case on consultation is *Haida Nation* v. *British Columbia (Minister of Forests)* ([2004] 3 S.C.R. 511), involving an Aboriginal title claim to the Queen Charlotte Islands and the surrounding waters and seabed. Despite this claim, the government of British Columbia had been issuing licenses to forestry companies, authorizing them to log on the islands. The court action was brought by the Haida to stop the logging until their claim was resolved. The Supreme Court decided that, although the Haida did not have a veto on resource development while their claim was pending, the government could not ignore the existence of that claim, observing that "[t]he Crown, acting honourably, cannot cavalierly run roughshod over aboriginal interests where claims affecting these interests are being seriously pursued in the process of treaty negotiation and proof" (p. 526). It has to engage in good faith consultation with them, take account of their concerns, and accommodate their interests in appropriate circumstances. Regarding the scope of the duty, it "is proportionate to a preliminary assessment of the strength of the case supporting the existence of the right or title, and to the seriousness of the potentially adverse effect upon the right or title claimed" (p. 531). Given the strength of the Haida claim and the serious impact of the logging, the Court held that the province had a duty to engage in meaningful consultation, which might result in a duty to accommodate. The Court found that the province had not fulfilled this duty, unlike in *Taku River Tlingit First Nation* v. *British Columbia (Project Assessment Director)* ([2004] 3 S.C.R. 550), where the Court decided that consultation over construction of a road to a mining site had been adequate.

The Supreme Court subsequently applied the concept of honor of the Crown in *Mikisew Cree First Nation* v. *Canada (Minister of Canadian Heritage)* in concluding that the Crown has a duty to consult and possibly accommodate before exercising its treaty right to take up lands for infrastructure and other purposes. Together, *Haida Nation* and *Mikisew Cree* amount to significant developments in the law, especially because they compel governments to involve Aboriginal peoples in decision-making in relation to lands that are subject to Aboriginal claims or covered by treaty.

## Conclusion

The focus here has been on Aboriginal title, other Aboriginal rights, treaty rights, fiduciary obligations, and constitutional issues. Other important matters, such as family relations, gender issues, status and citizenship, criminal justice, and the interpretation and application of the Indian Act have not been addressed, nor have regional matters received much attention. Modern land claims agreements and self-government arrangements generally have not been the subject of much litigation at the Supreme Court level; some of them have been presented elsewhere in the volume ("James Bay Cree," "Nisga'a," and "Nunavut").

For a comprehensive collection of case law relating to Aboriginal peoples, the University of Saskatchewan Native Law Centre, Saskatoon, has published a nine-volume compilation, entitled *Canadian Native Law Cases*, covering the period to 1978 (Native Law Centre 1980–1991). The Centre publishes the *Canadian Native Law Reporter*, a quarterly, on-going collection of decisions since 1979. Both these publications have very useful subject indexes and include summaries of the cases.

# Aboriginal Land Claims

SHIN IMAI

Modern land claims and self-government agreements attempt to bridge the gap between the desire of mainstream society to impose its laws and the actual experience of the Aboriginal party to the application of those laws. These Agreements have been controversial, being criticized from some Aboriginal people as a boondoggle for Aboriginal elites (T. Alfred 1999) and some non-Aboriginal people as a return to race-based government (G. Gibson 1999). Nonetheless, significant groups of Aboriginal people and Crown governments have negotiated several such Agreements (table 1). They provide exclusive rights to territory combined with varying degrees of control over the natural resources of a larger area. There are also provisions relating to the election of governments and jurisdiction to make laws over the territory. The three Agreements of the James Bay and Northern Quebec Agreement of 1977, the Nunavut Agreement of 1993 and 2000, and the Nisga'a Agreement of 2000 take very different approaches to land claims and self-governance.

## History

The term "land claim" is used when an Aboriginal group or nation is making a "claim" on land that is not recognized by the government as belonging to that group or nation. While there have been great strides made in recognizing that these claims are legitimate, there remains a fundamental difference between the perspectives of Aboriginal people and the government entering into negotiations.

For the settler societies, which in Canada were the French, English, and Scottish, land was viewed as a commodity that should be owned, traded, and sold. It was something to be exploited in order to create wealth. The settlement of Canada was premised, in part, on the view that Aboriginal peoples were "wasting" land that could be better put to productive use through agriculture, mining, and forestry. As late as 1982, a history text widely used in Canada celebrated the extermination of Indians for this reason (McInnis and Horn 1982:11). For most Aboriginal people the relationship to land was much different. Although the concept of territoriality was known—both family groupings and larger tribal groupings identified geographi-

cal boundaries—the concept of land as a commodity for sale for personal gain was not.

As the British military strength and the sheer number of settlers grew during the eighteenth and nineteenth centuries, the colonies spread farther into Indian country. The British signed treaties that generally involved the "surrender" of land. According to the text of Treaty 9, for example, the First Nations signed away all their rights to land in northern Ontario, in return for what one judge described as "an absurdly low consideration (even for that time)" (*R* v. *Battisse* [1978] 19 O.R. [2d] 145). The Indians were left with one square mile for every 400 square miles surrendered, $8 each on signing of the treaty, and a yearly treaty payment of $4 per person. Hunting and fishing would continue to be allowed on land that was not taken up by settlers for mining, lumbering, settlement, or other uses.

These treaties were not well respected. Promises were not fulfilled and the courts found that the federal government could unilaterally override treaty promises (*R* v. *George* [1966] S.C.R. 267). In *R* v. *Syliboy* ([1929]1 D.L.R. 307: 313–314), for example, the court discounted the validity of treaties completely. The judge wrote: "A civilized nation first discovering a country of uncivilized people or savages held such country as its own until such time as by treaty it was transferred to some other civilized nation. The savages' rights of sovereignty even of ownership were never recognized. Nova Scotia had passed to Great Britain not by gift or purchase from or even by conquest of the Indians but by treaty with France, which had acquired it by priority of discovery and ancient possession, and the Indians passed with it."

Although much of Canada was covered by treaties, there were large areas in the East, Quebec, British Columbia, and the North that were not ("The Department of Indian Affairs and Northern Development," fig. 5, this vol.). In those areas, the government set up reserves for the Indians and took control over the land ("The Evolution of Native Reserves," this vol.). The reserves were very small compared to those in the United States. The combined area of all the reserves in Canada would not cover one-half of the Navajo Reservation (Royal Commission on Aboriginal Peoples 1996, 2:423). Under the Indian Act the title for the reserves remained with the Crown and the land could only be alienated to the Crown. The Indian Act also provided for the election of Chief and Council, which had limited powers to pass laws concerning

**Table 1. Modern Land Claims and Self-Government Agreements**

| Agreement | Land | Monetary Settlement |
|---|---|---|
| James Bay and Northern Quebec Agreement, 1977 | 5,408 sq. miles | $225 million over 20 years |
| Northeastern Quebec, 1978 | 126 sq. miles | $9 million over 20 years |
| Inuvialuit Agreement, 1984 | 35,000 sq. miles | $152 million over 14 years |
| Gwich'in Agreement, 1992 | 9,258 sq. miles | $75 million over 15 years |
| Nunavut Land Claims Agreement, 1993 | 136,000 sq. miles | $1.17 billion over 14 years |
| Council for Yukon Indians Agreement, 1993 | 10,000 sq. miles | $242,673,000 over 15 years, divided among 14 First Nations |
| Sahtu Dene and Métis Agreement, 1993 | 16,000 sq. miles | $75 million over 15 years |
| Nisga'a Agreement, 2000 | 770 sq. miles | $190 million over 15 years |
| Tlicho Agreement, 2003 | 15,058 sq. miles | $98.6 million over 14 years |
| Labrador Inuit Land Claims Agreement, 2005 | 6,100 sq. miles | $140 million |
| Nunavik Inuit Land Claims, 2006 | Islands with area of 1,930 sq. miles | $54.8 million over 9 years |

SOURCE: Department of Indian and Northern Affairs.
NOTE: The effective date is given, which may be later than the date the treaty was signed.

local issues. Even then the Crown retained the right to disallow any law. For a period, First Nations could not even commence legal proceedings against the government because a section in the Indian Act made it a crime to raise funds to advance claims on behalf of Indians (Canada 1926–27:c. 32, s. 6).

The two other Aboriginal groups fared worse than the Indians. In the case of the Métis, most were offered "scrip," which was a right to an individual plot of land. These individual entitlements were soon dissipated amid allegations of fraud and deceit. With the exception of the province of Alberta, the Métis were left with no land base ("Métis," this vol.). In the case of the Inuit of the North no land arrangement was made at all.

The nadir of federal government relations with Aboriginal peoples and their lands came in 1969 with the release of the Statement of the Government of Canada on Indian Policy, commonly referred to as the White Paper. This document proposed an entirely new relationship with Indian people, which would permit "full and equal participation in the cultural, social, economic and political life of Canada" (Canada 1969:11). The new policy was to be implemented by dismantling Indian reserves and programs targeted for Aboriginal people and eventually phasing out treaties. What the government saw as "equality" Indian people saw as assimilation. The document was stunning in its misreading of the mood among Indians and the rising sense of consciousness of Canadians as a whole. It is ironic that the articulation of a vision that saw Indians disappearing became the defining moment for the resurgence of Aboriginal rights.

**Recognition of Aboriginal Rights After 1969: the James Bay Agreement**

Aboriginal people reacted strongly against the 1969 White Paper and their protests were soon followed by court decisions that forced the government to change its approach.

The first case was commenced by the Nisga'a in northern British Columbia asking for a declaration that they continued to have Native title. They had never signed a treaty, no legislation had been passed specifically extinguishing their rights, and hardly any land in their territory had been alienated to third parties. *Calder* v. *Attorney General of British Columbia* ([1973] S.C.R. 313) was heard by the Supreme Court of Canada in 1973. Three judges found that title had been extinguished when the government passed general legislation on land for the province. Three judges found that the Royal Proclamation's provisions requiring meetings of the nation before the transfer of land had not been followed and that there was no "plain and clear" legislation extinguishing rights. Therefore, Native title continued to exist. The seventh judge dismissed the case on a technicality, which did not address the issue of Aboriginal title. Consequently, the Court was evenly split on the existence of Aboriginal title in British Columbia.

At around the same time, the government of Quebec announced that it would commence a huge hydroelectric project in the North, which would require relocation of some communities and the damming of rivers. The Cree and Inuit living there had not been informed, let alone consulted about this project.

The Cree and the Inuit commenced a court case to stop the development and initially succeeded in getting an injunction to stop the development in 1973 (*Gros-Louis* v. *Société de développement de la Baie James* [1973], 8 C.N.L.C. 188). The injunction was overturned a few days later on appeal (*James Bay Development Corp.* v. *Kanatewat* [1973], 8 C.N.L.C. 414; *Société de développement de la Baie James* v. *Kanatewat* [1974], 8 C.N.L.C. 373), but it forced the parties to the negotiating table and resulted in the negotiation of Canada's first modern treaty on land and self-government ("James Bay Cree," this vol.).

For the rights and benefits contained within the Agreement, the James Bay Cree and Inuit of Quebec ceded, released, surrendered, and conveyed all their Native claims, rights, titles and interests, in and to land in the Northwest Territories and Quebec. The Cree and Inuit of Quebec renounced any claims against Quebec with respect to royalties, mining duties, taxes or equivalent derived from development and exploitation of the territory (Quebec 1976:s. 2, 25). The monetary settlement is $225,000,000 payable over 20 years (Quebec 1976: s. 25). The provisions were slightly different for the Cree and Inuit.

### Territory

The Agreement covers most of the land mass of the province—410,000 square miles (1,061,895 sq. km). The territory is divided into three categories of land. In each category, there is a different balance between rights of the Aboriginal parties, and the rights of the Crown.

Category I lands are for the exclusive use and benefit of the Inuit or the Cree. Title to approximately 3,250 square miles (8,417 sq. km) is transferred to the Inuit Community Corporation for Inuit community purposes, including commercial, industrial, and residential development. These lands, however, remain under provincial jurisdiction. Inuit cannot sell or transfer except to Quebec. Prior to the Agreement, Cree already lived on reserves, and these lands (with some additions) became the Category I lands that total 2,158 square miles. Because the reserves were under federal jurisdiction, some of the Category I lands of the Cree continue under federal jurisdiction. Quebec owns the mineral and subsurface rights on Category I lands, but it can extract these minerals only with the consent of the Aboriginal parties and on payment of compensation (Quebec 1976:s. 5).

About 35,000 square miles (90,650 sq. km), are set aside as Category II lands for the Inuit and 25,000 square miles (64,750 sq. km) for the Cree (Quebec 1976:s. 4). The title to these lands is in the province, and the province has the right to initiate development activities. However, Inuit and Cree have exclusive hunting, fishing, and trapping rights on these lands. If the land is expropriated by Quebec for development activities, the Aboriginal parties have a right to replacement land or to compensation (Quebec 1976:s. 5, 7).

The rest of the land is Category III. Both Native and non-Native people may hunt and fish there subject to regulations adopted in accordance with the Agreement. Aboriginal groups have the exclusive rights to harvest certain aquatic species and fur-bearing mammals and to participate in the administration and development of the land (Quebec 1976:s. 5, 7).

### Co-management

The participation of Inuit and Cree in decision-making on all three categories of land is an important aspect of the Agreement. Historically the federal or provincial governments have assumed that they have plenary authority to impose their own land regimes on Aboriginal nations. It was this attitude that led the government of Quebec to announce the James Bay Hydroelectric Project without consulting the Cree and Inuit who lived in the territory. The James Bay and Northern Quebec Agreement addresses Cree and Inuit interests through the creation of committees that include representatives of both the Aboriginal parties and the government parties. While these provisions were groundbreaking at the time, in later Agreements, these mechanisms were strengthened to provide greater input for the Aboriginal parties.

The Inuit and Cree also participate on a number of boards and committees related to resource use, environmental quality, and assessment of the impacts of proposed development projects. The Aboriginal participation on these committees goes beyond token representation. The committees are structured to provide a rotation in the balance of power between the government and the Aboriginal parties. For example, the James Bay Advisory Committee on the Environment has 13 members. Four members each will be appointed by the Cree, the federal government, and the provincial government. The final member is the chair of the Hunting, Fishing, and Trapping Co-ordinating Committee. The chair and vice-chair of the Advisory Committee on the Environment will alternate each year among the Cree and the government parties. In the first year, Quebec appointed the chair and Canada appointed the vice-chair. In the second year, the Crees appointed both the chair and vice-chair. In the third year, Canada appointed the chair and Quebec appointed the vice-chair. In the fourth year, the Cree appointed both the chair and vice-chair. This pattern recognizes that the Crees have an interest that is distinct from the two Crown governments. The makeup of the committee, with equal representatives from the three parties, recognizes the shared responsibilities of the three governments.

The co-management committees have fairly wide mandates to review matters, but their powers are limited to providing advice and making recommendations. For the James Bay Advisory Committee on the Environment, for example, the ultimate decision rests with the appropriate federal or provincial minister. If these ministers disagree with the recommendations of the committees, the only requirement is that the minister "consult" with the committee, and the Agreement provides that "failure to consult shall not invalidate the said regulations" (Quebec 1976:s. 22.3.31). Agreements signed in later years, such as for Nunavut, strengthened the authority of committees by requiring the minister to give reasons for not following advice of the committee.

### Government

The Inuit and the Cree negotiated different self-government arrangements. Each of the 13 Inuit communities is incorporated as a municipality under Quebec law, and specific powers are delegated to them by Quebec legislation. A regional government structure was established under a provincial act concerning the Kativik regional government (Kativik Act

1978, c. 87). Both Inuit and non-Inuit can vote in elections as long as they have resided in the area for at least 36 months (Quebec 1976: s. 12, sched. 2, s. 13). The regional government also administers the Kativik Health and Social Services Council (Quebec 1976:s. 15). The Kativik School Board has responsibility for developing and implementing culturally appropriate educational programs in elementary, secondary, and adult education (Quebec 1976:s. 17).

The Cree, as Indians under the Indian Act, negotiated a continuation of their basic governance structure where members of each of the eight Cree communities vote for their own Chief and Council. Only registered Crees can vote. The Cree also extracted a commitment by the federal government to exempt them from some of the strictures of the Indian Act by enacting a new Cree-Naskapi of Quebec Act (Canada 1984a, c. 18). The Agreement establishes a Cree Health and Social Services Board (Quebec 1976:s. 14) and a Cree Education Authority (Quebec 1976:s. 16).

## Constitutional Recognition: The Nunavut Land Claims Agreement

In 1974, the federal government received a proposal to build a gas pipeline across the Northwest Territories. Objections by Aboriginal and environmental groups to the pipeline resulted in the creation of the Mackenzie Valley Pipeline Inquiry chaired by Justice Tom Berger. The Inquiry concluded with a report that recommended that native claims be settled with the "establishment of new institutions and programs that will form the basis for native self-determination" (Canada 1977:1–2).

Before more Agreements were signed, there was an important constitutional change. For Aboriginal nations, the most important changes were made in 1982 and 1983 with the addition of section 35 of the Constitution Act, 1982, which provided:

(1) The existing aboriginal and treaty rights of the aboriginal peoples of Canada are hereby recognized and affirmed.

(2) In this Act, "aboriginal peoples of Canada" includes the Indian, Inuit and Métis peoples of Canada.

(3) For greater certainty, in subsection (1), "treaty rights" includes rights that now exist by way of land claims agreements or may be so acquired.

(4) Notwithstanding any other provision of this Act, the aboriginal and treaty rights referred to in subsection (19) are guaranteed equally to male and female persons.

Subsection (3) was significant for land claims agreements because it elevated treaty rights to the level of constitutional rights. This meant that the provisions in the James Bay and Northern Quebec Agreement were protected from unilateral extinguishment ("Native Rights and the Constitution in Canada," this vol.).

For the Inuit, subsection 35(2) was significant because it was the first time that the Constitution had recognized them as a distinct people. Because of their isolation, they had been largely ignored. There were no treaties signed with them, nor any legislation similar to the Indian Act. The first real intrusions of settlers came in the 1950s, when there were dramatic relocations of entire Inuit communities from Quebec, Inukjuak, and Baffin Island to the High Arctic. Often these communities were relocated for the convenience of government administration and a perceived need to industrialize and assimilate Inuit (Royal Commission on Aboriginal Peoples 1994).

The land claims movement among the Inuit began with the creation of the Inuit Tapirisat of Canada at around the time of the signing of the Alaska Native Claims Settlement Act in the United States in 1971. The proposal for a gas pipeline provided the impetus for a group in the Western Arctic, the Inuvialuit, to arrive at their own Agreement in 1984. The Inuvialuit Agreement (Canada 1984b) recognized title to approximately 35,135 square miles (91,000 sq. km) out of the 167,954 square miles (435,000 sq. km) that they traditionally occupied. Although some co-management committees were established, there were no provisions dealing with a separate governing body for the Inuvialuit people.

The main body of the Inuit, located in the eastern part of the Northwest Territories, negotiated a two-part Agreement. The first part dealt with land and other rights that were to benefit the Inuit exclusively. This part of the Agreement received protection in the Constitution in the same way the James Bay and Northern Quebec Agreement received constitutional protection, under subsection 35(3) of the Constitution Act, 1982.

The second part was an ambitious plan to create their own territory where Inuit would be the majority. This meant breaking apart the Northwest Territories and creating a new Territory of Nunavut in the Eastern Arctic. This part of the Agreement was implemented through federal legislation and the degree of constitutional protection may be less complete than the provisions on land.

### Territory

The Nunavut Land Claims Agreement covers 733,594 square miles (1,900,000 sq. km) of the Eastern Arctic, including seven of Canada's largest islands and two-thirds of the country's coastline (Canada 1993a). It constitutes one-fifth of Canada's total land mass. Under the land claim, Inuit title is recognized to approximately 136,000 square miles of land, of which 13,613 square miles (35,257 sq. km) include mineral rights (Art. 19). Monetary compensation includes a capital transfer payment of $1.148 billion payable to the Inuit over 14 years (Art. 29), a $13 million Training Trust Fund (Art. 37), and a share of federal government royalties from oil, gas, and mineral development on Crown land (Art. 25). Like the James Bay and Northern Quebec Agreement, the Nunavut Land Claims Agreement requires a surrender of Aboriginal rights.

Throughout Nunavut, the Inuit have the right to harvest wildlife on lands and water (Art. 5) and the right to the use of the water (Art. 20). Other provisions include the right of first refusal on sport and commercial development of renewable resources in the Nunavut Settlement area (Art. 5), rights to carving stone (Art. 19); and the creation of three new federally funded national parks, including provision for the involvement of the Inuit in the planning and management of parks (Art. 8).

*Co-management*

A number of wildlife management, resource management, and environmental boards were established to provide Inuit with a formal role in making recommendations to government decision-makers. These include the Nunavut Planning Commission, the Nunavut Water Board, the Nunavut Wildlife Management Board, and the Surface Rights Tribunal. The Boards are generally composed of the same number of representatives from the Tunngavik Federation of Nunavut as from the federal and territorial governments. Since the territorial government is dominated by Inuit, the majority of the members of a Board may be Inuit people.

For the most part the decisions of the co-management bodies remain advisory opinions for a government minister who will make the final decision. Nonetheless, the Agreement makes it more difficult to ignore the advice of the co-management board. The structured decision-making in the Nunavut Wildlife Management Board is illustrative. The Board is the main instrument for wildlife management in the Nunavut Settlement Area and the main regulator of access to wildlife. The purpose of the Board is to create a system of harvesting rights and priorities and privileges that reflect current and traditional Inuit harvesting (Art. 5). When the Board makes a decision, it is to convey the decision privately to the minister. If the minister decides to reject the advice of the Board, the minister must give his or her decision in writing within 30 days and permit the Board to reconsider its decision. The Board will then reconsider the matter and make its decision publicly. At that point, the minister is again in a position to accept or reject the decision of the Board (Art. 5). This process is more rigorous than that in the James Bay and Northern Quebec Agreement, which only required the minister to "consult" before reversing a recommendation of a board under that Agreement.

In some cases the Boards have more significant authority. The Nunavut Impact Review Board is the environmental assessment agency for Nunavut. The Board examines the impact of project proposals on the land, air, and water, and on the people of the area. They rely on traditional Inuit knowledge and recognized scientific methods to assess and monitor the environmental, cultural, and socioeconomic impacts of proposals. The Board determines whether project proposals should proceed to develop and, if so, under what conditions. If the Board decides that a development proposal needs to be reviewed the minister is required to refer the matter to a federal environmental assessment panel for socioeconomic and ecosystem impacts (Art. 12).

*Government*

The rights contained in the land claims Agreement are held by the Tunngavik Federation of Nunavut, an incorporated body representing the Inuit in the territory. This organization is not the government of Nunavut. That function is left to the legislative assembly, which is elected by both Inuit and non-Inuit voters who are residents of the territory ("Nunavut," this vol.).

The legislature has powers to make new laws over all matters of a local or private nature in Nunavut, similar to the Yukon and Northwest territories. An important power is the administration of justice in Nunavut, including the organization of territorial courts, and the establishment and maintenance of prisons. The legislature has authority to make laws for the preservation, use, and promotion of the Inuktitut language (Nunavut Act; Canada 1993a:c. 28, s. 23).

## Constitutional Recognition of Self-Government: The Nisga'a Agreement

A number of Agreements were signed at around the time of the Nunavut Land Claims Agreement. The Gwich'in (Kutchin) in the Northwest Territories signed in 1992; 14 First Nations signed the Yukon Indians Umbrella Final Agreement in 1993; and the Sahtu Dene (Bearlake) and Métis signed an Agreement in 1994. All these Agreements provided for constitutional protection of the land claims part of the Agreement but relied on federal legislation for the self-government aspects of their Agreements. The first break to this pattern came with the Nisga'a.

The negotiations for the Nisga'a were prompted by the decision in *Calder* v. *Attorney General of British Columbia*, and formal negotiations began in 1976. It took until May 11, 2000, for the federal government, British Columbia, and the Nisga'a to sign an Agreement ("Nisga'a," this vol.). It is very complex. There is intricacy involved in the crafting of the legal and cultural borders and bridges between mainstream society and the Nisga'a. One of the significant aspects of this Agreement is that both the land and the self-government rights receive constitutional protection (Canada 1998b).

While the Nisga'a and the federal and provincial governments were supportive of the Agreement, there was opposition from many sectors of the population. The leader of the opposition Liberal Party in British Columbia tried to stop the Agreement through a court action. The British Columbia Supreme Court rejected the challenge, finding, in fact, that the Constitution of Canada implicitly recognized the right to self-government of the Nisga'a (*Campbell* v. *British Columbia (Attorney General)*, [2000] B.C.J. No. 1524).

### Territory

The Agreement provides for 770 square miles (2,000 sq. km) of land, including mineral rights, to be granted in fee simple to the Nisga'a as a whole. This is several times larger than the land set aside as reservations under the Indian Act.

The land surrender provisions found in the James Bay and Northern Quebec Agreement and the Nunavut Land Claims Agreement were controversial because they emphasized the view that the Agreement was a real estate transaction. First Nations viewed the transaction as dealing with rights that were inalienable. One could not "surrender" one's right to free speech, for example. The Nisga'a Agreement uses somewhat different language to address this issue. The Agreement says that it "exhaustively sets out" Nisga'a rights including Aboriginal title and the jurisdictions of the Nisga'a government. This provision is fortified by a release and indemnity provided by the Nisga'a to the federal and provincial governments (Canada 1998:chaps. 2, 23, 26, 30).

The Agreement allows the Nisga'a to alienate any of their interest in the land as long as the rules are set out in the Nisga'a Constitution. The Constitution requires the approval of 70 percent of the Nisga'a who vote. Unlike surrendered reserve land under the Indian Act, the Nisga'a will continue to have jurisdiction and governing authority over those Nisga'a lands, even if they are entirely held in fee simple by non-Nisga'a (Canada 19998:chap. 3, s. 5).

### Co-management

The Nisga'a have rights outside their territory in a number of areas including forestry, wildlife, and fishing. The rights include access to the resource and participation in the management of the resource. The fishing provision, for example, provides for domestic and commercial harvest of salmon and the purchase of vessels and licenses (Canada 1998: chap. 8). A Joint Fisheries Management Committee is established to make recommendations and provide advice to the Minister of Fisheries. There are two representatives each from the Nisga'a, the province of British Columbia, and Canada, and they are to attempt to carry out their responsibilities by consensus. The powers of this management committee seem to be weaker than that of the Nunavut Wildlife Management Board, which required that, if the minister did not accept a recommendation of the Nunavut Committee, the minister had to given written reasons and refer the matter back to the Committee.

The environmental protection and assessment provisions are interesting. The Nisga'a can make laws on the environment as long as they are not inconsistent with federal and provincial laws. The three governments (Nisga'a, provincial, federal) agree to cooperate and avoid duplication. When a project is "reasonably expected to have adverse environmental effects" on the land under the jurisdiction of another government, there is a duty to give notice, consult and afford an opportunity for the other government to participate in the environmental assessment (Canada 1998: chap. 10).

### Government

The Nisga'a Agreement provides that members of government will be elected by secret ballot. The Nisga'a address the situation of those residing outside of the claim area by providing three seats on the Council for representatives of Nisga'a "urban locals." It is the first Agreement to provide for the formal participation of members who reside outside of the territory.

People who are not Nisga'a cannot vote or run for Council. This provision was controversial, with some non-Native people complaining that a "race-based" government was counter to the Canadian Charter of Rights and Freedoms. The matter was addressed by the Supreme Court of British Columbia, which found that the restriction on voting for political office was necessary in light of the "communal nature of aboriginal rights" (*Campbell* v. *British Columbia (Attorney General)*). The judge also pointed out that there were provisions in the Agreement that allowed for the participation of non-Nisga'a in public institutions.

The Nisga'a government has three types of law-making authority. First, in limited areas relating internally to the Nisga'a, the laws of the Nisga'a would be paramount over federal or provincial legislation. Second, in other areas, Nisga'a can exercise authority, but where there is an inconsistency, federal or provincial laws on the same matter would be paramount (e.g., laws on the environment). And third, in some areas (e.g., criminal law), Nisga'a have no authority to make laws.

The jurisdictions recognized for the Nisga'a are much more circumscribed than for many American tribes. The Navajo, for example, have exclusive jurisdiction in all areas except where there is overriding federal legislation, primarily in the criminal law area; however, for the Nisga'a, the assumption is the opposite. All federal and provincial laws apply unless they conflict with a Nisga'a law, which is paramount. The areas where Nisga'a laws would be paramount over federal or provincial laws relate mainly to matters necessary for the internal governance of the nation and for cultural issues important for the preservation of the Nisga'a identity: the Nisga'a government and constitution (Canada 1998:chap. 11, s. 34), Nisga'a citizenship (chap. 11, s. 39), culture and language (chap. 11, s. 41), Nisga'a property (chap. 11, s. 47), use of Nisga'a lands (chap. 11, s. 89), child and family services (chap. 11, s. 100,103), education (chap. 11, s. 115), and cultural property. Areas where federal or provincial laws would be paramount include public order, safety (s. 59); buildings, structures, public works (s. 69); traffic (s. 72); marriages (s. 75); social services (s. 78); health services (s. 82); gambling (s. 108); intoxicants (s. 110); emergency preparedness (s. 122); and Nisga'a courts (chap. 12).

The Nisga'a jurisdictions may be more limited, but they are better protected than in the United States because the Nisga'a rights are incorporated into the Constitution as treaty rights. This prevents a unilateral override by Canadian governments. The Nisga'a jurisdictions have a constitutional status similar to the federal and provincial jurisdictions.

## Conclusion

Confrontations, some of which turn violent, occur regularly around fisheries, resource development, and claims to land. In some cases Aboriginal people cut trees in violation of provincial laws to claim a resource (R v. Bernard [2005] 2 S.C.R. 220). In other cases non-Native people fish in violation of federal laws to protest against Aboriginal fishing (R v. Kapp [2006] BCCA 277).

Solutions have not come quickly and Canada faces continuing challenges in negotiating future Agreements. Some progress is being made in the more populated southern parts of Canada, but First Nations with reserves near urban centers have a real problem finding land available for them as governments are unwilling to expropriate land from "innocent third-party purchasers." One less than ideal solution is to provide the First Nation with money to buy land on the open market, but it is difficult to purchase large blocks and there is resistance from non-Natives. The Métis, who are descendants of European fur traders and Indian women, have been recognized in section 35 of the Constitution as one of the Aboriginal peoples. While some Métis have joined in land claims by Indians (e.g., the Sahtu Dene and Métis Agreement), by and large, they have faced an uphill battle for recognition.

It is important to have an idea of what elements constitute a "good" agreement. There will be as many standards as there are interested parties, but from the perspective of Canada as a country that respects the uniqueness of its many communities, two related questions stand out. First, does the Agreement recognize the cultural integrity of the Aboriginal nation? Second, does the Agreement provide for the appropriate "interconnectedness" to the rest of Canada? The two questions are related because the "tradition" or "culture" of the Aboriginal nation is not static nor monolithic. It is as dynamic and multi-faceted as the "tradition" and "culture" of Canada as a whole. This seems a trite point to make but it is one that is a challenge to capture in the legal language of the Agreements.

The James Bay and Northern Quebec Agreement addressed the issue of culture and tradition obliquely through the creation of Aboriginal specific institutions in health, education, and justice. The lack of direct authority to make laws over those matters is highlighted in one section setting out powers of a municipality in the Kativik Act. The only law-making powers in the category of recreation and culture are over matters such as the regulation of swimming pools, public baths, privies and laboratories; the establishment of libraries; and the regulation of community radio.

By way of contrast, in the Nisga'a Agreement there is a general statement that Nisga'a have a right to make laws over those matters. These laws would be paramount over federal and provincial laws on the same matter: "Nisga'a Lisims Government may make laws to preserve, promote, and develop the Nisga'a culture and Nisga'a language, including laws to authorize or accredit the use, reproduction, and representation of Nisga'a cultural symbols and practices, and the teaching of Nisga'a language" (Canada 1998: chap. 11 s. 41). With respect to culture, for example, an entire chapter is dedicated to the return of artifacts and protection of heritage sites (chap. 16), and there are specific law-making powers over the devolution of cultural property (chap. 11, s. 115–120). With respect to tradition, there is a provision for the accreditation of Aboriginal healers (chap. 11, s. 86) and a role for "the Nisga'a elders, *Simgigat* [chiefs] and *Sigidimhaanak* [matriarchs], in providing guidance and interpretation of the *Ayuuk* [traditional laws and practices] to Nisga'a Government" (chap.11, s. 9).

But what of the dynamic aspects of culture, which encompass change, adaptation, and interaction with the mainstream society? In this respect, there has been some movement over time in the legal language. The provisions on alienation of land provide an example of the change. Under the James Bay and Northern Quebec Agreement and the Nunavut Agreement, the land can only be alienated to the federal or provincial Crown. There can be no direct alienation by the Aboriginal nation to a third party. These are good provisions in that they provide some protection to the land base. The Nisga'a negotiated a different arrangement, which is more flexible.

The Nisga'a Agreement provides that the land is initially owned in fee simple by the Nisga'a Nation. The Nation may then alienate the land to "any person" in fee simple, or "create, or dispose of any lesser estate or interest to any person" (chap. 3, s. 4). This approach allows the framework for the ownership and use of lands to develop in at least three different directions.

First, the Nisga'a may continue the landholding patterns that exist at the present time on Indian reserves. This is a mix of property owned by the Indian Band, with "private property" owned by individual Indians. The Band-owned property, on most reserves, includes housing lots that are reserved for the exclusive use of those occupying the house but that generally revert to the Band when the house is vacated. The "private" property is allocated to an individual by something called a "certificate of possession," which can only be transferred to other Indians. Lands may also be leased to non-Indians through a variety of mechanisms that provide for reversion of the land to the Band.

A second way that the Nisga'a land regime could develop is toward the fee simple system used off reserve. The provisions in the Agreement permit the Nisga'a Nation to alienate fee simple estates to Nisga'a or non-Nisga'a. Gordon

Gibson, a non-Aboriginal commentator, sees this as a good thing. He is critical of the Nisga'a Agreement for not establishing a system based on individual fee simple ownership of land and would like to see that changed (G. Gibson 1999). In contrast, John Borrows, Anishinabe (Ojibwa) commentator, sees this possibility as a danger, and regrets that the land could eventually be alienated in its entirety, and become "unavailable for Nisga'a use or possession at some time in the future" (Borrows 2001a:635).

Third, land use and occupation could develop in the opposite direction, accommodating traditional Nisga'a governance structures organized around the matrilineal houses (*wilp*). Under this system, individual Nisga'a would not have fee simple ownership of parcels of land, and the land could not be alienated to non-Nisga'a. Val Napoleon (Cree, Saulteaux, Beaver) would welcome this development, as a move in this direction would address the "discord between historic cultural systems and modern state-influenced entities" (Napoleon 2001:130).

Whichever way the framework on land develops, it will be under the control of the Nisga'a. The framework could adapt organically in response to internal dynamics and external pressures. In these circumstances, the Nisga'a would not feel that a foreign law was being imposed, and it would be much less likely that this law would become the source of alienation from Canada.

It may seem somewhat counterintuitive, but those laws and institutions that are locked into the mainstream laws and institutions may drive Aboriginal nations further away from feelings of "common belonging" with Canadians. Even under the Nisga'a Agreement mainstream courts and institutions retain so much power: "Therefore, though the treaty represents some of the highest aspirations of Aboriginal peoples and Canadians in creating a relationship of mutuality and respect, it also contains a number of elements that potentially make Canadian visions of law, politics, and development the standard by which Nisga'a life may ultimately be judged" (Borrows 2001a:636). A sense of "common belonging" is more likely to be enhanced when internally generated organic change and adaptation are possible. It is true that this may result in Aboriginal nations looking "different." But perhaps the degree of "difference" is not a good way to judge the degree of "interconnectedness." A better place to focus concerns about the connection to Canada may be the administrative, judicial, political, social, and economic links set out in the self-government Agreements.

The Nisga'a Agreement, for example, consists of 22 chapters and is 252 pages long, with an additional 462 pages of appendices. Its length is a result of the intricate tuning necessary for creating an appropriate interface between mainstream society and the Nisga'a. It has chapters detailing the roles of the Nisga'a and Crown authorities on lands (ownership, registration, access, roads), resources (forestry, fisheries, wildlife), environmental assessment, administration of justice, taxation, and legislative jurisdiction. In addition, there is an entire chapter detailing how disputes are to be addressed and resolved.

The extent and quality of these types of links between the Aboriginal nation and the surrounding society are the real test for "interconnectedness" with Canada. Whether it is an Agreement to have a local municipality supply water or an arrangement to enhance regional economic development, success will depend in great part on the strength of the mechanisms set out in the self-government Agreements. If these mechanisms do their job, a "sense of common belonging" need not be imposed: it will emerge organically from the joint endeavors of Aboriginal nations and the larger Canadian community.

# Native Governments and Organizations

YALE D. BELANGER

Native governments and Native organizations in Canada are unique entities that at times collaborate to press the federal government for the recognition of Aboriginal rights. Yet outside the constitutional arena they, for the most part, remain separate and work apart, promoting unique political agendas despite possessing what at times appear to be parallel concerns. This separation of interests has historically resulted in diminished political influence. Native organizations are largely lobby groups, acting on behalf of constituents with specialized needs.

## Band Government and Tribal Councils

Hereditary councils that guided the political processes in Aboriginal communities since prior to European contact were replaced with the band council, modeled after municipal governments elsewhere in Canada. Band councils are elected bodies consisting of a chief and council that are responsible for the day-to-day activities on the reserve. According to section 74 of the Indian Act, the council of a band consists of one chief and one councillor for every 100 members of the band, although the number of councillors cannot be less than two or more than 12. The Act distinguishes the realm in which bands may pass by-laws, which in turn must conform to federal regulations. Indian leaders in the 1870s were not consulted during the creation of the Indian Act's governance section.

Band council operations are overseen by officials of Indian and Northern Affairs Canada, a department created in 1880 specifically to manage the federal assimilation program. The implementation of the band council model and the rise of Native political organizations dates to 1869 and the passage of the Gradual Enfranchisement Act, an attempt on the part of the newly established Canadian government to facilitate Native assimilation into the country's cultural mosaic. Born of the same legislation, band governments (fig. 1) were designed to distance Native leaders from customary governing institutions and smooth their overall transition from a traditional lifeway to a more civilized way of life, while Native organizations emerged in direct response to what Native leaders considered restrictive federal legislation.

Deriving their powers exclusively from the federal government and lacking independent administrative authority, bands are a form of self-administration as opposed to true self-governing bodies. Bands may pass by-laws in certain limited areas such as the control or prohibition of public games, the regulation of public wells, regulation of livestock, and the management of game, for instance. By-laws related to taxation of the land may be passed, including the rights to occupy, possess, or use land. These powers are limited, for according to the Indian Act, all by-laws must be accepted by the Minister of Indian Affairs prior to local implementation, and it is estimated that the Minister disallows more than 60 percent of all by-laws. This is in contradiction to the Inherent Rights Policy of 1995, acknowledging the right to Aboriginal self-government.

The guidelines established by the Musqueam Indian Band (Central Coast Salish) in British Columbia are instructive. The Musqueam Indian Band elects officials to its council according to section 74 of the Indian Act. Section 81 of the Act grants the council the powers to make by-laws over reserve lands, and the band council is entrusted by the band membership to represent the band's views and aspirations at the district, provincial, and national levels. Ultimately, the council is answerabale to the band membership and the Minister of Indian Affairs. At the beginning of each term, the Musqueam band council is required to swear an oath of service the band for its welfare.

In an effort to provide greater decision-making authority in First Nations communities, the federal government has at times established initiatives such as amending the Indian Act to expand band control in elections, membership, and health and family services by transferring revenue to the band councils. This transfer of program management in order to grant greater local control to First Nations is at variance with the federal responsibility to ensure the well-being of Aboriginal peoples articulated in the Indian Act and the Numbered Treaties of 1871–1877 and 1899–1921. In 1996 the government transferred one billion dollars designed for service delivery to 300 First Nations through multiyear financial transfer agreements.

Tribal councils were created in the early 1970s to provide advisory services for program delivery in an effort to assist with the devolution of control. Blending cultureal boundaries representing multiple treaties, various bands

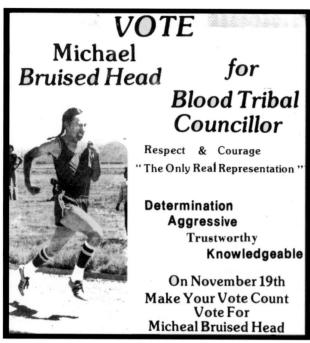

Fig. 1. Advertisement for an election for government of the Blood Band, Alta., 1980, in the *Kenai News*, Standoff, Alta.

joined to organize as a tribal council. Tribal councils take a lead role in First Nations governance by accepting responsibility for program and service delivery to member First Nations that have agreed to share to maximize their resources. Protections of Aboriginal and treaty rights and assistance to First Nations in management and in dealings with federal and provincial governments are key responsibilities. Tribal councils in certain regions are assigned the task of promoting economic development. The goal is to grow a tribal council into a self-sufficient, revenue-generating entity that can take on and guide economic development initiatives on behalf of its member nations, a strategy that is tied directly to self-government policy. Tribal councils promote bilateral and tripartite negotiation with federal and provincial governments.

**Earliest Political Action**

The Gradual Enfranchisement Act took direct aim at dismantling Native customary governance, considered by colonial and later Canadian administrators an obstacle to Indian assimilation. The Act's implementation meant that all internal decisions pertaining to band matters were "subject to confirmation by the Governor in Council." In response to this increasingly restrictive political environment, Native leaders across Canada began to consider forming political organizations to contest similar initiatives. If successful, Native leaders surmised that these organizations could aid their

nations in reasserting the desire to participate as partners in Canada's evolution (Belanger 2006). The first concerted attempt at political organizing occurred in 1870, following the gathering of Native leaders from 21 Anishinaabe (Ojibwa) and Haudenosaunee (Iroquois) communities from Ontario and Quebec (Shields 2001; Lueger 1977). The council was established to discuss the rapid settler immigration that was negatively influencing local economic endeavors. Historically, various council formats had been utilized by Native groups in Canada to help resolve internal and external diplomatic issues, which included treaty and economic councils. The Grand General Indian Council of Ontario and Quebec was formed to stem the further loss of political influence manifest in Indian legislation and policies being developed and implemented without Native cooperation.

During the next seven decades, the Grand Indian Council worked with government officials, occasionally guiding federal policy decisions. The Council was a response by primarily enfranchised southern Ontario Native leaders to government indifference concerning their political, social, and economic concerns. The Council was unable to reconcile traditional Iroquoian and Algonquian organizational models and political ideologies into one, workable political association, which failure lead to its demise.

Native political mobilization was not a new phenomenon. From the start of cross-cultural contact in the early seventeenth century, Native peoples participated economically as well as politically with European and British settlers. Initially, Native nations were powerful enough to influence these political relationships. Yet from the end of the eighteenth century until Confederation in 1867, colonial and later Canadian officials largely ignored Native leaders, who struggled to maintain political continuity and to preserve existing political relationships. One obstacle was colonial society's paternalistic attitude toward Indians, which had as of the 1850s become the fundamental value guiding the federal Indian policy process (Milloy 1983; Tobias 1983). This consequently led to both federal and provincial leaders abandoning indigenous concerns in lieu of more pressing national issues. Since it was assumed that Native people were destined to cultural absorption and physical disappearance, dealing with Indian issues was considered be a waste of valuable political resources (Francis 1992).

Native leaders rightly anticipated that additional, non-beneficial alterations would occur (Dyck 1991). A second obstacle emerged in the form of federal refusal to accept Native leaders' allegiance to what were perceived to be foreign, albeit historic, organizing institutions and political philosophies. To better cope, Native men who understood the ideological inner workings of Canada's parliamentary tradition slowly began to generate support for political organizing. Altering their traditional or customary organizational formats was deemed essential for those seeking to influence the creation and implementation of federal Indian policy and legislation. In the case of the Grand Indian Council and many later associations, their leaders allied with men of like mind and education, inclined to choosing elective institutions that embraced regularized, structured meetings where minutes were kept. This was the model that would become the norm in Native political organizing, the foundation of which is still evident in twenty-first century associations such as the Assembly of First Nations and Federation of Saskatchewan Indian Nations.

Despite the rise in political organizing, responsibility for Native peoples remained vested with the Secretary of the State Responsible for the Provinces until 1873 following its transfer to the Department of the Interior. The Department of Indian Affairs, a branch office of the Department of the Interior, was created in 1880 and operated until 1935, when it was dissolved as a cost cutting measure; responsibility for Indian Affairs was transferred to the Department of Mines and Resources, and a subdepartment established—the Indian Affairs Branch ("The Department of Indian Affairs and Northern Development," this vol.). Ottawa's failure to recognize Natives as self-governing nations led organizational leaders to call for meetings with federal officials; these men never wavered in their belief that their communities were nations connected to Canada through a shared political history manifested in numerous treaty relationships, economic agreements, military relationships, and other political activities. Canadian officialdom reacted by implementing the Indian Act of 1876, legislation founded on the notion that Native people were little more than wards of the state, and designed specifically to hasten Indian assimilation. Further resistance to the band council model led to Indian Act revisions in 1880 that established the Department of Indian Affairs, empowering Indian Affairs officials to impose band council elections. The Indian Advancement Act of 1884 further consolidated federal powers by authorizing the superintendent general of Indian affairs to depose chiefs considered unfit for duty (Milloy 1983; Tobias 1983; J.R. Miller 1997). Band councils were provided with limited powers that included establishing their own community bylaws whose operations were overseen by Indian agents stationed on reserves to ensure the transition of customary governance to responsible government. With the exception of removing Indian agents from reserves in the 1950s, this model remains in place throughout Canada in the twenty-first century.

British Columbia Native leaders attempted to organize in 1879. More than 1,200 Coast and Interior Salish from the Fraser and Thompson rivers, the Nicola Valley, and the Similkameen area met that year at Lytton. The goal was to force Canada's recognition of tribal land ownership and to demand treaties with the provincial government. The council took one year to plan, a feat that, in the eyes of one provincial official, demonstrated the ability of the Thompson Indians (Nlakapamux) to self-govern (D. Harris 1996; C. Harris 2002). Delegates adopted a hierarchical approach to organizing, named their organization the Confederation of the Tribes of the Mainland, and selected a Lower Thompson, Michael, as head chief and spokesman. Thirteen coun-

cillors were chosen by acclamation for three-year terms. The councillors determined that hereditary tribal chiefs would hold office until their deaths, albeit not be replaced, while also empowering themselves to formulate rules and regulations concerning issues including schools, health, hunting and fishing, and personal conduct. An additional committee of the council consisting of at least three councillors was selected to act as a judiciary responsible to arbitrate perceived violations.

In their attempt to forge an alliance with the Queen, community members felt compelled to abandon many of their traditional ways. No distinction was made between new and old; rather, this represented a unique fusion of "Victorian propriety, Canadian paternalism, and indigenous tradition" (D. Harris 1996:9). The Confederation of the Tribes of the Mainland collapsed after delegates failed to agree on an organizational mandate essentially because they were unable to formalize operational guidelines that could reconcile traditional and modern political desires. Specifically, the younger delegates resolved to abolish the potlatch, a move they believed would impress Canadian officials. The older leaders resisted, forcing the Confederation's dissolution. The Grand Indian Council and the Council of the Mainland attempts to form political organizations are important, for they represent a Native political response to government inaction. Both groups attempted to engender federal acceptance of a Native organization that embraced the parliamentary tradition. In the end, these two organizations failed to attain a desired level of influence.

Many of these same issues influenced the development of later Native organizations. From 1870 to 1946, 24 Native political organizations were established, and each one immediately faced federal and community-based legitimacy challenges. The legitimacy of the political community is based on the consent of those who are governed, something the Grand Indian Council failed to generate even if federal officials considered it to be a legitimate organization. To the chagrin of organizational leaders, most community leaders failed to accept the Grand Indian Council as the legitimate voice of provincial Native interests. All organizations to emerge faced similar issues, which resulted in a complex balancing act that stressed working with Canadian officials while representing community needs. As most leaders discovered, without legitimacy an organization lacked the influence needed to foster change and could be rendered ineffective. This eventually led organizations to become both financially and ideologically dependent upon the Canadian government for their continued existence. In the Grand Indian Council's case, government funding was required to maintain operations. For the other organizations, it was difficult to generate and maintain organizational support if the federal government refused to cooperate. As organizations attempted to become legitimate representatives of Native people in Canada, in many cases they inadvertently undermined community councils that were also fighting the government to improve local conditions.

As Ontario, Quebec, and British Columbia Native leaders discovered, engendering federal acceptance of their initiatives was challenging, and nearly three decades passed before Native leaders again attempted to organize. They in turn adopted a number of organizational strategies anticipated to secure Native political influence in Canada in the early 1900s. West coast Native groups led the charge during this period. Influenced by labor activism, traditional political techniques predicated on face-to-face meetings (councils) were still employed to facilitate interaction with federal, provincial, and British officials. In 1906, for example, Joe Capilano, a Squamish (Central Coast Salish), Basil David (Shuswap), and Chief John Chillihitza (Thompson) traveled to Britain where they were granted an audience with King Edward VII. This represented an attempt to renew the political relationship dating to the treaties fashioned by Gov. James Douglas, 1850–1854 (J.R. Miller 2004; Carlson 2005). All claims were rejected by the British monarch on the grounds that it was a uniquely Canadian matter (Patterson 1978:189; Tennant 1990:85). In August 1910, members of the Interior tribes met with Prime Minister Sir Wilfrid Laurier to discuss the issue of land title. The leaders complained that "we have been told there is no issue, but we think there is a very clear issue, and our reason for being here is to press for an equitable settlement of the same with an adjustment or every question concerning us and our relationship with your Government and that of British Columbia." One chief concluded that the "whole country has been taken from us without treaty or agreement, and without compensation of any kind, and the cities have come later, and the railways later, and these things have been built on our land" (Belanger 2006:111–112). With the exception of a promise to investigate the situation further, Native political concerns were ignored.

By the end of the first decade of the twentieth century, most Native leaders reluctantly came to acknowledge that the British Crown would not enter the political arena and that political change was dependent upon successfully engaging the federal government. Three issues during this period came to drive this second wave of organizing. The first was the British Columbia land question, which, until the late 1920s, was a source of alarm for Native leaders (C. Harris 2002). Second was Native participation in the organized labor movement. Finally, a pan-Indian consciousness developed resulting from interaction among leaders such as Andrew Paull (Squamish) from British Columbia and John Tootoosis (Plains Cree) from Saskatchewan ("The Department of Indian Affairs and Northern Development," fig. 1, this vol.), Fred O. Loft (Mohawk) from Ontario, John Calihoo (Plains Cree) from Alberta, and Métis leaders Malcolm Norris and James Brady (vol. 13:664). Their frequent interactions led to the understanding that Native peoples in Canada were being treated poorly and that they shared overlapping political concerns.

Born of this political activism was what could perhaps be considered the first modern Native political organization:

the Indian Rights Association. Established in 1909 following a meeting of 20 coastal tribal representatives in Vancouver, the Association's leaders chose an intricate and hierarchical organizing structure unlike the Nisga'a Land Committee, formed in 1907, which was based upon tradition and structured to represent clans and local committees, or the Interior Tribes of British Columbia, formed by Coast Salish chiefs in 1909. Those two groups competed in their attempts to stimulate government awareness of their concerns. The Indian Rights Association was the only one of the three to provoke a government response to their demands, due likely to the organizing structure that "owed a good deal to 'White' models. At the centre was a small executive, whose functions included fund-raising, organizing conferences, circulating information to local representatives and maintaining links with legal counsel" (Galois 1992:34). The Association for the first time brought together north and south coast tribal groups while consciously adopting an organizing format that was "intended as something White politicians and the White public could readily understand and would take more seriously than they had been taking traditional chiefs in traditional roles" (Tennant 1990:86).

After several years of political wrangling, and following the implementation of a royal commission in 1913, the McKenna-McBride Commission, to investigate the Indian land question, members of the Interior Tribes of British Columbia, the Nisga'a Land Committee ("Nisga'a," fig. 3, this vol.), and the Indian Rights Association met in 1916 to form a new organization called the Allied Tribes of British Columbia. In reality, the Association absorbed the Nisga'a Land Committee and the Interior Tribes. The Allied Tribes made a name for itself by hounding federal officials to resolve British Columbia land claims. Unable to sway the Royal Commission, the Allied Tribes pressured Premier Frank Oliver in 1919 to assign the organization the duty of preparing a response to the McKenna-McBride report (vol. 7:160). Despite recommendations to alter the report making it more acquiescent to Native concerns, federal officials ignored Native pleas. The Allied Tribes and their leader Andrew Paull persisted in lobbying Parliament to call an inquiry into the land question, and on 8 March 1927, a formal hearing was held to keep the land claims out of the courts. The Committee rejected the Allied Tribes claims and treaty requests (Tennant 1990).

## Political Organizing, 1918–1960

Upon his return from action overseas, World War I veteran Lt. F.O. Loft called a December 1918 meeting at the Six Nations Reserve near Brantford, Ontario. Intent on establishing an organization that was politically focused and forceful enough to inveigle Canadian officials to accept political guidance, Loft relied upon Native dissatisfaction with federal programs to stimulate support for his League of Indians of Canada. Writing in 1919, he claimed that "the unseen tears of Indian mothers in many isolated Indian reserves have watered the seeds from which may spring those desires and efforts and aspirations which will enable us to reach the stage when we will take our place side by side with the white people, doing our share of productive work and gladly shouldering the responsibility of citizens in this, our country." He concluded, "we have the right to claim and demand more justice and fair play as a recompense for we, too, have fought for the sacred rights of justice, freedom and liberty so dear to mankind" (Belanger 2006:157). Loft anticipated the League cooperating "with the Government, but we must have its sympathy, encouragement and assistance to make good. To force or coerce us will do no good; justice and fair dealing is what we ask for." According to Loft, cultural interaction was required to facilitate dialogue prior to Native people reclaiming political influence. League support was immediate, especially in Saskatchewan, convincing Loft that "union then has started." He publicly stated that it was the duty of Indians Canada-wide "to join with the forces to create a permanent national brotherhood" (Belanger 2006: 158). Loft proposed using a collective bargaining strategy to help create a productive Native-Canada relationship (Kulchyski 1988:101).

The League held conventions in Manitoba in 1920 and Saskatchewan in 1921. Loft wrote to Blood Chief Shot Both Sides of the Blackfoot Confederacy (Alberta) in 1920 about joining the League. The chief was unimpressed, responding that he "had made his treaty with the Queen and would remain faithful to it. He did not know what kind of treaties the eastern Indians had and he had no interest in Indian matters outside his own treaty area" (Dempsey 1986:108). Leaders from other tribes joined Loft, specifically Plains Cree and Stoney. Meetings were held in 1920 "to promote religious freedom and the right to travel without passes" (Cuthand 1991:382). Yet Prairie Native response was impressive, as evidenced by a June 1922 conference in Alberta attended by more than 1,500 delegates. When the League was formally established as a national Native organization later that year, it boasted a total membership of more than 9,000 (Goodwill and Sluman 1984:132). Despite this success, the 1920s was a difficult period for Loft. In particular Deputy Superintendent General of Indian Affairs Duncan Campbell Scott made repeated attempts to enfranchise Loft, actions aimed at discouraging his organizing efforts. This proved to be the League's downfall, ultimately limiting Loft from raising the required operating expenses (Titley 1986). When Loft died in 1934, the League had become dormant. Nevertheless, historian Hugh Dempsey claims that Loft's main impact "was to engender an awareness of the possibilities of Indian associations as protest and pressure groups among bands on the Prairies and for this he has justly been called the 'Father of Western Canadian Indian Associations'" (Lueger 1977:145).

That Saskatchewan and some Alberta Native leaders should so readily engage in political organizing should not be considered an anomaly. For example, in February 1872, members of Treaty 1 and 2 petitioned the government, claiming unfulfilled treaty promises (Titley 1997). Plains Cree leaders farther west, who were upset with the government's slow pace in establishing reserves and the constant distribution of substandard rations, decided to unite to force a treaty revisions. Activism was considered an effective political tool to generate collective support; Plains Cree leaders Big Bear and Chief Piapot "understood the need for a united front and the futility of armed action" (J.R. Miller 1991:176). The Plains Cree leader Poundmaker, upset with local crop failures and government inaction, also made an unsuccessful "effort to secure a large Indian gathering to press demands upon the Government for further concessions." In 1883, he again tried to convince Native leaders from neighboring communities to lobby the government for change. Among his more interesting demands: "complete control of the reserve should be turned over to himself and his councillors" (Stanley 1992:284). This stipulation was accompanied by a request for Aboriginal self-government. The next June, Poundmaker (vol. 4:92) organized a Thirst Dance, attended also by Big Bear, Lucky Man, Strike-Him-on-the-Back, and Red Pheasant. Although the Northwest Mounted Police broke up the gathering, the Plains Cree reassembled at the end of July in a meeting attended by Big Bear, Lucky Man, and all the Carleton district chiefs, including Beardy, Okemasis, One Arrow, Mistawasis, Attackakoop, Petequaquay, John Smith, James Smith, and Badger, all Plains Cree (J.R. Miller 1991:176).

Little came from the council. Following the Northwest Rebellion of 1885, Canadian officials reacted by impounding Plains Cree horses, guns, and carts, while instituting a prairie-wide pass system intended to confine Native leaders to their reserves (vol. 13:317–318). Further restrictions included a ban on the Thirst Dance, all of which lasted well into the twentieth century and briefly retarded political engagement (Dickason 1994:314–315). Saskatchewan Natives decided to confront these restrictive measures, and in 1909 they met at Valley River to discuss the deteriorating reserve living conditions (Lueger 1977:148). The following year, a collection of 16 Plains Cree and Northern Ojibwa bands met at the Cowessess Reserve and formed the Allied Bands of Qu'Appelle, "to discuss their growing concern over the manner in which the government of Canada was exercising their power over Indian people and lands and the way in which promises made in Treaty 4 were being violated" (in Wheaton 1999). This organization was guided by politically experienced individuals including Louis O'Soup, Zac LeRat, Alex Gaddie, and Kanaswaywetung (all Cowessess First Nation), all of whom had been present at the signing of Treaty 4 in 1874. All were concerned that their way of life was being threatened. With O'Soup in the lead, a five-man delegation was dispatched to Ottawa to meet with senior officials from the Department of Indian Affairs, including Superintendent General Frank Oliver. The leaders expressed several concerns: the Department had not appointed enough chiefs and headmen; young aspiring farmers needed assistance to begin operations; the indigent, old, and young needed assistance; Indian agents were using treaty annuities to settle Native debts; and the ban on the Thirst Dance should be lifted. The delegation was unsuccessful and an attempt by the group's lawyer to engage Oliver was also ignored (Belanger 2006). Although it is difficult to pinpoint when, this political organization dissolved prior to 1920.

Native political mobilization in Saskatchewan continued to mount during the 1920s. In the south, the Pasqua, Piapot, and Muscopetung reserves once again combined forces to protect remaining reserve lands from the forced surrenders federal officials deemed necessary to satiate settler desires and government demands. After this meeting, Pasqua band member Andrew Gordon formed the Allied Bands, which was followed by a succession of meetings held from 1922–1924. Two military veterans, Harry Ball and Abel Watetch, both Plains Cree from the Piapot Reserve, combined forces with Pat Cappo and Charles Pratt, Plains Crees from the Muscopetung Reserve to form the organization's executive. A regional group whose influence did not extend beyond southern Saskatchewan, the Allied Bands sent a delegation to Ottawa in 1928 to protest reserve living conditions, and the Indian agent's behavior, and to lobby federal officials to establish a royal commission to investigate Indian administration (Opekokew 1980:34). Little came of these efforts. Following a 1933 conference, the Allied Bands changed its name to the Protective Association for Indians and their Treaties, while altering its mandate to focus on protecting treaty rights, Native lands and resources, and the enhancement of Native education.

In British Columbia during this period, the Allied Tribes continued to lobby federal officials for change, specifically for the recognition of Aboriginal title and formally negotiated treaties. A joint committee of the Senate and House of Commons previously denied both demands in 1927. This was a significant blow, and the Allied Tribes quickly disbanded. Several of the Allied Tribes's non-Native advisors were considered agitators (Titley 1986:157). The Indian Act was again revised, this time making it illegal for Indians to use band funds for hire lawyers to pursue land claims. Despite the implicit suggestion that using band monies for political purposes was also illegal, William Benyon and Ambrose Reid formed the Native Brotherhood of British Columbia in 1931 (vol. 7:166–167). Reflecting upon the Indian Rights Association's and Allied Tribes's failed attempts to establish a politically legitimate group, the two men established the Native Brotherhood as a labor union that would furtively double as a political organization. This made sense considering that most Native Brotherhood delegates were employed in the province's resource industries, in particular as cannery workers and fishers. After a decade of effective bargaining activities, the Native Brotherhood morphed into a political organization, moving gradually from local to provincial political matters into federal politics as the Northwest Coast's representative Native organization by the 1940s (Belanger 2006).

The 1930s was an active period for prairie Native political activists and community leaders. Métis organizers James Brady and Malcolm Norris influenced many if not the majority of prairie Native leaders seeking to establish political organizations (Dobbin 1981). Norris and Brady worked with John Calihoo and John Tootoosis, both of whom were leading the Alberta and Saskatchewan sects of the struggling League of Indians of Western Canada, respectively. A falling out between the two men led to the League of Indians's demise. Nevertheless, Tootoosis and Calihoo went on to form the Union of Saskatchewan Indians and the Indian Association of Alberta with James Gladstone in 1939 (vol. 13:324). Brady in particular remained involved by writing the Indian Association of Alberta's constitution, which was utilized by the Union of Saskatchewan Indians (Meijer Drees 2002). Saskatchewan in particular was a hotbed of Native political activity. The Association of Indians of Saskatchewan was established in 1944, following the formation of the Protective Association for Indians and Their Treaties in 1933. Led by Dan Kennedy, Assiniboine, from Carry the Kettle Reserve and non-Native supporter Zachary Hamilton, the Association of Indians of Saskatchewan included World War I veteran Joseph Dreaver (Plains Cree), the Mistawasis Band chief who sought enhanced education, augmented political authority over reserve matters, improved health care, and a formal investigation into Native veterans's concerns. Dreaver was elected president, Hector Brass (Plains Cree) from Peepeekisis Reserve was selected vice-president, and Hector's wife, Eleanor, was chosen secretary-treasurer. The group offered associate memberships to non-Native supporters but restricted memberships to Status Indians and bands that paid an organizational fee. Provincial Lt.-Gov. A.P. McNabb was an associate member who was named honorary president (Deiter 1999).

When Tommy C. Douglas led the socialist party, the Co-operative Commonwealth Federation, to power in Saskatchewan in 1944, one of its primary goals was to improve Native living conditions. Douglas and his party believed that Native people should integrate into Saskatchewan society (Pitsula 1994). The Federation endorsed the creation of one Native political organization to act as a unifying force, and he provided funding to assist in its operations (D.E. Smith 1992). The Union of Saskatchewan Indians lobbied for the establishment of reserve day schools as well as Native access to higher education. They also demanded equivalent old-age pensions and better treatment for Native war veterans (Barron 1997). The first elections saw Tootoosis elected president, John Gambler and Earnest Goforth elected first and second vice-presidents, and Joe Dreaver's daughter, Gladys, selected secretary-treasurer.

The Manitoba Indian Association was formed in 1934. The Association's first major conference was in 1946 in Winnipeg. On hand were more than 100 Manitoba chiefs and councillors. Returned from action overseas, war hero Tommy Prince (Plains Ojibwa), the great-great grandson of Chief Peguis, was selected vice president and chairman, a

190

position that enabled him to negotiate on the organization's behalf (Special Joint Committee 1948). Founders anticipated that Prince would center the fledgling organization and unite Native people to fight for treaty rights, improved educational facilities, better on-reserve sanitary conditions, and a revised agricultural policy. Prince himself observed, "my job is to unite the Indians of Canada so we can be as strong as possible when [we] go to the House of Commons for better education, sanitation, and other things on reserves" (B. Larsen 1946). With the exception of treaty rights, Manitoba Indian Association delegates were unable to establish a mandate. John Tootoosis was at the conference, applauding the delegates' work on behalf of their individual communities. He stressed that every community must join as a unit while also seriously considering the possibility of creating a single, national Native organization in Canada.

As former Allied Tribes leader Andy Paull discovered, this was a difficult task, for he had on many occasions unsuccessfully tried to establish a national Native political organization. Paull managed to enlist the help of the increasingly influential Tootoosis, and the Ontario Huron (Wendat) political activist Jules Sioui. The three men conceived of the Committee for the Protection of Indian Rights in 1943, devised to "resist the inclusion of Indians under the Canadian conscription act and government attempts to tax them" while impressing upon federal officials the need to protect "aboriginal rights and the principle of self-determination" (in Shewell 1999:221). Paull, Sioui, and Tootoosis had radically divergent ideas concerning the Committee's role. Tootoosis advocated treaties as the foundation of any Canada-Native relationship, Paull promoted a nationalistic vision that had all Indians uniting under an umbrella organization (Patterson 1962, 1978), and Sioui was more interested in pursuing militant activity (Goodwill and Sluman 1984; Shewell 2004, 1999). Sioui was eventually forced out, and the Committee's mandate came to resemble Paull's concerns. Tootoosis returned to Saskatchewan to concentrate on building the Union of Saskatchewan Indians. Paull then founded the Brotherhood of Canadian Indians, which almost immediately changed its name to the North American Indian Brotherhood in 1944.

Within one year, the North American Indian Brotherhood under Paull's guidance promoted itself as the leader of "the Indian Nation within the Sovereignty of the British Crown, a nation, by treaty obligation, under a protective agreement," seeking national recognition from the government of Canada of a united Native Nation as one established body within the sovereignty powers of the Dominion of Canada and extending a welcoming hand to White people, offering them a chance to cooperate with the Native people to strengthen the bonds of racial unity (Special Joint Committee 1947:853). The organization urged Native voting rights, the elimination of liquor laws resulting in fewer liquor-related offenses, and the implementation of pensions and an appropriate welfare system. Similar Native political mobilization combined with increasing media exposure, which led the federal govern-

ment to establish a Special Joint Parliamentary Committee in 1946 to investigate the Indian Act's continued validity. Native leaders representing the North American Indian Brotherhood, Indian Association of Alberta, Union of Saskatchewan Indians, Native Brotherhood of British Columbia, and Manitoba Indian Association testified. During its two-year run, it held 128 sessions and heard from 122 witnesses (Mackay 1947).

For the first time since the creation of Canada's civilization policy in the 1830s, Indians were sitting down collectively with federal officials in a forum where they could present their views and complaints about Indian policy and administration (Leslie 1999:122). Native leaders considered the Special Joint Committee an opportunity to re-establish political relationships with the federal government, and organization leaders offered impassioned testimony. Members of various groups and Native nations not affiliated with the core five Native organizations, including the Six Nations Confederacy Council and the Six Nations Band Council, also appeared. In all, 31 Native leaders representing 17 organizations and associations testified while six organizations additionally submitted written briefs. The Special Joint Committee's final recommendations did not alter the band council model, leading one commentator to state that, "in essence the joint committee approved the goal of Canada's previous Indian policy—assimilation—but disapproved some of the earlier methods to achieve it" (Goikas 1996).

The reaction from Native leaders upon hearing news of the recommendations was mixed. Tommy Prince, one of the most decorated noncommissioned officers in Canadian military history, was distressed with what he perceived to be government inaction. He abandoned the Manitoba Indian Association and politics generally to re-enlist in the army during the Korean War in 1951 (Dohla 2001). Malcolm Norris, a motivating force in Métis politics, retired from politics and moved north to become a full-time prospector (Dobbin 1981). John Calihoo continued as the Indian Association of Alberta president (Mejier Drees 2002). John Tootoosis remained politically active for the rest of his life, although he limited his concerns to Saskatchewan issues (Goodwill and Sluman 1984). Andy Paull, whose efforts were hindered by a lack of national Native support, continued to guide the Brotherhood until his death in 1959, remaining a vocal proponent of Aboriginal rights while promoting the need for a united Canadian Native political organization (Manuel and Posluns 1974; McFarlane 1993). In all, the reaction of Native leaders to the Special Joint Committee ranged from complete disgust to optimism that they had at least been consulted.

## From Wards to Self-Governing Nations, 1960–1982

For Native people in Canada, 1960 was a promising year. First, the Canadian Bill of Rights was introduced, prohibiting discrimination on the basis of race, color, and creed, *191* legislation that protected Native interests; the federal franchise and full citizenship rights both were extended permitting Native people to vote in a federal or provincial elections without compromising an individual's status or making participation "conditional upon complete assimilation into Canadian society" (Ponting 1997:29); and a second Special Joint Committee was established to once again study the Indian Act. The federal government suggested that the time was right for Native people to "assume the responsibility and accept the benefit of full participation as Canadian citizens." The Special Joint Committee was mandated to develop recommendations that were "designed to provide sufficient flexibility to meet the varying stages of development of the Indians during the transition period" (Canada 1961:605). It appeared that federal officials had determined to improve the social, political, and economic standing of Natives in Canada. All the same, responsibility for Indian affairs vested with the Department of Citizenship and Immigration in 1950 remained centered in Ottawa, and little thought was given to devolving any authority or jurisdiction to the band councils. In 1966, an independent Department of Indian Affairs and Northern Development was established that continues to oversee the financing of and overall band council operations.

The National Indian Council was created in 1961 to represent three of the four major groups of Native people in Canada: treaty and Status Indians, non-Status Indians, and the Métis (the Inuit were not involved). Established largely due to the efforts of prairie Native leaders, the Council's goal was to promote "unity among all Indian people," although the organization's leaders soon discovered the difficulty in reconciling the interests of all of the various Native groups nationally. Nevertheless, these lobbying efforts helped generate awareness of what could be described as the federal government's benign neglect of Native peoples. Media reports of poor reserve socioeconomic and living conditions became commonplace, and pressure soon came to bear on provincial and federal politicians to improve the situation. The minister of the Department of Citizenship and Immigration responded in 1963 by commissioning one of a number of studies to review the situation of the Natives with a view to understanding the difficulties they faced. University of British Columbia sociologist Harry Hawthorn set up a research team to study Native socioeconomic conditions in Canada and to make recommendations for improvement (Hawthorn 1966–1967). The report focused on reserve conditions and federal programs that were economic, political, and administrative in nature. The report rejected assimilation as a certainty, proposing instead the concept of "citizens plus" to emphasize that Natives should benefit from Canadian citizenship while also maintaining those rights guaranteed as a result of status and treaty arrangements. They were to be included as "charter members of the Canadian community" as commissioners stressed "a common citizenship as well as the reinforcement of difference" (Cairns 2000:8).

In 1968, the Council became "troubled by tensions between treaty Indians, principally from the prairie provinces, and Metis and non-status Indians over the strategy to be followed." Specifically, "Indians with treaties preferred to pursue claims on the basis of treaty promises, but those without treaties (both Indians and Métis) found it more attractive to argue from a basis of Aboriginal rights" (J.R. Miller 1991:337). The National Youth Council (vol. 13:324) split into the National Indian Brotherhood (fig. 2) and the Canadian Métis Society. Also in 1968 a new Liberal government led by Pierre Trudeau and his promise of a "just society" took federal office. This "new government was imbued with a strong liberal ideology that stressed individualism and the protection of individual rights . . . that emphasized individual equality and de-emphasized collective ethnic survival" (Ponting 1997:31). Trudeau opposed the direction Hawthorn had charted, and in 1969 he and his minister of Indian affairs, Jean Chrétien, introduced in the House of Commons their policy proposal entitled *A Statement of the Government of Canada on Indian Policy*, referred to as the White Paper. Claiming the legislation once passed would "enable Indian people to be free to develop Indian cultures in an environment of legal, social and economic equality with other

Dept. of Ind. Affairs and Northern Development, Que.:11-10-05-00.

Fig. 2. Indians of Quebec Association meeting in March 1971. George Manuel (b. 1921, d. 1989), Shuswap, elected first president of the National Indian Brotherhood in 1970, is at left. Educated at the Kamloops Indian residential school, Manuel was treated at an Indian tuberculosis hospital on a reserve near Chilliwack, B.C., and worked for the Dept. of Indian Affairs as a community development officer among the Cowichan (Central Coast Salish) people in the early 1960s. In 1959 he became president of the North American Indian Brotherhood of British Columbia. In 1975 Manuel helped found and became the president of the World Council of Indigenous Peoples. From 1979 to 1981 he was president of the Union of British Columbia Indian Chiefs. Others at the meeting are Max Gros-Louis, Huron of Lorette, executive secretary-treasurer of the Indians of Quebec Association; Andrew Delisle, Mohawk of Caughnawaga, chairman; and Mike MacKenzie, chief of the Kipawa Algonquin band and vice-chair. Photographed at Ste. Foy, Que.

Canadians," it was clear that the federal government was seeking to transfer its federal responsibilities by devolving bureaucratic control over social programs to the provinces (Canada 1969:3).

The Liberal government further argued that it was this status and the resulting policies that "kept the Indian people apart from and behind other Canadians" and that this "separate road cannot lead to full participation, to better equality in practice as well as theory" (Canada 1969:5). All references to special and separate status of Indians were to be removed from Canada's Constitution to promote equality among all citizens. Epitomizing this unique status was special consideration over land and title that resulted from treaty negotiations (i.e., reserves), and provisions would be made enabling Native individuals to gain control and acquire title to these lands in addition to determining who would share in its ownership. Native resistance to the White Paper proposal was pronounced, in particular because the policy took aim at dismantling the unique legal relationship that existed between Natives and the federal government. The first written response to the White Paper came from the Indian Chiefs of Alberta, which at the time was attempting to resolve difficulties posed by the ethnic and linguistic discreteness of bands, highly localized band identities, and the geographical separation of reserves (Dyck 1983). Entitled *Citizens Plus*, also known as the Red Paper, the authors chastised the government for its lack of vision and its use of the Hawthorn report's recommendations to repudiate Native concerns (Indian Chiefs of Alberta 1970:4). *Citizens Plus* presented a Native political vision of the nature of the Native-federal relationship.

The Liberal government formally withdrew the White Paper in 1970, albeit still convinced of their Native policy. Native leaders were nonetheless still concerned with consistent federal dismissal of their nationhood claims. Ottawa promoted Indians as one of several multicultural ethnicities in need of federal assistance to boost their political participation in Canadian society. This resulted in part from an increase in the number of immigrants to Canada. As a way of maintaining Canadian national character, immigrant selection criteria included the "absorptive capacity" of various nations and races of people within a country endeavoring to establish a bilingual partnership between French and English Canadians (Newhouse, Fitzmaurice, and Belanger 2005). With anticipation that the new "multicultural mosaic" would be able to accommodate cultural diversity as well as Quebec's demands for greater autonomy; this policy became official in 1971. It was designed to foster a national identity in two ways. First, it was a manner of distinguishing Canada as an independent nation separate from the cultural "melting pot" of the United States. Second, it sought to cultivate a Canadian cultural plurality by assisting ethnic groups to participate within Canadian society.

Notwithstanding state aspirations for plurality, within one unified Canada existed the problematic notion of a diversity of cultures and their contributions to one nation. Even though it promoted ethnic participation in Canadian society, the new

multicultural policy functioned to transform ethnic groups such as Natives into political clientele. As a result Native cultural expressions could be managed without the need to change the dominant federal system in any significant way. This federal desire for increased levels of Native participation in Canadian society can be further understood in terms of the concerted resistance to the 1969 White Paper proposal to rescind the aforementioned unique legal relationship. Native leaders were reiterating their longstanding treaty message of a nation-to-nation relationship of equal coexistence with the Crown that of which contrasted sharply with the view of Natives as one multi-cultural ethnicity among many in need of federal assistance if they were to contribute to Canadian society. Simply put, the Canadian government view had Natives differing insubstantially from other minorities albeit uniquely impoverished and disorganized. The official Canadian position read that Native peoples constituted "an ethnic group in the functional sense but they have not reached the level of organizational structure (European style) which would make it possible for government to deal with them through the same approach as would be effective with other ethnic groups" (Newhouse, Fitzmaurice, and Belanger 2005:5).

In 1973, the Supreme Court of Canada in *Calder* v. *The Attorney General of British Columbia* recognized the existence of Aboriginal rights. Acknowledging the impact of the *Calder* decision and the Aboriginal right to land, the Indian Claims Commission was established in 1974 followed in 1975 by the first modern-day treaty signed between Canada and the James Bay Cree ("James Bay Cree," this vol.). The federal government also initiated the devolution of social control to Native peoples by instigating the transfer of responsibility for programs such as education to Native organizations and communities in the mid-1970s (Pompana 1997).

As the 1970s came to a close Native peoples had begun their transition from "wards of the state" reliant upon federal handouts, to political players focused on educating the Canadian public and federal politicians about Canada's treaty obligations (Newhouse, Fitzmaurice, and Belanger 2005:9). Native organizations were increasingly influential; this was directly attributable to federal programming resulting in Native concerns becoming more visible thereby attracting parliamentary attention. This influence could be seen during the constitutional discussions of the late 1970s that led to the entrenchment of existing Aboriginal and treaty rights in Section 35 of the Constitution Act of 1982. Native activists had become effective, which led to greater political influence. By 1978, for example, the National Indian Brotherhood, the Native Council of Canada, and the Inuit Committee on National Issues were invited to participate in the constitutional discussions. Not satisfied to watch from the periphery, 11 additional Native organizations initiated an influential lobby effort (Sanders 1983). It was during this period that Native groups such as the Federation of Saskatchewan Indians, formed in 1958, started to articulate the foundational ideas that would eventually become known as Aboriginal self-government.

## The Road to Self-Government, 1982–

As Native organizational influence grew, band councils remained under the watchful eyes of the Department of Indian Affairs, their operations specified by the Indian Act. By 1979 Native leaders again were battling to secure constitutional inclusion. At the community level, leaders of band councils were valiant (albeit in most cases unsuccessful) in their efforts to offer basic services to reserve populations. This was due in part to the limited success of federal economic development programs implemented beginning in the 1960s. Yet nationally the 1980s was the most significant political period for Native peoples since Confederation in 1867, and it appeared that their leaders were up to the task based on their successful lobbying efforts, which resulted in the federal government initiating the Parliamentary Task Force on Indian Self-Government in 1982 (the Penner report), recognizing Aboriginal self-government; the inclusion of section 37 in the Constitution Act mandating the conferences of provincial premiers between 1983 and 1987 to define Aboriginal self-government; the Ministerial Task Force on Program Review (Nielsen report) in 1986; and the Indian Self-Government Community Negotiations policy statement in 1986 (Boldt 1993). These developments were viewed as a way to "partially reverse hundreds of years of oppressive government policies and neglect, and to improve their intolerable socio-economic condition" (Hawkes 1987:1).

It was clear that the provincial premiers would be reluctant to constitutionally entrench the right to self-government, for it represented a departure from the legal and political history of dealing with Native people (Long, Little Bear, and Boldt 1982:192–194). Native groups had through a succession of reports been developing the common doctrines that would coalesce into what is today understood as Aboriginal self-government. One may conclude that much of this resulted from Prime Minister Pierre Trudeau's pronouncement that "we are not here to consider whether there should be institutions of self-government, but how these institutions should be brought into being . . . [and] how they fit into the interlocking system of jurisdictions by which Canada is governed" (Dickason 1994:408). Providing a sense of legitimacy was the *Report of the Special Committee on Native Self-Government*, known as the Penner report, the result of a mandate "to review all legal and related institutional factors affecting status, development, and responsibilities of band councils on Indian reserves, and to make recommendations in respect to establishing, empowering and funding Indian self-government" (Boldt 1993:88). The committee traveled across Canada to obtain testimony from Native people and presented its findings in October 1983.

The Penner report argued for a new federal relationship with Native peoples based on Trudeau's commentary at the First Ministers' Conference on Native Constitutional Matters: "Clearly, our aboriginal peoples each occupied a special place in history. To my way of thinking, this entitles them to special recognition in the Constitution and to their own place in Canadian society, distinct from each other and distinct from other groups who, together with them comprise the Canadian citizenry" (Canada 1983:39). The report recommended that "the federal government establish a new relationship with Indian Natives and that an essential element of this relationship be recognition of Indian self-government" (Penner 1988:141). Further, "the right of Indian peoples to self-government [should] be explicitly stated and entrenched in the Constitution of Canada. The surest way to achieve permanent and fundamental change in the relationship between Indian peoples and the federal government is by means of a constitutional amendment. Indian Natives would form a distinct order of government in Canada, with their jurisdiction defined." The report indicated that "virtually the entire range of law-making, policy, program delivery, law enforcement and adjudication powers would be available to an Indian Native government within its territory" (Canada 1983:39–40).

The federal government of Canada responded to the Penner report in March 1984: "The Committee's recommendations have a special importance because they were unanimously supported by Committee members of all Parties. It agreed with the need to establish a new relationship with Indian peoples." In all, "the effect . . . is to call for the Government and Indian Natives to enter into a new relationship . . . many of the details of the restructured relationship will have to be worked out after careful consideration and full consultation with Indian people." Furthermore, "the Government agrees with the argument put forth by the Committee that Indian communities were historically self-governing and that the gradual erosion of self-government over time has resulted in a situation which benefits neither Indian people nor Canadians in general" (Belanger and Newhouse 2004:154). However, the government did not accept the idea of constitutional entrenchment, although within a decade government officials reluctantly read the constitution in such a way as to include the right to self-government within it.

The idea of Aboriginal self-government, "as a component in the existing paradigm, was accepted" (Mawhiney 1994: 125–126). Despite this optimistic pronouncement, the implementation problems that followed from the recommendations were not addressed (Peters 1986:23). For the first time not only were Native leaders embracing the concept of a right to self-government but so too was the Canadian government. The result of the Penner report's recommendations had they been implemented "would be that Indian people would determine their own form of government, establish criteria for the self-identification of membership in Indian communities, and exercise jurisdiction in such fields as resources, social services, taxation, and education" (Hawkes 1986:10). Many Native leaders interpreted this to mean that jurisdiction for economic development, the key ingredient to any successful administration, had been effectively transferred to Native interests ("Aboriginal Economic Development," this vol.).

## The Assembly of First Nations

The most recognizable of the estimated 4,000 Native political organizations operating in Canada is the Assembly of First Nations, which was originally known as the National Indian Brotherhood. Initially influential, by the end of the 1970s internal factionalism took its toll. Complaints that the Brotherhood was not accountable to the nation's chiefs were politically destabilizing as was the debate over whether members should continue to be appointed, or whether an elected council would be more appropriate. Uncertain that the Brotherhood could effectively represent their interests, 300 Status Indians and chiefs arrived in London, England, in 1979 to try and halt the repatriation of the Constitution, causing even greater dissension among First Nations leaders. First Nations confidence in the Brotherhood failed after a number of questionable moves by the founder, Del Riley, which were followed by calls for organizational reform. Restructuring debates focused largely on the need to create an organization that was representative and accountable to First Nations community leaders. It was at this point that the Brotherhood began its transition, and in 1982, the Assembly of First Nations was born. The organization is open to the chiefs representing all the Status Indian bands in Canada, as opposed to being an organization of regional representatives. The new structure permitted First Nations leaders to formulate and administer policies.

In response to First Nations lobbying efforts, Canada revised its Constitution in 1982 to acknowledge formally the existence of Aboriginal rights. The Constitution recognized Aboriginal people as the Métis, Inuit, Status Indians, and non-Status Indians of Canada, while affirming "existing aboriginal and treaty rights" ("Native Rights and the Constitution in Canada," this vol.). From 1983 to 1987, the Assembly met with the provincial premiers at their conferences in an attempt to define Aboriginal self-government. The Assembly began working closely with other prominent lobby groups and organizations such as the United Nations in an attempt to convince Canada to uphold the spirit and intent of treaties. By the mid-1980s the Assembly had become an influential lobby group and contributor to the ongoing constitutional debates, as well as a critic of the United States-Canada Free Trade Agreement and other proposed legislative changes and issues affecting Canada's First Nations (fig. 3). Assembly resistance helped scuttle the Meech Lake Accord in 1990, which proposed constitutional amendments recognizing Quebec's distinct society while simultaneously ignoring distinctive First Nations cultures. This, in turn, resulted in the federal government openly consulting with First Nations

Federation of Sask. Ind. Nations, Saskatoon.

Fig. 4. Gathering hosted by the Federation of Saskatchewan Indian Nations, called the National Day of Action, 2007. About 200 people marched through Regina to the Saskatchewan legislature, where the First Nations and provincial political leaders spoke about the circumstances of First Nations communities in the province. At the podium is Federation First Vice Chief Morley Watson (Ochapowace-Chacachas Cree). At the table, right to left, are: Federation Chief Lawrence Joseph (Big River Cree), Saskatchewan Premier Lorne Calvert, Opposition Leader Brad Wall, and Wascana member of the federal parliament Ralph Goodale. Standing behind them are, right to left, Federation Fourth Vice Chief Lyle Whitefish (Big River Cree), Witchekan Lake First Nation Chief Steven Jim (Cree), and Federation Third Vice Chief Glen Pratt (George Gordon First Nation, Cree-Saulteaux). Second Vice Chief Guy Lonechild (White Bear First Nation) is not in the picture.

Dept. of Ind. Affairs and Northern Development, Que:20-08-12-00.

Fig. 3. George H. Erasmus, Dene (Dogrib), right, presenting the land claims of the Dene Nation to the federal government, 1976. George Kurszewski is at left, representing the Métis. From 1976 to 1983 Erasmus was president of the Indian Brotherhood of the Northwest Territories. He was the principal chief of the Assembly of First Nations from 1985 to 1991. In 1996 he was appointed co-chair of the Royal Commission on Aboriginal Peoples. In 2007 he was the head of the Aboriginal Healing Foundation in Ottawa.

leaders prior to drafting the Charlottetown Accord in 1992. Had the Accord been successful, Aboriginal self-government would have been realized. The Charlottetown Accord was rejected by Canadians in a national referendum in 1992.

Throughout the 1990s, the Assembly of First Nations continued working with the federal government while zealously lobbying for the formal recognition of Aboriginal self-government and the expansion of Aboriginal rights. In 2001, the Canadian government tabled proposed changes to legislation known as the First Nations Governance Initiative. Minister of Indian Affairs Robert Nault informed those in attendance at the Kainai High School located on the Blood Reserve in Alberta that he was instituting new legislation that would become recognized as the First Nations Governance Act. This proposal generated significant opposition from the Assembly of First Nations as well as other Aboriginal organizations. Soon thereafter, two additional bills were tabled: Bill C-6, known as the Specific Claims Resolution Act, and Bill C-19, known as the First Nations Fiscal and Statistical Management Act. Without consulting First Nations leaders, federal officials proposed changes that many Assembly delegates considered analogous to the termination policy embodied in the White Paper policy of 1969. After years of Assembly-led resistance, the Liberal government in 2004 rescinded its unpopular initiatives.

## Conclusion

Native organizations (fig. 4) in Canada continue to agitate against the Canadian government for political change. The Special Joint Committee of the 1940s, the resistance to the White Paper of 1969, and the opposition to legislation in the 2000s are evidence of effective Native political lobbying; however, the early Native political organizations were more than political activism. They represent a considered effort by Native leaders to force federal officials to once again listen to Native concerns and to impress upon federal representatives the importance of incorporating into Canadian politics the concerns of what Saul (2002) described as the third tier of confederation—Native along with Francophone and Anglophone. No doubt Native leaders consider Canada a permanently incomplete experiment built on a triangular foundation.

Notwithstanding the impressive political activity of Native political organizations and their leaders' demonstrated understanding of the Canadian legislative and policy arena as it relates to Indian Affairs and the parliamentary tradition, the federal government refuses to abandon its band government model, delegating political authority to municipal-style councils that are in many ways impotent to effect positive change in reserve communities. Band councils continue to agitate for increased local authority, which has slowly been forthcoming in the form of the gradual devolution of federal control over socioeconomic programs to reserve communities. Yet the federal Indian and Northern Affairs Canada bureaucracy remains responsible for the overall political direction of most communities. The system that resulted in the imposition of the band government model and the corresponding rise of Native political organizations remained largely in place in 2007.

# The Evolution of Native Reserves

YALE D. BELANGER, DAVID R. NEWHOUSE, AND HEATHER Y. SHPUNIARSKY

The British North America Act of 1867, through section 91 (24), assigned "Indians, and lands reserved for Indians" to the Canadian federal government. The Indian Act of 1876 sets out the legislative framework for the management of these responsibilities. Here are found the definitions of Indian and Indian reserve as used in the contemporary Indian reserve policy. An Indian is a "person who pursuant to this *Act* is registered or entitled to be registered as an Indian." An Indian reserve is a "tract of land, the legal title to which is vested in Her Majesty, that has been set apart by Her Majesty for the use and benefit of a band" (Indian Act, Revised Statutes 1985). In 2003, 633 Indian Bands making up 50 nations with an equal number of language groups occupied or utilized 2,597 reserves across Canada, comprising roughly 6.7 million acres of land and approximately 0.2% of the land base of Canada (fig. 1) (Statistics Canada 2003a). In 2005, there were 397,980 registered Indians living on-reserve, or 53 percent of the Canadian Indian population (Department of Indian Affairs and Northern Development 2006:70). The largest reserve by population in 2005 was the Six Nations of Grand River community in Ontario, with 22,349 residents (vol. 15:525–536) (Department of Indian Affairs and Northern Development 2006:xi). The largest reserve by size of land was the Blood Reserve in southern Alberta, at 547.5 square miles (350,400 acres). The Indian Act provides the regulatory framework that guides the governance of Indian reserves, including land regulation, taxation, and personal property. Most Indian reserve communities are governed by an elected band council, ranging in size from 3 to 12 councillors and one chief. Band members may not own reserve land in fee simple but they may be given a form of near ownership through a certificate of possession. This certificate allows individuals to use the land as if they owned it; however, sale is restricted to other band members or Indians.

Unlike Indian nations, where communal landholding was by and large the norm, European and British newcomers had conceptions of land ownership centered on private land ownership. The English and the French justified their territorial claims to Indian lands based on the theories of discovery and terra nullius. To secure title, the French, for example, would establish an alliance with the local inhabitants, followed by all parading together. To maintain French authority on the land it was necessary "to envision themselves to be creating a consensual colonialism that they termed 'alliance'" (Seed 1995:62). Only Christian Indians were considered subjects of the French Crown. Contrarily, the English did not consider gaining Indian political or cultural allegiance necessary. Rather, erecting a fence or a hedge established ownership, while a permanent house located upon an enclosed site signified a legal right to own that property. Seasonal movements that took Indian peoples to their hunting sites resulted in their often returning to lands occupied by English settlers reluctant to acknowledge Indian title. Accordingly, "lacking settled habitation . . . domestic animals, and fences, Indians . . . did not institute full dominion over their land," Indian title could be "extinguished by the arrival of those who had a civil right through the clear action of improvement" (Seed 1995:39). Such "ceremonies of possession" conveyed meaning and the intent to control land, ideologies that came to inform ideas about land and the resulting reserve policies that followed.

It was here that the notion of separating Indians and settlers became prominent, and the practice of establishing reserves accomplished a number of colonial objectives, including protecting Indians while obtaining land for settlers. Most importantly, removal of Indians from the land desired by settlers combined with the outright separation of Indians from settler society was an important goal. Homelands for the growing settler populations were subsequently created. The third goal was to promote the civilization of Indians. During this era, Europeans believed that the Indian "did not live in an ordered way, nor did he possess the kind of manners that a proper education would have bestowed upon him." Further, "his mode of living lacked 'industry' which, for the European of that period, was a description of the moral qualities a person would gain from laborious work or toil" (Francis 1992:56). Finally, the fourth goal was to create Christian religious communities, for civilization was seen as intimately linked with Christianity, and in new reserve communities, the church and religious officials became the centers around which life was organized. It was necessary, so the missionaries believed, to separate Indians who wished to become Christians and live a Christian life from their relations not inclined to convert. The children born into these communities' reserves would know only the Christian life, receive a Christian education, and interact with Christian people, acting as role models to future generations.

197

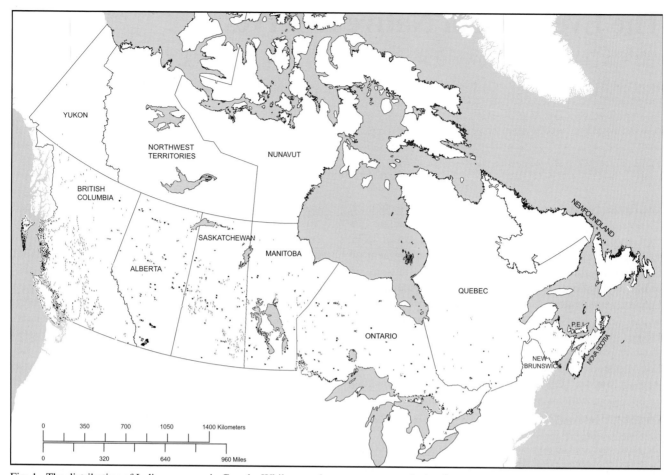

Fig. 1. The distribution of Indian reserves in Canada. While some larger reserves are depicted as areas, most reserves are tiny and cover less area than the representative dots.

## Colonial Policies

The French and British both regularly engaged Indian leaders in political negotiations at extended councils. Escalating cultural and political interaction led European settlers "to recognize in practice, and later in law, the capacity of Aboriginal nations not only to govern their own affairs" but to "possess their own lands" (Royal Commission on Aboriginal Peoples 1996). Indian leaders came to accept and adopt certain colonial practices such as living in permanent settlements and engaging in the fur trade to help maintain peaceful relations. French and British colonial officers in particular learned the importance of gift-giving, agreed to discuss matters in councils to try to establish working relationships, and generally established cooperative Indian-settler relations (J.R. Miller 2000).

Indian nations had a history of treaty-making among themselves before the arrival of Europeans, which was expanded to include European powers. Indian leaders embraced the treaty process as a means of establishing the interactive protocol that, if respected by all involved, would act to stabilize the political, military, and economic environment. European movement into Indian-held territories had a destabilizing ef-

fect, resulting in Indian leaders regularly attempting to engage settlers in treaty negotiations as they tried to restore balance. Treaty councils were utilized to try to protect Indian interests threatened by increased settlement. Hundreds of treaties were signed between French and British representatives and the various Indian nations throughout Canada, suggesting that hundreds of councils were established to forge these political relationships. This form of cross-cultural interaction resulted in Indian leaders engaging new political players in an evolving political landscape. French treaty-making practices (vol. 15:356) adopted an "Indian diplomatic protocol including constant renewal of the treaty by means of gift distributions accompanied by feasting and speeches" (Opekokew 1996), whereas the British maintained that written treaties were more effective, even though they often engaged in consensual negotiations.

At the same time, the colonial settlement of the New World was underway. Continued Indian claims to territorial ownership and the slow legal recognition of Indian title emerging in the British and French legal discourse of the period notwithstanding, the expressed desire to see Indians removed from resource-laden lands became palpable. Establishing reserves for Indian use that would permit European access to fertile farmland and interior fur stocks was motivational. Early French Recollets and later French Jesuits considered reserves an effective missionary tool that kept Indian populations in one area for an extended period of time. Conventional thought of the day held that separating Indian peoples from their families and villages to live among the French newcomers would result in augmented Christian conversions. The first Indian reserve in Canada dates to 1637 and was established by Jesuit priests at Sillery, Quebec. Land grants from the French Crown established Iroquoian Indian reserves at Kahnawake (Caughnawaga) and Saint Regis (vol. 15:469–471), Kanesatake, Odanak, Lorette (vol. 15:389–392), and Becancour (Bartlett 1990:8). Over time the French altered their separation strategy, promoting and accepting marriages between French farmers and fur traders, and Indian women (Brown 1980).

At the same time, the French eventually came to embrace Indian populations as political contemporaries, albeit never renouncing the reserve policy. In the summer of 1701, 1,300 representatives of 40 Indian Nations from the Maritimes to the Great Lakes to James Bay to southern Illinois met with French officials at Montreal to establish peaceful relations. Indian leaders considered peace a "natural law state of communication, connection, solidarity, and trust between all people, linked together in reciprocating relations of trade, friendship, and goodwill" (R.A. Williams 1999:59). At Montreal, an elaborate, month-long ceremony took place in a general council observed by over 4,000 people. The negotiated agreement between the Iroquois and the French established a Great Peace that extended from the Maritimes, throughout the southern half of Quebec and Ontario, down into Illinois (Brandao 1997). The negotiations were meant "to maintain and renew the good thoughts linking the five tribes of the confederacy to each other" while also renewing relations between the Iroquois and the French (R.A. Williams 1999:59–60).

The British did not believe in establishing reserves for Indians. They needed Indians to act as middlemen in the fur trade, and unlike the French the British clergy had yet to significantly penetrate the Canadian interior. The British rather attempted to establish political relationships with local tribes and until the 1750s remained unmoved by increasing Indian complaints of settler encroachment.

## The Royal Proclamations of 1761 and 1763

British colonial policy in North America acknowledged Indian land title framed by a policy of Indian protection. The policy also resulted in an attempt to situate the Crown between Indians and the westward-moving settler population, a doomed policy due primarily to the failure of Crown officials to accept, even in the face of mounting evidence, that their directives were prone to being ignored by colonial officials more concerned with fulfilling both their desires for in-

creased land holdings and those of their constituents. Indian complaints directed at the Crown were two-pronged. First, the Crown was censured for failing to deal with Indians as political equals. Also, Indian leaders were concerned with the increasing prevalence of shady land deals that were resulting in escalating conflict on the frontier. If the Crown would not listen, emphasizing the potential for violence became an effective way to propel local colonial officials to establish alliances of peace and friendship with neighboring Indian populations (Bartlett 1990:9).

Upon receiving word of territorial incursions and the resultant animosities, King George III issued a Royal Proclamation in 1761 to the governors of Nova Scotia, New Hampshire, New York, North and South Carolina, and Georgia. No longer was it permissible to grant lands to settlers or permit settlements that could potentially interfere with the Indian populations. Settlers found on Indian land were to be immediately removed. Finally, the Commissioner of Trade and Plantations of London became responsible for all applications from Indians seeking to sell their land (Dickason 1997:187). Indian leaders soon found local officials ignoring the Crown edict by narrowly interpreting the line that read ". . . those treaties and compacts which have been heretofore solemnly entered into with the said Indians by our Royal predecessors Kings and Queens of this realm" as suggesting that the Proclamation applied to previous Crown-Indian agreements and was not applicable to all Indian-held lands (Bartlett 1990:9).

Recognizing these inconsistencies, King George III issued a Royal Proclamation in 1763 demarcating all lands west of the Appalachian Mountains as territory reserved for the Indians' use and benefit by prohibiting settlement expansion into the Ohio Valley. Acknowledging "that the several Nations or tribes of Indians with whom we are connected, and who live under our protection, should not be molested or disturbed in the possession of such parts of our Dominion and Territories as," and that those lands had not "been ceded to or purchased by us," the Crown reserved those lands for the use and benefit of the Indian population, particularly for hunting. The 1763 Proclamation employed the Appalachians to separate "Indian territory" from eastern seaboard settler lands, the result being that lands falling west of the mountains were reserved for Indians. Similar to the 1761 Proclamation, land purchases had to go through the Crown, and private purchases were prohibited. Indian leaders expressed their unwillingness to permit colonial officials to arbitrarily ratify legislation affecting their political autonomy, and they lobbied for a meeting with the Crown to offer their interpretation of the Royal Proclamation. The Crown acquiesced and invited Indian leaders of the Great Lakes and the upper Ohio River valley to attend a conference at Niagara in 1764 to discuss principles that would govern Indian-Crown relations (Borrows 1997).

The council was held to help set "the framework by which the parties would relate to one another" (Borrows 2002:

125). Between July and August 1764, approximately 2,000 leaders representing more than 24 Indian nations from as far east as Nova Scotia and west to the Hudson's Bay watershed convened at Niagara Falls (Borrows 1997:155). The headmen read the Royal Proclamation's provisions and then commented on its provisions through speeches. This process served to renew old political relationships as each party promised to maintain the existing peace and friendship. The principles agreed upon included Crown recognition of "Aboriginal governance, free trade, open migration, respect for Aboriginal land holdings, affirmation of Aboriginal permission and consent in treaty matters, criminal justice protections, military assistance, respect for hunting and fishing rights, and adherence to principles of peace and friendship" (Borrows 2002:125). To Indian leaders, the two-month long council was a treaty negotiation, at which time they reaffirmed their allegiance to the spirit of the two-row wampum, which recognized the Crown and Indian nations as equals. British officials were expected to do the same. Accordingly, the principles symbolized in the two-row wampum belt, "together with Johnson's speech . . . are important because they testify to the foundational treaty of alliance and peace between First Nations and the Crown in Canada" (Borrows 2002:127). This 1763 Proclamation is frequently cited as an "indigenous bill of rights," due to its explicit recognition of Indian title that reserved the majority of the western North American continent to Indians. This is a somewhat dubious claim considering that the Proclamation also asserted British sovereignty to the whole of North America, and that notwithstanding Indian claims to the land, these former homelands in law were now the exclusive domain of the British Crown.

## Atlantic Region

Due to the nature of the Royal Proclamation of 1763's provisions, Canada's Atlantic region was exempt from having either to enter into treaties of surrender with Indians in order to extinguish Indian title or to establish reserves. In keeping with British colonial policy of Indian protection and settlement, reserves were still created, albeit through an executive order in council or by the issuance of a license of occupation. Local control over Indian lands and reserves was established in New Brunswick and Nova Scotia in 1848 and in 1851, respectively, and in Prince Edward Island. In Nova Scotia, for instance, the order in council stated that the lands were to be held in trust by the province for Indian peoples, "to whom they are to be hereafter considered as exclusively belonging." Colonial officials acknowledged that "trespasses are committed upon the Indian reserves with the most daring impunity" and the corresponding need to protect Indian resource reserves, although these encroachments were never dealt with by the Commissioner of Indian Affairs (Bartlett 1990:21). Prior to Confederation in 1867, officials from Britain's Colonial Office placed few restraints on the settler governments regarding their power to administer Indian lands and reserves. But according to the Enfranchisement Act of 1869 and the Indian Act of 1876, the newly formed federal government encouraged Indian leaders' surrenders of land as a means to expedite disputes between settlers and Indian populations.

It became common practice to add to or establish reserves by purchasing private lands. Between 1874 and 1910, 14 reserves comprising 630 acres were set aside (Bartlett 1990:33). Some of these purchases were to rectify past inadequacies in the quality of reserve lands, while others, completed between 1900 and World War II, were a means to settle claims with squatters or to open the region to additional settlers. In Nova Scotia, the federal government purchased small areas near towns to provide room for Indian settlement, followed by the purchase of large tracts of land (6,000 acres) in the 1940s to "further the economic self-sufficiency" of the Indian population. In New Brunswick, the reserve allocation model required a license of occupation, which would then be confirmed by an order in council followed by lands being set aside. All the land in Prince Edward Island was granted to absentee British proprietors in 1767, a process that failed to take into account Mi'kmaq (Micmac) interests, which resulted in no land allocation. In 1772, officials discovered that Lennox Island had been overlooked in the original survey, and this land was granted to a landowner who permitted local Indian populations to live there.

Newfoundland and Labrador did not enter Confederation until 1949, though it operated under responsible local government beginning in 1855. No legislation during this period was passed relating to Indian peoples or their lands in the province. Indian lands did not exist within Newfoundland and Labrador's boundaries, treaties were never entered into with Indian peoples, and provincial officials did not acknowledge an obligation to do so. The Province of Newfoundland-Labrador continues to deny the existence of Indian title, although it has been suggested by some that "in 1870 a reserve was set apart for the [Mi'kmaq] of Conne River." The reserve lands were surveyed in 1872 and later subdivided into 30-acre blocks for individual Mi'kmaq. But Indian people and their lands were not mentioned in Newfoundland's terms of union in 1949. By the mid-1950s, it was agreed that the federal government would assume financial responsibility for the province's Indian peoples. It would be 1973 before administrative responsibility was transferred, at which time federal funding was extended to the Conne River residents. In 1983, the Conne River Indian Band recommended that all federal funds be transferred directly to them, and the next year it was declared a band under the Indian Act. In 1987 Canada and Newfoundland reached an agreement that allowed the Conne River lands to be recognized as a reserve (Bartlett 1990:34). Since that time, Naskapi, Innu (Montagnais), and Inuit land claims in Labrador have been accepted.

## Quebec

Colonial officials in Quebec did not deem it necessary to adhere to the Royal Proclamation of 1763's surrender requirements. Instead the local Indian commissioners appointed to protect and supervise Indian land transactions were empowered to dispose of reserve land without Indian consent. The reserves in Quebec were established by grants from the French Crown to missionary orders, on the theory that the Crown had exclusive right and title to the land. As a result, protective legislation was passed in the nineteenth century to deal with these and related problems, including the 1851 passing of an act to authorize the setting apart of lands for the use of certain Indian tribes in Lower Canada (fig. 2). As the population spread from the Saint Lawrence area, more pressure was exerted upon Indian lands and the need for more reserves was increased. By 1854, 230,000 acres of land had been set aside for reserves in Quebec (Bartlett 1990:14). That same year, imperial control over Indian lands and reserves was given up, and it was extinguished by 1860. Following Confederation, the amount of land set aside for reserves was minimally altered. Few occasions existed in which the province set aside lands, and these were usually for the settlement of disputed boundaries, to affect an exchange, or to confirm existing arrangements. Two boundary extensions in 1898 and 1912 resulted in the transfer of territorial title to the Province of Quebec, the second of these promising to recognize the rights of the Indians inhabiting the lands. In return, the Indians were to release their rights to the Province and any agreements would then have to be approved by Order in Council, a commitment that was never honored.

Indian people continued to utilize the vast region because the only non-Indian presence consisted of Hudson's Bay Company employees, missionaries, and some members of the federal department responsible for Indian affairs. This continued occupation eventually led to the the James Bay and Northern Quebec Agreement signed in 1975, representing the first in what has become Canada's modern treaty period ("James Bay Cree," this vol.).

Inuit communities were incorporated as municipalities under Quebec law, and municipal powers are delegated to them by Quebec legislation. The Kativik regional government was established according to a provincial act. Cree and Inuit school boards were established as part of the Agreement, with a special mandate and unique powers enabling them to adopt culturally appropriate educational programs. Canada and Quebec jointly fund the school boards, with Canada paying 25 percent of the Inuit budget, and three-quarters of the Cree budget. A coordinating committee of federal and provincial representatives and Indian delegates was established to administer, review, and regulate wildlife harvesting, while ensuring that Indian rights to hunting acknowledged in the Agreement are not abused.

## Ontario

The influx of Loyalist settlers to Ontario following the American Revolution resulted in amplified claims to an already dwindling land base still held by Indian leaders by virtue of Indian title. In response to these expressed desires for more land, colonial officials in Ontario aggressively pursued treaties and agreements with Indian leaders. Officials adhered to the principles of the Royal Proclamation of 1763 requiring public meetings be held to ensure both appropriate negotiations leading to lawful surrenders. The first regional treaties and agreements resulted in cash payments for the surrender of Indian title. In return, reserves were created outside the boundaries of surrendered land (vol. 15:450). As settlement pressure increased and the corresponding amount of available land diminished, an "express provision" was implemented for the creation of reserves; nevertheless, "the language of the treaties and agreements customarily purported merely to reserve a tract of land from surrender" (Bartlett 1990:11). During this period, Ontario officials did not establish a formula to aid in their reserve allocations, although it does appear that administrators and government officials reserved on a case-by-case basis land deemed necessary to meet the agricultural needs of an individual Indian community. However, rights such as hunting, trapping, and fishing were not protected despite colonial promises to do so. Imperial control over Indian lands and reserves was rescinded in 1854, and in 1860 the Act Respecting the Management of Indian Lands and Property established the provincially appointed commissioner of crown lands as the chief superintendent of Indian Affairs. The Act gave this individual the authority "to apply the public lands legislation to the sale of Indian lands, but stipulated that a surrender from the Indians must entail the assent of a majority of the chiefs of the tribe" (Bartlett 1990:22).

Natl. Geographic Society, Washington, D.C.:neg. no. 115934.

Fig. 2. Montagnais family at Pt. Bleue Res., Que., 1938, where Montagnais had been residing since 1856. Photograph by Harrison H. Walker.

Treaties and agreements were not the only means to establish reserves. Following the end of the Revolutionary War, the British Crown purchased a tract of land from the Mississaugas in 1784 in recognition of Haudenosaunee (Iroquois) loyalty, the land that was granted in 1788 and integrated into the 1793 Simcoe Deed as the Six Nations Reserve. Oftentimes lands were set aside for Indians by orders in council. There were also instances where Indian leaders were forced to purchase land with annuities in order to establish an adequate reserve. For example, the Mnjikaning (Rama, Ojibwa) First Nation near modern-day Orillia, Ontario, occupies a resource-rich region that includes the regional transportation hub. The Mnjikaning people supplemented their fishing activities by hunting and trading with local Indian and British and French entrepreneurs. The movement of settlers into Ontario resulted in their encroachment into and the eventual occupation of Mnjikaning territory. Settlers desired the region for its abundance of fish and good hunting. Most importantly, the Mnjikaning land base was considered to be rich farmland with unlimited agricultural potential. In 1818, colonial administrators decided to open Ontario up to settlement and approached Mnjikaning leaders to propose an exchange. In return for a perpetual annuity of £1,200 in both currency and goods, Mnjikaning Chief Mesquakie (William Yellowhead) agreed to cede 1,592,000 acres to the colonial government to be opened up for settlement. Colonial officials upheld their end of the deal but the Mnjikaning were soon contending with unchecked colonial settlement. Such was the case of much of eastern Ontario, and the threat of hostilities began to take root. Wary of the near-constant threat of war and settler complaints, Lt.-Gov. John Colborne created a plan in 1829 aimed at settling all of the "nomadic tribes" into two settlements located at Coldwater and the Narrows (near Orillia). Upon his arrival at the Narrows, Chief Mesquakie and his people were ensured that this was the last time they would have to relocate, and they were encouraged to take up farming. Again, unchecked settler movement into the region and pressure to open up the Narrows to large-scale farming operations resulted in Chief Mesquakie and his followers once again relocating, this time to Ramara Township where 1,600 acres of land were purchased and assigned reserve status (Belanger 2006).

The ramifications of this reserve policy became evident in 1924, following the *Star Chrome* decision of 1921, which sought to determine whether the Quebec provincial government or the federal government held land title and the right to issue resource patents. The case concerned lands surrendered in 1882 by Western Abenakis of Becancour. Federal officials argued title was vested with Canada because the land in question was set aside under the Lower Canadian Protection Act of 1851. They claimed that Quebec was not permitted to claim title notwithstanding the fact that Confederation had not yet occurred. Quebec argued that the British North America Act protected their interests, citing section 109, which "assigns all lands vested in the Crown to the government of the province in which they are situated." Therefore, the contested territory became provincial lands, and the provincial interest was "subject to" the Indian interest pending a treaty and purchase. Despite excessive amounts of surrenders of Indian reserve land, the Judicial Committee of the Privy Council determined Quebec, and by extension Ontario, was not required to direct revenues from the sale of surrendered reserve land to Indian interests. Further, according to the *Saint Catherines Milling* decision of 1888 (Privy Council, 14 App. Cas. 46), the federal government had "neither authority nor power to take away from Quebec the interest which had been assigned to that Province by the Imperial statute of 1867" (Bartlett 1983:262).

Canada found itself in a difficult position due primarily to the number of illegal land sales that had taken place both prior to and following Confederation. Accordingly, Canada had a number of avenues to choose from, which included "selling out the interests of First Nations," the path that federal officials in the end chose (Telford 1996:312). This was followed by enactment of the Canada-Ontario Indian Reserve Lands Agreement (S.C., 1924, c. 48) in 1924, which "sought to provide for the disposition of reserve lands upon a surrender" that granted Ontario a "statutory entitlement to a half-share of mineral proceeds on reserves" (Bartlett 1983:268). According to Indian leaders, the Agreement "assumed that the Indian Tribes of Canada have not and never had tribal title to their territories" and that it was "assumed that a province has reversionary title to all Indian reserves" (Belanger 2006:85–86). They further complained that the agreement was structured to eliminate treaty fishing, hunting, and trapping rights, that the Judicial Committee of the Privy Council did not fully comprehend the *Saint Catherines Milling* case, and that all Indian rights court cases from 1888–1920 failed to consider the treaties established from 1780–1906. This was a significant failing, for the treaties recognized "tribal title to Indian territories, and show intention to have been that lands reserved should be completely, permanently, and beneficially lands of the Indian Tribes" (Belanger 2005:86). Ontario proceeded to implement the Agreement, ignoring all concerns to the contrary (vol. 15: 764). For Mohawk reserves in Ontario, see volume 15:471.

### British Columbia

British Columbia's Indian policy was simply to deny Indian title to land, to allocate small reserves close to White settlements, all accomplished without engaging Indian leaders in a dialogue or establishing formal arrangements (Bartlett 1990:15). This policy ran contrary to the Royal Proclamation of 1763, although this did not deter colonial officials from establishing a localized reserve policy that was dependent upon colonial needs and desires. In particular, the Hudson's Bay Company charter was extended to Vancouver Island in 1849, which meant that the company colony could develop internal policies. However, it was the arrival of James Douglas in British Columbia that unleashed a significant impact upon the local political cultures. Douglas began construction of a trading post at Victoria in 1843 and was eventually appointed the Hudson's Bay Company chief factor in the province and later colonial governor, 1850–1864 (Sage 1930:121). As colonial governor, Douglas was given the responsibility for opening up the island to settlement "in accordance with the terms of the Crown's Grant of Vancouver Island to the Company" (Madill 1981:8). He quickly entered into 14 treaties with Indian nations of southern Vancouver Island (Tennant 1990:37). Douglas also attempted to engage Indian leaders in political negotiations and treaty councils.

Douglas entered into the first treaties with Vancouver Island Indian leaders in May 1850 (vol. 7:161–162). A number of councils followed, resulting in nine purchases. The chiefs surrendered their lands in their entirety with the understanding that each treaty would make their "village sites" and "enclosed fields" available for their use and that they would be able to freely "hunt over the unoccupied lands, and to carry on fisheries as formerly" (British Columbia 1875:5–11). Reserve sites were established with the promise that traditional means of subsistence would be permitted to continue, even if the treaties and the accompanying deeds of conveyance were "short, murky documents open to many interpretations" (D. Harris 2002:26). The chiefs' goal was to secure political permanence by securing economic stability, thus the mention of fishing sites, hunting, and continued access to enclosed fields. Following the signing of the treaties, Douglas endeavored to maintain peaceful relations with Indian leaders by establishing a protectionist policy while also preserving Indian reserve lands from settler encroachment. In 1859, when settlers tried to buy a portion of one reserve, Douglas ran a statement in a local newspaper informing residents the land, in fact, could not be sold. Later, when the Legislative Council of Vancouver Island wanted to remove Indian people from the reserves, Douglas asserted that such removal was unjustified (R. Fisher 1978:111–115).

Until his retirement as colonial governor, Douglas was able to rebuff repeated attempts to obtain additional land from Indians. His political successor changed the situation drastically within a few years. Douglas appointed Joseph Trutch to the position of chief commissioner of lands and works for British Columbia in 1864 and Trutch acted promptly: "where reserves exceeded the supposed ten-acre 'rule' established by Douglas, Trutch reduced them; the Kamloops reserve was cut on his instructions to less than half its former extent, reducing reserve sizes while simultaneously denying Aboriginal title, actions he considered appropriate, and a way to eliminate the need for treaties or agreements of extinguishment" (D.C. Mitchell and P. Tennant 1996). Although both levels of government seemingly had the same goal, Indian assimilation, federal officials recognized the need to enter into treaty negotiations in order to legally extinguish Indian

territorial title. Trutch ignored federal requests to initiate treaty negotiations with Indian leaders. The colonial governor expressed a desire to do little more than grant reserve lands that were sufficient to "fulfil all their reasonable requirements for cultivation and grazing" (La Violette 1961: 108–111). Indian leaders complained about the provincial government's failure to interface politically and raised concerns regarding Trutch's decision to ignore Indian title to land or to grant reserves large enough to accommodate their needs.

Following British Columbia's entry into Confederation in 1871, provincial officials maintained that the Royal Proclamation of 1763 never extended into its territory, and the terms of union agreed to by provincial officials do not state specifically that the province was required to treat with Indian peoples. Nevertheless, article 13 of the terms of union recognized a need to set aside reserves (fig. 3) while non-Indian settlement continued throughout the province, though in a very general way (Bartlett 1990:35). Negative Indian response to Trutch's arbitrary changes to colonial policy, which reduced reserve size, led to the joint 1876 decision by

top, Film and Video Centre of Canada, Ottawa:66-12380; bottom, B.C. Prov. Mus., Victoria:13866–13.

Fig. 3. Haida reserves on Queen Charlotte Is., B.C., which were laid out in 1882. In 1984 the Haida had 37 reserves, with about 4,000 acres. top, Massett Res., 1966. The population in 2001 was 707. Photograph by Chris Lund. bottom, Skidegate village on Skidegate Res., 1978. For a picture of the town in 1878, see vol. 7:242. The population in 2001 was 743. Photograph by Peter McNair.

British Columbia and Canada to form a joint commission of inquiry. Commissioner G.M. Sproat recommended the province take a lead role in the investigation; furthermore, it was suggested the province retain final say as to whether to accept the Indian Reserve Commission's interpretation of the concept of Indian title. The Commission, nevertheless, failed to resolve all outstanding questions related to Indian title beyond Vancouver Island's confines. Sproat immediately began corresponding with his superiors and Indian affairs officials in Ottawa, although his support for Indian title went ignored. Indian requests to revisit the land question were ignored, with Premier William Smithe rejecting these claims.

The McKenna-McBride Commission sought to settle this dispute. And while it was supposed to also provide for the adjustment of acreage of reserve lands and for the conveyance of reserves to the federal government, an agreement signed by J.A.J. McKenna and former provincial premier, Richard McBride, proposed that the Commission be appointed "with power to adjust the Acreage of Indian reserves," thereby "taking away where the Indians have too much land, and adding where the lands are insufficient" (Belanger 2005:116). Indian peoples were not part of this agreement and no surrender was obtained, though it was necessary according to the Indian Act since there was a reduction of acreage. The McKenna-McBride Commission in 1916 recommended adding 136 square miles, appraised at $5.10 an acre, to British Columbia reserves while cutting off 74 square miles, land that was appraised at upward of $27 an acre (Tennant 1990:98; C. Harris 2002:241–246). Superintendent General of Indian Affairs W.J. Roche reaffirmed that the support of Indian leaders was required prior to any land allocations taking place. The Commission's final recommendations removed reserve land desired by local settlers for farming and ranching in lieu of adding land of little economic value.

The newly formed Allied Tribes of British Columbia in 1916 began an aggressive lobby campaign demanding resolution of the land question. Their efforts led Prime Minister Robert A. Borden to establish a committee to evaluate the McKenna-McBride Commission's failure to consider Indian title, followed by provincial Premier John Oliver's request that the Allied Tribes prepare a formal response to the McKenna-McBride report (Belanger 2006:116). In April 1920, a team composed of Maj. J.W. Clark and Chief Inspector W.E. Ditchburn was proposed to evaluate the McKenna-McBride report, completing their task in 1923 while minimally altering the report's final recommendation. Two delegations to Ottawa opposing the report followed later that year. In official channels, however, scepticism remained that Indian land title existed. Finally, in 1924 the Dominion government arbitrarily ratified the report even though no surrender was ever obtained for the lands that were removed from the reserves, breaking an earlier promise to consult the Allied Tribes (C. Harris 2002:261–262). This was a significant blow to the Allied Tribes. The group

continued to lobby Parliament for resolution of the Indian land question (see Tennant 1990). On 8 March 1927, a formal hearing was called, and the Allied Tribes' claims and the desire for treaties were rejected. In 1969 the federal government recognized that the consent of Indian peoples was necessary for the reduction of reserve lands, and as of "1982 the first settlement was reached, which provided for the return of unalienated land (except for land that the province wished to retain upon payment of compensation), and for the payment of compensation by the federal government for alienated land" (Bartlett 1990:39).

## Prairie Provinces—Alberta, Saskatchewan, and Manitoba

In the talks preceding Confederation, the British Crown insisted that Canada accept legislative and financial responsibility for Indian peoples. The British North America Act (section 91, subsection 24) ultimately assigned "federal jurisdiction over 'Indians and Lands reserved for the Indians'" as a mechanism "to protect Indians and Indian lands from local interests" (Bartlett 1990). That year, the Secretary of State was Superintendent General of Indian Affairs, and all lands vested in the commissioners of the four provinces were transferred to the Crown. In addition, no part of a reserve could be surrendered without going through the Crown. This protected lands from local interests and maintained the imperial principle created by the Royal Proclamation of 1763. The nation-building project was well under way, and Canada set its sights on what was then the frontier known as the Northwest Territories. These lands fell within the demarcated region called Ruperts Land, which was ceded to Canada by Great Britain in 1868 for £300,000 sterling silver. In 1870, by Imperial Order-in-Council, Crown officials agreed to obtain Indian title to the lands through treaties and that "any claims of Indians to compensation for lands required for purposes of settlement shall be disposed of by the Canadian Government in communication with the Imperial Government; and the Company shall be relieved of all responsibility of them" (Cumming and Mickenberg 1974:148). The consideration of Native peoples as little more than barriers to westward expansion was explicit when newly appointed Lt. Gov. Adams George Archibald of Manitoba was then directed to "ascertain and report to His Excellency the course you may think most advisable to pursue, whether by treaty or otherwise, for the removal of any obstruction that may be presented to the flow of population into the fertile lands that lie between Manitoba and the Rocky Mountains" (Oliver 1914–1915, 2:974).

From 1871 to 1877 over 100 Prairie Indian leaders signed seven treaties with the Canadian government. Four more treaties were signed with northern Indian leaders from 1899 to 1921. In all 11 treaties, in exchange for ceding Indian title to vast expanses of land, Indians were to receive small but economically manageable reserves (vol. 13:831) for their use and benefit in perpetuity. The treaties were nation-to-nation agreements establishing the rules of conduct that guided cultural interaction that included territory sharing provisions (Daniel 1980). This position is substantiated in the writings of the numbered treaty's primary negotiator and Treaty Commissioner Alexander Morris (1991). Legal scholar J. Henderson (1994) has deconstructed the wording of the main provision in all the numbered treaties as showing the Crown's intent of establishing working relationships with Indian leaders to promote cultural interaction for the purposes of opening tribal lands to settlers wishing to *share* the territory with its original inhabitants. Treaties were also a means of extending the protective arm of the monarchy to western Indians battling an influx of settlers and whiskey bootleggers (Dockstator 2001).

Soon thereafter Canadian officials were intent on eliminating the reserve system, the goal according to Deputy Superintendent General of Indian Affairs Duncan Campbell Scott being to absorb all Indians "into the body politic" until "there is no Indian question, and no Indian Department" (Leslie and Maguire 1978:114). The Oliver Act was passed in 1911 and amended in 1914, permitting the federal government to relocate reserves situated next to growing municipalities. This was followed by the presentation of nine bills to amend the Indian Act to the Canadian House of Commons from 1914 to 1930, to increase the powers of the deputy superintendent general of Indian affairs while permitting greater access to Indian lands in western Canada (S.D. Grant 1983:29). This included implementation of the Greater Production Campaign, designed to permit the transfer of dormant agricultural lands to non-Indian farmers, and an amendment established to permit further acquisition of reserve lands to enable the Soldiers Settlement Act of 1919. In that case, Indian war veterans were ineligible for consideration because of conflicting Indian Act legislation that excluded Indians from acquiring private land holdings on reserves. Indians were able to benefit from commercial dealings on their reserves (fig. 4).

The Department of Indian Affairs and Northern Development supplied modern housing on reserves (fig. 5), but this provision was not enough to keep people on the reserves.

## Yukon, Northwest Territories, and Nunavut

Canada's North is sparsely populated, and with the exception of Treaty 11, few treaties have been negotiated with the local populations. In 2007, there were six reserves comprising 1,233 acres in the Yukon Territory and two reserves comprising 1,386 acres in the Northwest Territories. The national average is 2,907 acres per reserve. There are no reserves in the territory of Nunavut.

## Self-Government and Urban Reserves

Indians have been moving into Canadian cities since the 1950s. The 2001 census showed that approximately 43 percent of the Indian population resided in urban centers, while about 50 percent of the total Aboriginal population resided in cities and towns. This movement has led to the development of urban aboriginal communities and institutions in many Canadian urban centers.

### Urban Aboriginal Self-Government

With the movement of Indian peoples into urban centers since the 1980s, there has been some attention paid to establishing urban Aboriginal self-government for these populations. Aboriginal peoples living in urban centers have consistently expressed a desire for more input and improved jurisdiction over aspects of their lives such as social services, employment, and cultural institutions (Calliou 1998; Peters 1992). This desire has been seen as problematic for both reserve communities and municipal governments. Some suggest that the establishment of urban Aboriginal self-government could lead to difficulty and uncertainty on reserves resulting in significant emigration of Indian people to urban centers. The majority of municipal governments consider urban Indian self-government as irrelevant, placing the onus upon urban Aboriginal populations to devise their own responses, plans, and decisions (Blakeney 1994).

Urban Aboriginal populations consist of individuals from a variety of cultural backgrounds as well as differing legal statuses. These differences are not normally an issue in reserve governance. Cultural differences and differing municipal circumstances argue for a significant degree of flexibility approaching urban Aboriginal self-government development (Peters 1995). The Canadian government (1998a) concurred with this approach in its official response to the Royal Commission on Aboriginal Peoples findings and recommendations. It determined that the approach to urban Aboriginal governance must be multidimensional and developed around "communities of interest." Furthermore, non-Indian governments should consider providing resources that facilitate consultation, consensus, and community building and that financial strategies should be places at the top of the list when it comes to what is required to establish urban Indian self-government in Canada. The Urban Aboriginal Working Group developed three possible approaches to improving governance for urban Aboriginal people. These include establishing self-governing Aboriginal institutions in urban areas to be responsible for key services, promoting an Aboriginal authority that would enter into agreements with a public government, and reforming municipal governments and other local public authorities to make them more representative to Aboriginal residents (K. Graham 1999). Some First Nations support extending the jurisdiction of land-based governments to urban citizens (Opekokew

top, Glenbow Arch., Calgary, Alta.: ND-8-398.

Fig. 4. Stoney Res., Alta. top, Stoney Indians receiving lease payments from an oil company for the right to drill on their reserve. Chief of the Chiniki band Hector Crawler (Calf Child) takes the $10 per capita. Behind him, left to right, are: Philip Adams, Tom Kaquitts, Dan Wildman, Sr., William Soldier, and John Twoyoungmen. The contract also called for a 12.5% royalty to be paid to the tribe, but the company did not make any profit. Photograph by William J. Oliver, Morley, Alta., 1929. bottom left, Tribal adult education building. Built in 1968, it was the administration building until 1976. bottom right, Stoney tribal building, including the health center. bottom left and bottom right, Photographs by Ian Getty, 1998.

Fig. 5. Dogs bringing in firewood at Brochet Res., Man. The modern housing was built by the Dept. of Indian Affairs and Northern Development. The reserve was about half Cree and half Chipewyan, but by 1976 all the Chipewyan had moved away to establish a new settlement at Lac Brochet (vol. 6:282). The reserve had been built outside the best range for the caribou that the Chipewyan men needed to hunt for months in the bush. The Barren Land band of Cree continues to live at Brochet Res. Photograph by James G.E. Smith, 1967.

1996), arguing that their jurisdiction over their citizens doesn't stop at the reserve boundaries. They proposed the establishment of urban Indian reserves that would provide a government center, commercial development, and residences.

*Urban Indian Reserves*

Some Indian reserves were established adjacent to urban centers while, over the years, others have seen municipal boundaries extend to reserve boundaries. Urban Indian reserves, as extensions of rural reserves or as an entity in their own right, are a phenomenon that emerged in the 1990s. In 2007 there were 31 urban reserves in western Canada, with Lethbridge, Alberta, considering the idea as Winnipeg, Manitoba, took the required steps to establish one. Urban reserves are considered an effective mechanism to help alleviate social and economic problems of urban Indian populations. There are three facts that influence urban reserve development: urban Indian people do not enjoy the same level of services available on reserve or in their communities, many find it increasingly difficult to obtain access to provincial programs available to all urban residents, and there is a lack of culturally appropriate programming in urban centers (Royal Commission on Aboriginal Peoples 1996). Most programs were produced in the absence of policy, suggesting that they were little more than ad hoc measures resulting in urban Aboriginal programming that is "largely disjointed and at times incoherent" (Hanselmann 2002a:11, 2002). Despite federal acknowledgement of a desperate need for coordination and collaboration between different levels of government to ameliorate the difficulties being experienced by urban Aboriginal populations, "there is no sign that basic issues

of jurisdiction and responsibility are being addressed" (K. Graham and E. Peters 2002:18).

Things may be changing in this regard. In 2002, the federal court decision *Canada* v. *Misquadis* determined that Human Resources and Skills Development Canada discriminated against the urban Indian community. Specifically, the court defined off reserve Indian people as a group of self-organized, self-determining, and distinct communities, analogous to that of a reserve community. *Misquadis* reinforced the political connection between on- and off-reserve Indian people articulated in the Supreme Court of Canada's *Corbière* v. *Canada* (1999) decision, which compelled Indian Bands holding elections or referendums under the Indian Act to permit members living off-reserve to vote. Off-reserve members living in urban centers were provided political voice in on-reserve decision making. More specifically, *Corbière* determined all Band members must be provided with equality of access to programs and services, regardless of residence. The political lines between reserve and urban residence were made nonexistent. Following *Corbière*, the court in *Misquadis* determined that Indian organizations can represent urban Indian interests, and that the federal department called Human Resources and Skills Development Canada is responsible to provide funding to aid in the establishment of the infrastructure needed to effect service delivery and the creation of representative Indian governance.

**Conclusion**

The governance of Indian reserves and the management of Indian lands are still by and large determined by the 1876 Indian Act. The Act, based upon the premises of protection and civilization, is inconsistent with the emerging needs of Indian communities, both on and off reserve. Indian band councils have agitated for changes to the land management regimes to facilitate the use of land in economic development projects; some have been successful. An example of this was the Sechelt Indian Band Self-Government Act of 1986, which transferred, in fee simple, all Sechelt Indian Reserve land to Sechelt Indian Band jurisdiction. The legislation created the Sechelt Indian Government District as a municipality within the province of British Columbia. In 1985 the federal government enacted an amendment to the Indian Act that removed its gender discriminatory aspects while permitting Indian Bands to define their own rules for determining membership and residency. The implementation of The First Nations Land Management Act in 1999 enabled Indian Bands to develop and implement land management codes that provide for increased local control and decisionmaking over reserve land by removing the need for the minister of Indian affairs to approve land transactions and decisions. Indian reserves have evolved into homelands for many Indian people, far different from their original conception as places where Indians could be protected and civilized.

# The Department of Indian Affairs and Northern Development

JOHN F. LESLIE

The Department of Indian Affairs and Northern Development is one of the oldest Canadian government departments, established in 1755. The Department's administrative apparatus, policy mandates, and programs and services have expanded to meet both domestic challenges and political realities. The Department's utility has often been questioned, and its demise predicted with regularity.

Since the mid-twentieth century, the federal government has developed a wide variety of social welfare programs and policies for Canadians including health care, child care, care of the elderly and the challenged, and services for war veterans. The federal government of Canada has recognized the need to provide such programs to Aboriginal peoples and to develop policies that meet the specific needs of Aboriginal groups across Canada.

## Special Joint Parliamentary Committee, 1946–1948

At the close of World War II the plight of Canada's Indian peoples became a matter of national concern. A House of Commons Special Committee on Reconstruction and Re-establishment was struck in 1944 (Shewell 2004:145–146). This committee was charged with assessing the nature of postwar Canadian society and the nature and scope required for new social welfare programs. The Reconstruction Committee recommended that Parliament investigate living conditions on Indian reserves as well as Indian policy and administration (Shewell 2004:166–170). The investigation by a Special Joint Committee of the Senate and House of Commons was the first public scrutiny of departmental operations since pre-Confederation times.

The Special Joint Committee held hearings from 1946 to 1948. During its tenure, it heard testimony from witnesses representing the Indian Affairs Branch, select Indian groups, and interested third parties (Shewell 2004:173–206). The resulting report recommended several significant policy changes including: a reduction in the Minister's discretionary powers; granting permission for Indian bands to develop their own constitutions and charters for "self-government;" legislation to enable Indian bands to incorporate and hold title to reserve lands; the creation of an Indian Claims Commission; and granting Indian people the right to vote in federal elections. The Special Joint Committee also recommended that registered Indians receive pensions and social services that were available to non-Indians. Perhaps most significantly, the Committee recommended modifying the policy of Indian separation, favoring social, economic, and political integration of Indian peoples into post-war Canadian society (Leslie 1999:179).

*Government Reorganization*

In January 1950, the Indian Affairs Branch was transferred from the Department of Mines and Resources to the newly created Department of Citizenship and Immigration (Canada 1982:109). The transfer underlined the federal government's perception that Indian peoples were still in the process of becoming citizens of Canada and would benefit from programs and services directed at immigrants. To politicians and bureaucrats, it seemed that Indian administration and the process of Indian integration had been set on a productive and conciliatory course.

*A Revised Indian Act, 1951*

A revised Indian Act that specifically excluded Eskimos from its ambit came into effect in September 1951, after consultations with Indian leaders (fig. 1) (Canada 1981:3). The new Indian Act contained virtually none of the Special Joint Committee's recommendations, although it lifted prohibitions on dances and traditional ceremonies and permitted the investigation of land claims. The Act contained a new legal definition of "Indian," which departed from previous definitions that were founded in part on communal acceptance (Canada 1981:1). Based on this new definition, a central Indian Membership Registry, containing the names of Status Indians eligible to receive government benefits, was created at headquarters in Ottawa (Canada 1981:3). A new category of individuals was excluded from this Membership Registry, as section 12(1)(b) of the revised Act stated that an Indian woman who married a non-Indian lost her Indian status. This loss of status extended to the woman's children. If she resided on an Indian reserve at the time of her marriage to a non-Indian, then she had to leave the reserve (Canada 1981:5). This provision affected thousands of Indian women. These women have sought registration of

Fig. 1. Representatives of First Nations convened to discuss provisions of the Indian Bill to amend, consolidate, and clarify the Indian Act. front row, left to right: S. Knockwood, chief, Shubenacadie Band (Micmac), N.S.: Gus Mainville, president, Grand Council of Treaty No. 3, Ont.; A.C. Moses, secretary, Six Nations Band Council, Ohsweken, Ont.; Prime Minister Louis St. Laurent; Joseph Beauvais, councillor, Caughnawaga Band, Que.; T. Gideon, chief of Restigouche Band, Que.; and G. Faries, chief, Moose Factory band, Ont. second row: T. Favel, chief, Poundmaker Band and representative of the Queen Victoria Treaty Protective Association, Sask.; Joseph Dreaver, Mistawasis Band (Plains Cree), Sask.; John Tootoosis, president, Union of Saskatchewan Indians; Rev. F.P. Kelly, chairman, legislative committee, Native Brotherhood of B.C.; Dan Manual, chief, Upper Nicola Band, B.C.; James Gladstone (Blood), president, Indian Association of Alberta; Andrew Paull (Squamish), president, North American Indian Brotherhood; W. Scow, president, Native Brotherhood of B.C.; W. Cory, legal advisor, Department of Citizenship and Immigration; J. Thompson, president, Indian Association of Manitoba; G. Barker, chief, Hollow Water Band, Man.; L. Pelletier, Manitoulin I. Unceded Band, Ont. third row: Walter Harris, minister of the Department of Citizenship and Immigration; D. Mackay, director of the Indian Affairs Branch of the Department; Paul Martin, minister of National Health and Welfare; Laval Fortier, deputy minister of Citizenship and Immigration; Albert Manyfingers, Blood Indian Res., Alta.; L.L. Brown, solicitor, Indian Affairs Branch; T.R.L. MacInnes, secretary, Indian Affairs Branch. The Indian Affairs Branch was under the Department of Citizenship and Immigration until 1966, when the Department of Indian Affairs and Northern Development was established. Photographed in Ottawa, Ont., Feb. 1951.

their Indian status under the federal government's reconciliation policy in 1985.

## Policy Alternatives, 1948–1970

### Integration

From 1948 to 1970, there was public interest in improving living conditions on Indian reserves and enhancing government funding for Indian social programs. By the early 1950s, registered Indians were receiving the same social welfare benefits that were available to all Canadians, including mothers' allowances, pensions for disabled and blind persons, old age security, and old age assistance (Shewell 2004:228–259).

During this period, federal intervention in the North led to many changes in Inuit lifeway. Two large housing projects were established with the goal of having all Inuit settled in permanent communities by 1971 (Bruce 1969:3). A system of federal day schools with church-run hostels was implemented during the 1950s and secondary schools were constructed in the 1960s (Duffy 1988:97–105, 118–121; Hobart and Kupfer 1974:13–17; King 2006; Simpson and Wattie 1968:1; Welsman 1976:35–37). Permanent housing and increased access to medical services lowered the incidence of tuberculosis and other diseases (Barsh 1994:17; Duffy 1988: 67–71). Acculturation of Inuit to southern Canadian culture, and to wage labor in particular, was seen as a way to improve the Inuit standard of living (Chartrand 1987:241; Rockwood 1955:1–3). Beginning in 1945, Inuit were given disks with identification numbers ("E" or Eskimo numbers) to facilitate administration of the Family Allowance program. E-numbers were discontinued in 1968 when Inuit were registered federally according to surnames that they selected (Alia 1994:51–55; Roberts 1975:24–31; D.G. Smith 1993:41–58; Canada 1993:iv).

*209*

Beginning in 1953, senior branch officials conducted a series of regional and national consultation meetings with selected Indian leaders and Indian Affairs field staff. The actors in the Indian policy community were social scientists, adult education experts, and community development specialists, who were consulted to improve the content and strategy of the program to integrate Indian peoples into Canadian society (Leslie 1999:244–261). Under contract by the Indian Affairs Branch, Dr. Harry Hawthorn and a group of anthropologists from the University of British Columbia prepared a study that provided insights into Indian acculturation and social adjustment (Hawthorn, Belshaw, and Jamieson 1958). The National Commission on the Indian Canadian (the forerunner of the 1960 Indian-Eskimo Association) was established. This organization informally provided Indian Branch officials and the public with information on Indian history, languages, and cultures, social welfare issues, education, and community planning measures (Leslie 1999:268–269).

During the 1950s, for the first time since the Depression, the Indian Affairs Branch underwent a significant reorganization and expansion through the addition of new divisions. These were: Reserves and Trusts, Education, Welfare, Economic Development, Construction, and Administration. The Indian Affairs Branch also began to decentralize its operations and established new regional offices, mainly in western Canada (Canada 1959:4–34).

Increased government funding, structural reorganization of the branch, and insights from outside experts nudged the Indian Affairs Branch in new directions. Social workers and community development officers were hired to improve living conditions on Indian reserves. Roads, housing, and buildings on reserves were either repaired or rebuilt. A revolving economic development fund was established within the Economic Development Division to provide short-term loans to Indians wishing to establish new businesses or other economic ventures. Finally, a new strategy for Indian education was adopted that involved, wherever possible, the integration of Indian children into the local provincial school system (Canada 1959:1–27).

It was during the 1950s that the Indian Affairs Branch began to rethink its philosophy and longstanding approach to Indian issues. The branch had traditionally guarded its jurisdictional turf from what it regarded as provincial encroachment. However, the expanded postwar Indian policy community recognized that the help of outside experts, academics, federal government departments and agencies, and provincial departments was essential if Indian reserve living conditions, as well as Indians' social, political, and economic integration, was to proceed.

Coupled with an emerging partnership approach to Indian administration, Indian Affairs officials recognized that elected and traditionally organized Indian band councils needed to have expanded authority and powers over local affairs; the term used was "self-government." Branch officials viewed the jurisdiction of Indian band councils as similar to rural non-Indian municipalities. For example, section 80 of the 1951 Indian Act conferred powers on band councils to develop by-laws in areas such as the: regulation of traffic; observance of law and order; prevention of trespass; construction and maintenance of roads, bridges, fences and local works; health; subdivision of reserve lands; protection of fish and game; and the construction, repair, and use of reserve buildings. Under section 82, those chiefs and councils of Indian bands that were in "an advanced stage of development" could license local businesses, trades, and occupations; levy taxes; appoint and pay officials to conduct band business; and authorize the expenditure of band funds (Canada 1959:7–9). In official circles, the rationale was that providing additional powers for band councils in combination with reducing the discretionary powers of the Minister of Citizenship and Immigration and increasing government funding for infrastructure and social programs would encourage band councils to assume control and management of their reserves.

The advent of Prime Minister John Diefenbaker's Progressive Conservative government in June 1957 ushered in a period of policy innovation designed to advance Indian integration. In January 1958, James Gladstone, a Blood Indian from Alberta (vol. 13:324), was appointed to the Senate to represent the interests of Indian people in Parliament (Leslie 1999:311). In 1960, qualified Indian people received the federal vote (Inuit received the federal vote in 1950). In early 1961, all provisions for compulsory Indian enfranchisement were removed from the Indian Act (Leslie 1999:324–325).

A second Joint Committee of the Senate and House of Commons was struck between 1959 and 1961 to investigate Indian policy and administration. In its 1961 final report, the Joint Committee issued a number of policy recommendations. The Indian Affairs Branch actively promoted some of its recommendations including the establishment of an Indian Claims Commission and major Indian Act revisions (Leslie 1999:304–392). The Progressive Conservative government was defeated at the federal election of 1963. The Liberal government headed by Lester B. Pearson pursued the creation of an Indian Claims Commission but decided to defer reforming the Indian Act.

*Citizens Plus*

Lester Pearson's government decided that the time was right to study "the Indian problem" as a part of its war on poverty. In the government's view, Indian integration was not proceeding so fast as expected and revised program strategies were required. In 1963, the federal government, with the support of the Indian Affairs Branch, turned to Dr. Harry Hawthorn, Dr. M.-A. Tremblay, and a team of experts to examine existing arrangements and to suggest new policy directions. The team produced a study titled *A Survey of the Contemporary Indians of Canada: Economic, Political, Educational Needs and Policies* (Canada 1966, 1967).

This study was the most comprehensive nongovernmental analysis of Indian conditions and Indian policy and administration in Canadian history. The report contained over 90 recommendations, including a proposal that the Indian Affairs Branch should gain departmental status and assume a greater advocacy role in government for Indian peoples (Canada 1966–1967:13–20). The most important policy recommendation departed from traditional thought regarding Indian integration and suggested instead that Indian people be considered "citizens plus" (Canada 1966–1967:13). This term affirmed the notion of an asymmetrical citizenship and recognized that Indian people possessed special rights and privileges arising from the provisions of historic Indian treaties, the Indian Act and various government programs. For a short while, the recommendations seemed to provide insights on how to deal with the "Indian question."

In 1966, just as the Hawthorn-Tremblay team was in the process of its investigation, the Indian Affairs Branch gained departmental status when it was linked with the Northern Affairs Branch to form the new Department of Indian Affairs and Northern Development. The Hawthorn report's recommendations seemed to provide a philosophy and blueprint for the new department's operations. Political events, however, intervened and sharply turned the course of Aboriginal policy.

*Termination*

In April 1968, Pierre Trudeau replaced Lester Pearson as Prime Minister of Canada. For a number of years, Canadian federal politicians had been faced with demands from political leaders in the province of Quebec for either special provincial status within Confederation or for political separation from Canada. Pierre Trudeau was vehemently opposed to both concepts. Trudeau's political philosophy stressed traditional liberal-democratic values that emphasized the rights of the individual, equality before the law, and equal opportunity. His opposition to special status for Quebec was reflected in his opposition to the concept of Indian people possessing special rights as "citizens plus," as well as to the continuation of the Department of Indian Affairs and Northern Development as an agency for addressing and promoting the needs of Indian peoples within government.

*The Statement of the Government of Canada on Indian Policy, 1969*

In the summer of 1968, meetings were held across Canada with a view to revising the Indian Act. A national meeting of Indian leaders and government officials was scheduled for spring 1969 to discuss legislative amendments. In June 1969, instead of convening a national policy forum, the federal government presented recommendations for Indian policy in a document titled *Statement of the Government of Canada on Indian Policy*, popularly known as the White Paper. The theme of the White Paper was "termination": termination of Indian status, termination of the existing Indian reserve system, and termination of the Department of Indian Affairs and Northern Development (Canada 1969:1–13). In the document, Indian claims to Aboriginal title (or ownership of land) were rejected. Claims involving lawful obligations in regard to land and treaty issues were referred to an Indian Claims Commissioner, Dr. Lloyd Barber, for adjudication. Neither Métis nor Inuit was mentioned in the White Paper.

Indian peoples, their leaders, their political associations, and Canadian supporters were outraged by the White Paper proposals. The new Indian policy recommendations did not reflect the proposals broached at the earlier consultation meetings. A "termination psychosis" gripped Indian communities across Canada (Weaver 1981:171–189). Indian political associations and band councils mobilized immediately. Assisted by federal government funding, a series of Indian counter-proposals appeared from the Indian Association of Alberta, the Manitoba Indian Brotherhood, the Federation of Saskatchewan Indians, and other interested groups (Drees 2002:166–171). The National Indian Brotherhood, a national Indian political organization whose membership contained representation from provincial organizations, was the successor to the National Indian Council that had been organized a decade earlier. A subcommittee of the National Indian Brotherhood, the National Committee on Indian Rights and Treaties, was established to investigate claim-related issues.

In the face of stiff Aboriginal and non-Aboriginal opposition, the federal government formally withdrew its policy proposals in July 1970. Prime Minister Pierre Trudeau introduced a conciliatory note by requesting suggestions for policy direction from Aboriginal associations (Weaver 1981:198–204). To deflect Indian anger, the Privy Council Office began funding the National Committee on Indian Rights and Treaties to research claim-related issues. An indirect consequence of this government funding was the gradual emergence of an Indian "rights" agenda.

Between 1945 and the withdrawal of the White Paper in 1970, living conditions of Aboriginal people, and Aboriginal policy and administration, underwent intensive Parliamentary and academic scrutiny. The direction of Indian policy, in particular, had shifted from emphasizing the socioeconomic and political integration of Indian peoples to promoting Indian peoples as "citizens plus" and, finally, to recommending the termination of Indian legal status, Indian reserves, and the Department of Indian Affairs and Northern Development. The White Paper left a bitter legacy; Aboriginal peoples' trust in government integrity and intentions was severely shaken.

**Policy Fragmentation: the 1970s**

The withdrawal of the White Paper (fig. 2) left a number of unanswered policy questions for Canadians. What was the

Fig. 2. Minister of Indian and Northern Affairs Jean Chrétien speaking to Indian delegates concerning their response—the Red Paper—to the Canadian government in Ottawa, 1970. Prime Minster Pierre Trudeau is seated to the left of Chrétien. At this meeting the White Paper on Indian policy was withdrawn. Photograph by Duncan Cameron, 1970.

future for the Department of Indian Affairs and Northern Development, and what would be the department's goal for Indian policy? Did Aboriginal people want to integrate into Canadian society, or did they wish to retain their cultural, social, economic and political institutions? Could Canadian society accommodate political, economic, and social diversity from its first citizens?

## A New Environment for Development of Aboriginal Policy

The early 1970s witnessed two major developments that fundamentally altered the course of Canadian Aboriginal policy. In the absence of political and bureaucratic leadership, the Supreme Court of Canada and, to a lesser degree, the Federal Court of Canada emerged as major players in Aboriginal policy development. The influence and authority of the courts was inadvertently strengthened in 1982 by Section 35(1) of the Constitution Act, which affirmed the existing Aboriginal and treaty rights of Canada's Aboriginal peoples—Indians, Métis, and Inuit.

Aboriginal policy making was also affected by the federal government's multiculturalism policy that celebrated the ethnic diversity of Canadian society and encouraged cultural minorities to retain aspects of their heritage. The multiculturalism policy encouraged Aboriginal peoples to reject assimilation and to rediscover their respective histories, languages and cultural practices. Cultural renaissance and pride was reflected by the adoption of the term "First Nations" to replace Indian bands.

During the 1960s, Inuit became concerned over the federal government's development and exploitation of Northern nonrenewable resources. In 1971, Inuit created Inuit Tapirisat of Canada (changed to Inuit Tapiriit Kanatami in 2001) to represent their concerns to the federal government

(Nunavut 1999). During the 1970s, Aboriginal organizations, such as the National Indian Brotherhood and Inuit Tapiriit Kanatami, became significantly involved in the development of an Aboriginal policy agenda that focused on the settlement of land claims, the assertion of treaty and Aboriginal rights, the recognition of Aboriginal self-government, and the devolution of federal programs to Aboriginal governments.

## An Indian Claims Policy, 1973

In 1973, the issue of Indian claims suddenly came to the fore again in *Calder* v. *Attorney-General of British Columbia*. In this case, the Supreme Court of Canada dealt with the continued existence of Aboriginal title and rights of the Nisga'a tribe in the Nass River valley in northern British Columbia (Isaac 2004:32–39). Although the Supreme Court justices were evenly split on the issue, their historical analysis and legal reasoning prompted the federal government to issue a "Statement on Claims of the Indian and Inuit People" in August 1973 ("Nisga'a," this vol.) (Canada 1973:1–6).

The claims policy document recognized two categories of claims—comprehensive and specific claims. Comprehensive claims involved unextinguished Aboriginal interests to lands and resources that arose in nontreaty areas. Comprehensive claims were geographically located in Quebec, the Maritimes, northern Canada, and British Columbia. The second category, specific claims, involved unresolved treaty issues including treaty land entitlement, irregularities surrounding reserve land surrenders, and improper administration of Indian band assets. Government funding, in the form of contribution and loan funds, was provided to Aboriginal researchers to document claim submissions. In 1974, the Office of Native Claims was established within the Department of Indian Affairs and Northern Development to validate and negotiate land claim agreements. The first comprehensive claim agreement (these agreements are referred to as modern treaties) was the 1975 James Bay and Northern Quebec Agreement, among the federal government, the provincial government of Quebec, and the Cree and Inuit of northern Quebec (fig. 3) ("James Bay Cree," this vol.).

Ten Comprehensive Claims settlement agreements have been signed ("Aboriginal Land Claims," this vol.). These are: the James Bay and Northern Québec Agreement (1975), the Northeastern Québec Agreement (1978), the Inuvialuit Final Agreement (1984), the Gwich'in Agreement (1992), the Nunavut Land Claims Agreement (1993), the Sahtu Dene and Métis Agreement (1994), the Nisga'a Agreement (2000), the Labrador Inuit Association Agreement (2004), the Tlicho Agreement (2005), and the Council for Yukon Indians Umbrella Final Agreement (1993).

## Efforts to Improve Indian-Government Relations

In April 1975, in an effort to rebuild trust and confidence in Indian-government relations, the federal government and

Fig. 3. Signing ceremony of the agreement-in-principle between the governments of Canada and Quebec and publicly owned Hydro-Quebec, the Grand Council of the Cree, and the Northern Quebec Inuit Association, Nov. 15, 1974. The final accord, the James Bay and Northern Quebec Agreement, was signed on Nov. 15, 1975. Present are, from right, Chief Billy Diamond of the James Bay Cree; Jean Chrétien, president of the Treasury Board; John Ciaccia, member of the Quebec Assembly and representative of Premier Bourassa on the James Bay negotiation; Premier Robert Bourassa of Quebec; Charlie Watt, president of the Quebec Inuit Association, and Judd Buchanan, Minister of Indian Affairs and Northern Development.

the National Indian Brotherhood established a policy consultation process that included Joint Working Groups focusing on: government funding, rights and claims, Indian Act revision, economic development, and housing. The Minister of Indian Affairs, senior Cabinet officials, and Indian representatives were active participants. As part of the consultation process, a new government agency, the Canadian Indian Rights Commission was formed to study land claims and treaty rights issues (INAC 1997).

In 1976, as part of the policy consultation process, the Department of Indian Affairs and Northern Development issued a directive titled, "Approach to Government-Indian Relationships." The directive focused on elements essential to clarifying and strengthening the "Indian identity within Canadian society," a policy blueprint for future decades (Buchanan 1976). Polices and programs that were identified for joint National Indian Brotherhood and government investigation included: Indian Act revision, settlement of land claims and treaty issues, devolution of programs and ministerial powers to First Nation governments, environmental protection of Indian lands, expansion of social services, assured access to provincial government programs, improved reserve housing, economic development measures, and education and skills training. The agenda was ambitious; however, the Brotherhood-government consultation process foundered in April 1978. There were disagreements concerning power sharing, levels of funding, setting the policy agenda, and personality clashes. At the close of the 1970s,

the quest for an appropriate forum for the joint development of Aboriginal policy remained as elusive as ever.

## 1980–2000

From 1980 to 2005 the federal government responded to the Aboriginal policy agenda that had emerged in the 1970s and 1980s. There was a shift in the federal government's perception and conception of Aboriginal policy issues: "the old paradigm [up to1970] is characterized by a preoccupation with law, formality, and control over First Nations peoples. The new paradigm is more concerned with justice, adaptation and workable inter-cultural relations. And it conceptualizes relations between the state and First Nations as going beyond 'lawful obligations' to incorporate the historical and moral obligations in an attempt to put increasingly hostile and unproductive state-aboriginal relations onto a new and useful footing" (Weaver 1990:12–15).

The major policy components of the new Aboriginal agenda focused on land claims, treaty and Aboriginal rights issues, self-government, and the devolution of programs to First Nation governments. A theme of reconciliation was introduced with the investigation of residential school abuse claims, and the reinstatement of First Nation women who had been forced to enfranchise under Section 12(1)(b) of the 1951 Indian Act. The legitimacy of the Aboriginal policy agenda was indirectly strengthened by the Constitution Act of 1982; the creation of a Royal Commission on Aboriginal Peoples (1991); issuance of the Inherent Right to Self-Government Policy (1995); and the federal government's response to the Royal Commission, "Gathering Strength: Canada's Aboriginal Action Plan (1998)."

### The Constitution Act, 1982

In 1980, the Liberals returned to power under Pierre Trudeau. During the election campaign, Trudeau had promised to patriate the Canadian constitution, meaning that the ultimate government authority would be in Canada, not the United Kingdom (fig. 4). This was accomplished via the Constitution Act, 1982, with an accompanying Charter of Rights and Freedoms. Section 35(2) of the Constitution Act stated that the Indians, Métis, and Inuit were the Aboriginal peoples of Canada. Section 35(1) affirmed the existing treaty and Aboriginal rights of Aboriginal peoples (Isaac 2004:370–371). These constitutional arrangements posed something of a conundrum for the Department of Indian Affairs and Northern Development, as it had never assumed full jurisdictional responsibility for either the Métis or Inuit.

### Government Relations with the Métis

The Métis people are of mixed Indian and European ancestry. In the late nineteenth century, during the negotiation of

213

AP Images.

Fig. 4. Signing of the constitution. Queen Elizabeth II, center, signing Canada's constitutional proclamation in Ottawa on April 17, 1982, as Prime Minister Pierre Trudeau, seated left, looks on. Photograph by Ron Poling.

numbered Treaties 1 to11 in western Canada, the Department of the Interior issued money and land scrip to those Métis who did not wish to adhere to treaty (Spry and McCardle 1993). The Department of Indian Affairs dealt with the issue of Indian status by discharging and re-admitting Métis to the numbered Indian treaties. Those Métis who took money or land scrip did not receive benefits from the numbered Indian treaties, nor were they under the jurisdiction of the Indian Act. They became Canadian citizens.

Until the patriation of the Constitution, and the designation of Métis as one of Canada's Aboriginal peoples, the Department of Indian Affairs regarded the Métis as a provincial responsibility (Isaac 2004:277–285). Their inclusion suggested that the federal government, in particular the Department of Indian Affairs and Northern Development, had some constitutional responsibility for their well-being. In response to this situation, the position of Federal Interlocutor for Métis and Non-Status Indians was created.

The role of the Federal Interlocutor was created in 1985 to provide a point of contact between the federal government of Canada and national Aboriginal organizations that represent Métis, non-Status Indians, and urban Aboriginal people to discuss their priority issues (INAC 2006). Since 2004, the Minister of Indian Affairs and Northern Development has assumed the Interlocutor's role. In 2003, the Supreme Court of Canada began to map out the nature of existing Aboriginal rights of the Métis under Section 35(1), Constitution Act, 1982. In two cases, *R* v. *Powley* [2003] 2 S.C.R. 207, 2003 SCC 43, and *R* v. *Blais* [2003] 2 S.C.R. 236, 2003, SCC 44, the hunting rights of the Métis were clarified and affirmed (Isaac 2004:277–285). The Supreme Court is expected to be active in identifying and defining additional Métis Aboriginal rights as well as the extent of federal jurisdiction over Métis and non-Status Indians under Section 91 (24), Constitution Act, 1982.

Inuit, the primary inhabitants of the Arctic, live in Nunavut, the Northwest Territories, northern Quebec, and Labrador. Historically, the Department of Indian Affairs and Northern Development has had limited responsibility for Inuit administration and policy. There is no separate legislation, such as the Indian Act, for Inuit as there is for Indians. There are no Inuit reserves and no departmental registry for issuing certificates of status to Inuit. Indeed, the federal government has studiously avoided linking Indian and Inuit policy and administration.

In 1939, the Supreme Court of Canada held that, in *Re: Eskimo* Inuit were constitutionally classed as Indians (Diubaldo 1981). This distinction, based on historical documents dating from the 1700s, made Inuit the legal responsibility of the federal government. After World War II, federal authorities determined that Inuit policy and administration should remain distinct from Indian administration. The Indian Act of 1951 specifically excluded Inuit from its ambit (S.C. 1951, c. 29 s. 4).

Inuit received programs and services from various levels of government. In 1941, the federal government adopted the E [Eskimo]-number system to identify Inuit who were eligible to receive government-funded medical services and social welfare benefits. It was administered by the Department of Resources and Development, 1950–1953, and by the Department of Northern Affairs and National Resources, 1953–1968. Between 1945 and 1972, all Inuit interaction with the federal, territorial, and provincial governments required the use of E-numbers (D.G. Smith 1993:41–74). In 1968, the Northwest Territories Council launched Project Surname, requesting Inuit to provide given and family names in order to acheive standardized spellings. By 1972, Inuit enumeration was complete (Alia 1994:51–55; Canada 1993; Roberts 1975:26–31).

Since the 1980s, the Department of Indian Affairs and Northern Development has played an important role in the affairs of Aboriginal peoples north of 60° north latitude. As part of the initiatives to foster a northern renaissance, the Department has taken the lead in negotiating comprehensive land claim agreements that have facilitated northern political evolution and resource development. Inuit now play a major role in the government of Nunavut and will play major roles in the Nunatsiavut government in eastern Labrador. They are also in charge of framing policies and programs for the sustainable development of the North.

In May 2005, the Inuit Relations Secretariat was established within the Department of Indian Affairs. The Secretariat plays a coordinating role in advancing important policy areas for Inuit such as housing, health care, and education. The role of the Secretariat is designed to form an important part in the proposed partnership agreement with Inuit Tapiriit Kanatami to improve Inuit living conditions in the north (Inuit Tapiriit Kanatami 2004).

*Settlement of Comprehensive and Specific Land Claims*

Both the Federal and Supreme courts were active in establishing the acceptance criteria for comprehensive claims (*Baker Lake* v. *Minister of Indian Affairs and Northern Development*, 1979), in defining the spectrum of Aboriginal rights (*Delgamuukw* v. *British Columbia*, 1997), demonstrating the importance of oral histories as evidence in the proof of Aboriginal title (*Delgamuukw* v. *British Columbia*, 1979), establishing a test for the existence of Aboriginal rights (*R*. v. *Van der Peet*, 1996), and clarifying Aboriginal title issues in Quebec and the Atlantic Provinces (*R*. v. *Côté*, 1996). The high courts were equally active in providing guidance in Specific Claims issues and setting guidelines for the interpretation and implementation of historic Indian treaties (Isaac 2004:71–184). Although some claims have been settled, others remain (fig. 5).

For contemporary Indian administration, perhaps the most important Supreme Court decision was *R* v. *Guerin* (1984), a case that dealt with the nature of Aboriginal rights in respect to reserve land (Isaac 2004:8–9). In its decision, the Supreme Court summarized the two essential characteristics of Aboriginal title as being its inalienability, except to the Crown; and the Crown's fiduciary duty relating to issues surrounding the alienation of the Indian interest in their lands. This enforceable, equitable, and fiduciary obligation placed a high onus on the Crown, particularly on the Minister of Indian Affairs and Northern Development when acting and making decisions on behalf of Indians. The *Guerin* decision made departmental administration of Indian assets more problematic and opened the door to a new set of Indian claims based on alleged breaches of fiduciary obligations.

The Specific and Comprehensive Claims policies were updated and amended in 1982 and 1986, respectively (Canada 1998:9). In 1991, in the wake of the Oka, Quebec, crisis, the Specific Claims acceptance criteria were broadened to include the negotiation of valid pre-Confederation claims. In 1991, the federal government established an independent body, the Indian Specific Claims Commission, to hold public inquiries into specific land claim disputes (Canada 1998:iii). The Commission was mandated to hold inquiries at the request of Indian bands when the federal government had rejected a claim or where a dispute had arisen over the compensation criteria applied to settle a claim. It could also assist in mediating disputes between First Nations and the Department of Indian Affairs and Northern Development (Canada 1998:iii–iv). The Commission, which operated in tandem with the Specific Claims Branch, could only make recommendations to the federal government regarding the settlement of claims.

On 13 June 2002, Bill C-60, the Specific Claims Resolution Act, was introduced into Parliament. The purpose was to replace the Indian Specific Claims Commission with the Canadian Centre for the Independent Resolution of First Nations Specific Claims to facilitate the settlement of specific claims across Canada. There was a provision for the creation of a tribunal that could make binding decisions on the Crown. The Act was passed in November 2003, but the Centre for Claims Resolution had yet to be established in 2007.

*The British Columbia Treaty Commission Process*

The comprehensive claims situation in the Province of British Columbia is a special case. The only land cession treaties in British Columbia are Treaty 8 in the northeastern portion of the province and 14 small treaties negotiated between 1850 and 1854 on Vancouver Island. Aboriginal rights to land and resources remain unextinguished throughout the remainder of the province. The issue of unresolved land claims has complicated provincial resource development.

In 1991, a task force on land claims recommended the creation of a British Columbia Treaty Commission to negotiate comprehensive land claim settlements involving components such as self-government, sharing access to natural resources, and resource revenue sharing. A Federal Treaty Negotiation Office was established within the British Columbia Regional Office of Indian Affairs to participate claim negotiations. In 2003, 57 First Nations, two-thirds of the Aboriginal people in British Columbia were negotiating land claims as modern treaty agreements (Canada 2003:16). As of 2005, there were no final settlement agreements. The Nisga'a claim settlement in northwest British Columbia in April 2000 was settled outside the British Columbia Treaty Commission process.

*Inherent Right to Self-Government*

Historically, the Department of Indian Affairs viewed the powers accorded to Indian band councils under the Indian Act as similar in nature to those of rural municipalities (Daugherty and Madill 1983:Part Two, 10–26). This municipal government model remained in vogue until the 1970s when Native leaders sought increased jurisdiction and government funding for reserve-based Indian governments.

In December 1982, a Special Parliamentary Committee on Indian Self-Government was formed. The committee traveled across Canada hearing 567 witnesses and 215 presentations. Committee members even made excursions to Washington State and the American Southwest to examine American arrangements. When the Minister of Indian Affairs and Northern Development appeared before the Special Parliamentary Committee, he proposed a new system of First Nations government involving the transfer of powers to First Nations in such areas as health, housing, social assistance, band membership, and management and control of reserve land and trust accounts.

The Special Committee presented its final report (the Penner report) to Parliament in November 1983 (Canada 1983). The Committee's report endorsed the establishment of a "new relationship" with First Nations and the entrenchment of Aboriginal self-government in the Constitution. As

215

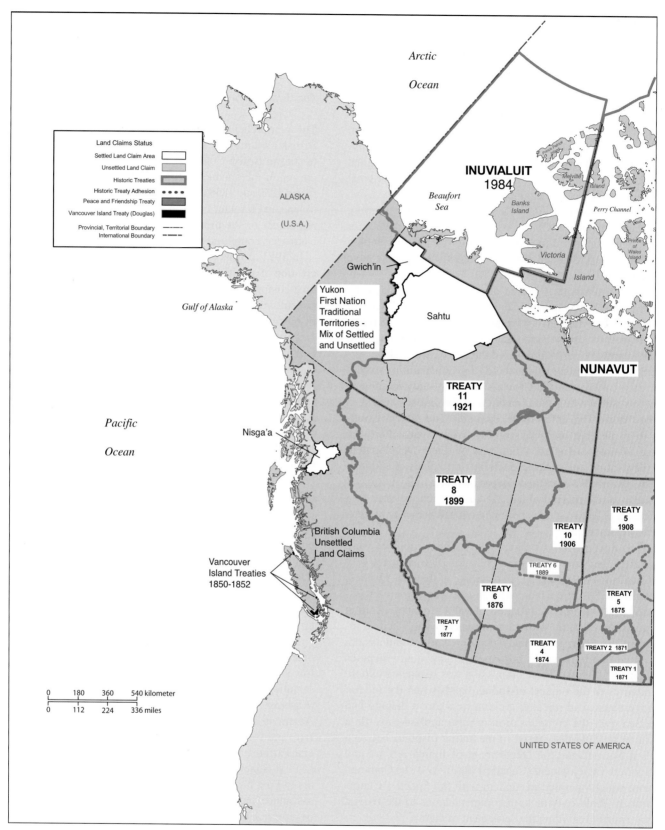

Fig. 5. Treaties and comprehensive land claims in Canada. Comprehensive land claims are based on the assertion of continuing aboriginal rights and claims to land that have not been dealt with by treaty or other means. An Indian treaty, as understood by the government of Canada and the courts, is an agreement between the Crown and a specified group or groups of Indian people (Treaty First Nations) in which the parties

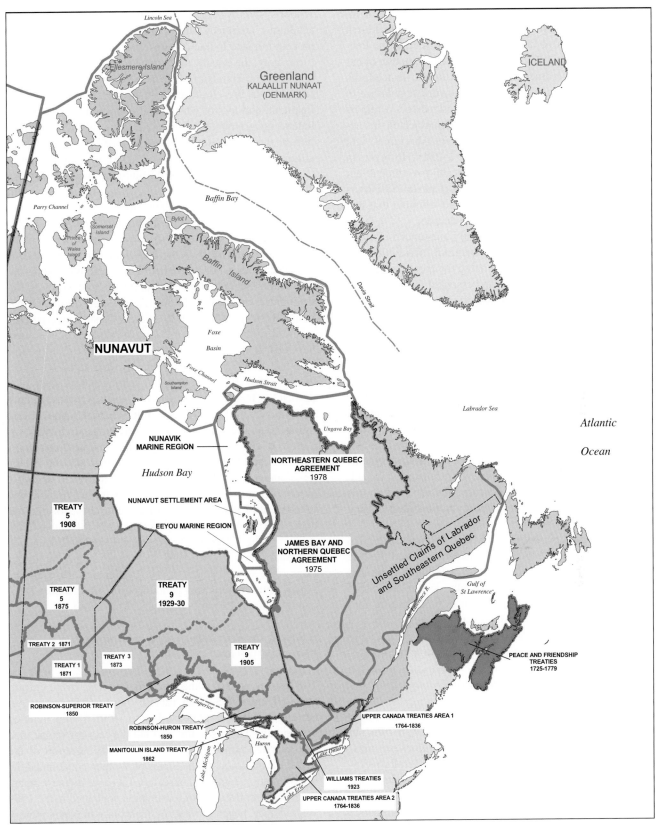

created mutual binding obligations that were to be solemnly respected. Settled land claims for the Nisga'a (Nishga), Gwich'in (Kutchin), and Sahtu (Bearlake) show only the land claim areas, not the finalized parcels within those areas. A final agreement is the outcome of successful land claim negotiations (Natural Resources Canada 2007).

an interim measure, the Penner report recommended the introduction of a "First Nation Recognition Act." In March 1984, the Minister of Indian Affairs responded to the Penner report (Canada 1984:1–7). He rejected the notion of enshrining self-government in the Constitution. Instead, the Minister proposed to introduce framework legislation to establish First Nation governments whose powers would be delegated from the minister. Indian leaders rejected this approach, arguing that they had an inherent Aboriginal right to self-government (Tennant 1984:211–224). However, in 1985, the federal government enacted self-government legislation for the Sechelt First Nation (Coastal Salish), a small, well-organized group in British Columbia that had been requesting such legislation for a decade.

The Inherent Right policy, formally announced in 1995, recognized that the scope of Aboriginal jurisdiction extended to matters that were internal to the group, integral to its distinct Aboriginal culture, and essential to its operation as a government institution. Under this approach, First Nations could negotiate for control of constitutions and internal governing structures; membership; marriage; adoption and child welfare; education; health; social services; housing; business licensing; language; culture and religion; policing; agriculture; reserve land management; taxation; and hunting, fishing and trapping on Aboriginal lands. There were other subject matters, for example, divorce, gaming, fisheries co-management, and environmental issues, where there would be shared jurisdiction with federal and provincial governments. First Nation Self-Government agreements could be implemented by a variety of mechanisms including existing historic treaties, comprehensive land claims agreements, legislation, or memoranda of understanding (INAC 1995).

The Inherent Right policy, in different formats, extended to the Métis and the Inuit. The policy recognized that the fiduciary obligations of the Minster of Indian Affairs and Northern Development would gradually decline and disappear as First Nations, Métis, and Inuit assumed greater control over their own affairs. What was not clear is where a "third order" of Aboriginal government will fit in relation to existing municipal, provincial, and federal structures.

## Settlement of Residential Schools Abuse Claims

The Indian residential school system existed in Upper Canada (Ontario) before Confederation. In part, it grew out of Canada's missionary experience with religious organizations ministering to Indians. In 1874, the federal government began to play a role in the development and administration of this system to meet legal obligations under the Indian Act. In 1879, the federal government commissioned a study of American Indian schools. The American models were adopted and modified, and in the 1880s, industrial and boarding schools were established in western Canada. The Department of Indian Affairs operated nearly every school in partnership with a religious organization. The residential school system was designed to teach Indian boys and girls academic, technical, and home making skills and, in the process, replace Indian cultures with Canadian culture. Unfortunately, the organization of the school system left operations open to claims of physical, sexual, and mental abuse, cultural loss, breach of treaty fiduciary duties, forcible confinement, and loss of educational opportunity. In 1969, the federal government assumed total responsibility for operation of the Indian day, residential, and boarding schools, although the churches were still active in many instances (Indian Residential Schools Resolution Canada 29 January 2001). Most residential schools ceased to operate in the 1970s, as provincial school integration progressed. The last federally run residential school closed in 1996.

In 1990, the first claim of alleged residential school abuse was received. In 1996, some 200 claims were received. In response to allegations from both First Nations and Inuit, the Residential School Unit at Indian Affairs and Northern Development was created. In 2001, a new government Office, Indian Residential Schools Resolution Canada, emerged and reported to the Minister of Public Works and Government Services. It was estimated that 80,000 Aboriginal people who had attended residential schools were still alive. From them, 16,687 Indian residential school claims were filed against the federal government of Canada. Of these claims, 3,910 have been resolved (Indian Residential Schools Resolution, Canada June 2006). Many claimants are included in a series of class action lawsuits against churches, missionary societies, and the federal government. In 2005, the federal government appointed a special representative to negotiate an out of court settlement. An Agreement in Principle was reached with legal counsel for the churches, former students, and the Assembly of First Nations in November 2005. As part of the settlement, an Aboriginal Healing Foundation was established in April 1998, and related support organizations were soon formed. A final settlement of residential school abuse claims was announced in 2006 (Indian Residential Schools Resolution Canada, May 2006).

## Bill C-31, the Reinstatement of Enfranchised Aboriginal Women

The historic goal of Canadian Indian policy was to enfranchise all Indians. Section 12(1)(b) of the 1951 Indian Act automatically enfranchised Indian women who married non-Indians. However, this was not the case for Indian men who married non-Indian women. In 1970, a report of the Royal Commission on the Status of Women condemned the discrimination contained in section 12(1)(b). Indian women, upset at the philosophy of termination contained in the 1969 White Paper, began to focus on their place in contemporary Aboriginal society. In the early 1970s, two Indian women, Jeannette Corbière Lavell (Ojibwa from Wikwemikong Reserve) and Yvonne Bedard (Iroquois from Six Nations Reserve), legally challenged section 12(1)(b) of the Indian Act as discriminatory (Isaac 2004:511–513). Their court cases brought national attention to the plight of enfranchised Indian women and attracted support from national and provincial Aboriginal women's organizations. In 1977, Sandra Lovelace, a Maliseet from the Tobique Reserve, New Brunswick, brought the issue of Indian Act discrimination to the attention of the United Nations Human Rights Committee. The recently established Canadian Human Rights Commission became involved. In 1981, Canada was found to be in contravention of the United Nations Covenant on Civil and Political Rights (Isaac 2004:514–516). In 1982, a Parliamentary Sub-Committee on Indian Women and the Indian Act recommended that section 12(1)(b) be repealed. The situation became more perilous for the federal government because section 15 of the Charter of Rights and Freedoms, which would become effective on 1 April 1985, condemned all forms of discrimination. The federal government had only three years to rectify the situation.

The federal response was Bill C-31. It was introduced into Parliament in 1984 and became law in June 1985 (Isaac 2004:508–509). The legislation was designed to remove discrimination against Indian women by creating a nondiscriminatory legal concept for defining "Indian" under the Indian Act.

The legislation was not popular with male-dominated First Nations governments or with First Nations political organizations. Many First Nations leaders felt that the reinstatement of Indian women to band lists and the potential return of these women to their reserves would strain already limited education, health, housing, and social welfare services. There was concern that traditional Indian cultures would be disrupted by the arrival of newcomers. There were also arguments that Bill C-31 just perpetuated discrimination against Indian women in a different form. Children of Indian men, for example, could be registered and automatically be accorded full band membership under section 6(1). On the other hand, children of reinstated Indian women fell under section 6(2). This meant that they were only conditional band members who were subject to First Nation approval (Isaac 2004:508–509).

To ease the situation, band membership codes that accompanied Bill C-31 allowed First Nation governments to maintain their own membership lists. Bands were also given the authority to restrict reserve residency.

Bill C-31 was an effort to establish an acceptable compromise that would eliminate sexual discrimination in the Indian Act, while still allowing bands some control over their own membership. By the end of 1999, 133,134 applications had been received. Fifty-five percent of applications were approved, amounting to 73,554 reinstatements. In 1990, the Status Indian population of Canada stood at 478,355, 15 percent of whom were Bill C-31 reinstatements.

The reinstatement of Indian women put pressure on both the federal government and on First Nations administrations. For example, in 1990, in addition to regular Indian program funding, $338,000,000 was spent on Bill C-31 registrants for health, housing, and postsecondary educa-

tion. First Nations wanted the Department of Indian Affairs and Northern Development to create new bands and reserves to accommodate the reinstated population. Officials replied that new reserves would be created only if there was a legal requirement and so long as no additional financial expenditures were required. This approach put pressure on the existing Indian reserve land base. The only way that many Indian reserves could physically expand their territory was through specific and comprehensive claim negotiations, or by Treaty Land Entitlement settlements in the Prairies. Thus, Indian policy in one sector drove policy considerations in another.

### The Royal Commission on Aboriginal Peoples, 1991–1996

In the summer of 1990, the issue of land rights at Oka, Quebec, made international news when the First Nation at Kanesatake and their supporters blockaded a road and occupied a building to prevent the local municipality from expanding a golf club onto lands claimed by the Kanesatake First Nation (York and Pindera 1992). The federal government attempted to resolve the immediate issue by purchasing a portion of the land in question for the people of Kanesatake.

However, the broader question of the place of Aboriginal peoples in modern Canadian society remained. Prime Minister Brian Mulroney responded by establishing a Royal Commission on Aboriginal Peoples in 1991, chaired by Georges Erasmus (former president of the Dene Nation in the Northwest Territories) and Judge René Dussault. The Royal Commission issued its five-volume report in November 1996 after an extensive consultation and research process that investigated almost every aspect of Aboriginal life in Canada. The Royal Commission made 440 recommendations (Library of Parliament 2000). Among the major proposals, the commission called for massive increases in government spending to address housing and health problems and to promote economic development. The commissioners recommended that a House of First Peoples be created to function as a parliament for Aboriginal peoples across the country and to provide advice to the federal parliament. The commission sought formal recognition of an Aboriginal third order of government, subject to the Charter of Rights and Freedoms and with authority over matters related to the good government and welfare of Aboriginal peoples. This recommendation included recognition of Métis self-government, provision of a land base, and recognition of Métis rights to hunt and fish on Crown land.

Another set of recommendations suggested that the Department of Indian Affairs and Northern Development be replaced by two new departments. One department would implement the proposed new relationship with Aboriginal peoples while the other would provide services for non-self-governing Aboriginal communities. The objective of the commission's 20-year action plan was to improve Aboriginal living conditions and to establish productive relationships 219 among Aboriginal peoples, non-Aboriginal peoples, and the federal government.

## Gathering Strength: Canada's Aboriginal Action Plan, 1998

The Royal Commission report was well received by Aboriginal groups and generated expectations for a government response. In December 1996, the Prime Minister said that the federal government needed time to study the recommendations. The Minister of Indian Affairs stated that it would be difficult to increase spending to the levels proposed by the commission. In April 1997, the Assembly of First Nations held a national day of protest to express its anger over government inaction.

In January 1998, the Minister of Indian Affairs responded to the Royal Commission study with "Gathering Strength: Canada's Aboriginal Action Plan." This plan set out a policy framework based on four objectives: renewing the partnership, strengthening Aboriginal governance, developing a new fiscal relationship, and supporting strong communities, people, and economies. Many of the initiatives were aimed at developing the capacity of Aboriginal peoples to design, negotiate, and finance self-governing institutions. Resources were earmarked for improving reserve infrastructure including housing, fresh water, and sewer systems. In addition, a $350 million Aboriginal Healing Fund was established to address the legacy of abuse in the residential school system.

## The Twenty-First Century

### Aboriginal People

In 2005 there were 458,600 on-reserve Status Indians and 285,200 who resided off-reserve. Status Indians living on reserve represented about 62 percent of the Status Indian population. In total, there were 614 First Nation communities, comprising 52 nations or cultural groups and more than 50 languages. About 61 percent of First Nation communities had fewer than 500 residents, and only 6 percent had more than 2,000. Overall, 35 percent of on-reserve Status Indians lived in urban areas, while 45 percent lived in rural areas (Treasury Board of Canada Secretariat 2005).

The on-reserve Status Indian population is projected to increase by 53 percent from 2004 to 2021, compared with 11 percent for the Canadian population as a whole. It should be noted that 40 percent of the Status Indian population is under the age of 20, compared with 25 percent for the overall Canadian population. These demographic figures, coupled with generally poor living conditions on many reserves, demonstrate some of the socioeconomic challenges facing the Department (Treasury Board of Canada Secretariat 2005).

Of the 976,305 people who identified themselves as Aboriginal in the 2001 Canadian census, about 5 percent, or 45,070, reported they were Inuit. Fully one-half of the Inuit population, about 22,560, lived in the territory of Nunavut. Quebec is second with 9,535, or 21 percent of the total, followed by Labrador with 10 percent of the Inuit population, and the Northwest Territories with 9 percent (Statistics Canada 2001).

According to the 2001 Canadian Census, the Métis population from Ontario westward was 262,785. In September 2002, the Métis people adopted a national definition for citizenship within the Métis Nation. Based on this definition, it is estimated that there are 350,000 to 400,000 Métis in Canada. The Métis do not live on reserve lands. There are a number of Métis settlements in the province of Alberta ("Métis," this vol.). The provinces and municipalities are generally responsible for Métis programs and services (Métis National Council 2006).

### The Department

The mandate of the Department of Indian Affairs and Northern Development is derived from the 1985 Department of Indian Affairs and Northern Development Act, the Indian Act, territorial acts, and legal obligations arising from section 91(24) of the Constitution Act, 1867. The Department is responsible for administering over 50 regulations and statutes. Consequently, its mandate is complex, and its responsibilities encompass a wide range of services and overlap responsibilities with other federal departments.

The Department has three major "business lines": Indian and Inuit Affairs, Northern Affairs, and Departmental Management and Administration. The Department of Indian Affairs and Northern Development is a decentralized government department. Its headquarters are in Ottawa, and there are 10 regional offices located in the provinces and the territories. They are: Amherst, Nova Scotia, for the Atlantic region; Quebec City for Quebec; Toronto for Ontario; Winnipeg for Manitoba; Regina for Saskatchewan; Edmonton for Alberta; Vancouver for British Columbia; Whitehorse for the Yukon; Yellowknife for the Northwest Territories, and Iqaluit for Nunavut. In 2004–2005, the Department's annual budget amounted to $5.9 billion. Within the federal government, Aboriginal programming is shared among 14 federal departments and agencies with total expenditures of $8.8 billion. As of 1 April 2006, the Department had 3,839 employees, of whom 1,150 were Aboriginal (Daniel Ricard, personal communication 2006).

In 1999, the First Nations Land Management Act was passed by Parliament. This legislation was an initiative of 14 First Nations who wished to escape the land management provisions of the Indian Act in order to improve their capacities and opportunities for economic development. Under the Land Management Act, First Nations can develop their own land management codes. The Act is regarded as a major step in the continuing devolution of the Department of Indian Affairs's administrative responsibilities to First Nations.

The search for policies to put an end to the cycle of Aboriginal dependency has been the quest of the Indian Department since the nineteenth century. Between 1828 and 1858 there were six commissions of inquiry into Indian conditions and government administration. The 1858 report observed that the government was "groping in the dark" in its attempt to frame a viable policy for meeting the challenges (Leslie 1984:133). The report of the Royal Commission on Aboriginal Peoples (1996) offered new solutions to old problems. Will efforts at achieving an Indian-government relationship based on the settlement of land claims, the implementation of Aboriginal self-government, and the devolution of programs and services achieve a renewed relationship?

THE DEPARTMENT OF INDIAN AFFAIRS AND NORTHERN DEVELOPMENT

# Health and Health Care in Canada

JAMES B. WALDRAM

Within Canada's publicly funded health care system, citizens receive a variety of services at no or marginal cost, and the provinces control health spending and program delivery. The situation of Canada's Indian and Inuit populations is unique in that the federal government plays a prominent role in service delivery. The various provinces have only a peripheral relationship to "registered" Indians, and most matters pertaining to health and health care are handled by federal government agencies. National health standards are designed to ensure comparable services across the country. Changes in health status and health services delivery since 1980 can be related in part to broader, positive political developments in the relationship between Native peoples and federal, provincial, and territorial governments, and, paradoxically, to ongoing social, cultural, and economic marginalization.

The quality and extent of health data for Native peoples has improved immeasurably since the 1980s. However, the majority of aboriginal health research remains focused on registered Indians (referred to as First Nations individuals). These can be recognized in health data bases by a unique registration number designed initially by the federal government to keep track of those individuals for whom it had taken on a fiduciary right. Similarly, much research remains focused on relatively small Indian communities or reserves, politically bounded tracks of land that provide researchers with relatively easy access to culturally synonymous populations. The Inuit, still living primarily in the northern territories, have seen a dramatic increase in health research and, therefore, available information. In contrast, other groups, including Métis, non-Status Indians (individuals of Native heritage not included under the other three terms), and all Native peoples in urban areas, still represent significant gaps in knowledge. Particularly with respect to urbanization, knowledge has not kept pace with demographic shifts; it is not appropriate to generalize across the nation, or from reserve to urban contexts, or from cultural group to cultural group with respect to health status or health service delivery.

## Contemporary Health Profile

The earliest years, even centuries, of postcontact health history were dominated by infectious diseases and their impact (Decker 1998, 1999; Lux 2001). It was only in the late twentieth century that the impact of infectious diseases on the aboriginal population was surpassed by new scourges such as chronic, noncommunicable diseases and the effects of accidental and intentional injury and death. Infectious diseases are by no means eradicated, of course, and problems such as pneumonia, tuberculosis, and various sexually transmitted diseases certainly remain, and in some areas have seen a resurgence in incidence. These have been joined by the incidence of HIV/AIDS (Craib et al. 2003; Myers et al. 1993; Public Health Agency of Canada 2004a). However, these problems have come to be overshadowed somewhat by the more traumatic problems of self-inflicted and external injury and death. While infectious diseases have long been the target of government intervention, both to treat infected individuals and to eradicate the sources of these problems, with some measure of success, the new plague of injuries and accidents, suicide, and homicide have proven resistant to intervention efforts. Comorbidity with alcohol and substance abuse is a well recognized pattern (Kirmayer, Brass, and Tait 2000).

There have been significant gains in increasing the life expectancy of aboriginal people but only a slight reduction in the gap between them and the national population. In 1960, Aboriginal male life expectancy was around age 60, and by 2000 it was close to 70, whereas the national male population lived seven to eight years longer in each era. Aboriginal females had a 1960 life expectancy of around 65 compared to close to 75 in 2000, in comparison to the national female population with expectancies of 73 and 81 respectively (DIAND 2002; Norris 1990). A significant reduction in infant mortality over this period, the result of improvements in health service delivery and prenatal care, can explain much of this change in life expectancy. The live birth rate for Indians stood at 6.4 per 1,000, close to the national rate (Health Canada 2003a).

The demographic profile for the Native population has changed as the result of both this increase in live birth rate and a baby boom that coincided with it. The contemporary age-sex structure of the aboriginal population demonstrates a significant bulge in the 15 to 44 age brackets, compared to the more top-heavy profile for Canada as a whole. The 2001 census showed that 35 percent of Indians were under the age of 15, as were 39 percent of the Inuit and 29 percent of the

222

Métis. In contrast, only 19 percent of the national population was under age 15 (Waldram, Herring, and Young 2006:20). Conversely, only 4 percent of the Indian population was over age 65, compared to 12 percent nationally. This demographic profile explains many of the health and social issues faced by the Native population.

Overall, infectious diseases have declined considerably since the introduction of wide-spread vaccination programs in the 1950s. The virulent diseases of the past, such as measles, mumps, and poliomyelitis, no longer result in significant morbidity or mortality. Tuberculosis, a significant problem in the early and mid-twentieth century, declined steadily as well, the result of vaccinations and other antituberculosis measures (T.K. Young and R.I. Casson 1988). The impact of tuberculosis treatment on the aboriginal population was profound, with many patients forcefully removed from their homes and communities and relocated to urban sanitaria for lengthy periods (vol. 5:684–685). Individuals sometimes died in these institutions and were buried nearby, children were sometimes adopted into nonaboriginal homes, and programs of assimilation often accompanied treatment (Grygier 1994; Hader 1990; G.J. Wherrett 1965). Despite assumptions that the disease was under control and largely eliminated in most areas, in the 1980s new cases emerged, especially in the north. The tuberculosis incidence rate for First Nations stood at approximately 37 per 100,000 and at 62 per 100,000 for the Inuit, compared to the national rate of 1.4 per 100,000 for Canadian-born residents (Public Health Agency of Canada 2004; Waldram, Herring, and Young 2006:86).

The link between housing conditions and sanitation that appears to explain the persistence of infectious diseases such as tuberculosis is related to problems such as impetigo, scabies, and gastroenteritis. Contaminated water supplies and poor sewage treatment in many communities have lead to deadly outbreaks of gastroenteritis due to *Escherichia coli* (Rowe et al. 1998).

HIV/AIDS made inroads into the Native population, and, due to its links to behavior choices, is believed to be a health issue especially for urban individuals engaged in drug use and sex trade activities (Canadian Aboriginal AIDS Network 2003; Culhane 2003; Downe 2003, 2006). The number of AIDS cases in the aboriginal population— about 3 percent in 2006—is proportional to its population size but represents a significant increase over previous years (Public Health Agency of Canada 2004a). In comparison to the national population, three times more HIV/AIDS diagnoses are made for aboriginal women, and the majority of these are related to use of injected drugs (Health Canada 2000, 2003a).

Despite the overall improvement in the infectious disease situation, greater gains in health have not been made, due to increasing morbidity and mortality resulting from an increase in chronic, degenerative diseases such as cancer, heart disease, and diabetes on one hand (vol. 3:795), and sudden, traumatic death on the other hand. While there has been a steady decline in overall mortality rates since 1950, these scourges have dramatically changed the health profile of the population.

Cardiovascular diseases have emerged since the 1970s as a particular problem for aboriginal people. Ischemic heart disease, in the form of heart attacks, and stroke mortality and morbidity in particular are believed to be linked to changes in behavior, such as tobacco smoking and lack of physical activity, and diet. The age-standardized mortality rate for all cardiovascular diseases among the First Nations population was slightly higher than for the national population in 1999–2000, and while the rate for ischemic heart disease alone was on par with the national population, for stroke specifically it was 1.4 times higher in First Nations women and 1.7 times higher in First Nations men (Health Canada 2003a; Waldram, Herring, and Young 2006:93). Age-specific hospitalization rates for all cardiovascular diseases combined are also higher among the Indian population in many regions than among Canadians as a whole. The Inuit consistently demonstrate lower rates than other aboriginal peoples of such "lifestyle" diseases. Hypertension, a risk factor for cardiovascular disease, appears to be higher in aboriginal populations. A national health self-report survey determined that Indian men had a prevalence rate 2.8 times the national and that Indian women had a rate 2.5 times higher (NAHO 2004; Waldram, Herring, and Young 2006:95).

Diabetes rates among the aboriginal Canadian population, as is the case for many other indigenous populations in the world, reached alarming levels since the 1970s. This is particularly the case for type 2 diabetes. Overall prevalence in most areas of Canada appears to be two to five times the national rates (vol. 3:794–795). Certain groups, such as the Mohawk (Montour, Macaulay, and Adelson 1989) and Oneida (Evers et al. 1987) in the south, and the Cree-Ojibwa (T.K. Young et al. 1985) in the north, have particularly high rates (fig. 1). Other groups, such as the Inuit and northern Athapaskans, appear to have prevalence rates that are much lower. Generally, rates are lowest in the Northwest Territories and highest in the Atlantic provinces (T.K. Young et al. 1990). A link may exist between genetic susceptibility and environmental factors in understanding differential prevalence rates; for instance, prevalence seems to vary by language family and latitude. Many confounding factors exist, such as increased urbanization in southern areas and differing histories of colonization. Self-report data indicate that the prevalence of diabetes for First Nations populations around 2000 exceeded that of both women and men in the national population. Hospitalization data confirm these figures. Like heart disease, lifestyle factors, such as diet and physical activity, appear alongside heredity as explanatory factors. Obesity as a risk factor for diabetes and other health problems emerged, all the more alarming given that some aboriginal populations at mid-twentieth century, notably Inuit in the High Arctic, were starving (Waldram, Herring, and Young 2006).

Alta. Health and Wellness, Edmonton.

Fig. 1. Diabetes education. Kathleen Cardinal, Goodfish Lake Cree (Plains Cree), a diabetes nurse educator, explains blood sugars to Rose Vermillion, Mikisew Cree First Nation, at the Aboriginal Wellness Program, Capitol Health. Photograph by Josie Auger, Edmonton, Alta., 2005.

Cancer appears to be one disease that is less common within the aboriginal population than nationally. Aboriginal oral traditions suggest that this disease was rare as late as the mid-twentieth century, but it has become more prominent since the 1980s as the population's lifespan has increased. While the aboriginal population appears to have lower overall cancer incidence rates—that is, across all sites (Gallagher and Elwood 1979; T.K. Young and J.W. Frank 1983; T.K. Young and N.W. Choi 1985)—they appear to have higher rates in specific sites, such as the cervix for women and kidney for men. Further, the high prevalence of tobacco smoking among the aboriginal population does not bode well for their health (Northwest Territories 2004; Reading 1996), and an increase in lung and other cancers due to smoking can be expected.

Morbidity and mortality due to accidents and violence pose a significant challenge to health and social planners in much of aboriginal Canada. As of 2000, the age-standardized mortality rate from accidental injury and violence was roughly three times higher than for the national population (Waldram, Herring, and Young 2006:103).

Injury and death due to motor vehicle accidents, fire, drowning, and suicide are particularly problematic. The problem is acute in the younger age brackets. While to a significant extent these problems are explainable by the life circumstances of many Native people—the northern lifestyle involving guns for hunting and overland and water travel, for instance—they also speak to broader social problems and mental health issues. Alcohol use in particular is linked with many accidental injuries and deaths (Jarvis and Boldt 1982; Kirmayer et al. 1994). Suicide, which has reached alarming proportions in some aboriginal communities, has been clearly linked to alcohol and substance abuse. One study in Manitoba, for instance, demonstrated that not only were Indian suicides younger than the national population—27 years to 45 years—but also blood alcohol levels among the suicides were twice as high as among non-Indian suicides (Malchy et al. 1997). The spontaneous nature of many of these suicides may be reflected in the fact that they were much less likely to seek out counseling or other assistance.

For many health professionals, alcohol and other substance use remain the most pernicious health issues in many Native communities. Research that has attempted to link such abuse to a unique aboriginal genetic susceptibility has proven methodologically and conceptually problematic, and most researchers focus more on issues of social, cultural, and economic disruption to traditional lifestyles as the root of the problem (Waldram 2004). Co-morbidity with other health problems is extensive, from liver disease to accidents and violence. Young people have gravitated to gasoline sniffing.

A thread that clearly weaves throughout this section is the link between health problems and social, cultural, and economic conditions. Despite many years of government programming and improvements, Natives lag behind national standards on income and education levels and employment rates (Statistics Canada 2003). For instance, while 62 percent of Canadians were employed according to the 2000 census, only 50 percent of the Native population had jobs. Forty-three percent of the Native population had an income under $10,000, compared to 28 percent of Canadians. While 31 percent of the national population had not completed high school, 48 percent of the aboriginal population had not. Housing conditions in both aboriginal communities and urban centers failed to achieve most national standards. A federal government assessment in 2000, for instance, rated the adequacy of housing on reserves to be only 56 percent, that is, not requiring renovations; the adequacy of water and housing were much better, at 98 percent and 95 percent respectively, significant improvements from a decade earlier but still factors in many health problems (DIAND 2002a). Tuberculosis, for instance, has been related to poor housing conditions and income among some First Nations (M. Clark, P. Riben, and E. Nowegesic 2002).

Personal behavior can contribute significantly to health problems among the Native population just as it does nationally. The high rate of tobacco use, in particular, which exceeds that of the national population in all age groups, is noteworthy (Reading 1996). Similarly, significant dietary changes, as recent as the 1950s for some Inuit populations, are implicated in many health problems. Store-bought foods of inferior quality have come to replace many of the wild foods and farmed crops. The high cost of imported store foods in many areas exacerbates the problem (Abonyi 2001). This, in turn, has contributed to dramatically increased consumption of saturated fats, while many vitamin and fiber levels remain low. Finally, while intense physical activity was central to survival in the past, the trend toward a sedentary lifestyle contributed to soaring rates of obesity and other health problems. National campaigns directed at smoking, diet, and exercise appear to have had minimal impact among aboriginal people. Similarly, preventive services are underutilized by aboriginal people relative to Canadians as a whole. For instance, in Manitoba it was found that immunization rates for Native children in the early years were substantially less than for non-Natives. Breast-feeding of newborns was also less likely. Preventive diagnostic procedures, such as mammography, were also substantially underutilized (Martens and Young 1997; Martens et al. 2002). The messages about the importance of healthy lifestyles have simply not impacted the Native population in the same way they have for other Canadians.

Overall, the health of Native Canadians is seen as much poorer than for Canadians as a whole. This poorer health status is evident in broad-based statistics, such as hospitalization rates. In several western provinces, the hospitalization rate for Indians is often twice that of other citizens, and sometimes more (Waldram, Herring, and Young 2006). There is evidence that Indians utilize physician services at a higher rate as well. In a Manitoba study, it was determined that Indian patients averaged 6.1 physician visits per year, compared to 4.9 visits by other Manitobans (Martens et al. 2002). These statistics are only suggestive of differential health problems, of course, since utilization patterns and access are also important. Medical folklore suggests that aboriginal people overutilize some services, underutilize others, and otherwise use services inappropriately, despite the lack of hard data or the existence of data to the contrary (DeCoster et al. 1999; Waldram 1990a:227). Cultural differences certainly explain some differential use, as does the higher degree of morbidity for some problems. Access to available resources is quite variable across the country, and there is evidence that attitudes associated with racial stereotyping may affect utilization (Sherley-Spiers 1989). Under aboriginal control, health service utilization may improve (M. Moore, H. Forbes, and L. Henderson 1990). Nevertheless, the health of aboriginal people remained an inconsistency in a country that routinely ranks among the most healthy in the world.

## Government Health Services

Despite advances in the devolution of health services to Indian and Inuit communities and organizations, various levels of government in Canada continued to play an important role in the delivery of services. Prior to the 1980s, almost all health services were in fact provided to Native peoples by government (vol. 5:674). Canada maintains responsibility for Indian health care, while the provinces continue to provide services for their Métis, non-Status Indian, and non-Aboriginal citizens. The Inuit and Indian residents

of the Northwest Territories saw responsibility for their health transferred to the territorial government in the late 1980s (Waldram, Herring, and Young 2006).

Although there have been many precursors, the main federal agency involved in the delivery of health care to Natives is the First Nations and Inuit Health Branch of the federal agency Health Canada. The main goals of the Branch are: to ensure the availability of and access to health services for First Nations and Inuit communities, to assist First Nations and Inuit communities to address health barriers and disease threats, to achieve health levels comparable to other Canadians, and to build strong, collaborative partnerships to improve health and health care delivery (Waldram, Herring, and Young 2006). The administrative structure for service delivery involves various regions across the country, often with a hospital or major health facility at the center. The degree of services varies, of course, in part due to the vast size of the country and the often remote location of many communities, some of which remain without all-weather road access (fig. 2). By the late 1980s, the federal government was operating over 500 health facilities of various kinds (fig. 3), including eight hospitals. Since then, there has been an effort to scale back, especially on hospitals, and to utilize provincial services where possible. For example, James Bay General Hospital, Moosonee, Ontario, serves 3,300 Crees. It evolved from a Roman Catholic hospital, but today the facility built in 1985 is largely federally funded. Depending on geographic residence, First Nations and Inuit individuals in the 2000s can expect to receive varying services. All receive a variety of health benefits

Fig. 2. Sioux Lookout Zone Hospital, serving a population of 15,000 Cree and Ojibwa people in western Ont., from the Canadian National Railway line to Hudson Bay. The helicopter lands on the hospital grounds to deliver emergency patients from outlying communities during spring "break-up" and fall "freeze-up" when regular float planes or ski-planes cannot land on water. Photograph by Dr. Kue Young, 1980–1985.

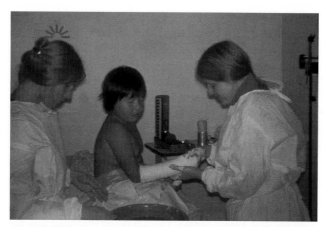

Fig. 3. Ojibwa boy getting a cast on a fractured arm at Weagamow Lake Nursing Station, Ont. Outpost nurses P. Salata, left, and C. McKellar, right, are performing duties that are usually done by physicians, one aspect of Aboriginal health care in the Canadian North. Photograph by Dr. Kue Young, 1980–1985.

including prescription drugs and dental and vision care. Individuals living on reserves have access to a variety of health services and medical transportation to larger centers where needed. Those living in more isolated areas can expect to receive primary health care services, usually delivered by nurses with periodic visits by physicians and medical specialists. Most such services are delivered on a contractual basis, often involving personnel from regional, nonaboriginal centers and university medical schools. In urban areas, Indians and Inuits are usually required to access health services through provincial and municipal agencies, which then bill the federal government for the services rendered. Other aboriginal peoples are required to access these provincial and municipal services regardless of residence. Responsibility for their health care rests with the provinces, just as it does for other citizens, and these individuals therefore are impacted by provincial policies on medical insurance and coverage restrictions.

Why has the federal government accepted responsibility for health delivery to First Nations and Inuit individuals? The answer lies within a web of policy decisions, legislative initiatives, treaties, and court cases. The Royal Proclamation of 1763, and then the British North America Act of 1867, established that the Crown should be responsible for Indian peoples, a fact substantiated with the Indian Act in 1876, the first Canadian legislation to indicate that Indian peoples were wards of the government. In the 1870s, treaties were signed between Canada and the Indian bands in the west. While the Indian oral tradition suggests that health care was often discussed, specific reference to health care is found only in Treaty Six, signed in 1876. At the insistence of the Indians, two relevant clauses were added to the written text: "That in the event hereafter of the Indians comprised within this treaty being overtaken by any pestilence, or by a general famine, the Queen, on being satisfied and certified thereof by her Indian Agent or Agents, will grant to the Indians assistance of such character and to such extent as her Chief Superintendent of Indian Affairs shall deem necessary and sufficient to relieve the Indians from the calamity that shall have befallen them" and "that a medicine chest shall be kept at the house of each Indian Agent for the use and benefit of the Indians, at the discretion of such Agent" (Morris 1880:355). There has been considerable debate since that time on the meaning of these two clauses, and the extent of their reach. While First Nations have generally argued that the clauses meant free, comprehensive medical care in perpetuity, available to all Indians in Canada, the federal government has promoted a literal and geographically restricted interpretation. The medical services that the government does provide to First Nations people is seen, in this context, as a matter of government policy, subject to review and alteration. The fact that by the late 1960s Canada as a whole had moved toward publicly funded, comprehensive health services for all citizens rendered the issue somewhat moot, at least for purposes of determining fiscal responsibility.

Health care costs for the country as a whole have risen substantially since the 1960s, and not surprisingly the costs of delivery to the Aboriginal population are substantial. The total cost of health services (including capital costs for facility construction and maintenance) for aboriginal groups in 2002–2003 was about 1.5 billion dollars (Waldram, Herring, and Young 2006:215). This amount includes funds transferred directly to aboriginal groups as part of programs to transfer control over the delivery of services to aboriginal control, an amount that has increased steadily since the 1980s. This does not include expenditures on aboriginal peoples who fall under provincial jurisdiction, a figure difficult to discern as these jurisdictions tend not to enumerate their aboriginal citizens.

### Self-Determination in Health Care

The initial impetus for self-determination in health care came from broader changes in the Canadian political climate vis-à-vis Aboriginal peoples. While certainly there is a long history to aboriginal claims to self-determination, including claims to health care (Weaver 1972), political changes in Canada beginning in the late 1960s opened the door for increased Native control. In the first modern treaty, the James Bay Cree and Inuit negotiated health care as part of the James Bay and Northern Quebec Agreement in 1975 (Salisbury 1986). Unlike most Indians, the Cree in James Bay saw the responsibility for their health care pass from federal hands to the province of Quebec, with whom they would negotiate on-going funding arrangements. But it was a variety of federal policies and legislation dating to the late 1970s that sparked acceleration in demands by aboriginal groups that their special status—as "citizens plus"—and their inherent rights to govern themselves be recognized. A new Indian health policy in 1979 declared that the answer to on-going and emerging health problems was not to be found in more money for clinical programs and services; rather, it was concluded that more direct Native control was needed. In 1982, when Canada's first homemade constitution was passed, one section noted that the "existing aboriginal and treaty rights" were "recognized and affirmed," and the door to self-determination swung wide-open. This was followed the subsequent year by the report of the federal Special Committee on Indian Self-Government, which established health care as a negotiable entity between government and First Nations (Penner 1983). In 1986 the Sechelt group of Northern Coast Salish in British Columbia obtained control over health care through passage of the Sechelt Indian Band Self-Government Act.

Discourses of self-government eventually gave way to that of self-determination, as the transfer of responsibility from Canada and the provinces to specific aboriginal groups moved past what might be thought of as issues of governance and jurisdiction and into special spheres of community activity. Social welfare, education, and economic development led the way, as many aboriginal groups, sometimes as separate entities and sometimes through larger, regional organizations, progressively gained some degree of control over the shape of services to be delivered and the budgets with which to deliver them. Health care was a relatively late arrival on this scene, receiving little attention from emerging aboriginal governments until the late 1980s, at which time other changes on the national level, combined with relative success in taking control of those spheres just mentioned, rendered the delivery of health services an imminent possibility for jurisdictional transfer.

The first step in the transfer of health services was taken in 1982, with the federal Community Health Demonstration Program (D.E. Young and L.L. Smith 1992). The purpose of this program was to generate a variety of models of health care delivery at the local and regional levels involving differing degrees of local control, and some 30 projects were funded (Garro, Roulette, and Whitmore 1986). When the program ended a few years later, First Nations were met with the formation of a new branch of government, the Program Transfer and Development Directorate, and a new Indian Health Transfer policy. This 1986 policy established the procedures under which individual First Nations, or regional organizations, could progressively gain control over the delivery of health services (Lynch 1991). Different types of transfer were supported under this initiative, which allowed communities to determine the extent and pace of service transfer, thereby proving attractive to both communities with well-developed self-governing structures and those earlier on in the more general process of gaining greater control over their lives.

Initially, there were some concerns expressed about the health transfer process. For instance, the Assembly of First Nations, a national association representing all First Nations in the country, challenged the program on the grounds that on one hand it seemed designed primarily to reduce government costs for health care delivery, a violation of treaty and fiduciary rights, and on the other hand failed to support the notion of an inherent right to self-determination by virtue of the dominant role of the federal government in setting and policing the policy (Assembly of First Nations 1988; Culhane Speck 1989). First Nations themselves began to see the merits in the transfer policy and an opportunity to gain increased self-determination no matter the legal underpinnings. Within a couple of years of the announcement of the policy, over 200 First Nations communities were already involved in the various stages of transfer planning and implementation. The 1990s saw an acceleration of this trend. By 1992, 23 transfer agreements were in place involving more than 70 First Nations (DNHW 1992). In 2002, 284 First Nations had concluded transfer agreements, almost half of those eligible, and 81 percent of all eligible communities were active in some phase of the transfer process (Health Canada 2002). While criticism has continued to surface, for instance that the program offloads the cost of service delivery to the local level (Jacklin and Warry 2004), the program has been extremely successful.

Unlike the Indians, the Métis people in Canada have had considerable trouble in attaining meaningful control over health services. This no doubt relates to their somewhat anomalous position in Canada as an "aboriginal" population within the meaning of the Constitution but primarily the responsibility of the provincial governments (Lemchuk-Favel and Jock 2004). As such, health service delivery to the Métis is governed in largely the same fashion as it is for non-aboriginal peoples under Canada's publicly funded health care system. With the exception of Alberta, which has several Métis settlements, the Métis lack the land base that Indians have in the reserves, a logical locus for self-determination initiatives because of their special legal status and geographical boundedness. In contrast, the Inuit road to health self-determination has been much smoother. With residence in Canada's northern territories, the Inuit (and other Indians) were not eligible for the Indian health transfer program and deal directly with the federal government on such matters. In the new territory of Nunavut the Inuit have achieved a public form of self-determination by virtue of their majority population.

The training of Native health professionals has been a cornerstone of the self-determination movement. Across Canada, professional colleges such as medicine, dentistry, nursing, and allied health fields have developed programs to attract and retain Aboriginal students. In 1984 the federal government launched the Indian and Inuit Health Careers program to support the education of aboriginal health professionals (Waldram, Herring, and Young 2006). This program was moved to the National Aboriginal Achievement Foundation in 1998, with a health careers budget over one-half million dollars. Successes are everywhere evident. Estimates place the number of aboriginal physicians in 1991 at 25 individuals; by 1998 this had increased to 67. By the same time there were some 800 aboriginal nurses. Certain specialties, such as psychiatry, remain unpopular (Commission on the Future of Health Care in Canada 2002:220). For many years there have been associations advocating on behalf of the training of aboriginal health professionals, including the Aboriginal Nurses Association of Canada, the Canadian Native Mental Health Association, and the Canadian Native Physicians Association. Organizations have been formed to promote self-determination through both education and research. The National Aboriginal Health Organization, which produces the *Journal of Aboriginal Health*, and the Aboriginal Healing Foundation have considerable influence over both aboriginal health research agendas and policy. The Aboriginal Health Foundation, funded after a royal commission into the state of aboriginal peoples in the country, has seen its initial mandate to develop programs for survivors of residential schools expand into broader research and policy areas. However, vetting and funding "healing" projects has remained its core function, and by 2004 the Foundation had approved more than 1,300 grants totaling $375 million (Waldram, Herring, and Young 2006: 287). Finally, the formation in 2002 of the Institute of Aboriginal People's Health as part of the Canadian Institutes of Health Research placed aboriginal health research, especially with significant aboriginal input and control, on the national agenda of politicians and health researchers.

While self-determination in health care is a laudable and logical goal in its own right, many proponents have also assumed that health status would improve once First Nations had gained such control; however, the evidence for this is not readily available. A study in British Columbia suggests that the greater the degree of self-determination generally, including in the area of health services, the lower the suicide rate (Chandler and Lalonde 1998). After health transfer at the William Charles First Nation (Western Woods Cree) in Saskatchewan, which included substantial education and preventive as well as clinical services, it was reported that the people began to take more responsibility for their health, including increased home management of minor problems, increased immunizations for children, and increased regular care for elders who were now able to access services in their Cree language (M. Moore, H. Forbes, and L. Henderson 1990). Hospitalization for ear infections and upper respiratory infections declined, as did overall utilization of emergency out-patient facilities. A primary health care program was developed as part of health transfer at the Eskasoni First Nation in Nova Scotia. Improved service delivery for these Micmac (Mi'kmaq) peoples through an arrangement with Dalhousie University medical school, Halifax, Nova Scotia, contributed to an overall decline in physician and hospital emergency department visits, a reduction in the use of prescription medicines, improved prenatal care, and a corresponding reduction in costs (Health Canada 2003; Lemchuk-Favel and Jock 2004).

The transfer process has contributed to the development of services more appropriate to the communities involved, including services in local languages and following local ethical protocols. Increased awareness of health issues among residents and aboriginal politicians has also been noted. Finally, there appears to have been a decline in the use of medical services (Health Canada 1999). Most evidence for the benefits of the Indian transfer program specifically, and increased aboriginal self-determination in health more generally, remains qualitative and somewhat anecdotal. Nevertheless, there is a strong sense that both health and healthcare delivery have improved.

## The Resurgence of Aboriginal Healing

Since the 1980s there has been a renewed interest in what is referred to as traditional healing. Research suggests that aboriginal healing traditions in the precontact period not only survived but also adapted to the arrival of Europeans (Waldram, Herring, and Young 2006). Nevertheless, colonization had a significant impact. New epidemic diseases not only caused a loss in population, including a loss of medical specialists, but also they created an opening for a nascent European medicine in part through a crisis in confidence in Native abilities to stem the scourges. Missionization, and later government programs aimed at assimilation, directly challenged the spiritual beliefs that underlay aboriginal healing approaches. The development of biomedical services into all areas of aboriginal Canada posed a threat to traditional services. Some healing activities went underground, beyond the eyes of missionaries and government agents, as some aspects of Native spiritual traditions were outlawed for a time. This is true, for instance, of the Ojibwa healing tradition known as the Midewiwin, as well as the shaking tent, Plains Indian Sun Dance, and the Salish *tamananawas* (Waldram, Herring, and Young 2006) or spirit dancing ceremony on the Northwest Coast (Cole and Chaikin 1990; Jilek 1982; Pettipas 1994). Other practices and knowledge, less threatening to the national goal of assimilation, were simply retained even as the number of specialists declined. Rather than eliminating traditional knowledge, elements of Christianity and biomedicine fused with Native traditions to form syncretic approaches to treatment.

What is meant by "traditional healing" in the contemporary context is anything but clear, and it would be a mistake to view various beliefs, knowledge, and practices as if they represented a precontact medical tradition in a pristine, unaltered way, despite pronouncements by new age gurus and raconteurs (Aldred 2000; Churchill 1990; Kehoe 1990). The Royal Commission on Aboriginal Peoples (1996, 3:348) offers a definition that promotes such a view: "traditional healing has been defined as practices designed to promote mental, physical and spiritual well-being that are based on beliefs which go back to the time before the spread of western 'scientific' bio-medicine. When Aboriginal Peoples in Canada talk about traditional healing, they include a wide range of activities, from physical cures using herbal medicines and other remedies, to the promotion of psychological and spiritual well-being using ceremony, counselling and the accumulated wisdom of elders."

It is best to consider traditional healing, in a contemporary sense, as an approach to wellness and treatment that embraces flexibility and change in an effort to serve peoples and communities whose health issues in turn reflect both ages-old and very recent problems. Indeed, many of the most serious issues to affect Native people historically, such as infectious diseases, and later, such as alcohol and substance abuse, suicide, and HIV/AIDS, have represented profound challenges to the traditional forms of knowledge. In fact, it has only been through change and adaptation to these new problems that aboriginal healing has likely been able to persist and even to mount somewhat of a comeback.

While much Native healing is believed to be based in the more remote areas of the country, or on reserves, its greatest gains have come in urban and institutional contexts. Healing philosophies, practices, and practitioners have made their way into a variety of mainstream treatment facilities and programs, such as medical clinics, hospitals and prisons. Early efforts to do so were often met with ignorance and hostility. Some Native peoples argued that traditional healing was based on secret knowledge that could not be shared with others or that practicing it in nontraditional contexts would be a violation of its basic ethos and would invite spiritual sanction. Hospitals, for their part, had difficulty with the use of burning substances such as sage or sweetgrass during healing ceremonies because of bans on smoking, and, of course, the lack of scientific evidence supporting claims of efficacy. While Native healers often expressed concerns that patients could not be effectively treated while on medication or attached to medical equipment, clinicians refused to facilitate healing activities if patients were not monitored closely and remained on whatever medications or procedures had been deemed necessary. Eventually, accommodations on all sides were made. Aboriginal medical interpreters, often advocating for patients who wished traditional services, began to join clinics and act as culture brokers (Kaufert, O'Neil, and Koolage 1985; O'Neil 1988). Healers began to rethink the essentialness of certain aspects of their practices to accommodate the concerns of clinicians, and the clinicians did likewise. The need to employ covert action to bring traditional healing into facilities such as hospitals, as D.E. Young, G. Ingram, and L. Swartz (1988) described in the work of one Cree healer, seems tempered by honest efforts on the part of health care administrators to be culturally sensitive and serve the needs of Native patients. Aboriginal people have come to recognize the value of, and need for, traditional style services within institutional settings (Waldram 1990).

Nevertheless, insofar as Native healing has made inroads into the biomedical world, there has been a tendency to marginalize it within the realm of mental health services, broadly understood. Traditional counseling services, in-

cluding ceremonies, have proven both attractive and safe in the eyes of the clinical directors who hold the power. In the communities themselves, in contrast, traditional services continue to be offered in those communities that have healers. The federal government has sometimes funded the activities of healers, including travel costs to bring them into communities from outside or to transfer patients to the healers (Gregory 1989; Health Canada 2003b). Several provinces and territories have developed policies that provide some support for aboriginal healing activities. The 1990 Health Act in the Yukon, for instance, includes provisions pertaining to "Aboriginal control over traditional Aboriginal nutrition and healing practices and to protect these healing practices as a viable alternative for seekers of health and healing services" (World Health Organization 2001:47). In the mid 1990s, Ontario presented a policy that included as a fundamental principle that "traditional Aboriginal approaches to wellness, including the use of traditional resources, traditional healers, medicine people, midwives and elders, are recognized, respected and protected from government regulation" (Ontario Ministry of Health 1994:15).

Two such examples of the contemporary uses of aboriginal healing have required considerable adaptation: forensic treatment of offenders and substance abuse treatment.

Initiatives to introduce aboriginal healing into prisons came through its appearance as religious or spiritual practice protected within the Canadian constitution (Waldram 1993, 1997). Inmate advocates, and supporters on the out-

Fig. 4. Fire ceremony after completion of counselor training at Nechi Inst., St. Albert, Alta., led by Dr. Jane Simington, third from right. Nechi trains people of all ethnicities, but the majority of students are Cree. Photograph by Gaston Gabarro, 2007.

side, argued that inmates do not lose the right to religious freedom by virtue of their incarceration. In response, the federal and provincial agencies responsible for corrections began to allow the use of sweetgrass for prayer, followed by sacred circles (a form of group therapy involving sharing of experiences, thoughts, and emotions), sweatlodge ceremonies and, eventually, supervised release passes to allow inmates to attend fasts and healing ceremonies beyond the prison walls. These activities were facilitated by Native liaison staff working for the correctional facilities and, eventually, healers and elders on contract. Problems resulted when elders and healers and their spiritual paraphernalia were subject to searches, which desecrated the sacred pipes and medicine bundles they were bringing in for ceremonies. Sweatlodge ceremonies were disrupted for security procedures. Prison schedules forced healers to curtail activities to ensure that inmates were in their cells at the appropriate times. And spiritual and healing activities were required to work around other forensic programming, usually by occurring in the evenings or on weekends. The resolve of the elders and healers to educate and demonstrate the value of their approaches eventually lead to reduced restrictions and more Native staff. In 2006, it was even common for a correctional case manager to suggest that an inmate consult an elder. Several federal correctional facilities specifically for Native inmates, men and women, have been constructed with programming predicated on aboriginal understandings of rehabilitation, involving elders and healers as core treatment staff rather than as ancillaries (Waldram, Herring, and Young 2006).

Native-controlled alcohol and drug abuse treatment centers were among the first facilities to be native run. Poundmaker's Lodge, located near Edmonton, Alberta, is perhaps the most famous of these. Along with its affiliated alcohol and substance abuse training facility, the Nechi Institute (fig. 4), the treatment philosophy is to provide the best of both aboriginal and mainstream biomedical and psychotherapeutic approaches in a complementary fashion (Waldram, Herring, and Young 1995). Poundmaker's Lodge, and other such facilities, have lead the way in integrated care for both in-patient and out-patient care. Anchored by Alcoholics Anonymous and similar models on one side, often adapted to be more compatible with aboriginal philosophies, and traditional models involving sweatlodge ceremonies and sacred circles on the other side, patients are provided with the opportunity to engage in treatment in a manner most compatible with their beliefs and worldviews. Most of these facilities accept that some clients will be considerably more Euro-Canadian in outlook than others, and some more Christian than others. Predicated on an understanding of substance abuse problems as rooted in processes of cultural change and loss, these centers are usually also able to accommodate the differing aboriginal cultural backgrounds of their clients. Although the treatment models vary from center to center, aboriginal approaches and philosophies remain central to the overall treatment approach; they are not simply add-ons.

Across Canada, the revitalization of aboriginal healing continues in both urban and rural areas. This process has coincided with the movement toward self-determination and demonstrates that, when in control, aboriginal people tend to opt for an integrated, holistic model: contemporary traditional philosophies and approaches combined with Western biomedical and psychotherapeutic approaches. The challenge remains the need to anchor treatment in local sociocultural contexts and to adapt to an increasing demand for traditional services while facing a shortage of practitioners. The broad process of aboriginal cultural rejuvenation that is occurring in the country suggests that there may ultimately be an increase in the number of individuals with the knowledge to be elders and healers.

## Conclusion

The Native peoples of Canada have experienced new health problems since the 1960s even as they have escaped the historical scourges of infectious diseases. Their most pressing health problems relate to their anomalous position as a marginalized minority in a wealthy nation with an extensive social and health services network. Health problems related to poor living conditions and behavior choices have risen to the forefront. Epidemiologically, as the incidence of cancer and cardiovascular disease approaches national levels, especially as the population ages, and problems related to alcohol and substance abuse, and suicide, target the younger individuals. Self-determination in health service delivery has been an important step in combating the new health and social problems, parallel to the resurgence of traditional aboriginal health philosophies and treatment approaches.

# Aboriginal Economic Development

CARL BEAL

Since the mid-1970s, a combination of political activism, court decisions recognizing Aboriginal and treaty rights, Aboriginal demands for comprehensive rather than piecemeal approaches to economic development, and government commitment of significant financial resources to support the Aboriginal development institutions has created a new dynamic for Aboriginal economic development.

There are persistent and substantial disparities between the economic circumstances of Aboriginal and non-Aboriginal populations in Canada. This generalization masks very different outcomes for different communities. In some instances, Aboriginal communities have achieved substantial gains in employment, income, and assets, with corresponding improvements in community well-being. In others, the results have been deeply discouraging. In part, these different outcomes can be traced to different endowments of land and resources, access to markets, technology and financial capital, an educated and skilled labor force and management capacity, and the well-being of the community.

An analysis of Aboriginal communities that have achieved a notable measure of economic success suggests that the key to economic development is not doing business, but creating the institutional climate that is conducive to business development. Good governance institutions need to be in a position to exercise effective self-government and to assume responsibility for community outcomes. This requires the capacity to make and carry out decisions effectively, to ensure that there are appropriate institutions in place to create a stable climate for business development, to provide education and skills development to the members of the community, and to articulate a vision that finds an appropriate match between the history and culture of the community and business development. Often, the last requires a kind of "retraditionalization" that articulates cultural values of independence, self-reliance, and personal responsibility in place of the dependency values inculcated under the lengthy tutelage of federal and provincial policies.

## The Human Resources

In 2004, the registered (Status) Indian population numbered 733,626, nearly half (43%) residing off-reserve (Canada 2005:xiii). The on-reserve population lived on some 2,675 reserves of widely varying size and population. Sixty percent of 612 recognized Bands under the Indian Act have on-reserve populations of less than 500; the largest 20 bands account for more than 20 percent of the registered Indian population (Canada 2005).

The Métis population was counted at 292,370 in 2001 ("Native Populations of Canada," table 4, this vol.). The Métis lack a land base, except in Alberta, where eight Métis settlements have been entrenched in the provincial constitution.

*R* v. *Powley* set out to define Métis rights and brought the issue of Métis harvesting rights to the fore. Another case with potentially important economic ramifications was the land claims case heard in 2006, *Manitoba Métis Federation et al.* v. *Attorney General of Canada and Attorney General of Manitoba* (Manitoba Métis Federation Inc. 2004). The land claims case contends that the Métis were unconstitutionally deprived of the promises related to 1.4 million acre land grant and protection of river lots under sections 31 and 32 of the Manitoba Act of 1870. This case could have a substantial impact on the recognition of Métis treaty rights and could create significant economic opportunities.

The Inuit numbered 45,075 in the 2001 census; there were some 55 small Inuit communities across the North in 2005. The Inuit and Innu (formerly called Montagnais and Naskapi) were gathered in permanent settlements by the federal government in the 1950s and 1960s, in a process of "relocation, sedentarisation and supervision," resulting in loss of livelihood and negative social and cultural consequences (Usher 2003:372; Samson 2003).

Data from the 2001 census show the economic disparities between Aboriginal people and Canadians in general (table 1). Aboriginal Canadians earn less, have lower rates of participation in the labor force, unemployment rates as much as three times those of other Canadians, lower educational attainment, and a wide range of health and social inequities (Adelson 2005).

A study of employment growth in approximately 400 Indian reserves over the periods 1991–1996 and 1996–2001 examined the relative impact of changes in population growth, participation rates, and unemployment rates on Aboriginal employment. It found that from 1991 to 1996, there was real employment growth arising from both

**Table 1. Labor and Income in 2000**

| | | | | Identity | | | | |
|---|---|---|---|---|---|---|---|---|
| | Total National Population | Total Aboriginal Identity Population | North American Indian Only | Métis Only | Inuit Only | Multiple Aboriginal Identities | Aboriginal Responses Not Included Elsewhere | Total Non-Aboriginal Population |
| Total population over 15 years by employment income and work activity | 23,901,360 | 652,350 | 395,325 | 207,615 | 27,605 | 4,535 | 17,270 | 23,249,010 |
| Labor force participation rate | 66.4 | 61.4 | 57.3 | 69.1 | 62.5 | 60.7 | 60.2 | 66.5 |
| Unemployment rate | 7.4 | 19.1 | 22.2 | 14.0 | 22.2 | 16.4 | 17.4 | 7.1 |
| Average income in $ | 29,769 | 19,132 | 17,376 | 22,213 | 19,878 | 19,557 | 20,673 | 30,062 |
| Employment income % | 77.1 | 75.1 | 72 | 79.8 | 76.5 | 73.6 | 73.1 | 77.1 |
| Government transfer payments % | 11.6 | 20.8 | 24.3 | 15.7 | 20.3 | 19.9 | 19.4 | 11.5 |
| Other % | 11.3 | 4.1 | 3.6 | 4.6 | 3.2 | 6.5 | 7.5 | 11.4 |
| Incidence of low income in % | 12.9 | 31.2 | 37.3 | 24.5 | 21.9 | 30.3 | 35.8 | 12.4 |

SOURCE: Statistics Canada 2003:Census of 2001.

increased labor force participation and reduced unemployment rates, due in part perhaps to devolution of government programs to Indian administration. However, from 1996 to 2001, the rate of employment growth was 7.8%, less than the growth of the working-age population (Damus and Liljefors 2004). The situation in Canada's north showed that ground was lost in terms of employment and participation in both periods; over the period 1991–2001, 8,230 jobs were created "even though the growth in population could have produced 11,843 jobs without any change in unemployment and participation rates" (Damus and Liljefors 2004:8). Significantly, disparities grew among Indian and northern communities, half experiencing employment growth due to rising participation rates and falling unemployment rates between 1996–2001 and the rest experiencing relative employment decline.

Aboriginal economic development in Canada incorporates a wide variety of approaches, in urban and rural/remote locales, in resource-rich and resource-poor areas. As a result, the case study remains a valuable tool for exploring the diversity of ventures and institutional arrangements in place for development (Elias 1995; R.B. Anderson 1999; Atlantic Canada Opportunities Agency 2003). The great diversity of approaches to development, the greatly differing circumstances of Aboriginal groups, the opportunity to build business partnerships on the basis of local resource development, and the navigation of local, regional, national, and global markets, has led to a suggestion that Aboriginal economic development initiatives in Canada may flourish in the regime of capitalist accumulation characterized by flexible specialization (R.B. Anderson 2005). Others have suggested that soliciting Aboriginal participation in the expanding resource frontier can reduce Aboriginal resistance to development initiatives and facilitate incorporation of traditional lands into the capitalist system, while undermining traditional pursuits based on renewable resources.

In the context of opposition to the termination policy proposed by the federal government in its White Paper on Indian Policy (Canada 1969), Aboriginal organizations framed economic development activities within a broader context of cultural and social development, self-government and self-determination, characterized as a comprehensive approach to development (Elias 1991). In the ensuing decades, this approach has been further articulated and lessons drawn from experience.

Aboriginal economic development is informed by, and to a greater or lesser extent incorporates and accommodates traditional Aboriginal values in a modern organization or enterprise. This blending is found in many Aboriginal communities and organizations, beyond the strictly economic, including domains of education, governance, and community action (Newhouse 2000). Indigenous entrepreneurship by definition entails reconciliation of tradition and innovation and requires a consideration of how "Indigenous worldviews and values impact upon enterprise" (Hindle and Lansdowne 2005:131).

This definition of economic development excludes some economic activities and programs that, although addressed to and utilized by Natives, and possibly involving Native-owned enterprises, may not qualify as Aboriginal development for the lack of the critical interface with Aboriginal traditions, the interests of the collective, and social and cultural issues. Many job placement services, employment equity hiring programs, and training and education initiatives do not qualify on this account as Aboriginal development, even though they contribute to the employment of Aboriginal individuals. There is no single template that lists "the" traditional values, and how they mesh with business practice. This varies from community to community, from culture to culture, and the particular traditions and values that are prominently positioned will vary from case to case. As a result, the analysis of the role of cultural values in enterprise management are either expressed in a global way (Hindle and Lansdowne 2005; Hindle et al. 2005), or find concrete expression in case studies (Atlantic Canada Opportunities Agency 2003). The emphasis on an appropriate cultural fit of development activities goes to the legitimacy of development initiatives in the participating communities. The appropriate balance in reconciliation of business principles and tradition is often contested as Aboriginal communities undertake development initiatives.

The articulation of the fit between traditional and modern values varies from community to community. The Membertou First Nation (Micmac) in Sydney, Nova Scotia, articulated a "First Nation Progression Model," a three-stage process from capacity building, to preparation, to economic development. The approach is portrayed as resting on two traditional values (conservation and sustainability) and two business values (innovation and success). Most importantly, the overall objective of development is not articulated in terms of corporate growth and profitability alone, but rather in terms of social objectives of community development (J.T. Scott 2004).

The Osoyoos Indian Band, one group of Northern Okanagan in British Columbia, created an economic development corporation in 1988. In 2007 they operated nine businesses, including a golf course (fig. 1), construction company, vineyard, and a winery, Nk'mp (Inkameep) cellars, a joint venture with Vincor International. The Osoyoos Indian Band stressed the importance of businesslike operation for community success, with economic self-sufficiency seen as integral to "honouring culture and tradition" (Graham and Edwards 2003:25).

The importance of creating an institutional environment conducive to successful enterprise development has led to emphasizing good governance practices, with an appropriate relationship among governing bodies, development institutions, and business enterprise. Political leadership needs to be visionary, carefully constructing a space within which both their constituencies and business enterprises are able to thrive on the basis of stable "rules of the game." Developing institutions to create a stable climate for business, management capacity, labor force development, finance, negotiating access to lands, resources, technology, and markets has been the focus of successful Aboriginal development initiatives since the 1970s.

Osoyoos Indian Band Development Corporation, Oliver, B.C.

Fig. 1. Quentin Baptiste, Osoyoos Indian Band member, maintaining the course at the NK'MIP Canyon Desert Golf Course, Oliver, B.C., one of the businesses operated by the Band. In 1961 the Band leased the land to investors to build a golf course and then a mobile home park. In 1994 the business was sold back to the Band. In 1999 the Band undertook expansion, with the construction employing not only Osoyoos but also other Natives and some Whites. In 2007 the golf course employed over 50 people. Photograph by Russell Zubeck, 2007.

## 1945–2005

The economic circumstances of Indians worsened in the decade after World War II, even as the Canadian economy entered an unprecedented period of growth. Many Aboriginal people who had found employment in industrial establishments during the war found themselves "squeezed out of regular long-term employment" by returning veterans (Lithman 1984:40). Prairie reserve agriculture was faced with an inadequate land base and lack of capital to participate in the rapid postwar mechanization of agriculture. The Department of Indian Affairs, unwilling to countenance an expanded reserve land base or significant investment in agriculture, encouraged Bands to lease field and pasture to land-hungry White farmers. Mechanization led to a reduction in off-reserve agricultural employment (Buckley 1992:67–68). In more northern communities, family allowances, payable as long as children attended schools, and later, the extension of other social welfare expenditures to Indians, undermined the subsistence economy and reshaped family social relations (Buckley 1992:72).

Indian economic circumstances on reserves were greatly influenced by the policies and programs of the Department of Indian Affairs. Yet, economic development had never been a preoccupation of the Department. There was no economic development branch of the department prior to 1949. A Departmental review of the economic development function for the decade 1948–1958 revealed a two-pronged approach of encouraging and supporting the traditional industries that were on the wane, while "supporting an increasing movement of Indians into other fields of employment," through measures such as the Indian Placement Program, established in 1957, to facilitate movement of Indian workers from the reserve to urban and industrial work settings (Canada 1958). The department enlarged a revolving loan fund that had been established in 1938, the number of loans growing 12 times, and the value of loans seven times, in 1948–1958 over the previous decade, principally in support of industries such as agriculture and handicrafts, which the Department rightly saw as a providing little basis for reserve or even household self-sufficiency. The revolving loan fund was soon supplemented by a rotating herd program on the prairies as a means of aiding marginal farm operations. The Department urged Indian farmers and small resource-based and handicraft enterprises to take advantage of programs offered under the Agricultural Rehabilitation and Development Act of 1961 and the Prairie Farms Rehabilitation Act of 1935 (Canada 1964). By the mid-1960s, the low level of resources and staffing for economic development had become abundantly clear. The Hawthorn report, a two-year study of Indian economic and social conditions and government policy, found that the economic development programs in the Department of Indian Affairs "inadequate and inappropriate," a program made up of bits and pieces–projects—with most of the personnel engaged in recordkeeping. Hawthorn pointed to the necessity for massive investment, on the order of hundreds of millions a year, in order to close the social and economic gaps between Indians and other Canadians, an undertaking the Department was then incapable of carrying out (Hawthorn 1966–1967, 1:164–165).

The Department of Indian Affairs pursued first one, then another, and sometimes overlapping approaches to economic development. The approaches identified by the Royal Commission on Aboriginal Peoples were: migration to areas with wage employment opportunities, especially cities; business enterprise development; development in mining, forestry, and fisheries; human resource development; and community economic development (Royal Commission on Aboriginal Peoples 1996, 2, part 2:791). These approaches appear to have been informed by the idea that where possible, viable enterprises would be encouraged. Marginal and submarginal enterprises, especially in remote areas, would be supported in low-income and low productivity ventures in order to supplement incomes, while the main thrust of policy was to encourage migration to wage employment, with transition to the labor market facilitated by education and training and job placement services.

If economic development did not figure prominently in the Department's priorities up to the mid-1960s, neither was it a major public concern. The issue of economic development was barely mentioned in the briefs to the 1946–1947 Joint House Senate Committee on the Indian Act, including the briefs from Indian organizations across the county. However, in the joint committee hearings on Indian Affairs,

1959–1961, economic disparities between the Indian and non-Indian populations were exposed. Briefs from Indian organizations, both band and provincial level organizations, highlighted the dismal economic circumstances on reserves. These views were echoed in provincial government briefs and in briefs from church and other non-governmental organizations. Some briefs to the committee, notably that of the government of Saskatchewan, quantified the income gap between on-reserve Indians and the general population, as well the much greater importance of government transfer payments in on-reserve Indian incomes.

Since then, "gap analysis" has become the standard approach for measuring the disparity between Aboriginal and White socioeconomic conditions. The Hawthorn (1966–1967) report estimated the gap between average annual earnings of Indians and non-Indians at $1,361 compared to $4,000, or a ratio of 1:3. This analysis of gaps, and estimates of job creation, capital investment, educational attainment, and occupational distribution has become sophisticated. Yet the gaps remain (Royal Commission on Aboriginal Peoples 1996, vol. 2, part 2:chap. 5; CTV.ca News Staff 2005).

The idea that economic development, spearheaded by Aboriginal people and organizations, might be an alternative to the policies of subsidized marginalization on-reserve, combined with relocation to urban and industrial wage-economies, came to the forefront in the political reaction of Indian leaders to the 1969 federal White Paper proposing the overhaul of Indian policy. The White Paper proposed a termination policy that would remove constitutional recognition of federal responsibility for Indians and land reserved for Indians, eliminate Indian status, Indian reserve lands, and provide educational, health, social and economic programs to Indians on the same basis as other Canadians. The reaction of Indian leadership across the country was strongly opposed to any proposal that would derogate from Aboriginal and Treaty rights (vol. 4:281–282). In the course of articulating that opposition, significant proposals were advanced proposing a comprehensive approach to economic development.

The Indian Association of Alberta (1970) issued a reply to the White Paper entitled *Citizens Plus*, a phrase taken from the Hawthorn report. It advanced a proposal for a "framework for development" that would coordinate action on employment with self-government, education, housing and a sense of socio-cultural identity. It argued that capital, human and educational resources were essential, and that "capital and educational resources are evident more by their lack than their presence." The brief argued that participation by private enterprise was essential to the success of Aboriginal economic development, as long as it was "in tune with the life and spirit of the reserve communities" (Indian Association of Alberta 1970:39, 41). The approaches proposed by the Indian Association of Alberta, the Manitoba Indian Brotherhood, the Council of Yukon Indians, and others in response to the White paper were comprehensive, including economic, social, and cultural development and self-government (Elias 1991).

This comprehensive approach was explicitly framed in opposition to the kind of piecemeal projects and programs that had been criticized by the Hawthorn report. In 1970, implementing a recommendation of the 1969 White Paper, the Department of Indian Affairs announced a $50 million Indian Economic Development Fund, providing "three main types of financial assistance: direct loans to finance business Enterprises; guaranteed loans from normal sources of commercial credit and grants to help Indian people meet special problems in developing business enterprises" (Canada 1972:38). The fund was sharply criticized by Indian leadership on the grounds that it was "project rather than program oriented," not grounded in any philosophy or approach to economic development, was so small as to "bear no relation to the magnitude of need," did not invest in much needed social capital, and failed to involve Indian leadership in the design, development and implementation of programs" (Manuel 1972:21). An audit concluded that the Indian Economic Development Fund was inadequately managed, and its operation made it unclear whether its role was to finance enterprise, create short-term jobs, or train entrepreneurs (Auditor General of Canada 1980:188).

Throughout the 1970s, the National Indian Brotherhood worked on the elaboration of a comprehensive approach to development. A working paper, *A Strategy for the Socioeconomic Development of Indian People,* was prepared under a joint steering committee of the National Indian Brotherhood and the Department of Indian Affairs and Northern Development. The lasting imprint of opposition to the 1969 termination policy proposal is found in the articulation of a comprehensive approach to economic development:

> . . . emphasis has been placed upon the need for Indian people to determine their own goals and objectives respecting socioeconomic development; for a renaissance of Indian culture looking to an entry into the Canadian mosaic as equals and to an end to forced assimilation; for the restoration of Indian feeling of continuity with their past while bringing forward to the Euro-Canadian society cultural contributions that may assist us as we struggle to adapt our value system to the postindustrial era; and for the protection and retention of Indian land as the most essential element of their cultural and physchological [sic] well-being and their existence as Indian people (National Indian Brotherhood 1977: ii).

The strategy articulated both sociocultural and economic elements, called for the strengthening of Indian institutions and community-based Indian control, and identified self-determination for Indian people as the objective of socioeconomic development. A year later, the National Indian Brotherhood completed the national report of the socioeconomic development strategy. Approved by the Brotherhood's executive council, the strategy called for the transfer of program funds from the Department of Regional Economic Expansion, for its various agricultural development and Northlands agreements, and funds from other government programs, to be transferred to the Department of Indian Affairs (National Indian Brotherhood 1977).

The federal Department of Regional Economic Expansion became involved in Aboriginal economic development from the early 1970s through the Special Agricultural and Rural Development Act, federal-provincial agreements aimed principally at Manitoba, Saskatchewan, and British Columbia. Despite the desire of the National Indian Brotherhood to see Regional Economic Expansion program funds transferred to the control of the Department of Indian Affairs and Northern Development, the Native Economic Development Program, announced in 1981, would be administered through several departments, with much of the program delivery outside Indian Affairs.

The Native Economic Development program was launched in 1984, departing fundamentally from initiatives within other federal departments. It was open to all native persons–status and non-Status Indian, Métis, and Inuit—extending its reach beyond the constitutionally restricted definition of Aboriginal groups. The strategy was developed out of a consultative process with a specially constituted Advisory Board. The four elements of the program showed that the recommendations made by the National Indian Brotherhood (renamed the Assembly of First Nations in 1982) and other organizations were being heeded.

The program made significant investments in the creation of a national network of financial and economic institutions. Through its special projects portfolio, funding was provided to establish university-level Aboriginal business management, public administration, and economic development programs, as well as to support community-based economic development and Aboriginal-owned business development (Kanary 1986). Since the establishment of the Native Economic Development Program, many federal government programs and services to support Aboriginal economic development have been created. In 1989, the program was refashioned as the Canadian Aboriginal Economic Development Strategy, involving three federal departments—Indian Affairs and Northern Development; Industry, Science and Technology Canada (known as Industry Canada in 2005); and Employment and Immigration (known as Human Resources and Skills Development Canada in 2005).

One billion dollars was allocated over the first five years of the strategy for implementation. The Department of Indian Affairs assumed full responsibility for four programs: community economic development, commercial development, resource access negotiations, and regional opportunities. The human resource development component was assumed by Employment and Immigration in collaboration with Aboriginal groups. Industry, Science and Technology implemented the Aboriginal Business Development and Joint Ventures program as well as the Aboriginal capital corporations program.

These major program directions have remained in place under new names, such as the Aboriginal Human Resource Development Strategy, announced in 1999, which has entered into agreements with Indian, Métis, urban Native, and Inuit organizations for human resource development and

235

skills training programs across the country. The Industry Canada programs are delivered as Aboriginal Business Canada. In addition, Fisheries and Oceans became involved in the implementation of an Aboriginal Fisheries strategy to increase First Nation access to and participation in commercial fisheries as a result of the Supreme Court decision in *R* v. *Marshall* (1999 3 S.C.R. 456).

The combined federal financial resources for these programs were $300 million in 2003–2004. These resources supported a wide array of development initiatives, delivered through many agencies and contracting Aboriginal organizations, with the result that application and reporting requirements are byzantine and overwhelming for many businesses and organizations. Despite the financial and professional resources in place, lack of access to natural resources and capital and business support for economic development pose significant barriers (Auditor General of Canada 2003).

## The Métis

Before 1984, the main programs available to the Métis were the special agricultural development and Northlands agreements, as well as agreements with provincial governments related to economic development programming. One of the biggest obstacles to Métis development has been the absence of a land and resource base. The method of administering the Métis land grant in Manitoba and the scrip process in the Northwest Territories did not secure a Métis land base (Sprague and Frye 1983; Hatt 1983; Barron 1990).). It was not until the Native Economic Development Program supported the capitalization of Aboriginal capital and economic development corporations that Métis development activities gained momentum.

In 1989, the Métis Settlements Accord was reached, setting the stage for the confirmation of a Métis land base and Métis self-government in Alberta. Eight Métis settlements have a land base of 528,000 hectares. The province provided more than $310 million between 1990 and 2007 for infrastructure, housing, economic development, and local government under the terms of the accord. One aim of the province of Alberta was to quiet an oil and gas lawsuit based on Aboriginal rights claims of the Métis. The funding for Métis settlement development has been eclipsed by provincial royalties from oil and gas resources taken from Métis lands. Investment in economic development initiatives has been limited (Metis Settlements Accord Implementation Act 1990 [c. M-14.5]; Joint Steering Committee 2005).

## The North

Although Treaties 8 (1899) and 11 (1911) covered much of the present-day Northwest Territories, the northern resource frontier was undeveloped and government interest in the Aboriginal peoples in the north was slight before 1945. After World War II economic conditions in the north deteriorated (Stabler and Howe 1990). The circumstances of the Inuit and Indians in the north presented the government with an administrative crisis:

> The old policy of leaving them to lead their traditional way of life, independent of government, was becoming unsustainable. Fur prices were in decline, the Hudson's Bay Company was closing posts, and independent traders were leaving the country. The cost of trade goods was rising rapidly with postwar inflation, and the need for them was increasing. Bands of Inuit began living, in miserable conditions, around military bases and weather stations for security and material goods. Reports of distress and starvation of isolated bands were reaching the southern media (Usher 2003a:193–194).

The response of the government was relocation of bands, sedentarization, and supervision to fit the needs of administration and delivery of services. Those settled were left with neither their traditional livelihoods nor accommodation and incorporation into a wage economy. Similar policies were carried out among the Innu; between two worlds, these communities have been described as "a way of life that does not exist" (Samson 2003:173). Development was slow in coming to the north; mining industries were capital intensive and relied on southern labor. There were opportunities in the maintenance of defense installations and weather stations and there were employment opportunities in the public sector, including public sector construction. A mixed economy, with cash gained from wages, fur sales, and government transfer payments included the balance of livelihood gained from domestic harvesting (Stabler and Howe 1990).

## Institution Building

Sound institutional arrangements are decisive for sustained economic development. Such arrangements "set the framework for economic development" and include political, governmental and partnership organizations and structures, as well as institutional rules, policies, and procedures. A study of First Nations institutional arrangements for economic development found that "[good] practices include developing a vision to guide economic development, establishing institutional arrangements to ensure that development is sustainable, and partnering with others to benefit from economies of scale and expertise" (Auditor General of Canada 2003:1).

Development opportunities for Aboriginal people are being created as a result of provincial, territorial, and comprehensive claim agreement regulatory regimes, such as requirements for Aboriginal employment and local contracting in surface lease agreements to mining and other companies. First Nations participate in casino gaming in some jurisdictions (R.B. Anderson 1999).

Capacity creation and institution building emerged as themes in Aboriginal economic development in the early 1980s. In contrast with the previous decades of failed experience in labor market strategies and business development initiatives, these development institutions focused explicitly on creating the institutional capacity to support a broad range of Aboriginally controlled development initiatives (D. McArthur 1988).

One of the first institutions in Canada to embody this approach was Kitsaki Development Corporation (later Kitsaki Management Limited Partnership, KMLP), the economic development arm of the 8,000-member La Ronge Indian Band (Western Woods Cree) in northern Saskatchewan (fig. 2). From the outset, KMLP placed "heavy emphasis on capacity building and self-sufficiency. The investment strategy utilized by Kitsaki on behalf of the Band has emphasized institution building and participation in all sectors of the economy" (Decter and Kowall 1989:i). The role of the development institution is distinct from that of a business

Northern Lights Foods, La Ronge, Sask.

Fig. 2. The business of wild rice. top, Tom Charles, Lac La Ronge Band member, checking the maturity of the wild rice on Bigstone Lake, Sask., 2006. bottom, Walter Ratt, Lac La Ronge Band member, harvesting the rice by mechanical means on the Mercer River, 2006. Then the grain is cured and roasted. Both Charles and Ratt work for Northern Lights Foods, the largest exporter of certified organic wild rice in the world, exporting to Europe and Asia. Northern Lights Foods is one of the Kitsaki Management Limited Partnership businesses.

enterprise. At KMLP, the task was articulated in terms of constructing "the necessary infrastructure which provided it with the capacity to 'plan, design, finance, implement and operate economic development programs'" (Decter and Kowall 1989:11). The lessons drawn from the Kitsaki experience as early as 1989 identified the importance of: an arm's length corporation separate from political structures, focusing on long-run capacity building, joint ventures for accessing expertise and equity capital, rigorous project appraisal, a "business minded, profit-oriented approach," and key individuals (Decter and Kowall 1989:42). These lessons have shown some durability. The 92 employees in operational businesses in 1989 had increased to nearly 450, plus harvester and seasonal workers who supplied the KMLP enterprises in 2003 (Hindle and Lansdowne 2005). Some of the very factors that have made for KMLP success pose challenges, for example, in terms of potential vulnerability to leadership succession and enterprise life cycles that may necessitate exiting or strategically redirecting enterprises in response to economic conditions (Hindle et al. 2005).

Similar principles, recognizing the importance of creating an environment conducive to successful business development, rather than a primary emphasis on business management and job creation, have been followed in the creation of Aboriginal economic development institutions across the country. For Aboriginal economic development, "dual leadership" is important: technical, business leadership and political, cultural leadership that is compatible with the communities in which the institution is active (Hindle et al. 2005).

*Capital Corporations*

Since the early 1980s, a network of Aboriginal Capital Corporations and Aboriginal economic development institutions has been created. They typically provide business services, technical assistance and a revolving loan fund to support Aboriginal business development. Some, such as Peace Hills Trust (Samson Cree First Nation [Plains Cree]) and First Nations Bank of Canada (Saskatchewan Indian Equity Foundation and TD Canada Trust), are privately backed. A large number of institutions received core funding through the Native Economic Development Program, and others have established development or holding companies created with compensation from comprehensive land claims agreements. The National Aboriginal Capital Corporation Association, established in 1996, had 59 members at the beginning of 2006, including Aboriginal Capital Corporations, Community Futures Development Centres, and Development Corporations. The member institutions had a collective capitalization of $200 million and had provided more than $1 billion in loans between 1985 and 2005 (NACCA 2005).

*Human Resource Development*

In the 1980s, the federal "Pathways to Success" program established a five-year, billion dollar, Aboriginal human resource development strategy that was administered by provincial or local Aboriginal organizations. The funding for Aboriginal human resource development continued in the post-pathways period. In 1999, the Aboriginal Human Resources Development Strategy began and was renewed until 2009. Agreements have paid explicit attention to the issue of urban employment. These agreements have assisted more than 80 organizations to develop and deliver education and training services leading to employment.

The efforts to develop Aboriginal postsecondary institutions have met with limited success, in large part because of the reluctance of both federal and provincial governments to recognize and acknowledge Aboriginal institutions. Only two provincial jurisdictions, Saskatchewan (Saskatchewan Indian Institute of Technologies) and British Columbia (Nicola Valley Institute of Technology), have acknowledged the right of Aboriginal institutions to issue degrees, certificates, and diplomas. The federal government was unwilling as of 2006 to exercise its prerogative to grant educational charters to Aboriginal institutions. Aboriginal organizations are obliged to enter into partnership arrangements with provincially chartered universities, colleges and institutes. Both Métis and First Nation organizations across Canada have entered into such arrangements, with varying degrees of Aboriginal involvement in institutional governance, program and curriculum design and development. In some instances, these arrangements are made on a program-by-program basis, in other cases on an institutional basis, such as the First Nations University of Canada, which has a federated college arrangement with the University of Regina, Saskatchewan. Federal and provincial governments, despite avowed support for the principle of Indian control of Indian education as enunciated by the National Indian Brotherhood in 1972, have been unwilling to provide enough financial and policy support for this aspect of Aboriginal institution-building. Yet these institutions are vital both for human capital development and for research and other support for Aboriginal efforts at economic development (Aboriginal Institutes Consortium 2004).

*Land and Resources*

Access to resources is a major limiting factor for development, especially outside of areas covered by comprehensive land claims agreements in the north. The reserve land base is often insufficient for economic support of the resident population. Some successful Aboriginal-provincial and Aboriginal-territorial agreements have provided increased access to forest, fish, oil and gas, and mineral resources outside reserve lands and settlement areas.

There are provisions under the Indian Act related to on-reserve timber harvesting, although on-reserve timber resources are typically insufficient for operations on a scale that could provide community self-sufficiency (Parson and Prest 2003). In addition to the management and harvesting of on-reserve timber, several provinces have fostered greater First Nation and Métis participation in the forestry industry. Several provinces have taken steps to allocate forest lands to increase First Nation participation in the industry, including New Brunswick and British Columbia. Although timber allocations are made to First Nations under legislation in British Columbia, the allocations are often too small for viable utilization, and during the first years of the twenty-first century, forest revenues were in decline. The Saskatchewan provincial government was a pioneer in the use of forest harvest licenses and mine surface leases in northern Saskatchewan, requiring investors to maximize northern and Native labor and contracting. First Nations in northern Saskatchewan are involved in joint ventures; in 2005, the Meadow Lake Tribal Council, comprised of nine First Nations in the northwest of the province, had sizable stakes in milling operations and reportedly had 500 forest sector jobs. Profits from its forestry operations have been used to finance on-reserve education and recreation programs, and to provide capital for investments in other industries, such as aviation and hotels. But with the non-Aboriginal pulp mill in Meadow Lake under creditor protection, and the closure of the Weyerhauser pulp mill in Prince Albert, the Meadow Lake Tribal Council forest ventures are vulnerable to these and other changes in the industry (Lyons 2006). Similar challenges face other Aboriginal development initiatives that rely heavily on success in one industry. In Ontario and Alberta, Native participation in forestry has been limited. Growth of Aboriginal participation in the industry will depend on the ability of Indian and Métis development corporations to position themselves as preferred partners with existing industry players (J. Wilson and J. Graham 2005).

The Indian Oil and Gas Act (1974-75-76, c. 15; R.S. 1985, I-7) lays down federal regulations for these resources on-reserve. First Nations have negotiated agreements for pipelines traversing their lands. Indian Oil and Gas Canada, reporting to the Lands and Trusts division of the Department of Indian and Northern Affairs, administers the oil and gas agreements of 60 First Nations. It reports having collected over $1 billion from oil and gas activities for them.

The Fort McKay First Nation (Chipewyan) in Alberta negotiated participation in the oil sands development at Fort McMurray. The tribe provided services to the oil sector since 1996 and operated several companies under the banner of the Fort McKay Group of Companies, with revenues of as much as $50 million a year. A 2003 treaty land entitlement claim has allowed it to develop leases on 8,200 acres of prime oil sands land, which will be strip-mined and hauled to the nearby Shell refinery. There are plans to build a 400-unit hotel as a joint venture that will serve oil patch workers. There are a number of privately owned companies operating out of the Fort McKay First Nation. Participation in the oil sands development may offset the losses of traditional livelihood, such as hunting and trapping, as animal populations have suffered as a result of the oil developments (Harding 2006; Hutchinson 2006).

Treaty and Aboriginal rights for subsistence harvesting do not provide substantial support to development initiatives. Commercial treaty rights to fish have been recognized in the case of *R* v. *Marshall*, but the extension of those rights to other resources is in serious doubt as a result of the decision in *R* v. *Bernard* and *R* v. *Marshall* (2005 S.C.C. 43). The Aboriginal right to commercial harvesting was affirmed in *Gladstone* (1996 2 S.C.R. 723), but both *Marshall* and *Gladstone* so closely circumscribed the right that it appears to provide little scope for expanded access to resources in competition with other, established, commercial harvesters. In the case of the 34 Mi'kmaq (Micmac) and Maliseet communities in the Maritimes and Gaspé region of Quebec, the federal Department of Fisheries and Oceans negotiated agreements with First Nations to provide increased access to the fisheries and develop fishing capacity.

By early 2004, these First Nations were involved in more than 400 fishing enterprises with licenses to fish for several species, with a harvest constrained to ensure that the court-imposed limitation imposed on the commercial right, the right to a "moderate" livelihood is not exceeded. The federal government committed $325 million for this initiative from 1999 to 2004. Fisheries and Oceans Canada is involved in programs to increase the participation in commercial activity by Indians through a communal commercial license reallocation from retiring commercial license holders.

Building institutions and negotiating effective institutional arrangements have supported a range of development efforts. Aboriginal capital corporations face serious limitations in the amount of resources they are able to commit to any enterprise, and they risk exposure to significant losses that can erode the capital base of these small institutions. Although the federal and provincial governments both provide significant resources for Aboriginal human resource development, education, and skills training, in 2005 there was no policy or financial commitment to building Aboriginal higher education institutions. In the area of forestry, oil and gas, mining and other resources, Aboriginal participation can be enhanced or hindered by the legislative, regulatory, and policy measures on Indian and Métis participation in the industries.

## Governance

The quality of governance is recognized as crucial to successful Aboriginal economic development. The Harvard Project on American Indian Economic Development concluded that the key factors for successful development are essentially political, including "practical sovereignty," "capable governing institutions," and "cultural match." Two other factors that led to development success are "*a strategic orientation* (an ability to think, plan, and act in ways that support a long-term vision of the nation's future) and *leadership* (some set of persons who consistently act in the nation's interest instead of their own and can persuade others to do likewise)" (Cornell, Curtis, and Jorgensen 2004:7).

Case studies of Aboriginal communities, such as Meadow Lake Tribal Council, Saskatchewan; Niigon Industries at the Moose Deer Point First Nation, Ontario; and Osoyoos Indian Band, have confirmed these conclusions (Graham and Edwards 2003). The conventional wisdom that business "must be kept completely separate from politics" has been found to be difficult to achieve in practice in small communities. Revising their views, Graham and Edwards (2003a:9) concluded from further studies that: "So it is not the clear separation of business from politics that counts. Rather, commercial enterprises should be established and operate in a manner that respects good governance principles–performance, direction, legitimacy and voice, fairness and accountability."

Businesses must operate as businesses, but must also give back to the community and its members in tangible ways that contribute to the community objectives. Critically, enterprises cannot be developed as ends in themselves, "jobs and income," but must be part of the strategic orientation of "nation building."

Diversifying revenue sources, and finding increased "own sources" of revenue is important for reducing dependence on federal and provincial transfer payments. Osoyoos Indian Band, Membertou First Nation, and other nation-builders have shown that it is possible to generate significant returns that can, in time, dwarf the necessary and legitimate program dollars delivered through Indian Affairs, thereby enhancing its capability, as well as its accountability to the community.

The Indian Act and associated regimes for the management of lands, resources, and assets, and the lack of a regulatory regime for dealing with commercial and industrial enterprises on reserve lands has begun to be addressed through legislation.

The First Nations Commercial and Industrial Act (SC 2005 c. 53) of 2006 allows First Nations to select a process that leads to a provincially monitored regulatory regime of on-reserve commercial and industrial development, with the intention of encouraging investment in large on-reserve projects. The First Nations Fiscal and Statistical Management Act (SC 2005, c. 9) is legislation for First Nations wishing to establish a real property taxation regime on-reserve; it will provide a facility for those First Nations to use pooled resources to issue bonds and raise long-term capital for reserve infrastructure projects. The First Nations Oil and Gas and Moneys Management Act (SC 2005 c. 48) allows First Nations to opt into arrangements that will give them authority to administer and oil and gas code and a financial code that will regulate the oil and gas development and money management. Together, these acts arise out of 20 years of negotiations and discussions on matters related to lands, resources, and taxation. They may provide opportunities for First Nations to pursue on-reserve development opportunities, gaining access to their own financial resources in a timely way and with less direct government oversight.

The constitutional entrenchment of Aboriginal and treaty rights in section 35 of the 1982 Constitution Act evoked discussion of the extent to which both Aboriginal and treaty rights convey a right to livelihood (Henderson 2004). Treaties 1–7 from northwestern Ontario through the grasslands and parklands of present-day Manitoba, Saskatchewan, and Alberta, contained guarantees of assistance for the transition to a viable and productive economy, comparable to that of incoming settlers. Despite the record of treaty negotiations, which gave specific assurances of effective development assistance (A. Morris 1880:92, 213, 216), the federal government has generally interpreted the economic provisions as a promise of agricultural assistance rather than as a promise of economic development. In later and more northern treaties, such as Treaty 8, Crown negotiators guaranteed protection to the Indians in their securing of a living from hunting and trapping forever (Fumoleau 2004).

Since the 1970s, Comprehensive Land Claims Agreements, sometimes called "modern treaties," have been negotiated with Indians and Inuit in Northern Quebec and across much of the Canadian north. These agreements typically include lands with various degrees of ownership and control by the Aboriginal party, financial compensation, limited resource revenue sharing, and participation in land use planning and resource management. These are explicitly intended to provide a foundation for economic development and self-government, although the implementation of agreements has had mixed results (Rynard 2000).

Distinctions made by the courts between renewable resource harvesting for traditional domestic and for commercial purposes have seriously circumscribed Aboriginal participation in renewable resource development, despite the initial expectations of greatly expanded resource harvesting rights generated by the *Marshall* decision (Coates 2000). Canadian courts have demonstrated a bias favoring industrial resource development over traditional use of lands (Christie 2004).

Specific claims, arising out of the Crown's breach of treaties, and the treaty land entitlement process in Saskatchewan, Alberta, and Manitoba, have resulted in sizeable financial and land settlements that have supported economic development initiatives, including the development of urban reserves in Saskatchewan (Martin-McGuire 1999). The British Columbia Treaty Commission process, established in 1992 to facilitate the settlement of outstanding land claims arising from unceded Aboriginal title throughout most of British Columbia, saw 48 federal–provincial–First Nation negotiations underway in 2007, involving 58 First Nations. In 2007, seven had reached agreement-in principle stage, and no final agreements had been settled, the 1999 Nisga'a agreement having been negotiated outside the British Columbia Treaty Commission ("Nisga'a," this vol.). The sole final agreement was rejected by the First Nation membership in 2007.

The 1973 Supreme Court decision in *Calder* v. *Attorney General of British Columbia* recognized that Aboriginal title had existed in British Columbia. The court was split on whether or not it had been extinguished. Meanwhile, an injunction was obtained by the James Bay Cree briefly halting the James Bay Hydroelectric project, and a *caveat*, claiming Aboriginal title, was placed on 400,000 square miles of the western Arctic, creating uncertainty for the proposed McKenzie Valley Pipeline (vol. 4:282). This led to the negotiation of comprehensive land claims agreements. In 1974, the James Bay and Northern Quebec Agreement was signed ("James Bay Cree," this vol.); in 1984, the agreement on the western Arctic was signed. Other final agreements, or agreements in principle, encompassing most of the north—with the exception of the Deh Cho (Slavey) and the Innu, have been signed ("The Department of Indian Affairs and Northern Development," fig. 5, this vol.). These included the Nunavut final land settlement agreement and the creation of the territory of Nunavut as the self-government mechanism ("Nunavut," this vol.).

The agreements typically include: full ownership, often fee simple, over narrowly defined settlement rights; rights to wildlife harvesting; co-management of resources over a larger area of traditional lands, including participation in environmental measures, and land use planning; financial transfers and compensation; and limited participation in sharing of resource revenues (Agreements, Treaty and Negotiated Settlements Project 2004). These agreements create structures and resources to leverage significant economic development (Saku and Bone 2000).

Analysis of the differential economic impacts of land the Inuvialuit Final Agreement in 1984 and the James Bay and Northern Quebec Agreement in 1974 has suggested that the emphasis on market development in the Inuvialuit region and the emphasis on the traditional resource sector in the James Bay agreement may account for the different economic impacts (Saku 2002). Based on the status of the Inuvialuit corporate portfolio as of 2000 as an exemplar of a land claim generating economic development, "Aboriginal entrepreneurship and economic development building on this foundation [land claims agreements] is the key to achieving such prosperity" (R.B. Anderson et al. 2004:644). The prospects for sustainable resource management of the extensive land base covered under land claims agreements are better under a co-management regime, yet in the absence of sustained economic development, and an emphasis on human resource development to spur innovation and enterprise, the agreements may end up creating desolate *"rentier"* economies, whereby people live on interest and settlement distributions, do not participate in the economy, and lack both innovativeness and education (Usher 2003).

By 2006, the James Bay Northern Quebec Agreement and the Inuvialuit Agreement were the only two with a lengthy implementation history. The legacy of the first quarter-century of the James Bay Agreement was one in which the promise of development for the Cree was largely unrealized, and the federal government failed to follow through on its treaty promises (Rynard 2001). In 2002, the Cree and the Province of Quebec entered into a 50-year agreement that provided $810 million in contracts for the Cree to participate in construction activities; a minimum of $70 million per year for 49 years (subject to increase depending on the value of mineral, timber and hydroelectric realized from the land claims area), and provisions to support expanded Cree participation in forestry, mining, and other economic development activities (The Crees of Quebec and Le Gouvernement de Québec 2002).

The Inuvialuit Final Agreement (1984) was more generous and more focused on economic development than the James Bay Agreement. The Inuvialuit Agreement provided for $512 million in 1984 dollars, control of 91,000 square kilometers of land (13,000 with subsurface rights), and consultative participation in wildlife management. The agreement provided for the creation of the Inuvialuit Development Corporation to foster participation in the economy, the Inuvialuit Petroleum Corporation, and the Inuvialuit Investment Corporation, intended to preserve the capital for future generations through the maintenance of a conservative investment portfolio. "In the case of the Inuvialuit at least, a just settlement of land claims has provided the capital for successful entrepreneurship and business development and has contributed to significant improvement in socioeconomic conditions" (R.B. Anderson et al. 2004:644). Under the terms of the agreement, the federal government's financial contributions could cease if it deemed that satisfactory progress had been made. The review of the economic measures section of the agreement found that:

> The results of the review have not been overly positive. Among other things, the review found that the economy of the ISR [Inuvialuit Settlement Region] lost ground compared to its northern neighbours during the period 1984–1999. There is high unemployment in the ISR, income from employment is low, and use of social assistance remains high. Additionally, the report identified some IFA economic measures that have been implemented, but are generally not effective.
>
> The review found that low levels of academic achievement and capacity across the ISR have been major factors in preventing the Inuvialuit from participating in the northern economy. While there has been growth of the economy in some areas, the lack of overall capacity has meant that the Inuvialuit have not been able to take full advantage of the associated opportunities (Inuvialuit Final Agreement Implementation Coordinating Committee 2002:3).

This calls into question the effectiveness of land claims agreements as vehicles for successful Aboriginal economic development. Even with significant resources for development capacity and with substantial financial resources, there may remain very difficult development challenges arising from the distance from markets, level of education and skills training, the difficulty of leveraging efficiencies of scale in a large, but sparsely populated area, the heavy reliance on the development of the resource frontier, and the limitations to entrepreneurial economy of a *rentier* economy relying heavily on the infusion of outside resources, or annual distributions from the settlement fund. Similar issues and concerns have been expressed with respect to constraints on development in the Northwest Territories (DiFrancesco 2000).

In 1974, the Mackenzie Valley inquiry recommended that development of the natural gas resources of the region be deferred until outstanding land claims had been settled. In 1999, there was renewed interest in development of a natural gas pipeline through one of two routes: Prudhoe Bay or Mackenzie Delta. Representatives of signatories to major land claims agreements, including Inuvialuit and Gwi'chin (Kutchin), formed an Aboriginal Pipeline Group to maximize economic benefits through ownership in a northern pipeline. In 2001, the Group signed a memorandum of agreement with Imperial Oil, Shell Canada, ExxonMobil Canada, and Gulf Canada with respect to equity participation in the development of a pipeline. Hopes have been raised that the one-third Aboriginal participation in this venture could significantly enhance employment and incomes for people of the region. This would be a collaborative corporate-Aboriginal venture to share in the development of the resource. The challenging issue yet to be addressed is how the net returns from the project, and the economic spinoffs that it generates, may lift the region out of the staple trap that has characterized the exploitation of the resource frontier of Canada since first European contact (Watkins 1977).

The 1930 Natural Resource Transfer Agreement, transferring constitutional jurisdiction over lands and resources from the Crown in right of Canada to the provinces of Manitoba, Saskatchewan, Alberta, and British Columbia, recognized outstanding treaty land obligations (except in the case of British Columbia); the three prairie provinces were obliged to ensure that Crown lands were reserved to fulfill them. The 1976 Saskatchewan Formula agreement foundered because of the lack of available Crown lands in the vicinity of First Nations with land entitlements. In 1992, an agreement was reached that provided a financial settlement based on outstanding land obligations, with provision for bands to purchase lands and to use residual financial resources for development purposes. The entitlement of 25 First Nations was recognized in the 1992 tripartite treaty land entitlement agreement, and by 2005, another four First Nations had signed agreements. These involve payment of $539 million and the addition to reserves of another two million acres in Saskatchewan, doubling the land base of reserves in Saskatchewan to about 2 percent of the area of the province. Although the process of selection of lands by First Nations has proceeded on schedule, the federal government has failed to act in a timely way to transfer the subject lands to reserve status. The Auditor General of Canada (2005) found that the Department of Indian Affairs lacked a plan to expedite the transfer of lands to reserve status. This problem was pronounced in Manitoba; a comparative analysis of the Saskatchewan and Manitoba framework agreements showed that there were disincentives for municipalities to enter into agreements related to tax and service arrangements, and no incentives for the federal government to expedite the conversion of purchased lands to reserve status (Pankratz and Hart 2005).

In Manitoba, 19 First Nations entered into treaty land entitlement agreements in 1997; another seven First Nations have entered into individual agreements. In Manitoba, most entitlement agreements were being fulfilled by Crown lands; there is provision for land acquisition monies for purchasing non-Crown lands.

In Alberta, between 1986 and 2000, 11 land entitlement claims were settled involving more than 190,000 acres and financial compensation of nearly $161,000,000, as well as additional commitments for $65,000,000 in new capital construction, and $3 million for a special employment and education program.

Thus, in the three prairie provinces, 66 First Nations have received (or will receive) significant additions to their land and resource base through the treaty land entitlement process, and compensation of $900 million dollars (although in the case of Saskatchewan, a large part of the financial package is for land acquisition). In Alberta the province, and in the case of 2,500 acres, the federal government, provided the land as part of the settlement. In Manitoba northern treaty land claims are being settled with Crown lands, while in the south, there is some provision for purchase. These have contributed significant financial and land resources to support development initiatives.


## Development Initiatives

### Urban Reserves

One significant development initiative has been the creation of urban reserves in urban centers and in towns and villages in the Northern Administrative District of Saskatchewan. The existence of federal crown lands in some communities created an initial opportunity for First Nations to select urban lands for addition to reserves. The early urban reserves were created by the transfer of federal lands to First Nation ownership: 41 acres in Prince Albert to Peter Ballantyne Cree Nation (1982); 55 acres in Lebret to Starblanket First Nation (Cree) (1983); jointly to Beardy's and Okemasis and One Arrow First Nation (Cree), 681 acres at Duck Lake (1992), among others. The land entitlement framework agreement among the First Nations, the province, and the federal agreement anticipated a process for the creation of urban reserves. The process allowed for urban land selection, agreement with the municipality, and completion of the "addition to reserves" process of the Department of Indian Affairs.

Urban reserves in Saskatchewan represent an experimental approach to economic and social development and capitalizing on urban opportunities without compromising Aboriginal and treaty rights (Barron and Garcea 1999). Although there have been discussions around creating urban reserves in other provinces, for example, in the cities of Winnipeg, Manitoba, Calgary, Alberta or Vancouver, British Columbia, by 2005 urban reserves had been established only in Saskatchewan, where there were 28. Nine had been created in the cities of Saskatoon, North Battleford, Prince Albert, and Yorkton.

Urban reserves contribute to the achievement of several objectives. They take advantage of the economic potential of valuable urban lands and access to urban markets. They offer a place for urban Aboriginal people to access health, education, social, and cultural services. Urban reserves enter into municipal services agreements as an alternative to taxation, ensuring no tax loss to the cities, while First Nations businesses and organizations operating on reserve have the benefit of tax-relieved status on on-reserve property and services, including Indians' individual employment earnings.

The Muskeg Lake Cree Nation urban reserve occupies 33 acres on the east side of the city of Saskatoon. It houses 40 businesses and organizations, including offices of the Federation of Saskatchewan Indian Nations, the Saskatchewan Indian Gaming Authority, the Saskatoon Tribal Council and the Saskatchewan Indian Institute of Technologies. Together, more than 300 people are employed on the Muskeg Lake Cree Nation urban reserve. The three First Nation urban casinos in Saskatchewan are on reserves in the cities of Prince Albert, North Battleford, and Yorkton; together these establishments employed approximately 1,000 people in 2006. There are two other urban reserves in Prince Albert, the site of the former residential school complex, and undeveloped lands just to the south of the school grounds. An administrative complex has been built, housing First Nation administrative offices and businesses (Western Economic Diversification Canada 2005).

In 2005, it was estimated that 1,356 people were employed on the nine urban reserves in Saskatoon, Prince Albert, Yorkton, and North Battleford. Many of these jobs might have been created even without establishing urban reserves; but arguably, the urban reserves have fostered a conducive climate for First Nation businesses and administrative operations in urban centers. These urban reserves contribute to employment of Aboriginal people in these cities, and they are contributing to the economic success of the host municipalities (Western Economic Diversification Canada 2005).

### Cooperatives

The first Aboriginal cooperative in Canada was created in northern Saskatchewan in 1945 for fish marketing (Belhadji 2001). In 2001, there were approximately 133 predominantly Aboriginal cooperatives across Canada (Ketilson and MacPherson 2001). A survey of the 50 cooperatives formed in the 1990s found that they were mainly operating in the handicraft and arts, consumer retail, and housing sectors. In 2001, there were 50 Aboriginal cooperatives in the North- west Territories and Nunavut, 23 in Quebec, and 21 in Saskatchewan, these regions accounting for 70 percent of these cooperatives in Canada. Three-quarters of coopera- tives are in the retail sector.

Cooperatives play an important role in coping with high transportation and storage costs, and the network of Arctic Coops achieves important economies of scale. Cooperatives in the provinces are more likely to be single-product, serv- ing particular markets. There are two main co-operative "centrals": Arctic Co-Operatives Ltd., formed in 1985 out of a merger of Canadian Artic Co-Operatives Federation Ltd. and the Canadian Arctic Producers, serving the Northwest Territories and Nunavut; and la Féderation des Co-opéra- tives du Nouveau-Québec.

The estimated volume of business by Aboriginal coopera- tives in 2001 was $250 million, with more than 90 percent accounted for in the retail sector. Marketing cooperatives account for only a small part of the Aboriginal cooperatives sector; these are concentrated in forest products, fisheries, and arts and handicrafts. Although the main activities of northern co-operatives are concentrated in the retail sector, many cooperatives provide other services, such as hotel, fuel sales, cable television distribution, and hardware.

Cooperatives are major employers in the north; 77 Abo- riginal cooperatives reported 1,410 employees in 1997 (Belhadji 2001:90), with 44 percent reporting more than 10 full-time employees. Thus, the cooperatives make signif- icant economic contributions to their communities.

*Joint Ventures and Partnerships*

Joint ventures and partnerships are important instruments for Aboriginal economic development in Canada. Ab- original partners may gain access to managerial expertise, technological knowledge, marketing capability, financial capital, and other resources that complement their own re- sources, financial capacity, and human resources. Business enterprises may gain access to natural resources within com- prehensive claim, reserve, or traditional Aboriginal lands; may be better able to comply with provincial and territorial regulatory requirements that mandate regional or Aboriginal employment or contracting targets; may gain access to Abo- riginal capital, such as the resources flowing from compre- hensive and specific claims processes, or from provincial and federal Aboriginal financial and human resource dev- elopment programs; and for major national and international procurement bids, can show social benefits of Aboriginal participation.

The Kitsaki Development Corporation is an example of partnerships arising out of a provincial regulatory regime. The Saskatchewan provincial government required uranium

companies in northern Saskatchewan to maximize northern and Native employment as a condition of its surface leases (fig. 3). Brodsky Construction of Saskatoon approached the La Ronge Indian Band to establish a joint venture partner- ship that would allow the company preferential access to construction contracts in the north (Decter and Kowall 1989). The regulatory regime was subsequently used by Kit- saki to develop other joint ventures (fig. 4).

In 1996, the federal Department of Indian Affairs an- nounced a preferential procurement policy for Aboriginal businesses, where contracts are to provide services to Abo- riginal populations, and, in some cases, more widely. With Aboriginal businesses defined as 51 percent Aboriginal owned and controlled, this has created further incentives for joint ventures between Aboriginal and non-Aboriginal businesses.

Membertou First Nation in Sydney, Nova Scotia, reor- ganized its band operations in the mid-1990s and obtained internationally recognized quality management certification for its management systems. The Membertou Corporate Di- vision provides strategic advice to chief and council regard- ing band business ventures and has leveraged important partnerships with industrial corporations. In addition to local businesses, including video lottery terminals, fisheries, and food and gasoline retailing, the Band has entered into corporate partnerships that secure profit participation and training for Band members, with SNC-Lavalin, Lockeed Martin/Fijutisu, and others (J.T. Scott 2004). Membertou has established an economic development fund to support entrepreneurship among Band members.

Kitsaki Management Limited Partnership, Saskatoon, Sask.

Fig. 3. Testing the water, part of environmental monitoring dur- ing economic development. Kelly Wells, left, an aquatic toxicolo- gist, and Jason Toutsaint, right, Black Lake Denesuline First Nation (Chipewyan), are doing sediment coring on Smith Bay of Hatchet Lake, Sask., 2003. They work for Canada North Environ- mental Services Limited Partnership, Saskatoon, whose clients include mining companies and municipal, federal, provincial, and First Nations governments. Canada North is owned by Kitsaki Management Limited Partnership.

Kitsaki Management Limited Partnership, Saskatoon, Sask.

Fig. 4. John Charles, Lac La Ronge Band member, picking chanterelles for Northern Lights Foods Limited Partnership, in the Wapawekka Lake area, Sask. The wild mushrooms, which are certified organic, are sold fresh, dried, and frozen. Photographed in 2005.

The Moose Deer Point First Nation (descendents of Potawatomis and Beausoleil Island Ojibwas) in Ontario established Niigon Technologies, an injection molding company, with technical support from Husky injection molding systems. The company has become certified as a minority company in Canada and the United States by the Canadian Aboriginal and Minority Supplier Council, as a means to increase its supplier opportunities with major corporations in Canada and the United States. It obtained internationally recognized certification of its management system as a supplier of parts to the automotive industry (Niigon Technologies Ltd. 2006).

Corporate-Aboriginal alliances "take various forms ranging from employment access programs at one extreme to true business joint ventures at the other" (R.B. Anderson 1999:98) and may include consultation processes, such as environmental and social impact studies, co-management regimes, and procurement and contracting opportunities among others. In addition to corporate partners, some Aboriginal communities have entered into partnerships with local governments in order to develop joint regional economic development opportunities (Atlantic Canada Opportunities Agency 2003).

*Casino Gaming*

In 1985, amendments to the federal criminal code made provincial governments "the sole legal providers and regulators of gambling in Canada" (R. Kelly 2001:43). In *R* v. *Pamajewon* (1996 2 S.C.R. 821), the Supreme Court ruled that the right to regulate gaming activities rests with the provinces, as the defendants were unable to prove to the Court's satisfaction that for-profit gambling was a distinctive feature of Aboriginal culture prior to contact (Morse 1997). As a result, gambling on Indian reserves is subject to agreement of the provinces and territories.

On-reserve charitable gaming, including bingos, pull-tickets, and raffles, are carried out in every province and are generally subject to provincial gaming regulations. In Manitoba, New Brunswick, and Nova Scotia, First Nations may enter into gaming agreements with the provinces to license on-reserve charitable activities. First Nations are allowed to have video lottery terminals on-reserve in Manitoba, Quebec, New Brunswick, and Nova Scotia, with varying provisions related to revenue-sharing and the number and location of the terminals (R. Kelly 2002). In Saskatchewan, the Indigenous Gaming Regulators, an institution of the Federation of Saskatchewan Indian Nations, license and regulate the on-reserve charitable gaming activities of First Nations who request it. It works with the Saskatchewan Indian Gaming Authority as a regulator of First Nations casinos' table games.

Casino gaming is found in five provinces. In British Columbia, the "Casino of the Rockies" is run by the Saint Eugene Mission Resort Limited Partnership, which comprises the Ktunaxa (Kootenai), Samson Cree (Hobbema, Alberta), and Rama Mnjikining (Chippewas of Rama, Ontario) First Nations. In Alberta, several First Nation casinos have been, or are in the process of being, licensed. These include a proposal by the Stoney Nakoda First Nations near Kananaskis; the Tsuu T'ina First Nation (Sarcee) near Calgary; the Enoch Cree Nation (Plains Cree) near Edmonton, and four other proposed casinos in central Alberta. In Saskatchewan, there are four Indian casinos, and approvals have been given by the province for two more, one to be built by the Whitecap Dakota First Nation (Sioux) near Saskatoon, and another in Swift Current. In Manitoba, as of 2005, two First Nation casinos were in operation, one at Opaskwayak Cree First Nation, near The Pas, Manitoba, and one at the Brokenhead First Nation (Ojibwa) in southeast Manitoba. In Ontario, there are two First Nation charity casinos. Casino Rama, Canada's largest Indian Casino, is one of four commercial casinos in Ontario.

In general, the provinces have controlled the approval process, requiring the First Nation applicants to meet strict criteria. In addition, a percentage of gaming revenues are typically appropriated by the province, part by casino operator, part by the host First Nation, and part to a development or trust fund to support social and economic development (R. Kelly 2001). Arrangements can be complex and controversial. The Rama/Mnjikaning First Nation casino proposal was more generous to all Ontario First Nations than other proposals. The chiefs of Ontario struck a committee to work out a revenue-sharing proposal. The split was 65 percent for 133 Ontario First Nations and 35 percent to the host First Nation, Rama/Mnjikining. The 65 percent would be split 50 percent by population, 40 percent by Band, and 10 percent to remote First Nations. The moneys were to be allocated for the five purposes of: community development, health, education, economic development, and cultural development. In 2001, the chiefs of Ontario voted for an equal distribution of net proceeds for all First Nations, including Rama/Mnjikaning. Rama/Mnjikining rejected the proposal and went to court to retain its 35 percent share, which has been held in escrow since 2001 pending resolution of the suit.

First Nation casino arrangements are subject to changing policies of the provinces. The Ontario government elected in 1996 imposed a 20 percent win tax, an amount estimated to return $100 million to the province. The previous government had ruled that Casino Rama returns would be tax-exempt. The imposition of a win tax on an on-reserve facility was strongly opposed by the chiefs, but the province withheld financing for Casino Rama until the Rama/Mnjikaning First Nation signed an agreement to turn over the 20 percent tax (Union of Ontario Indians 2006). At the end of March 2006, a deal was struck between Ontario and the Chiefs of Ontario that would have provided 1.6% of total gross gaming revenues over 20 years. In June 2007 the chiefs rejected the proposal, as it included restrictions on the use of their money and involved the loss of jurisdiction and sovereignty. The lawsuit by Mnjikaning First Nation and the Chiefs of Ontario continued.

Despite the legal entanglements of the several parties—Rama/Mnjikaning First Nation, the chiefs of Ontario, and the province of Ontario—the casino has been an engine for economic development, employment and income, especially for Rama/Mnjikaning and other nearby First Nations and the Orillia, Ontario, region. The casino has reportedly created 6,000 direct and indirect jobs, increased the occupancy rates in Orillia area hotels, despite having built its own major resort hotel and entertainment center. Approximately 500 Indian employees from some 52 communities work at Casino Rama. The annual payroll of the casino was reported at $95.8 million, and hundreds of millions of dollars have been made available to distribution to First Nations across Ontario (Union of Ontario Indians 2005).

In other jurisdictions where Indian casino gaming is permitted, issues related to revenue sharing, provincial shares of revenue, and compliance with the provincial regulatory regime abound. In Manitoba, the 2005 gaming report to the Assembly of Manitoba Chiefs pointed to the regulatory obstacles to the expansion of First Nation participation in gaming beyond the two small casinos that have been established.

Gaming has proven a source of jobs, income, and significant revenues for First Nations. In some jurisdictions, such as the Calgary, Alberta, area, market saturation is possible. Not all casinos are as well-placed as Casino Rama, in the Toronto area market. Some casinos are struggling, and some may fail.

The direct economic impacts, in terms of employment and incomes, can be substantial. The indirect, or multiplier effects, of the gaming industry are likely small (Dubois, Loxley, and Wuttunee 2002). The strategic issue for First Nations benefiting from casino gaming is to maximize the economic development benefits for further development. Objections based on the morality of the gaming industry, or the vulnerability of members of the host community to the dangers of gambling addiction, are often raised (Belanger 2002). Less often discussed are the ways to transform the short-term and limited returns from gaming into the creation of a diversified and vibrant economic foundation. The allocation of the revenues from gaming to purposes such as health, education, and community development represent real social returns to Aboriginal communities, but a review of the terms of trusts in various jurisdictions indicates that establishing long-term economic viability of communities is not a top priority.

# Nunavut

KIRT EJESIAK

Inuit went to the polls twice to determine if they wanted to create their own territory. The first referendum was in April 1982, when a majority of Inuit in Nunavut agreed to move along the road to self-government. The second referendum was held in May 1992, where 69 percent of residents of the Northwest Territories agreed that the Inuit should create a territory of their own (Amagoalik 1999).

On April 1, 1999, the Territory of Nunavut and its government came into existence. Nunavut, an area of 1.9 million square kilometers, is both a political Territory of Canada and a region legally defined by an aboriginal land claims agreement (fig. 1). In 1993 the Nunavut Land Claims Agreement Act was ratified by the Canadian Parliament, defining Inuit rights within what was then the eastern part of the Northwest Territories. Nunavut Tunngavik Inc. (NTI), the organization mandated to implement the Nunavut Land Claims Agreement, superseded Tunngavik Federation of Nunavut, the organization that had had the responsibility for reaching a land claim settlement for the Inuit of what is now Nunavut. As part of this agreement the government of Canada agreed to create a new Territory with its own separate government. For the Inuit of Nunavut there are two distinct entities—the territorial government of Nunavut and Nunavut Tunngavik Inc.

The government of Nunavut, with its capital at Iqaluit on southern Baffin Island (fig. 2), is in most ways like all other territorial and provincial governments in Canada. There is an elected 19-member legislative assembly from which the premier and other cabinet ministers are selected (fig. 3). The legislature is a consensus-style system without party politics where the government (premier and ministers) forms a minority. This style of governing forces everyone to discuss the root of the problems and ensures that every member is heard on a particular issue.

In addition to territorial governance, the territory elects one member of the Canadian parliament and has one appointed member of the Senate. There are some unique differences and problems. The territory covers a vast portion of the Canadian Arctic. Although Nunavut covers almost 20 percent of Canada, it has a population of only slightly more than 26,665 (2001 Aboriginal Peoples Survey), with a population density of only .01 persons per square kilometer. The Inuit population of 22,625—about half the Inuit In Canada—constitutes over 85 percent of the total, the remainder being nonaboriginal Canadians. Although all adult resident Canadian citizens can vote in territorial elections, the Inuit are the dominant political force in the territory. The vast majority of elected officials are Inuit. The territory has three official languages—Inuit (called Inuktitut), English, and French.

Although technically a corporation, NTI can be considered a shadow government working to keep both the government of Nunavut and the government of Canada accountable in implementing their responsibilities under the Nunavut Land Claims Act. NTI maintains a list of all Inuit beneficiaries of the agreement and is governed by a 10-member board of directors elected by beneficiaries (Inuit covered by the agreement) who are 16 years of age and older. The primary responsibility of NTI is the implementation of the Act as well as management of all Inuit-owned lands and income. Under the terms of the Act the Inuit have legal title to approximately 136,000 square miles of land and have a share of the royalties on minerals, oil, and gas developed within the 14,285 square miles. In addition, the act provided for compensation of $1.148 billion to be paid into a trust fund from 1993 to 2007. NTI provides a wide range of social and economic programs for the Inuit that are currently not provided by either the territorial or federal governments.

## What Nunavut Means

Nunavut means 'our land' in the language of the Inuit. However, the real implication is 'taking back what was taken from us'. This is what the Inuit faced when exploration companies and the federal government wanting to take the land Inuit have occupied and used for their subsistence lifeway for a millennium. Filmmaker Norman Cohn said it well: "Why people would take a sophisticated, 4,000-year-old intellectual and spiritual system that worked and had [them] at the top of the food chain and suddenly replace it with a completely foreign system, and end up 40 or 50 years later at the bottom of the food chain. Why would these people do this?" (Giese 2006).

The Inuit of Canada became organized formally in 1971. They began to question activities of exploration companies in their homelands, wanting to stop the environmental

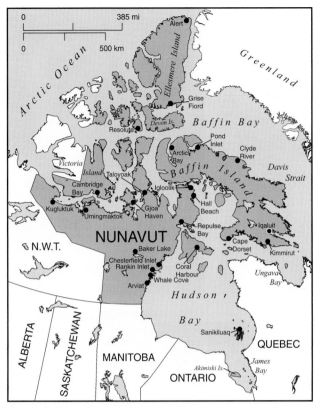

Fig. 1. Nunavut territory.

degradation that threatened the Inuit way of life. Through this struggle they began the process of creating their own territory.

Inuit were "passengers" in relations with government agencies for most of the period leading to the 1970s, and it was time for them to change places and be the driving force of change. There were many casualties along the way. Nunavut means many things to the Inuit. It means hope for a better future. It means opportunity that the Inuit can provide

AP Images.

Fig. 2. Iqaluit, which lies 200 miles south of the Arctic Circle, capital of Nunavut. The population is about 7,000 people. Photograph by Beth Duff-Brown, 2007.

for their families for years to come. It also means that Inuit can begin to govern themselves within the political structure of Canada (fig. 4).

Today's generation of young adult Inuit requires a unique plan for the future, particularly for those educated Inuit who do not live fully the traditional lifeway of their grandparents and for those who have a worldview. This is Nunavut, a political gamble with high stakes for its citizens. "By now the Inuit have had enough and are taking things into their own hands, not an easy task when you consider just how few they are compared to the countries (not one but four) they are subject to. But they are getting on, somewhat better than might be expected, although with a lot further to go" (P.K. Stern 2004).

**Inuit Political Activities and Organizations**

Inuit in Canada were permitted to vote in federal elections in 1950 (Stern 2004); however, prior to that time, the Inuit were full Canadians without access to benefits available to other Canadians. "Unlike the Indian policies that evolved in British North America after the Royal Proclamation of 1763, no official Inuit policy—neither British nor later Canadian—existed until after the Second World War. Although recognized as 'Natives,' the Inuit were not included in the Indian Act, nor was legislation passed to make them wards of the federal government. As a consequence, they were technically full fledged Canadians without any privileges—no access to health or educational services, and no vote" (Grant 2002).

Native Greenlanders were only permitted to elect representatives to the Danish Parliament in 1953 (P.K. Stern 2004); prior to that they were considered Danish citizens without a political voice. Since the Eskimoan peoples have become able to participate in democracy within their national states, they have accomplished much in a short time. Because of these changes that have happened in such a short period, many have had their lives transformed with the westernization of their daily lives and the dramatic shift to a wage economy.

Starting in the 1950s, with the collapse of the fox fur trade, and in the 1960s with the introduction of the snowmobile, economic and settlement patterns were radically altered. In 1953 the Canadian government reversed its Arctic policy and encouraged Inuit to settle in permanent communities (P.K. Stern 2004), where schools, nursing stations, housing, and the family allowance were all available. From the 1950s to the 1970s periodic canine epidemics and the Inuit movement into settlements revolutionized lifeways (RCMP 2006:6). The belief that the Mounted Police were responsible for the loss of their dogs circulated among the Inuit.

The Russian Yupik have had to live without state assistance and with near starvation even in the twenty-first century

AP Images.

Fig. 3. Nunavut government. top left, Hunter Tootoo, right, waiting to vote in the legislative assembly election for premier, on March 5, 1999. Photograph by Stephan Savoia. top right, 19 members of the legislature being sworn in on April 1, 1999. Photograph by Carlo Allegri. bottom left, Nunavut Premier Paul Okalik, center, a lawyer, signing a declaration of celebration at the inaugural ceremonies. bottom right, Okalik speaking at the inaugural ceremonies, while Prime Minister Jean Chrétien and Gov.-Gen. Romeo LeBlanc applaud. Photographs by Tom Hanson, Iqaluit, 1999.

because of neglect. Hunting was the only way to supplement their food source. However, some of the state-sanctioned hunting grounds were areas near nuclear waste sites. The Inuit Circumpolar Conference was able to drop ship food, medicine, and hunting supplies to assist their fellow Inuit from starving in 2001 (Rideout 2001).

Since the 1970s agreements between the Eskimoan peoples and their nations over land and harvesting rights have been developed. At the same time the Inuit became aware of the need to organize at the international level, mainly to combat industries that wanted to take control of the mineral-rich lands occupied by the Inuit in the circumpolar world.

The Inuit political history in Canada began in 1971 with the formation of the Inuit Tapirisat of Canada. This was done

out of necessity as Inuit were not involved with the large- and small-scale projects that affected their communities and their lands (Inuit Tapiriit Kanatami 2006). Inuit communities were being exploited, and the Inuit were more and more desiring to stop the exploitation. Oil companies wanting to drill large reserves, mining companies wanting to extract rich minerals, and tourists wanting to enjoy the wonderful scenery—all were affecting the Inuit environment.

In 1977, the Inuit Circumpolar Conference was formed to bring together all Eskimoan peoples—Yupik, Inupiat, Inuit, and Greenlanders—of Greenland, Canada, Alaska, and the Soviet Union (Chukotka), in recognition of the importance of international cooperation on issues and interests in national and international forums (vol. 5:724–728). The Inuit Circumpolar Conference is an organization that

AP Images.

Fig. 4. Members of the Arctic Rangers raising the first Nunavut flag on April 1, 1999. The colors blue and gold symbolize the riches of land, sea, and sky, and red stands for Canada. The red cairn in the center represents those that mark special and sacred places throughout the territory. The North Star in the upper right-hand corner (not visible) invokes the traditional guide for navigation. Photograph by Tom Hanson.

represents 130,000 Native people in the four countries (Lynge 1993). In 1983 the Inuit Circumpolar Conference passed a resolution requesting that each of the governments remove all restrictions and provide free and unrestricted travel. Resolution 83-30, section 7 stated: "THAT the Inuit Circumpolar Conference initiates and supports exchange programs among the Inuit, and the Inuit Circumpolar Conference requests from the governments of Canada, the United States of America and Denmark that all restrictions for a free and unrestricted travel throughout the Inuit homeland be removed; further that the Inuit Circumpolar Conference be the initiator of establishing central education and information centers, accessible for all Inuit and aimed at studies relevant to Inuit requirements" (Inuit Circumpolar Conference 1983).

The Russian Inuit homelands were not included in the resolution. At that time, it was impossible to travel outside Russia without approval from the Soviet regime in Moscow.

**Economic Situation**

The groups of Inuit who live in Nunavut are those traditionally called Caribou, Netsilik, Copper, Iglulik, Sallirmiut, and Baffinland, and many continue to live on the land (fig. 5). There were very few Inuit who owned and operated their own businesses before 1999. The government of the Northwest Territories conducted business using their business incentive policy, which favored northern-owned businesses over southern-owned businesses. Those existing non-Inuit-owned businesses were established mostly with the help of government in some way. Either they received large capital grants to start up or they received government contracts. Inuit businesses lacked the expertise in financial matters and skilled workers. This was in addition to the lack of financial institutions, the high costs of shipping goods, and the delays in payment for the services rendered. Payment could sometimes take as long as three to six months.

In the 1950s the federal government of Canada introduced a policy to have health care provided to Inuit living in the Arctic. The government wanted to educate the children and prepare them for a future with Canadian society. Residential schools were set up all across the north where the children were forced to attend. The children were not permitted to speak their traditional language.

The Inuit culture has survived assimilation, forced relocations, and the imposition of the residential school system on their children. These human rights violations against the Inuit happened over a span of 70 years, a mere two generations, creating a host of social ills. Among these problems are broken families, low employment, higher than usual suicide rates, and threatened identity and cultural values. It can be argued these acts of injustice of the Canadian state require them to provide for Inuit (and First Nations) until the healing is completed, in one or two generations, and there is mutual respect and understanding between both parties (Ejesiak 2004:17).

**Unresolved Issues**

Inuit of Nunavut have many unresolved issues that must be addressed in order to move forward and reach their full potential. It seems that today Inuit live from one crisis to another. This could range from tragic deaths of family members (from suicide, hunting accidents, or natural causes) to loss of jobs or housing. In order to deal with the real problems, which stem from the rapid changes in Inuit life, one must have relative stability with respect to housing, health,

AP Images.

Fig. 5. Traditional life in Nunavut. left, Caribou on Baffin I. Caribou remain a major source of food and clothing for Inuit living both on the land and in town. Photograph by Stephan Savoia, 1999. right, Polar bear hunting, Meeka Mike in her hunting cabin near Tuungait, Frobisher Bay. Photograph by Kevin Frayer, 2003.

food, and an adequate support system. However, many Inuit live in a state of flux, which does not result in these important factors being realized. Inuit therefore are suffering constantly without a way out of their situations. A solution must be found to break this vicious cycle that threatens to destroy several generations of otherwise productive members of Nunavut society.

The forced residential school program among the Inuit was responsible for pervasive sexual and physical abuse, isolation, neglect, and servitude (Blackstock et al. 2004). Lawsuits were brought in the courts, and the government is making restitution ("The Department of Indian Affairs and Northern Development," this vol.). With the abuse that occurred to a generation of Inuit (who make up the majority of Inuit leaders in the 2000s), this has bound to have had a serious impact in how Nunavut has been shaped. The suffering of those who were victims of abuse did not stop at the individuals who attended the federal schools but continued with their dysfunctional families. These traumas must be addressed in order for the Inuit to regain their self-sufficient attitudes of life.

*Housing*

According to the Centre on Housing Rights and Evictions in Geneva, Switzerland, housing is a human right (COHRE 1993), but for the Inuit of Nunavut this is more an aspiration than a right. In 1953 the government of Canada promised Inuit housing for each family. This is the time when the Department of Indian Affairs and Northern Development implemented a policy that encouraged the Inuit to settle in permanent communities (P.K. Stern 2004). Only about 25 families live away from the urban communities.

The housing crisis has slowly increased in Nunavut since the 1940s. The Inuit are in dire straits when it comes to housing. While efforts by both the federal and territorial government have included a range of programs and services over the years, "the end result remains the same: Inuit in Nunavut currently experience among the highest levels of overcrowded, inadequate housing in the country" (Government of Nunavut 2004).

When comparing levels of housing with the rest of Canada, there is an equity issue for the Inuit. Funding allocations have been distributed unequally among Aboriginal peoples. In Nunavut, 54 percent of Inuit were living in overcrowded conditions. Multiple families sleep in shifts within homes that average less than 1,000 square feet (Government of Nunavut 2004).

Unlike on-reserve First Nations people, Inuit pay taxes. However, Article 2 of the constitutionally protected Nunavut Land Claims Agreement states that nothing in the Agreement shall: "(a) be construed so as to deny that Inuit are an aboriginal people of Canada . . .; (b) affect the ability of Inuit to participate in and benefit from government programs for Inuit or aboriginal people generally as the case may be." Yet social housing programs for Nunavut ceased even while on-reserve housing programs for other Aboriginal Canadians were maintained and, in some cases, improved. Since 1993, over $3.8 billion has been invested in housing for First Nations, while Inuit, clearly recognized as Aboriginal people, were specifically excluded.

*Health*

An important issue related to the right housing is the health of the Inuit. Overcrowding is the norm in Inuit communities. This has negative consequences to health among the Inuit. "Aboriginal people more likely to live in crowded conditions. Health experts maintain that inadequate housing can be associated with a host of health problems. For example, crowded living conditions can lead to the transmission of infectious diseases such as tuberculosis and hepatitis A, and can also increase risk for injuries, mental health problems, family tensions and violence" (O'Donnell and Tait 2003).

The life expectancy for the Inuit of Nunavut is 10 years lower than the rest of Canada at 68.7 years. The infant mortality for the Inuit of Nunavut is 3.5 times higher than the Canadian average, at 15.6 per 1,000 live births (Healey et al. 2004). According to the Nunavut Ten Year Housing Action Plan, "Inadequate, unsuitable, overcrowded housing has long been linked to community and social well being. Although specific causal relationships remain elusive, there is increasing evidence, for example, that overcrowded conditions can have direct health effects upon household members—especially infants. According to Health Canada, overcrowded housing conditions are associated with the transmission of infectious diseases such as tuberculosis" (Health Canada 1999:14).

Human rights are interdependent and it is evident and clear that health and education are linked to adequate hous-ing. Lack of adequate housing contributes to poor health and low levels of education among the Inuit. Respiratory synctitial virus and tuberculosis are two contagious respiratory diseases that are known to spread more easily in cramped quarters.

*The Future*

The expectations of Inuit prior to the creation of the Territory may have been too high for the political leaders to manage. Inuit may not have understood how long it would take to create a fully functioning government and the time it takes to change the laws to fully reflect the people's wishes. Thus, many people in Nunavut were disappointed. There now exists a split of ideology between those who have government jobs who are non-Inuit and those who are leading the political changes to increase the number of Inuit in government. The non-Inuit employees are slowly working themselves out of a stable job to make way for newly trained Inuit.

# James Bay Cree

COLIN H. SCOTT

The Cree east of James Bay in northern Quebec are a hunting people who have undergone rapid and dramatic social change, while accumulating enough power in their relations with the Canadian state to significantly influence the course of that change. The Crees of Quebec (East Main Cree) were the first indigenous nation in Canada, since the numbered treaties of land cession and surrender concluded between the 1870s and 1920s, to negotiate a comprehensive claims settlement, the James Bay and Northern Quebec Agreement signed in 1975 ("The Department of Indian Affairs and Northern Development," fig. 5, this vol.) (Anonymous 1976).

They did so at the beginning of an era of rising consciousness of the human rights dimension of Canada's dealings with indigenous peoples, consciousness that their regional representative body, the Grand Council of the Crees, has done much to promote. The Crees of Quebec have remained at the leading edge of indigenous rights discourse, both within Canada and in international arenas, ever since. Notwithstanding a series of southern-initiated industrial activities on their lands and waters, they have managed to defend workable if diminished conditions for what remain some of the most active hunting, fishing, and trapping communities in northern Canada. At the same time, their negotiation of rights to a share of modern economic benefits has enabled the development of a relatively affluent cash economy, which became the primary occupational setting for the majority of Cree people.

The James Bay and Northern Quebec Agreement, along with the Agreement Concerning a New Relationship between Le Gouvernement du Québec and the Crees of Quebec (Anonymous 2002), remain the primary legal expressions of the relationship established by the Cree with the provincial government of Quebec and the federal government of Canada. The Agreement is a major amendment, regarding Quebec's undertakings, to the 1975 treaty. These treaty arrangements are protected under the Canadian Constitution (Canada 1982a, 1983a), such that the terms of treaty cannot be changed unilaterally by either provincial or federal governments. But the gains made by the Cree stem as much from the circumstances under which and the strategies with which Cree rights together with other political resources have been wielded, as from the terms of treaty per se. Behind treaty agreement lie sustained political action and a social history that this chapter seeks to outline.

## Circumstances Prior to Industrial Intrusions and Treaty-Making

In the 1950s, as they had done for generations, the great majority of the East Main Cree of eastern James Bay primarily hunted, fished, and trapped for their survival (vol. 6:193–207). They spent the fall, winter, and spring of each year on extended family hunting territories, nearly 300 in number, with a total area of about 375,000 square kilometers. Each territory (*nituuhuu aschii* 'hunting ground') was occupied by a core group of kin by descent and marriage, sometimes joined by friends and neighbors, under the leadership of a hunting group leader and territory steward on behalf of the group, known as the *nituuhuu uchimaau* ('hunting boss'). Within major watersheds, regional bands of these Cree families converged for several weeks each summer on fur trading posts at major estuaries along the James Bay coast, or on major lakes and rivers inland, where they fished, socialized, and exchanged their furs for imported items they would need when they returned to their hunting territories by summer's end. The economic value of the furs exchanged remained, in a real sense, supplementary to the value of subsistence production for home consumption, as it had throughout the nearly 300 years of Cree engagement with European fur traders (Scott 1984). While there existed a transregional Cree identity rooted in shared culture and language, and ties of intermarriage between neighboring bands, there was no James Bay territory-wide political organization.

The 1950s brought the beginning of major changes to Cree society. A new expectation was imposed on parents that their children should be in school, not on the hunting grounds, which meant in the majority of cases that they had to be sent to residential schools in the south, outside Cree territory. Federal social assistance programs were systematically extended to northern indigenous communities. By the end of the 1950s, permanent villages with nursing stations and year-round housing (even if these houses were routinely vacant for most of the year, when people were in the bush for hunting) were being provided by the government. To manage the widening spectrum of interactions with southern governments, elected band councils as stipulated by Canada's Indian Act were regularized in the villages (Morantz 2002; Preston 2002). Through the 1960s, construction work in housing and other community infrastructure projects offered seasonal employment, supplementing income from hunting, fishing, furs, and social assistance payments. On the southern edge of Cree territory, there were seasonal (and sometimes year-round) employment opportunities in forestry, mining, and guiding. These diversifying forms of cash income became important for the maintenance of the hunting way of life, because the long-term trend in fur value relative to the material costs of imported technology and supplies was downward, and because hunters were incorporating new technologies, such as air charter service to get their families to and from their hunting territories. Hunting, fishing, and trapping remained the principal occupational focus for the majority of Cree households in all Cree villages into the 1970s, though the rising costs of hunting forced some families to spend more extended periods in the village to find employment and raise cash for their next season in the bush.

Notwithstanding these changes, most evident in the villages, the institutional and symbolic organization of life in hunting camps endured in a distinctively Cree mode (Tanner 1979). Cree hunters were in charge of activities on their territories, according to indigenous systems of knowledge, resource management, and customary tenure (Feit 1973, 1992; Scott 1988, 1996). The exceptions to this general picture of Cree possession of their lands and waters were on the southern edge of Cree territory, where mining, approaching industrial forestry, and some interference from provincial game wardens were experienced. These were early instances of encroachment on what mainstream Quebecers and Canadians regarded as their own untapped northern resource hinterland.

## Hydroelectricity and the James Bay and Northern Quebec Agreement

The defining episode of the 1970s was set in motion with the announcement by the government of Quebec, in 1971, of plans for three phases of massive hydroelectric development that would transform all major watersheds of Cree territory (fig. 1). The first of these, to be undertaken by Hydro-Quebec, a provincial crown corporation, would dam and divert a large portion of the Eastmain River and its tributaries, northward through Boyd and Sakami lakes, into the La Grande River, whose valley would be flooded with a chain of massive power generating reservoirs. This development would impose severe impacts on the Cree communities of Chisasibi, Eastmain, and Wemindji. Other Cree communities were scheduled for similar hydroelectric projects on

their territories, in Phases II and III of Hydro-Quebec's plans (figs. 2–3).

Phillip Awashish, a Cree man from Mistassini who was then a university student in Montreal, read about the announcement of the La Grande River project in the newspapers. He contacted another man, soon to become a prominent Cree leader, Billy Diamond. The two were among that generation of Crees who had received institutional education at residential schools in southern Quebec and Ontario. They used their knowledge of mainstream Canadian society, as well as the network of their peers from other Cree communities, to organize a meeting of community leaders and to inform the people in all James Bay Cree villages about the project. Village leadership had been neither consulted nor informed by the governments of Quebec or Canada about the engineering plans for their territory. The assumption of government officials of the day was that no such procedure was required.

In 1969, the federal Liberal government of Prime Minister Pierre Elliott Trudeau had announced in its White Paper policy that Indian special status, and treaty-making to resolve matters of outstanding aboriginal claims, were aberrations in a modern liberal state, best consigned to the past. The resulting outrage from indigenous communities throughout Canada had forced the government to back down from this position, but the ramifications of this retreat had not yet penetrated to most governmental arenas, either federal or provincial (Weaver 1981).

The initial reaction of older people in the Cree communities to Hydro-Quebec's plans was incredulity that they were not regarded as the rightful possessors of their traditional territories; that such massive transformation of lands and waters would be physically feasible; or that if it were, governments could be foolish enough to intervene so drastically in the natural order of things. As people became informed that the plans were serious and that similar projects had been undertaken elsewhere, a consensus developed throughout the Cree communities to oppose the La Grande project. The early organizing and local consultations were undertaken with the support of the Indians of Quebec Association. But a divergence of interest led the eight Cree communities to go their own way, incorporating themselves politically as the Grand Council of the Crees of Quebec, which would assume control of the process of litigation and negotiation.

The demands of engaging state institutions in an oppositional manner precipitated not only a new regional political identity and organization but also for some purposes reconfigured leadership locally. There was now a premium on electing band council chiefs and councilors with strong oral and literate competence in either English or French. Although elders and other Crees with little exposure to formal schooling were still to be found on local councils, their ratio declined. Elder chiefs were replaced with younger individuals schooled in southern residential schools, people who could represent communities to the outside world, and

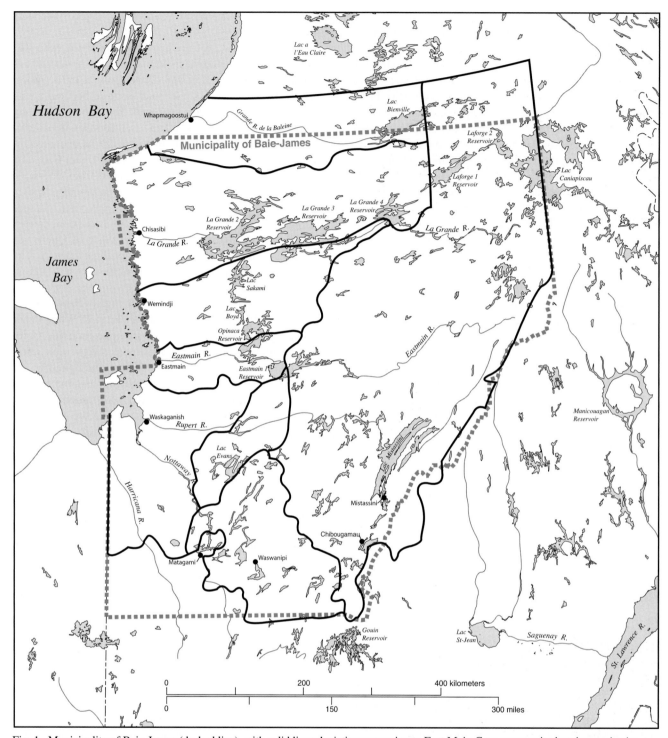

Fig. 1. Municipality of Baie-James (dashed line), with solid lines depicting approximate East Main Cree community hunting territories. Reservoirs indicate submerged Cree lands.

interpret the outside world for community members. On the hunting territories, meanwhile, customary leadership anchored in knowledge of the land, and the relationships with humans and animals deemed necessary to effectively direct the enterprise of hunting, remained intact.

The Cree leadership turned to the federal government of Canada for support, given its constitutional jurisdiction for Indians and Indian lands. But the federal (Liberal Party) government sought to avoid entanglement in the issue. Natural resources were constitutionally a provincial jurisdiction, and it was feared that federal interference in the provincial government (also Liberal Party) plans for hydroelectric development would inflame Quebecois nationalism and add fuel to a separatist movement within the

AP Images.

Fig. 2. Cranes and other earth-moving equipment used to create the dam for La Grande 2 reservoir, which is part of Quebec's James Bay Hydroelectric project. Because no permanent roads existed, over 1,500 km of highway was constructed to reach the site. The largest hydroelectric project at the time, it affected a land area the size of France. Photograph by Jeffrey Ulbrich, 1990.

province. The Cree did, however, receive funding assistance through the federal government's Comprehensive Land Claims Policy, formulated in 1972 in response both to its retreat from the 1969 White Paper, and the Supreme Court of Canada's groundbreaking *Calder* v. *Attorney General of British Columbia* decision in 1971 in regard to the claim of the Nisga'a, which recognized the strong possibility that aboriginal rights in areas not previously covered by treaty had survived the acts of colonial and post-Canadian Confederation legislators.

The Cree in Quebec had signed no treaties because the government of Quebec, during the era in which Canada's Treaty Commissioners negotiated the numbered treaties of

AP Images.

Fig. 3. Spillway at the Robert-Bourassa dam (formerly La Grande 2), part of Canada's largest hydroelectric system. The terraced diversion channel is carved 100 feet into the side of a mountain. The power station has a generating capacity of 16,000 megawatts, three times that of all stations at Niagara Falls. Photograph by Jeffrey Ulbrich, 1990.

land cession and surrender in several other provinces, had refused to be a party to the process. This era of provincial refusal to acknowledge aboriginal title was a legacy that now favored the Cree. It was not only that the Cree were unbound by the terms on which land cession and surrender was secured, or at least later interpreted, by the Crown under the numbered treaties. In addition, Canada had stipulated, as a condition of its Quebec Boundaries Extension Act (Canada 1912), which added to Quebec's territory lands north of the Eastmain River, that Quebec would recognize the rights of Indian inhabitants of the newly granted provincial lands and obtain "surrenders" acceptable to the federal government. This Quebec had never done. In a bid to halt construction activities associated with the James Bay hydroelectric project, the Cree in November 1972 launched an action in Montreal Superior Court seeking an injunction against the development.

Hundreds of hours of testimony were heard from Cree leaders, hunters, and elders, as well as expert witnesses from a range of academic and professional disciplines. Evidence introduced on matters of Cree economy, culture, and history stemmed largely from the research of scholars at McGill University's program in the Anthropology of Development. In 1973 the judge declared that the Cree had a prima facie case for title, rights, and interests in the territory that would be compromised were the construction allowed to continue, and he ordered a temporary injunction (Richardson 1979).

Quebec appealed this decision to the Quebec Court of Appeals, which summarily reversed the temporary injunction on an argument of "balance of convenience," that the interests of 6,000 Cree were outweighed by the interests of 6,000,000 Quebecers. Construction could resume, while the Court of Appeals would render its decision on the actual merits of the case in a year's time. The Cree in turn appealed to the Supreme Court of Canada, which refused to hear the case until the Quebec Court of Appeals had ruled on the merits. Hence, the project would be a fait accompli by the time the Cree could have recourse to the Supreme Court. They were left little option but to negotiate.

The judicial decision did push Quebec into negotiating seriously with the Cree. Quebec and its investors were jittery about the prospect of massive reparation that might eventually be ordered by the Supreme Court. Quebec and the Canadian government commenced negotiations with the Cree as well as the Inuit, whose most southerly communities would be impacted by the proposed Great Whale River phase of development, and to whom the same federal expectations of Quebec would apply as to the Cree under the 1912 Quebec Boundaries Extension Act.

Here only the most general summary of the processes and terms of the resultant James Bay and Northern Quebec Agreement is possible (La Rusic et al. 1979; Salisbury 1986; Feit 1989; Vincent and Bowers 1988; Scott 2001). One may say that what occurred was an exchange of general and unspecified aboriginal title for the rights and benefits spelled out in the agreement. There is indication in the language of the agreement that the provincial and federal governments thought they were achieving the extinguishment of aboriginal title in exchange for treaty rights, rather in the vein of the old numbered treaties, albeit at the price of more substantial treaty entitlements. Cree leaders have since declared themselves against such interpretation, arguing that inherent aboriginal rights, like fundamental human rights, cannot be extinguished. This is not the place to argue the legal issues involved, but it is important to recognize, in building an account of the aftermath of the original James Bay and Northern Quebec Agreement, that the political possibilities for Cree control of their traditional territory overflow the letter of the agreement.

Expressed in surface areas, the land regime of the James Bay and Northern Quebec Agreement does not seem very advantageous for the Cree. Category I lands are those to which Cree communities have ownership in inalienable collective fee simple, and on which Cree villages are located. They are only 5,500 square kilometers, or about 1.5% of the territory occupied by the Cree. Category II lands, comprising an additional 65,000 square kilometers (17.3% of Cree territory), are lands on which the Cree have exclusive rights to hunting, fishing, trapping and certain other traditional subsistence resources, but from which Quebec also has the right to remove land for development, subject to replacement with similar lands from Category III lands. Category III lands, the remainder and substantial majority of Cree territory, are deemed public lands to which general provincial legislation and regulations apply. However, the Cree do retain preferential rights to subsistence resources in general, as well as exclusive rights to fur animals and certain other species.

What Crees were forced to yield in terms of outright ownership they retained in some measure through co-management arrangements for the governance of lands, waters, and resources. Their participation in the Hunting-Fishing-Trapping Coordinating Committee (Anonymous 1976:section 24) affords a role in wildlife management, and their participation in the various environmental assessment and review bodies of the environmental regime (section 22) involves them in the evaluation of development projects, throughout the whole of their territory. The numbers of aboriginal members in the co-management bodies roughly balance those of provincial and federal government members. However, these bodies remain, for the most part, advisory and consultative in nature, inasmuch as their advice, while normally providing the basis for policy and regulations, may be accepted or declined by the provincial or federal ministry responsible in a given area of jurisdiction.

Self-government was enhanced through the creation of a regional Cree School Board, a regional Cree Board of Health and Social Services, and provisions for local government to be elaborated in later negotiations, culminating in the Cree-Naskapi of Quebec Act (Canada 1984a). The Cree School Board and the Cree Board of Health and Social Services, like the Grand Council of the Crees and its administrative arm, the Cree Regional Authority, enabled the Cree to command more resources in the form of transfers for public administration from provincial and federal governments, to exercise more authority than they could have done as individual communities, and to strengthen the regional coordination of services. The existence of the regional bodies stimulated pro-active self-governance at the local community level, sometimes in competition with the regional level. Substantial social learning has occurred, since the James Bay and Northern Quebec Agreement was signed, about those situations and contexts in which authority is best vested at the local level, and those in which the collective interest is best served through strong regional institutions.

The James Bay and Northern Quebec Agreement provided compensation to the Cree, in the order of $240 million. While it seemed a large settlement in 1975, and provoked accusations of "sell-out" from some other indigenous groups and from environmentalist allies of the Cree who were disgruntled that a campaign of uncompromising opposition could not be sustained, it would prove inadequate to the needs for services and economic development of a rapidly expanding Cree population.

## Gathering Power

From a population of about 6,000 in 1975, the Quebec Cree population grew to roughly 14,000 in 2005. At first, growth in the young adult labor force could be accommodated, through the rapid expansion of Cree-controlled local and regional administration and services for those who sought jobs, and through a new Income Security Program (established as a James Bay and Northern Quebec Agreement benefit to promote continuity in the hunting way of life) for those who chose hunting as their primary occupation. As a result, the Cree enjoyed a condition of virtually full employment by the early 1980s (Salisbury 1986).

The increase in employment opportunities, mainly through growth in public administration and services and some successes in local and regional entrepreneurial development, did not keep up with growth in the labor force. By the early 1990s, local communities were reporting unemployment rates approaching 30 percent, borne largely by young adult sectors of the population. There were ecological limits to accommodating increased population in occupational hunting, exacerbated by the fact that the communities of Eastmain, Chisasibi, and Wemindji lost a large percentage of their prime large river, lake, and wetland habitat to hydroelectric diversions and reservoirs. The new reservoirs and diversion corridors were largely unsuitable for hunting and fishing, due to navigational hazards and methyl-mercury contamination of fish. In the southern portion of Cree territory, meanwhile, industrial forestry was steadily eroding Cree hunting territory, and sport hunters from the south were competing heavily for moose, thanks to vehicular access afforded by highways and forestry roads.

While the number of households on the Income Security Program for Cree hunters had stabilized at a level comparable to that of the late 1970s (when the program increased participation in occupational hunting compared with the years immediately prior to implementation of the James Bay and Northern Quebec Agreement; Feit 1991), this number by the early 1990s represented a steadily diminishing percentage, on the order of 25–30 percent, of the Cree population. The economic growth generated by compensation monies combined with transfers of provincial and federal funding for various services and programs administered by the Cree was not enough. The Cree found themselves in the position of having to balance their opposition to large-scale hydroelectric developments to protect the hunting way of life with their need to negotiate additional income from resource development.

Although cash resources were all too finite, they were nevertheless of sufficient magnitude, in combination with the organizational capacity of the burgeoning Cree Nation, to enable Cree to maintain an effective political presence vis-à-vis the provincial and federal governments. Thanks to their ability to sustain costly processes of litigation, of lobbying central governments, and of media connection to the public, the Cree achieved court victories in actions undertaken to remedy breaches of the James Bay and Northern Quebec Agreement, and they used the institutional arrangements of the James Bay and Northern Quebec Agreement as tools to enhance their political effectiveness in opposing unwanted developments. In the early 1990s, the provincial Liberal government attempted to develop the Great Whale River hydroelectric complex as Phase II of Hydro-Quebec's engineering plans for the James Bay region. The government argued that the Cree had already agreed not to oppose these plans on social grounds as part of the James Bay and Northern Quebec Agreement, and that the project could proceed subject to assessment of natural environmental impacts. Premier Robert Bourassa's government went further in an attempt to make the Great Whale River project another fait accompli, through an attempt to separate the building of road and airport infrastructure from the environmental assessment of the project as a whole, so they could begin public investment on construction before the Great Whale River project had passed the environmental review process stipulated by the James Bay and Northern Quebec Agreement. The Cree successfully blocked this maneuver in the federal court of Canada.

The requisite process of environmental assessment gave the Cree time to pursue other strategies in opposition to the Great Whale River project (McCutcheon 1991; Barker and Soyez 1994; Mulrennan 1998; Tanner 1999). They allied themselves with a variety of environmental, indigenous rights, and public policy organizations as well as economic nationalists and energy industry competitors who were opposed to Quebec's commitment to hydroelectric power as energy source and economic development tool. They pursued the international law angle, taking their case to the International Water Rights Tribunal in The Hague. They argued against the project in the media, in community assemblies, and in legislatures throughout the northeastern United States, on environmental, human rights, and economic grounds. These efforts were effective; the combination of their appeals and the uncertainties associated with a protracted environmental review process led power authorities in New York State to cancel key energy purchase contracts required to finance the Great Whale project.

In autumn 1994, a newly elected Parti Quebecois nationalist government took over from the Liberal government and indefinitely suspended the project. It was argued by some observers in the wake of this suspension that the economics of various energy options had shifted, and that the cancellation of key contracts was not solely the result of Cree political action. Notwithstanding this observation, the project would have been well underway before this shift occurred, in the absence of Cree resistance. Their victory established the fact that the pursuit of development plans on Cree territory without Cree consent could have unpredictable political and economic costs for governments. Recognition of this fact was reinforced by confrontation between the Grand Council of the Cree and the new Parti Quebecois government, over its 1995 referendum on Quebec sovereignty.

The Parti Quebecois government argued that in the event of a majority vote by the provincial population authorizing it to establish Quebec as a sovereign state, the provincial borders were indivisible and would become the borders of the new state. The Cree argued, along with other indigenous nations in Quebec, that this position was based in a spurious double standard: that if the boundaries of Canada were divisible, so were the boundaries of Quebec; and that if the people of Quebec could exercise sovereign rights as a people to determine their political future, certainly the indigenous nations on their traditional territories were entitled to no less (Coon-Come 1996). The Cree, along with several other indigenous nations in the province, held their own referenda, all of which affirmed by very large majorities their communities' determination to decide for themselves whether to remain with Canada, to go with Quebec, or to establish themselves independently. The votes of the Cree and Inuit and other northern indigenous people were sensitive for Quebecois nationalists, because the northern groups occupied territories that were conferred by the federal government on the province subsequent to Canadian Confederation in two boundary extension acts (Canada 1898, 1912).

In the event of a "yes" vote in its referendum on sovereignty, the Parti Quebecois government was aware, and indeed argued, that recognition by the world community of nations would be an important condition for establishing itself as independent of Canada. The Parti Quebecois government was confident that it could get this recognition. The

Grand Council of the Crees set to work to shake this confidence. They were active on the international stage, generating sympathy in European countries, in particular, for the argument that their own rights to aboriginal Cree territory trumped Quebec's claim. The Grand Council commissioned international law experts to assemble a publication titled *Sovereign Injustice*, which was followed by a condensed and popularized version (Grand Council of the Crees 1995, 1996).

The referendum vote was "no" by the most slender of margins, narrowly avoiding a crisis of Canadian federal disintegration. But the legacy of the failed Great Whale River project, together with the Parti Quebecois' realization that its posture toward indigenous nations had an impact on international perception of the legitimacy of its own nationalist aspirations, prompted a major shift in the provincial government's northern development policy. New hydroelectric developments would not be entertained without Cree cooperation and consent. This became stated policy in the late 1990s, an important condition for a major extension of the terms of the James Bay and Northern Quebec Agreement, in the form of the Agreement Concerning a New Relationship between Le Gouvernement du Québec and the Crees of Quebec (Anonymous 2002).

## Agreement Concerning a New Relationship

The new Agreement, dubbed the Paix des Braves ('Peace of the Braves') agreement in the francophone media, was attractive to Quebec as a means of opening a path for redesigned hydrodevelopment plans that departed from the engineering specified in the James Bay and Northern Quebec Agreement and that therefore needed Cree consent. Due to a pattern of rainfall lower than anticipated, over a period of years, Hydro-Quebec was encountering difficulty in maintaining optimum reservoir levels in the La Grande River Complex. Their solution would be to dam and divert a portion of the Rupert River northward through the Eastmain system and onward into the reservoirs of the La Grande. There were initial efforts by Hydro-Quebec to deal individually with the Cree communities affected, but communities were wise to this maneuver, and in any case the Quebec government was ultimately obliged to negotiate with the Grand Council of the Crees, as signatory to the original James Bay and Northern Quebec Agreement. The Rupert River diversion held some appeal for the Cree. It would result in only 10 percent as much flooding as the planned Phase III Nottaway-Broadback-Rupert Complex, and would greatly reduce the feasibility of that complex for the longer term. The Grand Council of the Crees was not content to negotiate the Rupert River diversion independent of more inclusive concerns over forest clear-cutting, proliferating mining activity, Cree economic and social development, and revenue sharing from resource extractive indus-

tries, none of which was satisfactorily resolved by the original James Bay and Northern Quebec Agreement.

Extensive clear-cutting by industrial forestry companies, and other unsustainable forest management practices, were grievances of the Cree. Facilitated by the highway infrastructure established to service the La Grande River hydroelectric complex, in the course of three decades a rapidly proliferating network of secondary and tertiary roads had been established by forest companies to clear-cut large areas on hunting grounds in the southern third of Cree territory.

The Cree had no voice in forest management, and they had been unable to apply environmental review procedures established under the James Bay and Northern Quebec Agreement to this form of development. They had been in litigation with Quebec over this issue, in the Mario Lord forestry case (Quebec Superior Court) since 1998 (Penn 1997; Grand Council of the Crees 2000; Feit and Beaulieu 2001; Scott 2005). As it had done in its opposition to the Great Whale River project, the Grand Council of the Crees sought allies, and they pursued a number of concurrent strategies. In environmentalist arenas, they appealed to public disillusionment over the destruction of forest habitats and resources, relating their own actions to wider public values and interests. They again geared up for an active publicity campaign in the United States, seeking the support of legislators, organizing boycotts of Quebec forest products, and calling attention to the endangerment of their own rights.

These sources of power, together with legal action and lobbying in Canada, spurred Quebec to negotiate the forestry issue as part of the new Agreement. Once Grand Chief Ted Moses of the Grand Council of the Crees and Premier Bernard Landry of the Quebec government resolved to pursue negotiations, these were concluded in a matter of weeks. All pending lawsuits and countersuits were dropped by both sides as a condition of the new Agreement. The Grand Council of the Crees accepted the Rupert River Diversion, subject to acceptable environmental review, in exchange for a variety of concessions by Quebec, including the "definitive suspension" of the Nottaway-Broadback-Rupert Complex.

A new Cree-Quebec Forestry Board was created to comanage forestry, together with Joint Working Groups in each Cree community to coordinate forest management plans with the management of family hunting territories. While these co-management bodies are, like others under the James Bay and Northern Quebec Agreement, consultative and advisory in nature, they were given power by having spelled out in the Agreement a series of standards for forest management in relation to the needs of Cree hunting territories. These may or may not prove sufficient and workable in the longer term, but they represent a considerable improvement over the former situation. They include, for example, the ability of hunting territory stewards to designate areas that for cultural and wildlife management purposes are exempt from forestry, or where cutting is kept

258

within stricter limits than in other areas; the replacement of clear-cutting with mosaic cutting generally, to mitigate impacts on forest habitat, wildlife and Cree hunting; and a specified minimum percentage area of hunting territories that must remain in mature forest, after forestry and forest fires are taken account of.

Because these standards are explicitly incorporated into the Agreement, they have the force of constitutionally protected treaty arrangements. Therefore, although the co-management bodies remain consultative and advisory, the discretionary latitude of the provincial ministry responsible for forestry is strictly circumscribed. A major element of the new Agreement is the roughly $3.5 billion to be paid by Quebec to the Cree over the 50-year life of the Agreement.

From 2005 forward, the base value of $70 million annually will be indexed to increases in the value of hydro-electric, mining, and forestry production throughout the territory of the East Main Cree. This amount fulfills, in part, Quebec's commitment to support the community and economic development of Cree communities and the Cree region. At the same time, it is a means to share revenue from resource extractive industries, recognition of a Cree stake in ownership of the territory amounting to something more than mere compensation for lands and resources surrendered. The cash component of the new Agreement is also an index of the negotiating strength accumulated by the Cree in the decades following the original James Bay and Northern Quebec Agreement. It is an order of magnitude greater than compensation received under the original James Bay and Northern Quebec Agreement, in exchange for Cree acceptance of a hydroelectric project that will yield a fraction of the generating potential of the original La Grande River Complex. Further, this is not a "final" settlement. It meets Quebec's obligations under the James Bay and Northern Quebec Agreement and the new Agreement only for the 50-year term of the Agreement, after which it will be revisited.

Monies will be used in part to support community infrastructure and services, but the primary challenge will be its use to achieve a sustainable regional Cree economy. A newly established Cree Development Corporation is to promote opportunities and expertise for economic development, through job creation, enterprise development, and partnership initiatives with non-Cree public and private enterprises. At the same time, the new Agreement includes undertakings by Quebec to support Cree economic development through provision of employment, contracts and joint ventures in forestry, hydro-electricity, mining, tourism, transportation, and regional infrastructure.

The new Agreement, then, represents a consolidation of political gains achieved in the 28 years since the signing of the original James Bay and Northern Quebec Agreement (fig. 4). It involves compromise among the multiple goals of sustaining hunting as an occupational and part-time pursuit for Cree; of generating a viable regional cash economy that will enable most East Main Cree to stay in their home

AP Images.

Fig. 4. Cree Grand Chief Matthew Mukash, right, and Quebec Premier Jean Charest, left, announcing another hydroelectric project in northern Quebec, which calls for the diversion of the Rupert River and 4 new dams. It will be beneficial for the economy by providing jobs and business opportunities for the Cree, but some sacred sites may be flooded. Some Cree and Inuit groups had opposed the plans. Photograph by Paul Chiasson, Montreal, 2007.

communities or region, where kin ties and attachment to local environments are strong; and of managing a politically viable relationship with state governments and citizens of the mainstream. It is too early to predict how effectively the terms of the new Agreement will enhance the ability of Cree to protect local and regional environments and to provide economic alternatives for all their people who wish to remain in Eeyou Istchee.

After concluding the Paix des Braves agreement, the Grand Council of the Cree focused on reached a separate agreement with the federal government, to resolve long-standing differences and litigation over the fulfillment or nonfulfillment of federal obligations under the 1975 James Bay Agreement. Negotiations were completed in July 2007, and a Cree nation referendum was scheduled for late 2007.

## Conclusion

What can be stated with assurance is that the East Main Cree have been among the most successful of indigenous peoples in organizing themselves politically for cultural survival. They have maintained substantial control of their

259

traditional territories, though the pressures from outside are unrelenting and there have been difficult losses and hard compromises. They have maintained hunting as an important component of their economy and a living cultural practice. They are building local and regional economies that have so far enabled the majority of their young people to stay at home, and they have developed in their villages a level of infrastructure and services that rival or surpass those in towns of comparable size elsewhere in rural Canada. While there are challenges to be met in employment, health, education, and cultural adjustment to village life, the general spirit of confidence and well-being in the communities of Eeyou Istchee stands in marked contrast to the poor circumstances against which many indigenous communities struggle.

In a span of four decades the Cree have forged an indigenous national identity and a regional society with a significant degree of autonomy within the Quebec and Canadian state. They have significantly increased their power to influence the terms on which southern industry makes increasing use of their home lands and waters. They have not been spared the conundrum of the mainstream's growth imperative, in which they are now implicated as a growing population of wage employees, entrepreneurs, and consumers of industrial goods and services. The expansive pressure of hydroelectric, forestry, and sport hunting and fishing industries will continue, and the Cree were experiencing in the first decade of the twenty-first century a wave of gold and diamond exploration that has resulted in major finds in the heart of their territory. At the same time, they have powerful vested interests as the original and permanent inhabitants of Eeyou Istchee, reinforced by a culture of environmental stewardship, to curb and modulate the demands of the mainstream society for their territorial resources and to set their own agenda for cultural and environmental sustainability.

# Nisga'a

MARGARET SEGUIN ANDERSON

The Nisga'a (Nisga'a, Nisgha, Nishga) have lived in the Nass River valley for millennia, and throughout that time they have defended their rich territories and resources from rival nations such as the Tlingit, Haida, Tsetsaut, Gitksan, and Coast Tsimshian. Their most valiant struggle was waged in courtrooms and at negotiating tables against the Crown of Canada and British Columbia, and their success is recorded in the Nisga'a Treaty of 1998, the first modern treaty signed by a First Nation in British Columbia. The lengthy fight by the Nisga'a people to secure their land and resources ultimately reshaped the province of British Columbia and the nation of Canada, marking a watershed in relations between aboriginal peoples and the state.

## Identification and Location

The territories of the Nisga'a comprise the rich, rain-forested watershed of the Nass River, from the glacial headwaters among interior mountains to the estuary where the river meets the Pacific (fig. 1). The Nisga'a share a common ancient heritage with their closest neighbors, the Coast Tsimshian and Gitksan, whose languages comprise the only other members of the Tsimshianic family. Although community size and location have varied, the present villages remain, for the most part, within a few kilometers of ancient settlements. Over the millennia there have been many villages in the valley; two were buried by a volcanic eruption around 1700. The Nisga'a are situated in four main villages along the river: Kincolith at the mouth of the river; Lax-galt'sap (formerly known as Greenville) 30 kilometers from the coast; Gitwinksihlkw (formerly known as Canyon City); and New Aiyansh, the most inland of the four villages. Until 1958 the villages were connected to one another and to the outside exclusively by the river or by overland trails (later replaced by logging roads). In 2005 there were 5,980 Nisga'a citizens, living in over 70 communities in British Columbia, other Canadian provinces, Alaska, and other states; the largest number lived in Prince Rupert and Terrace, while the four Nass Valley communities comprised about 28 percent of Nisga'a citizens (Nisga'a Final Agreement Implementation Report 2004–2005).

## History of the Tribe

The Nass Valley provides abundant resources, including rich runs of salmon and other foods; the mouth of the Nass is renowned as the most abundant source of the rich oil of the eulachon, which return in great abundance each year, and this resource has shaped the culture and history of the Nisga'a. These small smeltlike fish are valued primarily for their oil, which is traded to the inland and coastal peoples (vol. 7:269–270). The quality of the Nass River eulachon is particularly rich, and this has traditionally forced the Nisga'a to defend their homeland and resources from invaders while at the same time enabling them to trade widely. The early spring eulachon season at the mouth of the Nass River has been described as a great trade fair where as many as 14,000 Tlingit, Haida, Tsimshian, Nisga'a and other people converged to trade (journal of trader John Work in 1835). This figure is notable in part because there was a smallpox epidemic in 1836 that reduced the population, which had also been affected by earlier epidemics. The ancient migrations by which this region was populated created a network of communities whose common heritage is commemorated in family histories (adaawak) and the related crests depicted on totem poles and house fronts. It was this network that facilitated the development of a complex system of commodity exchange, a trading system that became one of the most important factors in the sophisticated and thriving economy of the Northwest Coast.

When the Northwest Coast was first visited by explorers and traders in the late eighteenth century they were quick to join the trade at the mouth of the Nass. Capt. George Vancouver entered the Portland Canal in Nisga'a territory in 1793. When Russian, European, and American fur traders visited the area, the coastal groups had direct access to the trade while interior groups traded furs through coastal middlemen. When the sea otter were depleted, inland furs became the main product of exchange, and the Nisga'a communities played a key role in the trade by capitalizing on their direct access to the furs of the Tahltan and Tsetsaut to the north and east, as well as to the markets among the Tsimshian on the coast. This enriched the Nisga'a and provided the wealth that supported a period of exceptional artistic productivity.

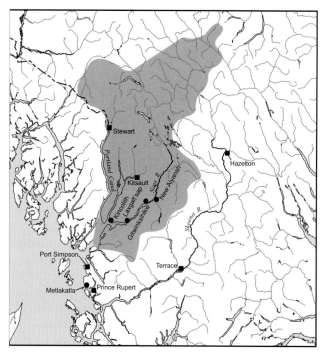

Fig. 1. Traditional Nisga'a territory, B.C. See also vol. 7:268.

The establishment of Fort Saint James in 1806, Fort Babine in 1822, Fort Simpson in 1831–1834, and the Hagwilget post at Hazelton in 1866 did not undercut the control of the trade by the Nisga'a and neighboring coastal groups, since links of kinship and longstanding trading relationships drew trade to native partners resident near the posts and forced the trading companies to deal with coastal middlemen. The Hudson's Bay Company moved Fort Simpson in 1834 from the Nass mouth to the present site of Port Simpson (Lax Kw'alaams) in Coast Tsimshian territory about 30 miles southwest. The eulachon fishery and trade remained an important part of the regional economy, and the products of the Nass valley continued to be traded at Fort Simpson and via the traditional grease trails to the interior. The impact of the emphasis on land furs, as with the earlier sea-otter trade, was an escalation of resource extraction, increased wealth in foreign goods, and a fluorescence of ceremonial and artistic activity. As the European and Chinese markets for furs declined and the Hudson's Bay Company consolidated its monopoly on the coastal trade at the mouth of the Nass and Skeena rivers and at the interior posts, the enormous profits from the trade in furs were replaced by modest returns. A status quo developed in which trapping for furs to exchange for European goods, and later for cash, was integrated into the economies of the groups in the area. The traders were far from genteel, and alcohol abuse and violence involving both company personnel and their neighbors were not uncommon. The first missionary to enter the area was William Duncan, an Anglican lay preacher from the Church Missionary Society, who began his work among the Coast Tsimshian at Fort Simpson in

1857 and who by 1862 had moved with several hundred followers to establish the mission village of Metlakatla at the site of an old winter village. Duncan visited the Nass in 1860, and in 1864 Robert Doolan and Robert Cunningham arrived on the Nass as missionaries to the Nisga'a, though Cunningham returned to Metlakatla after a short stay and Robert Tomlinson replaced Cunningham, remaining for the rest of his life. By this time, traders and military and government personnel who had become familiar in the area had been joined by gold seekers en route to the Cariboo. From this period to the middle of the twentieth century there was a small but steady flow of newcomers, who came to prospect, log, pack fish, mine, farm, or establish new communities, and whose resource extraction activities forced the Nisga'a people to engage in political and legal battles to defend their territories, at great expense in terms of money, time, and lost economic opportunities as resources were extracted by outsiders.

While the territory abounds in wildlife, and the temperate rainforest of the coast provided the Nisga'a with an abundance of shellfish and salmon, the climate and isolation of the valley were inhospitable to the sporadic attempts that were made at agricultural settlement during the nineteenth century. The presence of traders, missionaries, and Indian agents did not radically alter the ancient way of life as trade goods, along with new foods and ideas, were added to the existing cultural repertoire without rending the fabric of society. Over time, as settlers entered British Columbia in larger numbers, efforts to impose White institutions were followed quickly by legislation and regulations specifically intended to replace native practices. Eventually, small reserves were laid out, but their inadequacy—comprising less than 1 percent of the traditional territory—led the Nisga'a to engage in a lengthy struggle for their land rights. After British Columbia joined the Canadian confederation in 1871, systems of government, land tenure, justice, education, and resource management as well as religion and family structures were all attacked by laws enforced with escalating rigor. The period from the 1860s to the 1880s was a watershed marked by the influx of foreigners and their weapons; ultimately, a show of military force was used against several communities to quell their attempts to exercise their rights, though the only gunboat to enter the Nass, in 1866, shot off blank rounds from four 24-pound guns as a demonstration (Gough 1984:194). Once Euro-Canadian institutions became pervasive, the Nisga'a entered a period during which communities outwardly accommodated themselves to the new regime while developing strategies of resistance. After the federal government passed antipotlatch legislation in 1885—legislation that was revised and enforced in the 1920s—communities with resident Indian agents hid their activities in various ways.

In 1873, the first salmon canneries on the Skeena and Nass rivers brought non-Native residents to the area in substantial numbers for the first time, and shortly after this the federal government began interfering with aboriginal fisheries. Though some missionaries in the area attempted to support the rights of the original inhabitants to their traditional territories, the combined forces of church hierarchies, provincial administrators, federal Indian administrators, and land speculators were arrayed against them.

By the late nineteenth century an economic pattern had developed in each community involving a mix of seasonal trapping and hunting; salmon, shellfish, berry, and eulachon harvest and preservation; spring and fall trade; and winter ceremonies. Many families combined this pattern with annual moves to the commercial canneries on the coast to work in the fishing industry, the women in the processing plants and the men as gillnetters and shoreworkers (vol. 7:288). By the 1950s large forestry companies and commercial canneries were the key players in the economy of the Northwest, and the way of life of all of the residents was changed. As with the fur-trade period, there was a time of increased prosperity followed by consolidation of industries, depletion of resources, softening of foreign markets, and a marked decline, beginning in the early 1980s. Of the many thriving coastal canneries, only two remained in 2006, with their workforces shrinking. Many Nisga'a people were still employed in the industry, but much of the labor force resided in Prince Rupert where the surviving canneries are located, and this circumstance weakened the economies of the native villages. Forestry also saw consolidation, and the pulp mill near Prince Rupert was shut down, making it less remunerative to harvest the old fiber supply of the coastal rainforest. A molybdenum mine at Kitsault on Alice Arm was closed during the 1970s because of protests, spearheaded by the Nisga'a, about the impact of dumping mine tailings into the sea, but mining has a foothold in the northern part of Nisga'a territory and there is a small non-Native community at Stewart. Unlike other northwestern British Columbia First Nations, the Nisga'a people have remained the majority of the population on their territories. The entire northwestern part of the province was largely First Nations until the coming of the railroad and the building of Prince Rupert and Terrace in the first decade of the twentieth century (vol. 7:267–297).

In the twenty-first century the economy of the Nisga'a people continued to adapt. Forestry, fishing, harvesting of forest products such as pine mushrooms, sale of art, management of resources, government services, and a growing tourism industry were the major sources of income. The rate of unemployment in some communities was over 50 percent, especially seasonally, related to the cycles of commercial fishing and logging. The cash economy was paralleled by a continuation of age-old patterns of fishing for salmon, halibut and cod, harvesting shellfish and berries, and hunting and trapping, supplemented by some gardening, especially potatoes and berries.

Federal and provincial initiatives have been underfunded and sporadic, and it has been difficult to establish long-term community-based responses to local needs. In some communities, the systems of social control that have been in place for many generations have held through the stress of the twentieth century; in others, these have been severely damaged and nothing effective has been put in their place. The results—high levels of substance abuse and family violence, and large numbers of suicides and attempted suicides—have been tragic and are issues of great concern.

Until the Nisga'a Treaty was signed in 1998, provision of educational, health, and social services to Nisga'a communities had been uneven and, on average, below national norms. While there were increasing numbers of well-educated people from these communities working in the resource-industry, government, and professional sectors, there were also many people who were marginalized by lack of access to critical services. The movement for self-government was stimulated by acute awareness of these issues.

In the twenty-first century, the sociopolitical system of the Nisga'a persists in spite of efforts on the part of government agencies to replace it with the Euro-Canadian system. For example, although the Indian Act banned the potlatch in the nineteenth century, the Nisga'a continued to feast. During the era of repression, defiance of the potlatch ban was relatively open in more remote communities in which agents of the state did not reside. In the communities where police, Indian agents, and missionaries resided, people feasted in their homes and in some places covered their windows to avoid detection if the feast lasted into the night. Some charges were laid under the antipotlatch law, but they were not effective in ending the practice.

A fundamental fact of life for the Nisga'a, as for all First Nations in British Columbia, is the nonrecognition of their land rights by non-Native society. The only treaties signed with the native people of the province were those on Vancouver Island in the early 1850s and Treaty 8, which covers territory on the eastern side of the Rocky Mountains in the northeast Peace River country, and which is an extension of the nineteenth-century numbered prairie treaties. Natives in other parts of the province had never entered into treaty with the Crown and continued to assert their ownership of their territories, while the British Columbia government claimed that aboriginal land title had been extinguished through successive pieces of provincial legislation. Obtaining formal recognition of their rights to their land and self-government was a constant concern of the Nisga'a, and they played a leading part in reshaping the political landscape of the province for all aboriginal groups.

## The Land Question

The Nisga'a fight for their land and resources took generations and was punctuated by a number of dramatic events. The Nisga'a repeatedly demanded justice and called on the honor of the Crown, which was not always forthcoming despite the language of the 1763 Royal Proclamation:

And whereas it is just and reasonable, and essential to our Interest, and the Security of our Colonies, that the several Nations or Tribes of Indians with whom We are connected, and who live under our Protection, should not be molested or disturbed in the Possession of such Parts of Our Dominions and Territories as, not having been ceded to or purchased by Us, are reserved to them, or any of them, as their Hunting Grounds—We do therefore, with the Advice of our Privy Council, declare it to be our Royal Will and Pleasure, that no Governor or Commander in Chief in any of our Colonies of Quebec, East Florida or West Florida, do presume, upon any Pretence whatever, to grant Warrants of Survey, or pass any Patents for Lands beyond the Bounds of their respective Governments. as described in their Commissions: as also that no Governor or Commander in Chief in any of our other Colonies or Plantations in America do presume for the present, and until our further Pleasure be known, to grant Warrants of Survey, or pass Patents for any Lands beyond the Heads or Sources of any of the Rivers which fall into the Atlantic Ocean from the West and North West, or upon any Lands whatever, which, not having been ceded to or purchased by Us as aforesaid, are reserved to the said Indians, or any of them (Brigham 1911:212–218).

Early indications were that the British would deal with Indians on the west coast of Canada in the spirit of the Royal Proclamation but this did not prove to be the case. The first government authority in the area was the Hudson's Bay Company, represented by the factors at each of the forts, who in general maintained a laissez-faire approach intended to encourage trade. As settlers entered the area, there was pressure to acquire land. The Crown Colony of Vancouver Island was established in 1849, and in 1851 James Douglas, the chief factor of the Hudson's Bay Company, became the second governor of the Crown Colony. Over the next three years he made 14 agreements with tribes on Vancouver Island, which have been enforced as treaties by the courts. In 1858 the mainland Crown Colony of British Columbia was proclaimed, and Governor Douglas had sole authority to allocate land in the territory and to establish Indian reserves. By the 1860s, the climate of opinion had shifted; the governing class of former Hudson's Bay factors was displaced by newcomers, and no funds were made available for treaty-making. British Columbia Lands Commissioner Joseph Trutch denied the existence of aboriginal rights or the need for treaties with Indians and prohibited the pre-emption of Crown lands by aboriginal people. In 1866 the two Crown Colonies were united, and in 1871 British Columbia joined the Dominion of Canada, which had been established under the British North America Act in 1867. Under the terms of the agreement, the federal government was responsible for Indians, while Crown lands and resources came under the authority of the provincial government. In the 1870s, Israel Wood Powell, the federal Indian superintendent responsible for British Columbia, attempted to establish a standard

of 80 acres per family for reserves, while the government of British Columbia had a 10-acre policy. There was considerable turmoil: in 1872 the Gitksan closed the Skeena River and the government sent a military expedition to quell the trouble. In 1875 the British Columbia Land Act set a formula of 20 acres per family for Indian reserves, while allowing 160-acre land grants for individual settlers at no charge, though Indians were still prohibited from pre-empting land. In 1884 Parliament revised the Indian Act, including a provision to outlaw the potlatch, undermining the ability of the Nisga'a to govern themselves through their system of feasts.

In 1886 Nisga'a chief Israel Sgat'iin (fig. 2) led his people as they pulled out the stakes of government land surveyors in the upper Nass, and in 1887 Chief Mountain lead a delegation of Nisga'a chiefs who traveled along with Tsimshian chiefs to Victoria to press for a settlement to their land and resources and for the right to govern themselves. Their claims of Indian title and their request for a treaty were dismissed. In 1890 the first Nisga'a Land Committee was established and the leaders of the matrilineal families began to articulate the philosophy that made it possible for

Royal B.C. Mus. and Arch., Victoria:E-07668.

Fig. 2. Chief Israel Sgat'iin, Nisga'a chief from Nass River. Photographed in the 1890s.

ANDERSON

them to work together effectively to pursue their land rights. In 1908 the Nisga'a issued a petition asserting their ownership of their territories and requested that they be reserved for their use.

In 1910 Prime Minister Wilfrid Laurier met with Nisga'a and Tsimshian chiefs in Prince Rupert, and Laurier promised to take steps to address the land question. In 1913 the province and federal governments set up the McKenna-McBride Commission to settle the dispute about Indian affairs and lands (Canada. Royal Commission on Indian Affairs for the Province of British Columbia 1916). Also in 1913 the Nisga'a Land Committee (fig. 3) sent a petition to Ottawa requesting that it be heard by the Privy Council in London, which was refused. The 1916 report of the McKenna-McBride Commission didn't address most of the issues, focusing on reserve size only. In 1927 Parliament amended the Indian Act to prevent land claims from going to court and making it illegal to accept money to pursue land claims. In 1949 British Columbia extended the vote to include male Indians, and two years later the province dropped property requirements to vote (vol. 7:159–168). In 1951 the sections of the Indian Act banning the potlatch and prohibiting activities for land rights were removed. In 1955 the Nisga'a Land Committee was re-established; it is now known as the Nisga'a Tribal Council. In 1960 Indians got the right to vote in federal elections.

From ancient times Nisga'a lands were divided into over 60 autonomous territories held by matrilineal families (*wilp*) and jealously guarded against trespass and encroachment. Each *wilp* was responsible for taking care of its land and safeguarding its productivity for future generations. Disputes were resolved through the feast system. Early in the history of the Nisga'a land question the *wilp* leaders realized that the distributed system of authority over land and resources undermined their strength in confronting external forces, and realized that they had to present a united front to

Royal B.C. Mus. and Arch., Victoria:D-7858.

Fig. 3. Members of the Nisga'a Land Committee at Aiyansh, B.C., 1913. front row, left to right: Paul Mercer, John Wesley, Stephen Allan, Arthur Calder, Charlie Barton, William Foster, Sam Pollard, William McNeil. 2d row, left to right: Benjamin Munroe, Peter Calder, William Lincoln, George Woodfield, Lazarus Moody, Andrew Mercer, William Angus, Alfred McKay, George Eli, Johnny Moore. 3d row, left to right: Matthew Russ, Jeremiah Clayton, Charlie Davis, Leonard Douglas, Benjamin Benson, George Pollard. 4th row, left to right: Charlie Elliot, Mark Smith, Brian Peal, Charlie Brown, William Stevens.

succeed in defending their territories. To achieve unity they articulated the philosophy of the "common bowl," which extended the traditional principle of sharing within each *wilp* so that the Nisga'a would stand united and speak with one voice. Under traditional Nisga'a law each *wilp* territory was for the sole use of one group, but after all *wilp* leaders worked together in the land struggle, all Nisga'a lands were considered to be for all Nisga'a.

In the late 1960s the Nisga'a accelerated their ongoing political and legal struggles to secure control over their territories and their very existence as a nation. A pivotal incident that marks a shift in the relations between the Canadian First Nations and governments occurred in 1968 when the Nisga'a Tribal Council hired lawyer Thomas Berger and went to court over the land question in the *Calder* case, named for Frank Calder, then president of the Nisga'a Tribal Council and the lead plaintiff in the case. In 1973 the Supreme Court of Canada decision in the case finally acknowledged that aboriginal rights might indeed exist, and even still be valid, though the court did not make a decision on Nisga'a title because the court split 3-3 over whether aboriginal title still existed, and the seventh justice ruled that the case should not be decided because the Nisga'a had not gotten a fiat from the provincial government authorizing them to sue. The potential implications had the decision gone the other way were huge; around the same time the James Bay Cree had also managed to get an injunction against the building of a massive hydroelectric project in northern Quebec (though that injunction was overturned within a few days and the issue was ultimately settled by negotiation rather than in court). By 1976 the government of Canada had reversed its opposition to treaty negotiations in British Columbia, established a treaty negotiating policy, and begun the decades-long negotiating process to establish a treaty with the Nisga'a. Until 1990, the Nisga'a negotiations were conducted on a bilateral basis between the national government and the Nisga'a Tribal Council. In 1990 the government of British Columbia joined the negotiations, which was a key to eventual success since the province had control of Crown lands and resources in the province. A tripartite agreement was signed in 1991 among Canada, the Tribal Council, and British Columbia.

In 1993 the number of aboriginal rights and title cases looming lead to the establishment of the British Columbia Treaty Commission involving many of the Native groups of British Columbia, when the province finally came to the table. Negotiations with the Nisga'a Tribal Council predate the British Columbia Treaty Commission and were conducted outside the Treaty Commission process. During the 1990s the three sets of negotiators (Nisga'a, provincial, and federal) signed interim protection measures and participated in hundreds of meetings to inform and consult with communities throughout northwestern British Columbia. An Agreement-in-Principle, reached in 1996, was ratified by all three parties. It was ratified by the Nisga'a people and signed on March 22, 1996, in New Aiyansh. It provided for a financial

AP Images.

Fig. 4. Nisga'a hereditary chiefs Jacob Nyce and Gordon McKay entering the Gitlakdamiks recreation facility for the signing of the Nisga'a treaty in New Aiyansh, B.C., Aug. 4, 1998. The signing of the treaty signified the end of the tribe's quest for land rights and self-government. Photograph by Nick Procaylo/Canadian Press.

transfer of more than $190 million over a 15-year period and the establishment of a Nisga'a central government with ownership of, and jurisdiction over, approximately 2,000 square kilometers of land in the Nass River valley. It outlined Nisga'a ownership of surface and subsurface resources on Nisga'a lands and spelled out entitlements to Nass River salmon stocks and Nass area forestry and wildlife harvests.

By 1998 a final agreement had been hammered out, which was initialed in New Aiyansh on August 4, 1998 (figs. 4–5). Throughout the process of the Nisga'a negotiations, all three parties kept the public and third parties informed through public consultations and meetings and through briefings to both the Treaty Negotiation Advisory Committee, comprising 31 members representing various third-party interests, and regional advisory committees. Some 250 consultation meetings and public events concerning the Nisga'a negotiations took place between late 1991 and the close of negotiations on the final agreement on July 15, 1998 (Hurley 1999, 2001).

## The Treaty of 1998

The final agreement mirrors the Agreement-In-Principle. The final agreement includes provisions regarding environmental regulation, Nisga'a language and culture, repatriation of artifacts, substantial upgrading of the roads in the Nass Valley, a framework for the development of Nisga'a government and the administration of justice, and an eventual phase-out of the taxation exemptions available under

AP Images.

Fig. 5. Nisga'a President of the Tribal Council Joe Gosnell addressing the crowd after the historic signing of the treaty in 1998. Photograph by Nick Procaylo/Canadian Press.

the Indian Act. Although the Nisga'a final agreement is not a prototype, it has been reviewed closely for its implications for the 51 Native groups in negotiations under the British Columbia Treaty Commission process. To make the final agreement into law, the Canadian government and the province of British Columbia each had to pass legislation, while the Nisga'a ratified it by presenting the final agreement at an assembly, followed by a referendum.

*Political Responses*

British Columbia has traditionally had a highly polarized electorate, with a solid conservative bloc that re-formed and coalesced from the old Social Credit and Reform parties into the provincial Liberal party, and a strong social democratic movement with support from trade unions, under the banner of the New Democratic Party. Reaction to the Nisga'a final agreement was strongly politicized, with considerable reaction, both positive and negative. The New Democratic Party, which was in power during the final negotiations, signed the

final agreement. The new provincial Liberal leader, Gordon Campbell, argued that the treaty created an unconstitutional third order of government and thereby undermined the rights of British Columbians. He joined a court action to try to stop the treaty and called for a provincial referendum on the issue. When his party won the next election such a referendum was in fact held. Many critics of this action objected to the use of a provincial referendum to address issues of minority rights, calling it a fundamentally flawed process, and argued that the federal and provincial governments had the right to negotiate treaties and the Nisga'a final agreement should not be subject to a referendum. The eventual referendum question focused on what the Liberals called principles for treaty negotiation. The questions asked for a simple yes or no response to eight sometimes confusing statements such as: "private property should not be expropriated for treaty settlements" (though there had been no proposals for such expropriation in the treaty process) and "aboriginal self-government should have the characteristics of local government, with powers delegated from Canada and British Columbia" (though the Canadian courts had already recognized broader self-government rights). Another statement was "the existing tax exemptions for aboriginal people should be phased out," which ignores the fact that taxation is a federal responsibility that could not be changed by the provincial legislature, and the existing taxation exemptions had long been part of the Indian Act, and that "existing aboriginal and treaty rights" had been entrenched in the Canadian Constitution when it was repatriated in 1982.

Criticism was vocal and scathing. Thomas Berger, a former judge and a Vancouver lawyer and New Democratic party leader, who had represented the Nisga'a in the landmark *Calder* case (Berger 1981), accused the Liberals of putting "minority rights up for auction" and of undermining aboriginal self-government rights already established by the courts. "It is essential to avoid conferring the slightest legitimacy on this abuse of the referendum process," he wrote in the Vancouver *Sun* (April 15, 2002).

The response rate for the mail-in referendum ballot was low (about one-third), and over 80 percent of respondents favored the provincial government's position. The Liberal government, which remained in power, modified its initial stance on aboriginal rights and treaties. Between 2000 and 2006 that government put forward a number of what might be seen as conciliatory initiatives towards First Nations, including negotiation of interim agreements on forestry and land use while a First Nation is in the treaty negotiation process.

In addition to the debate about the treaty referendum, there was a great deal of media coverage and more serious legal and academic debate about the Nisga'a final agreement. Some argued that the self-government powers included in the treaty were unconstitutional, and there was a court case attempting to test this (eventually dropped). Some commentators argued that the final agreement was contrary to the Canadian Charter of Rights and Freedoms. This debate focused on the fact that only Nisga'a citizens can vote for the Nisga'a government even though that government can pass laws that affect non-Nisga'a people residing on Nisga'a lands. Supporters of the agreement point out that the treaty does not prohibit the Nisga'a from extending citizenship under Nisga'a law to non-Nisga'a residents, and there are provisions for consultation with all residents of the Nass Valley on decisions that affect them.

Some critics argued that the treaty would create a "race-based" government. Other critics deplored the fact that the treaty provides for the Nisga'a nation to exercise its inherent right of self-government, which they saw as a dangerous precedent. Others reacted to the cost of the provisions in the treaty, which some estimated would amount to over a billion dollars though it had been originally quoted at $190 million. Finally, some commentators argued that the Nisga'a treaty would become a template for the settlements yet to be negotiated with other First Nations of British Columbia, which they stated would be costly and would bestow broad powers of self-government on other Native groups.

Another set of concerns was voiced by several First Nations whose territories border the Nisga'a. The Gitanyow (Kitwancool) band of Gitksan to the east sought an injunction because they argued that the Nisga'a had claimed some of the land properly belonging to the Gitanyow and argued that it was a breach of fiduciary responsibility for the government to negotiate with the Nisga'a over those lands before the Gitanyow claim was negotiated. The Coast Tsimshian made a similar argument regarding territories at the mouth of the Nass. The attempt to force a resolution of overlaps in court ultimately proved unsuccessful. Other First Nations leaders have been critical because under the final agreement they had to abandon future claims, ceding and surrendering their aboriginal rights, and in 12 years they would lose the tax-exempt status of income earned on reserve, though this is a benefit shared by all Status Indians in Canada. Some have argued that the province gained virtually all its goals and that there are insufficient resources on which the Nisga'a can build a future.

The Nisga'a final agreement has been criticized internally by some members of the Nisga'a nation as well. The Nisga'a acquired control of almost 2,000 square kilometers of land, powers of self-government, fishery, forestry and other resource rights, and hundreds of millions of dollars. However, the Nisga'a lands included in the agreement are a fraction of the original territories—about 8 percent. Some Nisga'a critics were opposed to the Nisga'a lands being clustered in the middle of the original territories; this omits territory that was claimed as overlap by the Gitanyow and by the Allied Tribes of Tsimshian but also leaves out most of the lands belonging to some Nisga'a *wilp*. For some, the omission of any of the territories of their own grandfathers was a bitter blow. Other Nisga'a critics argued that the land and money were simply not sufficient or that the benefits would not be evenly distributed among Nisga'a people.

*Impacts*

The identity and pride of the Nisga'a people in 2006 was strong. During the first half of the twentieth century there was a period of low visibility and, for some, a loss of commitment, but in all communities since the 1960s and 1970s language, culture, feasts, and art gained renewed prominence and were highly valued. People sought creative new ways of expressing their identity and worked to revitalize their language skills and to exercise ownership of their resources. The Nisga'a treaty was viewed as a route to ensuring a future for the Nisga'a people (A. Rose 2001). In September 1998, President of the Tribal Council Joseph Gosnell, Sr. (fig. 5), said:

> The Nisga'a Treaty stands as a symbol of hope and reconciliation between aboriginal and non-aboriginal Canadians.
>
> . . . By reconciling the aboriginal rights of the Nisga'a Nation with the sovereignty of the Crown, the Treaty is intended to be a just and equitable settlement of the Nisga'a Land Question that spells out a new relationship based on mutual recognition and sharing.
>
> To the Nisga'a people, a treaty is a sacred instrument, the legal framework for a new society based on self-reliance and self-actualization. Fairly and honourably negotiated, the Treaty represents a major breakthrough for aboriginal self-determination—one of the most pressing issues in contemporary Canada and around the world (A. Rose 2001:15).

The treaty brought concrete opportunities to the valley. The Nisga'a Highway reached to Kincolith and was upgraded to provincial standards; it was given the provincial highway number 113 to commemorate the years of the land struggle. The Wilp Wilxo'oskwhl Nisga'a sought official status as a provincial postsecondary educational institution governed by its own legislation. The provision on fisheries enabled the Nisga'a to take over much of the responsibility for management of the stocks on the Nass River; a successful inland fishery permits each Nisga'a adult to take up to 500 sockeye salmon for commercial sale each year, providing a valued source of income and employment in fishing, processing and stock assessment, and management. Although economic and social challenges confront the Nisga'a and the treaty is not a panacea, many Nisga'a people hope that it will give their nation an opportunity to be responsible for themselves.

# United States Native Population

RUSSELL THORNTON

The area of the present-day United States had a large aboriginal population before White contact. It declined drastically following European arrival—officially with Ponce De Léon's journey from the Caribbean to *La Florida* in 1513—and subsequent colonization. How drastic the decline was is debated, since estimates of aboriginal population size for the area vary widely, ranging from 879,400 in the coterminous United States area (Mooney 1928) or 720,000 plus 72,600 for Alaska (Kroeber 1939) at first "extensive European contact" to assertions of 8.5 million or more (Dobyns 1966, 1983). For scholars' analysis of the numbers see volume 3:694–711.

The Native American population of the United States reached a nadir population of perhaps less than 250,000 at around 1900 (Thornton 1987:42–43), although it may have been significantly higher (vol. 3:694–701). In any event, there was an actual demographic collapse, albeit one that varied from region to region, from century to century. In other words, population size was reduced drastically due to increases in mortality (and decreases in fertility) so that the Native American population was unable to reproduce itself demographically.

## Recovery of Native Population

Following these almost four centuries of population decline, the Native American population of the United States started to increase around the beginning of the twentieth century and has continued into the twenty-first century (vol. 3:702–711). The United States Census decennial enumerations indicate a Native American population growth for the United States that has been nearly continuous since 1900, to 291,000 by 1910, to 362,000 by 1930, to 1.4 million by 1980, to 2 million by 1990, to 2.5 million by 2000, plus 1.6 million self-reported "racially mixed Native Americans (table 1). The exception is in 1920 when the U.S. census enumerated the Native American population at only about 261,000, because of the 1918 influenza pandemic that caused serious population losses worldwide. (Changing definitions and procedures for enumerating Native Americans used by the Bureau of the Census also had an effect on the enumerated population size from census to census during the twentieth century.)

This 2.5 (or 4.1 million) Native American population in the United States in 2000 represents an increase of 26 percent (or 110 percent) from the almost 2 million in 1990. It represents an increase of 1,000 percent (or over 1,600 percent) from the nadir population of some 250,000 at around 1900. The 2000 census reported a total United States population of 281.4 million; subtracting 2.5 million Native Americans only or 4.1 Native Americans and other race produces a non-Native American population of either about 279 million or 277 million; thus, Native Americans represent either 0.9 percent or 1.5 percent of the total United States population.

This population recovery during the twentieth century was in part a result of lower mortality rates and increases in life expectancy, particularly after 1950, although the picture is complicated (Thornton 1987:168). The mortality differences between Whites and Native Americans narrowed after the 1980s; however, "the American Indian population still experiences substantially higher mortality than other Americans, notably the White population" (Snipp 1996:30).

In 1967, by way of example, the age-adjusted death rate for Native Americans was 10.5 per 1,000 as compared with 7.4 per 1,000 for the total United States population; in 1982, it was 5.7 per 1,000 for Native Americans and 5.5 for the total population (5.3 for the White population) (Thornton 1987:171); in the mid-1990s, it was 6.1 for only those Native Americans served by the Indian Health Service—those more likely living on or near reservations or traditional Native American areas—and only 5.0 for the total United States population (4.8 for the White population) (U.S. Department of Health and Human Services, Indian Health Service 2001:76, table 4.11). Native Americans continue to have higher mortality rates than Whites at all age levels except the very old, where a "mortality crossover" occurs and Whites have the higher mortality rates (Thornton 1995, 2004).

Particularly important in narrowing the mortality differential between Native Americans and other Americans was a narrowing of the infant mortality rates, from 60.9 per 1,000 live births of Native Americans compared with only 26.4 per 1,000 live births for the total population in 1955 to

**Table 1.  U.S. Census Enumerations of Native Americans, 1900 to 2000**

| U.S. Census | Population |
| --- | --- |
| 1900 | 237,000 |
| 1910 | 291,000 |
| 1920 | 261,000 |
| 1930 | 362,000 |
| 1940 | 366,000 |
| 1950 | 377,000 |
| 1960 | 552,000 |
| 1970 | 827,000 |
| 1980 | 1,420,000 |
| 1990 | 1,959,000 |
| 2000 | 4,119,000 |
|    Native American Alone | 2,476,000 |
|    Native American and Other Race | 1,643,000 |

SOURCES: Thornton 2000:32, table 2-7; U.S. Department of Commerce 2002:3, table 1.

13.2 per 1,000 live births of Native Americans compared with 12.6 per 1,000 live births for the total population in 1980 (Thornton 1987:169, table 7-5)! In 2000, the mortality rate for Native Americans under 1 year of age was 6.99 per 1,000 (7.6 per 1,000 for those served by the Indian Health Service) as compared with 6.47 per 1,000 for Whites (Thornton 1995; U.S. Department of Health and Human Services, Indian Health Service 2001:56, table 3.8).

A similar pattern occurred in changes in life expectancy at birth, with the difference narrowing from about 20 years in 1939 to three years by 1980, when Native American life expectancy was about 71 years for Native Americans and 74 years for the total United States population (Thornton 1987:172). In 2000, Native American life expectancy at birth was 71.0 for males and 78.7 for females, as compared with 72.3 for males and 79.1 for females in the total population and 73.2 for males and 79.8 for females in the White population (Hahn and Eberhardt 1994:table 2; U.S. Department of Health and Human Services, Indian Health Service 1997:10–11, table 1).

The population recovery of Native Americans also resulted from adaptation through intermarriage with nonnative peoples and from changing fertility patterns, whereby Native American birth rates have remained higher than those of the average North American population (Thornton, Sandefur, and Snipp 1991; Snipp 1996:24–28).

Early in the twentieth century, at around the point of the Native American population nadir in the United States, the fecundity and fertility of Native Americans—particularly the "full bloods"—was of considerable concern to government officials as they predicted that Native Americans were disappearing (U.S. Bureau of the Census 1915:157–159): They noted that only 56.5 percent of American Indians were enumerated as "full blood" in the 1910 census, and the census data indicated the "full bloods" were reproducing at lower rates than the "mixed bloods." For example, 10.7 percent of the marriages between "full bloods" had no children while only 6.7 percent of the marriages between "mixed bloods" and 5.8 percent of the marriages between "mixed bloods" and Whites had no children. Similarly, the average number of children born in "full blood" marriages was 4.5 compared with 5.1 in "mixed blood" marriages and 4.9 in "mixed blood" and White marriages, with "full blood" marriages having 69.7 percent of their children surviving while "mixed blood" marriages and "mixed blood" and White marriages having 79.0 percent and 83.0 percent, respectively, of their children surviving (U.S. Bureau of the Census 1915:157–158; Thornton 1987:177–179, tables 7-9, 7-11, and 7-12). By the 1930 census, the percentage of American Indians enumerated as "full bloods" had dropped to 46.3 percent (Thornton 1987:175).

Despite the concerns, the twentieth-century recovery of the Native American population of the United States was eventually driven by Native American fertility increases and Native American fertility levels higher than the total United States population. In 1980, for example, married American Indian women 35 to 44 years of age had a mean number of children ever born of 3.61 in comparison to 2.77 for the total population and only 2.67 for White women (Thornton, Sandefur, and Snipp 1991:390). Intermarried American Indian women generally had lower fertility rates in 1980 than American Indian women married to American Indian men; yet, intermarried American Indian women still had higher fertility than the total United States population. This figure is important considering that over 50 percent of all married Native Americans in 1980 were married to non-Native Americans: "in 1980, 119,448 out of 258,154 married American Indian, Eskimo and Aleut couples were married within the same racial group" (Thornton 1987:236), a decrease from less than 40 percent a decade earlier (Sandefur and Liebler 1996: 212, fig. 9-3; Sandefur and McKinnell 1986).

Both Native American intermarriage and fertility rates remain high. Only some 40 percent of Native Americans had a Native American spouse in 1990 (Sandefur and Liebler 1996:212, table 9-3). In 1999, the birth rate for Native Americans was 16.8 per 1,000 as compared with 14.5 per 1,000 for the total population and only 13.9 per 1,000 for the White population (National Center for Health Statistics 2001:25, table 1). In this regard "a key to explaining the high rates of American Indian fertility is that American Indian women begin their childbearing at a relatively early age. Women who begin childbearing at an early age typically have more children than those who defer motherhood until they are older" (Snipp 1996:24–25). Therefore, the very nature of Native American population history and demographic recovery has had and continues to have profound effects upon the Native American population, particularly who Native Americans are and how they might be defined, not only on individual levels but also on population and tribal levels.

## Definitions of Native American

For legal definitions of Indian status, from various tribal and governmental points of view, see "Native American Identity in Law," this volume.

The twentieth-century increase in the Native American population reflected in successive censuses of the United States was due in part to changes in the identification of individuals as "Native American." The United States Census has in the past typically enumerated individuals as of only one race. Since 1960 the census has relied on self-identification to ascertain an individual's race. Much of the increase in the American Indian population—excluding Eskimo and Aleuts—from 523,591 in 1960 to 792,730 in 1970 to 1.37 million in 1980 to 1.9 million in 1990 resulted from individuals not identifying as American Indian in an earlier census but identifying as such in a later census (Passel 1976; Passel and Berman 1985, 1986; Eschbach 1993; D. Harris 1994). It is estimated that about 25 percent of the population "growth" of American Indians from 1960 to 1970, about 60 percent of the "growth" from 1970 to 1980, and about 35 percent of the "growth" from 1980 to 1990 may be accounted for by these changing identifications (Thornton 2000:32). Generally, the observed increase reflects changes in self-identification of individuals affiliated loosely, if at all, with actual Native American tribes.

The 2000 census was the first national census in which the population could identify itself as having more than one race—some 6.8 million people did so, about 2.4 percent of the total population (U.S. Department of Commerce 2001).

In the census, 2.5 million people identified themselves as Native American and another 1.6 million identified themselves as Native American and another race. The other race was generally White: 66 percent of those listing another race listed "White;" 11 percent listed "Black or African American;" and 6.8 percent listed "White" and "Black or African American;" while 5.7 percent listed "Some other race" (U.S. Department of Commerce 2002:3). Thus, 37 percent of those with a Native American identification were self-identified as "racially mixed." Seemingly, this allowed individuals formerly indicating they were White to indicate they were both White and Native American, thereby increasing the numbers of Native American, something Native Americans have launched public campaigns about, through, for example, United States Census posters urging people with only partial Native American ancestry to identify as "Native American." Not surprisingly, the percentage of Native Americans identifying as "racially mixed" far exceeds the percentages for other groups. For example, only about 5 percent of African-American—1.8 million out of 36.4 million—indicated mixed ancestry (typically with White), although there is considerably more mixed ancestry in that population (U.S. Department of Commerce 2001). To report White and another race for African-Americans would simply act to reduce the numbers of African Americans. And,

too, most mixed people of African American and other "race" are defined by society solely as African-American, unlike the case with Native Americans whereby "mixed" individuals can be accepted as Native American or White.

Certainly, the Native American population could not have recovered to the extent it has without intermarriage (Shoemaker 1999:63–66, 87–97) and the resulting creation of "mixed bloods" as an increasing segment of the Native American population. However, intermarriage has created identity issues for the offspring of such marriages as they sought to define who they were and get others to accept it. Children of Native American and African-American intermarriages have had difficulty getting others to accept their Indian status, generally much more difficulty than those of Native American and White intermarriages.

## Distribution of Population

Native Americans were not evenly distributed within the United States in 2000. The majority of those identifying either as Native American alone or with another race lived in the western United States (table 2), with California ranking first in number of Native Americans, followed by Oklahoma (table 3). As shown in table 4, New York City had the largest number of Native Americans, followed by Los Angeles.

**Table 2. Native American Population by Regions in 2000**

| Region | Total | Native American Alone | Native American and Other |
|---|---|---|---|
| Northeast | 374,035 | 162,558 | 211,477 |
| Midwest | 714,792 | 399,490 | 315,302 |
| South | 1,259,230 | 725,919 | 533,311 |
| West | 1,771,244 | 1,187,980 | 583,255 |

SOURCE: U.S. Department of Commerce 2002:5, table 2.

**Table 3. States with over 100,000 Native Americans in 2000**

| State | Total | Native American Alone | Native American and Other |
|---|---|---|---|
| California | 627,562 | 333,346 | 294,216 |
| Oklahoma | 391,949 | 273,230 | 118,719 |
| Arizona | 292,552 | 255,879 | 36,673 |
| Texas | 215,599 | 118,362 | 97,237 |
| New Mexico | 191,475 | 173,483 | 17,992 |
| New York | 171,581 | 82,461 | 89,120 |
| Washington | 158,940 | 93,301 | 65,639 |
| North Carolina | 131,736 | 99,551 | 32,185 |
| Michigan | 124,412 | 58,479 | 65,933 |
| Alaska | 119,241 | 98,043 | 21,198 |
| Florida | 117,880 | 53,541 | 64,339 |

SOURCE: U.S. Department of Commerce 2002:5, table 2.

271

**Table 4. Cities with over 15,000 Native Americans in 2000**

| City | Total | Native American Alone | Native American and Other |
|------|-------|-----------------------|---------------------------|
| New York City | 87,241 | 41,289 | 45,952 |
| Los Angeles | 53,092 | 29,412 | 23,680 |
| Phoenix | 35,093 | 26,696 | 8,397 |
| Tulsa | 30,227 | 18,551 | 11,676 |
| Oklahoma City | 29,001 | 17,743 | 11,258 |
| Anchorage | 26,995 | 18,941 | 8,054 |
| Albuquerque | 22,047 | 17,444 | 4,603 |
| Chicago | 20,898 | 10,290 | 10,608 |
| San Diego | 16,178 | 7,543 | 8,635 |
| Houston | 15,743 | 8,568 | 7,175 |
| Tucson | 15,358 | 11,038 | 4,328 |
| San Antonio | 15,224 | 9,584 | 5,640 |

SOURCE: U.S. Department of Commerce 2002:8, table 3.

## Native American Tribalism

Many separate criteria may be used to delimit the Native American population, defining who is an Indian. Language, residence, cultural affiliation, recognition by a community, degree of blood, genealogical lines of descent, and self-identification have all been used at some point in the past to define both the total Native American population and specific tribal populations. Each measure produces a different population, and which measure is ultimately employed to define a population can be an arbitrary decision; however, the implications for Native Americans can be enormous.

The United States Census has long collected tribal affiliation on the Native Americans it enumerated (table 5). This dates from when Native Americans were first enumerated separately in the census. In 2000, those identifying as Native Americans, that is, "American Indian or Alaskan Native," were asked to also "Print name of enrolled or principal tribe." Out of the total 4.1 million Native Americans enumerated, 74.4 percent did so; however, 79.3 percent of those identifying as Native American only did so, while only 66.9 percent of those identifying as Native American and another race did so (U.S. Department of Commerce 2002:10, table 4). As shown in table 6, more Native Americans identified as Cherokee than any other tribal group, followed by Navajo.

Native Americans are unique among contemporary ethnic and racial groups in the United States in that many still have formal tribal affiliations and have both formal individual and tribal relationships with the federal government. This is one way to define the population. Thus, most, but not all, individuals who may be considered as Native Americans are official Native Americans; that is, Native Americans who are enrolled members of Native American entities recognized by the federal government, as it is often phrased, "for the purposes of having a relationship." This possibility is reflected in the 2000 census question asking for the "'enrolled or principal tribe."

In 2006, there were 563 American Indian groups in the United States that were legally recognized by the federal government and received services from the Bureau of Indian Affairs. These encompass 338 American Indian tribes and 225 Alaska Native groups and 1.7 million people in 2000 who were formal members of these tribes and groups (Thornton 2004a:appendix 1). In addition, there are numerous Native American groups seeking federal recognition and many others who may do so in the future. Since 1978, some 150 petitions for federal recognition were submitted to

**Table 5. Comparisons of Tribal Enrollments with U.S. Census Enumerations, 1950 to 2000**

| Year | Tribal Enrollments | Census Enumeration | "Percent Enrolled" | Percent in Census Not Listing a Tribal Affiliation |
|------|--------------------|--------------------|--------------------|----------------------------------------------------|
| 1950 | | 357,499 | 112.75[a] | |
| 1952 | 403,071 | | | |
| 1960 | | 523,591 | | |
| 1970 | | 792,730 | | 21.2 |
| 1980 | | 1,366,676 | 65.21 | |
| 1981 | 891,208 | | | |
| 1985 | 950,055[b] | | | |
| 1990 | | 1,937,391 | | 11.6 |
| 1999 | 1,698,483 | | | |
| 2000 | | | | |
|   Native American only | | 2,475,956 | 68.60 | 20.7 |
|   Native American and other | | 1,643,345 | | 33.1 |
|   Total | | 4,119,301 | 41.23 | 25.6 |

[a]This undoubtedly reflects a census undercount as well as the 2-year difference in time.
[b]Excludes Alaska.

SOURCES: Thornton 1987:160, table 7-1; Ubelaker 1988:292, 293, table 4; U.S. Department of the Interior 1999:i; U.S. Department of Commerce 2001:8, table 6, 2002:10, table 4.

**Table 6. Native American Tribal Affiliations of over 50,000 in the 2000 Census**

| Tribe[a] | Total | Native American Alone | | Native American and Other | |
| --- | --- | --- | --- | --- | --- |
| | | One Tribe | 2 or More Tribes | One Tribe | 2 or More Tribes |
| Cherokee | 729,533 | 281,069 | 18,793 | 390,902 | 38,769 |
| Navajo | 298,197 | 269,202 | 6,789 | 19,491 | 2,715 |
| Choctaw | 158,774 | 87,349 | 9,552 | 50,123 | 11,750 |
| Sioux | 153,360 | 108,272 | 4,794 | 35,179 | 5,115 |
| Chippewa | 149,669 | 105,907 | 2,730 | 38,635 | 2,397 |
| Apache | 96,833 | 57,060 | 7,917 | 24,947 | 6,909 |
| Blackfeet | 85,750 | 27,104 | 4,358 | 41,389 | 12,899 |
| Iroquois | 80,822 | 45,212 | 2,318 | 29,763 | 3,529 |
| Pueblo | 74,085 | 59,533 | 3,572 | 9,943 | 1,082 |
| Creek | 71,310 | 40,223 | 5,495 | 21,652 | 3,940 |
| Lumbee | 57,868 | 51,913 | 642 | 4,934 | 379 |

[a]180,940 indicated they were "Latin American Indian," 54,790 said they were Eskimo, and 16,978 said they were Aleuts; 195,902 did not specify a tribe.
SOURCE: U.S. Department of Commerce 2002:11, table 5.

the Bureau of Indian Affairs, a dozen of which were granted along with some "clarification" and "recognition" of another nine. There are other groups recognized as Native American by states but not by the federal government. Most of the nonrecognized groups have relatively small populations, but the Lumbee of North Carolina have a population in excess of 55,000 ("Recognition," this vol.).

Many but not all of these tribes and groups have some land base administered as an Indian reservation. In 2006 there were about 275 such land areas, known as reservations, pueblos, rancherias, communities or even "statisti-cal areas" with a total Native American population of 538,300, according to the 2000 census. The largest is the Navajo Reservation, encompassing about 16 million acres surrounded by the states of Arizona, New Mexico, and Utah, and with a resident Native American population in 2000 of 175,228 plus 5,234 non-Native Americans (table 7).

The process of enrollment in a Native American tribe has historical roots that extend back to the early nineteenth century. As the U.S. government dispossessed native peoples, treaties established specific rights, privileges, goods, and

**Table 7. Reservations and Trust Lands with over 10,000 Native Americans in the 2000 Census**

| Reservation and Trust Land | Total Population[a] | Native American Alone | Native American and Other |
| --- | --- | --- | --- |
| Navajo Reservation and trust land, Ariz., N. Mex., Utah | 180,462 | 173,987 | 175,228 |
| Cherokee, Okla. | 462,327 | 76,041 | 104,482 |
| Creek, Okla. | 704,565 | 51,296 | 77,273 |
| Lumbee, N.C. | 474,100 | 58,238 | 62,327 |
| Choctaw, Okla. | 224,472 | 29,521 | 39,984 |
| Cook Inlet, Alaska[b] | 364,205 | 24,923 | 35,972 |
| Chickasaw, Okla. | 277,416 | 22,946 | 32,372 |
| Calista, Alaska[b] | 23,032 | 19,617 | 20,353 |
| United Houma Nation, La. | 839,880 | 11,019 | 15,305 |
| Sealaska, Alaska[b] | 71,507 | 11,320 | 15,059 |
| Pine Ridge, S. Dak., Nebr. | 15,521 | 14,304 | 14,484 |
| Doyon, Alaska[b] | 97,190 | 11,182 | 14,128 |
| Kiowa-Comanche-Apache-Fort Sill Apache, Okla. | 193,260 | 9,675 | 13,045 |
| Fort Apache Reservation, Ariz. | 12,429 | 11,702 | 11,854 |
| Citizen Potawatomi Nation-Absentee Shawnee, Okla. | 106,624 | 6,733 | 10,617 |
| Gila River Reservation, Ariz. | 11,257 | 10,353 | 10,578 |
| Cheyenne-Arapaho, Okla. | 157,869 | 7,402 | 10,310 |

[a]Includes non-Native Americans.
[b]Alaska Native Regional Corporation.
SOURCE: U.S. Department of Commerce 2006:38, No. 36.

money to which those party to a treaty—both tribes as entities and individual tribal members—were entitled. The practices of creating formal censuses and keeping lists of names of tribal members evolved to insure an accurate and equitable distribution of benefits. Over time, Native Americans themselves established more formal tribal governments, including constitutions, and began to regulate their membership more carefully, especially in regard to land allotments, royalties from the sale of resources, distributions of tribal funds, and voting. In the twentieth century, the federal government established further criteria to determine eligibility for benefits such as educational aid and health care.

To be enrolled, individuals must meet various criteria for tribal membership, which vary from tribe to tribe and are typically set forth in tribal constitutions approved by the Bureau of Indian Affairs (Thornton 1997). Upon membership, individuals are typically issued tribal enrollment (or registration) numbers and cards that identify their special status as members of a particular American Indian tribe. To be enrolled in some tribes, individuals must first receive a Certificate of Degree of Indian Blood from the Bureau specifying a certain degree of Indian blood, that is, a blood quantum.

Each tribe has a particular set of requirements—generally requiring a minimum degree of Indian blood or lineal descent from a tribal member—for membership (enrollment) of individuals in the tribe (see "Native American Identity in Law," this vol.). Typically, a blood quantum is established by tracing ancestry back through time to a relative or relatives on earlier tribal rolls or censuses where the relative's proportion of Native American blood was recorded. In such historic instances, more often than not it was simply self-indicated. Minimal blood quantum requirements for membership in a tribe or village vary widely. Most tribes require a one-fourth minimal amount of Native American blood; around two dozen tribes require more than one-fourth; several tribes require less than one-fourth; and somewhat more than 100 tribes do not specify a minimal requirement, only that one must have a documented tribal blood quantum in order to be enrolled in the tribe (Thornton 1997).

Thus, Native American tribal populations are defined tribally by the particular tribe itself and racially by the federal government whereby the Bureau of Indian Affairs issues cards certifying a Native American tribal blood quantum. However, tribes may, and some have at times, changed their enrollment criteria. Often, the change has been to establish minimum blood quantum requirements; in 1931, the Eastern Band of Cherokee Indians established a one-sixteenth blood quantum requirement for those born thereafter (Cohen 1942:5). Sometimes the change has been to establish higher requirements: the Confederated Salish and Kootenai Tribes have tightened their membership requirements since 1935; in 1960 they established that only those born with a one-quarter degree or more blood quantum could be tribal members (Trosper 1976:256). A question that has yet to be fully re-solved is the tribal membership status of the Freedmen, individuals of African-American ancestry, allotted as citizens of one or another of the Five Civilized Tribes (vol. 14:753–759; "The Freedmen," this vol.). The economic prosperity for some tribes through gaming and other enterprises has introduced another element into the issue of tribal membership. Restrictions on membership are occurring more frequently as the economic benefits of tribal membership increase.

## Implications of Population Recovery

The nature of the population recovery of Native Americans has produced distinctive Native American population segments, ones distinguished along both racial and tribal lines. Racial heterogeneity has been produced through intermarriage whereby many individuals with few Native American genes are within the Native American population, defined either tribally or by self-reporting in the census (or by most other methods). Tribal heterogeneity has been produced through different membership requirements of tribes and, particularly, if an individual is a formal tribal member. A dichotomy exists between Native Americans as only Native American and tribal Native Americans; that is, between Native Americans not enrolled in tribes and Native Americans enrolled in tribes.

Table 5 lists percentages of enumerated Native Americans in censuses actually enrolled in federally recognized tribes. Only certain percentages of those indicating American Indian race in the censuses are official tribal members. Thus, of the 2.5 million indicating Native American race only in the 2000 census, only 68.6 percent could have been actual members of federally recognized tribes; of the 4.1 million indicating Native American and another race, only 41.2 percent were actual members of federally recognized tribes, although some 3.1 million or 75.6 percent of Native Americans enumerated said they had a tribal "identification."

These differences varied by tribe: For example, there were 241,054 people enrolled in the Navajo Nation about 2000 and 220,710 enrolled Cherokees: 200,628 enrolled in the Cherokee Nation, 12,139 enrolled in the Eastern Band of Cherokee, and 7,953 enrolled in the United Keetoowah Band of Cherokee. The 2000 census enumerated 298,197 people of some Navajo identification, and 729,533 people of some Cherokee identification (U.S. Department of the Interior 1999; U.S. Department of Commerce 2002:10, fig. 5). Therefore, only about 80 percent of people identifying as Navajo could have been enrolled whereas only about 30 percent of people identifying as Cherokee could have been enrolled. It should also be noted that 269,202 out of the 298,197 Navajo identifiers, or 90.3 percent, identified as Native American only, whereas only 281,069 out of the 729,533 Cherokee identifiers, or 38.5 percent, identified as Native American only.

# The Freedmen

CIRCE STURM AND KRISTY J. FELDHOUSEN-GILES

## Historical Origins

The Freedmen's origins lie in the first encounters among Africans, Europeans, and Native Americans in the Southeast. Since the arrival of Africans in North America in the 1500s, people of African descent have forged long and complex relationships with Indian peoples in the region. During much of the seventeenth century, Africans worked alongside Indians as slaves taken by White colonists, forming familial and cultural bonds with Indian individuals (Forbes 1993:56). As the slavery continued to develop into the eighteenth century, free Blacks and runaway slaves joined Native communities (Nash 1974:289), with some of these people achieving full status as tribal citizens through clan adoption. In the early period of contact between Africans and Southeast Indians, race was not a factor in determining tribal membership. Most native peoples in the Southeast defined tribal citizenship on the basis of a matrilineal clan system, so that any person whose mother was a clan member was also a native citizen, regardless of race. Kinship was the basis of tribal belonging and identity. In this way, tribal towns in the Southeast—those that would later become the Cherokee, Chickasaw, Choctaw, Creek Confederacy, and Seminole Nations, also known as the Five Civilized Tribes—were already multiracial communities by the mid-eighteenth century (vol. 14:753–759).

Racial and cultural diversity in the Southeast was a source of both conflict and cooperation. Slave-owning colonists and their American descendants experienced firsthand the effects of African and Native American collusion during slave revolts. As a result, they came to fear broader and more systematic forms of cooperation between the two groups and, in many cases, did what they could to foster discord between Natives and African-Americans (Willis 1963). For example, Southeast tribes were encouraged to round up runaway slaves, while African-Americans were used in military campaigns against Indian nations in the region (Nash 1974:286–288). At the same time, many Africans and Native Americans established close relationships that led to cultural exchanges between the two groups, particularly in terms of foodways, music, artwork, medicinal knowledge, and folklore—a case in point being African-American tales of Br'er Rabbit that closely resembled Southeast Indian stories of Rabbit, the trickster (Miles 2005:29; Wright 1981:262–271).

As Europeans and later Americans gained a foothold in the Southeast, government programs were established that encouraged tribes to adopt farming as their primary subsistence activity, a shift that most Euro-American colonists believed would help Indian people along the road toward "civilization," as it was defined according to Euro-American standards at the time. In this climate, citizens of the Five Civilized Tribes noted that Black slaves were critical to the economic success of Southern agriculture as well as a symbol of prestige and wealth to their owners. Accordingly, each of the Five Civilized Tribes began implementing forms of African slavery by the late eighteenth century (Littlefield 1978, 1979, 1980). The nature of these forms varied considerably over time and place. Early slavery among the Five Civilized Tribes was much like traditional Native systems of slavery, in which war captives or criminals would become indentured servants. In some cases, captives would be adopted into clans and become fully incorporated into Native societies as free people. In others, they would remain in bondage yet work alongside those to whom they were indentured and share in the products of their labor. Also in contrast to American slavery, captives were allowed to marry noncaptives, and their children did not inherit their status as servants. For the most part, early African slavery in the tribes followed this pattern (Perdue 1979:3–18). However, as attempts to "civilize" Southeast Indians took hold, with large-scale agriculture and extensive intermarriage with Whites becoming more common, the Cherokee, Creek Confederacy, Choctaw, and Chickasaw increasingly adopted dominant slave-holding practices.

The Seminole adopted slavery in a manner qualitatively different from what was practiced in the other four tribes. African people who came to live with Seminoles, often referred to as Seminole Maroons, were largely former slaves who had fled Euro-American plantations to form their own independent towns bordering Seminole Indian communities in what is today Florida (Littlefield 1977; vol. 14:65–77). Seminole Indians and Seminole Maroons shared a long history of social association, cultural exchange and military cooperation, but in the late eighteenth and early nineteenth century, some Seminole Indians began to take ownership of some Seminole Maroons, a practice that developed as Seminoles noted the prestige associated with slave ownership in Southern society. Some began to steal African slaves from

275

plantations; others, to buy them from slave dealers. Still, Black slavery among the Seminoles differed significantly from what was practiced in the other four tribes and much of the American South in that Seminole slaves lived in autonomous communities and paid tribute to their owners mainly in exchange for protection against slave raiders. The tribute was not unlike what Seminole townspeople provided to their town mico or chief (Mulroy 1993:17–23; Porter 1996:5–7).

As the Seminole case illustrates, slave-owning practices among Southeast Indians varied considerably according to tribal, historical, and local contexts, but there was common ground as well. In general, Black slavery was the exception rather than the rule for citizens of the Five Civilized Tribes, and in the early nineteenth century, the number of slaves in Indian communities relative to those in the broader American society was quite small. Most slaves were owned by "progressive" Indian elites, who often found themselves in conflict with tribal "traditionalists" who did not approve of slavery as a practice. These political tensions continued well after the 1830s and 1840s, when all Five Civilized Tribes were forcibly removed from their traditional homelands to Indian Territory, what is now Oklahoma (Jahoda 1975). Though Black slaves accompanied their Indian owners on these notorious "Trails of Tears" (vol. 14:163) and helped to rebuild Indian communities in their new lands, all Five Civilized Tribes increased both the magnitude and severity of their African slaveholding in the period after removal and leading up to the Civil War (Halliburton 1977; Littlefield 1979).

The American Civil War saw increased antagonism between Indian progressives and traditionalists over the practice of slavery and its associated cultural values. Tribal nations, communities, and families were divided along political and ideological lines, much as was the case in the broader American conflict. Among the various tribes, and even within individual Indian families, some fought on the side of the South and others on the side of the North (Abel 1915). After the Union victory, most of the Five Civilized Tribes freed their slaves; in fact, the Cherokee Nation had freed their slaves in 1863. However, certain Chickasaw and Choctaw slaveholders attempted to keep their slaves in bondage until October 1865, six months after the close of the war (Krauthamer 2000; Littlefield 1980). In the end, the Civil War brought about a great change in American societies: the Thirteenth Amendment to the Constitution and the formal emancipation of all slaves, including those that had once been owned by Indians.

## Citizenship Conflicts After the Civil War

At the end of the Civil War, federal officials ignored the factionalism that had long existed among the former slaveholding tribes in Indian Territory. During reconstruction negoti-

ations, they heard Southern sympathizers demanding the removal of their former slaves, while some pro-Union factions asked for their partial inclusion within their respective tribal polities. In the end, the Cherokee, Creek Confederacy, and Seminole Nations signed treaties with the federal government that provided for the emancipation and adoption of their former slaves, or Freedmen, as tribal citizens (Kappler 1904–1941, 2:910–915, 918–937, 942–950; Littlefield 1977, 1978, 1979). These treaties, known as the Treaties of 1866, guaranteed that Freedmen and their descendants would have rights of native citizens, including rights to land and national funds. These reconstruction era treaties would become the basis of social, political, and legal controversy, framing debates about tribal belonging and citizenship into the future.

Though the 1866 treaties held great promise that the Seminole, Creek, and Cherokee Freedmen would enjoy tribal rights in abundance, certain conditions had to be met before those rights would go into effect. The Creek and Cherokee treaties specified that Freedmen had to be resident within the nation, or to return within a certain time frame to be granted status as citizens. The Cherokee treaty limited citizenship to those Freedmen who returned within six months, whereas the Creek granted a period of one year. Unfortunately, these deadlines disenfranchised many former slaves who had been taken out of the nations by their owners during the Civil War, as well as those who had relocated outside of the nations to avoid the war. Because of their geographic distance, many Freedmen were unaware that they might be granted tribal citizenship or that a deadline to that effect was looming. For those who did know, the residency requirements often proved impossible to meet, particularly given their state of impoverishment as newly emancipated slaves. With limited resources for returning to their homelands, they often arrived too late or not at all. As a result, many Freedmen of the Cherokee and Creek Nations came to be known as "too lates" and were never admitted as tribal citizens (vol. 14:757).

Creek Freedmen who met the residency requirements had a different experience altogether. They were granted full tribal citizenship and in the decades immediately following emancipation enjoyed rights in the Creek Nation, including receiving tribal annuities, voting in tribal elections, and even holding political office. Three new Creek tribal towns were created for the representation of Creek Freedmen: Arkansas Colored, North Fork Colored, and Canadian Colored. Thus, Freedmen were fully incorporated into the Creek government, and they had a good deal of political power through their sheer numbers (May 1996:96, 171–173). They attended tribal schools and churches with local Creek Indians, with only a handful of these institutions becoming racially segregated as Oklahoma statehood loomed (Sameth 1940). In the decades after Reconstruction, the Seminole Freedmen experienced a pattern of political incorporation much like that of the Creek Freedmen. Seminole Freedmen were able to share in tribal citizenship, funds, and political rights. Like the Creeks, they were integrated into the traditional system of government, being represented in two of the 14 Seminole bands: the Caesar Bruner and Dosar Barkus bands, which remain part of the Seminole National Council (Bateman 1990:51).

During the same era, the Cherokee Freedmen did not fare so well as the Seminole and Creek Freedmen. Cherokee Freedmen who met the residency requirements imposed during Reconstruction were granted full tribal citizenship within the Cherokee Nation, but they faced an uphill battle in trying to secure their political rights, as the Cherokee government fought to exclude them from citizenship, annuity payments, and eventually land allotments. Though a few Cherokee Freedmen held national offices, Cherokee Freedmen in general were racially segregated and not afforded the same opportunities as most other Cherokee citizens. They were unable to attend schools with non-Black Cherokees, and continually struggled for access to payments, schools, and orphanages. In response, Cherokee Freedmen soon began to form activist networks across the Cherokee Nation, writing letters to the federal government and to the Cherokee Nation government in order to try and secure their rights as tribal citizens (Littlefield 1978).

After emancipation, the conditions of Choctaw and Chickasaw Freedmen citizenship were far more contested and uncertain than what was experienced by Freedmen in the other three tribes. During reconstruction, the Choctaw and Chickasaw Nations were racially hostile areas; consequently, the federal government gave them the option of adopting their Freedmen as tribal citizens or having them removed from their territories at the expense of the federal government. The nations were given two years to decide whether they would adopt the Freedmen. The Chickasaws chose not to adopt their Freedmen, but in the Choctaw Nation, the deadline passed with no decision being made. Because the Freedmen had no citizenship rights under tribal law, they were subject to violence, theft, destruction of property, and had no means of attaining justice. Like the Cherokee Freedmen, Choctaw and Chickasaw Freedmen became politically active early on in an effort to secure a footing within their nations, mobilizing and organizing mass meetings to petition Congress about their situation. The Chickasaw Freedmen united in the Chickasaw Freedmen's Association in 1894, trying to garner the attention of the president and Congress through petitions and statements of grievances. The Choctaw Nation adopted their Freedmen as citizens in 1883, although they experienced segregation and continued to struggle for access to national funds and schools (Krauthamer 2000:237–291). The Chickasaw Nation never adopted its Freedmen as citizens, and the United States never removed them from the nation, despite repeated appeals from the Chickasaw government. They were not granted citizenship of any sort and were people without a country until 1906, when all Indian Territory inhabitants became United States citizens (Littlefield 1980).

## Race and Oklahoma Statehood

While most Freedmen were citizens of their nations without question of their race, as time passed and race consciousness grew, some native families began to hide their African roots and to disassociate from their Black relatives (Saunt 2005). Race became important in framing tribal identity as Native polities adopted racial hierarchies and as pressures to incorporate the Five Civilized Tribes into the state of Oklahoma mounted. In preparation for the transition to statehood, the federal government formed the Dawes Commission, which was given the task of enumerating all the citizens of the Five Civilized Tribes in order to divide and allot the tribal land base to individual tribal citizens (Debo 1940:31–91). Produced between 1898 and 1906, the Dawes Rolls were actually made up of separate rolls for "Indians," "Intermarried White Citizens," and "Freedmen" (table 1). Most citizens with any degree of African ancestry were listed on the Freedmen Rolls regardless of any known Indian ancestry. All others with Indian ancestry, including those with predominant White ancestry, were assigned to the Indian Rolls. Racial categorizations at the time worked in such a way that most people of African ancestry were designated as Black or Freedmen, regardless of Indian ancestry. The foremost problem for Freedmen in the creation of the Dawes Rolls would be in the recording of an Indian blood quantum. Those who were listed on the Indian Rolls were listed with a degree of Indian blood, while Freedmen and Black Indians on the Freedmen Rolls were listed with no blood quantum at all (Carter 1999:49, 92–94). The end result of the Dawes enrollment process was that it divided the citizens of each of the Five Civilized Tribes along racial lines and stripped Black Indians of their status as Indians—something that would have devastating effects on their future rights as tribal citizens.

After the divisive effects of the Dawes enrollment, Freedmen continued to face obstacles. In 1907, the state of Oklahoma was admitted to the union, and the Oklahoma state legislature immediately passed Jim Crow laws, including a grandfather clause that disenfranchised African-Americans. Indians, by contrast, were legally categorized as Whites. Black Indians and Freedmen found themselves in a new racial category, legally and socially separated from the people with whom they had formed close relationships over

**Table 1. Dawes Commission Rolls**

|                | Indians | Intermarried Whites | Freedmen |
| -------------- | ------- | ------------------- | -------- |
| Seminole       | 2,141   | 0[a]                | 996      |
| Muskogee Creek | 11,952  | 0[a]                | 6,809    |
| Cherokee       | 36,619  | 286                 | 4,919    |
| Choctaw        | 19,148  | 1,651               | 6,029    |
| Chickasaw      | 5,659   | 645                 | 4,662    |

[a]The Seminole and Muscogee Creek Nations chose not to extend citizenship to intermarried Whites (Debo 1940:47).

the years. Many Freedmen who had enjoyed the rights of Indians were awakened to the injustices that segregation brought. The rigid new racial hierarchy divided friends and families and changed the social fabric of the Five Civilized Tribes (Bateman 1990; Miles 2005; Saunt 2005).

Although all Freedmen on the Dawes Rolls had been allotted reservation land as citizens of the Five Civilized Tribes, restrictions were lifted from their lands in 1904. Consequently, Freedmen allotments could be sold and otherwise alienated from Freedmen ownership. The same would be true for other tribal citizens who were not designated as three-quarters Indian blood or more (Debo 1940:179). The federal government lumped these two groups of people together with the rationale that race was a measure of one's competency in understanding and administering economic transactions. Thus, "Fuller-blood" Indians were designated as "incompetent" and in need of guardianship, while "lesser-blood" Indians and Freedmen were viewed as "competent" and thus able to sell their own property. The Freedmen, like other tribal citizens, became vulnerable to theft, murder, and graft (Debo 1940:61–125). Despite these obstacles, most Freedmen continued to keep small farms as they did in the Indian Territory era. Some moved to metropolitan areas when these farms became nearly impossible to maintain during the Depression of the 1930s.

Even as Freedmen were struggling against racial discrimination, African-Americans from other states went to Oklahoma in large numbers to participate in land runs and to find economic and political opportunities. Culturally different from these newcomers, Freedmen frequently regarded them with contempt, referring to them as "State Negroes," and among the Creek Freedmen as *wacína* 'American', the usual term for White people, glossed by Grinde and Taylor (1984:218) as "White man's Negro." Initially, the two

groups lived in separate communities (Sameth 1940). In time, their common experiences as Blacks brought them together. As a result, most Freedmen descendants in the twenty-first century have ancestors that are a mixture of Freedmen, Indians, Whites, and other Blacks (fig. 1).

## Struggles for Citizenship and Equal Rights

During the first half of the twentieth century, one legal battle after another attempted to remedy the injustices of the allotment era. Yet, tribal citizens were often divided on Freedmen issues: for example, many Indians believed that the Freedmen should never have been included on the tribal rolls. A case in point was in 1933 when the Seminole Nation sued the federal government in the United States Court of Claims to reclaim lands issued to the Seminole Freedmen during allotment. The Seminole Nation argued that they had been forced against their will to adopt Seminole Freedmen as tribal members and had lost valuable property in the process. Freedmen, on the other hand, believed they had been discriminated against during the allotment process and that they had generally received lands far inferior in quality to those granted other tribal citizens. At least three such suits were filed after 1933, all resulting in denial of the Seminole claims (vol. 14:474).

In the Creek Nation, federal law provided that unequal allotments would be redressed through payment in land or money to individual allottees. Creek Freedmen who had received unequally valued allotments and no compensation formed the Creek Freedmen Association and brought their case to the Indian Claims Commission in 1948 (*Creek Freedmen Association* v. *U.S. Indian Claims Commission*,

AP Images.

Fig. 1. Researching family history. left, Ruth Adair Nash, Cherokee Freedwoman (foreground), and her brother Everett Adair and his wife Susie examining family history paperwork at Ruth's home in Bartlesville, Okla., while her granddaughter Rudi Thompson looks on. Photograph by Brandi Simons, 2006. right, Johnny Toomer, Cherokee Freedman, with genealogical documents in Muskogee, Okla., 2006.

Docket 25). The case was dismissed as the complaint was against the Creek Nation, of which the Freedmen were citizens, and according to the court it was an internal tribal affair over which it had no jurisdiction. As a general rule, Freedmen faced a bitter predicament. As tribal citizens, they could not seek justice in federal and state courts, since sovereign immunity meant that internal tribal conflicts had to be decided by tribes themselves. Yet, Freedmen felt they had no other choice but to pursue external legal remedies, since they believed anti-Black sentiment within the tribes would prevent them from getting fair hearings within the tribal courts.

Similar legal contradictions and political conflicts continued to plague the Freedmen in the second half of the twentieth century. Despite the fact that the civil rights legislation of the 1950s and 1960s had brought an end to overt forms of racial segregation in Oklahoma, the era had an enduring legacy, one that in fact separated many Black Indian families and fostered further racism throughout the Five Civilized Tribes. De facto segregation continued well into the 1970s, when each of the Five Civilized Tribes began to reassert their sovereignty and reorganize their tribal governments. As each of the Five Civilized Tribes created new tribal constitutions, they limited citizenship to those who could prove tribal blood; the exceptions were the Seminole and Cherokee Nations.

In the late 1960s, as the Seminole Nation reorganized, 12 Seminole and two Seminole Freedmen bands were called upon to elect representatives to a constitutional committee. Though some Seminoles proposed excluding the Freedmen from citizenship, in the end the Freedmen were included as tribal citizens in the Seminole Nation's constitution of 1969. Only seven years later, the Seminole Nation government tried to exclude the Freedmen from a $16 million award the tribe had received from the Indian Claims Commission. The monies were intended to compensate the tribe for loss of communal lands in Florida, under treaties dating to 1823 and 1832. Prior to the allocation of these funds, the Seminole Nation of Florida filed an injunction, and the two Seminole Freedmen bands of the Seminole Nation of Oklahoma also intervened, stating they should not be excluded from the funds. In 1991, Congress passed the Seminole Judgment Fund Act, stating that approximately 75 percent of the fund would be awarded to the Oklahoma Seminoles and the remaining 25 percent to the Florida Seminoles. Unfortunately, the Seminole Freedmen were excluded from receiving any share of the payment, even though they were citizens of the Seminole Nation of Oklahoma. A 1976 Bureau of Indian Affairs memorandum explained the rationale behind this decision. It stated that although Seminole Freedmen were instrumental in Seminole society, holding high-ranking positions as civil and war leaders, living in adjacent communities and intermarrying with other Seminoles, they were not entitled to benefits from the settlement because they were property-less slaves at the time of the treaties. In order to receive benefits from the fund, the Freedmen would have to prove a Seminole Indian lineage dating back to 1823, an impossible task given the scarcity of records from this period (vol. 14:474).

In the 1970s and 1980s, the Muskogee Creek, Cherokee, Choctaw, and Chickasaw Nations each created new tribal constitutions limiting tribal citizenship to those with Indian blood whose ancestors were listed on the Dawes Rolls. Some tribes also passed citizenship codes specifying that citizens must prove descent from the Dawes Indian Rolls, a practice that specifically excludes Freedmen from citizenship and has been the focus of several legal battles. The contemporary perspective of the tribal governments—whether it is expressed explicitly in tribal laws or implicitly in tribal practices—has been one of limiting tribal citizenship to those people who are eligible for a Certificate Degree of Indian Blood. Yet, proof of Indian blood is still taken from the Dawes Rolls, where Freedmen were not listed with any blood quantum regardless of their actual Indian ancestry.

Prior to the adoption of these new constitutions and continuing even into the early 1980s, some Freedmen remember voting in tribal elections, having tribal registration cards and even being considered tribal citizens. They were able to vote in tribal elections one year and then were turned away from the polls the next. In the case of Reverend Roger H. Nero, a Cherokee Freedmen descendent, the seemingly arbitrary shift was not something he was willing to abide. Between 1984 and 1989, Reverend Nero and several other elderly Cherokee Freedmen descendents fought numerous legal battles in the state and federal courts to have their rights as Cherokee citizens reinstated. These efforts proved unsuccessful as the courts once again upheld tribal sovereignty, determining that they had no jurisdiction over internal Cherokee affairs and that the matter had to be settled within the tribal courts (Sturm 2002:178–186).

After this bitter lesson, Cherokee activists reorganized, and in 1997 they brought a case before the Cherokee Judicial Appeals Tribunal. Bernice R. Riggs, an elderly Cherokee Freedman descendant, had applied for citizenship in the Cherokee Nation in 1996 and been denied in 2001. Riggs could prove her Cherokee ancestry using various tribal and federal documents, and she had Cherokee Freedmen ancestors listed on the Dawes Rolls. Representatives for Riggs argued that it was impossible for Freedmen to meet the Certificate Degree of Indian Blood standard imposed by the tribal government, that the practice excluded Freedmen on a categorical basis and that it was inherently racially discriminatory (*Bernice Riggs* v. *Lela Ummerteskee*, JAT 97-03-K). In 2002, the court concluded that although Riggs possessed Cherokee blood and her ancestors were on the Dawes Roll, the Cherokee Nation had the authority to decide who was a citizen and who was not, and in their opinion Bernice Riggs was not a Cherokee citizen. The decision upheld tribal sovereignty, and although it was a blow to Cherokee and Cherokee Freedmen activists, they formed new coalitions. They used the arguments in the Riggs case to help frame a new case before the Cherokee tribal courts, one that would bring them success several years later.

## Changes in Freedmen Cultural Practices and Identity

Over the course of the twentieth century, Freedmen experienced dramatic cultural and social shifts, just as other citizens of the Five Civilized Tribes. In the first half of the century, many Freedmen used their knowledge of the medicinal properties of roots and herbs, a unique blend of Native and African-American folk culture, to "doctor" themselves and others. Many Freedmen cooked and ate traditional tribal foods. A majority of Freedmen spoke English as well as their tribal languages prior to statehood and in the early twentieth century (T.L. Baker and J.P. Baker 1996; Naylor-Ojurongbe 2002). Many Seminole Freedmen spoke the Creek language, but many also spoke their own ancestral language, an English-based creole called Afro-Seminole, which contained words of African, Spanish, and Creek origin (Hancock 1980). Unfortunately, as with other tribal citizens, many Freedmen lost the ability to speak their tribal languages over the generations, particularly as compulsory schooling outside of tribal contexts became more common (Bateman 1990:292–293). In 2006, very few Seminole and Creek Freedmen retained any knowledge of their tribal languages, and this is even less common among the Cherokee, Choctaw, and Chickasaw Freedmen.

Due to segregation before and after statehood, many Freedmen communities consisted mainly of Freedmen and "State" Blacks, residing separately from the majority of Indians and Whites. Nonetheless, there was some intermarriage across racial lines, and day-to-day life involved inter-actions among all three groups. Throughout most of the twentieth century, Freedmen life centered on rural living, small farm ownership, and social events in small-town churches (fig. 2). Many of these churches were Southern Baptist in their orientation, though some were also Holiness and African Methodist Episcopal. Prince Hall Masonic lodges were also a central part of most Freedmen communities. Many Creek and Seminole Freedmen participated in traditional tribal ceremonies and church systems alongside Indian people. Cherokee, Choctaw, and Chickasaw Freedmen did not participate in native ceremonial life or church systems as frequently and usually attended their own churches. Besides regular church functions, people gathered at community picnics held at different points throughout the summer. In the Cherokee Nation, these great picnics would be held on August 4 to commemorate the emancipation day of Cherokee slaves. Whatever the occasion, picnics lasted for several days, with Freedmen and African-Americans from throughout the county, as well as Whites and Indians attending (Feldhousen-Giles 2003–2005).

Most historic Freedmen communities have experienced considerable population loss as younger generations moved to the cities. Even though Freedmen communities are smaller, and many traditional social events are no longer practiced, many Freedmen still reside on their ancestors' allotments and organize much of their lives around family-based social networks. Yet, one of the effects of segregation is that many Freedmen no longer identify themselves primarily as such, but as African-American or Black with "Freed-

Mt. Triumph Missionary Baptist Church, Ft. Coffee, Okla.

Fig. 2. Congregation and visitors outside Mt. Triumph Missionary Baptist Church, Ft. Coffee, Okla., a Choctaw Freedmen town. Photographed in 1947.

men" being a part of their ancestry and their history. Many Seminole Freedmen do continue to identify themselves primarily as Seminole, Black Seminole, Seminole Freedmen, or use the Creek term Estelusti (*Eisti-lásti* 'Black person'. In some contexts, other Freedmen descendants do identify as Freedmen, or use the terms Black Indian, Black Cherokee, Black Creek, or simply their particular tribal affiliation without "Black" preceding it. Still others take offense at the term Freedmen because their ancestors were never actually held as slaves but were instead individuals of African, or African and Indian descent who later came to be misidentified as Freedmen (Feldhousen-Giles 2003–2005).

## Political Activism After 2001

In 2000, the Seminole Nation held an election that amended its constitution to exclude the Freedmen Bands from citizenship in the Seminole Nation. This event ignited a firestorm of political and legal controversy among all Five Civilized Tribes, Freedmen descendants, Black Indian activists, and other interested parties around the United States. Accused of anti-Black racism, the Seminole Nation maintained that it was not acting out of racism in its exclusion of Freedmen from citizenship. Rather, the choice to limit citizenship to those with Seminole blood was an act of sovereignty, even if outsiders viewed that choice as unfair or even racially discriminatory. The Seminole Nation argued that because the Seminole Freedmen were not Seminoles by blood, they should not be entitled to Seminole citizenship. Of course, this argument, a legacy of the Dawes enrollment era, excludes Seminole Freedmen with Indian ancestry whose ancestors fail to appear on the Seminole Indian rolls, but even Freedmen without Seminole Indian ancestry believe that they are entitled to citizenship because of their long history of social and political association with the tribe.

Whether they did or did not have Seminole ancestry, many Seminole Freedmen contested the election results, but it passed at the Seminole national level and would have become tribal law if not for external intervention. The Seminole constitution, like others of the Five Civilized Tribes, contains a clause that states that constitutional amendments cannot be made without the approval of the Bureau of Indian Affairs—something that considerably undermines tribal sovereignty. Because the Freedmen were not allowed to vote in the election, and because of the nature of the constitutional amendment, the Bureau of Indian Affairs refused to validate the election. Although the Seminole Nation contested this decision in *Seminole* v. *Norton* (2001), the tribe lost the case and the Freedmen bands retained their tribal citizenship rights. The bands have not fared so well concerning other rights within the tribe and do not have access to equal housing, education, and health care benefits. Sylvia Davis, a representative of the Dosar Barkus Band of Seminole Freedmen, addressed the inequities in court, by filing

several cases and appeals to have the Bureau of Indian Affairs grant Certificate Degrees of Indian Blood to the Seminole Freedmen—the idea being that such a practice would undermine the Dawes legacy of race-based discrimination tied to blood descent (*Davis* v. *United States*). Her case was dismissed in 2003 when the 10th Circuit Court of Appeals found that it had failed to include the Seminole Nation as an indispensable party and that the Seminole Freedmen had not exhausted their administrative appeals within the tribe. Although the Seminole Freedmen remained active in their quest for equality in the Seminole Nation, the Seminole Nation, along with others of the Five Civilized Tribes, is moving to eliminate the clause from its constitution that requires Bureau of Indian Affairs oversight concerning constitutional amendments. In doing so, the tribe is fighting for its sovereignty, but many Freedmen expect this shift to affect their future rights to citizenship.

Because it received a great deal of national media attention, the case of the Seminole Freedmen became a catalyst for Freedmen activism throughout the state of Oklahoma. In 2002, a small group of Freedmen assembled in Oklahoma City to form the Descendants of Freedmen of the Five Civilized Tribes Association. Their goals have been to educate people on Freedmen history in the Five Civilized Tribes and to regain their tribal rights and citizenship. In 2003, several former members formed a separate activist group called the Freedmen Descendants of the Five Civilized Tribes. Based in Kansas, this second group has been responsible for making many Freedmen records accessible over the internet and for accomplishing a great deal of Black-Indian genealogical research. The original group is larger and has a greater political presence. This group continues to meet on a monthly basis in Oklahoma City and in other cities in Oklahoma to attract Freedmen descendants and supporters from across the state. It holds an annual academic conference on Freedmen history and legal issues and raises money to support legal actions to reinstate Freedmen as citizens of the tribes. While many Freedmen attend the meetings of this association to learn more about their possible rights in the Five Civilized Tribes, many other Freedmen in Oklahoma are not very concerned with these legal and political issues. For some, the desire to learn more about family histories and genealogies outweighs legal struggles (fig. 3). Especially since the early 1980s, Freedmen descendants have been trying to rediscover their past and to document their individual histories. Sometimes the quest is about finding proof of Indian blood—a significant part of many Freedmen oral histories—so they can enroll in their tribes without having their rights to citizenship questioned. Others only want to know about their origins and their role in tribal history.

The Descendants of Freedmen Association provides information about Freedmen history and attempts to recruit Freedmen from all Five Civilized Tribes. They are responsible for two current lawsuits by Cherokee and Creek Freedmen in federal and tribal courts, and they support other legal actions by Freedmen, whenever and wherever they can. The

left, Roscoe Foreman, Chicago.

Fig. 3. Freedmen descendants. left, Zack Foreman, former slave, wealthy cattleman and business owner, and founder of the Cherokee Freedmen town of Foreman, Cherokee Nation, Indian Terr. Photographed about 1900. right, Reunion of the Foreman family. Roscoe Foreman, grandson of Zack, second from left, brought his sons Ghian (left) and Javin (fourth from left), from Chicago to Foreman, Okla., his birthplace. Damon Foreman (right), a cousin, guided the family around the town and introduced them to Benjamin "Skinner" Benton (center), the town's oldest continuous resident. Photograph by Kristy Feldhousen-Giles, 2005.

president of the association, Marilyn Vann, brought the first of these lawsuits to federal court in 2003. That year the Cherokee Nation held elections for principal chief and other political offices and proposed a constitutional amendment that would remove the clause requiring Bureau of Indian Affairs oversight of future constitutional reforms. Marilyn Vann and other Cherokee Freedmen attempted to vote in this election and were denied. Citing the Seminole case in which the Bureau refused to recognize an election in which Freedmen were not included as voters, Vann and others (fig. 4) filed a lawsuit against the federal government challenging the election (*Marilyn Vann, et al.* v. *Norton*). In 2005, the Cherokee Nation intervened in the lawsuit, filing a motion to dismiss. In 2006, a judge denied the motion, stating that the Cherokee Nation's sovereignty is abrogated by the Thirteenth Amendment to the Constitution. As of April 2007, the case was not decided.

The second case supported by the Descendants of Freedmen of the Five Civilized Tribes Association involved the Creek Nation and Creek Freedmen descendants. Ronald Graham and Fred Johnson, whose ancestors had been enrolled as Creek Freedmen, attempted to enroll as tribal citizens on several occasions between 1980 and 2004 and were repeatedly denied. In 2005, the men appealed the decision in the Creek Nation courts, arguing that they had proof of Creek blood from documents other than the Dawes Roll,

and had always been culturally Creek—given that their families spoke Creek, participated in Creek ceremonial life, foodways, and other cultural traditions (fig. 5). Their attorneys argued that the Creek Nation citizenship board had illegally disenfranchised countless Creek Freedmen by limiting citizenship to people whose ancestors were on the Dawes Indian (Creek by blood) Rolls. More specifically, they argued that the 1979 Creek constitution states only that citizens must be Creek by blood and that they must have an ancestor on the Dawes Roll. In fact, many Freedmen descendants meet these criteria, yet the Bureau of Indian Affairs and the Creek Nation citizenship office have denied all applications from people whose ancestors were listed on the Freedmen Rolls since the 1980s. The Creek Nation citizenship board changed its citizenship criteria in 2001 to explicitly limit Creek citizenship to those who could prove descent from the Dawes Creek Indian Rolls. The plaintiffs argued that this change targeted Freedmen applicants and made their citizenship impossible and that this new citizenship code was contrary to the Creek constitution. In March 2006, the Creek Nation District Court ruled in favor of Graham and Johnson, ruling that the Creek Nation Citizenship Board had acted illegally when it denied them citizenship according to the existing citizenship code that was in place prior to 2001 (*Ron Graham* v. *Muscogee (Creek) Nation Citizenship Board, Fred Johnson* v. *Muscogee (Creek) Na-*

Fig. 4. Hattie Cullors, center, a plaintiff in *Marilyn Vann et al.* v. *Norton*, her companion Wade Milton, Jr., and her grandson Jordan in Tulsa, Okla. Photograph by Kristy Feldhousen-Giles, 2006.

*tion Citizenship Board*); the Citizenship Board appealed. While a significant victory against historical and institutional discrimination, only Graham and Johnson can be enrolled in the Creek Nation because they had evidence that they had applied for citizenship and were rejected prior to the passage of the new citizenship code. Those Creek

Freedmen who cannot document when they were turned away, who are not Creek by blood, and the many others who are Creek but can find no proof of this fact in the historical documents must search for justice in some other venue.

Freedmen seeking legal remedies have fared far better in tribal than in federal courts, given that federal judges have maintained that they have no jurisdiction over internal tribal affairs. The most successful Freedmen case to be decided in the tribal courts is that of *Lucy Allen* v. *Cherokee Nation Tribal Council*. Filed in 2004 before the Cherokee Judicial Appeals Tribunal, the Allen case is in many respects similar to the Riggs case first brought before the courts in 1997. Like Riggs, Lucy Allen is a Cherokee Freedman descendant (fig. 5) who wished to enroll as a citizen in the Cherokee Nation. Her representative argued that she and all Cherokee Freedmen should be admitted to Cherokee citizenship according to the Cherokee national constitution. In a change from current and past lawsuits based on Freedmen possession of Indian blood, Allen's representative argued that she should be admitted to citizenship not on the basis of having Cherokee blood, but based on the fact that Freedmen had been granted citizenship in the 1866 treaty. The Allen case argued that a tribal citizenship code limiting citizenship to those who could prove Cherokee blood was unconstitutional according to the 1975 tribal constitution. As such, this case fought for all Cherokee Freedmen descendants, regardless of provable Indian ancestry. In March 2006, in what for many Cherokee citizens and Freedmen activists was a dramatic turn of events, the Cherokee Judicial Appeals Tribunal ruled in

left, AP Images.

Fig. 5. Seeking tribal membership. left, Lucy Allen, Cherokee Freedwoman, and plaintiff in *Lucy Allen* v. *Cherokee National Tribal Council* during an interview in Tulsa, Okla., 2006. right, Fred Johnson and Ronald Graham at the Muscogee Creek Nation headquarters, Okmulgee, Okla., during their trial for citizenship, Aug. 2005. Photograph by Vashti Butler.

favor of Lucy Allen, making Cherokee Freedmen eligible for enrollment as Cherokee citizens. However, their rights were still very much threatened, as many Cherokee citizens, including the chief of the Cherokee Nation, Chad Smith (2007), wished to pass a constitutional amendment that would explicitly exclude Freedmen from citizenship. In March 2007, the Cherokee nation held a special election by which Cherokee voters overwhelmingly approved an amendment to the Cherokee Nation constitution: "the amendment limits citizenship in the Cherokee Nation to descendants of people who are listed on the Final Rolls of the Cherokee Nations as Cherokee, Delaware, or Shawnee and excludes descendants of those listed on Intermarried White and Freedmen rolls taken at the same time" (Cherokee Nation 2007). Approximately 2,770 Cherokee Freedmen were affected. The new amendment was called "racist and discriminatory" by members of the Descendants of Freedmen of the Five Civilized Tribes (Kate 2007). By April 2007 about 60 Cherokee Freedmen had appealed the action.

In 2007 there was no litigation, in either federal or tribal courts, for Freedmen citizenship in the Choctaw and Chickasaw Nations. Future Chickasaw Freedmen citizenship is especially precarious, as the Chickasaw Nation never adopted them as citizens. Despite these different histories, and the Cherokee Nation vote, Freedmen descendants in the other Five Civilized Tribes continued to apply for citizenship in their tribal nations and to seek rights in federal and tribal courts. Tribal sovereignty and race lie at the crux of these contests. Tribes argue that they should be able to determine their own citizenship and that citizenship is not based on race but on specific social and political linkages, some of which are measured by the possession of Indian blood. However, because the Five Civilized Tribes use racially separate rolls to determine eligibility for citizenship, Freedmen descendants believe that their exclusion from the tribes is inherently race-based. Despite these longstanding issues, and the Cherokee Nation vote of exclusion, in the first decade of the twenty-first century, Freedmen in all Five Civilized Tribes shared a renewed interest in their distinctive history, a sense of Black Indian self-identification, and the hope of being able to reconnect with their tribal communities in some meaningful way.

# Native Populations of Canada

C. VIVIAN O'DONNELL

Estimates of the population of indigenous peoples who were living in the area now known as Canada at the time of contact with European newcomers have been the subject of considerable debate among experts. Generally, these estimates have increased "with better understanding of Native subsistence bases and with greater awareness of the effect of imported diseases in the sixteenth century" (Dickason 1992: 26–27). The Royal Commission on Aboriginal Peoples (1996) cites an early scholarly estimate of 210,000 people, as well as another estimate that exceeds two million people, and concludes that the figure of 500,000 people living in the Canada at the time of initial sustained contact is the most widely accepted estimate.

A number of diverse indigenous nations with distinctive cultural practices, economies, ways of life, languages, and traditions resided (and continue to reside) across the continent. Population concentrations were found largely on the Northwest Coast and in parts of what is now southern Ontario, where abundant resources and agricultural economies allowed for relatively dense concentrations of sedentary and populous settlements. However, in many regions of Canada, including the Plains, Plateau, Arctic, and Subarctic, Native peoples lived according to a land-intensive economy, that is, one requiring a large territory, resulting in relatively sparse populations over vast territories (Dickason 1992).

After sustained contact with European newcomers there were major population decreases in Native populations, perhaps up to a 93 percent loss (Dickason 1992:26–27). Rampant infectious diseases such as smallpox and measles and armed conflicts and starvation were the causes (Royal Commission on Aboriginal Peoples 1996; Thornton 1987; R. Wright 1992; Sioui 1992). The Native population in Canada has since experienced a surge in growth, particularly in the late twentieth century.

## The Term "Aboriginal"

In Canada, the term aboriginal is used to refer to all indigenous people collectively. The aboriginal population comprises three groups—Indians, Métis, and Inuit—each recognized in the Canadian Constitution.

## Indians

North American Indians, sometimes referred to as First Nations people or Indians, make up the largest group of aboriginal people in Canada. There are many diverse nations of North American Indian people, such as the Cree, Haida, and Blackfoot. North American Indians are further divided into Status or non-Status Indians (the term 'registered Indian' is also commonly used). Status Indians have certain rights and benefits that non-Status Indians do not, such as on-reserve housing benefits, education benefits, and certain tax exemptions (Indian and Northern Affairs Canada 2003). According to the 2001 census, there were approximately 558,000 Status Indians and 104,000 non-Status Indians. The Department of Indian Affairs and Northern Development maintains the "Indian Register," which is the list of Status Indians. In 2001 this list recorded a population of approximately 690,000 Status Indians (Indian and Northern Affairs Canada 2006:vi). North American Indian people are also divided into those who are members of First Nations or Indian bands and those who are not. Most, but not all, Status Indians are First Nation band members. According to the Assembly of First Nations, there were 633 First Nations bands, representing 52 nations or cultural groups and more than 50 languages, in 2006 (Assembly of First Nations 2006).

## Métis

The Métis are a distinct group whose early ancestors were of mixed heritage (North American Indian and European descent). This is the second largest and fastest growing aboriginal group in Canada. According to the Métis National Council, Métis communities are found in Manitoba, Alberta, Saskatchewan, parts of Ontario, British Columbia, and the Northwest Territories, as well as parts of the northern United States (North Dakota, Montana). Censuses have shown that Métis populations are growing at substantial rates in other parts of Canada, particularly in the eastern provinces.

## Inuit

The Inuit are the indigenous people of the Canadian Arctic. Inuit have been referred to as Eskimos, although this term is not commonly used in the Canadian context. This is the smallest of the aboriginal groups in terms of population size, although the Inuit comprise the vast majority of residents in the Canadian Arctic, an area that makes up about 40 percent of Canada's land.

There are many ways to define the Native population in Canada. Some aboriginal people affiliate themselves with specific nations (e.g., Mohawk or Ojibway) or specific bands (e.g., the Red Rock Indian band or the Siksika Nation), while others choose legal definitions (such as Status or registered Indian) or more broadly based terms (e.g., Native Canadian or Indian). Other ways to identify aboriginal people—such as blood quantum, physiological traits, or cultural characteristics such as language abilities—are also used. While acknowledging the complexities surrounding aboriginal identity in Canada, the following examination of the Native populations is based for the most part on information collected in the Canadian census of population.

In Canada, the census is carried out every five years, and four concepts are used to define the aboriginal population: ethnic or cultural origins of one's ancestors, registered Indian status, membership in a First Nation or Indian Band, and aboriginal identity. Each of these concepts relies upon "self-reporting" on the part of the respondent.

## Aboriginal Ancestry Population

During the census, Canadians are asked about the ethnic or cultural origins of their ancestors. In 2001, just over 4 percent of Canada's population (about 1.3 million) reported that their ancestors were of aboriginal ancestry. The numbers and proportions of Canadians who reported Native ancestry were not uniform across the country. In Ontario, Canada's most populous province, 308,000 persons reported being of aboriginal ancestry. While this was the largest number of any province, the aboriginal ancestry population represented only 3 percent of the total population living there. By contrast, in Manitoba and Saskatchewan, the aboriginal origin population represented 15 percent and 14 percent of the total populations, respectively. Much higher percentages of people living in the northern territories also reported having aboriginal ancestry—one-quarter of the population of the Yukon Territory, half of the population of the Northwest Territories, and 86 percent of the population of Nunavut (table 1).

The majority of those who reported having aboriginal ancestry reported having multiple ancestries; that is, in addition to aboriginal origins, they reported having nonaboriginal origins. The Métis were the most likely of the three aboriginal groups to report multiple origins—only 23 percent reported being of Métis origins only. Given that the very definition of Métis refers to the "mixing" of ancestries, this is perhaps not surprising. By contrast, two-thirds of Inuit reported being of Inuit origins only. This is likely due

**Table 1. Aboriginal Ancestry Population, Canada, 2001**

| | Aboriginal Ancestry Population | % of Total Population Reporting Aboriginal Ancestry |
|---|---|---|
| Canada | 1,319,890 | 4.5 |
| Newfoundland and Labrador | 28,070 | 5.5 |
| Prince Edward Island | 2,720 | 2.0 |
| Nova Scotia | 33,420 | 3.7 |
| New Brunswick | 28,465 | 4.0 |
| Quebec | 159,905 | 2.2 |
| Ontario | 308,105 | 2.7 |
| Manitoba | 160,250 | 14.5 |
| Saskatchewan | 135,035 | 14.0 |
| Alberta | 199,010 | 6.8 |
| British Columbia | 216,110 | 5.6 |
| Yukon Territory | 6,985 | 24.5 |
| Northwest Territories | 18,955 | 51.1 |
| Nunavut | 22,865 | 85.7 |

SOURCE: Statistics Canada 2003:2001 Census.

to the homogeneity of many Inuit communities in the Arctic, where the majority of Inuit live.

Among those with North American Indian ancestry, about 46 percent reported being of North American Indian origins only. Among North American Indian people who were living on-reserve, 90 percent reported that their ancestors were North American Indian only. By contrast, in urban areas where cultural and ethnic heterogeneity is common, only 28 percent of North American Indians reported that their ancestors were North American Indian exclusively. In other words, the majority (72%) of North American Indians living in urban areas reported that their ancestors were a mix of North American Indian and other ethnic or cultural groups. The same was true of rural nonreserve areas, where again the majority of North American Indians (73%) reported having multiple ancestries.

The aboriginal ancestry population has significantly increased since 1970 (fig. 1). Following a slow rate of growth in the first part of the twentieth century, from 1951 until

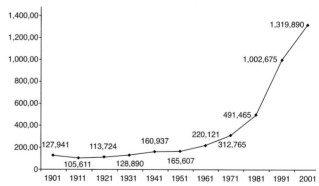

Fig. 1. Populations with Native ancestry, 1901–2001 (Statistics Canada 2003:2001 Census).

2001, the aboriginal ancestry population grew an astounding 700 percent, from 165,000 to 1,320,000. The slow growth rate in the first part of the century has been attributed to high mortality rates, which more than offset high birth rates. This began to change in the late 1960s when a declining infant death rate combined with high fertility rates led to a baby boom in the Native population (Statistics Canada 2003; Royal Commission on Aboriginal Peoples 1996). Indeed, the fertility rate for Native people in the 1966 to 1971 period was 5.5 children per woman (Ram 2004).

While demographic factors account in part for the rapid growth since the 1960s, there are other factors at play. Legislative, political, historical, cultural, and social changes resulted in an increased willingness on the part of many Canadians to acknowledge aboriginal ancestors and to report them in the census. Many events in the post-World War II period, including several successful aboriginal rights court cases, changes to the Canadian Constitution that recognized aboriginal and treaty rights, a Royal Commission on Aboriginal Peoples, and a general renaissance of aboriginal cultures led many Canadians to acknowledge their aboriginal ancestors. The phenomenon of more people reporting such ancestry over time has been coined "ethnic mobility" by some researchers. This phenomenon has also been observed and studied in the Native populations of the United States, New Zealand, and Australia (Eschbach 1993, 1995; Eschbach, Supple, and Snipp 1998; Guimond 1999, 2003; Hoddie 2002; Nagel 1996; K. Ross 1996; Siggner 2003a).

## Registered Indians and First Nation and Band Members

In 2005, there were approximately 748,000 persons on the Indian Register (Indian and Northern Affairs Canada 2006c). The Indian Register, maintained by the Department of Indian Affairs and Northern Development, acts as the official record of those recognized as status or registered Indians under the terms of the Indian Act. While the Indian Register was officially established in 1951, it was as early as 1850 that the colonial government maintained records to identify individual Indians and their bands to determine eligibility for treaty benefits (Indian and Northern Affairs Canada 2003). Among the rights and privileges that come with legal Indian status and First Nation band membership are the right to vote in band elections and access to certain programs and services, including some health, education, and housing benefits.

Approximately 100,000 people have been added to the Indian register since amendments to the Indian Act were made in 1985 under Bill C-31 (Indian and Northern Affairs Canada 2003; Furi and Wherret 2003). These amendments served to remove some of the provisions in the Indian Act that caused many to be stripped of their registered Indian status. Prior to Bill C-31, for example, if a Status Indian

woman married a non-Status man (aboriginal or nonaboriginal) she was removed from the Indian Register and lost membership in her First Nation band. Further, she could no longer pass registered Indian status on to her children. The opposite was true for a Status Indian man; he automatically conferred registered Indian status to his spouse, regardless of whether she was non-Status (aboriginal or nonaboriginal). Other ways to lose Indian status included the "enfranchisement" process according to which a Status Indian could apply to relinquish Indian status in exchange for, among other rights and benefits, the right to vote in federal elections. In 1960 the law was changed to allow Status Indians to vote in federal elections (Indian and Northern Affairs Canada 2003).

The Bill C-31 legislation enabled many who had voluntarily or involuntarily lost their Indian status through certain provisions of the Indian Act to be reinstated as registered Indians. As a result, the registered Indian population grew significantly after 1985 (table 2). Women and those living off-reserve accounted for a disproportionate share of this growth (O'Donnell 2006:25).

Bill C-31 introduced new inheritance rules regarding the passing of registered Indian status from parents to children (Sprague 1995; Furi and Wherret 2003). It is now the case that both parents must have registered Indian status in order to ensure that Indian status will be passed to their children. Two generations of "out-marriage" (or parenting children with non-Status individuals) leads to the termination of legal Indian status for that line of descendents. It is certain that because of out-marriage, there will be a decline in the proportion of births eligible for registration. One study has predicted that the proportion of births eligible for Indian registration on reserve could decrease from around 99 percent in 2000 to 87 percent by 2021. Among the off-reserve population, the predictions were even lower—79 percent in 2000 to 52 percent by 2021 (Indian and Northern Affairs Canada 2006b:11).

Bill C-31 amendments allowed First Nations bands the opportunity legally to take control of their own membership codes. Whereas prior to 1985, Indian registration was virtually

**Table 2. Registered Indian Population, 1981, 1991, and 2001**

|  | 1981 | 1991 | 2001 | Growth rate 1981–2001 (%) |
|---|---|---|---|---|
| On-reserve | 170,055 | 184,710 | 274,215 | 61.3 |
| Males | 87,835 | 95,055 | 139,185 | 58.5 |
| Females | 82,220 | 89,660 | 135,030 | 64.2 |
| Off-reserve | 119,120 | 201,090 | 283,955 | 138.4 |
| Males | 54,940 | 89,870 | 129,245 | 135.2 |
| Females | 64,180 | 111,225 | 154,715 | 141.1 |
| Total | 289,175 | 385,805 | 558,175 | 93.0 |
| Males | 142,770 | 184,920 | 268,430 | 88.0 |
| Females | 146,400 | 200,885 | 289,745 | 97.9 |

SOURCE: O'Donnell 2006:205.

**Table 3.   The 20 Largest Native Indian Bands in Canada, Dec. 31, 2005**

| Band | Indian Register Population |
|---|---|
| Six Nations of the Grand River, Ont. | 22,349 |
| Mohawks of Akwesasne, Ont. | 10,217 |
| Blood, Alta. | 9,842 |
| Kahnawake, Que. | 9,392 |
| Saddle Lake, Alta. | 8,404 |
| Lac La Ronge, Sask. | 8,030 |
| Peguis, Man. | 7,846 |
| Peter Ballantyne Cree Nation, Sask. | 7,740 |
| Mohawks of the Bay of Quinte, Ont. | 7,533 |
| Wikwemikong, Ont. | 6,880 |
| Bigstone Cree Nation, Alta. | 6,557 |
| Fort Alexander, Man. | 6,486 |
| Samson, Alta. | 6,478 |
| Cross Lake First Nation, Man. | 6,470 |
| Norway House Cree Nation, Man. | 6,229 |
| Siksika Nation, Alta. | 6,012 |
| Sandy Bay, Man. | 5,164 |
| Oneida Nation of the Thames, Ont. | 5,127 |
| Nisichawayasihk Cree Nation, Man. | 4,882 |
| Opaskwayak Cree Nation, Man. | 4,815 |

SOURCE: Department of Indian Affairs and Northern Development 2006:xi.

synonymous with First Nation band membership, these two concepts became separate with the enactment of Bill C-31. Approximately 37 percent of First Nations bands elected to devise their own membership codes (Indian and Northern Affairs Canada 2006). Table 3 lists the 20 largest bands in Canada.

## Aboriginal Identity Population

The Canadian census asks a very pointed question regarding aboriginal status: "Is this person an Aboriginal person?" The respondent checks off any of the following: North American Indian, Métis, and/or Inuit. Unlike the question dealing with aboriginal ancestry, this question refers specifically to the individual as opposed to their ancestors. In 2001, 976,000 Canadians reported that they were aboriginal (table 4). This was a 22 percent increase from five years earlier, which is a remarkable level of growth considering that the Canadian population as a whole increased by only 3 percent in the same period.

While 1.3 million Canadians reported that they have Native ancestry, only 976,000 Canadians reported that they are Native persons. In other words, not every person with Native ancestors considered themselves to be Native, even though in some cases they were reported to have registered Indian status or First Nations membership or both. Perhaps the aboriginal ancestor was too distant in the past and the individual no longer felt connected to the Native community. This theory is supported by the fact that in areas of Canada where contact with nonaboriginal peoples has been sustained over longer time periods or where aboriginal people represent only a small minority, higher percentages of people were found who reported aboriginal ancestry but not aboriginal identity. For example, figure 2 shows the percentage of the North American Indian ancestry population who also identify as aboriginal. In the eastern Atlantic provinces, about half of those with North American Indian ancestry identified themselves as aboriginal persons. In Saskatchewan, the overwhelming majority of those with

**Table 4.   Total Population by Aboriginal Identity Group, 2001**

| | Aboriginal Identity Population | North American Indian | Métis | Inuit | Belongs to More Than One Aboriginal Group | Other[a] | Total Non-aboriginal Population |
|---|---|---|---|---|---|---|---|
| Canada | 976,310 | 608,850 | 292,310 | 45,075 | 6,660 | 23,415 | 28,662,725 |
| Newf. and Labr. | 18,775 | 7,035 | 5,485 | 4,555 | 195 | 1,510 | 489,300 |
| P. E. I. | 1,350 | 1,035 | 220 | 20 | — | 60 | 132,040 |
| N. S. | 17,010 | 12,920 | 3,135 | 350 | 50 | 560 | 880,560 |
| N. B. | 16,990 | 11,495 | 4,295 | 160 | 165 | 885 | 702,720 |
| Que. | 79,400 | 51,125 | 15,850 | 9,535 | 595 | 2,300 | 7,046,180 |
| Ont. | 188,315 | 131,560 | 48,340 | 1,375 | 1,695 | 5,345 | 11,097,235 |
| Man. | 150,045 | 90,340 | 56,795 | 340 | 500 | 2,060 | 953,655 |
| Sask. | 130,185 | 83,740 | 43,695 | 235 | 895 | 1,625 | 832,965 |
| Alta. | 156,225 | 84,995 | 66,060 | 1,090 | 1,100 | 2,980 | 2,784,930 |
| B.C. | 170,025 | 118,290 | 44,265 | 805 | 1,170 | 5,490 | 3,698,850 |
| Yukon Terr. | 6,540 | 5,600 | 535 | 145 | 100 | 165 | 21,980 |
| N.W.T. | 18,730 | 10,615 | 3,575 | 3,905 | 180 | 445 | 18,375 |
| Nunavut | 22,720 | 95 | 50 | 22,560 | 10 | 10 | 3,945 |

[a]Includes those who did not identify with an aboriginal group but who reported having registered Indian status and/or First Nations membership.
SOURCE: Statistics Canada 2003:2001 Census.

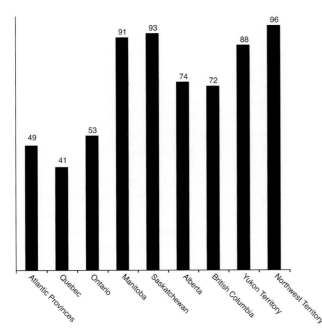

Fig. 2. Percentage of persons with Native ancestry who identified as Aboriginal in 2001 (Statistics Canada 2003:2001 Census).

North American Indian ancestry reported that they identify as aboriginal persons (93%). While there are many potential ways to define the aboriginal population in Canada, the aboriginal identity population is generally the most commonly used definition for research and policy and program planning. It is this population definition that will be used here to explore the characteristics of Native people in Canada.

*Age Structure*

One of the defining characteristics of the Native population is its youthfulness. In 2001, the median age of the Native population (the point at which half the population is older and half the population is younger) was 24.7 years. By comparison, the median age of the nonaboriginal population had reached an all-time high of 37.7 years (Statistics Canada 2003).

Of the three Native groups, the Inuit were the youngest population. In 2001, about 57 percent of Inuit were under the age of 25. In fact, more than one in three Inuit were

under the age of 15. The Métis were the oldest of the Native groups with about 47 percent of their population under the age of 25, yet they remained significantly younger than the nonaboriginal population, where only 32 percent were under the age of 25, and more than 10 percent were 65 years and over. By comparison, only 3 percent of Inuit and 4 percent of Métis were in their senior years (table 5).

In 2001, just over half of North American Indian people were under the age of 25. This varied according to area of residence. In reserve communities, the young and the old represented higher percentages of the population than among North American Indians living off-reserve. Specifically, 42 percent of North American Indian people living on-reserve were either children or seniors. In urban areas, 36 percent of North American Indians were either children or seniors (33% under the age of 15 and 3% 65 years and over) (fig. 3).

Compared to the nonaboriginal population, aboriginal people have more children, and they tend to have their children at younger ages. For the 1996 to 2001 period, the aboriginal fertility rate (the number of children that a woman could expect to have in her lifetime) was 2.6 children, compared to 1.5 children for the total Canadian population. Among the three Native groups, the Inuit have the highest fertility rate at 3.4 children, compared to 2.2 children for the Métis population, and 2.9 children for the North American Indian population (Statistics Canada 2005).

Because of the population's youthful nature, native people tend to make up much larger proportions in the younger cohorts. For example, in 2001, 14 percent of Saskatchewan's total population was Native; however, 25 percent of the province's children were Native. In Nunavut, while Aboriginal people made up 85 percent of the total population, 94 percent of all children were Aboriginal.

Youthful as the population is, it is slowly aging. This is due in large part to a gradually improving life expectancy and to the declining birth rate among Native peoples (Statistics Canada 2003). While life expectancies have improved over time, they remain lower than those of other Canadians (fig. 4). In 2001, the estimated life expectancy for men in the general population was 77 years; however it was 71 for North American Indian men, 72 for Métis men, and 63 for Inuit men. Women in both the aboriginal and nonaboriginal populations have higher life expectancies than their male counterparts. In 2001, the estimated life expectancy at birth

**Table 5. Age Structure, by Ethnic Group, Canada, 2001**

| | Total Aboriginal Identity Population | Indian On-reserve | Indian Off-reserve | Métis | Inuit | Total Non-aboriginal Population |
|---|---|---|---|---|---|---|
| 0–14 years | 33% | 3% | 34% | 29% | 39% | 19% |
| 15–24 years | 17 | 17 | 17 | 18 | 18 | 13 |
| 25–44 years | 30 | 28 | 31 | 31 | 29 | 31 |
| 45–64 years | 15 | 14 | 15 | 17 | 11 | 25 |
| 65 years+ | 4 | 5 | 3 | 4 | 3 | 13 |

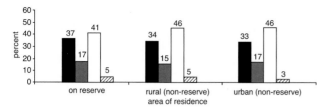

Fig. 3. Age distribution of Native identity population in Canada, 2001 (Statistics Canada 2003:2001 Census).

for the total Canadian female population was 82 years, compared to 77 years for North American Indian women, 78 years for Métis women, and 72 years for Inuit women (Statistics Canada 2005).

Even with improving life expectancies, seniors continue to make up a very small percentage of the Native population. In 2001, while half the Native population was under the age of 25 years, only 4 percent were 65 years and over. Aboriginal seniors are a small group and they are quite distinct from their younger counterparts: they tend to reside in communities where the majority of people are Natives (such as reserves or remote northern communities), whereas higher percentages of young people choose to live in urban areas; seniors are more likely than their younger counterparts to speak a Native language, and they are much less likely than their younger counterparts to have high levels of formal schooling.

*Population Projections*

The growth of the Aboriginal population is projected to continue to outpace that of the nonaboriginal population. Statistics Canada's (2005:8) projections for 2001 to 2017 indicate that the average annual increase for the Native population will be more than double the rate projected for the total population of Canada (1.8% and 0.7% respectively) and that the Native population will represent a greater proportion of the total Canadian population.

The median age of the Native population was projected to increase from 24.7 years in 2001 to 27.8 years by 2017. In the same time period, the median age of the total Canadian population would increase from 37.1 years to 41.3 years.

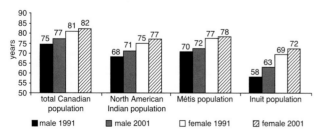

Fig. 4. Life expectancy at birth by sex, 1991 and 2001 (Statistics Canada 2005; Norris, Kerr, and Nault 1995).

The number of aboriginal seniors was projected to more than double, although their proportion in the population will only increase from 4 percent in 2001 to 6.5 percent in 2017 (Statistics Canada 2005:8–9).

Native youth remain the most important component of the population in terms of size and policy implications. According to Statistics Canada, the number of young adults (aged 20 to 29 years) entering the labor market was projected to increase from 170,300 in 2001 to 241,700 in 2017 (Statistics Canada 2005:9).

Accurate aboriginal population projections are notoriously difficult to produce, largely due to the fluid nature of affiliation with the aboriginal population. The accuracy of population projections is generally dependent upon the degree to which underlying assumptions on future fertility, mortality, and migration prove to be correct. In the case of the Native population, additional nonconventional components of growth add to the uncertainty. The "permeability and fuzziness" of ethnic boundaries (as opposed to an "inherited and permanent" nature) are a major challenge in creating Native population projections (Kerr, Guimond, and Norris 2003:57–58).

As an illustration of these challenges, consider the Métis population, which grew by 43 percent from 1996 to 2001. In contrast, the total Canadian population increased by 3 percent. Demographic features commonly used to explain growth in populations, such as the interaction of natural increase and migration, cannot adequately explain the dramatic increases in the Métis population. Demographers maintain that the maximum rate that a population may increase by natural increase is 5.5% per year; the growth rate of the Métis populations far surpassed this maximum rate in several regions of Canada. For example, the Métis populations of New Brunswick, Nova Scotia, and Ontario grew by 352, 280, and 125 percent respectively within five years. One may conclude that a significant portion of these increases may be explained by people reporting Métis identity in the census when they had not done so before. Reasons for doing so may be the result of increased awareness of Métis culture, rights, history, and issues. Some Métis leaders have accounted for this growth as an indication of pride in the Métis nation (Métis National Council 2003).

*Regional Distribution*

The Native population has become urbanized since the 1980s (Newhouse and Peters 2003). Statistics Canada reported that from 1996 to 2001, the percentage of aboriginal people living in urban areas increased from 47 to 49 percent and that one-quarter of the total aboriginal population lived in the 10 largest cities (Statistics Canada 2003).

Winnipeg, Manitoba, Edmonton, Alberta, and Vancouver, British Columbia, topped the list of census metropolitan areas with the largest aboriginal populations in 2001. From 1981 to 2001, the Native population of Winnipeg grew by 247 percent to 55,760, in Edmonton by 205 percent to

40,930, and in Vancouver by 140 percent to 36,860 (Siggner and Costa 2005). Yet these were not the most dramatic cases of aboriginal population growth in metropolitan areas. Saskatoon, Saskatchewan, recorded an aboriginal population of approximately 20,000 in the 2001 census, an increase of 382 percent since 1981. While Toronto also had an aboriginal population of about 20,000 in 2001, that population represented less than one-half of one percent of its total. In contrast, in Saskatoon almost 10 percent of the population is aboriginal.

When considering aboriginal population counts in cities, it is important to note that aboriginal people are highly mobile, particularly in urban areas. In 2001, 65 percent of aboriginal people living in urban areas reported that they had moved at least once in the five years prior to the census (39% had moved within their town or city, and 26% had moved from outside their town or city or province), compared to 45 percent of nonaboriginal people. The large numbers of people moving within and between communities may have implications on service providers and policy makers that are not immediately evident when simply looking at static population counts.

In 2001, 45 percent of North American Indians were living on reserve. "A reserve is land set apart and designated for the use and occupancy of an Indian group or band" (Indian and Northern Affairs Canada 2006a). Generally speaking, only those with registered Indian status and First Nation or Band membership are eligible to live on reserve. Therefore, when registered Indian status is taken into consideration, about 53 percent of North American Indians with registered Indian status were living on reserve, compared to only 4 percent of non-Status Indians.

The popular notion that there is a mass exodus underway from reserve communities to urban areas is somewhat of a misconception. From 1991 to 1996 reserve communities actually experienced net gains in population as a result of inflows of migrants. In other words, more registered Indians were moving to reserve communities from rural and urban areas than the number of registered Indians who were leaving reserve communities for other areas. Although there was positive growth in the reserve population as a result of migration, this growth was relatively small. Conversely, urban areas experienced net losses due to migration of registered Indians, although again the impact was small. It was in rural areas, which experienced population losses of registered Indians through migration mainly to urban areas, where the impact of the loss of population was felt most significantly (Norris and Clatworthy 2003:60–61). The constant turnover between reserves and urban areas may lead to social challenges: "It is the frequency of population movement between reserves and cities, not an exodus from the former, that has the greatest implications for the well-being of Aboriginal people and communities" (Norris and Clatworthy 2003:73).

In 1951, 7 percent of North American Indian people were living in urban areas; by 2001, this had increased to about one-half the population (Newhouse and Peters 2003:6).

High birth rates continue to contribute to the growth of the North American Indian population in urban areas, as well as the effects of "ethnic mobility" (that is, increasing numbers of people who are already living in urban areas who are beginning to report themselves as North American Indian whereas they had not done so before).

Of the three aboriginal groups, the Métis are the most urbanized population. In 2001, 68 percent of the Métis population was living in urban areas (39% in census metropolitan areas and 29% in smaller cities). By comparison, 43 percent of North American Indians and 27 percent of Inuit were living in urban areas. In contrast, 80 percent of the nonaboriginal population in Canada resided in urban areas. In fact, 29 percent of Métis were living in rural communities, compared to only 19 percent of the nonaboriginal population. While the Métis do not have reserves as do North American Indians, there are eight constitutionally protected Métis settlements in Alberta.

Of the approximately 45,000 Inuit, the vast majority live in the Canadian Arctic in one of the four Inuit self-governing land claim regions: Nunatsiavut, the region along the northern coast of Labrador, home to 5 percent of all Inuit; Nunavik, which lies primarily north of the 55th parallel in Quebec, where 19 percent of the Inuit population lives; the territory of Nunavut, home to about one-half the Inuit population; and the Inuvialuit region in the northwestern Northwest Territories, where about 7 percent of the Inuit population lives. About 20 percent of Inuit live outside the Arctic, mostly in large cities in southern Canada (Statistics Canada 2006:5–6).

Inuit represent the majority of people in these Arctic regions, and many continue to live according to their unique culture. "Most live in coastal communities in the north, and rely on marine life and land animals for a significant portion of their diet. The majority of Inuit in the Arctic speak Inuktitut . . . this language family, along with a common technology and culture, extends from Siberia to Greenland" (Statistics Canada 2006:6). Unlike Native populations in other areas, Inuit are less likely to move between and within communities than the nonaboriginal population. The 2001 Aboriginal Peoples Survey showed that the majority (64%) of Inuit adults had lived in the same community all their lives. Although Inuit communities in the North face many challenges and issues (such as high unemployment) the majority (71%) of Inuit adults had not considered leaving their community. The main reason given for wanting to stay was to be close to family members (Statistics Canada 2006:14–15).

*Aboriginal Language Use*

Undoubtedly the use and intergenerational transmission of aboriginal languages has been in decline. "During the past 100 years or more, nearly ten once flourishing languages have become extinct; at least a dozen are on the brink of extinction. When these languages vanish, they take with them unique ways of looking at the world, explaining the unknown

**Table 6.  Native Identity Population with Knowledge of a Native Language of 2,000 or More Speakers, Canada, 1996 and 2001[a]**

| Aboriginal Language Sets[b,c] | 1996 | 2001 | Percentage change 1996 to 2001 |
|---|---|---|---|
| Cree | 95,555 | 92,630 | −3.1 |
| Inuktitut (Eskimo) | 29,400 | 31,945 | 8.7 |
| Ojibwa | 29,735 | 27,955 | −6.0 |
| Dene (Chipewyan) | 9,525 | 10,500 | 10.2 |
| Montagnais-Naskapi | 9,335 | 10,285 | 10.2 |
| Micmac | 7,975 | 8,625 | 8.2 |
| Oji-Cree (Northern Ojibwa) | 5,480 | 5,610 | 2.4 |
| Attikamek | 4,075 | 4,935 | 21.1 |
| Sioux | 4,710 | 4,875 | 3.5 |
| Blackfoot | 5,530 | 4,415 | −20.2 |
| Salish languages other than Shuswap and Thompson | 2,285 | 2,675 | 17.1 |
| Algonquin | 2,555 | 2,340 | −8.4 |
| Dogrib | 2,430 | 2,265 | −6.8 |
| Carrier | 2,930 | 2,000 | −31.7 |

[a]Data adjusted for incompletely enumerated Indian reserves.
[b]Data for 4 reserves in Man. for Cree, Ojibwa, and Oji-Cree have been excluded.
[c]Due to changes in reporting patterns, North Slave (Hare) and South Slave (Slavey) are not shown.
SOURCE: Statistics Canada 2003:2001 Census.

and making sense of life" (Norris 1998:8). As of 1996, only three of Canada's 50 aboriginal languages—Inuktitut, Cree, and Ojibway—had large enough populations to be secure from extinction in the long-run (Norris 1998:10).

In 2001 the Inuit languages, sometimes called Inuktitut, remained the healthiest of the aboriginal languages. About 71 percent of Inuit reported that they could speak Inuktitut well enough to carry on a conversation; however, there is evidence that their use and transmission is decreasing. For example, in 2001, 78 percent of Inuit seniors reported that they spoke and understood Inuktitut and 73 percent reported using Inuktitut as their primary language in the home. By comparison, 69 percent of Inuit children under the age of 15 reported speaking and understanding Inuktitut, and about 66 percent reported Inuktitut as the primary home language.

Comparatively, much smaller percentages of Métis reported having knowledge of an aboriginal language. In 2001, 5 percent of the Métis population reported that they could speak an aboriginal language well enough to carry on a conversation. The percentages of aboriginal language speakers were higher among older Métis people. For example, about 16 percent of Métis aged 65 years and over reported that they could speak and understand an aboriginal language, while only 3 percent of Métis children and youth could carry on a conversation in an aboriginal language. The Métis historically developed a unique and distinctive language called Mitchif, a mixed language that blends mainly French nouns with Cree verbs. The number of Mitchif speakers was estimated as less than 1,000 (Bakker 1997).

In 2001, 30 percent of North American Indians reported that they could speak an aboriginal language well enough to carry on a conversation. By far the vast majority of aboriginal language speakers in the North American Indian popula-tion could also speak English or French; only 1 percent reported speaking only a Native language. Not surprisingly, higher percentages of older North American Indians can speak an aboriginal language compared to their younger counterparts. In 2001, over half (54%) of North American Indian seniors reported an aboriginal mother tongue (this is the language first learned in childhood and still understood), while the percentages of North American Indians with an aboriginal mother tongue declined with each younger age group—41 percent of North American Indians aged 45 to 64, 29 percent of those 25 to 44 years, and 18 percent of those under 25 years.

There were significant differences in the language characteristics of North American Indians who lived on reserve and off reserve. The expression of culture, such as the use of one's aboriginal language, is presumably easier in areas where most people are culturally similar. The vast majority of residents of Indian reserves are North American Indian (85%), whereas in urban centers North American Indians often represent a small minority within a larger mosaic of cultures. In 2001, half the on-reserve population could carry on a conversation in an aboriginal language, compared to only 13 percent of the urban North American Indian population. Further, 41 percent of North American Indians on-reserve reported using an aboriginal language as their primary home language, compared to 8 percent of those living off-reserve.

Nonetheless, the 2001 Aboriginal Peoples Survey revealed that aboriginal languages remain an important priority to many aboriginal people living in off-reserve areas. According to the 2001 Aboriginal Peoples Survey, 64 percent of North American Indian adults living off-reserve reported that learning, relearning, or maintaining their aboriginal language was "very" or "somewhat" important, as did 50 percent of Métis adults and 87 percent of Inuit adults. Most encouragingly, similar levels of aboriginal youth reported that their languages were very or somewhat important (O'Donnell and Tait 2003).

Not all aboriginal languages showed a decline in the number of speakers; indeed, eight out of 14 languages and language groupings with at least 2,000 speakers increased from 1996 to 2001. Those showing an increase in the number of speakers were: Inuktitut (Eskimoan), Dene (Chipewyan), Montagnais-Naskapi, Micmac, Oji-Cree (Northern Ojibwa), Attikamek, Sioux, and a grouping of Salishan languages (table 6). In 2001, Cree was the language with the most speakers, just over 92,000, although there was a 3.1% decrease in the number of Cree speakers since 1996 (Statistics Canada 2003).

# Métis

JOE SAWCHUK

In Canada, it is important to distinguish between the Métis Nation and the more generic usage of the term Métis. In the 2001 Canadian census, 292,310 people self-identified as Métis, a 43 percent increase from 204,120 five years earlier (Statistics Canada 2003). More than half reside in Saskatchewan, Manitoba, and Alberta ("Native Populations of Canada," table 4, this vol.). Statistics Canada does not attribute this growth to demographic factors alone. An increased awareness of Métis issues coming from court cases related to Métis rights and constitutional recognition has undoubtedly contributed to the increase in the population identifying as Métis. These census figures also do not distinguish between the different groups in Canada that have begun to apply the term Métis to themselves. For years, the term was used to refer to any person of mixed First Nations and European descent. In this popular sense, the term is growing in scope. It has been appropriated by mixed-blood populations in Labrador and portions of the eastern United States, including Maine. The Métis Nation, on the other hand, more properly refers to the aboriginal people descended from the historic Métis population that occupied the area of land in west-central North America, encompassing present-day Manitoba, Saskatchewan, Alberta, eastern parts of Ontario, and the Upper Great Lakes region, Montana, and North Dakota (vol. 13:661–676). In this chapter, unless otherwise noted, the term "Métis" is used in the specific sense of members of either the historic or the contemporary Métis Nation.

## The Historic Métis Nation

There have been many names associated with the Métis as political and social circumstances have changed over the years: *michif, bois brûlé, chicot*, half-breed, country-born in the eighteenth and nineteenth centuries; and mixed blood, half-breed, and non-Status Indian in the twentieth and twenty-first centuries. Much of the confusion over who, when, or where is a Métis comes from the mistaken belief that the term refers mainly to biological race mixture (*métissage*). But Métis is a social and cultural term rather than a racial one: it refers not to biology, but to culture, ethnicity, and nationhood. One of the greatest misconceptions about

the Métis is that they are "simply" mixed bloods. If that were true, the origins of the Métis could be traced back much farther than the eighteenth century, when they were first noted in the Upper Great Lakes and on the western Plains. But the children of early-contact unions were not or did not become Métis. Prior to the emergence of the Métis, mixed-blood individuals were absorbed either into the native or the White population. What set the Métis apart is that they were the first group of mixed bloods who became a distinct community: who were seen as and who chose to see themselves as separate from both the Indian population and the White population that surrounded them.

Historic, economic, and political factors contributed to the emergence of the Métis as a politically and culturally distinct group (Foster 1985, 2001; Peterson 1985). The traditional origins of the Métis have usually been characterized as centering around the Red River colony during the seventeenth and eighteenth centuries—that is, separate groups of French, Scottish, and English mixed-blood populations that evolved from marriages between European fur traders and aboriginal women, in the Red River basin of southern Manitoba (vol. 6:150, 361–371, 685, 688–689). Much of this familiar analysis concerns the Louis Riel resistance movements of 1869–1870 and 1885 (vol. 4:91). But many other Métis groups, with distinct characteristics and separate local histories, have existed, such as the ones found in the Grande Cache area of Northern Alberta (Nicks and Morgan 1985), in areas south of the Great Lakes (Peterson 1985), and in northern Ontario. Contemporary characterization of the Métis tends to amalgamate these separate histories and populations of English, French, and Scottish "half-breeds" into a single entity known as Métis, but this is definitely an oversimplification.

The term Historic Métis Nation is a contemporary one, representing the present-day interpretation of the historical background of the Métis by the Métis Nation itself, as represented by the Métis National Council. This emphasizes that "Métis," as the term has come to be understood in Canada, does not have its roots solely in the nineteenth century but also in the dynamics of government-imposed identities and policies and in the renewed and revitalized native political activism of contemporary society. A major influence is the existence of the many Métis political organizations and pressure groups that pursued Métis nationalism and aboriginal rights with vigor from the 1960s through the 1980s. Their actions resulted in the recognition of the Métis as one of Canada's aboriginal peoples in the Canadian Constitution in 1982 and in court cases that have recognized aboriginal rights of the Métis in various provinces. So, although twenty-first century Métis share the origins and the same name as the "New Nation" of the nineteenth century and celebrate their history, it should be remembered that "Métis" is very much a modern concept and population.

## Government Definitions of Métis

In addition to the historical confusion over the name Métis, it is important to recognize that Canada has many other designations of native, including: Indian, Status Indian, non-Status Indian, Inuit, and C-31. Three of these—Indian, Inuit, and Métis—have been recognized in Canada's constitution, but there are no official definitions for any of these terms. There is a definition for "registered" or "Status" Indian; the Indian Act defines "Indian" as someone who, pursuant to the Act, is registered as an Indian or is entitled to be registered as an Indian. But it is not clear that Status Indian is synonymous with "Indian" as mentioned in Section 35 of the Constitution. Since the definition for Status Indian makes no mention of Indian ancestry, for many years it was possible for an individual with no Indian ancestry whatsoever to be registered as an Indian. Furthermore, the very fact that a registry exists means that some people of Indian ancestry are on the list and some are left off. Hence, Canada has a large number of nonregistered or non-Status Indians (i.e., people of Indian ancestry not registered under the Indian Act). There is no corresponding registry or definition for either the Métis or the Inuit, although the Métis National Council proposed a centralized registry of Métis citizens. The situation is complicated by the existence of the C-31 category: non-Status Indians or Métis who have successfully applied for reinstatement into Indian status under government legislation introduced in 1985. There is a certain amount of resentment against these individuals among Status Indians, and many of the C-31s face problems in claiming band services or membership. Their growing numbers have caused some shrinkage in the ranks of Métis, as many have "taken C-31" because Indian status brings with it benefits such as medical care, education benefits, housing, and tax free income if earned on reserves. Because not all C-31s can pass their status on to their offspring, it is likely that this attenuation of Métis membership may only last for a generation or two.

It is surprising that no federal governmental definition of Métis exists, considering the long history of federal government legislation specifically recognizing the Métis as an aboriginal people separate and distinct from Indians. This legislation includes the Manitoba Act of 1870, which recognized the "Indian title" of certain "half-breeds"; the Domin-ion Lands Act of 1879, which also dealt with the extinguishment of the "Indian title" for mixed-blood residents in the Northwest Territories outside the limits of Manitoba; the adhesion to Treaty 3 of the mixed-bloods of Rainy River (whereby they "surrendered all claim, right, title, or interest which they, by virtue of their Indian blood, have or possess"); and Section 35(2) of the 1982 Constitution Act, which states that "aboriginal peoples of Canada" includes the Indian, Inuit, and Métis peoples of Canada.

There is one example of a provincial governmental definition; in 1938 the province of Alberta passed the Métis Population Betterment Act, which established several Métis "colonies" or settlements in the province and contained a definition of Métis. Alberta is the only Canadian government body to have such a definition. Originally the definition stated "a Métis means a person of mixed white and Indian blood but does not include either an Indian or a non-treaty Indian as defined in The Indian Act." A later version of the act that appeared in 1940 defined a Métis as a person with "a minimum of one quarter Indian blood" (Bell 1994:6). This definition was an anomaly: unlike in the United States, blood quantum has almost never been used to determine aboriginality in Canada. The Alberta definition was only used for administrative purposes, to determine if an individual was eligible to live on one of the provincial Métis settlements. It was of no practical use in identifying whether a person was Métis or not, since most Métis did not regard the definition as a legitimate criteria of identification. The idea of blood quantum was eventually dropped, due in no small part to the objections of the Métis themselves. The subsequent version of the act, the Métis Settlements Act (1990) defines Métis as "a person of aboriginal ancestry who identifies with Métis history and culture." This definition, which depends primarily on the basis of self-identification and acceptance from the Métis population, is more in keeping with the way political organizations have defined Métis since the late twentieth century.

## Aboriginal Organizations and Definition of Métis

The nature of contemporary Métis society in Canada cannot be understood without a consideration of the role Métis and non-Status Indian organizations have played in promoting their cultural and legal identity. This is true not only for the Métis; in Canada, government-native relationships are almost totally defined by the many provincially and federally based Native pressure organizations that have become a permanent part of the political scene. The four most important national organizations are the Assembly of First Nations representing Status Indians; the Inuit Tapiriit Kanatami (formerly the Inuit Tapirisat of Canada), representing the Inuit; the Métis National Council representing Métis from the western provinces and Ontario; and the Congress of Aboriginal Peoples (formerly the Native

Council of Canada), representing a variety of Métis, non-Status, and other aboriginal groups. Funded for the most part by government grants, these lobbying organizations define the relationship between Canada and its aboriginal populations. The national organizations are augmented by many powerful associations organized on the provincial and sometimes regional level. Other countries boast similar organizations, particularly Australia and Norway, but Canada is unique in the breadth and depth of these organizations and in the amount of public funding that supports them.

The role the Métis organizations have played in negotiating contemporary Métis identity in Canada is considerable. The most obvious example is the recognition of the Métis as one of Canada's aboriginal peoples under Section 35(2) of the Constitution Act of 1982, which came about as a direct result of lobbying by Métis and non-Status Indian groups (particularly the Native Council of Canada), and some of the more active provincial organizations such as the Association of Métis and Non-Status Indians of Saskatchewan. However, Constitutional inclusion has set the stage for several conflicts between different groups of Métis. Two of these conflicts were the dissolution of a longstanding political union between Métis and non-Status Indians and the growing separation between the western or "historic" Métis (the descendants of the Métis population having origins in the Red River basin area of southwestern Manitoba) and other Métis populations in Ontario, Labrador, and elsewhere.

In the 1960s and 1970s, the early days of Native political organizations in Canada, a political union existed between Métis and non-Status Indians. The definition of who was a Métis and who was allowed to join a Métis organization was broadly based. Most Métis organizations defined a Métis as someone of mixed White and Indian ancestry (or of mixed non-Indian and Indian ancestry) and generally, non-Status Indians were welcomed to join regardless of their racial background. No distinction was made between Métis with roots in Red River and those Métis whose ancestry was founded in other parts of Canada. For example, Section V(1) of the Constitution of the Métis Association of Alberta, dated August 13, 1977, simply defined a Métis as "any person of mixed Indian and Non-Indian blood." Membership was also open to "any non-status Indian, or their [sic] spouse, as the case may be, sixteen years of age or older." However, in 1984 the same organization changed the definition to "a Métis is an aboriginal person who declares himself/herself to be a Métis person, and can produce satisfactory historical or acceptable legal proof that he/she is a Métis, or has traditionally held himself/herself to be a Métis, and is accepted by the Métis people as a Métis" (AMMSA 1984). All mention of non-Status Indians was dropped as well as references to mixed ancestry. The term "Métis" was broadened to include those who trace their descent to English and Scottish mixed-blood populations of the Red River area of the nineteenth century, as well as of the French.

The Métis Association of Alberta is now known as the Métis Nation of Alberta. Its constitution requires that a prospective member produce an ancestor from up to five generations back who was recorded as a Métis by the government or a church or ancestor who received scrip under either the Manitoba Act or the Dominion Lands Act. Scrip was the method used by the Canadian government to attempt to settle Métis land claims in the Northwest between the 1870s and 1920s. Scrip could be in one of two forms: land scrip that could be redeemed for a specific amount of Dominion lands (80, 160, or 240 acres) open for homesteading, or cash scrip ($80, $160, or $240). The Métis Association of Alberta will also accept a statutory declaration from another Métis. As in the previous definition, the member must "hold himself/herself to be a Métis, and be accepted by the Métis people as a Métis" (Fuller 1993). An appointed 14-member Métis senate has, among other duties, the ability to decide on a person's eligibility to claim Métis status and join the organization.

Both the inclusion of the term "aboriginal" and the dropping of the term "non-Status" are undoubtedly references to Section 35(2) of the Constitution Act of 1982. Prior to 1982, Métis and non-Status Indians stood in the same relation to the Canadian government, as people with an aboriginal background, but with no special rights as recognized by the government. The political status of the two groups drastically changed when the new constitution recognized Métis but did not recognize non-Status Indians (Sawchuk 1992). All the Métis organizations subsequently changed their definitions to either eliminate or at least no longer specifically to recognize non-Status Indians as potential members.

By the late 1980s the idea of a separate, historically definable group of Métis, one that was limited to people descended from Red River Métis (that is, distinct from other mixed-blood populations in Canada), and the only one entitled to use the name "Métis," was beginning to take hold. This sentiment led to the formation of the Métis National Council in 1983 (fig. 1). Despite its name, the Métis National Council is not a national organization in the strict sense of the word, nor does it pretend to represent all Métis across Canada. It is the umbrella organization for Métis organizations from Ontario, Manitoba, Saskatchewan, Alberta, and British Columbia. The definition adopted on September 7, 2002, states that "Métis means a person who self-identifies as Métis, is of historic Métis Nation Ancestry, is distinct from other Aboriginal Peoples and is accepted by the Métis Nation." The Council further defines "Historic Métis Nation" as the aboriginal people then known as Métis or Half-Breeds who resided in Historic Métis Nation homeland; the "Historic Métis Nation Homeland" as the area of land in west-central North America used and occupied as the traditional territory of the Métis or Half-Breeds as they were then known; and "Métis Nation" as the aboriginal people descended from the Historic Métis Nation, and one of the aboriginal peoples of Canada within Section 35 of the Constitution Act of 1982 (MNC 2002).

The Métis National Council has proposed the establishment of a national Métis registry, to be used to identify those

St.-Laurent Community Development Corporation, Man.

Fig. 1. W. Yvon Dumont O.M. (Order of Manitoba). He was president of the Métis National Council, 1988–1993; founding vice-president of the Native Council of Canada, 1972–1973; president of the Manitoba Métis Federation, 1984–1993; and lt.-gov. of Manitoba, 1993–1999. Standing in front of the Métis flag, a white infinity symbol on a blue field, he holds a Métis sash. Photographed in the 1980s.

eligible to participate in the electoral process governing Métis political institutions and to receive benefit from the programs and services delivered by Métis organizations. The registrar would have the legal responsibility to add or delete individuals from the registry. This invites parallels to the federal government's registry system for Status Indians, which could lead to a new category in Canada: "registered Métis" and (inevitably) "nonregistered Métis."

### The "Other Métis"

Not all people who describe themselves as Métis fit the criteria or history of the Historic Métis Nation. There are people of mixed aboriginal-White ancestry in several parts of Canada who have adopted, or are in the process of adopting, the name Métis to describe themselves, even though the term was not used historically for them. Ontario offers an

instructive example. As late as the 1960s, the name Métis was almost unknown in northern Ontario, the most common designation being "half-breed." Métis became the more commonly used designation after the formation of the Ontario Métis and Non-Status Indian Association in 1971 (McGuire 1997). Another group adopting the name is the mixed-blood population in Labrador, who did not use the name until being politicized by the Native Council of Canada (Dumont 1995). The Congress of Aboriginal Peoples claimed in 2006 to represent several mixed-blood groups, including "Bush Cree-Métis, Bay-Métis in Northern Ontario; and Gwitchin Métis in the northern McKenzie" as well as the Labrador Métis (CAP 2006).

This split between the "Métis Nation" from the Prairie Provinces and other groups claiming a Métis identity in the rest of Canada was addressed by the Royal Commission on Aboriginal Peoples (1996), which acknowledged that the appropriateness of applying the term Métis to everyone is problematic and that many members of the Historic Métis Nation believe that, because the term has been associated most often with them and their ancestors, they have a right to its exclusive use. These Métis believe that other Canadians of mixed aboriginal and nonaboriginal ancestry and culture should be described in some other way. But other mixed-blood populations in Canada point out that in terms of a dictionary definition, "Métis" simply means "mixed." They contend that when the term was inserted in the constitution in 1982, it was intended to apply to all Métis people. This definition of Métis attempts to accommodate both groups by recommending that every person who (1) identifies himself or herself as Métis, and (2) is accepted as such by the nation of Métis people with which that person wishes to be associated, on the basis of criteria and procedures determined by that nation, be recognized as a member of that nation for purposes of nation-to-nation negotiations and as Métis for that purpose (Royal Commission on Aboriginal Peoples 1996:4.5:2).

This definition obviously takes much of its inspiration from earlier organizational definitions, particularly in terms of self-identity and acceptance from the community. Where it breaks new ground is in its inference that there may be more than one Métis community. The Royal Commission on Aboriginal Peoples report (1996:4.5:1.3) explicitly acknowledges that there are many distinctive Métis communities across Canada, with more than one culture:

> [I]n deference to the legitimate concerns of Métis Nation members who trace their roots to the western fur trade, we have tried to differentiate these two Métis worlds as much as possible by referring to one as the Métis Nation and to the other by terms such as other Métis, Labrador Métis, and so on. . . . There are many distinctive Métis communities across Canada, and more than one Métis culture as well. Geographically, the homeland of the Métis Nation embraces the three prairie provinces as well as parts of Ontario, the Northwest Territories, British Columbia, and the north central United States. Another Métis people, at least as old as the Métis

Nation, is located in Labrador and has maritime traditions. Although the origins of that population are venerable, the application of the term Métis to it is relatively recent. Other Métis communities are found in Quebec, Ontario, Nova Scotia, New Brunswick, British Columbia, and the North. Some have significant links to the western Métis Nation while others do not.

## Provincial Courts and the Definition of Métis

Métis identity became an issue in several court cases involving either aboriginal title or aboriginal rights. The courts accepted self-definition as sufficient proof of Métis identity. In *Manitoba Métis Federation* v. *Attorney General of Canada* (2 C.N.L.R. 19 [S.C.C., 1990]), a case concerning the land rights of the Métis under the Manitoba Act of 1870, the court accepted that "all half-breeds of 1870 were 'Métis'; that the Métis of 1870 were a distinct people; and that all their descendants are included within the undefined group of persons constitutionally recognized today as 'the Métis people.'"

In *R* v. *Blais* (3 C.N.L.R. 109 [Man. Provincial Court 1997]), the judge commented that an appropriate definition of Métis might be taken from the wording of the Métis Nation Accord, which was accepted by federal, provincial, and aboriginal leaders in 1992 as part of the Charlottetown Accord. The Charlottetown Accord, a wide-ranging agreement that dealt with issues such as recognition of Quebec as a distinct society and the right to self-government of aboriginal peoples, was rejected in a national referendum and is not legally binding. But the judge felt that the definition contained in the Métis Nation Accord was a useful political answer to a political question. The definition is as follows: Métis means an aboriginal person who self-identifies as Métis, who is distinct from Indian and Inuit, and who is a descendant of those Métis who received or were entitled to receive land grants and scrip under the provisions of the Manitoba Act of 1870 or the Dominion Lands Act as enacted from time to time (para. 26). Note that this definition is very similar to that of the various prairie Métis organizations and the Métis National Council: that is, it refers specifically to the "Historic Métis Nation." Mentioning scrip, the Manitoba Act, and the Dominion Lands Act automatically excludes the Labrador and other Métis.

The most significant case for defining both aboriginal rights and the nature of Métis society has been *R* v. *Powley* (O. J. No. 5310 [Ont. Provincial Court 1998]). The case concerned Steve and Roddy Powley, who shot a bull moose north of Sault Sainte Marie, Ontario. One of the men was in possession of an Ontario Métis and Aboriginal Association card. This card indicated that he claimed aboriginal rights to hunt under the Robinson Huron Treaty of 1850, as well as "the right to harvest natural resources as my family has done since time immemorial." It was necessary for the court to determine if the Powley family was indeed "Métis" for the purposes of Section 35(2) of the Constitution Act of 1982. In that light, the judge reviewed earlier cases, particularly *R* v. *Blais*. The court then proposed its own definition of Métis: "a person of aboriginal ancestry; who self-identifies as a Métis; and who is accepted by the Métis community as a Métis." The Métis Accord definition was considered, but the section limiting Métis to those who had or were eligible to receive scrip was dropped. Had that criterion not been dropped, the definition would automatically have eliminated Powley and all other Métis from northern Ontario. The court found in favor of the Métis. The case was upheld by the Supreme Court of Canada on September 19, 2003.

The Supreme Court ruling is likely to have profound effects on the place of Métis in Canadian society, going to the heart of Métis identity. While the court stopped short of defining who was or was not a Métis, it did define Métis communities as "a group of Métis with a distinctive collective identity, living together in the same geographical area and sharing a common way of life." The court went on to state that in addition to demographic evidence, proof of shared customs, traditions and a collective identity is required to demonstrate the existence of a Métis community that can support a claim to site-specific aboriginal rights. One of the implications of this ruling is that it leaves the door open for any group of mixed bloods in Canada that can demonstrate a collective identity, shared geographical area and common way of life to lay claim to being a Métis community. Indeed, shortly after the Supreme Court's decision was announced, Métis in the Maritimes Provinces, as well as some Acadians, announced that they were considering making claims to aboriginal rights based on the criteria specified in the Supreme Court's decision.

## Cultural Considerations

Legal and political boundaries are not the only way the Métis distinguish themselves from the rest of Canadian society. Ethnicity, and an individual's sense of belonging to a group, are routinely maintained and rationalized through the use of symbols of belonging; flags, dress, ritual, written and oral history. The Métis are no exception. Like many modern ethnic or aboriginal groups, the Métis are striving to demonstrate that they are "human communities so 'natural' as to require no definition other than self-assertion" (Hobsbawm 1983:14). But there is some irony in the symbols of ethnicity available to them, since the Métis, by their very definition, are biologically diverse and the product of at least two cultures or traditions (European and aboriginal) or many (French, Scottish, English, Saulteaux, Cree, etc.) depending on the criteria used. Furthermore, the historic accouterments and symbols available to the Métis are not rooted in some mythic past but can be traced to specific, and relatively recent, historic occurrences. Still, this has not prevented the contemporary Métis from developing a system of cultural and political symbols to distinguish them from both other natives and mainstream society.

Some of these symbols, like the Métis themselves, demonstrate a mixed heritage: the Red River cart, the L'Assomption sash, Métis fiddle music, the Mitchif language. Some, like the Métis National Council's discussion over which date best represents the birth of the Métis nation (either December 8, 1869, the date of the proclamation of the Provisional Government of the Métis in the Northwest Territories, or the proclamation of the Métis Nation at the Battle of Seven Oaks in 1816) are used to distinguish the Métis from White society; other symbols and values are used to distinguish the Métis from other natives, in particular, from other mixed-ancestry groups who have laid claim to the name Métis.

A defining characteristic of any ethnic or aboriginal group is a collective sense of history. The Métis have a particularly strong sense of their own history, centering round the idea of an historic Métis homeland, and culture heroes Louis Riel and Gabriel Dumont (fig. 2). The basic sentiment is partly a pride in being Métis, but it is also strongly informed by a sense of aggrievement, injustice, and being victims of Canadian imperialism, particularly through the martyrdom of Louis Riel in 1885. Scrip is another issue. Almost all Métis families in the northern parts of the prairie provinces have stories of how their great grandparents or grandparents had been given scrip in recognition of their aboriginal rights, and how in most cases, the scrip was subsequently lost, stolen, or swindled from them. A related grievance centers round the lack of recognition of hunting and fishing rights. This connection with the past has its echoes in the various land claim cases the Métis take to court. The loss of a land base is closely associated with the idea of a historic Métis homeland. This concept is so central to the idea of being Métis that the Métis National Council incorporated the definition of a historic Métis nation homeland as part of its definition of Métis.

No symbol or artifact from their past is more closely associated with the Métis than the wooden, two-wheeled Red River cart (vol. 4:344, vol. 13:670–671) used by the Métis in their buffalo hunts and general transportation. The carts are still being built in 2006 by Métis craftspeople, to be used for Métis ceremonies or as museum pieces. Many logos of the provincial Métis organizations have featured the cart as an emblem of the Métis. In the 1960s and 1970s, the logo of the Métis Association of Alberta featured a Red River cart in silhouette, along with a dedication to "Louis Riel, a great Métis leader." The Manitoba Métis Federation's logo, developed in the same time period and in use in 2006, features a Red River cart wheel with a buffalo head and two rifles superimposed over it (fig. 3).

Another common emblem Metis identity is the Assomption or arrowhead sash, commonly referred to as the Métis sash (vol. 6:368, vol. 13:672–673). The Métis sash has become one of the most important symbols of Métis identity. The Métis National Council, the Métis Nation of Ontario,

Lib. and Arch. Canada, Ottawa: PA-178147.

Fig. 2. Gabriel Dumont (b. 1837, d. 1906), military commander of the Métis during the Northwest Rebellion of 1885. Photograph by Harvey J. Strong, at his studio in Winnipeg, Man., 1880s.

Man. Métis Federation, Inc., Winnipeg.

Fig. 3. Logo of the Manitoba Métis Federation, designed in the 1970s.

the Manitoba Métis Federation, and many other Métis organizations feature the sash in their promotional literature and web sites, usually giving a brief description and history of the sash, discussing its evolution from a simple and practical article of clothing to a contemporary piece of regalia to be worn at formal Métis cultural and political events. As such, it is a perfect example of an "invented" tradition; the Métis organizations are completely forthright about the adaptation of the sash as symbol and its use in the development of contemporary tradition. "The sash has acquired new significance in the 20th century, now symbolizing pride and identification for Métis people. Manitoba and Saskatchewan have both created 'The Order of the Sash' which is bestowed upon members of the Métis community who have made cultural, political or social contributions to their people" (Métis Nation of Ontario 2006). This association of the sash with the historic Métis Nation has not prevented the sash from being adapted by other mixed-blood groups. For example, the Confederacy of Nova Scotia Métis lists the sash as part of their cultural heritage, and a web site produced by the craft coordinator of the province not only listed the Métis sash as one of the emblems of the eastern "Métis" but also reproduced in toto the symbolism of the colors developed by the Plains Métis, including the contemporary black thread pattern developed in Manitoba (although the "dark period" the black thread refers to, the days following the formation of Manitoba, when the Métis people had to endure dispossession and repression, has little relevance for the mixed bloods of the Maritimes).

Another symbol that has been retrieved from the past, and used both in Ontario and on the Plains, is the Métis flag (vol. 13:674). Although historically there were many Métis flags, the one most commonly used in the 2000s consists of a white infinity sign on a blue background. The flag was given to the Métis as part of a ceremonial exchange between the Métis and the North West Company in 1814, although the original flag had a red background, not blue. The infinity sign has two meanings: the "joining of two cultures, and the existence of a people forever" (C. Racette 1987:6).

Métis music and dance, especially fiddling and jigging, and other aspects of Métis culture entered a period of revitalization in the 1990s. Used as cultural markers, they enter school curricula as well as organizational literature and web sites. The Métis and their organizations are adopting and manipulating many more symbols. The Métis National Council website, for example, has discussions on the following symbols: the Mitchif language, contributions by Métis; the Métis flag; Louis Riel; Louis Riel Day; the sash; the voyageurs; Métis voyageur games; beading; jigging; the fiddle; York boats; Red River cart; the buffalo hunt; and National Aboriginal Day. What all these symbols have in common is that they address the present by referring to the past. They define the Métis of today, and their attempts to deal with contemporary society on their own terms, in a way that allows them to remain a distinct sector of Canadian society, very much like a "strand in the sash."

The Métis lay claim to a special set of values distinguishing themselves from the rest of Canada. They rely on supposed "native" values such as generosity, willingness to share, affinity with nature, and living off the land to distinguish themselves from Whites. They distinguish themselves from Status Indians and other natives by drawing attention to their long history of independence and their ability to survive without recourse to government assistance. Although many Métis are eligible to take C-31, and reap the benefits of extended health care, housing, and tax-free income earned on reserves, a significant number refuse to do so. The reason for this was stated by a Métis from near Thompson, Manitoba, who, when asked why he and his nine children refused to apply for status under C-31 replied, "I always paid for my own gas," referring to the benefits received by Treaty Indians he felt he could do without.

It is misleading to conclude that specific attempts at "reinventing" or "objectifying" various traditions, cultures, or communities (such as the selection of one date over another as the "origin" of the historic Métis Nation) are insincere or contrived. The creation of an identity is always self-conscious to some degree, but there is little heuristic value in labeling such events as concoctions or inventions. The various Métis Days events and other celebrations of Métis ethnicity that are held throughout the prairies (usually including Métis dancing, fiddling, contests of strength, races, and the like), Back to Batoche Days in Saskatchewan, and other celebrations held in Métis communities across Canada fill an important need, especially for the 68 percent of the Métis population who, according to the 2001 census, live in urban areas, far from their traditional communities.

Office of Paul Martin, Ottawa.

Fig. 4. First ministers meeting on aboriginal issues, Nov. 2005. At the opening ceremonies Prime Minister Paul Martin (left) was presented with a Métis buckskin jacket and Métis sash by the Métis National Council. Photograph by Dave Chan, at Kelowna, B.C.

## Twenty-first Century

The contemporary Métis look very different from the historic Métis of the eighteenth and nineteenth centuries. They differ in terms of cultural boundaries, cultural markers, relations with the wider society, and even in their name ("Métis" did not originally refer to all the mixed-blood populations in the Red River area, and certainly not to groups in Labrador and the Maritimes). The sense of Métis nationalism, and of who is or who is not a Métis, is both reflected in, and fueled by, the success in fighting for aboriginal rights and being recognized by the Canadian government and public. Perhaps their greatest achievement was the inclusion of "Métis" under Section 35 of the Canadian Constitution, recognizing them as one of Canada's aboriginal peoples. This recognition was by no means easily won; it was the result of years of struggle and political effort. The Métis faced opposition not only from nonnatives but also from a sizable proportion of Status Indians.

Of course, Constitutional recognition was not the end of their struggles. Problems centered around whether "Métis" as defined constitutionally includes all populations of Métis in the country, or only the Historic Métis Nation. Statistics Canada has made no effort to distinguish between the historic Métis and other groups of Métis in Canada when gathering census data.

Métis have made legal and political gains besides Constitutional recognition. In Manitoba, the Métis have initiated legal action to pursue land claims under the Manitoba Act; in northwestern Saskatchewan, a similar historic Métis land claim under the Dominion Lands Act has been initiated. Métis aboriginal rights have been recognized in Ontario with the *Powley* case. In Alberta, Premier Ralph Klein's government signed an interim deal in October 2004 with the Métis Nation of Alberta and the Métis Settlement General Council, permitting Métis to hunt on unoccupied Crown lands, privately owned lands with permission, and in protected areas where there is a hunting designation. In Saskatchewan, the Métis Nation encouraged its members to exercise hunting rights in order to force an agreement with the Saskatchewan government, and the Manitoba Métis Federation launched a campaign aimed at forcing the province to recognize the Métis right to hunt and fish as aboriginal people. The courts have recognized not only Métis aboriginal rights but also Métis organizations as the legitimate representatives of the Métis people.

Federal government recognition includes a Métis Interlocutor, a government representative who is the point of contact to discuss issues. Since 2004, the office of Interlocutor has been held by the minister of Indian affairs, the federal minister who is responsible for Indians and Inuit. Of particular symbolic value to the Métis was referral to "the Métis Nation" by Prime Minister Paul Martin (fig. 4) in his address at the Canada-Aboriginal Peoples Roundtable on April 19, 2004.

Although many Métis have refused Bill C-31, it is still having the effect of thinning their ranks, particularly in the northern reaches of the Prairie Provinces. But this attrition is likely limited to one or two generations at the most. Through the vagaries of the C-31 program, many C-31 Métis have been classified as "Section 6(2)" and cannot pass their status on to their offspring if they marry a non-registered person. Thus, in all likelihood, the Métis will begin to see their ranks swell again within a few years, as the children of Section 6(2) parents, without Indian status, begin to seek an identity.

What is the major trait of Métis existence in Canada in the early twenty-first century? Perhaps of premier importance is the persistence of their identity. For over 100 years, the Métis were told that they "didn't exist," "weren't native," or that they had no special rights as aboriginal peoples, but the Métis refused to die out, go away, or hide their identity. Eventually they won Constitutional recognition as one of Canada's aboriginal peoples.

# Native American Identity in Law

EVA MARIE GARROUTTE

The United States decennial census is not a source to which readers commonly look for intriguing stories. Nevertheless, in the case of individuals identified as American Indians, it suggests a complex and compelling tale. The first year in which census respondents were allowed to identify their own race, as opposed to being classified according to the enumerator's judgment, was 1960. Since then, there have been large reported increases in the American Indian population in every decade. Significant gains appeared between 1970 and 1980, which showed a surge of more than 72 percent and the period from 1990 to 2000, which indicated a swell of more than 100 percent.

Although changes from 1990 to 2000 in the way census data on race are compiled render comparison to earlier figures problematic, the apparent increases in the American Indian population are so large that demographers argue they probably do not reflect simply an increase in births or a decline in death rates. Instead, a substantial part of the numerical changes are almost certainly the result of individuals who once identified themselves as White (or another race) and switched to identifying themselves as American Indians (Nagel 1996; Snipp 1986; Passel 1996; Thornton 1997).

Comparison of census figures over time foregrounds the contested issue of racial "identity." Which individuals may appropriately claim to be Indian people? What contexts or purposes might demand different answers to such questions? Whereas the United States census allows people to describe their racial identity based on any criteria they choose, many other contexts are regulated by formal, legal definitions of Indian status.

## Individual Identity

### Tribal Law

According to historic court cases, including *Cherokee Nation* v. *Georgia* (1831) and *Worcester* v. *Georgia* (1832), American Indian tribes constitute "domestic dependent nations" invested with a range of governmental powers (S. O'Brien 1989, 1991). One of the most fundamental of such powers is the right to define the criteria that individuals must satisfy in order to be eligible for formal, tribal membership. Tribes are free to craft such definitions in any way they choose, and

different tribes have accomplished the task in many different ways.

The most common tribal requirement for determining citizenship revolves around "blood quantum," or degree of Indian ancestry. About two-thirds of all federally acknowledged tribes of the conterminous United States specify a minimum blood quantum in their legal citizenship criteria, with one-quarter blood degree being the most frequent requirement. (In the simplest instance, an individual has a one-quarter blood quantum if any one of her four grandparents was of exclusively Indian ancestry and the other three were non-Indian.) The remaining one-third of Indian tribes specify no minimum blood quantum (Garroutte 2003:15).

Tribal legal requirements for citizenship may include other factors in addition to, or instead of, a particular degree of ancestry. A number of tribes require only lineal (direct) descent from another tribal member. Others require not only that their members possess tribal ancestry but also that this ancestry comes from a particular parent. Thus, the Santa Clara Pueblo (New Mexico) requires paternal descent, while other nearby Pueblos require maternal descent. By contrast, among the Miami Nation (Oklahoma), children may become eligible for citizenship either through the mother's or father's ancestral line, but when only one parent is a tribal member a vote of the tribal council is required. The Swinomish Indian Tribal Community (Washington) and Cheyenne River Sioux Tribe (South Dakota) ignore both the source and degree of tribal ancestry; they instead consider residency definitive, automatically admitting to citizenship all children born to parents living on the reservation. Tribes such as the Nez Perce (Idaho) accept only applicants whose parents submit the necessary paperwork within a limited time after a child's birth, while tribes including the Native Tribe of Koyukuk (Alaska) and the Lumbee Tribe (North Carolina) require members to fulfill certain minimal duties, such as maintaining regular contact with the tribal council. (For tribal constitutions and their citizenship requirements, see University of Oklahoma Law Center and National Indian Law Library 2005.)

Tribally specified legal definitions regulate individuals' right to vote in tribal elections, to hold tribal office, and generally to participate in the political, and sometimes the cultural, life of the tribe. The ability to satisfy legal definitions of identification may also determine the right to share in certain tribal revenues (such as income generated by tribally controlled businesses). Perhaps most significantly, it may determine the right to live on a reservation or to inherit land interests thereon.

## Federal Law

Although tribes possess the right to formulate legal definitions for the purpose of delimiting their citizenship, the federal government has many purposes for which it, too, must distinguish Indians from non-Indians, and it uses its own, separate legal definitions for doing so. More accurately, it uses a large array of legal definitions. Although the United States Constitution uses the word "Indian" in two places (in passages regarding the regulation of commerce and the taking of a federal census), it nowhere defines this category. Accordingly, Congress has made its own definitions on an ad hoc basis. A 1978 congressional survey discovered 33 separate definitions of Indians in use in different pieces of federal legislation, and more have been crafted since that time (S. O'Brien 1991). These may or may not correspond with those any given tribe uses to determine its citizenship.

Most federal legal definitions of Indian identity specify a particular minimum blood quantum—frequently one-quarter but sometimes one-half—but others do not. Some require or accept tribal citizenship as a criterion of federal identification, and others do not. Some require reservation residency or ownership of land held in trust by the government, and others do not. Other laws affecting Indians specify no definition of identity, such that the courts must determine to whom the laws apply. One important law that provides no definition of "Indian" is the Major Crimes Act of 1885 (23 Stat. 385, U.S.C. § 1153). It subjects Indians who commit crimes against other Indians on a reservation to federal prosecution for offenses that would expose non-Indians only to state prosecution. Because of the wide variation in federal legal identity definitions and their frequent departure from specific tribal ones, individuals who are recognized by their tribes as citizens may be considered non-Indian for some or all federal purposes. The converse can be true as well (Cohen 1982).

There are various contexts in which one or more federal legal definitions of Indian identity become important. The matter of economic resource distribution, involving access to various federally sponsored social services and educational incentives, comes immediately to mind. Many people are aware, for instance, that citizens of Indian tribes can receive medical care without charge at special facilities and may be eligible for certain types of scholarships and education loans. The particular legal situation of Indian people, with its attendant opportunities and responsibilities, is the result of historic negotiations between tribes and the federal government. In these, the government agreed to compensate tribes in various ways for the large amounts of land and other resources that tribes surrendered, often by force (Washburn 1971). Benefits available to those who can sat-

isfy federal definitions of Indian identity are administered through a variety of agencies, including the Bureau of Indian Affairs in the Department of the Interior, the Indian Health Service in the Department of Health and Human Services, the Department of Agriculture, the Department of Education, and the Department of Labor (Walk 1991).

Legal definitions affect specific economic rights deriving from treaties or agreements that some tribes made with the federal government. These may include rights such as the use of particular geographic areas for hunting, harvesting, fishing, or trapping, as well as certain water use rights (Washburn 1971). Those legally defined as Indians under federal law may be exempted from certain requirements related to state licensure and state (but not federal) income and property taxation (Sandefur 1991).

Legal definitions determine the applicability of a number of protections available to individual Indians from the federal government. Notable among these are an Indian parent's rights under the Indian Child Welfare Act of 1978 (25 U.S.C. 1901 et seq.). Responding to the unusually high numbers of American Indian children who were being removed from their families and tribes, this law requires that efforts be made to place endangered children with another family member, or at least with another Indian family, rather than with non-Indians (Harjo 1993; Redbird and Melendey 1978).

Just as important, federally specified legal definitions provide for certain religious freedoms. They allow Indian people to seek protection from prosecution for the possession of specific ceremonial objects that are otherwise restricted by law. For instance, some Indian people own eagle feathers that they use in prayer and ceremonies, although non-Indians are not permitted to possess any part of this endangered species. Similarly, Indian members of the Native American Church ingest peyote, legally classified as a hallucinogen, as a sacramental substance in closely controlled worship settings; non-Indians are forbidden to possess it (H. Smith and R. Snake 1996). Since the passage of the Native American Graves Protection and Repatriation Act of 1990 (25 U.S.C. 3001 et seq.), federal law allows Indian people to claim sacred ceremonial objects, as well as to receive and rebury the remains of their ancestral dead, if these are being held in federally funded museums for display or study (Fine-Dare 2002; Grose 1996).

Federal legal definitions of Indian identity can even affect some individuals' ability to pursue their livelihood. A controversial protection available to those legally defined as Indians revolves around the Indian Arts and Crafts Act of 1990 (25 U.S.C. 305 et seq.). Recognizing that much art marketed as made by American Indians was actually produced by non-Indians (often being imported from other countries), this legislation forbids any artist who is not a citizen of a federally or state-acknowledged tribe from marketing work as "Indian produced" (J. Barker 2003; Sheffield 1997).

Finally, federal legal definitions allow Indian people, as a class, to claim certain privileges, in relation to the larger society, that others do not enjoy. One such privilege is the right to benefit from "Indian preference" in federal employment. This policy means that the Bureau of Indian Affairs and the Indian Health Service are permitted a bias in favor of Indian applicants, and it has helped ensure a significant presence of Indian employees in governmental bodies primarily responsible for administering programs affecting tribes.

Although Indian preference may appear to constitute an example of racism, or favoritism extended to a racial group, the courts ruled otherwise in *Morton* v. *Mancari* (417 U.S. 535, 1974). Their reasoning was that "Indian" refers, in this context, to a political, rather than to a racial status. It refers, that is, to rights and obligations vis-à-vis the United States that an individual possesses not by virtue of his specific biological (racial) characteristics but by virtue of his conformity to a particular set of legal criteria. In the case of Indian preference, these criteria include citizenship in a federally acknowledged tribe or documentation of a blood quantum of at least one-half degree from any tribe.

## Negotiating Legal Identities

All these legal rights and protections offer their significant advantages only to those who are able to make claims to Indian status that are judged as meaningful within particular definitions of identity. However, many Indian people cannot manage to pass successfully through the definitions of identity imposed by the federal government, or even by their own tribes. (And there is no guarantee that those definitions correspond.) Who is able to negotiate a legal identity and who is not?

Tribal citizenship requirements usually require documentation of a minimum blood quantum of one-fourth, and the federal government does the same for at least some of its various purposes. If this requirement seems fairly obvious in theory, in practice it can throw many claimants to a tribal identity into legal limbo.

One group of people who are likely to find themselves in such circumstances are individuals of tribally mixed ancestry. Consider, for instance, the hypothetical case of a child who possesses one-half Indian ancestry and one-half White ancestry, meaning that she has one parent who is exclusively White and one parent who is exclusively Indian. Her identity claim is likely to meet with approval from both the federal government and her tribe—so long as her Indian ancestry comes from a single tribe. But compare her potential fortunes with those of another child whose half-Indian heritage derives from several different tribes. If this second child, in addition to his one-half White ancestry, is also one-eighth Blackfeet (Montana), one-eighth Turtle Mountain Chippewa (North Dakota), one-eighth Sicangu Lakota (South Dakota), and one-eighth Cheyenne-Arapaho (Oklahoma), he is, like the first child, one-half Indian. But each tribe of his ancestry requires its citizens to document a one-quarter blood degree, from that tribe only. From the perspective of each individual tribe, this child possesses only one-eighth tribal blood and is therefore ineligible for citizenship. As far as his several tribes are concerned, he is simply non-Indian within their legal definitions of identity.

Indeed, even children of exclusively Indian ancestry can find themselves denied citizenship through a similar set of circumstances. The repeated intertribal marriages implied by the foregoing example are not even necessary. A mother with exclusively Indian ancestry in a tribe that reckons descent through the paternal line only and a father with exclusively Indian ancestry in another tribe that reckons descent through the maternal line only will produce children who are non-Indian according to the legal requirements of both tribes. It is even possible, in some cases, for children whose parents belong to the same tribe, but who are from different reservations, to encounter similar enrollment prohibitions (D.R. Miller 1994).

Some people of Indian ancestry fall afoul, in tribal legal definitions of identity, of still another potential snare. This entanglement has to do with one's ability to establish relationship to a tribal community in the way that many legal definitions require. Although a few tribes have no written records of citizenship even today (some Pueblos, for instance, depend upon their oral traditions), the majority of tribes maintain written documents, usually called "tribal rolls" (Thornton 1987). Applications for citizenship are evaluated with reference to certain "base rolls," or written records of tribal citizenship in a particular year. Individuals seeking tribal or federal identification as Indian must typically establish that one or more of their ancestors appears on such a roll.

Unfortunately, many people who clearly conform to any other definition of Indian identity do not have ancestors who appear on the base rolls. Consider the example of the Dawes Rolls of 1899–1906, from which applicants for citizenship in a number of tribes must show descent, including those seeking citizenship in one of the largest tribes, the Cherokee Nation (Oklahoma). In this instance, the process that would-be registrants endured took so long that some died before the paperwork was completed. Even when applicants did manage to live long enough to complete the process, they frequently found themselves denied. Dawes commissioners enrolled only a small fraction of all those who applied, and they readily agreed that they had denied many people of indubitable tribal ancestry (K. Carter 1999).

Other Indian people, including many of the most culturally conservative tribal members among the Cherokee and other Oklahoma tribes, resisted census enumeration (Debo 1940; Otis 1973). But regardless of the reason for the absence on the Dawes records, no Cherokee—even a person of exclusively Cherokee ancestry, who speaks his language fluently, participates fully in the social and cultural life of his tribe, and may even have ancestors on other historic censuses—can become a tribal citizen if he fails to identify an ancestor on this one, specific document.

*Manipulating Identities*

The reverse situation involves people who may have tenuous ancestral connections to tribes—or none at all—but who have nevertheless managed to have themselves legally defined as Indians at various times. For example, in the late nineteenth and early twentieth centuries, when registration on the Dawes census implied eligibility for distribution of tribal lands in Oklahoma, it was not uncommon for individuals with no Indian ancestry, but with active homesteading ambitions and perhaps an unscrupulous lawyer in tow, to seek a place on the rolls through dishonest means. Thousands of them succeeded (J. Barker 2003; Debo 1940; Perdue 1981). Although it is far more difficult to manipulate the legal requirements for tribal citizenship in the twenty-first century, there is considerable resentment in Indian communities against individuals perceived as inventing or resurrecting distant or previously disowned ancestry—often in the form of a romantically imagined Cherokee great-grandmother—in order to establish tribal ties and their legal (or even simply social) benefits (J. Barker 2003; Garroutte 2003).

Such controversies notwithstanding, one must not assume that attempts to manipulate racial classifications are limited to individuals. The federal government has likewise had many opportunities to tailor legal definitions of Indian status. For instance, in 1892, Commissioner of Indian Affairs Thomas Jefferson Morgan urged the federal government to adopt "a liberal and not technical or restrictive construction" of Indian identity when distributing property and other government benefits (ARCIA 1892:37). Morgan's proposal allowed many individuals of varying degrees of ancestry to qualify for these benefits.

Prior to 1892, agents of American government had judged "mixed bloods" more cooperative than "full bloods" on a variety of issues, particularly in the signing of legal instruments allowing for land cessions. The agents had therefore specifically sought them out for such purposes (Meyer 1999; T.P. Wilson 1992). By the end of the nineteenth century, to deny the Indian status of mixed bloods, Morgan argued, would have been disastrous to government interests because it "would unsettle or endanger the titles to much of the lands that have been relinquished by Indian tribes and patented to citizens of the United States" (ARCIA 1892:36). At other times, and in arenas involving different types of interests, the federal government found it useful to formulate more restrictive legal definitions. It often strictly insisted on a standard of one-quarter, or even one-half, blood quantum before it would legally define individuals as Indians. This can be the case in the first decade of the twenty-first century for determining eligibility for Indian preference in hiring.

Internal political interests can favor attempts by tribal governments to adjust identity criteria for specific purposes. Such accusations have been made, for instance, in regard to events occurring in the Keweenaw Bay Indian Community of Chippewas (Michigan). There, contested elections in 1994 were followed by the disenrollment of a substantial portion of the electorate—the majority of whom were reportedly supporters of a faction opposing the tribal chairman, Fred Dakota. New elections were held and produced results more favorable to Dakota's alleged interests. A portion of the disenrolled individuals were later re-enrolled as adopted citizens. As such, they were barred from voting or from holding political office in the tribe. The chairman's critics pointed out that "once [the chairman] . . . manipulates the 'adoption' process in his favor, he will be politically situated to banish his opponents permanently, effectively foreclosing even the possibility of political change" (Melmer 1996:A2). In 1999, the Bureau of Indian Affairs determined that the disenrollments were a violation of the Indian Civil Rights Act of 1968 (Morin 1999). By this time, Chairman Dakota had been convicted and imprisoned on various federal charges (Dietz 1997; Melmer 1996, 1996a, 1996b). J. Barker (2003) discusses other intratribal disputes related to citizens' disenrollment, making clear that such controversies are not necessarily related to corrupt interests and can be handled responsibly. Yet there is clearly nothing that renders tribal political bodies, any more than the federal government, immune from the temptation to manipulate the criteria of individual Indian identity.

## Collective Legal Definitions

Identity definitions are a concern not only for individuals but also for entire groups. The federal government formally classifies certain groups as "acknowledged" Indian tribes and invests them with specific rights and responsibilities unshared by other entities. By acknowledging a group of claimants as an Indian tribe, the federal government extends "government-to-government" relations to it, legally constituting it as a sovereign power. This is an extremely powerful status. In fact, the legal case of *Native American Church* v. *Navajo Tribal Council* (1959) made clear that tribal sovereignty is superior to that of any state government. It is argued, on the basis of this case, that tribes retain all national powers that they have not been explicitly required to surrender by the United States (S. O'Brien 1989).

Federal acknowledgment extends government "trust responsibility" to tribal nations. The interpretation of the precise meaning of this concept has changed significantly over time, but one current definition describes trust responsibility as "the responsibility to act in the best interests of Indians in managing Indian-owned land and other resources" (Sandefur 1991:213–214). In present practice, the extension of trust responsibility usually implies individual and collective eligibility for federal governmental services and programs. In some cases, acknowledgment creates a government obligation to provide land for a reservation or allows the tribe to seek compensation for land judged to have been improperly taken from it. Federally acknowledged tribes have the right to establish political and legal institutions, and they are exempt from various kinds of taxation and legislation (including certain environmental protection laws) on the reservation. In addition, they can operate businesses that others cannot, such as gambling establishments (Canby 2004).

### Negotiating Identities

As with definitions operating at the individual level, there are many difficulties that a group faces in establishing a legitimate definition of itself as an Indian tribe. The application of the federal criteria for acknowledging a group of claimants as a tribe is frequently described in scholarly literature with words such as "woefully inconsistent," "serendipitous," and "an accident of history" (T. Anderson 1978). Until the 1970s, the federal government did not even have a formalized criterion for distinguishing acknowledged and unacknowledged tribes. It issued lists, from time to time, of tribes that it defined as acknowledged. But the list could change on the basis of congressional or executive decision. Indian people could suddenly become non-Indians, at least for a range of extremely consequential legal purposes.

In general, historic tribal groups that were large, showed serious resistance to White settlement, signed treaties with the federal government, or were otherwise hard to ignore have been treated as tribes by the federal government. They enjoy unquestioned acknowledgement status and have not been required formally to demonstrate the legitimacy of their collective identity. Smaller or less aggressive groups, groups that moved around a great deal, and many groups that were colonized early (including many of the groups in the eastern United States) have been much easier to neglect. They have frequently remained without federal acknowledgment.

Since the mid-1970s, unacknowledged groups have a mechanism by which they may create or establish a legal definition of themselves as an Indian tribe: the Federal Acknowledgment Process. This process, administered by the Branch of Acknowledgement and Research in the Bureau of Indian Affairs, requires that petitioners satisfy the seven criteria set out in "Procedures for Establishing that an Indian Group Exists as an Indian Tribe" (Code of Federal Regulations 2003, 1:257–258) and accompanied by a set of "official guidelines" consisting of another 80 pages. The criteria can be summarized as requiring "that a single Indian group has existed since its first sustained contact with European cultures on a continuous basis to the present; that its members live in a distinct, autonomous community perceived by others as Indian; that it has maintained some sort of authority with a governing system by which its members abide; that all its members can be traced genealogically to an historic tribe; and that it can provide evidence to substantiate all of this" (Quinn 1990; U.S. General Accounting Office 2001).

If these criteria sound relatively straightforward and sensible, it is not the case that all petitioners—even those who might seem to have a reasonable claim on a tribal identity—can satisfy them. Although some tribal groups lack formal acknowledgement because they decline to seek it, financial considerations prohibit others. The process of filing an application is expensive, potentially requiring the hiring of genealogists, historians, anthropologists, and other experts. Moreover, petitioners may confront difficulties in meeting the criteria for historical reasons beyond their control. The Branch of Acknowledgment and Research concedes that tribes may be denied acknowledgment due to conditions that they did not choose but that the federal government deliberately created. Maintenance of a distinct community, for example, is not always strictly a matter of members' preferences. Communities can be (and have been) destroyed by circumstances imposed upon them. Even in such instances, petitioners can be denied federal acknowledgement as tribes.

### Manipulating Identities

For all its difficulties of application, federal acknowledgment of tribes helps prevent non-Indian groups from improperly exploiting the advantages of tribal status. This is an effort in which certain claimants have shown themselves to be quite ambitious, with consequences from the appalling to the bizarre. For instance, a company claiming the title of the Sovereign Cherokee Nation Tejas (and using a seal sufficiently similar as to be mistaken for that of the federally acknowledged Cherokee Nation) was the subject of a 1991 Senate subcommittee hearing. The subcommittee alleged that the company had misrepresented itself as an Indian tribe for the purpose of perpetrating a variety of business frauds.

The tribal head, "Chief Bear Who Walks Softly" (also known as William M. Fry, Jr.) testified that the Sovereign Cherokee Nation Tejas had been created by an act of God. The subcommittee offered the somewhat humbler interpretation that it was the product of Col. Herbert M. Williams, a retired Air Force officer. He had birthed the idea of creating (as he put it) an "'offshore tax haven'" on a sand bar in the middle of the Rio Grande, to which he would lure a variety of businesses. By the time of the "tribe's" encounter with the Senate subcommittee, it had contracted to underwrite a number of corporate insurance policies that it possessed inadequate assets to guarantee. The subcommittee expressed concern that the Sovereign Cherokee Nation Tejas had the potential to cause massive business failure because some of America's largest corporations, such as Dow Chemical, had done business with it (Senate Subcommittee on Governmental Affairs 1991).

The federal government, too, has shown considerable creativity in its application of the criteria for defining Indian tribes. For instance, in the late 1960s, the Department of Justice went to considerable lengths to exclude Alaska

Native communities from the benefits of the 1946 Indian Claims Commission Act, a bill that created a special tribunal to hear tribal claims against the federal government for violations of treaties and agreements. The effort ignored a long series of court decisions holding that any of the aboriginal peoples of the Americas, regardless of nomenclature, should be included under legislation written to apply to American Indians. The Justice Department pressed the effort to exclude Native Alaskans, although it was ultimately unsuccessful (Washburn 1971:167).

In other cases private, financial interests may intervene in negotiations over tribal status. For instance, in 1993, businessman Donald Trump publicly protested the competitive advantages that had accrued to the Mashantucket Pequot Tribal Nation (Connecticut) in the gaming industry. In testimony offered during congressional hearings on the Indian Gaming Regulatory Act, Trump questioned the legitimacy of the Pequot's status as a federally acknowledged tribe. Referring to the fact that the Mashantucket Pequots are a highly intermarried tribe with many members showing obvious phenotypic relationship to other racial groups, Trump informed Congress, "They don't look like Indians to me. They don't look like Indians to Indians" (U.S. Congress 1994:242).

A few years later, Trump undertook an entrepreneurial move that suggested considerable flexibility in his thinking about tribal authenticity and federal acknowledgment. In 1999, he entered a deal with the Paucatuck Eastern Pequot Tribal Nation, a then unacknowledged group who are relatives and immediate neighbors of the Mashantuckets. Under the terms of the agreement, Trump reportedly funded the Paucatucks' petition for federal recognition in exchange for a share in any gaming operations that their anticipated acknowledgement status would allow them to establish. He later sued the group for breach of contract when they withdrew from the agreement and aligned themselves with a rival backer (Elvin 1999; J. Adams 2003). Such ironic situations shed stark light on the many forces that may intrude into the federal acknowledgment process, attempting to manipulate the success or failure of tribal petitioners, even while just observing the legal punctilios.

## Conclusion

Legal claims to an Indian identity emerge out of complex negotiations occurring within the context of competing, often contradictory, definitions formulated by tribes and the federal government. They are vulnerable to manipulations by a range of interests from within and without the tribal camp. All the available definitions, while often strikingly different from each other, can exclude some people who are by any common-sense criteria Indian, while including some with dubious claims.

Although it is widely agreed that legal definitions of Indian status have an imperfect relationship to tribes' pre-contact standing, contemporary Indian people often take proof of legal definitions of identity with great seriousness even in everyday interaction (J. Barker 2003:31, 71; Meyer 1999). At the same time, because the process of establishing legal status is fraught with difficulties, Indian communities also often use other, less formal definitions of their boundaries for the purposes of everyday interaction. These may include factors such as individual or collective cultural characteristics, community participation, and family relationships (Garroutte 2003).

# Urban Communities

JOAN WEIBEL-ORLANDO

Sixty-six percent of the people who identified themselves as Native American in the 2000 U.S. census and 49 percent of the Native population of Canada in their 2001 census lived in metropolitan areas (U.S. Census Bureau 2003:2; Canada Analysis Series 2006:18), that is, places of at least 2,500 people (Thornton, Sandefur, and Grasmick 1982:4). This dramatic statement both underscores and masks the full significance of a sociocultural and historic truth. That two of every three American Indians and virtually one in two Canadian natives were urban dwellers in 2000–2001 strongly indicates that Native North American loci, lifeways, and cultures have changed as significantly in the second half of the twentieth century as they had in the previous 300 years of western European contact.

The urbanization of the Native population of the United States and Canada developed after about 1950. Until the mid-twentieth century the native population in both countries was overwhelming rural. In fact they were the most rural population of any of the major ethnic groups in these countries. As late as 1950–1951 only 13.4 percent of the American Indian and Alaska native population in the United States and only 7 percent of Canadian Natives were urban dwellers.

For such a dramatic shift of Native Americans to occur in only 50 years major and concerted social and political forces had had to have been marshaled. This chapter chronicles the major national issues and programs that encouraged, facilitated, or forced hundreds of thousands of Native Americans from rural and reservation lands into urban centers. Secondly, this chapter examines the creation and employment of other social and political mechanisms that allowed for the development of a twenty-first-century cultural entity as well as identity—the urban Indian.*

Urban residence is neither novel to nor nontraditional for Native Americans. Great city centers had been established throughout North (Cahokia, Chaco Canyon), Central (the great Mayan, Toltec, and Olmec complexes), and South (Incan urban centers) America long before Western European contact (Thornton, Sandefur, and Grasmick 1982:2–3, 6–12). Urbanism should not be thought of as purely a European contribution to the "civilizing of the Americas." Rather, Native Americans, throughout the western hemisphere and to the extent that climate, topography, and carrying power allowed, had experienced and acted upon similar impulses to congregate, aggregate and settle in larger and larger population densities—to create urban spaces for themselves and all that meant in terms of modifying the structures of its social institutions for hundred of years before western European contact.

Sixteenth and early seventeenth-century European assumed that Native Americans were "living in the countryside, in jungles, forests, on the plains and pampas, or in small villages." Yet "the Americas witnessed a greater process of urban development" before 1500 "than did any other continent, with the growth of the most elaborate planned cities found anywhere. . . . The First Americans have, in fact, gone through periods of deurbanization and reurbanization on various occasions in their history and . . . urban life has been a major aspect of American life from ancient times" (Forbes 2001:5).

While it is important to be aware of the glories that were urban, precontact America, it is equally insightful to recall that in the 300 years after European contact, the Native North American population, through the ravages of disease and warfare, was reduced by an estimated 90 to 95 percent (D.S. Jones 2004:9). As a result of such loss of life, indigenous North American expressions of, even the need and/or human resources capable of sustaining urban cultures, largely, had been extinguished or destroyed by 1700. By 1900 the indigenous peoples of the United States (except for a reported 1,000) were confined to rural and, largely, federally administered reservation lands (Thornton, Sandefur, and Grasmick 1982:14). The coincidence of Native Americans and the rustic, "uncivilized" rural had been made complete.

## Early Incursions into Twentieth-century Urban America

Native American rural-urban population change statistics demonstrate the slow but inevitable increase in the percentage of American Indians in urban settings with each census count after 1900 (Sorkin 1978). A number of reasons for the

---

* Eugene Herrod (Creek) conducted the initial archival review that provided supporting documentation for this chapter.

steadily increasing presence of Native Americans in urban centers between 1900 and 1950 have been proposed.

Propinquity of certain metropolitan complexes to rural reservation lands could have facilitated regular movement for periods of time from tribal lands to urban centers (J.A. Price 1978:136). (For a list of such proximal arrangements in both the United States and Canada see J.A. Price 1978:157.)

Squads of Native American workers left their tribal homes to work for the Atlantic and Pacific Railroad Company, members of the Laguna Pueblo in New Mexico beginning as early as 1880. Those work contracts eventuated in the development of a Laguna colony at "the end of the line" in Richmond, California, in 1922. In fact, by World War II, there were several settlements of Laguna families along the Atchison, Topeka, and Santa Fe lines between Albuquerque and Richmond (Peters 2001:117–126).

Canadian and American Mohawks filled a skilled craftsman niche as steelworkers at high rise construction sites all over the country, which necessitated their regular movement off their Six Nations Reserve. The largest colony of Mohawks settled in Brooklyn, New York, starting in the late 1920s (vol. 4:458) (J. Mitchell 1960:3).

The poverty and lack of economic opportunity on remote reservations, particularly during the 1930s and the early years of the Depression, provided a "push" off tribal lands (J.A. Price 1978:147). The expectation of locating gainful employment in burgeoning industrial centers provided the urban "pull" (Kerri 1976).

Enlistment into the armed services during World Wars I and II brought groups of young Native American men and women to urban ports of embarkation. Many would spend sufficient periods of time there before being shipped off to the various theatres of war to develop a taste for urban life (Bernstein 1991:150–151).

Certain work contract commitments brought other cadres of Native Americans into the urban, mainstream American work force during, between, and even before the World Wars. The urbanization of American Indians was also "a phenomenon of differential fertility and mortality of American Indians in urban and non-urban areas *and* of differential migration between these areas" (Thornton, Sandefur, and Grasmick 1982:5). With all these influences, in 1950, American Indians were still securely located, both geographically and conceptually, in rural places.

## Termination and Relocation

Although rural to urban migration of Native Americans had increased with each census count since 1900, in 1950 Native North Americans still constituted a predominantly (86.6%) rural population (Thornton, Sandefur, and Grasmick 1982:14). Two federal political initiatives in the 1950s profoundly changed that population profile. During the 1960s, "the rural American Indian population grew only 16 percent, whereas the urban Indian population grew by 144 percent" (Thornton, Sandefur, and Grasmick 1982:13). Clearly, influences beyond naturally occurring and evolving mortality and migration patterns were at work during this historical period to bring about such residential shifts.

### Termination

Introduced on August 1, 1953, House Concurrent Resolution 108 declared the policy of the United States to be the abolishment of federal supervision over the tribes as soon as possible and the subjection of Indians to the same laws, privileges, and responsibilities as other citizens of the United States. As a result of this resolution, the government began the process of "termination" of the tribal relationship. The resolution aroused immediate and virulent opposition among Native Americans (Prucha 1990:223). Nonetheless, from 1954 through 1960, 61 tribes, groups, communities, rancherias, or allotments were terminated by withdrawing federal services and protection (Driver 1969:499).

After tremendous and continuous outcries against the termination policy, termination was ultimately expunged from the federal record in 1980. However, Native Americans had transformed themselves from being largely (86.6%) rural and reservation-based societies to having, in 1970, 44.5 per cent of its citizenry voluntarily living off reservation and in urban settings (Thornton, Sandefur, and Grasmick 1982:15). See "Termination and Relocation," this volume.

### Relocation

When thousands of Native American veterans trained as mechanics and machinists during World War II returned to their reservation homes and families in the late 1940s and early 1950s they found the opportunity for gainful employment on their home reservations as elusive as it had been before they enlisted. Reservation unemployment rates, especially among the returning veterans were the highest in the nation in the postwar period. Coincidentally, alcohol abuse and its associated accident, suicide, homicide, and physical violence rates also spiked on the reservations during this period (Bernstein 1991:141, 137). The Bureau of Indian Affairs, Indian Health Service providers, the United States Congress, and tribal officers and members all knew postwar reservation economic conditions were untenable. Something had to be done to provide viable employment opportunities for Native Americans who wished (and many who now had the training) to be gainfully employed.

An urban relocation test case was initiated in 1947. For the first time, federal funds were appropriated for a Labor Recruitment and Welfare program for the Navajo and Hopi reservations. Indians on those reservations desirous of locating gainful employment were to be relocated to Denver, Los Angeles, Phoenix, and Salt Lake City (Bahr 1972:407).

When the regional trial program was a success, an expanded program of relocation assistance entitled the Voluntary Relocation Program was established in 1950 (Bernstein 1991:168). In 1952 the program went national. The Bureau of Indian Affairs was awarded a modest line item in that year's federal budget to be used to "relocate, [provide] financial assistance, to cover all or part of the costs of transportation to the place of relocation and short-term temporary subsistence to Indians, in addition to relocation services" (Prucha 1990:237).

Branch relocation offices of the Bureau of Indian Affairs were established in 12 target cities where the economy was thriving. Entry-level jobs were there for the asking for anyone who had even the most minimal of training or for all able-bodied men and women who were willing to learn.

Bureau of Indian Affairs administrator Glenn L. Emmons fairly glowed about the success of the fledgling program in the 1954 annual report of the commissioner of Indian affairs. "During the 1954 fiscal year, 2,163 Indians were directly assisted to relocate under the Bureau's relocation program. . . . In addition, over 300 Indians left reservations without assistance to join relations and friends who had been assisted to relocate. . . . The total number of relocations represented a substantial increase over relocations during the previous fiscal year. On the reservations there was continued interest in relocation throughout the year. Relocation assistance funds were used up in almost every area, and at the end of the year there was a backlog of applications for relocation. Letters from relocated Indians to friends and relatives back on the reservation, describing their experiences and new standards of living, served to stimulate interest as did a decrease in employment opportunities in the vicinity of some of the reservations. . . ." (Prucha 1990:237).

With such enthusiasm for and apparent early success of the program, it was expanded further in 1957 (Bahr 1972:407). In 1962 the Voluntary Relocation Program was renamed the Employment Assistance Program. Its activities were broadened to include job placement on or near reservations, as well as in certain metropolitan areas. Still later, educational and vocational training components were added to the list of services provided by the program (Officer 1971:49).

The urban relocation program officers stressed the voluntariness and positive results of the program. Yet "economic pressures force the Indian to relocate. . . . The [relocation program, in effect said] to the Indian, either conform to the Anglo way and move several hundred miles away from the reservation or stay . . . and live at substandard levels" (Bahr 1972:408). The 1980 census determined that approximately 63.8 percent of the Native American population lived in urban centers (D.M. Bahr 1993:54). Four years earlier, the operations of the Los Angeles Bureau of Indian Affairs relocation branch office had been suspended (Weibel-Orlando 1999:15). The urban relocation assistance centers in the other target cities had already experienced similar fates

(Oswalt 2006:480). By 1980, it appears, the urban relocation Employment Assistance Program's work had been done (Fixico 1986).

Just how successful was the relocation program? If the sheer number of Native Americans the program assisted in their efforts to relocate from rural unemployment to urban work opportunity is the criterion of program effectiveness, then the program was an unequivocal success. In 1957 one *Saturday Evening Post* editorialist even asserted that "Indian reservations may someday run out of Indians" (Bernstein 1991:168).

Other observers were not so optimistic about having solved the problem of chronic unemployment on Indian reservations. Although the relocation program had paid the relocatee's travel costs to the city (among other things), the free ticket had never been for a round trip. It had been assumed that, once ensconced in the urban milieu, no right-minded Native American would ever want to leave, and, having been brought to the city at very little personal expense, the Native American relocatee was, henceforth, on his or her own. Neither of these assumptions always held true (Weston 1996:101).

Over the years the program admitted to a 30 percent return rate. But other estimates ran as high as 60 percent (Bernstein 1991:169). Individuals who had volunteered to "check out what the city had to offer" soon found that more skills than they acquired were needed to secure meaningful employment or to command a living wage in the city. Numbers of people would take advantage of the changes in levels and kinds of assistance offered by the program over the years a number of times before making the final decision to stay in one place or another. Additionally Native Americans routinely travel back and forth from reservation kin households to their urban residences as work and school schedules permit or necessitate or family dynamics dictate (Lobo 2003; Oswalt 2006:481). Bahr (1972:408) labeled this intermittent residential relocation the "rurban" life style.

As individuals acquired higher education or as administrative and social service delivery positions were established in reservation communities, especially during the Great Society period of parallel social service program development in ethnic communities in the 1960s and with President Richard Nixon's promise to help "Indians become independent of Federal control without being cut off from Federal concern and Federal support" (Prucha 1990: 258), numbers of Native Americans who had honed their administrative skills in urban public service programs returned to their reservation communities to take on federally funded service positions "for the good of our people" (Weibel-Orlando 1988). Finally, a number of early relocatees, after having spent a good portion of their adult lives in urban centers, upon retirement, made the decision to "go home." Therefore, if a major vacation of tribal lands was the ultimate intent of the program, Native Americans continued to find ways and reasons to mitigate that outcome.

Nonetheless, and as national census figures bear out, the rural-urban distribution of the Native American population shifted dramatically after 1950. And though, from 1980 on, the shift to urban centers appeared to have leveled off from its increases between 1950 and 1980, the preponderance of Native Americans in urban centers is a contemporary demographic reality. As Bahr (1972:409) noted "even if a large proportion of the urban Indian people eventually leave the city, it cannot be denied that the urban experience has become a major, if not dominant, element determining the attitudes, behavior, and values of Native Americans. In fact, it seems probable that in terms of long-term consequences for Indian culture, the movement of Indians to cities that began in mid-century may be as significant as their earlier forced removal to reservations."

*Twenty-first Century Urban Communities*

In 2000, 4,119,301 people identified themselves as American Indian and Alaska Native alone or in combination with one or more other races (table 1). Three and a half million (66 percent) of that total population is reported to have been living in urban settings at that time (U.S. Census Bureau 2003).

Of the 10 largest places in total population and in American Indian and Alaska Native populations in 2000 (table 2), four cities—Los Angeles, Chicago, Dallas, and Phoenix—were among the original 12 relocation program target cities. Three other, smaller cities with disproportionate percentages of Native American residents in 2000, Tulsa (7.7%), Oklahoma City (5.7%), and Albuquerque (4.9%) were also original relocation program sites (table 3). Other major

### Table 1. Urban and Rural American Indian Population in the United States, 1900–2000

| Year | Total | Urban | Rural | Percentage Urban |
|------|-------|-------|-------|------------------|
| 1900 | 237,000 | 1,000 | 236,000 | 0.4 |
| 1910 | 266,000 | 12,000 | 254,000 | 4.5 |
| 1920 | 244,000 | 15,000 | 229,000 | 6.1 |
| 1930 | 332,000 | 33,000 | 299,000 | 9.9 |
| 1940 | 334,000 | 24,000 | 310,000 | 7.2 |
| 1950 | 343,000 | 56,000 | 287,000 | 13.4 |
| 1960 | 524,000 | 146,000 | 378,000 | 27.9 |
| 1970 | 764,000 | 340,000 | 424,000 | 44.5 |
| 1980 | 1,420,400 | 906,215 | 514,185 | 63.8 |
| 1990 | 2,015,143 | 1,128,991 | 886,152 | 56.0 |
| 2000 | 4,119,906 | 2,719,138 | 1,400,768 | 66.0 |

SOURCES: 1900 through 1970 data are from Thornton, Sandefur, and Grasmick 1982:14. The 1980 urban data are from D.H. Bahr 1993:54; 1980 total population data are from U.S. Census Bureau Internet Release Data September 12, 2002: table 1. United States—Race and Hispanic Origin: 1790 to 1990. The 1990 data are from U.S. Census 1990 U.S. Summary: Social and Economic Characteristics, Table 8. The 2000 data are from Table 1 in the Census 2000 Brief The American Indian and Alaska Native Population: 2000 and U.S. Census Press Release 3/16/2006:2.

### Table 2. Ten Largest Places in Total Population and in American Indian and Alaska Native Population, 2000

| Place | Total Population | | American Indian and Alaska Native Alone or in Combination | |
|-------|------|--------|------|--------|
| | Rank | Number | Rank | Number |
| New York, N.Y. | 1 | 8,008,278 | 1 | 87,241 |
| Los Angeles | 2 | 3,694,820 | 2 | 53,092 |
| Chicago, Ill. | 3 | 2,896,016 | 8 | 20,898 |
| Houston, Tex. | 4 | 1,953,631 | 10 | 15,743 |
| Philadelphia | 5 | 1,517,550 | 21 | 10,835 |
| Phoenix, Ariz. | 6 | 1,321,045 | 3 | 35,093 |
| San Diego, Calif. | 7 | 1,223,400 | 9 | 16,178 |
| Dallas, Tex. | 8 | 1,188,580 | 18 | 11,334 |
| San Antonio, Tex. | 9 | 1,144,646 | 12 | 15,224 |
| Detroit, Mich. | 10 | 951,270 | 25 | 8,907 |
| Oklahoma, OK | 29 | 506,132 | 5 | 29,001 |
| Tucson, Ariz. | 30 | 486,699 | 11 | 15,358 |
| Albuquerque, N.Mex. | 35 | 448,607 | 7 | 22,047 |
| Tulsa, Okla. | 43 | 393,049 | 4 | 30,227 |
| Anchorage, Alaska | 65 | 260,283 | 6 | 26,995 |

SOURCE: U.S. Census Bureau, Census 2000:Summary File 1.

American cities with significant Native American populations but not among the 12 original relocation program destination cities include: New York City, Houston, Philadelphia, San Diego, San Antonio, and Detroit. Only Anchorage, Alaska (10.4% of its population identified as Native American in 2000) among the smaller cities with disproportionately large percentages of Native American residents was not an original relocation program site. Table 3 indicates other smaller cities that have, since the 1950s, developed sizable Native American populations. They include: Green Bay, Wisconsin; Tacoma, Washington; Minneapolis, Minnesota; Spokane, Washington; and Sacramento, California.

The nationwide distribution of Native Americans in urban centers other than the original relocation program target

### Table 3. Ten U.S. Places of 100,000 or More Population With the Highest Percentage of Native Americans, 2000

| Place | Percent of Total Population Are Native Americans |
|-------|------------------------------------------------|
| Anchorage, Alaska | 10.4 |
| Tulsa, Okla. | 7.7 |
| Oklahoma City, Okla. | 5.7 |
| Albuquerque, N. Mex. | 4.9 |
| Green Bay, Wis. | 4.1 |
| Tacoma, Wash. | 3.6 |
| Minneapolis, Minn. | 3.3 |
| Tucson, Ariz. | 3.2 |
| Spokane, Wash. | 3.0 |
| Sacramento, Calif. | 2.8 |

SOURCE: U.S. Census Bureau, Census 2000:Summary File 1.

cities is explained in several ways. From its earliest days and although certain cities had been targeted, the program was quite flexible in its placement of the voluntary relocatees. In 1952 the commissioner of Indian affairs reported that the 2,163 Native Americans who had been assisted in their relocation efforts in the previous two years had traveled "to 20 different States" (Prucha 1990:238). Secondly, certain urban centers evolved into major industrial areas after the urban relocation Program had been initiated and its recipient cities identified. Houston and its aerospace development in the 1960s is a prime example of this later and unanticipated urban, industrial development.

Other cities with major concentrations of Indians can be thought of as second stage urban residences in a multistage Native American rural-to-urban migration pattern. The lively San Diego, California, Native American community, for instance, is led and its social service programs administered by a number of people whose first assisted urban relocations were to Los Angeles before making moves to San Diego years later and as opportunities presented themselves.

The San Diego Indian community illustrates another aspect of Native American urbanization. Many Native Americans are there, not necessarily as the result of federally assisted, long-distance, and cross-cultural migrations, but because their reservations and traditional tribal lands abut, if not are incorporated, into their host metropolitan areas. Other examples are those in the metropolitan areas of Phoenix, Oklahoma City, Tulsa, Tucson, and Anchorage. Even Los Angeles, one of the first and most distanced target cities of the relocation program and with more than 200 distinct tribal groups represented in its 2000 population of 53,092 Native Americans, the second largest urban Indian concentration in the United States, boasted an existing Indian population of around 6,000 in 1955 as the urban relocation program began its encouragement of tribal people from all over America to seek economic opportunity in Los Angeles (Price 1968:169).

Other cities targeted as relocation assistance center sites (Cleveland, Denver, Oakland, San Jose, and Salt Lake City) do not appear on either list of American cities with significant numbers of Native American residents. Given the amount of documentation and political activism of the Native Americans in Denver, Minneapolis, and San Francisco Bay areas, it was surprising to discover the comparatively low numbers of Native Americans in these cities in 2000.

The reverse can be said about the unexpectedly high number of Native Americans in New York City (its 2000 Native American population of 87,241 makes it the largest urban concentration of Native Americans in the United States) and the relative paucity of information about this community. Save for the excellent accounts of the concentrations of Mohawk high rise steel workers in New York (Blumenfeld 1965), there are few ethnographic accounts written after 1950 about American Indians living in New York. The same is true for Philadelphia.

## Major Urban Communities

### United States

Los Angeles, the second largest urban Indian community in the United States, enjoyed continuous observation and discussion during the first 25 years of the federal relocation program (J.A. Price 1968, 1978; Frost 1973; Guilmet 1976, 1979; Bramstedt 1977; Weibel 1978). Other original sites were studied: Denver (Graves 1966, 1967, 1970, 1974; Graves and van Arsdale 1966; Lave, Mueller, and Graves 1978; Snyder 1973; Weppner 1971, 1972), Albuquerque (W. Hodge 1969), Phoenix (Liebow 1991), San Francisco (Ablon 1964, 1971), Seattle (Bahr, Chadwick, and Stauss 1972; Chadwick and Stauss 1975; Stauss and Chadwick 1979; Stauss et al. 1979), Spokane (Roy 1962; Chadwick and White 1973), and Tucson (Ferguson 1968, 1976; Stull 1973, 1977; Uhlmann 1972; Waddell 1975). Individual studies of Sioux in Midwestern cities were conducted (Hurt 1962; Kemnitzer 1973; Kuttner and Lorincz 1967).

The earliest accounts of urban Indian communities were as much attempts to test certain sociological models and theories about social change, assimilation, acculturation, and accommodation as they were ethnographic descriptions of the creation and evolution of urban American Indian life. The earliest accounts were, almost to a one, concerned with what were assumed to be problems inherent in the rural-to-urban migration of people little experienced with the vagaries of urban life (see Waddell and Watson 1971). Certain of the Denver, Phoenix, and Albuquerque studies dealt with outcomes of alcohol use and abuse among Native Americans in the focal cities. Early articles about the Native Americans who had elected the San Francisco Bay area as their urban destination asserted that the Native Americans who had migrated to the Bay area were in danger of losing their sense of tribal identity and integrity and of becoming recognized (by others as well as themselves) as members of an urban ethnic (pan-Indian) category.

Popular literature and films of the 1960s and 1970s emphasized the more negative aspects of urban relocation for Native Americans. In the 1972 film based on his Pulitzer Prize-winning novel, *House Made of Dawn*, Scott Momaday places his protagonist in postrelocation Los Angeles as the social setting best suited for the plumbing of the depths of a displaced Indian's despair and degradation (Kilpatrick 1999:181). The docudrama, *The Exiles* (K. MacKenzie 1961), also presents American Indians newly migrated to Los Angeles as socially uncertain, lonely victims of their own false hopes and dreams and culturally lost in the forgivingly cold, black and white anonymity of the urban landscape.

While urban Indian communities continued to be of research interest during the 1980s (Weibel-Orlando 1999; D.M. Bahr 1993; Danziger 1991), the level of scholarly reportage about the urban Native American experience waned for about a decade. Since the late 1980s, important restudies, reassessments, and reconsideration of the urban Native

American experience have occurred. These research projects have been influenced by the development of subdisciplines—feminist and gender studies, ethnic relations, political agency—and fresh perspectives of revisionist history and interpretive anthropology (Fixico 2000; Lobo and Peters 2001; Lawrence 2004). Monographs such as T. Strauss's (1990) on the Chicago area, Weibel-Orlando's (1999) on Los Angeles, and D. Jackson's (2002) on a mid-sized city in the Upper Great Lakes area provide in-depth ethnographic as well as historical accounts of how Native Americans have found ways of making contemporary urban complexes tenable cultural milieus for themselves.

*Canada*

The 1971 Canadian census indicated that the residence of Indians was classified as: "reserve 62 per cent, rural non-reserve 16 percent, small urban centers (Canadian under 100,000) 11 per cent, and large urban centers (1000 or more) 11 per cent" (J.A. Price 1988:228). That only 22 per cent of the Canadian Indian population lived in urban centers of any size in 1970 contrasts sharply with the 44.5 percent (Thornton, Sandefur, and Grasmick 1982:14) of Indians in the United States who did.

Just over 1.3 million Canadian people reported having at least some Native ancestry in 2000. This group represents 4.4 percent of Canada's total population (Canada Analysis Series 2006:1). By contrast, the 4.5 million Native Americans in the United States comprised only 1.5 percent of the United States total 2000 population (U.S. Census Bureau 2002:1).

The relatively greater proportion of tribal peoples in urban centers in the United States (U.S. Census 2003:2) as opposed to Canada (Canada Analysis Series 2006:8) continued to hold true with the 2000 censuses. These population figures are especially intriguing given the fact that, as J.A. Price (1978:137) asserted: "It was a conscious design in the planning of Canadian reserves to make them small and to scatter them among the White communities, rather than to provide large separately viable territories. This was done to encourage Indian-White interaction and Indian adoption of White culture." The percentage of Natives living in urban areas went from 5.1 in 1901 to 6.7 in 1951 (Kalbach 1987:102), about 12 in 1961, about 30 in 1971, and 38 in 1981, 44 in 1991, and 49 in 2001 (E. Peters 2004).

Winnipeg has the greatest Native population (55,755) of any Canadian city (Canada Analysis Series 2006:8). Other major concentrations of aboriginal peoples are in shown in table 4.

## Urban Native American Institutional Parallels

A review of the ethnographic information provided as cultural context in the various works about the urban Native American experience reveals certain institutional and historical parallels across the various communities in both the United States and Canada. Urban Native populations continue to be characterized by tribal heterogeneity (Ablon 1964; Snyder 1973; Lobo 2001a:79). Los Angeles is the probably the most heterogeneous of the urban Indian communities (Weibel-Orlando 1999:310–314). A few exceptions to this pattern should be noted. J.A. Price (1978:136–137) reported that three-fourths of the 1,000 Natives in "a city in Kansas" are Potawatomi or Kickapoo from nearby reservations and that "80% of the 3,000 or so Indians in Boston are Micmacs." (For excellent ethnographic accounts of the Boston Micmac see Guillemin 1975.)

Although there were a few exceptions (the concentration of Native Americans in Chicago's "Uptown" District, LaGrand 2002, and the Mohawk colony in Brooklyn, J. Mitchell 1960), most of the urban Indian populations were and continue to be characterized by a lack of concentration in ethnic enclaves (Weibel-Orlando 1999; Lobo 2001a:71). With each census count, even early patterns of central city, residential concentrations gave way to centrifugal residential migration. Those urban Indians who can afford it continue to move to middle-class communities at the periphery of metropolitan regions in which homes are still within the economic reach of those gray and white collar, administrative and managerial middle class urban Indians wishing to trade homeownership for the rigors of one to four hours of daily commuting (Weibel-Orlando 1999:29–31; S. Williams 2002:2–3).

There are a number of parallels across the Canadian and United States urban Indian institutions (J.A. Price 1978, 1988). The most prevalent ethnic institutions in cities were "bars that develop a significantly Indian clientele" (J.A. Price 1978:159). The Indian bar phenomenon, while still viable in certain smaller and reservation-bordering cities such as Albuquerque, Gallup, and Flagstaff, has all but disappeared from cities such as Los Angeles (Weibel-Orlando 1999:320).

**Table 4.  Ten Largest Canadian Urban Areas, 1991**

| Place | Population | Aboriginal People | % of City |
|-------|-----------|-------------------|-----------|
| Toronto | 5,148,750 | 20,595 | .4 |
| Montreal | 3,758,333 | 11,275 | .3 |
| Vancouver | 2,070,288 | 37,265 | 1.8 |
| Ottawa-Hull | 1,141,250 | 13,695 | 1.2 |
| Calgary | 960,869 | 22,110 | 2.3 |
| Edmonton | 918,069 | 41,295 | 4.3 |
| Winnipeg | 682,561 | 55,970 | 8.2 |
| Halifax | 352,500 | 3,525 | 1.0 |
| Saskatoon | 232,493 | 20,455 | 8.8 |
| Regina | 197,375 | 15,790 | 8.0 |

SOURCES: 1991 Census and Aboriginal Peoples Survey, 1991 Statistics Canada Catoalgue #94-327; E. Peters 2004; www.statcan.ca/english/Pgdb/demo43b.htm.

The social significance of urban Indian bars was eclipsed by a number of other Native American urban institutions and volunteer associations across both the United States and Canada (J.A. Price 1978:160–161). These other urban Indian social forms are Indian centers and elaborated kinship-friendship networks—the second stage.

Tribal as well as occupational (Mohawk steel workers, Navajo silver jewelry workers) networks are other forms of social institutions that function to sustain and facilitate social, cultural, and economic ties among tribal people in urban centers as well as in rural and reservation locations. Other personal ethnic networks and involvements that operate throughout North America include powwow dancing ("Powwows," this vol.), Indian political activism, and Indian athletic leagues and sporting events. Other urban institutions are educational programs and centers that take on the function of receiving and assisting in the adaptation of newcomers to the urban environment.

By 1978, a third stage of urban ethnic institutionalization had occurred in both the United States and Canada. This stage included the development of ethnic institutions that cover a broad range of common interest associations such as Indian athletic leagues, Indian Christian churches (vol. 4:458), powwow clubs, and political organizations. In this stage the Indians developed unique ethnic institutions, typically related to positive ethnic identity and expressions. Similar developments were chronicled in Los Angeles (Bramstedt 1977; Weibel 1978; Weibel-Orlando 1999). (For a comprehensive list of Native American organizations and urban Indian centers in both Canada and the United States see http://www.nativeculturelinks.com/organizations.html).

In Toronto, Vancouver, Chicago (fig. 1), San Francisco, and Los Angeles, J.A. Price (1978:161–162) found a fourth stage in which Indians become involved in "creating academic, entrepreneurial, and professional institutions," such as Native Studies programs. A number of United States colleges and universities established such programs in the late 1960s and throughout the 1970s. Many of the programs continue to flourish as undergraduate and graduate programs ("Native American Studies Programs," this vol.). The University of California in Los Angeles offers a joint degree program that allows students to earn both an M.A. in Native American Studies and a law degree. The law school there developed a specialization in Native American tribal law by the 1970s. Another example of this development is the Indian Community School of Milwaukee (Krouse 2004:533–547). In this case, the institution is an Indian-administered, culture-sensitive, educational program for elementary and middle school-aged Native American children.

Starting in the late 1960s, urban Indian centers and other urban Indian coalitions and self-help groups perceived the rural-to-urban shift in the Native American population as a rationale for establishing spokesperson and lobby groups that functioned as mediating voices between the urban Native American communities and the larger urban entities in which they are embedded. The creation of the Los Angeles City/County Native American Indian Commission in 1976 exemplifies this paradigm of liaison-facilitation organization (Weibel-Orlando1999:178–198).

## Urban Relocation Outcomes

In the first decades after the initiation of the urban removal assistance program, those concerned with predicting outcomes of the massive reordering of American Indian lives were convinced that the Native Americans who elected to move to urban centers would, for the most part, be negatively impacted by the shift in cultural context. Loss of tribal identity, culture, and language; assumption of drug and alcohol addiction as coping strategies; and an inevitable adherence to other, more ambiguous social categories of ethnic group (American Indian) or place (Los Angeles Indian) identity were all seen as possible negative outcomes of Native American urban relocation.

Later findings point to the urban experience as having offered Native Americans novel, career enhancing opportunities and as the context in which new beginnings, new educational and employment opportunities, new statuses and roles and more positive self identities could be forged by those (both men and women) intellectually and psychologically prepared for and equal to the challenges.

"The migration of tens of thousands of Native Americans to the cities had enormous political ramifications" (Olson and Wilson 1984:165). The tribal heterogeneity that characterized most urban Indian communities led to increased pan-Indian political activity. In turn, the emerging political activism in urban-based groups like the United Native Americans, the American Indian Movement, and the National Indian Youth Council also helped inspire a resurgent nationalism on the reservations. Since 1969 and the Alcatraz Island occupation, even modest-sized urban Indian communities have been the training grounds of Native American political leadership. As an example, Russell Means (1995), American Indian Movement leader, received his formal education and developed his political voice and skills in Los Angeles.

Cities have been the loci of some of the most dramatically effective Native American political actions of the last 50 years. The battlegrounds on which Native Americans wage their fiercest struggles to sustain their ways of life are no longer solely on the rolling plains west of the Mississippi River. Rather, the federal and tribal court buildings in urban centers throughout the nation and especially in Washington, D.C., are where contemporary Native Americans make their cases known and have their voices heard (Beck 2001). Even though the 1978 Longest Walk demonstration crossed the entire width of the United States, the trek began in San Francisco (from Alcatraz Island to be precise). Six months later, it reached its destination—Washington, D.C. (Deere 1978:4–5).

Fig. 1. American Indian Center of Chicago, founded in 1953. top left, Christmas dinner buffet 2006 in Diane Maney Tribal Hall. An orchestra plays at the annual event. The mural *The Three Sisters*, painted by Robert Wapahi, Santee Sioux, is an allegorical representation of corn, beans, and squash, the mainstays of precontact Northeast agriculture. top right, Samantha Selby, Choctaw, the Indian Center's 2007 Junior Miss, leading fancy dancing at the annual June celebration of the graduations of all community members, from kindergarten to graduate school. bottom left, Art opening in 2006 at the American Indian Center's Trickster Gallery, located in Schaumburg, Ill. Musicians Mark Cleveland (left), Cherokee, and Grammy award winner Bill Miller (right, seated), Mohican, provide a concert. bottom right, Rita Hodge, Navajo, in 2007 sewing a fancy dance outfit as part of the Enter the Circle program, which teaches young people, 11–18 years old, to design and make their own regalia and to dance and learn about powwows. Photographs by Warren Perlstein.

The Native American mascots controversy is essentially an urban-based phenomenon. The fight originated in Atlanta (Kilpatrick 1999:121). And the loci of the offenses, more often than not, have been on high school, college, and university campuses in urban centers such as Minneapolis and Saint Paul, Palo Alto, California, and Urbana, Illinois ("Activism Since 1980," this vol.). (For a full discussion of this issue see King and Springwood 2001).

A wealth of ethnographic documentation about the range of political power, family authority, clan leadership, and economic control women commanded in traditional and contemporary tribal societies amply supports the assertion that tribal Native American women were and are not solely and stereotypically the tenders of hearth and home (Klein and Acker-

man 1995). Therefore, those women who availed themselves of the Bureau of Indian Affairs urban relocation assistance, accompanied their husbands or fathers who did, or migrated to cities on their own after 1952 found that the urban environment was not a total novelty but, rather, its variety of opportunity served to expand their choices of economic statuses and roles as did the proliferation of emerging urban Indian community institutions and their staffing needs.

One issue of *The American Indian Quarterly* is devoted entirely to the topic of urban American Indian women's activism (Krouse and Howard-Bobiwash 2003). Would the remarkable Native American female activists in Chicago, San Francisco, Milwaukee, and Anchorage as well as Toronto, Vancouver, and Thunder Bay in Canada whose community

315

grass roots activities are described in this journal have had such social effect had they or their families remained economically, geographically, and psychically tied to their rural and tribal communities? There is no way to answer that rhetorical question with any certainty.

In the urban setting, the intrepid community leaders discovered issues that demanded resolution and summoned the personal agency by and space and circumstances in which, to address, effectively those community needs. There, in their urban Indian communities of choice, the women were able to complete their educations, develop service careers, involve themselves in community and national Native American causes, and find constituent supporters of their causes and clients who could be advantaged by the provision of their services and self-help programs.

## Economic Strategies

As in 1952, Native American economic opportunity continues to be intrinsically associated with the urban milieu. Native Americans living on reservations have for decades been identified as the poorest groups in the United States (Kalt and Taylor 2005:1). Though American Indians on reservations made substantial gains, both economically and socially, during the final decade of the twentieth century, studies have shown that unemployment rates still exceed 40 percent on many reservations, few jobs are available, and there is often intense competition for whatever jobs there are (Hillabrant, Earp, and Rhoades 2004:1).

The most successful and still operating Native American casinos are those within easy car, bus, or train rides of major urban centers. As examples, the highly successful casinos in Barona and Pechanga are within an hour's drive of San Diego, California (Darian-Smith 2004); all eight of the casinos in New Mexico are an hour or two from Albuquerque, Santa Fe, or the tourist destination town of Taos (New Mexico Indian Casinos 2006:1). The same can be said for the propinquity of the enormously successful Foxwoods Casino and the New England urban centers of Boston, Providence, Hartford, and New Haven, and the placement of the Morongo Casino two hours east of Los Angeles and a half hour from the tourist destination of Palm Springs ("Gaming," this vol.).

## Urban Indians or Tribal Americans in Urban Spaces?

Even after 50 years and up to three generations of city living, Native Americans in urban environments have not necessarily experienced either a total break with the rural, reservation Indian lifeway or complete assimilation into mainstream urban American culture. Rather, Native Americans who live in urban centers view themselves as contemporary practitioners of an ancient and pragmatically quasi-nomadic lifestyle. The urban environment is a resource to be experienced, learned, used, but not to be taken on as a separate reality and identity. One does not necessarily become less Navajo, Lakota, Micmac, Chippewa, or Choctaw with movement to the city. Rather, experiencing city life creates a tribesperson who has widened his or her cultural and economical options. Similarly, long-term urban residence does not necessarily mean the loss of talent, energy or economic contributions to the rural reservation community. Rather, regular visits to the reservation, periodic movement from the urban to the rural and back as personal circumstances dictate, and the possibility of a return to full-time reservation residence upon retirement characterize the urban Native American experience.

Native Americans who live in urban centers would like federal agencies charged with subsidizing and administering Native American entitlement programs to realize and accept their continuing sense of tribal membership. Treaty-mandated Indian entitlements, it is argued, should be matters of documented or verifiable tribal membership and not individual location.

The problem with long-term absence and distance from one's tribal land and cultural core (the reservation) is that individuals find it increasingly difficult to retain those linguistic skills, tribal lore, and lifeways that constitute cultural identity. A second concern is the increasing propensity for intertribal, interethnic and interracial marriage in the city. How being one-quarter or less of any one tribal group effects tribal or ethnic identity is yet to be determined. Given these mitigating influences, Native Americans living in urban spaces for whom continuity of tribal membership and participation is important face the challenge of working conscientiously to provide a continuing sense of cultural connectedness, especially for the urban dwellers in their children's and grandchildren's generations.

# The Native American Church

DANIEL C. SWAN

For thousands of American Indian people, the Peyote religion provided the spiritual and social basis to create meaningful lives amid the economic, social, and political disruptions of the nineteenth century. In the twentieth century the Peyote religion grew from its origins in northern Mexico and the southern Plains and spread throughout the United States (vols. 10:558–569, 11:673–681) and beyond to Canada. In the early twenty-first century, in large urban centers as well as in rural Indian communities, the various organizations of the Native American Church comprised about 300,000 members in North America (Mead, Hill, and Atwood 2005) and continue to evolve to meet the changing circumstances and needs of their membership.

While Peyote had been a part of the native pharmacopoeias of numerous tribes for thousands of years (Furst 1996:141; La Barre 1989:291; Michael 1994:8A), it was in the late eighteenth century that a new religion, based on the ritual consumption of the Peyote cactus, began to coalesce among lower Rio Grande groups called Carrizos, who passed it to the Lipan Apache around 1800. It was through Lipan sources, in the 1860s–1870s, that the religion was introduced to the reservations of southwest Indian Territory, modern-day Oklahoma. In the following decade the religion gained converts among the Plains Apache, Kiowa, and Comanche, and quickly spread to surrounding tribal communities (Stewart 1987:45–46, 49, 61).

The Peyote religion shares a number of features with the Ghost Dance, the Drum religion, Christianity, and other religious movements among Plains Indian societies in the late nineteenth and early twentieth centuries (vol. 13:996–1010). In many tribal communities this was a time of accelerated and often cataclysmic change in their social, economic, and political systems. The tribal religions that had previously provided a spiritual charter for the formation and perpetuation of these societies and a moral code of conduct for their members were often at odds with the realities of confinement to reservations and the collapse of native economies. The adoption of new religious forms often resulted from the conscious efforts of American Indians to adapt their traditional values and religious practices to these new circumstances and conditions. The story of the Native American Church is one of cultural survival, social adaptation, and moral revitalization.

## The Peyote Plant

Peyote (*Lophophora williamsii*) is a small, spineless cactus (fig. 1) that grows in the arid chaparral environment of the Rio Grande valley in Texas and the northern plains of Mexico. Peyote is generally referred to as "the medicine," "the sacrament," or "this holy herb" by members of the Native American Church. The top portion of the cactus is harvested for use by members of the Native American Church, and when dried it is referred to as a "button" (vol. 13:1006–1007) (LaBarre 1989:82; E.F. Anderson 1996:159, 207). Considerable confusion regarding the identification of Peyote has existed in both scholarly and popular discussions of the plant and its uses. Often referred to as "mescal," peyote has been confused with both the alcoholic drink distilled from the century plant (*Agave angustifolia*), and the hard shell beans (mescal) of the Texas mountain laurel (*Sophora secundiflora*). Early anthropologists, government officials, and missionaries often used the term "mescal buttons" to refer to the dried tops of the peyote cactus (E.F. Anderson 1996:155–163; Stewart 1987:4–8).

The range of peyote in the United States is a thin strip of habitat that extends from the Big Bend region of west Texas along the Rio Grande valley to Brownsville. The density of peyote is much more extensive in northern Mexico, extending from the international border south to San Luis Potosi between Monterrey and Torreón. The primary source of peyote for members of the Native American Church is an area that extends from near Oilton, Texas, south to Rio Grande City on the Mexican border (E.F. Anderson 1996: 168–175; G.R. Morgan 1983:73–79).

The Peyote cactus contains a complex set of alkaloids and related compounds. The most important chemical ingredient, in terms of physical and mental effects, is mescaline. The concentration of mescaline in a dried peyote plant is approximately one percent (E.F. Anderson 1996:145). Mescaline causes a wide range of effects in humans, including a slight increase in blood pressure and heart rate, dilation of the pupils, increased motor action, a rise in blood sugar, flushed skin tone, increased salivation, and sweating. Mescaline is psychoactive in the brain and central nervous system, effecting synaptic function and the action of neurotransmitters, specifically serotonin (E.F. Anderson 1996:120–127).

317

Fig. 1. Peyote cactus (*Lophophora williamsii*) growing in Starr County, Tex. Photograph by Joe Hermosa, 2004.

The effect of peyote consumption among the members of the religion is a complex matter that involves a highly defined environment of reverence and reflection, a psychoactive plant, and each individual's sense of faith and belief. Peyote is viewed by members of the Church as a gift from God that facilitates physical healing, spiritual guidance, and moral instruction.

The anti-Peyote campaigns of the late nineteenth and early twentieth centuries were based on allegations of the deleterious effects of peyote on the Indian people who used it. The issues of addiction, tolerance, and genetic damage with respect to the religious use of peyote by members of the Native American Church have received extensive chemical, medical, and psychological investigation. These studies support the conclusion that such usage does not lead to addiction, mental illness, chromosomal damage, or increased tolerance (E.F. Anderson 1996:128, 185–187).

As the religious use of Peyote spread to communities farther from the natural habitat of the plant, Native Americans began to augment their harvests of green plants by purchasing dried tops of the cactus from Hispanic traders. Called *Peyoteros*, these individuals were responsible for the development of a system that involved harvesting, processing, and distributing peyote to members of the Native American Church. Once processed, the peyote was packed in wooden barrels for wagon transport to Laredo, Texas, where it was shipped to Oklahoma and other regions by rail (G.R. Morgan and O.C. Stewart 1984:273–279).

In the first half of the twentieth century the peyote trade between *Peyoteros* and Native Americans continued much as it had from its beginning. Numerous states passed laws prohibiting the shipment of the plant to Native Americans within their boundaries, including Texas in 1937, but the activities of the *Peyoteros* and their Native American clients largely went unhindered. It was not until 1953, when a well known *Peyotero* was arrested, that the Texas law was enforced. The Native American Church retained a lawyer for his defense and, on the recommendation of the prosecuting attorney, the grand jury failed to act on the warrant. In 1954, peyote was officially exempted from the Texas Narcotic Drug Act. Regulation of the Peyote trade was established in 1969, when Peyote dealers were required to obtain licenses, to keep sales records, and to sell only to individuals with membership credentials from the Native American Church (G.R. Morgan and O.C. Stewart 1984: 290–291).

The natural population of peyote has diminished since the 1950s, largely due to increased demand for the plant among members of the Native American Church and destruction of its habitat in south Texas. Increased regulation of the legal trade in Peyote has prevented the majority of Church members from harvesting peyote for themselves. In the key area of south Texas in which an abundant supply of peyote can be found, the overwhelming majority of the land is in private ownership. Strict laws regarding trespassing and frequent patrols by a number of federal, state, and local law enforcement agencies combine to make unauthorized access something to be avoided. *Peyoteros* and Native Americans found their access to private land restricted in the last quarter of the twentieth century. Increased commerce in sport hunting leases has caused land owners to protect access to their properties and to erect tall chain link fences to inhibit game movement. Competition among *Peyoteros* for access to peyote has led them to lease the harvesting rights to particular tracts of land from the owners at considerable cost (E.F. Anderson 1996:181; G.R. Morgan 1983:83).

While the demand for Peyote has increased since the 1960s, the northern extent of its range in the United States has receded dramatically (G.R. Morgan 1983:83). An estimated 1.1 million plants were sold between September 1972 and August 1973 (G.R. Morgan 1972–1974). In 1993, the State of Texas, which requires *Peyoteros* to report the amount of peyote sold, revealed that 1.9 million plants were harvested and sold through the legal peyote trade (Michael 1994:9A). This upward trend continued until 1997, when a record 2.3 million plants were reported sold (Swan 1996–1998). In the late 1990s legal sales of Peyote to members of the Church began to decline slightly, with *Peyoteros* stating that the available supply could no longer meet demand (E.F. Anderson 1995:2). The spread of Peyote to the Navajo Reservation and its rapid adoption has made the Navajo people the largest consumers in the Peyote trade with estimates suggesting that 80 percent of the Peyote sold is going to the Navajo Nation (G.R. Morgan 1983:85).

An additional, and perhaps more immediate, threat to Peyote is the destruction of its habitat through the conversion of land to commercial pasturage. The use of this region as animal pasturage began in the 1750s and quickly led to overgrazing and an increase in brush vegetation (G.R. Morgan 1983:80). In the 1930s increased use of brush eradication through chopping and dragging temporarily disrupted the natural growth pattern of peyote. Dragging the land as a means of brush eradication has been replaced by the practice of root plowing and sowing of native and non-native grasses. This is a much more destructive practice, with peyote growth continuing only in those areas that evade plowing. Government incentives, in the form of cost sharing, to promote root plowing were halted in the late 1980s when peyote was placed on the endangered species list in the state of Texas (E.F. Anderson 1996:181; G.R. Morgan 1983:83–84).

The future of the peyote plant lies in increased conservation of its habitat, the promotion of harvesting techniques that stimulate its growth, and most importantly, increased cooperation among members of the Church, *Peyoteros*, and land owners. Officials of the Native American Church have explored alternate methods of insuring an adequate supply of peyote, including importation from Mexico and cultivation, with both avenues finding no support from federal and state officials in the United States (*New York Times* 1995:8A). The leading botanist in the field of peyote studies remained optimistic that peyote will continue as a species but considered its future in sufficient quantity to support current demand questionable (E.F. Anderson 1996: 180–181).

## The Development of the Peyote Religion

In its earliest documented use Peyote was employed by Native Americans to cure illnesses, to foresee future events, to combat fatigue, and to lead to spiritual instruction and knowledge (La Barre 1989:25–29; Stewart 1987:24–30). A number of origin stories are perpetuated for the manner in which the powers of Peyote and its associated ceremony were revealed to the members of Native American communities. The Kiowa version (Mooney 1897:330) centers on the grief of a young woman over the supposed death of her brothers when they failed to return from a war expedition. During her seclusion to mourn her loss she was visited by the "Peyote Spirit" and informed that her brothers were in fact alive and that peyote would restore her health and spirit and provide for the safe return of her brothers. She also received instructions on the ceremonial use of Peyote. Upon awaking from her dream she returned to her camp with a supply of peyote plants and shared the instructions she had received regarding the details of the ceremony and the religious use of peyote. During the religious service, visions of her brothers wandering in the desert were received, and a large party was organized to search for the men. After several days of journey they were located and safely returned to their family.

Although a number of stories are recorded for the mythical origin of the Peyote religion, certain consistent themes emerge, including someone lost, usually a woman, who experiences spiritual distress, hunger, and thirst, and finds comfort through Peyote and guidance in its ceremonial use (E.F. Anderson 1996:25–31; Petrullo 1975:34–41). The role of this "Peyote Woman" in the origin of the religion is ven-

erated among Peyotists and symbolized by the woman who brings the water into the tepee at dawn (La Barre 1989:51).

The development of the Peyote religion has received considerable attention from anthropologists (La Barre 1989; Opler 1938; Stewart 1974, 1987; P.M. White 2000), and generalizations regarding its early history and diffusion can be made. The use of Peyote by the Carrizo is well documented in the late seventeenth century. Their ceremonies incorporated several features of the religion that emerged on the southern Plains in the late nineteenth century, including an all-night ceremony, rounds of individual singing and drumming, and a ritually maintained fire (Stewart 1974: 214–219, 1987:47–51).

The Carrizo taught their form of the Peyote religion to the Lipan and Mescalero Apache in the late eighteenth and early nineteenth centuries where the ceremony underwent additional innovation and change, including the use of a tepee as the place of worship, a ceremony that focused on meditation and quiet prayer, and the incorporation of Christian elements and symbols. The Lipan Apache, perhaps as early as the 1860s, are widely regarded as the source of the modern Peyote religion on the reservations of the Oklahoma Territory (McAllester 1949:14–17; Stewart 1987:48, 51, 58–61). The Comanche, Kiowa, and Apache reservation of southwestern Oklahoma quickly became the "Cradle of Peyotism" (Stewart 1987:53), where a ready number of converts adapted the religion to local traditions and circumstances. By 1880, the ceremonial structure, ritual instruments, and core theology of Peyotism became more uniform; and the religion spread to neighboring reservations. The growth of Peyotism was influenced and impacted by a number of factors including the development of a trade system that insured a dependable and affordable supply of Peyote, increased knowledge of English as a common language, new forms of intertribal contact through prisoner of war camps and boarding schools, and increased exposure to Christianity (E.F. Anderson 1996:34–37, 39–42; Slotkin 1956:8–19; Stewart 1987:61–65; Swan 1990:484–494).

While it is important to note that Peyotism spread through innumerable personal contacts and multiple sources in any given tribe, there were some groups and individuals who significantly contributed to the rapid and continued growth of the religion. The Comanche and the Kiowa were primary in proselytizing the religion, introducing it to the Otoe, Southern Cheyenne, Caddo, Southern Arapaho, Pawnee, Wichita, Ponca, and Shawnee by 1890. The Caddo were important for their development of the Big Moon variant of the religion and its introduction among the Delaware, Osage, Quapaw, Oklahoma Seneca-Cayuga, and Oklahoma Band of the Modoc (La Barre 1989:112–122). By 1900, the Peyote religion had spread to the majority of the reservations in Indian Territory (Oklahoma), greatly facilitated by patterns of intertribal visiting and intermarriage. The greatest factor in the early diffusion of Peyotism, and the rationale often given for its acceptance at the individual level, was the role of Peyote in curing illness. By 1915, Peyotism had spread to Indian reservations in Colorado, Iowa, Kansas, Nebraska, Montana, New Mexico, South Dakota, Wisconsin, Wyoming, and Utah (Stewart 1987: 148). In the 1920s and 1930s the Peyote religion continued to gain converts among the Indian people of the Northern Plains, Great Basin, and the Southwest. Important events in this period were the diffusion of the religion into Canada and the adoption of Peyote by the Navajo (Stewart 1987:248, 252, 257, 265, 273, 294).

In each reservation and community not all the members adopted Peyotism, and some were violently opposed to it. Many individuals maintained strong ties to tribal religions and continued their participation in traditional ceremonies. Others became strong supporters and members of Christian denominations and still others participated in several religions simultaneously, including Peyotism. As Peyotism spread to new communities local traditions, practices, and variations were incorporated into the ceremony while its basic structure and ideology remained consistent, proof that the religion was highly flexible and adaptable and thus readily adopted in new settings and situations (Stewart 1987:97).

A number of individuals can be identified who were significant figures in the diffusion of Peyotism. Quanah Parker (vol. 13:1006–1007) may well have been the most influential and effective leader among early Peyotists. The son of a Comanche father and a White mother, Quanah was a Peyote leader of considerable reputation and is credited with introducing the religion among a number of groups. Quanah was one of the first and most prominent intertribal leaders to emerge in the effort to gain legal protection for the use of Peyote as a religious sacrament (La Barre 1989:113; Stewart 1987:79). The second individual of considerable stature among the early missionaries of Peyotism was John Wilson, a Caddo-Delaware with some French ancestry (vol. 14:621). Wilson was responsible for the development of the Big Moon form of Peyotism, with converts among the Caddo, Delaware, Osage, Quapaw, Wichita, Shawnee, Seminole, Oklahoma Seneca-Cayuga, and Oklahoma Band of the Modoc (La Barre 1989:158; Stewart 1987:93). Other individuals, most without any formal recognition, played important roles in the introduction and adoption of the Peyote religion in its diffusion throughout the North American continent.

## The Ritual Practice of the Peyote Religion

The ritual ceremony of the Peyote religion has remained amazingly consistent over both time and space. Although there is room for the incorporation of local customs and practices, the basic structure and content of the service are quite similar throughout North America (Aberle 1982:124; Stewart 1987:209). The ceremonies of the Native American Church, or "meetings" as often referred to by members, can generally be described as conforming to two major types

with minor variations within each group. The standard form is that of the Kiowa and Comanche, referred to as Little Moon, or more commonly by members as the Half Moon or Tepee Way ceremony (La Barre 1989:43–53). Throughout the history of the modern Peyote Religion the majority of Peyotists in the United States and Canada have practiced the Half Moon ceremony. The most significant variant of the standard Half Moon ceremony is the "Big Moon" form of Peyotism as conceived, developed, and proselytized by members of the Caddo tribe. The name of this form of Peyotism is derived from the size and nature of the ceremonial altar or "moon" and involves a number of changes in ritual structure and content (La Barre 1989:151–161; Petrullo 1975:92–101; Swan 1990:170–175).

Typical reasons for holding services of the Native American Church include the desire to cure illness, birthdays, Christian holidays, New Years Day, Veterans Day, entrance and graduation from school or military service, funerals and memorials, marriages, and any other significant events in the lives of the participants. A stated purpose is not required to hold a church service. Many times they are held for the same reasons people worship in any religion: to seek guidance and direction to lead better lives, to give thanks for blessings, and to ask for forgiveness and deliverance. As more Native Americans became involved in the economy of Western society, religious services of the Church were commonly held on Saturday evening to facilitate the work schedules of participants. Meetings typically have sponsors, who ask a Roadman to conduct a service for a specific event or need and bear the financial costs for meals and the sacramental peyote that will be consumed by the worshipers (La Barre 1989:58).

Four individuals serve as officials during the Half Moon Peyote ceremony (fig. 2). The chief official is the Roadman or leader, who is responsible for conducting the service. The authority and credentialing of Roadmen varies among communities, and each is generally free to exercise some latitude in the nuances and details of the ceremony. The Drum Chief and Cedarman assist the Roadman in the conduct of the religious service. The fourth official is the Fireman, who usually sits on the north side of the doorway and is responsible for maintaining the ritual fire through out the ceremony (La Barre 1989:63–66).

Meetings are generally held in a Plains style, canvas tepee that is erected for this specific purpose. The tepee has become strongly associated with the Native American Church and has diffused into areas where it has no prior use as a residential or ceremonial structure (vol. 11:676). Individual homes can also be used as the place of worship, particularly during the winter and in emergency situations. Frame structures are used as the place of worship in several communities including the use of hogans among the Navajo, octagonal church houses among practitioners of Big Moon Peyotism (fig. 2) and rectangular buildings among the HoChunk (Winnebago) of Wisconsin and the Sioux of South Dakota. Meetings are also held in the open, with only

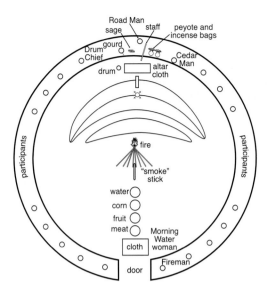

left, after La Barre 1989; right, Preston Morrell, Hominy, Okla.

Fig. 2. Worship spaces. left, Diagram of the ceremonial arrangement for the general Little Moon style of Peyote religious service. right, Congregation of Osage Peyotists in front of the Kipp Family Church, Hominy, Okla., an example of the octagonal teepeelike church houses associated with Big Moon Peyotism. In 2006 the Osage were the only community to practice the Big Moon form of Peyotism. Photograph by Tom Fields, about 1980.

a windbreak to delineate the place of worship (Aberle 1982:173; E.F. Anderson 1996:52, 66; La Barre 1989:61).

The tepee is generally erected the day of the meeting, usually in the afternoon, oriented so that the door faces east. Once the tepee has been set up the ritual altar, or "moon" as referred to by Peyotists, is constructed. The altar is hand formed from clean soil, sand or clay, and ranges in shape from a horseshoe to a crescent moon (vol. 11:674, 13:490). A line is incised along the top of the altar from tip to tip, symbolic of the "the Peyote Road" or the "Path of Life," that each person travels as his knowledge increases through the religious use of Peyote (vol. 10:561). Big Moon Peyote altars are larger in scale and exhibit an elaborated set of symbolic markings and designs. These attributes led to the use of dried pond clay and commercial cement to create permanent altars (La Barre 1989:48–47, 74–77; Swan 1990: 157–166).

The ritual instruments used to conduct the ceremony have remained amazingly consistent throughout the history of Peyotism (vol. 13:1006–1007). The core set of instruments owned by each Roadman includes a "chief peyote," a ritual staff, several fans made from bird feathers, a gourd rattle, a whistle made from the wing bone of an eagle, and the necessary components to assemble a water drum with a deer hide head that is attached to a cast iron kettle through the use of drum bosses and a length of rope. The participants of a religious service gather for an evening meal and then enter the tepee around dark. The Roadman removes his ritual instruments from a carrying case and places them near the altar. A large, dried peyote, referred to as the "chief peyote," is placed on a cross made from sprigs of wild sage (*Artemisia*

spp.) at the center of the crescent altar. This "chief" is the object of great respect and worshipers focus their attention on it during the service. The eagle-bone whistle of the Roadman is propped against the altar, in back of the chief peyote (La Barre 1989:46, 66).

The service begins with a statement of its purpose, the acknowledgment of the sponsors, and the smoking of ceremonial cigarettes of tobacco in a cornhusk wrapper. The Roadman leads a prayer with other members praying silently or aloud. Cedar is burned in the fire, and the Roadman incenses a bunch of sage and a bag of dried peyotes. When the medicine has completed the circuit the Roadman takes his staff, rattle, and gourd, incenses them with cedar, and sings four songs, the first being the prescribed Opening song, with the Drum Chief drumming for him. He then passes the staff to the Drum Chief and drums for him while he sings four songs. The Cedarman then sings four songs and the staff and drum begin a clockwise circuit with each man drumming for the person to his left. In general it is common for only the men to sing, although in some communities women are permitted to participate in this aspect of the ceremony according to local customs (La Barre 1989:47–50).

The ceremony continues in this manner with rounds of singing and prayer until midnight, when water is taken in a ritual manner. This event is marked by the singing of the Midnight Water Song by the Roadman and incorporates the use of cedar incense, a ritual cigarette, prayers, and other preparations that are undertaken prior to the consumption of the water that is brought into the tepee by the Fireman (vol. 13:918). The rounds of individual signing and prayer continue until dawn when the Roadman sings the Daylight

Song. The religious service ends with the morning water ritual and the consumption of a ceremonial breakfast. A woman, often the wife of the Roadman or sponsor, brings the morning water into the tepee according to ritual procedures, and when all have had a drink the morning water woman takes the bucket and exits the tepee. The Roadman then sings the Quitting song and three others. While doing this the woman enters the tepee with a breakfast of corn, fruit, and meat; and the bowls are lined up in order between the fire and the doorway. The ceremonial breakfast is passed clockwise around the circle, starting with the person sitting just south of the doorway. When all have eaten the worshipers leave the tepee in a prescribed order. Following this the participants rest in the tepee and its vicinity, socialize, and tell stories that recount aspects of the prior night's service. The drum may be re-tied and informal "sings" held to practice and learn new songs. A noon meal attended by both the participants and other family and community members concludes the service (La Barre 1989:50–53).

While this sketch has provided the basic structure and events that characterize a religious service of the Native American Church, a number of variants can be found with differences significant enough to merit distinction by Peyotists themselves. The major differences are often denoted by the name of the ceremony or "way," including, Cross Fire Way, Navajo Star-Way, Navajo V-Way, Morning Star Way, and others. These variations often focus on the configuration of the altar, as in the Navajo V-Way in which the crescent-shaped earth altar is replaced with a V-shaped altar made from coals and ashes (E.F. Anderson 1996:68–69). In the Cross Fire and Morning Star Ways the altar is intermediate between the Little Moon and Big Moon forms, with a cross design created by the addition of lines from the Chief Peyote to the east and a perpendicular north-south line (Stewart 1987:339). The religious ceremony has been modified in a number of settings to include local practices such as the incorporation of traditional healing ceremonies, the use of a Plains-style catlinite pipe, various methods of shaping the ashes from the fire, and a prohibition on smoking. In some communities additional Christian elements have been adopted, including the rites of baptism and marriage, the reading of Bible passages, and the confession of sins (Aberle 1982:157–169; J.H. Howard 1956:433–434; La Barre 1989:162–166; Radin 1914:5, 1970:341, 369–370, 373; Steinmetz 1990:94–96; Slotkin 1952:579–580, 592, 599; Wagner 1975:166–168).

## Peyote and Religious Freedom

Members of the Native American Church have been the target of numerous, organized efforts to deprive them of their use of peyote as a religious sacrament. Much of this campaign stems from the classification of peyote as a dangerous drug by the dominant society, associating peyote with recreational or pleasure drugs and the toll that their illicit trade takes on American society. Despite the overwhelming medical, scientific, and cultural information that exists to support the safe use of peyote by members of the Native American Church, Peyotists have endured an almost continuous assault on their basic freedom of free exercise with respect to religious pursuits.

The first recorded efforts to prohibit the use of Peyote by Native Americans came quickly on the heels of European knowledge of its existence. In the sixteenth century Mexican officials of the state and church placed the use of Peyote on the same level as human sacrifice and cannibalism. In 1620 they banned the use of peyote (E.F. Anderson 1996:10; Leonard 1942:326).

The first concerted campaign to prohibit the religious use of peyote in the United States began in the late nineteenth century in Oklahoma Territory when various Indian agents and missionaries attempted to extend the federal laws prohibiting liquor on Indian reservations to include peyote and other "intoxicating" substances. These early efforts failed as the courts upheld the claim that the federal laws related solely to liquor and that individual Indian agents had no authority to enforce their decrees without the backing of appropriate legislation (Stewart 1987:75–76).

Ignoring the rulings of the courts, the commissioner of Indian affairs, through his Indian agents, continued efforts to suppress the Peyote religion into the early twentieth century (Johnson 1909:1). Anti-Peyote legislation was introduced in Congress each year between 1912 and 1916 without success. In 1918, hearings were held on the religious use of peyote before a subcommittee of the House of Representatives. Testimony was taken from Native Americans, missionaries, chemists, physicians, Indian agents, and anthropologists. While the defenders of Peyotism won this battle by a narrow margin, they realized that a new strategy was needed if they hoped to end the continued efforts to pass a federal ban of the religious use of peyote (Stewart 1987: 214–219).

## The Native American Church

Peyotists began to view formal organization as a religious defense as early as 1906 when a number of loosely defined organizations emerged on the local level. Fashioned after fraternal and denominational organizations, they included the Mescal Bean Eaters, the Union Church, the Peyote Society, the American Indian Church Brotherhood Association, and the Kiowa United American Church. The next step in the evolution of organized Peyotists took place in 1914, among the Otoe of Red Rock, Oklahoma. Following the example of the Indian Shaker Church of the Northwest Coast, Jonathan Koshiway filed an application for the incorporation of the First Born Church of Christ in Oklahoma City (La Barre 1989:170; Slotkin 1956:57–58).

The effort to gain a federal anti-Peyote bill in 1918 prompted greater communication and cooperation among Peyotists and brought them into contact with sympathetic Whites, including a number of anthropologists from the Smithsonian Institution. After a series of intertribal conferences, Peyote leaders from the Comanche, Kiowa, Cheyenne, Ponca, Kiowa Apache, and Otoe tribes, with the assistance of James Mooney, a Smithsonian ethnologist, filed an application with the Oklahoma Secretary of State for incorporation. The Native American Church of Oklahoma was granted a charter on October 10, 1918 (Slotkin 1956:58–62).

In an effort to reflect its rapidly expanding, national membership the charter of the Native American Church of Oklahoma was amended in 1934, to permit affiliation with chapters in other states. The formal name of the organization changed in 1944, to the Native American Church of the United States. In 1946, a split developed in the organization over the issue of a further expansion to reflect the growing number of Peyotists in Canada. In 1955, The Native American Church of the United States filed a new charter to incorporate Peyotists in Canada and renamed their organization as the Native American Church of North America (Slotkin 1956:62).

In the 1990s a number of formal organizations of Peyotists, including the Native American Church of Oklahoma, the Native American Church of the United States, the Native American Church of North America, Azee' Bee Nahagha of Diné Nation (former Native American Church of Navajoland) and numerous state and local chapters accounted for over 250,000 registered members (H. Smith and R. Snake 1996:9). In 2006, there were at least 100 separate international, national, state and local organizations of the Native American Church in North America. The heaviest concentrations were in Oklahoma and on the Navajo Nation.

While the Peyote religion remains a largely rural, reservation-based religion, urban chapters located in Denver, Colorado; Chicago, Illinois; Saint Paul, Minnesota; and Memphis, Tennessee provide opportunities for intertribal congregations to participate in the religion while living away from their reservation communities (Stewart 1987: 319; Swan 1998, 2005–2006). The expansion of the Native American Church in the late twentieth century also included the organization of Native peoples from Mexico who resided in the United States and used Peyote in their religious ceremonies. Largely located in Texas, and concentrated in the El Paso and San Antonio areas, these organizations maintain diverse memberships of Indian people from communities in Mexico and the United States (Swan 2005–2006).

While incorporation brought significant improvements in the organization of Peyotists it had little effect on local, state, and federal efforts to prohibit the religious use of Peyote, and efforts to pass federal anti-Peyote legislation continued during the period of 1919 to 1934. In this same period several state legislatures enacted anti-Peyote laws, leading to the arrest and prosecution of many individuals. Additional bills calling for federal anti-Peyote legislation were introduced in Congress in 1939 and 1963, although neither gained passage. The period of 1963 to 1990 was relatively successful for Peyotists, who gained exemptions from the expanded and modified federal drug policies of the era on religious grounds. The arrest and convictions of Native Americans for violation of state laws for the possession of Peyote were all overturned on appeal to higher courts on the grounds of First Amendment protection (Peregoy, Echo-Hawk, and Botsford 1995:11–14). Peyotists also gained protection in certain states through court rulings or legislative actions that exempted them from state drug laws (E.F. Anderson 1996:200; Peregoy, Echo-Hawk, and Botsford 1995:18).

The enactment of the American Indian Religious Freedom Act of 1978 provided a federal law for the protection of American Indians in the practice of traditional religions and their right to access and use of sacred sites and objects. It was assumed that this federal law would extend to members of the Native American Church and thus support previous federal rulings on the religious use of peyote (S.C. Moore and J. Trope 1989:4). This sense of calm was disrupted in 1990, with the ruling of the United States Supreme Court in the case of *Employment Division of Oregon* v. *Smith*. The case in question was one in which two members of the Native American Church were fired from their jobs as drug and alcohol counselors, based on their religious use of peyote. When denied unemployment benefits on the basis that their membership in the Native American Church was a direct violation of the Oregon law prohibiting the use of peyote, one individual sued the State of Oregon. On appeal to the Supreme Court the ruling went in favor of Oregon, arguing that a state could enforce their laws even if in doing so they infringe upon the religious freedom of a minority interest in that state. This effectively established a constitutional precedent for states to prohibit the religious use of peyote. Despite protests from constitutional law experts and religious organizations, the Court refused to reconsider its decision (E.F. Anderson 1996:203–204; H. Smith and R. Snake 1996:134–139).

In 1993, Congress reacted to the *Smith* ruling with passage of the Religious Freedom Restoration Act, to require the government to refrain from limitations on the religious freedom of the citizens of the United States. In a 1994, an amendment to the American Indian Religious Freedom Act passed by Congress included explicitly worded legislation that protects the members of the Native American Church in the religious use of peyote (E.F. Anderson 1996:204–204; Peregoy, Echo-Hawk, and Botsford 1995:19–23; H. Smith and R. Snake 1996:145–153). In 1997 the Supreme Court ruled that the legislation exceeded the authority of Congress and rendered it unconstitutional on the grounds that included the majority opinion that the act favored religion over nonreligion and thus violated the First Amendment of the Constitution. In 1996, Congress reaffirmed the previous exemptions for members of the Native American Church from federal code regarding the possession and use of peyote in bona fide religious services within traditional Indian cultures and communities (U.S. Code 1996:Title 42).

The activities of the formal organizations of the Native American Church remain largely focused on the legal status of the Church and regulation of the legal trade in Peyote by federal and state agencies. The organizations were largely uninvolved in the business of individual chapters and members. Just as in any organized religion, Peyotists exhibit a diverse range of opinions and attitudes with reference to religious and secular matters. In certain communities, including the Teton Sioux and Navajo, the Native American Church has evolved toward administrative authority in the development of membership requirements and the credentialing of Roadmen (Swan 2005–2006).

The legal status of the Native American Church is a complicated situation that involves a wide range of federal and state jurisdictions and legislative bodies. Leaders of the Church work diligently to maintain dialogue and cooperation with religious, government, and secular representatives and organizations to monitor and protect the free pursuit of religion among its members (fig. 3). The Native American Church has survived more than 100 years of criticism, persecution, and legal attack, largely due to the deep conviction that allowed its leaders and members to tenaciously cling to their religious beliefs and practices in the face of adversity and opposition.

Fig. 3. The official emblem for the Native American Church of North America, which is used on Veterans Affairs headstones and grave markers for servicemen and women.

## The Expressive Culture of Peyotism

The Peyote religion has achieved prominence in the development of contemporary Native American expressive culture, particularly in the arenas of visual arts and music. A wide range of traditional and contemporary artistic forms evolved in association with the Peyote religion to produce a distinct genre of Native American art (Archuleta and Strickland 1991:7–8; Cartwright 1950; Fintzelberg 1969:22–23; J. King 1986:90; La Barre 1989:203; Lessard 1984:24; Slotkin 1956:72; Sturtevant 1986:33).

The traditional artistic forms of beadwork, carving, metalwork (vol. 13:1058–1059), and featherwork combine to produce exquisite fans, rattles, drumsticks, jewelry, ritual staffs and other objects used during the services of the Church (vol. 10:560). The material culture of the religion provides both the earliest media for aesthetic expression and important themes and elements that dominate later works of fine art. The emergence of key symbols of religious practice and belief is inherently tied to the physical setting of the ceremony and its associated ritual objects. The accomplishments of individual artists contribute to the collective tradition of Peyote art and to its continued vitality through innovations in design, technique, and composition (Swan 1999: 35–47).

The majority of the traditional and fine art works produced by Peyotists are intended for use by the members of the religion in the local community. Gifts of ritual instruments are common for both initiates and Roadmen on the occasion of their ordination. The objects associated with the religion are not generally found in shops and galleries, and the few objects that are made for sale are often of insufficient quality to meet local standards (Lessard 1984:24; Wiedman 1985:44).

A rich symbolism has evolved in association with these art forms to produce an iconography for the natural, theological, and ritual elements of the Peyote religion. The rendering of ceremonial scenes and religious experiences through the medium of easel painting (fig. 4) (vol. 10:561), drawing, and sculpture comprises an important aspect of the Native American fine arts movement. An examination of the cultural and historical contexts in which these diverse works were created can provide a basis for their interpretation as symbolic representations of the theology and doctrine of the Native American Church (Swan 1999:72–81).

An important aspect of the symbolism associated with the art of the Native American Church is that it is by nature multivocal, evoking a number of alternate interpretations and meanings. Much of the theology and spiritual belief of Peyotism is highly individualized with the conservative ritual structure and content providing a setting for introspection and meditation. A basic moral creed of almost universal nature and a desire for right living, health, and happiness are general characteristics of the common doctrine and purpose of the religion. Peyotism is a religion of diffusion and accommodation that incorporates a wide range of community

Gilcrease Mus., Bartlesville, Okla.: left, 0127.249; right, 0127-2498.

Fig. 4. Peyote experiences depicted in art. left, *Touched by the Spirit* by Kevin Connewerdy, oil on canvas, about 1992. right, *Cactus Men* by Ben Adair Shoemaker, acrylic on board, about 1981.

and individual traditions and practices. It is no surprise that the art forms that developed in connection with the religion elicit a similarly diverse set of interpretations and meanings. In discussing the inspiration and motivation for their works artists often speak of the complex set of factors that articulate between individual creativity and collective tradition, their deep conviction as representatives of the Church and the role that their works assume as ritual instruments and sources of spiritual inspiration. A sense of responsibility and commitment is evident in their reflections on their artwork and its relationship to the Native American Church (Swan 1999:93–95, 99–100).

The Peyote religion has inspired the development of a distinct genre of Native American music, commonly referred to as "Peyote songs" (vol. 10:612, vol. 13:1008). The development of a Peyote musical tradition shares historical features with other ceremonial and ritual aspects of the religion with its style and technical qualities reflecting aspects of indigenous music from the Southwest and influences from the Southern Plains. The musical content of Peyote ceremonies may also have been influenced by other intertribal religious movements of the nineteenth century, including the Ghost Dance. Peyote songs exhibit great variability and range with respect to their melodic structure, additional evidence of the ability of the religious ceremony to incorporate local and individual innovations. In general, Peyote songs are fast paced, driven by the rapid beat of the water drum (fig. 5) and gourd rattle, exhibit descending melodies, and consist of four refrains. Early examples of Peyote songs among the Comanche, Apache, and Kiowa communities contain lyrical passages that refer to the approaching dawn, birds, and the sacrament Peyote (McAllester 1949:29–31, 82–83, 85–88).

As the Peyote religion diffused to other communities the original words in songs were often submerged and replaced with meaningless vocables (Nettl 1953:161–164). In other instances words from local native languages were inserted into songs, and there are numerous examples of Peyote songs that incorporate English language phrases. Peyote music was influenced in both melody and lyrical content by Christian hymns and the Bible (Densmore 1938:175–177, 1941:79–82; La Barre 1989:82–84). Given that the ritual service is largely comprised of singing, song acquisition and composition have been central to the Peyote religion since its inception. Members of the Native American Church

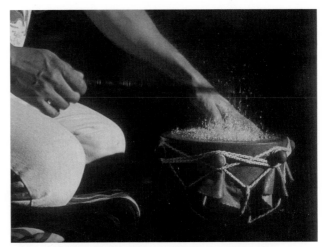

Fig. 5. *The Little Drum Calls*, a visualization of the fast pace of Peyote songs driven by the water drum. Silver gelatin print copyright by Tom Fields, 1996.

expend great time and energy to acquire and refine their skills at drumming, movement of the gourd rattle, and song performance.

Members of the Native American Church have accessed a wide range of technologies to document and perpetuate the musical traditions of their religion, including phonograph, wire, and tape recordings. The availability of commercial recordings of Native American Church music in the 1960s and 1970s elevated Peyote music to new levels of public access and interest. Digital recording technology contributed to the quantity and diversity of commercial and amateur recordings of Peyote music in the late twentieth and early twenty-first centuries.

## Conclusion

In contrast to other nativistic religious movements in the nineteenth century, the divine gift of Peyote to Native Americans provided a mythological charter that was inherently intertribal and anonymous in nature. The basic theology and doctrine of Peyotism provided an essentialist, philosophical foundation upon which Indian people could build meaningful lives in a time of economic and social upheaval. The most often articulated tenets of the Church reflect its largely ecumenical and generalized propensities, comprised of "Faith, Hope, Love, and Charity."

Academic research on the Peyote religion has focused on its ceremony and history and often failed to acknowledge the social dimensions of the religion. Peyotists engage in a range of meaningful activities and interactions beyond the ceremonial practice of their religion. Informal "Sings" are a common event among Peyotists to practice and learn Peyote songs and hone their skills to play the water drum accompaniment. The acquisition of the techniques and skills necessary to produce ritual instruments is an important aspect in the social life of Peyotists, who teach and learn from one another and spend time discussing the aesthetic and functional aspects of their works. Peyotists gather for picnics, birthday parties, and other recreational pursuits.

Peyotists invest time and effort traveling to attend religious services in diverse communities and settings, contributing to the longstanding desire to establish and maintain a broad network of Church members. In the twenty-first century Peyotists continued to travel to the Peyote Gardens in South Texas, to visit the natural habitat of the medicine, to conduct religious services, and to attend annual meetings of various Native American Church organizations.

In the early twenty-first century the Native American Church continued to be a vital component in the lives of hundreds of thousands of indigenous people in North America, providing a source of individual spiritual enrichment, a focus for community life, and the emergence of a hemispheric identity for indigenous people. The Peyote religion is one of the most successful modern religious movements among the indigenous people of North America. The growth and florescence of the Peyote religion provides testament to the voracity of Native American cultural traditions and their propensity for survival and perpetuation through adaptation and change. Despite continuous efforts to ban and inhibit the religious use of Peyote, the members of the Native American Church have gained access to the medicine and to perpetuate its ceremonial use.

# Powwows

THOMAS W. KAVANAGH

Powwow is a major institution of community and inter-community interaction among twenty-first-century Native Americans. In contemporary usage, a powwow is a "secular event featuring group singing and social dancing by men, women, and children. The elements of the powwow originate from both tribal functions and non-Indian influences" (Powers 1970:271), the "tribal functions" being the Hethuska complex (vol. 13:1012) of the Dhegiha Siouans of the central Plains—Omaha, Ponca, Osage, Kansa, and Quapaw. Although it does not have overt religious functions, elements of the powwow—particularly the drum and eagle feathers—are often considered sacred, and there are often prayers and blessings, in English or a native language (Kracht 1994). There are also a variety of "honorings"—of veterans, of elders, of knowledge, of symbols of identity—that give the event an aura beyond the merely secular.

Although powwows are widespread, there is no standardization of terminology with which to discuss them; sometimes the same term is used for different aspects, and different terms may refer to the same aspect. For example, the term "special" can refer to both tribal-specific but nonpowwow dances (such as the Navajo Basket Dance) done in a powwow context, as well as to the honoring giveaways done in the course of a powwow (vol. 13:429).

Unlike many traditional Native American events that are sponsored by specific portions of their communities for specific ritual purposes, powwows may be sponsored by a variety of groups for a variety of purposes. Participation is usually open to any individual or family wishing to take part. In size and number of participants, powwows range from small community events involving only a few dozen individuals to large intertribal events with thousands of participants. Although the number of powwows held annually is impossible to determine with any precision, during the course of a normal year several hundred such events may be held in the United States and Canada. With increasing intertribal marriages and with the increasing urbanization of native populations, powwows have emerged as a critical social institution. Participation in powwows serves to reinforce and expand the social obligations between families and individuals, while at the same time serving as an arena in which these families and individuals publicly acknowledge and demonstrate their social identity as either a member of a native community or as an "Indian" in general (vol. 14:331). Col-lectively powwow has created informal social networks linking native families and individuals from throughout the United States and Canada.

## Pan-Indianism and Intertribalism

In the late 1940s, when anthropologists began to focus on powwow, particularly in Oklahoma, their discussions were often linked to the hazy concept of "pan-Indianism" (J.H. Howard 1955). This offspring of the acculturation studies of the 1920s and 1930s (Powers 1990:87) proposed that the propinquity of disparate tribes thrown together in Oklahoma (Indian Territory) was inevitably leading to a blending of cultures, with pan-Indianism as "an attempt to create a new ethnic group . . . the American Indian" (Thomas 1968:134), as a final stage in the assimilation of Indians to the dominant culture (J.H. Howard 1955:220).

Those early pan-Indianist analysis of powwow confused several issues. Pan-Indianism was originally defined as the "process by which socio-cultural entities such as the Seneca, Delaware, Yuchi, Ponca, and Comanche are losing their tribal distinctiveness and in its place developing a non-tribal 'Indian-culture'" (J.H. Howard 1955:215). This assumed that "tribes" and tribal cultures were somehow "distinct" and that in native North America cultural diffusion was somehow unique to the powwow. The argument that there were processual differences between the formal transfer of ceremonies through gift and purchase and the informal diffusion of "pan-Indian" powwow traits (J.H. Howard 1983) failed to address the problem that the specific listing of pan-Indian "entities" conflated the nineteenth- and early twentieth-century "formal" diffusions of the Hethuska complex with later "informal" pan-Indian powwow diffusions. Of those groups on the powwow list, the Poncas were among the originators of the Hethuska, while the Comanches received it early in the twentieth century. Moreover, Howard's (1955:216) list included groups, such as Yuchi, who never were powwowers and whose own traditions were still maintained; indeed, the Stomp Dance traditions of eastern Oklahoma were being maintained with an equal strength to the powwow in western Oklahoma (Bailey and Ashworth 1990:2; J.B. Jackson

2005). At the same time, scholars noted that even in multi-tribal urban settings, "tribal identity [is] inseparable from Indian identity" (Lurie 1970:309). This was due, in part, to the fact that "tribe"—not "Indian"—is the point of articulation with the federal and state governments.

Beginning in the 1980s, analyses of the powwow moved beyond the acculturationalist approaches to an approach that views powwows as identity performances, serving as an arena in which individuals and families publicly acknowledge and demonstrate their social identity as a member of a native community (Kavanagh 1980, 1982; Browner 2002; Goertzen 2001). In addition, network analyses of powwows have shown that participation in powwows serves to reinforce and expand social obligations (Kavanagh 1982; Ashworth 1986). Collectively, powwows have created social networks linking Native and non-Native individuals, families, and communities throughout the United States and Canada. Thus, powwow is not so much "pan-Indian" as "intertribal" (fig. 1).

Moreover, since powwows are generalized "Indian" events, anything identified as "Indian" may be incorporated. For instance, in the East, Iroquois have combined their traditional Smoke Dance choreography and music into the powwow format. New cultural elements derived from different cultural traditions may be adapted and incorporated into powwow. New songs are being made, new dance forms and clothing styles are evolving, and new oral traditions are being created. As a result of the dynamic nature of the powwow, there is a great deal of variability in cultural elements that may be drawn upon for inclusion in a particular powwow. It is in the cultural traditions associated with powwow that contemporary Native American culture fully demonstrates that it is not inert, let alone dead or dormant.

At the same time, despite centuries of acculturative pressures, many tribes still hold "traditional" secular and religious events. These events differ from powwows in several critical ways. Traditional activities are under the control of formal groups of individuals, usually religious leaders, who have full authority over their performance. Often these activities can only be performed at certain times of the year and at specific locations. Finally, these "traditional" activities are usually closed events, with only specific community members allowed to participate.

However, the distinction between a "traditional" event and a "powwow" is not always readily apparent. For instance, the powwow Straight Dance choreography and clothing evolved from the Hethuska societies of eastern Oklahoma. However, the three Osage Inloshka society events are not powwows, and conversely, powwow Straight Dancers might not be members of the societies. Thus, although the Straight Dance choreography may appear the same at a powwow event and at an Osage Inloshka Society event, there are significant cultural differences between the two (Duncan 1997:22). Similarly, although Gourd Dances are often held during powwows, the Comanche Little Pony Society annual event is not a powwow. There may also be mixed events, such as Kiowa Ohoma society events, in which "afternoons are often given over to dances conducted according to the society's protocols and rules. Evenings are often given over to social powwow dancing" (Ellis 2003:35). But the same songs may be used in both phases. Thus it is primarily the context, not the songs, dances, or clothing that defines a particular event as a powwow as opposed to a "traditional" ceremony. There is one ritual element that distinguishes a Hethuska event from a powwow: dancing the "tail."

## History

Three cultural-historical processes characterize the history of powwow: diffusion, secularization, and elaboration, often occurring simultaneously. The basic elements of powwow probably derive from the western branches of the late Mississippian cultural tradition, A.D. 1200–1700, perhaps with elements as early as Hopewellian times (Bailey 1995; Duncan 1997). Since that was a multiethnic, multilinguistic tradition, it is not useful to assign a specific tribal origin for the ancestral elements. However, that tradition did include ancestors of the Osage, Omaha, Ponca, Kansa, Quapaw, and possibly the Iowa, Otoe, and Missouria. Some of this commonality is shown by the shared historic name of the complex: Inloshka (Osage) and Hethuska (Omaha-Ponca), sometimes written Heloshka. At the same time that origins of the powwow are sought in the Hethuska or War ceremonial, that ceremonial was itself paired with the Wawathan Peace ceremony, also known as the Pipe or Calumet Dance, which diffused widely and was a mode of establishing intertribal peace. Because the Omahas were of primary importance in the diffusion, the Omaha name, Hethuska, will be used here as generic for the complex.

The role of Caddoans in the historical trajectory is problematic. A watercolor painting of 1821 or 1822 entitled *Danse Militaire* shows a group of bustled dancers, possibly including the Pawnee chief Petalasharo the Elder as well as Omahas and Otoes, performing for President James Monroe in Washington (Little 1957:152–153). There is little evi-

Thomas W. Kavanagh, Netcong, N.J.

Fig. 1. Posters announcing powwows in different parts of the country, varying in style and detail. top left, the 26th Annual Powwow in Costa Mesa, Calif., 1994; top right, the Tunica-Biloxi Powwow in Marksville, La., 1997. bottom, Three events in Okla.: bottom left, the 50th Annual Pawnee Indian Homecoming in Pawnee, 1996. bottom top right, the Creek Nation Annual Powwow in Okmulgee, 1994; bottom lower right, 19th annual Powwow of Champions in Tulsa, 1996.

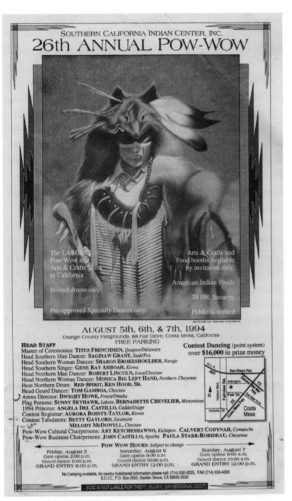

## SOUTHERN CALIFORNIA INDIAN CENTER, INC.
## 26th ANNUAL POW-WOW

The LARGEST Pow Wow and Arts & Crafts Show in California

Invited drums only

Pre-approved Specialty Dances only

Arts & Crafts and Food booths available by invitation only.

American Indian Foods

24 HR. Security

Public is invited

AUGUST 5th, 6th, & 7th, 1994
Orange County Fairgrounds, 88 Fair Drive, Costa Mesa, California
FREE PARKING

**HEAD STAFF**
Master of Ceremonies: TITUS FRENCHMEN, Quapaw/Delaware
Head Southern Man Dancer: SAGINAW GRANT, Sauk/Fox
Head Southern Woman Dancer: SHARON BROKESHOULDER, Navajo
Head Northern Singer: GENE RAY AHBOAH, Kiowa
Head Northern Man Dancer: ROBERT LINCOLN, Iowa/Choctaw
Head Northern Woman Dancer: MONICA BIG LEFT HAND, Northern Cheyenne
Host Northern Drum: RED SPIRIT, KEN HOOD, SR.
Head Gourd Dancer: TOM GAMBOA, Choctaw
Arena Director: DWIGHT HOWE, Ponca/Omaha
Flag Persons: SUNNY SKYHAWK, Lakota, BERNADETTE CHEVELIER, Menominee
1994 Princess: ANGELA DEL CASTILLO, Caddo/Osage
Contest Registrar: AURORA BOINTY-TAYLOR, Kiowa
Contest Tabulators: BETTY GAYLORD, Sycamore
MELODY McDOWELL, Choctaw
Pow-Wow Cultural Chairpersons: ART KETCHESHAWNO, Kickapoo, CALVERT CODYNAH, Comanche
Pow-Wow Business Chairpersons: JOHN CASTILLO, Apache, PAULA STARR-ROBIDEAU, Cheyenne

**Contest Dancing** (point system)
over $16,000 in prize money

**POW WOW HOURS:** Subject to change

| Friday, August 5 | Saturday, August 6 | Sunday, August 7 |
|---|---|---|
| Gate opens 2:00 p.m. | Gate opens 9:00 a.m. | Gate opens 9:00 a.m. |
| Gourd dance 6:00 p.m. | Gourd dance 10:00 a.m. | Gourd dance 10:00 a.m. |
| GRAND ENTRY 8:00 p.m. | GRAND ENTRY 12:00 p.m. | GRAND ENTRY 12:00 p.m. |

No Camping available, for nearby hotel/motel information please call: (714) 530-0225, FAX (714) 636-4226
S.C.I.C, P.O. Box 2550, Garden Grove, CA 92642-2550

SCIC IS NOT LIABLE FOR THEFT, INJURY, OR PERSONAL COST.

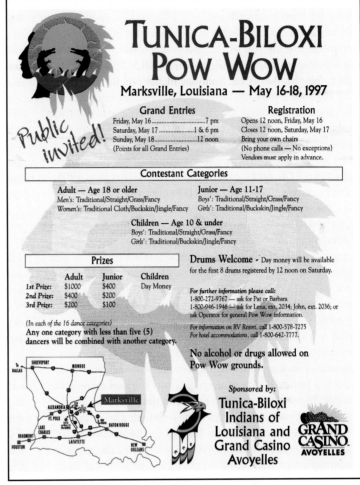

# TUNICA-BILOXI POW WOW
## Marksville, Louisiana — May 16-18, 1997

**Public invited!**

### Grand Entries
Friday, May 16 .................................. 7 pm
Saturday, May 17 ...................... 1 & 6 pm
Sunday, May 18 .......................... 12 noon
(Points for all Grand Entries)

### Registration
Opens 12 noon, Friday, May 16
Closes 12 noon, Saturday, May 17
Bring your own chairs
(No phone calls — No exceptions)
Vendors must apply in advance.

### Contestant Categories

**Adult — Age 18 or older**
Men's: Traditional/Straight/Grass/Fancy
Women's: Traditional Cloth/Buckskin/Jingle/Fancy

**Junior — Age 11-17**
Boys': Traditional/Straight/Grass/Fancy
Girls': Traditional/Buckskin/Jingle/Fancy

**Children — Age 10 & under**
Boys': Traditional/Straight/Grass/Fancy
Girls': Traditional/Buckskin/Jingle/Fancy

### Prizes

| | Adult | Junior | Children |
|---|---|---|---|
| 1st Prize: | $1000 | $400 | Day Money |
| 2nd Prize: | $400 | $200 | |
| 3rd Prize: | $200 | $100 | |

(In each of the 16 dance categories)
Any one category with less than five (5) dancers will be combined with another category.

**Drums Welcome** - Day money will be available for the first 8 drums registered by 12 noon on Saturday.

For further information please call:
1-800-272-9767 — ask for Pat or Barbara
1-800-946-1946 — ask for Lena, ext. 2034; John, ext. 2036; or ask Operator for general Pow Wow information.

For information on RV Resort, call 1-800-578-7275
For hotel accommodations, call 1-800-642-7777.

No alcohol or drugs allowed on Pow Wow grounds.

**Sponsored by:**
Tunica-Biloxi Indians of Louisiana and Grand Casino Avoyelles
GRAND CASINO AVOYELLES

**50th Annual**     **July 4, 5, 6 & 7, 1996**

# PAWNEE INDIAN HOMECOMING
Sponsored by PAWNEE INDIAN VETERANS
Memorial Field • Pawnee, Oklahoma

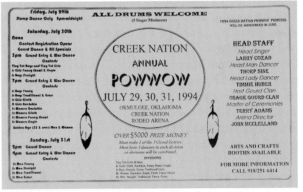

**Friday, July 29th**
Stomp Dance Only 8pm-midnight

**Saturday, July 30th**
Noon Contest Registration Opens
Gourd Dance & All Specials
3pm Grand Entry & War Dance Contest
7pm Grand Entry & War Dance Contest

**Sunday, July 31st**
2pm Gourd Dance
4pm Grand Entry & War Dance Contest

**ALL DRUMS WELCOME** (5 Singer Minimum)

## CREEK NATION ANNUAL POWWOW
JULY 29, 30, 31, 1994
OKMULGEE, OKLAHOMA
CREEK NATION RODEO ARENA

OVER $5000 PRIZE MONEY
Must make 2 of the 3 Grand Entries.
Must have 5 dancers in each division or divisions will be combined.

1994 CREEK NATION POWWOW PRINCESS WILL BE ANNOUNCED IN JUNE

**HEAD STAFF**
Head Singer LARRY COZAD
Head Man Dancer THORP SINE
Head Lady Dancer TIMMIE HUBER
Host Gourd Clan OSAGE GOURD CLAN
Master of Ceremonies TERRY ADAMS
Arena Director JOHN McCLELLAND

ARTS AND CRAFTS BOOTHS AVAILABLE

FOR MORE INFORMATION CALL 918/251-6414

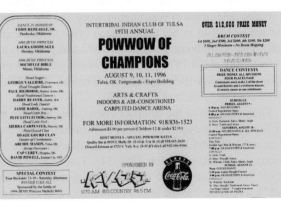

INTERTRIBAL INDIAN CLUB OF TULSA
19TH ANNUAL

# POWWOW OF CHAMPIONS
AUGUST 9, 10, 11, 1996
Tulsa, OK Fairgrounds - Expo Building

ARTS & CRAFTS
INDOORS & AIR-CONDITIONED
CARPETED DANCE ARENA

FOR MORE INFORMATION 918/836-1523
Admission $3.00 per person (Children 12 & under $2.00)

OVER $12,000 PRIZE MONEY

Sponsored by Coca-Cola
KVOO 1170 AM BIG COUNTRY 98.5 FM

dence that Wichita or Arikara had elements of the complex before the nineteenth century.

The shared basic elements of material culture of the Hethuska include the use of the hair roach (vol. 13:455) and the bustle or crow-belt (vol. 13:1014–1015, bottom right). While the roach was used independently of the complex (J.H. Howard 1960), the bustle apparently does not occur in any other cultural context. The original bustle was of crow feathers and was said to represent the crows flocking over a battlefield (Fletcher 1892:138). The braid of sweetgrass worn in the crow-belt was either an "emblem of abundance and charity" (de Smet, in Crittenden and Richardson 1905, 3:1059), representative of scalps (Fletcher 1892:138), or "of the lives of men" not only of the enemy but of the people being protected (La Flesche 1939:75).

The common social structural elements of the sodality complex are sets of officers, including but not limited to the leader, a small number (2–8) of bustle wearers who must have earned specified war honors, a whip man, a pipe keeper, and a drum keeper (La Flesche 1939; Wissler 1916:862). Ritual elements of the event included the acting out of war deeds (hence the occasional name "war dance"), scouting of a kettle of food (sometimes a dog stew), counting coup on it, and retrieving meat either with the bare hands or with a pointed stick or a spoon (thus the nickname Hot Dance). This "trick" was also related to the Teton Heyoka or "contraries" (vol. 13:833), a term linguistically linked to Hethuska. Another common feature is the giveaway, of prestige accrued through generosity. However, the specific meanings associated with specific elements varied from group to group and through time.

The Hethuska ritual passed to many other tribes by gift, actively sought, as well as "sold." Omaha oral tradition states that after a period of war with the Arikara, they made peace through the Wawathan ceremony and they gave the Hethuska to the Arikara (Duncan 1997:33). When the Teton received the complex dance is unclear; Catlin (1844:pl. 103) painted hints of dance bustles at a village on the Teton River about 1833. An unnamed Teton winter count gives 1860 as the time of adoption. The Yankton may have received it in the 1830s during their brief alliance with the Ponca (Duncan 1997:73); certainly by 1867 it was the "principal" dance among them (de Smet, in Crittenden and Richardson 1905, 3:1058–1059). That same year, Long Foot, a member of a Yankton delegation to Washington, wore a bustle, but with a fur hat or turban rather than a roach (vol. 13:1014, center left). The Assiniboine got it about 1872 and passed it to the Gros Ventre about 1875 (Flannery 1947:41); Santees passed it to the Mandan-Hidatsa that year (Duncan 1997:73). The Northern Cheyenne had it by 1877.

The recipients of the complex often called it by the name of the giving group. Thus the Teton initially called their dance the Omaha Dance while the Chippewa called it the Sioux dance (Rynkiewich 1980:34). Tetons also called it $p^{h}ež\acute{i}$ $ip^{h}\acute{i}yaka$ $ogn\acute{a}$ $wa\breve{o}^{h}\acute{i}pi$ ('the dance with grass in the belt'), a reference to the braids of sweetgrass in the bustle.

At that same time, the 1880s, various entrepreneurs—both national, such as Buffalo Bill, and local, including Indians such as Quanah Parker (Comanche) and Henry Spybuck (Shawnee)—were hiring Indians to dance for paying non-Indian audiences. As early as 1883, Joe Miller of the 101 Ranch in Oklahoma took more than 100 Poncas to the Alabama State Fair for a dance exhibition (Collins and England 1937:136). It has been estimated that between 1880 and 1930 "thousands of Indians joined dozens of shows" (Ellis 2003: 79). One result of this employment was that dance styles diffused even faster and farther. It has also been suggested that the contest dances of contemporary powwows evolved from the auditions required of participants in the shows.

Meanwhile, the complex diffused to the Great Lakes region as both the War Dance or Sioux Dance, and the Dream Dance and Drum Dance, probably in the 1860s or early 1870s (Rynkiewich 1980:39). This Drum Dance was accompanied by a mythological sanction attributing the dance, and particularly the drum, to the vision of a young girl. It was proselytized, with groups passing drums, songs, and other cultural and material presents to other groups (Vennum 1982; Ellis 2003:46, citing G. Young 1981).

The dates and routes of the diffusion of the Hethuska complex into western Oklahoma are not clear. The Kiowa call their version Ohoma, but it was not a direct introduction from the Omaha. According to some accounts it was received from the Southern Cheyenne about 1880 (Gamble 1952:97) or 1883 (Kracht 1994:330), or from the Northern Cheyenne in "the 1880s" (Boyd 1981:65). A watercolor by the Kiowa artist Etahdleuh, about 1875–1878, while a prisoner at Fort Marion, Florida, is titled *Omaha dance* (Pratt 1980); however, that caption is typewritten and it is not known when or by whom it was added.

In the summer of 1891, Grant Left Hand returned to the Southern Arapaho from Carlisle Indian School and organized a Crow Dance held in conjunction with the incipient Ghost Dance (Mooney 1898:901); it is not known from whom he learned it. Comanches probably did not receive the Hethuska as a formal sodality ritual before the end of the reservation in 1906, although they probably did know of its counterpart, the "pipe dance" (Attocknie 1964; Kavanagh 2007). It is not clear what choreography Quanah Parker's dance troupe used; photographs show his dancers wearing contemporary "Indian clothes" but without bustle. A group of Poncas visited the Comanches in 1919 and give them a version (Duncan 1997:85). By the late 1920s, some Comanches had learned the choreography such that in 1931, Joe Attocknie won the title of "Champion Indian Dancer of the World" at the Craterville Park Indian Fair, Oklahoma (Ellis 2003:117). The contemporary Comanche War Dance Society received another version of the ritual from Poncas in the 1960s. In many of these diffusions, the Hethuska complex was integrated into existing ceremonial forms. For instance, it was taken as the ritual form of the Gros Ventre Wolf society (Kroeber 1908:235–239; Flannery 1947:42; Fowler 1987:57).

The spread of the Hethuska complex beyond the Plains–Great Lakes area is less well known and less well documented. Many of the Pueblos of New Mexico and Arizona have long had "Comanche" dances, but these were integrations of the image of Comanches into their own choreographic and symbolic forms, not diffusions of the Hethuska sodality or choreography. Although many contemporary Pueblo individuals participate in powwows, few Pueblo communities themselves sponsor powwows; notable exceptions are Jemez, San Felipe, Zuni, and the Hopi Intertribal Powwow Association at Shongopavi village on Second Mesa, Arizona. The role of Taos Pueblo is problematic. Taos had long been an entrepôt for Plains Indians into New Mexico, and elements of Plains culture such as clothing (vol. 9:258) were integrated into Taos culture. But exactly when Taoseños began to utilize Plains style choreography is unclear, though perhaps it was as early as 1895 (D.N. Brown 1961:35). The likely origin of the Hoop Dance is at Taos.

As early as 1913, Indian peoples in the Plateau—Coeur d'Alene, Flathead, Nez Perce, Umatilla—were using Plains-inspired dance clothes at the First National Indian Congress, Spokane Interstate Fair (Kavanagh 1995). They continue to do so (vol. 12:218, 432).

With the cessation of Indian-White hostilities, participation in the complex lost immediate association with participation in war. According to McClintock ([1898] 1937), "anyone who had a suitable outfit could take part" in the Blackfeet Hairparters society (P.E. Goddard 1914). The ritual parts of the ceremony–the actual feast and its accompanying rituals—were dropped, while the choreographic motions of scouting the kettle were retained. Other innovations were added from the protocol of the Wild West shows, such as the Grand Entry.

In the 1870s the Omaha, Ponca, Osage, Kansa, and Pawnee were relocated from Kansas and Nebraska to Oklahoma. This lead to the development of two general areas of powwow development, the "Southern" area—Oklahoma—and the Northern area—the Dakotas, Montana, Wyoming, and the prairie provinces of Canada. While there are commonalities, there are also cultural alternatives and regional differences in choreography, song styles, and social traditions. Since World War II, there has been renewed cultural diffusion between those areas.

## Types of Powwows

Within the Plains and Great Lakes regions of powwow development, a continuum of powwows can be recognized. Corrigan (1970) distinguished three types of powwows on the Canadian Plains; Kavanagh (1980) applied this typology to Oklahoma. Bailey and Ashworth (1990) expanded this to five types and also suggested that powwows could be typed by sponsorship: tribal, intertribal, and institutional clubs. Albers and Medicine (2005:28) recognized the extremes of the continuum as "in-group" and "pan-Indian."

*Local Events*

Local events are limited to "the winter when travel is difficult" (Corrigan 1970:254). That may have been true of Canadian powwows in the 1960s, but these are year-round events in Oklahoma. There are several variations of local events: "honorings," the public acknowledgment of a rite of passage or other special occasion such as graduation from high school, college, or graduate school (Schneider 1981; Kavanagh 1979–2007); memorial and holiday, such as Christmas (Albers and Medicine 2005); changes of residence ("farewell" and "return") (Albers and Medicine 2005:29); and "benefit or donation" powwows, to raise money for an annual summer powwow. Most of these are simple one-day dance events with no contests. These may be what Gamble (1952) called "sings" or "singings." An Oklahoma variant is the "descendant powwow." These are annual one-day events sponsored by the descendants of some notable ancestor, "to honor our deceased grandfather for all the good things he's left us. Besides a good name, a good family, material things, and the talents that are found in this family" (Kavanagh 1980:100).

In some Plains communities, for example, Northern Arapahoe, this type of local powwow does not exist. There are only two powwows each summer, both tribally sponsored, and family (honorings" are done in other formats (vol. 13:856).

*Annual Summer Powwow of Several Days, Intertribal or Interband*

The summer powwows (fig. 2) are related to various historic forms of intertribal "visitations" (Riggs 1893:225; Mooney 1898:351, 379; Blaine 1982) as well as to the summer ceremonials such as the Sun Dance. The oldest of these seems to be the Ponca powwow, begun as a secular version of their Hethuska. Many reservation communities have official powwow committees that organize the annuals. Tribal clubs may also sponsor annual dances, such as the various Homecoming Committees. Pawnee Homecoming (fig. 1) was organized in 1946 by World War I veterans to honor the returning World War II veterans (vol. 13:542); Comanche Homecoming was organized in the early 1950s to honor returning Korean War veterans. The largest of these annuals is the Crow Fair, begun in 1906 (vol. 13:710–711).

*Public Demonstration of Indian Dancing to a Largely non-Indian Paying Audience*

The commercial public shows are derived from the Wild West shows of the nineteenth century. Variations on these included the dance troupes organized by individual Indian entrepreneurs such as Quanah Parker and Henry Spybuck.

A number of annual commercial events began in the 1920s: the Gallup, New Mexico, "Ceremonial" (1921–present); the Craterville Park, Oklahoma, Indian Fair (1924–1933), and the Anadarko, Oklahoma, Indian Exposition, about 1930–present (Ellis 2003:135).

AP Images.

Fig. 2. Powwows, an integral part of tribal life. top left, Hundreds of Indian dancers assembling at the Greyhound Park and Events Center for the Coeur D'Alene Tribes Julyamsh Powwow, held annually in July. Photograph by Jason Hunt, Post Falls, Idaho, 2002. top right, Chris Bussey (Grand Traverse band of Ottawa and Chippewa) performing his dance at the reservation in Peshawbestown, Mich., in 2000. Photograph by John Flesher. bottom left, Powwow in Charles City County, Va., in May 2002, the first time that 6 state-recognized tribes convened in 400 years. Participants are gathered around the drum for a "warm up" sing. Photograph by Cindy Blanchard. bottom right, Zade Morsette, age 13 months, dancing with his father at the United Tribes International Powwow in Bismarck, N. Dak., 1n 1999. Photograph by Will Kincaid.

In the 1980s and 1990s, these events were transformed into megapowwows, events with thousands of participant dancers and singers, tens of thousands of paying spectators, and $1,000 or more in juried prize money for outstanding dancers and singers. These include the Gathering of Nations in Albuquerque, the Denver Powwow, Red Earth in Oklahoma City, and Schemitzun Powwow hosted by the Mashantucket Pequots of Connecticut.

A primary point of distinction of the public shows (besides the large prizes awarded in the mega-powwows), is that admission is charged for all spectators. In the local events and summer powwows, admission is free (contestants pay an entry fee). A variation on the public powwows are what Bailey and Ashworth (1990) call institutional clubs: in urban centers, as well as universities with large Indian populations, admission-based powwows are sponsored by the local Indian clubs, with the proceeds going to fund special charitable projects.

## Powwow Statuses and Roles

Despite the differences in size and overt function, there are five statuses in any powwow, derived from the original officers of the Hethuska societies: sponsor, principal, singer, dancer, and spectator.

### Sponsors

The sponsor, also called "the committee," is the group or individuals who plan the event. The group may be a extended family planning an honoring event or it may be a formally organized powwow committee. The sponsors plan the event, provide the facilities and rations for participants, and select the head staff or principals.

### Head Staff or Principals

The principals are an announcer or master of ceremonies, a head man dancer and a head lady dancer, and an arena director. Since the 1970s, the head dancer positions have been expanded to sometimes include a head Straight dancer, a head Fancy dancer, and a head Gourd dancer. Some of the larger powwows have a princess (vol. 13:562, 14:767), a young lady chosen to represent the sponsors at other powwows.

Inasmuch as the principals are often chosen from a tribal group other than that of the sponsors, powwows automatically set up intertribal reciprocity networks. These are the basis for the "powwow circuit" or "powwow trail," the rotation of personnel from one event to another. On the Northern Plains, where tribal committees might sponsor only one event a year, dancers and singers from that community must travel to other communities in order to participate. Since the 1950s, summer and public powwows have increased their prizes. With the establishment of the megapowwows, some champion dancers have been able to earn significant income on the circuit.

The announcer, in conjunction with the sponsors and the arena director, keeps the whole affair running smoothly by alternative dances so that "no one gets tired . . . so we keep their attention" (Kavanagh 1980). The announcer is sometimes called upon to be the "talker" at honoring specials.

The arena director manages the dance ground. At powwows with contest dances, a group of judges would be appointed by the sponsors.

### Singers

The term "drum" is used to refer not only to the musical instrument, since the 1880s often a commercial marching band bass drum, but also to the people who sit around it to sing and drum (vol. 13:859). One of the Hethuska society statuses was that of "drum keeper." In Oklahoma, this has evolved into the position of head singer. Most Oklahoma powwows have an "open drum": anyone who wishes may ask the head singer for permission to sit at the drum and help sing. Sometimes there are so many singers that a second drum may be brought out. During "honorings" gifts may be given "to the drum" and divided among all the singers.

In the north, more formalized singing groups called "named drums" have evolved. These are groups of singers who practice together and who travel to powwows together. Whereas Oklahoma powwows advertise their head singer, Northern powwows advertise their "host drum." With named drums has come the proliferation of singing contests, and the increasing availability of easily reproduced recording technologies has lead to their professionalization (W.K. Powers 1981).

Structurally, Northern and Southern songs are similar, although there are internal differences within those regional differences (Vennum 1982; Hatton 1986; W.K. Powers 1990; Browner 2000). A major point of difference in song style is the vocal register: Northern style songs are sung in a higher register than are Southern songs. In both traditions, songs are started (called the "first push" or "push up") by a lead singer—often but not always the head singer as the lead may rotate around the drum—with the rest of the singers joining in ("seconding") in monophony to complete a song-section. This is followed by a second song-section, and the whole may be repeated several times. Most powwow drumming is a straight beat, although at certain points in the songs—the point varies North and South—there are louder "honor beats." To end the song, after a repetition of the second song-section, there is a break after which the second song-section is sung again. This last repetition is called the "tail." Many songs, particularly honoring songs, have individual words or short phrases; however, many, if not most, songs are sung "straight," with just vocables.

There are also regional differences in the social traditions around the drum. In the original Hethuska societies, the role of women was as "supporters" rather than active participants. Moreover, with the incorporation of the religious connotations of the Drum Dance into the powwow (vol. 13:562), the drum became a medicine object and subject to the basic taboos of association with menstruating women. Thus Southern women do not drum; they might sit behind their husbands or other relatives in a ring of "chorus girls" but are not at the drum. However, since the 1970s, women have been allowed to sit at Northern drums; there are some all-female drums (Hatton 1986).

### Dancers

The head dancers lead the dancing. The head male dancer has the responsibility to begin; everyone else follows his lead. The head male dancer and head lady dancer often lead Two-Steps as a couple (vol. 13:1017).

At most powwows, the question of whether or not to dance is a purely individual choice. The primary restriction on

333

dancing is the amount of money an individual and his or her family is able to put into the preparation of the dance clothes. For women, the choice is somewhat simplified; in all dances, the minimum lady's costume is a fringed shawl. It does not matter whether she is wearing the finest heirloom buckskin dress or the latest designer pant suit; as long as she has a shawl she is properly dressed. The only comparable situation for men is the Round Dance, the Two-Step "lady's choice," and the special song during an honoring. In all other cases, a specific dance outfit is necessary. It has been suggested (J.H. Howard 1976) that one reason for the popularity of the Gourd Dance is the inexpensive minimum outfit: a rattle.

Powwow dances (choreography) may be classified into two types, "basic" and "specials." The "specials" are those non-Hethuska-related dances that are interspersed in a pow-wow program. These include round dances, Two-Steps (called Owl Dance in the north), Snake-and-Buffalo Dance, Trot Dance, Smoke Dance (in the East). The "basic" pow-wow choreographies are those that developed from the Het-huska complex. These can be further classified by gender and region. All of these have distinctive "regalia" and chore-ography but are generally performed to the same music al-though there are special songs associated with these choreo-graphies that are used for contests.

## Spectators

The majority of the people present at a powwow are spec-tators. It is rare for a singer or dancer to attend a powwow as an individual, and most have relatives and friends in at-tendance. However, except for family honoring events, powwows do not explicitly recognize kinship relations. In a sociological sense, spectators include everyone present whenever they are not participating in another status.

## Southern Men's Dance Styles

There have been stylistic changes in dance choreography and clothing since 1900. The following is intended as a basic outline of styles and is not inclusive.

### Straight Dance

The Southern Straight Dance developed out of the Het-huska society dances but dropped the honorific bustle. Its dance clothing reflects its Prairie Plains origins: roach and spreader (some Straight dancers wear an otter-fur turban), cloth "ribbon shirt," crossed hair pipe bandoliers, a "drop" or "trailer" of cloth-backed otter fur, ribbon appliqué breechclout, cloth leggings tied with finger-woven garters, bells, and moccasins. Straight dancers carry a fan and either a dance mirror or a staff (vol. 13:936–937). Some western Oklahoma Straight Dancers wear their own tribal-specific clothing of buckskin leggings and black shawl apron.

The Straight Dance itself is often referred to as "digni-fied." The dancer holds himself erect or slightly bent for-ward. The footwork is the basic toe-heel step. The staff is sometimes used as a prop.

### Fancy or Feather Dance

The Southern Fancy or Feather dance style was developed and spread in the 1920s and 1930s by the Ponca Gus McDonald and the Kiowa Five artists (vol. 13:923). To the single waist (or "back") bustle of the Hethuska, a smaller bustle was added at the back of the neck. The trend since the 1970s has been to elaborate the length of the tassels on the tips of the feathers. Accoutrements include arm bustles, beaded cuffs, a beaded belt and harness (or "suspenders") in matching pattern, and angora-skin anklets were soon added (vol. 13:510, 429). Until the 1960s most Fancy dancers were bare-chested; many now wear cloth shirts. Fancy dancers usually carry whistles or "whip sticks."

Fancy Dance steps are much more athletic than those of the Straight Dance. In the past they have included gymnastic movements, flips, and splits, although those are now frowned upon.

### Gourd Dance

The Gourd Dance is not strictly a powwow dance, having evolved from a different sodality tradition. Its origins are in the non-Hethuska men's societies of the Kiowa, Co-manche, and possibly Cheyenne (from whom the Kiowa and Comanche are sometimes said to have gained it by capture in the late 1830s). It is distinct in choreography, music, and clothing. It is now done in the afternoons and early evenings, often beginning with a "Brush Dance" to Gourd Dance songs leading from outside the arena (vol. 13:921, 1018–1019).

There is no specific "Indian" clothing standard, although sometimes tribe-specific clothing is worn; contemporary "good clothes" are accepted. The minimum "outfit" needed for Gourd Dancing is a rattle, and beyond that, a velveteen sash, mescal bean bandolier, and a fan; sometimes a red and blue blanket is worn (with a veteran's service decorations), or of it is too hot for the blanket, a white cloth "apron."

The Gourd Dance step is a bobbing in place, on the balls of the feet alternating with a forward toe-heel step. Tradi-tionally, women danced in place behind the men; however, in the 2000s, some female combat veterans from the Iraq and Afghanistan wars have attempted to "dance with the gourd" to some opposition.

## Southern Women's Dance Styles

Southern women's dance clothing is divided into "buckskin" and "cloth" dress categories. The former are the modern versions of traditional Southern three-skin dresses, often with exaggerated sleeve fringes, while the latter are versions of cotton cloth "camp" dresses. In some groups, for example, Caddo and Osage, tribal-specific cloth dress styles are worn. In buckskin and cloth, a wide leather belt (often with German silver conchos) is worn. Attached to the belt are the woman's tools, an awl case, a bag, and a silver drop (vol. 13:892). The silver drop evolved from the leather strop that women carried to sharpen their knives. Southern Plains high-top moccasins are worn with both cloth and buckskin. Women carry a shawl over one arm.

The woman's dance step is a toe-heel forward bob, slightly bent forward. A goal is to get the shawl and buckskin dress fringes to sway in time.

## Northern Men's Dance Styles

With the geographic separation of the Northern Plains from the Southern Plains, and with their much greater geographic area, the Northern "Omaha" dances developed into several regional variants: Grass Dance in North Dakota and Montana, Prairie Chicken Dance in Canada, and Traditional Dance in South Dakota.

### Grass Dance and Prairie Chicken Dance

The Prairie Chicken Dance (also called Round Bustle) is the oldest of the modern Northern styles. The basic difference between the dances is that the contemporary Grass Dance clothing, like the Southern Straight Dance, has dispensed with the bustle. However, both the Grass Dance and the contemporary Chicken Dance clothes are characterized by fringe. Whereas Southern Fancy Dancers wear a matched beaded harness and belt, Grass and Chicken Dancers wear matched fringed shoulder yokes and aprons with a matching beaded belt and side tabs. Some older, as well as some new-style Chicken Dancers wear dyed long underwear; others wear fringed "pants," shirts with beaded rosettes or "rondels," and sleeve garters rather than arm bustles.

Grass and Chicken dance choreography is characterized by high bent-knee fancy steps, toe taps, and side steps, often alternating between the side and bottom of the foot.

### Northern Traditional

Meanwhile, those Grass Dancers in South Dakota who retained the single bustle began to call themselves "Old Time" or "Traditional" (vol. 13:1014–1015). They have elaborated their clothing to incorporate more "natural" items such as full bird wings and animal skins. Northern Traditional dancers also include full face paint. In place of the Hethuska toe-heel step, Northern Traditional choreography is "flatfooted."

## Northern Women's Dance Styles

The Northern women's traditional dancing styles parallel the Southern styles, taking into account the regional differences in buckskin and cloth dress styles. One particular area of difference is in the development of women's "Fancy" dance styles in the north.

The original Hethuska and its descendant choreographies were initially all male dances, with women playing a supportive role or not dancing at all. As early as the 1950s, a few young women in Oklahoma were attempting to Fancy Dance (J.H. Howard 1955) but were generally unsuccessful, in part because of implicit cultural sanctions on women contact with eagle feathers. In the late 1960s and 1970s, two new styles developed that allowed women to do the fancy steps while remaining in the women's dress (fig. 3).

The jingle dress (vol. 13:1022) originated in the Great Lakes region, and like the earlier Dream Dance, has a sanctioning myth relating the clothing and the associated choreography with healing. The cloth jingle dress is decorated with metal cones, preferably made from snuff can lids. The Jingle Dress Dance step is often done on tiptoe point rather than the flat foot. Jingle Dress Dancers carry feather fans in their right hands and during the "honor beats" of the song, they raise them to "bless the crowd" or to "honor the drum." A variant of the Jingle Dress Dance step is called the "side step" in which dancers keep their feet together rather than alternating feet, rotating the feet on the balls of the foot.

The Northern Shawl Dance originated on the Northwestern Plains and Plateau (vol. 12:560). Its characteristic is the fringed and yoked shawl worn over the shoulders. Like the Jingle Dress Dance, it features fancy steps, with high bent knees, and twirling to highlight the shawl's fringes.

Several other dance features are unique to the Northern Plains area. Powwow dancing was called "solo dancing en masse" (J.H. Howard 1955:216), but "team dancing" has developed. This involves groups of two or more dancers, in all categories, who synchronize their choreography, from Jingle Dress dancers in a line to groups of Traditional Dancers performing figures such as in a Scottish reel. In the "All Around" category, dancers must compete, in proper outfit, in all their gendered categories over the course of a powwow. In the Switch Dance dancers participate in their opposite gender's category. This is related to clowning activities of the Heyoka.

## Program of Events

While some Southern powwows begin with an afternoon Brush Dance and Gourd Dance, most powwows begin with an evening Grand Entry. This is a formal parade of the participants into the arena, lead by military service flags carried

Fig. 3. Women performing a Northern Cloth dance at the 3d Annual Sacred Circle Powwow of the Little River Band of Ottawa in July in Onekema, Mich. Photograph by Andy Klevorn, 1998.

by veterans, followed by the dancers according to category. This may be followed by a Flag Song, an Honoring Song specifically relating to the national flag, and a Christian or Native invocation. In some powwows these are followed by a Victory or Scalp Dance (round dances).

The majority of choreographic dances at most powwows are called "intertribals;" all dancers in the arena participate, no matter what style of clothing they are wearing. During these Intertribals, the arena is ablaze with swirls of color and sound, from the drums and singing to the announcer's, "Come on folks, let's evvv'ry body dance!"

Interspersed with the intertribals may be other choreographic dances called "specials." In some non-Plains areas where indigenous traditions are still practiced, such as Albuquerque, intertribal dances may be interspersed with a Pueblo Buffalo Dance or a Navajo Basket Dance.

In Oklahoma, the term "special" also refers to the specific honoring giveaway that is the reason for the event (vol. 13:1023–1024). At some point the sponsors have a speaker recount the reasons for the event and give away gifts to selected spectators. A variant of this is to spread gifts around the arena and ask spectators to come in and pick them up. At summer powwows, each of the principals will have a special. The principals and head staff at summer powwows also host a giveaway during the event.

Contest dances are often a feature of both summer powwows and public events. Powwow contests may derive from the auditions held by Wild West show producers. Initially, there were only Fancy Dance contests, but the categories have expanded to include the various age (tiny tots, junior, senior), gender, and choreography categories. Contest judging is often subjective but one objective feature is that dancers must stop on the last beat of the song's tail. Special contest songs often end abruptly without the usual format of regular songs. There are also drum contests and "49 Dance" contests.

After the main activities of a powwow, after-hours dance activities known as "49 Dances" are held away from the powwow grounds. This is a round dance that generally involves couples holding hands, linking arms, or sharing a blanket. It is possibly derived from the trysting sessions that accompanied war expedition preparations. The name may be derived from a "Days of '49" carnival show. Many of the songs have English words.

### Economics

Powwows are the nexus of several economic networks. In 1979, a small one-night "descendants" powwow in western Oklahoma distributed $500–1,000 in giveaway goods and food rations; the funds were raised by the family (Kavanagh 1980:88).

Weekend-long annual powwows have commensurately larger budgets; a 2005 Comanche Homecoming powwow had a budget of $10,000. Expenses included the contest prizes as well as a payment to the head staff. Although the Homecoming committee is not an official "tribal" institution, the Comanche Business Committee did appropriate funds for its support. Committees might also hold local "benefit" dances. They have raffles, "50–50" drawings, and auction various donated items such as shawls or Pendleton blankets. Funds also come from contest entry fees. Some powwow committees run concession stands during their events, taking a profit from refreshment sales. Cash and foodstuffs (a whole beef) are sometimes donated to the sponsors by participants.

Honoring giveaways by groups other than the sponsors occur during summer annual powwows, although giveaways occur at other types of events (Weist 1973; Kehoe 1980; Grobsmith 1981; Schneider 1981; vol. 13:856; J.H. Moore 1993). Each of the principals, supported with donations from their families, hosts a giveaway, called a "special" in Oklahoma, thanking the sponsors for the "honor" of serving in their role. Gifts are given to respected members of the community in attendance as well as to the other principals. Their overt social function, as with the sponsoring of the event itself, is that of prestige accrued through generosity; covert functions include establishing and maintaining social networks (Grobsmith 1981) and redistributing wealth (J.H. Moore 1993).

Participating in powwows as a dancer can be costly, not only in money but also in time. For a Gourd Dancer, the refinements—sash, bandolier, fan, or more traditional clothes—are acquired through one's own crafting, by purchase, or as gifts from relatives. The other dance styles require more elaborate outfits, and with the constant evolution of styles, clothing must be reworked from year to year, although parts may be recycled. However, there is no general market of finished powwow clothing parts. Some individuals, Indian and non-Indian, operate "Indian stores" that sell raw materials such as leather, beads, trade cloth, and feathers. Ultimately, except for eagle feathers (which are, by federal law, legally obtained by Indians only through inheritance or from a federal repository), while most of the basic raw materials for a powwow outfit are produced outside of the Indian community, most of a powwow clothing set is self-produced.

Some retail vendors participate in the powwow circuit. For a small concession fee to the sponsors, vendors can set up a booth or table around the perimeter of the dance arena, back from the viewing area, but not so far away as to be unnoticed by spectators. The most common items sold are cassette and compact disk recordings of powwow singers.

## Politics

Powwow is not an uncontested arena, and powwow and politics intersect on several levels. From the 1880s to the 1930s, the federal government, allied with Christian churches, tried to suppress dancing (Ellis 2003). There have been other intrusions of non-Indian politics into powwow.

In the late 1970s, when the northern "Traditional" style of dancing was first filtering into Oklahoma, one dancer at a Comanche Homecoming wore an American flag as part of his outfit. Conservative Comanches—well aware of the anti-Vietnam War protests of the recent past—were outraged at what they first saw as a desecration of the American flag. After some behind-the-scenes negotiations among the dancer, the outraged spectators, and the sponsors, the dancer was allowed time on the microphone to explain that he, too, was a veteran and wore the flag not to desecrate it, but to honor it. He gave a donation to the drum.

Intratribal politics have intruded into the powwow arena in other ways. On the one hand, as a public event, powwows have been a venue for appearances by tribal politicians; "every candidate in tribal elections makes the rounds these days to the dances because they recognize that there's a constituency there they need" (Lassiter, quoted in Ellis 2003: 163). Candidates' signs and handouts appear at powwows. Elected positions on powwow Committees can be the focus of debate.

Conversely, from the mid-twentieth century, powwow people have been tribal politicians. For much of the 1950s, the Kiowa chairman of the American Indian Exposition was also chairman of the joint Kiowa-Comanche-Apache Business Committee. At the same time, several of his political opponents were instrumental in the re-establishment of Kiowa warrior society dances (events and sodalities) in opposition to the Anadarko Fair (Levy 1961). In 2006, the chairmen of both the Comanches and Kiowas were prominent powwow people. Non-Indian politicians have appeared at powwows.

Mere attendance at, let alone participation in, powwows can identify oneself as a member of a particular portion of the community, and as such, in opposition to other community groups. In the early 1900s the Ponca Peyotist faction forced the Hethuska groups to secularize the ceremony (Duncan 1997). In the late 1970s, one Comanche "descendant group" that sponsored an annual powwow split into two rival committees, each sponsoring an event (Kavanagh 1979–2007). The Northern Arapahoe Powwow Committee successfully prevented the establishment of a second Committee (Fowler 1982).

# Native Museums and Cultural Centers

LISA J. WATT AND BRIAN L. LAURIE-BEAUMONT

Museums are among North America's important educational institutions. The collections housed in museums not only preserve the tangible legacy of the past but also, through exhibits and displays of material objects, educate the general public. Starting in the mid-nineteenth century museums and collectors throughout North America systematically collected Native American cultural materials in large quantities (Archambault 1996:408). Native American life was changing rapidly, and it was assumed that these items and the cultures that created them would soon disappear. Museums and collectors aggressively acquired all types of objects, even important sacred and ceremonial items, and preserved them far from their places of origin (Feest 1993; Ewers 1967:49–72).

By the mid-twentieth century the vast majority of Native American sacred and cultural materials were owned by local, city, state, provincial, national, and private museums and historical societies in the United States and Canada. Within these institutions, public displays of Native American life and culture were assembled by non-Native staff, with rare exceptions. Just as the national governments of the United States and Canada had claimed authority over the Native future, museums and their curators and researchers claimed authority over the material expressions of the Native past.

As a consequence, museums were often criticized as presenting a Eurocentric view of Native American culture and history, with Native objects seen merely as curiosities and trophies and scientific data. Some observers thought that interpretation was based too much on current academic ideas (Maurer 2000:25), with little regard for a broader cultural context, often resulting in inaccuracies. Museums were seen as reinforcing prevailing Euro-American and Euro-Canadian stereotypes through the selective use of information, images, and objects. Foremost among these was the view that Native American peoples belonged to a historic past and lived in a simple state of nature, outside the flow of Western culture.

Some critics objected to the fact that major collections like those in the American Museum of Natural History in New York, the Field Museum in Chicago, and the National Museum of Natural History of the Smithsonian were housed and displayed together with wildlife and geological collections and exhibits. Local, state, and provincial historical museums often followed suit. The notion of a conquered or vanishing race has fed popular misconceptions and stereotypes about Native people that have cut deeply across the American, Canadian, and Native experience (Karp and Levine 1991; Erasmus 1992; Assembly of First Nations 1992, 1992a; M.F. Brown 2003; Trigger 1980; Swidler et al. 1997; R. McLaughlin 1976; Trennert 1974; Watkins 2000).

Since the 1960s and 1970s, Native museums and cultural centers have become significant ingredients in the cultural renaissance taking place in Native communities throughout North America. As an expression of self-determination, they may be considered an alternative voice to the often inaccurate and staid representations of Native people while simultaneously working to preserve and protect living Native cultures. No longer is the Native voice absent or passive in museum settings; the Native voice is growing and so are Native museums (Doxtator 1985; Herle 1994; Horse Capture 1981; Maxwell 2005; Secakuku 2006; M.G. Simpson 1996; R.W. Hill 1977; Lester 1972).

The Western museum model is not a traditional institution within Native societies, but museums are highly desirable institutions to Native people. They have taken on a broad range of interpretive and educational facilities that include cultural centers, heritage centers, history centers, archeological repositories, research centers, and interpretive centers. While the definitions and functions of these terms vary by degree, all of them, for Native purposes, are concerned with the interpretation, preservation, protection, or perpetuation of Native cultures and cultural materials.

A native museum is a community-based, community-focused cultural and educational institution that is owned and operated by a native community (K.C. Cooper 1998:6). It is difficult to determine the exact number of these institutions since these facilities vary greatly. Some have their own museum building staff and collections, while others consist of a few display cases in tribal offices. Native museums open and close frequently, depending on funding availability. Given these dynamics, there are approximately 150 tribal museums in the United States alone. Other estimates suggest 200 in the United States, Canada, and Mexico combined (K.C. Cooper 2006:8–9).

## The United States

In the 1930s and 1940s, five tribally controlled museums opened. In the 1950s and 1960s, 21 more opened (vol. 7:578). In the 1970s, tribal museum development surged when 45 new museums opened their doors, followed by another 35 in the 1980s (Brascoupé 1981). In the 1990s, another 40 tribal museums opened (K.C. Cooper 2006:8–9; Sadongei 2005; American Association for State and Local History 1999).

In the 1960s and 1970s federal funds were critical to the establishment of tribal museums, through the Economic Development Administration of the Department of Commerce, which viewed tribal museums as vehicles to alleviate high unemployment on reservations by creating jobs, increasing tourism, and stimulating and diversifying tribal economies. The Economic Development Administration provided construction funds for scores of tribal museums, including the Daybreak Star, Seattle; the Makah Cultural and Research Center, Washington; the Native American Center for the Living Arts, Niagara Falls, New York; the Pueblo Indian Cultural Center, Albuquerque, New Mexico (fig. 1); the Seneca Iroquois National Museum, Salamanca, New York; and the Yakama Nation Cultural Center, Toppenish, Washington, among others. Although the Economic Development Administration stopped awarding construction funds after 1979, new tribal museums continued to open (Horse Capture 1981; Risser 1979), built by a combination of private, public, and tribal dollars.

In addition to construction funds, the federal Comprehensive Employment and Training Act provided employment and job training for Native people in museum management (Hanson 1980). It was a vital funding source that enabled many new tribal museums to operate, and in many cases it was the sole source of operations funding.

Important change took place as a result of federal legislation. In 1975, the Self-Determination and Education Assistance Act was passed, followed three years later with the passage of the American Indian Religious Freedom Act, and in 1979 by the Archeological Resources Protection Act. These important pieces of legislation enabled tribes to have a louder voice in their affairs and guaranteed religious freedom and site protections. These and other political victories galvanized a resurgence in cultural pride and tribal identity, which in turn sparked a dialogue between Native peoples and museums (T. Johnson 1994; Champagne 1999; DeLuca 1983; Ames 1986:1–11; Archambault 1992). Museums were becoming open to community involvement in

AP Images.

Fig. 1. The Pueblo Indian Cultural Center in Albuquerque, N. Mex., owned and operated by the 19 Indian Pueblos of N. Mex., which hosts community events. top, Discussion concerning a proposed coal mine project near Zuni Salt Lake. Presenting the issue are, left to right, Zuni Pueblo Councilman Edward Wemytewa; Councilman Carlton Albert, Sr.; Zuni Pueblo governor Arlen Quetawki; and Ron Solimon, president of the Center. Photograph by Susan Montoya Bryan, 2003. center, Book signing by world War II veterans, the Navajo code talkers. Bill Toledo accepts a book to autograph his photograph, while fellow code talker John Brown (center) and Chester Nez (left) look on. Photograph by Jake Schoellkopf, 2002. bottom, Tunte Vigil of Pojoaque Pueblo, 1997 Miss Indian New Mexico, before relinquishing her crown to the 1998 winner during a ceremony at the Center. Photograph by Kitty Clark, 1997.

their practices. Tribal people demanded the return of sacred objects and human remains from museums nationwide and insisted on their removal from display. They also expected involvement in the interpretation and representation of Native people and cultures in museum exhibitions and programs (Erasmus 1992; Goforth 1993). The demand for accurate representation and interpretation was not relegated to mainstream museums alone; tribes wanted their own museums to interpret their stories and for cultural preservation and continuity in their communities (Biddle 1977).

By the 1990s, another wave of significant legislation was passed that would have a tremendous impact on tribal cultural concerns: the Indian Arts and Crafts Board Act (1990), the Native American Graves Protection and Repatriation Act (NAGPRA 1989), the National Museum of the American Indian Act (1989), and the Native American Languages Act (1990). Each of these acts signified the importance of respecting Native cultures and of Native efforts to preserve tribal heritage.

More tribes are planning and opening new or replacement museums as a result of their increased financial resources, in part due to gaming revenues. Where tribes have the money, resources, knowledge, and desire, they are creating museums and cultural centers. One of the more remarkable efforts is The Museum at Warm Springs, a 25,000-square-foot project owned and operated by the Confederated Tribes of the Warm Springs Reservation, Oregon, which opened in 1993. The museum represented a decades' long dream of the three tribes that make up the confederacy—Warm Springs, Wasco, and Northern Paiute. The tribes' efforts included the creation of an artifact acquisition fund resulting in the formation of one of the finest and largest collections of Native artifacts in tribal hands and a significant appropriation of tribal dollars toward the construction of an award-winning building (Carnes 1993).

These facilities are not small attractions but sophisticated, well-conceived educational institutions. In 1998, the Confederated Tribes of the Umatilla Reservation opened the 45,000-square-foot Tamástslikt Cultural Institute in Pendleton, Oregon (fig. 2). In 2002, the Saginaw Chippewa Indian Tribe opened the 32,000-square-foot Ziibiwing Center of the Anishinabe Culture and Lifeways in Mount Pleasant, Michigan. In 2004, the Gila River Indian Community opened the 40,000-square-foot Huhugam Heritage Center in Chandler, Arizona. In 2006 Acoma Pueblo opened the Sky City Visitor Center and Haak'u Museum. In 2007 the Tohono O'odham Nation opened a cultural center and museum.

Other tribes are planning replacement buildings, such as Suquamish Tribe, Washington (Caldwell 1987), the Southern Ute Tribe of Colorado, and the Agua Caliente Band of Cahuilla Indians, California, whose new facility will replace their 1,600-square-foot building with one that is 110,000 square feet, expected to open in 2010. The Tulalip Tribes of Washington and the Confederated Tribes of Siletz in Oregon are planning new facilities. Both will be more than 20,000 square feet.

The tribal museum and cultural center movement will grow as will the demand for professional training in operations, exhibitions, and collections. Tribes are paying closer attention to other cultural concerns, such as language preservation, repatriation, cultural resources protection, intellectual property rights, research protocols, historic preservation of structures and sites, archives, and libraries (Circle of Tribal Advisors 2004; T.F. King 1998; National Association of Tribal Historic Preservation Officers 2005; P. Parker 1990; Stapp and Burney 2002).

## Canada

Prior to the 1970s there were two aboriginal-operated museums in Canada: 'Ksan Historical Village and Museum, outside Hazelton, British Columbia (vol. 7:292); and, the Musée des abenakis d'Odanak (Western Abenaki) in Quebec. 'Ksan's collection began in 1957 as a project of the Hazelton library association and moved into its first building—the Skeena Treasure House (so-named because the word "museum" indicated lifeless objects)—in 1959. Rather than build a larger museum as growth required, additional buildings were added as the years went by to create a traditional Gitksan village. The Musée des abenakis d'Odanak, established in 1962 with major renovations in 2005, is found along the Saint Lawrence River north of Montreal. It occupies a historic house and has strong ties to the First Nation community.

Beginning with Canada's centennial in 1967, a series of events created the drive and the opportunity for aboriginal communities to take control of the preservation and interpretation of their cultures. The centennial celebrations helped to foster Canadian national pride and a search for a "Canadian identity." This in turn led to an explosion in museum and other cultural facilities for the centennial and in subsequent years. Although none of these new museums was owned by Natives, their heritage was part of what was on display. The paradox of having others interpret their cultural heritage—and benefiting from it—was not lost upon aboriginal leaders.

Following the centennial, the federal government inaugurated the first National Museum Policy in 1972, which included financial assistance programs to help establish museums and make them more professional. Among the First Nation projects to make use of the new source of federal government funding was the Woodland Cultural Centre in Brantford, Ontario. Located in a former residential school, the Centre in 1972 transformed a school building on the property into a museum whose mandate is to serve several Six Nations communities in southern Ontario. It has a considerable collection of art along with over 25,000 artifacts. Programming includes traditional and contemporary cultural expression (Doxtator 1988).

The Province of Quebec has a long history of cultural support of First Nations. The Huron-Wendat, just north of

top and bottom right, AP Images.

Fig. 2. Cultural centers in the U.S. top and bottom left, Tamástslikt Cultural Center, built by the Confederated Tribes of the Umatilla Indian Res., east of Pendleton, Oreg., the first museum on the Oregon Trail to tell the story from the Indian point of view. Photographs by top, Jeff Barnard, 1998; bottom left, Lisa J. Watt, 2001. bottom right, Ziibiwing Center for Anishinabe Culture and Lifeways in Mt. Pleasant, Mich., which opened in 2004. On display are objects from the Caleb E. Calkin Collection, including a Potawatomi beaded shirt. Photograph by Melanie Maxwell, 2004.

Quebec City, operate a museum in a historic house, the Maison Tsawenhohi, which is part of the Centre Culturel Ti-Yarihuten. In 1977, The Native Museum of Mashteuiatsh was created to preserve the culture of the Pekuakamiulnu-atsh of the Montagnais First Nation in the Lake Saint John area.

The National Museum Policy of 1972 was just one part of a wider federal initiative that sought to create what was termed "a just society." There was a perceived need to deal with the circumstances of the country's aboriginals if this just society was to exist. One key result of this initiative was the intensification of land claims negotiations. Related to this was the aboriginal demand for inclusion in discussions of environmental impacts and economic development that would alter their way of living. Many realized change was coming fast and there was a need to preserve traditional culture and knowledge.

Overall, Canadians have generally sympathized with aboriginal people. Aboriginal leaders became more adept at marshalling that sympathy for practical gains. Many aboriginal representatives realized the land claims and treaty negotiations presented an opportunity to deal with their cultural interests. It became the norm for such discussions to involve cultural protection and development and in some cases cultural regeneration.

The Glenbow Museum played a role in this development during the 1988 Winter Olympics in Calgary. The Museum chose to highlight aboriginal culture in its exhibition, "The Spirit Sings: Artistic Traditions of Canada's First Peoples," and the related "Celebration of Native Cultures," a varied mix of traditional and contemporary Native artistic expressions. The event became intertwined with land claim and mineral exploration issues when the Lubicon Lake First Nation (Western Woods Cree) called for a boycott, noting the exhibit was sponsored by the oil company seeking to drill on land claimed by the band. The problem was exacerbated by what some felt was a lack of direct First Nation input on an exhibit about First Nations, even though there had been Glenbow-First Nation consultations. Although the actual impact of the boycott is open to question, the event highlighted the need for museums to be collaborative in projects about aboriginal culture.

In 1992, the report *Turning the Page: Forging New Partnerships Between Museums and First Peoples* (Task Force 1992) was released from a federally sponsored task force of the Assembly of First Nations and the Canadian Museums Association, a follow-up to a wider Canadian museum review in 1988 called "Challenges and Choices" and the subsequent new National Museum Policy of 1990. Some of the issues raised by "The Spirit Sings" exhibit at the Glenbow were fresh in the minds of the writers of the 1988 document. The new Museum Policy introduced an Aboriginal Assistance Program within the museum funding programs of the Department of Communications and clearer direction for federal cultural agencies to ensure aboriginal interests are more clearly included in activities affecting their cultural heritage.

The report made a number of recommendations, among them: the need for more involvement of First Peoples in museum activities involving their culture, especially interpretation; the need for greater access to collections and cultural information by the communities from which the material is derived; the repatriation of human remains, sacred objects, and other objects of special significance; training and job opportunities for First Peoples to become directly involved in the preservation and management of their cultural material; and assistance in the creation of their own museums.

The interest created in aboriginal communities across the country resulted in an unprecedented wave of proposals for new cultural heritage institutions (vol. 12:216). Many of these proposals are equal parts social projects and economic development. The social project aspect involves creating a sense of pride and community. It involves healing the spirit in the hopes of making a stronger person more able to cope with the issues of modern society. An excellent example of this is the proposed Residential School Museum of Canada, based in a former residential school outside Portage-la-Prairie, Manitoba. And there are attempts to bridge the divide between aboriginal and non-aboriginal communities living side-by-side, such as the Membertou Heritage Centre (Micmac) where the Elders Advisory Committee specifically noted that the project goal to serve "the local community" includes the nonaboriginal population of adjacent Sydney, Nova Scotia. Economic development includes employment in nonprofit museums as well as for-profit activities in tourism. The aim of the proposed Northern Plains Museum in Brandon, Manitoba, is not to be simply a museum and art gallery but a center for learning heritage and tourism skills as well as traditional and contemporary Native arts and business.

Although there are many projects being planned or proposed, there have been few new aboriginal-operated museums or heritage interpretation centers opened since the 1970s. There is a real challenge in creating viable institutions in often economically disadvantaged communities where rural population and tourist numbers are low, meaning few opportunities for self-generated revenue. In Canada, federal and provincial operating support programs for heritage have declined in real dollar terms. Municipal governments are the primary source of operating funds for most museums. But most band councils have so many other social needs to deal with that they normally cannot match that type of assistance. Staff training and retention is a problem. There is a need to create a long-term training plan to develop among aboriginals the skills required to manage their own institutions. The desire to repatriate collections must balance cultural ownership and control with attendant costs. And almost all projects developed or in planning are outside urban areas, even though half of Canada's aboriginal population in the 2000s lives in urban centers.

These problems do have a silver lining. Those aboriginal museums built in the twentieth century for the most part have developed along Eurocentric museum models: an emphasis on collections and exhibits. Financial restraints and the difficulties encountered in repatriation have caused many communities to focus more on noncollection-based programming, often more reflective of traditional learning models, which may well resonate more with changes in nonaboriginal population information acquisition interests. An example would be the proposed Honekwē (House of Stories) in Thompson, Manitoba, planned to collect oral histories and to emphasize story-telling programs. It is also leading to beneficial partnerships, such as the planned Torngasok Cultural Centre in Nain, Labrador, where the federal Parks Canada agency is developing a nature center nearby and will put its exhibits and offices in the Inuit cultural center, both helping to tell their own story with the land as well as providing rent revenue. The Blackfoot Crossing Heritage Park, which opened in July 2007 in Siksika, Alberta, provides both education and entertainment.

## The Mission of Native Museums

Native museums and cultural centers are not unlike mainstream museums in that they exist for many of the same basic reasons: to educate, preserve, and protect a collective cultural heritage. For most Native groups, however, Native museums have a larger goal: to strengthen indigenous cultures and identities. Native communities view their museums as vehicles to tell their stories from their perspective, as conduits to protect and preserve cultural knowledge, systems, and materials, and as a means to perpetuate living cultures and traditions through the collections they hold and the resources and services they provide. Nearly all Native museum staff consider their primary mission as preserving and perpetuating Native culture and traditions (Abrams 2004:7).

Native museums are also symbols. They are important cultural, historical, and artistic expressions of sovereign nations. They serve as reminders to the mainstream world of a tribe's presence and of their historic and cultural connections and rights to place and resources. They help to define original homelands and contemporary territory. They communicate a tribe's self-understanding and what is important to them. They can serve as a public relations tool (Watt 2002).

An example that displays all these characteristics is the Mashantucket Pequot Museum and Research Center, owned by the Mashantucket Pequot Tribal Nation of Connecticut. This 308,000 square-foot facility opened to the public in 1998. It is the largest Native museum in North America and one of the few full-service indigenous cultural facilities, providing ongoing research, exhibitions, and educational programming; storage for ethnographic and archeological collections; an archive and two libraries with reading rooms; an auditorium where a professionally produced film on the Pequot War of 1637 is shown; a restaurant; and other services. Situated within the 85,000 square feet of exhibition space depicting 18,000 years of Native and natural history is an extraordinary 22,000-square-feet Pequot village of the sixteenth century. Visitors may walk among traditional dwellings and observe scenes of Pequot life. This museum has been very successful in celebrating the Pequots' reemergence for tribal members while reminding the general public of their ancestral ties to the land and region.

Native museums face a unique opportunity and challenge. They have two distinct audiences: the Native community and the general non-Native public (K.C. Cooper 2006:1). Theoretically, the first priority is the Native community where activities focused on cultural perpetuation and preservation can take place. The secondary audience is the non-Native public, where the goals are more obvious: to educate visitors about the history, art, and culture of a particular community. Similar to all small museums, when Native museums have the resources and staff, they can provide educational opportunities and services not found anywhere else.

Meeting the needs of two distinct audiences is a delicate and often difficult balance to achieve, sometimes unintentionally resulting in the sacrifice of the primary audience for the secondary one. This is not by design or desire but by default, and most often due to the lack of funding. Native communities have been working through these issues. Some have been more successful than others.

One of the more successful strategies for meeting the needs of both audiences has been the creation of partnerships to help offset operating costs. One of the most successful partnerships is between the Southeast Alaska Indian Cultural Center and the Sitka National Historical Park of the National Park Service in Alaska. The Center is dedicated to the arts and culture of the Tlingit, Haida, and Tsimshian. Over 300,000 visitors pass through their doors each year. In 1969, the park visitor center opened, including a wing for a tribal cultural center as a place to pass on tribal traditions to the Native community and to educate the public about these living cultures. Today, the visitor center is operated by the National Park Service while the cultural center is managed by an independent, all-Native board of trustees as a non-profit organization. Much of the funding is provided by the Park Service, enough for a full-time cultural center director and a summer arts program featuring four Native artists who demonstrate traditional arts. The Park Service funded a building expansion in 2002 for four new artist studios and a larger exhibition area.

The Ak-Chin Him-Dak Ecomuseum, Maricopa, Arizona (fig. 3), utilizes the concept that the land and territory replace the building, and tribal members are both the curators and the audience, thereby creating a seamless interface among museum, territory, and community (Fuller 1992). The Poeh Arts and Cultural Center of Pojoaque Pueblo, New Mexico, provides instruction on traditional and contemporary native arts for enrolled tribal people combined with a small museum.

## Collections

By 2000, after almost two centuries of aggressive collecting by museums and collectors, much of Native peoples' material culture was held in private collections and public institutions worldwide. With the exception of a few tribal museums such as The Museum at Warm Springs, the Makah Cultural and Research Center, and the Navajo Nation Museum, most Native communities possess but a small fraction of their cultural materials (Hartman and Doyel 1982). For many communities, acquiring objects has become a priority, and they have been active in acquiring donations and purchasing objects and archival materials with their own funds.

It would have been impossible to imagine in the 1970s the prices Native objects command on the national and international art markets in the twenty-first century. In 2006, in an auction of American Indian art at Sotheby's, New York, one object—a Tsimshian mask—sold for $1.8 million, a record for a single Native North American item (Sotheby's 2006).

As the availability of objects becomes scarcer, prices will continue to climb, thus making the acquisition of cultural objects for display and education a problem facing most Native museums. One successful example has been the purchase of the Breazeale Collection by the Gila River Indian Community, Arizona. This well-documented collection of 84 Pima baskets was purchased at a cost of $75,000 in 1997 and rests in the Huhugam Heritage Center. Had the collection gone to auction, chances were very high that the collection would have landed out of their reach.

The passage of the Native American Grave Protection and Repatriation Act (NAGPRA) in 1989 played an important role in building collections. The Act provides for the repatriation of human skeletal remains, sacred objects,

top, Makah Cultural and Research Center, Neah Bay, Wash.

Fig. 3. Museums in the West. top, Makah Cultural and Research Center, Neah Bay, Wash. Opened in 1979, the Center displays material from the 50,000 objects excavated at the Ozette archeological site (vol. 7:412–421), which are the basis for ongoing research by tribal members and scholars. The Center has an active language program (vol. 7:429) and works in local school districts on cultural programming. Photographed in 1981. bottom left, The Museum at Warm Springs, a 25,000-sq.-ft. structure located on the Warm Spring Res., in central Oreg. Through the efforts of the Confederated Tribes—Warm Springs, Wasco, and Paiute—it possesses one of the largest and finest collections of cultural treasures and family heirlooms in tribal hands. Architectural details on the building symbolize many aspects of the tribes' cultures, including the roofing that echoes forms of traditional dwellings, a man-made stream representing water, and a large lava rock that represents a drum. Photograph by Lisa J. Watt, 2002. bottom right, Ak-Chin Him-Dak Eco-Museum, Maricopa, Ariz. The Ak-Chin Indian Community consists of both Tohono O'odham (Papago) and Pima Indians. Eco-museums explore the identity of place, rely on local community involvement, and aim to enhance community welfare and development. These concepts are reflected in the exhibitions that the Ak-Chin has created, including the topics diabetes prevention, community archeology, veterans, and community quilters. Photograph by Lisa J. Watt, 2002.

funerary objects, and items of cultural patrimony housed in institutions receiving federal funding. Most of the repatriated collections have been human remains and funerary objects, which have been most often been reburied. Other times, repatriated sacred objects have been returned to religious leaders for use in ceremonies, properly disposed of according to tradition bearers, or accessioned into tribal museum collections.

One example is the return of the Sacred Pole of the Omaha. About 1900, Francis LaFlesche, Omaha, an anthropologist, persuaded the last religious leader of the Omaha to place the tribe's Sacred Pole, together with other material items, in the Peabody Museum at Harvard. After long negotiations, the Peabody voluntarily repatriated these items to the Omaha in 1989. Later, the Omaha persuaded the Nebraska State Historical Society, Lincoln, to repatriate their Omaha collections. Today, both collections are housed at the Nebraska State Historical Society, awaiting the construction of the New Moon Moving Interpretive Center and Museum (Ridington and Hastings. 1997).

While Canada does not have a repatriation law, there are two instances in which repatriated materials have been a source of collections for First Nations. In 1884, the Canadian government passed Anti-Potlatch laws, laws that were not rescinded until 1951. In 1921 a large Kwakwaka'wakw (Kwakiutl) potlatch was raided by federal officers and the masks and other items being used were confiscated. Most of the seized property was deposited with the federally owned Victoria Memorial Museum (now the Canadian Museum of Civilization) in Ottawa and the Royal Ontario Museum in Toronto. However, some pieces found their way into the George Heye collection (now the National Museum of the American Indian, Smithsonian Institution, Washington, D.C.), the British Museum in London, and personal collections. After a long repatriation process, and with financial assistance from the government of Canada, the collection at the Museum of Civilization was returned to the Namgis and Cape Mudge bands in 1975. The U'Mista Cultural Centre at Alert Bay and the Kwagiulth Museum at Cape Mudge, British Columbia, were built to display the collection (vol. 7:382, 389). The Royal Ontario Museum returned the material they held in 1988, and over the years many items have been returned from the National Museum of the American Indian (Cole 1985; C.H. Carpenter 1981).

For those items that have been returned and reintroduced through ceremony to communities, toxic chemical contamination of repatriated materials is a concern. Pesticides and arsenic, mercury, and lead were used as preservatives. The Iroquois faced this issue when some of their 455 repatriated False Face masks were covered with arsenic (Jemison 2001:38–40). Detection and mitigation are the priorities for many; for others, contamination is reason enough not to undertake a repatriation process (J.S. Johnson 2001; Nason 2001; Odeden 2004; Odegaard and Sadengei 2005). Toxic chemicals for preservation are no longer used in museums.

The Smithsonian has played a leading role in working with Native museums. In the 1970s the National Museum of Natural History lent artifacts to new tribal museums. In the 1990s that Museum provided the museum at Zuni with 3,000 historical photographs, which are used in their education and exhibits. The National Museum of the American Indian (NMAI) provided 80 long-term loans to the Seminole Ah-Tah-Thi-Ki Museum (vol. 14:445) for their permanent exhibition. Since it opened in 1997, the Ah-Tah-Thi-Ki Museum has met the professional climate control and security standards required to receive museum loans. Not all Native museums meet these standards but for those that do, loans help fill in their collection gaps and enable the community to have ancestral objects in their midst for educational and artistic purposes.

In addition to acquiring objects and archival materials, greater emphasis is being placed on traditional care policies and culturally sensitive storage. Perhaps the most impressive and unique example is the Makah Cultural and Research Center in Neah Bay, Washington. Their collection of 55,000 beautifully preserved objects came as a result of a mudslide that buried the Makah village of Ozette in the 1700s. In 1970, water-eroded areas of the site and artifacts were exposed. The tribe, in cooperation with Washington State University, Pullman, excavated the site over 11 years and in the process developed new techniques for underwater excavations (R. Kirk and L. Kirk 1980:5). The tribe was advised by university archeologists that in order to preserve, display, and make available for study this world-class collection, a first-rate museum would be needed. The tribe agreed, and in 1979 the Makah Tribe opened their facility (Erikson, Ward, and Wachendorf 2002).

Because of the nature of the objects and the opportunities the Ozette Collection presented, staff organized the collection by a traditional system of property ownership, which grouped objects by family and household and as associated objects in units. Gender restrictions applied to some objects, such as whaling gear, so those items have been flagged. All objects are identified in the Makah language, which "encouraged analysis of the cultural meanings and affinities between artifacts in the collection and provides insight into both Makah language and thought" (Mauger and Bowechor 2006). While a non-Western view and usage of collections in their storage and handling are in place, professional collections management and care are followed, thereby combining western and non-Western museological practices.

## Libraries and Archives

Archives are considered essential sources for documenting tribal history and traditional knowledge and as repositories for historic and contemporary legal documents, photographs, maps, oral histories, and sound recordings among other documentary items (fig. 4). The model of a western archive is not meant to replace oral histories, once the primary method of transmitting history between Native people, but to supplement them (Fleckner 1984:1).

An archive can help to improve the administration of tribal government by promoting a more efficient and controlled management of information. An archive may also contain the documents to substantiate legal claims and rights or clarify legal challenges. Through an archive, a tribe is better able to protect information and control research and the study of itself by others. An archive may also contain valuable cultural information and documentation, thereby strengthening cultural self-determination efforts. An archive could well be one of the most important elements in sustaining the living memory of a people and as the foundation for development of a society (Warren 1984:viii).

As of 2006, there were approximately 200 tribal libraries in the United States (Lotsee Patterson, personal communication 2006) and others in Canada. Like Native museums, libraries are seen as vehicles for cultural perpetuation and as community gathering places. The greatest need is for trained personnel, who are being prepared at tribally controlled colleges.

Fig. 4. The Akwesasne Library and Cultural Center, Hogansburg, N.Y. top, Exterior of the center built for the Mohawk in 1971. bottom, Reading room. The library's collection of 28,000 books includes 2,400 volumes on Indians. The cultural center, on the lower level, features exhibits on the Mohawk. Photographs by Lisa J. Watt, 2001.

Since 1984, in the United States, the Institute of Museum and Library Services, a federal agency, has managed a program devoted to tribal libraries. Tribes are collaborating with area universities, libraries, and archives more frequently. One example is the Southwest Oregon Research Project, a collaboration among the Coquille Indian Tribe, the University of Oregon, and the American Indian Museums Program of the National Museum of Natural History. Starting in 1995, Coquille tribal and university scholars discovered and retrieved over 110,000 ethnographic and military documents, maps, and microfilm located in the National Anthropological Archives and the National Archives, both major repositories for materials related to western Oregon tribes. Through the collaboration, copies of these important documents are now housed in the university's special collections library and accessible to tribal members, scholars, and the general public. In two potlatch ceremonies, the Coquille Tribe presented 44 regional tribes with copies of the printed inventory and seven Oregon tribes with copies of relevant manuscripts and reference materials for their own tribal libraries.

In 2002, the Coquille Tribe was honored by the Honoring Nations: Tribal Governance Success Stories Program of the Harvard Project on American Indian Economic Development, which recognizes innovative tribal programs. Honoring Nations stated that the collaborative program "has enhanced cultural education, resulted in valuable institutional partnerships, improved intertribal relations, rekindled community traditions, and strengthened the tribal government's ability to function as a self-determined sovereign" (Harvard Project on American Indian Economic Development 2002).

The gathering and building of cultural and intellectual resources is a new priority within tribal governments, but with them come new responsibilities and opportunities to define ways in how they will be represented and by whom. In this regard, tribes are concerned about intellectual property rights and research protocols.

## Exhibits

Native people are storytellers, so it is not surprising that they would adopt the exhibition format as a vehicle to convey tribal histories and stories. The variety of exhibition designs is diverse. They range from the million-dollar permanent installations found in many of the newer facilities, organized with the help of professional design firms, to exhibits that are not professionally designed nor thematically arranged but instead create an eclectic mix of imagery and ideas.

Aside from the vast cultural and historical diversity among the Native peoples, there are a few common themes found in Native museum exhibitions in the United States. They are: pride in tribal heritage; a reverence for their homelands, and for their reservation in particular; a sense of accomplishment in their government and community; and pride in their communal perseverance and resiliency (Watt 2002). These are the stories tribes wish to convey.

More often than not, tribal museum exhibitions replicate a conventional linear approach similar to other museums. Often depicted as a journey through time, most tribes will describe their stories as: precontact (prehistory), contact (history), the treaty era, reservation era, the boarding school experience, self-determination, tribal government, contemporary life and achievements, languages including loss and preservation efforts, and the future. "Culture" is often expressed in the seasonal calendar. Tribal veterans nearly always have a place of honor. Objects are used to illuminate the text wherever possible. Few United States tribal museum exhibitions diverge from this formula (Watt 2002).

Some subjects are generally not found in native museum exhibitions. Overt political statements are rare or, if stated, are gently implied. Detailed discussions of treaties and their impact on tribal life are often absent, or when discussed are usually brief or void of a larger historical context. Traditional creation stories, when they appear in tribal museums (and many times they do not), are conveyed most likely as text on panel or through a single narrative painting. Traditional ceremonies, for obvious reasons having to do with cultural and intellectual property rights and proprietary concerns, are rarely discussed. In most cases, social conditions such as health issues and poverty are not addressed at all. There is rarely any acknowledgement of the surrounding border towns (Watt 2002).

Why conventional exhibitions? Native people may have preconceived notions about how information ought to be conveyed in professional museum settings, that the linear, thematic approach may be more legitimate or valuable in the eyes of academia, the museum world, and the general public. Tribal people may also assume that this conventional approach is what their audiences desire. For many years the Smithsonian and now the National Museum of the American Indian's American Indian Museum Program workshops on exhibition development have emphasized culturally appropriate, community-based approaches and voice, but few museums have diverged from the standard linear formula.

## Training

With the growth in number and sophistication of Native museums, training in professional museological practice became a priority. One of the first museum training programs for native people was founded in 1971, at the Institute of American Indian Arts Museum, Sante Fe, New Mexico (Dailey 1977). The Museum possesses the most important collection of contemporary Native American art in the world, known as the National Collection of Contemporary Indian Arts. This 7,000-piece collection is available for study by Institute students and is the foundation of their museum training. The training program is aimed at skill-building for Native students and the needs and problems of small museums. Combining theoretical and practical coursework for either certificate or degree, the program, which includes a work practicum, introduces students to all aspects of museum management and operations. The goal is to cultivate Native personnel prepared to work in either Native museums or mainstream ones.

In 1973, the American Indian Cultural Resources Training Program was founded by the National Anthropological Archives and Herman J. Viola in the National Museum of Natural History. Its primary purpose was to inspire American Indians to become professional archivists and historians (Viola 1978). Through this program, native people gained access to cultural and intellectual resources they did not know existed or know they had access to at the Smithsonian and other federal agencies. The program formally ended in 1979 but the relationships were by then established and Indian people kept accessing these and other repositories.

In 1977, the Smithsonian's Office of Museum Programs began offering tribal museum training, including workshops and internships. The National Museum of the American Indian developed their first museum training program in 1997 in partnership with the existing program. In 2003 the American Indian Museum Training Program was moved to the National Museum of American Indian Community Services Department. This program is the largest provider of museum training for tribal people in the United States. Since 1991, over 600 Native people from the United States and Canada have received museum training (Cooper, personal communication 2006). The program offers internships, visiting professional opportunities, guided research, technical assistance, and workshops. The program has emphasized culturally appropriate and culturally relevant training approaches and practices that can be translated to specific tribal contexts. Created to meet the specific needs of small museums and advocating a native perspective, participants recognize the value and its unique emphasis, where they can speak openly about common concerns.

The Smithsonian has two other Native-related programs: the American Indian programs at the National Museum of American History and the National Museum of Natural History, which were established in 1984 and 1986, respectively. Both programs have worked with dozens of Native museums and personnel by providing access to collections and resources and organizing research projects and internships. The Canadian Museum of Civilization offers a training program in museum practices to aboriginals. The Museums Association of Saskatchewan developed a certificate course in First Nations museum studies.

## Native Museum Associations

Despite the growth of the Native museum movement since the 1970s, there is no national association serving the needs of these institutions. However, there have been at least two attempts. The first effort occurred in 1978 when the North American Indian Museums Association was founded by a small group of Native Americans working in about 100 museums. Its mission was to address the training needs of the tribal museum field. Staff at the Smithsonian's museum training program helped to organize the association. The goals were: "to preserve, perpetuate and enhance the traditional culture, history and art of the North American Indian; counteract the negative stereotypes of Pan-Indianism by recognizing the diversity of tribal identities; assist tribal elders and religious leaders, without interfering with spiritual teachings, in the instruction of Indian children as to the proper respect for their traditional culture; assist Indian museums in the development of their institutions, staff, resources, collections, marketing and promotion, research, information exchange, interpretive programs and other mutual concerns; act as a resource center on museum services and a clearinghouse on museum information; and, provide a united voice to address the concerns, achievements and goals of North American Indian museums" (NAIMA 1979). Association members, concerned about the display and storage of human remains and sacred objects in museums worldwide, were early proponents of repatriation.

It was an inspiring agenda. Members were concerned about the display and storage of human remains and sacred objects in museums nationwide. They were early proponents of repatriating these materials to tribal communities. In its first few years of operation, the Association conducted a national needs survey and a repatriation inventory. They organized workshops to help administrators deal with issues of management, collections care, conservation, funding, and research. Internships with major museums were created regionally. Funding for much of this work was provided by the Smithsonian and the Department of Labor. Despite these early successes the Association could not sustain itself and ceased operations around 1989.

The second attempt to create a national association occurred in 1995 when a group of Native museum professionals approached the American Association for State and Local History and asked their leadership to serve as an umbrella organization until they could establish an independent, national association of their own. In 2000, the Institute of Museum and Library Services awarded the advisory committee a leadership grant to conduct a national survey on the state of Native museums and cultural centers. The goal was to use the information as the statement of needs to create the association. In the meantime, the advisory committee was the driving force behind the creation of a new federal funding program within the Institute devoted to the improvement of tribal museums. The program, started in 2005 with an appropriation of $830,000, is now the only source of federal funding devoted exclusively to Native museums in the United States. At the conclusion of the survey in 2004, a national association was not formed.

If not at the national level, then greater tribal museum participation is being seen in regional museum associations. The American Association of Museums has a professional interest committee for Native museum professionals, the Native American and Museum Collaboration Network. The Western Museums Association recruits Native museum professionals for both board and committee memberships and seeks tribal participation in all its programming. In 2001, the regional Mountain-Plains Museums Association created the Tribal Museums Network as a professional standing committee. The network covers 11 western states and serves as an information clearinghouse while providing a forum for the tribal museum community to advocate and promote the highest curatorial standards for museum collections. Museums Alaska, the state-wide museum association, has Native participation.

## National Museum of the American Indian

Since passage of the National Museum of the American Indian legislation in 1989 (P.L. 101-185), the Museum board and staff have made the Native voice in interpretation and representation their highest priority. This commitment is not only reflected in its mission statement, which is committed to advancing knowledge and understanding of the Native cultures of the western hemisphere in partnership with Native people and others, but also extends to facility designs, traditional care and storage of the collections, exhibitions, and all its programming. Indian people have moved from the position of an absent or near-absent native voice in the interpretation in many museums to an active and passionate voice of survival and cultural self-determination on a national stage (Blue Spruce 2004; McMaster and Trafzer 2004; West 2000). The Museum opened in 2004 (fig. 5).

Aside from its physical structures—the Heye Center in New York City; the Cultural Resources Center in Suitland, Maryland; and the museum on the Mall—perhaps the Museum's most important work is embedded in the idea of the Fourth Museum. Recognizing that most tribal people may not visit any one or more of their three facilities, the Fourth Museum is designed to extend access and use of the Museum's many collections and cultural resources to Native communities, not just in the United States and Canada, but throughout the Americas (Horse Capture 2004:43). It is an ambitious educational outreach program that includes traveling exhibitions, artifact loans, collections research and access, training programs, internships, and a workshop series that provides scholarship support for a limited number of participants, thereby making this program extremely valuable. The use of technology, including radio, plays a significant role in the Fourth Museum so as to extend its reach.

## Challenges

In his address at the first national conference of the North American Indian Museums Association in 1979, coordinator Richard Hill (Tuscarora) provided a summary of 30 respondents to a brief survey. He said: "Basically, we are very small organizations with small facilities.... Usually we are grossly understaffed, underpaid and underfunded.... Your urgent needs are to keep the doors open, develop your staff, your exhibits and your programs. We can see from this [survey] that funds and fund raising, as always, are a major concern and immediate need" (Risser 1979:3–5). The issues that challenged development of tribal museums in the 1970s are the same issues that exist at the start of the twenty-first century: namely, sustainability and funding, staffing and training, and governance. These issues are common for many

top left, AP Images.

Fig. 5. The National Museum of the American Indian, in Washington, D.C., which opened to the public on Sept. 21, 2004. Design and construction involved Indians from the U.S. and Canada. top left, Exterior of the 5-story curvilinear building, clad in Kasota dolomite limestone from Minn., evoking stratified rocks carved by wind and water. Features include an entrance facing east, prism windows, and, top right, a soaring interior circular space, called the Potomac. Photographs by, top left, J. Scott Applewhite, 2004; top right, Michael Hamady, 2007. bottom left and right, Opening of the museum with the Parade of Nations, a procession of Natives from the western hemisphere, many wearing traditional regalia. Colo. Sen. Ben Nighthorse Campbell addressed the crowds, bottom left, while dancers from a Northwest Coast delegation performed. Photographs by Laura Stafford, 2004.

mainstream, predominantly smaller, institutions nationwide, not just Native museums.

Sustainability and funding have been and continue to be the most significant issues. In the early days of the tribal museum movement, tribes considered museums as money-making ventures or, at minimum, had hoped to generate enough revenues through admission fees and gift shop sales to be self-sustaining. It rarely happened. Tribes have had a somewhat easier time constructing the buildings, but once opened, their operating costs sometimes took communities by surprise. The reality is, most tribal museums are found in rural reservation communities, far from other tourism attractions and population centers. There is a lack of local public funding from tax revenues as well as a pool of wealthy donors (Hanson 1980).

Although successful with federal grants, tribes have not sufficiently tapped charitable dollars from nonfederal sources. For example, from among the 900 largest American foundations, contributions to all Native causes totaled $91.9 million in 2002, or just 0.3% of total giving (Hicks and Jorgensen 2005). To counter the situation, tribes are seeking training in fundraising and assigning staff to work with nonfederal funding sources.

Staffing and training are two of the greatest needs. Salaries for tribal museum personnel are low, making it difficult to attract and keep qualified tribal members. Staff turnover is high due to inadequate resources. The result can leave a museum static in time and providing few services to the Native community.

The one area that has generated the most confusion in Native museums is governance. Since United States tribes are sovereign nations, there are more mechanisms to receive charitable contributions ranging from tribally chartered nonprofits to direct giving to the tribe to 501c3 nonprofit status and 7871 designations, among other vehicles. The main concerns are control, sovereign immunity, and taxation (Secakuku 2006:43). Tribal governments are becoming better versed in governance in order to best serve the interests of the museum while protecting tribal control and sovereignty.

Community politics is another challenge. A change in administration can have devastating effects on Native museum operations. Depending on the circumstances, the consequences may include staff cuts or replacements, budget reductions or elimination, or recurring governance issues. The ideal is to have the museum immune to Native politics, but it sometimes does not occur. More community participation and volunteerism in museum programs may help shield the institution, since members of a Native community can be advocates to tribal leadership, but so far, Native member visitation is low at many Native museums.

For Alaska Natives, the challenges are more pronounced. The majority of facilities are seasonal because of the long winters and short tourism season, making sustainability next to impossible. Construction costs are high and complicated by the short building season and isolation of Native villages. Acquiring professional training is difficult since Native (and non-Native) museum professionals often have to travel and invest both considerable time and money. Distance learning is limited due to the lack of a technology infrastructure, especially in the bush where many Native villages are located (Watt 2002).

Finally, native governments have many priorities. For groups with new financial resources, they may have a backlog of delayed community improvement projects. Native governments' focus has been on improvement of community members' health, housing, and education, diversifying their economies and acquiring traditional lands, among other important needs. Thus, for the first time, many communities are able to achieve their long-term development objectives. In this context, it is easy to understand why creating and operating museums are low on funding priority lists, thus often falling short of serving the membership in ways the community might have hoped or demanded.

The question remains as to whether the museum model is an appropriate one for the perpetuation of living Native cultures in the first place. When describing five Arizona tribes' efforts to create tribal museums, curator Ann Hitchcock states, "Each tribe has traditional means for dealing with the preservation of its customs, whether it be through a medicine man, a ceremonial society, or some other mechanism. The concept of a museum is a fairly ineffective substitute for the traditional means of preservation" (A. Hitchcock 1973:191).

The formal and informal sharing of cultural and traditional knowledge is widespread in Native communities. There are no set limitations; four walls and a formal structure do not guarantee effective knowledge sharing and identity strengthening (Doxtator 1985:25). Museums can facilitate the perpetuation and preservation of living cultures to a certain degree, but they are not replacements or substitutes for the intergenerational relationships that can cultivate pride in one's heritage, identity and culture and the desire to see them passed on to future generations. Museums may not be an answer to perpetuating living cultures after all, just one minor vehicle of many.

# Languages and Language Programs

LEANNE HINTON

Surveys in the mid-1990s found that 209 Native languages were spoken in North America, but that children were learning only 49 of them, more than half of these in Canada; 120 known languages were no longer spoken by anyone, as well as scores for which there were no data at all (vol. 17:3; Michael E. Krauss, personal communication 1997). Even where some children were being raised as speakers, they were often a dwindling minority under peer pressure to shift to the national language. Seventy-two Indian languages were then down to their last few elderly speakers, and year by year the number of language extinctions has increased while the number of children who are speakers has continued to drop.

The decline of the indigenous languages of North America is mourned by linguists and even more by the indigenous communities themselves. With the loss of the languages and the knowledge of human language that could be derived from them, worlds of knowledge, belief systems, and rich oral literatures are also lost to posterity. A community whose language disappears suffers a loss of identity, personal history, and community belonging.

After centuries of indifference and efforts at suppression, by the beginning of the twenty-first century societal attitudes toward Native languages had changed. But despite the self-determination of Native Americans in economics and education, for example, the aftermath of past policies, combined with the realities of modern life such as television, jobs, and school, created a situation where dozens of languages were in their last generation of existence. Even Navajo, with the largest number of speakers, showed a huge decline in the percentage of children who spoke it, with less than five percent of children fluent in their ancestral tongue at the time they entered school (Ted Fernald, personal communication, 2006). By the early years of the century, there were hardly any Indian communities where an Indian language could typically be heard in public, with the exception of some of those in remote areas. Very few Native Americans were monolingual in their heritage languages, and most who did know them were dominant in English. As the speakers of most American Indian languages were predominantly elderly, such languages seemed destined to have no native speakers left in a few decades. In this context efforts burgeoned to create new generations of native speakers by language revitalization.

## Language Revitalization

By the year 2000 language revitalization was a strong movement among indigenous groups in the United States and Canada. Native language activists generally saw each indigenous language as the key to the continuation of a Native people. Many expressed the feelings toward their languages that led to this movement, emphasizing that language was the key to their unique cultures and their sense of identity:

> Our languages mean much. They encompass whole linguistic solar systems of spiritual expression, whole galaxies that express universal human values like love, generosity and belonging, and whole universes of references that enable us to cope with an ever-changing world. Because our elders are moving on, it is up to us to help strengthen our languages. When one elder journeys to the spirit world, a whole Smithsonian Institution's worth of information goes with him or her. We have to retain that information in our languages, and that is why language is so vitally important (Littlebear 2005:7).
>
> The importance of language as an expression of culture, of who we are as a people, must be upheld by each individual, each family, each community, and each nation (Kirkness 2002).
>
> I am really worried if we lose our language we won't be able to think in the Arapaho way. If we lose our language we will lose our ceremonies and ourselves because our life is our language, and it is our language that makes us strong (Greymorning 1999).

Cheyenne educator Richard Littlebear (1999) emphasized the "spiritual relevance" of Native languages in the contemporary world. Ojibwa anthropologist Mindy J. Morgan (2005) stressed language as empowerment, a symbol of sovereignty and self-determination.

The consciousness leading to the desire for language revitalization probably began in the 1960s during the civil rights movement. At the time, language issues were not part of the agenda of Native American activists, but what was reborn at that time was a sense of pride of being Indian, and with it a sense of the right of Indian people to maintain their own cultures—and by extension their languages.

In the late 1960s, with the advent of government-sponsored bilingual education programs, Native peoples had their first real opportunity to look toward language maintenance and revitalization. Language maintenance applies when a threatened minority language can be maintained as a living language with some assistance, such as school programs. Language revitalization is needed in the more urgent cases in which a language has suffered a major decline or may even have very few or no remaining speakers. Language maintenance was the main goal at first: in the 1960s and 1970s it was not clear to many communities that their languages were disappearing. Many children still spoke the language, and many believed that by supporting the languages in the schools, the languages could be maintained. Only in subsequent decades did it become widely recognized that the languages were truly dying out, so that programs began to have the goal of the revitalization of the languages, rather than simply their maintenance.

## The Role of Linguists

Linguists studying the indigenous languages of North America have long been aware of their decline, and throughout the twentieth century and even before, linguists tried to document languages before they disappeared. The goal was to preserve the knowledge of each language by publishing "a grammar, a dictionary and a body of texts," as the ideal was formulated by Mary Haas, who trained generations of linguists in this work at the University of California at Berkeley (Hinton and Munro 1998). This sort of linguistic documentation declined in the 1970s and 1980s under the influence of modern theoretical linguistics, which tended to focus on what was thought to be the abstract universal "language faculty" shared by speakers of all languages. In the 1990s, it began to come back into favor in the field of linguistics with the awareness of the plight of endangered languages, a change of attitude reflected in an influential article in the journal *Language* (Hale et al. 1992) and further impelled by adamancy in the communities where linguists worked about maintaining or regaining their languages. The language revitalization movement has had a strong effect on the depth and breadth of documentation, with a focus on conversation and the recording of situational speech, essential material for bringing a language back into daily use.

The documentation work that linguists and other scholars have done over the years has been very important in the revitalization process, especially so for languages that have lost all their native speakers and that can be reclaimed only from documents. Archives of field notes and tapes are visited regularly by Native Americans collecting the materials for use in their efforts to revive indigenous language use.

Linguists have played a direct role in language revitalization projects and have worked closely with indigenous groups on orthography design and the development of dictionaries, grammars, and other materials for community use. Part of any linguist's bargain with communities involving field research in the United States and Canada now includes the development of materials directly for use by the community. In some cases, a young linguist's first paying job is with a tribe rather than a university.

However, Native communities are the prime movers in language revitalization, and for many revitalization projects, linguists play little or no role. There is tension between the agendas of linguists and tribes, in particular involving issues surrounding publication. Furthermore, as indigenous peoples move toward autonomy in their affairs, there is often an aversion to depending too much on outside experts; and linguists often lack training in many of the important aspects of revitalization anyway (in particular, the theory and methods of effective language teaching). Darrell Kipp, cofounder of the Piegan Institute in Browning, Montana, which runs the Cuts Wood immersion school (Blackfeet) (fig. 1), warned about reliance on linguists: "Don't hire linguists. They can speak the language but the kids won't" (Kipp 2000:4) and "It depends on the individual linguist about whether you want them to get involved with the immersion programs. I would caution you to ensure that they not be the primary resource or supplant anything that we should be doing for ourselves. I don't want us to sit back and become reliant upon them" (Kipp 2000:35).

Nevertheless, as language revitalization gathers steam, the linguists who document and research the indigenous languages of North America are learning more about how to make relevant contributions to this movement, and their work in this area is often of great value to community efforts. More and more linguists are seeing their contribution to community language revitalization as an important and satisfying part of their careers. However, this takes time and energy away from the publication of scholarly articles, and universities have not always recognized these applications of linguistics as counting toward hiring and promotion.

## Community Classes

The emphasis on language as an essential part of Native American identity and culture came into focus slowly after the 1960s. The earliest and still the most common effort at language revitalization involves informal get-togethers of interested members of a community, sometimes with a linguist present and often without, where native speakers teach the language to other community members. These informal classes may occur once a week or so, tend to focus on vocabulary and short phrases, and usually involve writing. If a linguist or a community member who knows about writing is present, the speaker may say the words, the writing expert writes it on the blackboard, and the learners copy it down. Sometimes the learners will just make a attempt at writing it down using their understanding of English orthography as a guide. Often the learners guide the speaker by asking how to say certain words or phrases. Few people have ever really learned to speak the language

Fig. 1. The Piegan Institute, Browning, Mont. left, Darrell Kipp. Photograph by Herb Luthin, 2006. right, Nizipuhwahsin or Cuts Wood School for Blackfeet language immersion. Photograph by Leanne Hinton, 2006.

through this means; the classes are too short and far between, and the method is not one that leads to conversational proficiency. However, these informal classes, which virtually every Native community has experienced, can result in increased awareness and knowledge that is valued greatly by the participants.

Indigenous language classes modeled after foreign language classes in schools began to develop in educational facilities with sizable indigenous populations in the 1970s if not before; they were common in the 1990s and 2000s. Methodology and focus varied depending on the fluency, educational background, and imagination of the instructors, ranging from the translation method of teaching words and their English equivalents, through a formal presentation of grammar and writing, to full immersion methods. Immersion methods have the best results in terms of producing students who can carry on a conversation in the target language (vol. 12:78), although their ultimate degree of proficiency will be determined largely by the amount of time they can spend with the language. Many schools, if they allow Native language instruction at all, will allow only an hour or two a week, whereas some schools may allow as much as five hours, an investment that can result in a fairly high degree of proficiency.

## Bilingual Education

An important step in language maintenance and revitalization was the advent of bilingual education, set up nationally in the United States in 1968 by the Bilingual Education Act,

and later mandated for schools with non-English speakers in as a result of the *Lau* v. *Nichols* Supreme Court decision. Bilingual education was established mainly with immigrants in mind, not American Indians, the idea being that children who did not know English would progress faster in their education if they began learning the basics in their mother tongue at the same time they were learning English. But Native Americans immediately pounced on the opportunity to start programs of their own. With grants under this act, many communities began programs that brought the languages into the schools. Before the Bilingual Education Act, the Rough Rock bilingual demonstration school was established in 1966 (vol. 10:665–667), the first Native American bilingual school in the United States (J. Crawford 1995:187). By 1969, just a year after the Bilingual Education Act was passed, there were already several American Indian bilingual education programs, and by the early 1970s, there were scores of programs.

When the Bilingual Education Act was passed, the government had in mind a transitional model of bilingual education. The goal was to switch to English-medium education when the children were sufficiently fluent to do so. However, most indigenous groups saw bilingual education as a tool for language maintenance, in addition to being a way to make education more relevant to Native children's culture and worldview. Thus, the goal was to develop bilingual education programs in as many grades as a community had resources to teach, regardless of the degree of student fluency in English. Indeed, in many Native communities where the language was already moribund, in the early years of bilingual education there were bilingual programs started where children did not know their heritage languages, and teaching the language to the children was part of the program. In the late 1980s Secretary of Education William Bennett terminated dozens of such programs in Native American communities.

Indian bilingual education also focused on Native cultural practices. Traditional foods, crafts, and oral arts were stressed along with the schoolhouse topics of reading, writing, and science. Studies show that bilingual education, with its culturally sensitive approach, has positive educational results for Native American students in comparison with mainstream public schools (A. Holm and W. Holm 1995; Demmert 2001; Kratochwill et al. 2004).

One of the earliest indigenous bilingual education programs to be founded was the Rock Point Bilingual Education Program, Arizona, begun in 1967. At the time, the majority of students entering the school system were dominant in Navajo. From the start, the first reading language was Navajo, taught starting in kindergarten. English reading was not started until the second grade. English consumed a greater portion of the day each year, until by grades seven and eight students had only one period a day in Navajo and a quarter each year of Navajo writing (Reyhner 1990). Throughout the grades, Navajo social studies and cultural instruction were also given. Standardized tests showed that these students did very well in their studies, and by eighth grade the students were performing considerably better than the students attending English-only schools. Yet by 1995, a majority of Navajo children were coming to kindergarten not knowing their heritage language, and so programs had to be devised at Rock Point to teach the Navajo language to the students. Bit by bit, the language goals of bilingual education programs shifted from maintenance to revitalization.

## Literacy

American Indian languages north of Mesoamerica were not written before European contact. Literacy first emerged in the context of Christian missions, and to varying degrees members of some tribes acquired the ability to read and write their languages, beginning in the seventeenth century (vol. 17:158–184). In the late twentieth century a number of Indian groups sought the development of practical writing systems that could be used in language education and in the production of written materials, bilingual education programs being a major impetus. Vocabulary for things and concepts encountered in school, such as "triangle" and "subtract," had to be standardized. Literacy development also demanded the development of a literature and genres of writing. These needs resulted in a large number of Native Americans pursuing degrees in education and the enlisting of professional linguists and educators as consultants to help in the special training, planning, and material needs of communities.

*Orthography*

Orthographic design has been and continues to be an important and hotly debated issue both between linguists and within Native American communities. Existing traditional writing systems were usually kept and used in the new school curricula. The syllabaries used to write Cherokee, Cree, and Inuit have been taught in schools since the advent of school language classes. However, alphabetic systems have been devised for some of those languages as well. For example, in the Canadian territory of Nunavut, both the syllabary and the alphabetic system exist side by side, with some communities using one and some the other; both are taught in school. Similarly, the Cherokee language has both the old syllabary and an alphabetic system, and if anything, the alphabetic system is used more. The Montagnais (Innu) orthography developed by Roman Catholic missionaries in the eighteenth century was standardized for all dialects in a series of conferences that brought together representatives from all Montagnais-speaking communities.

In the twentieth century, some North American languages adopted phonemic writing systems similar or identical to those used by linguists working on those languages. The fact that linguistically based phonemic alphabets often have symbols that cannot be typed on a normal typewriter or a computer does not always deter communities from adopting them. For example, the speakers of Montana Salish (Flathead) have adopted an alphabet based largely on the phonetic notation used by linguists. Conversely, where linguists have worked with community members interested in language development, the practical orthographies developed for speakers and learners have sometimes been used in linguistic documentation. This was the case, for example, with the Navajo orthography standardized in 1937 (vol. 10:666–667, vol. 17:178), and the Diegueño orthography that was developed by the linguist Margaret Langdon in the early 1970s while working with Northern Diegueño speaker Ted Couro, who ran a weekly language class.

The advent of bilingual education heralded a movement toward the development of practical writing systems. The technical orthographies used by linguists for documentation used letters and accents in values that were unfamiliar to anyone literate only in English, as well as special characters that were difficult to type or print but were required by the linguists' guiding principle of "one sound, one letter." Typical accommodations to English spelling are the use of multiletter combinations to write single sounds, such as "sh," "ch," and others developed for specific languages. (The orthographic footnotes in the tribal chapters in vols. 5–15 have many examples.) Where non-English symbols were deemed necessary, often new ones were designed that could readily be typed, such as the use of the number "3" in Arapaho orthography to write the "th" sound in "three" (technical symbol /θ/). The main orthographic problems tend to concern the representation of vowel quality and vowel length, and how to spell sounds not found in English.

Also playing a role in orthography are social and political issues, such as the desire of different groups who speak the same or very similar languages to display their independence by having different orthographies. For example, the Havasupais and Hualapais (Walapai), who are differentiated only by minor dialect differences, insisted on having different writing systems to reflect their political separation (Crook, Hinton, and Stenson 1977). Some orthographies are used in different degrees of precision, for example, when accents that mark tones are customarily omitted, as in the Arapaho orthography. In other cases, several competing orthographies have been developed over the years for a particular language, and the differing origins and associations (such as a system created in connection with a religious organization, versus a linguistic system, versus a system developed by activists within the community) have created or increased factionalism within some communities. One problem with the development of a new writing system is that if there is not a strong educational program to support it, the community has no way to get the training necessary to understand and utilize it. Thus even when a good writing system exists, people often revert to nonstandard and highly variable "folk writing" systems based on English spelling rules.

These problems are minor compared to the benefits that can derive from the development and use of writing systems by American Indian communities. Native literacy has tremendous value for the documentation of languages. A language with sufficient documentation has the potential for revitalization even if all the speakers are gone. A literate community need not rely on outsiders to document their language; the local community can do it too, and are in fact likely to document aspects of the language that linguists may miss. Furthermore, if a community can avoid using the dominant language for many of their reading and writing needs, then the local language gains new functionality, a necessary part of revitalization.

*Literacy Development*

Bilingual education allowed the development of publications and new genres of literature. Children's books have been the main focus of literary development, ranging from mimeographed copies of handwritten compositions to highly professional volumes. For example, the Navajos produced translations of the *Time-Life* series of lavishly illustrated science books for young people, such as *Náshdóí Yáázh*, about lions in Africa (Bił Hazí'ąądi Nooyééł 1972). For several years, until government funding was terminated, the Navajo Reading Project produced a great deal of reading material for students and the community in general. Among the many books published by the Hualapai program, under the leadership of Lucille Watahomigie, was the excellent *Hualapai Reference Grammar* (Watahomigie, Bender, and Yamamoto 1982) and the beautiful *Kathad Ganavj* (Mapatis et al. 1981)—a compilation of stories told by the elders.

Havasupais were among the many groups who developed stories written and illustrated by school children, and then reproduced them for class reading. As the focus on native-language school curriculum has evolved, books and materials on all topics have developed for math and the social and physical sciences. Also being produced by tribal language organizations are dictionaries, reference grammars, pedagogical language learning materials, volumes of texts, newspapers (usually in the dominant language but also usually with at least a column in the indigenous language), and a myriad of other publications. For several years, the Navajos had a linguistic journal (*Diné Bizaad Náníl'įįh*) written mostly in Navajo.

Functionally, writing in Native American languages is primarily used in the schoolroom, and in the case of some individuals, for the continuation of writing genres introduced in the schools (such as poetry or short stories). Given that most indigenous people of the United States and Canada are native speakers of English or French, most practical literacy needs outside the classroom are filled by reading and writing in the dominant language. Rarely are the new writing systems used for correspondence (other than as part of the school curriculum), shopping lists, or other practical matters, or for official matters such as council meeting minutes. Yet some official uses of the new orthographies have occurred, such as the development of maps showing aboriginal territory, or the translation of a new constitution into the language (Bunte and Franklin 2001). Important symbolic usage of the writing systems includes street and store names, publication titles, and tribal logos, as well as the less formal use of the orthography on tee shirts, for example. But more importantly, for communities where the language is rarely heard, the writing system stimulates the development of materials and books that allow members access to their language. As an example, attractive pocket-size phrasebooks published by several northern California tribes and the Sac and Fox of Oklahoma and Missouri have met with great appreciation by members of those tribes (N. Richardson and S. Burcell 1993; Hupa Indian Language Classes, Golla, and Fletcher 1994; Bommelyn 1995; Whittaker 1996).

*The Computer and the Internet*

With the advent of e-mail and the internet, the functionality of writing has taken a new turn in all languages. The internet has vastly increased the potential accessibility of linguistic materials to indigenous people, and as more communities develop mass computer literacy, the use of the internet for language revitalization purposes is exploding. E-mail can potentially be used for indigenous language communication and practice, especially between people who are far apart. As one example, Phil Cashcash runs a Nez Perce listserv where he puts out a "word of the day" in writing and with a sound file, and a discussion of the meaning; he carries on regular correspondence in Nez Perce off the listserv with several people.

As archives at universities and museums put their collections on line, indigenous people can have those materials at their fingertips. However, there are issues developing over how free access should be. Some tribes are nervous about letting nontribal people have unrestricted access to their language materials, and both sacred texts and gossip can be injurious in the wrong hands. The need to be selective about what actually goes on line is recognized, and password protection is used in many cases.

One project of interest is the digitization of the J.P. Harrington materials, headed by Martha Macri at the University of California at Davis. Native people are being trained to input Harrington's materials on their own languages, and primary use of the materials will be by the interested people of the community. The language materials are being entered into a well-designed database, as well as scanned so that the original page can be seen beside the entries. When completed, users will be able to look up materials by English gloss, indigenous language form, subject (plants, relatives, colors, etc.), name of the speaker, date collected, and so forth.

One of the important internet projects directed at language revitalization is Canada's First Voices project, operated by the First Peoples' Cultural Foundation in Victoria, British Columbia. The heart of the First Voices project is an online language archiving tool, where indigenous people can input language data for the creation of an alphabet, dictionary, and phrase book, along with sound files and images. Dozens of Canadian languages are already represented at the First Voices website. At the site are brief descriptions of the languages' histories and their language revitalization efforts, along with children's games and activities. More and more Native groups have their own language websites, with online dictionaries and other materials. The website of the Nunavut government allows users to select a language (English, French, Inuit), and for Inuit either Roman letters or syllabary.

## From Language Maintenance to Language Revitalization

Bilingual education in the United States served as an important first step toward community-driven language revitalization, by helping to stimulate many Native Americans to get degrees in education and become experts in language-teaching theory and methods. It helped reverse the negative attitudes toward the languages that had been developed during the boarding school era, and it got communities started on literacy development.

Despite the educational benefits of bilingual education, by 1990 it was clear to most communities that bilingual education was not turning language loss around. Even in places with the best bilingual education programs, such as the Navajo programs, children coming to kindergarten speaking

Navajo became a tiny minority. Bilingual education is generally not designed to successfully teach the language to community people who do not know it. It is at best a tool for language maintenance, not language revitalization. As Christine Sims (2001:69) put it for her own community, "these programs had not produced what was most critical to Acoma language stability and vitality: new generations of Acoma speakers." Furthermore, the federal government's interest in bilingual education diminished. There are still excellent bilingual education programs in some Native communities, but the number is declining. And for declining languages, bilingual education is simply not enough.

The main goal of language revitalization of North American Indian languages is getting new speakers of the languages. Thus, while indigenous literacy will always remain a necessary component of language development and of Native-run schools, the focus of language revitalization in North America is shifting from literacy to spoken language acquisition.

### Immersion Schools

The most radical and effective movement toward language revitalization has been the development of language immersion schools. The Maoris of New Zealand led the way to early childhood immersion learning with the development of "language nests," where preschool-aged children spent the day at centers where the fluent grandparent generation communicated with them full-time in the Maori language. Hawaiians developed their own language nests, and eventually Hawaiian as the medium of instruction in some schools all the way through twelfth grade (W.H. Wilson and K. Kamana 2001) and Hawaiian-medium classes at the University of Hawaii at Hilo. The Maoris and Hawaiians have been important role models for North American indigenous groups, who have often visited Hawaii and New Zealand for inspiration and instruction in the development of their own programs. In immersion schooling the primary language of instruction is the Native language, with a strong emphasis on the development of oral proficiency. English instruction begins in the later grades or not at all. The grandparent generation forms a large part of the teaching force, and parental involvement is intensive. In addition to language, the schools emphasize native values, ceremonialism, and traditional skills.

The development of language immersion schools has been a strong movement in the United States and Canada since the 1980s. By the early 2000s there were 50 immersion schools in the United States (Pease Pretty-On-Top 2005). Many of the schools that began bilingual education programs when the children were still coming to school speaking the indigenous language shifted focus in response to the decline of childhood fluency and became immersion schools themselves. For example, the Window Rock School District on the Navajo Reservation transitioned from bilingual education to immersion in 1986 (Margaret Benally, personal communication 2006). The Yupik (Yup'ik) language and culture education programs of the Lower Kuskokwim School District in Alaska have several different programs for the broad range of communities in the district. There is one kind of schooling for communities who are dominant in Yupik (the Yup'ik First Language Program), another for communities where about half the children are dominant in Yupik and half in English (the Yup'ik Two-Way Immersion Program); and a third for communities where most are dominant in English (the Yup'ik One-Way Immersion program) (Norris-Tull 1999). Just to name a few of the many immersion school programs extant in 2006, there was the Mohawk Akwesasne Freedom School, Rooseveltown, New York (founded in 1979 becoming an immersion school in 1985), which is operated by the parents; the Navajo Tséhootsooí Diné Bi'ólta' at Window Rock Unified School District in Fort Defiance, Arizona, also known as the Diné Language Immersion School, serving 250 students from kindergarten to sixth grade; the Blackfeet Cuts Wood School in Browning, Montana; Nḱʷusm School, a Salish immersion school, on the Flathead Reservation, Montana (fig. 2); Waadookodaading, an Ojibwa language immersion charter school, in Hayward, Wisconsin; Nikaitchuat Ilisagviat, an Inupiaq language immersion preschool, opened in 1998, serving 20 children ages 3–5, at the Native Village of Kotzebue, Alaska; Grande Ronde School, teaching Chinuk Wawa (Chinook Jargon), Grande Ronde, Washington; Chief Atahm School, a Secwepemc (Shuswap) language immersion school in Chase, British Columbia; and the Cayuga and Mohawk Language Immersion School at Six Nations of the Grand River, in Ontario.

Some immersion schools are located within the public school system, where they are sometimes subject to laws and regulations that conflict with the mission of language revitalization. Other immersion schools are private or charter schools, allowing them to go their own way more than the public schools. The first principle of immersion schools is that all basic subjects are taught in the Native language. The strategy is often to start with a "lead group" who enters the immersion program at the preschool level, and then is carried forward into the elementary years and possibly even high school. The teachers and supporting staff develop the next year's curriculum ahead of the lead group, developing materials for reading, math, science, and social studies as they go. Frequently the curriculum is informal and in the early years of a program may be experimental and opportunistic. Children tend to thrive in these schools and emerge from them better adjusted, more confident, and more prepared to go on to higher education than many of their counterparts in the English-medium public schools (Pease Pretty-On-Top 2005).

In some areas different communities may be dominant either in the indigenous language or in English or French. This is the case in Nunavut territory, where many schools practice immersion through the early grades and then switch to English instruction. Nunavut has communities at all stages of language shift or maintenance; nevertheless, there is concern that the Inuit language (Inuktitut) is losing ground. The Nunavut government has declared the goal of having 85 percent of its workforce use the Inuktitut language at work by the year 2020.

As the last fluent native-speaking generation in most cases, the "grandparent teacher" has a major presence in the classroom. Typically, the grandparents do not have teaching credentials, and so the classrooms also make use of younger teachers who are second language learners. Since most or all of the children coming to the school for the first time know only English, the first educational hurdle is to get them to the point of understanding and speaking the Native American heritage language. The strategy is to immerse them totally in the language, which means no English is allowed in the classroom. All school lessons, informal patter, classroom management language, and playground interaction must be in the target language. The teachers must be trained to curb any temptation to break into English or to translate into English when a child doesn't understand.

But learning the language does not take place by the unstructured "sink or swim" method. Lessons and all talk are accompanied by gestures, visual aids, actions, and activities that allow the children to understand what is going on even before they understand the words. Among the most popular tools is the Total Physical Response method (Asher 1982), based on the notion that language learning is facilitated by physical activity in connection with the words and phrases being learned (fig. 3). This method focuses first on verbal commands, where learners are given commands in the target language and then do what they are told. Action-based drills are central to the method, and comprehension is stressed before production. Krashen and Terrell's (1983) "Natural Approach" to language learning is also followed by a number of schools. The "natural approach" takes lessons learned from first language acquisition and applies them to second language acquisition as well.

The schools are strongly committed not only to language immersion but also to teaching Native values and cultural traditions. For example, the Akwesasne Freedom School has school holidays during its 15 traditional ceremonies, and children are expected to attend the ceremonies during those days. The Cochiti summer school ties its teaching to the summer ceremonies. In almost all the immersion schools, traditional prayer and song are important. Learning traditional ways of dealing with natural resources and issues of conservation are also a big part of education in most immersion schools, as well as Native arts and Native-oriented social studies and history. At the same time, the immersion schools aspire to the educational standards of the state and nation to bring technology, including multimedia learning, to the classroom.

While the idea of an immersion school is to have all instruction take place in the heritage language, English plays a role both officially and unofficially. The official role of English in the immersion schools differs depending on the philosophy of the school. Most of the children who attend

the Native language immersion schools have learned and use English as the primary language of home, so oral fluency in English is already established by the time they attend school. The only issue is when to introduce English literacy. The Navajo immersion school Tséhootsooí Diné Bi'ólta' brings in more English each year until sixth grade when 50 percent of the classes are English and 50 percent in Navajo. Cuts Wood School allows English signage and some English-language books informally in the classroom, but it gives no formal English-medium instruction until late spring of the eighth grade, when it provides a several-week-long intensive class in English grammar, just before they go to the English-medium high school. The Shuswap-run Chief Atahm School, on Adams Lake Reserve, Chase, British Columbia, allows no English at all.

Unofficially, English "sneaks" into the classroom and onto the playground fairly often, as might be expected in a situation where everyone in the school is fluent in English. The staff has to maintain constant vigilance of their own speech in order to keep English at bay, and also design their programs so that the children continue to speak in the indigenous language during break periods as well as in the classroom. Many immersion programs are within schools that also have English-medium tracks, and it creates a particular problem at recesses and in the halls, where immersion students find themselves surrounded by English.

A frequent question is whether the children who go to immersion schools are being educated as well as children in English-medium schools, and in particular whether they are being prepared for higher education and work in the English-speaking world. One common answer to that is that the goal of the immersion school is to make children fluent in their language and able to function in the Native environment, not to make them do better in school. As Darrell Kipp (2000:1) put it: "Keep in mind that the language is the key. There is nothing else. There is no other priority. There are no other issues. There is no reason to defend your motives, your actions, or your vision. You do not defend yourself, your own language fluency, or lack of fluency. You do it.

Fig. 2. NƛʷK̓usm, a Salish language immersion school in Arlee, Mont., funded primarily by the Confederated Salish and Kootenai Tribes. Founded in 2002, NK̓ʷusm taught 45 students, ages 3–14, in 2007. All academic subjects are taught in the Salish language to bring the students to a high level of fluency. In addition, adult speakers become fluent as teachers and aides. top, Stephen Small Salmon, elder, teaching a preschool class about preparing choke-cherries by pounding them with a rock. Amy Plante is holding the rock. Photograph by Antoine Sandoval, 2006. center, Elder teacher Patrick Pierre with 3d to 8th grade students, left to right, Daniel Moran, Darien Parker, Nichole Perry holding the camas flower and stem, Shandiin "Maii" Pete, Siliye Pete holding the whole plant with bulb, Aspen Smith, Stsa Pete with camas flower, Jordan Plant, and Kayenta Pete at a camas site where they were digging the edible root. The camas is baked in a pit in the ground, a process that takes 3 days. Photograph by Antoine Sandoval, 2007. bottom, Sign inside the school. Photograph by Leanne Hinton, 2006.

Action is the key. Native children who are actively speaking the language are your only result."

But another, equally true answer is that evidence from the less than two decades that Native language immersion schools have been developing indicates that children do as well or better than their counterparts in the English-immersion schools. For example, testing shows that when the children from the Cayuga Mohawk Immersion School enter the English-medium grades, they may test below average at grade 9, but by grade 10 they test at grade level, and by grade 12 they are beyond grade level (Michelle Davis, personal communication 2006). The reason is probably in part that the immersion schools build self confidence in their children by creating a school environment relevant to the home and community, respectful of Native traditions and values rather than in conflict with them, as is the case with most of the public schools. Furthermore, there is a good deal of research showing that bilingualism confers cognitive advantages and appears to enhance school performance (Hakuta and Diaz 1985).

*Immersion Camps*

Developing and maintaining an immersion school is a major community effort: it is expensive, and it takes an enormous amount of work, often by too few people with too little funding and too little space, and facing a plague of laws and regulations. Few communities have the financial, human, and linguistic resources necessary to run a full-scale immersion school. Many communities focus instead on summer immersion sessions. Cochiti Pueblo, in Cochiti, New Mexico; Chief Dull Knife College Northern Cheyenne Language Immersion Camp, Montana (fig. 3); Little Big Horn College, Land and Water Migration Camp, Montana; and the Fond Du Lac Community College Teacher Training and Language Immersion Camp, Minnesota, are four of literally hundreds of indigenous language and cultural immersion camps that take place around North America annually.

*Adult Language Facility*

One major obstacle in language revitalization is the problem of the "missing generation." Intensive revitalization projects tend to focus on bringing children to language proficiency, and it is the parents of those children who are motivated enough to choose immersion schools or send them to immersion camps. Yet the parents themselves typically do not know the language well or at all. The "missing generation" is the generation that could become the teachers in immersion schools or bring the language back into the

Chief Dull Knife College, Cultural Affairs Dept., Lame Deer, Mont.

Fig. 3. Conrad Fisher, center, dean of cultural affairs at Chief Dull Knife College, teaching at the Northern Cheyenne immersion language camp run by the Cultural Affairs Dept. of the college, at Crazy Head Springs campground near Lame Deer, Mont., on the Northern Cheyenne Res. It is for ages 9 to 16; children younger than that may attend if a parent accompanies them. Living in tents or tepees for 12 days, the students hike, do crafts, and listen to adults in small groups for 4–7 hours a day. The Northern Cheyenne language is the means of discussion. The children are wearing tags that give their names in both English and Cheyenne. Fisher is using the Total Physical Response method of teaching. Photographed probably 2003.

home, if only they knew the language. Instead, finding qualified teachers of professional age who can teach in Native-language medium schools is a daunting task. For example, the Akwesasne Freedom School cannot go higher than eighth grade in 2007 primarily because of the lack of teachers who know the language. And in many immersion schools around North America, English often enters the classroom more than desired, because the teachers are not fluent in the Native language. Native-speaking elders are always in the classroom in most of the immersion schools, but because in most Native American groups the native speakers are past retirement age and not trained as teachers, much of the teaching falls to second-language learners. Many communities have no adequate means for adults to learn their heritage language. The development of oral fluency for adult second-language learners is an important component of immersion schooling, which can make the difference between a truly successful immersion environment and a less successful situation where teachers—and therefore the children as well—frequently slip into English.

Since immersion schools depend on parental involvement and cooperation in the stimulation of language revitalization, parent language training is considered very important. Parent volunteers in the classroom need to learn basic interactional language such as greetings and instructions. Programs may provide phrase lists to the parents, or evening lessons. Children also take their language home with them, and parents and siblings learn from them. Often school assignments are designed with this in mind.

*College Classes*

By 2007 language classes for adults were often available in colleges near indigenous population centers. The University of Minnesota, Minneapolis; the University of Oklahoma, Norman; the University of Alaska, Fairbanks; the University of New Mexico, Albuquerque; the University of Arizona, Tucson; Michigan State University, East Lansing; the University of British Columbia, Vancouver; Simon Frasier University, Burnaby, British Columbia; and the University of Toronto were among the universities that offered regular language classes in indigenous languages. Tribally run colleges usually provide some courses in the local languages. For example, Diné College, Tsaile, Arizona, offers courses in Navajo; Little Priest Tribal College, Winnebago, Nebraska, offers one semester of Ho-Chunk (Winnebago); Fort Belknap College, Harlem, Montana, offers two semesters of Assiniboine (Nakota) and Gros Ventre; Salish Kootenai College, Pablo, Montana, offers three semesters each of Montana Salish and Kootenay; and Blue Quills First Nations College, Saint Paul, Alberta, offers intensive immersion classes in Cree. How intensive these courses are and what teaching methods are used varies a good deal. Many of them are linguistically based, with writing and structure as the primary focus. Others might be mainly vocabulary-based. Only a few are conversationally based, the kind of course that actually leads to people being able to use the language orally.

*The Master-Apprentice Model*

Despite the fact that there are many indigenous language courses taught in colleges and universities, most North American languages are not taught in classes at all. It is impossible, for example, for California Indians to find classes that would teach them their languages of heritage. The very linguistic diversity of North America, and the tiny populations claiming those languages, makes it impossible to teach most of the languages in colleges. Effective learning of one's language of heritage must therefore take place in some other way. California's Master-Apprentice Language Learning Program provides a model for "bootstrap" language learning (Hinton 2002). Developed and run by the nonprofit Advocates for Indigenous California Language Survival, the Master-Apprentice method trains teams consisting of a speaker (the "master") and an adult learner (the "apprentice") to immerse themselves in the speaker's language by using only that, and no English, for at least 10 hours a week while engaged together in real-life activities. The successful teams are able to develop conversational proficiency over a period of two to three years. These apprentices go on to teach the language themselves and sometimes begin raising children in the language. This method and other similar mentored language learning programs are also being used in some communities around the United States and Canada for teacher training, to bring them to sufficient proficiency to be able to run the classroom without lapsing into English.

*Training*

Staff for bilingual programs, immersion programs, and community programs outside the school system all require training in how to plan and run their programs. There are few opportunities to get this training, much less opportunities to get any kind of degree or certificate in language revitalization. A few programs emerged to fill this need, most of them summer programs for people already involved in language teaching in their communities. One of the oldest is the American Indian Languages Development Institute at the University of Arizona, Tucson, which was founded in 1978 for indigenous bilingual education teachers. The University of Oregon, Eugene, has run the summer Northwest Indian Language Institute since 1997.

In Canada, too, there were opportunities for training. A program leading to a bachelor's in education specifically oriented to indigenous language education was established in 1989 at the Memorial University of Newfoundland, Saint John's (Johns and Mazurkewich 2001). In British Columbia the University of Victoria and University of British Columbia, Vancouver, both developed summer programs of certification in language revitalization, granting credit for relevant courses in language revitalization, language documentation, linguistics for language revitalization, curriculum development, and so forth, as well as classes on the structure of the specific languages of the participants.

There are also university programs in linguistics for indigenous people planning to work in their communities. The University of Arizona has an master's program in community linguistics, and Massachusetts Institute of Technology, Cambridge, offers a master's program for indigenous linguists, the Indigenous Language Initiative. While some of these programs may do less to prepare their students for the field of language education, the students come out with great knowledge of linguistics in general and their language in particular, and how to analyze and utilize the linguistic documentation of their language.

### Spreading the Language to the Community

Since the languages in question are all endangered, the same situation exists outside the school that existed before: the language is silent, and nothing is heard around town and in the family but English or French. One challenge is to get the community involved and using the language; another is to keep the children using the language after they graduate from the immersion school and go on to English-medium schooling. Leaders in the immersion schools try to tackle both these problems in various ways. Public performances in the Native tongue by students and even simply training students to greet others and speak in the language at ceremonials and elsewhere have elicited interest and support from community members. An emphasis on Native ceremonialism at the Piegan Institute's Cuts Wood immersion school means that ceremonial leaders take on some of the students as apprentices and helpers as they get older, keeping them involved in the language even after they graduate and go on to the English-medium high school. The Mohawks and other communities similarly report that children who have gained proficiency in their school programs go on to play important roles in the ceremonies, providing a strong venue for continued language use.

Commitment by the leadership of the community can play a big role. For example, the Cochiti tribe decided to be a model for the rest of the community by using the language as much as possible at the tribal office. It was decreed that anyone who can speak Cochiti should speak it and teach it; and any tribal employee that cannot speak Cochiti should learn it. A half-hour language session was set up at the beginning of every workday to this end (Pecos and Blum 2001).

### Bringing the Language Home

Many parents trying to bring their heritage language into the home faced barriers of unconscious language choice. Even parents fluent in their heritage language had to overcome lifelong habits of using English as their main language of communication. Margaret Peters, a fluent speaker of Mohawk and member of the staff at Akwesasne Freedom School, gave an honest assessment of how hard it is. She did not use Mohawk at home with her first four children, even though she sent them to the immersion school. She finally realized that she and her peers all had a pattern of language use at home such that they would speak Mohawk to each other, but switch to English whenever the children would come into the room. She and her husband then made a strong conscious effort to speak Mohawk to their children, and especially to their youngest child, who was acquiring Mohawk as his first language. There are enormous barriers to home language use: lack of fluency, lack of other speakers to reinforce the language, schools that teach only in the dominant language and do not support minority language use, and peer groups speaking English, leading children to come home saying "I'm not going to speak that other language any more." It takes a strong community effort to help a family work through these stumbling blocks to raise fluent speakers of an endangered language.

## Languages Without Speakers

Even when a language lacks speakers entirely, Native language activists refuse to concede that all is lost. A number of individuals from these defunct speech communities took it upon themselves to learn their heritage languages from documentation and to bring it into their homes. Among these were Daryl Baldwin (Miami) and Jessie Little Doe Baird (Wampanoag). Both obtained master's degrees in linguistics in order to increase their ability to understand and use the documentation, and both were raising young children as speakers of their languages. Both have also been leaders in community-wide language revitalization programs.

The University of California at Berkeley runs a biennial program specifically for Indians whose languages lack speakers, the Breath of Life Language Workshop, cosponsored by the Advocates for Indigenous California Language Survival (fig. 4). The participants learn how to find their materials in the archives, how to read phonetic writing, and how to glean useful language out of the materials for language learning and revitalization purposes. In fact, archives are increasingly visited by Native people. At Berkeley, over 90 percent of the visitors to the archives of Native American languages are the Native Americans themselves, seeking copies for their own archives and for language revitalization purposes.

The Department of Linguistics at the University of Washington, Seattle, runs a similar workshop biennially. Salish, Klamath, and Chinookans learn to use the archives while educating linguists and librarians in the needs of their language communities.

Even when a language is poorly recorded, there may be some way that a people can regain their linguistic identity. In some cases, a closely related language may be used as a

Fig. 4. Breath of Life workshop at the University of California at Berkeley. Virginia Carmelo, left, is learning Tongva (Gabrielino, a Takic language). Her mentor is linguist Pam Munro, right. Photograph by Leanne Hinton, 2006.

source. For example, Juaneño (a Uto-Aztecan language of California) has no fluent speakers and very little in the way of documentation. The closely related Luiseño language, on the other hand, has a good deal of documentation as well as a number of speakers, and Juaneño language activists such as Kelina Lobo utilized Luiseño documentation in the development of Juaneño language lessons. With some knowledge of linguistics, regular sound differences between the two languages were utilized to convert Luiseño words into the shape the corresponding Juaneño words would have had. The same technique was used by David Costa to recover Mohegan-Pequot words based on those in other Southern New England Algonquian languages.

## Language Change and Development

Most of the young speakers of indigenous languages in North America in 2007 did not learn their languages in the normal manner of language transmission across generations that would take place in a thriving speech community. Instead, they have learned in schools and colleges, as adults in a Master-Apprentice program, or at home from parents who are themselves second-language speakers of the heritage language. Thus, the language known by these new speakers may be quite different from that spoken by their native-speaking ancestors; in most cases people honestly say that they or their students or offspring are "proficient but not fluent." New speakers may be comfortable speaking in some situations and about some topics, but not in others. Their pronunciation may be influenced by English, and they may make substitutions for some sounds. They may have areas of faulty grammar and lack some of the complex sentence structures and less-often-used affixes (Hinton 2000). The difference in the degree of knowledge between the last fully fluent native speakers and the young new speakers is

still very great. These new speakers realize that language learning will be a lifetime project for them, and that when they are the primary speakers carrying on the language to future generations, the language may be quite different than it was in generations past.

In some cases, dialect differences may ultimately disappear, even though they may be strongly defended by those that have them and some language programs have accommodated the speakers of more than one variety of the language by teaching all variant usages. Dictionaries can have multiple versions of the same word, and language teachers who understand the dialect situation may often simply teach all the variants. Language learners sometimes make a special effort to learn the varieties of all the speakers they can work with. All this may result in dialect mixing and, in the end, a loss of the current dialect variations, which is not surprising given that the social divisions that created the differences are obsolete.

For languages being brought into new situations, there is the issue of vocabulary development. Something as mundane as going shopping may involve many items and activities for which no words are known in a moribund language that has never been used for the activities of modern life. For immersion schools, where math and science are taught along with other subjects, whole new areas of scientific vocabulary are needed. And for the written language, new genres such as essays must also be developed. Thus, language revitalization also requires language development. Learning and using the language again means creating new language. It may be informally done, as with master-apprentice teams who will develop descriptive terms for the things in daily life, or more formally, by the establishment of a committee that sanctions new words.

## Institutional Assistance

A number of nonprofit organizations had developed by the early 2000s to assist in funding, training, or materials development in language revitalization. Among these were the Advocates for Indigenous California Language Survival, the Indigenous Language Institute, the First Peoples' Cultural Foundation and its First Voices project, Terralingua, and the Language Conservancy (run by the Lakota Language Consortium in Bloomington, Indiana). By the 1990s and 2000s, public and private foundations had begun to devote funding to the documentation of endangered languages with a revitalization component, which resulted in assistance for many revitalization programs in North America.

### Conferences

Conferences have been important in the United States and Canada for language revitalization projects. All over North America there are several conferences every year in various regions where people from indigenous communities gather to discuss their language revitalization projects and learn from each other. For example, there is the annual Sweetgrass Conference in London, Ontario, the biennial Revitalizing Algonquian Languages conference sponsored by the Mashantucket Pequot Tribal Nation in Mashantucket, Connecticut, and the biennial Language is Life Conference for California languages run by the Advocates for Indigenous California Language Survival. One of the most important conferences is the Stabilizing Indigenous Languages Symposium, which takes place at a different venue each year, and publishes annual proceedings.

While these conferences are of use to all people involved in language revitalization, they may play an especially important rule to people whose tribes do not have revitalization programs. There are many individuals who are trying to do something for their language on their own—to learn to speak their language from their elders or from materials in archives, or at least to begin to have gatherings of interested people for language learning. For such people the indigenous language conferences give them ideas, encouragement, and a network of like-minded people. In many cases what they learn at conferences can help them to take a leadership role in developing language programs for their own communities.

Language revitalization plays a role in conferences with a broader subject matter, such as the American Indian Sovereignty Conference in Tulsa, Oklahoma, as well as in regional and national linguistics and anthropology conferences. There are papers about language revitalization every year at the American Anthropological Association and the Linguistic Society of America (LSA) conferences, and especially at the conference of the Society for the Study of the Indigenous Languages of the Americas, held in conjunction with the LSA. The LSA also has a committee on endangered languages.

*Language Policy*

Throughout the years, language policy has both driven and responded to language issues for indigenous peoples. The repressive boarding-school policies were the earliest and most destructive language policies of the federal governments of Canada and the United States.

In the United States, until 1975, most Indian education was in the hands of the Bureau of Indian Affairs in the Department of the Interior. Probably the most important policy development for Native American education (and ultimately for bringing the languages into the schools) was the Indian Self-Determination and Education Assistance Act of 1975, which allowed Native American communities to take greater control of their schooling (J. Crawford 1995:186). Then, starting in the 1990s, policies encouraging the use of indigenous languages began to appear in North America. In the United States, the Native American Languages Act of 1990 turned around years of unfriendly policies toward Na-

tive American languages and proclaimed that the United States government has a responsibility to act in concert with Native American communities to maintain their languages. The Native American Languages Act of 1992 provided funding to the Administration for Native Americans in the Department of Health and Human Services to give grants to tribes and Native non-profit organizations for language revitalization programs. This funding, though small in amount, had a positive impact on the development of language revitalization programs. It is short-term funding, with a maximum of three years for a given project. The Esther Martinez Native American Languages Act of 2006 funded grants to support Native American language immersion programs, including "language nests" for children and language survival schools.

In Canada, there was no national law protecting aboriginal languages in 2007. The 1969 Official Languages Act of Canada recognizes English and French as the official languages and makes no mention of the indigenous languages. However, in 1998 the Minister of Heritage established the Aboriginal Languages Initiative, whose objective was to maintain and revitalize aboriginal languages by increasing the number of speakers, encouraging the transmission of these languages from generation to generation, and expanding language usage. Twenty million dollars was set aside for use in language revitalization by aboriginal communities.

Several Canadian provinces have their own policies. For example, British Columbia passed the First Peoples' Heritage, Language, and Culture Act in 1990; and the Northwest Territories and Nunavut have an Official Languages Act. Quebec and the Yukon both have active programs encouraging the use and revitalization of aboriginal languages.

While the Native American Languages Act protects American Indian, Hawaiian, and Alaska Native languages in the United States, there are other movements in language and educational policies that undermine them. Some members of Congress wish to make English the official language of the United States, and many states passed official language bills and initiatives, some of which have a negative impact on Native American language programs. The No Child Left Behind Act of 2001 was criticized for gaining "(any) success . . . at the expense and diminishment of Native language and culture" (National Indian Education Association 2005a:7). Pressures to attain good scores in English proficiency caused some Native schools to drop the language programs (National Indian Education Association 2007:11).

## Sources

The first decade of the 2000s saw the rapid development of a literature documenting and supporting language revitalization. The father figure in the field is Joshua Fishman, whose classic Graded Intergenerational Disruption Scale was developed in 1991. Fishman's (1991, 2000) prolific writings include the indigenous languages of the New World. Literacy planning for indigenous communities was developed by Hornberger (1997). The proceedings from the Stabilizing Indigenous Languages Symposia, dating from 1994, are a very important resource. *The Green Book of Language Revitalization in Practice* (Hinton and Hale 2001) was the first major comprehensive volume on the topic. *Keeping Your Language Alive* (Hinton et al. 2002) is more specifically about the bootstrap methods for developing proficiency in an endangered language. Grenoble and Whaley (2006) provide excellent introduction to language revitalization. The Indigenous Language Institute has been publishing a series of manuals on specific aspects of language revitalization that will be of great value to Native communities.

# News Media

DAN AGENT

From newspapers and broadcast to the world wide web and the internet, tribal media outlets and audiences have expanded, informing a greater diversity of people and strengthening a sense of community among many different tribes, having an impact on blending that community with the global village. The future appears bright for tribal media, yet, as exciting as the new technologies may be, the history of tribal media includes obstacles and remaining challenges. The degree to which they continue into the future will determine the degree at which the sense of community—tribal and global—will solidify and expand. For Native American journalists and tribal media, the primary challenge is achieving accurate coverage, not only in the mainstream media but also in tribal media.

American Indian communication, whether in print, radio, television, or any other venue or medium, has been created within a political dimension. Expression is the breath of life for Native Americans. When asked about his songs, Netsilik poet Orpingalik explained, "My breath—this is what I call my song, for it is just as necessary for me to sing as it is to breathe" (Wiget 1985:28–29). In her anthology of the works of American Indian women writers, Rayna Green, Cherokee, notes that "The political dimension . . . is an inherent part of their writing because it is an inherent part of their lives" (Green 1984:9–10).

Understanding Native American communication within the perpetual political dimension, whether in the oral tradition of storytelling, poetry, song, or journalism and the media, is extremely important. The perception of Native Americans is largely shaped by what people read, see, and hear in the media. Unfortunately, most of what has been communicated in the past 500 years has been through the eyes of non-Native journalists for non-Natives (Hirschfelder and de Montaño 1993:195). At a media conference in Kotzebue, Alaska, in 1978, Clifford Black of the Alaska Federation of Natives complained that Alaska Natives had received "lousy coverage, sick coverage, and in some cases despicable coverage" in the non-Native press (Littlefield and Parins 1986:xiv). The negative reporting continued through the early 1980s (Siegenthaler 1995), and it, along with the attempt to develop professionalism in the Native press, was one of the primary forces that resulted in the establishment of the Native American Press Association in 1984 (Littlefield and Parins 1986:xiv). Known as the Native American

Journalists Association since 1986, the organization continues its efforts today.

In addition to the perpetuation of stereotypes and inaccurate information in print, radio, television, the internet, in spite of its great promise for communication and change for Native Americans, has become the tool of many non-Indians who have appropriated Native cultures for business purposes, including the marketing of art, healing, and religion. Although the "problem will never be solved . . . it can be minimized by the increased proliferation of Indian-created content on the Web" (Twist 2006:12).

## The First Amendment and the Native Press

Native American journalism began with the publication of the *Cherokee Phoenix* on February 21, 1828 (vol. 4:44, 14:358). The first editor, Elias Boudinot, named the paper for the bird in Egyptian mythology that consumes itself in fire every 500 years and is reborn from the flames. That analogy has proven appropriate, not only for the Cherokee Nation and its newspapers, but also for Native American journalism and media since then. The first biweekly issue included the goals of the publication: to publish laws and documents of the nation; accounts of Cherokee customs and customs, and progress in education, religion and life; the news of the day; and articles to promote literature, civilization, arts, and religion (Perdue 1983:15). The goals are not unlike those of nearly all tribal media, from print to the internet.

Six years after making history as the first Indian newspaper, the *Cherokee Phoenix* made history as the first Indian newspaper to be shut down because of its content. Political conflict and factionalism over the proposed removal of the Cherokees to Indian Territory led to the termination of the publication on May 31, 1834. Although it was a relatively short-lived publication, it proved to be the foundation for the newspapers and tribal media that would follow. After the forced removal on what became known as The Trail of Tears, the Cherokees established a new national capital of the Cherokee Nation at Tahlequah. On October 25, 1843, Chief John Ross called for the establishment of a Cherokee-English press. The National Council approved his request and the *Cherokee Advocate* began on September 26, 1844, making it the first newspaper in Indian Territory.

Other Native newspapers were begun in Indian Territory and elsewhere, but Indian journalism, for the most part, was interrupted by the Civil War (J. Murphy and S. Murphy 1981:36–52). Since then, Native American journalism has risen like the mythical phoenix to become a significant force. In 1998 there were "approximately 280 reservation newspapers and bulletins, and 320 urban publications, about 100 magazines, 28 radio stations and one television station" (Richard La Course, personal communication 1999). From 1921 to 1970, "probably no more than 600 titles were established, most in the 1960s," while during the period from 1971 to 1985, more than 1,000 were begun (Littlefield and Parins 1986:xi–xiii). Limited funding, reliance on federal or tribal funding, politics, and staff strong on commitment but with no journalism experience resulted in publications that were "inexpensively produced" and reflected those limits, graphically, technically, and editorially.

The American Indian Press Association, established in 1971, provided a forum for a discussion of common problems and attempted to raise the level of Indian journalism and publishing. It operated a news service that distributed news releases for republication, offering readers greater variety and analysis from the Indian perspective. As a news source for three years, "it did much to reshape the content of Native publications" (Littlefield and Parins 1986:xiii–xiv).

Such progress did not overcome the problem of funding. Because they depended on tribal or federal sources for funding, editors were often not free to print what they wished. Many publications lacked continuity because they became political issues in tribal affairs. Editors changed frequently as they fell out of favor with the people who held the purse strings. Whether federally or tribally funded, publications were at risk of censorship because of their lack of independence. That censorship—whether overt, implied, or imagined—was debilitating to the American Native press (Littlefield and Parins 1986:xiv).

In July 2000 and October 2003, the Cherokee Nation and the Navajo Nation, respectively, took action that may have a lasting impact on the establishment of a free press in Indian Country, including print, broadcast, and the internet. The Cherokee Independent Press Act of 2000 was approved by the tribal council and signed by Cherokee Nation Principal Chief Chad Smith (August 2004 issue of the *Cherokee Phoenix*). In 2003, the Navajo Nation Council approved the establishment of the Navajo Times Publishing Company and the independent publication of *The Navajo Times* separate from the Navajo tribal government. These are the two largest tribes in the country. From 1852 to 1968, a total of 64 tribes adopted written constitutions that included provisions for a free press within their sovereign reservation boundaries. The Indian Civil Rights Act of 1968 specifically extended the rights of the United States Constitution to Indian peoples under tribal governments, including the guarantee of freedom of the press. Title II of that act stated:

"No Indian tribe in exercising powers of self-government shall make or enforce any law prohibiting the free exercise of religion, or abridging the freedom of speech, or of the press, or the right of the people peaceably to assemble and to petition for a redress of grievances." La Course (1998:3) identified problems that tribal newspapers have faced, including a "wide variety of interfering actions: political firings before or after tribal elections; political cutoff or selective reduction of publication funds; prior censorship and removal of news story copy by political officials or administrative personnel; placing of unqualified persons on news staffs by reason of blood kinships or political loyalties;" and "restrictions on press access and withholding of governmental documents from publication or broadcast [and] punitive political firings by incoming or outgoing tribal administrations."

The Cherokee Independent Press Act of 2000, also known as the Cherokee Free Press Act, calls for the publication of all the news of the Cherokee Nation without fear of political recriminations. The news staff must still follow standards of conduct and ethics required of all employees of the Cherokee Nation. However, the staff is protected from dismissal for reporting the news, fairly and evenhandedly (Agent 2004:12).

Other tribes have made the same effort. One success was recorded by the Eastern Band of Cherokee Indians. In April 2006, the tribal council of the Eastern Band of Cherokee Indians, Cherokee, North Carolina, passed the Eastern Band Free Press Act of 2006, reaffirming a commitment to the free press provisions of the federal Indian Civil Rights Act. It made the tribally owned press "independent from any undue influence and free of any particular political interest [with] the duty . . . to report without bias the activities of the tribe, the tribal government and any and all news of interest to have informed citizens."

## Newspapers

In 2007 there are about 250 Native-run newspapers publishing in the United States. *The Navajo Times*, established by the Navajo Tribal council in 1959, is the largest financially independent tribal newspaper. It publishes weekly as well as online, with 21,000 paid subscriptions. The staff is 40–45 employees.

The *Cherokee Phoenix* (fig. 1) was revived in 1977.

The national newspaper *Indian Country Today*, founded by Tim Giago (Oglala Lakota) as *Lakota Times* in 1981, publishes weekly (fig. 2) and claims readership of over 64,000.

*News From Indian Country*, published biweekly by Indian Country Communications, Inc., since 1986, is an independent, Indian-owned, reservation-based business, located at the Lac Courte Oreilles Reservation, Hayward, Wisconsin. In 1997 the company began publishing the regional

## Hall of Fame

Tee Woolman is inducted into the ProRodeo Hall of Fame.
Sports Page 26

## Warriors Memorial

First phase of construction done, dedication planned for Nov. 10
News Page 5

## Museum opening

National Museum of the American Indian opens Sept. 21.
News Page 21

CHEROKEE PROTECTION PHOENIX
ᏣᎳᎩ ᏧᎴᎯᏌᏅᎯ

VOLUME XXVIII, NO. 9 · CELEBRATING 176 YEARS OF NATIVE AMERICAN JOURNALISM · SEPTEMBER 2004

# Tribal cancer detection program helps women

By Christina Good Voice
Staff Writer

TAHLEQUAH, Okla. – The Cherokee Nation's Breast and Cervical Cancer Early Detection Program budget is for $1.1 million for fiscal year 2004-2005, and this amount covers all of the program's costs including screenings, diagnostic tests, case management, office supplies and travel.

Kym Cravatt, CN director of cancer programs, said the core component of the program is the screening tests, which include clinical breast and cervical exams.

"We follow up through diagnosis and we serve as a resource to help put women and their families in touch with outside resources – local and otherwise – if cancer is diagnosed," Cravatt said.

To qualify for the BCC program the patient must be 40 years or older for breast cancer screening or 18 years or older for the cervical cancer screening. The patient must not have Medicare Part B, Medicaid, no private insurance and must be a member of a federally recognized tribe and at or below 250 percent of federal poverty guidelines. (See income guidelines Page 9)

Cravatt said what makes the CN's program distinctive is that it is one of the two tribal BCC programs in the state, with the other program being managed by the Kaw Nation.

"Ours is the largest tribal program in Oklahoma, and I think that we have the opportunity to serve a larger area of women," Cravatt said. "We're really reaching a unique population in that it's an Indian population in a rural setting. It's been a very successful program."

She said since the program began, over 15,000 mammograms and more than 15,000 cervical tests have been administered.

Cravatt said it is important for women to be screened because the earlier cancer or any abnormality is detected, the sooner the

ᏓᎵᏆ, ᎣᎦᎵᎰᎻ. ᏣᎳᎩ ᎠᏰᎵ Ꭰ
ᏂᎨᏯ ᏧᏂᎪᎵᏰᏗ ᎤᎾᏙᏢᏒᎢ Ꮷ
ᏂᎤᏗ ᎠᎴ ᏧᎾᏍᏗ ᎠᎾᏚᏅᏍᎬ
ᎤᏂᏣᎯᏍᏗ ᎤᎬᏨᏟ ᎯᎠ ᎢᎬᏱ
ᏣᏂᏨᏛᎯ ᎠᏓᏰᏍᎩ ᎡᎵᏬᏍ
ᎨᏥᎤᏬᏗ ᎨᏦᎢ. ᎾᏍᎩᏃ ᎠᏕᎳ
ᎤᎾᏁᏝᎤᎯ ᎢᏕ ᏤᏬ ᎢᏳᏆᏗᎤ
Ꮣ ᎤᏣᏒᏍᏗ
ᎢᏕᎢ ᎾᏍᎩ 2004,2005
ᏚᏚᎫᏴᏤᎫᏒ ᏂᏕᏓ ᎤᎤᏔᏂᏓᏍ
Ꮧ ᎨᏥᎪᎵᏰᏍᎩ ᎠᏂᎨᏯ.
ᎰᏨᏃ ᏣᏂᏨᏛᎯ ᎠᏓᏰᏍᎩ ᎤᏓᏂ
ᏄᎢ ᎠᎨᏯ ᎢᎤᏂᏘᏍᏗ ᎠᎴ ᎤᏂᏨ
ᏛᏗ ᎢᎨᏎᏍᏗ
ᎤᏣᎫᏂ ᏚᎪᏢᏒ ᎾᏍᎩ ᎠᏂᎨᏯ
ᎨᏥᎪᎵᏰᏗᎢ ᎠᏗᏍᎨ Kym Cravatt
ᏄᎬᏫᏳᏒ
ᎾᏍᎩ ᎤᎾᏙᏢᏒᎢ.
ᎾᏍᎩᏃ ᎡᎵᏬ ᏗᎬᏨᏂᏍᏚᏄᏗ
ᎨᏒ ᎤᎩᏍᎪᎯ ᎢᏧᎾᏚᎫᏴᏓ ᏨᎴ
ᏂᏍᏕ Ꮎ
ᏧᏂᎤᏗ ᏗᎨᏥᎪᎵᏰᏗ ᎠᎴ ᏁᎳᏚ
ᎢᏧᎾᏚᎫᏴᏓ ᏨᎴᏂᏍᏕ Ꮎ ᏧᎾᏍ
Ꮧ ᎠᎾᏚᏅᏎᎬ
ᎤᏂᏣᎯᏍᏗᎢ. ᎾᏍᎩᏃ ᎯᎠ ᎪᏪ
Ꮅ ᏳᏂᎾᎢ Medicare part B,
Medicaid, ᎠᎴ ᎤᎤᏤ
ᎢᏳᎾᏓᏚᏓᎵ Ꮭ ᏱᎬᏂᏍᏚᎵ ᎾᏗᏕ
ᎵᏍᏙᏗᏃ ᏕᎳ ᎡᎵᏬ ᎡᏳᏍᏚᎵ
ᏍᎬᎢ. ᏖᎢᏃ
ᎨᏒ ᏨᏥᎾ ᎠᏰᎵ ᏚᏙᏢᏒ ᎠᏁᎵ
ᏱᎩ, ᏃᎴ ᏧᎬᏨᏣᏗ ᎠᏃᏢᏍᎬ
ᏕᏄᎳᏗᏢ ᏂᎨᏒᎾ ᏱᎩ ᎾᏃ
ᎠᏟᏣᎥᎢ.
CravettᏄᏪᏖᎢ ᎯᎠ ᎤᎵᏍᎨᏗ Ꮔ
ᏨᏁ ᎾᏍᎩ ᎳᎵᏬ ᎠᏰᎵ ᏚᏙᏢ
Ꮢ ᎨᏒ ᎤᏂᏖ Ꮎ BCC ᎤᎾᏙᏢ
Ꭿ, ᏖᎢᏃ Ꮎ Kaw
ᎠᏰᎵ ᎤᎾᏙᏢᏒᎢ.
ᎠᏖᏂᏃ ᏊᎳᎤ ᎠᏰᎵ ᎤᎾᏙᏢᏅ
Ꮎ ᎣᎦᎵᎰᎻ ᎨᏒᎢ ᎠᎴ ᎠᏙᎯᏳ
ᎤᏂᎪᏗ ᎠᏂᎨᏯ ᎤᎤᏙᏗ
ᎾᏍᏬᎴ ᎤᎾᎵᏍᏚᏄᏙᏗ. ᎾᏍᎩ
Ꮓ ᎤᏛᎬᏨᏓᎴᎤᏓ ᏕᎳ ᎤᏂᎪ
Ꮧ ᎠᏂᎨᏯ ᎨᏥᎪᎵᏰᏓ ᎠᎴ ᎨᏥᏍ
ᏚᏄᏓ.
ᎤᎵᏍᎨᏗᏳᏃ ᎾᏍᎩ ᎠᏂᎨᏯ Ꭸ

See Tribal Page 9.

Drawings by Sam Watts-Kidd, used with permission of Rich-Heape Films. Graphic composition by Lisa Hicks.

# Rich-Heape Films producing Trail of Tears documentary

By Dan Agent

DALLAS – "Families at dinner were startled by the sudden gleam of bayonets in the doorway and rose up to be driven with blows and oaths along the weary miles of a trail that led to the stockade."

That statement from James Mooney's "Myths of the Cherokees" describes how families were treated in preparation for the "Trial of Tears," the forced march that began on June 8, 1838, that the Cherokees called ᏅᏃᎯ ᏚᎾᏠᏱᏄ or the "trail where they cried."

Soldiers were following the orders of U.S. Gen. Winfield Scott, who was following the orders of President Martin Van Buren, who succeeded the champion of removal, President Andrew Jackson.

The words that have been written about the tragedy of the Trail of Tears evoke heartbreaking images, but the evil work is not much more than a footnote in history courses in most high schools and colleges. Cherokee-owned Rich-Heape Films Inc. of Dallas plans to change that with the production of a two-hour docudrama. Bringing those images to the film screen will be diffi-

See Rich Page 8.

PRSRT STD
U.S. POSTAGE
PAID
TULSA OK
PERMIT #2146

*Cherokee Phoenix*, Tahlequah, Okla.

Fig. 1. Front page of the *Cherokee Phoenix*. The paper began in 1977 as the *Cherokee Advocate*. It was known as the *Cherokee Phoenix and Indian Advocate* from 2000 to 2005, when it became again the *Cherokee Phoenix*. The paper publishes monthly, with a circulation of 35,000, 25,000 in Okla. and 10,000 mailed elsewhere. In 2007 the staff of 10 consisted of 8 Cherokees, 1 Muskogee Creek, and 1 Quapaw. Between 2001 and 2007 the *Phoenix* was awarded 46 awards by the Native American Journalists Association. Some of the text is in the Cherokee syllabary invented by Sequoya in 1819 (vol. 17:162–166).

*Indian Country Today*, Canastota, N.Y.

Fig. 2. Lea Gonyea, Onondaga, graphic designer with *Indian Country Today*, laying out editorial copy and photographs in InDesign. The weekly has published since 1981, with journalists based in key regions of North America. In 1998 the paper was purchased by the Oneida Nation of New York State through Four Directions Media, which also publishes quarterly magazines on specific topics, such as powwows or education, maintains a website, and provides podcasts. Photographed in Canastota, N.Y., 2007.

*Akiing* monthly, covering stories from Algonquian-speaking nations.

The *Sho-Ban News* is published and owned by the Shoshone-Bannock Tribes, Fort Hall, Idaho. Established in 1970, *Sho-Ban News* has a circulation of 1,750. It is shipped to Wind River, Northern Ute, and Duck Valley reservations. The staff of eight are all Shoshone-Bannock.

The *Seminole Tribune* is the official newspaper of the Seminole Tribe of Florida, based in Hollywood, Florida. It began as *Smoke Signals* in 1963. Published bimonthly, with a circulation of more than 5,000, it is distributed throughout the United States.

Established in 1979, the *Wotanin Wowapi*, Fort Peck, Montana, with a distribution list of 1,200, is an important publication for the 10,000 citizens of the Fort Peck Reservation. It is published with partial funding from the Fort Peck Tribes, supplemented with advertising and sales revenue. It serves as the newspaper of the city of Poplar, Montana (Lisa Perry, personal communication, 2007).

## The Internet

Newspapers are the foundation from which all media have grown to include radio, television, and the Internet. Progress has been made and is continuing in print and broadcast, but the internet has become the medium for possible resolution. "The Internet is the medium of choice for the distribu-

tion of Native media. Broadband, in particular, alleviates the cost barrier of radio and television broadcast distribution. Streaming media applications also provide a dynamic means of distributing content via real-time broadcast. Native web portals are devoted to news, entertainment, arts and culture, and tribal government information and are typically for-profit enterprises operated by tribally-owned subsidiaries. These portals provide culturally relevant content and offer non-Indians opportunities to learn about the contemporary Indian experience. Importantly, they create a sense of inter-tribal community and an identifiable 'Indian space' on the Internet" (Twist 2004:20).

In 1998 the Gates Foundation began an effort to increase internet access for native Americans as a component of a comprehensive partnership with libraries to give millions access to the internet. The foundation provided computers to tribes in the Southwest, primarily the Navajo Nation, the Pueblos of New Mexico, and to tribes in the Four Corners area of New Mexico, Arizona, Utah, and Colorado.

Indianz.com is a key source of information for national newspapers, offering two or three features daily. It is operated by the Winnebago Tribe of Nebraska and Noble Savage Media. Based on the reservation in Nebraska, it maintains an office in Washington, D.C.

## Radio

In 2007, there were 32 Native American radio stations, all west of the Mississippi River, in 14 states, including Alaska. Many broadcast programs in English and Native languages. Although few in number they have created a sense of community and serve as a source of information the Native American audience does not get otherwise (Hirschfelder and de Montaño 1993:196–197).

In 1972 KTDB-FM went on the air in Ramah, New Mexico. It was the first Indian-owned and operated noncommercial station in the country. Now broadcasting from Pine Hill, New Mexico, 5 A.M. to 11 P.M., it offers local, state, and national news, about 80 percent spoken in Navajo, to approximately 5,000 people in its 45-mile area. It is funded by the Bureau of Indian Affairs and the Corporation for Public Broadcasting (Barbara Maria, communication to editors 2007).

In 1975, KRNB-FM began service to the Makah people of Neah Bay, Washington, and KEYA-FM began service to the Turtle Mountain Chippewa at Belcourt, North Dakota. More were established, primarily in the Southwest, in the 1970s and 1980s (Hirschfelder and de Montaño 1993:196). There are at least 12 native-controlled radio stations in Canada (fig. 3).

In 1987, National Native News, Anchorage, Alaska, began broadcasting by satellite. It is the only daily radio news service covering Native American issues. Produced in Albuquerque, New Mexico, it provides one five-minute news

Aboriginal Multi-Media Society, Edmonton, Alta.

Fig. 3. Wally Desjarlais, Métis, host of the Morning Show on CFWE, broadcasting from Edmonton, Alta. The station was established in 1987 in Lac La Biche and moved to Edmonton in 1994. All First Nations and Métis settlements in the province receive CFWE, which is on air from 7am to 6pm with live programming and with automated music the rest of the day. Cree broadcaster Norman Quinney, now retired, hosted a Word of the Day feature, in which an English word would be translated into the various Indian languages spoken among the listening audience. The station is owned and operated by a nonprofit aboriginal-controlled organization, which receives some funds from a federal government program focused on Aboriginal language promotion. The rest of the station support is derived from advertising revenues and twice-weekly bingo. Photograph by Bert Crowfoot, Edmonton, Alta., 2003.

summary daily to 123 public and tribal radio stations that reach 254 rural and urban communities in the United States and Canada. It provides Native and non-Native public radio listeners with a regular, timely and balanced source of news about Native issues. National Native News covers the social, economic, and cultural issues that affect every community, and helps radio listeners understand the interconnectedness between Native people and their non-Native neighbors.

In addition to broadcast on the airwaves, programming is available in cyberspace at Native Voice One (www.nv1.org). Based in Albuquerque, NV1 distributes programming 24 hours a day to a network of Native and public radio stations throughout the United States and to listeners worldwide via the website. Native Voice One provides programs from a Native point of view about Native American news, culture, music, events, and life. Many Native stations and independent radio producers contribute Native-oriented programs to Native Voice One, a division of Anchorage-based Koahnic Broadcast Corporation, which has since the early 1990s brought Native voices to Alaska, the nation, and the world. Koahnic produces the daily programs, including National Native News, Native America Calling, Earthsongs, and Stories of Our People. It also operates KNBA-FM, the first Native radio station located in an urban market. Koahnic runs training programs to prepare people for employment in the media.

The Native Voice One program roster includes a variety of information and entertainment programs by, of, and for Native Americans. Those include Reach the Rez Radio, UnderCurrents, Voices from the Circle, and Rezervations. Native America Calling, one of the most popular and longest running, is a daily one-hour call-in program, linking public radio stations, the internet, and listeners in a national conversation about issues specific to Native communities. It is broadcast on 52 stations and the internet to an estimated 500,000 listeners in the United States and Canada. The audience can call in and speak with experts about issues of concern to Native Americans. Established in 1995, and funded by the Corporation for Public Broadcasting, Native America Calling is one of the most popular Native-produced programs in the country (www.nativeamericacalling.com). Native America Calling "has produced about 2,600 shows and featured more than 7,000 guests. Anybody of importance in Native America has been on" (Tirado 2005:13–16).

The stations' primary challenge is the lack of financial resources. Many stations are located in small communities with few businesses. Native stations generally have no success with pledge drives, underwriting, and other sources of support. Of the 32 Native stations, seven stations raised 93 percent of their budget. Stations rely on "substantial in-kind support from tribes, but most don't receive significant amounts of direct funding. The exception is Alaska Native stations, which receive annual operating grants from the state" (Theriault and Tilin 2004).

## National Museum of the American Indian

The Smithsonian Institution's National Museum of the American Indian in 2001 began a Native Radio Program, to produce programs for radio and web broadcasts that are informative, educational, and entertaining. The program was designed to produce audio segments of Native communities to support language preservation and oral history projects. It includes two radio series—Living Voices and Time. The initial Living Voices series offered 15 individual profiles of contemporary tribal leaders. The Time radio series showcases culturally based stories centered in time and communicating a contemporary personal story.

## Television

Since it began in 1977, Native American Public Telecommunications has served as the major contributor and facilitator of Native American television, radio, and film productions. The mission is to support the creation, promotion, and distribution of Native public media. Major funding has been provided from the Corporation for Public Broadcasting. Nebraska Educational Telecommunications has been a major supporter, providing office space in its Lincoln, Nebraska, headquarters, as well as other administrative support functions. The organization was formed in 1976 as the Native American Public Broadcasting Consortium to be a national organization for production development, distribution, and to serve as a library for public television and radio. Its mission broadened to include production and distribution of programming to National Public Radio.

Native America Television, known primarily as NATV Online, is the digital online portal for news, commentary, history and culture about Indian Country from rural and urban Indian tribal communities and from their studio in Washington, D.C. NATV plans to train students in multimedia technology in a Washington Semester program, offering web development, studio production, and technology management along with fundamental journalism practices. NATV has covered numerous Native American events, such as powwows held on the National Mall in Washington, D.C., the opening of the National Museum of the American Indian, and the American Indian Inaugural Ball of 2001. NATV has provided video production assistance to other organizations, such as the American Indian Society and the National Congress of American Indians. When NATV was formed, television was the primary medium for viewing news. Its sole mission was to train Native American students in television broadcasting, news reporting, and studio production. With more and more news organizations moving toward 24-hour-a-day, multimedia coverage, NATV is using the internet to provide online video, news, and commentary about issues, history, and culture (Randolph Flood, personal communication 2007).

According to the American Society of Newspaper Editors, in their 2007 newsroom census on the ethnicity of more than 57,000 journalists, less than one percent were Native American, which is slightly less than the percentage of Natives in the population. Recognizing the need for a greater Native presence at all levels of communications, in both Native and non-Native communities, the Native American Journalists Association supports the involvement of Native Americans in the media. There are more than 450 Native media organizations and approximately 700 Native journalists in the United States and Canada.

Native journalists employed by publications and radio and television stations that serve the general public (Hirschfelder and de Montano 1993:195) include Mark N. Trahant (Shoshone-Bannock), editorial page director at the *Seattle Post-Intelligencer*. Jon Shurr (Cherokee) was a reporter, photographer, and editor for 35 years at the Associated Press. George Benge (Cherokee) was a corporate news executive with Gannett Company of McLean, Virginia. Derrick Henry (Navajo) is a senior web producer at the *New York Times*. Hattie Kauffman (Nez Perce), an Emmy Award-winning reporter, has been a correspondent for both CBS and ABC television.

In spite of ongoing issues of funding and limited freedom of the press within the political dimension, the Native American Journalists Association and related professional organizations have made an impact in the status of Native American journalism and tribal media. This includes the employment of Indian journalists in mainstream media because each represents, in a very real way, tribal media. One of the primary goals of the Journalists Association is to provide training and education to young journalists (fig. 4) with hope that, eventually as professional journalists, they can impact the lack of accurate coverage in the mainstream and the tribal media. Since 1985, the Association has sponsored an annual journalism and education training convention for its members and other journalists. The convention offers training and education workshops, on-the-job critiques for publications, radio and television programs, and awards for the best of Native press. In 1990 the Association started what became Project Phoenix (High School Workshop)—in honor of the *Cherokee Phoenix*—an effort to recruit Native American students into the field of journalism. The Student Scholarship Program assists Native American students pursuing a degree in journalism or a related field. The organization aims to recruit more Native people into journalism careers, develop outreach to tribal colleges, and support Native editorial and opinion by lobbying news organizations to carry Native opinion writers.

### The Internet Drumbeat

Seizing the potential of the internet, websites have been established for Native youth, each in its own way providing an education in journalism, as well as being viable news and information sources. NativeYouth Magazine.com., begun in 2005, offers news and resources for Indian youth, as well as

Native Amer. Public Telecommunications, Lincoln, Nebr.

Fig. 4. Kade Twist (Cherokee) and Dustinn Craig (White Mountain Apache/Navajo) presenting a workshop on New Media at the Native American Journalists Association conference in Tulsa. Photograph by Shirley K. Sneve, 2006.

sections for elders and adults who can share their wisdom and encouragement. The website features commentaries, profiles, photos, and artwork submitted by Native youth that can be used by educators, tribal leaders, parents and those who work directly with Native youth to experience their perspective. The website includes general Native news and happenings in Indian country (Titla 2006).

Perhaps the most impressive use of the internet in producing stories and training Native youth as journalists is reznetnews.com, the online student newspaper written by and for Native American college students. Reznet provides young Native American journalists with an education, professional experience, and a forum for news and information about tribal governments, people, and culture. Denny McAuliffe, an Osage tribal member and associate professor of journalism at the University of Montana, Missoula, is reznet's creator. He worked at *The Washington Post* as an editor for 16 years, primarily on the Foreign Desk, and wrote occasionally for the paper, including articles on Native issues. McAuliffe says "Reznet's most important work is as a classroom behind the computer screen. By subjecting stories to an editing process more demanding than those at many of the newspapers where the reznetters intern, students receive training that they do not often receive in schools." Reznet news was the first program to try "this nationwide and year-round approach to train Native journalism students" (Denny McAuliffe, personal communication 2007).

Reznet employs professional newspaper editors and reporters as teachers. In addition to the menus of stories, photos, columns, and reviews, the website features blogs, podcasts, and audio slide shows. Along with the extensive

Freedom Forum, Vermillion, S. Dak.

Fig. 5. The American Indian Journalism Institute, sponsored by the Freedom Forum at the U. of S. Dak. at Vermillion. The program began in 2001. Participants in the program in June 2007: seated, left to right, Jack Marsh, a vice-president of the Freedom Forum and executive director of the American Indian Journalism Institute; Breanna Roy, Blackfeet/Cree; Charles Pulliam, Aleut; Neda Spotted Wolf, Hidatsa/Chippewa; Candace Begody, Navajo; Devin Wagner, Crow; Jordan Dresser, Northern Arapahoe. standing, left to right: George Benge, Cherokee, guest speaker; Andrea Murphy, Navajo; Janine Harris, staff; Nancy Kelsey, Little River Band of Ottawa; Chuck Baldwin, teacher for basic newswriting; Princella Parker, Omaha; Amanda Teller, Navajo; Ellen Feuerhelm, Turtle Mountain Chippewa/Métis; Darlene Schieffer, staff; Christie Cooke, Navajo; Troy Doney, Assiniboine; Melissa Morgan, Ely (Western) Shoshone; Victor Merina, teacher for basic newswriting; Sandra White Shield, Rosebud Lakota; Tesina Jackson, Cherokee; Denny McAuliffe, Osage, teacher for basic newswriting; Martina Lee, Navajo; Jasa Santos, Salish; Lina Miller, non-Native; Michael Downs, teacher for advanced reporting; Jacquelyne Taurianen, Sault Ste. Marie Chippewa; Bill Elsen, teacher for basic newswriting and editing; Victoria Jackson-Dick, Ft. McDermitt Paiute-Shoshone; Craig Henry, Cherokee, teacher for basic newswriting; Kelly Johnson, teacher for editing; Val Hoeppner, Cherokee, teacher for multimedia classes. Most students went directly from graduation to summer internships, before returning to their undergraduate colleges in the autumn.

Freedom Forum, Vermillion, S. Dak.

Fig. 6. Guest lecturer Keith Woods, dean of the faculty at The Poynter Institute, St. Petersburg, Fla., speaking on "Talking Across Difference," to students at the American Indian Journalism Institute in 2007.

use of computer digital and internet technology, journalism at reznet is taught the "old-fashioned way—publishing stories and photos after they pass through editors who, at each step, teach more professional and effective ways to report, write and shoot" (Denny McAuliffe, personal communication 2007).

Reznet began online publishing in 2002 and has annually hired about 30 students as reporters, editors, photographers, podcasters, and multimedia journalists to cover their tribal communities or colleges during the academic year. Most staff members have been graduates of the Freedom Forum's American Indian Journalism Institute, a three-week training program each June at the University of South Dakota, Vermillion (figs. 5–6). Professional journalists, most from the mainstream media, teach reporting, editing, and web production at the Institute. Of 21 graduates in 2007, 17 went directly to paid internships at large and small newspapers. Graduates also become the subsequent academic year's reznet staff. Reznet pays students for each story, podcast, or photo assignment and for labor-intensive audio slide shows, a monthly requirement for all photographers. Staff members can contribute commentary or personal accounts to a reznet blog, and reznet publishes news releases from tribes and Native organizations and groups. Student copy editors

edit Associated Press wire stories nightly, as well as contributing movie and music reviews. Staff stories and photos are published at a rate of one each weekday during the academic year.

Reznet's philosophy has evolved from an initial focus on the tribal colleges to being committed to help any Native student with an interest in journalism. From 2002 through 2006, reznet brought 85 Native college students onto the staff. They were from 47 tribes in 17 states and Canada and attended 35 colleges in 17 states. They attended public and private colleges around the country, ranging from journalism programs such as Syracuse University in New York and the University of Nebraska at Lincoln to tribal colleges such as Haskell Indian Nations University in Lawrence, Kansas, and Turtle Mountain Community College in Belcourt, North Dakota.

Reznetters have interned and been employed by mainstream and tribal newspapers, including *The Washington Post*, the *Los Angeles Times*, *The Seattle Times*, Minneapolis *Star Tribune,* and *The Kansas City Star*, as well as The Associated Press news bureaus. Reznet is a project of the University of Montana School of Journalism and the Robert C. Maynard Institute for Journalism Education; it is funded by foundations (McAuliffe 2006).

As the potential of true mass communication is being realized by the internet and the world wide web, it is important for the future of tribal media that the barriers of misinformation be overcome, not only for Native Americans but for better understanding and a sense of community for all ethnicities that comprise the fabric of America. No one has said it better than Kade Twist (Cherokee) in his Viewpoint in *Native Peoples* magazine. "The digital era enables Indian people to place our stories, our ideas, our identities and our worldview on a global stage of 800 million people connected to the Internet. Any one of us can step up to the keyboard and make a remarkable contribution to Indian people, America and the world. The big-picture implications of the medium are significant: self-actualized empowerment. The Web enables us to correct a Western history that has spoken on our behalf for far too long—misrepresenting us; casting us as subjects, commodifying us—and always focusing on the negative. Now we can juxtapose our narratives, our histories and our experiences against that which has been delivered from the Western imagination—and displace myth with accuracy" (Twist 2006:12).

# Theater

HANAY GEIOGAMAH

Out of the tumult of tribal life starting in the 1960s, a new American Indian theater and performing arts movement emerged, punctuated by bursts of optimism and periods of uncertainty and struggle. This Native theater encompasses a range of subject matter and performance styles from ceremonial and ritual forms to comedy, tragedy and tragicomedy, to experimental and hybrid genres. It comprises a loose network of performing artists, writers, directors, presenters, designers, and others interested in theater of, by, and for American Indians.

Since the 1800s, plays and historical pageants about Indians or containing Indian characters have been presented on the American stage and in outdoor settings. These works have overwhelmingly been written, directed, produced, and for the most part acted by non-Indians. After long and unabated exposure to this mass misrepresentation, serious distortions of Indian images and identities led to harmful misconceptions and the propagation of egregious stereotypes in American theater as well as in other cultural, educational, social, and political institutions. This kind of "Indian" theater is outside the scope of this chapter, which is dedicated to the examination of stage plays and performances conceived, written, directed, produced and acted by Indians themselves. It could legitimately be argued that the history of the contemporary, new Indian theater really begins in the 1960s. Why did it take so long?

From the American Indian viewpoint, the short answer is lack of education, opportunity, and interest. Tribal people's losses in the Indian wars, the outlawing of tribal languages and ceremonial gatherings, and other forced restrictions near the end of the nineteenth century excised the vital creative energy from Indian life and created an abiding demoralization, a sense of alienation, and a fragmentation that made it difficult to recognize common interests and to enjoy any cultural exchange. Even the grant of citizenship and the right to vote in 1924 did little to rouse the tribes from their political anomie and cultural hibernation or to build Indian confidence in the political process or belief in the good will of the dominant culture. The struggle for mere survival had left little room for the finer aspects of social and artistic progress.

## The Plays

Some writers have argued that the first significant American Indian play to be performed or reviewed in New York City was Lynn Riggs's *The Cherokee Night*, first performed and reviewed in 1934. This is because Riggs was part Oklahoma Cherokee, and all the characters in his play are Oklahoma Indians. This obscure, experimental, and enigmatic drama has not been produced since its original production and remains a curious, albeit intriguing, depiction of the complex hardships of Indian life in Oklahoma in the 1920s (L. Riggs 2003).

Partly because of the social and economic change during and after World War II, the late 1940s and early 1950s saw significant advances in education, social justice, and the acquisition of wealth by minorities. Both the federal government and the private foundations opened their coffers, stimulating among Indians a drive toward self-government and participation in the arts. The late 1940s also witnessed the development of the modern powwow movement ("Powwows," this vol.). Tribal fairs began to flourish, and intertribal communication improved. A greater sense of self-worth and responsibility for their own destiny stirred among Native peoples. Pride in tribal traditions joined with a forward-looking and hopeful attitude. The nascent cultural revitalization in the late 1940s, fueled anew by the political and economic resurgence of the late 1950s and early 1960s ("Literature," this vol.), forged an invigorating sense of momentum, of dedication, and of self-responsibility and renewed acknowledgment of the value of tradition.

A query circulated to various funding agencies in early 1970 by the organizers of the American Indian Theater Ensemble exuded passion and determination:

> What are the reasons for forming an all-Indian theater ensemble? For decades American Indians have been portrayed in films and on television in a manner entirely derogatory to the cultural and mental well-being of this most maligned and isolated of American minority groups. Who on this earth can enjoy seeing themselves and their race portrayed as fiendish savages and murderers who hurl forth blood-curdling yelps as seemingly their only form of vocal communication? It is thought by many American Indian leaders and activists that this unabated corrupt use of American Indians by the American dream makers has been a major factor contributing to the deepening cultural and spiritual malaise of American Indians.
>
> Those of us working to establish the American Indian Theater Ensemble believe the audience for Indian plays should

be primarily Indians themselves and only secondly whites and others. Plays for and about Indians, their past, their despairing present, their hopes and dreams and daily lives, presented by Indian artists, could be of inestimable value in uniting and uplifting Indian people.

Enough talent exists in the Indian world to assure that all (creative) materials used by the ensemble would be produced by Indian people, from scripts to sets to music. Indian people want and need Indian actors, writers and directors to produce entertainments about them, and the Ensemble will train Indians to achieve this (National Indian Youth Council 1970).

In the mid-1960s the Bureau of Indian Affairs boarding school in Santa Fe, New Mexico, which had for decades served the basic educational needs of the northern New Mexico Indian Pueblos, was converted to the Institute of American Indian Arts to provide training for American Indian students in the visual, written, and performing arts. Roland Meinholtz, playwright (*Place Where Bear Dances*) and trained theater professional, was appointed in 1964 to develop the theater arts department. He recruited students from reservations in many parts of America to bring them to Santa Fe to form a reservoir of talent for an Indian theater.

By 1969, Meinholtz and his students had progressed sufficiently in the experimental phase of their theater work to outline their impressions, theories, and projections in a manifesto entitled *Indian Theater: An Artistic Experiment in Progress*. In its introduction, headed "Credo for American Indian Theatre," the Institute's director, Lloyd H. New (1969) wrote:

We believe that an exciting American Indian theatre can be evolved out of the framework of Indian traditions. We think this evolution must come from the most sensitive approaches imaginable in order not to misuse or cheapen the original nature of Indian forms, most of which are closely tied to religion. We believe that young Indian people must be trained in the fullest degree regarding all aspects of theatre: the history of universal forms, the technical aspects, acting, speech and movement. Against this understanding they must then be led to examine Indian culture for that which is theatrical, and then find ways to interpret those unique aspects for contemporary audiences in true theatre settings. *Indian theatre* ultimately will be born from this group of sophisticated Indian artists. Until their statement is made and a heretofore (sic) new theatrical form is evolved we can only view present dramatic manifestations of Indian life, the religious ceremony, the grandstand performance, the Indian powwow as raw material from which Indian theatre will evolve.

Indian theatre cannot be developed overnight, but will come only as a result of an educational process in which Indian artists are created who can then make their own statements. To understand this point fully, one must acknowledge the fact that no pure traditional form of Indian theatre presently exists—one must be created. New ethnic cultural forms must result from the forces and ideas within the ethnic group itself.

In a separate statement, New described these goals for the Institute's theater arts department: cultural enrichment of international scope to the contemporary arts world; an identifying vehicle for a group who sorely needed constructive rebuilding of group pride; a dam to the dissipation of Indian cultural values; and an interpreter of cultural values to the world at large.

While it is unquestioned that the Institute of American Indians Arts served as the crucible for forging an Indian theater, its description in the Meinholtz manifesto remains remote, rigid, and difficult to translate into actual stage production. Accompanying the document were the texts of six short plays, four of which were written by Indian student playwrights and given their first productions by the Santa Fe troupe. These plays, variously described in their title pages as a "coyote play" or a "mystical play" or an "action play" are characterized by a density of poetic imagery and a lack of narrative clarity. Only two of them were given a full production by the Indian theater companies that appeared in the early 1970s.

Meinholtz mentored the students in how to use their minds, bodies, and performance skills to create Indian characters and to portray them on stage in their own, original theatrical productions. A 1,000-seat outdoor amphitheater on the western edge of the Institute of American Indian Arts campus, designed by architect Paolo Soleri, was fitted out with the most modern technical equipment for presenting the widest possible range of theater styles and productions. The Santa Fe program began to lose its vitality in the early 1970s. Although the project lasted only a few years, it is significant primarily as an early training ground for talents such as actor-director Keith Conway (Blackfeet) and Jane Lind (Aleut), one of the leading actresses in native performing arts today. Among the young writers in the program was Bruce King (Oneida), who became one of the pillars of Indian theater in the late 1990s.

The first professional Indian theater project, and one of the most influential, was the American Indian Theater Ensemble, later the Native American Theater Ensemble, founded in New York City in 1972. This project arose as part of a drive by young Indian intellectuals working in politics or active in the Red Power movement to define what "being Indian" meant and implied. They began lively discussions of the need for constructive change without losing their cultural heritage, for belonging to the American dream without being swallowed by it, for finding new forms of self-expression without being mired in a romanticized past or seeking sympathy and compensation for the "plight" and "vanishing" status to which all Indian tribes had been consigned.

The American Indian Theater Ensemble began at the facilities of the La Mama Experimental Theater (fig. 1). The troupe took lessons in acting, directing, speech, lighting, and stage design. Ellen Stewart, the founder of the theater, agreed to sponsor the new company in its first year and helped acquire grants for the project from the National Endowment for

Fig. 1. The original members of the American Indian Theater Ensemble Company in front of Café La Mama, New York, prior to their engagement in 1972. Standing, left to right, are Keith Conway, Blackfeet; Debra Key, Cheyenne; Gerald Bruce Miller, Skokomish/Yakima; Marie Antoinette Rogers, Mescalero Apache; Phil Wilmon, Cherokee; Michael Trammel, Sac and Fox/Shawnee; Geraldine Keams, Navajo; David Montana, Tohono O'odham; Richard Camargio, Yaqui; Debbie Finley, Colville; Robert Shorty, Navajo; Bernadette Track Shorty, Taos Pueblo; Timothy Clashin, Navajo; and Grace Logan, Osage. Kneeling is Jane Lind, Aleut, with the son and daughter of Debbie Finley. Hanay Geiogamah is not in the picture. Photograph by Amon Ben Nomis.

the Arts and the Ford and Rockefeller Foundations. Sixteen young Indian artists were invited to New York for a nine-month training program. The first public performances by the troupe, given on October 25, 1972, included *Na Haaz Zaan,* a Navajo creation narrative developed by Robert Shorty in collaboration with Timothy Clashin and Geraldine Keams and the ensemble, accompanied by English translation, and *Body Indian* by Hanay Geiogamah (K.R. Brown 1973). Clive Barnes, drama critic of the *New York Times*, in a favorable review, declared that the company "offers a new kind of theater, and I welcome it."

One of the principal contributions of the American Indian Theater Ensemble was its widespread touring program, which traveled to many of the major tribal reservations and urban communities in the country. The troupe also performed in Europe, including an engagement at the Theater im Reichskabarett in Berlin, where their production of Geiogamah's *Foghorn* (fig. 2), a collage of scenes that examines stereotypes, received its world premiere. Touring was essential to the company's mission, which was formed to take its work to Indian audiences wherever they might reside. The reaction and interaction of Indian audiences was a key element in the conceptualization and creation of the group's repertoire.

News of the company's successful New York debut spread quickly over the "moccasin telegraph" network

Hanay Geiogamah, Los Angeles.

Fig. 2. *Foghorn*, written and directed by Hanay Geiogamah. The play received its world premiere in Berlin in 1973. In this scene, Princess Pocahontas (Jane Lind, Aleut) is describing her encounter with Capt. John Smith to her friends, played by, left to right, Irene Toledo (Navajo), Maggie Geiogamah (Kiowa), Denise Hernandez (Potawatomi), and Marie Antoinette Rogers (Mescalero Apache). Photograph by Chris Spotted Eagle, Berlin, 1973.

within the American Indian community. A favorable review of the two plays written by Richard La Course, then Washington correspondent for the American Indian Press Association, was reprinted in nearly 100 tribal newspapers, and a trickle of inquiries and tentative requests for the company to perform at reservations, in urban Indian centers, and for American Indian Studies programs began arriving at the La Mama office. A three-week tour of the new plays was organized after the end of the New York run. The tour was organized for two main purposes: to test the proposition that Indian people would respond positively to an all-Indian theater company and to provide a performing laboratory with on-the-job study of touring logistics.

Tour stops were made at Chickasha, Oklahoma, where an audience of 950 saw the plays at Oklahoma College of Liberal Arts; at the University of New Mexico in Albuquerque; at Saint John's College in Santa Fe; at Lawrence, Kansas, where the 1,200-member student body of Haskell Indian Junior College attended the performance; at Fort Thompson, South Dakota, for an audience of students at Flandreau Indian School; at the Walker Arts Center in Minneapolis, where over 1,000 persons attended, spread over three days of performances; and at Chicago, Illinois, where there was standing room only on two successive evenings at the Chicago American Indian Center.

The first date on the second tour was a three-day engagement at the Museum of Natural History, Smithsonian Institution, March 4–6, where 15 troupe members from 13 tribes performed *Na Haaz Zan* and *Body Double* to near-capacity houses and earned good notices from the two major newspaper reviewers in Washington (Rosenfeld 1973:B11). The

performance itinerary of the second tour also included Rough Rock Demonstration School in Chinle, Arizona; Navajo Community College High School in Many Farms, New Mexico; Springfield College, Massachusetts; University of Massachusetts at Amherst; University of Michigan at Ann Arbor; Saginaw Valley College, Saginaw, Michigan; University of Wisconsin at Milwaukee; Dartmouth College, Hanover, New Hampshire; and New York State University at Buffalo.

In 1974 the Ensemble chose to move to Indian Country, specifically to Oklahoma City, where a large Indian community lived. One of the company's most significant productions, *49*, a jubilant musical celebration by Geiogamah, was created there. After four years of activity, the company members disbanded temporarily. They had brought to life some vivid aspects of Indian character and mores, dramatized Indian strengths and weaknesses of character and community, and enacted situations of Indian-to-Indian perfidy and of confused identity. They gave wild comic life to Coyote.

The initial success of the American Indian Theater Ensemble encouraged other native theater companies to form. A strong body of work was produced by the Red Earth Performing Arts Company in Seattle, and a major native theatrical project was launched in Tulsa, Oklahoma, under the title of the American Indian Theater Company of Oklahoma.

Red Earth was especially active in the late 1970s under the direction of John Kauffman, a Nez Perce actor and director who was one of the first university-trained Native performing artists to head a Native theater company. Kauffman's artistic leadership guided the Red Earth group in producing several seasons of innovative and colorful works. Their production of *Changer*, by the multi-talented artist Gerald Bruce Miller, also known as Sobiyax (Skokomish-Yakima), was an expertly staged and sophisticated synthesis of tribal myth, music, dance, storytelling, and costumes, an early example of Native drama as ceremonial literature. The Red Earth performers, including the Assiniboine actress Phyllis Brisson and Tewa performer Terry Tafoya, toured extensively in tribal communities in the Pacific Northwest, hosting numerous guest artists from other Native performing groups around the country.

The American Indian Theater Company of Oklahoma, founded in 1976 in Tulsa, was headed by artistic director J.R. Matthews (Seneca) for several seasons. This troupe sought to develop Indian actors' performing skills and to cast these actors in productions of new plays by Native playwrights (fig. 3). The company is noted for its development of the plays of Choctaw dramatist Wallace Hampton Tucker, who worked full time as a professor of astrophysics at the University of California, San Diego. Tucker's work included *At the Sweet Gum Bridge*, *Now! Walk Through the Dawn*, and *Bonesmoke*. One of this company's acting alumni is Wes Studi (Cherokee), who gained fame in *Dances with Wolves*.

One of the notable companies that debuted in the 1970s is Spiderwoman Theater, which started out as a multiracial

Fig. 3. *A Song of Winter "Thlufoh Yahegeedah!"*, written and directed by Will Hill, and presented by the American Indian Theater Company of Tulsa, Okla., at the Tulsa Performing Arts Center, Dec. 2006. The play, a Christmas comedy, is set in contemporary America, and features songs in the Creek language. Jehnean Washington (Cherokee, Yuchi, Seminole) plays Lowiza Coachman, and Will Hill (Muscogee) is Ebenezer Screechowl. Photographed by Wilburn Hill, 2006.

feminist performance collective but transformed into a showcase for the Miguel sisters of New York City's Native American community. Muriel Miguel, Gloria Miguel, and sister Lisa Mayo (Kuna-Rappahanock) collaborated on numerous productions that they performed and toured with both nationally and internationally during the 1980s and 1990s. *Sun, Moon, and Feather, Winnetou's Snake Oil Show from Wigwam City,* and *The Lysistrata Numbah* are among their more popular creations. Their work entails a process of creating designs and weaving stories with words and movement.

## The Playwrights

Among the more active and productive playwrights who made important contributions to the emergence of a Native American theater movement are Bruce King, William Yellow Robe Jr. (Assiniboine-Sioux), and Marcie Rendon (White Earth Anishinaabe). The plays of these contemporary theater artists break new ground in their eschewal of conventional modes of theatrical storytelling, their experiments with nonlinear as well as realistic plot lines and dialogue, and their embrace of traditional iconography, dance, humor, and narrative structures. Their works frequently situate contemporary issues in the context of both current and past Native history and culture and present more realistic images of modern Native American life. This diverse cohort has per-

sonal roots and community ties in all areas of Indian Country, and their plays have been performed in or near their tribal communities.

Not one of the 20 or more individuals who identify themselves in 2007 as Indian playwrights manages to make a living solely by writing for the theater, or for film or television either.

Bruce King was one of Roland Meinholtz's students in Santa Fe, and a member of the Native American Theater Ensemble. He founded the Indian Time Theater at the Chicago American Indian Center in the late 1970s, then moved back to Santa Fe to work in Indian theater at the Institute of American Indian Arts in an effort to continue the movement there. His next move was to the Turtle Cultural Center in Niagara Falls, New York, in the 1980s. All this time he continued to write and stage Indian plays any place and under any circumstances available. His plays were produced in front of mainly Indian audiences across Indian Country. Five of King's plays were published in *Evening at the Warbonnet and Other Plays* by the American Indian Studies Center at the University of California at Los Angeles. The plays whirl audiences and readers "from the barbaric, drug-drenched trenches of Vietnam . . . to a supernaturally challenged Indian home on a reservation in upstate New York, to the hip, familiar sounds and smells of an Indian bar located just this side of the other side" (Geiogamah 2006:ix).

*Dustoff*, a dramatic retelling of King's service in Vietnam, premiered on January 22, 1982, at the Westside Mainstage Theater in New York City. It is a contemporary version of the back-from-battle warrior tales that the fighting men shared with each other in isolated locales way from the main camp and told with colorful, mimetic gesturing and shocking details as a means of relieving the fear and stress of the battle, the deaths and close brushes with death, the maiming and bloodshed. The play contains some of the most intense Native American storytelling ever written, and its 20-year-old single Native American character, Breed, has pretty much gone off the deep end in the bloodlust of battle. Breed, in his war-induced madness, wants to stay on in the hell of Vietnam so as not to have to go back to the hell of his South Dakota reservation homeland where, he tells his stunned buddies, just as much death and destruction occurs. Breed is an alcoholically zonked-out reminder of the miserable anomie that gripped so many young American Indian men in the 1960s and 1970s. The language of *Dustoff* is dead-on, electrifying, written by an American Indian who definitely had been there.

It is signally characteristic of King, in his most widely produced play, *Evening at the Warbonnet*, to present the Creator as assigning anthropomorphic versions of Coyote and Loon to preside over a scenario that closely resembles what happens in Christian purgatory. The parable is set in an Indian bar complete with a jukebox and pool tables and located near the entry points to both Heaven and Hell. The play's self-deluded characters represent an end-of-the-trail lineup of the most representative of internal Indian stereotypes from the 1960s and 1970s. Alternately dark, outrageous, sharply humorous, sad, and provocative, this play deftly mixes all the theatrical techniques and motifs that King employs in his writing: varyingly surreal settings; human characters blended with spiritual, mythic, and legendary characters; characters who have made utter fools of themselves and are seeking redemption; ghostly, supernatural atmospheres; a lurking, amorphous sense of threat and dread; and an Indian version of Good versus a kind of mixed-Indian version of Evil.

Another playwright who emerged as a considerable talent in the 1980s is William Yellow Robe Jr., whose plays reflect the courage and commitment required to dramatize the hard and nasty realities of contemporary Indian life. In 2005, Yellow Robe's exploration of racial mixing and its uglier ramifications in his play, *Grandchildren of the Buffalo Soldiers*, was presented jointly by the Penumbra Theatre of Saint Paul (fig. 4) and the Trinity Repertory Theater of Providence, where he was playwright in residence. His most challenging play, *Sneaky*, written and first performed in 1985, presents one of the most shocking scenes in the new Indian theater and exemplifies his thematic experimentations throughout his career. Yellow Robe is the first Native American dramatist to write about homosexuality in a reservation community, in his early one-act play, *Wink-Dah*. Many critics and scholars have noted that Yellow Robe's plots are mostly based on highly sensitive aspects of contemporary Indian life that have been ignored or denied by traditionalists and purists. Few of his plays offer easy, comfortable theater. They are intense, perfervid dramas, undeni-

Penumbra Theater, St. Paul, Minn.

Fig. 4. *Grandchildren of the Buffalo Soldiers*, produced at Penumbra Theater, St. Paul, Minn., Sept. 23–Oct. 15, 2005. left to right, Jake Hart as Brent Robe, James Craven as Knobby Coles, freedome bradley as Elmo Robe, and George A. Keller as Carol Robe. This play was the second of four dealing with the issue of "blood quantum" that tribes use to identify members. The question arises whether the fraction of genetic inheritance can measure a person's identity. Photograph by Ann Marsden.

ably strong specimens of the new Indian theater. Yellow Robe's (2000) five-play collection, *Where the Pavement Ends*, includes *The Star Quilter, The Body Guards, Rez Politics, The Council, and Sneaky*. Having written more than 45 plays in his career, Yellow Robe is almost certainly the most prolific Indian dramatist. He is an actor, director, poet, and has taught at universities.

Indian America's most active female dramatist is Marcie R. Rendon, a mother, grandmother, writer, and occasional performance artist. Most of her theatrical experiences have taken place in the Minneapolis area and the Great Lakes region. She is widely respected for her focus on younger audiences, but her body of work includes several highly original theater pieces that reflect her commitment to experimenting with new forms and approaches to storytelling.

The themes and concepts of the collected body of plays in the new Native theater are dramatized in many styles and forms. Theatrical influences are eclectic: traditionalism, spirituality, experimentalism, nonlinear plotting, solo performance, historical pageantry, tribal oral traditions, Brechtian theater, poetic ceremonialism, Gothic (Native Gothic), and realism. Spiderwoman Theater's *Sun, Moon, and Feather* and Geiogamah's *Foghorn* reflect Brechtian influences; Bruce King's *Evening at the Warbonnet* is a mixture of realism, mysticism, and Indian humor; Riggs's *Cherokee Night* is written in nonlinear sequence and is very clearly experimental; and Diane Glancy's *The Truth Teller* is a complex example of poetic ceremonialism.

Indian dramatists have chosen as subject matter such issues and questions as tribal loyalty, the destructiveness of alcoholism, cultural loss, human fallibility, self and group deception, numerous facets of identity, and the seeking and creating of new sources of strength, creativity, and faith.

To qualify as bona fide Native drama, the new Indian theater must have been written by a tribal playwright and performed by an all-Indian cast in their original productions. The plays should be reflective of Indian life and must speak effectively and logically to Indian audiences. The messages should be communicated clearly and effectively in Indian terms, and characters and dialogue should be culturally authentic.

A persistent question regarding the plays of the new Indian theater is their presentation of dramatic conflict in the Western theater sense of the term. Much of the new Indian theater consists of works that are structurally different from plays of non-Native playwrights and may not contain dramatic conflict in the same forms as Western theater. Native stories often are narrative and descriptive in form and do not reflect human and spiritual conflict in ways that are easily adaptable to strong theatrical scenes and action.

Dramatic conflict is present in many plays in the new Native American theater, but it is made manifest in more gradual and accumulative build-ups of actions, responses, revelations, reversals, contrasts, discoveries, weaknesses, and confrontations. The characters in *Evening at the Warbonnet* are not aware that they are poised on the precipice of Heaven and Hell, though the audience knows it. The Indians in *Body Indian* would almost certainly deny that their taking of Bobby Lee's money is morally wrong and that they are actually harming his person. They would deny this because they consider themselves to be his friends, his pahbes (Kiowa for 'brother, close friend'), his relatives, his family, and Bobby Lee relates to them on similar terms. The irony present in this denial generates the energy for the play's dramatic action and conflicts. Betrayal and disrespect, in intense activation, and the unawareness and denial of these transgressions, are at the core of the play's dramatic actions.

Between 1999 and 2003, four multiauthor collections of Native plays were published in the United States: *Keepers of the Morning Star: An Anthology of Native Women's Theater*, edited by Jaye T. Darby and Stephanie Fitzgerald (Cree), 2003; *Seventh Generation: An Anthology of Native American Plays*, edited by Mimi D'Aponte (1999); *Stories of Our Way: An Anthology American Indian Plays*, edited by Hanay Geiogamah and Jaye T. Darby (1999); and a collection of children's plays, *Pushing Up the Sky: Seven Native American Plays for Children* (2000), adapted and edited by Joseph Bruchac (Abenaki) (Haugo 2005).

## Conclusion

In 2006, Native American communities across the United States remained the most underserved and underrepresented in arts funding and support. The Native theater of the twenty-first century has come alive in an Indian America that is home to hundreds of young Native Americans who dream of careers as professional performers, directors, playwrights, screenwriters, and television producers. This generation of Native creative artists is shaped significantly by the stunning developments in media and communications since the 1980s. But the lack of opportunities for Native performing talent, coupled with inadequate funding, has impeded the full realization of Native performing arts and the establishment of a greater presence in the American cultural landscape.

A handful of experiments of direct tribal support and participation in Native performing arts has produced mixed results. Tribes are able to provide not only money but also other resources: housing, production materials, and even spiritual support. With financial and other forms of support from the tribe, with fair and adequate funding from foundations, businesses, and institutions, with cooperation from other segments of the American theater and the entertainment industry, colleges and universities, and American Indian studies programs, the new Indian theater can thrive. It is an enterprise that—unlike films, which require millions of dollars in financing—can be produced on much smaller budgets and can be conducted fully in Indian hands and under Indian and tribal direction.

Mark Rolo, Madison, Wis.

Fig. 5. Poster for *What's an Indian Woman to Do?*, which premiered on June 28, 2007, starring DeLanna Studi (Cherokee). Inspired by a poem of the same title, the play was written by Mark Anthony Rolo and directed by Kenneth Martines. It is a solo play to be performed by a Native American actress. Part of the narrative is concerned with the character's confrontation of her future as a modern urban Indian who nonetheless feels deep spiritual connections to her traditional culture.

The contemporary Native American theater and performing arts movement can be an important means for renewal, self-determination, and creative development of contemporary Native communities, both tribal and urban (fig. 5). It is clearly evident that, of all the twenty-first-century Native art forms, Native American theater and performing arts are the most rooted in tribal traditions. Being community-based and oriented, Native theater integrates storytelling, music, choreography, costuming, and speech. It draws upon the spirituality, myth, ceremony, and ritual that embody tribal traditions. It serves as an effective forum for creating and nurturing intergenerational continuity, community development, and the sharing of unique tribal cultures that will provide opportunities for introspection, examination, and celebration of the tribal community in a cultural and theatrical context.

Collectively, the women and men who write for the Indian theater are seeking to help Indian people to know who they are and how their lives are being affected by the changes occurring in the first decade of the twenty-first century. Their plays confront and help clarify the endless confusions that have resulted from non-Indian beliefs and misconceptions of Indian life and also help to untangle the mass of confusion that stereotyping, assimilation, and acculturation have created in many Indian minds. The Indian playwrights face failure, ostracism, ignorance, and misbegotten envy. The Indian theater they are creating, day by day, one difficult step at a time, slowly but steadily, is a vigorous new wing of tribal arts and culture.

# Film

MARK ANTHONY ROLO

After nearly six decades of depictions of the American Indian in moving pictures, Hollywood believed it had finally reinvented its own image from that of perpetrator of visual violence to pop cultural advocate of racial understanding in Kevin Costner's film *Dances With Wolves* (1990). This story of a renegade Civil War soldier's social and spiritual integration into a Sioux Indian community was lauded by critics for its earnest strides toward achieving racial sensitivity and cultural accuracy. "The movie makes amends, of a sort, for hundreds of racist and small-minded Westerns that went before it. By allowing the Sioux to speak in their own tongue, by entering their villages and observing their ways, it sees them as people, not as whooping savages in the sights of an Army rifle" (Ebert 1990).

To add to Hollywood's copacetic celebration, American filmgoers were equally enchanted by Costner's historical "realism." It was a unique theatrical experience. In Costner's revisionist take on the Wild West, gone were the wagon-burning "red devils," those bloodthirsty savages bent on raping, murdering, and pillaging the brave pioneers trying to settle the West. Instead, consumers of American commercial films saw a different Indian on the big screen in *Dances With Wolves*. This time, Indians were the innocents, and the White man was the "White devil." In the subsequent films about American Indians that Hollywood produced, going to the movies became an educational experience—seeing a new race of people, discovering a never-before-seen slice of the frontier past.

Not surprisingly, at a time when America had several decades to reflect on the significance of the civil rights movement, Costner's movie generated a measure of collective guilt and sympathy to the historical plight of Indian people. Not surprisingly, Hollywood interpreted the success of their new-found racial advocacy by the sounds of box office cash registers. By the time *Dances With Wolves* ran its course in movie houses it had raked in over $180 million, joining the list of the 100 largest-grossing films of all time (worldwide, the film nearly doubled its domestic earnings). In 2007, *Dances With Wolves* was the highest-grossing film of the western genre (Box Office Mojo 2007).

But as Hollywood extended the celebration of their "breakthrough" film—honoring *Dances With Wolves* with the Best Picture award of 1990, along with six other Oscars—some American Indians were not so moved by Cost-

ner's redemptive crusade, his reinvention of the ignoble savage into the "human" savage (Aleiss 2005:145–146). In fact, to many Native people the only change *Dances With Wolves* instigated was a renewed interest among the dominant society in seeing nineteenth-century Indians on the screen again. No matter how earnest the intent, Indian stories were still told by non-Indians. "But these are not Native American histories. These are the histories of white colonists, military leaders, government workers, and missionaries whose lives intersected with Native Americans. Like the Hollywood film, *Dances with Wolves,* a movie purportedly about Indians, but really a love story about a white couple who interacted with the Cheyenne, historical accounts that rely heavily on outside interpretations of Native events, should more aptly be called *Dances with History*" (Loew 2005:2).

Still, with Costner's blockbuster, Hollywood understood it could get back into the lucrative business of mining mythological gold by freeze-framing American Indians as relics of the past—by feeding America's need to explore, to find a sense of identity through the indigenous inhabitants of the land (Jay 2000:3). If Hollywood was at all stunned to learn that Costner's "contribution" toward eliminating intolerance and ignorance was by and large publicly rejected by Indian activists, community leaders, and scholars, the comprehension was short-lived. In the years following the release of *Dances With Wolves,* Hollywood endeavored to capitalize on "humanizing" the Indian in films such as *The Last of The Mohicans* (1992) and Disney's animated commercial success, *Pocahontas* (1995).

## Irreconcilable Views

While the success of *Dances* raised a new awareness of America's first peoples, it also raised the objections by Native people to a higher level within and beyond Indian Country. For many Indians the gulf between the Indians of the past and those of the present remained just as wide as it was during the age of the westerns directed by John Ford.

What Hollywood failed to hear, perhaps, is that for those Native American dissenters there is no such thing as a "dead past." Even more to the point, there is no such ideal as atonement or healing if in fact the sins, the wounds inflicted upon tribal people by institutions such as the film industry, remain open. No film speaks to the argument that Hollywood westerns have and continue to assert racism against Native Americans as well as John Ford's *The Searchers* (1956). John Wayne portrayed an angry ex-soldier in pursuit of finding and rescuing his niece from a band of Comanche; it is one of the most racist and complex antiheroes of the western (Cameron and Pye 1996:229). The character of Ethan Edwards unapologetically shoots eyes of dead Indians, slaughters buffalo, imagining they are Indians, and is trigger-happy enough to consider killing his niece for becoming a "squaw."

Much of the appeal of the film is the director's fearless attempt to wrestle down the theme of racism. But Ford's racist protagonist (clearly more driven by hatred toward Indians than in saving his niece) continues to be problematic, in spite of the fact that the director attempted to create a more accurate portrayal of Native people with this film. Beyond analysis by film critics and academics, who conclude that Ford failed to draw genuine sympathy to a hero who hates Indians (Ebert 2001), there are those Native Americans who continue to assert that whether the film is *The Searchers* or *Dances With Wolves* the Hollywood western is an inherently racist genre of filmmaking.

Not surprisingly, adding to the Indian furor over the rebirth of the western, which was re-ignited by the visibility of *Dances With Wolves*, came more critical dialogue among Native people about how to counter Hollywood's obsessive affair with their past (Deverell 1993:1189). Accurate or not, historical depictions of Native Americans clouded the dominant society's perception of modern Native life. Perhaps due in part to the fact that Native Americans remain one of the smallest in number of minority groups, and to the reality that tribal reservations are set in rural, isolated geographic locations, the only persistent images of Native people among the rest of the country were those in popular culture. If Hollywood believed it could solve the Indian celluloid race problem with newer films, many Native people refused to buy it. And with the explosion of the independent film movement in the 1980s—a movement that embraced telling stories of those who were ignored, marginalized, or falsely portrayed in institutionalized production companies—it only seemed logical that the best hope in presenting Hollywood's Indian would be Native Americans telling their own stories.

## The Model Villain

One year before *Dances With Wolves* there was another Indian film that broke free from the clasp of Hollywood image-making. In 1989 art house audiences across the country were intrigued by a low-budget film about two Northern Cheyennes who venture on a mystical road trip from their reservation in Montana to Santa Fe. *Powwow Highway*, with its comedic tone and surreal visual depiction of contemporary reservation life, offered a startling contrast to the romanticized savage characters deeply embedded in the psyches of film audiences. Based on the novel of the same title by David Seals, a writer of Huron descent, living in South Dakota, the movie brought up close the damage inflicted on Native people by the tragedies of the past—loss of connection to traditional tribal culture and custom (Maslin 1989).

*Powwow Highway* succeeded in charming a niche movie audience—garnering just a small measure of exposure compared to Costner's *Wolves*. Though Seals rejected the movie producers' adaptation of his novel, the film did more than give audiences something different to consider about Native people. It provided a new lens on Hollywood. In one memorable scene, Philbert, the free-spirited Indian who calls his used car a "war pony," stares into a television screen, mesmerized by a classic cowboy and Indian movie. It is a scene loaded with pathos (short as it is) in that it reveals a disturbing statement on how integral Native Americans were in helping to build Hollywood's movie-making empire. This tragic irony of a modern-day Indian looking at Hollywood's savage Indian of the past is a reminder of how the industry effectively exploited the American Indian as a mythic, model villain for numerous protagonists. It is a model that is still used—whether the villains be aliens, sociopaths, or foreign terrorists.

Even before the creation of Hollywood the Native American served as a source for captivating storytelling. Beginning in the eighteenth century, the bloodthirsty savage as threat to civilized people searching for the promise of prosperity remained widespread throughout popular culture (Bird 1999:62). From dime novels to songs, poems, and photography, Native people have been a major subject of media culture. Many of the first motion pictures, those crude silent films of the early 1900s, found abundant "savage" fodder (vol. 4:609–610).

D.W. Griffith, known for his depictions of Black Americans in *Birth of A Nation* (1915), honed his craft and built his reputation as a racist film director on short silent pictures featuring Native American characters and themes: *The Last of the Mohicans* (1909), *Massacre* (1912), and *The Battle of Elderbush Gulch* (1914). His violent vision of race in America was shaped through his exploration and use of the Indian. "Since the camera loved action, the Indian-white conflict offered countless possibilities with which we are now all too familiar: the chase (whether on horseback or in canoe), the battle, hand-to-hand combat, the circling of the wagons, the burning of the settler's home, the scalping of the victim, the terrorizing of the innocent white woman, and the bashing of babies' heads" (Jay 2000:5–6). Of course, in all of Griffith's films the goal was to portray Whites as victims who rise up against the Indian savage—becoming heroes.

On balance, there were some silent movies that did not exploit the bloodthirsty savage. In *The Silent Enemy* (1930), a band of Ojibwas struggle against hunger. The director,

Henry P. Carver, borrowed artifacts from the American Museum of Natural History, New York, and the film featured an Ojibwa cast from Canada (Aleiss 2005:41). In fact, it was not uncommon for filmmakers to employ Native actors and directors; Chickasaw director Edwin Carewe made over 60 Hollywood feature films before his retirement in 1934 (Aleiss 2005:25). But as film technology evolved, when moving pictures became more than a curious fad for a few, when movies became a commodity to be marketed to the masses, the appeal of Indian as savage villain proved to be a more appealing storyline than those few culturally authentic silents.

The "Indian villain" formula became the standard of nearly all Hollywood westerns for decades (vol. 4:607–616). This popularity of the western grew even more with the advent of sound in motion pictures. But it was John Ford's *Stagecoach* (1939) that propelled the genre to marquee status. "This revolutionary, influential film—a story of redemption—is considered a landmark quintessential film that elevated westerns from cheaply-made, low-grade, Saturday matinee "B" films to a serious adult genre—one with greater sophistication, richer Western archetypes and themes, in-depth and complex characterizations, and greater profitability and popularity as well" (Dirks 2006).

Throughout the 1940s and 1950s the Indian villain dominated film, radio, and television. Especially in radio and television, a parallel Indian character was imagined. Perhaps not so fondly referred to by many Native people, the "Fort Indian" is that kind of Indian who attaches himself to Whites and their ways. Tonto of the long-running *Lone Ranger* serial is the classic example of the "Fort Indian."

Typical of many westerns of that era that were based on people and events, stories were framed to glorify the White man at the expense of historical reality. In 1941 Errol Flynn starred as George Custer in the *They Died With Their Boots On*. As the title suggests, Custer and the United States Calvary are depicted as defenders of a nation warring with savage tribes. The historical inaccuracies within the film were not just limited to Native Americans. Custer was not at the First Battle of Bull Run, nor did he lead the Union soldiers to victory over the Confederates.

Clearly the paramount concern of Hollywood was creating an engrossing story at any cost even if it involved blatant distortions of Native culture and history. Nothing served this purpose better than vilifying the American Indian to mythic status.

Yet, even though the cliché plot formula would go virtually unchanged until the 1970s the push for greater realism (specifically filming on location) meant more sophisticated characterizations of the Indian villain. But these roles went to established or emerging non-Indian actors such as Anthony Quinn who played Crazy Horse in *They Died With Their Boots On* (1941), Jeff Chandler as Cochise in *Broken Arrow* (1950) (vol. 4:613), Sal Mineo as White Bull in *A Horse Named Comanche* (1958), and Robert Blake as Willie Boy in *Tell Them Willie Boy Is Here* (1969). Often, these Indian characters spoke either in stoic, broken English or used a combination of Native languages that sounded like pure gibberish. This "slaughtered tongue" was never an issue with audiences given the fact that most filmgoers were, for the most part, culturally illiterate about Indians.

The Indian villain as legitimate character was not invented to bring into focus the forced plight of Indians, nor was it meant as a device to raise questions about the conquest of Indian tribal lands. As the western evolved, villain as character was intended to heighten moral conflict within the cowboy hero. In *The Searchers* the character of Scar, the Comanche leader who marries the White girl who was abducted by the tribe as a child, is a mirror character of John Wayne's Ethan Edwards. Played by German actor Henry Brandon, the character of Scar is developed by the filmmakers in order to reveal the internal war within the movie's anti-hero. "For the white Ethan Edwards (John Wayne), the Comanche Scar is the 'Other' that he can stare at but cannot see. Worse, he is Ethan's doppelgänger, everything in himself that he despises . . . thus Ethan must kill Scar in order to destroy the complexity of violence within himself" (Gallagher 1993:70).

## Villain to Victim

The 1970s ushered in a new era of how Native Americans would be depicted in film. In a decade that brought mass confusion about identity, it is not surprising that this questioning of what it means to be American would extend to rethinking the past. This "lost innocence" was, no doubt, a threat to the Hollywood western. America would no longer buy the godlike caricatures created by John Wayne and Gary Cooper. War, as in Vietnam, was no longer about protecting and preserving the American dream. Therefore, the western as a profitable genre of filmmaking clearly was in danger of becoming extinct. The nation was no longer enamored with the glorious, mythic history that Hollywood and other mass culture had promoted. America was a country that was built on stolen lands through the violent subjection of tribal nations.

But reinvention has always been Hollywood's greatest asset. And if America no longer had an appetite for good old-fashioned cowboy and Indian movies, then Hollywood would imagine a new story for the western film. Though the savage Indian became passé, the film studios found a different look for the Native American of the Old West, one that suited the rage and guilt that was plaguing American hearts and minds. And no image was more appeasing to the jaded American spirit than that of the Indian as helpless victim, prey to the willful, violent onslaught of cruel, rogue United States Calvary generals, corrupt politicians, and greedy, land-grabbing corporations. *Little Big Man* (1970) and *The Outlaw Josey Wales* (1976) would become two of the most significant films that portrayed Native people in the light of victimhood. Though the characterizations may have drawn more pity than sympathy—Indians as defeated and not surviving—the point was well-served: who were the real savages of the Old West?

This new western became more than a revisionist take on history. It was more than an outright rejection of the cowboy hero and a denunciation of the "good versus evil" formula. Clint Eastwood, as Josey Wales, captured the anti-American sentiment in his self-directed story about an ex-Union soldier's revenge over the slaying of his family by extending a conspicuous "shame" for the Indian. "Eastwood's *The Outlaw Josey Wales*, in its radical reworking of the pattern of social intolerance established in Ford's *The Searchers*, is more than just another typical western of its era. Instead, the film is a substantial revision of the conventional story form, providing a far more enlightened view of race and gender than is evident in *The Searchers* and thus illuminating perhaps more than any other film of its time the differing cultural values of America in the 1950s and America in the 1970s" (Sickels 2003:227).

## Appropriating Story

While Hollywood may have found a renaissance of sorts by re-imagining the western in terms of more disturbing, contradictory realities as in Eastwood's *The Outlaw Josey Wales*, there remained a core problem with stories involving Native Americans. To many Native people the concern about Hollywood making movies about Indians—no matter how many reforms had been instituted—lay in the issue of appropriation (Weatherford 1995:48). Should non-Natives have the right to create images, characters, and stories about Indians on film?

Aside from the fact that there were few visible Native American actors (even fewer behind-the-scenes personnel) working in the industry other than Will Sampson, a Muskogee Creek from Oklahoma (*One Few Over The Cuckoo's Nest*, 1978), and Chief Dan George, a Salish from British Columbia (*The Outlaw Josey Wales* and *Little Big Man*), one of the most telling examples of Hollywood's continual cultural appropriation of Native American life was the basic, fundamental storytelling problem of Point of View.

In director Arthur Penn's critically acclaimed *Little Big Man* starring Dustin Hoffman, the viewers' point of entry into a Cheyenne village comes from the White character of Jack Crabb. Crabb (played by Hoffman), recounts his story as one of the only living survivors of the Battle of Little Bighorn. As a boy Crabb was adopted into a Cheyenne family. Hence, the Cheyenne are seen entirely through Crabb's eyes. Though the film had reinterpreted the cliché "captivity" plot of White people kidnapped by savage Indians (Zeinert 1995), emphasizing a more endearing and sympathetic portrayal of the Indian, *Little Big Man* was first and foremost a story about a White man's coming of age. In spite of showing "humanized" Cheyennes, they served merely as contextual background for the growth of the film's main character.

There is perhaps no more indicting evidence that spoke to the need for an independent Indian film movement than Indians having to be seen through White eyes. Maybe knowing that the audience would no longer buy a White actor dressed up in a braided wig and a dark tan, Hollywood created the notion of a half-breed protagonist as a way of selling the White actor as Native in the *Billy Jack* films. Though he was clearly Anglo in physical appearance, Tom Laughlin's 1971 portrayal of vigilante Jack was popular. The film was one of the biggest box office hits of its time. And in fact, no matter how determined Hollywood may have been in trying to crawl inside an Indian's skin, it was becoming painfully clear to many Native people that nothing could ever replace an Indian telling an Indian story.

If the concern about cultural "theft" proved difficult for the film industry to fully grasp, it was because the very real issue of appropriation ran much deeper than the literary license argument. Native people have understood for a long time that cultural and spiritual appropriation are acts of violence against American Indian tribes. In 1992, multimedia Hopi artist Victor Masayesva, Jr., produced and directed the landmark documentary *Imagining Indians* to protest, in large part, the widespread praise of *Dances With Wolves* and a less successful film *The Dark Wind* (1991). Masayesva was especially perturbed by *The Dark Wind*, which was based on the novel by serial mystery writer Tony Hillerman. Hillerman, who is White, has long been at the center of the cultural appropriation war for financially profiting from his mysteries based on Navajo and Hopi people and culture (Aleiss 2005:152).

In referencing his *Imagining Indians* Masayesva writes: "Coming from a village which became embroiled in the filming of *Dark Wind*, a Hollywood production on the Hopi Reservation, I felt a keen responsibility as a community member, not an individual, to address these impositions on our tribal lives. Even as our communities say no, outsiders are responding to this as a challenge instead of respecting our feelings . . . I have come to believe that the sacred aspects of our existence which encourage the continuity and vitality of Native peoples are being manipulated by an aesthetic in which money is the most important qualification. This contradicts the values intrinsic to what's sacred and may destroy our substance. I am concerned about a tribal and community future which is reflected in my film and I hope this challenges the viewer to overcome glamorized Hollywood views of the Native American, which obscure the difficult demands of walking the spiritual road of our ancestors" (Documentary Education Resources 2007).

Ironically, the opportunity for Masayesva's voice to be heard by an audience beyond his own community was made possible by the complex ripples created by Kevin Costner. It should be noted that the idea of Native people making their own movies—telling their own stories—was not new since

*Dances With Wolves*. In 1975 the American Indian Film Institute began its annual film festival in Seattle. In 1977 it moved to San Francisco (fig. 1). The purpose of the institute was, and is, to promote and screen films made by members of the Native American communities of the United States and Canada. Phil Lucas (Choctaw), George Burdeau (Blackfeet), and Bob Hicks (Creek/Seminole) were just a few of these pioneer filmmakers.

To the degree that Costner's film was dismissed and ridiculed by some Native people it was also embraced by others—an obvious testament to the diversity among Native peoples. *Dances With Wolves* raised an awareness, a consciousness among Native Americans about their portrayals in film. If it was clear that Hollywood could never do justice to past and present depictions of Native people, if it was just as obvious that the pursuit of accurate portrayals would have to demand the full participation of Native people on all levels of filmmaking. More importantly, if the industry had no clue about how Native people should be seen on film, then how should they be portrayed?

In a very curious twist, *Dances With Wolves* stirred a level of dialogue that resulted in an explosion of Native-produced films. In the years that followed *Wolves* Native film festivals appeared in Minneapolis, New York, Phoenix, and other cities with urban Indian populations. From short autobiographical sketches to attempts at feature-length narratives, Native people were taking advantage of an artistic climate that sought authentic Native American voices. State arts boards, national private foundations, and even Hollywood offered funds for equipment, training, and development.

One of the most ambitious efforts to support aspiring Native performers was the creation of the American Indian Registry for the Performing Arts, which was based in Hollywood. Though the organization formed in 1983 with the support of Will Sampson, the Registry gained greater visibility by seizing on a new-found interest by Hollywood in wanting to attract more Native actors. But the Registry's mission was to do more than provide access to actors who could skillfully ride a horse, speak a Native tongue, and look the part of an authentic Indian without a tan or braided wig. The Registry sought to encourage the industry to consider developing more contemporary roles for Indians (B.R. Singer 2001:21).

Curiously, the concept of an Indian acting agency was not a new attempt to advocate on behalf of Native actors. During the 1930s the Indian Actors Workshop was created for the same reasons as the American Indian Registry. Native actors were tired of non-Native actors playing their roles. Jay Silverheels, an Iroquois from Ontario, frustrated with being typecast as the stoic, obedient sidekick Tonto in the *Lone Ranger* television series (1949–1957), revived the Workshop for a short period in 1966, offering peer support and training for Native actors.

In addition to advocating for more diverse Native roles one of the main thrusts of the Registry was to promote tribally affiliated actors. With the growing number of "wannabe" Native actors competing for the same roles, the Registry sought to convince the industry to adopt strict blood-quantum standards as defined by the federal government. This demand was perceived by Hollywood as a political ploy and it soured many in the industry. Like its predecessor, the Indian Actors Workshop, the Registry ultimately proved to have little impact on the industry. The agency closed its doors in 1993 due to a lack of financial support (Aleiss 2005:149).

In fact, the larger reality was that Hollywood was not interested in modern Native roles any more than they were in tribal affiliation. Hollywood simply was not done exploiting the American Indian of the Old West. The institution was stubbornly committed to promoting the "savage" of the west because it was a financially profitable formula. Ironically,

Native Amer. Public Telecommunications, Lincoln, Nebr.

Fig. 1. American Indian Film Institute. left, Chief Dan George (Salish) holding an award. right, Actor, producer, and board member Michael Horse (Zuni) and founder and president Michael Smith (Sioux), at the 29th American Indian Film Festival in San Francisco in 2004.

some of the most notable tribally affiliated actors secured the biggest roles at the time. Irene Bedard (Inupiat/Cree) was the voice of Disney's animated *Pocahontas* (fig. 2), which also starred Lakota activist Russell Means. Wes Studi (Cherokee), who had played the lead in Turner's *Geronimo*, actually found parts in non-Native themed pictures. And Gary Farmer (Cayuga), who played Philbert in *Powwow Highway*, found work in John Jarmusch's *Dead Man* (1995).

## Recreating the Past

Key to the new interest in discovering who the Native Americans truly were in America's past was the documentary, with a specific emphasis on dramatic recreations—a storytelling approach that was just beginning to influence the form. Riding on his success, Kevin Costner's production company produced an ambitious eight-part documentary series, *500 Nations* (1995), which aired on CBS. CNN and PBS also created and aired documentary programs. Ted Turner embarked on a multipicture project that included both documentary and fictional films on the historical Native experience. The documentary project consisted of a three-part, six-hour television series titled *The Native Americans* (1994).

Despite an obvious attempt to "correct" a history that either vilified Natives or ignored them, and despite bringing on Natives in pivotal research and technical positions (Kiowa producer and playwright Hanay Geiogamah played a key producing role in all of Turner's Indian projects), they received less than favorable reviews by the critics. Some were lambasted by critics who surmised that the producers

were not so much interested in a balanced retelling the past as in exploiting Native Americans to the point of romanticizing actual history (Goodman 1994).

Turner's five made-for-television movies, *The Broken Chain* (1993), *Geronimo* (1993), *Lakota Woman: Siege at Wounded Knee* (1994), *Tecumseh, The Last Warrior* (1995), and *Crazy Horse* (1996) fared just as poorly in the eyes of the press. The producers took a noble (and what some might describe as even honorable) approach by filming nearly all of these projects on location. Native actors and actresses starred in both principal and supporting roles. Native consultants were extensively used. Authenticity in culture and language were paramount, perhaps more vital than the actual stories, which were formulaic. In fact, the scripts were noticeably Hollywood in that the Native characters were "westernized"—having that good guy, bad guy aesthetic. Like the primetime documentary series by Costner, CNN, and PBS, these films were met with the same degree of disdain and dismissal because of their overt sympathy toward the Indian as victim.

As for Native audiences, what was most troubling was a lack of an American Indian sensibility in storytelling. The Turner films were especially disturbing in this realm. Here, the giants of tribal history, the warriors of old, were little more than White men in feathers all over again. For example, Crazy Horse appeared to be more like a fallen Greek god than the quasi-primal, spiritual warrior that he was to the memory of many Lakota Indians. The plot in *Crazy Horse* looked like a John Ford western. Only this time, the enemy was not a marauding band of wild savages, but a politically savvy family known as the Red Clouds.

By and large, Hollywood continued to snub any projects involving the contemporary Native American, unless the script read like a modern-day cowboy and Indian story. The conflict between American Indian Movement activists and FBI officials during the 1970s was recaptured in *Thunderheart* (1992). Val Kilmer, who is of Cherokee descent, starred as a federal agent torn between his duty to his country and his loyalty to his tribal family in this story based on actual events that occurred on the Pine Ridge Reservation in South Dakota (Pack 2001:105). For all its commercial budget efforts *Thunderheart* failed at the box office. The movie garnered a mere $22.7 million in receipts (Box Office Mojo 2007a).

What few modern roles available came from network television programming. *Northern Exposure*, the story of a medical doctor's life and times in Alaska that aired for five seasons on CBS, featured regular Native characters such as Elaine Miles (Umatilla). Still, the majority of Native roles on television were small parts. Often the Indian character was portrayed as mystical, as having some control over the supernatural. In the television science fiction series *The X-Files*, Native American mythology was re-imagined in the context of an alien abduction plot (Hersey 1998:109).

Clearly, Hollywood was not going to embrace the notion that there existed a very diverse world of contemporary

AP Images.

Fig. 2. Actress Irene Bedard (Inupiat/Cree), voice of Pocahontas in the Disney film of the same name, at the Thunder in the Desert powwow in Tucson, Ariz. Photograph by John Miller, 2004.

American Indian experiences. Perhaps, more simply put, Hollywood had no faith that American audiences could be attracted to an Indian on film who did not wear buckskin or speak in broken English. Once again, the struggle to get Hollywood to rethink portrayals of Native people seemed futile. It seemed clear that if Native Americans wanted to be portrayed on the screen in the way that reflected their own modern realities they would have to find ways to make their films outside of Hollywood.

## Sundances with Redford

At the beginning of the 1980s one of Hollywood's biggest moneymaking stars recognized that the creative vision of individual filmmakers was being sacrificed in order to make a living within the industry. Robert Redford gambled on the conviction that under the right conditions artists and financial underwriters could form partnerships toward creating independent film projects—projects that would allow the filmmaker autonomous artistic control. The Sundance Institute has become the premiere home and venue for independent filmmakers. In 1994, Redford, known for his environmental convictions and his concern for the American Indian plight (he produced and narrated the 1992 documentary on incarcerated activist Leonard Peltier titled *Incident at Oglala*) created a forum within the Institute's annual film festival—a venue that exclusively showcased work by Native film artists. The venue allowed for the inclusion of video projects. This was significant considering that the majority of Native projects were created using the less expensive technology (B.R. Singer 2001:64).

The goal of the Native program at Sundance was to expose Hollywood to a new generation of Native filmmakers. Despite the debacle of *The Dark Wind* movie, in which Redford was an executive producer, the actor and activist charged Sundance to mentor Native writers and directors with the hope that full-feature projects could be created and succeed at the box office.

The hope of an independent Native film movement came at a time when self-determining efforts to tell a story from a Native perspective were seen and heard throughout Indian Country. The timing seemed surreal. A new political climate that valued and supported multicultural voices proved to be a ripe season for Native filmmakers. Tribal media exploded on the scene in forms of newspapers and radio stations. Due in large part to new forms of tribal revenue such as gaming, the demand for Native-produced forms of communication was on the rise. Nontribal sources of funding were also available for the new Native communicators. In regard to television, the Native American Public Telecommunications (NAPT), which had been in existence since the 1970s as the Native American Public Broadcasting Consortium, found opportunities to help documentary filmmakers (fig. 3). Under the leadership of Frank Blythe (Eastern

Native Amer. Public Telecommunications, Lincoln, Nebr.

Fig. 3. Angelique Midthunder, self-taught documentary filmmaker, filming a close up of Stanford Addison, a Northern Arapaho quadriplegic horse tamer, on the set of *Silent Thunder*, which aired on PBS in 2006. Photograph by Teresa Neptune.

Cherokee) NAPT formed a partnership with the Public Broadcasting System (PBS). Along with a consortium of African-American, Asian-American and Hispanic telecommunication boards, NAPT awarded funds to documentary productions that showed promise of airing on PBS.

But the dream of offering PBS a plethora of shows was not realized as originally envisioned. The reality proved to be that what Native filmmakers had in mind for a "quality" film did not equal the specific expectations of PBS programmers. Even the highly ambitious and expensive documentary series *Storytellers of the Pacific Rim* (1996) could not break into the primetime schedule of PBS. In fact, programs funded by NAPT ended up either on local PBS affiliate stations or made the rounds at the numerous Indian film festivals.

This was the same result for filmmakers at Sundance. Despite the prestige of getting screened at the Sundance Film Festival, concerns about the lack of craftsmanship kept Native filmmakers in a marginalized world. It became quite clear to many Native filmmakers that what Sundance and PBS meant by "independent" was in reality nothing more than a euphemism for "must appeal to White audiences."

However, Native filmmakers' frustration over differing views of creative and technical quality spoke to a deeper problem than Sundance and PBS. At a time when there was a significant amount of funds available to artists of color, a number of Native people began to question, even challenge, who was actually receiving this money. Ava Hamilton (Arapaho), whose documentary *Everything Has A Spirit*, premiered at the 1994 Sundance Film Festival, helped form the Native American Producers Alliance at the Deadwood Film

Festival in 1993 in an effort to support tribally affiliated Native filmmakers. Concerned about the growing number of non-Native filmmakers receiving funding to make films about Native people, the Producers Alliance was not shy in vocalizing accusations of unfairness and inequity. Particularly, Hamilton and her colleagues charged that NAPT funded non-Native artists. In fact, NAPT stipulated that non-Native filmmakers could receive support only if they collaborated with Native artists (B.R. Singer 2001:40). Like the American Indian Registry, the Producers Alliance was mostly shunned by the industry and funders from both the public and private sectors; unlike the Registry, it remains visible. In addition to a membership of Native filmmakers from over 20 tribes, prominent film director Chris Eyre (Cheyenne/Arapaho) is an active member.

By the late 1990s the independent Native American film movement seemed to dissipate as if it were no more than a novelty. Many artists never made a second short film. For those who had invested in feature projects, those who had hoped to find distribution, the opportunity never came. After multiple screenings of the same films most of the urban Indian festivals closed their curtains for good. The few that kept their festivals on the yearly calendar, such as the Native Film and Video Festival at the National Museum of the American Indian in New York, reached out to filmmakers in South America—supporting an indigenous video movement that includes festival screenings and training (Weatherford and Seubert 1988:8).

While Native filmmakers struggled against a history of Hollywood image-making, in Canada it has not historically been so severe. This, of course, is not to suggest Aboriginal peoples in Canada have not faced violent racism, loss of land, and culture. In fact, Aboriginals of Canada have suffered many of the same ills brought on through generations of mistreatment. The immense diversity of film and video programs involving Aboriginal peoples testify to an artistic environment that is significantly supported by the Canadian government and the public.

Beginning in the 1970s the National Film Board of Canada provided training to Aboriginal documentary filmmakers. Provinces have offered training in both television and radio (Weatherford and Seubert 1988:7). Since 1999 the Aboriginal Peoples Television Network has aired across Canada, providing news and arts programming by and about its First peoples. *Dance Me Outside* (1995) remains one of the most recognized contemporary films about the lives of Aboriginal youth. However, though the cast starred Aboriginal actors (it propelled the Hollywood career of Ojibwa actor Adam Beach) and it created a CBC spin-off entitled *The Rez*, the creative control was in the hands of a White producer and director.

At Sundance the commitment toward nurturing the Native American voice remained steadfast. The Institute continued to recruit promising Native writers and directors to their prestigious workshops. And despite the waning amount of films made since the mid-1990s, the showcase venue of Native projects continued to be a hallmark at the annual Sundance festival. To Redford and programmers at Sundance the real obstacle that emerging Native filmmakers faced was not so much an issue of different aesthetics and creative approaches to storytelling; the problem Native artists had to overcome was in convincing film distributors of the marketable merit of their work. The reason distributors had little interest in taking on an independent Native film was simply because they did not believe there was a viable market (R. Martin 2003).

But the cost of convincing the industry that there was a market for contemporary Native stories carried a high price—the danger of cultural exaggeration and exploitation. Such was the case with a 1996 miniseries called *Grand Avenue*. Determined to prove that a modern American Indian story could attract a mainstream audience, Robert Redford's company convinced HBO to take on a project that was based on a series of short stories by a Pomo writer named Greg Sarris. With Robert Redford's name attached as an executive producer, HBO decided to encourage the production. This was to be a feature narrative about a single Native mother struggling to raise her children and struggling to break free from alcohol. The principal leads were Native characters led by newcomer Sheila Tousey (Menominee/Stockbridge Munsee). What was unique about *Grand Avenue* was that it was a modern tale of a Native family living in urban America.

Specifically, what disappointed some Native critics was the familiar imposition of a White aesthetic into the script. HBO had taken a Native text and compromised its cultural soul. The characters in *Grand Avenue* were nothing more than White people in brown skin. The attempt to endear audiences to the plight of contemporary Indians was at the expense of Native cultural reality. Still, in many ways *Grand Avenue* served as a crossroads for independent Native filmmakers. Should Native artists negotiate cultural representation—accuracy—in order to appease and assure Hollywood that Indian films can appeal to White audiences and become a commercial success? Or do Native artists find financial backing outside the system entirely in order to retain cultural and creative authority?

**Documenting New Histories**

In the mid-1970s, long before the idea of using video technology as a political and social means to tell stories from an American Indian perspective was realized, Sandra Osawa (Makah) was clashing heads with commercial broadcast programmers over who had the right to document current Native histories.

Curiosity about American Indians had hit the national evening news when activists of the American Indian Movement began to call attention to the continued mistreatment of Indian people. Osawa convinced the NBC affiliate in Los

Angeles that a proposed series on contemporary American Indian life needed a Native writer (B.R. Singer 2001:37). *The Native Americans Series*, which also aired in markets outside of Los Angeles in 1975, was a rare opportunity, and Osawa knew it. If American Indians wanted full creative control over their projects they would have to work outside the system. Later Osawa produced some of the most acclaimed documentaries on modern Indian life—*Lighting the 7th Fire* (1995) and *Pepper's Pow Wow* (1996).

Phil Lucas (fig. 4) was another pioneer who, like Osawa, knew that if he was going to make films his way he would have to find ways to fund his projects. Best known for his five-part series, *Images of Indians*, Lucas's career was almost entirely devoted to making documentaries. By the time of his death in 2007 Lucas had made over 100 films and won 18 awards, including an Emmy for directing an episode of *The Native Americans*.

The documentary has always been the most accessible and adaptable form of storytelling for American Indian filmmakers. The visual form of telling the stories of those whose voices may never have been heard has been a powerful way to speak against both past and current oppression. Noted broadcast journalists such as Hattie Kaufman (Nez Perce), Conroy Chino (Acoma Pueblo), and Patty Loew (Bad River Ojibwa) have worked and remained in either mainstream or public news because they have opportunities to tell stories of the American Indian for the smaller screen.

Native Amer. Public Telecommunications, Lincoln, Nebr.

Fig. 4. Phil Lucas (Choctaw, d. 2007), who produced or directed more than 100 television shows, film and documentaries, with Hawaiian filmmaker Lurline McGregor at a planning session. Photographed in the 1990s.

With the growth of tribal radio stations, a nationally syndicated radio call-in program, *Native America Calling*, the new media has continued to offer diverse venues for Native stories.

But the realization of a full-length narrative film making it to the big screens remained elusive. The deeply held perception that Hollywood was not interested in a story told purely from an Indian perspective turned to reality. Though pioneer narrative filmmakers were celebrated for their daring attempts to break into the industry—George Burdeau (Blackfeet) was the first American Indian to gain membership into the Director's Guild of America, and Bob Hicks was the first Indian to graduate from the Director's Program at the American Film Institute (B.R. Singer 2001: 44)—their vision and projects were marginalized as "experimental"—acceptable for film schools and audiences with avant garde tastes, but not appealing enough for mainstream America.

## Signals of Change

At the close of the 1998 Sundance Film Festival, Robert Redford had every reason to believe that his vision, his tenacity toward the realization of a hit independent film written and directed by American Indians, was at last fulfilled. *Smoke Signals*, directed by Chris Eyre, garnered the biggest buzz of the festival's line up. Picked up and distributed by Miramax, *Smoke Signals* became one of the cinema darlings of 1998.

At last, America was looking at a film made by a Native writer and director.

Not since the surprise hit of *Powwow Highway* had there been a more offbeat narrative film about everyday Indians. *Smoke Signals*, based on the short stories of Coeur D'Alene writer Sherman Alexie ("Literature," this vol.)—quirky, tragic life on the Coeur D'Alene Indian reservation—offered American audiences one of the most original stories of Indians on the screen.

Alexie's high-energy screenplay follows Victor and Thomas Builds-the-Fire on their journey from an Idaho reservation to the desert outside Phoenix, Arizona. Victor reluctantly lets Thomas join him on his quest to recover his father's ashes, to bring closure to a lifetime of abandonment.

Though the film earned a paltry $6.7 million, it was nonetheless as groundbreaking as Costner's epic. And like *Wolves* no other film challenged and continues to challenge celluloid images of American Indians like *Smoke Signals*.

But as highly touted as *Smoke Signals* was for being a truly independent Indian-created project, the reality is that the film could never have been made without the support and investment of the Sundance Institute. Eyre, a film school graduate, and Alexie developed their script at the Sundance Director's Lab before going into production. With a sizeable production grant through Sundance, Eyre and Alexie secured a Seattle-based production company's commitment to make the film. Once the film was made it was given a prominent spot at the Sundance Festival (J. Kilpatrick 1999:239).

Neither Eyre nor Alexie had written or directed a full-length film prior to *Smoke Signals*. But programmers at Sundance gave their support to the project because they believed both artists had the right formula for at least a marginal commercial success.

What sets *Smoke Signals* apart from Hollywood's Indian is its upbeat, light humor. Though alcoholism and poverty are integral to the film's plot (Mihelich 2001:131), the focus of the story is on the relationship between the two protagonists. The film's high stakes are not wrapped around White and Indian tension. Rather, it is a basic, universal theme, that of coming to emotional terms with the loss of a loved one.

Aesthetically (and perhaps intentionally), *Smoke Signals* makes the creative decision to exploit the "otherness" of its characters and setting. Victor and Thomas come from a hidden world inside America. They travel like lost immigrants in a new land. This "otherness" is key to giving a non-Indian audience an entry point into the film. By constructing the characters and physical place as uniquely different from the audience's frame of reference, they are relieved from trying to reconcile stereotypical images with what they are seeing on the screen. At its best, the approach allows for play on Hollywood stereotypes—a humorous exchange between Victor and Thomas on just what an Indian warrior is supposed to be. At its worst, because of the distance created away from Hollywood imagery, the story cannot delve into deeper layers of an Indian experience.

But keeping *Smoke Signals* light and universal is what the producers needed in order to make the film marketable (Aleiss 2005:159). The success story of *Smoke Signals* is one of creative compromises. For the producers concerned with selling a film about a world of people who are virtually invisible in America, *Smoke Signals* succeeds in reinforcing an undeniable reality of America's diversity. For the Indian director and writer, *Smoke Signals* holds true to a strong sense of cultural authenticity and integrity.

For the first time in American cinema, Native people recognized their fictional selves on the silver screen.

And yet, in the years that have passed since the release of *Smoke Signals*, there has not been another film so commercially successful, although *The Fast Runner* (*Atanarjuat*), a 2001 Canadian feature film based on an Inuit legend and shot entirely in the Inuktitut language, won numerous awards, and worldwide grossed nearly $6 million (Box Office Mojo 2007c). Both Eyre and Alexie have made more films. Eyre has found considerable work, but his biggest success has been in finding a niche in reworking the Redford adaptations of Tony Hillerman's Navajo mystery novels for PBS's *American Mystery!*

But the fact that the achievements of *Smoke Signals* may appear to be another Hollywood aberration is not entirely accurate. *Smoke Signals*, like all films that find resonance with audiences, had that one intangible ingredient that cannot be learned, cannot be manufactured. *Smoke Signals* had screen magic.

## Reflections and Considerations

It is not uncommon to read a national news story about a new American Indian film project in the works. It is not uncommon for Hollywood to premiere another revisionist tale of the past. (James Fenimore Cooper's literary saga *The Last of the Mohicans* has been made into five film versions.) In 2005, a live action drama about Pocahontas, *The New World*, was released by New Line Cinema. The film, which starred Peruvian-German actress, Q'orianka Kilcher and featured dialogue in the reconstructed Virginia Algonquian language, attempted to debunk the longstanding myth that the young Powhatan woman was romantically involved with Capt. John Smith (Chagollan 2005). *The New World* earned over 30 million dollars worldwide (Box Office Mojo 2007d).

Native filmmakers still attend the Sundance labs and festival each year. Actors continue to find work, mostly in historical pictures, but on occasion, as in the case of the 2003 ABC miniseries *Dreamcatcher*, or Clint Eastwood's drama about World War II in *Flags of our Fathers* (2006), there are some non-Western roles. The First Americans in the Arts, based in Los Angeles, recognizes the best in Native film performances at their annual awards show no matter the genre.

After nearly three decades of funding independent projects, the Native American Public Telecommunications produced their own two-part documentary series exclusively for PBS. *Indian Country Diaries* aired nationally in November 2006.

Collectively, the new scripts and roles are changing world perception of American Indians. Perhaps this body of work demonstrates that a blockbuster film is not Indian Country's only hope for social change. The funding outside the Hollywood machine is as difficult as ever to attract. Despite what may seem like the obvious to non-Native people, the tribes are not seen as a viable source of financial support. Part of the reason why gaming profits are not widely tossed at ambitious film projects might simply be that movies are not seen as a critical means to saving or recovering Indian culture.

Not yet.

Of course, this poses the question: what is the relationship between film and community? Obviously, the aged question of just what defines success for a filmmaker arises. Is there any less success in creating a 10-minute video that documents community elder stories for the local tribal museum or school? Is there any less success in making a short film about rediscovering one's own connection to ceremony, culture, language?

The American filmgoer does not look at the Indian through the same lens that John Ford did. Much of that change of view has come through the increased participation of American Indians in film. But the power of visual storytelling among American Indian communities has not yet been clearly understood, measured in terms of social change within tribal communities. And as the twenty-first century unfolds the question of what impact Native-produced films may have in shaping, in defining, the American Indian experience may very well be one of the most important questions facing the American Indian.

# Literature

KATHRYN W. SHANLEY

## Defining Native American Literature

Through many thousands of years on the North American continent, Native Americans have produced a deep and rich linguistic and literary legacy. The fewer than 200 Native American languages alive in 2007, less than half the number that existed when Christopher Columbus reached the western hemisphere (vol. 17:3), reflect myriad ways of looking at the world—ways based on indigenous experience in particular places. Europeans, Africans, and Asians brought new languages and worldviews to North America, leading to exchanges with and adaptations by the Native peoples residing here. One of the most significant adaptations has involved the technology of writing.

What often falls into the category of Native American (or American Indian literature) takes shape in all identifiable Western European genres from oral chants and sermons, to poetry, to fictional and historical texts. Including as it does specific literatures from the more than 1,000 indigenous groups in the United States and Canada, Native American literature may seem impossibly broad; nonetheless, a general rubric distinguishes the literature from other traditions by its rootedness in indigenous North American experience and its historical responses to encounters with European peoples and settler movements. Because writers of American Indian literature hail from all over the continent, from many walks of life, socioeconomic levels, and so forth, the literature will itself take on a wide range of subjects in a wide range of forms. In this chapter, particular themes do arise and repeat: indigenous roots, "homing in" motif, a search for identity, the importance of building strong Native communities, and coming of age in postcolonial Indian Country.

Defining the field first by its indigenous roots, even when tribal descendants no longer speak their Native tongues, need not result in a Noble Savage past. Just as the study of Puritan theology, and their vision of building a "city on a hill" according to biblical dictates, leads to viewing contemporary America better, understanding the linguistic and philosophical roots of contemporary American Indian expressive cultures expands the knowledge of particular histories at the same time as it extends the visions of where those histories fit in a common humanity.

Despite a persistence of stereotypes of and about American Indian peoples in the American popular mind (vol. 4:587–616), literature by Indian individuals needs to do more than respond to pressures to counter false or simplistic images; these writers offer a look at the colonial past and Indian perseverance. The tyranny of false representations of Indian life and peoples has always played a part in spawning and shaping Indian writing, but the very best of the writing draws on fact, circumstance, representation, and imagination.

Regarding stereotypical portrayals, all writers can fall prey to them; American Indians are no exception. While European Americans, like James Fenimore Cooper and Mark Twain and other writers up to the present, portrayed American Indians through biased lenses (vol. 4:573–581), American Indians themselves fall prey to distorted representation, albeit for different reasons. Serious attention to the study of texts requires looking past both the nostalgic and the political manifesto strains on the part of both non-Indian editors and Indian writers in the body of Native American works. To mark this pitfall, literary critic Arnold Krupat commented, in his study of Native American autobiography, on the prevalence of pieces of "the past": most of what appears in anthologies of Indian literature was collected after the Civil War, roughly from 1887 to 1934, "inscribed by anthropologists determined to preserve this vanishing heritage in the name of science" (Krupat 1985:6). In contrast with this nostalgic trend, imagining, recovering, revitalizing, and inventing Native literary traditions took on tremendous momentum after 1945.

A popular identification with and focus upon indigenous thought has slowly led to a interest in the survival of indigenous peoples and languages in a way that goes beyond what is frequently referred to as "salvage anthropology," the movement to which Krupat refers. That movement sought to save tribal knowledge and artifacts, rather than saving tribal peoples, because the people were often seen as doomed to disappear. The "vanishing Indian" stereotype had a long life in American thought. Whether in the form of Henry Wadsworth Longfellow's "Hiawatha" or in Edward Curtis's staged portraits of Indians from a pristine past. Americans tended to mourn American Indians of a romanticized, "closed" world. It was termed "imperialist nostalgia," which was defined as "yearning for what was destroyed as a form of mystification" (Rosaldo 1989, 1993:71). Curtis's sepia romantic photographs from around 1900, like all photographs, "give the illusion of motion in abeyance, as if everything visible was holding its breath. Curtis's went further. He made stillness palpable, a living presence in a silent landscape, the atmospheric equivalent of the simple epochal idea of 'vanishing race' that governs his great quixotic project" (Trachtenberg 2004:180).

In the United States the Indian Reorganization Act of 1934 increased American Indian self-governance, and with that policy shift came a greater Indian voice. American indigenous peoples began in a measured sense to put their communities back together, and after being subject to a system of education in English in existence for over half a century, American Indians began to put their literacy to use for their own good. Since that time the environmental movement as well as the political upheavals of the 1960s and 1970s have helped to shape scholarly attempts to re-envision indigenous thought. Particularly among anthropologists, ways of seeing indigenous knowledge and practices as valid in their own right began to develop. Literary production has been at the center of that effort.

As American Indian writers asserted their voices, they reaffirmed their communities, as Jace Weaver describes well the search for community in *That the People Might Live* (1997). Louis Owens (1992, 1992a) describes how writers shaped fiction to portray a Native search for identity, balancing Indian and White worlds.

Edited texts such as Dennis Tedlock's *Finding the Center* (1972, 1978), Jerome Rothenberg's *Technicians of the Sacred* (1968, 1985), Jerome and Diane Rothenberg's *Symposium of the Whole* (1984), and Rothenberg's *Shaking the Pumpkin* (1972, 1991) influenced thinking regarding the complexity of "primitive" poetries during the emergence of a postmodern American Indian literature. Eventually that thinking filtered into broader forums and encouraged American Indian people themselves to write out of their own experiences. Tedlock and Rothenberg's journal, *Alcheringa,* which ran 1970–1980, presented tribal literatures in their own terms. A reissue of *Black Elk Speaks: Being the Life Story of a Holy Man of the Ogalala Sioux,* originally published in 1932 (vol. 13:1073), furthered the growth of Native American literature in the 1960s, even though it was not actually written by Black Elk. An as-told-to (or "through") autobiography written with John G. Neihardt, *Black Elk Speaks* was regarded by some as serving a function for the young Indian generations similar to the Christian Bible; the younger generations of Indians from all tribes turned to tribal ways of knowing, seeing, and being (Neihardt 1932, 1961, 1979; see also DeMallie 1984). As American Indian writers and scholars matured away from initial nostalgic and romantic posturing, they moved toward theory, analysis, and more nuanced fictional renderings of Native life. The calling into question of the means of production of texts such as *Black Elk Speaks* increased the diligence of people working with American

Indians to record their life stories and increased the attention to preserving indigenous worldview perspectives, languages, and consciousnesses in ways that dictate fidelity to indigenous literary forms. Archival recovery of texts has fostered a greater depth of understanding of past writers, heretofore little known, such as Samson Occom, William Apess, and Alice Callahan. A. LaVonne Brown Ruoff (1990) provided a valuable bibliographic and overview for launching critical studies in the field with her book *American Indian Literatures.*

The increase in the number of Western-educated American Indians affected a cross-influence among literature, politics, history writing, cultural preservation, and religious revitalization. As Joy Harjo states, "We are still here, still telling stories, still singing whether it be in our native languages or in the 'enemy' tongue" (Harjo and Bird 1997:31).

An overview of themes in those American Indian stories across time reveals a movement that begins with efforts to inform and preserve Indian ways and lives, continues with attempts to unwrite images of the Noble (or Ignoble) Savage, and eventually leads to uniqueness in individual expression and perspective. In early periods, writing histories represented an urgent attempt to record information being lost or overlooked by the dominant culture and to correct false records, while making a case for the continuance of Indian people, if not cultures. As more writers moved fully into self-generated autobiography, poetry in modern idioms, and fiction writing, their themes and subgenres have also expanded, while furthering the imperative of seeing the literature as continuous with its indigenous roots. "Assimilation" rings colonial in Indian Country, and since many writers arising from the 1960s and 1970s were university students or had university educations (N. Scott Momaday received a Ph.D. in English from Stanford University in 1963), their identities as Indians have been interrogated. Some writers and their work tend to be pushed out of the definitions of American Indian, if their indigenous roots or perspectives are questionable. While questions persist of who is Indian and how readers judge such matters in the written works, the increased freedom with which Indian people practice their traditions, determine their political and economic futures, and intersect with education empowers the people to arbitrate somewhat in those discussions and to write their own stories, their own versions of truth.

## Tribal Histories, Life Stories, and Autobiographies

For centuries, writing seemed antithetical to being American Indian, until the modern period, when education in English became mandatory for children on the reservation and in off-reservation boarding schools. Yet, the truth is that American Indians have been writing in English since at least the eighteenth century, with the best-seller publication of Samson Occom (Mohegan, vol. 15:182), *Sermon Preached at the Execution of Moses Paul*, in 1772 (Hochbruck and Dudensing-Reichel 1992; also in Jaskoski 1996:1–14). (In fact, Occom learned at Harvard to write in Greek and Latin.) Prior to the sermon's publication, Occom wrote *A Short Narrative of My Life* (1768), which one critic sees as representing "the social fabric that is literarily repressed, and literally oppressed" (D. Nelson 1996:62). Christian Indians often found voice in the form of testimony to faith and conversion in the eighteenth century, in what may be labeled "rituals of subordination and strategies of resistance" (Murray 1996:15).

The earliest book-length, self-generated autobiography, *A Son of the Forest* (1829), also comes from a Christian minister, William Apess (Pequot), but Apess's work does not engage a posture of subordination. In some ways, the text reads like fiction, in that he develops themes, characters, and motifs to guide the telling of his life story of poverty, abuse, indentured servitude, conversion to Christianity, his Christian ministry, and his devotion to the cause of racial justice (O'Connell 1992). Apess embraced Methodism after abuse at the hands of his own kin and many sad years as a foster child, more aptly termed indentured servant. He writes about the abuses he and other minorities suffered at the hands of Americans; his narrative compares to conversion narratives of the time but also differs in its insistence on calling Christians to practice the Golden Rule by loving people unlike themselves.

Other Natives who wrote about their lives, their tribes' histories, and their cultures in the nineteenth century most notably include David Cusick (Tuscarora), George Copway (Ojibwa), Peter Jones (Ojibwa), Sarah Winnemucca Hopkins (Northern Paiute), Francis La Flesche (Omaha), Charles Eastman (Santee Sioux), Carlos Montezuma (Yavapai), and Gertrude Bonnin, also known as Zitkala-Ša (Yankton Sioux). The speaking, even performing, of Indianness that many of these writers engaged in became part of the ritual of making America. Indian intellectuals of the time were caught in that cultural ambiguity and pressed into community service as public intellectuals in ways that limited their time for writing. Philip J. Deloria (Yankton Sioux) describes well the audience for articulate, educated Indians back then: "The indeterminacy of American identities stems, in part, from the nation's inability to deal with Indian people. Americans wanted to feel a natural affinity with the continent, and it was Indians who could teach them such original closeness. Yet, in order to control the landscape they had to destroy the original inhabitants" (P.J. Deloria 1998:5). The double-bind of having to testify about Indianness and advocate for Indian causes truly left many early writers stranded between worlds. Going "home" was not always easy for them. The identity problems persist with Indian writers, while the association of American Indians with the land adds a further moral imperative to honor Native traditions.

American Indian autobiography, over 80 percent of which comes about through an editor or collaborator who is not Native, has always been a popular form of American Indian literature, probably because of the non-Indian desire to know what a "real" Indian is like or to puzzle over what remains of indigenous "otherness" (Brumble 1988:72). Depending on how much the amanuensis—the person recording, editing and contextualizing the story of the Native person—values retaining the spoken qualities and cultural details, the autobiography can be fairly representative of the person's life.

The first autobiography by an American Indian woman, Sarah Winnemucca Hopkins (vol. 11:458, 601–602), was *Life Among the Piutes* (1883, 1994), which arose by popular demand from her success in the eastern United States on the lecture circuit. Winnemucca became a prominent public speaker in the women's movement, and she used the platform given her by White women to advocate for her own people. Mary Peabody Mann helped Hopkins with the writing of the text. Charles Eastman (Ohiyesa) wrote two autobiographies, *Indian Boyhood* (1902, 1991) and *From the Deep Woods to Civilization* (1916, 1936), as well other works on Plains Indian life. As a medical doctor who had experienced a move from "the deep woods to civilization," Eastman had many stories to tell, and he did so with his wife Elaine Goodall's editorial help. Luther Standing Bear (Teton Sioux), with the editorial assistance of E.A. Brininstool, settled into writing after many adventures, such as performing with Buffalo Bill's Wild West Show, being a movie star, public speaking, and advocating for American Indian political causes. *Land of the Spotted Eagle* (1933, 1978, 2006) was his most fully realized work. Francis La Flesche's story of his youth spent in an on-reservation Presbyterian boarding school, *The Middle Five* (1900, 1963), poignantly depicts the dilemmas of that generation of Indians who obtained a Western education in order to serve their people (S.L. Smith).

In the 2000s, almost two centuries after the first as-told-to American Indian autobiography was written, similar stories continue told through non-Native collaborators contain a mixture of history, storytelling, and autobiography with varying levels of involvement by the editor (Krupat 1985: xiii). Examples include Ron Paquin's (1992) *Not First in Nobody's Heart* (with Robert Doherty), Frances Manuel's (2001) *Desert Indian Woman* (with Deborah Neff), and Rudy Wiebe and Yvonne Johnson's (1998) *Stolen Life: The Journey of a Cree Woman*. Literacy issues continue to figure into the choices of the Native autobiographers to work with non-Indian collaborators to produce texts, and most often it is the editor-collaborator who seeks out the Indian whose story is deemed worthy of being told. Given the wide differential latitude of works that pass as Indian autobiography, a genre overlap persists with what is generally considered fiction. The texts stand between the oral tradition and literary tradition, and a sense of indigeneity can and does survive into the twenty-first century through these texts.

## Early Fiction

In the last decade of the nineteenth century and the first two decades of the twentieth century, many American Indians educated in off-reservation boarding schools published short fiction in periodicals, as they began reflecting on both their experiences as educated Indians and the beauty and truth in their besieged cultures. Crafting adaptations of traditional stories for reconsideration constituted a transitional form that moved from oral and traditional literatures. "[T]he Indian writers of this period wrote almost entirely for the non-Indian reader (Creek poet and journalist Alex Posey is a notable exception; see Littlefield 1992), it is not surprising to find popular stereotypes sometimes reflected in their short stories. . . . It should be remembered, however, that a nostalgic view of the past was also a sincere expression of the Indian writers' own feelings on the matter, not simply the adoption of an imposed stereotype" (Peyer 1989:xii). Despite the apologia regarding the nostalgic, romanticized tone of many of the stories, a goodly number of stories in the collection describe "contemporary Indian life, and . . . represent a conscious effort on the part of the authors to educate their readers concerning everyday Indian existence and the problems resulting from cultural contact" (Peyer 1989:xii). Among the contributors, only John Milton Oskison, John Joseph Mathews, and D'Arcy McNickle went on to write longer fiction.

In the beginning years of the growth of the field of Native American literary studies—the late 1970s and early 1980s—critic after critic misidentified the first novel by an American Indian. The honors for being the first novel by an American Indian male, until a new text is discovered, go to *The Life and Adventures of Joaquín Murieta: The Celebrated California Bandit*, published in 1854 by John Rollin Ridge (Cherokee) with the pseudonym Yellow Bird; and by an American Indian female to *Wynema: A Child of the Forest* (1891, 1997), by S. Alice Callahan (Muskogee). Joaquín Murieta, a protagonist-hero, an outlaw with a Robin Hood heart, avenges the underdog and pursues one adventure after another in the process; originating from the oral traditions in California, the novel is the prototype for the character of Zorro in subsequent television and film. Ridge's novel dramatizes by allegory the dispossession his own Cherokee people experienced in the forced relocation from the Southeast to Indian Territory. *Wynema* revolves around the friendship between two women, one White and one Indian, whose conversations involve the Indian issues of the day: allotment of land, interracial tolerance, and political reform.

Christine Quintasket (Southern Okanogan, vol. 12:269), using the pen name Mourning Dove, wrote what was long thought of as the first novel by an American Indian woman, *Cogewea, the Half-Blood: A Depiction of the Great Montana Cattle Range* (1927, 1981), with help from Lucullus Virgil McWhorter. Combining the features of the romance and the western, the novel plays out a somewhat innovative view of frontier intercultural relations. It is a brave attempt to take up the issue of interracial marriage between Native women and White men.

With the increased use of the novel as a form among American Indian writers in the first decades of the twentieth century, the troubled status and experience of people of mixed-blood ancestry gained more full treatment as a theme. The two most prominent American Indian writers of this period, John Joseph Mathews (Osage) and D'Arcy McNickle (Cree/adopted Flathead), wrote both fiction and nonfiction. As Indian intellectuals they shared many perspectives regarding life as educated Indians, including the importance of advocating for tribal empowerment. Mathews's novel *Sundown* (1934, 1988) and McNickle's *The Surrounded* (1936, 1978) both involve mixed-blood protagonists. These novelists' styles and themes meshed "neatly with the popular naturalism of the twenties and thirties" (Owens 1992:49). The novels bear resemblance to one another in multiple ways: they are both situated on the authors' respective reservations, one on the Osage and the other the Flathead; their protagonists are caught between Native mothers and non-Native fathers in reservation politics; and the natural world speaks in muted tones that echo the voices of the people—the people and nature suffer oppression under the newcomers.

Historical happenings, such as when the Flathead of Montana sent delegations to Saint Louis, Missouri, 1831–1839, to implore Jesuits to come among them with their powerful spiritual ways, have since been viewed as ironic, given that the priests then required the Indians to bring their spiritual and ritual objects of great power to the mission to be burned (vol. 12:306). In that vein, both Mathews and McNickle evoke Native spiritual affinity with Christianity, as well as ambivalence and revulsion. Mathews's protagonist Chal feels too dark-skinned for keeping company with Whites, yet attracted to a young White woman named Blo. The narrator suggests such affinities need not be seen as antithetical: "He wondered why he had a feeling that was something like a religious emotion when he thought of Blo. Of course it never occurred to him that it might be the tribal heritage of religion associated with beauty and dreams" (Mathews 1934:155). McNickle's protagonist Archilde finds himself pulled into the Roman Catholic mission, attracted to a painting behind the altar, then when he touches it, as if it were forbidden, a bat flies out from behind the painting, startling him, as fear and dread make him feel as if the forces of the cosmos were bearing down upon him. The church becomes associated with alienation, just as the idea of sin relates to alienation from God. The transplanted faith signifies alienation from indigeneity. The protagonists find themselves displaced, if not replaced, by the White man and his religion, in their own homeland.

The period identified as the Native American Renaissance (K. Lincoln 1983), starting in the 1960s, was a blossoming of talent and hope in new expression. A Choctaw critic concludes that "In *Sundown*, Mathews leaves open the possibility of 'another destiny, another plot' for the American Indian, refusing any romantic closure that would deny the immense difficulties confronting the displaced Native American" (Owens 1992:60). "In *The Surrounded*, McNickle's mixed-ancestry Archilde becomes an even more interesting and innovative device . . . [McNickle] builds a tension between a popular stereotype and evidence that it is baseless, and this tension takes the reader far beyond the conventional 'clash between two civilizations' that was the basis of most popular fiction about Native people in McNickle's time and since" (Purdy 1990:67–68). McNickle aimed to "re-educate both native and non-Native readers so that they could better understand each other's cultural codes. *Wind from an Enemy Sky* (1978a) was his last and some say best attempt to illuminate the cognitive structures in this cross-cultural dynamic, reflecting years of personal experience and his refined literary talent" (Ruppert 1995:110). Re-educating people to understand each other's cultural codes also involves encouraging people to understand their own codes. American Indian writers needed a community conversation to foster a depth of self-understanding of what makes them collectively similar and individually distinct. In the decades after Mathews and McNickle's period of relative intellectual isolation, a new generation addressed anew the difficulties of "carrying the dream wheel" (from a poem by N. Scott Momaday) of American indigenous survival forward (Niatum 1975).

**Renaissance After 1968**

Between the mid-1940s and the mid-1960s, a new American Indian writing movement took root. Excitement reverberated throughout Indian Country, in literary circles and academic settings, because Indians were speaking out. This movement was triggered in 1969 when, along with the publication of Vine Deloria, Jr.,'s *Custer Died for Your Sins: An Indian Manifesto* (1969) and the occupation of Alcatraz Island by American Indian activists, N. Scott Momaday's (Kiowa) *House Made of Dawn* (1968) won the Pulitzer Prize. As part of efforts symbolically to reclaim lost territory, the novel helped launch a public awareness of American Indian life and issues (vol. 4:580–581). In *House Made of Dawn*, the protagonist Abel must come back to his indigenous roots if he hopes to heal. He returns home to the reservation from the armed forces, and while he is drinking, he kills an albino man, an act that symbolically locates the menace as "white." From there, he drifts to Los Angeles until his grandfather's death forces him to return home again. The impression is given that, through his running as in rituals of old, he has reconnected with a deeper self, has begun a healing process, and located himself where he is supposed to be—among his people.

Although parts of Momaday's *Way to Rainy Mountain* (1969) were published before *House Made of Dawn*, the full text came out afterward. As a text, it sits between periods and amalgamates literary and historical forms as well as oral and written traditions, to bring an American Indian person's voice into relation with his world in a way that values the interconnectedness of all things. The text's narrator relies on nature to be his teacher and guide as he follows the ancient journey of his Kiowa people from Montana to Oklahoma (vol. 13:907). Themes of tribal identity as it ties to the geography of place inform all of Momaday's work.

*Storyteller* (1981) by Leslie Marmon Silko (fig. 1) similarly presents a many-voiced story through photographs by her father, family stories, contemporary stories that incorpo-

Tulsa City-County, Lib., Okla.

Fig. 1. Leslie Marmon Silko, Laguna Pueblo, signing one of her many publications during the 2005 Festival of Words, at the American Indian Resource Center's event at the Tulsa City-County Lib., Okla. Silko was the 2005 recipient of the American Indian Festival of Words Award, established in 2001 and given biannually. The award recognizes literary contributions of outstanding American Indian authors. Other honorees are Joy Harjo in 2001; Vine Deloria, Jr., in 2003; and Carter Revard, Osage, in 2007. Photograph by John Fancher.

rate her Laguna Pueblo's traditional myths, and poetry. Both the tradition of storytelling and the innovation of writing celebrate the power of language. The Southwest landscape unites all the pieces—verbal, written, and visual. Such a mingling of forms characterizes Momaday's *The Names* (1976) as well, complete with a genealogical chart in the front of the book. Connections to a lineage empower writers to speak with authority about their tribal histories. Irvin Morris followed in the mixed-genre tradition of Silko and Momaday with *From the Glittering World* (1997), a text he describes as a fictional autobiography. Morris opens his text with an untranslated Navajo prayer, and the work divides into four sections under Navajo titles with English translations. By the end of the book, as Morris enters the glittering world (the fourth world since creation), the stories take only English titles. It is as if the indigenous world mingles with the Anglo world, in multicolored and multilayered ways. The last story or chapter, "Meat and the Man," begins with mention of "a fragment of music" from the Navajo Blessingway ceremony and ends with a conversation about a man who speaks Navajo "barely" but seems to be trying to steal stories from them (Morris 1997:257). From the inside looking out, the family sustains itself. The text, as a work of fictional autobiography, adapts to the author's need to establish and maintain himself within two traditions, as a writer and as a member of the Navajo community. For all those reasons, the text eludes easy classification.

The works of Ray A. Young Bear (Meskwaki), *Black Eagle Child: The Facepaint Narratives* (1992) and *Remnants of the First Earth* (1996), connect a story across two books, depart significantly from previous forms of American Indian autobiography or fiction, and claim new representational turf. Neither imitative nor imitable, neither fully fictional nor fully autobiographical, the work is unique. For all its gritty realism, Young Bear disguises the characters and the place, and presents the events as if they took place in a mythical timelessness, from when the protagonist, Edgar Bearchild, attended the surreal Peyote religious ceremony to his firing his rifle at UFOs. *Black Eagle Child* was published as part of *Singular Lives: The Iowa Series in North American Autobiography*, edited by Albert E. Stone; the veracity of "plot" features is contained in introductory passages to chapters. In the text, "The Facepaint narratives" becomes a metaphor for a kind of medicine power inherent in writing, a ceremonial outward sign; it also refers to the name of Edgar's best friend, Ted Facepaint. The first text largely takes the form of poetry; the second is largely prose. Told in the third person, Edgar Bearchild chronicles life in the Black Eagle Child Settlement (the Meskwaki Settlement at Tama, Iowa) in a timeless way that suggests myth more than life history. Yet, within the text he outlines his writing influences that originate in family stories: "Along with new poems I began / writing stories as told to me by my great / uncle, Carson Two Red Foot, and my maternal / grandmother, Ada Principle Bear. These stories were recorded and then translated and revised back into English. It was a

momentous winter. The fingers would hit the keys all day" (Young Bear 1992:142). The passage ends with an unpleasant exchange between him and an employee of an arts agency that does not send him information he requests and calls him "Mr. Bear Butt." Finally, he makes an entry in an imaginary journal: " 'After so much hate talk at the golf course, / church, and business breakfasts,' I recorded in *Journal of a Woodland Indian*, 'there has to be a subtle transference / of bigotry in the genes from one Why Cheer / generation to the next' " (Young Bear 1992:142–143). The humor in names such as that of the town, Why Cheer, dovetails with his whimsical and playful naming of characters based on real Meskwaki families: "Bearchild," for Young Bear, and "Principle Bear" for Old Bear.

The literature of writers such as Momaday, James Welch (Blackfeet/Gros Ventre), Simon J. Ortiz, Jr. (Acoma Pueblo), Silko, Joy Harjo (Creek), and Paula Gunn Allen (Laguna/Lakota/Lebanese), from the beginning of the Native American Renaissance, no doubt made the work of Morris and Young Bear possible. In American Indian literature, the autobiography often comes in tandem with the fiction, as if each legitimizes the other. Writers may have also felt they need to reveal their tribal roots as a way of establishing their Indianness or out of a "need to say" or even a need to confess the ways in which they depart from expectations (Shanley 2001:3–16). Two important anthologies in that period capture individual differences among American Indian writers: *Survival This Way: Interviews with American Indian Poets* (1987), edited by Joseph Bruchac, and *I Tell You Now: Autobiographical Essays by Native American Writers* (1987), edited by Arnold Krupat and Brian Swann.

During the early part of the Native American Renaissance, three novels became foundational in their influence: Momaday's *House Made of Dawn*, Welch's *Winter in the Blood* (1974), and Silko's *Ceremony* (1977). All three develop indigenous senses of time and place and themes involved with valuing community and circularity. As Paula Gunn Allen states, "The way of the Imagination is the way of continuity, circularity, completeness." Allen then reiterates the phrase for which Momaday is perhaps best known: "an Indian is an idea which a given man has of himself" (Allen 1987:563). William Bevis refers to the way the protagonists in those three novels (and three others) return to or remain in their tribal homelands for healing as "homing in" (Bevis 1987:584). Of the "regressive" pattern Bevis identifies, he writes: "most Native American novels are not 'eccentric,' centrifugal, diverging, expanding, but 'incentric,' centripetal, converging, contracting. The hero comes home. . . . In Native American novels, coming home, staying put, contracting, even what we call 'regressing' to a place, a part where one has been before, is not only the primary story, it is a primary mode of knowledge and a primary good" (Bevis 1987:582). The appeal of the "homing in" plot structure was immense in the late 1960s, when civil rebellion of American ethnic minorities was breaking out all over the United States ("Activism, 1950–1980," this vol.).

Welch's *Winter in the Blood* held both popular appeal as the voice of a contemporary American Indian and the lyrical beauty of its prose pushed it to the fore. Welch's book of poetry, *Riding the Earthboy 40* (1971, 1976) was reissued, and he became a literary sensation. As the title of the novel implies, *Winter in the Blood* depicts the harsh, cold circumstances in the life of the protagonist, a nameless narrator on Highway 2 across Montana. His life is presented in the first person, mimicking autobiographical form, which adds immeasurably to the story's appeal, as the novel draws the reader into the hauntingly intimate voice of a man who does not know what to do with his life. The depth of humor in the work distinguishes the novel and the fact that readers can never be certain of closure—it does not tie itself up neatly with its "homing in." The protagonist, though riddled with grief over the deaths of his father and brother and aware of the racism around him, does not project blame; instead, he sees the world as "cockeyed." Welch's second novel, *The Death of Jim Loney* (1979), continues the theme of a young man with a serious drinking problem caught between worlds, but it shapes the plot around epochs before and after Christ, darkness before the dawn, and does so with considerably more seriousness than in *Winter*. Each of Welch's five novels builds itself around a male protagonist searching to establish himself as a man in a world that is off-kilter.

Silko's *Ceremony* centers around similar themes: continuity and change on the cultural level and alienation and loss along with healing on the individual level. The novel's mixed-blood protagonist, Tayo, goes to fight in World War II with his brother Rocky, who dies in a prisoner of war camp with Tayo by his side. Racked by grief, guilt, and war trauma, Tayo must find ways of healing himself. Ironically, "home" for Tayo means a comfort zone he has never known, a place to live as a person in-between—becoming a new breed like the spotted Mexican cattle in the novel who are better adapted to survive the drought on the land. Tayo's problems stem from the cosmos gone awry. The central story the author uses to explain the sad state of current affairs begins at a witches conference: "Long time ago / in the beginning / there were no white people in this world. . . ." The witches try to outdo one another, so the last witch invents "white skin people" who "grow away from the earth" and become destroyers (Silko 1977:135). Restoring harmony becomes a central concern in the vision of this novel, and while Tayo does find stability through a mysterious mountain spirit woman, a dancer, and Navajo medicine man named Betonie, who draws power eclectically from those things around him, the world is only in balance "for now."

Like Momaday's Abel in *House Made of Dawn* and Welch's nameless narrator in *Winter in the Blood*, Tayo must deal with the cruelty of his people, particularly members of his own family, as well as with prejudices against Indians in the world at large. Silko's mammoth novel *Almanac of the Dead* (1991) continues the idea of witchery and disharmony, but it develops the prophetic and historical dimensions to the playing out of a corruption let loose in the world. Fundamental to Silko's vision is the idea that new ceremonies are needed to battle the wickedness in the world and that growth and change are not only inevitable, but necessary for strong ceremonies and healthy people. An ordinary person, like Tayo, can center himself by simple prayers to the earth powers; the kachina spirit inspires him to pray: "He repeated the words as he remembered them, not sure if they were the right ones, but feeling they were right, feeling the instant of the dawn was an event which in a single moment gathered all things together—the last stars, the mountaintops, the clouds, and the winds—celebrating this coming" (Silko 1991:182). Applying Bevis's terminology, Tayo would have had an "incentric" moment, when all things in the universe come together in one place.

Although mostly known as a fine poet, Simon J. Ortiz, Jr., played an important role in the Native American Renaissance. His two collections of stories, *Howbah Indians* (1978) and *Fightin': New and Collected Stories* (1983), assured his place as a relentless voice in pressing for recognition of the losses of land, water, human rights, and all that American Indian people suffered under European American domination. He calls on America to own its own vision of democracy. In Ortiz's work, aesthetics and politics come together synergistically to present a stunning view of the power of indigenous ways.

Another best-selling book during the 1970s, *Seven Arrows* (1972) by Hyemeyohsts Storm (Cheyenne), presented a vision of the power of medicine wheels, but the roots of Cheyenne knowledge that the author employed were questioned, and as a result, the text fell into disfavor with academics and American Indians (vol. 4:580). Nonetheless, the text and its sequel, *The Song of Heyoehkah* (1981), are sold in museum or national park bookstores, a fact that points to the various communities of readers of Native American literature.

Beginning as a journalist, Gerald Vizenor (Chippewa) has been one of the most prolific American Indian writers, having published dozens of books: Ojibwa oral history, nonfictional essays, haiku poetry, autobiography, stories, and novels. Vizenor's *Darkness in Saint Louis Bearheart* (1978), his first novel, presents an apocalyptic vision of the future, a satire on society with sexually outrageous transgressions of mainstream mores. The trickster figure in the novel serves as a prototype for future tricksters in Vizenor's next several books, one of which is influenced by the time he spent in China: *Earthdivers: Tribal Narratives on Mixed Descent* (1981), *Griever: An American Monkey King in China* (1987), *The Trickster of Liberty* (1988), *The Heirs of Columbus* (1991), and *Dead Voices: Natural Agonies in the New World* (1992).

Vizenor has greatly influenced academic thinking about the field of American Indian literature through his creation of terms such as "survivance" (the opposite of dominance, and a more triumphant term than "surviving"), "terminal creeds" (writings that doom tribal people to vanish by representation in flat, stereotypical images), "manifest manners" (a term that plays off the idea of Manifest Destiny, the belief that America's growth and imperialism are divinely ordained), and "cultural striptease" (the pop-culture demand that American Indians "take it all off," to reveal the depths of their being and experience). His views, clearly radical readings of politics, writing, and language, serve as a reminder of false representation and the power of language to shape reality. Vizenor moves significantly beyond the "homing in" impulse in the literature: "Most non-historical Native American novels relate a story of the healing, initiation or reinitiation, personal growth, or gradual coming to tribal awareness of the protagonist. . . . Vizenor's prose . . . resists these standard patterns of a romantic or tragic identity search. Whenever possible he inverts the expected stories" (Blaeser 1996:202–203). Describing Vizenor as the "most ambitious and radically intellectual of American Indian writers," Louis Owens asserts that Vizenor maintains a belief in "ethics beyond aesthetics, upon the immutable values of spirit and heart articulated by Proude Cedarfair [the protagonist of *Darkness*], and though he celebrates the liberated play of postmodernism, he nonetheless goes beyond the 'contrived depthlessness' that has been defined as 'the overwhelming motif in postmodernism'" (Owens 1992:254).

Paula Gunn Allen grew up in Laguna Pueblo, like Silko, and found her voice through traditional stories. She began writing poetry in the 1970s and went on to write in many forms—as a literary critic (*The Sacred Hoop,* 1986), editor (*Studies in American Indian Literature*, 1983, and *Spider Woman's Granddaughters*, 1989), and novelist (*The Woman Who Owned the Shadows*, 1983). Feminist concerns are central to her work.

The 1980s brought many new voices to the American Indian writing scene. Louise Erdrich (Turtle Mountain, Plains Ojibwa) framed her first novel (or a collection of interconnected stories) *Love Medicine* (1984), around a large extended family and their struggles to understand one another. The novel draws the "homing in" themes together through a remarkable cast of characters who get caught up in fantastic plot elements. Unlike *Ceremony, Love Medicine*'s structure jumps around in time and through multiple voices. Set mostly on or around the reservation, the story comes together as community views of events often do—without a single authoritative voice. The roots of intergenerational grief, religious belief, and mystery hinge on piecing together many bits of history, as contemporary Indians reach for greater truth to guide them. Erdrich's next novels follow many of the same characters and stories: *The Beet Queen* (1986) and *Tracks* (1988). She has since written novels in which characters from her first novels reappear, with the exception of *The Crown of Columbus* (with Michael Dorris 1991): *The Bingo Palace* (1994), *Tales of Burning Love* (1996), *The Antelope Wife* (1998), *The Last Report on the Miracles at Little No Horse* (2001), *The Painted Drum* (2005). Erdrich has written two award-winning children's books, *The Birchbark House* (1999) and *The Range Eternal*

(2002), and a reflection on child-bearing, *The Blue Jay's Dance: A Birth Year* (1995).

Erdrich states that her early work was written in collaboration with her husband, Michael Dorris (Modoc), a novelist and academic, founder of the Native American Studies Program at Dartmouth. His own first novel *A Yellow Raft in Blue Water* (1987) broke new ground in many ways, presenting a protagonist of mixed-blood African American and American Indian heritage (from Montana, though no tribal affiliation is specified). His nonfiction book, *The Broken Cord: A Family's Ongoing Struggle with Fetal Alcohol Syndrome* (1989), opened up difficult discussions about the legacy of poverty and social ills on reservations and about Indian alcoholism; he writes honestly and agonizingly about his role as the adoptive parent to a child with fetal alcohol syndrome.

In his novel *Medicine River* (1989), Thomas King (Cherokee) provides scenes and images of how tribal communities function, through the interconnectedness of kinship, the glue of which is gossip and humor. The novel, set among Blackfoot people in Canada, was adapted for the screen by Thomas MacNaughton, and although the film takes a decidedly less political track, it depicts well how the importance of place and kinship function. The protagonist Will comes home for his mother's funeral; in the book, his life in Toronto as a photographer had not been going well anyway, but in the movie, he is a world-class photographer just returned from a civil war in Africa. The novel revolves around the fact that Canadian Indian women who married White men were no longer considered Status Indians and could not live on the reservation where their relatives live. Will's mother suffered the alienation from her homeland, but Will also suffered from not having a father; his father being a ne'er-do-well whom his mother divorced. "Homing in" is a primary theme in the novel, especially in regard to extended family and returning to geographic tribal homelands.

In *Green Grass, Running Water* (1993), King's second novel, he develops an elaborate pun through a series of peculiar events and oddball characters whose names echo American historical figures. A fabulous read, the plot does not give itself away until the end. King's third novel continues the theme of water: *Truth and Bright Water* (1999), which are the names of two border towns on the Canada-United States border. King has had a weekly radio program, called the Dead Dog Café, as well as written short stories, literary criticism, and a children's book.

Linda Hogan (Chickasaw) began as a poet but made her debut as a novelist with *Mean Spirit* (1990), which is set in Oklahoma during the 1920s, when oil made the Osage prosperous. The novel details the traumatic and tragic experiences of Osage people when greedy Whites tried everything to get their oil money away from them. Each Osage held a headright to a share in oil revenues, and Osage women who married White men were being murdered after they had had children, so the men could own the family's headrights. Since Mean Spirit, Hogan has published two novels, *Solar*

*Storms* (1995) and *Power* (1998). Both works have to do with environmental justice, Native women's power, and indigenous people. Hogan, like Beth Brant (Mohawk), author of *Mohawk Trail* (1985), *Food and Spirits* (1991), and editor of *A Gathering of Spirit* (1984), focuses upon the lives of women. Both present female characters and relationships between women in realistic and unique ways. Although both could be referred to as feminist, they do not conform to mainstream feminist goals that focus on individual change; rather, Hogan and Brant treat women's subjects and use female characters to highlight community concerns.

## Gender Issues and Portrayals

The work of many women, taken together, opened the field of American Indian studies to broader gender issues and concerns, a move that paralleled the mainstream feminist movement of the 1960s and 1970s. The work of Native writers and scholars such as Rayna Green (Cherokee), Paula Gunn Allen, Beatrice Medicine (Standing Rock Sioux), Wesley Thomas (Navajo), and Beth Brant, in particular, influenced thinking about gender in American Indian cultures and literatures. Each contributed in unique ways to explorations of the intersections between gender and race. In her seminal essay, "The Pocahontas Perplex: Images of American Indian Women in American Culture," Rayna Green (1998) discusses the central role that distorted representations of American Indian women, such as that of the Princess and the Squaw, play in the American popular mind. Non-native women such as Gretchen Bataille, Kay Sands, and Patricia Albers contributed to making American Indian women's literature accessible and available. Bataille and Sands co-authored *American Indian Woman: Telling Their Lives* (1984), an important study of American Indian autobiography that attempted to give women's voices more play, since scholars often focused on male leaders and warriors. Patricia Albers collaborated with Bea Medicine in the study of Plains Indian women's autobiography (1983).

Janet Campbell Hale's second novel *The Jailing of Cecilia Capture* depicts a woman who gets picked up from driving under the influence of alcohol, and while in jail considers the events of her life. Writers such as Debra Earling (Flathead) have taken up topics that relate to women's lives; her novel *Perma Red* (2002) develops the story of Earling's Aunt Louise, who suffered a needless death. Silko's *Garden in the Dunes* (1999), set in the Victorian era, develops a touching relationship between an older White woman Hattie and a young Indian girl from the Southwest who travel to Europe to smuggle citrus scions. Global consciousness and connections to nature make up the core of the novel. Diane Glancy (Cherokee) presents parts of the story of the Trail of Tears through a woman character's eyes, Maritole, in *Pushing the Bear* (1996).

*Living the Spirit*, an anthology of gay Indian literature, edited by Will Roscoe, appeared in 1988, and since then many gay and lesbian writers have come to the fore. The Creek writer and scholar, Craig Womack, wrote *Drowning in Fire* (2001), which focuses on a gay Indian's story. The film *The Business of Fancydancing* (2002), written by Sherman Alexie (Spokane) and only loosely associated with his book of poems by the same title (1991), follows its central character Seymour home to the reservation for a friend's funeral; as a poet, as a gay man, and as a successful person in the White world, Seymour finds he no longer fits in. Alexie presents a homosexual encounter in his novel *The Toughest Indian in the World* (2000), between a young Spokane Indian professional and a Lummi hitchhiker he picks up. Although the Spokane is quick to tell the Lummi he is not gay, the poetic imagery at the end suggests he has returned to first beginnings, "traveled upriver toward the place where I was born and will someday die" (Alexie 2000:34).

Gender issues in American Indian literature and studies examine new understandings of traditional male roles. *Fools Crow* (1986) by James Welch is an example of a plot focused on the roles on Indian men in conflict with White men, where the women play secondary roles. Set in Montana among Blackfeet people in the 1860s, the novel follows the growth and development of two young men—one who turns out to be a leader and one who goes wrong and becomes a renegade who puts his people in jeopardy. The culmination of the conflict pulls the visionary thread together with the historical, as the protagonist Fools Crow ponders the end of his people's way of life after the Army carried out the Baker's Massacre on the Marias River in January 1870.

Louis Owens (Choctaw/Cherokee/Irish), well-known as a scholar for his work on John Steinbeck, began publishing fiction with *Wolfsong* (1991), a story with a "homing in" plot involving environmental justice as well. In his other novels, he moves more intricately into character and plot development: *The Sharpest Sight* (1992), *The Bone Game* (1994), *Nightland* (1996), and *Dark River* (1999). His book, *Mixedblood Messages: Literature, Film, Family, Place* (2001), maps an autoethnographic journey through his family stories, readings, reviews of films, and other means of expression in the mixed-genre mode.

James Welch's *Indian Lawyer* (1990) in some ways represents a departure from the "homing in" motif but, in other ways, refines it. The novel's Blackfeet protagonist, Sylvester Yellowcalf, is a young lawyer with potential to become a United States senator, but he gets involved in an intrigue with the wife of an inmate while he himself sits on the parole board. In the end, he decides to abandon his hopes of an American mainstream political career and focus on Indian land claims issues. He returns to Indian Country as a successful professional Indian, an uncommon character in American Indian fiction. In Welch's last novel, *The Heartsong of Charging Elk* (2000), a young Sioux warrior had been performing with Buffalo Bill's Wild West Show but became ill on the overseas tour and was stranded in France. Through a twist of fate, he murders a man and goes to prison. By the time he gets out, he has almost lost his desire to go home and instead settles down with his French wife who is expecting a child. Out of cultural time and place, away from his tribal nation, Charging Elk reconciles himself as best he can in the very different world that has become his lot. Identity becomes the daily choices of being.

Sherman Alexie regarded James Welch as a mentor and friend, and Alexie's work reflects that influence, except that Alexie's ribald humor and penchant for the outrageous come more with his generation than with those beginning writers of the Native American Renaissance. Alexie's collection of poems *The Business of Fancydancing* (1991) prompted a publisher to pursue him for other possible publications. In a very short period of time, Alexie wrote an entire series of collections of short stories and poems, novels, and films, including *The Lone Ranger and Tonto Fistfight in Heaven* (1993). Overall the angry and sorrowful perspectives of the stories in the collection bespeak loss of homeland and familial stability, corruption at all turns, and hope being hard to find. The deeply troubled Victor, Junior, and a collection of friends move in and out of the stories, along with Victor's family. The movie *Smoke Signals* (1998), with the screenplay written by Alexie, is based primarily on the story in *Lone Ranger* entitled "This is What it Means to Say Phoenix, Arizona."

## Expanding Genres, Diversified Themes

The place-centered theme in American Indian literature persists, whether it involves being at home in a place, looking for the way back, or mourning the possibility of return, perhaps because without communities, the future of the tribes does not seem possible. "Home" becomes a metaphor for belonging among a larger group of people, a place one can harken back to for comfort, identity, and support.

Writing since the Native Renaissance often involves weaving histories and imagined ancestral lives with contemporary people. This is the past left out of history books and American literature written by James Fenimore Cooper, author of the Leatherstocking Tales series, and Henry Wadsworth Longfellow, the poet who absorbed the legendary Iroquois Hiawatha into American identity. James Welch's third novel, *Fools Crow* (1986), and Simon Ortiz's *From Sand Creek* (1981), a collection of poems written while Ortiz was being treated in a Veterans Administration hospital in Colorado, seek historical reckoning by providing more full histories of atrocities. Both involve massacres and reconciling such wrongs, first by acknowledging the traumatic events in Indian history.

David Treuer (Leech Lake, Plains Ojibwa) breaks with the "homing in" theme, in an effort to free up Indian literature to what he sees as more accurate portrayal, as more focused on the works as literature rather than ethnography. His novels include: *Little* (1995), *The Hiawatha* (1999), and *The Translation of Dr. Apelles* (2006).

In some instances, enough writers from the same tribal heritage have arisen to constitute study with a more focused look at their regional histories. Craig Womack's book *Red on Red* (1999) is a study of Creek literary traditions. The award-winning novel *Shell Shaker* (2001) by Leanne Howe (Choctaw) and the novels and stories by D.L. Birchfield (Choctaw)—*Oklahoma Basic Intelligence Test* (1998), *Field of Honor* (2004), and *Black Silk Handkerchief* (2006)—suggest new directions in American Indian literature, especially as writers move into mystery, detective, fantasy, and science fiction, in addition to whatever imaginative directions their paths take them. Indigenous rootedness, homing in, life histories, identity conflicts and searching, and mixed-genre writing remain part of American Indian literature.

# Tribal Colleges and Universities

WAYNE J. STEIN

The founders of the native-controlled colleges and universities recognized that they could not only prepare Native students to be proficient in their own cultures but must also prepare them to be proficient in the non-Indian world. They had to prepare their students to live productively in two very different worlds. It had to be that way if their peoples were to survive with their Indian identity and to protect what they had retained of their homelands and sovereign rights into the twenty-first century (Stein, Shanley, and Sanchez 2003:2–3).

In both the United States and Canada these founders developed a philosophy in the late 1960s and early 1970s that would support a dual mission, protecting and enhancing their own cultures and at the same time embracing many of the tools of standard postsecondary education. Native-controlled colleges continue their effort of exploration, initiative, and development that began in the summer of 1968 with the founding of Navajo Community College in Tsaile, Arizona, and in 1971 with the establishment of Blue Quills Education Center in Saint Paul, Alberta. These schools can best be described as small, tenacious institutions of higher education, which serve the smallest and poorest minority group in the United States and Canada under challenging circumstances. Native-controlled colleges and universities are chronically underfunded, with overworked administrators, faculties, and staffs; they are viewed by the rest of American and Canadian higher education with some wonder at their ability not only to survive but also to survive with panache (Stein 1999:259).

World War II had a major impact upon Native American peoples by exposing thousands of young men, and many young women, to a world away from their home communities. These Native Americans, upon returning home after the war, had much higher expectations from life, were less inclined to endure overt or covert racism, wanted greater freedom from the authoritarian government interference in their daily lives, and wanted educational opportunities for themselves and their children.

Education was deemed as one of the most important areas targeted by Native people returning home. In the United States it started slowly with a number of veterans taking advantage of the Veterans Readjustment Act (GI Bill of Rights) to pursue higher and vocational education. During the 1950s the number of Indian students enrolled in college jumped dramatically, from only 200 enrolled in 1950 to 3,500 by the fall of 1957 (The Editor 1958–1959:1). At the same time young Indian leaders were demanding day schools for their children (about half of American Indian children were still attending federal and mission boarding schools at this time) as were available in the rest of the United States. In the 1960s and 1970s Congress developed the opportunities through new laws that allowed Indians to gain a measure of self-determination over their daily lives. Since the beginning of the twentieth century some Americans such as August Breuninger believed that American Indians should control their own educational institutions and he went on to propose in 1911 to the Bureau of Indian Affairs that they have their own university. In the mid-1950s Tribal Chairman Robert Burnette of the Rosebud Sioux (Sicangu Teton) proposed total tribal control of education on the Rosebud Sioux Reservation and the development of a college. In the early 1960s Dr. Jack Forbes (Powhatan/Delaware) pulled together a small group of American Indian intellectuals and forwarded to the federal government a plan to develop and found an American Indian university (Stein 2003:30). While none of these efforts came to fruition, each illustrates the ongoing and continuous desire of American Indian people to control their education.

While the movement toward Indian self-determination was taking place across the United States during the 1960s, it was on the Navajo Reservation that events were moving most quickly. Raymond Nakai had promised during his election campaign for Navajo tribal chairman to work toward Navajo control of education. When elected in the early 1960s, he gave the go-ahead to several Navajo leaders who set out to fulfill those promises. The first real success came at Rough Rock, Arizona, when Allen Yazzie, Guy Gorman, Robert and Ruth Roessel, and Dr. Ned Hatathli formed Dine, Inc., and incorporated and created Rough Rock Demonstration School. They had strong support in this effort from the Tribal Council and two allies, Graham Holms, Bureau of Indian Affairs Navajo Area Director, and Buck Benham, Assistant Area Director for Education.

Dr. Robert Roessel, a non-Navajo with strong ties to the Navajo people through his Navajo wife, Ruth, went to the Navajo Reservation to direct Rough Rock Demonstration School. The two major goals of the school were to provide a quality education to the children and to prove that Navajos could run their own schools. During the mid-1960s, this effort was a success, and the group turned the school over to the local community for governance in 1967 (vol. 10:665–667). Concurrently, the same group of individuals began talking of a community college for the Navajo (Gorman 1986).

## The Community College Model

The junior college, or community college, developed at the beginning of the twentieth century. American higher education leaders advanced the idea of separating the lower and upper divisions of studies into separate institutions. This would be the model for the development of tribal colleges.

As the demand for higher education led to the founding of junior colleges, so too did it lead to the expanding role those colleges began assuming in the 1920s and 1930s. A new functional development was taking place in the colleges. They were "aiming to prepare students by means of a two-year course for positions of usefulness to society, particularly in the so-called semi-professions" (Eells 1931:5).

The growth of two-year junior colleges was steady through the 1940s and 1950s with the major changes coming in their curriculum as they continued to add occupational education programs to their offerings and emphasized the importance of guidance and counseling as a function.

The 1960s era was one of expansion in higher education with community colleges playing a major role. Toward the end of the decade a new community college opened its doors each week somewhere in the United States. It is within this historical tradition that tribally controlled community colleges made their appearance on the United States higher education scene (Ramirez 1987).

Though there is a visible separation between non-Indian community colleges and tribally controlled colleges, they function much more alike than differently. Both strive to serve their communities as comprehensive institutions providing programs that respond to community and students' needs. Their differences lie in funding sources, jurisdiction, and cultural factors, not educational goals.

Where the tribal colleges have flourished, they have found state governments either benign or supportive. Arizona, California, Washington, Alaska, Montana, North Dakota, Wisconsin, Nebraska, and South Dakota all have stated policies that allow cooperation between their institutions and the tribal colleges, but take no fiscal or policy responsibility. They have left it to the tribes and federal government to assume these important duties. In the twenty-first century, the tribal colleges and their sister non-Indian institutions remain separate in the political, educational, and fiscal arenas, but not in spirit. A growth of mutual trust and appreciation does exist between the two systems.

## The United States

The individuals who formed Diné, Inc., developed a plan for a Navajo-controlled community college and gained the support of the Navajo Nation during the mid-1960s, which led to the Navajo Nation founding and chartering Navajo Community College in July 1968. Though underfunded and forging a completely new path in higher education, Navajo Community College (now called Diné College) survived and succeeded (vol. 10:668–670), encouraging more than 30 other tribes to charter their own institutions starting in the 1970s.

Tribal colleges have made significant progress and gained much sophistication as institutions of higher education since 1968 in their effort to improve the educational opportunities of American Indian people. This was illustrated at a February 1996 gathering of higher education administrators convened in Albuquerque by the W.K. Kellogg Foundation's Native American Higher Education Initiative Project, where the consensus of the attendees was that everyone in higher education had much to learn from these newest members of the higher education community. The administrators of higher education present agreed that the tribal colleges' ability to serve students and communities under very difficult circumstances holds many lessons for other higher education institutions. This change in attitude is significant when it is remembered that many such administrators believed that the tribal college movement was doomed to fail because of the harsh economic status of the American Indian reservations of the early 1970s.

That tribal colleges have contributed to mitigating some of the harsh economic realities of their home reservations clearly demonstrates the positive impact a college can have on an American Indian reservation. Tribal colleges, tribal governments, tribal institutions such as tribal schools and tribal businesses, and local privately owned reservation-based businesses have done much work together to improve the economies of their reservations. Most tribal colleges have as a part of their mission a statement that says in some form that they will do what they can to promote the economic well being of their community. To carry out this aspect of their mission statement tribal colleges have done economic assessment studies to determine the needs of the community, designed and implemented specific training programs to meet the job skill requirements of employers of the community, and developed specific programs and or institutes to explore and develop certain aspects of the community's resources, whether natural or human.

Because the economic reality on many Indian reservations is persistent poverty, tribal colleges have become important to the economic revitalization of their reservations. A study of American Indian reservations having a college in 1980–1990, before any reservation in the study had a successful gaming operation, showed that women's income saw an increase of 49 percent over the 10 years. A similar gain in income was noted among Indian males. Overall the poverty rate for families went down on reservations with a tribal college. In contrast, families living on a reservation without a college were 20 percent worse off than their neighbors living on reservations with tribal colleges (D.D. Harris 1997:19–25).

In 2007 there were 36 tribal colleges in the United States (table 1) and 12 in Canada (table 2). These colleges served numerous American Indian tribes, but all adhered to several basic principles in their mission statements. Each has stated that the need to preserve, enhance, and promote the language and culture of its tribe is central to its existence. The colleges serve their communities as resources to do research on economic development, human resource development, and community organization. Each provides quality academic programs for students seeking two-year degrees for transfer to senior institutions. Wherever possible, each college provides vocational and technical programs that help

assure that students can find decent jobs in their communities upon completion of their studies (P. Boyer 1989).

The continuous development efforts of the college presidents, boards of trustees, and the American Indian Higher Education Consortium (AIHEC), the national organization of tribal colleges, has led to many innovative and productive outcomes. One, the passage of the Equity in Education Land Grant Status Act of 1994, provides land grant status to the tribal colleges. This important piece of legislation helps to preserve and expand a solid agriculture, programmatic, and financial base for all tribal colleges (AIHEC 1995b). Second, executive orders signed by Presidents William Clinton and George W. Bush are an important reminder that the colleges are constituents of the entire federal government and are part of a federal mandate to American Indian education. President Clinton signed Executive Order No. 13021 on October 19, 1996, which promoted tribal college access to all federal programs and instructed those same agencies to explore ways in which they might assist tribal colleges carry forward their mandate to serve American Indian communities (R.L. Robbins 2002:88). On July 3, 2002, President Bush signed an executive order creating two advocacy tools for tribal colleges, which are the President's Board of Advisers on Tribal Colleges and Universities and the White House Initiative on Tribal Colleges and Universities (R. Morgan 2002).

### American Indian Higher Education Consortium (AIHEC)

One of the most important aspects of the tribal college movement is the founding and development of the American Indian Higher Education Consortium. It is a contemporary Native American story that can be captured and personalized because many of the key characters in the story were able to tell their own part in its early history.

In 1972, the American Indian Higher Education Consortium was born of political necessity. Leaders of the tribally controlled community college movement recognized that

**Table 1. Tribal Colleges and Universities in the United States, 2007**

Bay Mills Community College, Brimley, Mich.
Blackfeet Community College, Browning, Mont.
Candeska Cikana Community College, Ft. Totten, N. Dak.
Chief Dull Knife College, Lame Deer, Mont.
College of Menominee Nation, Keshena, Wis.
Comanche Nation College, Lawton, Okla.
Crownpoint Institute of Technology, Crownpoint, N. Mex.
D-Q University, Davis, Calif.
Diné College, Tsaile, Ariz.
Fond du Lac Tribal and Community College, Cloquet, Minn.
Ft. Belknap College, Harlem, Mont.
Ft. Berthold Community College, New Town, N. Dak.
Ft. Peck Community College, Poplar, Mont.
Haskell Indian Nations University, Lawrence, Kan.
Institute of American Indian Arts, Sante Fe, N. Mex.
Keweenaw Bay Ojibwa Community College, Baraga, Mich.
Lac Courte Oreilles Ojibwa Community College, Hayward, Wis.
Leech Lake Tribal College, Cass Lake, Minn.
Little Big Horn College, Crow Agency, Mont.
Little Priest Tribal College, Winnebago, Nebr.
Nebraska Indian Community College, Macy, Nebr.
Northwest Indian College, Bellingham, Wash.
Oglala Lakota College, Kyle, S. Dak.
Saginaw Chippewa Tribal College, Mount Pleasant, Mich.
Salish Kootenai College, Pablo, Mont.
Sinte Gleska University, Mission, S. Dak.
Sisseton Wahpeton College, Sisseton, S. Dak.
Si Tanka University, Eagle Butte, S. Dak.
Sitting Bull College, Ft. Yates, N. Dak.
Southwestern Indian Polytechnic Institute, Albuquerque, N. Mex.
Stone Child College, Box Elder, Mont.
Tohono O'odham Community College, Sells, Ariz.
Turtle Mountain Community College, Belcourt, N. Dak.
United Tribes Technical College, Bismarck, N. Dak.
White Earth Tribal and Community College, Mahnomen, Minn.
Wind River Tribal College, Ethete, Wyo.

**Table 2. Tribal Colleges in Canada**

Blue Quills First Nations College, St. Paul, Alta.
Bullhead Adult Education Centre, Tsuu T'ina, Calgary, Alta.
En'owkin Centre, Penticton, B.C.
First Nations University of Canada, Regina, Saskatoon, and Prince Albert, Sask.
Kayas College, Fox Lake, Alta.
Old Sun Community College, Siksika, Alta.
Piikani Postsecondary Education Centre, Brocket, Alta.
Maskwachees Cultural College, Hobbema, Alta.
Nakoda Nation Education, Morley, Alta.
Red Crow Community College, Cardston, Alta.
Yellowhead Tribal College, Edmonton, Alta.
Yellow Quill College, Winnipeg, Man.

unity among the small number of tribal colleges was imperative in promoting them as a viable option for Indian people in higher education. Gerald One Feather of the Oglala Sioux Community College, Kyle, South Dakota; David Reisling, Jr., of D-Q University, Davis, California; Pat Locke of the Western Interstate Commission for Higher Education, and Helen Schierbeck of the United States Office of Education organized a meeting and convened all those interested in such a national organization (Reisling 1986). Representatives of all existing Indian postsecondary institutions met in Washington, D.C., to discuss the founding of a national organization. Institutions represented at the meeting were: Hehaka Sapa College, D-Q University; Navajo Community College, Many Farms, Arizona; Oglala Sioux Community College; Sinte Gleska College, Rosebud, South Dakota; Standing Rock Community College, Fort Yates, North Dakota; Turtle Mountain Community College, Belcourt, North Dakota; and three Bureau of Indian Affairs institutions: Haskell Junior College, Lawrence, Kansas; Institute of American Indian Arts, Santa Fe, New Mexico; and Southwestern Indian Polytechnic Institute, Albuquerque, New Mexico. The decision was reached that the colleges could agree on several principles by which to form a national organization (Reisling 1986; One Feather 1974). The colleges found they had many traits in common that bonded them: they were located on or near Indian reservations, which were isolated geographically and culturally; they were governed by boards with a majority of Indian administrators and faculty; their student bodies were small, with enrollment ranging from 75 to 800; their financing was meager and unpredictable; and their students and communities were demonstrably from the lowest income areas in the United States (One Feather 1974:72).

The colleges called their organization the American Indian Higher Education Consortium. With the encouragement of Helen Schierbeck, the newly founded organization pursued funds to finance its operation from Title III of the 1965 Strengthening and Developing Higher Education amendment to the Higher Education Act. The decision to pursue federal funds from the federal Department of Education set into motion the rules that excluded federally controlled institutions from being a part of AIHEC. Shortly after the meeting it was discovered that one federal program could not benefit financially from another. The finding necessitated the excluding of Haskell Junior College, Southwestern Indian Polytechnic Institute, and the Institute of American Indian Arts from the initial founding of the fledgling national Indian education organization because each was a federally funded postsecondary Indian institution. Each remained associated with AIHEC until it no longer had to rely on Title III funds for its survival and became a full member of AIHEC.

The six founders of AIHEC (D-Q University, Standing Rock Community College, Navajo Community College, Turtle Mountain Community College, Sinte Gleska College,

and Oglala Sioux Community College) held their second meeting in Phoenix, Arizona, where the written drafts from each participant were brought together for submission of a proposal to the Department of Education. Gerald One Feather was chosen AIHEC's first president. Navajo Community College staff person, Gerald Brown, a member of the Montana Flathead Tribe, was selected as acting executive director (Gipp 1986; C. Davis 1987; Wilke and Gailfus 1987).

The AIHEC Board consciously chose to honor traditional Indian ways as Sinte Gleska College's Board Chairman, Stanley Red Bird (Teton), offered prayers on AIHEC's behalf. AIHEC's founders realized the difficulty of the task they were assuming with the creation of tribal colleges on the depressed Indian reservations of the West. They understood that a major spiritual uplift would be needed to see them through the many hard times ahead (Wilke and Gailfus 1987).

Navajo Community College was chosen to be the sponsoring institution of the Title III proposal. This arrangement established an often abrasive but successful relationship between the first colleges and AIHEC. Navajo Community College representatives understood their part in setting a precedent for tribal colleges and serving as a role model for other tribes to follow. They also recognized that, as the movement spread throughout Indian country, competition would grow for limited fiscal resources (Gorman 1986; Gipp 1987).

In June 1973, AIHEC was formally organized when it received its Incorporation Certification from the State of Colorado and established corporate headquarters in Denver as a nonprofit organization. It had received notice of federal Education Act funding, and Steve Little, attorney, and Gerald Brown, developed a set of articles and by-laws for the Board's approval (AIHEC 1973). The Board chose as its guiding priorities: the establishment of an American Indian Higher Education accreditation agency, the establishment of a financial and institutional resource office, the establishment of a human resource development program, the establishment of an American Indian education data bank, and the establishment of an American Indian curriculum development program (One Feather 1974:73).

On September 14–15, 1973, the Board met in Davis, California, as guests of D-Q University to make the important selections of its first full-time staff. David M. Gipp, a Standing Rock Lakota, was selected as first executive director of AIHEC (AIHEC 1973). Gipp and the core staff selected at the meeting received the assignment of implementing the policies of the Board, organizing activities to carry forward the priorities established by the Board, and establishing AIHEC as a credible national organization. All these tasks were ongoing while they sought out and developed the necessary funding resources to carry forward these vital organizational tasks.

Many of the newer members of AIHEC had little or no funding, administrative infrastructure, development experience, or concept of what was needed to survive as a community college. The tribal colleges benefited from help in curriculum development, human resource development, administration, board training, fund raising, and regional accreditation preparation that the AIHEC staff provided. The role played by the staff became more important as the organization expanded from six members to 16 by 1978. Jack Barden of Standing Rock (now Sitting Bull College), stated that without AIHEC, several of the colleges he worked with, as a consultant, would have failed (Barden 1987). Carty Monette of Turtle Mountain Community College stated that AIHEC was the glue that held the tribal college movement together from 1973 to 1978 (Monette 1986). AIHEC gained a reputation among the colleges as a first-class technical assistance agency during its first five years of existence, but it was in Washington, D.C., that it made its national reputation (Stein 1992).

In 1973, AIHEC's Board of Directors identified the single most difficult problem facing the tribal colleges as the chronic shortage of financial resources. The colleges continually pursued funding from every source coinciding with their mission, but were often denied funding from many seemingly logical sources of support for reasons beyond their control, such as not yet being candidates for accreditation or fully accredited institutions of higher education. The constant shortage of funding retarded the natural growth and development tribal colleges should have experienced in the early 1970s. This led the Board to choose as its number one task the securing of a solid, stable funding source for its membership. This decision set the course that would dominate AIHEC for the next decade, often overriding the other priorities set by the Board (AIHEC 1977; Bordeaux 1987).

Executive Director Dave Gipp and AIHEC's second Board President, Lionel Bordeaux of Sinte Gleska College, began a series of trips to Washington, D.C., in 1974 for the purpose of securing support from the federal government. They made it a point to visit each of the congressmen from the tribal colleges' districts. They received help and assistance from many, but it was Helen Schierbeck of the federal Office of Education who extended herself on AIHEC's behalf. She helped draft the first legislation for tribally controlled colleges, patterned somewhat after Navajo Community College's legislation (Gipp 1986).

The initial strategy was to amend the Indian Self-Determination and Education Assistance Act, as it was being written in 1975. President Bordeaux and David Gipp offered testimony on behalf of AIHEC that requested the amendment to authorize the Secretary of the Interior to grant planning, development, and operational funds for member colleges of the consortium. The testimony explained to Congress the unique qualities of the tribal colleges and articulated their needs in meeting the demands placed upon them to provide higher education on the reservations. However, the kinds of institutional data needed to realistically portray the operational, facilities, and maintenance cost estimates of the tribal colleges had not yet been fully developed by AIHEC or its members (AIHEC 1976).

The effort did partially succeed, by getting language added to the bill that instructed the Secretary of the Interior to prepare a specific program together with detailed legislation recommendations, to assist the development and administration of Indian controlled community colleges. Perry Horse, AIHEC Director of Research and Data, developed a system of data collection and instigated a number of research projects that answered the data needs of AIHEC when called upon to testify before Congress and various national councils. Furthermore, the ability of AIHEC to provide accurate data for testimony on behalf of American Indian education became well known in Washington, D.C., and from 1975 to 1978 they were called upon to testify on many Indian education issues (AIHEC 1976).

While AIHEC and the tribal colleges developed alliances in Congress and with other national Indian organizations, the Black College Consortium, church leaders, the American Associaiton of Community and Junior Colleges, and several national philanthropic foundations as it sought legislation, the Bureau of Indian Affairs emerged as an antagonist (Gipp 1986). When asked by Sen. James Abourezk, Chairman of the Senate Subcommittee on Indian Affairs, who had written and submitted the Indian Postsecondary Educational Assistance Act of 1975, to comment on the bill, they replied negatively. Commissioner of Indian Affairs Morris Thompson recommended that it not be enacted. He stated the existing programs in the Department of Health, Education, and Welfare and the Bureau of Indian Affairs would better serve the educational needs of Indians. He maintained the authorization to fund the tribal colleges was already in place under the Snyder Act of 1921 (25 U.S.C. 13), which generally authorized funds "for the benefit, care, and assistance of the Indians throughout the United States" (M. Thompson 1976). This pattern of antagonism continued for the next several years, leading to the irony of the Bureau's representative testifying against the Tribally Controlled Community College Act of 1978.

The tribal colleges found a staunch supporter in Senator Abourezk of South Dakota, who from 1975 to 1978 introduced several pieces of legislation to support the tribal colleges. He had grown up on the Rosebud Sioux Reservation and had firsthand knowledge of the hardships Indian people faced in their daily lives and had to overcome if they were to pursue a higher education (Gipp 1986; Bordeaux 1987). He rallied Senate support and kept the issue of support of the tribal colleges before the Senate each session. This active support combined with the work of AIHEC eventually won the Senate's support for tribal college legislation.

In 1977, the AIHEC Board selected Leroy Clifford (Oglala Lakota) to succeed David Gipp, and James Shanley (Assiniboine) to be president of the AIHEC Board for 1978. These two joined staff members Horse and Richard Nichols in seeking tribal college legislation. A key to getting a piece of legislation all AIHEC members could agree upon, including Navajo Community College, were the negotiations among congressional staff, representatives of colleges other than Navajo Community, and officials of Navajo Community College. The Navajo officials had a major stake in any new legislation because it would immediately affect them financially. On October 17, 1978, President Jimmy Carter signed into law the Tribally Controlled Community College Assistance Act (Public Law 95-471). Almost exactly five years after the new organization calling itself AIHEC hired a staff and instructed them to work on legislation to bring fiscal stability to tribally controlled colleges, it was accomplished.

The members of the AIHEC Board of Directors brought their individual professionalism to the Board, which gained it respect as a national Indian board. Without AIHEC, it is possible there would be no legislation, many fewer tribal colleges, and poorer prospects of continued success for even the stronger tribal colleges. AIHEC continued to fulfill multiple roles as the national representative of the tribal colleges with its first priority as advocate in Washington on behalf of the tribal colleges, charged with securing and maintaining the principal funding source of the colleges. The tribal colleges continue to interact with the federal government much as state-supported institutions do with their state governments. The Tribally Controlled Community College Act of 1978 has had a stabilizing influence on the tribal college movement, although the tribal colleges have never been funded through the congressional appropriation process at the level ratified by the Act. AIHEC is an organization that met the challenges set before it, not always fully successfully, but it won the battles necessary to secure the future of the tribal colleges.

## Students

Tribal colleges continue to focus on their students and the special abilities and needs these students bring to their colleges. Diné College and all subsequent tribal colleges recognized that mainline institutions of higher education were not adequately serving American Indian students, especially those from geographically isolated reservations. The reasons were many: the social isolation of Indian students on off-reservation campuses, culture shock, and poverty were some of the main contributors to the near 90 percent attrition rate experienced by Indian students in mainstream colleges and universities for much of the twentieth century.

Tribal college students are generally older; often female heads of households; may speak English as a second language; are poor; and, prior to their tribal college experience, have found formal educational settings to be a hostile environment for them. In 2004, the enrollment of all undergraduates was 11,510 women and 5,899 men (AIHEC count).

College personnel work closely with each student to help that student design a program that will fit his or her individual needs and abilities. This concern for the individual student has played an important role in the high retention rates of first-generation American Indian students within the tribal colleges. Retention rates for the tribal colleges can be measured in two ways. The conventional method counts as a dropout any student who leaves college before completion of a degree program, in which case tribal colleges have a retention rate of approximately 45 percent. The method begun by the tribal colleges labels as "stop-outs" those who leave and then return within a quarter to continue their studies. By measuring in this fashion, the colleges' retention rate is 75–80 percent. Students who stop-out generally do so because of financial difficulties or because they have been put on academic probation (A. Three Irons, personal communication 1991).

In a study conducted in 1990, researchers from the AIHEC gathered data from six colleges with large enough enrollments and long enough track records to accurately assess the effectiveness of tribal colleges in educating their students. The colleges were Oglala Lakota College (vol. 4:299); Sinte Gleska University; Standing Rock College, Fort Yates, North Dakota; Turtle Mountain Community College; Salish Kootenai College, Pablo, Montana (vol. 12:236); and Blackfeet Community College, Browning, Montana. The data collected for the period 1983–1989 revealed that the six colleges graduated 1,575 students with 210 earning one-year vocational certificates, 1,198 earning associate degrees, 158 earning bachelor's degrees, and 9 earning master's degrees (Houser 1991). In all AIHEC schools, associate degrees awarded in 1998 were 1,076; in 1999, 831; in 2000, 984, in 2001, 918; and in 2002, 1,146. Bachelor's degrees earned in 1998 were 48, in 1999, 62; in 2000, 98; in 2001, 112, and in 2002, 159 (IPEDS peer analysis system in Voorhees 2003:9).

An AIHEC survey taken in 1982 found that Indian students who completed a course of study at a tribal college went on to complete a four-year degree program at a senior institution with a 75 percent greater success rate than Indian students who bypassed tribal colleges and went directly to four-year institutions. Another interesting set of data from the survey found that about 85 percent of tribal college graduates who stayed on the reservation were employed; contrast this with unemployment rates on American Indian reservations that are usually 45 to 80 percent (Stein 1992).

## Governing Boards and Personnel

Tribal colleges are a reflection of their communities at the board of trustees level. Boards of trustees that are nearly 100 percent local American Indian community members control all tribal colleges. Boards of trustees for tribal colleges play the important role of buffers between tribal politics and the colleges. They also often act as mediators among policy makers and as personnel selection committees, and they are the local watchdogs of and for the colleges. These important responsibilities make the boards of trustees unique in Indian country because of the autonomous nature of their authority as granted by the tribal charters founding the tribal colleges. Most American Indian decision-making entities (including tribal governing councils) must seek the approval of the Secretary of the Interior for their important decisions, but the boards of trustees of tribal colleges. However, board members do keep in mind how their decisions will impact their communities and their long-term relations with their chartering tribal governments.

Administrators and faculty of tribal colleges are a mixture of American Indians and non-Indians; most administrators are American Indian, but many faculty members are non-Indian. Whatever the ethnicity of an administrator or faculty member, the strongest characteristic of both groups is dedication to their students and to the missions of their colleges. The accreditation associations evaluating the tribal colleges in almost every report made since the 1970s have written about the importance of the dedication of the administrators and faculty.

Faculty problems experienced by tribal colleges generally fall into three main areas. First is the difficulty in finding and keeping science and mathematics instructors. Second is the high turnover among faculty who find life on Indian reservations too isolated and culturally different. Third and toughest to solve is the fact that, as the colleges mature and their student populations grow, salaries generally remain low among the faculty. The financing issue facing the tribal colleges is a serious one, but nowhere is it more serious than in recruiting, hiring, and keeping good faculty, administrators, and support staff (Stein 1999: 262–265).

## Curricula

Areas of special concern to tribal colleges are those of curricula and programs that have been developed in response to tribal community needs. A typical academic and teaching curriculum offered at a tribal college would be for two-year associate of applied science degrees, associate of arts degrees, associate of science degrees, and one-year certification programs.

Associate of applied science degrees combine practical course work and general education designed to prepare students for immediate entry into the world of work. Typical disciplines for associate of applied science degrees would be human services, computer science and information systems (fig. 1), tribal language arts, office technology, tribal administrative practices, and dental assisting technology.

Associate of arts degrees are academic programs designed to prepare students to transfer to a four-year higher education institution. Typical areas of study include general and liberal arts studies, business administration, tribal or Native American studies, psychology, and the social sciences.

Associate of science degrees are also designed to prepare students wishing to transfer to four-year colleges or universities. Typical courses of study are business administration, health sciences, environmental science, elementary education, information technology, nursing, and pre-engineering.

One-year certificate programs are designed by the tribal colleges to respond to local community employment opportunities. Students are prepared within a sharply focused vocational program with much hands-on practical experience. General office skills, health sciences, hospitality, automotive trade skills, medical office clerk, digital arts and design, and manufacturing assembly are examples of certificate programs (Bay Mills Community College 1994–1996; Salish Kootenai College 2006).

Four tribal colleges, Sinte Gleska University, Oglala Lakota College, Haskell Indian Nations University, and Salish Kootenai College, have instituted four-year baccalaureate programs in human resources, social sciences, business and entrepreneurship, nursing, information technology, environmental science, tribal management, and education. Sinte Gleska University led the way for tribal colleges beyond the baccalaureate by developing and receiving accreditation for the first master's degree program in education at a tribal college. By 1998 Oglala Lakota also offered a master's (vol. 13:827). This achievement marks a major stride in curriculum development. This growth is illustrated by the fact that in 1972, Sinte Gleska University, then Sinte Gleska College, offered 22 undergraduate and one-year certificate courses in disciplines from psychology to math with 13 part-time administrators and faculty making up the college staff (Stein 1992).

Sinte Gleska University, Oglala Lakota College, Salish Kootenai College, and Haskell have demonstrated that advanced degrees are possible. Many tribal colleges are researching advanced curriculum options for their students and are preparing to become four-year institutions (Stein 1999:266). This latest focus of tribal colleges, expanding to become four-year colleges, is a strong indication of how optimistic these institutions are about their future growth and development.

The colleges have made receiving full accreditation for every tribal college from their respective sanctioning agencies an AIHEC goal. Each college has had to travel the accreditation path alone, but morale and expertise have been liberally shared among AIHEC members. This accreditation effort has so far resulted in 34 of the 36 American colleges gaining full accreditation as institutions of higher education. The two remaining colleges are new colleges in the process of gaining candidacy status and full accreditation.

Turtle Mt. Community College, Belcourt, N. Dak.

Fig. 1. Students in a computer science class at Turtle Mountain Community College, Belcourt, N. Dak., in 2005.

## Funding and Development

The Tribal College Act of 2000 authorized $6,000 per American Indian full-time equivalent student. The actual amount appropriated in the 2005 federal budget was $4,447 per full-time student for funding. To keep the funding of tribal colleges in perspective, these figures need to be compared to the national average for nonresident community colleges. These received approximately $7,000 per student from states and local non-Indian communities during the 1990s according to the National Association of Colleges and Business Officers (Tiger 1995).

The tribal colleges do seek funding vigorously from a number of other sources such as federal agencies (other than the Bureau of Indian Affairs and the Tribally Controlled College Act), philanthropic organizations such as the W.K. Kellogg Foundation and the Bush Foundation, corporate foundations such as U.S. West, and their own foundation,

the Tribal College Fund. These additional funds are targeted to specific high priority tasks by the individual tribal colleges as they are identified and funds are secured. Upon occasion AIHEC will also seek grants from these sources to carry out membership projects needed by all the tribal colleges or by the central office of AIHEC itself to improve its infrastructure. The W.K. Kellogg Foundation provided 25 million dollars that focused on: strengthening the faculties and internal programs of tribal colleges; cultural, language, and sovereignty issues of tribal communities; and improving the relationships between tribal colleges and other institutions of higher education (Stein 1999:263).

An important effort by the tribal colleges to build a diversified funding base began in 1989 with the founding of the American Indian College Fund, which has an independent board of directors yet is answerable to AIHEC as its chartering agent. It has raised significant amounts of money and has allowed the College Fund to award each tribal college, from the interest earned on its endowment, a sum for scholarships. A major capital fundraising effort has committed building funds to be distributed to the tribal colleges for much-needed facilities (Robbins 2002:87). Fitting these additional funding sources into the tribal colleges' fiscal designs allows the colleges to begin examining new programs, new curricula, new forums, new buildings, and additional and advanced degrees for their students and communities.

Another achievement of the tribal colleges and AIHEC is the development and publishing of the *The Tribal College Journal*. The *Journal* has led the way in informing the world about the tribal college movement, played a vital role in spreading the news among the colleges of innovative programs they can share, and begun an important research agenda on behalf of the colleges (R.L. Robbins 2002:84).

Tribal colleges have reached out to non-Indian institutions of higher education, since the founding of the tribal college movement. In the early days of the movement to found tribal colleges, non-Indian institutions would act as funding conduits to the tribal colleges who had not yet earned accreditation candidacy. Non-Indian institutions also participated in cross-registration of students and lent faculty to the tribal colleges when requested. This tradition has blossomed into full partnerships between tribal colleges and four-year mainstream institutions, partnerships that provide to both kinds of institutions innovative science and mathematics opportunities, two-plus-two teacher training programs, distance learning and other telecommunications programs, and course transfer agreements. The land-grant status bestowed on tribally controlled colleges in 1994 by the federal government enhanced the opportunities for tribal colleges and non-Indian institutions to continue their mutually beneficial partnerships.

Even with all the positives that have transpired, there are major obstacles facing American Indian tribes who desire to develop and found a new college. The two major obstacles are funding for such efforts and maintaining the community will to persevere in the face of all the difficulties that appear when trying to start such institutions.

Tribal colleges and AIHEC have embarked on an aggressive outreach program and share regular communication with indigenous-controlled institutions around the world, such as the three Maori-controlled campuses of Te Wañanga o Aotearoa in of New Zealand, the Saami college in Norway, the Aborigine-controlled college of Australia, and four Indian colleges in Canada. Each of these institutions reflects the same principle of "indigenous control of education," thus making them natural allies. At the 2002 World Indigenous Peoples Conference on Education held on the Nakoda Reserve west of Calgary, Alberta, the World Indigenous Higher Education consortium was founded, with control of the postsecondary education of their peoples its focus. AIHEC is at the forefront of the development of this worldwide organization that will bring the international indigenous institutions together as a research entity, program development entity, and political force in the international affairs of the world.

## Canada

Eleven First Nations of western Canada have chosen a path parallel to that of the tribal colleges of the United States in addressing social problems. They are working through their own postsecondary institutions to reverse and eliminate those problems.

The effort to gain control of First Nations people's postsecondary education began in 1971 in the town of Saint Paul located 200 kilometers northeast of Edmonton, Alberta. A group of people from seven Western Woods Cree communities founded the Blue Quills Education Center, Canada's first indigenous-controlled education center. Blue Quills First Nation College, a college since 1998, chose as its primary mission the promotion of indigenous heritage and the reclamation of traditional knowledge and practices. A secondary but important part of their mission is the preparation of their students to succeed in the non-Native world of Canada. To carry forward its second prime objective it has since the 1970s invested in building relationships with other Native and non-Native institutions of higher education to bring educational programs to its students. The example of Blue Quills led to the founding of several other Native learning centers and First Nations colleges throughout western Canada (Blue Quills 2006).

Like their counterparts in United States the First Nations colleges and learning centers of Canada desire to protect and enhance their own cultures and languages. Though taking differing tracks from one another, and Blue Quills, two First Nations colleges, First Nations University of Canada and Red Crow Community College, have chosen more direct routes to becoming accredited institutions of higher education.

First Nations University of Canada was established in 1976 as Saskatchewan Indian Federated College in Regina, Saskatchewan, to serve the Cree, Saulteaux, Chipewyan, Sioux, and Assiniboine. It was closely affiliated with the University of Regina. The federation with the University of Regina granted the tribal college in 1976 the normal privileges and responsibilities accorded any other higher education institution of its stature within the province of Saskatchewan. The exception was that the college had to secure its own funding from the federal and provincial governments (Wasacase 1979). First Nations University of Canada grew into a multicampus institution serving thousands of Indians and other Canadian students, graduating more than 200 students in spring and fall convocations each year. The most popular majors are Indian social work and indigenous studies. Both master's and doctorate degrees are offered. The university has campuses at Regina, Saskatoon, and Prince Albert, Saskatchewan, while offering its programs and services in several other First Nation communities. University President Dr. Eber Hampton stated in 1999 that this education "is one way to prepare First Nation people to exercise self-determination. Realistically, Canadian universities have not and cannot fulfill this role. Indian control of Indian education is not just for elementary and secondary education. It is even more important that we seize our responsibility for university education as an expression of self-government" (Wells 1999/2000).

Red Crow Community College, serving the Blood Reserve (members of the Blackfeet Confederacy), located in Cardston, Alberta, was founded as an adult education center in 1986. Its mission was to provide quality education training opportunities and to meet the cultural needs of students of the Blood tribe. The center experienced rapid growth through the late 1980s and early 1990s. The governing board hired Marie Smallface Marule (Blood), an experienced administrator, in 1992 as their first president with instructions to bring the college to accredited community college status. Red Crow is the only Native college in Canada to be a member of the American Indian Higher Education Consortium. In 1995 Red Crow Community College was chartered by the Blood Tribe Chief and Council; it is located within the boundaries of that nation.

Ten of the First Nation tribal colleges and learning centers have formed a postsecondary consortium called the First Nations Adult and Higher Education Consortium, which serves the Canadian institutions much the same way AIHEC serves the colleges of the United States. Its mission statement declares that it will nurture and protect the First Nations' identity and cultures while promoting indigenous based initiatives to maintain and perpetuate their ways of knowing.

## Conclusion

The need for Native-controlled colleges and universities is borne out by the fact that more that 50 percent of the Native American population of the United States and Canada is under 24 years of age. Native Americans as a group are among the economically poorest minority groups. Formal education is critical in overcoming the income disparity between them and other segments of the population. Unfortunately, a large percentage of this youthful population either lives in isolated rural areas or lacks the economic resources to attend state or private colleges and universities. However, possibly of equal importance is the fact that these institutions, through the inclusion of Native cultural, linguistic, and historical materials in their curriculum serve to enhance the Native student's identity as a Native person. Tradition is not the enemy of progress, but rather the basis for progress.

The period from 1968 to 2006 has seen the number of Native-controlled colleges and universities grow from one to 48, a remarkable movement in the history of higher education that has spread to indigenous communities well beyond the borders of United States and Canada. The positive impact of Native institutions on the Native American peoples and communities they serve is phenomenal, particularly as represented by the successes of their students in the workplace and in the mainstream institutions to which they transfer. The impact is even more powerful considering the pride and hope these institutions have spread throughout the Native American world.

# Native American Studies Programs

CLARA SUE KIDWELL

Native Americans have long been the subjects of academic study in colleges and universities, primarily in the disciplines of anthropology and history. During the 1960s Native people began to reject the status of passive subjects of study and demand the right to control knowledge about Native cultures and what was taught about them. Native American and American Indian Studies programs in colleges and universities first appeared in 1970. They emerged in a time of social activism in American society that was fueled by the civil rights movement and antiwar activism. Native Americans occupied an ambivalent position in the era as both savages and victims. In Vietnam, enemy territory was referred to as "Indian country," while in the movie *Little Big Man* the massacre of a Cheyenne encampment on the Washita River was seen as a representation of the massacre of civilian inhabitants of the Vietnamese village of My Lai by American troops (Kasden and Tavernetti 1998:125).

For many Native peoples living in Minneapolis, Minnesota, in 1968, police brutality and frequent arrests for drunkenness were facts of life, and they led to the formation of the American Indian Movement in Minneapolis. The takeover of Alcatraz Island in San Francisco Bay by groups of Indian college students in November 1969 focused national attention on their demands for redress for broken treaties and for the creation of a cultural center and Indian-controlled university on the island (P.C. Smith and R.A. Warrior 1996:1–35; Josephy, Nagel, and Johnson 1999:39–43; Johnson, Nagel, and Champagne 1997:19–31). Although Alcatraz received most of the attention in terms of political protest, Indian "fish-ins" in Washington state had begun in the early 1960s to protest the state's attempt to regulate Indian fishing rights guaranteed by treaties signed in 1854 (Deloria 1977:160–176).

Confrontational tactics were used in some educational institutions as well to pressure administrators to meet student demands for curricular changes. The result was the creation of American Indian or Native American Studies programs. Although these programs began in an atmosphere of confrontation and were perceived by many administrators as rising from political advocacy rather than legitimate scholarly concerns, some of the programs survived into the early twenty-first century and achieved respectable academic status in major institutions. Their development has been marked by the evolution of intellectually coherent curricula,

adaptation of disciplinary methods to work in Indian communities, and theoretical concerns regarding culture, identity, and community. One of the key debates that marked the evolution of such programs has been over their status as a discipline (Jaimes 1985:15–21, 1987:1–16; Thornton 1978: 10–19, 1998a:87–98; T.P. Wilson 1979:217–223). Expanding curricula based on new scholarship and the growing number of Native Americans with scholarly credentials have contributed to the evolution of the field of American Indian Studies and Native American Studies into forms that may be characterized as an academic discipline.

## Political and Academic Activism in the Origins of Native American Studies

While American Indian Movement and United Indians of All Nations (the name of the group that organized the Alcatraz takeover) engaged in confrontational politics, Indian students at the University of Minnesota, Minneapolis; the University of Arizona, Tucson; and the University of California at Berkeley joined general student protests over lack of access to higher education for minority students. Indian students and faculty challenged misconceptions about Indian cultures that discouraged Indian people from attending college. They proposed to tell truths that had not been included in academic studies of Indians. They wanted to create their own knowledge rather than simply being the subjects of study.

The rhetoric of demands for academic programs and curricular change focused on challenging stereotypes. It was based on resistance to the power that academic institutions exercised in American society through their control of knowledge. The knowledge that they produced perpetrated negative images of Native Americans. The beginning of formal academic programs was thus in large part a response to existing curricula rather than a positive statement of Indian epistemology. The programs did give Native students access to colleges and universities in unprecedented numbers. Most provided special student counseling services, and curricula often included experiential learning and outreach activities for Native communities.

The beginnings of the programs, associated as they were with political activism and advocacy for Indian students, made them suspect in the academy. When students and faculty challenged the presumed objectivity of traditional disciplinary knowledge in history and anthropology and proposed that the institutions validate Native oral traditions as history, institutions reacted with suspicion and delayed the approval of programs. Debate arose among faculty over the nature of the new programs. Were they disciplines in the traditional academic sense? Were they multidisciplinary programs similar to area studies programs such as Latin American Studies or Middle Eastern Studies? Those questions have been underlying issues in the intellectual development of American Indian and Native American Studies programs since their inception.

## Intellectual Roots

Although the academic programs of the early 1970s were based on political advocacy and countering stereotypes, they have matured by drawing on a rich intellectual heritage as well as generating new scholarship. In the early twentieth century, members of the Society of American Indians, a group of educated American Indians organized in 1911, were speaking out on Indian rights issues, critiquing federal Indian policy, debating issues of American Indian identity, and seeking to preserve Indian cultures, all activities that generally characterize contemporary programs (vol. 4:306–309) (Hertzberg 1971:88, 145, 151, 178). Its members included Charles Eastman, a Dartmouth-educated Dakota (Sioux), Gertrude Bonnin, also Dakota, and Carlos Montezuma, Yavapai, all of whom saw it as their mission to advocate for Native concerns by educating the American public about Indian culture and Indian political issues. Eastman's books about Dakota culture and history, published under his Dakota name Ohiyesa, became immediate best sellers (Eastman 1902, 1911, 1916). Bonnin published Dakota stories under the name Zitkala-Ša (Zitkala-Sa 1901, 1911). Montezuma, generally regarded as the most politically outspoken of the group, published a newspaper, *Wassaja* (which appeared in Chicago between 1916 and 1922), in which he advocated the abolition of the Bureau of Indian Affairs and the full assimilation of American Indians into American society (Montezuma 1915). Although the Society of American Indians largely ceased to function by the late 1920s, primarily because of the sharply divided opinions of its members on the issues of citizenship for American Indians and the role of the Bureau of Indian Affairs in Indian life, its existence attests to the longevity of issues that are still addressed in contemporary Native American Studies programs.

Some Natives became ethnographers by some times collecting and providing information to non-Native researchers and at other times by producing their own publications. George Hunt, a Kwakiutl, worked with Franz Boas (Cole 1985:156–163). Francis LaFlesche, Omaha (vol. 17:58), first worked with Alice Fletcher before becoming an ethnologist for the Bureau of American Ethnology and publishing

his own research on the Osage (Bailey 1995). Arthur Parker, Seneca, was employed as an archeologist by the New York State Museum and as an ethnologist by the New York State library (Parker 1922, 1935). John N.B. Hewitt, a Tuscarora who was associated with the Bureau of American Ethnology at the Smithsonian Institution, published extensively on Iroquoian cultures (Deserontyon 1928; Hewitt 1903, 1928; Rudes and Crouse 1987). James Murie, a Pawnee (vol. 17: 251), both as a collaborator with non-Native scholars and as an independent researcher, is responsible for most of the published materials on the Pawnee (Murie 1989). Ella Deloria, a Yankton Sioux, encouraged by Franz Boas, collected an extensive body of Lakota language materials (E.C. Deloria 1944, 1992). In 1904 William Jones, a one-quarter Meskwaki raised among the Sac and Fox in Oklahoma, became the first Native American to receive a Ph.D. in anthropology (vol. 17:57, 250). The works of these Native scholars (Liberty 1978) and others preserved information that might otherwise be lost to communities if it were entrusted only to living memory, and they have become part of the curricula of contemporary American Indian Studies programs.

In the same year as the takeover of Alcatraz Island, N. Scott Momaday, Kiowa, won a Pulitzer Prize for his novel, *House Made of Dawn* (1968), the story of a young Pueblo veteran who is an outsider in his own society. The novel is generally considered the beginning of the so-called Native American Renaissance in American Indian literature (K. Lincoln 1983:13–14), but novels written in the 1930s, notably *The Surrounded* (1936), by D'Arcy McNickle (Flathead) (vol. 4:555), and *Sundown* (1934), by John Joseph Mathews (Osage), had already established the theme of the mixed-blood alienated from his own culture but still aware of his Indian identity ("Literature," this vol.). Mathews, a Rhodes scholar, documented the history of his tribe in *Wahkon-tah* (1932) and *The Osages: Children of the Middle Waters* (1961). These works demonstrated the failure of the federal policy of assimilating Indians completely into American society.

The policy remained in place, and it thwarted an early attempt to establish a college-level academic program at the University of Oklahoma. In 1929, Joseph Brandt, editor of the newly created University of Oklahoma Press, Norman, wrote to William Bizzell, president of the university, proposing the creation of an "American Institute of Indian Civilization," which would comprise a new building for a library of Indian materials, annual conferences on Indian policy, and academic courses on Indian art, culture, and history. Bizzell's attempt to obtain funding from the Bureau of Indian Affairs failed because the establishment of a program specifically for the study of American Indians contradicted the Bureau's policy of assimilation (Crum 1988:179).

In 1934, the Indian Reorganization Act reversed that policy, ended the practice of allotting Indian land to individuals, and provided the mechanism for the establishment of constitutionally based tribal governments. It also provided college scholarships for Indian students, although only in vocational areas. John Collier, commissioner of Indian affairs from 1934

413

to 1944, and primary author of the original legislation, encouraged the preservation of Indian cultural practices through the Indian Arts and Crafts Act (Philp 1977:185; Deloria and Lytle 1984:250; Schrader 1983:xi–xii). The Indian Reorganization Act established the basis for tribal political sovereignty, and the establishment of the National Congress of American Indians in 1944 fostered a new sense of political activism. Its executive director from 1964 to 1967, Vine Deloria, Jr., emerged as one of the leading intellectuals of the new era of Indian political activism (Cowger 1999).

In 1961, a conference organized at the University of Chicago by Sol Tax, a faculty member in the Anthropology Department, formulated a new political agenda for American Indians. That meeting produced a document entitled "Declaration of Indian Purpose," which provided guidelines for changes in federal policy, that is, the end of the policy of terminating the federal relationship with Indian tribes, greater involvement of Indians in setting federal policy, and systematic attention to improving the socioeconomic conditions in Indian communities (Lurie 1961:478–500; Josephy 1971:37–40). In 1964, Jeannette Henry (Cherokee) and Rupert Costo (Cahuilla) established the American Indian Historical Society in San Francisco and published a journal, *The Indian Historian*, which appeared from 1968 through 1982. The goal was "to promote the culture, education, and general welfare of the American Indian: To inform and educate the general public concerning America's Native, original people; To preserve the philosophy, culture and languages of this land's First People."

The 1960s also saw the rise of the National Indian Youth Council, an organization of young, mostly college educated, politically active Indians who articulated the concerns of Indians across the Nation. Melvin D. Thom (Northern Paiute), Herbert Blatchford (Navajo), and Clyde Warrior (Ponca) were leaders of this new movement and, with Vine Deloria, Jr., they became identified as the new intellectuals in Indian Country (Steiner 1968:26–27, 29–30). Deloria's book, *Custer Died for Your Sins* (1969), was a scathing critique of American society's attitudes toward Indians, and it marked the emergence of a powerful Indian intellectual voice. *Custer* is still widely read in introductory American Indian Studies classes.

Native American Studies programs, then, did not arise simply as a result of political activism evident in the takeover at Alcatraz. They represented the evolution of Indian traditions of questioning the relationship between Indian nations and the United States government and of trying to define the unique place of Indians in American society.

## Growth of the Programs

College-level programs focusing on American Indians are associated primarily with major universities in the early 1970s, but in 1961 the Bureau of Indian Affairs established a post-baccalaureate program focused solely on American Indian art at the Santa Fe Indian School in Santa Fe, New Mexico. The program became known as the Institute of American Indian Arts. Although the purpose of the Institute was primarily vocational, it did include a college preparatory curriculum, and it gave young Indian students an opportunity to explore new media and to break out of the model of so called "traditional" Indian art (Garmhausen 1988:62–71). Fritz Scholder, T.C. Cannon, and Alan Houser taught at the Institute, broke new ground in their own works, and trained a generation of Indian artists, many of whose works reflected the political themes emerging in Indian country. The curriculum of the Institute now includes literature, and the school offers an associate of arts degree.

The takeover of Alcatraz Island in San Francisco Bay in 1969 was spearheaded by college students from San Francisco State University, where an American Indian Studies program had been established in 1968 (De la Torre 2001: 11–20), and the University of California at Berkeley, emphasizing the confrontational aspect of Indian activism, but confrontation had already occurred on the Berkeley campus in the form of a Third World Strike led by African-American students. The strike resulted in violent confrontation between students and administrators. It was sparked when Black students invited Black Panther leader Stokeley Carmichael to speak on the campus. University administrators decided to cancel his appearance, fearing violence. The Black students indeed launched a protest that resulted in the Third World strike that shut down the campus. It involved Hispanic, Asian, and American Indian students as well as Black students, and they demanded the establishment of an academic program.

The Academic Senate, the faculty governing body on the campus, passed a resolution creating an Ethnic Studies Department that comprised Black, Chicano, Asian-American, and Native American Studies programs. Courses were offered for the first time in the spring of 1969. The Department answered directly to the chancellor (T.P. Wilson 1979: 214–215). Although the situation seemed to promise special attention for the new department, in actuality, it was cut it off from access to the usual processes by which academic programs were funded and staffed, and the administration adopted a policy of benign neglect while a newly recruited faculty struggled to master the intricacies of academic politics. Since the San Francisco Bay area was a center of urban relocation for Indian families in the 1950s, the curriculum emphasized contemporary issues, and the concept of tribal sovereignty was one of its core components.

The American Indian Studies program at the University of Minnesota emerged as a result of a long process of negotiation. A report by an ad hoc committee to the university administration in 1966 outlined a curriculum for an American Indian Studies program that would give Indian students academic and practical skills. It also called for an outreach program aimed at the Indian reservations in the state. The administration finally took note of the proposal in January 1969 when a group of Black students occupied the administration building, and in March an ad hoc committee was convened to plan a program. An important aspect of the plan was an emphasis on teaching the Dakota and Ojibwa languages. The new department established connections with some of the Indian communities in the state by recruiting native speakers from communities to work with university linguists to structure teaching materials. The American Indian Studies Department offered its first courses in 1970 as part of a bachelor's degree program. From its beginning, the department had the same status as other university departments (F. Miller 1971:318–334).

The University of Arizona, Tucson, had a longstanding interest in the sizable Indian population within the boundaries of the state. Its Bureau of Ethnic Research, precursor of the present Bureau of Applied Research and Anthropology, was established in 1952, and in 1958 the president of the university appointed an Indian Advisory Committee. In 1968, Dr. Edward Dozier, a Santa Clara Pueblo anthropologist and a member in the Anthropology Department at the university, proposed the development of an American Indian Studies academic program and became its chair in 1970. Internal disputes and the failure of the university to hire American Indian faculty derailed the program, but in 1976 it was reorganized under the leadership of Jay (Joseph H.) Stauss (Jamestown Band S'Klallam, a faculty member in the Sociology Department). In 1978 the university hired Vine Deloria, Jr., who became head of a graduate program in the Political Science Department that emphasized federal Indian policy. Deloria envisioned the program as a training ground for future American Indian leaders. In 1982, the university approved an interdisciplinary M.A. program (Stauss, Fox, and Lowe 2002:85–88).

The development of an American Indian Studies program at the University of California at Los Angeles followed a similar trajectory as that at the University of Arizona. American Indian Studies began with the establishment of the American Indian Culture and Research Center as one of four centers in a multiethnic Institute of American Cultures. The four programs in the Institute had external funding from the Ford Foundation to create new faculty positions in academic departments that would hire appropriate candidates. The American Indian Center's main activities were research-related conferences, externally funded research projects, and publication of a journal, *The American Indian Culture and Research Journal*. The Center's director in 1977, Dr. Charlotte Heth (Cherokee) initiated a proposal for a master's degree, which was implemented in 1982 as an interdisciplinary program administered by a faculty committee (Champagne 2002:42–53). Other programs began during the 1970s at the University of California at Davis (Forbes et al. 2002), at Harvard (Graham and Golia 2002:123–144), at Dartmouth (Calloway 2002:17–28), the University of Minnesota at Duluth (Powless 2002:183–190), and at the University of North Carolina at Pembroke (Knick and Oxendine 2002:203–228).

Cornell University, Ithaca, New York, began a small program in 1981 (Usner 2001:97–102). The University of Oklahoma, Norman, established a committee in 1974 to plan an academic program but did not commit any funding to its establishment. In a state with 39 federally recognized tribes and a total Indian population usually ranked as first or second in total numbers in federal census counts, Oklahoma did not establish a Native American Studies bachelor's degree program until 1994 (Kidwell 2002:271–294). The Applied Indigenous Studies at Northern Arizona University, Flagstaff, emphasized environmental management; it was approved in 2001 (Trosper 2001:97–102).

The academic programs at tribally controlled community colleges are another venue for Native American Studies programs (Benham and Stein 2003:167–175). These programs are generally tribally specific in their content and include languages and courses taught by elders in the tribe (Boyer 1997:62–67). In 1968 the Navajo Nation established its own tribally controlled community college, the first such institution in the country ("Tribal Colleges and Universities," this vol.). Sinte Gleska college was founded on the Rosebud Reservation in South Dakota. As the number of colleges grew, the American Indian Higher Education Consortium (AIHEC) was established in 1972 (vol. 13:827–828). Among the colleges is Haskell Indian Nations University, which was run by the Bureau of Indian Affairs. Haskell was established in 1884 as a Bureau boarding school with vocational programs, part of the assimilation program of the federal government. In 1970, the Bureau established an associate of arts degree program to change the school into a community college. It established a four-year, American Indian Studies academic program in 1978 (Chenault 2001:77–86). In 2006, AIHEC had 35 members and published the *Tribal College Journal* as an outlet for scholarship in the field of education as well as reports on its member institutions.

The emergence of Native Studies programs in Canada follows a similar path as that in the United States, with less intense political activism (Price 1978:6). The rights of Native peoples in Canada were at issue largely in terms of threats to their lands and subsistence posed by the development of hydroelectric projects around the Hudson's Bay region and the McKenzie Valley Pipeline (Berger 1977). Trent University in Petersborough, Ontario, established the first degree-granting program in Canada in 1968 (Newhouse, McCaskill, and Milloy 2002:61–82; Price 1978:9). The University of Lethbridge, Alberta, established a program in 1974, and Saskatchewan Indian Federated College emerged in the 1970s from Native-oriented vocational and academic programs associated with the University of Regina, Saskatchewan (Stonechild, Asikinack, and Miller 2002:165–82; Price 1978:9). Harold Cardinal and George Manuel became eloquent spokesmen for Native people through their published writings. In the late twentieth century, Taiaiake Alfred became a leading voice in Canada and the United States explicating an indigenous political philosophy. The *Canadian Journal of Native Studies*, published at Brandon University, Manitoba, and the *Native Studies Review*,

415

published by the University of Saskatchewan, Saskatoon, provide outlets for scholarship.

The early promise of Native American and American Indian Studies programs in the United States was not sustained in terms of numbers. The early 1970s saw a proliferation of programs designated as Native American or Native American Studies in colleges and universities. In 1974, 100 institutions that responded to a survey commissioned by the Western Interstate Commission for Higher Education reported having such a program. The programs ranged in scope from one or two courses taught in history or anthropology or education departments, and perhaps a counselor with some special responsibility for Indian student concerns, to departments with their own faculty and degree programs such as the American Indian Studies Department at Minnesota and the Native American Studies program in the Ethnic Studies Department at the University of California at Berkeley.

A survey in 1978 elicited 99 responses. It is interesting to note that the overlap between responses to the two surveys was only 56 institutions, which may say something about shifting definitions of Indian Studies programs, or something about their demise (Locke 1974, 1978). By the early 1980s many of the programs that had begun with such optimism and potential promise in the early 1970s had shrunk considerably or disappeared entirely. It appears that many programs that existed in 1976–1977 had changed or disappeared by 1981 (Guyette and Heth 1985:5).

Programs at major universities have suffered from the vagaries of academic politics. The American Indian Studies Department at the University of Minnesota was dismantled in the mid-1970s after a period of turmoil in the urban Indian community over the appointment of a new director, and its faculty was distributed to other departments; it regained its standing first as a subset of the American Studies program and finally its autonomy in the early 1990s. At the University of California at Davis, the Native American Studies degree program was suspended for a time when faculty retirements seemed to threaten the stability of the department. It too regained its status and has gone on to develop into one of the largest full departments in the country. At Berkeley, the Native American Studies program, like the rest of the university, suffered from the effect of a frozen state budget for education. In the mid-1990s, as a result of budget cuts and internal turmoil, the administration suspended the search for two vacant faculty positions in Native American Studies. Although Berkeley offers a bachelor's degree in Native American Studies, the faculty is less stable than it was during the 1980s and 1990s.

Native American Studies academic programs follow two basic structural models in universities. One model used in the establishment of early programs at the University of California at Los Angeles and the University of Arizona was interdisciplinary in that faculty and courses were housed in academic departments (English, history and anthropology were most common) and that courses were taught from disciplinary perspectives. The other model was that of a regular department (Minnesota, University of California, Berkeley) with its own faculty and courses. An assessment of the two models concluded that the multiple discipline model was more effective than the department model because it was structurally connected to the university as a whole, whereas the departmental model could be easily isolated (Washburn 1975:266–267). In the early twenty-first century, there were a wide variety of models, some using both dedicated core faculty and joint appointments (Arizona, Oklahoma, University of California at Davis, Montana), some operating as subsets within Ethnic Studies (Berkeley) or American Studies Departments (Michigan, Minnesota), and some being interdisciplinary programs (UCLA). The variety of structural arrangements is a matter of individual institutional resources and internal politics.

The survival of Native American studies programs during the 1970s and 1980s depended generally on strong leadership by individual faculty and active support by at least one university administrator. New deans often find a program to foster in order to develop their own reputations for nurturing new fields of scholarship, and some Native American studies programs have grown because of this fact.

In 2006 there were 87 United States programs and 11 Canadian programs listed on the internet directory maintained by Robert M. Nelson, professor of English at the University of Richmond, Virginia: 36 granted the bachelor's degree, 64 had a minor program, and 24 listed a concentration. Twenty-one institutions listed a graduate degree in Native American Studies, although nine indicated that such a degree was a concentration in a discipline such as history or American Studies (R.H. Nelson 2006).

The persistence of Indian Studies programs and Ethnic Studies programs in general has been sustained as much by political rhetoric as by institutional recognition of their intellectual contributions. During the 1970s such programs were viewed largely in term of affirmative action, intended to address the significant underrepresentation of American Indian and other "minority" students in higher education. By the late 1980s the rhetoric in higher education focused on the manpower needs of American society, especially in math and science fields. In a technological society, it was necessary to educate American students, including minority students, to meet shortages of people available for skilled jobs. The emphasis in minority recruitment to college programs shifted rather markedly to science majors (Commission on Minority Participation in Education and American Life 1988). By the 1990s, enrollments of minority students, including American Indians, had risen in higher education, and colleges and universities realized that their curricula should also reflect the diversity of their student bodies. The emergence of new voices in the academy also challenged the established notion of the canon. The replacement of Shakespeare by Momaday on college reading lists and the ensuing scholarly debates demonstrated the effect that Native American Studies and other such programs have had on the academy.

Allan Bloom (1987), Dinesh D'Souza (1991), and Arthur M. Schlesinger (1992) were among the most outspoken critics of the curriculum reforms of the 1980s.

## New Scholarship

The challenge to the established canon of the academy came from a body of scholarship that had emerged, if not in Native American Studies programs per se, certainly in the disciplines associated with the study of American Indians. These disciplines were themselves undergoing significant change. In the field of history, Francis Jennings's (1975) *The Invasion of America* provided a revisionist reading of colonial American history that examined the reasons for American Indian responses to European colonization and examined the attitudes of Europeans that inspired their treatment of Indians. Merrell (1989) revealed that the Catawba Indians had not disappeared from South Carolina despite their disappearance from the history of the state in the early nineteenth century. Rather, they had found ways to preserve a sense of community although they hid their identity as Indians. Anthropologists became more self-reflexive about their research. Jean Briggs's (1970) *Never in Anger* examined the influence of her presence in a Canadian Inuit community and her own responses to situations during her fieldwork. Clifford (1988) and Geertz (1973) ushered in new ideas in the study of culture, challenging accepted anthropological materialist and functionalist definitions of culture.

In the field of literature, Momaday's novel *House Made of Dawn* (1968) opened the door for other Indian writers. In college classrooms, two anthologies, Hobson's (1979) *The Remembered Earth*, and Velie's (1979) *American Indian Literature* offered new access to Native literature. They were not the usual collections of Indian myths and legends presented in English translation but included prose and poetry by contemporary Indian writers.

Literary scholarship about American Indians generally proceeded from a basic premise that Native languages are essential to cultural identity and an understanding of American Indian world views. A corollary is that knowledge in Indian communities was transmitted through oral means, shaping Native world views in particular ways. Indian oral traditions—origin stories and stories of historic events—have long constituted subjects of study by non-Indian scholars. Studies of oral traditions have had a long academic history in the field of folklore. In the 1970s a body of scholarship emerged under the rubric of "ethnopoetics." Its focus was the performance aspects of oral traditions (Hymes 1981; Tedlock 1972) Ethnopoetics has informed the development of native literary criticism.

Literary criticism took its cue from a new intellectual approach, cultural studies, which in turn derived from trends appearing in academia at large—postmodernism, deconstruction, the New Historicism. In general, these ideas challenged notions of absolute knowledge and authority that existed in the academy. Literary scholars became concerned with the context in which texts were produced. Owens (1992) adopted Mikhail Bakhtin's ([1975] 1982) theory of heteroglossia in his study of American Indian novels. Womack (1999) demonstrated the existence of a body of literature expressing the national identity of the Creek (Muskogee) people and argued that Creek literature should be critiqued in cultural terms. Weaver (1997) argued that loyalty to community was the highest value in Native American cultures. Sarris (1993) explored the complex interaction of story teller and audience and the significance of oral traditions. Vizenor (1989) introduced "trickster hermeneutics" as a uniquely Indian critical stance. Drawing from trickster figures in Indian traditions, who violate human norms by their excessive behavior, Vizenor participates in that decentering of knowledge that characterizes postmodern literary criticism (Radin 1956).

Historians began to pay attention to the voices of ordinary people. The "New Western History" produced controversial studies that focused on Indians, African-Americans, Asian-Americans and Hispanics as agents in the development of the west. Such intellectual trends gave latitude for American Indian scholars to develop their own ways of knowing. It was fashionable to pay attention to the voices of those who had not been heard before. Biographies became respectable academic sources of information for Native American Studies, not only those published as ethnographic studies (*Black Elk Speaks, Plenty Coups, Pretty Shield, Son of Old Man Hat, Dezba, Woman of the Desert*) but also works that reflected more contemporary sensibilities (*Half Breed* by Maria Campbell 1973 and *Lame Deer, Seeker of Visions* by Lame Deer and Erdoes 1972). Historians considered approaches such as ethnohistory, gender-based history, oral history, and environmental history (Fixico 1997:11, 43, 73, 87, 101).

As Native American nationalism has become a theme in literary criticism, tribal sovereignty has also become a topic of scholarship. Intellectual and political sovereignty have become conjoined in the work of Robert Warrior (1994, 1999). The major theme in studies of tribal sovereignty is the federal relationship, which has been defined by congressional action and case law rather than the United States Constitution (Deloria and Lytle 1984; Wilkins 1997; Wilkins and Deloria 2000; Wunder 1996).

## Native American Studies as a Discipline

In its broadest scope, and in its beginning, Native American Studies may be defined as research and teaching focused on Native Americans. Some scholars would limit the field further to define it as studies of Natives done by Native people, both those operating in the academy and those based in communities. From the inception of the programs there has

*417*

been debate over whether they constitute a discipline or are interdisciplinary programs, that is, using a variety of disciplinary techniques united by their common focus on Native American populations. Since there is no generally accepted definition in academia for what constitutes a discipline, and new departments emerge within universities on a regular basis, particularly in the biological sciences, it is unrealistic to expect that Native American Studies programs will fit a single model. There are a multitude of ways to organize knowledge, and ongoing debate over the very nature of knowledge is inherent in the academy (Thornton 1978:10).

If one were to venture a definition of an academic discipline, it could be that scholars in the field share a set of assumptions about their subject matter. An early critique of the field defined American Indian Studies as expressing an endogenous expression of knowledge and suggested a number of elements assumed to be essential in American Indian Studies programs—oral tradition, treaties and treaty rights, tribal government, forms of social organization, group persistence, American Indian epistemology, and contemporary issues (Thornton 1978:15–17). These themes continued to be key in the curricula of Indian Studies programs, although they can be formulated in a number of different ways.

Premises that seem to appear in all programs are the following. The first is that Native American identity is associated with land. Cultural identity comes from spiritual beliefs and ceremonies in Native cultures that arise from an intimate relationship between people and the land on which they live. Obviously, the political identity of tribes, that is, their ability to govern themselves and their recognition by the United States government, depends on the existence of a land base. The second is that the history of intercultural contacts must present the viewpoints of both cultures. This assumption has arisen from past historical studies that posited the "empty land" theory of European conquest of North America and the disappearance of Native Americans from history. Although some scholars might reject academic history altogether (C. Martin 1987:27–34), Native American Studies programs do not exist in a vacuum, especially with regard to their teaching mission. The analysis of conflicting views in history is an intellectual enterprise that challenges both scholars and students. The third assumption basic to Native American Studies is that tribes are sovereigns who have inherent rights of self-government. The unique status of American Indian tribes is an essential component of their political identity and a source of their cultural identity. Although the federal government and the United States court system might dispute the notion of sovereignty, it is accepted as a given in Native American Studies curricula. The fourth assumption is that language is essential to an understanding of culture and that Native languages must be preserved. The final assumption is that art, music, dance, and other forms of expressive culture are forms of adaptation of culture to changing circumstance. These forms draw upon cultural forms and ideas and express them in new media as an assertion of Indian identity (Kidwell and Velie 2005).

Underlying all these assumptions is a deeper question: Who is an Indian? This question becomes the intellectual linchpin of Native American Studies. In the field of literature, the theme of the mixed blood, the individual who is not fully integrated into the community, has been significant. The notion of community is another basic assumption of Native American Studies—that communal values are the basis for Indian identity.

## Methodological Concerns

The field has spawned a set of methodological concerns. These grow out of the effects of methods of academic disciplines that assume some ultimate and absolute standard of truth that is purely objective. Scholarly disciplines in contemporary society have largely acknowledged that knowledge is generated in cultural ways and at specific points in history. The disciplines generally do not admit openly that knowledge privileges and empowers certain groups over others. Anthropologists seek universal human values and have developed racial categories based on evolutionary principles that imply superiority and inferiority. They have appropriated knowledge from native communities to prove their own theories. Historians have compiled master narratives celebrating the triumph of western civilization over inferior people. Edifices of knowledge have been built on Native knowledge while Native people themselves have been excluded from the edifices of academic institutions.

The basic methodological premise of Native American Studies is that knowledge is generated by and belongs to the community. It is the community, that is, the cultural and social group, that has to control knowledge and thus exercise power over its own affairs. The community must ask its own questions in order to gain information from research that will address its needs to preserve its culture and provide those things that it defines as benefiting itself. The basic premise of research methodology is to consult the community. The significance of knowledge must be defined from the grass roots level. Knowledge is not purely objective. It must be formulated within cultural bounds and for cultural ends.

Scholars have critiqued the exploitation of Native communities by non-Native scholars working for their own academic advancement (Mihesuah 1998; Mihesuah and Wilson 2004). Weaver's (1997:xi–xiii) formulation of "communitism" (the concept that identity derives from association with a Native community) deals with the ethical issues of scholarship that Mihesuah and Wilson raise.

## Theoretical Issues

Academic disciplines are informed by basic assumptions, methodological concerns, and theoretical frameworks. The challenge of defining Native identity points to the need for a theoretical stance. Two ideas regarding Native knowledge are prominent in the current literature in the field. One, some scholars maintain that there is an Native point of view or a Native voice that is culturally distinct from American society (Momaday 1976:55–56; Vizenor 1981, 1989, 1999).

The theory of colonialism first proposed by Thomas (1966–1967, 1966–1967a) argues that this voice has been suppressed and silenced by the colonialism that has characterized American treatment of Indians. Advocates of this viewpoint wish to recover that voice (Mihesuah and Wilson 2004:69–87). Other scholars argue that Indians are still a colonized people in their relationship with the United States government and that postcolonialism is simply a western academic construct that justifies continued oppression (Cook-Lynn 1997:13–28). A basic assumption in this view is that communities have remained culturally intact over time and that they must throw off the influences of colonial society in order to reveal their cultural integrity. Taken to an extreme, this thinking is described as essentialist. It presupposes ways of thinking and acting that are culturally bound in such a way that communication with other cultural groups becomes impossible. This stance makes it impossible to define the essence of Native identity in academic terms because there is no common basis for understanding with other groups (C. Martin 1987:27). Given the diversity of Native cultures, the essential values of each are unique; however, there seems, in this formulation, to be some universal idea of Native voice that remains to be defined.

The second theoretical stance is that cultural adaptation represents a form of Native agency. Native people are not helpless victims of overpowering forces; rather, they make choices based on cultural values that allow them to deal with new external forces in their lives. This approach has become apparent particularly in historical studies such as Hoxie (1995). This stance has been supported by debates in the field of anthropology over the nature of race and racially based distinctions. Anthropologists have also given up an older theoretical paradigm of acculturation, that is, the idea that culture is a set of traits and that when two cultures come into contact, the values of the superior or dominant culture replace those of the subordinate culture. In the field of history, the term "agency" has become widely used to indicate that peoples (including Natives) who were formerly viewed as victims of the historical process have actually played a role in bringing about changes to their own benefit. This idea gives historical causality a much more human dimension than earlier formulations.

The idea that cultures adapt and change in historical circumstances involves the idea of agency and the power of choice. Taken to an extreme, this position may, indeed, lead to the idea that Natives will assimilate wholly into American and Canadian society. The challenge is to find ways in which cultures change and yet remain distinctive, and to define the distinction.

Native American scholars have borrowed from theories that have emerged in the field of cultural studies, particularly as these have informed literary studies. An important theoretical concept in the general field of cultural studies is the subaltern. Drawn from the East Indian colonial experience, the idea of the subaltern explains the total suppression of Native voices by a European colonizer. The leading proponent of subaltern studies is Gayatri Spivak (1994), whose intellectual enterprise is to find the voice of the subaltern. Edward Said (1978) introduced the concept of cultural discourse theory in order to discuss how colonizers have imposed identities on indigenous populations. He describes the way in which Asian natives were characterized as weak, effeminate, and exotic in order to reduce them to a subject status. Said maintains that the rhetoric of Orientalism reveals more about the colonizer's values and attitudes than it does about the subject population.

Native scholars have used these ideas in their work. Philip Deloria (1998) played on these themes, exploring the way in which American society has historically used Indians as the counterpoint to a unique American identity. The term heteroglossia characterizes the many voices in dialogue in Native American literature. The notion of hereoglossia challenges the idea of a singular, authoritative voice in any text, thus allowing Native voices to be heard equally with others. Other Native American scholars have contributed the new vocabulary that usually characterizes theory: "survivance" (Vizenor's 1999 term for the persistence of Native identity in contemporary society); "communitism" (Weaver 1997:xi); "memory in the blood" (Momaday's 1968:129 statement about the essential nature of Native identity), and "intellectual sovereignty" (Warrior's 1994:87 assertion of the right of Native scholars to speak for themselves).

Another intellectual trend appears in the language of colonialism and postcolonialism. Cherokee anthropologist Robert K. Thomas (1966–1967, 1966–1967a) placed Indian reservations as internal colonies in America and discussed strategies of resistance for Indian communities. Thomas used the Pine Ridge Reservation in South Dakota as an example of a community existing in a colonial relationship with the United States government. In the larger academic world, postcolonial studies emerged as a significant intellectual trend, and some American Indian scholars adopted the model. Postcolonial studies asserts that formerly colonized peoples can recover their own voices, which had been systematically oppressed by colonizers who sought to exploit the resources and the labor of indigenous people. Theory provides overarching themes through which oppressed peoples can understand the tactics of oppressors and develop strategies for resistance. These strategies depend on new theories that "decenter" existing ideas that knowledge constitutes a body of absolute and unalterable truth.

The philosophical ideals of logical positivism and human progress that emerged in late eighteenth-century Europe as part of the Enlightenment laid the foundation for the idea of modernity, which in turn led to the contemporary intellectual concept of postmodernism. The notions of evolution and perfectibility in human societies are products of the Enlightenment, and cultural, intellectual, and economic imperialism derives from those. The subjects of that imperialism have rebelled against it and challenged it with their own ideas. Native American Studies programs have evolved within this intellectual milieu. Their presence in academic institutions has been part of the challenge to academic establishments and the power that they have exerted as arbiters of knowledge and culture.

One of the debates in the development of Native American Studies has concerned the importance of knowledge about Indians generated by non-Indian scholars. Much of the political rhetoric of the 1960s and 1970s was a rejection of the knowledge generated in academic disciplines such as history and anthropology. This outright rejection was tempered by changes in those disciplines and the greater sophistication in framing questions. Warrior's (1994, 1999) formulation of intellectual sovereignty privileges the writings of Native authors over those of non-Indians, maintaining that Native American intellectuals were ignored in academic scholarship in the past. Womack (1999) has taken this idea in the direction of national, that is, tribally specific, literature with his work on Creek, maintaining that distinct cultural differences among Native nations should inform writings of authors who are members of those nations.

The theme of national identity accompanies the call for a sense of responsibility to community. The concept of "communitism" places Native identity in the sense of belonging to a community, with the concomitant responsibility to other members of that community. American Indian Studies is an expression of tribal sovereignty and nationalism and as a discipline based in "a body of intellectual information" that is "internally organized, normatively regulated, and consensually communicated" (Cook-Lynn 1997:10).

## Conclusion

American Indian and Native American Studies programs have grown and matured in their intellectual approaches. The early concern with stereotypes evolved into a much more sophisticated consideration of Native American identity that questions both external and internal perceptions of who is a Native American.

The definitions of Native American literature and art are moving beyond the simple question: is it Native literature or Native art because it is done by Natives? Scholars are formulating critically defined standards that define art and literature by quality rather than simply the identity of the creator. The establishment of the National Museum of the American Indian created an educational venue within which the scholarship produced in Native American studies programs can help shape perceptions of American Indians in the minds of the general public (Cobb 2005:361–383).

A number of academic journals provide forums for the exchange of ideas and the self-reflexivity that characterizes an academic discipline. The longest standing are the *American Indian Culture and Research Journal*, published by the American Indian Research Center at the University of California at Los Angeles, and the *American Indian Quarterly*, published by the University of Nebraska Press, Lincoln. *Wicazo Sa Review*, published by the University of Minnesota Press, Minneapolis, provided an outlet for scholarly research and creative activity by faculty and graduate students in Native American Studies programs and in other academic programs throughout the country. The *Indigenous Nations Studies Journal* is published by the Indigenous Nations Studies program at the University of Kansas, Lawrence. *Ethnohistory*, the journal of the American Society for Ethnohistory, has provided a venue for scholarship on Native Americans since 1954. It is an example of the joining of political activism and scholarship since the Society was formed by scholars who were engaged in research on Indian claims cases before the United States Court of Indian Claims in the 1950s (Tanner 1991:65–68).

# Lawyers and Law Programs

RENNARD STRICKLAND AND SHARON BLACKWELL

At the time of contact, Native Americans were engaged in sophisticated legal systems that varied substantially from tribe to tribe. Indian communities often had important law-givers, legislators, judges, clan spokesmen, and advocates who fulfilled roles in tribal legal systems that were similar to their contemporaries in European common law and civil jurisdictions.

The earliest Native American known to have been admitted to practice law in a state jurisdiction was John Rollin Ridge, the mixed-blood Cherokee newspaperman and poet who fled to California during the Gold Rush and founded *The Sacramento Bee*. In 1855, Ridge wrote his uncle Stand Watie about studying and practicing the law. "I will not practice the law unless I am driven to it. The general science of the law I admire—it's every day practice I dislike. But for the sake of having something upon which to rely in case of necessity, I have patiently burned the midnight oil" (Strickland 1977:7). Like many Native American lawyers, Ridge found a place in politics and struggled to resolve Indian issues, including efforts to negotiate the tribal treaty at the end of the American Civil War (vol. 14:365).

Adaptation to change is central in the life of contemporary Native Americans. The histories of the tribes' societal and governmental changes are contained in the journals and letters of European explorers and merchants, federal documents maintained in the United States National Archives, and in tribal records. An overview of those changes during the twentieth century is found in the evolution of federal policies and implementing statutes that apply to all tribes and Native communities (vol. 4:230–237; "The Federal-Tribe Relationship," this vol.).

Indian historians, legal scholars, and political scientists suggest that the twentieth century may be usefully divided into four policy periods: allotment and assimilation (1871–1928), Indian reorganization (1928–1945), termination (1945–1961), and self-determination (1961–present). The contours of the first three policy periods were formed almost exclusively by legislative fiat as the federal government defined, considered, and redefined the trust doctrine. In contrast, the present era of self-determination had its beginnings in that dynamic time when national legal services were made available in regions designated as poverty stricken, including Indian reservations; when western communities experienced phenomenal population growth and began to

nudge tribal lands; and when renewed competition for the nation's natural resources focused attention on tribal water and energy reserves.

This present policy era is characterized by the dramatic repositioning of the tribes and individual Indians from the passive role of "ward," described by the Supreme Court in *United States* v. *Kagama* (118 U.S. 375 [1886]), to that of competent participants in commercial enterprises on tribal homelands, and in capital ventures beyond tribal borders ("Tribal Sovereignty and Economic Development," this vol.). The "modern era" in federal policies began in 1959 when the Supreme Court (*Williams* v. *Lee*, 358 U.S. 217 [1959]) held that, because of the right of the Navajo Nation to self-government, the Navajo, and not the state of Arizona, had jurisdiction to hear contract matters that had been entered into on the reservation between a non-Indian and an Indian. The acknowledgment by the Court of the concepts of tribal sovereignty and self-government, concepts that had been raised and systematically ignored in protest of congressional actions to disable and terminate tribal governments, gave new resolve to the tribes to explore, and test, the extent of tribal authority. In the years following *Williams*, the practice of Indian law rapidly moved from discrete real property title matters handled in private law offices to the broader realms of constitutional law cases litigated in federal courts. From what began as essentially a handful of governmental lawyers and legal scholars who were self-educated in Indian law principles in 1960, there emerged a substantial body of highly trained attorneys and firms who specialize in Indian law.

The genesis of the modern Indian lawyer dates back at least to the New Deal and the establishment of the Indian Claims Commission. A significant role was played by the growing discipline of ethnohistory and legal anthropology, including the work of pioneers E. Adamson Hoebel and Karl Llewellyn. The creation of an identifiable body of organized legal concepts by Felix Cohen (1942), in the original *Handbook of Federal Indian Law* and the subsequent revisions, provided a standard for Indian law. Contemporary federal legislation that addresses Indian civil and social matters, such as foster care and adoption of Indian children, probate of Indian estates and Indian civil rights, has engaged attorneys who might not have otherwise been involved with Native peoples and their law. In 2007, there are a number of specialized firms who limit their practice to issues of Native law. A number of large firms have added special Indian law practice groups focusing upon tribal economic development and resource utilization.

Legal institutions, programs, and organizations devoted to the development of Indian law and Indian lawyers have shaped the twenty-first century world of Indian law and refined the principles including sovereignty, the trust doctrine, self-governance, and economic sustainability in Indian Country.

## American Indian Law Center

In 1966 Dean Tom Christopher of the University of New Mexico School of Law, Albuquerque, and faculty member Frederick M. Hart conducted a survey of law schools and state bar associations. They determined that there were only 25 Indian attorneys and 15 Indian law students nationwide. Christopher enlisted Hart to develop an initiative for the University of New Mexico to increase the number of Indian law students, and ultimately, the number of Indian lawyers. The outcome was the American Indian Law Center, housed at the University of New Mexico, charged with the administration of an intensive pre-law summer session for Indian students. The Pre-Law Summer Institute (PLSI), begun in 1967, is designed to replicate the first-year law school experience. Unlike many law school "headstart" initiatives that admit only low-score-range applicants, many of the students in the summer program have already been admitted to one or more law schools.

One of the great strengths of the PLSI is that the classes mirror regular law school classes, and participants are similarly graded. Upon successful completion of the summer session, approximately 30 students each year matriculate to law schools across the country. Students that have not been admitted to a law school prior to attending the PLSI are assisted to gain admission based upon their performance. The American Indian Law Center reports that approximately 1,140 potential Indian lawyers completed the Pre-Law Summer Institute between 1984 and 2006 (fig. 1). Over the decades the collegiality fostered by the program has created a cadre of Indian lawyers who share a sense of purpose and responsibility to the refinement of Indian legal principles.

Professor Kevin Gover, Pawnee, former assistant secretary of the Department of the Interior, a graduate of the PLSI, reported that in 2007 "there are approximately 4,000 Native attorneys and an estimated 25 percent of them have completed the PLSI program. It's been extraordinarily successful" (Missoulian.com, Monday, May 21, 2007). Data from the American Law School Admissions Council shows that in a typical year about 750 or so Alaskan Natives and American Indians apply to law school and about 400 or so are admitted.

American Indian Law Center, Albuquerque, N. Mex.

Fig. 1. Participants at the 2004 Pre-Law Summer Institute program at their graduation from the University of New Mexico Law School, Albuquerque. left to right, David Adams (Sault Tribe of Chippewa), Dana Cleveland (Colville Confederated Tribes), and Casey Douma (Laguna Pueblo). Photographed in 2007.

The first Director of the American Indian Law Center was Robert LaFollette Bennett, Oneida Tribe of Wisconsin, who earned his law degree in the evenings while working in Washington, D.C. Bennett served as the commissioner of Indian affairs from 1965 to 1969. During his confirmation hearings in 1966 the Senate Committee had tried to force Bennett to take a stand favoring termination, which he refused to do. Under Commissioner Bennett's leadership, the mission of the Center expanded beyond the pre-law summer sessions to providing legal education and service to the broader Indian community. Bennett began to engage tribal leaders nationwide in dialogues concerning good governmental practices and to assist them in developing tribal codes, and in providing legal training to tribal judges, court personnel, and law enforcement officers. When Bennett retired in 1972, Philip S. Deloria, Standing Rock Sioux, was named his successor. Deloria had worked in the Office of Economic Opportunity legal services program on his reservation and in Indian programs in Washington. During his tenure he worked to establish the Center as an independent and informed policy voice in national Indian affairs as well as in international indigenous peoples' matters.

## Native American Rights Fund

By the mid-1960s, Indian issues were becoming an integral part of the broader national social and economic agenda. The Office of Economic Opportunity in 1964 established government-funded programs on or near many Indian reservations to provide legal services to poor and disadvantaged Indians. It quickly became apparent that Indian legal matters were uniquely complex, governed by a myriad of discrete federal statutes, treaties, regulations, administrative rulings, and court decisions. This highlighted the need for a national Indian litigation organization to monitor and provide litigation support in significant Indian cases. In 1970 California Indian Legal Services obtained a Ford Foundation grant to implement a pilot project to provide legal services to Indians on a national level. The project was referred to as the Native American Rights Fund (NARF) and is generally known to this day by these initials. A year later NARF incorporated with an all-Indian board of directors and moved its office to Boulder, Colorado.

That same year NARF obtained funding from the Carnegie Corporation to establish the National Indian Law Library, a public law library devoted exclusively to federal Indian and tribal law materials. The library is available for all practitioners in the field as well as scholars in the area of Indian history and policy. The integrity of the library has made it the repository for tribal donations of unique and valuable documents. In turn, this has inspired the creation

of other major Indian law collections, particularly the Shleppey Collection at the University of Tulsa; the Strickland Collections at the University of Oklahoma, Norman, and the University of Oregon, Eugene; and collections at the University of New Mexico and the University of Minnesota. Additionally, the University of Washington, Seattle, and the University of California at Los Angeles have extensive tribal materials.

NARF's staff of approximately 13 attorneys, two-thirds of whom are tribal members (fig. 2), seek involvement in high-profile Indian cases that will establish precedent in the areas of preservation of tribal existence, protection of tribal natural resources, assertion of tribal treaty rights, rights to adequate education, health, housing and religious freedom, and accountability from federal and state governments. Almost immediately after incorporation in 1971, NARF attorneys became involved in the most controversial Indian case in the nation (*United States* v. *Washington*, 384 F. Supp. 312 [W.D. Wash. 1974], *aff'd* 520 F.2d 676 [9th Cir. 1975], *cert. denied*, 423 U.S. 1086 [1976]), universally referred to as the Boldt case, after Judge George Boldt (vol. 7:177–178). In 1970 the United States on its own behalf, and as trustee for

Native Amer. Rights Fund, Boulder, Colo.

Fig. 2. Native American Rights Fund attorneys conducting a moot court for a public defender from Wyoming. left to right, Public defender Sylvia Hackl; NARF staff attorneys Mark Tilden, Navajo; Kim Gottschalk; Don Wharton; David Gover, Pawnee/Choctaw; and Walter Echo Hawk, Pawnee. Photograph by Ray Ramirez, Boulder, Colo., 2007.

several western Washington tribes, filed the action against the state, its game and fish regulatory agencies, and the Washington Reef Net Owners Association to enforce off-reservation treaty rights for the Indians. These treaty rights were the recognition of the historic power to take fish at their usual and accustomed grounds (various watersheds in western Washington, including the American portion of the Puget Sound watershed, some Olympic Peninsula watersheds, and the offshore waters adjacent to those areas) free from state and private infringement. Attorneys for NARF represented five additional "treaty tribes" who intervened as plaintiffs in the case.

In his decision, Judge Boldt stated that his objective was to finally settle what he characterized as more than a century of frequent and often violent controversies between state officials, commercial and sport fishing officials, and non-Indians, all on one side, and the Indians on the other. In an extraordinary decision for the time, Judge Boldt held that state officials may only regulate Indian fishing *after* the federal court was satisfied that: (1) the regulation of Indian fishing is reasonable and necessary for conservation of the fish species, and (2) *only after* the state's conservation measures had not been attained by first restricting non-Indian fishing. The Boldt decision was upheld by the federal Ninth Circuit Court of Appeals and tacitly by the Supreme Court when it denied certiorari. Far from alleviating, or even mitigating, the dangerous situation, following the Boldt decision, the community remained volatile for decades and with it NARF's long term involvement with the tribes. Thus, from the very beginning, the Native American Rights Fund established the value of a public interest, independent, not-for-profit law firm to the Indian community.

## Federal Bar Association

The Indian law renaissance of the 1960s and 1970s was national in scope with issues being contested in courts from Washington to Maine and California to Florida. In 1975, J. Thomas Rouland, then Executive Director of the Federal Bar Association (FBA), watched the practice of Indian law moving from a relatively small group of specialized lawyers and administrative judges employed by the federal government, mostly located in Western states, to legal services attorneys across the entire nation, including a sizable number in the East. He identified the need for quality education programs that addressed relevant common issues in Indian cases for Federal Bar members and the growing number of potential new members. He asked for the assistance of former Commissioner of Indian Affairs Robert L. Bennett to help create a relevant Indian law curriculum and secure teachers who could present it at a national conference sponsored by the FBA.

This first national conference on Indian law was held in May 1976 in Phoenix, Arizona. The topics included tribal,

state, and federal jurisdiction, development of energy resources on reservations, water rights, and the Indian Self-Determination and Education Assistance Act of 1975. Attendance was about 150 people. The annual conference has become the largest and most important Indian law conference in the nation with 750–1,000 attendees from federal and state and local governments, private practitioners, law students, tribal leaders and advocates, and court personnel. The first conference topics continue to have relevance in the annual sessions.

In 1990 the FBA acknowledged the significance of Indian law to the legal profession by making it a part of the FBA's permanent organizational structure. The FBA created an Indian Law Section that, in addition to assuming responsibility to continue the standard of excellence at the annual seminars, engaged members in setting professional and ethical standards for the development of the discipline. Two important committees within the Indian Law Section exemplify the FBA's commitment to the sound and fair administration of Indian legal issues. The Committee on the Development of Federal Indian Law has responsibilities to monitor and report critical developments in federal Indian cases and draft positions that may be taken as *amicus curiae* in federal appellate courts. The Committee on Public Education has responsibilities to respond to and correct misinformation about Indian law issues in the media.

Since the 1980s, the Oklahoma Supreme Court has worked with interested groups to host an annual "Sovereignty Symposium" under the direction of Supreme Court Justice Yvonne Kauger. This conference is second only to the FBA in terms of attendance and longevity. State bar associations and special interest national legal associations like the Rocky Mountain Mineral Law Institute have followed the FBA example and incorporated Indian law in annual legal education seminars. During this time tribal and Indian bar associations were formed, and they offer Indian law programs that are unique to tribal laws and codes, as well as federal and state cases. The result is that there are excellent seminars that feature outstanding lawyers, judges, and professors for the practicing attorney in Indian law.

## American Bar Association

Historically, the American Bar Association (ABA), the nation's largest lawyers association, has been slow in addressing issues of diversity and membership for minority lawyers, as was illustrated by the creation of the National Bar Association by African-Americans who were not welcomed into the ABA until after the Second World War. In the twenty-first century, the ABA has pursued greater involvement of Native Americans in the Association's leadership positions and its professional activities. In 1999 William G. Paul, Chickasaw, was elected the president of the organization (fig. 3). Paul committed the ABA to estab-

AP Images.

Fig. 3. Incoming president of the American Bar Association, William Paul, Chickasaw, at right, receiving the gavel from outgoing president Philip Anderson, at the organization's convention, Aug. 10, 1999. Photograph by Alan Mothner, Atlanta.

lish a minority scholarship fund and to encourage more minority recruitment of law clerks in private law offices. Kirke Kickingbird, Kiowa, was elected to the ABA Board of Governors in 1996. Native American lawyers and educators have served on the ABA Section on Legal Education and Admission to the Bar. A number of American Indian lawyers have been awarded the ABA "Spirit of Excellence" Award for their contributions to the rule of law and the rights of Native peoples. Lawrence Baca, Pawnee, Deputy Director of the Office of Tribal Justice, Department of Justice, received the 2007 award.

## Native American Bar Associations

Approximately half of the states have Indian law sections in the state bar associations. Many states have Indian bar associations formed exclusively for Indian law practitioners. Oklahoma has both levels of Indian law association.

The oldest and most important association is the National Native American Bar Association, which was founded in 1973 as the American Indian Lawyers Association to promote social, cultural, political, and legal issues among Indian lawyers, judges, professors, and students. Regular membership is available only to lawyers or law school graduates who are enrolled members of Indian tribes. Special membership is available to Indian law practitioners who are not eligible for regular membership. The annual meeting is generally devoted to current political and legal issues that may infringe on the welfare of Indian communities.

## American Law Schools and Indian Law Curricula

The first Indian law courses were not generally about tribal policies, constitutional rights, or the unique jurisdictional aspects of Indian affairs but were essentially "Indian land title" courses offered as part of the real property law studies. The first course was at the University of Oklahoma School of Law, and it dealt exclusively with the discrete federal statutes that govern the alienation and inheritance of Indian allotted lands in the state. It was generally offered on Saturdays so that lawyers practicing in real property and probate matters in various parts of the state could attend. It was not until Professor Ralph Johnson at the University of Washington School of Law taught an Indian seminar that the modern course was even envisioned. In 1975, working in association with the American Indian Law Center, Professor Monroe E. Price of the University of California at Los Angeles developed the first Indian law course book, *Law and the American Indian* (1973). The text was adopted for use generally by western law schools, but usually for a seminar course offering taught by an adjunct faculty member from the private sector. In 2007 Indian law is an established area of academic study. Many law schools have established chairs and professorships, some of which are funded by tribes, to attract and encourage scholars in the field. Harvard Law School, University of California at Los Angeles, the University of Oregon, the University of Arizona, Tucson, and Arizona State University, Tempe, are among the universities that have received substantial tribal, foundation and public support to build educational programs for Indian lawyers.

The increased significance of Indian law is reflected in the curriculum of American law schools. A review of law school course offerings reveals that at least one course in Native American law is offered in about 85 percent of the ABA approved law schools at least every three years. The law school curriculum data demonstrate not only the increasing numbers of Indian law students, but also non-Native law students who desire Indian law courses. There are 37 Native American Law Students Association chapters at ABA-approved law schools with both Native and non-Native members. A growing number of law schools have established clinical education programs that provide legal services to tribal governments and to individual Indians.

Further, Indian lawyers are found on both sides of the law school desk. In 2006 there were 21 law professors who were recognized Indian tribal members. The Association of American Law Schools Indigenous Law Section has approximately 200 legal educators that subscribe to the

Section's listserv to stay current on Indian law issues and cases. Native American law professors have been named to national leadership positions in legal education. Since the 1980s Native law professors have served as the President of the Association of American Law Schools and Chair of the Law School Admissions Council. One Native professor has served as dean of four law schools.

In addition to the professional association that sponsors Indian law seminars, law schools have become primary continuing legal education providers on Indian law issues and offer professional credit hours to lawyers to maintain annual state bar certification requirements. In a number of states, particularly those states with significant Indian communities, there is a movement to add a question on Indian law to the state bar examination. New Mexico and Washington have done this. Additionally, a number of law schools offer graduate work in Indian law and award either an LL.M. or a masters of comparative law degree. These include the University of Tulsa, the University of Arizona, and the University of California at Los Angeles.

## Law-Trained American Indian Leaders

Legal educators argue that the kind of decision-making skills taught in law school are designed to help formulate policy and address social and cultural issues. Richard West, Jr., was the director of the National Museum of the American Indian from 1990 to 2007, and lawyer Kevin Gover succeeded him in the post. Indian lawyers have become de facto political leaders as well as important legislative and judicial figures. Substantial numbers of tribal heads of state (presidents, chiefs, governors) are lawyers. Indian lawyers have served in key congressional staff positions, solicitor ap-

pointments, and members of congress. Since the 1970s, the assistant secretary of the Interior and the deputy commissioner of Indian affairs, both key federal officials in the administration of the federal trust responsibility, have most often been Indian lawyers. Most federal departments and commissions, for example, the Department of Commerce, the Department of Housing and Urban Development, the Environmental Protection Agency, and the Federal Communication Commission, have established "Indian desks," frequently administered by Indian lawyers who work with tribal leaders and tribal business executives to achieve programmatic and cultural goals.

In the 1990s Attorney General Janet Reno and Counsel to the Attorney General Gerald A. Torres held "listening conferences" between Department of Justice officials and Indian tribal leaders across the nation. One outcome of this federal outreach effort was the appointment of Indian lawyers in United States Attorney offices throughout the nation with a special charge to address Native issues and strengthen law enforcement on Indian lands.

## Conclusion

In the twenty-first century, "briefcase warriors" are widely represented in decision-making positions in almost all facets of modern Indian affairs. With book in hand, Indian lawyers move effortlessly from their reservations and Indian communities to the committee rooms of the Congress of the United States and the chambers of state and federal courts. The experience of thousands of "briefcase warriors" is proof that the adaptation and revitalization of the traditional law can serve as a vital weapon in the preservation of Native people and values.

426

# Repatriation

C. TIMOTHY McKEOWN

Repatriation is the process of returning someone, or in the case of cultural property, something to its nation of origin. Cultural property is generally defined as any object that is specifically designated by a nation as being of importance. The acquisition of objects of importance from the indigenous nations of North America began with the arrival of the first Europeans. It reached a peak in the late nineteenth and early twentieth centuries as public and private collections were established in North America and Europe (Cole 1985; Bieder 1990, 1992; Krech and Hail 1999; D.H. Thomas 2000). The return of Native American cultural property to its indigenous nations of origin began with isolated efforts during the late twentieth century. Later, state, provincial, and national legislation and policy reforms defined the relationship between indigenous nations and museums (Greenfield 1996; Fforde, Hubert, and Turnbull 2002).

## Early Efforts, 1890–1990

One of the earliest and most protracted efforts by indigenous nations to repatriate cultural property was initiated in the 1890s by the Six Nations Confederacy of the Cayuga, Mohawk, Oneida, Onondaga, Seneca, and Tuscarora. At issue were a number of wampum belts, woven strips of cylindrical white or purple shell beads, used by the confederacy to memorialize significant agreements and traditionally kept by a designated Onondaga leader for the confederacy as a whole. The American Revolution precipitated a split within the confederacy as groups chose to ally with the American or British causes. With the American victory, many Loyalist communities resettled from the United States to the Six Nations Reserve in Ontario, Canada, and the confederacy belts were divided between the American and Canadian communities. In 1891, the wampum keeper in New York was persuaded to sell four belts, which were ultimately acquired by Albany mayor John Boyd Thacher (Fenton 1971:450). When the wampum keeper in Ontario died in 1893, his heirs assumed control of the wampum and began to sell pieces to museums. The two indigenous communities quickly tried to recover the belts (Fenton 1989:403).

In Ontario, the confederacy was successful in gaining the return of several belts in 1894, but others continued to be sold by the late wampum keeper's heirs, despite a reward posted by the confederacy for their return. In 1909, the confederacy requested the assistance of the governor general of Canada in securing the return of the belts, but when in 1915 the Indian Department requested affidavits affirming that the belts were not individual property and could only be disposed of with the consent of the confederacy as a whole, they declined to identify who had sold them and the matter was dropped. Eleven wampum belts were eventually acquired by the Heye Museum in New York, now the Museum of the American Indian (Fenton 1989:401–407).

In New York, the Onondaga Nation filed suit in 1897 to recover the four belts that had been sold by the wampum keeper to John Thacher. The following year, realizing that eight other belts were in danger of being dismantled or lost, the Onondaga Nation elected the University of the State of New York as the wampum keeper and, by bill of sale, sold and transferred all interest in the wampum. The State of New York, in turn, enacted legislation in 1899 identifying the university as the wampum keeper with authority to acquire additional wampum to which the Six Nations Confederacy was entitled. Though the university joined the Onondaga's suit to recover the four belts, the case was dismissed, with the court ruling that while the wampum keeper had authority to sell the four belts, the Onondaga Nation did not have authority to unilaterally select the university as wampum keeper (*Onondaga Nation* v. *John Boyd Thacher*, 29 Misc. 428, 61 N.Y.S. 1027 [1899], aff'd 169 N.Y. 584, 62 N.E. 1098 [1901], aff'd 189 U.S. 306 [1903]). After nearly 15 years of administrative and judicial struggle in the United States and Canada, most of the belts sold by the wampum keeper or his heirs in the 1890s remained in museum or private collections.

One of the first successful repatriation efforts began in 1958 when residents of several Kwakiutl villages at the north end of Vancouver Island, British Columbia, began to campaign for the return of a collection of items they argued had been illegally confiscated by the Canadian government. In 1921, government officials arrested 45 participants for violation of section 149 of the Indian Act, which made engaging in or assisting in a potlatch a misdemeanor punishable by up to six months in jail. Twenty-two participants from Village Island, Alert Bay, and Cape Mudge were given suspended sentences if they surrendered their potlatch regalia to the government official. Over 250 items were surrendered, including 20 coppers, scores of hamatsa whistles, and dozens of masks for which the government claimed it paid $1,495. Several of the pieces ended up in private collections of government officials. Thirty three pieces were sold directly to George Heye for the Museum of the American Indian in New York, and other pieces were subsequently donated to that museum. The greater part of the collection was shipped to the Victoria Memorial Museum in Ottawa, now the Canadian Museum of Civilization in Gatineau, Quebec, and to the Royal Ontario Museum in Toronto. Kwakiutl requests for repatriation argued that the 1921 alienation of the ceremonial objects in exchange for dropping criminal charges was contrary to principles of Canadian law. The Canadian Museum of Civilization began negotiations regarding repatriation of the portion of the potlatch collection under its control in 1967, while insisting that they would only be repatriated to the Kwakiutl people as a whole and not to the individuals from whom they were taken, and then only when proper climate and security controls for the collection could be ensured. Separate cultural societies were established in Alert Bay and Cape Mudge. The potlatch collection was transferred from Ottawa for temporary residence to the Royal British Columbia Museum, Victoria, in 1978, where an agreement was reached on division of the collection between the Alert Bay and Cape Mudge communities, and by 1980 the collections were installed in the U'Mista Cultural Centre in Alert Bay and the Kwagiulth Museum in Cape Mudge ("Native Museums and Cultural Centers," this vol.). The Royal Ontario Museum returned the portion of the potlatch collection in its possession to the cultural centers in 1988 (Jacknis 1996, 2002).

The birth of the movement to protect Native American graves and repatriate human remains from museum collections can be traced to a 1971 Iowa road construction project that encountered a historic cemetery containing graves of 27 individuals. Under the direction of the state archeologist, the 26 individuals identified as Caucasian were placed in new caskets and reburied. The remaining body, a Native American adult female, was taken to the state archeologist's office for study. Maria Pearson (fig. 1), the Yankton Sioux wife of one of the highway engineers, was outraged when she learned of the disparate treatment of the Native American remains and confronted the Iowa state governor, who agreed that the Native American remains should also be reburied (Pearson 2005). Pearson then set out to change the state law governing treatment of Native American human remains. The 1976 revision made the state archeologist responsible for reburying all prehistoric human remains at designated state cemeteries following the recovery of physical and cultural information (Iowa State Code 1976). The Iowa reburial statute served as inspiration for other legislation, with 27 states enacting laws specifically protective of Native American remains by 1990 (Price 1991; R.C. Echo-Hawk and W.R. Echo-Hawk 1994).

AP Images.

Fig 1. Maria Pearson (Yankton Sioux), holding a photograph of her maternal grandmother Minnie Flute. Pearson fought for the protection and preservation of Native gravesites. Photograph by Michael L. Palmieri, Ames, Ia., 2002.

In 1978, the Pueblo of Zuni began a concerted campaign to recover ahayu:da (ʔahayu· ta 'war gods') that had been wrongfully removed from shrines on the Zuni Reservation in New Mexico. The Zuni Deer and Bear clans each prepare one figure during ceremonies at the winter solstice. The twin figures, carved from cylindrical pieces of cottonwood or pine, with stylized face, torso, and hands, and bundles of prayer feathers fastened around the base, are placed at a shrine on the mesa near the Pueblo. Figures from the previous year are placed on a pile of "retired" images that are left to gradually return to the earth. Over the years, scores of the figures were stolen from their shrines, with many ending up in museum collections around the world. Zuni religious leaders believed that removal of the ahayu:da from the shrines had unleashed wanton destruction and mayhem and that restoring them to the shrines was necessary to restore harmony to the world. When an ahayu:da was advertised for sale at a New York auction house, the Zuni asked the Department of Justice to investigate. The figure was identified as stolen tribal property and seized by federal agents. Zuni claims for return were based on three principles: ahayu:da are sacred items whose presence at Zuni is needed for spiritual purposes in the longstanding Zuni religion; to the degree that ahayu:da can be regarded as property, they are owned communally by the Pueblo of Zuni; once placed at their shrine, the ahayu:da could not legally be removed. Following the auction, Zuni leaders decided to use a culturally appropriate nonconfrontational approach in subsequent requests for the return of ahayu:da, viewing legal action as a last resort. By 1990, 34 ahayu:da had been recovered from 28 institutions and individuals in the United States and Canada (Merrill, Ladd, and Ferguson 1993; Ladd 2001).

One of the most comprehensive repatriations of cultural property to an indigenous nation occurred in Greenland when, following establishment of home rule in 1979, the National Museum of Denmark, Copenhagen, signed a repatriation contract with the Greenland National Museum and Archives, Nuuk. In 1981, the National Museum of Denmark repatriated the information in its archives regarding Greenlandic prehistoric monuments. This was followed the next year by the repatriation of 204 nineteenth-century watercolor paintings by Greenlandic artists. Ethnographic and archeological collections were then repatriated on a regional basis, with items from East Greenland repatriated in 1986,

the Thule District in 1990, and West Greenland in 1992 (Haagen 1995). Ultimately, Denmark transferred 35,000 objects to the Greenland National Museum and Archives (Pentz 2004). Ownership of the remains of 1,646 individuals, of both Eskimo and Norse origin, was also transferred to Greenland, though most remained in the possession of the Panum Institute in Copenhagen (Thorleifsen 2006; Berglund 2003). Some human remains were transferred to Greenland, including the six mummies found in 1972 near Qilakitsoq, which are on exhibit in Nuuk (Nunatta Katersugaasivia Allagaateqarfialu 2007).

Efforts to reclaim the Six Nations Confederacy wampum belts began again in the 1960s. In 1967, a New York State Assembly proposal to revise or eliminate all state laws more than 50 years old used the 1899 ordinance establishing the university as wampum keeper as a case in point. With tribal representatives demonstrating before the state capitol, the New York State Assembly passed legislation in 1971 to return five wampum belts to the Onondaga, though not without provisions specifying how the belts would be cared for, which tribal representatives rejected as paternalistic. The wampum remained in the museum vault. During the

Woodland Cultural Centre, Brantford, Ont.

Fig. 2. Return of wampum belts to the Six Nations Confederacy, Grand River Res., Ont., on May 6, 1988. left to right, Chief Bernard Parker (Seneca), Chief Arnold General (Onondaga), Chief Allen McNaughton (Mohawk), Chief Jake Thomas (obscured) (Mohawk), and Chief Harvey Longboat (Cayuga).

mid-1980s Six Nations Confederacy delegations were meeting with representatives of both the New York State Museum, Albany, and the Museum of the American Indian to recover the wampum. In 1988 the 11 wampum belts held by the Museum of the American Indian were transferred to the traditional chiefs of the Six Nations Confederacy on the Grand River Reserve, Ontario (fig. 2) (Fenton 1989:393–397). The next year, amid ceremonies and feasting on their New York reservation, 12 wampum belts held by the State of New York, including four that had been donated by John Thacher's widow in the 1920s, were transferred to the Onondaga Nation with conditions of transfer including that the belts must be stored in a secure fireproof vault under the supervision of the wampum keeper whenever they are not in use and that the belts must never be destroyed, dismantled, or restrung in a way that would change their meaning (M. Sullivan 1992; R.W. Hill 2001, 2001a).

The period from 1890 to 1990 evinced slow but steady escalation of efforts by some indigenous nations to repatriate Native American cultural property from museums and private collections. The Onondaga's unsuccessful attempt to regain the four belts acquired by Thacher made it clear that the courts were generally not sympathetic to such claims in the 1890s. Many of the successful repatriations were based less on legal provisions and more on moral and ethical principles of equity. The resulting agreements often included conditions of transfer that guaranteed the perpetual care of the cultural property. Indian tribes in the United States began to have success in persuading state legislatures to enact provisions protecting Native American graves from desecration. In Greenland, repatriation of cultural property was part of a broader agreement establishing the home rule government and included not only archeological and ethnographic collections but fine arts and archives as well. By the late 1980s, the repatriation issue was actively debated among the museum, archeology, and indigenous communities.

**National Legislation and Policy Reform**

Efforts to enact federal repatriation legislation in the United States began in 1986 with the discovery by Cheyenne religious leaders that the Smithsonian Institution held the remains of thousands of Native American individuals (Spotted Elk 1989). The Cheyenne approached Sen. John Melcher, who introduced the Native American Cultural Preservation Act to resolve the controversy over the disposition of human skeletal remains and artifacts of a sacred nature (U.S. Congress, Senate 1986). This bill, while not enacted, was the first of 26 bills considered by the Senate or House of Representatives from 1986 to 1990 that contained repatriation or grave protection provisions (McKeown and Hutt 2003:155). Testimony at some of the legislative hearings highlighted previous efforts to repatriate wampum and ahayu:da.

Upon discovery of the estimated 18,500 Native American individuals held by the Smithsonian Institution, Sen. Daniel Inouye of Hawaii began exploring the possibility of establishing a memorial on the national mall in Washington, D.C., where the human remains could be interred. Inouye was approached by the board of the Museum of the American Indian in New York, who suggested that the Smithsonian Institution should acquire the financially troubled museum's collections and establish a new museum on the mall (U.S. Congress, Senate 1989:2). In 1987, Inouye introduced a bill to establish the National Museum of the American Indian, as well as to require the Smithsonian to determine the geographical and tribal origin of all skeletal remains of Indians and Alaska Natives in its control and to inter those remains that could not be associated with a specific Indian tribe or group of Alaska Natives or acquired from a specific archeological or burial site in a national memorial (U.S. Congress. Senate 1987). The idea of interring human remains on the national mall was opposed by many Indians (U.S. Congress. Senate 1988b:71), while the Smithsonian Institution considered the repatriation provisions of the bill to be inconsistent with both the Smithsonian's historic mandate for the increase and diffusion of knowledge and the precepts of modern scientific inquiry (Adams 1988a:87–88). The interment provision was deleted from a second version of Inouye's bill, with disposition of unidentifiable human remains being left for consideration by Congress at a later date (U.S. Congress. Senate 1988).

Congressional discussions regarding repatriation served as a catalyst. By late 1988, the museum communities in both the United States and Canada recognized the need to establish a formal dialogue with Native American groups. In November, the Canadian Museums Association cosponsored a national conference with the Assembly of First Nations to address issues raised by the exhibit "The Spirit Sings: Artistic Traditions of Canada's First Peoples," at the Glenbow Museum, Calgary, Alberta. The conference resulted in establishment of a task force to facilitate further discussions between museums and Native groups and the development of appropriate guidance. In 1988 a group of museum and tribal representatives, along with congressional staff, met in Phoenix to initiate a similar dialogue among American museums and Indian tribes.

In the United States, tribal representatives remained adamant that repatriation provisions must be included in any legislation authorizing the establishment of the new Indian museum. Faced with the prospect of having tribes oppose the bill, the Smithsonian agreed to include the repatriation provisions (Barringer 1989; Swisher 1989). When the National Museum of the American Indian Act became law in November 1989, repatriation provisions were included. While the Act was primarily devoted to establishing a new museum dedicated to the history and art of cultures indigenous to the Americas, it also directed the Secretary of the Smithsonian Institution to inventory and identify the origin of human remains and associated funerary objects in the Smithsonian's possession or control and expeditiously return them upon the request of lineal descendants or culturally affiliated Indian tribes and Native Hawaiian organizations (U.S. Public Law 1989). Sen. John McCain (1989) of Arizona undertook to enact similar legislation to expand repatriation requirements to all federal agencies and museums.

In January 1990, the American panel issued its final report (Panel for a National Dialogue on Museum/Native American Relations 1990). The majority of panelists found that the wishes of culturally affiliated Native American groups should be followed regarding the disposition of human remains or other materials. For human remains for which a culturally affiliated Native American group could not be identified, the majority of panelists believed that a process should be developed for their disposition with the permission of Native nations. A minority of panelists felt that scientific and educational values may predominate where cultural affiliation with a present-day Native American group does not exist. The majority of the panel believed that federal legislation was needed to implement their recommendations.

Congress continued work on several bills to extend repatriation provisions to all federal agencies and institutions that receive federal funds. In July 1990, Rep. Morris Udall introduced the Native American Graves Protection and Repatriation Act (NAGPRA) (U.S. Congress, House 1989). The bill provided a detailed set of definitions and processes to facilitate the repatriation of Native American cultural items. The purview of the bill included not only Native American human remains and funerary objects, as had the Museum of the American Indian Act, but also sacred objects and objects of cultural patrimony. Sacred objects were defined to include items that were needed by traditional religious leaders for the practice of traditional religion by present-day adherents. Objects of cultural patrimony were defined to include items of ongoing significance to a Native American group or culture itself, rather than property owned by an individual. The bill included deadlines by which federal agencies and museums would be required to provide documentation of their collections to affiliated Indian tribes and Native Hawaiian organizations. A federal advisory committee would be established to compile an inventory of human remains for which a culturally affiliated Indian tribe or Native Hawaiian organization could not be reasonably determined and make recommendations regarding their disposition. The advisory committee was charged with assisting in the resolution of disputes among lineal descendants, Indian tribes, federal agencies, and museums. A federal agency or museum was required to expeditiously repatriate cultural items meeting the definitions to lineal descendants and culturally affiliated Indian tribes or Native Hawaiian organizations unless it could be shown that the cultural items had been acquired with the voluntary consent of an individual or group with authority of alienation. The federal agency or museum could also temporarily retain cultural items if there was a dispute between multiple claimants or the cultural items were needed to complete an ongoing scientific study determined to be of benefit to the United States. The Act included provisions to protect Native American graves located on federal land, made trafficking of Native American cultural items a federal crime, and gave federal district courts jurisdiction over actions brought alleging violations of the Act (vol. 3:519–523). The bill was ultimately supported by all major museum, archeological, and Native American organizations and was enacted into law (U.S. Public Law 1990). "In the larger scope of history this is a very small thing," Udall commented. "In the smaller scope of conscience, it may be the biggest thing we have ever done" (Udall 1990).

In 1992, the Canadian Task Force Report on Museums and First Peoples issued its final report (Assembly of First Nations and the Canadian Museums Association 1992). The task force had studied the Native American Graves Protection and Repatriation Act and specifically rejected a legalistic approach to repatriation in favor of one based on moral and ethical criteria. The task force recommended that museums report aboriginal human remains in their collections to affiliated First Nations, communities, clans, tribes, and families. The task force agreed that human remains, burial objects, sacred and ceremonial objects, and other cultural objects of ongoing historical, traditional, or cultural import should be returned to First Nations that could demonstrate direct prior cultural connection and ownership to the collections. Museums could retain other remains for scientific investigation for a period agreed upon by the appropriate First Nation, after which the remains would be reinterred. The disposition of human remains that could not be affiliated with a First Nation would be decided through discussion and negotiation with an advisory committee of First Peoples. The task force recommended that museums return sacred and ceremonial objects to a community when they are judged by current legal standards to have been acquired illegally or when, even if obtained legally, they have ongoing historical, traditional, or cultural importance to a Native group or culture. Although the task force called for the Canadian Museums Association to establish a resource-documentation center, with a full-time staff position, to assist museums and First Nations in implementing the recommendations of the task force, none of the recommendations was funded.

The United States and Canada took different paths when faced with similar circumstances of indigenous nations requesting the return of Native American cultural property. The American approach was to formalize the controversy by means of legislation that defined the content and process of repatriation activities. The Canadian approach focused more on encouraging case-by-case negotiations leading to solutions acceptable to all parties (C.E. Bell 1992; C.E. Bell and R.K. Paterson 1999:196). This decision was in part due to the somewhat ambiguous status of aboriginal rights in Canada, which was changed by court cases in the 1990s

(*R* v. *Sparrow* [1990] 3 C.N.L.R 160; *R* v. *Van der Peer* [1996] 4 C.N.L.R. 177). In 1997, the Supreme Court of Canada rendered a decision in *Delgamuukw* v. *British Columbia*, which was brought by the Gitksan and Wet'suwet'en people seeking recognition of their aboriginal title to their traditional territories. Giving little weight to the Gitksan and Wet'suwet'en oral histories in favor of "learned treatises," the trial court ruled that the plaintiffs' aboriginal title to their traditional territories had been extinguished when British Columbia entered the Canadian Federation in 1871. On appeal, the court rejected the trial court's blanket extinguishment of aboriginal title but ruled that while the plaintiffs had unextinguished aboriginal rights, they did not include a right of property or ownership. Finally, the Supreme Court of Canada ordered a new trial, finding that aboriginal title is a right to the land itself and not just site-specific practices, customs, and traditions. The Supreme Court advised that the adjudication of aboriginal claims requires the courts to come to terms with aboriginal oral histories that are often the only record available (*Delgamuukw* v. *British Columbia* ([1997] 3 S.C.R. 1010). These court cases clarified the concept of aboriginal title at a time when many First Nations were negotiating treaties to resolve questions of ownership and use of land and resources and the application of law.

Repatriation of cultural property to indigenous nations has become a global phenomenon (Greenfield 1996). In 2007, the Declaration on the Rights of Indigenous Peoples was adopted by the United Nations Human Rights Council. The declaration affirms that indigenous peoples have the right to manifest, practice, develop, and teach their spiritual and religious traditions, customs, and ceremonies; the right to maintain, protect, and have access in privacy to their religious and cultural sites; the right to the use and control of ceremonial objects; and the right to the repatriation of human remains (United Nations Human Rights Council 2006).

## After 1990

Passage of the National Museum of the American Indian Act and the Native American Graves Protection and Repatriation Act in the United States and the adoption of the Task Force Report on Museums and First Peoples in Canada precipitated a flurry of activity as museums began to assess their collections and consult with tribes and First Nations. Over 1,000 United States institutions distributed summaries of their collections to Indian tribes and Native Hawaiian organizations with nearly as many providing more detailed inventories of Native American human remains and funerary objects (National Park Service 2006a). Though not required by law, many Canadian institutions provided tribes with documentation of their collections (C.E. Bell and R.K. Paterson 1999:196).

Statistics regarding the number of indigenous human remains in museum collections are available online, since each federal agency and museum provided its inventories not only to the affiliated Indian tribes but also to the National Park Service, which posted a summary of the data on its website (National Park Service 2006, 2006a). By 2007, 963 federal agencies and museums had prepared inventories accounting for the remains of 158,008 Native American individuals. Of these, a lineal descendant or culturally affiliated Indian tribe or Native Hawaiian organization had been identified for 41,392 individuals (26%), making those remains eligible for expeditious repatriation. The remaining individuals (74%) were determined to be "culturally unidentifiable," requiring a recommendation from the Secretary of the Interior or the finalization of new regulations in order to effect their disposition to a tribe.

The National Museum of Natural History, Washington, posted collection summaries on its website (National Museum of Natural History 2006a). By 2007, the remains of 18,568 individuals had been identified. Of these, the remains representing 5,435 individuals (29%) had been offered for repatriation to lineal descendants or culturally affiliated Indian tribes or Native Hawaiian organizations (vol. 13:691). By 1996, the National Museum of the American Indian had identified the remains of 524 individuals in its collection, of which 227 (43%) had already been repatriated (Rosoff 1998:34).

Statistics regarding the status of human remains in other institutions are more difficult to obtain. Museums in Canada, Greenland, and Europe, as well as several large American museums with collections from Canada and Greenland, identify the remains of another 13,974 Native American individuals. Compiling these data provides an estimated minimum of 192,636 Native American human remains that were once held by museums in the United States, Canada, Greenland, and Europe. Most human remains were originally excavated or removed from California, the Southwest, Northeast, Southeast, and Alaska.

Tracking actual repatriations is somewhat more difficult since neither NAGPRA nor the National Museum of the American Indian Act requires publication of documentation regarding the transfer of control from museum to Indian tribe. The National Museum of Natural History keeps a running list of repatriations on its website (National Museum of Natural History 2006). By 2007, the remains of 3,591 individuals had been repatriated (fig. 3), with over two-thirds of those being claimed by Alaska Native villages. In the largest of its repatriations, the museum returned the remains of 1,000 individuals to the village of Larsen Bay on Kodiak Island, Alaska. The remains had been excavated between 1931 and 1938 by physical anthropologist Aleš Hrdlička. When the tribe's 1987 request for repatriation was rebuffed, the tribal council enlisted the aid of the attorneys of the Native American Rights Fund to press its case by compiling additional evidence to demonstrate the connection between human remains and present-day tribal members as well as

Carotte, Inc., Kodiak, Alaska.

Fig. 3. Members of the Blackfeet tribe of Mont. smoking a pipe of sweetgrass and sage in a ceremony marking the transfer of remains of their ancestors from the Museum of Natural History, Smithsonian, Washington, D.C. Physical anthropology curator Douglas Ubelaker, who had been working with the Blackfeet for 2 years, determined that 17 bones had been removed from a Blackfeet cemetery in 1892 and received by the Smithsonian in 1898. Casts of the bones were made for study purposes. The elders are, clockwise, Ken Weatherwax (back to the camera), Gordon Belcourt (president of Blackfeet Community College, Browning Mont.), Mike Swims Under, Buster Yellow Kidney, Marvin Weatherwax, Tom Whitford, and Curly Bear Wagner. Harriet Skye (Standing Rock Sioux) of the National Museum of American History is at the far right. Photograph by Laurie Minor-Penland, 1988.

working with congressional offices in the development of repatriation legislation. Representatives of the village also testified before Congress supporting inclusion of repatriation provisions in the National Museum of the American Indian Act (Bray and Killion 1994; Pullar 1994; Sockbeson 1994). The human remains were repatriated to Larsen Bay in 1992 and reburied with a ceremony conducted by Russian Orthodox priests (fig. 4). Substantial numbers of human remains were repatriated by the National Museum of Natural History to the Alaska Native villages of Gambell (410 individuals), Savoonga (400 individuals), Point Hope (354 individuals), Barrow (184 individuals), and Golovin, White Mountain, Elim, and Koyuk (167 individuals).

One of the largest repatriations under NAGPRA occurred in 1999, when the Pueblo of Jemez received remains excavated from the pueblo at Pecos, New Mexico (fig. 5), whose last residents had gone to Jemez in 1838. Between 1915 and 1929, archeologist Alfred Kidder systematically excavated the site, recovering the remains of nearly 2,000 individuals and over 100,000 artifacts. Most of the archeological collections were curated by the Robert S. Peabody Museum of Archaeology in Andover, Massachusetts, while the human remains were sent to the Peabody Museum of Archaeology and Ethnology, Harvard University, in nearby Cambridge.

Further excavations were conducted at Pecos by the Museum of New Mexico, Santa Fe, between 1935 and 1965, with the recovered human remains curated by the Maxwell Museum at the University of New Mexico, Albuquerque. Consultations between the Pueblo and the four museums culminated in a historic reburial of the remains of 2,067 individuals at Pecos National Historical Park. Most of the 1,300 funerary objects that were transferred to the control of the Pueblo of Jemez, along with the remaining portion of the archeological collection from the site, were placed on loan to the park (Britton 1999; Gewertz 1999; National Park Service 2004). Another large repatriation took place in 2006 when the remains of 1,560 individuals and 4,937 associated funerary objects were reburied at Mesa Verde National Park in southwest Colorado. The remains were excavated from sites in the park and the surrounding area. The reburial culminated 13 years of negotiations between the park and 24 Indian tribes (Erickson 2006).

SI Arch., neg. 88-16362-15.

Fig. 4. Reburial of human remains at the Alutiiq Village of Larson Bay, Alaska. Officiating at the ceremony is Russian Orthodox priest Father Peter Kreta, standing closest to the trench. The remains were repatriated by the Smithsonian Institution, National Museum of Natural History, Washington, D.C. Photograph by Marion Owen, 1992.

Fig. 5. A clay bowl, one of many objects from the Pueblo of Jemez being returned to Raymond Gachupin, governor of Jemez Pueblo, left, and Ruben Sando, governor of Pecos Pueblo, right, by Dr. Rubie Watson, director of the Peabody Museum of Archaeology and Ethnology at Harvard. Photograph by Julia Malakie, Cambridge, Mass., 1999.

While large repatriations of human remains have been newsworthy, the efforts of the Haida of coastal British Columbia are more typical of most North American tribes. Between 1993 and 2004, the combined repatriation committees from the Haida villages of Skidegate and Old Massett visited museums across Canada and the United States, eventually repatriating all 441 Canadian Haida ancestral remains held by North American institutions (Vassallo 2005:1). Similar efforts are underway by many Indian tribes and First Nations (National Park Service 2006b; Bell and Napoleon 2007; Bell and Paterson 2007; Fine-Dare 2002; Mihesuah 2000).

Difference in legal traditions have presented complications to international repatriation. In 1989, Montana artist and collector Bob Scriver sold Blackfeet material to the Provincial Museum of Alberta, Edmonton (Stepney 1990). The buyer and the timing of the sale seemed to have been driven by the impending passage of NAGPRA, which would require an American museum recipient to give parts of the collection to the Blackfeet. The sale and publication of a catalog sparked a generational debate among the Blackfeet (W.E. Farr 1993; Noble 2002; White Wolf 2003). In 2000, the provincial legislature passed the First Nations Sacred Ceremonial Objects Repatriation Act to "harmonize the role museums play in the preservation of human heritage with the aspirations of First Nations to support traditional values" (Province of Alberta 2000). The first agreement under the act directed the repatriation of items vital to the practice of ceremonies to the Blood, Peigan Nation, and Siksika Nation of Canada, who, together with the American Blackfeet, comprised the Blackfoot Confederacy. Some bundles in the Scriver collection were transferred to Blackfeet traditional religious leaders (Johnsrude 2002; Hungry Wolf 2006). American museums repatriated bundles to the Blackfeet, acting on behalf of the Canadian members of the Blackfoot Confederacy (Federal Register 1994a, 1996, 1996a, 2000, 2000a).

Some Indian tribes have specifically chosen not to claim culturally affiliated human remains, often for cultural reasons such as proscriptions against handling the dead or lack of appropriate ceremonies for the reburial of unknown individuals. In 1990, the Zuni Tribal Council issued a resolution explaining that human remains that had been excavated and removed from the ancestral Zuni homeland had been desecrated to such an extent that there was no adequate way to reverse it. The council requested that ancestral Zuni remains be retained in museum collections to be cared for with respect (Ferguson, Anyon, and Ladd 1996:266–268). When contacted by the National Museum of the American Indian to repatriate remains, the Zuni requested that they be transferred to the National Museum of Natural History for appropriate care and curation (R.W. Hill 1996:73; Rosoff 1998:35). Other tribes have delayed repatriation of human remains because they do not have an appropriate ceremony to rebury ancestors that were removed from their original gravesite (D. O'Brien 2004).

Though individual repatriations and reburials of human remains have in some cases represented hundreds or thousands of individuals, claims for sacred objects and objects of cultural patrimony have been much more limited. By 2006, Indian tribes had made NAGPRA claims for 3,570 sacred objects, 281 objects of cultural patrimony, and 709 cultural items fitting both the sacred object and cultural patrimony categories (National Park Service 2006a). While the National Museum of the American Indian estimated that nearly 25,000 items in its collection might fall within the categories of funerary object, sacred object, or object of cultural patrimony, less than 10 percent of that total had actually been repatriated (National Museum of the American Indian 2006). The Museum of Natural History returned 89,848 funerary objects.

Some tribes were focused on repatriation of particular types of cultural items. Within weeks of NAGPRA's passage, the chairman of the Hopi Tribe had contacted the Heard Museum in Phoenix to indicate the tribe's intention to repatriate the *Katsina kwaatsi*, literally 'kachina friends', in the museum's collection (Clemmer 1995:287). Usually identified as "masks" by non-Hopi, the *Katsina kwaatsi* are living entities, and Hopi religious practitioners had repeatedly visited the Heard collections to provide them with the required religious care. In 1997, the Heard Museum agreed to repatriate 37 *Katsina kwaatsi* to the Hopi Tribe (*Federal Register* 1997). The Hopi Tribe identified more than 400 cultural items in museum collections that might meet the definition of sacred object or object of cultural patrimony, and 60 such items were returned to the tribe by 2001 (Loma'omvaya 2001:32).

The Six Nations Confederacy announced its policy on the status, sale, exhibition, and return of wooden and corn husk masks in 1995. The policy described the masks as representations of the shared power of the original medicine beings that are essential to the spiritual and emotional well-being of the Six Nations communities. The medicine mask society at each reservation has authority over the use of masks for individual and community needs. Individuals making masks for commercial purposes were advised to cease their activities. Since only the Grand Council of Chiefs had authority to alienate a mask, and such sanction had never been given, all museums, art galleries, historical societies, universities, commercial enterprises, foreign governments, and individuals were asked to return masks in their possession (Grand Council of the Haudenosaunee 1995). The large collection at the National Museum of the American Indian was made a priority. In November 1998 the Museum repatriated 450 masks to the Six Nations (Jemison 2001).

In 1999, the Cape Fox Corporation (Tlingit) filed repatriation claims with the Peabody Museum of Archaeology and Ethnology in Cambridge, Massachusetts; Cornell University in Ithaca, New York; Burke Museum in Seattle; Field Museum in Chicago; and National Museum of the American Indian in Washington. The requests were for the return of objects of cultural patrimony, including totem poles, house posts, and house fronts, all with elaborately carved clan crests, that had been taken in 1899 when the Edward H. Harriman scientific expedition visited the village. Assuming the village had been abandoned, the expedition members, including naturalist John Muir and photographer Edward Curtis, loaded items from the village onto their boat and sailed away. In fact, the cultural items remained the property of the village clans. Repatriation was scheduled to occur in conjunction with a centennial retracing of the expedition's path (Litwin 2005).

While the Hopi, Iroquois, and Tlingit have been readily able to use the statutory definitions of sacred object or object of cultural patrimony to reclaim cultural property in American museums, the statutory structure has proved more problematic for other tribes. Each tribe must negotiate its own fit between the statutory definitions and traditional concepts of property. Internal negotiations over the statute are also inevitable. The Makah Tribe in Washington State repatriated only human remains (Tweedie 2002). Discussions have arisen regarding tribal rights to repatriate recordings of ceremonial songs of an extremely sensitive nature (Farrer 1994). Folklorist Barre Toelken (1998) wrestled with the disposition of over 40 years of original Navajo field recordings that he made with the expressed agreement that they would only be played during the season in which they could properly be performed. The prospect of an archivist playing the tapes at the wrong time or year, or saying some words out loud in the wrong situation led the widow of Toelken's Navajo collaborator to request that the tapes be given to her. In 1997, he boxed up over 60 hours of tapes and sent them to the widow, where they were presumably destroyed.

On the heals of the *Delgamuukw* decision, Canadian federal and provincial governments and First Nations began to include repatriation provisions in several comprehensive land claims agreements (Lee 1997). Comprehensive agreements with the Nisga'a and Labrador Eskimo have identified specific artifacts in museum collections that were to be transferred to the respective First Nations and committed the federal and provincial governments to assist in providing the tribes with access to artifacts in other public and private collections (Nisga'a Final Agreement 1999; Labrador Inuit Comprehensive Land Claims Agreement 2003). Tom Hill, cochair of the Task Force on Museum and First Nations, believed that despite the pitfalls of legislation, repatriation agreements were moving in that direction (Bolton 2004:23).

Objects have been repatriated to Greenland from other countries, including perhaps the oldest kayaks in the world from Holland, a large archeological collection from Norway, and ethnographic documentation from France (Thorleifsen 2006). In 1993, the American Museum of Natural History in New York returned the remains of four Polar Eskimos. In 1897, Arctic explorer Robert E. Peary had arrived in New York with six Eskimo passengers, including Qisuk and his young son Minik. The six were initially housed at the American Museum of Natural History, where they were interviewed by anthropologists Franz Boas and Alfred L. Kroeber. Within a year, four Eskimos had died, one had returned to Greenland, and the orphaned Minik was adopted by a museum employee. The museum performed a funeral for Qisuk but, unbeknownst to Minik, his father's remains were not buried but were added to the museum collections. The subterfuge was discovered by the press in 1907, but the museum was unmoved by Minik's requests for the return of his father's remains. The story was again brought to light in *Give Me My Father's Body: The Life of Minik, the New York Eskimo* (Harper 1986). Bending to public opinion, the museum contacted Greenland authorities and eventually the remains of the four Polar Eskimos were buried in the Qaanaaq village cemetery, Greenland (E. Carpenter 1997; George 2000).

While NAGPRA and the Task Force Report on Museums and First Peoples recommendations were being developed, some argued that repatriation would be the harbinger of the end of archeology in North America. However, indigenous nations have turned to archeologists, anthropologists, historians, and other professionals to better understand aspects of their own history (Dongoske 1996; Ferguson, Watkins, and Pullar 1997). In 1999, a group of hunters found frozen human remains at the edge of a glacier in Tatshenshini-Alsek Park in far northern British Columbia, within the traditional lands of the Champagne and Aishihik Nations, Southern Tutchone-speaking people of southern Yukon Territory and northern British Columbia. The park was comanaged by tribal and provincial officials (Tatshenshini-Alsek Park 1996). The tribal council decided to allow full documentation of the frozen remains and associated objects. Dried fish and fish scales found with the remains indicated a coastal origin, and the spruce root hat found with the body was of a Tlingit style. A gopher-fur robe appeared to have come from the Canadian interior. The human remains were named Kwäday Dän T'sìnchį 'person of long ago that was found' in the Southern Tutchone language. Carbon dates from the hat and robe indicated the materials were gathered between A.D. 1415 and 1445 (vol. 3:222–223). DNA analysis indicated that the remains belonged to haplogroup A (vol. 3:846). About 300 members of the Champagne and Aishihik Nations and Tlingit groups volunteered DNA samples to compare with samples taken from the remains (Chandonnet 2001; C. Brown 2001). The remains were eventually cremated and spread over the discovery site, while the associated objects remain available for study (Bridge 2004).

By 2007, repatriation of cultural property was a major focus of many, though not all, Indian tribes (fig. 6). Several important issues remained to be resolved. The first concerned the disposition of Native American human remains for which no lineal descendant or culturally affiliated Indian tribe could be identified. In the early 1990s, the National Museum of the American Indian buried the remains of 31 undocumented and unaffiliated individuals at a tribal cemetery in upstate New York. The Museum board of trustees wanted these individuals to have a decent place of rest. The burial ceremony was conducted by tribal members who agreed to act as guardians for the remains as they returned to the earth (Rosoff 1998:36).

NAGPRA included language directing a federal advisory committee to compile an inventory of culturally unidentifiable human remains and make recommendations regarding a process for their disposition. The inventory of culturally unidentifiable human remains contained information regarding 118,400 individuals in federal agency and museum collections (National Park Service 2007). The federal advisory committee issued its recommendations regarding the disposition of culturally unidentifiable human remains in 2000 (Native American Graves Protection and Repatriation Review Committee 2000). The committee recommended that unidentifiable remains be treated with respect and that their disposition might be based on a range of cultural relationships or geographic affiliation. The committee recognized that appropriate disposition solutions might result from joint recommendations of museums and claimant tribes or through the recommendations of regional consortia. In 2007, draft regulations implementing the committee's recommendations were developed and published.

An unexpected consequence of repatriation was the discovery that some cultural property had been treated with potentially harmful substances while held in museum collections. Pesticides have long been used by museum staffs to protect leather, feathers, organic paints, fur, or grass items in the collections. The most common pesticides used were arsenic trioxide, mercuric chloride, and dichlorodiphenyl trichlorethane (DDT). All three have potentially severe health consequences. In 1998, the Six Nations Confederacy repatriated 455 medicine masks from the National Museum of the American Indian. The joy of the return was overshadowed by the news that some of the masks had tested positive for the presence of arsenic. Community members from the Six Nations Reserve in Ontario declined to take home their masks (Jemison 2001). Similarly, in 1999, the Hopi tribe tested three repatriated cultural items and found that two evidenced high levels of arsenic. The Hopi tribal chairman enacted a moratorium on further physical returns of cultural items to the reservation, though transfer of control of items to the Hopi tribe has continued (Loma'omvaya 2001).

In a survey of Indian tribes in the United States, most respondents were adamant that Native American human remains should not be stored indefinitely in museum collections and that repatriation was essential. However, many Indian tribes expressed ambivalence about reburial and were unsure of how to deal with disturbed remains. Many tribes also believed that scientific analysis of human remains may be useful and necessary (T.R. Hall and J. Wolfley 2003).

The benefits of repatriation to indigenous communities have perhaps best been described by the Skidegate Repatriation and Cultural Committee from British Columbia:

Bringing our ancestors home is a large and long process, requiring the support and efforts of the entire Haida communities. School children and volunteers make button blankets and weave cedar bark mats to wrap our ancestors in. Artists teach apprentices how to make traditional bentwood burial boxes and paint Haida designs on them. The Haida language has to be learned by more and more people so that the ancestors can be spoken and prayed to. Elders and cultural historians teach traditional songs, dances and rituals. Many more people have begun to look towards and embrace traditions that until Repatriation began, only a handful of people participated in. And perhaps most important, after each ceremony,

AP Images.

Fig. 6. Mark Jacobs, Jr., wearing a Killer Whale hat during a repatriation ceremony in Sitka, Alaska. The headdress, carved by Dick Yeilnaawu of the Raven House of the Deisheetaan (Beaver clan) of Tlingit in Angoon in the late 19th century, was sold around 1904 by a clan member. It was given to the clan by the National Museum of Natural History, Smithsonian. Photograph by James Poulson, 2005.

436

one can feel that the air has been cleared, that spirits are resting, that our ancestors are at peace, and one can see that healing is visible on the faces of the Haida community (Skidegate Repatriation and Cultural Committee 2004).

The long-term effects of repatriation to indigenous communities are more difficult to predict. Richard Hill, Sr. (Tuscarora), has put it most eloquently when speaking of the return of the wampum. "It has taken us one hundred years to undo a cultural crime committed against our people. As long as we remember our cultural mandate, to consider the seventh generation to come, those wampum will never leave our possession again. Our very future as a people rests within those tiny shell beads" (R.W. Hill 2001:136).

# The Global Indigenous Movement

RONALD NIEZEN

## Indigenous Transnationalism

The global movement of indigenous peoples involves transnational networks of peoples and organizations dedicated to protecting those who are the original inhabitants of distinct territories, who now live politically and economically on the margins of nation-states. Their networks and institutional supports within the United Nations system developed so quickly in the last decades of the twentieth century that both indigenous leaders and human rights experts have struggled to keep pace with them. In the first meeting of the Permanent United Nations Forum for Indigenous Issues in 2002 it was found that there were so many initiatives on behalf of indigenous peoples in the United Nations (U.N.) system that one of the first orders of business of the Permanent Forum was to make them known to those indigenous peoples and organizations that might benefit from them. These initiatives included information gathering on threats to indigenous peoples' health and survival by the World Health Organization and the Pan American Health Organization; processes for pursuing grievances through the International Labor Organization; human rights standard setting by the Commission on Human Rights and the Organization of American States; and the establishment of a position for a Special Rapporteur on the human rights and fundamental freedoms of indigenous people under the auspices of the Commission on Human Rights, whose task it is to investigate and report on conditions in indigenous communities worldwide, with particular attention to state compliance with human rights norms and standards.

Parallel with U.N. initiatives, the numbers and influence of indigenous representatives and organizations have expanded. Numerical estimates of the global population of those who can be considered indigenous vary enormously, from roughly 200 to 600 million (Baer 2000:223), with 370 million in 70 countries suggested by the U.N. (United Nations Permanent Forum for Indigenous Issues 2007). As the variability of these figures indicates, population estimates are not accurate measures of the influence of indigenous peoples as participants in a transnational movement. A more insightful way to consider the growth of the global indigenous movement can be found in the participation in transnational processes. The 1982 inaugural meeting of the United Nations Working Group on Indigenous Populations included roughly 30 indigenous participants, while in later years these meetings have consistently brought together approximately 1,000 delegates, making it the largest forum sponsored by the Commission on Human Rights. The rapid development of indigenous representation is also reflected in the rise in numbers of officially sanctioned nongovernmental organizations (NGOs) representing indigenous peoples or organizations. In 1985 there were eight indigenous nongovernmental organizations possessing consultative status with the United Nation's Economic and Social Council; by 1995 this number had grown to 14, and in 2005 it had jumped to 42, of which 16 represented Native North Americans, including the Assembly of First Nations, Grand Council of the Crees, Inuit Circumpolar Conference; Métis National Council, National Congress of American Indians, and the Native American Rights Fund. This degree of representation and recognition of indigenous peoples in the institutions of global governance developed suddenly, with most new initiatives being established during the last decades of the twentieth century.

The growth in numbers of NGOs representing indigenous interests at the United Nations runs parallel to the global currency of the term "indigenous peoples" and a corresponding awareness of the common history and interests of those marginalized and dispossessed peoples the term has come to represent. The ways that the public imagines those whose collective identity is grounded in subsistence ways of life, and the ways that they are themselves defining and defending their distinctiveness, have gone through dramatic changes, many of which center upon legal use of the term "indigenous peoples." The International Labor Organization Convention stated: "Peoples in independent countries are regarded as indigenous on account of their descent from the populations which inhabited the country, or a geographical region to which the country belongs, at the time of conquest or colonization or the establishment of present state boundaries and who, irrespective of their legal status, retain some or all of their own social, economic, cultural and political institutions" (ILO 1989). A definition more widely invoked in human rights circles is from a report by José Martínez Cobo (1987:48): "Indigenous communities, peoples and nations are those which, having a historical continuity with pre-invasion and pre-colonial societies that developed on their territories, consider themselves distinct from other sectors of the societies now prevailing in those territories, or parts of them. They form at present nondominant sectors of society and are determined to preserve, develop and transmit to future generations their ancestral territories and their ethnic identity, as the basis of their continued existence as peoples, in accordance with their own cultural patterns, social institutions and legal systems."

In a sense, the ownership of the term "indigenous" has since the 1980s changed hands from those who formally define the concepts and priorities of human rights and international organizations to those representatives of societies marginal to nation-states who have redefined and repositioned themselves to take up the designation "indigenous" as a source of political aspiration and strategy. This is part of a process in which claims of distinct status by those on the margins of nation-states are asserted through conceptual reverse engineering, through the creative use of dominant societies' terminologies and institutions of emancipation. The international movement of indigenous peoples is thus associated with many efforts by self-defining peoples or nations within nation-states to take control of their identity and, above all, to control the legal foundations of their collective being through assertions of "nationhood" or self-determination.

What are the more general background conditions that have made it possible for so many distinct peoples to take up the bureaucratically ponderous word "indigenous" as a source of identity and then to shape it into the legal category that is the focus of numerous human rights, health, and development initiatives in the U.N. system? What are the challenges faced by indigenous representatives as they engage in efforts to represent their people through transnational processes? And what social changes and challenges accompany these efforts? These questions point to unprecedented strategies of transnational resistance and collective representation inherent in the indigenous peoples' movement. But there are also significant antecedents to efforts by indigenous peoples to seek redress of grievances through the bureaucratic and legal mechanisms of nation-states, which situate the indigenous peoples' movement in a more complete historical perspective.

## Precursors

If the global indigenous movement seems to have burst onto the scene with little or no precedent in the 1980s, that impression has likely been reinforced by historical and ethnological conventions, which long downplayed the legal sophistication of "primitive" or tribal societies on the margins of states or empires. An emphasis on the pristine, picturesque, and exotic qualities of those who represented human difference long concealed from view these peoples' drive to defend their cherished values and better the conditions of their lives using almost any political tool at their disposal, including the quintessentially nonexotic tools of literacy and law.

There is a sense in which the indigenous peoples' movement of the twenty-first century is consistent with efforts in previous centuries by conquered and colonized peoples under the rule of expanding states and empires to express their grievances to the highest levels of the power that dominated them in the hopes that some form of recognition and redress might come their way. The strategy of petitioning a colonial, imperial, or national power that has established dominance and control from a remote capital follows the logic that if one cannot deal successfully with those unjust and unsympathetic local agencies or representatives with whom one is immediately negotiating, then it still remains possible to appeal to that remote higher power to which one's oppressors are, perhaps, answerable.

Petitioning the British monarch was a long-recognized strategy by those under British colonial rule, a strategy that usually resulted in nothing more than a polite hearing. On a few occasions, however, measures were taken to redress grievances, at least often enough to make these petitions worthwhile. In 1704, for example, the Mohegan sachem Owaneco submitted a formal petition to the English Crown that complained of his peoples' dispossession of lands at the hands of the Connecticut colonial government. In 1705 an imperial commission established by Queen Anne found that the lands in dispute had been unjustly appropriated and should be retuned to the Mohegans, a finding that placed the Connecticut authorities in a more tenuous position as they attempted to act upon plans for control of territory (Calloway and Salisbury 2003). This decision indicates a willingness on the part of the Crown to consider the presumably conquered Indians in their colonies as "peoples" with distinct rights to their reserved lands (Den Ouden 2005:1). At the same time, it indicates a readiness on the part of conquered peoples to subvert the claims of colonial powers to authority over them and their lands (Den Ouden 2005:146).

Beginning with the League of Nations in 1918 (which lacked the formal membership of the United States) and culminating in the institutions of the United Nations after 1945, the strategy of petitioning to a higher power than one's immediate oppressor could be applied in response to the unjust actions of nation-states. An effort in 1923 by Chief Levi General (Cayuga Deskahe) to seek a hearing at the League of Nations can be seen as a significant precursory event in the development of the indigenous peoples' movement. General traveled to Geneva, accompanied by a delegation of Six Nations representatives and a lawyer, in an effort to draw attention to the government of Canada's efforts to unilaterally restructure the political organization of the Six Nations. In the early 1920s Canada was promoting a system of elected chiefs and councils, in opposition to the informally recognized body of hereditary leaders, of which General was a leading representative. The central point of contention that he hoped to bring to the attention of the world community was in broad outline similar to the more contemporary concerns of indigenous peoples: the traditional leadership of the Six Nations wished to exercise sovereignty on its own terms, in opposition to the state's drive toward constitutional uniformity, realized through usurpation of the Six Nation's land and reduction of its political control over a diminished territory.

In response to Canada's denial of the legitimacy of the Six Nations' hereditary leadership (vol. 4:210), General made an offer to participate in the League of Nations, not as a powerless minority or tribe but as a representative of a nation, of equal standing with other members of the League: "The Six Nations are ready to accept for the purpose of this dispute, if invited, the obligation of membership in the League of Nations upon such just conditions as the Council may prescribe, having due regard to our slender resources" (Ames 1923:4). When the League did not take this suggestion seriously, General made use of his public appeal as an Indian in Europe, frequently appearing with his delegation dressed in buckskin and an eagle feather bonnet, finding his way into newspapers and newsreel footage, conforming in some ways with the popular image of the Indian (Niezen 2003:31–36).

Even though the Canadian and British governments were successful in obstructing General's efforts to get a hearing before the League of nations, General did manage to persuade the mayor of Geneva to convene a meeting of sympathetic states at the City Hall, where he was finally able to give his address. Not long after this, General was informed by an official letter from Canada that the hereditary body he represented had been replaced by a newly elected tribal council. He left Geneva in 1924 in low spirits and failing health and died in Six Nations territory in the United States a few months after his return (Rostkowski 1995:3).

A very general point of similarity between petitions to the monarch or international assemblies and the rise of indigenous representation in international forums can be found in the way that those threatened by loss of land and way of life acted to shape and make full use of their legal entitlements. These entitlements were built into the very systems of governance that were the sources of their oppression. A centralized yet far-reaching system of government provided the possibility of remedy through appeal to a level of authority beyond self-interested, unjust local or regional levels of government. These petitions were oriented toward specific grievances and aspirations and did not embody the broadly cooperative, transnational dimension of the contemporary indigenous peoples' movement. Awareness among indigenous groups of the global nature of the common kinds of oppression they faced developed significantly only through the expansion of networks of organization and communications in the second half of the twentieth century (Niezen 2000:123).

General's unsuccessful effort to make a formal appeal to the League of Nations indicates in particular that the readiness of aboriginal leaders to pursue their grievances through legal processes has been more historically constant that might be initially supposed. The main reason for the relative infrequency of such efforts and for their relative lack of success has more to do with the lack of receptiveness of colonial and international regimes of governance and law than with the legal abilities or political sophistication of peoples on the margins of states, empires, or systems of international governance. This lack of institutional receptiveness was to change with the development of human rights and the global movement toward decolonization in the second half of the twentieth century.

## Human Rights and Global Governance

The ability of indigenous leaders to successfully lobby at international forums developed more fully in the post-World War II era of global governance, with its greater openness to the rights of minorities in the wake of the Holocaust, and eventually with the process of decolonization leading to an elaboration of the collective rights of peoples. A collective orientation to human rights is embodied, for example, in the first article of the 1966 International Covenant on Civil and Political Rights, which declares that all peoples have the right to self-determination and to pursue freely their economic, social, and cultural development. The use of the term "indigenous peoples" in the context of the rights of peoples emerged in this period. During the first half of the twentieth century, the term "indigenous" most commonly described plants and animals native to a particular geographical region and was rarely used to designate human groups with a long-standing occupation of a particular territory. In international legal circles the term "native" usually designated the original inhabitants of colonial territories, while "Indian" was used to designate the descendants of the first inhabitants of the Americas. The legal language of "indigenous peoples" was established in the late twentieth century.

An early legal use of the term "indigenous" in reference to an original human society occurred in the International Labor Organization's (1953) report *Indigenous Peoples: Living and Working Conditions of Aboriginal Populations in Independent Countries.* The concerns reflected in this report were later given a legal foundation with the Organization's Convention No. 107 Concerning the Protection and Integration of Indigenous and Other Tribal and Semi-Tribal Populations in Independent Countries, first put into effect in 1957. This instrument was elaborated without the direct participation of self-representing indigenous peoples. In fact, one of its primary goals was to integrate or assimilate those seen to be left on the margins of nation-states, unable to benefit from the opportunities of industrial society. Convention No. 107 embodied the rather contradictory objectives of protecting those identifiable populations suffering from poor education and poverty, but at the same time doing so with the goal of integrating them into the dominant cultures and polities of nation-states or "independent countries" from which they had been unfairly excluded.

The assimilationist goal of Convention No. 107 in the historical context of decolonization soon lost much of its legitimacy, while the identification of a broad category of marginalized "indigenous" peoples or populations endured. Eventually the term "indigenous," once used to designate those living without the advantages of civilization, acquired subjects who used it to designate themselves. Starting with efforts in the 1970s to orient human rights toward the struggle against racism and, by extension, the dispossession of the Indians of the Americas of their land, the term acquired a significant number of people from many parts of the world who saw it as descriptive of themselves and their communities.

The United Nations added to the scope of participation of indigenous nongovernmental organizations in international concerns when it declared the years from 1973 to 1982 the Decade for Action to Combat Racism and Racial Discrimination. Under the auspices of this Decade, the Special NGO Committee on Human Rights established a Sub-Committee on Racism, Racial Discrimination, Apartheid and Decolonization, the principal task of which was to host a series of conferences. As part of this initiative, The Women's International League for Peace and Freedom was instrumental in creating an international space and a new sociopolitical reality for indigenous peoples when it organized the 1977 International NGO Conference on Discrimination against Indigenous Populations in the Americas, held at the Palais des Nations in Geneva. This pivotal meeting assembled representatives from more than 50 international NGOs, from some 60 indigenous peoples from North and South America, as well as observers from 40 member states of the United Nations. The International Indian Treaty Council, one of the first indigenous peoples organizations to be granted consultative status to the U.N.'s Economic and Social Council, organized the meeting's Native American delegation. Edith Ballantyne (1977:1), chairwoman of the conference, did not overestimate the significance of this conference when she stated that it represented "the emerging ability of the indigenous peoples, in a number of regions, to organize themselves, to make their situation known and to state their needs and aspirations through their own spokesmen to the national and international communities."

From this point forward, the participation of indigenous representatives in international meetings on issues of their immediate concern became part of the way business in the Human Rights Commission was conducted. An NGO meeting of the United Nations focusing specifically on indigenous populations and the land took place in Geneva in 1981. In 1982 the U.N. Working Group on Indigenous Populations was established, bringing together indigenous representatives from around the world in annual gatherings; and in 1989 an International Conference of NGOs on discrimination against indigenous peoples in the Americas declared the right of indigenous nations to submit to international law

and to be recognized as nations, "so long as they observe the fundamental conditions of every nation, as follows: (a) have a permanent population; (b) possess a defined territory; (c) have the capacity to relate to other nations" (France cited in Ramos 2002:254). Numerous meetings bringing together representatives of indigenous NGOs with consultative status in the U.N.'s Economic and Social Council took place through initiatives sponsored in the 1995–2004 International Decade of the World's Indigenous People, such as the Permanent U.N. Forum on Indigenous Issues.

The groundswell of indigenous participation in U.N. meetings provided impetus toward the development of international treaties that reflected the experience and aspirations expressed by indigenous spokespeople. From 1985 to 1993, the Working Group of the Sub-Commission on the Prevention of Discrimination and Protection of Minorities brought together a body of five international experts to collate and assess a massive collection of living and historical testimony of indigenous peoples from around the world, with the goal of developing a Draft Declaration on the Rights of Indigenous Peoples (Corbett 1996:1).

In 1989 the International Labor Organization provided a legal corrective to its earlier assimilationist orientation toward indigenous peoples with the ratification of Convention No. 169 Concerning Indigenous and Tribal Peoples in Independent Countries. This was the first international instrument oriented towards enhancing the ability of indigenous peoples to protect and develop their customs and institutions on their own terms. The shift in the orientation of international law reflected in Convention No. 169 would likely not have occurred without the active participation of indigenous representatives in international meetings. The term "indigenous peoples" as used in international law has since served as a starting point for claims of distinct identity and rights based upon the principles of original occupation of land and pursuit of traditional ways of life (Anaya 1996; Thornberry 2002).

Lee Swepston, who was active in drafting Convention No. 169, recalls that indigenous representatives from Canada, the United States, Australia, New Zealand, and northern Europe (namely, the Saami), were the most effective participants in negotiating the language and principles needed to draft the new legal instrument. "'Northern' indigenous peoples' representatives," Swepston observes, "were the most articulate and the best able to deal with the complex ILO structure, new to all the NGOs. They dominated, and were resented by, the few organizations of indigenous peoples from developing countries—the 'south'— who could afford to come to the Conference" (Swepston 1990:226). Much of the reason for this disparity can be attributed to the wider political settings in which indigenous peoples from various parts of the world were situated. The civil rights movement centered in the United States had a ramifying effect throughout the liberal democracies of "the North," encouraging Indian and aboriginal activists to organize and take up political causes, locally and nationally. *441*

At the same time, military dictatorships in "the South" were still actively repressing indigenous organizations, making it difficult for participants to travel to international conferences, and leaving them with a diminished organizational and legal capacity when they did.

The indigenous peoples' movement became truly global only after the transformations of world politics in the 1990s. The end of axial competition between the United States and the Soviet Union in 1989 made possible the emergence of newly (re)constituted indigenous peoples and organizations from the former Soviet bloc. At the same time, many states in the developing world were no longer so persistent or successful in creating obstacles to indigenous peoples' organizational development and transnational networking. The resurgence of indigenous movements in Latin America, for example, can be traced to the decline of military dictatorships with interests in maintaining loyalty to the state and defending constitutional uniformity and territorial control by all means possible. By the mid-1990s, with the momentum of the indigenous peoples' movement well established, African and Asian representatives of indigenous peoples had become prominent in U.N. meetings. African and Asian indigenous representatives seem to have been encouraged by the simple argument that the conclusion of struggles for national independence by those who were formerly colonized did not succeed in liberating those peoples who continue to depend on forests and pastures for their subsistence, whose land is expropriated by dominant groups in new nation-states, while those who have long depended on it are removed and left without economic alternatives, on the margins of nation-states that care little for their knowledge and cultures (Niezen 2003:75).

Since the 1990s, assisted enormously by the availability of the internet as a resource for information, publicity, and communication, several thousand NGOs concerned with the promotion of indigenous rights have been established. The kind of NGO referred to in international circles as the Indigenous Peoples Organization (or IPO) developed in immense variety in terms of the geography and culture of origin, but with the common denominators of attachments to subsistence economies and distinct territories, state-sponsored histories of dispossession and cultural assimilation and, of course, indigenous identity.

The World Council of Churches is an organization with particular significance for the indigenous peoples' movement. It participated in the initiatives of the 1970s and has since been actively involved in promoting the organizations and ideas associated with indigenous peoples. Gatherings of indigenous representatives at the Council headquarters in Geneva have regularly taken place during the days prior to formal U.N. meetings; and with the functionally necessary provision of translation services, these preliminary assemblies of the indigenous caucus have been instrumental in creating a space in which indigenous delegates define their common concerns, strategies, and identities. The Council's Justice, Peace, and Creation team has been involved in human rights standard setting at the U.N., including the Working Group on Indigenous Populations, the Inter-sessional Working Group on a Draft Declaration on the Rights of Indigenous Peoples, and the establishment of the Permanent Forum on Indigenous Issues. More than this, it has promoted discussion of issues that combine spiritual and ecological concerns. Following from the premise that the world is experiencing an "accelerating deterioration of the global economic and political situation," the Council has promoted a "dialogue of Indigenous spiritualities," between and among traditional elders and representatives of other faiths (with an emphasis on Christianity), in an effort "to identify common gifts and understandings and encourage healing and reconciliation with all creation." The World Council of Churches has therefore been engaged in both the human rights concerns surrounding such issues as intellectual property, sustainable development, biodiversity and climate change as well as the promotion of ideas about the distinct spirituality and environmental ethic of indigenous peoples, affirming their "ancestral knowledge, identity and contributions to caring for the earth and future generations, while challenging the wider society to follow their example" (WCC 2000).

Stan McKay (Cree) writes of a global link between indigenous peoples based on an awareness of "our relationship to the land and water of our territories . . . [and] the experience of having been driven out of our places or denied access to that which is ours for life" (McKay 1999). Te Rua Winiata, a Maori from New Zealand, articulates her distinct indigenous identity as following from a holistic approach to life, connected to "recognition of the relationship between the earth and the sky and all that comes between . . . I do not own the land nor do I have dominion over the land. I understand that my relationship with creation means that I have a responsibility to care for Papatuanuku (earth) who provides me with the resources I need for life" (Winiata 1999).

As some of the views expressed by the World Council of Churches suggest, the spectacular rise in the number of NGOs representing indigenous peoples or other cultural and minority interests is largely driven by the views and activities of intermediaries who are excluded from recognized membership in the communities on behalf of which they struggle, but who are motivated by appreciation or longing for the ways of life of those seen to be living closer to the natural world. The sympathies and interests of a wider public have bolstered the ambitions and political influence of those with previously unrecognized aspirations toward collective self-determination. The elaboration of distinct cultural identities, formed around the indigenous peoples' concept, is a strategy of cultural survival that makes use of lobbying—influencing public opinion and political decisions through organized media campaigns. The indigenous peoples' movement is thus closely associated with a rise of cultural activism, partly reflected in growing numbers of nongovernmental organizations and culturally oriented internet sites, commonly directed toward a global audience of cultural spectators (Niezen 2005:538).

The visibility of indigenous lobbying is in large part due to a growing public receptiveness toward the environmental and spiritual wisdom that often accompanies indigenous cultural representation. To many sympathizers, indigenous peoples incarnate values and goals seemingly beyond the reach of regular channels of political participation: environmental stewardship, an unhurried existence, social harmony, spiritual unity with the natural world, a secure sense of social place, and in general the survival of fragile ways of life that combine oral sophistication and virtuosity with simplicity of livelihood.

## The Indigenous Experience

Scholars who specialize in the colonial history of the Americas regularly point to the widely varying motivations, attitudes, and policies associated with different European powers in the exercise of their expansionist ambitions. "Contemporary struggles by indigenous communities to preserve themselves have taken distinct political directions in different regions of the Americas. These directions . . . derive from national legal systems that are the heirs to separate colonial cultural and legal traditions" (Seed 1995:15).

The scholarly emphasis on the particularity of historical experience is in contrast to the loose definition of indigenous peoples and the relative openness with which indigenous representatives are able to participate in international meetings. In the process of negotiating and drafting the contents of Convention 169, the International Labor Organization took the position that indigenous peoples should be "self-defining," that the criteria for inclusion in meetings and legal processes associated with indigenous peoples should follow a peoples' own expressions (through their leadership) of who they are and how they are to articulate their aspirations toward self-determination. The same is true of the criteria for participation in the Working Group on Indigenous Populations and other U.N. forums. The U.N. has never elaborated a formal, "gate-keeping" definition of indigenous peoples that might exclude some marginalized peoples from the protections and opportunities of its initiatives on behalf of indigenous populations.

The global indigenous movement would lack its transnational dimension without the elaboration of narratives of shared experience. It is founded on a global identification between seemingly distinct and disparate peoples who see themselves as suffering from the same destructive influences of nation-states, international agencies and private corporations. Therefore, one of the most important sources of impetus behind the international movement of indigenous peoples is the widespread perception that distinct forms of collective suffering and hope of renewal have a global dimension. Many indigenous people have expressed the importance of the perception that their people's experience is not isolated or unique but resonates with that of other "first peoples" from every hemisphere of the world.

Indigenous leaders cultivate transnational networks of cooperation. such networks are occasionally built into the structures and mandate of indigenous organizations themselves, as in the Inuit Circumpolar Conference, which connects Alaska Eskimo, Canadian Inuit, and Greenlandic Eskimo; the International Indian Treaty Council, which represents indigenous peoples of the Western Hemisphere and the Pacific. Cooperative transnationalism is evident in broadly based web sites, such as that of the Indigenous Peoples Caucus. Most concretely, common goals and experience are evident in joint statements made in international meetings. The 2007 meeting of the U.N. Permanent Forum on Indigenous Issues, for example, included an almost globally encompassing joint statement that brought together the American Indian Law Alliance; the Coordination Autochtone Francophone; the Indigenous Peoples' Center for Documentation, Research, and Information; the Indigenous Peoples of Africa Coordinating Committee; the Russian Association of Indigenous People of the North, Siberia, and the Far East; the Service for Peace and Justice in Latin America; and the Southern Diaspora Research and Development Centre. Patterns of common experience that are regional, hemispheric, or global in scope lead to far-reaching networks of indigenous nongovernmental organizations.

This common experience includes a history of subjection to state-sponsored policies of assimilation, some of which were directed toward restriction of language use in imposed systems of formal education, separating children from their families to be institutionally socialized in boarding schools or to be raised separate from their parents in the homes of "national" families. States often expressed the goals of such policies in terms of "social improvement," "education," "development," or "equal rights." Although the history of boarding schools in the United States and residential schools in Canada have been the focus of efforts to understand this socially destructive assimilation policy, there have been similar forms of removal of children into "total institutions" in other parts of the world, including Australia, New Zealand, India, and the former Soviet Union. In colonial Africa the implementation of compulsory education programs among nomadic peoples had effects similar to those of boarding schools, including removal of children from their families and from subsistence activities and thus interrupting the transmission of cultural knowledge.

More than this, the residential and boarding school experience has been an important part of the personal backgrounds of many indigenous leaders, particularly of those from the United States and Canada who, since the 1970s, have promoted the human rights of indigenous peoples as well as distinct aboriginal or native identities. The promotion of indigenous rights requires a new form of leadership that is able to communicate in the languages of dominant societies and to deal with the complexities of written law and formal procedures. The formalization of identity implies a transition from the authority of elders to a legally sophisticated, computer literate generation able to navigate complex bureaucracies and systems of knowledge. Seen with this transition in mind, the education that was once forced upon indigenous people in many parts of the world at the same time provided them with the skills necessary to promote their distinctiveness through the vehicle of "rights."

Although socially destructive assimilation policies are widely shared among representatives of indigenous peoples, the focus of their concern tends more often to be oriented to protection of distinct territories from unwanted development. Concerns about the effects of large-scale development on indigenous peoples have been included in broader conceptions of the negative impacts of globalization. According to the findings of the U.N. Working Group on Indigenous Populations (2003:21): "globalization in its present form prioritized profits above social concerns, increased disparities among States and within them, and had contributed to long-lasting damage to the environment . . . [The Working Group] noted . . . the concerns expressed about forced displacement of indigenous peoples due to natural resource extraction and other developments on their lands, [and] the unequal and unjust relations prevailing between indigenous communities and large corporations implementing projects on their territories."

From the first meetings of indigenous peoples in the late 1970s and early 1980s, one of the primary concerns was loss of land and the viability of subsistence, particularly as a consequence of large-scale resource extraction. For example, the Grand Council of the Crees, a nongovernmental organization that represents nine Cree communities in northern Quebec, took a leading role in resisting the imposition of large scale hydroelectric projects on their territory, and they found common cause in their efforts with other indigenous peoples who faced or experienced similar processes forced removal and environmental degradation following from megaproject development. The success of Cree lobbying was reflected in the shelving of the James Bay II project by Hydro-Quebec in 1996 ("James Bay Cree," this vol.). In 2006 the Crees resisted new plans by Hydro Quebec for hydroelectric megaproject construction with a counterproposal to generate energy through a "wind park" that would place 1,100 windmills along a 350-mile corridor of Cree land (*The Gazette* 2006) and that would at the same time situate the Crees in even closer ideological proximity with many environmental lobby groups.

As with the progressive inclusion of widely varying peoples from different regions of the world into the global movement of indigenous peoples, the process of defining the key issues of concern for indigenous peoples has involved a process of inclusion, in this case widening the range of forces of modernity and development that are seen to threaten indigenous peoples' distinct ways of life. There is, for example, recognition of a need to overcome the legacy and ongoing practice of using indigenous peoples and communities as research subjects without their in-

formed consent or their participation in formulating research questions, goals, or strategies. This issue came to the forefront through the much publicized abuses of the Human Genome Diversity Project, which for its detractors embodied ethically abusive research motivated by profit (H. Cunningham 2005). To some extent, concern about research relationships with indigenous peoples has moved outside the human rights arena and has more directly involved relationships between indigenous organizations and research institutions, though still maintaining the global rubric and rights perspective of indigenous peoples. The need expressed by indigenous people to overcome "colonial" research has focused largely on their rights to make decisions about why, how, and by whom research that affects or includes them is conducted. This area of concern has involved the elaboration of distinctly "indigenous" research methodologies that are sensitive to the languages, ceremonies, consensus decision-making, and forms of sociability of indigenous communities (L.T. Smith 1999; Mihesuah and Wilson 2004).

## Implications of Transnational Activism

An important quality of the global indigenous movement that clearly differentiates it from the petitions of earlier times is the way it has become transnational but at the same time oriented toward defending societies with a strong sense of place. This transnationalism was first built around the idea of a distinct form of society that could be called "indigenous." It became internationalized by being built into the agendas of nongovernmental organizations and institutions of global governance. This transnationalism is more broadly cooperative than any earlier aboriginal, Indian, or native form of resistance, involving global networks of peoples and nongovernmental organizations.

In more practical terms, another significant event in the formation of the indigenous peoples' movement has occurred through the confluence of indigenous interests and those of other transnational activists. The conditions under which an indigenous people finds a distinct place in its host state and in the institutions of global governance are not only outcomes of face-to-face political lobbying and negotiation but also results of a wider, less direct process of cultural negotiation and cooperation among indigenous peoples, allied organizations with parallel interests, and cultural consumers.

Bolstered by new forms of institutional and public support, indigenous peoples appear to be more assertive in their claims of distinct status and rights. The general point that all indigenous claims seem to converge upon is indigenous peoples' rights to self-determination. Control of the education of children, land, subsistence pursuits, and the production of knowledge are all closely connected to aspirations toward self-governance as distinct peoples. Defense of a distinct culture and form of subsistence does not prevent indigenous organizations from displaying their rights of self-determination in ways that purposefully represent the practices of nation-states. Indigenous peoples have drawn cultural boundaries, legally redefined themselves as peoples, and by implication redefined the foundation of belonging for their individual members as more than kinship or shared culture, but also as distinct citizenship, as belonging to a distinct regime of rights, entitlements, and obligations.

Pursuing claims and grievances that follow from violations of rights means defining in very particular terms who is the beneficiary of those rights and who is not. The formalization of social defenses by those with attachments to mobile and flexible subsistence economies can result unintentionally in a process of cultural enclosure. Those seeking to assert their rights as distinct societies are more frequently subjected to the complexities of formally articulating the boundaries of social inclusion and exclusion. Collective rights imply a community that is the subject of rights. Collective rights and claims, including treaties, are consequently inextricably connected to the processes of ethnic formalization or nation building.

To successfully make a claim to formal recognition and rights from a dominant power, indigenous peoples must to some extent conform to the concepts and categories of that power, including those categories that have to do with collective self-perception or "identity." If all peoples have a right of cultural development as an important component of their right of self-determination, then what is the culture that is to be developed? How is this right to be exercised? Does cultural development allow room for imprecision and contestation? Or is it to be built around a dominant ideal?

Despite the ambiguities and uncertainties associated with indigenous peoples' strivings toward self-determination and nation-building, the global movement of indigenous peoples is part of a wider transition that stands out with greater clarity. Global indigenism is associated with a trend toward reduction of the reach of the nation-state in favor of transnational associations of community identities. The indigenous peoples' movement represents a new terrain of cultural claims, in which transnational movements encourage more ambitious expressions of local identity and goals of autonomy. It presents challenges, which remain to be squarely met, for both the development of multicultural governance and of a research-based understanding of global transformations of the politics of identity.

# Contributors

This list gives the academic affiliations of authors at the time this volume went to press. The dates following the entries indicate when each manuscript was (1) first received in the General Editor's office; (2) accepted by the General Editor's office; and (3) sent to the author (or, if deceased, a substitute) for final approval after revisions and editorial work

AGENT, DAN (Cherokee-Choctaw), Tahlequah, Oklahoma. News Media: 6/4/07; 6/27/07; 7/25/07.

ANDERSON, MARGARET SEGUIN, First Nations Studies, University of Northern British Columbia, Prince Rupert. Nisga'a: 8/28/06; 10/30/06; 3/6/07.

BAILEY, GARRICK A., Department of Anthropology, University of Tulsa, Oklahoma. Introduction: 5/18/07; 5/21/07; 6/4/07.

BEAL, CARL, Department of Indigenous Studies, First Nations University of Canada, Regina, Saskatchewan. Aboriginal Economic Development: 5/14/06; 2/12/07; 6/29/07.

BELANGER, YALE D., Department of Native American Studies, University of Lethbridge, Alberta. Native Governments and Organizations: 6/9/06; 2/23/07; 9/21/07. Evolution of Native Reserves: 8/16/06; 3/5/07; 9/13/07.

BENNETT, PAMELA (Cherokee), Department of History, University of Arizona, Tucson. Indians in the Military: 11/27/06; 1/18/07; 3/27/07.

BLACKWELL, M. SHARON (Omaha) (retired), Bureau of Indian Affairs, Washington, D.C.. Lawyers and Law Programs: 6/18/07; 7/31/07; 8/30/07.

BORROWS, JOHN J. (Chippewas of the Nawash First Nation), University of Victoria Faculty of Law, British Columbia. Native Rights and the Constitution in Canada: 7/25/06; 3/1/07; 4/6/07.

BURT, LARRY W., Department of History, Missouri State University, Springfield. Termination and Relocation: 7/17/06; 10/17/06; 1/26/07.

CATTELINO, JESSICA R., Department of Anthropology, University of Chicago, Illinois. Indian Gaming: 7/12/06; 10/2/06; 3/1/07.

DELORIA, VINE, JR. (Standing Rock Sioux) (deceased), Departments of History and American Indian Studies, University of Colorado Law School, University of Colorado, Boulder. Activism, 1950–1980: 3/14/79; 1/22/07; 4/26/07.

EAGLEWOMAN, ANGELIQUE/WAMBDI A. WASTE WIN (Sisseton-Wahpeton Dakota Oyate), Hamline University School of Law, St. Paul, Minnesota. The Bureau of Indian Affairs and Reservations: 6/13/06; 7//11/06; 5/14/07. Tribal Sovereignty and Economic Development: 6/13/06; 2/6/07; 8/13/07.

EJESIAK, KIRT (Canadian Inuit), Iqaluit, Nunavut Nunavut: 10/23/06; 3/26/07; 6/14/07.

FELDHOUSEN-GILES, KRISTY J., Department of Anthropology, University of Oklahoma, Norman. The Freedmen: 4/25/06; 6/7/06; 4/9/07.

GARROUTTE, EVA MARIE (Cherokee), Department of Sociology, Boston College, Chestnut Hill, Massachusetts. Native American Identity in Law: 5/14/06; 6/20/06; 1/8/07.

GEIOGAMAH, HANAY (Kiowa-Delaware), American Indian Studies Center, University of California, Los Angeles. Theater: 10/23/06; 7/23/07; 8/30/07.

GOLDBERG, CAROLE, School of Law, University of California, Los Angeles. The State-Tribe Relationship: 10/30/06; 11/20/06; 2/28/07.

HINTON, LEANNE, Department of Linguistics, University of California, Berkeley. Languages and Language Programs: 8/23/06; 6/15/07; 8/23/07.

HOLM, TOM (Cherokee-Muskogee Creek), Department of American Indian Studies, University of Arizona, Tucson. Indians in the Military: 11/27/06; 1/18/07; 3/27/07.

IMAI, SHIN, Clinical Education Program, Osgoode Hall Law School, York University, Toronto, Ontario. Aboriginal Land Claims: 3/6/07; 5/15/07; 6/21/07.

JOE, JENNIE R. (Navajo), Family and Community Medicine and Native American Research and Training Center, College of Medicine, University of Arizona, Tucson. Health and Health Issues in the United States: 8/28/06; 11/14/06; 3/30/07.

KAVANAGH, THOMAS W., Department of Sociology and Anthropology, Seton Hall University, South Orange, New Jersey. Powwows: 6/26/06; 4/27/07; 9/14/07.

KEEN, TAYLOR (Cherokee-Omaha), Tulsa, Oklahoma. Tribal Sovereignty and Economic Development: 6/13/06; 2/5/07; 8/13/07.

KIDWELL, CLARA SUE (Choctaw-Chippewa), Native American Studies, University of Oklahoma, Norman. Native American Studies Programs: 6/19/06; 6/22/06; 8/9/07.

LAURIE-BEAUMONT, BRIAN L., Ottawa, Ontario. Native Museums and Cultural Centers: 8/10/06; 5/31/07; 8/23/07.

LESLIE, JOHN F. (retired), Department of Indian Affairs and Northern Development, Ottawa, Ontario. The Department of Indian Affairs and Northern Development: 7/14/06; 3/14/07; 8/9/07.

McKeown, C. Timothy, National NAGPRA Program, National Park Service, Washington, D.C. Repatriation: 8/8/06; 3/19/07; 9/26/07.

McNeil, Kent, York University, Osgoode Hall Law School, Toronto, Ontario. Native Rights Case Law: 12/14/06; 3/21/07; 5/10/07.

Newhouse, David R. (Onondaga), Department of Indigenous Studies, Trent University, Peterborough, Ontario. The Evolution of Native Reserves: 8/16/06; 3/5/07; 9/13/07.

Niezen, Ronald, Department of Anthropology, McGill University, Montreal, Quebec. The Global Indigenous Movement: 4/27/06; 4/24/07; 5/14/07.

O'Brien, Sharon, Department of Political Science, University of Kansas, Lawrence. Tribal Government in the United States: 8/16/06; 1/29/07; 7/27/07.

O'Donnell, C. Vivian (Anishinaabe), Department of Indigenous Studies, Trent University, Peterborough, Ontario. Native Populations of Canada: 6/4/06; 6/30/06; 1/9/07.

Rolo, Mark Anthony (Bad River Band of Lake Superior Ojibwe), Madison, Wisconsin. Film: 3/12/07; 4/26/07; 9/20/07.

Roth, George (retired), Office of Federal Acknowledgment, Department of the Interior, Washington, D.C. Restoration: 8/25/06; 12/19/06; 3/23/07. Recognition: 8/25/06; 11/27/06; 6/22/07.

Royster, Judith, Native American Law Center, University of Tulsa College of Law, Oklahoma. Indian Land Claims: 7/18/06; 10/19/06; 2/7/07.

Sawchuk, Joe, Department of Anthropology, Brandon University, Manitoba. Métis: 5/14/06; 6/12/06; 4/26/07.

Scott, Colin H., Department of Anthropology, McGill University, Montreal, Quebec. James Bay Cree: 9/27/07; 3/7/07; 8/22/07.

Shanley, Kathryn W. (Assiniboine), Native American Studies, University of Montana, Missoula. Literature: 12/14/06; 4/9/07; 5/14/07.

Shpuniarsky, Heather Y., Department of Native Studies, Trent University, Peterborough, Ontario. The Evolution of Native Reserves: 8/16/06; 3/5/07; 9/13/07.

Skibine, Alex Tallchief (Osage), S.J. Quinney College of Law, University of Utah, Salt Lake City. The Federal-Tribe Relationship: 6/13/06; 7/7/06; 2/16/07.

Stein, Wayne J. (Turtle Mountain Chippewa), Department for Native American Studies, Montana State University, Bozeman. Tribal Colleges and Universities: 6/23/06; 4/13/07; 9/20/07.

Strickland, Renard (Osage-Cherokee), University of Oregon School of Law, Eugene. Lawyers and Law Programs: 6/18/07; 7/31/07; 8/30/07.

Sturm, Circe, Departments of Anthropology and Native American Studies, University of Oklahoma, Norman. The Freedmen: 4/25/07; 6/7/06; 4/9/07.

Swan, Daniel C., Department of Anthropology and the Sam Noble Oklahoma Museum of Natural History, University of Oklahoma, Norman. Native American Church: 8/16/06; 4/3/07; 7/2/07.

Thornton, Russell (Cherokee), Department of Anthropology, University of California, Los Angeles. United States Native Population: 5/14/06; 6/21/06; 1/9/07.

Waldram, James B., Department of Psychology, University of Saskatchewan, Saskatoon. Native Health and Health Care in Canada: 6/9/06; 12/4/06; 7/27/07.

Warrior, Robert (Osage), Department of English, University of Oklahoma, Norman. Activism Since 1980: 8/16/06; 1/24/07; 6/5/07.

Watt, Lisa J. (Seneca), Portland, Oregon. Native Museums and Cultural Centers: 8/10/06; 5/31/07; 8/23/07.

Weibel-Orlando, Joan, Department of Anthropology, University of Southern California, Los Angeles. Urban Communities: 7/17/06; 10/10/06; 8/22/07.

Worl, Rosita (Tlingit), Sealaska Heritage Institute and University of Alaska Southeast, Juneau. Alaska Native Corporations: 4/25/06; 2/9/07; 3/23/07.

# Bibliography

*This list includes all references cited in the volume, arranged in alphabetical order according to the names of the authors as they appear in the citations in the text. It also includes works submitted by the contributors or consulted by the Handbook research staff but not cited in the chapters. Multiple works by the same author are arranged chronologically; second and subsequent titles by the same author in the same year are differentiated by letters added to the dates. Where more than one author with the same surname is cited, one has been arbitrarily selected for text citation by surname alone throughout the volume, while the others are cited with added initials; the combination of surname with date in text citations should avoid confusion. Where a publication date is different from the series date (as in some annual reports and the like), the former is used. Dates, authors, and titles that do not appear on the original works are enclosed by brackets. For manuscripts, dates refer to time of composition. For publications reprinted or first published many years after original composition, a bracketed date after the title refers to the time of composition or the date of original publication.*

AFN *see* Assembly of First Nations (AFN)

AIC *see* Aboriginal Institutes Consortium (AIC)

AIHEC *see* American Indian Higher Education Consortium (AIHEC)

AIM *see* American Indian Movement (AIM)

AIPRC *see* American Indian Policy Review Commission (AIPRC)

AMMSA *see* Aboriginal Multi-Media Society of Alberta (AMMSA)

ARCIA = Commissioner of Indian Affairs
1849–    Annual Report of the Commissioner of Indian Affairs to the Secretary of the Interior. Washington: U.S. Government Printing Office. (Reprinted: AMS Press, New York, 1976–1977; originally issued as both *House* and *Senate Documents*, and as Department of the Interior separate publications: *see* Key to the Annual Reports of the United States Commissioner of Indian Affairs, by J.A. Jones. *Ethnohistory* 2(1):58–64, 1955.)

ASIA = Assistant Secretary of the Interior. Indian Affairs *see* U.S. Department of the Interior. Assistant Secretary of Indian Affairs (ASIA)

Abbott, Lawrence
1994    I Stand in the Center of the Good: Interviews with Contemporary Native American Artists. *American Indian Lives*. Lincoln: University of Nebraska Press.

1995    A Time of Visions: Contemporary American Indian Art and Artists. *Canadian Journal of Native Studies* 15(1):129–161. Brandon, Man.

1996    Spiderwoman Theater and the Tapestry of Story. *Canadian Journal of Native Studies* 16(1):165–180. Brandon, Man.

Abeita, Louise
1939    I am a Pueblo Indian Girl. New York: William Morrow.

Abel, Annie H.
1915    The American Indian as Slave Holder and Secessionist. An Omitted Chapter in the Diplomatic History of the Southern Confederacy. *The Slaveholding Indians* 1. Cleveland, Ohio: Arthur H. Clark Company. (Reprinted: see Abel 1992.)

1919    The American Indian as Participant in the Civil War. *The Slaveholding Indians* 2. Cleveland, Ohio: Arthur H. Clark Company. (Reprinted: see Abel 1992a.)

1925    The American Indian Under Reconstruction. *The Slaveholding Indians* 3. Cleveland, Ohio: Arthur H. Clark Company. (Reprinted: see Abel 1992b.)

1992    The American Indian as Slave Holder and Secessionist. An Omitted Chapter in the Diplomatic History of the Southern Confederacy. Introduction by Theda Perdue and Michael D. Green. Lincoln: University of Nebraska Press.

1992a    The American Indian in the Civil War, 1862–1865. Introduction by Theda Perdue and Michael D. Green. Lincoln: University of Nebraska Press.

1992b    The American Indian and the End of the Confederacy, 1863–1866. Introduction by Theda Perdue and Michael D. Green. Lincoln: University of Nebraska Press.

Abel, Kerry, and Jean Friesen, eds.
1991    Aboriginal Resource Use in Canada: Historical and Legal Aspects. *Manitoba Studies in Native History* 6. Winnipeg: The Universtiy of Manitoba Press.

Aberle, David F.
1967    The Peyote Religion Among the Navaho. 2d printing. Chicago: Aldine. (Originally publ.: *Viking Fund Publications in Anthropology* 42, New York, 1966. Reprinted: University of Chicago Press, Chicago, 1982.)

1983    *see* Handbook Vol. 10 (1983:558–569)

Aberle, David F., and Omer C. Stewart
1957    Navaho and Ute Peyotism: A Chronological and Distributional Study. *University of Colorado Studies. Series in Anthropology* 6. Boulder, Colo.

Abernethy, Thomas Perkins
1959    Western Lands and the American Revolution. New York: Russell and Russell. (Originally publ. in 1937.)

Abler, Thomas S., and Sally M. Weaver
1974    A Canadian Indian Bibliography, 1960–1970. Toronto: University of Toronto Press.

Ablon, Joan
1964    Relocated American Indians in the San Francisco Bay Area: Social Interactions and Indian Identity. *Human Organization* 24(4):296–304. Washington.

1965    American Indian Relocation: Problems of Dependency and Management in the City. *Phylon* 26(4):362–371. [Atlanta, Ga.]

1971    Retention of Cultural Values and Differential Urban Adaptation: Samoans and American Indians in a West Coast City. *Social Forces* 49(3):385–393. [Chapel Hill, N.C.]

Abonyi, Sylvia
2001    Sickness and Symptom: Perspectives on Diabetes Among Mushkegowuk Cree. (Ph.D. Dissertation in Anthropology, McMaster University, Hamilton, Ont.)

Aboriginal Institutes Consortium (AIC)
2004    Aboriginal Institutions of Higher Education: A Struggle for the Education of Aboriginal Studies, Control of Indigenous

Knowledge, and Recognition of Aboriginal Institutions. An Examination of Government Policy. Toronto: Canadian Race Relations Foundation.

Aboriginal Multi-Media Society of Alberta (AMMSA)
1984 [MMA to Have Local Voting, 24 August 1984.] (Aboriginal Multi-Media Society of Alberta, Edmonton, Alta.)

Aboriginal Peoples Survey
[2001] 2003 *see* O'Donnell, Vivian, and Heather Tait 2003

Abrams, George H.J.
2004 Tribal Museums in America. Nashville, Tenn.: American Association for State and Local History.

Abu-Saad, Ismael, and Duane Champagne, eds.
2005 Indigenous Education and Empowerment: International Perspectives. Blue Ridge Summit, Pa.: AltaMira Press.

Adair, John
1947 The Navajo and Pueblo Veteran: A Force for Culture Change. *American Indian* 4(1):5–11. New York.

Adams, E. Charles
1984 Archaeology and the Native American: A Case at Hopi. Pp. 236–242 in Ethics and Values in Archaeology. Ernestine L. Green, ed. New York and London: The Free Press.

Adams, Hank
1973 The Wounded Knee Negotiations: A Glimpse of Bargaining Table Activities During the Wounded Knee Crisis. *Indian Voice* 3(4):5–7, 38–41, 44–46, 64. San Jose, Ca.

Adams, Howard
1975 Prison of Grass: Canada from the Native Point of View. Toronto: New Press. (Reprinted, rev. ed.: Fifth House Publishers, Saskatoon, Sask., 1989.)

1995 A Tortured People: The Politics of Colonization. Penticton, B.C.: Theytus Books.

Adams, James
2003 Trump Sues Eastern Pequots. *Indian Country Today*, May 30, 2003:A1. Canastota, N.Y. (Webpage: http://www.indiancountry.com)

Adams, Roxana, ed.
2001 Implementing the Native American Graves Protection and Repatriation Act (NAGPRA). Washington: American Association of Museums.

Adelson, Naomi
2005 The Embodiment of Inequity: Health Disparities in Aboriginal Canada. *Canadian Journal of Public Health* 96, Supplement 2:S45–S61. Ottawa.

Advisory Council on California Indian Policy (ACCIP)
1997 Final Report. Washington: U.S. Government Printing Office.

Agent, Dan
1991 Indian Journalism Began with Cherokee Phoenix. *Cherokee Advocate*, February 1991:4. Tahlequah, Okla.

2004 Progress Continues Toward the Free Press in Indian Country. *Cherokee Phoenix*, August 2004:12. Tahlequah, Okla.

2006 Eastern Band Passes Free Press Act. (NAJA and Cherokee Phoenix Staff Reports). *Cherokee Phoenix*, May 2006:5. Tahlequah, Okla.

Agreements, Treaties and Negotiated Settlements Project *see* Canada. Agreements, Treaties, and Negotiated Settlements Project

Ainsley, Kathy
2005 Possession is Nine-Tenth of the Law. *Indigenous Peoples' Journal of Law, Culture & Resistance* 2(1):1102–1103. Los Angeles.

Aks, Judith H.
2004 Women's Rights in Native North America: Legal Mobilization in the US and Canada. *Law and Society*. New York: LFB Scholarly Publishing.

Akwesasne Notes
1973 Trail of Broken Treaties: B.I.A. I'm Not Your Indian Any More. Rooseveltown, N.Y.: Mohawk Nation.

1974 Voices from Wounded Knee 1973: In the Words of the Participants. Rooseveltown, N.Y.: Mohawk Nation.

Alaska Federation of Natives (AFN)
1991 Making It Work: A Guide to Public Law 100-241 1987 Amendments to the Alaska Native Claims Settlement Act. Anchorage: Alaska Federation of Natives (AFN).

Albers, Patricia C., and Beatrice Medicine, eds.
1983 The Hidden Half: Studies of Plains Indian Women. Washington: University Press of America.

2005 Some Reflections on Nearly Forty Years on the Northern Plains Powwow Circuit. Pp. 26–45 in Powwow. Clyde Ellis, Luke Eric Lassiter, and Gary H. Dunham, eds. Lincoln: University of Nebraska Press.

Albers, Patricia C., et al.
2002 A Story of Struggle and Survival: American Indian Studies at the University of Minnesota—Twin Cities. Pp. 145–164 in Native American Studies in Higher Education: Models for Collaboration Between Universities and Indigenous Nations. Duane Champagne and Jay Stauss, eds. Walnut Creek, Calif.: AltaMira Press.

Alberta Federation of Métis Settlement Associations
1982 Métisism: A Canadian Identity. Alberta Federation of Métis Settlement Associations: Statement on Aboriginal Rights in the Constitution of Canada. Edmonton, Alta.: Alberta Federation of Métis Settlement Associations.

Aldred, Lisa
2000 "Plastic Shamans and Astroturf Sun Dances": New Age Commercialization of Native American Spirituality. *American Indian Quarterly* 24(3):329–352. Lincoln, Nebr.

Aleiss, Angela
1987 Hollywood Addresses Postwar Assimilation: Indian/White Attitudes in Broken Arrow. *American Indian Culture and Research Journal* 11(1):67–79. Los Angeles.

1991 The Vanishing American: Hollywood's Compromise to Indian Reform. *Journal of American Studies* 25(3):467–472. London.

1994 A Race Divided: The Indian Westerns of John Ford. *American Indian Culture and Research Journal* 18(3):167–186. Los Angeles.

1995 Native Americans: The Surprising Silents. *Cineaste* 21(3): 34–35. New York.

2005 Making the White Man's Indian: Native Americans and Hollywood Movies. Westport, Conn.: Praeger.

Alexie, Sherman
1991 The Business of Fancy Dancing: Stories and Poems. Brooklyn, N.Y.: Hanging Loose Press.

1993          The Lone Ranger and Tonto Fistfight in Heaven. New York: Atlantic Monthly Press.

1998          *see* Eyre, Chris, director 1998

2000          The Toughest Indian in the World. New York: Atlantic Monthly Press. (Reprinted in 2001.)

————, author and director
2002          The Business of Fancy Dancing: Sometimes Going Home Is the Hardest Journey of All. DVD. New York: Studio Fox Lorber.

2003          The Business of Fancy Dancing: The Screenplay. Brooklyn, N.Y.: Hanging Loose Press.

Alfred, Gerald R.
1995          Heeding the Voices of Our Ancestors: Kahnawake Mohawk Politics and the Rise of Native Nationalism. Don Mills, Ont.: Oxford University Press.

Alfred, Taiaiake
1999          Peace, Power, Righteousness: An Indigenous Manifesto. Don Mills, Ont.: Oxford University Press.

2006          Wasase: Indigenous Pathways of Action and Freedom. New York: Broadwood Press.

Alia, Valerie
1994          Names, Numbers and Northern Policy. Halifax, N.S.: Fernwood Publishing.

Allen, Anne E. Guernsey
1997          All the World's A Stage: The Nineteenth Century Kwakwaka'wakw (Kwakiutl) House as Theater. *American Indian Culture and Research Journal* 21(4):29–73. Los Angeles.

Allen, Paula Gunn
1975          The Sacred Hoop: A Contemporary Indian Perspective on American Indian Literature. Pp. 111–135 in Literature of the American Indians: Views and Interpretations: A Gathering of Indian Memories, Symbolic Contexts, and Literary Criticism. Edited, with an Introduction and Notes, by Abraham Chapman. New York: Meridian/New American Library. (Reprinted: see Allen 1976.)

1976          The Sacred Hoop. In: Native American Literature: A Critical Anthology. Abraham Chapman, ed. New York: Harper and Row.

————, ed.
1983          Studies in American Indian Literature: Critical Essays and Course Designs. New York: Modern Language Association of America.

1983a         The Woman Who Owned the Shadows. San Francisco: Spinsters, Ink.

1986          The Sacred Hoop: Recovering the Feminine in American Indian Traditions. Boston: Beacon Press.

1989          Spider Woman's Granddaughters: Traditional Tales and Contemporary Writing by Native American Women. Boston: Beacon Press.

1997          Life Is a Fatal Disease: Collected Poems, 1962–1995. Albuquerque: West End Press.

Amagoalik, John
1999          Looking Back . . . A Journey of Sorrow, Joy and Adventure. In: Nunavut '99: Changing the Map of Canada. Iqaluit, NU.: Nortext Multimedia, Inc., and Nunavut Tunngavik, Inc.

Ambler, Marjane
1990          Breaking the Iron Bonds: Indian Control of Energy Development. Lawrence, Kans.: University Press of Kansas.

1992          The Wealth of (Indian) Nations: Tribes Are Creating a New Model of Economic Development by Building on Old Strengths. *Tribal College Journal: Journal of American Indian Higher Education* 4(2):9–12. Sacramento, Calif.

2002          Sustaining Our Home, Determining Our Destiny. *Tribal College Journal: Journal of American Indian Higher Education* 13(3):8–9. Sacramento, Calif.

American Association for State and Local History
1999          Directory of Native American Museums and Cultural Centers. Nashville, Tenn.: American Association for State and Local History.

American Gaming Association
2006          Factsheets. (Webpage: http://www.americangaming.org/Industry/factsheets/[24 June 2006].)

American Indian Chicago Conference
1961          Declaration of Indian Purpose: The Voice of the American Indian. Chicago: University of Chicago Press.

1961a         The Voice of the American Indian: Progress Report no. 4, April 26, 1961. Chicago: University of Chicago Press.

American Indian Higher Education Consortium (AIHEC)
1973–1977     [Board of Directors Meetings: Minutes.] Denver: AIHEC, Inc.

1976          Testimony on Senate Bill Z 634: Indian Post-Secondary Educational Assistance Act of 1975. Submitted to Senate Subcommittee on Indian Affairs, Washington: AIHEC, Inc.

1994          Testimony to the Appropriations Subcommittee on Interior, March 8, 1994. Washington: U.S. House of Representatives.

1995          Tribal Colleges: Information Handout. Arlington, Va.: AIHEC.

1995a         Testimony to the House Subcommittee on Veterans' Affairs, Housing and Urban Development, and Independent Agencies Appropriations, April 5, 1995. Washington: U.S. House of Representatives.

1995b         Testimony to the Senate Agricultural, Rural Development, and Related Agencies Appropriations Sub-Committee. May 31, 1995. Washington: U.S. Senate.

2006          Map of Tribal College Locations and Addresses. [AIHEC Homepage.] Alexandaria, Va.: AIHEC.

American Indian Historical Society (AIHS)
1974          Indian Voices: The Native American Today. The Second Convocation of American Indian Scholars. (2d: 1971: Aspen Institute for Humanistic Studies.) San Francisco: Indian Historian Press.

American Indian Movement (AIM)
1979          [Letter to Membership, dated March 14, 1979.] (Photocopy in Robert Warrior's possession.)

American Indian Policy Review Commission (AIPRC)
1976          Report on Terminated and Nonfederally Recognized Indians. Task Force Ten: Terminated and Nonfederally Recognized Indians. Report to the American Indian Policy Review Commission.Washington: U.S. Government Printing Office.

1976a    Report on Tribal Government. Task Force Two: Tribal Government. Final Report to the American Indian Policy Review Commission.Washington: U.S. Government Printing Office.

1977    Final Report: Submitted to Congress, May 17, 1977. 2 vols. Washington: U.S. Government Printing Office.

American Indian Theater Ensemble, The
1970    An Inquiry, Presented for Consideration by the Arts and Communications Committee of the National Indian Youth Council in Association with La MaMa Experimental Theater Club. Washington: The American Indian Theater Ensemble.

1971    Operating Plans for an American Indian Theater Ensemble. Washington: The American Indian Theater Ensemble.

1973    A Proposal for a Tour of Indian Country by The American Indian Theater Ensemble. Washington: The American Indian Theater Ensemble.

Amerman, Stephen Kent
2003    Let's Get In and Fight: American Indian Political Activism in an Urban Public School System, 1973. *American Indian Quarterly* 27(3&4):607–638. Lincoln, Nebr.

2007    "I Should Not Be Wearing a Pilgrim Hat": Making an Indian Place in Urban Schools, 1945–75. *American Indian Culture and Research Journal* 31(1):39–62. Los Angeles.

Ames, Herbert
1923    [Letter to Right Hon. W.L. Mackenzie King, Ottawa, Canada, dated December 28, 1923.] (League of Nations Document No. 11/33556, League of Nations Archives, Geneva, Switzerland.]

Ames, Michael M.
1986    Museums, the Public, and Anthropology: A Study in the Anthropology of Anthropology. *Ranchi Anthropology Series* 9. New Delhi: Concept Publishing Company.

1992    Cannibal Tours and Glass Boxes: The Anthropology of Museums. Vancouver: University of British Columbia Press.

_____, ed.
2000    *see* West, W. Richard 2000

Anaya, James
1996    Indigenous Peoples in International Law. Oxford, England: Oxford University Press.

Anders, Gary C.
1998    Indian Gaming: Financial and Regulatory Issues. *Annals of the American Academy of Political and Social Science* 556(1):98–108. Philadelphia.

Anderson, Duane
1985    Reburial: Is It Reasonable? *Archaeology* 38(5):48–51.

Anderson, Edward F.
1995    The "Peyote Gardens" of South Texas: A Conservation Crisis? *Cactus and Succulent Journal* 67(2):67–73. Santa Barbara, Calif.

1996    Peyote: The Divine Cactus. 2d ed. Tuscon: University of Arizona Press.

Anderson, George E., W.H. Ellison, and Robert F. Heizer
1978    Treaty Making and Treaty Rejection by the Federal Government in California, 1850–1852. *Ballena Press Publications in Archaeology, Ethnology, and History* 9. Banning, Calif.

Anderson, Jack
1984    Lots of Smoke Rises Around This 'Indian'. *Kainai News*, March, 1984, No. 2:5. (Originally publ.: *The Washington Post*.)

Anderson, Marge
2005    Look Forward to the Dawn of a New Century. Pp. 40–43 in Sovereignty, Colonialism and the Indigenous Nations: A Reader. Robert Odawi Porter, ed. Durham, N.C.: Carolina Academic Press.

Anderson, Robert B.
1999    Economic Development Among the Aboriginal Peoples in Canada: The Hope for the Future. North York, Ont.: Captus Press.

2005    Aboriginal Economic Development in the New Economy. *Saskatchewan Institute on Public Policy. Briefing Note* 9. Regina, Sask.

Anderson, Robert B., and Robert M. Bone, eds.
2003    Natural Resources and Aboriginal People in Canada: Readings, Cases, and Commentary. Concord, Ont.: Captus Press.

Anderson, Robert B., et al.
2004    Indigenous Land Claims and Economic Development: The Canadian Experience. *American Indian Quarterly* 28(3–4): 634–648. Lincoln, Nebr.

Anderson, Terry
1978    Federal Recognition: The Vicious Myth. *American Indian Journal* 4(5):7–19.

Andrews, Tracy J., and Jon Olney
2007    Potlatch and Powwow: Dynamics of Culture Through Lives Lived Dancing. *American Indian Culture and Research Journal* 31(1):63–108. Los Angeles.

Angle, Jerry
1959    Federal, State and Tribal Jurisdiction on Indian Reservations in Arizona. *Bureau of Ethnic Research. American Indian Series* 2. Tucson: University of Arizona Press.

Angulo, Jaime de
1990    Indians in Overalls. San Francisco: City Lights Books. (Originally publ. in 1950.)

Anonymous
1967    [Interview with Joseph H. Cash, 25 August 1967 (restricted use).] (Recorded text in South Dakota Oral History Center, University of South Dakota, Vermillion, S.Dak.)

1976    *see* Quebec 1976

2002    Agreement Concerning a New Relationship Between Le Gouvernment du Québec and the Crees of Quebec (7 February 2002). Nemaska/Quebec City, Que.: SAGES.

2007    Proposed Agreement Concerning a New Relationship Between the Government of Canada and the Cree of Eeyou Istchee. (Consolidation of Final Draft Agreement, July 10, 2007; Nemaska/Ottawa.)

Anthes, Bill
2006    Native Moderns: American Indian Painting, 1940–1960. Durham, N.C., and London: Duke University Press.

Anyon, Roger, and Russell Thornton
2002    Implementing Repatriation in the United States: Issues Raised and Lessons Learned. Pp. 190–198 in The Dead and Their Possessions: Repatriation in Principle, Policy and Practice. Cressida Fforde, Jane Hubert, and Paul Turnbull, eds. *One World Archaeology* 43. New York and London: Routledge.

*451*

Apess, William
1829        A Son of the Forest. The Experience of William Apes, A Native of the Forest; Comprising a Notice of the Pequod Tribe of Indians, Written by Himself. New York: Published by the Author. (Revised in 1831; see also O'Connell, Barry, ed. 1992.)

Apted, Michael, dir.
1992        Incident at Oglala: The Leonard Peltier Story. Robert Redford, Executive Producer. Video. Lions Gate. (Available on DVD, 2004.)

Arbolino, Risa Diemond
2003        Assessment of a Repatriation Request for a Cayuse Dress in the National Museum of Natural History, Smithsonian Institution. Washington: Smithsonian Institution, National Museum of Natural History, Repatriation Office.

_____
2003a      Assessment of a Lineal Descendent Request for the Repatriation of Human Remains from the Big Hole Battle of the Nez Perce War at the National Museum of Natural History, Smithsonian Institution. Washington: Smithsonian Institution, National Museum of Natural History, Repatriation Office.

Arbolino, Risa Diemond, and Betsy Bruemmer
2006        Assessment of the Unassociated Funerary Objects from the Memaloose Islands, Washington and Oregon, at the National Museum of Natural History, Smithsonian Institution. Washington: Smithsonian Institution, National Museum of Natural History, Repatriation Office.

Arbolino, Risa Diemond, and Carrie Feldman
2006        Assessment of the Cultural Affiliation of Human Remains Potentially Affiliated with the Pueblo of Jemez at the National Museum of Natural History, Smithsonian Institution. Washington: Smithsonian Institution, National Museum of Natural History, Repatriation Office.

Arbolino, Risa Diemond, Stephen D. Ousley, and Erica Jones
2005        Reassessment of Human Remains and Funerary Objects from Seaside, Oregon at the National Museum of Natural History, Smithsonian Institution. Washington: Smithsonian Institution, National Museum of Natural History, Repatriation Office.

Archambault, JoAllyn
1992        American Indians and American Museums. *Zeitschrift für Ethnologie* 118(1993):7–22. Berlin: Dietrich Reimer Verlag.

_____
1996        Museums and Collectors. Pp. 407–410 in Encyclopedia of North American Indians. Frederick E. Hoxie, ed. New York: Houghton Mifflin Company. (Also available online, see: *Encyclopedia of North American Indians* 2006.)

Archuleta, Elizabeth
2005        "That's the Place Indians Talk About": Indigenous Narratives of Survivance. *Indigenous Peoples' Journal of Law, Culture & Resistance* 2(1):126–156. Los Angeles.

Archuleta, Margaret, and Rennard Strickland, eds.
1991        Shared Visions: Native American Painters and Sculptors of the Twentieth Century. Phoenix: The Heard Museum.

_____, eds.
1993        Shared Visions: Native American Painters and Sculptors in the Twentieth Century. 2d. ed. New York: New Press.

Arizona Department of Environmental Quality (ADEQ)
2006        Tribal Liason Fact Sheet. (Webpage: http://www.indianaffairs.state.az.us/agreements/tribal%20policy%20statement-1.doc [27 September 2006].)

Arizona State University. Center for Indian Education
1998        Selected Dissertations in Indian Education (1987 to 1997). Indian Education Resource Paper, Third Edition, March 1998.

Tucson, Ariz.: Arizona State University. Center for Indian Education. (Webpage: http://www.coe.asu.edu/cie/dis.html)

Armstrong, Orland Kay
1945        Set the American Indian Free! *Reader's Digest* 47(280):47–52. Pleasantville, N.Y.

Arnold, Robert D., ed.
1978        Alaska Native Land Claims. Rev. ed. Anchorage: Alaska Native Foundation. (Originally publ. in 1976.)

Aronsen, Gary P., and Javier Urcid
1996        Inventory and Assessment of Human Remains and Funerary Objects from the Puget Sound and Grays Harbor Regions of Washington State in the National Museum of Natural History. Washington: Smithsonian Institution, National Museum of Natural History, Repatriation Office.

Aronsen, Gary P., Javier Urcid, and Tamara L. Bray
1997        Inventory and Assessment of the Human Remains from the Lower Columbia River Valley, Oregon and Washington States, in the National Museum of Natural History. Washington: Smithsonian Institution, National Museum of Natural History, Repatriation Office.

Arrow, Kenneth J.
1971        Essays in Theory of Risk-Bearing. Chicago: Markham.

Arviso, Tom, Jr.
2002        Native Journalism Keeps With Tradition. *The Quill* 90(1):34–35. Chicago.

Asch, Michael
1993        Home and Native Land: Aboriginal Rights and the Canadian Constitution. Vancouver: University of British Columbia Press.

_____, ed.
1997        Aboriginal and Treaty Rights in Canada: Essays on Law, Equality, and Respect for Difference. Vancouver: University of British Columbia Press.

Asch, Michael, and Patrick Macklem
1991        Aboriginal Rights and Canadian Sovereignty: An Essay on *R. v. Sparrow. Alberta Law Review* 29(2):498–517. Edmonton, Alta.

Ash-Milby, Kathleen E.
2005        Contemporary Native American Art in the Twenty-First Century: Overcoming the Legacy. *European Review of Native American Studies* 19(1):49–54. [Vienna, Austria, etc.]

Asher, James J.
1982        Learning Another Language Through Actions. Los Gatos, Calif.: Sky Oaks Productions.

*Asheville Global Report (AGR)*
2005        Eddie Hatcher Still Sounding the Alarm. *Asheville Global Report*, October 11, 2005. Asheville, N.C. (Webpage: http://www.agrnews.org.)

Ashley, Jeffery S., and Secondy J. Hubbard
2004        Negotiated Sovereignty: Working To Improve Tribal-State Relations. Westport, Conn.: Praeger Publishers.

Ashworth, Kenneth A.
1986        The Contemporary Oklahoma Powwow. (Ph.D. Dissertation in Anthropology, University of Oklahoma, Norman.)

Assembly of First Nations (AFN)
1988        Special Report: The National Indian Health Transfer Conference. Ottawa: Assembly of First Nations.

_____
2006        [First Nations Bands, Cultural Groups, and Aboriginal Languages, 2006.] Ottawa: Assembly of First Nations.

2006a    Royal Commission on Aboriginal Peoples at 10 Years: A Report Card. Ottawa: Assembly of First Nations.

Assembly of First Nations (AFN), and The Canadian Museums Association (CMA)
1992, 1992a  *see* Task Force. Assembly of First Nations and the Canadian Museums Association 1992, 1992a

Assistant Secretary of the Interior. Indian Affairs (ASIA) *see* U.S. Department of the Interior. Assistant Secretary of Indian Affairs (ASIA)

Associated Press (AP)
2007    Black Caucus Seeks Federal Action on Cherokee Vote. *The Washington Post*, Wedn. March 14, 2007:A07. Washington.

Association of ANCSA Regional Corporation Presidents/CEOs
2005    Alaska Native Corporations Annual Economic Impact Report Based on 2003 Financial Data: A Look at Selected Data from 13 Native Regional Corporations and 28 Native Village Corporations. Anchorage: Association of ANCSA Regional Corporation Presidents/CEOs.

Atlantic Canada Opportunities Agency, Canadian Institute for Research on Regional Development
2003    Aboriginal Economic Development in Atlantic Canada: Lessons Learned and Best Practices: Understanding Conditions for Successful Economic Development in Aboriginal Communities. Moncton, N.B.: Atlantic Canada Opportunities Agency.

Attocknie, Francis Joseph
1964    The Life of Ten Bears. (Manuscript in T. Kavanagh's possession.)

Attwood, Bain
2003    Rights for Aborigines. Crows Nest, N.S.W., Australia: Allen and Unwin.

Attwood, Bain, and Andrew Markus, eds.
1999    The Struggle for Aboriginal Rights: A Documentary History. Crows Nest, N.S.W., Australia: Allen and Unwin.

Auditor General of Canada *see* Canada. Auditor General of Canada

Baca, Lawrence
1988    *see* Handbook Vol. 4 (1988:230–237)

2005    Ignore the Man Behind the Curtain: A Brief History of Thirty Years of the Indian Law Conference. *Federal Lawyer* 52:4.

Bachman, Ronet
1992    Death and Violence on the Reservation: Homicide, Family Violence and Suicide in American Indian Populations. Foreword by Murray A. Straus. New York, [etc.]: Auburn House.

Baer, Lars-Anders
2000    The Right of Self-Determination and the Case of the Sami. Pp. 223–231 in Operationalizing the Right of Indigenous Peoples to Self-Determination. Pekka Aikio and Martin Scheinin, eds. Turku, Finland: Institute for Human Rights, Abo Akademi University.

Bagley, Annette Traversie, ed.
1980    The Native American Image on Film: A Programmer's Guide for Organizations and Educators. Washington: The American Film Institute.

Bahr, Diana Meyers
1993    From Mission to Metropolis: Cupeño Indian Women in Los Angeles. Norman and London: University of Oklahoma Press.

Bahr, Howard M.
1972    End to Invisibility. Pp. 404–411 in Native Americans Today: Sociological Perspectives. Howard M. Bahr, Bruce A. Chadwick, and Robert C. Day, eds. New York: Harper and Row.

Bahr, Howard M., Bruce A. Chadwick, and Robert C. Day, eds.
1972    Native Americans Today: Sociological Perspectives. New York: Harper and Row.

Bahr, Howard M., Bruce A. Chadwick, and Joseph H. Stauss
1972    Discrimination Against Urban Indians in Seattle. *The Indian Historian* 5(4):4–11. San Francisco.

Bailey, Garrick A., ed.
1995    The Osage and the Invisible World: From the Works of Francis La Flesche. Norman: University of Oklahoma Press.

Bailey, Garrick A., and Kenneth A. Ashworth
1990    Pan-Indianism and Powwows in Oklahoma. (Paper presented at the American Anthropological Association Annual Meeting.)

Bailey, Garrick A., and Daniel C. Swan, eds.
2004    Art of the Osage. Seattle, Wash.: Saint Louis Art Museum, in association with University of Washington Press.

Baird-Olson, Karren
1994    Reflections of an AIM Activist: Has It All Been Worth It? Pp. 233–254 in Special Edition: Alcatraz Revisited: The 25th Anniversary of the Occupation, 1969–1971. *American Indian Culture and Research Journal* 18(4). Los Angeles.

Baird, W. David
1990    Are There 'Real' Indians in Oklahoma? Historical Perceptions of the Five Civilized Tribes. *Chronicles of Oklahoma* 68(1):4–23.

Baker, Angela, writer
2002    *see* Martin, Catherine Anne, director 2002

Baker, Joanne, ed.
2006    Sovereignty Matters: Locations of Contestation and Possibility in Indigenous Struggles for Self-Determination. Lincoln: University of Nebraska Press. (Copyright: 2005.)

Baker, T. Lindsay, and Julie P. Baker, eds.
1996    The WPA Oklahoma Slave Narratives. Norman: University of Oklahoma Press.

Bakhtin, Mikhail
1982    The Dialogic Imagination: Four Essays. Michael Holquist, ed.; Vadim Liapunov and Kenneth Brostrom, trans. *University of Texas Press Slavic Series*. Austin, Tex.: The University of Texas Press. (Originally publ. in Russian in 1975.)

Bakker, Peter
1997    A Language of Our Own: The Genesis of Michif, the Mixed Cree-French Language of the Canadian Métis. *Oxford Studies in Anthropological Linguistics* 10. New York and Oxford: Oxford University Press. (Originally issued as the Author's Ph.D. Dissertation in Linguistics, University of Amsterdam, The Netherlands, 1992.)

Ballantyne, Edith
1977    Foreword. In: Report of the International NGO Conference on Discrimination Against Indigenous Populations in the Americas. Geneva, Switzerland: United Nations.

Bancroft, Hubert H.
1886    History of Alaska, 1730–1885. *The Works of Hubert Howe Bancroft* 33. San Francisco: The History Company. (Reprinted: Antiquarian Press, New York, 1959.)

Bank, Rosemarie K.
1993    Staging the "Native": Making History in American Theatre Culture, 1828–1838. *Theatre Journal* 45(4):461–486. Washington.

Bankes, Nigel
1998 *Delgamuukw*, Division of Powers and Provincial Land and Resource Laws: Some Implications for Provincial Resource Rights. *University of British Columbia Law Review* 32(2): 317–351. Vancouver.

Banks, Dennis, with Richard Erdoes
2004 Ojibwa Warrior: Dennis Banks and the Rise of the American Indian Movement. Norman: University of Oklahoma Press. (Reprinted in 2006.)

Banner, Stuart
2005 How the Indians Lost Their Lands: Law and Power on the Frontier. Cambridge, Mass.: Belknap Press of Harvard University Press.

Banting, Keith, and Richard Simeon, eds.
1983 And No One Cheered: Federalism, Democracy, and the Constitution Act. Toronto: Methuen Publications.

Barbeau, C. Marius
[1939] Assomption Sash. *National Museum of Canada. Bulletin* 93; *Anthropological Series* 24. Ottawa. (Reprinted in 1972.)

Barden, John
1987 [Interview concerning Standing Rock Community College (SRCC), February, 27, 1987.] (Conducted by Wayne J. Stein, Fort Yates, N.Dak.; Text of interview in Department of Native American Studies, Montana State University, Bozeman, Mont.)

Barkan, Elazar, and Ronald Bush, eds.
2002 Claiming the Stones, Naming the Bones: Cultural Property and the Negotiation of National and Ethnic Identity. *Issues and Debates*. Los Angeles: Getty Research Institute.

Barker, Joanne
2003 Indian™ U.S.A. *Wicazo Sa Review* 18(1):25–79. Minneapolis.

2005 Sovereignty Matters: Locations of Contestation and Possibility in Indigenous Struggles for Self-Determination. Lincoln and London: University of Nebraska Press. (Reprinted in 2006.)

Barker, Mary, and Dieter Soyez
1994 Think Locally, Act Globally? The Transnationalization of Canadian Resource-Use Conflicts. *Environment* 36(5):12–20, 32–36.

Barlett, Donald L., and James B. Steele
2002 Indian Casinos: Wheel of Misfortune. *Time* 160(2), December 16, 2002:44–58. New York.

2002a Indian Casinos: Playing the Political Slots. *Time* 160(25), December 23, 2002:52–63. New York.

Barnaby, Joanne
2004 *see* Fumoleau, René 2004

Barnes, Patricia M., Patricia F. Adams, and Eve Powell-Griner
2005 Health Characteristics of American Indian and Alaska Native Adult Population: United States, 1999–2003. *Advance Data from Vital and Health Statistics* 356:1–24. Hyattsville, Md.: U.S. Department of Health and Human Services, Centers for Disease Control.

Barreiro, Jose, and Tim Johnson, eds.
2005 America Is Indian Country: Opinions and Perspectives from Indian Country Today. Golden, Colo.: Fulcrum Publishing.

Barringer, Felicity
1989 Major Accord Likely on Indian Remains. *The New York Times*, August 20, 1989. New York.

Barron, F. Laurie
1988 The Indian Pass System in the Canadian West, 1882–1935. *Prairie Forum* 21(1):25–42. Regina, Sask.: Canadian Plains Research Centre, University of Regina.

1990 The CCF and the Development of Métis Colonies in Southern Sasketchewan during the Premiership of T.C. Douglas, 1944–1961. *The Canadian Journal of Native Studies* 10(2): 243–271. Brandon, Man.

1997 Walking in Indian Moccasins: The Native Policies of Tommy Douglas and the CCF. Vancouver: University of British Columbia Press.

Barron, F. Laurie, and Joseph Garcea
1999 Introduction. Pp. 1–21 in Urban Indian Reserves: Forging New Relationships in Saskatchewan. F. Laurie Barron and Joseph Garcea, eds. Saskatoon, Sask.: Purich Publishers.

Barse, Harold
1980 [Interview with Tom Holm, June 18, 1980.] (Veterans Outreach, Oklahoma City, Okla.)

Barsh, Russel Lawrence
1975 Corporations and Indians: Who's the Villain? Seattle, Wash.: University of Washington, Graduate School of Business Administration.

1982 Indian Land Claims Policy in United States. *North Dakota Law Review* 58(1):1–80. Grand Forks, N.Dak.

1991 Federal Acknowledgment: Another Viewpoint. *European Review of Native American Studies* 5(1):64–65. [Vienna, Austria, etc.]

1994 Canada's Aboriginal Peoples: Social Integration or Disintegration? *Canadian Journal of Native Studies* 14(1):1–46. Brandon, Man.

2004 Indigenous Rights and the *Lex Loci* in British Imperial Law. Pp. 91–126 in Advancing Aboriginal Claims: Visions/Strategies/Directions. Kerry Wilkins, ed. Saskatoon, Sask.: Purich Publishing.

Barsh, Russel Lawrence, and James Youngblood Henderson
1976 Tribal Administrations of Natural Resource Development. *North Dakota Law Review* 52:307–347. Grand Forks, N.Dak.

1997 The Supreme Court's Van der Peet *Trilogy*: Naive Imperialism and Ropes of Sand. *McGill Law Journal* 42(4):993–1009. Montreal.

*Bartlesville Examiner-Enterprise*
2006 Delaware Tribal Headquarters Building Slated for Auction. *Bartlesville Examiner-Enterprise*, July 28, 2006. Bartlesville, Okla.

Bartlett, Richard H.
1983 Mineral Rights on Indian Reserves in Ontario. *Canadian Journal of Native Studies* 3(2):245–275. Brandon, Man.

1990 Indian Reserves and Aboriginal Lands in Canada: A Homeland. Saskatoon, Sask.: University of Saskatchewan, Native Law Centre.

Baskir, Lawrence M., and William A. Strauss
1978 Chance and Circumstance: The Draft, the War, and the Vietnam Generation. New York: Vintage Books.

Bass, Howard, producer
2004 Beautiful Beyond: Christian Songs in Native Languages. CD. *Smithsonian Folkways Recordings*. Washington: National Museum of the American Indian, Smithsonian Institution.

Bataille, Gretchen M., ed.; Laurie Lisa, ed. assistant
1993        Native American Women: A Biographical Dictionary. *Bio-graphical Dictionaries of Minority Women*. New York and London: Garland Publishing.

Bataille, Gretchen M., and Kathleen Sands
1984        American Indian Women: Telling Their Lives. Lincoln: University of Nebraska Press.

Bataille, Gretchen M., and Charles L.P. Silet, eds.
1980        The Pretend Indians: Images of Native Americans in the Movies. Ames, Ia.: Iowa State University Press.

_____, eds.
1985        Images of American Indians on Film: An Annotated Bibliography. New York: Garland.

Bateman, Rebecca
1990        "We're Still Here": History, Kinship, and Group Identity Among the Seminole Freedmen of Oklahoma. (Ph.D. Dissertation in Anthropology, Johns Hopkins University, Baltimore, Md. Facsimile reprint: University Microfilms International, Ann Arbor, Mich., 1991.)

Battiste, Marie, ed.
2000        Reclaiming Indigenous Voice and Vision. Vancouver: University of British Columbia Press.

Baugh, Timothy G., and Stephanie A. Makseyn-Kelley
1992        People of the Stars: Pawnee Heritage and the Smithsonian Institution. Washington: Smithsonian Institution, National Museum of Natural History, Repatriation Office.

Baugh, Timothy G., Stephanie A. Makseyn-Kelley, and John W. Verano
1993        With a Lock of Hair for Remembrance: Nakota and Central Dakota Legacy at the Smithsonian Institution. Washington: Smithsonian Institution, National Museum of Natural History, Repatriation Office.

Bay Mills Community College
1996        1994–1996 Catalog. Bay Mills, Mich.: Bay Mills Community College.

Baylor, Timothy
1994        Modern Warriors: Mobilization and Decline of the American Indian Movement (AIM), 1968–1979. (Ph.D. Dissertation in History, University of North Carolina, Chapel Hill.)

Bays, Brad A., and Erin H. Fouberg, eds.
2002        The Tribes and the States: Geographies of Intergovernmental Interaction. Lanham, Md.: Rowman and Littlefield.

Beals, David T.
1954        [Letter to Clyde Kluckhohn, dated December 9, 1954.] (Original in Folder 1, Box V, Glenn Emmons Papers, University of New Mexico General Library, Albuquerque.)

Beals, Ralph L.
1977        The Anthropologist as Expert Witness: Illustrations from the California Indian Land Claims Case. Pp. 139–155 in Irredeemable America: The Indians' Estate and Land Claims. Imre Sutton, ed. Albuquerque: University of New Mexico Press.

Beardslee, Lois
2004        Rachel's Children: Stories from a Contemporary Native American Woman. Blue Ridge Summit, Pa.: AltaMira Press.

Beck, David R. M.
2001        An Urban Platform for Advocating Justice: Protecting the Menominee Forest. Pp. 155–164 in American Indians and the Urban Experience. *Contemporary Native American Communities*. Susan Lobo and Kurt Peters, eds. Walnut Creek, Calif.: AltaMira Press.

_____
2005        The Struggle for Self-Determination: History of the Menominee Indians Since 1854. Lincoln and London: University of Nebraska Press.

Beckham, Stephen Dow
1990        *see* Handbook Vol. 7 (1990:180–188)

Bee, Robert L.
1982        The Politics of American Indian Policy. Cambridge, Mass.: Schenkman Publishing.

Beinart, Peter
1999        Lost Tribes: Native Americans and Government Anthropologists Feud over Indians' Identity. *Lingua Franca*, May/June 1999:33–41. Hammond, Ind.

Belanger, Yale D.
2002        The Morality of Aboriginal Gaming: A Concept in the Process of Definition. *The Journal of Aboriginal Economic Development* 2(2):25–36. Edmonton, Alta.

_____
2006        Seeking a Seat at the Table: A Brief History of Indian Political Organizing in Canada, 1870–1951. (Ph.D. Dissertation in Native Studies, Trent University, Peterborough, Ont.)

Belanger, Yale D., and David R. Newhouse
2004        Emerging from the Shadows: The Pursuit of Aboriginal Self-Government to Promote Aboriginal Well-Being. *Canadian Journal of Native Studies* 24(1):129–222. Brandon, Man.

Belhadji, Bachir
2001        Appendix A Part 1: Socio-Economic Profile of Aboriginal Co-Operatives in Canada. Pp. 61–121 in A Report on Aboriginal Co-Operatives in Canada: Current Situation and Potential for Growth. Lou Hammond Ketilson and Ian MacPherson. Saskatoon, Sask.: Centre for the Study of Co-Operatives, University of Saskatchewan.

Bell, Catherine E.
1992        Aboriginal Claims to Cultural Property in Canada: A Comparative Legal Analysis of the Repatriation Debate. *American Indian Law Review* 17(2):457–521. Norman, Okla.

_____
1994        Alberta's Métis Settlements Legislation: An Overview of Ownership and Management of Settlement Lands. Regina, Sask.: Canadian Plains Research Centre, Universtiy of Regina.

_____
1998        New Directions in the Law of Aboriginal Rights. *The Canadian Bar Review* 77(1–2):36–72. Toronto.

_____
2001        Protecting Indigenous Heritage Resources in Canada: A Comment on *Kitkatla* v. *British Columbia*. *International Journal of Cultural Property* 10(2):246–263. Berlin and New York.

Bell, Catherine E., and Clayton Leonard
2004        A New Era in Métis Constitutional Rights: The Importance of *Powley* and *Blais*. *Alberta Law Review* 41(2):1049–1083. Edmonton, Alta.

Bell, Catherine E., and Val Napoleon, eds.
2007        First Nations' Cultural Heritage and Law: Case Studies, Voices and Perspectives. Volume 1. Vancouver: University of British Columbia Press.

Bell, Catherine E., and Robert K. Paterson
1999        Aboriginal Rights to Cultural Property in Canada. *International Journal of Cultural Property* 8(1):167–211. New York and Berlin.

_____, eds.
2007        First Nations' Cultural Heritage and Law: Reconciliation and Reform. Volume 2. Vancouver: University of British Columbia Press.

Bell, Catherine E., Graham R. Statt, and Michael Solowan
2005        Protection and Repatriation of First Nation Cultural Heritage: A National Survey of Recent Issues and Initiatives. (Webpage: http://www.law.ualberta.ca/research/aboriginalculture-heritage/researchpapers.htmacc)

Bellafaire, Judith
2006        Native American Women Veterans. Women in Military Service for American Memorial Foundation, Inc. (Webpage: http://www.womensmemorial.org [19 July 2006].)

Bellecourt, Vernon
1976        American Indian Movement. Pp. 66–82 in Contemporary Native American Address. John R. Maestas, ed. Provo, Utah: Brigham Young University.

Benedict, Jeff
2001        Without Reservation: How a Controversial Indian Tribe Rose to Power and Built the World's Largest Casino. New York: Harper Perennial.

Benham, Maenette K., and Wayne J. Stein
2003        The Renaissance of American Indian Higher Education: Capturing the Dream. *Sociocultural, Political, and Historical Studies in Education.* Mahwah, N.J., and London: Lawrence Erlbaum Associates, Publishers.

Benitez, Fernando
1975        In the Magic Land of Peyote. John Upton, trans. Austin, Tex.: The University of Texas Press.

Bennet, Kay
1964        Kaibah: Recollections of a Navajo Girlhood. Los Angeles: Westernlore Press.

Bennett, E.F.
1958        Federal Indian Law. Washington: U.S. Department of the Interior; U.S. Government Printing Office.

Berger, Thomas R.
1977        Northern Frontier: Northern Homeland: The Report of the MacKenzie Valley Pipeline Inquiry. Ottawa: Minister of Supply and Services Canada.

———
1981        The Nishga Indians and Aboriginal Rights. Pp. 219–254 in Fragile Freedoms: Human Rights and Dissent in Canada, by Thomas R. Berger. Toronto: Clarke, Irwin.

———
1985        Village Journey: The Report of the Alaska Native Review Commission. New York. Hill and Wang.

———
2002        "Why I Won't Be Voting." *Vancouver Sun*, 15 April 2002. Vancouver, B.C.

Berglund, Joel
2003        Problems Surrounding the Repatriation, Collection and Displaying of Human Remains in Museums. Pp. 95–98 in Mummies in a New Millenium. *Proceedings of the 4th World Congress on Mummy Studies, Nuuk, Greenland, September 4th to 10th, 2001.* Niels Lynnerup, Claus Andreasen, and Joel Berglund, eds. Copenhagen, Denmark: Greenland National Museum and Archives, Danish Polar Center. (Title page has 2002 publication date; copyright date 2003.)

Bergman, Abraham B., et al.
1999        A Political History of the Indian Health Service. *The Milbank Quarterly* 77(4):571–604. New York.

Bergman, Robert L.
1983        *see* Handbook Vol. 10 (1983:672–678)

Berkhofer, Robert F., Jr.
1978        The White Man's Indian. New York: Random House.

———
1988        *see* Handbook Vol. 4 (1988:522–547)

Berlo, Janet C.
1992        The Early Years of Native American Art History. Seattle: University of Washington Press.

Berlo, Janet C., and Ruth B. Phillips
1998        Native North American Art. New York: Oxford University Press.

Bernstein, Alison R.
1991        American Indians and World War II: Toward a New Era in Indian Affairs. Norman: University of Oklahoma Press.

Berry, Mary Clay
1975        The Alaska Pipeline: The Politics of Oil and Native Land Claims. Bloomington, Ind.: University of Indiana Press.

Berthrong, Donald J.
1988        *see* Handbook Vol. 4 (1988:255–263)

Besaw, Amy, et al.
2004        The Context and Meaning of Family Strengthening in Indian America. A Report to the Annie E. Casey Foundation by The Harvard Project on American Indian Economic Development. Cambridge, Mass.: The Harvard Project on American Indian Economic Development, Harvard University.

Bevis, William
1987        Native American Novels: Homing In. Pp. 580–620 in Recovering the Word: Essays on Native American Literature. Brian Swann and Arnold Krupat, eds. Berkeley, [etc.]: University of California Press.

BIA = Bureau of Indian Affairs *see* U.S. Department of the Interior. Bureau of Indian Affairs (BIA)

Biddle, Lucy
1977        Keeping Tradition Alive. *Museum News* 55(5):35–42. Washington.

Bieder, Robert E.
1990        A Brief Historical Survey of the Expropriation of American Indian Remains. Boulder, Colo.: Native American Rights Fund.

———
1992        The Collecting of Bones for Anthropological Narratives. *American Indian Culture and Research Journal* 16(2):21–35. Los Angeles.

Bigsby, Christopher W. E.
1982        American Indian Theatre. Pp. 365–374 in A Critical Introduction to Twentieth-Century American Drama 3: Beyond Broadway. Cambridge and New York: Cambridge University Press.

Bił Hazíʼąądi Nooyééł
1972        *see* National Geographic Society 1972

Bilharz, Joy Ann
1998        The Allegany Senecas and Kinzua Dam: Forced Relocation Through Two Generations. Lincoln: University of Nebraska Press.

Billeck, William T.
1995        Comments of the Cultural Affiliation of the Steed-Kisker Phase. Washington: Smithsonian Institution, National Museum of Natural History, Repatriation Office.

Billeck, William T., and Betsy Bruemmer
2007        Assessment of a Lock of Hair and Leggings Attributed to Sitting Bull, a Hunkpapa Sioux, in the National Museum of Natural History, Smithsonian Institution. Washington: Smithson-

ian Institution, National Museum of Natural History, Repatriation Office.

Billeck, William T., and Stuart Speaker
2001        Assessment of Human Remains from Owens Valley, California, in the National Museum of Natural History. Washington: Smithsonian Institution, National Museum of Natural History, Repatriation Office.

Billeck, William T., and Javier Urcid
1995        Assessment of the Cultural Affiliation of the Steed-Kisker Phase for Evaluation by the National Museum of Natural History Native American Repatriation Review Committee. Washington: Smithsonian Institution, National Museum of Natural History, Repatriation Office.

Billeck, William T., Betsy Bruemmer, and Karen Mudar
2001        Inventory and Assessment of Human Remains from Fort Brady, Michigan, in the National Museum of Natural History. Washington: Smithsonian Institution, National Museum of Natural History, Repatriation Office.

Billeck, William T., et al.
1995        Inventory and Assessment of Human Remains and Associated Funerary Objects Potentially Affiliated with the Pawnee in the National Museum of Natural History. Washington: Smithsonian Institution, National Museum of Natural History, Repatriation Office.

_____, et al.
1996        Inventory and Assessment of Human Remains and Funerary Objects Potentially Affiliated with the Mandan and Hidatsa of the Three Affiliated Tribes in the National Museum of Natural History. Washington: Smithsonian Institution, National Museum of Natural History, Repatriation Office.

_____, et al.
1997        Inventory and Assessment of Human Remains and Funerary Objects Potentially Affiliated with the Ponca in the National Museum of Natural History. Washington: Smithsonian Institution, National Museum of Natural History, Repatriation Office.

_____, et al.
2005        Inventory and Assessment of Human Remains and Funerary Objects Potentially Affiliated with the Arikara in the National Museum of Natural History, Smithsonian Institution. Washington: Smithsonian Institution, National Museum of Natural History, Repatriation Office.

Billinghurst, Jane
1999        Grey Owl: The Many Faces of Archie Belaney. Foreword by Donald B. Smith. New York: Kodansha America.

Biolsi, Thomas
1992        Organizing the Lakota: The Political Economy of the New Deal on the Pine Ridge and Rosebud Reservations. Tucson: University of Arizona Press.

Biolsi, Thomas, and Larry J. Zimmerman, eds.
1997        Indians and Anthropologists: Vine Deloria, Jr., and the Critique of Anthropology. Tucson: University of Arizona Press.

Birchfield, D.L.
1998        Oklahoma Basic Intelligence Test: New and Collected Elementary, Epistolary, Autobiographical and Oratorical Choctologies. *Frank Waters Memorial Publication Series* 2. Greenfield Center, N.Y.: Greenfield Review Press.

_____
2004        Field of Honor. Norman: University of Oklahoma Press.

_____
2006        Black Silk Handkerchief: A Hom-Astubby Mystery. Norman: University of Oklahoma Press.

Bird, S. Elizabeth, ed.
1996        Dressing in Feathers: The Construction of the Indian in American Popular Culture. Boulder, Colo.: Westview Press.

Bird, S. Elizabeth
1999        Gendered Construction of the American Indian in Popular Media. *Journal of Communication* 49(3):61–83. New York.

Bixler, Margaret T.
1992        Winds of Freedom: The Story of the Navajo Code Talkers of World War II. Darien, Conn.: Two Bytes Pub. Co.

Black Elk
1932, 1961, 1979 *see* Neihardt, John G. 1932, 1961, 1979

Blackhawk, Ned
1995        I Can Carry On From Here: The Relocation of American Indians to Los Angeles. *Wicaso Sa Review* 11(2):16–30. Minneapolis.

Blackstock, Cindy, et al.
2004        Keeping the Promise: The Convention on the Rights of the Child and the Lived Experiences of First Nations Children and Youth. Ottawa: First Nations Child and Family Caring Society of Canada.

Blaeser, Kimberly M.
1996        Gerald Vizenor: Writing in the Oral Tradition. Norman: University of Oklahoma Press.

Blaine, Martha Royce
1982        The Pawnee-Wichita Visitation Cycle: Historical Manifestation of an Ancient Friendship. Pp. 113–134 in Pathways to Plains Prehistory: Anthropological Perspectives of Plains Natives and Their Pasts. Don G. Wycoff and Jack L. Hofman, eds. *Oklahoma Anthropological Society Memoir* 3. Norman, Okla.

Blair, Bowen
1979        Indian Rights: Native Americans versus American Museums—A Battle for Artifacts. *American Indian Law Review* 7(1):125–154. Norman, Okla.

Blakeney, Allan
1994        Urban Aboriginals and Self-Government. Pp. 356–357 in Continuing Poundmaker and Riel's Quest: Presentations Made at a Conference on Aboriginal Peoples and Justice. Richard Grosse, James Youngblood Anderson, and Roger Carter, eds. Saskatoon, Sask.: Purich Publishing.

Blankenship, Bob
1992        Cherokee Roots. 2 vols. Vol. 1: Eastern Cherokee Rolls, Members of the Cherokee Tribe Residing East of the Mississippi River during the Period 1817–1924 (2d ed.). Vol. 2: Western Cherokee Rolls. A Listing of the Members of the Cherokee Tribe Residing West of the Mississippi River (4th ed.). Cherokee, N.C.: Bob Blankenship.

Block, Ira
2000        At Rest, At Last! A Personal Account of the Assignment from Photographer Ira Block. (Webpage: http://www.nationalgeographic.com/ngm/0011/pov.html; see also: Tarpy, Cliff, and Ira Block 2000.)

Bloom, Allan D.
1987        The Closing of the American Mind. New York: Simon and Schuster.

Blu, Karen I.
1980        The Lumbee Problem: The Making of an American Indian People. *Cambridge Studies in Cultural Systems*. Cambridge, London, [etc.]: Cambridge University Press. (Reprinted: see Blue 2001.)

_____
2001        The Lumbee Problem: The Making of an American Indian People. With a New Afterword by the Author. Lincoln and London: University of Nebraska Press.

2001a    Region and Recognition: Southern Indians, Anthropologists, and Presumed Biology. Pp. 71–85 in Anthropologists and Indians in the New South. Rachel A. Bonney and J. Anthony Paredes, eds. Tuscaloosa, Ala., and London: The University of Alabama Press.

2004    *see* Handbook Vol. 14 (2004:319–327)

Blue Cloud, Peter
1972    Alcatraz Is Not an Island. Berkeley, Calif.: Wingbow Press.

Blue Quills First Nations College
2006    Our History. St. Paul, Alta.: Blue Quills First Nations College. (Webpage: http://www.Bluequills.ca/our_history.htm&memorandum.htm)

Blue Spruce, Duane, ed.
2004    Spirit of a Native Place: Building the National Museum of the American Indian. Washington: National Museum of the American Indian, Smithsonian Institution.

Blumenfeld, Ruth
1965    Mohawks: Round Trip to High Steel. *Transaction* 3(Nov./Dec.):19–22.

Bodinger de Uriarte, John J.
2003    Imagining the Nation with House Odds: Representing American Indian Identity at Mashantucket. Pp. 549–565 in Native Peoples and Tourism. Neil L. Whitehead, ed.; Larry Nesper, guest ed. *Ethnohistory* 50(3).

2006    Casino and Museum: Representing Mashantucket Pequot Identity. Tucson: The University of Arizona Press. (Originally presented as the Author's Ph.D. Dissertation under slightly different title, University of Texas at Austin, 2003.)

Bol, Marsha C.
1985    Lakota Women's Artistic Strategies in Support of the Social System. *American Indian Culture and Research Journal* 9(1):33–51. Los Angeles.

1989    Gender in Art: A Comparison of Lakota Women's and Men's Art, 1820–1920. 2 vols. (Ph.D. Dissertation in Art History, University of New Mexico, Albuquerque.)

Boldt, Menno
1982    *see* Long, J. Anthony, Leroy Little Bear, and Menno Boldt 1982

1993    Surviving As Indians: The Challenge of Self-Government. Toronto: University of Toronto Press.

Bolton, Stephanie
2004    An Analysis of the Task Force on Museums and First Peoples: The Changing Representation of Aboriginal Histories in Museums. (M.A. Thesis in Art History, Concordia University, Montreal.)

Bommelyn, Loren, and Victor Golla, eds.
1995    Now You're Speaking—Tolowa! Arcata, Calif.: Humboldt State University, Center for Indian Community Development.

Bonney, Rachel A.
1977    The Role of AIM Leaders in Indian Nationalism. *American Indian Quarterly* 3(3):209–224. Lincoln, Nebr.

Bonney, Rachel A., and J. Anthony Paredes, eds.
2001    Anthropologists and Indians in the New South. Tuscaloosa, Ala., and London: The University of Alabama Press.

Bonnin, Gertrude *see* Zitkala-Ša (Gertrude Bonnin)

Bordeaux, Lionel
1987    [Interview concerning Sinte Gleska College (SGC), February, 20, 1987.] (Conducted by Wayne J. Stein, Mission, S.Dak.; Text of interview in Department of Native American Studies, Montana State University, Bozeman, Mont.).

Borrows, John
1994    Contemporary Traditional Equality: The Effect of the Charter on First Nations Politics. *University of New Brunswick Law Journal* 43:19–48. Fredericton, N.B.

1997    Wampum at Niagara: The Royal Proclamation, Canada Legal History, and Self-Government. Pp. 155–172 in Aboriginal and Treaty Rights in Canada: Essays on Law, Equality, and Respect for Difference. Michael Asch, ed. Vancouver: University of British Columbia Press.

1997a    Frozen Rights in Canada: Constitutional Interpretation and the Trickster. *American Indian Law Review* 22(1):37–64. Norman. Okla.

1999    Sovereignty's Alchemy: An Analysis of *Delgamuukw v. British Columbia. Osgoode Hall Law Journal* 37(3):537–596. Toronto.

2001    Listening for Change: The Courts and Oral Tradition. *Osgoode Hall Law Journal* 39(1):1–38. Toronto.

2001a    Domesticating Doctrines: Aboriginal Peoples after the Royal Commission. *McGill Law Journal* 46(3):615–661. Montreal.

2001b    Indian Agency: Forming First Nations Law in Canada. *PoLAR: Political and Legal Anthropology Review* 24(2):9–24. Washington.

2001c    Uncertain Citizens: The Supreme Court and Aboriginal Peoples. *The Canadian Bar Review* 80(1–2):15–41. Toronto.

2002    Recovering Canada: The Resurgence of Indigenous Law. Toronto: University of Toronto Press.

2006    Indigenous Legal Traditions in Canada. Ottawa: Law Commission of Canada.

2006a    Ground-rules: Indigenous Treaties in Canada and New Zealand. *New Zealand Universities Law Review* 22(2):188–212. Wellington, New Zealand.

Boserup, Ester
1966    The Conditions of Agricultural Growth: The Economics of Agrarian Change Under Population Pressure. Chicago: Aldine Publishers.

Boutros Ghali, Boutros
1994    Preface. In: The International Decade of the World's Indigenous People. General Assembly Resolution 1994/214. Geneva, Switzerland: Office of the United Nations High Commissioner for Human Rights (Copyright 1996–2000).

Box Office Mojo
[2007]    "Dances with Wolves" (1990). (Webpage: http://www.boxofficemojo.com.)

[2007a]    "Thunderheart" (1992). (Webpage: http://www.boxofficemojo.com.)

[2007b]    "Smoke Signals" (1998). (Webpage: http://www.boxofficemojo.com.)

[2007c]    "The Fast Runner (Atanarjuat)" (2002). (Webpage: http://www.boxofficemojo.com.)

[2007d]    "The New World" (2005). (Webpage: http://www.boxoffice mojo.com.)

Boyd, Maurice, ed.
1981    Kiowa Voices: Ceremonial Dance, Ritual and Song. Vol. 1. Forth Worth, Tex.: Texas Christian University Press.

Boyer, L. Bryce, Ruth M. Boyer, and Arthur E. Hippler
1974    The Alaska Athabaskan Potlatch Ceremony: An Ethnopsycho-Analytical Study. *International Journal of Psychoanalytic Psychotherapy* 3(3):343–365. New York.

Boyer, LaNada
1994    Reflections of Alcatraz. Pp. 75–92 in Special Edition: Alcatraz Revisited: The 25th Anniversary of the Occupation, 1969–1971. Joane Nagel and Troy Johnson, eds. *American Indian Culture and Research Journal* 18(4). Los Angeles.

Boyer, Paul, comp.
1989    Tribal Colleges: Shaping the Future of Native America. *The Carnegie Foundation for the Advancement of Teaching.* Princeton, N.J.: Princeton University Press.

——    1997    Native American Colleges: Progress and Prospects. Princeton, N.J.: Carnegie Foundation for the Advancement of Teaching.

Braatz, Timothy
2003    Surviving Conquest: A History of the Yavapai Peoples. Lincoln and London: University of Nebraska Press.

Bramstedt, Wayne G.
1977    Corporate Adaptations of Urban Migrants: American Indian Voluntary Associations in the Los Angeles Metropolitan Area. (Ph.D. Dissertation in Anthropology, University of California, Los Angeles.)

Brand, Johanna
1978    The Life and Death of Anna Mae Aquash. Toronto: James Lorimer.

Brand, Stewart
1988    *see* Handbook Vol. 4 (1988:570–572)

Brandão, José António
1997    Your Fyre Shall Burn No More: Iroquois Policy Toward New France and Its Native Allies to 1701. Lincoln: University of Nebraska Press.

Brandon, William
1973    The Last Americans: The Indian in American Culture. New York: McGraw-Hill.

Brant, Beth E., ed.
1984    A Gathering of Spirit: A Collection by American Indian Women. Rockland, Me.: Sinister Wisdom Books. (Reprinted, rev. ed.: Firebrand Books, Ithaca, N.Y., 1988.)

——    1985    Mohawk Trail. Ithaca, N.Y.: Firebrand Books.

——    1991    Food and Spirits. Ithaca, N.Y.: Firebrand Books.

——    1994    Writing as Witness: Essay and Talk. Ithaca, N.Y.: Firebrand Books.

Brant, Johanna
1978    The Life and Death of Anna Mae Aquash. Toronto: James Lorimer and Company.

Brascoupé, Simon, ed.
1981    Directory of North American Indian Museums and Cultural Centers. Niagara Falls, N.Y.: North American Indian Museums Association.

Brask, Per, and William Morgan, eds.
1992    Aboriginal Voices: Amerindian, Inuit, and Sami Theater. Baltimore, Md.: Johns Hopkins University Press.

Brathovde, Jennifer, ed.
1992    American Indians on Film and Video: Documentaries in the Library of Congress. Washington: Library of Congress.

Bray, Tamara L., ed.
2001    The Future of the Past: Archaeologists, Native Amearicans, and Repatriation. New York and London: Garland Publishing.

Bray, Tamara L., and Thomas W. Killion
1994    Reckoning with the Dead: The Larsen Bay Repatriation and the Smithsonian Institution. Washington: Smithsonian Institution Press.

Bray, Tamara L., Gary P. Aronsen, and Javier Urcid
1996    Inventory and Assessment of Human Remains and Funerary Objects from Northwestern Oregon in the National Museum of Natural History. Washington: Smithsonian Institution, National Museum of Natural History, Repatriation Office.

Bray, Tamara L., Javier Urcid, and Gary P. Aronsen
1993    Inventory and Assessment of Human Remains from Upper and Lower Memaloose Islands and Adjacents Areas of the Middle Columbia River, Oregon, and Washington. Washington: Smithsonian Institution, National Museum of Natural History, Repatriation Office.

——    1994    Inventory and Assessment of Human Remains from Clallam County, Washington, in the National Museum of Natural History. Washington: Smithsonian Institution, National Museum of Natural History, Repatriation Office.

——    1994a    Inventory and Assessment of Human Remains from Northeastern Washington and Northern Idaho in the National Museum of Natural History. Washington: Smithsonian Institution, National Museum of Natural History, Repatriation Office.

Bray, Tamara L., et al.
1992    Inventory and Assessment of Native American Human Remains from the Western Great Basin, Nevada Sector, in the National Museum of Natural History. Washington: Smithsonian Institution, National Museum of Natural History, Repatriation Office.

Brehaut, Harry Baker
1971    The Red River Cart and Trails: The Fur Trade. *Manitoba Historical Society Transactions, Series* 3, No. 28(1971–72 Season). Winnipeg, Man.

Brenneman, G.R.
2000    Maternal, Child, and Youth Health. Pp. 138–150 in American Indian Health: Innovations in Health Care, Promotion, and Policy. E.R. Rhoades, ed. Baltimore, Md.: Johns Hopkins University Press.

Brescia, William, and Tony Daily
2007    Economic Development and Technology-Skill Needs on American Indian Reservations. *American Indian Quarterly* 31(1):23–44. Berkeley.

Brewer, Cynthia A., and Trudy A. Suchan, comps.
2001    Mapping Census 2000: The Geography of U.S. Diversity. Washington: U.S. Department of Commerce, Economics and Statistics Administration—U.S. Census Bureau.

*459*

Bridge, Maurice
2004 Iceman's Remains Now Complete: Hunters Return to the Site of Their Original Discovery and Recover the 560-year-old Man's Remaining Bones. *The Vancouver Sun*, October 21, 2004. Vancouver, B.C.

Briggs, Jean L.
1970 Never in Anger: Portrait of an Eskimo Family. Cambridge, Mass.: Harvard University Press.

Brigham, Clarence S., ed.
1911 British Royal Proclamations Relating to America. *Transactions and Collections of the American Antiquarian Society* 12. Worcester, Mass.

Brinker, Paul A., and Benjamin J. Taylor
1974 Southern Plains Indian Relocation Returnees. *Human Organization* 33(2):139–146. Washington.

British Columbia
1875 Papers Connected with the Indian Land Question, 1850–1875. Victoria, B.C.: Richard Wolfenden, Government Printer.

British Columbia Treaty Commission
2006 [Negotiations Update.] (Webpage: http://www.bctreaty.net/files_3/updates.html)

——
2007 [Negotiations Update.] (Webpage: http://www.bctreaty.net/files/updates.php)

Britten, Thomas A.
1997 American Indians in World War I: At War and at Home. Albuquerque: University of New Mexico Press. (Reprinted in 1999. Originally presented as the Author's Ph.D. Dissertation under title: American Indians in World War I: Military Service as Catalyst for Reform. Texas Tech University, Lubbock, Tex., 1994.)

Britton, Sharon
1999 The Andover-Pecos Repatriation: "They Wanted to Come Back Home." *Andover Bulletin* 92(4):21–23. Andover, Mass.

Brock, Kathy
1991 The Politics of Aboriginal Self-Government: A Canadian Paradox. *Canadian Public Administration* 34(2):272–285. Toronto.

Brodeur, Paul
1985 Restitution: The Land Claims of the Mashpee, Passamaquoddy, and Penobscot Indians of New England. Boston: Northeastern University Press.

Brook, Peter
1974 Some Notes on Our Theater. *The New York Times*, January 20, 1974. New York.

Brooks, James F., ed.
2002 Confounding the Color Line: The Indian-Black Experience in North America. Lincoln and London: University of Nebraska Press.

Brophy, William A., and Sophie D. Aberle
1966 The Indian: America's Unfinished Business. Norman: University of Oklahoma Press.

Brown, Cathy
2001 Giving Blood in a Search for History: Natives Participate in Tests Designed to Track Relatives of Man Discovered at Glacier. *Juneau Empire*, June 13, 2001. Juneau, Alaska.

Brown, Cathy, Lori Thomson, and Svend Holst
1999 Between Worlds: How the Alaska Native Claims Settlement Act Reshaped the Destinies of Alaska's Native People. A *Juneau Empire* Special Report. Juneau, Alaska: Morris Communications Corporation. (Webpage: http://juneaualaska.com/between/[Copyright: 2001])

Brown, Dee
1971 Bury My Heart at Wounded Knee: An Indian History of the American West. New York: Holt, Rinehart and Winston. (Copyright:1970.)

Brown, Donald N.
1961 The Development of Taos Dance. *Ethnomusicology* 5(1):33–41. Middletown, Conn.

Brown, Harry J.
2004 Injun Joe's Ghost: The Indian Mixed-Blood in American Writing. Columbia, Mo., and London: University of Missouri Press.

Brown, Jennifer S.H.
1980 Strangers in Blood: Fur Trade Company Families in Indian Country. Vancouver: University of British Columbia Press.

Brown, Kent R.
1973 Opening on the Education Scene: A Native American Theater Ensemble. *The Journal of American Indian Education* 13(1):1–6. Tempe, Ariz.

Brown, Michael F.
2003 Who Owns Native Culture? Cambridge: Harvard University Press.

Brown, Stuart E., Jr., Lorraine F. Mayer, and Eileen M. Chappel
1985 Pocahontas and Her Descendants (and Supplement, 1987). Berryville, Va.: The Pocahontas Foundation.

Brownell, Margo S.
2000–2001 Who Is An Indian? Searching for an Answer to the Question at the Core of Federal Indian Law. *University of Michigan Journal of Law Reform* 34(1–2):275–320. Ann Arbor, Mich.

Browner, Tara
2000 Making and Singing Pow-Wow Songs: Text, Form and the Significance of Culture-Based Analysis. *Ethnomusicology* 44(2):214–233. Middletown, Conn.

——
2002 Heartbeat of the People: Music and Dance of the Northern Pow-Wow. Urbana: University of Illinois Press.

Bruce, Jean
1969 Arctic Housing. *North* 16(1):1–9. Ottawa.

Bruchac, Joseph
1987 Survival This Way: Interviews with American Indian Poets. *Sun tracks* 15. Tucson: University of Arizona Press.

——
1995 Dawn Land. Golden, Colo.: Fulcrum Publishing.

——, ed.
2000 Pushing Up the Sky: Seven Native American Plays for Children. Illustrated by Teresa Flavin. New York: Dial.

Bruguier, Leonard R., and Scott E. White
2001 The Institute of American Indian Studies: A Tradition of Scholarly Pursuit. *Indigenous Nations Studies Journal* 2(1):3–10. Lawrence, Kans.

Brumble, H. David, III
1988 American Indian Autobiography. Berkeley, [etc.]: University of California Press.

Buchanan, Judd
1976 Judd Buchanan to George Manuel, President, National Indian Brotherhood, Ottawa: Approach to Government-Indian Relationship. Ottawa: Indian and Northern Affairs Canada, Treaties and Historical Research Centre.

Buckley, Helen
1992     From Wooden Ploughs to Welfare: Why Indian Policy Failed in the Prairie Provinces. Montreal: McGill-Queen's University Press.

Buckner, Philip, ed.
2004     Canada and the End of Empire. Vancouver: University of British Columbia Press.

Bunte, Pamela, and Robert Franklin
2001     Language Revitalization in the San Juan Paiute Community and The Role of a Paiute Constitution. Pp. 255–264 in The Green Book of Language Revitalization in Practice. Leanne Hinton and Kenneth Hale, eds. San Diego, Calif.: Academic Press.

Bureau of Indian Affairs (BIA) *see* U.S. Department of the Interior. Bureau of Indian Affairs (BIA)

Bureau of Justice Assistance
2006     Walking on Common Ground: Pathways to Equal Justice. (Webpage: http://www.walkingoncommonground.org/webcontent/wocg_report.pdf [27 September 2006].)

Burgess, Laurie E., and William T. Billeck
2004     Assessment of a Brass Patu Traded by Captain Cook in 1778 and an Anthropomorphic Stone Carving from Northeast Oregon in the National Museum of Natural History, Smithsonian Institution. Washington: Smithsonian Institution, National Museum of Natural History, Repatriation Office.

Burgess, Laurie E., et al.
2004     Inventory and Assessment of Human Remains and Objects from Southeast Washington and Northeast Oregon in the National Museum of Natural History. Washington: Smithsonian Institution, National Museum of Natural History, Repatriation Office.

Burke, Brian J.
2000     Left Out in the Cold: The Problem with Aboriginal Title Under Section 35(1) of the *Constitution Act*, 1982 for Historically Nomadic Aboriginal Peoples. *Osgoode Hall Law Journal* 38(1):1–37. Toronto.

Burnaby, Barbara Jane, and Roderic Beaujot
1986     The Use of Aboriginal Languages in Canada: An Analysis of 1981 Census Data. Prepared for the Social Trends Analysis Directorate and Native Citizens Directorate. Ottawa: Department of the Secretary of State; Minister of Supply and Services Canada.

Burnaby, Barbara Jane, and Marguerite Mackenzie
2001     Cree Decision Making Concerning Language: A Case Study. *Journal of Multilingual and Multicultural Development* 22(3):191–209. Antigonish, N.S.

Burnaby, Barbara Jane, and Jon Allan Reyhner, eds.
2002     Indigenous Languages Across the Community. *Proceedings of the Annual Conference on Stabilizing Indigenous Languages; 7th, Toronto, Ont., Canada, May 11–14, 2000.* Flagstaff, Ariz.: Center for Education Excellence, Northern Arizona University.

Burnette, Robert, and John Koster
1974     The Road to Wounded Knee. New York: Bantam Books.

Burns, Louis F.
1989     A History of the Osage People. Tuscaloosa: The University of Alabama Press.

Burt, Larry W.
1977     Factories on Reservations: The Industrial Development Programs of Commissioner Glenn Emmons, 1953–1960. *Arizona and the West* 19(4):317–332. Tucson, Ariz.

1982     Tribalism in Crisis: Federal Indian Policy, 1953–1961. Albuquerque: University of New Mexico Press.

1986     Roots of the Native American Urban Experience: Relocation Policy in the 1950s. *American Indian Quarterly* 10(2):85–99. Lincoln, Nebr.

Burton, Lloyd
1991     American Indian Water Rights and the Limits of the Law. Lawrence, Kans.: University Press of Kansas.

Butler, LaFollette
1974     [Letter from Acting Deputy Commissioner of Indian Affairs to Senator Henry Jackson, dated June 7, 1974.] (Office of Federal Acknowledgment Files, June 7, 1974, Bureau of Indian Affairs, Washington.)

Butler, Raymond V.
1973     [Memorandum from Acting Director, Office of Indian Services, to the Secretary of the Interior, dated June 13, 1973.] (Branch of Acknowledgment and Research Files, June 13, 1973, Bureau of Indian Affairs, Washington.)

1977     [Memorandum from Acting Commissioner of Indian Affairs to Department of the Interior Legislative Council.] (Branch of Acknowledgment and Research Files, Bureau of Indian Affairs, Washington.)

Button, H. Warren, and Eugene F. Provenzo
1983     History of Education and Culture in America. Englewood Cliffs, N.J.: Prentice-Hall.

Byrd, Jodi A.
2007     "Living My Native Life Deadly": Red Lake, Ward Churchill, and the Discourses of Competing Genocides. *American Indian Quarterly* 31(2):310–332. Lincoln, Nebr.

Cahn, Edgard S., ed.
1969     Our Brother's Keeper: The Indian in White America. Washington: New Community Press.

Cairns, Alan
2000     Citizens Plus: Aboriginal Peoples and the Canadian State. Vancouver: University of British Columbia Press.

Cajete, Gregory A.
1999     The Native American Learner and Bicultural Science Education. Pp. 135–160 in Next Steps: Research and Practice to Advance Indian Education. Karen Gayton Swisher and John W. Tippeconnic, III, eds. Charleston, W.Va.: ERIC Clearinghouse on Rural Education and Small Schools.

Caldwell, Carey T.
1987     Suquamish Tribal Cultural Center and Suquamish Museum: Development and History. (M.A. Thesis, University of Washington, Seattle.)

Callahan, S. Alice
1891     Wynema: A Child of the Forest. Chicago: Smith. (Reprinted: see Callahan 1997.)

1997     Wynema: A Child of the Forest. Edited, with an Introduction by A. LaVonne Brown Ruoff. Lincoln: University of Nebraska Press.

Calliou, George
1998     Urban Indians: Reflections on Participation of First Nation Individuals in the Institutions of the Larger Society. Pp. 222–243 in First Nations in Canada: Perspective on Opportunity, Empowerment, and Self-Determination. J. Rick Ponting, ed. Toronto: McGraw-Hill Ryerson Limited.

Calloway, Colin

1987    Crown and Calumet: British-Indian Relations, 1783–1815. Norman: University of Oklahoma Press.

_____, ed.

1990    Dawnland Encounters: Indians and Europeans in Northern New England. Hanover, N.H.: University Press of New England.

2002    Eleazar Wheelock Meets Luther Standing Bear: Native American Studies at Dartmouth College. Pp. 17–28 in Native American Studies in Higher Education: Models for Collaboration Between Universities and Indigenous Nations. Duane Champagne and Jay Stauss, eds. Walnut Creek, Calif.: AltaMira Press.

2006    The Scratch of a Pen: 1763 and the Transformation of North America. Oxford: Oxford University Press.

Calloway, Colin, and Neal Salisbury

2003    Reinterpreting New England Indians and the Colonial Experience. Boston: The Colonial Society of Massachusetts.

Cameron, Ian Alexander, and Douglas Pye, eds.

1996    The Book of Westerns. New York: Continuum.

Campbell, Maria

1973    Half Breed. New York: Saturday Review Press.

Campisi, Jack

1988    Testimony Before the Senate Select Committee on Indian Affairs, U.S. Senate, in Support of S.2672. 58-108; 100:2nd on S.2672, to Provide Federal Recognition of the Lumbee Tribe of North Carolina. *Senate Hearing* 100-881. Washington: U.S. Government Printing Office.

1991    The Mashpee Indians: Tribe on Trial. Syracuse, N.Y.: Syracuse University Press.

2004    *see* Handbook Vol. 14 (2004:760–768)

Canada

1898    The Quebec Boundary Extension Act, 1898. Ottawa: Queen's Printer.

1905–1912    Indian Treaties and Surrenders, from 1680–1890. 3 vols. Ottawa: B. Chamberlin, Printer to the Queen's Most Excellent Majesty. (Reprinted: Cole, Toronto 1971.)

1912    The Quebec Boundaries Extension Act, 1912. Ottawa: King's Printer.

1926–1927    (An Act to Amend the) Indian Act. *Statues of Canada*, 1926–27, c. 32, s. 6. Ottawa: Queen's Printer.

1959    A Review of Activities 1948–1958. Indian Affairs Branch, Department of Citizenship and Immigration. Ottawa: Citizenship and Immigration Department.

1961    The Report of the Joint Parliamentary-Senate Committee Hearings on Indian Affairs in Canada. Ottawa: Queen's Printer.

1966    Treaty 8 Made June 21, 1899 and Adhesions, Reports, etc. Ottawa: Queen's Printer. (Reprinted from the 1899 edition.)

1966–1967    A Survey of the Contemporary Indians of Canada. Economic, Political, Educational Needs and Policies. Parts 1–2. Ottawa: Queen's Printer.

1969    A Statement of the Government of Canada on Indian Policy. Ottawa: House of Commons; Indian and Northern Affairs Canada.

1973    Statement on Claims of the Indian and Inuit People. Ottawa: Indian and Northern Affairs Canada.

1977    The Report of the Mackenzie Valley Pipeline Inquiry. Ottawa: Minister of Supply and Services.

1981    Contemporary Indian Legislation, 1951–1978. Ottawa: Indian and Northern Affairs Canada.

1982    Guide to Canadian Ministries Since Confederation, July 1, 1867, to February 1, 1982. Ottawa: Ministry of Supply and Services.

1982a    The Constitution Act, 1982. Ottawa: Queen's Printer.

1983    Report of the Special Committee of the House of Commons on Indian Self-Government (Task Force). Ottawa: Queen's Printer.

1983a    The Constitution Amendment Proclamation. Ottawa: Queen's Printer.

1984    Response of the Government to the Report of the Special Committee on Indian Self-Government. Ottawa: Indian and Northern Affairs.

1984a    Cree-Naskapi (of Quebec) Act, 1984. Ottawa: Minister of Indian Affairs and Northern Development.

1984b    The Western Arctic Claim: The Inuvialuit Agreement. Ottawa: Indian and Northern Affairs Canada.

1985    Living Treaties: Lasting Agreements, Report of the Task Force to Review Comprehensive Claim Policy. Ottawa: Department of Indian Affairs and Northern Development.

1987    Aboriginal Constitutional Matters: Transcript of Proceedings, Ottawa, March 26–27, 1987. Ottawa: Parliament of Canada.

1993    Identification and Registration of Indian and Inuit People. Ottawa: Indian and Northern Affairs Canada.

1993a    Agreement Between the Inuit of the Nunavut Settlement Area and Her Majesty the Queen in the Right of Canada. Ottawa: Minister of Indian Affairs and Northern Development and the Tungavik.

1996    *see* Canada. Royal Commission on Aboriginal Peoples (RCAP) 1996

1998    Federal Policy for the Settlement of Native Claims. Ottawa: Indian and Northern Affairs Canada.

1998a    Gathering Strength: Canada's Aboriginal Action Plan. Canada: Minister of Indian Affairs and Northern Development.

1998b    [i.e. 1999] *see* Nisga'a Final Agreement 1999

2003    Canada (Attorney General) v. Misquadis. *F.C.A.* 473. Ottawa.

2003       Resolving Aboriginal Claims: A Practical Guide to the Canadian Experience. Ottawa: Indian and Northern Affairs Canada.

Canada. Aboriginal Peoples Survey
[2001]     2003 *see* O'Donnell, Vivian, and Heather Tait 2003

Canada. Agreements, Treaties and Negotiated Settlements Project
2004      Comprehensive Land Claims Agreement. (Webpage: http://www.atns.net.au/biogs/A001973b.htm)

Canada. Analysis Series
2006      Aboriginal Peoples of Canada: A Demographic Profile. (Webpage: http://www.12.statcan.ca/English/census01/Products/Analytic/companion/Canada.cfm)

Canada. Auditor General of Canada
1980      Report of the Auditor General of Canada to the House of Commons—Comprehensive Audit: Department of Indian Affairs and Northern Development. Ottawa: Minister of Supply and Services.

2003      Economic Development of First Nations Communities: Institutional Arrangements. Chapter 9 in: Report of the Auditor General of Canada to the House of Commons. Ottawa: Auditor General of Canada.

2005      Indian and Northern Affairs Canada—Meeting Treaty Land Entitlement Obligations. Chapter 7, November 2005 Report of the Auditor General of Canada to Parliament. Ottawa: Auditor General of Canada

Canada. Census and Aboriginal Peoples Survey
1991      Statistics Canada Catalogue # 94-327. Ottawa: Statistics Canada. (Webpage: http://www.statcan.ca/english/Pgdb/demo43b.htm [January 2003].)

Canada. Department of Citizenship and Immigration
1958      Report of Indian Affairs Branch. Ottawa: Queen's Printer.

1964      Report of the Department of Citizenship and Immigration, 1963–1964. Ottawa: Queen's Printer.

Canada. Department of Indian Affairs and Northern Development (DIAND)
1970      Linguistic and Cultural Affiliations of Canadian Indian Bands. G.W. Neville, ed. and comp. Ottawa: Department of Indian Affairs and Northern Development.

1972      Annual Report of the Department of Indian Affairs and Northern Development, 1970–1971. Ottawa: Department of Indian Affairs and Northern Development.

1975      Registered Indian Populaton by Sex and Residence, 1974. Ottawa: Department of Indian Affairs and Northern Development.

1985      Registered Indian Population by Sex and Residence, 1984. Ottawa: Department of Indian Affairs and Northern Development.

2000      Registered Indian Population Projections for Canada and Regions, 2002–2021. Ottawa: Department of Indian Affairs and Northern Development.

2002      Registered Indian Population of Canada by Sex and Residence, 2001. Ottawa: Department of Indian Affairs and Northern Development.

2002a     Basic Departmental Data, 2002. Ottawa: Department of Indian Affairs and Northern Development.

2003      Registered Indian Population by Sex and Residence, 2002. Ottawa: Department of Indian Affairs and Northern Development.

2005      Registered Indian Population of Canada by Sex and Residence, 2004. Ottawa: Department of Indian Affairs and Northern Development.

2006      Registered Indian Population by Sex and Residence, 2005. Ottawa: Minister of Public Works and Government Services Canada.

Canada. Department of Indian and Northern Affairs *see* Canada. Department of Indian Affairs and Northern Development (DIAND)

Canada. Department of Mines and Resources. Indian Affairs Branch
1945      Census of Indians in Canada, 1944. Ottawa: Edmond Cloutier.

Canada. Department of National Health and Welfare (DNHW)
1992      Health Transfer Newsletter. *Winter* 1992. Ottawa: Department of National Health and Welfare.

Canada. Government of Nunavut
1999, 2004   *see* Nunavut, Government of 1999, 2004

Canada. Health Canada
1999      Ten Years of Health Transfer: First Nations and Inuit Control. Ottawa: Health Canada, First Nations and Inuit Health Branch.

2000      Facts and Issues: The Health of Aboriginal Women. (Webpage: http://www.hc-sc.gc.ca/women/english/facts_aborig.htm [13 December 2004].)

2002      Annual Report. Ottawa: Health Canada, First Nations and Inuit Health Branch.

2003      Interim FNIHB Medical Transportation Policy Framework. Ottawa: Health Canada, First Nations and Inuit Health Branch.

2003a     A Statistical Profile on the Health of First Nations in Canada. Ottawa: Health Canada, First Nations and Inuit Health Branch.

2003b     Working Together To Closing the Gaps. *Health Policy Research* 5(1). Ottawa: Health Canada, Applied Research and Analysis Directorate.

Canada. Indian and Northern Affairs Canada (INAC)
1995      The Government of Canada's Approach to Implementation of the Inherent Right and the Negotiation of Aboriginal Self-Government. (Webpage: http://www.ainc-inac.gc.ca/pr/pub/sg/plcy_e.html [14 June 2006].)

1997      Resume Outlining the Historical Development of the Administration of Indian Affairs. (Webpage: http://www.collections.ic.gc.ca/treaties/text/rec_e_tx.htm [22 August 2001].)

2003      Comprehensive Claims Policy and Status of Claims. Ottawa: Indian and Northern Affairs Canada. (Webpage: http://www.ainc-inac.gc.ca/ps/clm/brieff_e_html [31 May 2006].)

2003a     The Indian Register: July 2003. Ottawa: Indian and Northern Affairs Canada. (Webpage: http://www.ainc-inac.gc.ca/pr/info/tir_e.html [31 March 2006].)

2004      First Nations Land Management Act. Ottawa: Indian and Northern Affairs Canada. (Webpage: http://www.ainc-inac.gc.ca/pr/pub/matr/fnl_e.html [2 July 2006].)

2004a     Words First: An Evolving Terminology Relating to Aboriginal Peoples in Canada. Ottawa: Communications Branch, Indian and northern Affairs Canada.

2006     Federal Interlocutor for Métis and Non-Status Indians. Ottawa: Indian and Northern Affairs Canada. (Webpage: http://www.ainc-inac.gc.ca/interloc/index_e.html [4 June 2006].)

2006a     Frequently Asked Questions About the Aboriginal Peoples. Ottawa: Indian and Northern Affairs Canada. (Webpage: http://www.ainc-inac.gc.ca/pr/info125_e.html [31 March 2006].)

2006b     Registered Indian Population Projections for Canada and Regions, 2000 to 2021. Ottawa: Indian and Northern Affairs Canada. (Webpage: http://www.ainc-inac.gc.ca/pr/sts/ipp_e.pdf [31 March 2006].)

Canada. Indian Residential Schools Resolution Canada
2001     Historical Overview, 29 January 2001. (Webpage: http://www.irsr-rqpi.gc.ca/english/info 1_29_01 [11 June 2006].)

2006     Indian Residential Schools Settlement, May 2006. (Webpage: http://www.residentialschoolsettlement.ca/English.html [28 June 2006].)

2006a     Indian Residential Schools Statistics. (Webpage: http://www.irsr-rqpi.gc.ca/english/statistics.html [11 June 2006].)

Canada. Inuit Circumpolar Conference (ICC)
1983     Iqaluit, Canada: 3rd General Assembly: The Arctic—Our Common Responsibility. Iqaluit, NWT: Inuit Circumpolar Conference.

Canada. Inuit Circumpolar Council (ICC)
2007     Inuit Circumpolar Council (Canada). (Webpage: http://inuit circumpolar.com/index.php?auto_slide=&ID=156&Lang=En&Parent_ID=&current)

Canada. Library of Parliament
2000     The Report of the Royal Commission on Aboriginal Peoples. (Webpage: http://www.parl.gc.ca/information/library/PRB pubs/prb9924-e.htm [13 June 2006].)

Canada. Natural Resources Canada
2007     [Treaties and Comprehensive Land Claims.] Ottawa: Natural Resources Canada.

Canada. Parliament of Canada
1969     Statement of the Government of Canada on Indian Policy, Presented to the First Session of the Twenty-eighth Parliament by the Honourable Jean Chrétien, Minister of Indian Affairs and Northern Development. Ottawa: Queen's Printer.

Canada. Public Health Agency of Canada
2004     Tuberculosis in Canada, 2002. Ottawa: Public Health Agency of Canada.

2004a     HIV/AIDS Among Aboriginal Peoples in Canada: A Continuing Concern. Ottawa: Public Health Agency of Canada.

Canada. Royal Canadian Mounted Police (RCMP)
2006     Final Report: RCMP Review of Allegations Concerning Inuit Sled Dogs. Ottawa: Royal Canadian Mounted Police. (Webpage: http://www.rcmp-grc.gc.ca/ccaps/sled_dogs_final_ehtm)

Canada. Royal Commission on Aboriginal Peoples (RCAP)
1993     Partners in Confederation: Aboriginal Peoples, Self-Government, and the Constitution. Ottawa: Minister Supply and Services Canada.

1994     The High Arctic Relocation: A Report on the 1953–55 Relocation. Ottawa: Minister of Supply and Services Canada.

1996     Report of the Royal Commission on Aboriginal Peoples. 5 vols. Ottawa: Minister of Supply and Services.

Canada. Royal Commission on Indian Affairs for the Province of British Columbia
1916     Report of the Royal Commission on Indian Affairs for the Province of British Columbia. 4 vols. Victoria, B.C.: Acme Press. (Commonly referred to as: The McKenna-McBride Commission.)

Canada. Special Joint Committee of the Senate and House of Commons
1947     Special Joint Committee of the Senate and House of Commons, Appointed to Continue and Complete the Examination and Consideration of the Indian Act. *Minutes of Proceedings and Evidence* 18. Ottawa: House of Commons.

1948     Special Joint Committee of the Senate and House of Commons, Appointed to Continue and Complete the Examination and Consideration of the Indian Act. *Minutes of Proceedings and Evidence* 30. Ottawa: House of Commons.

Canada. Statistics Canada
2001     *see* Canada. Statistics Canada 2003

2003     Aboriginal Peoples of Canada: A Demographic Profile: 2001 Census. *Statistics Canada Catalogue* 96F0030XIE2001007. Ottawa: Minister Responsible for Statistics Canada. (Webpage: http://www12statcan.ca/english/census01/Products/Analytic/companion/abor/groups3.cfm [25 June 2006].)

2003a     2001 Standard Geographical Classification (SGC) Manual, Volume I. *Catalogue No.* 12-571-XPB. Ottawa: Minister Responsible for Statistics Canada.

2005     Projections of the Aboriginal Populations, Canada, Provinces and Territories: 2001–2017. *Statistics Canada Catalogue* 91-547-XIE. Ottawa: Minister Responsible for Statistics Canada.

2006     Harvesting and Community Well-being Among Inuit in the Canadian Arctic: Preliminary Findings from the 2001 Aboriginal Peoples Survey—Survey of Living Conditions in the Arctic. *Statistics Canada Catalogue* 89-619-XWE. Ottawa: Minister Responsible for Statistics Canada.

Canada. Supreme Court of Canada
1999     Corbiere v. Canada (Minister of Indian and Northern Affairs): 2 S.C.R. 203. Ottawa: Supreme Court of Canada.

Canada. Treasury Board of Canada Secretariat
2005     2004–2005 Report on Plans and Priorities for Indian and Northern Affairs Canada and Canadian Polar Commission. (Webpage: http://www.tbs-sct.gc.ca/est-pre/20042005/INAC-AINC/INAC-AINCr4501_e.asp [16 June 2006].)

Canada. Tri-Council Working Group
1996     Code of Conduct for Research Involving Human Beings. Ottawa: Minister of Supply and Services.

Canadian Aboriginal AIDS Network (CAAN)
2003     HIV/AIDS and Aboriginal Women, Children and Families. Ottawa: Canadian Aboriginal AIDS Network.

Canadian Native Law Cases (CNLC)
1980–1991     *see* Native Law Centre [Brian Slattery and Sheila Stelck, comps. and eds.] 1980–1991

Canby, William C., Jr.
2004     American Indian Law in a Nutshell. 4th ed. St. Paul, Minn.: West Publishing Co. (3d ed. published in 1998.)

464

CAP *see* Congress of Aboriginal Peoples (CAP)

Cardinal, Harold
1969        The Unjust Society: The Tragedy of Canada's Indians. Edmonton, Alta.: Hurtig Publishers.

———
1977        The Rebirth of Canada's Indians. Edmonton, Alta.: Hurtig Publishers.

Cardinal, Harold, and Walter Hildebrandt
2000        Treaty Elders of Saskatchewan: Our Dream Is That Our Peoples Will One Day Be Clearly Recognized As Nations. Calgary, Alta.: University of Calgary Press.

Carlson, Keith T.
2005        Rethinking Dialogue and History: The King's Promise and the 1906 Aboriginal Delegation to London. *Native Studies Review* 16(2):1–38. Saskatoon, Sask.

Carlson, Leonard A.
1981        Indians, Bureaucrats, and Land: The Dawes Act and the Decline of Indian Farming. Westport, Conn.: Greenwood Press.

———
1985        What Was It Worth? Economic and Historical Aspects of Determining Awards in Indian Land Claims Cases. Pp. 87–109 in Irredeemable America: The Indian's Estate and Land Claims. Imre Sutton, ed. Albuquerque: University of New Mexico Press.

———
1994        Allotment. Pp. 27–29 in Native America in the Twentieth Century: An Encyclopedia. Mary B. Davis, ed. New York and London: Garland Publishing.

Carmean, Kelli
2002        Spider Woman Walks This Land: Traditional Cultural Properties and the Navajo Nation. Blue Ridge Summit, Pa.: AltaMira Press.

Carnegie Foundation for the Advancement of Teaching
1989        Tribal Colleges: Shaping the Future of Native America. Princeton, N.J.: Carnegie Foundation for the Advancement of Teaching.

Carnes, Carolyn
1996        Industry Working with AIHEC To Build Museums. *Tribal College Journal* 8(2):20–21. Mancos, Colo.

Carpenter, Carole Henderson
1981        Secret, Precious Things: Repatriation of Potlatch Art. *Art Magazine* 12(53–54):64–70. Toronto.

Carpenter, Edmund
1997        Dead Truth, Live Myth. *European Review of Native American Studies* 11(2):27–29. [Vienna, Austria, etc.]

Carpenter, Kristen A., and Ray Halbritter
2001        Beyond the Ethnic Umbrella and the Buffalo: Some Thoughts on American Indian Tribes and Gaming. *Gaming Law Review* 5(4):311–327. Larchmont, N.Y.

Carr, Robert K.
1947        [Executive Secretary, Memorandum to Members of the President's Committee on Civil Rights, dated June 6, 1947.] (Committee Documents, Folder: Indians, Civil Rights of; Truman Papers, Harry S. Truman Library, Independence, Mo.)

Carroll, Dennis
[1950]      Relocation and the American Indian. (Pp. 6–7 in Box: Urban and Rural Indians. Papers of the American Indian Policy Review Commission; Record Group 220, National Archives, Washington.)

Carter, Kent
1991        Deciding Who Can Be Cherokee: Enrollment Records of the Dawes Commission. *Chronicles of Oklahoma* 69(2):174–205. Oklahoma City.

———
1999        The Dawes Commission and the Allotment of the Five Civilized Tribes, 1893–1914. Orem, Utah: Ancestry.com Incorporated.

Carter, Sarah
1990        Lost Harvests: Prairie Reserve Farmers and government Policy. Montreal: McGill-Queen's University Press.

Cartwrigt, Willena D.
1950        The Peyote Cult: Ritual Equipment. *Denver Art Museum Leaflet* 106. Denver.

Case, David S., and David A. Voluck
2002        Alaska Natives and American Laws. 2d ed. Fairbanks: University of Alaska Press. (Originally publ. in 1984.)

Casey, Carolyn
1996        Industry Working with AIHEC to Build Museums. *Tribal College Journal: Journal of American Indian Higher Education* 8(2):21–22. Mancos, Colo.

Cash, Joseph H.
1967        *see* Anonymous 1967

Cash, Joseph H., and Herbert T. Hoover, eds.
1995        To Be An Indian: An Oral Story. Introduction by Donald L. Fixico. St. Paul, Minn.: Minnesota Historical Society Press. (Originally publ. in 1971.)

Castillo, Edward D.
1994        A Reminiscence of the Alcatraz Occupation. Pp. 111–122 in Special Edition: Alcatraz Revisited: The 25th Anniversary of the Occupation, 1969–1971. *American Indian Culture and Research Journal* 18(4). Los Angeles.

Castro, Arachu, and Merrill Singer, eds.
2004        Unhealthy Health Policy: A Critical Anthropological Examination. Walnut Creek, Calif.: Altamira Press.

Catlin, George
1844        Letters and Notes on the Manners, Customs, and Condition of the North American Indians. 3d ed. 2 vols. New York: Wiley and Putnam. (Also, 4th ed.: David Bogue, London, 1844. Reprinted: Crown Publishers, New York, 1975.)

Cattelino, Jessica R.
2004        Casino Roots: The Cultural Production of Twentieth-Century Seminole Economic Development. Pp. 66–90 in Native Pathways: American Indian Culture and Economic Development in the Twentieth Century. Brian C. Hosmer and Colleen O'Neill, eds. Boulder, Colo.: University Press of Colorado.

———
2006        Florida Seminole Housing and the Social Meanings of Sovereignty. *Comparative Studies in Society and History* 48(3):699–726. Cambridge, Mass.

———
2007        Florida Seminole Gaming and Local Sovereign Interdependency. In: Beyond Red Power: Rethinking Twentieth-Century American Indian Politics. Daniel M. Cobb and Loretta Fowler, eds. Santa Fe, N.Mex.: School of American Research Press.

———
2008        High Stakes: Florida Seminole Gaming, Sovereignty, and the Social Meanings of Casino Wealth. Durham, N.C.: Duke University Press.

Census and Aboriginal Peoples Survey
1991        *see* Canada. Census and Aboriginal Peoples Survey 1991

Center for Indian Education *see* Arizona State University. Center for Indian Education

Chadwick, Bruce A., and Joseph H. Stauss
1975        The Assimilation of American Indians into Urban Society: The Seattle Case. *Human Organization* 34(4):359–369. Washington.

Chadwick, Bruce A., and Lynn C. White
1973        Correlates of Length of Urban Residence among the Spokane Indians. *Human Organization* 32(1):9–16. Washington.

Chagollan, Steve
2005        The Myth of the Native Babe: Hollywood's Pocahontas. *The New York Times*, November 27, 2005. New York.

Chamberlain, J. Edward
1988        Aboriginal Rights and the Meech Law Accord. Pp. 11–19 in Competing Constitutional Visions: The Meech Lake Accord. Katherine Swinton and Carol Rogerson, eds. Toronto: Carswell.

Chambers, Reid Peyton
1971        A Study of Administrative Conflicts of Interest in the Protection of Indian Natural Resources. *91st Congress, 2nd Session. Senate Committee on the Judiciary*: Subcommittee Print. Washington: U.S. Government Printing Office.

Champagne, Duane, ed.
1994        The Native North American Almanac: A Reference Work on Native North Americans in the United States and Canada. Detroit, Washington, London: Gale Research, Inc.

——
1994a       Bureau of Indian Affairs. Pp. 80–84 in Native America in the Twentieth Century: An Encyclopedia. Mary B. Davis, ed. New York and London: Garland Publishing.

——
1999        Contemporary Native American Cultural Issues. Walnut Creek, Calif.: Altamira Press.

——
2002        American Indian Studies at the University of California—Los Angeles. Pp. 43–60 in Native American Studies in Higher Education: Models for Collaboration Between Universities and Indigenous Nations. Duane Champagne and Jay Stauss, eds. Walnut Creek, Calif.: AltaMira Press.

Champagne, Duane, and Joseph H. Stauss, eds.
2002        Native American Studies in Higher Education: Models for Collaboration Between Universities and Indigenous Nations. Walnut Creek, Calif.: AltaMira Press.

Champagne, Duane, Karen Jo Torjesen, and Susan Steiner, eds.
2005        Indigenous Peoples and the Modern State. Blue Ridge Summit, Pa.: AltaMira Press.

Chance, Norman A.
1990        The Inupiat and Native Alaska: Ethnography of Development. New York, [etc.]: Holt, Rinehart and Winston.

Chandhuri, Joyotpaul
1974        Urban Indians of Arizona: Phoenix, Tucson, Flagstaff. Tucson: University of Arizona Press.

Chandler, Michael, and Christopher Lalonde
1998        Cultural Continuity as a Hedge Against Suicide in Canada's First Nations. *Transcultural Psychiatry* 35(2):191–219.

Chandonnet, Ann
2001        DNA Study Seeks Relatives of 'Ice Man' Found in B.C.: Natives Get Chance This Week To See If They Are Related to Man Discovered in Canadian Glacier. *Juneau Empire*, June 10, 2001. Juneau, Alaska.

Chapman, Abraham, ed.
1975        Literature of the American Indians: Views and Interpretations: A Gathering of Indian Memories, Symbolic Contexts, and Literary Criticism. Edited, with an Introduction and Notes, by Abraham Chapman. New York: Meridian/New American Library.

——, ed.
1976        Native American Literature: A Critical Anthology. New York: Harper and Row.

Chartier, Clem
1978–1979   "Indian": An Analysis of the Term Used in Section 91(24) of the British North America Act, 1867. *Saskatchewan Law Review* 43(1):37–80. Saskatoon, Sask.

Chartrand, Jean-Philippe
1987        Survival and Adaptation of the Inuit Ethnic Identity: The Importance of Inuktitut. Pp. 241–255 in Native People, Native Lands: Canadian Indians, Inuit, and Métis. Bruce Alden Cox, ed. Ottawa: Carleton University Press.

Chartrand, Larry N.
2004        The Definition of Métis Peoples in Section 35(2) of the *Constitution Act, 1982. Saskatchewan Law Review* 67(1):209–233. Saskatoon, Sask.

Chartrand, Paul L.
2003        The Hard Case Defining "The Métis People" and Their Rights: A Comment on *R. v. Powley. Constitutional Forum* 12(3):84–93. Edmonton, Alta.

Chavers, Dean
2007        Modern American Indian Leaders: Their Lives and Their Work. 2 vols. Lewiston, N.Y.: The Edwin Mellen Press.

Chenault, Venida
2001        American Indian Studies Program at Haskell Indian Nations University. *Indigenous Nations Studies Journal* 2(1):77–86. Lawrence, Kans.

Cheng, Chilwin Chienhan
1997        Touring the Museum: A Comment on *R. v. Van der Peet. University of Toronto Faculty Law Review* 55(2):419–434. Toronto.

Cherokee Nation
2007        Cherokee Nation Special Election Results, March 3, 2007. *Cherokee Nation News Release*, Sunday, March 4, 2007. Tahlequah, Okla.

Cherry, Conrad
1971        God's New Israel: Religious Interpretations of American Destiny. Englewood Cliffs, N.J.: Prentice Hall.

Chiefs of Ontario
2007        Ontario Chiefs Reject Settlement Offer to a Share of Provincial Gaming Revenues. (Press release, June 18, 2007; Webpage: http://www.chiefs-of-ontario.org. [6 July 2007.]

Christie, Gordon
1998        Aboriginal Rights, Aboriginal Culture, and Protection. *Osgoode Hall Law Journal* 36(3):447–484. Toronto.

——
2000        Justifying Principles of Treaty Interpretation. *Queen's Law Journal* 26(1):143–224. Kingston, Ont.

——
2000–2001   *Delgamuukw* and the Protection of Aboriginal Land Interests. *Ottawa Law Review* 32(1):85–115. Ottawa.

——
2002        The Court's Exercise of Plenary Power: Rewriting the Two-Row Wampum. *The Supreme Court Law Review*, 2d ser., 16:285–301. Toronto.

2004      Aboriginal Resource Rights After *Delgamuukw* and *Marshall*. Pp. 241–270 in Advancing Aboriginal Claims: Visions/Strategies/Directions. Kerry Wilkins, ed. Saskatoon, Sask.: Purich Publishing Ltd., and Centre for Constitutional Studies, University of Alberta.

Christopher, Thomas W., and Frederick M. Hart
1970      Indian Law Scholarship Program at the University of New Mexico. *University of Toledo Law Review* 2:691.

Churchill, Ward
1990      Spiritual Hucksterism. *Z Magazine*, December 1990:94–98. Boston.

1994      The Bloody Wake of Alcatraz: Political Repression of the American Indian Movement During the 1970s. Pp. 253–300 in Special Edition: Alcatraz Revisited: The 25th Anniversary of the Occupation, 1969–1971. *American Indian Culture and Research Journal* 18(4). Los Angeles.

1994a      American Indian Movement. Pp. 35–38 in Native America in the Twentieth Century: An Encyclopedia. Mary B. Davis, ed. New York and London: Garland Publishing.

1999      A Breach of Trust: The Radioactive Colonization of Native North America. *American Indian Culture and Research Journal* 23(4):23–70. Los Angeles.

Churchill, Ward, and Jim Vander Wall
1988      Agents of Repression: The FBI's Secret War Against the Black Panther Party and the American Indian Movement. Boston: South End Press.

Ciaccia, John
2000      The Oka Crisis: A Mirror of the Soul. Dorval, Que.: Maren Publications.

Circle of Tribal Advisors
2004      A Guide to Visiting the Land of Many Nations and to the Lewis and Clark Bicentennial. St. Louis, Mo.: National Council of the Lewis and Clark Bicentennial.

Claiborne, William
1999      Military, Indian Church Agree on Peyote Policy. *The Washington Post*, Wednesday, June 30, 1999:A29. Washington.

Clark, Bruce
1990      Native Liberty, Crown Sovereignty: The Existing Aboriginal Right of Self-Government in Canada. Montreal: McGill-Queens University Press.

Clark, C. Blue
1994      *Lone Wolf* v. *Hitchcock*: Treaty Rights and Indian Law at the End of the Nineteenth Century. Lincoln: University of Nebraska Press. (Reprinted in 1999.)

2004      *see* Handbook Vol. 14 (2004:742–752)

Clark, Joan, and William Vickery
1969–1970      Vanishing Americans. *Film Library Quarterly* 3(Winter): 27, 46–47. Greenwich, Conn.

Clark, Michael, Peter Riben, and Earl Nowegesic
2002      The Association of Housing Density, Isolation and Tuberculosis in Canadian First Nations Communities. *International Journal of Epidemiology* 31(5):940–945. Oxford, England.

Clatworthy, Stewart
2001      Reassessing the Population Impacts of Bill C-31. Winnipeg, Man.: Four Directions Project Consultant.

Claypoole, Antoinette Nora
1999      Who Would Unbraid Her Hair: The Legend of Anna Mae. Bethel, Vt.: Anam Cara Press.

Clemmer, Richard O.
1995      Roads in the Sky: The Hopi Indians in a Century of Change. Boulder, Colo.: Westview Press.

Cleveland, Sarah H.
2002      Powers Inherent in Sovereignty: Indians, Aliens, Territories, and the Nineteenth Century Plenary Power over Foreign Affairs. *Texas Law Review* 81(1):1–284. Austin, Tex.

Clifford, James
1988      The Predicament of Culture: Twentieth-Century Ethnography, Literature, and Art. Cambridge: Harvard University Press.

Clifton, James A., ed.
1990      The Invented Indian: Cultural Fictions and Government Policies. New York: Transaction Publishers.

Clinton, Lawrence, Bruce A. Chadwick, and Howard M. Bahr
1973      Vocational Training for Indian Migrants: Correlates of "Success" in a Federal Program. *Human Organization* 32(1):17–28. Washington.

1975      Urban Relocation Reconsidered: Antecedents of Employment Among Indian Males. *Rural Sociology* 40(2):117–133. [Columbia, Mo.]

Clinton, Robert N.
1981      Isolated in Their Own Country: A Defense of Federal Protection of Indian Autonomy and Self-Government. *Stanford Law Review* 33(6):979–1068. Stanford, Calif.

1988      Statement of Robert N. Clinton in Opposition to H.R. 4469 Proposing the Nonconsensual Partition of the Hoopa Valley Reservation Between the "Hoopa Valley" and "Yurok" Tribes. Hoopa-Yurok Reservation Partition, Hearing Before the Committee on Interior and Insular Affairs. *100th Congress, 2d Session. Serial No.* 100-75. Washington: U.S. Government Printing Office.

1995      The Dormant Indian Commerce Clause. *Connecticut Law Review* 27(4):1055–1249. Hartford, Conn.

2002      There Is No Federal Supremacy Clause for Indian Tribes. *Arizona State Law Journal* 34(1):113–260. Tempe, Ariz.

Clinton, Robert N., and Margaret Tobey Hotopp
1979      Judicial Enforcement of the Federal Restraints on Alienation of Indian Land: The Origins of the Eastern Land Claims. *Maine Law Review* 31(1):17–90. Portland, Maine.

Clinton, Robert N., Carole E. Goldberg, and Rebecca Tsosie
2003      American Indian Law: Native Nations and the Federal System. 4th ed. Newark, N.J.: LexisNexis; Matthew Bender and Co.

2005      American Indian Law: Native Nations and the Federal System: Cases and Materials. 4th ed., revised. Newark, N.J.: LexisNexis; Matthew Bender and Co.

Clow, Richmond L., and Imre Sutton, eds.
2001      Trusteeship in Change: Toward Tribal Autonomy in Resource Management. Foreword by David H. Getches. Boulder, Colo.: University Press of Colorado.

Coates, Kenneth S., ed.
1992      Aboriginal Land Claims in Canada: A Regional Perspective. Toronto: Copp Clark Pitman.

2000 The Marshall Decision and Native Rights. Montreal: McGill-Queen's University Press.

Coates, Robert M.
1967 Indian Affairs, New Style. *The New Yorker*, June 17, 1967. New York.

Cobb, Amanda J.
2005 The National Museum of the American Indian: Sharing the Gift. *American Indian Quarterly* 29(3–4):361–383. Lincoln, Nebr.

Cobb, Daniel M., and Loretta Fowler, eds.
2007 Beyond Red Power: Rethinking Twentieth-Century American Indian Politics. Santa Fe, N.Mex.: School of American Research Press.

Code of Federal Regulations
1976, 1978, 1994 *see* U.S. *Federal Register* 1976, 1978, 1994

Cody, Iron Eyes
1982 Iron Eyes: My Life as a Hollywood Indian. New York: Everest House.

Coe, Richard L.
1973 A New and Lively Season. *The Washington Post*, February 16, 1973:B8. Washington.

Coffey, Wallace, and Rebecca Tsosie
2001 Rethinking the Tribal Sovereignty Doctrine, Cultural Sovereignty, and the Collective Future of Indian Nations. *Stanford Law and Policy Review* 12(2):191–210. Stanford, Calif.

Cohen-Cruz, Jan
2005 Local Acts: Community-Based Performance in the United States. New Brunswick, N.J.: Rutgers University Press.

Cohen, Felix S.
1942 Handbook of Federal Indian Law. Washington: U.S. Government Printing Office. (Reprinted, new annotated eds.: see Cohen 1971, 1982, 2005.)

1948 The Civil Rights Report. *Review of General Semantics* 4(Spring):161–167. Fort Worth, Tex.

1948a Breaking Faith With Our First Americans. *Indian Truth* 25(March):1–8. Philadelphia.

1971 Handbook of Federal Indian Law. Albuquerque: University of New Mexico Press.

1982 Felix S. Cohen's Handbook of Federal Indian Law: 1982 Edition. Rennard Strickland, editor-in-chief. Charlottesville, Va.: The Michie Company, Law Publishers.

2005 Cohen's Handbook of Federal Indian Law. 2005 Edition. Nell Jessup Newton, Editor-in-Chief; Editorial Board: Robert Anderson, Carole Goldberg, John LaVelle, Judith V. Royster, Joseph William Singer, Rennard Strickland. Newark, N.J., and San Francisco: LexisNexis, Matthew Bender.

2007 On the Drafting of Tribal Constitutions. David E. Wilkins, ed. Foreword by Lindsay G. Robertson. *American Indian Law and Policy Series* 1. Norman: University of Oklahoma Press.

COHRE = Centre on Housing Rights and Evictions
1993 Mission Statement. Geneva, Switzerland: Centre on Housing Rights and Evictions.

Cole, Douglas
1985 Captured Heritage: The Scramble for Northwest Coast Artifacts. Seattle: University of Washington Press. (Reprinted: University of Oklahoma Press, Norman, 1995.)

Cole, Douglas, and Ira Chaikin
1990 Iron Hand Upon the People: The Law against the Potlatch on the Northwest Coast. Vancouver: Douglas and McIntyre.

Collier, John
1942 The Indian in a Wartime Nation. Pp. 29–35 in Minority Peoples in a Nation at War. J.P. Shalloo and Donald Young, eds. *Annals of the American Academy of Political and Social Science* 223. Philadelphia.

1944 *see* ARCIA 1849–

1949 Beleaguered Nation. *The Nation* 169(17 September):276–278. New York.

1949a The Indian Bureau and Self-Government: A Reply [to John F. Embree]. *Human Organization* 8(3):22–26. Washington.

1963 From Every Zenith: A Memoir and Some Essays on Life and Thought. Denver: Sage Books.

Collins, Ellsworth, and Alma Miller England
1937 The 101 Ranch. Norman: University of Oklahoma Press.

Colonnese, Tom, and Louis Owens
1985 American Indian Novelists: An Annotated Bibliography. New York and London: Garland Publishing, Inc.

Colt, Steve
1991 Financial Performance of Native Regional Corporations. *Alaska Review of Social and Economic Conditions* 28(2):1–24. Anchorage: University of Alaska, Institute of Social and Economic Research.

Commission on Minority Participation in Education and American Life
1988 One Third of a Nation: A Report of the Commission on Minority Participation in Education and American Life. [Washington]: American Council on Education in Association with the Education Commission of the States.

Commission on the Future of Health Care in Canada
2002 Building on Values: The Future of Health Care in Canada—Final Report. Roy J. Romanow, Q.C., Commissioner. Ottawa: The Commission.

Commissioner of Indian Affairs
1849– *see* ARCIA = Commissioner of Indian Affairs 1849–; *see also* U.S. Commissioner of Indian Affairs

Confederacy of Nova Scotia Métis (CNSM)
[2006] The Sash. (Webpage: http://www.geocities.com/nsmetis/culture2.html [16 June 2006].)

Congress of Aboriginal Peoples (CAP)
2006 The Forgotten People and The Indian Act System. (Webpage: http://www.abo-peoples.org/background/indianact.html)

*Congressional Record* see U.S. *Congressional Record*

Connecticut, State of
2003 [Comments of the State of Connecticut, The Connecticut Light and Power Company, Kent School Corporation, and Town of Kent of the Proposed Finding on the Petition for Federal Acknowledgment of the Schaghticoke Tribal Nation Petitioner Group, August 8, 2003.] (Office of Federal Acknowledgment, Schaghticoke Tribal Nation Administrative Record, August 8, 2003, Bureau of Indian Affairs, Washington.)

Continental Congress
1774–1789    *see* U.S. Continental Congress 1774–1789

Cook-Lynn, Elizabeth
1966        American Indian Intellectualism. *American Indian Quarterly* 20(1):57–58. Lincoln, Nebr.

1991        The Radical Conscience in Native American Studies. *Wicazo Sa Review* 7(2):9–13. Minneapolis.

1991a       From the River's Edge. New York: Arcade.

1996        The Broken Cord. Pp. 11–16 in Why I Can't Read Wallace Stegner and Other Essays: A Tribal Voice. Madison: University of Wisconsin Press.

1997        Who Stole Native American Studies? *Wicazo Sa Review* 12(1):9–28. Minneapolis.

1999        Aurelia: A Crow Creek Trilogy. Boulder, Colo.: University Press of Colorado.

2001        Anti-Indianism in Modern America: A Voice from Tatekeya's Earth. Urbana, Ill.: University of Illinois Press.

Cook, Sherburne F.
1973        The Significance of Disease in the Extinction of the New England Indians. *Human Biology* 45(3):485–508. Detroit, Mich.

Coon-Come, Matthew
1996        Remarks of Grand Chief Coon Come. (Canada Seminar, October 28, 1996. Harvard Center for International Affairs and Kennedy School of Government, Cambridge, Mass. Webpage: http://www.ratical.org/ratville/Cree.html)

Cooper, Karen Coody
1998        Tribal Museum Directory. American Indian Museum Studies Program, Center for Museum Studies. Washington: Smithsonian Institution.

Cooper, Karen Coody, and Nicolasa I. Sandoval, eds.
2006        Living Homes for Cultural Expression: North American Native Perspectives on Creating Community Museums. Washington: Smithsonian Institution.

Corbett, Helen
1996        A History of the U.N. Draft Declaration on Indigenous Peoples. (Unpublished report; United Nations Archives, New York.)

Cornell, Stephen
1989        The Return of the Native: American Indian Political Resurgence. New York: Oxford University Press.

2006        What Makes First Nations Enterprises Successful? Lessons from the Harvard Project. Tuscon, Ariz.: Native Nations Institute for Leadership, Management and Policy, and The Harvard Project on American Indian Economic Development.

Cornell, Stephen, and Joseph P. Kalt
1991        Where's the Glue? Institutional Bases of American Indian Economic Development. Harvard Project on American Indian Economic Development. Cambridge, Mass.: Harvard University, John F. Kennedy School of Government.

_____, eds.
1992        What Can Tribes Do? Strategies and Institutions in American Indian Economic Development. Los Angeles: University of California, American Indian Studies Center.

1998        Sovereignty and Nation Building: The Development Challenge in Indian Country Today. Harvard Project on American Indian Economic Development. Cambridge, Mass.: Harvard University, John F. Kennedy School of Government.

2006        Two Approaches to Economic Development in American Indian Nations: One Works, the Other Doesn't. *Joint Occasional Papers on Native Affairs* 2005-02. Tuscon, Ariz.: Native Nations Institute for Leadership, Management and Policy and The Harvard Project on American Indian Economic Development.

Cornell, Stephen, and Marta Cecilia Gil-Swedberg
1995        Sociohistorical Factors in Institutional Efficacy: Economic Development in Three American Indian Cases. *Economic Development and Cultural Change* 43(2):239–269. Chicago.

Cornell, Stephen, and Jonathan Taylor
2006        Sovereignty, Devolution, and the Future of Tribal-State Relations. (National Congress of American Indians: Mid-Year Session. Webage: http://access.minnesota.publicradio.org/civic_j/native_american/tribalstaterelations1.pdf [18 October 2006].)

Cornell, Stephen, Catherine Curtis, and Miriam Jorgensen
2004        The Concept of Governance and Its Implications for First Nations: A Report to the British Columbia Regional Vice-Chief, Assembly of First Nations. *Joint Occasional Papers on Native Affairs, Native Nations Institute and Harvard Project on American Indian Economic Development*. Cambridge and Tucson.

Corrigan, Samuel W.
1970        The Plains Indian Powwow: Cultural Integration in Manitoba and Sasktachewan. *Anthropologica* 12(1):253–277. Ottawa.

Corrigan, Samuel W., and Lawrence J. Barkwell, eds.
1991        The Struggle for Recognition: Canadian Justice and the Métis Nation. Winnipeg, Man.: Pemmican Publications.

Costo, Rupert
1970        Alcatraz. *The Indian Historian* 3(1):4–12. San Francisco.

1972        "Seven Arrows" Desecrates Cheyenne. *The Indian Historian* 5(2):41–42. San Francisco.

Couture, G., and J. Fielding
1998        Economic Development: The Public's Role in Shaping Winnipeg's Economic Future. Pp. 25–48 in Citizen Engagement: Lessons in Participation in Local Government. Katherine A. Graham and S.D. Phillips, eds. Toronto: Institute of Public Administration of Canada.

Coward, John M.
1999        The Newspaper Indian: Native American Identity in the Press, 1820–1890. Urbana and Chicago: University of Illinois Press.

Cowger, Thomas W.
1999        The National Congress of American Indians: The Founding Years. Lincoln: University of Nebraska Press.

Cox, Bruce Alden, ed.
1973        Cultural Ecology: Readings on Canadian Indians and Eskimos. Toronto: McClelland and Stewart.

_____, ed.
1987        Native People, Native Lands: Canadian Indians, Inuit, and Métis. Ottawa: Carleton University Press. (Reprinted in 1992.)

Coyote, John
1976        Nightmares in the BIA Anyone? A Humorous Recollection of the BIA Takeover in Washington. *Indian Voice* 3(4):37, 48. San Jose, Calif.

Cozzetto, Don A., and Brent W. La Roque
1996    Compulsive Gambling in the Indian Community: A North Dakota Case Study. *American Indian Culture and Research Journal* 20(1):73–86. Los Angeles.

Craib, Kevin J. P., et al.
2003    Risk Factors for Elevated HIV Incidence Among Aboriginal Injection Drug Users in Vancouver. *Canadian Medical Association Journal* 168(1):19–24. Ottawa.

Cramer, Renée Ann
2005    Cash, Color and Colonialism: The Politics of Tribal Acknowledgment. Norman: University of Oklahoma Press.

Crawford, James
1995    Bilingual Education: History, Politics, Theory and Practice. 3d ed., revised and expanded. Los Angeles: Bilingual Educational Services.

Cree, Linda
1974    The Extention of County Jurisdiction Over Indian Reservations in California: Public Law 280 and the Ninth Circuit. *Hastings Law Journal* 25(6):1451–1506. San Francisco.

Crees of Quebec, The, Le Gouvernement de Québec
2002    Agreement Concerning a New Relationship (Paix des Braves). (Webpage: http://www.gcc.ca/pdf/LEG000000008.pdf)

Creighton, Donald
1964    Road to Confederation: The Emergence of Canada, 1863–1867. Toronto: Macmillian.

Crittenden, Hiram Martin, and Alfred Talbot Richardson, eds.
1905    *see* Smet, Pierre-Jean de 1905

Crook, Rena, Leanne Hinton, and Nancy Stenson
1977    Literacy and Linguistics: The Havasupai Writing System. Pp. 1–16 in *Proceedings of the 1976 Hokan-Yuman Languages Workshop*. James E. Redden, ed. *Southern Illinois University. Museum Studies* 11. Carbondale, Ill.

Crosby, Alfred W.
1972    The Columbian Exchange: Biological and Cultural Consequences of 1492. Westport, Conn.: Greenwood Publishing.

Cross, Raymond
2000    Tribes As Rich Nations. *Oregon Law Review* 79(4):893–980. Eugene, Oreg.

Cross, Terry
2006    Statement of the National Indian Child Welfare Association Presented Before the House Ways and Means Subcommittee on Human Resources, Regarding Bush Adminstration Foster Care Flexible Funding Proposal. (National Indian Child Welfare Association. Webpage: http://www.nicwa.org/policy/legislation/s672/IV-E_testimony.htm [27 September 2006].)

Crow, John
1972    [Deputy Commissioner's Letter of June 9, 1972, to Congressman Lloyd Meeds.] (OFA, Nooksack Washington 050, Upper Skagit Indian Tribe of Washington, Sauk-Suiattle Indian Tribe of Washington.)

Crowshoe, Chelsea, comp.
2005    Sacred Ways of Life: Traditional Knowledge. Ottawa: Prepared for the First Nations Centre, National Aboriginal Health Organization.

Crum, Steven J.
1988    Bizzell and Brandt: Pioneers in Indian Studies, 1929–1937. *Chronicles of Oklahoma* 66(2):178–191. Norman.

———
2007    Indian Activism, the Great Society, Indian Self-Determination, and the Drive for an Indian College or University,
1964–71. *American Indian Culture and Research Journal* 31(1):1–20. Los Angeles.

CTV.ca News Staff
2005    Aboriginals Promised $5 Billion To Solve Poverty. (Webpage: http://www.ctv.ca/servlet/ArticleNews/story/CTVNews/20051125/native_summit_051125/20051126/)

Culhane, Dara
2003    Their Spirits Live Within Us: Aboriginal Women in Downtown Eastside Vancouver Emerging into Visibility. Pp. 593–606 in Keeping the Campfires Going: Urban American Indian Women's Activism. Susan Applegate Krouse and Heather Howard-Bobiwash, eds. *American Indian Quarterly*, Special Issue 27(3–4). Lincoln, Nebr.

Culhane Speck, Dara
1989    The Indian Health Transfer Policy: A Step in the Right Direction, or Revenge of the Hidden Agenda? *Native Studies Review* 5(1):187–213. Saskatoon, Sask.

Cumming, Peter A., and Neil H. Mickenberg, eds.
1974    Native Rights in Canada. 2d ed. Toronto: Indian-Eskimo Association of Canada, in association with General Publishing Company.

Cunningham, Alisa F.
2000    Tribal College Contribution to Local Economic Development. Washington and Alexandria, Va.: American Indian Higher Education Consortium and the Institute of Higher Education Policy.

Cunningham, Hilary
2005    Colonial Encounters in Postcolonial Contexts: Patenting Indigenous DNA and the Human Genome Diversity Project. Pp. 292–300 in The Anthropology of Development and Globalization. Marc Edelman and Angelique Haugerud, eds. Oxford, England, and Malden, Mass.: Blackwell.

Custalaw, Linwood Little Bear, and Angela L. Daniel
2007    The True Story of Pocahontas: The Other Side of History. Golden, Colo.: Fulcrum Publishing.

Cuthand, Stan
1991    Indian Peoples of the Prairie Provinces in the 1920s and 1930s. Pp. 381–392 in Sweet Promises: A Reader in Indian-White Relations in Canada. James R. Miller, ed. Toronto: University of Toronto Press.

Dahl, Jens, Jack Hicks, and Peter Jull, eds.
2000    Nunavut: Inuit Regain Control of Their Lands and Their Lives. Copenhagen, Denmark: International Work Group for Indigenous Affairs.

Dailey, Charles A.
1977    Bringing a Unique Perspective to Museum Work. *Museum News* 55(5):53–54. Washington.

Daily, Robert
1995    The Code Talkers: American Indians in World War II. New York: F. Watts.

Dale, Edward Everett
1949    The Indians of the Southwest: A Century of Development Under the United States. Norman: University of Oklahoma Press.

Daley, Patrick J., and Beverly A. James
2004    Cultural Politics and the Mass Media: Alaska Native Voices. Urbana and Chicago: University of Illinois Press.

Damus, Sylvester, and Kristina Liljefors
2004    Analysis of Some Indicators of Economic Development of First Nations and Northern Communities. Ottawa: Institute on Governance.

Daniel, Richard C.
1980        A History of Native Claims Processes in Canada, 1867–1979. Prepared by Richard C. Daniel [. . .] for Research Branch, Department of Indian and Northern Affairs. Ottawa: Indian and Northern Affairs.

Daniels, Harry W.
1979        We Are the New Nation: The Métis and National Native Policy. Ottawa: Native Council of Canada.

——
1992        Keystone of Confederation: A Métis Gift to Canada. *Makekun Productions and Canada* 125. Winnipeg, Man.

Daniels, John D.
1992        The Indian Population in North America in 1492. *William and Mary Quarterly* 49(2):298–320. Williamsburg, Va.

Daniels, Robert E.
1970        Cultural Identities Among the Oglala Sioux. Pp. 198–245 in The Modern Sioux: Social Systems and Reservation Culture. Ethel Nurge, ed. Lincoln: University of Nebraska Press.

Danky, James P., and Maureen Hady
1984        Native American Periodicals and Newspapers, 1828–1982. Westport, Conn.: Greenwood Press.

Dannenberg, Anne Marie
1996        "Where, Then, Shall we Place the Hero of the Wilderness?": William Apess's *Eulogy on King Philip* and Doctrines of Racial Destiny. Pp. 66– in Early Native American Writing: New Critical Essays. Helen Jaskoski, ed. Foreword by A. LaVonne Brown Ruoff. Cambridge, Mass.: Cambridge University Press.

Danziger, Edmund
1991        Survival and Regeneration: Detroit's American Indian Community. Detroit, Mich.: Wayne State University Press.

D'Aponte, Mimi Gisolfi
1999        Seventh Generation: An Anthology of Native American Plays. New York: Theatre Communications Group.

——
1999a       Native Women Playwrights: Transmitters, Healers, Transformers. *Journal of Dramatic Theory and Criticism* 14(1):99–108. Lawrence, Kans.

Darby, Jaye T., and Stephanie Fitzgerald, eds.
2003        Keepers of the Morning Star: An Anthology of Native Women's Theater. Los Angeles: UCLA American Indian Studies Center.

Darian-Smith, Eve
2002        Savage Capitalists: Law and Politics Surrounding Indian Casino Operations in California. Pp. 109–140 in *Studies in Law, Politics and Society* 26. Austin Sarat and Patricia Ewick, eds. Amsterdam, The Netherlands: JAI Press.

——
2003        New Capitalists: Law, Politics, and Identity Surrounding Casino Gaming on Native American Land. Belmont, Calif.: Thomson-Wadsworth. (Reprinted in 2004.)

Davis, Carol
1987        [Interview concerning Turtle Mountain Community College, March 5, 1987.] (Conducted by Wayne J. Stein, Belcourt, N.Dak.; Text of interview in Department of Native American Studies, Montana State University, Bozeman, Mont.)

Davis, David D.
2001        A Case of Identity: Ethnogenesis of the New Houma Indians. *Ethnohistory* 48(3):473–494.

Davis, Goode, Jr.
1990        Proud Tradition of the Marines' Navajo Code Talkers: They Fought with Words—Words No Japanese Could Fathom. *Marine Corps League* 46(1):16–26. Arlington, Va.

Davis, Mary B., ed.
1994        Native America in the Twentieth Century: An Encyclopedia. New York and London: Garland Publishing.

Davis, Sia, and Aura Kanegis
2006        Improving State Tribal Relations: An Introduction. (National Conference of State Legislatures. Webpage: http://www.ncsl.org/programs/statetribe/tribalbrief4.htm [7 October 2006].)

Day, David
1997        The Visions and Revelations of St. Louis the Métis. Saskatoon, Sask.: Thistledown Press.

Day, Robert C.
1972        The Emergence of Activism As a Social Movement. Pp. 506–532 in Native Americans Today: Sociological Perspectives. Howard M. Bahr, Bruce A. Chadwick, and Robert C. Day, eds. New York: Harper and Row.

Dearborn, Mary V.
1986        Pocahontas's Daughters: Gender and Ethnicity in American Culture. New York: Oxford University Press.

Debenham, Diane
1988        Native People in Contemporary Canadian Drama. *Canadian Drama/L'Art Dramatique Canadien* 14(2):137–158. Waterloo, Ont.

Debo, Angie
1940        "And Still the Waters Run": The Betrayal of the Five Civilized Tribes. Princeton, N.J.: Princeton University Press. (Reprinted in 1972; also, University of Oklahoma Press, Norman, 1984.)

——
1941        The Road to Disappearance. Norman: University of Oklahoma Press.

——
1970        A History of the Indians of the United States. Norman: University of Oklahoma Press.

Decker, Jody
1998        Tracing Historical Diffusion Patterns: The Case of the 1780–88 Smallpox Epidemic Among the Indians of Western Canada. *Native Studies Review* 4(1–2):1–24. Saskatoon, Sask.

——
1999        "We Should Never Be Again the Same People:" The Diffusion and Cumulative Impact of Acute Infectious Diseases Affecting the Natives on the Northern Plains of the Western Interior of Canada, 1774–1839. (Ph.D. Dissertation in Anthropology, York University, Toronto.)

DeCoster, C., et al.
1999        Assessing the Extent to Which Hospitals Are Used for Acute Care Purposes. *Medical Care* 37, Supplement 6:JS151–166. Ottawa.

Decter, Michael B., and Jeffrey A. Kowall
1989        A Case Study of the Kitsaki Development Corporation, La Ronge Indian Band, La Ronge Saskatchewan. *Economic Council of Canada Local Development Paper* 5. Ottawa.

Deere, Phillip Summer
1978        "No more are we going to stand around. . . . This is not the end of the Longest Walk!" *Akwesane Notes* 10(3):4. [Rooseveltown, N.Y., etc.] (Webpage: http://www.umass.edu/legal/derrico/phillip_deere.html)

Deiter, Patricia
1999        Biography of Chief Walter P. Deiter. (M.A. Thesis in History, University of Regina, Regina, Sask).

De la Torre, Joely
2001        From Activism to Academics: The Evolution of American Indian Studies at San Francisco State University, 1968–

2001. *Indigenous Nations Studies Journal* 2(1):11–20. Lawrence, Kans.

**Deloria, Ella C.**
[1944]     Speaking of Indians. New York: Friendship Press.

1992     Deer Women and Elk Men: The Lakota Narratives of Ella Deloria. Julian Rice, ed. Albuquerque: University of New Mexico Press.

**Deloria, Philip J.**
1998     Playing Indian. New Haven, Conn.: Yale University Press.

2004     Indian in Unexpected Places. Lawrence, Kans.: University Press of Kansas.

**Deloria, Philip S.**
1994     The American Indian Law Center: An Informal History. *University of New Mexico Law Review* 24:285. Albuquerque.

**Deloria, Vine, Jr.**
1969     Custer Died for Your Sins: An Indian Manifesto. New York and London: Macmillan; also, Avon Books. (Several reprints, incl.: Avon Books, New York, 1970; University of Oklahoma Press, Norman, 1988. Issued also as a sound recording under title: Custer Died for Your Sins, Re Corw. Words and Music based on the Book of the Same Title by Vine Deloria, Jr. Words and Music by Jimmy Curtis and Floyd Westerman. Red Cross Production, Malibu, Calif., 1970, 1982.)

1970     We Talk, You Listen: New Tribes, New Turf. New York: Macmillan.

1971     The Country Was a Lot Better Off When the Indians Were Running It. Pp. 235–247 in Red Power: The American Indians' Fight for Freedom. Alvin M. Josephy, Jr., ed. New York: American Heritage Press.

1973     Interview [with] Vine Deloria, Jr.: A Review of Current Indian Affairs by a Prominent Lakota Writer. *The Indian Voice* 3(4):8–10, 55–60. San Jose, Ca.

1974     Behind the Trail of Broken Treaties: An Indian Declaration of Independence. New York: Dell Publishing. (Reprinted, Revised ed.: The University of Texas Press, Austin, Tex., 1985.)

1974a     Of Outmost Good Faith. San Francisco: Straight Arrow Books.

1974b     The Rise of Indian Activism. Pp. 184–185 in The Social Reality of Ethnic America. Rudolph Gomez, et al., eds. Lexington, Mass.: DC Heath.

1974c     The Indian Affair. New York: Friendship Press.

1975     Indian Humor. Pp. 152–169 in Literature of the American Indians: Views and Interpretations: A Gathering of Indian Memories, Symbolic Contexts, and Literary Criticism. Edited, with an Introduction and Notes, by Abraham Chapman. New York: Meridian/New American Library.

1976     A Better Day for Indians. New York: Field Foundation.

1977     Indians of the Pacific Northwest: From the Coming of the White Man to the Present Day. New York: Doubleday.

1978     Legislation and Litigation Concerning American Indians. Pp. 86–96 in American Indians Today. J. Milton Yinger and George Eaton Simpson, eds. *The Annals of the American Academy of Political and Social Science* 436 (March). Philadelphia.

1979     The Metaphysics of Modern Existence. San Francisco: Harper and Row.

1979a     A Brief History of the Federal Responsibility to the American Indian. *DHEW Publication* (OE) 79-02404. Washington: U.S. Department of Health, Education, and Welfare.

1979b     Introduction. In: Black Elk Speaks: Being the Life Story of a Holy Man of the Oglala Sioux; As Told Through John G. Neihardt (Flaming Rainbow). Lincoln: University of Nebraska Press.

1983     Review of: Talbot, Steve, *Roots of Oppression: The American Indian Question*. New York: International Publishers, 1981. *American Indian Quarterly* 7(2):104–105. Lincoln, Nebr.

1984     Aggressions of Civilization: Federal Indian Policy Since the 1880s. Philadelphia: Tempe University Press.

———, ed.
1985     American Indian Policy in the Twentieth Century. Norman: University of Oklahoma Press. (Reprinted in 1992.)

1991     Commentary: Research, Redskins, and Reality. *American Indian Quarterly* 15(4):300–306. Lincoln, Nebr.

1992     Comfortable Fictions and the Struggle for Turf: An Essay Review of *The Invented Indian: Cultural Fictions and Government Policies* [James A. Clifton, ed., 1990]. *American Indian Quarterly* 16(3):397–410. Lincoln, Nebr.

———, ed.
1993     Frank Waters: Man and Mystic. Athenes, Ohio: Swallow Press; Ohio University Press.

1994     God Is Red: A Native View of Religion. Golden, Colo.: North American Press. (Reprinted: see Deloria 2003.)

1994a     Identity and Culture. Pp. 93–102 in From Different Shores: Perspectives on Race and Ethnicity in America. Ronald Takaki, ed. New York: Oxford University Press.

1994b     Alcatraz, Activism, and Accommodation. Pp. 25–32 in Special Edition: Alcatraz Revisited: The 25th Anniversary of the Occupation, 1969–1971. Joane Nagel and Troy Johnson, eds. *American Indian Culture and Research Journal* 18(4). Los Angeles.

1995     Red Earth, White Lies: Native Americans and the Myth of Scientific Fact. New York: Scribner. (Reprinted: Fulcrum Publishing, Golden, Colo., 1997.)

1998     Intellectual Self-Determination and Sovereignty: Looking at the Windmills in Our Minds. *Wicazo Sa Review* 13(1):25–31. Minneapolis.

1999     Spirit and Reason: The Vine Deloria, Jr., Reader. Golden, Colo.: Fulcrum Publishing.

1999a     For This Land: Writings on Religion in America. New York: Routledge.

1999b     Singing for a Spirit: A Portrait of the Dakota Sioux. Santa Fe, N.Mex.: Clear Light Publishers.

2000     Foreword. Pp. xiii–xvi in Skull Wars: Kennewick Man, Archaeology, and the Battle for Native American Identity, by David Hurst Thomas. New York: Basic Books.

2003     God Is Red: A Native View of Religion. 3th Anniversary Edition. New Forewords by Leslie Marmon Silko and George E. Tinker. Golden, Colo.: Fulcrum Publishing.

2003a     Foreword. Pp. 11–15 in Genocide of the Mind: New Native American Writing. MariJo Moore, ed. New York: Thunder's Mouth Press/Nation Books.

2006     The World We Used To Live In: Remembering the Powers of the Medicine Men. Golden, Colo.: Fulcrum Publishing.

Deloria Vine, Jr., and Raymond J. DeMallie
1999     Documents of American Indian Diplomacy: Treaties, Agreements, and Conventions 1775–1979. 2 vols. Norman: University of Oklahoma Press.

Deloria Vine, Jr., and Clifford M. Lytle
1983     American Indians, American Justice. Austin, Tex.: The University of Texas Press.

1984     The Nations Within: The Past and Future of American Indian Sovereignty. New York: Pantheon Books. (Reprinted: University of Texas Press, Austin, Tex., 1998.)

Deloria Vine, Jr., and David E. Wilkins
1999     Tribes, Treaties, and Constitutional Tribulations. Austin, Tex.: The University of Texas Press. (Reprinted in 2000.)

DeLuca, Richard
1983     We Hold the Rock: The Indian Attempt to Reclaim Alcatraz Island. *California History* 62(1):2–23. San Francisco.

DeMallie, Raymond J., ed.
1984     The Sixth Grandfather: Black Elk's Teachings Given to John G. Neihardt. Introduction by Raymond J. DeMallie; Foreword by Hilda Neihardt Petri. Lincoln: University of Nebraska Press.

Demmert, William G., Jr.
2001     Improving Academic Performance Among Native American Students: A Review of the Research Literature. *ERIC Clearinghouse on Rural Education and Small Schools* ED463917. Charleston, W.Va.

Dempsey, Hugh A.
1986     The Gentle Persuader: A Biography of James Gladstone. Saskatoon, Sask.: Western Producer Prairie Books.

Dempsey, L. James
2007     Blackfoot War Art: Pictographs of the Reservation Period, 1880–2000. Norman: University of Oklahoma Press.

Denevan, William M.
1976     The Native Population of the Americas in 1492. Madison, Wis.: University of Wisconsin Press. (Reprinted: see Denevan 1992.)

_____, ed.
1992     The Native Population of the Americas in 1492. Second Revised Edition. Foreword by W. George Lovell. Madison, Wis.: University of Wisconsin Press.

Den Ouden, Amy
2005     Beyond Conquest: Native Peoples and the Struggle for History in New England. Lincoln: University of Nebraska Press.

Densmore, Frances
1938     The Influence of Hymns on the Form of Indian Songs. *American Anthropologist*, n.s. 40(1):175–177.

Dent, Thomas C., Richard Schechner, and Gilbert Moses, eds.
1969     The Free Southern Theater by the Free Southern Theater: A Documentary of the South's Radical Black Theater, with Journals, Letters, Poetry, Essays and a Play Written by Those Who Built It. Indianapolis, Ind.: The Bobbs-Merrill Company.

Department of Defense *see* U.S. Department of Defense

Department of Indian Affairs and Northern Development (DIAND) *see* Canada. Department of Indian Affairs and Northern Development (DIAND)

Department of National Health and Welfare (DNHW) *see* Canada. Department of National Health and Welfare (DNHW)

Department of the Interior *see* U.S. Department of the Interior

Desbiens, Caroline
2004     Nation to Nation: Defining New Structures of Development in Northern Quebec. *Economic Geography* 80(4):351–366. Worcester, Mass.

Deserontyon, John
1928     A Mohawk Form of Ritual of Condolence, 1782. J.N.B. Hewitt, trans. New York: Museum of the American Indian, Heye Foundation.

Deskaheh, Levi General
1923     Red Man's Appeal to Justice. (League of Nations Document No. 11/30035/28075, League of Nations Archives, Geneva, Switzerland.)

Deverell, William
1993     Imagining Indians. *The American Historical Review* 98(4): 1189–1190. Washington.

Dewing, Rolland
1984     Wounded Knee: The Meaning and Significance of the Second Incident. New York: Irvington Publishers. (Reprinted, rev. ed.: see Dewing 1995.)

_____, ed.
1986     The FBI Files on the American Indian Movement and Wounded Knee. Lanham, Md.: University Press of America.

1995     Wounded Knee II. Chadron, Nebr.: Great Plains Network.

Diamond, Billy
1977     Highlights of the Negotiations Leading to the James Bay and Northern Quebec Agreement. Val d'Or, Que.: Grand Council of the Crees (of Quebec).

1990     Villages of the Damned: The James Bay Agreement Leaves a Trail of Broken Promises. *Arctic Circle* 1(3/November–December):24–34.

Diamond, Jared M.
1997     Guns, Germs, and Steel: The Fates of Human Societies.: New York: W.W. Norton and Company.

DIAND = Department of Indian Affairs and Northern Development *see* Canada. Department of Indian Affairs and Northern Development (DIAND)

Dickason, Olive P.
1992     Canada's First Nations: A History of Founding Peoples from Earliest Times. Norman: University of Oklahoma Press. (Reprinted in 1994, 1997, 2001: see also Dickason 2002.)

1997     Canada's First Nations: A History of Founding Peoples from Earliest Times. Toronto: McClelland and Stewart.

2002     Canada's First Nations: A History of Founding Peoples from Earliest Times. 3d ed. Don Mills, Ont.: Oxford University Press.

Dietrich, Bill
1985    Washington's Indians: A Special Report. *The Seattle Times*, December 24, 1985. Seattle, Wash.

Dietz, Vanessa
1997    Protesters Renew Call for Dakota Ouster. *Daily Mining Gazette*, June 30, 1997:1, 8. Houghton, Mich.

DiFrancesco, Richard J.
2000    A Diamond in the Rough? An Examination of the Issues Surrounding the Development of the Northwest Territories. *The Canadian Geographer* 44(2):114–134. Toronto.

Dincauze, Dena
1985    Report on the Conference on Reburial Issues. *Bulletin of the Society for American Archaeology* 3(5):1–3. Washington.

Dinnerstein, Leonard, Roger L. Nichols, and David M. Reimers
1970    Natives and Other Strangers. New York: Oxford University Press.

Dippie, Brian W.
1982    The Vanishing American: White Attitudes and United States Indian Policy. Middletown, Conn.: Wesleyan University Press.

Dirks, Tim
[2006]    "Stage Coach" (1939). (Webpage: http://www.filmsite.org/stagec.html.)

Diubaldo, Richard
1981    The Absurd Little Mouse: When Eskimos Became Indians. *Journal of Canadian Studies/Revue d'études canadiennes* 16(1):34–40. Peterborough, Ont.

Dixon, Mim, and Yvette Roubideaux, eds.
2001    Promises To Keep: Public Health Policy for American Indians and Alaska Natives in the 21st Century. Washington: American Public Health Association.

DNHW = Department of National Health and Welfare *see* Canada. Department of National Health and Welfare (DNHW)

Doanmoe, Etahdleuh
[1878]    [Omaha Dance at St. Augustine, Florida.] (Undated painting by Kiowa artist Etahdleuh Doanmoe in Richard H. Pratt Papers, Series 4, Box 31 Number 245; Yale University, Beinecke Library, New Haven, Conn.)

Dobbin, Murray J.
1981    The One-And-A-Half Men: The Story of Jim Brady and Malcom Norris, Métis Patriots of the 20th Century. Vancouver: New Star Books.

———
1984    The Métis in Western Canada Since 1945. Pp. 183–193 in Making of the Modern West: Western Canada since 1945. A.W. Rasporich, ed. Calgary, Alta.: University of Calgary Press.

Dobyns, Henry F.
1966    Estimating Aboriginal American Population: An Appraisal of Techniques with a New Hemispheric Estimate. *Current Anthropology* 7(4):395–416. Chicago.

———
1983    Their Number Become Thinned: Native American Population Dynamics in Eastern North America. Knoxville, Tenn.: University of Tennesee Press.

Dockstader, Frederick J.
1977    Great North American Indians: Profiles in Life and Leadership. New York: Van Nostrand Reinhold Company.

Dockstator, Mark S.
2001    Toward an Understanding of the Crown's Views on Justice at the Time of Entering Into Treaty with the First Nations of Canada. Saskatoon, Sask.: Office of the Treaty Commissioner.

Documentary Education Resources
[2007]    "Imagining Indians" (1992). (Webpage: http://www.der.org/films/imagining-indians.html.)

Dohla, Lloyd
2001    Thomas Prince: Canada's Forgotten Aboriginal War Hero. *First Nations Drum*, Summer, 2001:Coverstory. Toronto and Vancouver. (Reprinted: see Dohla 2004.)

———
2004    Thomas Prince: Canada's Forgotten Aboriginal War Hero. In: Smoke Signals from the Heart: Fourteen Years of the *First Nations Drum*. Len O'Connor, Natasha Netschay Davies, and Lloyd Dohla, eds. Vancouver: Totem Pole Books.

Doll, Don, and Jim Alinder, eds.
1976    Crying for a Vision: A Rosebud Sioux Trilogy: 1886–1976. Dobbs Ferry, N.Y.: Morgan and Morgan.

———
1994    Vision Quest: Men, Women, and Sacred Sites of the Sioux Nation. New York: Crown Publishers.

Dongoske, Kurt E.
1996    The Native American Graves Protection and Repatriation Act: A New Beginning, Not the End for Osteological Analysis—A Hopi Perpective. *American Indian Quarterly* 20(2):287–296. Lincoln, Nebr.

Dongoske, Kurt E., Mark Aldenderfer, and Karen Doehner
2000    Working Together: Native Americans and Archaeologists. Washington: Society for American Archaeology.

Dorian, Nancy C.
1981    Language Death: The Life Cycle of a Scottish Gaelic Dialect. Philadelphia: University of Pennsylvania Press.

Dorris, Michael
1975    Native Americans: 500 Years Later. New York: Thomas Y. Crowell.

———
1987    A Yellow Raft on Blue Water. New York: Henry Holt. (Reprinted in 2003.)

———
1989    The Broken Cord: A Family's Ongoing Struggle with Fetal Alcohol Syndrome. Foreword by Louise Erdrich. New York: Harper and Row. (Reprinted in 1990.)

———
2004    Morning Girl. New York: Scholastic, Inc.

Dorris, Michael, and Louise Erdrich
1991    *see* Erdrich, Louise, and Michael Dorris 1991

Douaud, Patrick C.
1985    Ethnolinguistic Profile of the Canadian Métis. Canada. *National Museum of Man. Mercury Series. Ethnology Service Paper* 99. Ottawa.

Downe, Pamela J.
2003    "I Don't Know What the Hell It Is But It Sounds Nasty": Health Issues for Girls Working the Streets. Pp. 86–101 in Being Heard: The Experiences of Young Women in Prostitution. Kelly Gorkoff and Jane Runner, eds. Halifax, N.S.: Fernwood.

———
2006    Aboriginal Girls in Canada: Living Histories of Dislocation, Exploitation and Strength. Pp. 1–15 in Girlhood: Redefining the Limits. Yasmin Jiwani, Claudia Mitchell, and Candis Steenbergen, eds. Montreal: Black Rose Books.

Downes, Randolph C.
1945    The American Indian Can Be Free. *American Indian* 2(4): 8–11. New York.

Downey, Roger
2000       The Riddle for the Bones: Politics, Science, Race and the Story of Kennewick Man. New York: Copernicus Books.

Doxtator, Deborah
1985       The Idea of the Indian Development of Iroquoian Museums. *Museum Quarterly: The Journal of the Ontario Museum Association* 14(2):20–26. Toronto.

———
1988       Fluffs and Feathers: An Exhibit on the Symbols of Indianess: A Resource Guide. Brantford, Ont.: Woodland Cultural Centre.

Doyel, David E.
1982       Medicine Men, Ethnic Significance, and Cultural Resource Management. *American Antiquity* 47(3):634–642.

Dozier, Edward H.
1962       Cycles of Conquest: The Impact of Spain, Mexico and the United States on the Indians of the Southwest, 1533–1960. Tucson: University of Arizona Press.

Drees, Laurie
2002       The Indian Association of Alberta: A History of Political Action. Vancouver: University of British Columbia Press.

Driben, Paul
1985       We Are Métis: The Ethnography of a Halfbreed Community in Northern Alberta. New York: AMS Press. (Originally issued as the Author's Ph.D. Dissertation in Anthropology, University of Minnesota, Minneapolis, 1975.)

Driedger, Leo, ed.
1987       Ethnic Canada: Identities and Inequalities. Toronto: Copp, Clark, Pitman.

Driver, Harold
1969       North American Indians. Chicago: University of Chicago Press.

Drummond, Susan G.
1997       Incorporating the Familiar: An Investigation into Legal Sensibilities in Nunavik. Montreal: McGill-Queen's University Press.

D'Souza, Dinesh
1991       Illiberal Education: The Politics of Race and Sex on Campus. New York: Free Press.

Dubois, Alison, John Loxley, and Wanda Wuttunee
2002       Gambling on Casinos. *The Journal of Aboriginal Economic Development* 2(2):56–67. Edmonton, Alta.

Duffy, Diane, and Jerry Stubben
1998       An Assessment of Native American Economic Development: Putting Culture and Sovereignty Back in the Models. *Studies in Comparative International Development* 32(4):52–78. New Brunswick, N.J.

Duffy, John
1951       Smallpox and the Indians in American Colonies. *Bulletin of the History of Medicine* 25(4):324–341. Baltimore, Md.

Duffy, R. Quinn
1988       The Road to Nunavut: The Progress of the Eastern Arctic Since the Second World War. Montreal: McGill-Queen's University Press.

Dufraimont, Lisa
2000       From Regulation to Recolonization: Justifiable Infringement of Aboriginal Rights at the Supreme Court of Canada. *University of Toronto Faculty of Law Review* 58(1):3–30. Toronto.

Dumont, Yvon
1994       Métis Nationalism: Then and Now. Pp. 82–89 in Pt. 2 of The Forks and the Battle of Seven Oaks in Manitoba History. Robert Coutts and Richard Stuart, eds. 2 Pts. Winnipeg, Man.: Manitoba Historical Society.

1995       [Taped interview with Yvon Dumont, Lt. Governor of Manitoba, 11 September 1995, by Doug Racine and Joe Sawchuck.] (Recorded at the residence of the Lt. Governor in Winnipeg, Man.)

Duncan, Jim W.
1997       Hethuska Zani: An Ethnohistory of the War Dance Complex. (M.A. Thesis in Anthropology, Northeastern State University, Tahlequah, Okla.)

Dunlay, Thomas W.
1987       Wolves for the Blue Soldiers: Indian Scouts and Auxiliaries with the United States Army 1860–90. Lincoln: University of Nebraska Press.

Durham, Jimmie
1980       [Open Letter on Recent Development in the American Indian Movement/International Treaty Council, dated December 1980.] (Photocopy in Robert Warrior's possession.)

Dussias, Allison M.
1993       Geographically-Based and Membership-Based Views of Indian Tribal Sovereignty: The Supreme Court's Changing Vision. *University of Pittsburgh Law Review* 55(1):1–97. Pittsburgh, Pa.

Duthu, Bruce, ed.
1996       Symposium: Stewards of the Land: Indian Tribes, the Environment, and the Law. *Vermont Law Review* 21(1):353–403. South Royalton, Vt.

Dyck, Noel
1983       Representation and Leadership of a Provincial Indian Association. Pp. 197–305 in The Politics of Indianness: Case Studies and Ethnopolitics in Canada. Adrian Tanner, ed. St. John's, N.L.: Institute of Social and Economic Research, Memorial University of Newfoundland.

———
1991       What Is the Indian "Problem": Tutelage and Resistance. *Social and Economic Studies* 46. St. John's, N.L.: Institute of Social and Economic Research, Memorial University of Newfoundland.

———, ed.
1992       Indigenous Peoples and the Nation-State: "Fourth World" Politics in Canada, Australia, and Norway. *Social and Economic Papers* 14. St. John's, N.L.: Institute of Social and Economic Research, Memorial University of Newfoundland.

Dyck, Noel, and James B. Waldram, eds.
1993       Anthropology, Public Policy, and Native Peoples in Canada. Montreal: McGill-Queen's University Press.

Dyk, Walter, recorder
1938       Son of Old Man Hat: A Navaho Autobiography. New York: Harcourt Brace.

Eadington, William R., ed.
1998       Indian Gaming and the Law. Reno, Nev.: University of Nevada Press.

Eagle, Adam Fortunate
1992       Alcatraz! Alcatraz! The Indian Occupation of 1969–1971. Berkeley, Calif.: Heyday Books.

———
1994       Urban Indians and the Occupation of Alcatraz Island. Pp. 33–58 in Special Edition: Alcatraz Revisited: The 25th Anniversary of the Occupation, 1969–1971. *American Indian Culture and Research Journal* 18(4). Los Angeles.

Eaglestaff, Anthony
1993 Wooden Wannabe Drives Wedges Among People. *Indian Country Today*, October 6, 1993:A5. Canastota, N.Y. (Webpage: http://www.indiancountry.com)

EagleWoman, Angelique (*WasteWin, Wambdi, A.*)
2006 U.S. Politics and Tribal Nation Gaming: How It All Plays Out in Oklahoma. *Oklahoma Bar Association Journal* 77(6): 525–541. Oklahoma City.

Earling, Debra
2002 Perma Red. New York: Bluehen Books.

Easterly, William
2006 The White Man's Burden: Why the West's Efforts To Aid the Rest Have Done So Much Ill and So Little Good. New York: Penguin Press.

Eastman, Charles A. (Ohiyesa)
1902 Indian Boyhood. Illustrated by E.L. Blumenshein. Boston: Little, Brown. (Reprinted: Dover Publications, New York, 1971; see also Eastman 1991.)

———
1911 The Soul of the Indian: An Interpretation. Boston, New York: Houghton Mifflin. (Reprinted: University of Nebraska Press, Lincoln, 1980.)

———
1916 From the Deep Woods to Civilization: Chapters in the Autobiography of an Indian. Boston: Little, Brown. (Reprinted: see Eastman 1936.)

———
1936 From the Deep Woods to Civilization: Chapters in the Autobiography of an Indian. Foreword by Raymond Wilson. Boston: Little, Brown. (Reprinted: University of Nebraska Press, Lincoln, 1977.)

———
1991 Indian Boyhood. Illustrated by E.L. Blumenshein. Introduction by David Reed Miller. Lincoln: University of Nebraska Press.

Eastman, Oliver D.
1971 *see* Pratt, Vince E. 1971

Ebert, Roger
1990 "Dances With Wolves" (1990). (Webpage: http://rogerebert.suntimes.com [9 November 1990].)

———
2001 "The Searchers" (1956). (Webpage: http://rogerebert.sun times.com [25 November 2001].)

Echo-Hawk, Roger C., and Walter R. Echo-Hawk
1994 Battlefields and Burial Grounds: The Indian Struggle To Protect Ancestral Graves in the United States. Minneapolis: Lerner Publications Company.

Editor, The
1958–1959 *see* Lesser, Alexander 1958–1959

Editorial
2006 *see The Gazette* 2006

———
2006a Felix Cohen's 'Handbook of Federal Indian Law': Essential for All Libraries. *Indian Country Today*, August 24, 2006. Canastota, N.Y. (Webpage: http://www.indiancountry.com)

Edward, Newton
1961–1962 Economic Development of Indian Reserves. Pp. 197–202 in American Indians and Their Economic Development. Fred Voget, ed. *Human Organization*, Special Issue 20(4). Washington.

Edwards, Chris
2006 [Statement of Chris Edwards, Director of Tax Policy, Cato Institute, March 8, 2006: The Need for Tax Reform and the Possibility of a Flat Tax for the District of Columbia.] (Testimony Before the Senate Committee on Appropriations, Subcommittee on the District of Columbia, U.S. Congress, Washington.)

Eells, Walter Crosby
1931 The Junior College. Boston, Mass.: Houghton Mifflin.

———
1945 Educational Opportunities for the Indian Veteran. *American Indian* 2(4):17–21. New York.

Eicher, Carl K.
1961–1962 Income Improvement on the Rosebud Sioux Reservation. Pp. 191–196 in American Indians and Their Economic Development. Fred Voget, ed. *Human Organization*, Special Issue 20(4). Washington.

Eisler, Kim Isaac
2001 Revenge of the Pequots: How a Small Native American Tribe Created the World's Most Powerful Casino. New York: Simon and Schuster.

Ejesiak, Kirt
2004 Homelessness Inequality Among Aboriginal Peoples of Canada: A Case for the Inuit of Nunavut. *John F. Kennedy School of Government*. Cambridge, Mass.: Harvard University.

Elias, Peter D.
1991 Development of Aboriginal Peoples Communities. North York, Ont.: Captus University Press.

———
1995 Northern Aboriginal Communities: Economics and Development. North York, Ont.: Captus University Press.

Elkus, Ben
[1940] The Gallup Ceremonial. (Elkus Collection, California Academy of Sciences, San Francisco; Webpage: http://www.calacademy.org/researh/library/elkus/stories/gallup.htm)

Elliot, David E.
2003 Much Ado About Dittos: *Wewaykum* and the Fiduciary Obligations of the Crown. *Queen's Law Journal* 29(1):1–40. Kingston, Ont.

Ellis, Clyde
2003 A Dancing People. Lawrence: University of Kansas Press.

Ellis, Clyde, Luke Eric Lassiter, and Gary H. Dunham, eds.
2005 Powwow. Lincoln and London: University of Nebraska Press.

Ellis, Richard N., ed.
1972 The Western American Indian: Case Studies in Tribal History. Lincoln: University of Nebraska Press

Ellison, Rosemary
1969 Contemporary Southern Plains Indian Art. [Introduction by Rosemary Ellison.] Anadarko, Okla.: Oklahoma Indian Arts and Crafts Cooperative.

———
1972 Contemporary Southern Plains Indian Panting. With an Essay by Rosemary Ellison. Myles Libhart, ed. Anadarko, Okla.: Oklahoma Indian Arts and Crafts Cooperative.

———
1976 Contemporary Southern Plains Indian Metalwork. [Introduction by Rosemary Ellison.] Anadarko, Okla.: Oklahoma Indian Arts and Crafts Cooperative.

Elvin, John
1999 Trump To Aid Unrecognized Indians. *Insight on the News* 15(41, November 8, 1999):35.

Emerson, Haven
1945        Freedom or Exploitation: Is Mr. O.K Armstrong's Recent Solution of the American Indian Problem Sound? *American Indian* 2(4):3–7. New York.

Emmons, Glenn L.
1990        Extract from the Annual Report of the Commissioner of Indian Affairs in the Annual Report of the Secretary of the Interior [1954]. Pp. 237–238 in Documents of United States Indian Policy. Francis Paul Prucha, ed. Lincoln and London: University of Nebraska Press.

*Encyclopedia of North American Indians*
2006        Encyclopedia of North American Indians. Frederick E. Hoxie, ed. Boston, New York: Houghton Mifflin College Division—Online Study Center. (Webpage: http://college .hmco.com/history/readerscomp/naind/html/; Published volume, see: Hoxie, Frederick E., ed., 1996.)

Enloe, Cynthia H.
1980        Ethnic Soldiers: State Security in a Divided Society. New York: Penguin Books.

Environmental Protection Agency
2007        *see* U.S. Environmental Protection Agency

Erasmus, George
1992        We Want To Turn the Page. *Museum Anthropology* 16(2): 7–9. Tempe, Ariz.

Erdoes, Richard, and Alfonso Ortiz, eds.
1984        American Indian Myths and Legends. New York: Pantheon Books.

Erdrich, Louise
1984        Love Medicine: A Novel. New York: Holt, Rinehart, and Winston. (Several reprints, incl.: 1985, 1988, 1993, 2005.)

1986        The Beet Queen: A Novel. New York: Henry Holt and Company. (Several reprints, incl.: 1998, 1999, 2001, 2006.)

1988        Tracks. New York: Henry Holt and Company. (Reprinted in 2004.)

1994        The Bingo Palace. New York and London, [etc.]: Harper Collins. (Several reprints, incl.: 1995, 1998, 2001, 2006.)

1995        The Blue Jay's Dance: A Birth Year. New York: Harper Collins.

1996        Grandmother's Pigeon. New York: Hyperion Books for Children.

1996        Tales of Burning Love. New York: Harper Collins.

1998        The Antelope Wife: A Novel. New York: Harper Flamingo. (Reprinted in 2002.)

1999        The Birchbark House. New York: Hyperion Books for Children. (Reprinted in 2002.)

2001        The Last Report on the Miracles at Little No Horse. New York: Harper Collins.

2002        The Range Eternal. New York: Hyperion Books for Children.

2005        The Painted Drum. New York: Harper Collins.

Erdrich, Louise, and Michael Dorris
1991        The Crown of Columbus. New York: Harper Collins. (Reprinted in 1999.)

Erickson, Jim
2006        Ancient Puebloans Reburied at Park. *Rocky Mountain News,* May 5, 2006. Denver, Colo.

Erickson, Patricia Pierce
2003        Welcome to This House: A Century of Makah People Honoring Identity and Negotiating Cultural Tourism. Pp. 523–547 in Native Peoples and Tourism. Neil L. Whitehead, ed.; Larry Nesper, guest ed. *Ethnohistory* 50(3).

Erikson, Patricia Pierce, Helma Ward, and Kirk Wachendorf
2002        Voices of a Thousand People: The Makah Cultural and Research Center. Lincoln: University of Nebraska Press.

Eschbach, Karl
1993        Changing Identification Among American Indians and Alaska Natives. *Demography* 30(4):635–652. [Chicago, etc.]

1995        The Enduring and Vanishing American Indian: American Indian Population Growth and Intermarriage in 1990. *Ethnic and Racial Studies* 18(1):89–108. London and New York.

Eschbach, Karl, Khalil Supple, and C. Matthew Snipp
1998        Changes in Racial Identification and the Educational Attainment of American Indians, 1970–1990. *Demography* 35(1): 35–43. [Chicago, etc.]

Euler, Robert C., and Henry F. Dobyns
1961–1962   Ethnic Group Land Rights in the Modern State. Pp. 203–207 in American Indians and Their Economic Development. Fred Voget, ed. *Human Organization*, Special Issue 20(4). Washington.

Evers, S. E., et al.
1987        Prevalence of Diabetes in Indians and Caucasians Living in Southern Ontario. *Canadian Journal of Public Health* 78(4): 240–243. Ottawa.

Ewers, John C.
1943        Museum: The Blackfeet Indians Now Have a Word for It. *Museum News* 20(18):12. Washington.

1958        *see* 1959

1959        A Century of American Indian Exhibits in the Smithsonian Institution. Pp. 513–525 in *Annual Report of the Board of Regents of the Smithsonian Institution for 1958. Publication* 4354.Washington: Smithsonian Institution; U.S. Government Printing Office.

1967        William Clark's Indian Museum in St. Louis, 1816–1838. Pp. 49–72 in A Cabinet of Curiosities: Five Episodes in the Evolution of American Museums. Whitfield J. Bell, ed. Charlottesville, Va.: University of Virginia Press.

1978        Richard Sanderville, Blackfoot, ca. 1873–1951. Pp. 117–128 in American Indian Intellectuals. Margot Liberty, ed. *1976 Proceedings of The American Ethnological Society*. St. Paul, New York, etc.: West Publishing Co.

Eyre, Chris, director
1998        Smoke Signals. Screenplay by Sherman Alexie. New York: Miramax Films.

500 Nations
2006        New Mexico Indian Casinos. (Webpage: http://www.500 nations.com/New_Mexico_Casinos.asp)

Falkowski, James E.
1992        Indian Law/Race Law. New York: Praeger.

Farr, Moira
2002        Back to the Grave. *University Affairs/Affaires universitaires: Canada's Magazine on Higher Education*, May 2002:10–15. Ottawa.

Farr, William E.
1993        Troubled Bundels, Troubled Blackfeet: The Travail of Cultural and Religious Renewal. *Montana: The Magazine of Western History* 43(4):2–17. Helena, Mont.

Farrer, Claire R.
1994        Who Owns the Words? An Anthropological Perspective on Public Law 101-601. *Journal of Arts Management, Law and Society* 23(4):317–326. Washington.

Fauntleroy, Gussie
2005        Uniquely American. *Art and Antiques Magazine* 28(1):80–85. [New York, etc.]

Feder, Norman
1980        Notes on the Osage War Dance. *Moccasin Tracks*. November 4–7.

*Federal Register* see U.S. *Federal Register*

Federal Trade Commission, Bureau of Competition
1975        Report to the Federal Trade Commission on Mineral Leasing on Indian Lands. (Washington: Federal Trade Commission, Bureau of Competition. Unpublished staff report.)

Feest, Christian F.
1987        Indians and Europe: An Interdisciplinary Collection of Essays. Aachen, Germany: Ed. Herodot.

_____
1988        *see* Handbook Vol. 4 (1988:582–586)

_____
1993        European Collecting of American Indian Artifacts and Art. *Journal of the History of Collections* 5(1):1–11. Oxford.

Feit, Harvey A.
1973        The Ethno-ecology of the Waswanipi Cree: Or, How Hunters Can Manage Their Resources. Pp. 115–125 in Cultural Ecology: Readings on Canadian Indians and Eskimos. Bruce Alden Cox, ed. Toronto: McClelland and Stewart.

_____
1989        James Bay Cree Self-Governance and Land Management. Pp. 68–99 in We Are Here: Politics of Aboriginal Land Tenure. Edwin N. Wilmsen, ed. Berkeley: University of California Press.

_____
1991        Gifts of the Land: Hunting Territories, Guaranteed Incomes and the Construction of Social Relations in James Bay Cree Society. *Senri Ethnological Studies* 30:223–268. Osaka, Japan.

_____
1992        Waswanipi Cree Management of Land and Wildlife: Cree Ethno-Ecology Revisited. Pp. 75–91 in Native People, Native Lands: Canadian Indians, Inuit and Métis. Bruce Alden Cox, ed. Ottawa: Carleton University Press.

Feit, Harvey A., and Robert Beaulieu
2001        Voices from a Disappearing Forest: Government, Corporate and Cree Participatory Forestry Management Practices. Pp. 119–148 in Aboriginal Autonomy and Development in Northern Quebec and Labrador. Colin Scott, ed. Vancouver: University of British Columbia Press.

Feldhousen-Giles, Kristy
2003–2005    [Ethnographic fieldnotes from approximately 28 months' fieldwork among Oklahoma Freedmen, Oklahoma.] (Notes in K. Feldhousen-Giles's possession.)

Fenelon, James V.
2000        Traditional and Modern Perspectives on Indian Gaming: The Struggle for Sovereignty. Pp. 108–128 in Indian Gaming: Who Wins? Angela Mullis and David Kamper, eds. *Contemporary American Indian Issues* 9; *Native American Politics Series* 6. Los Angeles: UCLA American Indian Studies Center.

Fenton, William N.
1971        The New York State Wampum Collection: The Case for the Integrity of Cultural Treasures. *Proceedings of the American Philosophical Society* 115(6):437–461. Philadelphia.

_____
1989        Return of Eleven Wampum Belts to the Six Nations Iroquois Confederacy on Grand River, Canada. *Ethnohistory* 36(4):392–410.

Ferguson, Frances N.
1968        Navajo Drinking: Some Tentative Hypotheses. *Human Organization* 27(2):159–167. Washington.

_____
1976        State Theory as an Explanatory Device in Navaho Acoholism Treatment Response. *Human Organization* 35(1):65–78. Washington.

Ferguson, Leland G., and Gene J. Crediford
1986        Contemporary Native Americans in South Carolina. Columbia, S.C.: South Carolina Committee for the Humanities.

Ferguson, T.J., Roger Anyon, and Edmund J. Ladd
1996        Repatriation at the Pueblo of Zuni: Diverse Solutions to Complex Problems. Pp. 251–273 in Repatriation: An Interdisciplinary Dialogue. Devon A. Mihesuah, ed. *American Indian Quarterly, Special Issue* 20(2):251–273. Lincoln, Nebr.

Ferguson, T.J., Joe Watkins, and Gordon Pullar
1997        Native Americans and Archaeologists: Commentary and Personal Perspectives. Pp. 237–252 in Native Americans and Archaeologists: Stepping Stones to Common Ground. Nina Swidler, et al., eds. Walnut Creek, Calif.: AltaMira Press, and Society for American Archaeology.

Fforde, Cressida, Jane Hubert, and Paul Turnbull, eds.
2002        The Dead and Their Possessions: Repatriation in Principle, Policy and Practice. *One World Archaeology* 43. New York and London: Routledge. (Reprinted in 2004.)

Fiedler, Leslie A.
1988        *see* Handbook Vol. 4 (1988:573–581)

Fikes, Jay C.
1992        Obstacles and Issues Connected with Amending AIRFA. (Typescript; copy in J.C. Fike's possession.)

_____, ed.
1996        *see* Snake, Reuben 1996

Findley, Tim
1994        Alcatraz Recollections. Pp. 59–74 in Special Edition: Alcatraz Revisited: The 25th Anniversary of the Occupation, 1969–1971. *American Indian Culture and Research Journal* 18(4). Los Angeles.

Fine-Dare, Kathleen S.
2002        Grave Injustice: The American Indian Repatriation Movement and NAGPRA. Lincoln and London: University of Nebraska Press.

Finger, John R.
1991        Cherokee Americans: The Eastern Band of Cherokee Indians in the Twentieth Century. *Indians of the Southeast Series*. Lincoln: University of Nebraska Press.

Finger, John R., and Theda Perdue
2004        *see* Handbook Vol. 14 (2004:152–161)

Fintzelberg, Nicholas M.
1969        Peyote Paraphernalia. *San Diego Museum of Man. Ethnic Technology Notes* 4. San Diego, Calif.

First Nations Adult and Higher Education Consortium
2006        FNAHEC Mission Statement, List of Members, and Map. (Webpage: http://www.Fnahec.org/post.html)

First Nations University of Canada
2006        [Homepage.] Regina, [etc.], Sask.: First Nations University of Canada. (Webpage: http://www.firstnationsniversity.ca)

Fisher, Jean
2002        In Search of the "Inauthentic": Disturbing Signs in Contemporary Native American Art. Pp. 331–340 in Race-ing Art History: Critical Readings in Race and Art History. Kymberly N. Pinder, ed. New York: Routledge.

Fisher, Robin
1971        Joseph Trutch and Indian Land Policy. *BC Studies* 12(Winter):3–33. Vancouver.

_____
1978        Contact and Conflict: Indian-European Relations in British Columbia, 1774–1890. Vancouver: University of British Columbia Press.

Fishman, Joshua A.
1991        Reversing Language Shift: Theoretical and Empirical Foundations of Assistance to Threatened Languages. Clevedon, U.K.: Multilingual Matters.

_____
2000        Can Threatened Languages Be Saved? Clevedon, U.K.: Multilingual Matters.

Fitzpatrick, Jeremy R.
2004        The Competent Ward. *American Indian Law Review* 28(1):189–202. Norman, Okla.

Five Hundred Nations
2006        *see* 500 Nations 2006 [first entry under letter "F"]

Fixico, Donald L.
1986        Termination and Relocation: Federal Indian Policy, 1945–1960. Alburquerque: University of New Mexico Press.

_____
1996        The Struggle for Our Homes: Indian and White Values and Tribal Lands. Pp. 29–46 in Defending Mother Earth: Native American Perspectives on Environmental Justice. Jace Weaver, ed. Maryknoll, N.Y.: Orbis Books.

_____, ed.
1997        Rethinking American Indian History: Analysis, Methodology, and Historiography. Albuquerque: University of New Mexico Press.

_____
1998        The Invasion of Indian Country in the Twentieth Century: American Capitalism and Tribal Natural Resources. Niwot, Colo.: University Press of Colorado.

_____
2000        The Urban Indian Experience. Albuquerque: University of New Mexico Press.

_____
2001        The Indigenous Nations Studies Program and Center at the University of Kansas. *Indigenous Nations Studies Journal* 2(1):87–96. Lawrence, Kans.

_____
2001a       Foreword. Pp. ix–x in American Indians and the Urban Experience. *Contemporary Native American Communities*. Susan Lobo and Kurt Peters, eds. Walnut Creek, Calif.: AltaMira Press.

_____
2004        *see* Handbook Vol. 14 (2004:162–173)

Flanagan, Thomas E., ed.
1976        The Diaries of Louis Riel. Edmonton, Alta.: Hurtig.

_____
1996        Louis 'Devil' Riel: Prophet of the New World. Rev. ed. Toronto: University of Toronto Press.

Flanagan, Thomas E., and John E. Foster, eds.
1985        The Métis: Past and Present. *Canadian Ethnic Studies* 17(2) [Special issue].

Flannery, Regina
1947        The Changing Form and Functions of the Gros Ventre Grass Dance. *Primitive Man* 20(2):39–70. Washington.

Fleckner, John A.
1984        Native American Archives: An Introduction. Chicago: The Society of American Archivists.

Fleming, Lee
2001        Declaration of R. Lee Fleming, The Mashpee Wampanoag Tribal Council, Inc., Plaintiff, V. Gail A. Norton, Secretary of the United States Department of the Interior; and Neal McCaleb, Assistant Secretary. (Indian Affairs: United States Department of the Interior No. 1:01CV00111(JR), in the United States District Court for the District of Columbia, Washington.)

Fletcher, Alice C.
1892        Hae-thu-ska Society of the Omaha Tribe. *Journal of American Folk-lore* 5(17):135–144. [Boston, New York, etc.]

Fletcher, Matthew
2005        The Legal Fiction of Gridiron Cowboys and Indians. *Indigenous Peoples' Journal of Law, Culture & Resistance* 2(1):11–21. Los Angeles.

Flynn, Gillian
2003        Richard Dalton, Sr. (1926–2003). *Anthropolog*, Spring 2003:16. Washington: Department of Anthropology, National Museum of Natural History.

Fogelson, Raymond D.
1988        [Testimony of Raymond D. Fogelson.] Pp. 43–44 in Oversight Hearing on Federal Acknowledgment Progess: Hearing Before the Select Committee on Indian Affairs, May 26, 1988. *100 Congress, 2d Session*. Washington: U.S. Government Printing Office.

_____, vol. ed.
2004        *see* Handbook Vol. 14 (2004)

Foley, Douglas
2005        The Heartland Chronicles Revisited: The Casino's Impact on Settlement Life. *Qualitative Inquiry* 11(3):296–320. Thousand Oaks, Calif.

Forbes, Jack D.
1988        Black Africans and Native Americans. Urbana: University of Illinois Press. (Reprinted: see Forbes 1993.)

_____
1993        Africans and Native Americans: The Language of Race and the Evolution of Red-Black Peoples. 2d ed. Urbana: University of Illinois Press.

_____
1994        The Native Struggle for Liberation: Alcatraz. Pp. 123–130 in Special Edition: Alcatraz Revisited: The 25th Anniversary of the Occupation, 1969–1971. Joane Nagel and Troy Johnson, eds. *American Indian Culture and Research Journal* 18(4). Los Angeles.

2001    The Urban Tradition among Native Americans. Pp. 5–25 in American Indians and the Urban Experience. *Contemporary Native American Communities*. Susan Lobo and Kurt Peters, eds. Walnut Creek, Calif.: AltaMira Press.

2007    The American Discovery of Europe. Urbana and Chicago: University of Illinois Press.

Forbes, Jack D., et al.
2002    A Hemispheric Approach: Native American Studies at the University of California–Davis. Pp. 97–122 in Native American Studies in Higher Education: Models for Collaboration Between Universities and Indigenous Nations. Duane Champagne and Jay Stauss, eds. Walnut Creek, Calif.: AltaMira Press.

Foreman, Carolyn Thomas
1943    Indians Abroad, 1493–1939. Norman: University of Oklahoma Press.

Foreman, Grant
1932    Indian Removal: The Emigration of the Five Civilized Tribes of Indians. Norman: University of Oklahoma Press. (Reprinted in 1953; see also Foreman 1986.)

1934    The Five Civilized Tribes: Cherokee, Chickasaw, Choctaw, Creek, Seminole. Introductory Note by John R. Swanton. Norman: University of Oklahoma Press. (Reprinted in 1974 and 1982.)

1986    Indian Removal: The Emigration of the Five Civilized Tribes of Indians. Rev. ed. Foreword by Angie Debo. Norman: University of Oklahoma Press.

Forquera, Ralph A.
2001    Urban Indian Health, Issue Brief. Washington: The Henry J. Kaiser Family Foundation.

Fortuine, Robert
1984    Traditional Surgery of the Alaska Natives. *Alaska Medicine* 26(1):22–25. Anchorage.

Foster, Don C.
1955    [Report of Portland Area Director, Bureau of Indian Affairs, to the Commissioner of Indian Affaris, Washington, dated February 21, 1955.] (Copy in Records of the Bureau of Indian Affairs, Record Group 75, Portland Area Office: Folder 103.5, Government Withdrawal Program, 1953. General Correspondence, 1952–1968, Box 16; National Archives—Pacific Northwest Regional Branch, Seattle, Wash.)

Foster, John E.
1985    Some Questions and Perspectives on the Problems of Métis Roots. Pp. 73–91 in The New Peoples: Being and Becoming Métis in North America. Jacqueline Peterson, and Jennifer S.H. Brown, eds. *Manitoba Studies in Native History* 1. Winnipeg: University of Manitoba Press.

1986    The Plains Métis. Pp. 375–404 in Native Peoples: The Canadian Experience. R. Bruce Morrison and Antoine S. Lussier, eds. Toronto: McClelland and Stewart.

2001    Wintering, the Outsider Adult Male and the Ethnogenesis of the Western Plains Métis. Pp. 179–192 in From Rupert's Land to Canada: Essays in Honour of John E. Foster. Theodore Binnema, Gerhard J. Ens, and R.C. Macleod, eds. Edmonton, Alta.: University of Alberta Press. (Originally published in: *Prairie Forum* 19(1):1–13. Regina, Sask., 1994.)

Foster, Lenny
1994    Alcatraz Is Not an Island. Pp. 131–134 in Special Edition: Alcatraz Revisited: The 25th Anniversary of the Occupation, 1969–1971. *American Indian Culture and Research Journal* 18(4). Los Angeles.

Foster, Martha Harroun
2006    We Know Who We Are: Métis Identity in a Montana Community. Norman: University of Oklahoma Press.

Four Arrows (Don Trent Jacobs), ed.
2006    Unlearning the Language of Conquest: Scholars Expose Anti-Indianism in America. Austin, Tex.: The University of Texas Press.

Fowler, Loretta
1978    Bill Shakespeare, Northern Arapahoe, 1901–1975. Pp. 227–240 in American Indian Intellectuals. Margot Liberty, ed. *1976 Proceedings of The American Ethnological Society*. St. Paul, New York, etc.: West Publishing Co.

1982    Arapahoe Politics, 1851–1978: Symbols in Crises of Authority. Lincoln: University of Nebraska Press.

1987    Shared Symbols, Contested Meanings: Gros Ventre Culture and History, 1778–1984. Ithaca, N.Y.: Cornell University Press.

2001    *see* Handbook Vol. 13(2001:840–862)

Fox, Sandra J.
1999    Student Assessment in Indian Education or What Is A Roach? Pp. 161–178 in Next Steps: Research and Practice to Advance Indian Education. Karen Gayton Swisher and John W. Tippeconnic, III, eds. Charleston, W.Va.: ERIC Clearinghouse on Rural Education and Small Schools.

Francis, Daniel
1992    The Imaginary Indian: The Image of the Indian in Canadian Culture. Vancouver: Arsenal Pulp Press.

Franco, Jere' Bishop
1990    Patriotism on Trial: Native Americans in World War II. Ann Arbor, Mich.: University Microfilms International.

1997    Crossing the Pond: The Native American Effort in World War II. *War and the Southwest Series* 7. Denton, Tex.: University of North Texas Press.

Franklin, Marvin
1973    [Letter from Assistant to the Secretary of the Interior to Mr. Garrison.] (Office of Federal Acknowledgment Files, June 27, 1973, Bureau of Indian Affairs, Washington.)

Frantz, Klaus
1999    Indian Reservations in the United States: Territory, Sovereignty, and Socioeconomic Change. *University of Chicago Geography Research Papers*. Chicago and London: University of Chicago Press.

Freeman, J. Leiper
[1950]    The Bureau of Indian Affairs. (Chaper 9 in: Administrative History of the Bureau of Indian Affairs, Box 25–27, BIA-Histories, AIPRC, Record Group 220, National Archives, Washington.)

French, Philip
1973    Westerns: Aspects of a Movie Genre. New York: Viking Press.

Frenette, Jacques
2003    La petition montagnaise du 1er février 1843: chasse, peche et agriculture a la baie des Escoumins. *Recherches amérindiennes au Québec* 33(1):105–114. Montreal.

Freng, Adrienne
2007      American Indians in the News: A Media Portrayal in Crime Articles. *American Indian Culture and Research Journal* 31(1):21–37. Los Angeles.

Friar, Ralph, and Natasha Friar
1972      The Only Good Indian: The Hollywood Gospel. New York: Drama Book Specialists.

Frickey, Phillip P.
1996      Domesticating Federal Indian Law. *Minnesota Law Review* 81(1):31–95.

Frideres, James
1993      Native Peoples in Canada: Contemporary Conflicts. 4th ed. Scarborough, Ont.: Prentice-Hall.

Frideres, James S., and L.E. Krosenbrink-Gelissen
1998      Aboriginal Peoples in Canada: Contemporary Conflicts. 5th ed. Scarborough, Ont.: Prentice-Hall.

Friedberg, Lilian
2000      Dare to Compare: Americanizing the Holocaust. *American Indian Quarterly* 24(3):353–380. Lincoln, Nebr.

Friesen, John W., and Terry Lusty
1980      The Métis of Canada: An Annotated Bibliography. Toronto: Ontario Institute for Studies in Education.

Frizzell, Kent
1975      [Letter from Acting Solicitor, Department of the Interior, to Lewis Bell, dated February 25, 1975.] (Office of Federal Acknowledgment, Stillaguamish Files, February 25, 1975, Bureau of Indian Affairs, Washington.).

———
1976      [Letter from Acting Solicitor, Department of the Interior, dated October 8, 1976.] (Office of Federal Acknowledgment, Stillaguamish Files, October 8, 1976, Bureau of Indian Affairs, Washington.).

———
1976a      [Letter from Acting Secretary of the Interior to David Getches, Native American Rights Fund, dated October 27, 1976.] (Office of Federal Acknowledgment, Stillaguamish Files, October 27, 1976, Bureau of Indian Affairs, Washington.).

Fromson, Brett Duval
2003      Hitting the Jackpot: The Inside Story of the Richest Indian Tribe in History. New York: Atlantic Monthly Press.

Frost, Richard
1973      A Study of a Los Angeles Urban Indian Free Clinic and Indian Medical Problems. (Master's thesis, California State University, Long Beach.)

Fuchs, Estelle, and Robert J. Havinghurst
1983      To Live on This Earth: American Indian Education. Albuquerque: University of New Mexico Press.

Fuller, Nancy J.
1992      The Museum As a Vehicle for Community Empowerment: The Ak-Chin Indian Community Ecomuseum Project. Pp. 327–365 in Museums and Communities: The Politics of Public Culture. Ivan Karp, Christine Mullen Kreamer, and Steven D. Lavine, eds. Washington: Smithsonian Institution Press.

Fuller, Nancy J., and Susanne Fabricius
1992      Native American Museums and Cultural Centers: Historical Overview and Current Issues. *Zeitschrift für Ethnologie* 117:223–237. Berlin.

Fuller, Patty
1993      Mayhem Among the Métis: The Métis Nation of Alberta Faces Membership-Fixing and Corruption Charges. *Alberta Report/Western Report* 20(42):16.

Fumoleau, René
2004      As Long As This Land Shall Last: A History of Treaty 8 and Treaty 11, 1870–1939. Afterword by Joanne Barnaby. Calgary, Alta.: University of Calgary Press. (Originally publ. in 1973.)

Furst, Peter T.
1996      People of the Peyote: Huichol Indian History, Religion and Survival. Albuquerque: University of New Mexico Press.

Gabriel Dumont Institute
2001–2002  Drops of Brandy and Other Traditional Métis Tunes. Book and CD. Regina, Sask.: Gabriel Dumont Institute of Native Studies and Applied Research.

Gabriel, Kathryn
1996      Gambler Way: Indian Gaming in Mythology, History and Archaeology in North America. Boulder, Colo.: Johnson Books.

Gabriel, Mille
2002      Repatriering: en udfordring for fremtidens museum. *Arkaeologisk Forum* 7:13–17.

———
2004      Human Remains, Subjects or Scientific Specimens: A Danish Perspective on the Repatriation and Reburial Issue. (Paper presented at the Theoretical Archaeological Group [TAG] Conference, Glagsow, Scotland.)

Gaffen, Fred
1979      Forgotten Soldiers. Penticton, B.C.: Theytus Books.

Gahagan, Sheila, Janet Silverstein, and The Committee on Native American Child Health and the Section on Endocrinology
2003      Prevention and Treatment of Type 2 Diabetes Mellitus in Children with Special Emphasis on American Indian and Alaska Native Children. *Pediatrics* 112(4):328–347. Evanston, Ill.

Gallagher, R.P., and J.M. Elwood
1979      Cancer Mortality Among Chinese, Japanese, and Indians in British Columbia, 1964–73. *National Cancer Institute Monograph* 53(Nov.):89–94. [Washington.]

Gallagher, Tag
1993      Angels Gambol Where They Will: John Ford's Indians. *Film Comment* 29(5): 68–72. New York.

Galois, Robert M.
1992      The Indian Rights Association, Native Protest Activity and the 'Land Question' in British Columbia, 1903–1916. *Native Studies Review* 8(2):1–34. Saskatoon, Sask.

Gamble, John I.
1952      Changing Patterns of Kiowa Indian Dances. Pp. 94–104 in Vol. 2: Acculturation in the Americas. Sol Tax, ed. With an Introduction by Melville J. Herskovits. *Proceedings and Selected Papers of the 29th International Congress of Americanists* [New York, 1949]. 3 vols. Chicago: University of Chicago Press.

GAO = General Accounting Office *see* U.S. General Accounting Office (GAO) [now Government Accountability Office]

Gardner, Leigh, Joseph P. Kalt, and Katherine A. Spilde
2005      Annotated Bibliography: The Social and Economic Impacts of Indian and Other Gaming. Cambridge, Mass.: The Harvard Project on American Indian Economic Development, Harvard University.

Gardner, Michael R.
2002      Harry Truman and Civil Rights: Moral Courage and Political Risks. Carbondale, Ill.: Southern Illinois University Press.

*481*

Gardner, Susan, and Godfrey, Joyzelle Gingway
2000        Speaking of Ella Deloria: Conversations with Joyzelle Ging-
            way Godfrey, 1998–200, Lower Brule Community College,
            South Dakota. *American Indian Quarterly* 24(3):456–475.
            Lincoln, Nebr.

Garmhausen, Winona
1988        History of Indian Arts Education in Santa Fe. Santa Fe,
            N.Mex.: Sunstone Press.

Garro, Linda C., J. Roulette, and R.G. Whitmore
1986        Community Control of Health Care Delivery: The Sandy Bay
            Experience. *Canadian Journal of Public Health* 77(4):281–
            284. Ottawa.

Garroutte, Eva Marie
2003        Real Indians: Identity and the Survival of Native America.
            Berkeley: University of California Press.

Garrow, Carrie E., and Sarah Deer
2004        Tribal Criminal Law and Procedure. Blue Ridge Summit,
            Pa.: AltaMira Press.

Garvey, John, and Troy Johnson
1994        The Government and the Indians: The American Indian
            Occupation of Alcatraz Island, 1969–1971. Pp. 151–188 in
            Special Edition: Alcatraz Revisited: The 25th Anniversary
            of the Occupation, 1969–1971. *American Indian Culture and
            Research Journal* 18(4). Los Angeles.

Geertz, Clifford
1973        The Interpretation of Cultures: Selected Essays. New York:
            Basic Books.

Geiogamah, Hanay, ed.
1987        The Entertainment Industry Guide to American Indian Pro-
            ductions. Los Angeles: American Indian Registry for the
            Performing Arts.

1994        The New Native American Theater. Pp. 377–381 in Dictio-
            nary of Native American Literature. Andrew Wiget, ed. New
            York: Garland.

Geiogamah, Hanay, and Angela Aleiss
1994        Media: American Indian Tribes in the Media Age; Indians
            in Film and Theater. Pp. 763–800 in The Native North
            American Almanac: A Reference Work on Native North
            Americans in the United States and Canada. Duane Cham-
            pagne, ed. Detroit, Washington, London: Gale Research,
            Inc.

Geiogamah, Hanay, and Jaye T. Darby, eds.
1999        Stories of Our Way: An Anthology of American Indian
            Plays. Los Angeles: UCLA American Indian Studies Center.

2000        American Indian Theater in Performance: A Reader. Los
            Angeles: UCLA American Indian Studies Center.

Gélinas, Claude
1996        La premiére revendication territoriale des autochtones de la
            Haute-Maurice? Quelques commentaires sur une petition de
            1814–1815. *Recherches amérindiennes au Québec* 26(2):
            73–76. Montreal.

Gelo, Daniel J.
1999        Powwow Patter: Indian Emcee Discourse on Power and
            Identity. *Journal of American Folklore* 112(443):40–57.
            [Boston, New York, etc.]

General Accounting Office (GAO) *see* U.S. General Accounting Office
            (GAO) [now Government Accountability Office]

General Session
1956        Oklahoma, Kansas, Mississippi Conference. Minutes:
            Tribal Area Conferences, 1956. (Folder 8, Box III, Glenn
            Emmons Papers, University of New Mexico General Library,
            Albuquerque.)

Georgakas, Dan
1972        They Have Not Spoken: American Indians in Film. *Film
            Quarterly* 25(3):26–32. Berkeley, Calif.

George, Jane
2000        Americans Catch Iqaluit Historian's Passion for Minik Tale.
            *Nunatsiaq News*, April 28, 2000. Iqaluit, NU.

Gershuny, William
1971        Associate Solicitor, Indian Affairs, to Commissioner of
            Indian Affairs: Solicitor's Opinion M-36833, dated August
            13, 1971.] (Office of Federal Acknowledgment, Western
            Washington Files, 050: Nooksack; Bureau of Indian Affairs,
            Washington.)

Getches, David H.
1993        Negotiated Sovereignty: Intergovernmental Agreements with
            American Indian Tribes as Models for Expanding Self-
            Government. *Review of Constitutional Studies* 1(1):121–170.
            Edmonton, Alta.

Getches, David H., Charles F. Wilkinson, and Robert A. Williams, Jr.
1998        Cases and Materials of Federal Indian Law. 4th ed. *American
            Casebook Series*. St. Paul, Minn.: West Group.

Getty, Harry T.
1961–1962   San Carlos Apache Cattle Industry. Pp. 181–186 in American
            Indians and Their Economic Development. Fred Voget, ed.
            *Human Organization*, Special Issue 20(4). Washington.

Getty, Ian A.L., and Antoine S. Lussier, eds.
1983        As Long as the Sun Shines and Water Flows: A Reader in
            Canadian Native Studies. Vancouver: University of British
            Columbia Press.

Getty, Ian A.L., and Donald B. Smith, eds.
1978        One Century Later: Western Canadian Reserve Indians Since
            Treaty 7. Vancouver: University of British Columbia Press.

Gewertz, Ken
1999        The Long Voyage Home: Peabody Returns Native American
            Remains to Pecos Pueblo. *The Harvard University Gazette*,
            May 20, 1999. Cambridge, Mass.

Giago, Tim A., Jr. (Nanwica Kciji)
1978        The Aboriginal Sin: Reflections on the Holy Rosary Indian
            Mission School (Red Cloud Indian School). San Francisco:
            Indian Historian Press.

1986        Notes from Indian Country. [Rapid City, S.Dak.]: Cochran
            Publishing Co.

1991        The American Indian and the Media. Minneapolis: National
            Conference of Christians and Jews.

2002        Who Gave the Order to Kill Anna Mae Pictou-Aquash? *News
            from Indian Country*, October 6, 2002. Hayward, Wis.

2005        Respecting Cultural Traditions in a Newsroom. *Nieman
            Reports* 59(2):99–101. Cambridge, Mass.

2005a       Freedom of the Press in Indian Country. *Nieman Reports*
            59(3):13–15. Cambridge, Mass.

2006        Tribes Have Traded Sovereignty Rights for Casino Profits.
            Pp. 40–43 in Indian Gaming. Stuart A. Kallen, ed. Farming-
            ton Hills, Mich.: Greenhaven Press.

Gibson, Arrell M.
1988        *see* Handbook Vol. 4 (1988:211–229)

Gibson, Gordon
1999        Comments on the Draft Nisga'a Treaty. *BC Studies* 120
            (Winter):55–71. Vancouver.

Giese, Rachel
2006        Family Matters: The Tragic, Shattering Journals of Knud
            Rasmussen. CBC, September 29th, 2006. Toronto: Canadian
            Broadcasting Corporation.

Gipp, David
1986        [Interview concerning Standing Rock Community College and
            AIHEC, November 23, 1986.] (Conducted by Wayne J. Stein,
            Reno, Nev.; Text of interview in Department of Native Amer-
            ican Studies, Montana State University, Bozeman, Mont.).

Glancy, Diane
1996        Pushing the Bear: A Novel of the Trail of Tears. New York:
            Harcourt Brace.

──────
1999        Further (Farther): Creating Dialogue to Talk About Native
            American Plays. *Journal of Dramatic Theory and Criticism*
            14(1):127–130. Lawrence, Kans.

Gleach, Frederic W.
2003        Pocahontas at the Fair: Crafting Identities at the 1907
            Jamestown Exposition. Pp. 419–445 in Native Peoples and
            Tourism. Neil L. Whitehead, ed.; Larry Nesper, guest ed.
            *Ethnohistory* 50(3).

Glover, William
1971        American Indians Form Own Theater Company. *The Courier-
            Journal and Times*, December 4, 1971. Louisville, Ky.

Goddard, Ives, vol. ed.
1996        *see* Handbook Vol. 17 (1996)

──────
1996a       Native Languages and Language Families of North America.
            (Map, to accompany: *Handbook of North American Indians*,
            Vol. 17: Languages. Ives Goddard, vol. ed.; William C. Sturte-
            vant, gen. ed.) Washington: Smithsonian Institution. (Re-
            printed, rev. and enl. ed., with additions and corrections, 1998.)

Goddard, Pliny Earle
1916        Dancing Societies of the Sarsi Indians. *Anthropological
            Papers of the American Museum of Natural History* 11(Pt.
            14):461–474. New York.

Goertzen, Chris
2001        Powwows and Identity on the Piedmont and Coastal Plains of
            North Carolina. *Ethnomusicology* 45(1):58–88. Middletown,
            Conn.

Goetz, Meg
2005        AIHEC's Efforts Pay Off with '05 Funding. *Tribal College
            Journal* 16(3):34–35. Mancos, Colo.

Goikas, John
1996        The Indian Act: Evolution, Overview, and Options for the
            Amendment and Transition. In: For Seven Generations: An
            Information Legacy of the Royal Commission on Aboriginal
            Peoples (RCAP). CD-ROM. Ottawa: Libraxus. (Copyright:
            1996–2007.)

Goldberg-Ambrose, Carole E.
1991        Not "Strictly" Racial: A Response to "Indians as Peoples".
            *UCLA Law Review* 39:169–190. Los Angeles.

──────
1994        Of Native Americans and Tribal Members: The Impact
            of Law on Indian Group Life. *Law and Society Review* 28:
            1123–1148.

1997        Planting Tail Feathers: Tribal Survival and Public Law 280.
            Los Angeles: UCLA-American Indian Studies Center.

──────
1997a       Public Law 280 and the Problem of Lawlessness in Califor-
            nia Indian Country. *UCLA Law Review* 44(5):1405–1448.
            Los Angeles.

──────
1997b       Acknowledging the Repatriation Claims of Unacknowledged
            California Tribes. *American Indian Culture and Research
            Journal* 21(3):97–119. Los Angeles.

──────
1997c       Pursuing Tribal Economic Development at "The Bingo
            Palace". *Arizona State Law Journal* 29(1):97–119. Tempe,
            Ariz.

Goldberg, Carole E., and Duane Champagne
1996        A Second Century of Dishonor: Federal Inequities and Cali-
            fornia Tribes. A Report Prepared by the UCLA American
            Indian Studies Center for the Advisory Cuncil on California
            Indian Policy. Los Angeles: UCLA American Indian Studies
            Center.

──────
2002        Ramona Redeemed? The Rise of Tribal Political Power in
            California. *Wicazo Sa Review* 17(1):43–63. Minneapolis.

──────
2006        Is Public Law 280 Fit for the Twenty-First Century? Some
            Data at Last. *Connecticut Law Review* 38(4):697–729. Hart-
            ford, Conn.

Goldie, Terry
1989        Fear and Temptation: Images of the Indigene in Canadian,
            Australian and New Zealand Literatures. Montreal: McGill-
            Queen's University Press.

Goldman, Gustave
1994        The Shifting Ethnic Boundaries: Causes, Factors and Effects.
            Ottawa: Carleton University Press.

Goldman, Gustave, and Andrew J. Siggner
1995        Statistical Concepts of Aboriginal People and Factors
            Affecting the Counts in the Census and the Aboriginal Peo-
            ples Survey. (Paper presented at the 1995 Symposium of the
            Federation of Canadian Demographers, Ottawa.)

Golla, Victor
2007        North America. Pp. 1–95 in Encyclopedia of the World's
            Endangered Languages. Christopher Moseley, ed. London
            and New York: Routledge.

Golla, Victor, and Jill Fletcher, eds.
1994        Now You're Speaking—Hupa! Hoopa, Calif.: Hoopa Valley
            Tribal Council. Arcata, Calif.: Humboldt State University,
            Center for Indian Community Development.

Gonzales, Angela A.
2003        Gaming and Displacement: Winners and Losers in American
            Indian Casino Development. *International Social Science
            Journal* 55(175):123–133. Paris.

Gonzalez, Mario, and Elizabeth Cook-Lynn
1999        The Politics of Hallowed Ground: Wounded Knee and the
            Struggle for Indian Sovereignty. Urbana and Chicago: Uni-
            versity of Illinois Press.

Goodman, Doug, Daniel C. McCool, and F. Ted Herbert
2005        Local Governments, Tribal Governments, and Service Deliv-
            ery: A Unique Approach to Negotiated Problem Solving.
            *American Indian Culture and Research Journal* 29(2):15–33.
            Los Angeles.

Goodman, Walter
1994 Television Review: A Romantic Tribute to the First Americans. *The New York Times*, October 10, 1994. New York.

Goodwill, Jean, and Norma Sluman
1984 John Tootoosis: Biography of a Cree Leader. Winnipeg, Man.: Pemmican Publications. (Originally publ.: Golden Dog Press, Ottawa, 1982.)

Gorman, Guy
1986 [Interview concerning Navajo Community College, November 23, 1986.] (Conducted by Wayne J. Stein, Reno, Nev.; Text of interview in Department of Native American Studies, Montana State University, Bozeman, Mont.).

Gough, Barry M.
1984 Gunboat Frontier: British Maritime Authority and Northwest Coast Indians, 1846–1890. Vancouver: University of British Columbia Press.

Gover, Kevin
2000 [Statement of the Assistant Secretary of Indian Affairs, dated May 24, 2000.] In: Hearing Before the U.S. Senate Committee on Indian Affairs on S. 611, to Provide for Administrative Procedures to Extend Federal Recognition to Certain Groups. Washington: U.S. Government Printing Office.

———— 
2000–2001 Remarks at the Ceremony Acknowledging the 175th Anniversary of the Establishment of the Bureau of Indian Affairs. *American Indian Law Review* 25(1):161–163. Norman, Okla.

———— 
2007 Legal Infrastructure and Economic Development. In: Track 3: Infrascure for Economic Development. Prepared for the National Congress of American Indians Policy Research Center: National Native American Economic Summit, Phoenix, Arizona, May 15–17, 2007.

Government of Nunavut
1999, 2004 *see* Nunavut, Government of 1999, 2004

Gradwohl, David Mayer, Joe B. Thompson, and Michael J. Perry, eds.
2005 Still Running: A Tribute to Maria Pearson, Yankton Sioux. *Journal of the Iowa Archaeological Society* 52(1). Iowa City.

Graham, John, and Heather Edwards
2003 Options for Commercial Enterprises in First Nations. Ottawa: Institute on Governance.

———— 
2003a Business and Politics in Aboriginal Communities. *Institute on Governance Policy Brief* 17. Ottawa.

Graham, Katherine
1996 Report of the Urban Governance Working Group. Ottawa: Royal Commission on Aboriginal Peoples.

———— 
1999 Urban Aboriginal Governance in Canada: Paradigm and Prospects in Aboriginal Self-Government in Canada. John Hylton, ed. Saskatoon, Sask.: Purich Publishing.

Graham, Katherine, and Evelyn Peters
2002 Aboriginal Communities and Urban Sustainability. Ottawa: Canadian Policy Research Networks.

Graham, Lorie M.
1998 The Past Never Vanishes: A Contextual Critique of the Existing Indian Family Doctrine. *American Indian Law Review* 23(1):1–54. Norman, Okla.

———— 
2004 An Interdisciplinary Approach to American Indian Economic Development. *North Dakota Law Review* 80(4):597–656. Grand Forks, N.Dak.

Graham, Lorie M., and Peter R. Golia
2002 In Caleb's Footsteps: The Harvard University Native American Program. Pp. 123–144 in Native American Studies in Higher Education: Models for Collaboration Between Universities and Indigenous Nations. Duane Champagne and Jay Stauss, eds. Walnut Creek, Calif.: AltaMira Press.

Grand Council of the Crees
1995 Sovereign Injustice: Forcible Inclusion of the James Bay Crees and Cree Territory into a Sovereign Québec. Nemaska, Eeyou Astchee (Québec): Grand Council of the Crees.

———— 
1996 Never Without Consent: James Bay Crees' Stand Against Forcible Inclusion Into an Independent Quebec. Toronto: ECW Press.

———— 
2000 Submission to the Office of the U.S Trade Representative (Addressing the Issue of Softwood Lumber Trade between Canada and the U.S.A.). Ottawa: Grand Council of the Crees.

Grand Council of the Haudenosaunee
1995 Haudenosaunee Confederacy Announces Policy on False Face Masks. *Akwesasne Notes*, Spring, Vol. 1. Rooseveltown, N.Y.

Grant, Kenneth W., II, Katherine A. Spilde, and Jonathan B. Taylor
2004 Social and Economic Consequences of Indian Gaming in Oklahoma. *American Indian Culture and Research Journal* 28(2):97–129. Los Angeles.

Grant, Shelagh D.
1983 Indian Affairs Under Duncan Campbell Scott: The Plains Cree of Saskatchewan,1913–1931. *Journal of Canadian Studies/Revue d'études canadiennes* 18(3):21–39. Peterborough, Ont.

———— 
2002 Arctic Justice: On Trial for Murder, Pond Inlet, 1923. Montreal: McGill-Queen's University Press.

Graves, Theodore D.
1966 Alternative Models for the Study of Urban Migration. *Human Organization* 25(4):295–299. Washington.

———— 
1967 Acculturation, Access and Alcohol in a Tri-Ethnic Community. *American Anthropologist* 69(3–4):306–321.

———— 
1970 The Personal Adjustment of Navajo Indian Migrants in Denver, Colorado. *American Anthropologist* 72(1):35–54.

———— 
1974 Urban Indian Personality and the 'Culture of Poverty'. *American Ethnologist* 1(1):65–86.

Graves, Theodore D., and Minor van Arsdale
1966 Values, Expectations, and Relocation: The Navajo Migrant to Denver. *Human Organization* 25(4):300–307. Washington.

Green, Ernestine L., eds.
1984 Ethics and Values in Archaeology. New York and London: The Free Press.

Green, Norma Kidd
1969 Iron Eye's Family: The Children of Joseph La Flesche. Lincoln, Nebr.: Johnsen Publishing.

Green, Rayna, ed.
1984 That's What She Said: Contemporary Poetry and Fiction by Native American Women. Bloomington: Indiana University Press.

———— 
1988 *see* Handbook Vol. 4 (1988:587–606)

1998a    The Pocahontas Perplex: Images of American Indian Women in American Culture. Pp. 182–192 in Native American Voices: A Reader. Susan Lobo and Steve Talbot, eds. New York: Longman.

Greenfield, Jeannette
1996    The Return of Cultural Treasures. 2d ed. Cambridge: Cambridge University Press.

Greenland National Museum and Archives
2006    *see* Nunatta Katersugaasivia Allagaateqarfialu (Greenland National Museum and Archives) 2006

Gregory, David
1989    Traditional Indian Healers in Northern Manitoba: An Emerging Relationship with the Health Care System. *Native Studies Review* 5(1):163–174. Saskatoon, Sask.

Gregory, Hiram F.
2004    *see* Handbook Vol. 14 (2004:653–658)

Grenoble, Lenore A., and Lindsay J. Whaley
2006    Saving Languages: An Introduction to Language Revitalization Cambridge and New York: Cambridge University Press.

Greymorning, Stephen, ed.
1991    A Will To Survive: Indigenous Essays on the Politics of Culture, Language, and Identity. New York: McGraw-Hill.

1999    Running the Gauntlet of an Indigenous Language Program. Pp. 6–16 in Revitalizing Indigenous Languages. Jon Reyhner, et al., eds. Flagstaff, Ariz.: Northern Arizona University.

Griffen, William B.
1983    *see* Handbook Vol. 10 (1983:329–342)

Grinde, Donald A., and Bruce E. Johansen
1995    Ecocide of Native America: Environmental Destruction of Indian Lands and Peoples. Santa Fe, N.Mex.: Clear Light.

Grobsmith, Elizabeth S.
1981    The Changing Role of the Giveaway Ceremony in Contemporary Lakota Life. *Plains Anthropologist* 26(91):75–79. Lincoln, Nebr.

Grose, Theresa Olwick
1996    Reading the Bones: Information Content, Value, and Ownership Issues Raised by the Native American Graves Protection and Repatriation Act. *Journal of the American Society for Information Science* 47(8):624–631. New York.

Gross, Emma R.
1989    Contemporary Federal Policy Toward American Indians. *Contributions in Ethnic Studies* 25. New York, [etc.]: Greenwood Press.

Grosse, Richard, James Youngblood Anderson, and Roger Carter, eds.
1994    Continuing Poundmaker and Riel's Quest: Presentations Made at a Conference on Aboriginal Peoples and Justice. Saskatoon, Sask.: Purich Publishing.

Grossman, David C., et al.
1994    Health Status of Urban American Indians and Alaska Natives: A Population Based Study. *Journal of American Medical Association* 271(11):845–850. Chicago.

Grounds, Richard A., George E. Tinker, and David E. Wilkins, eds.
2003    Native Voices: American Indian Identity and Resistance. Lawrence, Kans.: University Press of Kansas.

Grygier, Pat Sandiford
1994    A Long Way from Home: The Tuberculosis Epidemic Among the Inuit. Montreal: McGill-Queen's University Press.

Guillemin, Jeanne E.
1975    Urban Renegades: The Cultural Strategy of American Indians. New York: Columbia University Press.

Guilmet, George M.
1976    The Nonverbal American Indian Child in the Urban Classroom. (Ph.D. Dissertation in Anthropology, University of California, Los Angeles.)

1979    Maternal Perceptions of Urban Navajo and Caucasian Children's Classroom Behavior. *Human Organization* 38(1): 87–91. Washington.

Guimond, Éric
1999    *see* 2006

2003    Changing Ethnicity: The Concept of Ethnic Drifters. Pp. 91–107 in Aboriginal Conditions: Research as a Foundation for Public Policy. Jerry P. White, Paul S. Maxim, and Dan Beavon, eds. Vancouver: UBC Press.

2003a    Fuzzy Definitions and Population Explosion: Changing Identities of Aboriginal Groups in Canada. Pp. 35–50 in Not Strangers in These Parts: Urban Aboriginal Peoples. David R. Newhouse and Evelyn J. Peters, eds. Ottawa: Policy Research Initiative.

2006    Ethnic Mobility and Demographic Growth of Canada's Aboriginal Populations from 1986 to 1996. Pp. 187–200 in Report on the Demographic Situation in Canada, 1998–1999: Current Demographic Analysis. *Statistics Canada Catalogue* 91-209-XPE. Ottawa: Minister Responsible for Statistics Canada.

Guinn, Jeff
2002    Our Land Before We Die: The Proud History of the Seminole Negro. New York: J.P. Tarcher/Putnam.

Gulick, John
1958    Language and Passive Resistance among the Eastern Cherokees. *Ethnohistory* 5(1):60–81.

1973    Cherokees at the Crossroads. Rev. ed. With an Epilogue by Sharlotte Neely Williams. Chapel Hill, N.C.: University of North Carolina Press. (Originally publ. in 1960.)

Gundlach, James H., and Alden E. Roberts
1978    Native American Indian Migration and Relocation: Success or Failure? *Pacific Sociological Review* 21(1):117–128. Berkeley.

Gunther, Erna
1961–1962    Indian Craft Enterprises in the Northwest. Pp. 216–219 in American Indians and Their Economic Development. Fred Voget, ed. *Human Organization*, Special Issue 20(4). Washington.

Gurian, Elaine Heumann
2006    Civilizing the Museum: The Collected Writings of Elaine Heumann Gurian. New York: Routledge.

Guyette, Susan, and Charlotte Heth
1985    Issues for the Future of American Indian Studies: A Needs Assessment and Program Guide. Los Angeles: American Indian Studies Center, University of California.

Haagen, Birte
1995    Repatriation of Cultural Objects in Greenland. *Yumtzilob, Tijdschrift over de Americas* 7(3):225–243. Rotterdam, The Netherlands.

Haas, Theodore H.
1947     Ten Years of Tribal Government Under I.R.A. *United States Indian Service. Tribal Relations Pamphlets* 1. Lawrence, Kans.: U.S. Indian Service, Haskell Indian School.

Haddock, David D., and Robert J. Miller
2004     Can a Sovereign Protect Investors from Itself? Tribal Institutions To Spur Reservation Investment. *Journal of Small and Emerging Business Law* 8(2):173–228. Portland, Oreg.

Hader, J.
1990     The Effect of Tuberculosis on the Indians of Saskatchewan, 1926–1965. (M.A. Thesis in Anthropology, University of Saskatchewan, Saskatoon, Sask.)

Hafford, William E.
1989     The Navajo Code Talkers. *Arizona Highways* 65(2):36–45. Phoenix.

Hagan, William T.
1966     Indian Police and Judges: Experiments in Acculturation and Control. New Haven, Conn.: Yale University Press.

Hahn, Robert A., and Steven Eberhardt
1995     Life Expectancy in Four U.S. Racial/Ethnic Populations: 1990. *Epidemiology* 6(4):350–355. Cambridge, Mass.

Hakuta, Kenji, and Rafael M. Diaz
1985     The Relationship Between Degree of Bilingualism and Cognitive Ability: A Critical Discussion and Some New Longitudinal Data. Pp. 319–344 in Children's Language, Vol. 5. Keith E. Nelson, ed. Hillside, N.J.: Lawrence Erlbaum Associates.

Hale, Janet Campbell
1985     The Jailing of Cecelia Capture. New York: Random House. (Reprinted: University of New Mexico Press, Albuquerque, 1987.)

Hale, Kenneth L., et al.
1992     Endangered Languages. *Language: Journal of the Linguistic Society of America* 68(1): 1–42. Washington.

Halewood, Michael
2005     Common Law Aboriginal Knowledge Protection Rights: Recognizing the Rights of Aboriginal Peoples in Canada to Prohibit the Use and Dissemination of Elements of Their Knowledge. (Juris Doctorate Dissertation, Osgoode Hall Law School, York University, Toronto.)

Haley, Brian D., and Larry R. Wilcoxon
2005     How Spaniards Became Chumash and Other Tales of Ethnogenesis. *American Anthropologist* 107(3):432–445.

Hall, Robert L.
1997     An Archaeology of the Soul. Urbana and Chicago: University of Illinois Press.

Hall, Teri R., and Jeanette Wolfley
2003     A Survey of Tribal Perspectives on NAGPRA: Repatriation and Study of Human Remains. *The SAA Archaeological Record*, March 2003:27–43. Washington.

Halli, Shiva S., Frank Trovato, and Leo Driedger, eds.
1990     Ethnic Demography: Canadian Immigrant, Racial and Cultural Variations. Ottawa: Carleton University Press.

Halliburton, Rudi, Jr.
1977     Red Over Black: Black Slavery Among the Cherokee Indians. Westport, Conn.: Greenwood Press.

Halpin, Marjorie M.
1978     William Beyon, Tsimshian, 1888–1958. Pp. 141–158 in American Indian Intellectuals. Margot Liberty, ed. *1976 Proceedings of The American Ethnological Society.* St. Paul, New York, etc.: West Publishing Co.

Halpin, Marjorie M., and Margaret Seguin
1990     *see* Handbook Vol. 7 (1990:267–284)

Hamby, Alonzo L.
1973     Beyond the New Deal: Harry S. Truman and american Liberalism. New York: Columbia University Press.

Hamilton, James, and Tadd M. Johnson
1995     Self-Governance for Indian Tribes: From Paternalism to Empowerment. *Connecticut Law Review* 27(4):1251–1279. Hartford, Conn.

Hancock, Gael
2005     Native Views: Influences of Culture Aboard Artrain U.S.A. *American Indian Art Magazine* 30(4):60–67. Scottsdale, Ariz.

Hancock, Ian F.
1980     Texas Gullah: The Creole English of Bracketville Afro-Seminoles. Pp. 305–333 in Perspectives on American English. Joseph L. Dillard, ed. The Hague and New York: Mouton.

————
1980a     The Texas Seminoles and Their Language. Austin, Tex.: The University of Texas African and Afro-American Studies Research Center.

Hanselmann, Calvin
2002     Enhanced Aboriginal Programming in Western Canada. Calgary, Alta.: Canada West Foundation.

————
2002a     Uncommon Sense: Promising Practices in Urban Aboriginal Policy-Making and Programming. Calgary, Alta.: Canada West Foundation.

Hanson, James A.
1980     The Reappearing Vanishing American. *Museum News* 59(2):44–51. Washington.

Hardin, Peter
2006     Indian Chief Cites "Paper Genocide." *Richmond Times-Dispatch*, June 22, 2006. Richmond, Va.

Harding, John
2006     Native Group Joins Boom: Oils and Development. Ft. McKay To Be Producer with $1B Project. *National Post*, March 21: FP 1. Toronto.

Harjo Joy, and Gloria Bird
1997     Reinventing the Enemy's Language: Contemporary Native Women's Writings of North America. New York and London: W.W. Norton and Company.

Harjo, Susan Shown
1993     American Indian Experience. Pp. 199–207 in Family Ethnicity: Strength in Diversity. Harriet Pipes McAdoo, ed. Newbury Park, Calif.: Sage.

Harper, Kenn
1986     Give Me My Father's Body: The Life of Minik, the New York Eskimo. Frobisher Bay, N.W.T: Blacklead Books. (Reprinted: Steerforth Press, South Royalton, Vt., 2000.)

Harring, Sidney L.
1994     Crow Dog's Case: American Indian Sovereignty, Tribal Law, and United States Law in the Nineteenth Century. *Cambridge Studies in North American Indian History*. Cambridge: Cambridge University Press.

Harris, Cole
2002      Making Native Space: Colonialism, Resistance, and Reserves in British Columbia. Vancouver: University of British Columbia Press.

Harris, David D.
1994      The 1990 Census Count of American Indians: What Do the Numbers Really Mean? *Social Science Quarterly* 75(3): 580–593. Austin, Tex.

———
1997      Do Colleges Promote Local Economic Development? Tribal College Census Data Shows Marked Improvement in Personal Income and Poverty Levels. (Ph.D. Dissertation, Cornell University, Ithaca, N.Y.)

Harris, Douglas C.
1996      The Nlha7kápmx Meeting at Lytton,1879, and the Rule of Law. *BC Studies* 108:5–25. Vancouver.

———
2000      Territoriality, Aboriginal Rights, and the Heiltsuk Spawn-on-Kelp Fishery. *University of British Columbia Law Review* 34(1):195–238. Vancouver.

Harris, Michael
1971      American Cities: The New Reservations. *City* 5(March-April):44–48.

Harrison, Julia D.
1985      Métis: People Between Two Worlds. Calgary, Alta.: The Glenbow-Alberta Institute, in association with Douglas & McIntyre, Vancouver/Toronto.

Harrison, K. David
2007      When Languages Die: The Extinction of the World's Languages and the Erosion of Human Knowledge. Oxford and New York: Oxford University Press.

Hartman, Russell P., and David E. Doyel
1982      Preserving a Native People's Heritage: A History of the Navajo Tribal Museum. *The Kiva* 47(4):239–255. Tucson.

Harvard Project on American Indian Economic Development
2002      Honoring Nations: Tribal Governance Success Stories. Cambridge, Mass.: Harvard University.

Harvey, Byron
1970      Thoughts from Alcatraz. Phoenix, Ariz.: Arequipa Press.

Harvey, Graham, and Charles D. Thompson, Jr., eds.
2005      Indigenous Diasporas and Dislocations. Aldershoot, England, and Burlington, Vt.: Ashgate Publishing Ltd./Co.

Harvey, Sioux
2000      Winning the Sovereignty Jackpot: The Indian Gaming Regulatory Act and the Struggle for Sovereignty. Pp. 14–34 in Indian Gaming: Who Wins? Angela Mullis and David Kamper, eds. *Contemporary American Indian Issues* 9; *Native American Politics Series* 6. Los Angeles: UCLA American Indian Studies Center.

Hasse, Larry J.
1974      Termination and Assimilation: Federal Indian Policy, 1943–1961. (Ph.D. Dissertation in History, Washington State University, Pullman, Wash.)

Hathorn, Ramon J., and Patrick Holland, eds.
1992      Images of Louis Riel in Canadian Culture. Lewiston, N.Y.: The Edwin Mellen Press.

Hatt, Ken
1983      The Northwest Scrip Commissions as Federal Policy—Some Initial Findings. *Canadian Journal of Native Studies* 3(1):117–129. Brandon, Man.

Hatton, Orin T.
1986      In the Tradition: Grass Dance Musical Styles and Female Pow-Wow Singers. *Ethnomusicology* 30(2):197–222. Middletown, Conn.

Haugo, Ann
1999      Colonial Audiences and Native Women's Theatre: Viewing Spiderwoman Theater's Winnetou's Snake Oil Show from Wigwam City. *Journal of Dramatic Theory and Criticism* 14(1):131–141. Lawrence, Kans.

———
2005      American Indian Theatre. Pp. 189–205 in The Cambridge Companion to Native American Literature. Joy Porter and Kenneth M. Roemer, eds. Cambridge: Cambridge University Press.

Hawkes, David C.
1986      Negotiating Aboriginal Self-Government: Developments Surrounding the 1985 First Ministers' Conference. Kingston, Ont.: Institute of Intergovernmental Relations, Queen's University.

———
1987      The Search for Accommodation. Kingston, Ont.: Institute of Intergovernmental Relations.

Hawkes, David C., and Bradford Morse
1991      Alternative Methods for Aboriginal Participation in Constitutional Reform. Pp. 166–168 in Options for a New Canada. Ronald L. Watts and Douglas M. Brown, eds. Toronto: University of Toronto Press.

Hawthorn, Harry B., ed.
1966–1967      A Survey of the Contemporary Indians of Canada: Economic, Political, Educational Needs and Policies. 2 vols. Ottawa: Indian Affairs Branch, Department of Citizenship and Immigration.

Hawthorn Report, The
1966–1967      *see* Hawthorn, Harry B., ed. 1966–1967

Haymond, Jack Harrison
1982      The American Indian and Higher Education: From the College for the Children of the Infidels (1619) to Navajo Community College (1969). (Ph.D. Dissertation in Higher Education, Washington State University, Pullman, Wash.)

Hays, Robert G., ed.
1997      A Race at Bay: New York Times Editorial on "The Indian Problem", 1860–1900. Foreword by Senator Paul Simon. Carbondale, Ill.: Southern Illinois University Press.

Head, Lesley
2001      Cultural Landscape and Environmental Change. New York: Oxford University Press.

Healey, Sylvia, et al.
2004      Nunavut Report on Comparable Health Indicators. Iqaluit, NU: Government of Nunavut, Department of Health and Social Services.

Health Canada *see* Canada. Health Canada

Heine, Michael K.
2006      Snowshoeing: A Resource and Instructional Manual. *Traditional Aboriginal Sport Coaching Resources* 4. Yellowknife, NWT: The Sport North Federation and MACA (GNWT).

Heizer, Robert F.
1972      The Eighteen Unratified Treaties of 1851–1852 Between the California Indians and the United States Government. Berkeley: University of California.

———
1978      *see* Handbook Vol. 8 (1978:701–704)

Henderson, Eric
1997        Indian Gaming: Social Consequences. *Arizona State Law Journal* 29(1):205–250. Tempe, Ariz.

Henderson, James (Sákéj) Youngblood
1994        Empowering Treaty Federalism. *Saskatchewan Law Review* 58(2):241–329. Saskatoon, Sask.

———
1994a       Implementing the Treaty Order. Pp. 5262 in Continuing Poundmaker's and Riel's Quest: Presentations Made at a Conference on Aboriginal Peoples and Justice. Richard Gosse, James (Sákéj) Youngblood Henderson, and Roger Carter, eds. Saskatoon, Sask.: Purich Publishing.

———
2000        *Ayukpachi*: Empowering Aboriginal Thoughts. Pp. 248–278 in Reclaiming Indigenous Voice and Vision. Marie Battiste, ed. Vancouver: University of British Columbia Press.

Hendricks, Steve
2006        The Unquiet Grave: The FBI and the Struggle for the Soul of Indian Country. New York: Thunder's Mouth Press.

Henige, David
1998        Numbers from Nowhere: The American Indian Contact Population Debate. Norman: University of Oklahoma Press.

Henkes, Robert
1995        Native American Painters of the Twentieth Century: The Works of Sixty-One Artists. Jefferson, N.C.: McFarland and Co.

Herle, Anita
1994        Museums and First Peoples in Canada. *Journal of Museum Ethnography* 6(October):39–66. Oxford, England.

Hernández-Avila, Inés, ed.
2005        Reading Native American Women: Critical/Creative Representations. Blue Ridge Summit, Pa.: AltaMira Press.

Hernández López, Pedro
[1992]      Revitalization, Development, and Diffusion of Indigenous Languages, Starting with Their Writing: The Experience of CEDELIO (Manuscript in P. Hernández López's possession.)

Hersey, Eleanor
1998        Word-Healers and Code Talkers: Native Americans in the X-Files: *Journal of Popular Film and Television* 26(3):108–119. Bowling Green, Ohio.

Hertzberg, Hazel W.
1971        The Search for an American Indian Identity; Modern Pan-Indian Movements. Syracuse, N.Y.: Syracuse University Press.

———
1978        Arthur C. Parker, Seneca, 1881–1955. Pp. 129–140 in American Indian Intellectuals. Margot Liberty, ed. *1976 Proceedings of The American Ethnological Society*. St. Paul, New York, etc.: West Publishing Co.

———
1988        *see* Handbook Vol. 4 (1988:305–323)

Hewitt, J.N.B. (John Napoleon Brinton)
1903        Iroquoian Cosmology. Part 1. Pp. 127–339 in *21 Annual Report of the Bureau of American Ethnology for 1899–1900*. Washington: Smithsonian Institution; U.S. Government Printing Office. (Rerpinted: AMS Press, New York, 1974.)

———
1928        Iroquoian Cosmology. Part 2. Pp. 449–819 in *43d Annual Report of the Bureau of American Ethnology for 1925–1926*. Washington: Smithsonian Institution; U.S. Government Printing Office. (Reprinted: AMS Press, New York, 1974.)

Hicks, Sara, and Miriam Jorgensen
2005        Large Foundations' Grantmaking to Native America. Harvard Project on American Indian Economic Development, John F. Kennedy School of Government. Cambridge, Mass.: Harvard University.

High, Ellesa C., and Daniel W. Mc Neil
2001        Native American Studies at West Virginia University: Continuing the Interactions of Native and Appalachian People. *Indigenous Nations Studies Journal* 2(1):43–54. Lawrence, Kans.

Hightower-Langston, Donna
2003        The Native American World. Hoboken, N.J.: J. Wiley and Sons.

Hilger, Michael
1986        The American Indian in Film. Metuchen, N.J.: Scarecrow Press.

———
1995        From Savage to Nobleman: Images of Native Americans in Film. Lanham, Md.: Scarecrow Press.

Hill, Dawn Martin
2003        Traditional Medicine in Contemporary Contexts: Protecting and Respecting Indigenous Knowledge and Medicine. Ottawa: National Aboriginal Health Organization (NAHO)/ Organisation nationale de la santé autochtone (ONSA).

Hill, Richard W., Sr.
1977        Reclaiming Cultural Artifacts. *Museum News* 55(5):43–46. Washington.

———
1996        Reflections of a Native Repatriator. In: Mending the Circle: A Native American Repatriation Guide. Understanding and Implementing NAGPRA and the Official Smithsonian and Other Repatriation Policies. Barbara Meister, ed. New York: American Indian Ritual Object Repatriation Foundation.

———
2001        Regenerating Identity: Repatriation and the Indian Frame of Mind. Pp. 127–138 in The Future of the Past: Archaeologists, Native Americans and Repatriation. Tamara L. Bray, ed. New York and London: Garland Publishing.

———
2001a       Repatriation: An Opportunity for Cultural Exchange. P. 135 in Implementing the Native American Graves Protection and Repatriation Act (NAGPRA). Roxana Adams, ed. Washington: American Association of Museums.

Hill, Tom
1988        First Nations and Museums. *Muse* 6(3):2. Ottawa: Canadian Museums Association.

Hillabrant, Walter, et al.
2004        Overcoming Challenges to Business and Economic Development in Indian Country. MPR Reference 8550-931. Princeton, N.J.: Mathematica Policy Research, Inc. (Webpage: http://www.aspe.hhs.gov/hsp/wtw-grants-eval98/tribal-dev04)

Hindle, Kevin, and Michele Lansdowne
2005        Brave Spirits on New Paths: Toward a Globally Relevant Paradigm of Indigenous Entrepreneurship Research. *Journal of Small Business and Entrepreneurship* 18(2):131–142.

Hindle, Kevin, et al.
2005        Relating Practice to Theory in Indigenous Entrepreneurship: Pilot Investigation of the Kitsaki Partnership Portfolio. *American Indian Quarterly* 29(1–2):1–23. Lincoln, Nebr.

Hinton, Leanne
1994        Flutes of Fire: Essays on California Indian Languages. Berkeley, Calif.: Heyday Books.

2000        Language Revitalization and Language Change. Pp. 233–246 in Quinto Encuentro de Linguistica del Noroeste, Tomo II. Hermosillo, Sonora [Mexico]: Editorial UniSon.

Hinton, Leanne, and Kenneth Hale, eds.
2001        The Green Book of Language Revitalization in Practice. San Diego, Calif.: Academic Press.

Hinton, Leanne, and Pamela Munro
1998        American Indian Languages: Description and Theory. Berkeley: University of California Press.

Hinton, Leanne, et al.
2002        Keeping Your Language Alive: A Common-Sense Approach to Language Learning and Teaching. Berkeley, Calif.: Heyday Books.

Hinton, Thomas B.
1983        see Handbook Vol. 10 (1983:315–238)

Hirschfelder, Arlene, and Martha Kreipe de Montano
1993        The Native American Almanac: A Portrait of Native America Today. New York: Prentice Hall General Reference. (Reprinted in 1998.)

Hitchcock, Ann
1973        Tribal Cultural Centers: An Attempt to Salvage Cultural Heritage. Museums of Mexico and the United States: Policies and Problems. Austin, Tex.: Texas Historical Foundation.

Hitchcock, Robert K., comp.
[2006]      Indigenous Peoples and International Human Rights: A Bibliography. (Webpage of the American Anthropological Association: http://www.aaanet.org/committees/cfhr/bib_hitchcock_indg.htm [11 June 2007])

Hobart, Charles W., and George Kupfer
1974        Impact of Oil Exploratory Work on an Inuit Community. (Report presented at the Canadian Sociology and Anthropology Association Meetings, Toronto.)

Hobsbawm, Eric
1983        Introduction: Inventing Traditions. Pp. 1–14 in The Invention of Tradition. Eric Hobsbawm and Terence Ranger, eds. Cambridge: Cambridge University Press.

Hobson, Geary, ed.
1979        The Remembered Earth: An Anthology of Contemporary Native American Literature. Albuquerque: Red Earth Press.

Hochbruck, Wolfgang, and Beatrix Dudensing-Reichel
1992        "Honoratissimi Benefactores": Native American Students and Two Seventeenth-Century Texts in the University Tradition. Studies in American Indian Literatures 4(23):35–47. (Reprinted, pp. 1–14 in Early Native American Writing: New Critical Essays. Helen Jaskoski, ed. Foreword by A. LaVonne Brown Ruoff. Cambridge University Press, Cambridge, Mass., 1996.)

Hoddie, Matthew
2002        Preferential Policies and the Blurring of Ethnic Boundaries: The Case of Aboriginal Australians in the 1980s. Political Studies 50(2):293–312.

Hodes, Ann, Jennie Joe, and Ann Hodes
1994        Health: Traditional Indian Health Practices and Cultural Views; Contemporary U.S. Indian Health Care; Canadian Native Health Care. Pp. 801–853 in The Native North American Almanac: A Reference Work on Native North Americans in the United States and Canada. Duane Champagne, ed. Detroit, Washington, London: Gale Research, Inc.

Hodge, William
1969        The Albuquerque Navajos. Tucson: University of Arizona Press.

Hogan, Lawrence J.
1998        The Osage Oil Murders: The True Story of a Multiple Murder Plot to Acquire the Estates of Wealthy Osage Tribe Members. Frederick, Md.: Amlex.

Hogan, Linda
1990        Mean Spirit. New York: Ballantine.

1995        Solar Storms. New York: Scribner.

1998        Power. New York: W.W. Norton.

Hoikkala, Paivi
1998        Feminists or Reformers? American Indian Women and Political Activism in Phoenix, 1965–1980. American Indian Culture and Research Journal 22(4):163–185. Los Angeles.

Hollinger, R. Eric
2002        Addendum to the Repatriation Office Report Inventory and Assessment of Human Remains and Associated Funerary Objects from the Post-Contact Period in Barrow, Alaska, in the National Museum of Natural History. Washington: Smithsonian Institution, National Museum of Natural History, Repatriation Office.

2003        Inventory and Assessment of Human Remains Potentially Affiliated to the Miami in the National Museum of Natural History. Washington: Smithsonian Institution, National Museum of Natural History, Repatriation Office.

2003a       Inventory and Assessment of Human Remains and Funerary Objects Potentially Affiliated to the Memonimee in the National Museum of Natural History. Washington: Smithsonian Institution, National Museum of Natural History, Repatriation Office.

Hollinger, R. Eric, and Stephen D. Ousley
2006        Inventory and Assessment of Human Remains Potentially Affiliated with the Pembina Chippewa in the National Museum of Natural History, Smithsonian Institution. Washington: Smithsonian Institution, National Museum of Natural History, Repatriation Office.

Hollinger, R. Eric, Cheri Botic, and Stephen D. Ousley
2005        Inventory and Assessment of Human Remains Potentially Affiliated with the Northwestern Band of Shoshone in the National Museum of Natural History, Smithsonian Institution. Washington: Smithsonian Institution, National Museum of Natural History, Repatriation Office.

2006        Inventory and Assessment of Human Remains Potentially Affiliated with the Goshute in the National Museum of Natural History, Smithsonian Institution. Washington: Smithsonian Institution, National Museum of Natural History, Repatriation Office.

Hollinger, R. Eric, Betsy Bruemmer, and Ann-Marie Victor-Howe
2005        Assessment of Tlingit Objects Requested for Repatriation as Objects of Cultural Patrimony and Sacred Objects in the National Museum of Natural History, Smithsonian Institution. Washington: Smithsonian Institution, National Museum of Natural History, Repatriation Office.

Hollinger, R. Eric, Elizabeth Eubanks, and Steven D. Ousley
2004        Inventory and Assessment of Human Remains and Funerary Objects from the Point Barrow Region, Alaska, in the National Museum of Natural History, Smithsonian Institution. Wash-

ington: Smithsonian Institution, National Museum of Natural History, Repatriation Office.

Holm, Agnes, and Wayne Holm
1995        Navajo Language Education: Retrospect and Prospects. *The Bilingual Research Journal* 19(1):141–167. (NCELA, George Washington University, Washington.)

Holm, Tom
1996        Strong Hearts, Wounded Souls: Native American Veterans of the Vietnam War. Austin, Tex.: The University of Texas Press.

_____
2005        The Great Confusion in Indian Affairs. Austin, Tex.: The University of Texas Press.

Hoover, Herbert
1970        [Interview with Alfred DuBray, 28 July 1970.] (Tape 0533, 26, South Dakota Oral History Center, University of South Dakota, Vermillion, S.Dak.)

_____
1971        [Interview with Gordon Jones, 2 June 1971.] (Tape 768, South Dakota Oral History Center, University of South Dakota, Vermillion, S.Dak.)

Hoover, William N.
2005        Kinzua: From Cornplanter to the Corps. Lincoln, Nebr.: iUniverse, Inc.

Hopkins, Sarah Winnemucca
1883        Life Among the Piutes: Their Wrongs and Claims. Mrs. Horace Mann, ed. New York: Putnam's Sons. Boston: Cuppler, Upham. (Reprinted: Chalfant Press, Bishop, Calif., 1969; see also: Hopkins 1994.)

_____
1994        Life Among the Piutes: Their Wrongs and Claims. Mrs. Horace Mann, ed. Foreword by Catherine S. Fowler. *Vintage West Series*. Reno: University of Nevada Press.

Hornberger, Nancy H., ed.
1997        Indigenous Literacies in the Americas: Language Planning from the Bottom Up. Berlin: Mouton de Gruyter.

Hornung, Rick
1991        One Nation Under the Gun. New York: Pantheon Books.

Horse Capture, George P.
1981        Some Observations on Establishing Tribal Museums. *History News* 36(1):1–7. *American Association for State and Local History Technical Leaflet* 134.

_____
1991        Survival of Culture. *Museum News* 70(1):49–51. Washington.

_____
1994        From the Reservation to the Smithsonian Via Alcatraz. Pp. 135–150 in Special Edition: Alcatraz Revisited: The 25th Anniversary of the Occupation, 1969–1971. Joane Nagel and Troy Johnson, eds. *American Indian Culture and Research Journal* 18(4). Los Angeles.

_____
2005        The Way of the People. Pp. 31–45 in Spirit of a Native Place: Building the National Museum of the American Indian. Duane Blue Spruce, ed. Washington: National Museum of the American Indian, Smithsonian Institution.

Hosmer, Brian C.
1999        American Indians in the Marketplace: Persistence and Innovation Among the Menominees and Metlakatlans, 1870–1920. Lawrence, Kans.: University Press of Kansas.

Hosmer, Brian C., and Colleen O'Neill, eds.
2004        Native Pathways: American Indian Culture and Economic Development in the Twentieth Century. Boulder, Colo.: University Press of Colorado.

House of Commons *see* Canada. House of Commons

House of Representatives *see* U.S. Congress. House of Representatives

Houser, Schuyler
1991        Under Funded Miracles: Tribal Colleges. *Indian Nations at Risk. Task Force Commission Paper* 8. Washington: U.S. Department of Education.

Howard, James H.
1951        The Dakota Indian Victory Dance, World War II. *North Dakota History* 18(1):31–40. Bismarck, N.Dak.

_____
1951a       Notes on the Dakota Grass Dance. *Southwestern Journal of Anthropology* 7(1):82–85. Albuquerque.

_____
1952        The Sun Dance of the Turtle Mountain Ojibwa. *North Dakota History* 19(4):249–264. Bismarck, N.Dak.

_____
1954        Plains Indian Feathered Warbonnets. *Plains Anthropologist* 2:23–26. Lincoln, Nebr.

_____
1955        Pan-Indian Culture of Oklahoma. *The Scientific Monthly* 81(5): 215–220. Washington.

_____
1956        An Oto-Omaha Peyote Ritual. *Southwestern Journal of Anthropology* 12(4):432–436. Albuquerque.

_____
1960        The Roach Headdress. *American Indian Hobbyist* 6(7–8): 89–94. Alton, Ill.

_____
1965        The Plains-Ojibwa or Bungi: Hunters and Warriors of the Northern Prairie; with Special Reference to the Turtle Mountain Band. *University of South Dakota. South Dakota Museum. Anthropological Papers* 1. Vermillion, S.Dak. (Reprinted: J&L Reprint Company, Lincoln, Nebr., 1977.)

_____
1965a       The Ponca Tribe. In collaboration with Peter Le Claire, Tribal Historian, and Other Members of the Tribe. *Bureau of American Ethnology Bulletin* 195. Washington: Smithsonian Institution: U.S. Government Printing Office. (Reprinted: University of Nebraska Press, Lincoln, 1995.)

_____
1976        The Plains Gourd Dance as a Revitalization Movement. *American Ethnologist* 3(2):243–259.

_____
1976a       Yanktonai Ethnohistory and the John K. Bear Wintercount. *Plains Anthropologist* 21(73, Pt. 1):281–307. Lincoln, Nebr.

_____
1978        The Native American Image in Western Europe. *American Indian Quarterly* 4(1):33–56. Lincoln, Nebr.

_____
1983        Pan-Indianism in Native American Music and Dance. *Ethnomusicology* 27(1):71–82. Middletown, Conn.

Howard, Rebecca
1999        The Native American Women Playwrights Archive: Adding Voices. *Journal of Dramatic Theory and Criticism* 14(1): 109–116. Lawrence, Kans.

Howe, LeAnne
1999        Tribalography: The Power of Native Stories. *Journal of Dramatic Theory and Criticism* 14(1):117–125. Lawrence, Kans.

_____
2001        The Shell Shaker. San Francisco: Aunt Lute Books.

Hoxie, Frederick E.
1984        A Final Promise: The Campaign to Assimilate the Indians, 1880–1920. Lincoln: University of Nebraska Press.

1985     The Indians Versus the Textbooks: Is There Any Way Out? *Perspectives: Newsletter of the American Historical Association* 23(4):18–22. [Washington.]

1995     Parading Through History: The Making of the Crow Nation in America 1805–1935. *Cambridge Studies in North American Indian History*. Cambridge: Cambridge University Press.

———, ed.
1996     Encyclopedia of North American Indians. New York: Houghton Mifflin Company. (Also available online, see: *Encyclopedia of North American Indians* 2006.)

Hubert, Jane, and Cressida Fforde
2002     Introduction: The Reburial Issue in the Twenty-First Century. Pp. 1–16 in The Dead and Their Possessions: Repatriation in Principle, Policy and Practice. Cressida Fforde, Jane Hubert, and Paul Turnbull, eds. *One World Archaeology* 43. New York and London: Routledge.

Huck, Susan L.M.
1973     Renegades: The Second Battle of Wounded Knee. Belmont, Mass.: American Opinion.

Hughes, Marja
1997     Literature and Effective Practices: Review of Municipal-Aboriginal Relations. Ottawa: Center for Municipal-Aboriginal Relations.

Huhndorf, Shari M.
2001     Going Native: Indians in the American Cultural Imagination. Ithaca, N.Y.: Cornell University Press.

Hungry Wolf, Adolf
2006     Pikunni Ceremonial Life. *The Blackfoot Papers* 2. Skookumchuck, B.C.: Good Medicine Cultural Foundation.

Huntsman, Jeffrey F.
1983     Native American Theatre. Pp. 335–385 in Ethnic Theatre in the United States. Maxine Schwartz Seller, ed. Westport, Conn.: Greenwood Press.

Hurley, Mary C., comp.
1999     Report on The Nisga'a Final Agreement. (Report dated 9 February 1999; Library of Parliament, Ottawa. Webpage: http://www.parl.gc.ca/information/library/PRBpubs/prb992e .htm.)

2001     Report on The Nisga'a Final Agreement. (Report revised 24 September 2001. Library of Parliament, Ottawa. Webpage: http://www.parl.gc.ca/information/library/PRBpubs/prb992e .htm.)

Hurt, Wesley R., Jr.
1961–1962     The Urbanization of the Yankton Indians. Pp. 226–231 in American Indians and Their Economic Development. Fred Voget, ed. *Human Organization*, Special Issue 20(4). Washington.

Hurtado, Albert L.
1988     Indian Survival on the California Frontier. New Haven, Conn.: Yale University Press.

Hushka, Rock
2004     Lewis and Clark Territory: Contemporary Artists Revisit Place, Race, and Memory. Tacoma, Wash.: Tacoma Art Museum.

Hutchinson, Brian
2006     "Money Isn't Everything." *National Post*, April 4: A9. Toronto.

Hutchinson, Elizabeth
2001     Modern Native American Art: Angel DeCora's Transcultural Aesthetics. *The Art Bulletin* 88(4):740–756.

Hutt, Sherry
1992     Illegal Trafficking in Native American Human Remains and Cultural Items: A New Protection Tool. *Arizona State Law Journal* 24(1):135–150. Tempe, Ariz.

Hymes, Dell
1981     In Vain I Tried to Tell You: Essays in Native American Ethnopoetics. Philadelphia: University of Pennsylvania Press.

Ickes, Harold L.
1944     Indians Have a Name for Hitler. *Collier's* 113(January 15): 58. Springfield, Ohio.

1951     Justice in a Deep Freeze. *New Republic* 124(21 May):17. New York.

INAC = Indian and Northern Affairs Canada *see* Canada. Indian and Northern Affairs Canada (INAC)

Index of Native American Media Resources on the Internet
2007     Index of Native American Media Resources on the Internet. (Webpage: http://www.hanksville.org/NAresources/indices/ NAmedia.html)

Indian and Northern Affairs Canada (INAC) *see* Canada. Indian and Northern Affairs Canada (INAC)

Indian Association of Alberta
1970     Citizens Plus. Edmonton, Alta.: Indian Chiefs/Association/of Alberta.

Indian Chiefs of Alberta
1970     *see* Indian Association of Alberta 1970

Indian Claims Commission (ICC) *see* U.S. Indian Claims Commission (ICC)

*Indian Country Today*
2006     2006 Indigenous Games Wrap Up in Denver. *Indian Country Today*, July 14, 2006. Canastota, N.Y. (Webpage: http:// www.indiancountry.com)

Indian Health Service (IHS) *see* U.S. Department of Health and Human Services, Public Health Service, Indian Health Service (IHS)

Indian Residential Schools Resolution Canada *see* Canada. Indian Residential Schools Resolution Canada

*Indian's Friend, The*
1888–1951     *see* National Indian Association 1888–1951

*Indian Voice, The*
1973     *see* Deloria, Vine, Jr. 1973

Indian Voices
[1971]     1974 *see* American Indian Historical Society 1974

Indigenous Language Institute (ILI)
2004     Awakening Our Languages. *ILI Handbook Series* 1. Santa Fe, N.Mex.: Indigenous Language Institute.

Inglis, Gordon B., et al.
1990     *see* Handbook Vol. 7 (1990:285–293)

Institute of American Indian Arts, The
1969     *see* Meinholtz, Rolland et al. 1969

Institute of Social and Economic Research (ISER)
1991     *see* Colt, Steve 1991

Interior Board of Indian Appeals (IBIA) *see* U.S. Department of the Interior. Interior Board of Indian Appeals (IBIA)

Interior Report
2001–2004    *see* U.S. Department of the Interior 2001–2004

International Labour Organization (ILO)
1953    Indigenous Peoples: Living and Working Conditions of Aboriginal Populations in Independent Countries. *Studies and Reports* 35. Geneva, Switzerland: International Labour Office.

_____
1989    ILO Convention (No. 169) Concerning Indigenous and Tribal People in Independent Countries, June 27, 1989. Geneva, Switzerland: International Labour Organization.

Inuit Circumpolar Conference (ICC)
1983    *see* Canada. Inuit Circumpolar Conference (ICC) 1983

Inuit Circumpolar Council (ICC)
2007    *see* Canada. Inuit Circumpolar Council (ICC) 2007

Inuit Tapiriit Kanatami
2004    Creation of Inuit Secretariat Important First Step in Addressing Inuit Issues in Specific Manner. Ottawa: Inuit Tapiriit Kanatami. (Webpage: http://www.itk.ca/media/press-archive-20040419b.php)

_____
2006    Backgrounder: Inuit Tapiriit Kanatami. Stephen Hendrie, ed. Ottawa: Inuit Tapiriit Kanatami. (Webpage: http://www.itk .ca/media/backgrounder-itk.php [31 March 2006].)

Inuvialuit Final Agreement Implementation Coordinating Committee
2002    Annual Report 2001–2002. Ottawa: Minister of Public Works and Government Services Canada.

Iowa State Code
1976    Ancient Remains, 263B.7; Cemetery for Ancient Remains, 263B.8; Authority to Deny Permission to Disinter Remains, 263B.9. Des Moines, Ia.: Iowa General Assembly.

Isaac, Barbara
2002    Implementation of NAGPRA: The Peabody Museum of Archaeology and Ethnology, Harvard. Pp. 160–169 in The Dead and Their Possessions: Repatriation in Principle, Policy and Practice. Cressida Fforde, Jane Hubert, and Paul Turnbull, eds. *One World Archaeology* 43. New York and London: Routledge.

Isaac, Thomas
2001    Aboriginal and Treaty Rights in the Maritimes: The Marshall Decision and Beyond. Saskatoon, Sask.: Purich Publishing.

_____
2004    Aboriginal Law: Commentary, Cases and Materials. 3d ed. Saskatoon, Sask.: Purich Publishing Ltd.

Isaac, Thomas, and Anthony Knox
2003    The Crown's Duty To Consult Aboriginal People. *Alberta Law Review* 41(1):49–77. Edmonton, Alta.

Ivison, Duncan, Paul Patton, and Will Sanders, eds.
2000    Political Theory and the Rights of Indigenous Peoples. Cambridge: Cambridge University Press.

Jacklin, Kristen, and Wayne Warry
2004    The Indian Health Transfer Policy: Toward Cost Containment or Self-Determination? Pp. 215–234 in Unhealthy Health Policy: A Critical Anthropological Examination. Arachu Castro and Merrill Singer, eds. Walnut Creek, Calif.: Altamira Press.

Jacknis, Ira
1996    Repatriation As Social Drama: The Kwakiutl Indians of British Columbia, 1922–1980. Pp. 274–286 in Repatriation: An Interdisciplinary Dialogue. Devon A. Mihesuah, ed. *American Indian Quarterly, Special Issue* 20(2). Lincoln, Nebr.

_____
2002    The Storage Box of Tradition: Kwakiutl Art, Anthropologists, and Museums, 1881–1981. Washington and London: Smithsonian Institution Scholarly Press.

Jackson, Deborah D.
2002    Our Elders Lived It: American Indian Identity in the City. Dekalb, Ill.: Northern Illinois University Press.

Jackson, Helen Hunt
1884    Ramona: A Story. Boston: Roberts Brothers.

Jackson, Henry
1973    [Letter from Senator Henry Jackson, Chairman Interior and Insular Affairs Committee, to Interior Secretary Rogers C.B. Morton, dated December 7, 1973.] (Office of Federal Acknowledgment, Western Washington Files 050, Bureau of Indian Affairs, Washington.)

Jackson, Jason Baird
2005    East Meets West: On Stamp Dance and Powwow Worlds in Oklahoma. Pp. 172–197 in Powwow. Clyde Ellis, Luke Eric Lassiter, and Gary H. Dunham, eds. Lincoln and London: University of Nebraska Press.

Jacobs, Don Trent
2006    *see* Four Arrows (Don Trent Jacobs) 2006

Jacobsen, Trond E.
2007    Accessing Capital, Building Prosperity. *Tribal College Journal: Journal of American Indian Higher Education* 18(3): 32–36. Sacramento, Calif.

Jahoda, Gloria
1975    The Trail of Tears: The Story of the American Indian Removals, 1813–1855. New York: Holt, Rinehart and Winston. (Reprinted in 1995.)

Jaimes, M. Annette
1985    American Indian Studies: An Overview and Prospectus. *Wicazo Sa Review* 1(2):15–21. Minneapolis.

_____
1987    American Indian Studies: Toward an Indigenous Model. *American Indian Culture and Research Journal* 11(3):1–16. Los Angeles.

_____
1992    The State of Native America: Genocide, Colonization, and Resistance. Boston, Mass.: South End Press.

Jaimes, M. Annette, and Theresa Haley
1992    American Indian Women: Center of Indigenous Resistance. Pp. 311–344 in The State of Native America: Genocide, Colonization and Resistance. M. Annette Jaimes, ed. Boston, Mass.: South End Press.

James Bay and Northern Quebec Agreement
1976    *see* Quebec 1976

Jamieson, Stuart
1961–1962    Native Indians and the Trade Union Movement. Pp. 219–225 in American Indians and Their Economic Development. Fred Voget, ed. *Human Organization*, Special Issue 20(4). Washington.

Jaroff, Rebecca
2006/2007    Opposing Forces: (Re)Playing Pocahontas and the Politics of Indian Removal on the Antebellum Stage. *Comparative Drama* 40(4):483–504. Kalamazoo, Mich.

Jarvis, George K., and Menno Boldt
1982    Death Styles Among Canada's Indians. *Social Science and Medicine* 16(14):1345–1352. Oxford, England, [etc.].

Jaskoski, Helen, ed.
1996      Early Native American Writing: New Critical Essays. Fore-word by A. LaVonne Brown Ruoff. Cambridge, Mass.: Cambridge University Press.

Jay, Gregory S.
2000      White Man's Book No Good: D.W. Griffith and the American Indian. *Cinema Journal* 39(4):3–26. Austin, Tex.

Jemison, G. Peter
2001      Poisoning the Sacred. Pp. 38–40 in Contaminated Collections: Preservation, Access and Use: Preservation of Native American and Historical Natural History Collections Contaminated with Pesticide Residues. *Proceedings of a Symposium Held at the National Conservation Training Center (NTC), Sheperdstown, West Virginia, April 6–9, 2001.* Jessica S. Johnson, ed. *Collection Forum* 17(1–2). [Pittsburgh, Pa.: Society for the Preservation of Natural History Collections.]

Jennings, Francis
1975      The Invasion of America. Chapel Hill, N.C.: University of North Carolina Press.

Jennings, Michael L.
2004      Alaska Native Political Leadership and Higher Education: One University, Two Universes. Blue Ridge Summit, Pa.: AltaMira Press.

Jevec, Adam
2001      Semper Fidelis, Code Talkers. *Prologue Magazine* 33(4): 1–8. Washington: National Archives.

Jilek, Wolfgang G.
1982      Indian Healing: Shamanic Ceremonialism in the Pacific Northwest Today. Surrey, B.C.: Hancock House.

Joe, Jennie R.
2003      The Rationing of Healthcare and Health Disparity for American Indians/Alaska Natives. Pp. 528–551 in Unequal Treatment: Confronting Racial and Ethnic Disparities in Healthcare. Brian Smedley, Adrienne Y. Stith, and Alan R. Nelson, eds. Washington: National Academy, Institute of Medicine.

Joe, Jennie R., and Sophie Frishkopf
2006      I'm Too Young for This! Diabetes and American Indian Children. Pp. 435–458 in Indigenous Peoples and Diabetes: Community Empowerment and Wellness. Mariana Leal Ferreira and Gretchen Chesley Lang, eds. Durham, N.C.: Carolina Academic Press.

Johansen, Bruce E.
2002      The New York Oneidas: A Case Study in the Mismatch of Cultural Tradition and Economic Development. *American Indian Culture and Research Journal* 26(3):25–46. Los Angeles.

Johansen, Bruce E., and Roberto Maestas
1979      Wasi'chu: The Continuing Indian Wars. New York: Monthly Review Press.

Johns, Alana, and Irene Mazurkewich
2001      The Role of the University in the Training of Native Language Teachers: Labrador. Pp. 355–366 in The Green Book of Language Revitalization in Practice. Leanne Hinton and Kenneth Hale, eds. San Diego, Calif.: Academic Press.

Johnson, Jessica S., ed.
2001      Contaminated Collections: Preservation, Access and Use: Preservation of Native American and Historical Natural History Collections Contaminated with Pesticide Residues. *Proceedings of a Symposium Held at the National Conservation Training Center (NTC), Sheperdstown, West Virginia, April 6–9, 2001. Collection Forum* 17(1–2). [Pittsburgh, Pa.: Society for the Preservation of Natural History Collections.]

Johnson, Karl E.
      Competitive Advantages of Reservation Business Enterprises. Pp. 79–84 in Doing Business in Indian Country—2005. 3d ed. Okmulgee, Okla.: Muscogee (Creek) Nation District Court.

Johnson, Laurence
1996      A l'origine de la réserve Viger, une requete malécite de 1826. *Recherches amérindiennes au Québec* 26(2):77–81. Montreal.

Johnson, Lyndon B. (President)
1968      The Forgotten American. (The President of The United States, Message to Congress on Goals and Programs for the American Indian, March 6, 1968. Copy in Lyndon B. Johnson Library and Museum, Austin, Tex.)

————
1968–1969      [Papers, 1968–1969.] (*Public Papers of the Presidents of the United States: Papers* 336. Lyndon B. Johnson Library and Museum, Austin, Tex.)

Johnson, Ralph W., ed.
1970–1971      Studies in American Indian Law. 2 vols. Seattle: University of Washington School of Law.

————
1972      The States Versus Indian Off-Reservation Fishing: A United States Supreme Court Error. *Washington Law Review* 47(2): 207–236. Seattle.

Johnson, Troy, ed.
1991      The Indian Child Welfare Act: Indian Homes for Indian Children. Conference Proceedings. Los Angeles: University of California Press.

————, ed.
1993      The Indian Child Welfare Act: Unto the Seventh Generation. Conference Proceedings. Los Angeles: University of California Press.

————
1994      The Occupation of Alcatraz Island: Roots of American Indian Activism. *Wicazo Sa Review* 10(2):63–79. Minneapolis.

————, ed.
1994a      Alcatraz: Indian Land Forever. Los Angeles: University of California, American Indian Studies Center.

————
1995      You Are on Indian Land! Alcatraz Island, 1969–1971. Los Angeles: University of California Press.

————
1996      The Indian Occupation of Alcatraz Island: Indian Self-Determination and the Rise of Indian Activism. Urbana: University of Illinois Press.

————
1997      Indian Land Forever: The Indian Occupation of Alcatraz, 1969–1971. San Francisco, Calif. : Golden Gate National Parks Association.

————, ed.
1999      Contemporary Native American Political Issues. Walnut Creek, Calif.: AltaMira Press.

Johnson, Troy, and Joane Nagel
1994      Remembering Alcatraz: Twenty-five Years After. Pp. 9–24 in Special Edition: Alcatraz Revisited: The 25th Anniversary of the Occupation, 1969–1971. Joane Nagel and Troy Johnson, eds. *American Indian Culture and Research Journal* 18(4). Los Angeles.

Johnson, Troy, Joane Nagel, and Duane Champagne, eds.
1994      American Indian Activism: Alcatraz to the Longest Walk. Los Angeles: Regents of the University of California.

(Reprinted: University of Illinois Press, Urbana and Chicago, 1997).

Johnson, William E.
1909    [Letter to Commissioner of Indian Affairs, dated May 4, 1909.] (Peyote Correspondence, File 2989-1908-126, Chief Special Officer, Part 1C, Record Group 75, Records of the Bureau of Indian Affairs, National Archives, Washington.)

Johnsrude, Larry
2001    Bundles of Contention: Blackfoot Lament. *Edmonton Journal*, March 18, 2001. Edmonton, Alta.

2002    Spirits Return Home: Natives Celebrate Return of Bundle. *Edmonton Journal*, July 7, 2002. Edmonton, Alta.

Joint Steering Committee: Métis Settlements General Council and Province of Alberta
2005    The Alberta-Métis Settlements Accord: Making Progress Sustainable. Stage 1 Report of the Transition Assessment and Planning Project. Edmonton, Alta.: Métis Settlements General Council and Province of Alberta.

Jojola, Ted
2007    Physical Infrastructure and Economic Development. In: Track 3: Infrastructure for Economic Development. Prepared for the National Congress of American Indians Policy Research Center: National Native American Economic Summit, Phoenix, Arizona, May 15–17, 2007.

Jolivétte, Andrew, ed.
2005    Cultural Representation in Native America. Blue Ridge Summit, Pa.: AltaMira Press.

Jones, David S.
2002    The Health Care Experiments at Many Farms: The Navajos, Tuberculosis, and the Limits of Modern Medicine, 1952–1962. *Bulletin of the History of Medicine* 76(4):749–790. Baltimore, Md.

2004    Rationalizing Epidemics: Meanings and Uses of American Indian Mortality Since 1600. Cambridge, Mass., and London: Harvard University Press.

Jones, Dorothy V.
1988    *see* Handbook Vol. 4 (1988:185–194)

Jones, Eugene
1988    Native Americans as Shown on the Stage 1753–1916. Metuchen, N.J.: Scarecrow Press.

Jones, Richard S.
1981    Alaska Native Claims Settlement Act of 1971 (Public Law 92-203): History and Analysis Together with Subsequent Amendments. *Library of Congress. American National Government Division. Report* 81–127 GOV. Washington.

Jones, William A.
1899    [Commissioner of Indian Affairs to Francis M. Morrison, dated July 10, 1899.] (Branch of Acknowledgment and Research, Narragansett Case Files, Rhode Island Attorney General; Record Group 75, Land Division 206(LB411): 184–185, National Archives, Washington.)

Jorgensen, Joseph G., ed.
1983    Native Americans and Energy Development II. Boston: Anthropology Resource Center and the Seventh Generation Fund.

1998    Gaming and Recent American Indian Economic Development. *American Indian Culture and Research Journal* 22(3): 157–172. Los Angeles.

Jorgensen, Miriam R., and Jonathan B. Taylor
2000    Patterns of Indian Enterprise Success: A Statistical Analysis of Tribal and Individual Indian Enterprise Performance, A Report to the National Congress of American Indians. Cambridge, Mass.: The Harvard Project on American Indian Economic Development.

2000a    What Determines Indian Economic Success? Evidence from Tribal and Individual Indian Enterprises. Cambridge, Mass.: The Harvard Project on American Indian Economic Development.

2000b    What Determines American Indian Economic Success? Evidence from Tribal and Individual Indian Enterprises. *Red Ink: A Native American Student Publication* 8(2):45–51. Tucson, Ariz.

Josephy, Alvin M., Jr.
1968    Cornplanter, Can You Swim? *American Heritage Magazine* 20(1):1–8. New York.

——, ed.
1971    Red Power: The American Indians' Fight for Freedom. New York: American Heritage Press; McGraw-Hill Books.

1982    The Great Northwest Fishing War: The Clashes Over Native American Fishing and Hunting Claims. Pp. 177–211 in Now That the Buffalo's Gone: A Study of Today's American Indian. New York: Alfred A. Knopf.

1992    America in 1492: The World of the Indian Peoples Before the Arrival of Columbus. New York: Knopf Publishers.

Josephy, Alvin M., Jr., Joane Nagel, and Troy Johnson, eds.
1999    Red Power: The American Indians' Fight for Freedom. 2d ed. Lincoln: University of Nebraska Press.

*Juneau Empire*
1999, [2001] *see* Brown, Cathy, Lori Thomson, and Svend Holst 1999, [2001]

Justice, Daniel Heath
2006    Our Fire Survives the Storm: A Cherokee Literary History. Minneapolis: University of Minnesota Press.

Justice, James W., comp.
1982    Bibliography of Health and Disease in North American Indians, Eskimos and Aleuts, 1969–1979. Tucson, Ariz.: U.S. Department of Health and Human Services, Public Health Service, Indian Health Service, Office of Research and Development.

Kalbach, Warren E.
1987    Growth and Distribution of Canada's Ethnic Populations, 1871–1981. Pp. 82–110 in Ethnic Canada: Identities and Inequalities. Leo Driedger, ed. Toronto: Copp, Clark, Pitman.

Kallen, Stuart A.
2006    Indian Gaming. Farmington Hills, Mich.: Greenhaven Press.

Kalt, Joseph, and Jonathan B. Taylor, eds.
2005    American Indians on Reservations: A Databook of Socioeconomic Change Between the 1990 and 2000 Censuses. Cambridge, Mass.: Harvard University, John F. Kennedy School of Government, Project on American Indian Economic Development.

2005a    The U.S. Census Data on American Indians: 1990 v. 2000. Report Compiles Economic and Social Indicators on a Decade of Striking Change. *News*, January 5, 2005:1–2. Cambridge, Mass.: Harvard University, John F. Kennedy School of Government.

Kanary, Joseph M.
1986    A Formula for Native Economic Self-Reliance: the Native Economic Development Program. (M.A. Thesis in Development Economics, Dalhousie University, Halifax, N.S.)

Kaplan, Michael J.
1985    Issues in Land Claims: Aboriginal Title. Pp. 71–86 in Irredeemable America: The Indians' Estate and Land Claims. Imre Sutton, ed. Albuquerque: University of New Mexico Press.

Kappler, Charles J., comp. and ed.
1904–1941    Indian Affairs. Laws and Treaties. 5 vols. (Vols. I–V). Washington: Government Printing Office. (Reprinted: AMS Press, New York, 1971; see also Kappler 1904–1979.)

_____, comp and ed.
1904–1979    Indian Affairs: Laws and Treaties. 7 vols.: Vols. I–IV, reprinted [plus:] Kappler's Indian Affairs: Laws and Treaties. 2 vols.: Vols. VI–VII, prepared under the direction of Deputy Solicitors Raymond C. Coutler and David E. Lindgren. Washington: U.S. Department of the Interior; U.S. Government Printing Office. (Reprinted 7 vols.: William S. Hein, New York, [1990].)

Karamessines, Susan
1976    United States Indian Tribal Courts: A Bibliography. *Social Science Notes* 6. Ottawa: Indian and Northern Affairs; Minister of Supply and Serivces Canada.

Karp, Ivan, and Steven D. Levine, eds.
1991    Exhibiting Cultures: The Poetics and Politics of Museum Dislpay. Washington: Smithsonian Institution Press.

Karr, Steven M.
2000    "Water We Believed Could Never Belong to Anyone": The San Luis Rey River and the Pala Indians of Southern California. *American Indian Quarterly* 24(3):381–399. Lincoln, Nebr.

Kasden, Margo, and Susan Tavernetti
1998    Native Americans in a Revisionist Western: *Little Big Man*. Pp. 121–136 in Hollywood's Indian: The Portrayal of the Native American in Film. Peter C. Rollins and John E. O'Connor, eds. Lexington, Ky.: The University Press of Kentucky.

Kashatus, William C.
2006    Money Pitcher: Chief Bender and the Tragedy of Indian Assimilation. University Park, Pa.: Pennsylvania State University Press.

Katz, Jane B.
1980    This Song Remembers: Self-Portraits of Native Americans in the Arts. Boston: Houghton Mifflin.

Katz, Marisa
2003    Staying Afloat: How Federal Recognition as a Native American Tribe Will Save the Residents of Isle De Jean Charles, Louisiana. *Loyola Journal of Public Interest Law* 4(1):1–25. New Orleans, La.

Katz, William Loren
1986    Black Indians: A Hidden Heritage. New York: Simon and Schuster. (Reprinted: Simon Pulse Publishing, 1997.)

2007    Racism and the Cherokee Nation. *The Black World Today*, Tuesday, March 08, 2007. (Webpage: http://tbwt.org)

Kaufert, Joseph M., John D. O'Neil, and William W. Koolage
1985    Culture Brokerage and Advocacy in Urban Hospitals: The Impact of Native Language Interpreters. *Santé, Culture, Health* 3(2):3–10. Montreal.

Kavanagh, Thomas W.
1979–2007    [Ethnographic Notes from Fieldwork among the Comanche, Oklahoma.] (Manuscript in T.W. Kavanagh's possession.]

1980    Recent Socio-Cultural Evolution of the Comanche Indians. (M.A. Thesis in Anthropology, George Washington University, Washington.)

1982    The Comanche Powwow: Pan-Indianism or Tribalism. *Haliksa'i: Journal of the University of New Mexico Anthropology Society* 1:1227. Albuquerque.

1991    Photographic Evidence of Ritual Context: Southern Arapaho Painted Clothing and the Ghost Dance/Crow Dance, 1892–1893. American Anthropological Association. Chicago.

1992    Southern Plains Dance: Tradition and Dynamics. Pp. 105–124 in Native American Dance: Ceremonies and Social Traditions. Charlotte Heth, ed. Washington: Smithsonian Institution, National Museum of the American Indian.

1995    More Than Meets the Eye: Photographs as Research Documents. *William Hammond Mathers Museum Occasional Paper.* Bloomington, Ind.

2007    [Comanche ethnography 1993.] (Fieldnotes of Gustav G. Carlson, E. Adamson Hoebel, and Waldo R. Wedel; edited copy in T.W. Kavanagh's possession.).

Kawahara, James K., and Michelle La Pena
2006    Indian Country: Federal Law Will Play a Role in Any Real Estate Transaction Involving a Tribal Government, Inside or Outside of Indian Lands. *Los Angeles Lawyer* 28(11):26–34. Los Angeles.

Kawano, Kenji
1990    Warriors: Navajo Code Talkers. Flagstaff, Ariz.: Northland Pub. Co.

Kehoe, Alice B.
1970    The Dakotas in Saskatchewan. Pp. 148–174 in The Modern Sioux: Social Systems and Reservation Culture. Ethel Nurge, ed. Lincoln: University of Nebraska Press.

1980    The Giveaway Ceremony of Blackfoot and Cree. *Plains Anthropologist* 25(87):17–26. Lincoln, Nebr.

1981    North American Indians: A Comparative Account. Englewood Cliffs, N.J.: Prentice-Hall.

1990    Primal Gaia: Primitivists and Plastic Medicine Men. Pp. 193–209 In The Invented Indian: Cultural Fictions and Government Policies. James A. Clifton, ed. New York: Transaction Publishers.

Kelly, Lawrence C.
1983    The Assault on Assimilation: John Collier and the Origins of Indian Policy Reform. Foreword by John Collier, Jr. Albuquerque: University of New Mexico Press.

Kelly, Robin
2001    First Nations Gambling Policy in Canada. Calgary, Alta.: Canada West Foundation.

2002    First Nations Gambling Policy in Canada. *The Journal of Aboriginal Economic Development* 2(2):41–55. Edmonton, Alta.

Kelsey, Cynthia
1968    [Interview with Naomi Warren LaDue, 14 August 1968.] (Recorded text in South Dakota Oral History Center, University of South Dakota, Vermillion, S.Dak.)

Kemnitzer, Luis
1973    Adjustment and Value Conflict in Urbanizing Dakota Indians Measured by Q-Sort Techniques. *American Anthropologist* 75(3):687–707.

_____
1994    Personal Memories of Alcatraz, 1969. Pp. 103–110 in Special Edition: Alcatraz Revisited: The 25th Anniversary of the Occupation, 1969–1971. Joane Nagel and Troy Johnson, eds. *American Indian Culture and Research Journal* 18(4). Los Angeles.

Kendall, Edward Augustus
1809    Travels Through the Northern Parts of the United States, in the Years 1807 and 1808. 3 vols. New York: I Riley.

Kerr, Don, Éric Guimond, and Mary Jane Norris
2003    Perils and Pitfalls of Aborginal Demography: Lessons Learned from the RCAP Projections. Pp 39–62 in Aboriginal Conditions: Research as a Foundation for Public Policy. Jerry P. White, Paul S. Maxim, and Dan Beavon, eds. Vancouver: UBC Press.

Kerri, James N.
1976    "Push" and "Pull" Factors: Reasons for Migration as a Factor in Amerindian Urban Adjustment. *Human Organization* 34(2):215–220. Washington.

Kersey, Harry A., Jr.
1996    An Assumption of Sovereignty: Social and Political Transformation Among the Florida Seminoles, 1953–1979. Lincoln and London: University of Nebraska Press.

Ketchum, Shanna
2005    Native American Cosmopolitan Modernism(s). *Third Text* 19(75, Pt.4):357–364.

Ketilson, Lou Hammond, and Ian MacPherson
2001    A Report on Aboriginal Co-Operatives in Canada: Current Situation and Potential for Growth. Saskatoon, Sask.: Centre for the Study of Co-Operatives, Universtiy of Saskatchewan.

Kew, J.E. Michael
1990    *see* Handbook Vol. 7 (1990:159–168)

Key, Amos
1992    Language Retention Rates Disturbing. *Wadrihwa: Quarterly Newsletter of the Woodland Cultural Centre* 6(2):18–19. Brantford, Ont.

Kickingbird, Kirke, and Karen Ducheneaux
1973    One Hundred Million Acres. New York: Macmillan.

Kidwell, Clara Sue
1999    The Vanishing Native Reappears in the College Curriculm. Pp. 271–294 in Next Steps: Research and Practice to Advance Indian Education. Karen Gayton Swisher and John W. Tippeconnic, III, eds. Charleston, W.Va.: ERIC Clearinghouse on Rural Education and Small Schools.

_____
2002    American Indian Studies at the University of Oklahoma. Pp. 29–42 in Native American Studies in Higher Education: Models for Collaboration Between Universities and Indigenous Nations. Duane Champagne and Jay Stauss, eds. Walnut Creek, Calif.: AltaMira Press.

Kidwell, Clara Sue, and Alan Velie
2005    Native American Studies. Edinburgh, Scotland: University of Edinburgh Press.

Killion, Thomas W., Scott Brown, and J. Stuart Speaker
1992    Naevahoo'ohtseme (We Are Going Back Home) Cheyenne Repatriation: The Human Remains. Washington: Smithsonian Institution, National Museum of Natural History, Repatriation Office.

Killion, Thomas W., Elizabeth Eubanks, and William T. Billeck
2002    Inventory and Assessment of Human Remains from the Salinas Pueblos of Gran Quivira and Quarai, New Mexico, in the National Museum of Natural History. Washington: Smithsonian Institution, National Museum of Natural History, Repatriation Office.

Killion, Thomas W., et al.
1994    Inventory and Documentation of Skeletal Remains from the Prince William Sound in the Physical Anthropology Collections of the Department of Anthropology, NMNH. Washington: Smithsonian Institution, National Museum of Natural History, Repatriation Office.

Kilpatrick, Jacquelyn
1999    Celluloid Indians: Native Americans and Film. Lincoln and London: University of Nebraska Press.

Kimber, Clarissa T., and Darrell McDonald
2004    Sacred and Profane Uses of the Cactus *Lophophora Williamsii* from the South Texas Peyote Gardens. Pp. 182–208 in Dangerous Harvest: Drug Plants and the Transformation of Indigenous Landscapes. Michael K. Steinberg, Joseph J. Hobbs, and Kent Mathewson, eds. New York: Oxford University Press.

King, Bruce
2006    Evening at the Warbonnet and Other Plays. Los Angeles: UCLA American Indian Studies Center.

King, C. Richard, and Charles Fruehling Springwood
2001    Team Spirits: The Native American Mascots Controversy. Lincoln and London: University of Nebraska Press.

King, David
2006    A Brief Report of the Federal Government of Canada's Residential School System for Inuit. Ottawa: Aboriginal Healing Foundation. (Webpage: http://www.ahf.ca/assets/pdf/english/king-summary-f-web.pdf [16 June 2006].)

King, Duane H.
1976    History of the Museum of the Cherokee Indian. *Journal of Cherokee Studies* 1(1):60–64. Cherokee, N.C.

_____, comp.
1982    Cherokee Heritage: Official Guidebook to the Museum of the Cherokee Indian. Cherokee, N.C.: Museum of the Cherokee Indian. (Reprinted in 1984 and 1988.)

King, Jonathan C.H.
1986    Tradition in Native American Art. Pp. 65–92 in The Arts of the North American Indian: Native Traditions in Evolution. Edwin L. Wade, ed. New York: Hudson Hills Press.

King, Thomas
1989    Medicine River. Toronto: Penguin Canada.

_____
1993    Green Grass, Running Water. New York: Houghton Mifflin.

_____
1999    Truth and Bright Water. Toronto: Harper Flamingo Canada.

_____
2003    The Truth About Stories: A Native Narrative. Toronto: House of Anansi Press, Inc. (Reprinted: University of Minnesota Press, Minneapolis, 2005.)

King, Thomas F.
1998    Cultural Resource Laws and Practice: An Introductory Guide. *Heritage Resource Management Series* 1. Walnut Creek, Calif.: Altamira Press.

Kinkade, M. Dale
1991    The Decline of Native Languages in Canada. Pp. 157–176 in Endangered Languages. Robert H. Robins and Eugenius M. Uhlenbeck, eds. Published with the authority of the Perma-

nent International Committee of Linguists (CIPL). Oxford and New York: BERG; distributed by St. Martin's Press, New York.

Kipp, Darrell R.
2000    Encouragement, Guidance, Insight and Lessons Learned for Native Language Activists Developing Their Own Tribal Language Programs. St. Paul, Minn.: Grotto Foundation.

Kipp, Woody
1994    The Eagles I Fed Who Did Not Love Me. Pp. 213–232 in Special Edition: Alcatraz Revisited: The 25th Anniversary of the Occupation, 1969–1971. Joane Nagel and Troy Johnson, eds. *American Indian Culture and Research Journal* 18(4). Los Angeles.

Kirk, Ruth, and Louis Kirk
1980    The Pompeii of the Northwest. *Historic Preservation* 32(2): 29. Washington.

Kirkness, Verna J.
1989    Aboriginal Languages Foundation: A Mechanism for Language Renewal. *Canadian Journal of Native Education* 16(2):25–41.

————
1998    Aboriginal Languages: A Collection of Talks and Papers. Winnipeg, Man.: Published by the Author.

————
2002    The Preservation and Use of Our Languages: Respecting the Natural Order of Things. Pp. 17–23 in Indigenous Languages Across the Community. *Proceedings of the Annual Conference on Stabilizing Indigenous Languages; 7th, Toronto, Ont., Canada, May 11–14, 2000.* Barbara Jane Burnaby and Jon Allan Reyhner, eds. Flagstaff, Ariz.: Center for Education Excellence, Northern Arizona University.

Kirmayer, Laurence J., G. Brass, and C. Tait
2000    The Mental Health of Aboriginal People: Transformations of Identity and Community. *Canadian Journal of Psychiatry* 45:607–616. Ottawa.

Kirmayer, Laurence J., et al.
1994    Suicide in Canadian Aboriginal Populations: Emerging Trends in Research and Intervention. *Culture and Mental Health Research Unit. Research Report* 1. Montreal: Institute of Community and Family Psychiatry, Sir Mortimer B. Davis-Jewish General Hospital, and Transcultural Psychiatry, McGill University.

Klein, Laura F., and Lillian A. Ackerman
1995    Women and Power in Native North America. Norman: University of Oklahoma Press.

Knick, Stanley, and Linda E. Oxendine
2002    Standing in the Gap: American Indian Studies at the University of North Carolina-Pembroke. Pp. 203–228 in Native American Studies in Higher Education: Models for Collaboration Between Universities and Indigenous Nations. Duane Champagne and Jay Stauss, eds. Walnut Creek, Calif.: AltaMira Press.

Koning, Hans
1993    The Conquest of America: How the Indian Nations Lost Their Continent. New York: Monthly Review Press.

Kotlowski, Dean J.
2003    Alcatraz, Wounded Knee and Beyond: The Nixon and Ford Administrations Respond to Native American Protest. *Pacific Historical Review* 72(2):201–227. Berkeley, Calif.

Kracht, Benjamin
1994    Kiowa Powwows: Continuity in Ritual Practice. *American Indian Quarterly* 18(3):321–348. Lincoln, Nebr.

Kramer, Jennifer
2006    Switchbacks: Art, Ownership, and Nuxalk National Identity. Vancouver: University of British Columbia Press.

Krashen, Stephen D., and Tracy D. Terrell
1983    The Natural Approach: Language Acquisition in the Classroom. Hayward, Calif.: Alemany Press.

Kratochwill, Thomas R., et al.
2004    Families and Schools Together: An Experimental Analysis of a Parent-Mediated Multi-Family Group Program for American Indian Children. *Journal of School Psychology* 42(5): 359–383. New York.

Krauthamer, Barbara
2000    Blacks on the Borders: African-Americans' Transition from Slavery to Freedom in Texas and the Indian Territory, 1836–1907. (Ph.D. Dissertation in History, Princeton University, Princeton, N.J.)

Krech, Shepard, III, and Barbara A. Hail
1999    Collecting Native America: 1870–1960. Washington: Smithsonian Institution.

Kremer, Gary R.
1980    For Justice and a Fee: James Milton Turner and the Cherokee Freedmen. *Chronicles of Oklahoma* 58(4):377–391. Oklahoma City.

Kroeber, Alfred L.
1908    Ethnology of the Gros Ventre. *Anthropological Papers of the American Museum of Natural History* 1(Pt. 4). New York.

————
1939    Cultural and Natural Areas of Native North America. *University of California Publications in American Archaeology and Ethnology* 38. Berkeley. (Reprinted: University of California Press, Berkeley, 1947, 1953, 1963; also, Kraus Reprint Company, Millwood, N.Y., 1965 and 1976.)

Krouse, Susan Applegate
2003    What Came Out of the Takeovers: Women's Activism and the Indian Community School of Milwaukee. Pp. 533–547 in Keeping the Campfires Going: Urban American Indian Women's Activism. Susan Applegate Krouse and Heather Howard-Bobiwash, eds. *American Indian Quarterly*, Special Issue 27(3–4). Lincoln, Nebr.

Krouse, Susan Applegate, and Heather Howard-Bobiwash, eds.
2003    Keeping the Campfires Going: Urban American Indian Women's Activism. *American Indian Quarterly*, Special Issue 27(3–4). Lincoln, Nebr.

Krupat, Arnold
1985    For Those Who Come After: A Study of Native American Autobiography. Berkeley, [etc.]: University of California Press.

————
1989    The Voice in the Margin: Native American Literature and the Canon. Berkeley, [etc.]: University of California Press.

Krupat, Arnold, and Brian Swann, eds.
1987    I Tell You Now: Autobiographical Essays by Native American Writers. Lincoln: University of Nebraska Press.

————, eds.
2000    Here First: Autobiographical Essays by Native American Writers. New York: The Modern Library.

Kulchyski, Peter
1988    A Considerable Unrest: F.O. Loft and the League of Indians. *Native Studies Review* 4(1–2):95–117. Saskatoon, Sask.

Kuntz, James W.
1997    Nuclear Incidents on Indian Reservations: Who Has Jurisdiction? Tribal Court Exhaustion Versus the Price-Anderson

Act. *American Indian Law Review* 21(1):103–129. Norman, Okla.

Kuttner, Robert E., and Albert B. Lorincz
1967        Alcoholism and Addiction in Urbanized Sioux Indians. *Mental Hygiene* 51(4):530–542. (Arlington, Va.: National Association for Mental Health.)

Kvasnicka, Robert M.
1988        *see* Handbook Vol. 4 (1988:195–201)

Kvasnicka, Robert M., and Herman J. Viola, eds.
1979        The Commissioners of Indian Affairs, 1824–1977. Lincoln: University of Nebraska Press.

La Barre, Weston
1989        The Peyote Cult. 5th Edition, Enlarged. Norman: University of Oklahoma Press.

Labrador Inuit Comprehensive Land Claims Agreement
2003        Labrador Inuit Comprehensive Land Claims Agreement. Ottawa: Government of Canada, the Government of Newfoundland and Labrador, and the Labrador Inuit Association (LIA).

La Course, Richard
1973        The Second Battle of Wounded Knee: Aftermath of Shooting Confrontation on the Pine Ridge Reservation. *Indian Voice* 3(4):20–22, 49–50. San Jose, Calif.

——— 1973a        The Beginning of the Trail. Pp. 23 in Trail of Broken Treaties: B.I.A. I'm Not Your Indian Any More. Rooseveltown, N.Y.: Mohawk Nation.

——— 1998        Protecting the First Amendment in Indian Country. (Unpublished article, Yakama Nation, Wash.)

——— 1998a        A Native Press Primer. *Columbia Journalism Review* 37(4): 51. New York.

Ladd, Edmund J.
2001        A Zuni Perspective on Repatriation. Pp. 107–116 in The Future of the Past: Archaeologists, Native Amearicans, and Repatriation. Tamara L. Bray, ed. New and London: Garland Publishing.

LaDue, Naomi Warren
1968        *see* Kelsey, Cynthia 1968

LaDuke, Winona
1983        The Council of Energy Resource Tribes. Pp. 59–67 in Native Americans and Energy Development II. Joseph G. Jorgensen, ed. Boston: Anthropology Resource Center and the Seventh Generation Fund.

——— 1996        Like Tributaries to a River: The Growing Strength of Native Environmentalism. *Sierra: The Magazine of the Sierra Club* 81(6):38–45. San Francisco.

——— 1999        All Our Relations: Native Struggles for Land and Life. Cambridge, Mass.: South End Press.

La Farge, Oliver, ed.
1942        The Changing Indian. Edited by Oliver La Farge; From a Symposium Arranged by the American Association on Indian Affairs, Inc. Norman: University of Oklahoma Press.

——— 1947        They Were Good Enough for the Army. *Harper's Magazine* 195:444–449. New York.

——— 1961        An American Indian Program for the Sixties. *Indian Affairs* 40(February):1–3. New York.

La Flesche, Francis
1900        The Middle Five: Indian Boys at School. Boston: Small, Maynard, and Co. (Reprinted: see La Flesche 1963.)

——— 1939        War Ceremony and Peace Ceremony of the Osage Indians. *Bureau of American Ethnology Bulletin* 101. Washington: Smithsonian Institution; U.S. Government Printing Office.

——— 1963        The Middle Five: Indian Schoolboys of the Omaha Tribe. Foreword by David A. Barreis. Madison, Wis.: University of Wisconsin Press. (Reprinted: University of Nebraska Press, Lincoln, 1978.)

——— 1995        *see* Bailey, Garrick A., ed. 1995

LaFontaine, Frank
1974        [Frank LaFontaine, Small Tribes Organization of Western Washington, to Paul Weston, BIA Portland Area Office, dated November 26, 1974.] (Office of Federal Acknowledgment, US v. Washington Files, Bureau of Indian Affairs, Washington.)

Lagassé, Jean H.
1961–1962    Community Development in Manitoba. Pp. 232–237 in American Indians and Their Economic Development. Fred Voget, ed. *Human Organization*, Special Issue 20(4). Washington.

LaGrand, James B.
2002        Indian Metropolis: Native Americans in Chicago, 1945–75. Champaign, Ill.: University of Illinois Press.

Lamb, Yvonne Shinhoster
2007        [Obituaries] American Indian Rights Activist Vernon Bellecourt. *The Washington Post*, Monday, October 15, 2007:B6. Washington.

Lambert, Valerie
2007        Political Protest, Conflict, and Tribal Nationalism: The Oklahoma Choctaws and the Termination Crisis of 1959–1970. *American Indian Quarterly* 31(2):283–309. Lincoln, Nebr.

Lambertus, Sandra
2004        Wartime Images, Peacetime Wounds: The Media and the Gustafen Lake Standoff. Toronto: University of Toronto Press.

Lame Deer, John (Fire), and Richard Erdoes
1972        Lame Deer, Seeker of Visions. New York: Simon and Schuster.

Lame Woman, Tim
2002        The Murder of Anna Mae Aquash. *News from Indian Country*, September 22, 2002. Hayward, Wis.

Landau, Patricia M., and D. Gentry Steele
1996        Why Anthropologists Study Human Remains. *American Indian Quarterly* 20(2):209–228. Lincoln, Nebr.

Lane, Ambrose I.
1995        Return of the Buffalo: The Story Behind America's Indian Gaming Explosion. Westport, Conn.: Bergin and Garvey.

Lane, Theodore, ed.
1987        Developing America's Northern Frontier. Lanham, Md.: University Press of America.

Lang, Gottfried O.
1961–1962    Economic Development and Self-Determination. Pp. 164–171 in American Indians and Their Economic Development. Fred Voget, ed. *Human Organization*, Special Issue 20(4). Washington.

Langellier, John P.
2002        American Indians in the U.S. Armed Forces, 1866–1945.
            *G.I.: The Illustrated History of the American Soldier, His*
            *Uniform and His Equipment* 20. Philadelphia: Chelsea House
            Publishers. (Originally publ.: Greenhill Books, London, and
            Stackpole Books, Mechanicsburg, Pa., 2000.)

Langston, Donna Hightower
2003        American Indian Women's Activism in the 1960s and 1970s.
            *Hypatia* 18(2):114–132. Bloomington, Ind.

Lansdowne, Michele Lynn
2004        American Indian Entrepreneurship: A Complex Web. (Ph.D.
            Dissertation in Management, Cultural Anthropology, Union
            Institute and University, Cincinnati, Ohio.)

Larsen, B.
1946        Indian War Hero Heads New Battle. *Winnipeg Tribune*, 4
            December 1946:1, 5. Winnipeg, Man.

Larsen, Clark Spenser
1994        In the Wake of Columbus: Native Population Biology in the
            Postcontact Americas. *Yearbook of Physical Anthropology*
            37:109–154. New York.

Larson, Charles R.
1978        American Indian Fiction. Albuquerque: University of New
            Mexico Press.

La Rusic, Ignatius, et al.
1979        Negotiating a Way of Life. Ottawa: Indian Affairs and North-
            ern Development Canada.

Lave, Charles A., James V. Mueller, and Theodore D. Graves
1978        The Economic Payoff of Different Kinds of Education: A
            Study of Urban Migrants in Two Societies. *Human Organi-
            zation* 37(2):157–162. Washington.

LaViolette, E. Forrest
1961        The Struggle for Survival: Indian Cultures and the Protestant
            Ethic in British Columbia. Toronto: University of Toronto
            Press.

Law School Admission Council
2007        Annual Data Report to the Dean's Conference, February
            2007. Newton, Pa.: Law School Admission Council.

Lawlor, Mary
2005        Identity in Mashantucket. *American Quarterly* 57(1):153–
            177. Baltimore, Md.

Lawrence, Bonita
2004        "Real" Indians and Others: Mixed-Blood Urban Native Peo-
            ples and Indigenous Nationhood. Lincoln and London: Uni-
            versity of Nebraska Press.

Lawrence, Jane
2000        The Indian Health Service and the Sterilization of Native
            American Women. *American Indian Quarterly* 24(3):400–
            419. Lincoln, Nebr.

Lawrence, Sonia, and Patrick Macklem
2000        From Consultations to Reconciliation: Aboriginal Rights and
            the Crown's Duty to Consult. *The Canadian Bar Review*
            79(1):252–279. Toronto.

Lawson, Michael L.
1982        Dammed Indians: The Pick-Sloan Plan and the Missouri
            River Sioux, 1944–1980. Norman: University of Oklahoma
            Press. (Reprinted, new. ed., 1994.)

Lawson, Paul E.
1995        When States' Attorneys General Write Books on Native
            Law: A Case Study of Spaeth's "American Indian Law

Deskbook." *American Indian Quarterly* 19(2):229–236.
Lincoln, Nebr.

Lawson, Paul E., and Patrick Morris
1991        The Native American Church and the New Court: The Smith
            Case and Indian Religious Freedoms. *American Indian Cul-
            ture and Research Journal* 15(1):79–91.

Lawson, Paul E., and Jennifer Scholes
1986        Jurisprudence, Peyote and the Native American Church.
            *American Indian Culture and Research Journal* 10(1):13–27.
            Los Angeles.

Lawson, Steven F., ed.
2004        To Secure These Rights: The Report of President Harry S.
            Truman's Committee on Civil Rights [1947]. Edited with an
            Introduction by Steven F. Lawson. *Bedford Series in History
            and Culture*. New York and Boston: Bedford Books.

Lazarus, Edward
1991        Black Hills/White Justice: The Sioux Nation Versus the
            United States, 1775 to the Present. New York: Harper
            Collins.

Leacock, Eleanor Burke, and Nancy Oestreich Lurie, eds.
1971        North American Indians in Historical Perspective. New
            York: Random House. (Reprinted: Waveland Press, Prospect
            Heights, Ill., 1988.)

Lee, Tanya
2006        Navajo Group Begins Process of Crafting a Constitution.
            *Indian Country Today*, June 19, 2006. Canastota, N.Y. (Web-
            page: http://www.indiancountry.com)

Leeds, Stacy L.
2004        Borrowing from Blackacre: Expanding Tribal Land Bases
            Through the Creation of Future Interests and Joint Tenancies.
            *North Dakota Law Review* 80(4):827–848. Grand Forks,
            N.Dak.

Légaré, André
2003        The Nunavut Tunngavik Inc.: An Examination of Its Mode
            of Operation and Its Activities. Pp. 117–137 in Natural
            Resources and Aboriginal People in Canada: Readings,
            Cases, and Commentary. Robert B. Anderson and Robert
            M. Bone, eds. Concord, Ont.: Captus Press.

Lemanczyk, Sarah
2007        Return of the Native. *American Theatre* 24(3):50–53. New
            York.

Lemchuk-Favel, Laurel
1996        Trends in First Nations Mortality, 1979–1993 Ottawa: Minis-
            ter of Public Works and Government Services, Canada.

Lemchuk-Favel, Laurel, and Richard Jock
2004        Aboriginal Health Systems in Canada: Nine Case Studies.
            *Journal of Aboriginal Health* 1(1):28–51. Ottawa.

Lemont, Eric D., ed.
2006        American Indian Constitutional Reform and the Rebuilding
            of Native Nations. Austin, Tex.: The University of Texas
            Press.

Leonard, Irving A.
1942        Peyote and the Mexican Inquisition, 1620. *American Anthro-
            pologist*, n.s. 44(2):324–326.

Lerch, Patricia Barker
1992        State-Recognized Indians of North Carolina, Including a His-
            tory of the Waccamaw Sioux. Pp. 44–71 in Indians of the
            Southeastern United States in the Late Twentieth Century.
            James Anthony Paredes, ed. Tuscaloosa and London: The
            University of Alabama Press.

2004 *see* Handbook Vol. 14 (2004:328–336)

2004a Waccamaw Legacy: Contemporary Indians Fight for Survival. Tuscaloosa: The University of Alabama Press.

Leslie, John F.
1982 The Bagot Commission: Developing a Corporate Memory for the Indian Department. *Historical Papers/Communications Historiques* 17(1):31–52. Ottawa.

1984 Commissions of Inquiry into Indian Affairs in the Canadas, 1828–1858: Evolving a Corporate Memory for the Indian Department. (M.A. Research Essay in Canadian Studies, Carleton University, Ottawa.)

1999 Assimilation, Integration or Termination? The Development of Canadian Indian Policy, 1943–1963. (Ph.D. Dissertation in History, Carleton University, Ottawa.)

2002 The Indian Act: An Historical Perspective. *Canadian Parliamentary Review* 25(2):23–27. Ottawa.

Leslie, John F., and Ron Maguire, eds.
1978 The Historical Development of the Indian Act. 2d ed. Ottawa: Indian and Northern Affairs Canada, Treaties and Historical Research Centre, Research Branch.

Lessard, Dennis
1984 Instruments of Prayer: The Peyote Art of the Sioux. *American Indian Art Magazine* 9(2):24–27. Scottsdale, Ariz.

Lesser, Alexander
1958–1959 Going to College. *The American Indian* 8(2):1. New York.

1961 Education and the Future of Tribalism in the United States: The Case of the American Indian. *The Social Service Review* 35(2):1–9. Chicago.

Lester, Joan
1972 The American Indian: A Museum's Eye View. *The Indian Historian* 5(2):25–31. San Francisco.

Letgers, Lyman H., and Fremont J. Lyden
1994 American Indian Policy: Self-Governance and Economic Development. Westport, Conn.: Greenwood Press.

Leuchtenburgh, William E.
1983 In the Shadow of FDR: From Harry Truman to Ronald Reagan. Ithaca, N.Y.: Cornell University Press.

Levine, Stuart, and Nancy O. Lurie, eds.
1968 The American Indian Today. Deland, Fla.: Everett/Edwards, Inc. (Reprinted: Penguin Books, Baltimore, Md., and Pelican Books, New York, 1970.)

Levy, Jerrold E.
1961 After Custer: Kiowa Political and Social Organization from the Reservation Period to the Present. (Ph.D. Dissertation in Anthropology, University of Chicago, Chicago.)

Lew, Alan A., and George A. Van Otten, eds.
1998 Tourism and Gaming on American Indian Lands. New York: Cognizant Communication Corporation.

Lewis, David R.
1995 Native Americans and the Environment: A Survey of Twentieth-Century Issues. *American Indian Quarterly* 19(3): 423–450. Lincoln, Nebr.

Liberty, Margot, ed.
1978 American Indian Intellectuals. *1976 Proceedings of The American Ethnological Society*. St. Paul, New York, etc.: West Publishing Co.

Library of Parliament *see* Canada. Library of Parliament

Liebow, Edward D.
1991 Urban Indian Institutions in Phoenix: Transformation from Headquarters City to Community. *Journal of Ethnic Studies* 18(4):1–27. Hayward, Calif.

Light, Steven Andrew, and Kathryn R.L. Rand
2005 Indian Gaming and Tribal Sovereignty: The Casino Compromise. Lawrence, Kans.: University Press of Kansas.

Light, Steven Andrew, Kathryn R.L. Rand, and Alan P. Meister
2004 Spreading the Wealth: Indian Gaming and Revenue-Sharing Agreements. *North Dakota Law Review* 80(4):657–679. Grand Forks, N.Dak.

Lightman, David
1993 Trump Criticized Pequots, Casino. *The Harford Courant*, October 6, 1993: A1, A12. Harford, Conn.

Lincoln, Kenneth
1983 Native American Renaissance. Berkeley: University of California Press.

1993 Indi'n Humor: Bicultural Play in Native America. London and New York: Oxford University Press.

2006 The Year the Sun Died. Baltimore, Md.: PublishAmerica.

Linderman, Frank B.
1930 Plenty-Coups: Chief of the Crows. New York: The John Day Company.

1932 Pretty Shield: Medicine Woman of the Crows. New York: The John Day Company.

Lindley, Mark Frank
1926 The Acquisition and Government of Backward Territory in International Law: Being A Treatise on the Law and Practice Relating to Colonial Expansion. London: Longmans, Green and Co.

Lippard, Lucy, ed.
2003 Path Breakers: The Eiteljorg Fellowship for Native American Fine Art, 2003. Indianapolis, Ind: Eiteljorg Museum of American Indians and Western Art in association with the University of Washington Press, Seattle and London.

Lippert, Dorothy T.
2002 Inventory and Assessment of Human Remains and Funerary Objects from Kauwerak, Akavingayak and Port Clarence, Alaska, in the National Museum of Natural History. Washington: Smithsonian Institution, National Museum of Natural History, Repatriation Office.

2004 Inventory and Assessment of Human Remains from the Nulato Area of Alaska, in the National Museum of Natural History. Washington: Smithsonian Institution, National Museum of Natural History, Repatriation Office.

Lippert, Dorothy T., and Betsy Bruemmer
2004 Inventory and Assessment of Human Remains from St. Michael Island, Alaska, in the National Museum of Natural History, Smithsonian Institution. Washington: Smithsonian Institution, National Museum of Natural History, Repatriation Office.

Lithman, Yngve
1984 The Community Apart: A Case Study of a Canadian Indian Reserve Commuity. Winnnipeg, Man.: University of Manitoba Press.

Little, Nina F.
1957 The Abby Aldrich Rockefeller Folk Art Collection: A Descriptive Catalog. Colonial Williamsburg and Boston: Little, Brown and Co.

Little Bear, Leroy
1982 1982 *see* Long, J. Anthony, Leroy Little Bear, and Menno Boldt 1982.

Littlebear, Richard
[2005] Introduction. Pp. 5–7 in Native American Language Immersion: Innovative Native Education for Children and Families, by Janine Pease-Pretty On Top. A Project of the American Indian College Fund. (Webpage: http://www.collegefund.org/downloads/ImmersionBook.pdf).

——— 1999 Some Rare and Radical Ideas for Keeping Indigenous Languages Alive. Pp. 1–5 in Revitalizing Indigenous Languages. Jon Reyhner, et al., eds. Flagstaff, Ariz.: Northern Arizona University.

Little Eagle, Avis
1993 Pete Catches: Respected Holy Man of the Lakota Journeys On. *Indian Country Today*, December 8, 1993:A1–A2. Canastota, N.Y. (Webpage: http://www.indiancountry.com)

Littlefield, Daniel F., Jr.
1977 Africans and Seminoles: From Removal to Emancipation. *Contributions in Afro-American and African Studies* 32. Westport, Conn.: Greenwood Press. (Reprinted: Banner Books/University Press of Mississippi, Jackson, Miss., 2001.)

——— 1978 The Cherokee Freedmen: From Emancipation to American Citizenship. *Contributions in Afro-American and African Studies* 40. Westport, Conn.: Greenwood Press.

——— 1979 Africans and Creeks: From the Colonial Period to the Civil War. *Contributions in Afro-American and African Studies* 47. Wesport, Conn.: Greenwood Press.

——— 1980 The Chickasaw Freedmen: A People Without a Country. *Contributions in Afro-American and African Studies* 54. Wesport, Conn.: Greenwood Press.

——— 1981 A Biobibliography of Native American Writers, 1772–1994. *Native American Bibliography Series*. Metuchen, N.J.: Scarecrow Press. (See also Littlefield and Parins, 1985.)

——— 1992 Alex Posey: Creek Poet, Journalist, and Humorist. *American Indian Lives Series*. Lincoln: University of Nebraska Press. (Reprinted in 1997.)

——— 1996 Seminole Burning: A Story of Racial Vengeance. Jackson, Miss.: University Press of Mississippi.

Littlefield, Daniel F., Jr., and James W. Parins
1985 A Biobibliography of Native American Writers, 1772–1994: A Supplement. *Native American Bibliography Series*. Metuchen, N.J.: Scarecrow Press.

——— 1986 American Indian and Alaska Native Newspapers and Periodicals, 1971–1985. New York: Greenwood Press.

Litwin, Thomas S.
2005 The Harriman Alaska Expedition Retraced: A Century of Change 1899–2001. New Brunswick, N.J.: Rutgers University Press.

Lobo, Susan
2001 Introduction. Pp. 3–4 in American Indians and the Urban Experience. *Contemporary Native American Communities*. Susan Lobo and Kurt Peters, eds. Walnut Creek, Calif.: AltaMira Press.

——— 2001a Is Urban a Person or a Place? Pp. 73–84 in American Indians and the Urban Experience. *Contemporary Native American Communities*. Susan Lobo and Kurt Peters, eds. Walnut Creek, Calif.: AltaMira Press.

——— 2003 Urban Clan Mothers: Key Households in Cities. Pp. 505–522 in Keeping the Campfires Going: Urban American Indian Women's Activism. Susan Applegate Krouse and Heather Howard-Bobiwash, eds. *American Indian Quarterly*, Special Issue 27(3–4). Lincoln, Nebr.

Lobo, Susan, and Kurt Peters, eds.
2001 American Indians and the Urban Experience. *Contemporary Native American Communities*. Walnut Creek, Calif.: AltaMira Press.

Lobo, Susan, and Steve Talbot, eds.
1998 Native American Voices: A Reader. New York: Longman.

Locke, Patricia
1974 A Survey of College and University Programs for American Indians. Boulder, Colo.: Western Interstate Commission for Higher Education.

——— 1978 A Survey of College and University Programs for American Indians. Boulder, Colo.: Western Interstate Commission for Higher Education.

Locklear, Arlinda
1983 [Letter from Native American Rights Fund to John Shappard [sic], Branch of Federal Acknowledgment.] (Office of Federal Acknowledgment, Correspondence Files, Bureau of Indian Affairs, Washington.)

Loew, Patty
2005 Dances With History: Historical Research Methodology in Indian Country. Madison, Wisc.: University of Wisconsin-Madison.

Loew, Patty, and Kelly Mella
2005 Black Ink and the New Red Power: Native American Newspapers and Tribal Sovereignty. *Journalism and Communication Monographs* 7(3):99–142. Columbia, S.C.

Loma'omvaya, Micah
2001 NAGPRA Artifact Repatriation and Pesticides Contamination: The Hopi Experience. Pp. 30–37 in Contaminated Collections: Preservation, Access and Use. *Proceedings of a Symposium Held at the National Conservation Training Center (NCTC), Shepherdstown, West Virginia, April 6–9, 2001. Collection Forum* 17.

Lomawaima, K. Tsianina
1999 The Unnatural history of American Indian Education. Pp. 1–32 in Next Steps: Research and Practice to Advance Indian Education. Karen Gayton Swisher and John W. Tippeconnic, III, eds. Charleston, W.Va.: ERIC Clearinghouse on Rural Education and Small Schools.

Long, J. Anthony, and Menno Boldt, eds.
1988 Governments in Conflict? Provinces and Indian Nations in Canada. Toronto: University of Toronto Press.

Long, J. Anthony, Leroy Little Bear, and Menno Boldt
1982 Federal Indian Policy and Indian Self-Government in Canada: An Analysis of a Current Proposal. *Canadian Public Policy* 8(2):1892–1899. Toronto.

Longstreth, George F.
2007    Bibliographic Essay: Southern California Indian Concepts of Illness and Healing from Antiquity to the Present. *American Indian Culture and Research Journal* 31(1):121–139. Los Angeles.

Loo, Tina, and Carolyn Strange
2000    Rock Prison of Liberation: Alcatraz Island and the American Imagination. *Radical History Review* 78:27–56. New York.

Lopach, James J., Margaret Hunter Brown, and Richmond L. Clow
1998    Tribal Governments Today: Politics on Montana Indian Reservations. 2d ed., rev. Boulder, Colo.: University Press of Colorado.

Lord, Nancy
1996    Native Tongues: The Languages That Once Mapped the American Landscape Have Almost Vanished. *Sierra: The Magazine of the Sierra Club* 81(6):46–49, 68–69. San Francisco.

Lowe, Truman T.
2004    Native Modernism: The Art of George Morrison and Allan Houser. Seattle: University of Washington Press.

Lozano Conde, Alejandro
[2005]   Diplomado en Educación Intercultural Bilingüe. Modulo VI: Métodos y materiales educativos. México: Universidad Pedagógica Nacional, Dirección General de Culturas Populares e Indígenas. (Webpage: http://interbilingue.ajusco.upn.mx/modules.php?name=News&file=article&sid=195)

Lueger, Richard R.H.
1977    A History of Indian Associations in Canada, 1870–1970. (M.A. Thesis in History, Carleton University, Ottawa.)

Lujan, Carol C.
2001    Strengthening the Next Seven Generations: American Indian Studies Program at Arizona State University. *Indigenous Nations Studies Journal* 2(1):103–112. Lawrence, Kans.

Luna-Firebaugh, Eileen
2006    Tribal Policing: Asserting Sovereignty, Seeking Justice. Tucson: The University of Arizona Press.

Lund, Karen C., ed.
1992    American Indians in Silent Film: Motion Pictures in the Library of Congress. Washington: Library of Congress.

Lurie, Nancy Oestreich
1961    The Voice of the American Indian: Report on the American Indian Chicago Conference. *Current Anthropology* 2(5): 478–500. Chicago.

———
1970    An American Indian Renascence. Pp. 295–327 in The American Indian Today. Stuart Levine and Nancy O. Lurie, eds. Baltimore, Md.: Penguin Books.

———
1976    American Indians and Museums: A Love-Hate Relationship. *The Old Northwest* 2(3):235–251. Oxford, Ohio.

———
1978    The Indian Claims Commission. Pp. 97–110 in American Indians Today. J. Milton Yinger and George Eaton Simpson, eds. *The Annals of the American Academy of Political and Social Science* 436(March). Philadelphia.

———
1988    *see* Handbook Vol. 4 (1988:548–556)

Lurie, Theodora
1991    Shattering the Myth of the Vanishing American. *The Ford Foundation Newsletter* 22(3):1–5. New York.

Lussier, Antoine S., and D. Bruce Sealy, eds.
1978–1980   The Other Natives: The-Les Métis. 3 vols. Winnipeg, Man.: Métis Federation Press.

Lux, Maureen K.
2001    Medicine That Walks: Disease, Medicine, and Canadian Plains Native People, 1880–1940. Toronto: University of Toronto Press.

Lyman, Stanley David
1991    Wounded Knee 1973: A Personal Account. Floyd A. O'Neil, June K. Lyman, and Susan McKay, eds. Lincoln: University of Nebraska Press.

Lynch, G.I.
1991    Movement Toward Professional Excellence—Medical Services Branch Indian Health. Pp. 173–176 in Circumpolar Health 90. *Proceedings of the 8th International Congress*. Brian Postl, et al., eds. Winnipeg, Man.: University of Manitoba Press.

Lynge, Aqqaluk
1993    Inuit: The Story of the Inuit Circumpolar Conference. New ed. Nuuk, Greenland: Atuakkiorfik.

Lynnerup, Niels, Claus Andreasen, and Joel Berglund, eds.
2003    Mummies in a New Millennium. *Proceedings of the 4th World Congress on Mummy Studies, Nuuk, Greenland, September 4th to 10th, 2001.* Copenhagen, Denmark: Greenland National Museum and Archives, Danish Polar Center. (Title page has 2002 publication date; copyright date 2003.)

Lyons, Maurice
2005    The Growing Power of Tribal Economic Diversification. Pp. 18–20 in America Is Indian Country: Opinions and Perspectives from Indian Country Today. Jose Barreiro and Tim Johnson, eds. Golden, Colo.: Fulcrum Publishing.

Lyons, Murray
2006    Fear in the Forest: Failure of Pulp Mills Could Mean Major Job Losses Across Northern Saskatchewan. *Saskatoon Star-Phoenix*, January 21, 2006: E1. Saskatoon, Sask.

McAllester, David P.
1949    Peyote Music. New York: Viking Fund Publications in Anthropology.

McArthur, Douglas
1988    The New Aboriginal Economic Development Institutions: What Are They? Can They Help? (Indigenous Studies Research Centre, First Nations University of Canada, Catalogue # 53062-BS; Regina, etc., Sask.)

McAuliffe, Dennis
2006    [Reznet: November 2006.] (Unpublished essay, Missoula, Mont., in D. McAuliffe's possession.)

McCain, John
1989    *see* U.S. *Congressional Record* 1989

———
2006    [Statement of Senate Indian Affairs Committee Chairman, June 21, 2006.] (Transcript of Hearing Before the Committee on Senate Bill S480. Washington: U.S. Senate.)

McCarthy, Robert
2004    The Bureau of Indian Affairs and the Federal Trust Obligation to American Indians. *Brigham Young University Journal of Public Law* 19(1). Provo, Utah.

McCarty, Teresa L., et al.
2001    Indigenous Educators As Change Agents: Case Studies of Two Language Institute. Pp. 371–383 in National Indian Education Association: Preliminary Report on No Child Left Behind in Indian Country. *The Green Book of Language Revitalization in Practice.* Leanne Hinton and Kenneth Hale, eds. San Diego, Calif.: Academic Press.

———
2002    A Place To Be Navajo: Rough Rock and the Struggle for Self-Determination in Indigenous Schooling. *Sociocultural,*

*Political, and Historical Studies in Education.* Mahwah, N.J., and London: Lawrence Erlbaum Associates, Publishers.

McCaskill, Donald
1994        Education: Primary and Secondary U.S. Native Education; U.S. Indian Higher Education; Canadian Native Education. Pp. 855–913 in The Native North American Almanac: A Reference Work on Native North Americans in the United States and Canada. Duane Champagne, ed. Detroit, Washington, London: Gale Research, Inc.

McClanahan, Alexandra J., and Jangila D. Hillas
2001        Native Corporations: Building a Foundation for Alaska's Economic Destiny. Anchorage: Association of ANCSA Regional Corporation Presidents/CEOs.

McClintock, Walter
1937        Dances of the Blackfoot Indians. *Southwest Museum Leaflet* 7. Los Angeles.

McCoy, Donald R., and Richard T. Ruetten
1973        Quest and Response: Minority Rights and the Truman Administration. Lawrence, Kans.: University of Kansas Press.

McCoy, Padraic I.
2002–2003   The Land Must Hold the People: Native Modes of Territoriality and Contemporary Tribal Justifications for Placing Land Into Trust Through 25 C.F.R. Part 151. *American Indian Law Review* 27(2):421– 502. Norman, Okla.

McCoy, Ron
1981        Navajo Code Talkers of World War II: Indian Marines Befuddled the Enemy. *The American West* 18(6):67–75. Tuscon, Ariz.

McCulloch, Anne Merline
1994        The Politics of Indian Gaming: Tribe/State Relations and American Federalism. *Publius: The Journal of Federalism* 24(3):99–112. Philadelphia.

McCullogh, David
1992        Truman. New York: Simon and Schuster.

McCutcheon, Sean
1991        Electric Rivers: The Story of the James Bay Project. Montreal: Black Rose Books.

McDonnell, Janet A.
1991        The Dispossession of the American Indian, 1887–1934. Bloomington: Indiana University Press.

MacDougall, Pauleena
2004        The Penobscot Dance of Resistance: Tradition in the History of a People. Durham, N.H.: University of New Hampshire Press.

McFadden David, and Ellen N. Taubman
2004        Changing Hands: Art Without Reservation 1-Contemporary Native American Art from the Southwest. London: Merrell Publishers.

McFarlane, Peter
1993        Brotherhood to Nationhood: George Manuel and the Making of the Modern Indian Movement. Toronto: Between The Lines.

McGaa, Ed (Eagle Man)
1990        Mother Earth Spirituality: Native American Paths to Healing Ourselves and Our World. New York, San Francisco: Harper and Row.

McGovern, Dan
1995        The Campo Indian Landfill War: The Fight for Gold in California's Garbage. Norman: University of Oklahoma Press.

Macgregor, Gordon
1946        Warriors Without Weapons: A Study of the Society and Personality Development of the Pine Ridge Sioux. Chicago: University of Chicago Press. (Reprinted in 1975.)

McGuire, Mike
1997        [Taped interview with Mike McGuire, President of the Ontario Métis Aboriginal Association (OMAA), June 17, 1997.] (Recorded at Thunder Bay, Ont.)

McInnis, Edgar, and Michael Horn
1982        Canada: A Political and Social History. 4th ed. Toronto: Holt, Rinehart and Winston of Canada.

Mackay, S.
1947        Indian Affairs State Revealed by Government Committee. *The Saskatchewan Prince Albert Herald*, 17 May, 1947. Prince Albert, Sask.

McKay, Stan
1999        The Earth As Mother Birthing and Sustaining Life. Echoes: Justice Peace and Creation News. World Council of Churches. (Webpage: http://www.wcc-coe.org/wcc/what/jpc/echoes-16-01.html [3 August 2006].)

McKenna-McBride Commission, The
1916        *see* Canada. Royal Commission on Indian Affairs for the Province of British Columbia 1916

McKenzie, Kent, director
1961        The Exiles. Berkeley: UC Extension.

McKeown, C. Timothy
2002        Implementing a 'True Compromise': The Native American Graves Protection and Repatriation Act After Ten Years. Pp. 108–132 in The Dead and Their Possessions: Repatriation in Principle, Policy and Practice. Cressida Fforde, Jane Hubert, and Paul Turnbull, eds. *One World Archaeology* 43. New York and London: Routledge.

McKeown, C. Timothy, and Sherry Hutt
2003        In the Smaller Scope of Conscience: The Native American Graves Protection and Repatriation Act Twelve Years After. *UCLA Journal of Environmental Law and Policy* 21(2): 153–212. Los Angeles.

Mackie, Cam
1986        Some Reflections on Indian Economic Development. Pp. 211–226 in Arduous Journey: Canadian Indians and Decolonization. J. Rick Ponting, ed. Toronto: McClelland and Stewart.

Macklem, Patrick
1997        The Impact of Treaty 9 on Natural Resource Development in Northern Ontario. In: Aboriginal and Treaty Rights in Canada: Essays on Law, Equality, and Respect for Difference. Michael Asch, ed. Vancouver: University of British Columbia Press.

————
2001        Indigenous Difference and the Constitution of Canada. Toronto: University of Toronto Press.

MacLaine, Craig, and Michael S. Baxendale
1990        This Land Is Our Land: The Mohawk Revolt at Oka. Montreal: Optimum.

McLaughlin, Robert
1976        Who Owns the Land? A Native American Challenge. *Juris Doctor*, September:17–28. New York.

McManamon, Francis P.
2002        Repatriation in the USA: A Decade of Federal Agency Activities Under NAGPRA. Pp. 133–148 in The Dead and Their Possessions: Repatriation in Principle, Policy and Practice.

Cressida Fforde, Jane Hubert, and Paul Turnbull, eds. *One World Archaeology* 43. New York and London: Routledge.

McMaster, Gerald, and Clifford E. Trafzer
2004 Native Universes: Voices of Indian America. Washington: Smithsonian Institution.

McMillan, Alan D., and Eldon Yellowhorn
2004 First Peoples in Canada. Vancouver: Douglas and McIntyre.

McNally, Michael David
2006 The Indian Passion Play: Contesting the Real Indian in *Song of Hiawatha* Pageants, 1901–1965. *American Quarterly* 58(1):105–136. Baltimore, Md.

McNeary, Stephen A.
1976 Where Fire Came Down: Social and Economic Life of the Niska. (Ph.D. Dissertation in Anthropology, Bryn Mawr College, Bryn Mawr, Pa.)

McNeel, Jack
2006 Lack of Funding Threatens Museum of the Plains Indian. *Indian Country Today*, December 4, 2006. Canastota, N.Y. (Webpage: http://www.indiancountry.com)

McNeil, Kent
1989 Common Law Aboriginal Title. Oxford: Clarendon Press.

1998 Defining Aboriginal Title in the 90's: Has the Supreme Court Finally Got It Right? Toronto: Robarts Centre for Canadian Studies, York University.

2000 Sovereignty on the Northern Plains: Indian, European, American and Canadian Claims. *Journal of the West* 39(3):10–18. Los Angeles.

2000a Aboriginal Title and Section 88 of the *Indian Act. University of British Columbia Law Review* 34(1):159–194. Vancouver.

2001 Emerging Justice? Essays on Indigenous Rights in Canada and Australia. Saskatoon, Sask.: University of Saskatchewan Native Law Centre.

2001–2002 Extinguishment of Aboriginal Title in Canada: Treaties, Legislation and Judicial Discretion. *Ottawa Law Review* 33(2): 301–346. Ottawa.

2002 Self-Government and the Inalienability of Aboriginal Title. *McGill Law Journal* 47(3):473–510. Montreal.

2003 Culturally-Modified Trees, Indian Reserves and the Crown's Fiduciary Obligations. *The Supreme Court Law Review*, 2d series, 21:105–138. Toronto.

2004 The Vulnerability of Indigenous Land Rights in Australia and Canada. *Osgoode Hall Law Journal* 42(2):271–301. Toronto.

2005 Aboriginal Rights, Resource Development, and the Source of the Provincial Duty to Consult in *Haida Nation* and *Taku River. The Supreme Court Law Review*, 2d series, 29:447–460. Toronto.

2006 Aboriginal Title and the Supreme Court: What's Happening? *Saskatchewan Law Review* 69(2):281–308. Saskatoon, Sask.

2007 Judicial Approaches to Self-Government Since *Calder*: Searching for Doctrinal Coherence. In: Let It Be Done: *Calder*, Aboriginal Title and the Future of Indigenous Rights.

Hamar Foster, Heather Raven, and Jeremy Webber, eds. Vancouver: UBC Press.

2007a Legal Rights and Legislative Wrongs: Maori Claims to the Foreshore and Seabed. In: Maori Property Rights in the Foreshore and Seabed: The Latest Frontier. Claire Charters and Andrew Erueti, eds. Wellington, New Zealand: Victoria University of Wellington Press.

McNickle, D'Arcy
1936 The Surrounded. New York: Dodd, Mead. (Reprinted: see McNickle 1978.)

1949 They Came Here First: The Epic of the American Indian. Philadelphia: J.B. Lippincott.

1961–1962 Private Intervention. Pp. 208–215 in American Indians and Their Economic Development. Fred Voget, ed. *Human Organization*, Special Issue 20(4). Washington.

1970 Indians and Other Americans: Two Ways of Life Meet. New York: Harper and Row. (Originally publ. in 1959.)

1971 Indian Man: A Life of Oliver La Farge. Bloomington, Ind.: Indiana University Press.

1973 Native American Tribalism: Indian Survivals and Renewals. New York: Oxford University Press.

1978 The Surrounded. Albuquerque: University of New Mexico Press.

1978a Wind from an Enemy Sky. New York: Harper and Row.

1987 Runner in the Sun: A Story of Indian Maize. Afterword by Alfonso Ortiz. Albuquerque: University of New Mexico Press. (Originally publ. in 1954.)

1992 The Hawk Is Hungry and Other Stories. Tucson: University of Arizona Press.

McNiven, Ian J., and Lynette Russell
2005 Appropriated Pasts: Indigenous Peoples and the Colonial Culture of Archaeology. Blue Ridge Summit, Pa.: AltaMira Press.

McRoberts, Kenneth
1988 Quebec: Social Change and Political Crisis. 3d ed. *Canada in Transition Series*. Toronto: McClelland and Stewart. (Originally publ. in 1976.)

Madigan, LaVerne
1956 The American Indian Relocation Program. New York: The Association on American Indian Affairs.

Madill, Dennis
1981 British Columbia Treaties in Historical Perspectives. Ottawa: Research Branch, Corporate Policy, Indian and Northern Affairs Canada.

Maestas, John R., ed.
1976 Contemporary Native American Address. Provo, Utah: Brigham Young University.

Magnaghi, Russell M.
1998 Indian Slavery, Labor, Evangelization, and Captivity in the Americas: An Annotated Bibliography. *Native American Bibliography Series* 22. Lanham, Md., and London: The Scarecrow Press, Inc.

504

Mainville, Robert
2001    An Overview of Aboriginal and Treaty Rights and Compensation for Their Breach. Saskatoon: Purich Publishing.

Makseyn-Kelley, Stephanie A.
1993    Shota (Smoke), an Oglala Lakota Chief. Washington: Smithsonian Institution, National Museum of Natural History, Repatriation Office.

_____
1994    Non-Skeletal Human Remains Pertaining to the Cheyenne River Sioux Tribe. Washington: Smithsonian Institution, National Museum of Natural History, Repatriation Office.

_____
1994a   Ish-ta Cha-ne-aha (Puffing Eyes), A Chief of the Two Kettles Lakota. Washington: Smithsonian Institution, National Museum of Natural History, Repatriation Office.

_____
1996    Inventory and Assessment of Associated Funerary Objects in the National Museum of Natural History Affiliated with the Assiniboine. Washington: Smithsonian Institution, National Museum of Natural History, Repatriation Office.

_____
1998    Addendum to the Inventory and Assessment of Human Remains and Funerary Objects Potentially Affiliated with the Oglala Sioux Tribe in the National Museum of Natural History. Washington: Smithsonian Institution, National Museum of Natural History, Repatriation Office.

_____
1999    Inventory and Assessment of Human Remains and Funerary Objects Potentially Affiliated with the Brule Sioux in the National Museum of Natural History. Washington: Smithsonian Institution, National Museum of Natural History, Repatriation Office.

Makseyn-Kelley, Stephanie A., and Beverly Spriggs Byrd
1995    Inventory and Assessment of Human Remains and Associated Funerary Objects Affiliated with the Cheyenne River Sioux Tribe in the National Museum of Natural History. Washington: Smithsonian Institution, National Museum of Natural History, Repatriation Office.

_____
1997    Inventory and Assessment of Human Remains and Funerary Objects Potentially Affiliated with the Oglala Sioux Tribe in the National Museum of Natural History. Washington: Smithsonian Institution, National Museum of Natural History, Repatriation Office.

Makseyn-Kelley, Stephanie A., and Erica Bubniak Jones
1996    Inventory and Assessment of Remains From the Historic Period Potentially Affiliated with the Eastern Dakota in the National Museum of Natural History. Washington: Smithsonian Institution, National Museum of Natural History, Repatriation Office.

Malchy, B., et al.
1997    Suicide Among Manitoba's Aboriginal People, 1988 to 1994. *Canadian Medical Association Journal* 156(8):1133–1138. Ottawa.

Malcomson, Scott L.
2000    One Drop of Blood: The American Misadventure of Race. New York: Farrar Straus Giroux.

Manitoba Métis Federation
2004    Amended Statement of Claim Between Manitoba Métis Federation Inc., et al., and Attorney General of Canada. Winnipeg, Man.: Queen's Bench, Winnipeg Centre.

Mankiller, Wilma
1993    Mankiller: A Chief and Her People. New York: St. Martin's Press.

_____
2004    Every Day Is a Good Day. Golden, Colo.: Fulcrum Publishing.

Mann, Rudy
1987    Bingo 'Craze' Rips Native Population. *Kainai News*, February 5, 1987:5. Standoff, Alta.

Manuel, Frances, and Deborah Neff
2001    Desert Indian Woman. Tucson: University of Arizona Press.

Manuel, George
1972    Indian Economic Development: A Whiteman's Whitewash. Ottawa: National Indian Brotherhood.

Manuel, George, and Michael Posluns
1974    The Fourth World: An Indian Reality. Toronto: Collier Macmillan Canada, Ltd.

Mapatis, Elnora, et al.
1981    Kathad Ganavj. Peach Springs, Ariz.: The Hualapai Tribe.

Marchand, Paul, ed.
1991    Our Home and Native Land: A Film and Video Resource Guide for Aboriginal Canadians. Winnipeg, Man.: National Film Board of Canada.

Marino, Cesare
1990    *see* Handbook Vol. 7 (1990:169–179)

_____
1994    Reservations. Pp. 544–557 in Native America in the Twentieth Century: An Encyclopedia. Mary B. Davis, ed. New York and London: Garland Publishing.

Marks, Jonathan
1995    Commentary: The Human Genome Diversity Project. *Anthropology Newsletter* 36(4):72. Arlington, Va.

Marrs, Carl H.
2001    A Word from the President: Good News for CIRI Shareholders. *CIRI [Cook Inlet Region, Inc.] Newsletter* (May). Anchorage.

_____
2003    ANCSA, An Act of Self-Determination: Harnessing Business Endeavors To Achieve Alaska Native Goals. *Cultural Survival Quarterly* 27(3):28–33. Cambridge, Mass.

Marsden, Michael T., and Jack Nachbar
1988    *see* Handbook Vol. 4 (1988:607–616)

Marsden, Susan, Margaret Seguin Anderson, and Deanna Nyce
1999    Aboriginals: Tsimshian. In: Encyclopedia of Canada's Peoples. Paul Robert Magocsi, ed. Toronto: University of Toronto Press.

Marshall, Daniel
1999    Those Who Fell from the Sky: A History of the Cowichan Peoples. Duncan, B.C.: Cultural and Education Centre, Cowichan Tribes.

Martens, Patricia J., and T. Kue Young
1997    Determinants of Breastfeeding in Four Canadian Ojibwa Communities: A Decision-Making Model. *American Journal of Human Biology* 9(5):579–593.

Martens, Patricia J., et al.
2002    The Health and Health Care Use of Registered First Nations People Living in Manitoba: A Population-Based Study. Winnepeg, Man.: Manitoba Centre for Health Policy, University of Manitoba.

Martin, Calvin
1987    The American Indian and the Problem of History. New York: Oxford University Press.

Martin, Catherine Anne, dir.
2002    The Spirit of Annie Mae. Angela Baker, writer. Montreal: National Film Board of Canada.

Martin, M.
1981    Native American Medicine: Thoughts for Post-Traditional Healers. *Journal of the American Medical Association* 245(2):141–143. Chicago.

Martin-McGuire, Peggy
1999    Treaty Land Entitlement in Saskatchewan: A Context for the Creation of Urban Reserves. Pp. 53–77 in Urban Indian Reserves: Forging New Relationships in Saskatchewan. F. Laurie Barron and Joseph Garcea, eds. Saskatoon, Sask.: Purich Publishers.

Martin, Reed
2003    Native American Films Attempt to Crossover. *USA Today*, January 28, 2003. New York.

Martínez Cobo, José
1987    Study of the Problem of Discrimination Against Indigenous Populations. Vol. 5: Conclusions, Proposals, and Recommendations. *United Nations Document* No. E/CN. 4/Sub.2/1986/7/Add. 4. New York: United Nations.

Maslin, Janet
1989    A Cheyenne Mystic Who Transmutes Bitterness. *The New York Times*, March 24, 1989. New York.

Mason, W. Dale
[1981]    You Can Only Kick So Longé:AIM Leadership in Nebraska 1972–79. (Webpage: http://www.dickshovel.com/lsa23.html; viewed 1 March 2007.)

———
1983    The American Indian Movement. (M.A. Thesis in Political Science, University of Cincinnati, Cincinnati, Ohio.)

———
1996    Interest Group Federalism: Indian Gaming and the Place of Tribal Goverments in the American Political System. (Ph.D. Dissertation in Political Science, University of New Mexico, Albuquerque; published, in revised form: see Mason 2000.)

———
2000    Indian Gaming: Tribal Sovereignty and American Politics. Norman: University of Oklahoma Press.

Masten, Sue
2001    Indian Tribal Good Governance Practices as They Relate to Economic Development. (Statement of Sue Masten, President, National Congress of American Indians, Before the Senate Committee on Indian Affairs, *107th Congress. Senate* 15–19. Washington.)

Mathews, John Joseph
1932    Wah'kon-tah: The Osage and the White Man's Road. Norman: University of Oklahoma Press.

———
1934    Sundown. New York: Longmans, Green. (Reprinted: see Mathews 1988.)

———
1961    The Osages: Children of the Middle Waters. Norman: University of Oklahoma Press.

———
1988    Sundown. Introduction by Virginia H. Mathews. Norman: University of Oklahoma Press.

Matthiessen, Peter
1983    In the Spirit of Crazy Horse. New York: Viking Press. (Reprinted, 2d ed. in 1991.)

Matuz, Roger, ed.
1998    St. James Guide to Native North American Artists. Detroit, Mich.: St. James Press.

Mauger, Jeffrey E., and Janine Bowechop
2006    Tribal Collections Management at the Makah Cultural and Research Center. Pp. 57–64 in Living Homes for Cultural Expression: North American Native Perspectives on Creating Community Museums. Karen Coody Cooper and Nicolasa Sandoval, eds. Washington: Smithsonian Institution.

Maurer, Evan
2000    Presenting the American Indian: From Europe to America. Pp. 15–28 in The Changing Presentations of American Indian: Museums and Native Cultures. Michael Ames, ed. Washington and Seattle: National Museum of the American Indian, and University of Washington Press.

Mauzé, Marie
2003    Two Kwakwaka'wakw Museums: Heritage and Politics. Pp. 503–522 in Native Peoples and Tourism. Neil L. Whitehead, ed.; Larry Nesper, guest ed. *Ethnohistory* 50(3).

Mawhiney, Anne Marie
1994    Toward Aboriginal Self-Government: Relations Between Status and Indian Peoples and the Government of Canada, 1969–1984. New York: Garland Publishing, Inc.

Maxwell, Steve
2005    Tribal Museums: Native Places, Native Stories. *National Museum of the American Indian*, Summer:16–28. Washington.

May, Katja
1996    African Americans and Native Americans in the Creek and Cherokee Nations, 1830s to 1920s: Collision and Collusion. New York: Garland Publishing.

Mead, Frank, Samuel S. Hill, and Craig D. Atwood
2005    Handbook of Denominations in the United States. 12th ed. Nashville, Tenn.: Abingdon Press.

Meadows, William C.
2002    The Comanche Code Talkers of World War II. Austin, Tex.: The University of Texas Press.

Means, Russell
1980    For America to Live, Europe Must Die [originally published in *Mother Jones*, 1980]. Pp. 545–554 in Where White Men Fear to Tread: The Autobiography of Russell Means, by Russell Means with Marvin J. Wolf. New York: St. Martin's Press, 1995. (Reprinted in 1996.)

———, with Marvin J. Wolf
1995    Where White Men Fear To Tread: The Autobiography of Russell Means. New York: St. Martin's Press. (Reprinted in 1996.)

Medicine, Bea
2001    Learning to Be an Anthropologist and Remaining "Native." Chicago: University of Illinois Press.

Meijer Drees, Laurie
2002    The Indian Association of Alberta: A History of Political Action. Vancouver: University of British Columbia Press. (Reprinted: University of Washington Press, Seattle, 2003.)

Meinholtz, Rolland, et al.
1969    Indian Theatre: An Artistic Experiment in Progress. Santa Fe, N.Mex.: Institute of American Indian Arts.

Meister, Alan
2005–2006  Casino City's Indian Gaming Industry Report. (A Casino City Press Publication; Webpage: http://www.CasinoCity Press.com.)

Meister, Barbara, ed.
1996        Mending the Circle: A Native American Repatriation Guide. Understanding and Implementing NAGPRA and the Official Smithsonian and Other Repatriation Policies. New York: American Indian Ritual Object Repatriation Foundation.

Meister, Cary W.
1976        Demographic Consequences of Euro-American Contact on Selected American Indian Populations and Their Relationship to the Demographic Transition. *Ethnohistory* 23(2): 161–172.

Melmer, David
1996        Enrollment Orphans: Does Adoption Help? *Indian Country Today*, March 25, 1996:A1–A2. Canastota, N.Y. (Webpage: http://www.indiancountry.com)

1996a      FFJ Leader Jailed. *Indian Country Today*, June 11–18, 2006:A1, A3. Canastota, N.Y. (Webpage: http://www.indiancountry.com)

1996b      Fred Dakota Pleads Not Guilty. *Indian Country Today*, July 29–August 5, 1996:A2. Canastota, N.Y. (Webpage: http://www.indiancountry.com)

2006        A Fallen Soldier Is Laid To Rest [Army National Guard Cpl. Nathan Goodiron, 25, Hidatsa]. *Indian Country Today*, December 8, 2006. Canastota, N.Y. (Webpage: http://www.indiancountry.com)

Meriam, Lewis
1928        The Problem of Indian Administration. Baltimore, Md.: Johns Hopkins Press. (Reprinted: Johnson Reprint, New York, 1971.)

Merrell, James H.
1989        The Indians' New World: Catawbas and Their Neighbors from European Contact Through the Era of Removal. Chapel Hill, N.C.: University of North Carolina Press.

Merrill, William J., Edmund J. Ladd, and T.J. Ferguson
1993        The Return of the Ahayu:da: Lessons for Repatriation from Zuni Pueblo and the Smithsonian Institution. *Current Anthropology* 34(5):523–567. Chicago.

Messenger, Phyllis M., ed.
1989        The Ethics of Collecting Cultural Property: Whose Culture? Whose Property? Albuquerque: University of New Mexico Press.

Messerschmidt, Jim
1983        The Trail of Leonard Peltier. Boston: South End Press.

Métis Nation of Ontario (MNO)
2006        Métis Sash. (Webpage: http://www.metisnation.org/culture/culture_links/sash.html [16 June 2006].)

Métis National Council (MNC)
1999        [Draft for Discussion—MNC Definition of "Métis" Submitted by the Métis Rights Panel.] (Métis National Council, Ottawa.)

2002        Who Are the Métis? National Definition of Métis. (Webpage: http://www.metisnation.ca/who/definition.html)

2003        Latest Census Data Shows Huge Increase in Reporting of Metis Population: MNC Calls on Government To Answer This Latest Wake-up Call. (Webpage: http://www.metisnation.ca/PRESS/release03_STATS.html [31 January 2003].)

2006        Who Are the Métis? (Webpage: http://www.metisnation.ca/who/index.html [31 March and 11 July 2006].)

Metzler, William
1963        Relocation of the Displaced Worker. *Human Organization* 22(3):142–145. Washington.

Meyer-Arendt, Klaus J., and Rudi Hartmann, eds.
1998        Casino Gambling in America: Origins, Trends and Impacts. New York: Cognizant Communication Corporation.

Meyer, Leroy
2001        In Search of Native American Aesthetics. *Journal of Aesthetic Education (U.S.A.)* 35(4):25–46. Champaign, Ill.

Meyer, Melissa L.
1999        American Indian Blood Quantum Requirements: Blood Is Thicker Than Family. Pp. 231–249 in Over the Edge: Remapping the American West. Valerie J. Matsumoto and Blake Allmendinger, eds. Berkeley: University of California Press.

Michel, Karen Lincoln
1994        Congress Considers Native American Church Pleas on Peyote Use. *Dallas Morning News*, June 20, 1994:1A, 8A–9A. Dallas, Tex.

1998        Repression on the Reservation. *Columbia Journalism Review* 37(4):48–50. New York.

Middleton, Beth Rose, and Jonathan Kusel
2007        Northwest Economic Adjustment Initiative Assessment: Lessons Learned for American Indian Community and Economic Development. *Economic Development Quarterly* 21(2):165–178. Newbury Park, Calif.

Mihelich, John
2001        Smoke Signals? American Popular Culture and the Challenge to Hegemonic Images of American Indians in Native American Film. *Wicaso Sa Review* 16(2):129–137. Minneapolis.

Mihesuah, Devon A.
1993        Aquash, Anna Mae Pictou (1945–1976). Pp. 11–12 in Native American Women: A Biographical Dictionary. Gretchen M. Bateille, ed.; Laurie Lisa, ed. assistant. *Biographical Dictionaries of Minority Women*. New York and London: Garland Publishing.

1996        American Indians: Stereotypes and Realities. Regina, Sask.: Clarity International.

1996a     , ed.      Repatriation: An Interdisciplinary Dialogue. *American Indian Quarterly, Special Issue* 20(2). Lincoln, Nebr.

1998        Natives and Academics: Researching and Writing About American Indians. Lincoln: University of Nebraska Press.

2000        Repatriation Reader: Who Owns American Indian Remains? Lincoln and London: University of Nebraska Press.

Mihesuah, Devon A., and Angela Wilson, eds.
2004        Indigenizing the Academy: Transforming Scholarship and Empowering Communities. Lincoln: University of Nebraska Press.

Miles, Jack I.
1980        [Interview with Tom Holm, May 8, 1980.] (Oscar Rose Junior College, Midwest City, Okla.)

Miles, Tiya
2002        Uncle Tom Was an Indian: Tracing the Red in Black Slavery. Pp. 137–160 in Confounding the Color Line: The Indian-Black Experience in North America. James F. Brooks, ed. Lincoln and London: University of Nebraska Press.

2005      Ties That Bind: The Story of an Afro-Cherokee Family in Slavery and Freedom. Berkeley: University of California Press.

Miles, Tiya, and Celia E. Naylor-Ojurongbe
2004      *see* Handbook Vol. 14 (2004:753–759)

Miller, Carol
2001      Telling the Indian Urban: Representations in American Indian Fiction. Pp. 29–45 in American Indians and the Urban Experience. *Contemporary Native American Communities.* Susan Lobo and Kurt Peters, eds. Walnut Creek, Calif.: AltaMira Press.

Miller, David R.
1994      Definitional Violence and Plains Indian Reservation Life: Ongoing Challenges to Survival. Pp. 226–248 in Violence, Resistance, and Survival in the Americas. William B. Taylor and Franklin Pease, eds. Washington: Smithsonian Institution.

Miller, Donald B.
1993      Catawba Tribe Approves Settlement with South Carolina. Summary of Agreement in Principle to Settle the Land Claim of the Catawba Tribe of South Carolina. Catawba Tribe v. South Carolina: A History of Perseverance. *NARF Legal Review* 18(Winter/Spring). Boulder, Colo.

Miller, Dorothy Lonewolf, David de Jong, and Frances Abele
1994      Urbanization and Non-Reservation Populations: Non-Reservation Indians in the United States; Canadian Native Urbanization and Non-Reserve Populations. Pp. 605– 631 in The Native North American Almanac: A Reference Work on Native North Americans in the United States and Canada. Duane Champagne, ed. Detroit, Washington, London: Gale Research, Inc.

Miller, Frank
1971      Involvement in an Urban University. Pp. 313–340 in The American Indian in Urban Society. Jack O. Waddell and O. Michael Watson, eds. Boston: Little, Brown.

Miller, James R.
1991      Skyscrapers Hide the Heavens: A History of Indian-White Relations in Canada. Rev. ed. Toronto: University of Toronto Press. (Reprinted: see Miller 2000.)

1996      Shingwauk's Vision: A History of Native Residential Schools. Toronto: University of Toronto Press.

1997      Canada and the Aboriginal Peoples, 1867–1927. *Canadian Historical Association. Historical Booklet* 57. Ottawa.

2000      Skyscrapers Hide the Heavens: A History of Indian-White Relations in Canada. 3d ed. Toronto: University of Toronto Press.

2004      Petitioning the Great White Mother: First Nations' Political Organizations and Lobbying in London. Pp. 299–318 in Canada and the End of Empire. Philip Buckner, ed. Vancouver: University of British Columbia Press.

Miller, Mark E.
2004      Forgotten Tribes: Unrecognized Indians and the Federal Acknowledgment Process. Lincoln: University of Nebraska Press.

Miller, Robert J.
2001      Economic Development in Indian Country: Will Capitalism or Socialism Succeed? *Oregon Law Review* 80(3):757–861. Eugene, Oreg.

2005      The Doctrine of Discovery in American Indian Law. *Idaho Law Review* 42(1):1–122.

Milloy, John S.
1983      The Early Indian Acts: Development Strategy and Constitutional Change. Pp. 56–64 in As Long As the Sun Shines and Water Flows: A Reader in Canadian Native Studies. Ian A.L. Getty and Antoine S. Lussier, eds. Vancouver: University of British Columbia Press.

1999      A National Crime: The Canadian Government and the Residential School System, 1879–1986. Winnipeg, Man.: University of Manitoba Press.

Mills, Antonia, ed.
2005      "Hang Onto These Words": Johnny David's Delgamuukw Evidence. Toronto: University of Toronto Press.

Minges, Patrick, ed.
2004      Black Indian Slave Narratives: Real Voices, Real History. Winston-Salem, N.C.: John F. Blair Publishers.

Mitchell, Donald Craig
2001      Take My Land, Take My Life: The Story of Congress's Settlement of Alaska Native Land Claims, 1960–1974. Fairbanks: University of Alaska Press.

2003      Sold American: The Story of Alaska Natives and Their Land, 1867–1959. Fairbanks: University of Alaska Press.

Mitchell, Donald Craig, and Paul Tennant
1996      Government to Government: Aboriginal Peoples and British Columbia. In: For Seven Generations: An Information Legacy of the Royal Commission on Aboriginal Peoples (RCAP). CD-ROM. Ottawa: Libraxus. (Copyright: 1996–2007.)

Mitchell, Joseph
1960      The Mohawks in High Steel. Pp. 1–36 in Apologies to the Iroquois, by Edmund Wilson. New York: Farrar, Strauss, and Cudahy. (Chapter originally publ. in: *The New Yorker* 25(30): 38–53, 1949.)

Mitchell, Nancy Marie
1993      The Negotiated Role of Contemporary American Indian Artists: A Study in Marginality. (Ph.D. Dissertation in Anthropology, Stanford University, Stanford, Calif.)

Mitten, Lisa, ed.
2005–2006 Native American Organizations and Urban Indian Centers. (Webpage: http://www.nativeculturelinks.com/organizations .html)

MNC *see* Métis National Council (MNC)

MNO *see* Métis Nation of Ontario (MNO)

Molloy, Paula, and Javier Urcid
1998      Human Remains in the National Museum of Natural History Associated with the Battle Near Emigrant Springs, Oregon. Washington: Smithsonian Institution, National Museum of Natural History, Repatriation Office.

Molloy, Paula, and Ashley Wyant
1997      Inventory and Assessment of the Funerary Objects in the Pierite Collection. Washington: Smithsonian Institution, National Museum of Natural History, Repatriation Office.

Molloy, Paula, Beverly Byrd, and John W. Verano
1995      Inventory and Assessment of Native American Human Remains from the State of Connecticut in the National Museum of Natural History. Washington: Smithsonian Institution, National Museum of Natural History, Repatriation Office.

Molloy, Paula, Juliet Cleaves, and John W. Verano
1995        Inventory and Assessment of Human Remains from North Central Montana in the Museum of Natural History. Washington: Smithsonian Institution, National Museum of Natural History, Repatriation Office.

Molloy, Paula, et al.
1996        Inventory and Assessment of Human Remains Identified As Nez Perce in the National Museum of Natural History. Washington: Smithsonian Institution, National Museum of Natural History, Repatriation Office.

————
1998        Addendum to Inventory and Assessment of Human Remains Identified As Nez Perce in the National Museum of Natural History. Washington: Smithsonian Institution, National Museum of Natural History, Repatriation Office.

————
2000        Inventory and Assessment of a Stone Pendant (A017905) Requested by the Mohegan Tribe. Washington: Smithsonian Institution, National Museum of Natural History, Repatriation Office.

Molloy, Tom
2000        The World Is Our Witness: The Historic Journey of the Nisga'a Into Canada. Foreword by John Ralston Saul. Calgary, Alta.: Fifth House Publishers.

Momaday, N. Scott
1968        House Made of Dawn. New York: Harper and Row. (See also: Morse, Richardson, dir., 1972.)

————
1969        Way to Rainy Mountain. Albuquerque: University of New Mexico Press.

————
1975        The Man Made of Words. Pp. 96–110 in Literature of the American Indians: Views and Interpretations: A Gathering of Indian Memories, Symbolic Contexts, and Literary Criticism. Edited, with an Introduction and Notes, by Abraham Chapman. New York: Meridian/New American Library.

————
1976        The Names: Memoir. New York: Harper and Row. (Reprinted: University of Arizona Press, Arizona, 1987, 1996.)

————
1992        Carriers of the Dream Wheel. Pp. 26–27 in In the Presence of the Sun: Stories and Poems, 1961–1991. New York: St. Martin's Press.

Monette, Gerald
1986        [Interview concerning Turtle Mountain Community College, November 23, 1986. Conducted by Wayne J. Stein, Reno, Nev.] (Text of interview in Department of Native American Studies, Montana State University, Bozeman, Mont.)

Monsalve, M. Victoria, et al.
2002        Molecular Analysis of the Kwäday Dän Ts'finchi Ancient Remains Found in a Glacier in Canada. American Journal of Physical Anthropology 119(3):288–291. [New York, etc.]

Montezuma, Carlos
1915        Let My People Go: Dr. Montezuma Speaking in the Interest of His Race, the American Indians. Chicago: Hawthorne Press.

Montour, Louis T., Ann C. Macaulay, and Naomi Adelson
1989        Diabetes Mellitus in Mohawks of Kahnawake, PQ: A Clinical and Epidemiologic Description. Canadian Medical Association Journal 141(6):549–552. Ottawa.

Monture-Angus, Patricia A.
1999        Journeying Forward: Dreaming First Nations' Independence. Halifax, N.S.: Fernwood Publishing.

Moodie, Douglas
2003        Thinking Outside the 20th Century Box: Revisiting Mitchell—Some Comments on the Politics of Judicial Law-Making in the Context of Aboriginal Self-Government. Ottawa Law Review 35(1):1–41. Ottawa.

————
2004        Aboriginal Maritime Title in Nova Scotia: An "Extravagant and Absurd Idea?" University of British Columbia Law Review 37(2):495–540. Vancouver.

Mooney, James
1897        The Kiowa Peyote Rite. Der Urquell, n.s. 1:329–333. Leyden, The Netherlands.

————
1898        Calendar History of the Kiowa Indians. Pp. 129–468 in Pt. 1 of 17th Annual Report of the Bureau of American Ethnology [for] 1895–'96. Washington: Smithsonian Institution; U.S. Government Printing Office. (Reprinted, with an Introduction by John C. Ewers: Classics of Smithsonian Anthropology, Smithsonian Institution Press, Washington, 1979.)

————
1928        The Aboriginal Population of America North of Mexico. John R. Swanton, ed. Smithsonian Miscellaneous Collections 80(7):1–40, (Publication 2955). Washington: Smithsonian Institution; U.S. Government Printing Office. (Photocopy: University Microfilms International, Ann Arbor, Mich., 1980. Microfiche: Lost Cause Press, Louisville, Ky., 1989. See also: Ubelaker, Douglas H. 1976.)

Moor, Paul
1973        Europe's First Sight of the American Indians. The Times of London, November 7, 1973. London.

Moore, John H.
1993        How Giveaways and Pow-wows Redistribute the Means of Subsistence. Pp. 240–269 in Political Economy of North American Indians. John H. Moore, ed. Norman: University of Oklahoma Press.

Moore, M., H. Forbes, and L. Henderson
1990        The Provision of Primary Health Services Under Band Control: The Montreal Lake Case. Native Studies Review 6(1):153–164. Saskatoon, Sask.

Moore, MariJo, ed.
2003        Genocide of the Mind: New Native American Writing. Foreword by Vine Deloria, Jr. New York: Thunder's Mouth Press/Nation Books.

Moore, Steven C., and Jack Trope
1989        An Unwanted Crusade: The State of Oregon's Persecution of the Native American Church. Indian Law Support Center Reporter 12(8/9):1–11. Boulder, Colo., [etc.]

Moquin, Wayne
1973        Great Documents in American Indian History. New York: Praeger.

Morantz, Toby
2002        The Whiteman's Gonna Getcha: The Colonial Challenge to the Crees in Quebec. Montreal: McGill-Queen's University Press.

Morehouse, Thomas A.
1988        The Alaska Native Claims Settlement Act, 1991 and Tribal Government. University of Alaska. Institute of Social and Economic Research. Occasional Paper 19. Anchorage.

————
1988–1989   The Alaska Native Claims Settlement Act, 1991. Alaska Native Magazine 6(3):34–45. Anchorage.

Morgan, George R.
1972–1974   [Recorded Sales of Peyote by Registered Dealers.] (Manuscript notes, courtesy of Omer C. Stewart.)

1983    Hispano-Indian Trade of an Indian Ceremonial Plant, Peyote (*Lophophora williamsii*), on the Mustang Plains of Texas. *Journal of Ethnopharmacology* 9(23):319–321. [Amsterdam, etc.]

Morgan, George R., and Omer C. Stewart
1984    Peyote Trade in South Texas. *Southwestern Historical Quarterly* 87(3):270–296. Austin, Tex.

Morgan, Mindy J.
2005    Redefining the Ojibwe Classroom: Indigenous Language Programs Within Large Research Universities. *Anthropology and Education Quarterly* 36(1):96–103. Washington.

Morgan, Richard
2002    [Executive Order Creates Advocacy Tools for Tribal Colleges.] *The Chronicle of Higher Education Daily News*, July 8, 2002.

Morin, Larry
1999    [Letter to the Honorable Wayne Swartz from Bureau of Indian Affairs, Minneapolis Area Office, dated May 13, 1999, re Williamson-Edward v. Babbitt, Case No. 2:96-CV-294 [W.D. Mich.], and Resolutions KB-467-95 and KB-501-95.) (Webpage: http://www.baragarose.tripod.com/bia-case/bia-answer.htm [25 March 2006].)

Morin, Michel
1997    L'usurpation de la souveraineté autochtone: le cas des peuples de la Nouvelle-France et des colonies anglaises de l'Amérique du Nord. Motréal: Boréal.

Morris, Alexander
1880    The Treaties of Canada with the Indians of Manitoba and the North-West Territories; Including the Negotiations on Which They Were Based, and Other Information Thereto. Toronto: Belfords, Clarke and Co. (Reprinted in 1971, 1979; see also: Morris 1991.)

1991    The Treaties of Canada with the Indians of Manitoba and the Northwest Territories. Toronto: Fifth House Publishers. (Originally publ. in 1880.)

Morris-Carlsten, Traci L.
2005    Trickster in Contemporary Native Amerian Art and Thought: The Indigenous Cultural Language of Bob Haozous. *American Indian Art Magazine* 30(4):78–85. Scottsdale, Ariz.

Morris, Irvin
1997    From the Glittering World: A Navajo Story. Norman: University of Oklahoma Press.

Morrison, Dane Anthony, ed.
1997    American Indian Studies: An Interdisciplinary Approach to Contemporary Issues. New York: Peter Lang.

Morrison, R. Bruce, and Antoine S. Lussier, eds.
1986    Native Peoples: The Canadian Experience. Toronto: McClelland and Stewart.

Morse, Bradford W.
1997    Permafrost Rights: Aboriginal Self-Government and the Supreme Court in *R. v. Pamajewon*. *McGill Law Journal* 42(4):1012–1042. Montreal.

Morse, Eric W.
1969    Fur Trade Canoe Routes of Canada: Then and Now. Ottawa: Queen's Printer. (Reprinted, 2d ed.: University of Toronto Press, Toronto, 1979.)

Morse, Jedidiah
1822    Report to the Secretary of War of the United States on Indian Affairs. New Haven, Conn.: S. Converse.

Morse, Richardson, director
1972    Screenplay: *House Made of Dawn*, by N. Scott Momaday (1968). New York: New Line Video.

Mourning Dove (Catherine Quintasket)
1927    Co-ge-we-a, the Half-Blood: A Depiction of the Great Montana Cattle Range. Boston: Four Seas Company. (Reprinted: see Mournig Dove 1981.)

1981    Cogewea, the Half-Blood: A Depiction of the Great Montana Cattle Range. Introduction by Dexter Fisher (Alice Poindexter). Lincoln: University of Nebraska Press.

Mudar, Karen M.
1998    Inventory and Assessment of Human Remains from Cape Denbigh, Bering Straits Native Corporation, Alaska, in the National Museum of Natural History. Washington: Smithsonian Institution, National Museum of Natural History, Repatriation Office.

1998a   Non-Skeletal Human Remains Requested by the Family of Mr. Jim Keki (Swanson Harbor Jim), Hoonah, Alaska in the NMNH. Washington: Smithsonian Institution, National Museum of Natural History, Repatriation Office.

Mudar, Karen M., Erica Bubniak-Jones, and Stuart Speaker
1995    Inventory and Assessment of Human Remains and Associated Funerary Objects from Wainright, Alaska, in the National Museum of Natural History. Washington: Smithsonian Institution, National Museum of Natural History, Repatriation Office.

Mudar, Karen M., Erica Bubniak-Jones, and John W. Verano
1997    Inventory and Assessment of Human Remains from the Hand Site (44SN22), Southhampton County Virginia, in the National Museum of Natural History. Washington: Smithsonian Institution, National Museum of Natural History, Repatriation Office.

Mudar, Karen M., Stuart Speaker, and Erica Bubniak-Jones
1996    Inventory and Assessment of Human Remains and Associated Funerary Objects from Point Hope, Arctic Slope Native Corporation, in the National Museum of Natural History. Washington: Smithsonian Institution, National Museum of Natural History, Repatriation Office.

Mudar, Karen M., Stuart Speaker, and Elizabeth Miller
1996    Inventory and Assessment of Human Remains from the Geographical Territory of the NANA Regional Corporation, Alaska, in the National Museum of Natural History. Washington: Smithsonian Institution, National Museum of Natural History, Repatriation Office.

Mudar, Karen M., et al.
1996    Inventory and Assessment of Human Remains and Associated Funerary Objects from Northeastern Norton Sound, Bering Straits Native Corporation, Alaska, in the National Museum of Natural History. Washington: Smithsonian Institution, National Museum of Natural History, Repatriation Office.

———, et al.
1996a   Inventory and Assessment of Human Remains and Associated Funerary Objects from the Post-Contact Period in Barrow, Alaska, in the National Museum of Natural History. Washington: Smithsonian Institution, National Museum of Natural History, Repatriation Office.

———, et al.
1997    Inventory and Assessment of Human Remains on St. Lawrence Island, Bering Straits Native Corporation, Alaska, in the National Museum of Natural History. Washington: Smithsonian Institution, National Museum of Natural History, Repatriation Office.

Mudd, John O.
1972 Jurisdiction and the Indian Credit Problem: Considerations for a Solution. *Montana Law Review* 33(2):307–316. Missoula, Mont.

Mullis, Angela, and David Kamper, eds.
2000 Indian Gaming: Who Wins? *Contemporary American Indian Issues* 9; *Native American Politics Series* 6. Los Angeles: UCLA American Indian Studies Center.

Mulrennan, Monica E.
1998 Great Whale: Lessons from a Power Struggle. Pp. 15–31 in A Casebook of Environmental Issues in Canada. New York: John Wiley and Sons. (Copyright: 1997.)

Mulroy, Kevin
1993 Freedom on the Border: The Seminole Maroons in Florida, the Indian Territory, Coahuila, and Texas. Lubbock, Tex.: Texas Tech University Press.

———
2004 *see* Handbook Vol. 14 (2004:465–477)

Murie, James R.
1914 Pawnee Indian Societies. *American Museum of Natural History Anthropological Papers* 11(7):543–644. New York. (Bound with other monographs in: Societies of the Plains Indians. Clark Wissler, ed., New York, 1916.)

———
1989 Ceremonies of the Pawnee. 2 Pts. Pt. I: The Skiri; Pt. II: The South Bands. Edited with an Introduction by Douglas R. Parks. Lincoln and London: University of Nebraska Press for the American Indian Studies Research Institute, Indiana University. (Originally publ. in 1981.)

Murphy, James, and Sharon M. Murphy
1981 Let My People Know: American Indian Journalism, 1828–1978. Norman: University of Oklahoma Press.

Murray, Laura J.
1996 "Pray Sir, Consider a Little": Rituals of Subordination and Strategies of Resistance in the Letters of Hezekiah Calvin and David Fowler to Eleazar Wheelock. Pp. 15–41 in Early Native American Writing: New Critical Essays. Helen Jaskoski, ed. Foreword by A. LaVonne Brown Ruoff. Cambridge, Mass.: Cambridge University Press.

Myer, Dillon S.
1951 The Program of the Bureau of Indian Affairs. *The Journal of Negro Education* 20(3):346–353.

———
1953 Indian Administration: Problems and Goals. *Social Service Review* 27(June):191–209.

Myerhoff, Barbara G.
1974 Peyote Hunt: The Sacred Journey of the Huichol Indians. Ithaca, N.Y.: Cornell University Press.

Myers, Robert
1997 Mayan Indian Women Find Their Place Is On the Stage. *New York Times*, September 28, 1997:4, 12. New York.

Myers, Ted, et al.
1993 The Ontario First Nations AIDS and Healthy Lifestyle Survey. Toronto: University of Toronto, Department of Health Administration.

Nabokov, Peter
1981 Indian Running: Native American History and Tradition. Santa Barbara, Calif.: Capra Press. (Reprinted: Ancient City Press, Santa Fe, N.Mex., 1987.)

———
2006 Where Lightning Strikes: The Lives of American Indian Sacred Places. New York: Viking Penguin.

Nagel, Joane
1996 American Indian Ethnic Renewal: Red Power and the Resurgence of Identity and Culture. Oxford and New York: Oxford University Press.

Nagel, Joane, and Troy Johnson
1994 Introduction. Pp. 1–8 in Special Edition: Alcatraz Revisited: The 25th Anniversary of the Occupation, 1969–1971. Joane Nagel and Troy Johnson, eds. *American Indian Culture and Research Journal* 18(4). Los Angeles.

NAHO *see* National Aboriginal Health Organization (NAHO)

NAIMA *see* North American Indian Museums Association (NAIMA)

Napoleon, Val
2001 Extinction by Number: Colonialism Made Easy. *Canadian Journal of Law and Society* 16(1):111–145. Montreal.

Nash, Gary B.
1974 Red, White, and Black: The Peoples of Early America. Englewood Cliffs, N.J.: Prentice-Hall.

Nash, Gerald D.
1977 The American West in the Twentieth Century: A Short History of an Urban Oasis. Albuquerque: University of New Mexico Press.

———
1979 The Great Depression and World War II: Organizing America, 1933–1945. New York: St. Martin's Press.

Nash, Philleo
1949 [Interview.] (White House File, 1946–1953, Box 44—Indians: Proposed Presidential Commission, Philleo Nash Papers, Harry S. Truman Library, Independence, Mo.)

———
1949a [Memorandum to David K. Niles, dated October 11, 1949.] (White House File, 1946–1953, Box 44—Indians: Proposed Presidential Commission, Philleo Nash Papers, Harry S. Truman Library, Independence, Mo.)

———
1988 *see* Handbook Vol. 4 (1988:264–275)

Náshdóí yáázh [Lions Cubs]
1972 *see* National Geographic Society 1972

Nason, James D.
2001 A New Challenge, A New Opportunity. Pp. 9–13 in Contaminated Collections: Preservation, Access and Use: Preservation of Native American and Historical Natural History Collections Contaminated with Pesticide Residues. *Proceedings of a Symposium Held at the National Conservation Training Center (NTC), Sheperdstown, West Virginia, April 6–9, 2001.* Jessica S. Johnson, ed. *Collection Forum* 17(1–2). [Pittsburgh, Pa.: Society for the Preservation of Natural History Collections.]

National Aboriginal Capital Corporation Association (NACCA)
2005 Annual Report, 2005. Ottawa: National Aboriginal Capital Corporation Association.

National Aboriginal Health Organization (NAHO)
2004 First Nations and Inuit Regional Health Surveys, 1997. Ottawa: National Aboriginal Health Organization.

National Association of Tribal Historic Preservation Officers (NATHPO)
2005 Tribal Consultation: Best Practices in Historic Preservation. Washington: National Association of Tribal Historic Preservation Officers.

National Center for Health Statistics (NCHS)
2001 *National Vital Statistics Reports* 49(April 17, 2001):1–99. Hyattsville, Md.

National Gambling Impact Study Commission, The
1999    Final Report. Washington: The National Gambling Impact Study Commission.

National Geographic Society
1972    Náshdóí yáázh: Bił Hazí'aadi Nooyééł [Lions Cubs: Growing Up in the Wild]. Washington: National Geographic Society. (In the Navajo language; also published in other languages, incl.: Chinese, German, Japanese, etc., under translated titles.]

National Indian Association
1888–1951   *The Indian's Friend* [Vols. 1–63]. Philadelphia, [etc.]: National Indian Association.

National Indian Brotherhood
1977    A Strategy for the Socio-economic Development of Indian People: Executive Summary of the National Report. Ottawa: National Indian Brotherhood.

National Indian Education Association (NIEA)
2005    Hearings on the "No Child Left Behind" Act in Indian Country. *National Indian Education Association* 34(11/Summer). Washington.

2005a   Preliminary Report on No Child Left Behind in Indian Country. Washington: National Indian Education Association.

National Indian Gaming Association (NIGA)
2004    An Analysis of the Economic Impact of Indian Gaming in 2004. Washington: National Indian Gaming Association.

2006    Homepage. (Webpage: http://www.indiangaming.org/index .shtml [24 June 2006].)

National Indian Gaming Commission (NIGC)
2006    Tribal Data. (Webpage: http://www.nigc.gov/TribalData/ tabid/67/Default.aspx [2 July 2006].)

National Indian Health Board (NIHB)
1998    Tribal Perspective on Indian Self-Determination and Self-Governance in Health Care Management. *National Indian Health Board Health Reporter* 8(2). Denver, Colo.

National Indian Youth Council (NIYC)
1970    Proposal for an American Indian Theater Company. [Albuquerque: National Indian Youth Council.]

National Museum of Natural History (NMNH) *see* Smithsonian Institution. National Museum of Natural History (NMNH)

National Museum of the American Indian (NMAI) *see* Smithsonian Institution. National Museum of the American Indian (NMAI)

National Park Service *see* U.S. National Park Service

Native American Contractors Association (NACA)
2005    Cultural, Social, and Economic Benefits of Government Contracting and the 8(a) Program for Alaska Natives and the Economy. (Unpublished document, Native American Contractos Association, Washington.)

Native American Graves Protection and Repatriation Review Committee
2000    Recommendations Regarding the Disposition of Culturally Unidentifiable Native American Human Remains. *Federal Register*, Vol. 65, No. 111:36462–36464. Washington: U.S. Government Printing Office.

Native American Organizations and Urban Indian Centers (Webpage)
2005–2006   *see* Mitten, Lisa, ed. 2005–2006

Native American Rights Fund (NARF)
1984    Catawba Tribe v. South Carolina: From Augusta to Richmond—One Tribe's Struggle Continues. *NARF Legal Review* 18(Winter/Spring). Boulder, Colo.

2001    Klamath Water Case Gets Slippery. *NARF Newsletter*, Spring 2001:1. Boulder, Colo.

Native American Theater Ensemble, The
1973    A Proposal for a Second Developmental Phase for the Native American Theater Ensemble. [New York.]

1974    Annual Report: June 1, 1973–May 31, 1974. [New York.]

1974a   Right Now About NATE. [New York.]

1975    A Proposal for Funding for the Native American Theater Ensemble Encompassing Two Years of Creative Work in Indian Country. [Oklahoma City.]

Native Law Centre
1979–   *Canadian Native Law Reporter*. Zandra L. Wilson, ed. Saskatoon, Sask.: University of Saskatchewan Native Law Centre.

1980–1991   Canadian Native Law Cases. 9 vols. Brian Slattery and Sheila Stelck, comps. and eds. Saskatoon, Sask. University of Saskatchewan Native Law Centre.

Natural Resouces Canada *see* Canada. Natural Resources Canada

*Navajo Times*
1960–1984   *Navajo Times*, Vol. 1–48. Window Rock, Ariz.: Navajo Tribe.

Naylor-Ojurongbe, Celia E.
2002    "Born and Raised among These People, I Don't Want to Know Any Other": Slaves' Acculturation in Nineteenth-Century Indian Territory. Pp. 161–191 in Confounding the Color Line: The Indian-Black Experience in North America. James F. Brooks, ed. Lincoln and London: University of Nebraska Press.

Naysmith, John K.
1976    Land Use and Land Policy in Northern Canada. *INA Publication* QS-8091-000-EE-A1. Ottawa: Indian and Northern Affairs; Minister of Supply and Services Canada.

Nebelkopf, Ethan, and Mary Phillips, eds.
2004    Healing and Mental Health for Native Americans. Blue Ridge Summit, Pa.: AltaMira Press.

Neely, Sharlotte
1991    Snowbird Cherokees: People of Persistence. Athens, Ga., and London: The University of Georgia Press.

Neihardt, John G.
1932    Black Elk Speaks: Being the Life Story of a Holy Man of the Ogalala Sioux; As Told to John G. Neihardt. New York: William Morrow. (Reprinted: see Neihardt 1961.)

1961    Black Elk Speaks: Being the Life Story of a Holy Man of the Oglala Sioux; As Told Through John G. Neihardt (Flaming Rainbow). Illustrated by Standing Bear. With a New Preface. Lincoln: University of Nebraska Press. (Reprinted: see Neihardt 1979.)

1979    Black Elk Speaks: Being the Life Story of a Holy Man of the Oglala Sioux; As Told Through John G. Neihardt (Flaming Rainbow). Illustrated by Standing Bear. With an Introduction by Vine Deloria, Jr. Lincoln: University of Nebraska Press. (See also: DeMallie, Raymond J., ed. 1984.)

Neils, Elaine M.
1971    Reservation to City: Indian Migration and Federal Relocation. Chicago: University of Chicago Geography Department.

Nelson, Dana D.
1996        ("I Speak Like a Fool But I Am Constrained"): Samson
            Occom's *Short Narrative* and Economies of the Racial Self.
            Pp. 42–65 in Early Native American Writing: New Critical
            Essays. Helen Jaskoski, ed. Foreword by A. LaVonne
            Brown Ruoff. Cambridge, Mass.: Cambridge University
            Press.

Nelson, Ralph
1970        Massacre at Sand Creek. *Films and Filming* 16(6):26–27.
            London.

Nelson, Robert M.
2006        A Guide to Native American Studies Programs in the United
            States and Canada. (Webpage: http://www.oncampus.rich-
            mond.edu/faculty/ASAIL/guide/guide.html)

Nesper, Larry
2003        Simulating Culture: Being Indian for Tourists in Lac du
            Flambeau's Wa-Swa-Gon Indian Bowl. Pp. 447–472 in
            Native Peoples and Tourism. Neil L. Whitehead, ed.; Larry
            Nesper, guest ed. *Ethnohistory* 50(3).

Nettl, Bruno
1953        Observations on Meaningless Peyote Song Texts. *Journal of
            American Folklore* 66(260):161–164. [Boston, New York,
            etc.]

Neuberger, Richard L.
1942        On the Warpath. *Saturday Evening Post* 215(17):79. New
            York.

1942a       The American Indian Enlists. *Asia and the Americas* 42
            (November):628–631. New York.

Neville, G.W., ed. and comp.
1970        *see* Canada. Department of Indian Affairs and Northern
            Development (DIAND) 1970

New, Lloyd H.
1969        Credo for American Indian Theatre. In: Indian Theatre: An
            Artistic Experiment in Progress, by Rolland Meinholtz et al.
            Santa Fe, N.Mex.: Institute of American Indian Arts.

New Mexico Indian Casinos (Webpage)
2006        *see* 500 Nations 2006 [first entry under letter "F"]

*New York Times, The*
1942–1945   [Articles on American Indian participation in World War II.]
            New York.

Newcomb, Steven T.
1993        The Evidence of Christian Nationalism in Federal Indian
            Law: The Doctrine of Discovery, Johnson v. M'Intosh, and
            Plenary Power. *New York University Review of Law and
            Social Change* 20(2):303–341. New York.

2005        On the Rightful Political Heritage of Native Nations. *Indige-
            nous Peoples' Journal of Law, Culture & Resistance* 2(1):
            1–10. Los Angeles.

Newhouse, David R.
2000        From the Tribal to the Modern: The Development of Mod-
            ern Aboriginal Societies. Pp. 395–409 in Expressions in
            Canadian Native Studies. Ron F. Laliberte, et al., eds.
            Saskatoon, Sask.: University Extension Press, University of
            Saskatchewan.

2005        Hidden in Plain Sight: Aboriginal Contributions to Canada
            and Canadian Identity: Creating a New Indian Problem. Pre-
            sentation: First Nations, First Thoughts, 5/6 May 2004. Edin-
            burgh, Scotland: Centre of Canadian Studies.

Newhouse, David R., and Evelyn J. Peters, eds.
2003        Not Strangers in These Parts: Urban Aboriginal Peoples.
            Ottawa: Policy Research Initiative.

Newhouse, David R., Kevin Fitzmaurice, and Yale D. Belanger, eds.
2005        Creating a Seat at the Table: Aboriginal Programming at
            Canadian Heritage. Ottawa: Canadian Heritage.

Newhouse, David R., Don McCaskill, and John Milloy
2002        Culture, Tradition, and Evolution: The Department of Native
            Studies at Trent University. Pp. 61–82 in Native American
            Studies in Higher Education: Models for Collaboration
            Between Universities and Indigenous Nations. Duane Cham-
            pagne and Jay Stauss, eds. Walnut Creek, Calif.: AltaMira
            Press.

Newman, Dwight G.
2005        *Tsilhqot'in Nation v. British Columbia* and Civil Justice:
            Analyzing the Procedural Interaction of Evidentiary Princi-
            ples and Aboriginal Oral History. *Alberta Law Review*
            43(2):433–449. Edmonton, Alta.

Newton, Nell Jessup
1980        At the Whim of the Sovereign: Aboriginal Title Reconsid-
            ered. *Hastings Law Journal* 31(1):1215–1285. San Francisco.

1992        Indians Claims in the Courts of the Conqueror. *American
            University Law Review* 41(1):753–854. Washington.

_____, ed.
2005        *see* Cohen, Felix S. 2005

Newton, Nell Jessup, and Shawn Frank
1994        Gaming. Pp. 205–207 in Native America in the Twentieth
            Century: An Encyclopedia. Mary B. Davis, ed. New York and
            London: Garland Publishing.

Niatum, Duane
1975        Carriers of the Dream Wheel: Contemporary Native Amer-
            ican Poetry. New York: Harper and Row.

Nicks, Trudy, and Kenneth Morgan
1985        Grande Cache: The Historic Development of an Indigenous
            Alberta Métis Population. Pp. 163–181 in The New Peoples:
            Being and Becoming Métis in North America. Jacqueline
            Peterson and Jennifer S.H. Brown, eds. *Manitoba Studies in
            Native History* 1. Winnipeg, Man.: The University of Mani-
            toba Press.

Niezen, Ronald
1998        Defending the Land: Sovereignty and Forest Life in James
            Bay Cree Society. *Cultural Survival Studies in Ethnicity and
            Change*. Boston, London, [etc.]: Allyn and Bacon.

2000        Recognizing Indigenism: Canadian Unity and the Interna-
            tional Movement of Indigenous Peoples. *Comparative Stud-
            ies in Society and History* 42(1):119–148. London and New
            York.

2000        Spirit Wars: Native North American Religions in the Age of
            Nation Building. Berkeley and Los Angeles: University of
            California Press.

2003        The Origins of Indigenism: Human Rights and the Politics
            of Identity. Berkeley and Los Angeles: University of Califor-
            nia Press.

2005        Digital Identity: The Construction of Virtual Selfhood
            in the Indigenous Peoples' Movement. *Comparative Stud-
            ies in Society and History* 47(3):532–551. London and New
            York.

Niigon Technologies Ltd.
[2006]     Competitive Advantages. (Located within the Community of Moose Deer Point First Nation, Ontario. Webpage: http://www.niigon.com/comp_adv.htm [19 June 2006].)

Nisga'a Final Agreement
1999 (rev. 2001) *see* Hurley, Mary C., comp. 1999 (rev. 2001)

Niver, Kent R., comp.
1971     Biograph Bulletins: 1896–1908. Bebe Bergsten, ed. Los Angeles: Locare Research Group.

Nixon, Richard M.
1970     [Special Presidential Message to Congress on Indian Affairs.] Washington: The White House.

Noble, Brian
2002     Nitooii—The Same That Is Real: Parallel Practice, Museums, and the Repatriation of Piikani Customary Authority. *Anthropologica* 44(1):113–130. Ottawa.

Norcini, Marilyn
2006     Edward P. Dozier: The Paradox of the American Indian Anthropologist. Tucson: The University of Arizona Press.

Norris, Mary Jane
1990     The Demography of Aboriginal People in Canada. Pp. 33–59 in Ethnic Demography: Canadian Immigrant, Racial and Cultural Variations. Shiva S. Halli, Frank Trovato, and Leo Driedger, eds. Ottawa: Carleton University Press.

_____
1998     Canada's Aboriginal Languages. *Statistics Canada Catalogue* 11-008; *Canadian Social Trends* 51(Winter):9–16. Ottawa: Minister Responsible for Statistics Canada.

Norris, Mary Jane, and Stewart Clatworthy
2003     Aboriginal Mobility and Migration Within Urban Canada: Outcomes, Factors and Implications. Pp. 51–78 in Not Strangers in These Parts: Urban Aboriginal Peoples. David R. Newhouse and Evelyn J. Peters, eds. Ottawa: Policy Research Initiative.

Norris, Mary Jane, Don Kerr, and F. Nault
1995     Projections of the Population with Aboriginal Identity in Canada, 1991–2016. Ottawa: Canada Mortgage and Housing Corporation and the Royal Commission on Aboriginal Peoples.

Norris-Tull, Delena
1999     Our Language Our Souls: The Yup'ik Bilingual Curriculum of the Lower Kuskokwim School District: A Continuing Success Story. Fairbanks: University of Alaska. (Webpage: http://www.ankn.uaf.edu/curriculum/Yupiaq/DelenaNorris-Tull/bLower%20Kuskokwim%20bilingual.htm)

North American Indian Museums Association (NAIMA)
1979     NAIMA Bylaws. Niagara Falls, N.Y.: North American Indian Museums Association.

Northrup, Jim
1995     Walking the Rez Road. New York: Voyageur Press.

_____
1999     Rez Road Follies: Canoes, Casinos, Computers, and Birch Bark Baskets. Minneapolis: University of Minnesota Press.

Northwest Territories, Government of
2004     Summary Report: 2002 NWT School Tobacco Survey. Yellowknife, N.W.T.: Government of the Northwest Territories.

Nostrand, Richard L., and Lawrence E. Estaville, eds.
2002     Homelands: A Geography of Culture and Place Across America. Baltimore, Md.: Johns Hopkins University Press.

Novick, Peter
1988     That Noble Dream: The "Objectivity Question" and the American Historical Profession. Cambridge: Cambridge University Press.

Nunatta Katersugaasivia Allagaateqarfialu/Greenland National Museum and Archives
2006     Qilakitsormiut, Timit Paniinnarnikut/Mummies from Qilakitsok. (Webpage: http://www.natmus.gl/gl/formidling/mumier/fmumier.html [6 August 2006].)

_____
2007     [The Museum. Electronic file.] (Webpage: http://www.natmus.gl/en/html/museumenl.html [28 April 2007].)

Nunavut, Government of
1999     The Road to Nunavut. Iqaluit, NU: Government of Nunavut. (Webpage: http://www.nunavut.com/nunavut99/english/road.html [6 November 2006].)

_____
2004     Nunavut Ten-Year Inuit Housing Action Plan: A Proposal to the Government of Canada. Iqaluit, NU: Government of Nunavut (Nunavut Housing Corporation) and Nunavut Tunngavik Inc. (Webpage: http://www.nunavuthousing.ca/i18n/english/PDF/10YearHousing%20Plan_Eng.pdf [28 May, 2007].)

Nurge, Ethel
1970     Dakota Diet: Traditional and Contemporary. Pp. 35–91 in The Modern Sioux: Social Systems and Reservation Culture. Ethel Nurge, ed. Lincoln: University of Nebraska Press.

_____, ed.
1970a    The Modern Sioux: Social Systems and Reservation Culture. Lincoln: University of Nebraska Press.

Nye, Russel B.
1970     The Unembarrassed Muse: The Popular Arts in America. New York: Dial Press.

Oakley, Christopher Arris
2001     Indian Gaming and the Eastern Band of Cherokee Indians. *The North Carolina Historical Review* 78(2):133–155. Raleigh, N.C.

_____
2005     Keeping the Circle: American Indian Identity in Eastern North Carolina, 1885–2004. *Indians of the Southeast.* Lincoln and London: University of Nebraska Press.

O'Brien, Dennis
2004     Returning Bones Is a Daunting Task. *Baltimore Sun*, January 12, 2004:11A. Baltimore, Md.

O'Brien, Sharon
1984     The Medicine Line: A Border Dividing Tribal Sovereignty, Economies, and Families. *Fordham Law Review* 53:315–325. New York.

_____
1989     American Indian Tribal Governments. Norman: University of Oklahoma Press. (Reprinted in 1993.)

_____
1991     Tribes and Indians: With Whom Does the United States Maintain a Relationship? *Notre Dame Law Review* 99:14–61. Notre Dame, Ind.

Occom, Samson
1768     A Short Narrative of My Life. Pp. 730–735 in The Heath Anthology of American Literature. Volume 1. Paul Lauter, ed. Lexington, Mass.: D.C. Heath, 1990.

_____
1772     A Sermon Preached at the Execution of Moses Paul, An Indian Who Was Executed at New-Haven on the 2nd of September 1772 for the Murder of Mr. Moses Cook, Late of

Waterbury, on the 7th of December 1771. New Haven, Conn.: Press of Thomas and Samuel Green, 1774. (Reprinted in: The Heath Anthology of American Literature. Volume 1. Paul Lauter, ed. Lexington, Mass.: D.C. Heath, 1990.)

O'Connell, Barry, ed.
1992    On Our Own Ground: The Complete Writings of William Apess, A Pequot. With an Introduction by Barry O'Connell. Amherst, Mass.: University of Massachusetts Press.

O'Connor, John E.
1980    The Hollywood Indian: Stereotypes of Native Americans in Films. Trenton, N.J.: New Jersey State Museum.

O'Connor, Len, Natasha Netschay Davies, and Lloyd Dolha, eds.
2004    Smoke Signals from the Hearth: Fourteen Years of the First Nations Drum. Vancouver: Totem Pole Books.

Odegaard, Nancy, and Alyce Sadongei
2005    Old Poisons, New Problems: A Museum Resource for Managing Contaminated Cultural Materials. Walnut Creek, Calif.: AltaMira Press.

Odier, Pierre
1982    The Rock: A History of Alcatraz, The Fort/The Prison. Eagle Rock, Calif.: L'Image Odier.

O'Donnell, Vivian
2005    Women in Canada. Pp. 181–209 in Women in Canada: A Gender-Based Statistical Report. Statistics Canada Catalogue 89-5030-XPE. Ottawa: Minister Responsible for Statistics Canada.

O'Donnell, Vivian, and Heather Tait
2003    Aboriginal Peoples Survey 2001—Initial Findings: Well-Being of the Non-Reserve Aboriginal Population. Statistics Canada Catalogue 89-589-XWE. Ottawa: Minister Responsible for Statistics Canada; Housing, Family and Social Statistics Division.

OFA = Office of Federal Acknowledgment see U.S. Department of the Interior. Bureau of Indian Affairs (BIA). Office of Federal Acknowledgment (OFA)

Office of Federal Acknowledgment (OFA) see U.S. Department of the Interior. Bureau of Indian Affairs (BIA). Office of Federal Acknowledgment (OFA)

Office of Indian Affairs see U.S. Department of the Interior. Bureau of Indian Affairs (BIA)

Officer, James E.
1971    The American Indian and Federal Policy. Pp. 8–65 in The American Indian in Urban Society. Jack O. Waddell and O. Michael Watson, eds. Boston: Little, Brown.

Ogeden, Sherelyn, ed.
2004    Caring for American Indian Objects: A Practical and Cultural Guide. St. Paul, Minn.: Minnesota Historical Society Press.

Ogunwole, Stella U., et al., comps.
2006    see U.S. Census Bureau 2006

Oklahoma Indian Gaming and Tourism Magazine
2006    Chickasaw Enterprises: Transforming Presence. Oklahoma Indian Gaming and Tourism Magazine 2:4. Oklahoma City, Okla.

Oliva, Judy Lee
1995    Te Ata—Chickasaw Indian Performer: From Broadway to Back Home. Theatre History Studies 15(June):3–26. Grand Forks, N.Dak.

Oliver, E.H.
1914–1915    The Canadian North-West: Its Early Development and Legislative Records. Minutes of the Councils of the Red River Colony and the Northern Department of Ruperts Land. 2 vols. Publications of the Canadian Archives 9. Ottawa: Government Printing Bureau.

Olson, James S., ed.
1997    Encyclopedia of American Indian Civil Rights. Mark Baxter, Jason M. Tetzloff, and Darren Pierson, Associate eds. Westport, Conn., and London: Greenwood Press.

Olson, James S., and Raymond Wilson
1984    Native Americans in the Twentieth Century. Urbana and Chicago: University of Illinois Press.

One Feather, Gerald
1974    American Indian Community Colleges. In: Indian Education Confronts the Seventies: Future Concerns. Vol. 5. Vine Deloria, Jr., ed. Oglala, S.Dak.: American Indian Resource Associates; Washington: ERIC Document Reproduction Services, ED 113-092.

O'Neil, John D.
1988    Referrals to Traditional Healers: The Role of Medical Interpreters. Pp. 29–38 in Health Care Issues in the Canadian North. David E. Young, ed. Edmonton, Alta.: Boreal Institute for Northern Studies.

O'Neill, Colleen
2005    Working the Navajo Way: Labor and Culture in the Twentieth Century. Lawrence, Kans.: University Press of Kansas.

Ontario. Ministry of Health
1994    New Directions: Aboriginal Health Policy for Ontario. Toronto: Ontario Ministry of Health.

Opekokew, Delia
1980    The Natives: Indian Government and the Canadian Federation. Saskatoon, Sask.: Federation of Saskatchewan Indians.

——
1996    The Nature and Status of the Oral Promises in Relation to the Written Terms of the Treaties. In: For Seven Generations: An Information Legacy of the Royal Commission on Aboriginal Peoples (RCAP). CD-ROM. Ottawa: Libraxus. (Copyright: 1996–2007.)

Opler, Morris E.
1938    The Use of Peyote by the Carrizo and Lipan Apache Tribes. American Anthropologist, n.s. 40(2):271–285.

Ortel, Jo
2005    Exhibition Review of Continuum: Twelve Artists at the George Gustav Heye Center, Part 2. American Indian Art Magazine 30(2):58–65. Scottsdale, Ariz.

Ortiz, Alfonso, vol. ed.
1979    see Handbook Vol. 9 (1979)

——, vol. ed.
1983    see Handbook Vol. 10 (1983)

Ortiz, Simon J., Jr.
1978    Howbah Indians. Albuquerque: Blue Moon Press.

——
1981    From Sand Creek. Tucson: The University of Arizona Press. (Reprinted in 2000.)

——
1983    Fightin': New and Collected Stories. Chicago: Thunder's Mouth Press.

Oswalt, Wendell H.
2006    This Land Was Theirs: A Study of Native North Americans. 8th ed. New York: Oxford University Press.

Otis, Delos S.
1973      The Dawes Act and the Allotment of Indian Lands. Francis Paul Prucha, ed. Norman: University of Oklahoma Press. (Reprinted in 1978.)

Ourada, Patricia K.
1979      Dillon Seymour Myer, 1950–53. In: The Commissioners of Indian Affairs, 1824–1977. Robert M. Kvasnicka and Herman J. Viola, eds. Lincoln: University of Nebraska Press.

Ousley, Stephen D., William T. Billeck, and R. Eric Hollinger
2005      Federal Repatriation Legislation and the Role of Physical Anthropology in Repatriation. *Yearbook of Physical Anthropology* 48:2–32. New York: Wiley-Liss.

Owens, Louis
1991      Wolfsong. Norman: University of Oklahoma Press.

1992      The Sharpest Sight: A Novel. Norman: University of Oklahoma Press.

1992a      Other Destinies: Understanding the American Indian Novel. Norman: University of Oklahoma Press.

1994      Bone Game. Norman: University of Oklahoma Press.

1996      Nightland: A Novel. New York: Dutton Press.

1999      Dark River. Norman: University of Oklahoma Press.

2001      Mixedblood Messages: Literature, Film, Family, Place. Norman: University of Oklahoma Press.

Oxendine, Joseph S.
1995      American Indian Sports Heritage. With a New Afterward by the Author. Lincoln: University of Nebraska Press.

Pack, Sam
2001      The Best of Both Worlds: Otherness, Appropriation, and Identity in Thunderhart. *Wicaso Sa Review* 16(2):97–114. Minneapolis.

Painter, John S.
1981      Congressional Conservatism and Federal Indian Policy, 1928–1950. (Paper presented at the Annual Meeting of the Organization of American Historians, Detroit, Mich., 2 April 1981.)

Paisano, Edna, et al., comps.
1984, 1991   *see* U.S. Census Bureau 1984, 1991

Panel for a National Dialogue on Museum/Native American Relations
1990      Update on Repatriation: Report of the Panel for a National Dialogue on Museum/Native American Relations. *Museum Anthropology* 14(1):6–13. Tempe, Ariz.

Pankratz, Curt J., and Bryan A. Hart
2005      Comparative Analysis of TLE Implementation in Manitoba and Saskatchewan, With Focus on Solutions for Manitoba First Nations. Winnipeg, Man.: Paskanake Project Management for South Chiefs Organization Inc.

Panoff, Thomas V.
2004      Legislative Reform of the Indian Trust Fund System. *Harvard Journal on Legislation* 41(2):517–540. Cambridge, Mass.

Paquin, Ron, and Robert Doherty
1992      Not First in Nobody's Heart: The Life Story of a Contemporary Chippewa. Ames, Ia.: Iowa State University Press.

Paredes, James Anthony, ed.
1992      Indians of the Southeastern United States in the Late 20th Century. Tuscaloosa and London: The University of Alabama Press.

1992a      Federal Recognition and the Poarch Creek Indians. Pp. 120–139 in Indians of the Southeastern United States in the Late Twentieth Century. James Anthony Paredes, ed. Tuscaloosa and London: The University of Alabama Press.

1997      In Defense of the BIA and the NPS: Federal Acknowledgment, Native American Consultation, and Some Issues in the Implementation of the Native American Graves Protection and Repatriation Act in the Southeastern United States. *St. Thomas Law Review* 10(1):35–43. Miami, Fla.

Parins, James W.
1991      John Rollin Ridge: His Life and Works. Lincoln: University of Nebraska Press.

2006      Elias Boudinot: A Life on the Cherokee Border. Lincoln: University of Nebraska Press.

Parker, Alan F.
1972      State and Tribal Courts in Montana: The Jurisdictional Relationship. *Montana Law Review* 33(2):277–290.

Parker, Arthur C.
1922      The Archaeological History of New York. Albany, N.Y.: The New York State Museum.

1935      Indian Episodes in New York: A Drama-Story of the Empire State. Rochester, N.Y.: Rochester Museum of Arts and Sciences.

Parker, Linda S.
1989      Native American Estate: The Struggle Over Indian and Hawaiian Lands. Honolulu: University of Hawaii Press.

Parker, Patricia
1990      Keepers of the Treasures: A Report on Tribal Preservation Funding Needs Submitted to Congress. National Park Service. Washington: Department of Interior.

Parman, Donald L.
1994      Indians and the American West in the Twentieth Century. Bloomington, Ind.: University of Indiana Press.

Parson, Reginald, and Gordon Prest
2003      Aboriginal Forestry in Canada. *The Forestry Chronicle* 79(4):779–784. Saint-Anne-de-Bellevue, Que.

Pasquaretta, Paul
1994      On the "Indianness" of Bingo: Gambling and the Native American Community. *Critical Inquiry* 20(4):694–714. Chicago.

2003      Gambling and Survival in Native North America. Tucson: The University of Arizona Press.

Passel, Jeffrey S.
1976      Provisional Evaluation of the 1970 Census Count of American Indians. *Demography* 13(3):397–409. [Chicago, etc.]

1997      The Growing American Indian Population, 1960–1990: Beyond Demography. *Population Research and Policy Review* 16(1–2):11–31. Amsterdam: Springer Netherlands.

Passel, Jeffrey S., and Patricia A. Berman
1985      An Assessment of the Quality of 1980 Census Data for American Indians. (Paper presented at the 1985 Meetings of the American Statistical Association, Las Vegas, Nev.)

1986   Quality of 1980 Census Data for American Indians. *Social Biology* 33(3–4):163–182. Madison, Wis.

Patrick, Mary
1973   Indian Urbanization in Dallas: A Second Trail of Tears? *Oral History Review*, 1973:54–65. Fullerton, Calif.

Patterson, E. Palmer
1962   Andrew Paull and the Canadian Indian Resurgence. (Ph.D. Dissertation in Anthropology, University of Washington, Seattle.)

1978   Andrew Paull and the Early History of British Columbia Indian Organizations. Pp. 43–54 in One Century Later: Western Canadian Reserve Indians Since Treaty 7. Ian A.L. Getty and Donald B. Smith, eds. Vancouver: University of British Columbia Press.

Paul, Doris A.
1973   The Navajo Code Talkers. Philadelphia: Dorance and Company.

Payment, Diane Paulette
2001   *see* Handbook Vol. 13 (2001:661–676)

Pearce, Roy H.
1965   The Savages of America: A Study of the Indian and the Idea of Civilization. Revised ed. Baltimore, Md.: Johns Hopkins University Press.

Pearson, J. Diane
2004   Medical Diplomacy and the American Indian: Thomas Jefferson, the Lewis and Clark Expedition and the Subsequent Effects on American Indian Health and Public Policy. *Wicazo Sa Review* 19(1):105–130. Minneapolis.

Pearson, Maria D.
2005   Give Me Back My People's Bones: Repatriation and Reburial of American Indian Skeletal Remains in Iowa. Pp. 7–12 in Still Running: A Tribute to Maria Pearson, Yankton Sioux. David Mayer Gradwohl, Joe B. Thompson, and Michael J. Perry, eds. *Journal of the Iowa Archeological Society, Special Commemorative Issue* 52(1). Iowa City.

Pease-Pretty On Top, Janine
[2005]  Native American Language Immersion: Innovative Native Education for Children and Families. A Project of the American Indian College Fund. (Webpage: http://www.collegefund.org/downloads/ImmersionBook.pdf)

Pecos, Regis, and Rebecca Blum
2001   The Key to Cultural Survival: Language Planning and Revitalization in the Pueblo de Cochiti. Pp. 75–82 in The Green Book of Language Revitalization in Practice. Leanne Hinton and Kenneth Hale, eds.: San Diego, Calif.: Academic Press.

Peltier, Leonard
1996   Peltier Pleads: Please Don't Forget Me. *Akwesasne Notes*, n.s. 2(1):9–11. [Rooseveltown, N.Y.]

1999   Prison Writings: My Life Is My Sun Dance. New York: St. Martin's Press.

Penman, Sarah, comp. and ed.
2000   Honor the Grandmothers: Dakota and Lakota Women Tell Their Lives. St. Paul, Minn.: Minnesota Historical Society Press.

Penn, Alan
1997   The James Bay and Northern Quebec Agreement: Natural Resources, Public Lands, and the Implementation of a Native Land Claim Settlement. In: For Seven Generations: An Information Legacy of the Royal Commission on Aboriginal Peoples (RCAP). CD-ROM. Ottawa: Libraxus. (Copyright: 1996–2007.)

Penner, Keith
1983   Indian Self-Government in Canada: Report of the Special Committee on Indian Self-Government. Ottawa: House of Commons.

1988   Their Own Place: The Case for a Distinct Order of Indian Native Government in Canada. Pp. 31–37 in Governments in Conflict? Provinces and Indian Nations in Canada. J. Anthony Long and Menno Boldt, eds. Toronto: University of Toronto Press.

Penney, David W.
1996   Native American Art Masterpieces. New York: Hugh Lauter Levin Associates.

Pennington, Robert
1961   Oscar Owe: Artist of the Sioux. Sioux Fall, S.Dak.: Dakota Territorial Commission.

Pentz, Peter, ed.
2004   Utimut—Return: The Return of More Than 35,000 Cultural Objects to Greenland. *National Museum of Denmark, Greenland National Museum and Archives, and UNESCO*. Gylling, Denmark: Narayana Press.

Perdue, Theda
1979   Slavery and the Evolution of Cherokee Society, 1540–1866. Knoxville: The University of Tennessee Press. (Originally presented as the Author's Ph.D. Dissertation in Anthropology, University of Georgia, Athens, Ga., 1976.)

1981   Nations Remembered: An Oral History of the Five Civilized Tribes, 1865–1907. Westport, Conn.: Greenwood Press.

———, ed.
1983   Cherokee Editor: The Writings of Elias Boudinot. Athens, Ga.: University of Georgia Press. (Reprinted in 1996.)

2003   "Mixed Blood" Indians: Racial Construction in the Early South. *Mercer University Lamar Memorial Lectures* 45. Athens, Ga., and London: The University of Georgia Press.

Perdue, Theda, and Michael D. Green, eds.
2001   The Columbia Guide to American Indians of the Southeast. New York: Columbia University Press.

Peregoy, Robert M.
1991   [Letter from Native American Rights Fund to Assistant Secretary of Indian Affairs.] (Office of Federal Acknowledgment, 1994 Regulations Files, Bureau of Indian Affairs, Washington.)

Peregoy, Robert M., Walter R. Echo-Hawk, and James Botsford
1995   Congress Overturns Supreme Court's Peyote Ruling. *Native American Rights Fund Legal Review* 20(1): 1, 6–25. Boulder, Colo.

Peroff, Nicholas C.
2006   Menominee Drums: Tribal Termination and Restoration, 1954–1974. Reprint ed. Norman: University of Oklahoma Press. (Originally publ. in 1982.)

Perry, Richard Warren
2006   Native American Tribal Gaming as Crime Against Nature: Environment, Sovereignty, Globalization. *PoLAR* 29(1): 110–131. Washington.

Peters, Evelyn J.
1986   Aboriginal Self-Government in Canada: A Bibliography. Kingston, Ont.: Institute of Intergovernmental Relations, Queen's University.

———
1992   Self-Government for Aboriginal People in Urban Areas: A Literature Review and Suggestions for Research. *Canadian Journal of Native Studies* 12(1): 51–74. Brandon, Man.

———
1995   The Geographies of Aboriginal Self -Government. Pp. 411–431 in Aboriginal Self-Government in Canada: Current Trends in Issues. J. Hylton Book, ed. Saskatoon, Sask.: Purich Publishing.

———
2004   Three Myths About Aboriginals in Cities. *Breakfast on the Hill Seminar Series*. Ottawa: Canadian Federations for the Humanities and Social Sciences. (Webpage: http://www .fed.ca)

Peters, Kurt
2001   Continuing Identity: Laguna Pueblo Railroaders in Richmond, California. Pp. 117–126 in American Indians and the Urban Experience. *Contemporary Native American Communities*. Susan Lobo and Kurt Peters, eds. Walnut Creek, Calif.: AltaMira Press.

Peterson, Jacqueline
1985   Many Roads to Red River: Métis Genesis in the Great Lakes Region, 1680–1815. Pp. 37–71 in The New Peoples: Being and Becoming Métis in North America. Jacqueline Peterson and Jennifer S.H. Brown, eds. *Manitoba Studies in Native History* 1. Winnipeg, Man.: University of Manitoba Press.

Petrullo, Vincenzo
1975   The Diabolic Root: A Study of Peyotism, the New Indian Religion Among the Delawares. New York: Octagon Books.

Pettipas, Katherine
1994   Severing the Ties That Bind: Government Repression of Indigenous Religious Ceremonies on the Prairies. Winnipeg, Man.: University of Manitoba Press.

Pevar, Stephen L.
1992   The Rights of Indians and Tribes: The Basic ACLU Guide to Indian and Tribal Rights. Second Edition Completely Revised and Updated. *An American Civil Liberties Union Handbook*. Carbondale, Ill.: Southern Illinois University Press.

Peyer, Bernd C., ed.
1989   The Singing Spirit: Early Short Stories by North American Indians. Tucson: University of Arizona Press.

Phillips, McCandish
1972   Indian Theater Group, Strong Beginning. *The New York Times*, November 9, 1972. New York.

Philp, Kenneth R.
1977   John Collier's Crusade for Indian Reform, 1920–1954. Tucson: University of Arizona Press.

———
1985   Stride Toward Freedom: The Relocation of Indians to Cities, 1952–1960. *Western Historical Quarterly* 16(2):175–190.

———, ed.
1986   Indian Self-Rule: First-Hand Accounts of Indian-White Relations from Roosevelt to Reagan. Salt Lake City: Howe Brothers.

———
1999   Termination Revisited: American Indians on the Trail to Self-Determination, 1933–1953. Lincoln: University of Nebraska Press.

Pickering, Kathleen, and David Mushinski
2001   Making the Case for Culture in Economic Development: A Cross-Section Analysis of Western Tribes. *American Indian Culture and Research Journal* 25(1):45–64. Los Angeles.

Pico, Anthony
2005   Putting Indian Realities in Context for the Media. *Indian Country Today*, April 7, 2005. Canastota, N.Y. (Webpage: http://www.indiancountry.com)

Pine Ridge Meeting
1956   [Pine Ridge Meeting with Glenn Emmons.] (Minutes, Tribal Area Conferences, 1956, Folder 2, Box III, Glenn Emmons Papers, University of New Mexico General Library, Albuquerque.)

Pitsula, James M.
1994   The CCF Government and the Formation of the Union of Saskatchewan Indians. *Prairie Forum* 19(2):31–51. Regina, Sask.

Plamondon, Pun
2004   Lost from the Ottawa: The History of the Journey Back. A Memoir. Detroit Bootleg Edition. Cloverdale, Mich.: Plamondon, Inc.

Pommersheim, Frank
1991   Tribal-State Relations: Hope for the Future? *South Dakota Law Review* 36(2):239–276. Vermillion, S.Dak.

Pompana, Yvonne
1997   Devolution to Indigenization: The Final Path to Assimilation of Natives. (M.A. Thesis in Social Work, University of Manitoba, Winnipeg, Man.)

Ponting, J. Rick, ed.
1986   Arduous Journey: Canadian Indians and Decolonization. Toronto: McClelland and Stewart.

———
1986a   Economic Development Provisions of the New Claims Settlements. Pp. 194–210 in Arduous Journey: Canadian Indians and Decolonization. J. Rick Ponting, ed. Toronto: McClelland and Stewart.

———
1997   Historical Overview and Background, Part I: 1867–1969. Pp. 19–34 in First Nations in Canada: Perspectives on Opportunity, Empowerment, and Self-Determination. J. Rick Ponting, ed. Toronto: McGraw-Hill Ryerson.

———, ed.
1997a   First Nations in Canada: Perspectives on Opportunity, Empowerment, and Self-Determination. Toronto: McGraw-Hill Ryerson.

———
2000   Public Opinion and Canadian Aboriginal Issues, 1976–1998: Persistence, Change, and Cohort Analysis. *Canadian Ethnic Studies* 32(3):44–75.

Ponting, J. Rick, Roger Gibbons, and Andrew J. Siggner
1980   Out of Irrelevance: A Socio-Political Introduction to Indian Affairs in Canada. Toronto: Butterworths.

Poplar, Mildred
2003   We Were Fighting For Nationhood, Not Section 35. In: Box of Treasures or Empty Box: Twenty Years of Section 35. Ardith Walkem and Halie Bruce, eds. Penticton, B.C.: Theytus Books.

Porter, Joy, ed.
2007   Place and Native American Indian History and Culture. *American Studies: Culture, Society & the Arts* 5. Oxford, [etc.]: Peter Lang.

Porter, Kenneth Wiggins
1996        The Black Seminoles: History of a Freedom Seeking People. Revised and edited by Alcione M. Amos and Thomas P. Senter. Gainesville: University Press of Florida.

Porter, Robert B.
2002        Two Kinds of Indians, Two Kinds of Indian Nation Sovereignty: A Surreply to Professor LaVelle. *Kansas Journal of Law and Public Policy* 11:629–656.

Posluns, Michael
1974        The Fourth World: An Indian Reality. Toronto: Collier Macmillan Canada, Ltd.

Powell, Eric A.
2001        Old Canuck No Kennewick Man. *Archaeology* 54(5):17. Long Island City, N.Y.

Powers-Beck, Jeff
2004        The American Indian Integration of Baseball. Lincoln: University of Nebraska Press.

Powers, William K.
1970        Contemporary Oglala Music and Dance: Pan-Indianism Versus Pan-Tetonism. Pp. 268–290 in The Modern Sioux: Social Systems and Reservation Culture. Ethel Nurge, ed. Lincoln: University of Nebraska Press.

1981        Have Drum Will Travel: The Professionalization of Native American Singers. *Ethnomusicology* 25(2):343–346. Middletown, Conn.

1988        *see* Handbook Vol. 4 (1988:557–561)

1990        War Dance: Plains Indian Musical Performance. Tucson: University of Arizona Press.

Powless, Robert E.
2002        *O'ezhichigeyaang* (This Thing We Do): American Indian Studies at the University of Minnesota-Duluth. Pp. 183–190 in American Studies in Higher Education: Models for Collaboration Between Universities and Indigenous Nations. Duane Champagne and Jay Stauss, eds. Walnut Creek, Calif.: AltaMira Press.

Pratt, Richard H. *see* Doanmoe, Etahdleuh

Pratt, Vince E.
1971        [Interview with Oliver D. Eastman, 3 August 1971.] (Tape 768, 16, South Dakota Oral History Center, University of South Dakota, Vermillion, S.Dak.)

Preston, Jennifer
1992        Weesageechak Begins to Dance: Native Earth Performing Arts Inc. *TDR: The Drama Review* 36(1):135–159. Cambridge, Mass.

Preston, Richard J.
2002        Cree Narrative: Expressing the Personal Meaning of Events. 2d ed. Montreal: McGill-Queen's University Press.

Preucel, Robert W., et al.
2003        Out of Heaviness, Enlightenment: NAGPRA and the University of Pennsylvania Museum of Archaeology and Anthropology. *Expedition: The Journal of the University of Pennsylvania Museum of Archaeology and Anthropology* 45(3): 21–27. Philadelphia.

Price, Darby Li Po
2001        Red Wit in the City: Urban Indian Comedy. Pp. 231–246 in American Indians and the Urban Experience. *Contemporary Native American Communities*. Susan Lobo and Kurt Peters, eds. Walnut Creek, Calif.: AltaMira Press.

Price, David H.
2004        Threatening Anthropology: McCarthyism and the FBI's Surveillance of Activist Anthropologists. Durham, N.C., and London: Duke University Press.

Price, H. Marcus, III
1991        Disputing the Dead: U.S. Law on Aboriginal Remains and Grave Goods. Columbia, Mo.: University of Missouri Press.

Price, John A.
1968        The Migration and Adaptation of American Indians to Los Angeles. *Human Organization* 27(2):168–175. Washington.

1973        The Stereotyping of North American Indians in Motion Pictures. *Ethnohistory* 20(2):153–171.

1978        Native Studies: American and Canadian Indians. Toronto: McGraw-Hill Ryerson Limited.

1988        Indians of Canada: Cultural Dynamics. Salem, Wis.: Sheffield Publishing Company. (Originally publ. in 1979.)

Price, Monroe E.
1973        Law and the American Indian: Readings, Notes and Cases. *Contemporary Legal Education Series*. Indianapolis, Ind.: The Bobbs-Merrill Company

Price, Richard, ed.
1987        The Spirit of Alberta Indian Treaties. Edmonton, Alta.: Pica Pica Press.

Primeaux, Martha H.
1977        American Indian Health Care Practices: A Cross-Cultural Perspective. *The Nursing Clinics of North America* 12(1):55–65. Philadelphia.

Province of Alberta
2000        First Nations Sacred Ceremonial Objects Repatriation Act, R.S.A. 2000 c. F-14. Edmonton, Alta.: Province of Alberta.

Prucha, Francis Paul
1962        American Indian Policy in the Formative Years: The Indian Trade and Intercourse Acts, 1790–1834. Cambridge, Mass.: Cambridge University Press; Lincoln: University of Nebraska Press.

1984        The Great Father: The United States Government and the American Indians. 2 vols. Lincoln: University of Nebraska Press.

1988        *see* Handbook Vol. 4 (1988:238–244)

1990        Documents of United States Indian Policy. 2d ed., expanded. Lincoln: University of Nebraska Press. (Originally publ. in 1975.)

1990a       Atlas of American Indian Affairs. Lincoln: University of Nebraska Press.

1994        American Indian Treaties: The History of a Political Anomaly. Berkeley: University of California Press.

Public Health Agency of Canada
2004, 2004a  *see* Canada. Public Health Agency of Canada 2004, 2004a

Pullar, Gordon L.
1994        The Qikertarmiut and the Scientist: Fifty Years of Clashing World Views. Pp. 15–25 in Reckoning with the Dead: The Larsen Bay Repatriation and the Smithsonian Institution. Tamara L. Bray and Thomas W. Killion, eds. Washington: Smithsonian Institution Press.

Purdy, John Lloyd
1990          Word Ways: The Novels of D'Arcy McNickle. Tucson: University of Arizona Press.

Pye, Douglas
1996          Double Vision: Miscegenation and Point of View in The Searchers. Pp. 229–235 in The Book of Westerns. Ian Cameron and Douglas Pye, eds. New York: Continuum.

Quebec
1976          The James Bay Northern Quebec Agreement. Québec: Éditeur officiel du Québec.

Quesenberry, Steven
1995          [Testimony on S. 479 Before the United States Senate Committee on Indian Affairs, May 23 1995.] Pp. 187–200 in Hearing Before the Senate Committee on Indian Affairs on S. 479, To Provide for Administrative Procedures to Extended Federal Recognition to Certain Indian Groups. *104th Congress, 2d Session*. Washington: U.S. Government Printing Office.

Quinn, William W., Jr.
1990          The Southeast Syndrome: Notes on Indian Descendant Recruitment Organizations and Their Perceptions on Native American Culture. *American Indian Quaterly* 14(2):147–154.

Quintasket, Catherine *see* Mourning Dove (Catherine Quintasket)

Racette, Calvin
1987          Flags of the Métis. Regina, Sask.: Gabriel Dumont Institute.

Racette, Sherry Farrell
1991          The Flower Beadwork People. Regina, Sask.: Gabriel Dumont Institute.

Racine, Doug, and Joe Sawchuk, interviewers
1995          *see* Dumont, Yvon 1995

Radin, Paul
1914          A Sketch of the Peyote Cult of the Winnebago: A Study in Borrowing. *Journal of Religious Psychology* 7(1):1–22.

————
1956          The Trickster. New York: Greenwood Press.

————
1991          Road of Life and Death: A Ritual Drama of the American Indians. Princeton, N.J.: Princeton University Press.

Raento, Paulina, and Kate A. Berry
1999          Geography's Spin at the Wheel of American Gambling. *The Geographical Review* 89(4):590–595. New York.

Ragsdale, John W., Jr.
1989          The Movement to Assimilate the American Indians: A Jurisprudential Study. *University of Missouri–Kansas City Law Review* 57(3):417–439. Kansas City, Mo.

Rahall, Nick J.
2005          Indian Health Care: An Outdated Federal Partnership, Congressional Flyer. Washington: United States Congress Committee on Resources Democrats.

Ram, Bali
2004          New Estimates of Aboriginal Fertility, 1966–1971 to 1996–2001. *Canadian Studies in Population* 31(4):179–196. Edmonton, Alta.

Ramirez-Shkwegnaabi, Benjamin
1987          Roles of Tribally Controlled Community College Trustees: A Comparison of Trustees' and Presidents' Perception of Trustee Role. (Ph.D. Dissertation in School Administration, University of Wisconsin, Madison.)

Ramos, Alcida R.
2002          Cutting Through State and Class: Sources and Strategies of Self-Representation in Latin America. In: Indigenous Movements, Self-Representation, and the State in Latin America. Kay Warren and Jean Jackson, eds. Austin, Tex.: The University of Texas Press.

Rand, Kathryn R.L., and Steven Andrew Light
2006          Indian Gaming Law and Policy. Durham, N.C.: Carolina Academic Press.

Rave, Jodi
2005          Challenges Native and Non-Native Journalists Confront. *Nieman Reports* 59(3):7–9. Cambridge, Mass.

Ray, Arthur J.
1998          Indians in the Fur Trade: Their Role as Trappers, Hunters, and Middlemen in the Lands Southwest of Hudson Bay, 1660–1870. 2d ed. Toronto: University of Toronto Press.

Ray, Arthur J., Jim Miller, and Frank J. Tough
2000          Bounty and Benevolence: A History of Saskatchewan Treaties. Montreal: McGill-Queen's University Press.

RCAP = Royal Commission on Aboriginal Peoples *see* Canada. Royal Commission on Aboriginal Peoples (RCAP)

RCMP = Royal Canadian Mounted Police *see* Canada. Royal Canadian Mounted Police (RCMP)

Reading, Jeff
1996          Eating Smoke: A Review of Non-Traditional Uses of Tobacco Among Aboriginal People. Ottawa: Health Canada.

Redbird, Aileen, and Patrick Melendey
1978          Indian Child Welfare in Oregon. Pp. 43–46 in The Destruction of American Indian Families. Steven Unger, ed. New York: Association on American Indian Affairs.

Redbird, Duke
1980          We Are Métis: A Métis View of the Development of a Native Canadian People. Willowdale, Ont.: Ontario Métis & Non Status Indian Association.

Red Crow Community College
2006          Mission and History. Cardston, Alta.: Red Crow Community College. (Webpage: http://www.Redcrowcollege.com/mission.htm.)

Reddy, Marlita A., ed.
1993          Statistical Record of Native North Americans. Detroit, [etc.]: Gale Research Inc.

Red Paper (on Indian Policy)
1970          *see* Indian Association of Alberta 1970

Red Star, Wendy
2005          The Last Thanksgiving. *Indigenous Peoples' Journal of Law, Culture & Resistance* 2(1):22–24. Los Angeles.

Reeves, Shiela
1995          Native American Journalists: Finding a Pipeline Into Journalism. *Newspaper Research Journal* 16(4):57–73. Memphis, Tenn.

Reichard, Gladys A.
1939          Dezba: Woman of the Desert. New York: J.J. Augustin.

Reid, Gerald F.
2004          Kahnawà'ke: Factionalism, Traditionalism, and Nationalism in a Mohawk Community. Lincoln and London: University of Nebraska Press.

Reinhardt, Akim D.
2007 Ruling Pine Ridge: Oglala Politics from the IRA to Wounded Knee. Foreword by Clara Sue Kidwell. *Plains Histories Series*. Lubbock, Tex.: Texas Tech University Press.

Reisling, David
1986 [Interview Concerning D-Q University, November 23, 1986.] (Conducted by Wayne J. Stein, Reno, Nev.; Text of interview in Department of Native American Studies, Montana State University, Bozeman, Mont.)

Reyes, Lawney L.
2006 Bernie Whitebear: An Urban Indian's Quest for Justice. Tucson: University of Arizona Press.

Reyhner, Jon, ed.
1990 A Description of the Rock Point Community School Bilingual Education Program. Pp. 95–106 in Effective Language Education Practices and Native Language Survival. Jon Reyhner, ed. Choctaw, Okla.: Native American Language Issues.

Reynolds, James I.
2005 A Breach of Duty: Fiduciary Obligations and Aboriginal Peoples. Saskatoon, Sask.: Purich Publishing.

Reynolds, Jerry
2007 [Kevin] Gover To Take Helm at NMAI. *Indian Country Today*, September 14, 2007. Canastota, N.Y. (Webpage: http://www.indiancountry.com)

Rhoades, Russell F.
1997 Arizona Department of Environmental Quality, 0003.001. (Webpage: http://www.indianaffairs.state.az.us/agreements/DEQTribalPolicy.pdf [7 October 2006].)

Richardson, Boyce
1979 Strangers Devour the Land. Vancouver: Douglas and McIntyre.

Richardson, Nancy, and Suzanne Burcell
1993 Now You're Speaking—Karuk! Arcata, Calif.: Humboldt State University, Center for Indian Community Development.

Richland, Justin B., and Sarah Deer
2004 Introduction to Tribal Legal Studies. Blue Ridge Summit, Pa.: AltaMira Press.

Richter, Daniel K.
2001 Facing East from Indian Country: A Native History of Early America. Cambridge, Mass.: Harvard University Press.

Rideout, Denise
2001 [Article.] *Nunatsiaq News*. Iqaluit, NU.

Ridge, John Rollin (Yellow Bird)
1854 The Life and Adventures of Joaquin Murieta: The Celebrated California Bandit. San Francisco: W.B. Cooke and Company. (Reprinted, 3d ed., rev. and enl.: Fred MacCrellish and Co., San Francisco, 1871, 1874. See also Ridge 1955.)

————
1955 The Life and Adventures of Joaquin Murieta: The Celebrated California Bandit. Introduction by Joseph Henry Jackson. Norman: University of Oklahoma Press. (Reprinted in 1969.)

Riding In, James
1992 Without Ethics and Morality: A Historical Overview of Imperial Archaeology and American Indians. *Arizona State Law Journal* 24(1):11–34. Tempe, Ariz.

Ridington, Robin, and Dennis Hastings (*In'aska*)
1997 Blessing for a Long time: The Sacred Pole of the Omaha Tribe. Lincoln: University of Nebraska Press.

Riggs, Lynn
2003 The Cherokee Night and Other Plays. Foreword by Jace Weaver. Norman: University of Oklahoma Press.

Riggs, Stephen Return
1893 Dakota Grammar, Texts and Ethnography. *Contributions to North American Ethnology* 9. James Owen Dorsey, ed. Washington: Department of the Interior, U.S. Geographical and Geological Survey of the Rocky Mountain Region.

Riley, Mary, ed.
2004 Indigenous Intellectual Property Rights: Legal Obstacles and Innovative Solutions. Blue Ridge Summit, Pa.: AltaMira Press.

Risling, David
1999 [Memorandum from Superintendent, Central California Agency, to Director, California Regional Office, Bureau of Indian Affairs, Sacramento.] (Office of Federal Acknowledgment, California Special Project Files, 1999, Bureau of Indian Affairs, Washington.)

Risser, Madeline, ed.
1979 Proceedings of the First National Conference of the American Indian Museums Association (aka North American Indian Museums Association), April 30–May 3, 1979. Washington: Smithsonian Institution.

Ritzenthaler, Robert
1943 The Impact of the War on an Indian Community. *American Anthropologist*, n.s. 45(2):325–326.

Robbins, Lynn Arnold
1975 The Impact of Power Developments on the Navajo Nation. *Lake Powell Research Project Bulletin* 7. Los Angeles: University of California.

Robbins, Rebecca L.
2002 Tribal College and University Profiles. Pablo, Mont.: Salish Kootenai College.

Roberts, Barry
1975 Eskimo Identification and Disc Numbers: A Brief History. Ottawa: Social Development Division, Indian and Northern Affairs Canada.

Robertson, Lindsay G.
2005 Conquest by Law: How the Discovery of America Dispossessed Indigenous Peoples of Their Lands. Oxford: Oxford University Press.

————
2007 Foreword. Pp. 7–8 in On the Drafting of Tribal Constitutions, by Felix S. Cohen. David E. Wilkins, ed. *American Indian Law and Policy Series* 1. Norman: University of Oklahoma Press.

Rockwood, Walter C.
1955 Memorandum on General Policy in Respect to the Indians and Eskimos of Northern Labrador. St. John's, N.L.: North Labrador Affairs, Department of Public Welfare.

Rolde, Neil
2004 Unsettled Past, Unsettled Future: The Story of the Maine Indians. Gardiner, Maine: Tillbury House Publishing.

Rollins, Peter C., and John E. O'Connor, eds.
2003 Hollywood's Indian: The Portrayal of the Native American in Film. Expanded edition. Lexington, Ky.: The University Press of Kentucky. (Originally publ. in 1998.)

Roness, Lori Ann, and Kent McNeil
2000 Legalizing Oral History: Proving Aboriginal Title in Canadian Courts. *Journal of the West* 39(3):66–74. Los Angeles.

Roos, Philip D., et al.
1980  The Impact of the American Indian Movement on the Pine Ridge Indian Reservation. *Phylon* 41(1):89–99. Atlanta.

Rosaldo, Renato
1989  Culture and Truth: The Remaking of Social Analysis. Boston: Beacon Press. (Reprinted: see Rosaldo 1993.)

1993  Culture and Truth: The Remaking of Social Analysis. With a New Introduction. Boston: Beacon Press.

Roscoe, Will, ed.
1988  Living the Spirit: A Gay American Indian Anthology. New York: St. Martin's Press.

Rose, Alex
2001  Spirit Dance at Meziadin: Chief Joseph Gosnell and the Nisga'a Treaty. Madeira Park, B.C.: Harbour Publishing.

Rosenfeld, Megan
1973  An Evening of Indian Carrousel. *The Washington Post*, March 2, 1973:B11. Washington.

Rosenstein, Jay
1995  In Whose Honor? American Indian Mascots in Sports. Film: 46 minutes, color. Ho-Ho-Kus, N.J.: New Day Films.

Rosenthal, Harvey D.
1990  Their Day in Court: A History of the Indian Claims Commission. *Distinguished Studies in American Legal and Constitutional History* 21. New York and London: Garland Publishing.

Rosenthal, Nicolas G.
2004  The Dawn of a New Day? Notes on Indian Gaming in Southern California. Pp. 91–111 in Native Pathways: American Indian Culture and Economic Development in the Twentieth Century. Brian C. Hosmer and Colleen O'Neill, eds. Boulder, Colo.: University Press of Colorado.

Rosier, Paul C.
2003  Native American Issues. Westport, Conn.: Greenwood Press.

Rosoff, Nancy B.
1998  Integrating Native Views into Museum Procedures: Hope and Practice and the National Museum of the American Indian. *Museum Anthropology* 22(1):33–42. Tempe, Ariz.

Ross, Kate
1996  Population Issues, Indigenous Australians, 1996. *Australian Bureau of Statistics. Occassional Paper* 4708.0. Canberra, Australia.

Ross, Michael Lee
2005  First Nations Sacred Sights in Canada's Courts. Vancouver: UBC Press.

Ross, Norman A., comp. and ed.
1973  Index to the Expert Testimony Before the Indian Claims Commission: The Written Reports. New York: Clearwater Publishing.

    , ed.
1973a  Index to the Decisions of the Indian Claims Commission. New York: Clearwater Publishing.

Rosser, Ezra
2005  This Land Is My Land, This Land Is Your Land: Markets and Institutions for Economic Development on Native American Land. *Arizona Law Review* 47(2):245–312. Tucson.

Rostkowski, Joelle
1995  Deskaheh's Shadow: Indians on the International Scene. *European Review of Native American Studies* 9(2):1–4. [Vienna, Austria, etc.]

Roth, Christopher F.
2002  Without Treaty, Without Consent, Without Conquest: Indigenous Sovereignty in Post-Delgamuukw British Columbia. *Wicaso Sa Review* 17(2):143–165. Minneapolis.

Roth, George
1988  Comment in Reply. *Practicing Anthropology* 10(2):21–22. Oklahoma City, Okla.

1989  Interdisciplinary Research in the Federal Acknowledgment Process. *High Plains Applied Anthropologist* 9(1):156–164.

1992  Overview of Southeastern Indian Tribes Today. Pp. 183–202 in Indians of the Southeastern United States in the Late Twentieth Century. James Anthony Paredes, ed. Tuscaloosa and London: The University of Alabama Press.

2001  Federal Tribal Recognition in the South. Pp. 48–70 in Anthropologists and Indians in the New South. Rachel A. Bonney and James Anthony Paredes, eds. Tuscaloosa and London: The University of Alabama Press.

Roth, Lorna
2005  Something in the Air: The Story of First Peoples Television Broadcasting in Canada. Montreal: McGill-Queen's University Press.

Rothenberg, Jerome, ed.
1968  Technicians of the Sacred: A Range of Poetries from Africa, America, Asia, Europe, and Oceania. New York: Doubleday. (Reprinted: see Rothenberg 1985.)

    , ed.
1972  Shaking the Pumpkin: Traditional Poetry of the Indian North Americans. New York: Doubleday. (Reprinted: see Rothenberg 1991.)

    , ed.
1985  Technicians of the Sacred: A Range of Poetries from Africa, America, Asia, Europe, and Oceania. 2d ed., Revised and Expanded. New York: Doubleday.

    , ed.
1991  Shaking the Pumpkin: Traditional Poetry of the Indian North Americans. Revised Edition. Albuquerque: University of New Mexico Press.

Rothenberg, Jerome, and Diane Rothenberg, eds.
1984  Symposium of the Whole: A Range of Discourses Toward Ethnopoetics. Berkeley: University of California Press.

Rotman, Leonard Ian
1996  Parallel Paths: Fiduciary Doctrine and the Crown-Native Relationship in Canada. Toronto: University of Toronto Press.

1997  Taking Aim at the Canons of Treaty Interpretation in Canadian Aboriginal Rights Jurisprudence. *University of New Brunswick Law Journal* 46:11–50. Fredericton, N.B.

2000  "My Hovercraft Is Full of Eels": Smoking Out the Message in *R. v. Marshall. Saskatchewan Law Review* 63(2):617–644. Saskatoon, Sask.

2003  Crown-Native Relations as Fiduciary: Reflections Almost Twenty Years After Guerin. *The Windsor Yearbook of Access to Justice* 22:363–396. Windsor, Ont.

Roubideaux, Yvette
2004  A Review of the Quality of Health Care for American Indians and Alaska Natives. Silver Spring, Md.: The Commonwealth Fund.

522

Rountree, Helen C.
1990    Pocahontas's People: The Powhatan Indians of Virginia
        Through Four Centuries. Norman: University of Oklahoma
        Press.

Rourke, Constance
1942    The Roots of American Culture, and Other Essays. Van
        Wyck Brooks, ed. New York: Harcourt Brace. (Reprinted:
        Kennikat Press, Port Washington, N.Y., 1965.)

Rowe, Peter C., et al.
1994    Epidemic *Escherichia coli* 0157: H7 Gastroenteritis and
        Hemolytic-Uremic Syndrome in a Canadian Inuit Commu-
        nity: Intestinal Illness in Family Members as a Risk Factor.
        *Journal of Pediatrics* 124(1):21–26.

Roy, Prodipto
1962    The Measurement of Assimilation: The Spokane Indians.
        *The American Journal of Sociology* 67(5):541–551. Chicago.

Royal Commission on Aboriginal Peoples (RCAP) *see* Canada. Royal
    Commission on Aboriginal Peoples (RCAP)

Royal Proclamation of 1763
1763    [1763, October 7: By the King. A Proclamation. George r.]
        London: Mark Baskett, King's Printer. (Text available on
        line; webpage: http://www.ainc.inac.gc.ca/ch/rcap/sg/sga4_
        e.html; see also: Brigham, Clarence S., ed. 1911.)

Royster, Judith
1995    The Legacy of Allotment. *Arizona State Law Journal* 27(1):
        1–78. Tempe, Ariz.

Rubin, Paul
2004    Indian Givers. *Phoenix New Times*, May 27, 2004. Phoenix.

Rudes, Blair A.
1999    John Napoleon Brinton Hewitt: Tuscarora Linguist. *Anthro-
        pological Linguistics* 36(4):467–481.

Rudes, Blair A., and Dorothy Crouse
1987    The Tuscarora Legacy of J.N.B. Hewitt: Materials for the
        Study of Tuscarora Language and Culture. 2 vols. *Canadian
        Museum of Civilization. Mercury Series. Ethnology Service
        Paper* 108. Ottawa.

Rundstrom, Robert A.
1994    American Indian Placemaking on Alcatraz, 1969–1971.
        Pp. 189–212 in Special Edition: Alcatraz Revisited: The 25th
        Anniversary of the Occupation, 1969–1971. Joane Nagel and
        Troy Johnson, eds. *American Indian Culture and Research
        Journal* 18(4). Los Angeles.

Ruoff, A. LaVonne Brown
1990    American Indian Literatures: An Introduction, Bibliographic
        Review, and Selected Bibliography. New York: Modern
        Language Association of America. (Reprinted in 1999.)

_____, ed.
1997    *see* Callahan, S. Alice 1997

Ruppert, James
1995    Mediation in Contemporary Native American Fiction. Nor-
        man: University of Oklahoma Press.

Rushing, W. Jackson, III, ed.
1999    Native American Art in the Twentieth Century: Makers,
        Meanings, Histories. New York: Routledge.

Rushing, W. Jackson, III, and Claire Wolf Krantz
1990    Another Look at Contemporary Native American Art. *New
        Art Examiner* 17(6):35–37. Chicago.

Russell, Peter H.
1992    Constitutional Odyssey: Can Canadians Become a Sovereign
        People? Toronto: University of Toronto Press.

Rynard, Paul
2000    "Welcome In, But Leave Your Rights at the Door": The
        James Bay and Nisga'a Agreements in Canada. *Canadian
        Journal of Political Science/Revue canadienne de science
        politique* 33(2):211–243. Toronto.

_____
2001    Ally or Colonizer? The Federal State, the Cree Nation and
        the James Bay Agreement. *Journal of Canadian Studies/
        Revue d'études canadiennes* 36(2):8–48. Peterborough, Ont.

Rynkiewich, Michael A.
1980    Chippewa Powwows. Pp. 31–100 in Anishnabe: Six Studies
        of Modern Chippewa. J. Anthony Paredes, ed. Tallahassee:
        University Presses of Florida.

Sadongei, Alyce
2005    National Directory of Tribal Archives, Libraries, and Muse-
        ums. Tucson: University of Arizona.

Sage, W. N.
1930    Sir James Douglas and British Columbia. Toronto: Univer-
        sity of Toronto Press.

Said, Edward W.
1978    Orientalism. New York: Pantheon Books.

Saku, James C.
2002    Modern Land Claim Agreements and Northern Canadian
        Aboriginal Communities. *World Development* 30(1):141–
        151. Montreal.

Saku, James C., and Robert M. Bone
2000    Looking for Solutions in the Canadian North: Modern
        Treaties As a New Strategy. *Canadian Geographer* 44(3):
        256–270. Toronto.

Salisbury, Richard F.
1986    A Homeland for the Cree: Regional Development in James
        Bay, 1971–1981. Montreal and Kingston, Ont.: McGill-
        Queens' University Press.

Salish Kootenai College
2006    Catalog. Pablo, Mont.: Salish and Kootenai College. (Web-
        page: http://www.skc.edu/)

Sameth, Sigmund
1940    Creek Negroes: A Study of Race Relations. (M.A. Thesis in
        Sociology, University of Oklahoma, Norman.)

Sampsel, Roy H.
1982    [Testimony of Deputy Assistant Secretary, Indian Affairs,
        dated July 30, 1982.] In: House Committee on Interior and
        Insular Affairs, Hearing on H.R. 6588, to Provide Recogni-
        tion of the Cow Creek Band of Umpqua Indians. Washing-
        ton: U.S. Government Printing Office.

_____
1982a   [Letter from Deputy Assistant Secretary, Indian Affairs, to
        William S. Cohen, Chairman, Select Committee on Indian
        Affairs, U.S. Senate, dated September 27, 1982.] (Office of
        Federal Acknowledgment, Cow Creek Umpqua Files, Sep-
        tember 27, 1982, Bureau of Indian Affairs, Washington.)

Samson, Colin
2003    A Way of Life That Does Not Exist: Canada and the Extin-
        guishment of the Innu. St. John's, N.L.: Institute of Social
        and Economic Research, Memorial University of Newfound-
        land.

Sandefur, Gary D.
1991    Economic Development and Employment Opportunities for
        American Indians. Pp. 208–222 in American Indians: Social
        Justice and Public Policy. *Ethnicity and Public Policy Series*
        9. Donald E. Green and Thomas V. Tonneson, eds. Milwau-

kee: University of Wisconsin System Institute on Race and Ethnicity.

Sandefur, Gary D., and Carolyn A. Liebler
1996    The Demography of American Indian Families. In: Changing Numbers, Changing Needs: American Indian Demography and Public Health. Gary D. Sandefur, Ronald R. Rindfuss, and Barney R. Cohen, eds. Washington: National Academy Press. (Reprinted in: *Population Research and Policy Review* 16(1–2):95–114. Amsterdam: Springer Netherlands, 1997.)

Sandefur, Gary D., and Trudy McKinnel
1986    American Indian Intermarriage. *Social Science Research* 15(4):347–371.

Sandefur, Gary D., Ronald R. Rindfuss, and Barney R. Cohen, eds.
1996    Changing Numbers, Changing Needs: American Indian Demography and Public Health. Washington: National Academy Press.

Sanders, Douglas
1983    The Indian Lobby. Pp. 301–333 in And No One Cheered: Federalism, Democracy, and the Constitution Act. Keith Banting and Richard Simeon, eds. Toronto: Methuen Publications.

———
1988    The Constitution, the Provinces, and Aboriginal Peoples. Pp. 151–174 in Governments in Conflict? Provinces and Indian Nations in Canada. J. Anthony Long and Menno Boldt, eds. Toronto: University of Toronto Press.

———
1988a   *see* Handbook Vol. 4 (1988:276–283)

Sarris, Gregg
1993    Keeping Slug Woman Alive: A Holistic Approach to American Indian Texts. Berkeley: University of California Press.

Sasaki, Tom T., and Harry W. Basehart
1961–1962   A Comparison of Income in Two Indian Communities. Pp. 187–190 in American Indians and Their Economic Development. Fred Voget, ed. *Human Organization*, Special Issue 20(4). Washington.

Satz, Ronald N.
1975    American Indian Policy in the Jacksonian Era. Lincoln: University of Nebraska Press.

Saul, John Ralston
2002    Rooted in the Power of Three. *The Globe and Mail*, March 8, 2002. Toronto.

Saunt, Claudio
2005    Black, White, and Indian: Race and the Unmaking of an American Family. New York and Oxford: Oxford University Press.

Sawchuk, Joe
1992    The Métis: Non-Status Indians and the New Aboriginality: Government Influence on Native Political Alliances and Identity. In: Readings in Aboriginal Studies, Vol. 2: Identities and State Structures. Joe Sawchuk, ed. 2 vols. Brandon, Man.: Bearpaw Press. (Revision of an article originally publ. in: *Canadian Ethnic Studies* 17(2):135–146. 1985.)

Sawchuk, Joe, Patricia Sawchuk, and Theresa Ferguson
1981    Métis Land Rights in Alberta: A Political History. Edmonton, Alta.: Métis Association of Alberta.

Sayer, John William
1991    Social Movements in the Courtroom: The Wounded Knee Trials, 1973–1975. (Ph.D. Dissertation in History, University of Minnesota, Minneapolis.)

———
1997    Ghost Dancing the Law: The Wounded Knee Trials. Cambridge, Mass.: Harvard University Press.

Scheckel, Susan
1998    The Insistence of the Indian: Race and Nationalism in Nineteenth-Century American Culture. Princeton, N.J.: Princeton University Press.

Schlesinger, Arthur M., Jr.
1992    The Disuniting of America. New York: W.W. Norton.

Schneider, Andy, and JoAnn Martinez
1997    Native Americans and Medicaid: Coverage and Financing Issues, Policy Brief. Washington: Kaiser Family Foundation.

Schneider, Mary Jane
1981    Economic Aspects of Mandan/Hidasta Giveaways. *Plains Anthropologist* 26(91):43–51. Lincoln, Nebr.

———
1983    Woman's Work: An Examination of Woman's Roles in Plains Indian Arts and Crafts. Pp. 1–121 in The Hidden Half: Studies of Plains Indian Women. Patricia C. Albers and Beatrice Medicine, eds. Washington: University Press of America.

Schrader, Robert F.
1983    The Indian Arts and Crafts Board: An Aspect of New Deal Indian Policy. Albuquerque: University of New Mexico Press.

Schwartz, Brian
1986    First Principles, Second Thoughts. Montreal: Institute for Research on Public Policy.

Schwechten, John L.
1972    In Spite of the Law: A Social Comment on the Impact of Kennerly and Crow Tribe. *Montana Law Review* 33(2):317–320. Missoula, Mont.

Scott, Colin
1984    Between 'Original Affluence' and Consumer Affluence: Domestic Production and Guaranteed Income for James Bay Cree Hunters. Pp. 74–86 in Affluence and Cultural Survival: Proceedings of the Spring Meeting of the American Ethnological Society. Washington, D.C., March 20–21. Richard, Salisbury, ed. Washington: American Ethnological Society.

———
1988    Property, Practice and Aboriginal Rights among Quebec Cree Hunters. Pp. 35–51 in Vol. 2 of Hunters and Gatherers-Property, Power and Ideology. 2 vols. James Woodburn, Tim Ingold, and David Riches, eds. London: Berg Publishers Ltd.

———
1996    Science for the West, Myth for the Rest? The Case of James Bay Cree Knowledge Construction. Pp. 69–86 in Naked Science: Anthropological Inquiries into Boundaries, Power, and Knowledge. Laura Nader, ed. London: Routledge.

———, ed.
2001    Aboriginal Autonomy and Development in Northeren Quebec and Labrador. Vancouver: University of British Columbia Press.

———
2005    Co-Management and the Politics of Aboriginal Consent to Resource Development: The Agreement Concerning a New Relationship Between Le Gouvernement du Québec and the Crees of Quebec (2002). Pp. 133–163 in Re-Configuring Aboriginal-State Relations: An Examination of Federal Reform and Aboriginal-State Relations. Canada: The State of the Federation, 2003. Michael Murphy, ed. Montreal: McGill-Queen's University Press.

Scott, Jacquelyn T.
2004 Doing Business with the Devil: Land, Sovereignty, and Corporate Partnerships in Membertou, Inc. Halifax, N.S: Atlantic Institute for Market Studies.

Scott, James C.
1985 Weapons of the Weak: Everyday Forms of Peasant Resistance. New Haven, Conn.: Yale University Press.

Sealaska Corporation
2005 Annual Report: 2005. Juneau: Sealaska Corporation.

Seale, Doris, and Beverly Slapin, eds.
2005 A Broken Flute: The Native Experience in Books for Children. Blue Ridge Summit, Pa.: AltaMira Press.

Sealy, D. Bruce
1975 Statutory Land Rights of the Manitoba Métis. Winnipeg, Man.: Manitoba Métis Federation Press.

Sears, Priscilla F.
1982 A Pillar of Fire to Follow: American Indian Dramas 1808–1859. Bowling Green, Ohio: Bowling Green University Popular Press.

Seaver, James E.
1995 Captured by Indians: The Life of Mary Jemison. Karen Zeinert, ed. North Haven, Conn.: Linnet Books.

Secakuku, Susan
2006 Creating Museums Within a Tribal Government. Pp. 43–55 in Living Homes for Cultural Expression: North American Native Perspectives on Creating Community Museums. Karen Coody Cooper and Nicolasa Sandoval, eds. Washington: Smithsonian Institution Press.

Seed, Patricia
1995 Ceremonies of Possession in Europe's Conquest of the New World, 1492–1640. Cambridge: Cambridge University Press.

Seigenthaler, John
1995 Foreword. Pp. iii–iv in Pictures of Our Nobler Selves: A History of Native American Contributions to News Media, by Mark N. Trahant. Nashville, Tenn.: The Freedom Forum First Amendment Center.

Seller, Maxine S., ed.
1983 Ethnic Theatre in the United States. Westport, Conn.: Greenwood Press.

Senate Subcommittee on Governmental Affairs *see* U.S. Congress. Senate Subcommittee on Governmental Affairs

Sergeant, Elizabeth Shepley
1942 The Indian Goes to War. *The New Republic* 107(Nov. 30):708–709. New York.

Sevilla, Graciela
2000 20 Years of Research for What? Tribe Asks. *Arizona Republic*, October 31, 2000. Phoenix.

Shaffrey, Mary M.
2006 Lumbee Bill Gets Panels' OK, Stalls. *Wall Street Journal*, August 8, 2006. New York.

Shank, Theodore
1982 Beyond the Boundaries: American Alternative Theatre. Ann Arbor, Mich.: University of Michigan Press.

Shanley, Kathryn W.
2001 Born from the Need To Say: Boundaries and Sovereignties in Native American Literary and Cultural Studies. *Para-doxa: Studies in World Literary Genres* 6(15):3–16. Vashon Island, Wash.

Shays, Christopher
2002 Testimony of Congressman Christopher Shays Before Hearing of the Energy Policy, Natural Resources, and Regulatory Affairs Subcommittee of the House Government Reform Committee. Subject: Problems with the Bureau of Indian Affairs' Tribal Recognition Process; February 7, 2002. Washington: U.S. Government Printing Office.

Sheffield, Gail K.
1997 The Arbitrary Indian: The Indian Arts and Crafts Act of 1990. Norman: University of Oklahoma Press.

Shelton, Brett Lee
2004 Legal and Historical Roots of Health Care for American Indians and Alaska Natives in the United States, Issue Brief. Washington: The Henry J. Kaiser Family Foundation.

Shemluck, Melvin
1982 Medicinal and Other Uses of the *Compositae* by Indians in the United States and Canada. *Journal of Ethnopharmacology* 5(3):303–358. [Amsterdam, The Netherlands, etc.]

Sheppard, Mary Jane
1999 Taking Indian Land Into Trust. *South Dakota Law Review* 44(3):681–698. Vermillion, S.Dak.

Sherley-Spiers, Sandra K.
1989 Dakota Perceptions of Clinical Encounters with Western Health Care Providers. *Native Studies Review* 5(1):41–51. Saskatoon, Sask.

Shewell, Hugh E.
1999 Jules Sioui and Indian Political Radicalism in Canada, 1943–1944. *Journal of Canadian Studies/Revue d'études canadiennes* 34(3):211–242. Peterborough, Ont.

————
2004 Enough To Keep Them Alive: Indian Welfare in Canada, 1873–1965. Toronto: University of Toronto Press.

Shields, Norma D.
2001 Anishinabek Political Alliance in the Post-Confederation Period. (M.A. Thesis, Queen's University, Kingston, Ont.)

Shively, JoEllen
1990 Cowboys and Indians: Perceptions of Western Films Among American Indians and Anglo Americans. (Ph.D. Dissertation in Sociology, Stanford University, Stanford, Calif.)

————
1992 Cowboys and Indians: Perceptions of Western Films Among American Indians and Anglos. *American Sociological Review* 57(6):725–734. Columbus, Ohio.

Shoemaker, Nancy
1999 American Indian Population Recovery in the Twentieth Century. Albuquerque: University of New Mexico Press.

————
2002 Clearing a Path: Theorizing the Past in Native American Studies. New York: Routledge Press.

Sickels, Robert C.
2003 Clint Eastwood's The Outlaw Josey Wales. *Journal of Popular Film and Television* 30(4):220–227. Bowling Green, Ohio.

Sider, Gerald M.
1993 Lumbee Indian Histories: Race, Ethnicity and Indian Identity in the Southern United States. *Culture and Class in Anthropology and History* 2. Cambridge and New York: Cambridge University Press.

Sievers, Maurice L., and Jeffrey R. Fisher
1981 Diseases of North American Indians. Pp. 191–252 in Biocultural Aspects of Disease. Henry R. Rothschild, ed. New York: Academic Press.

Siggins, Maggie
1995        Riel: A Life of Revolution. 1st Harper Perennial ed. Toronto: HarperCollins Publishers. (Copyright: 1994.)

Siggner, Andrew J.
2003        Urban Aboriginal Populations: An Update Using the 2001 Census Results. Pp. 15–21 in Not Strangers in These Parts: Urban Aboriginal Peoples. David R. Newhouse and Evelyn J. Peters, eds. Ottawa: Policy Research Initiative.

2003a       Impact of 'Ethnic Mobility' on Socio-Economic Conditions of Aboriginal Peoples. *Canadian Studies in Population* 30(1):137–158.

Siggner, Andrew J., and Rosalinda Costa
2005        Aboriginal Conditions in Census Metropolitan Areas,1981–2001. *Statistics Canada Catalogue* 89-613-MIE. Ottawa: Minister Responsible for Statistics Canada.

Silko, Leslie Marmon
1977        Ceremony. New York: Viking. (Reprinted: Signet, New York, 1978.)

1981        Storyteller. New York: Seaver Press.

1991        Almanac of the Dead. New York: Simon and Schuster.

1999        Gardens in the Dunes: A Novel. New York: Simon and Schuster.

Siminoski, Ted
1979        Sioux Versus Hollywood: The Image of Sioux Indians in American Films. (Ph.D. Dissertation, Fine Arts/Performing Arts Department, University of Southern California, Los Angeles.)

Simmons, Rob
2002        Testimony of Congressman Rob Simmons Before Hearing of the Energy Policy, Natural Resources, and Regulatory Affairs Subcommittee of the House Government Reform Committee. Subject: Problems with the Bureau of Indian Affairs' Tribal Recognition Process. February 7, 2002. Washington: U.S. Government Printing Office.

Simpson, A.
2000        Paths Toward a Mohawk Nation: Narratives of Citizenship and Nationhood in Kahnawake. Pp. 113–136 in Political Theory and the Rights of Indigenous Peoples. Duncan Ivision, Paul Patton, and Will Sanders, eds. Cambridge: Cambridge University Press.

Simpson, D.W., and D.K.F. Wattie
1968        The Role and Impact of the Educational Program in the Process of Change in Canadian Eskimo Communities. Ottawa: Education Division, Northern Administration Branch, Indian and Northern Affairs Canada.

Simpson, Moira G.
1996        Native American Museums and Culture Centres. Pp. 135–169 in Making Representations: Museums in the Post-Colonial Era. New York: Routledge Press.

Sims, Christine P.
2001        Native Language Planning. Pp. 63–73 in The Green Book of Language Revitalization in Practice. Leanne Hinton and Kenneth Hale, eds. San Diego, Calif.: Academic Press.

2005        Tribal Languages and the Challenges of Revitalization. *Anthropology and Education Quarterly* 36(1):104–106. Washington.

Sinclair, Kathryn
1996        Maka Sitomniya Teca Ukiye Oyate Ukiye: The American Indian Movement. *Political Expressions* 1(2):33–52. Victoria, Australia.

Singer, Beverly R.
2001        Wiping the War Paint Off the Lens: Native American Film and Video. Minneapolis: University of Minnesota Press.

Singer, Joseph W.
2003        Canons of Conquest: The Supreme Court's Attack on Tribal Sovereignty. *New England Law Review* 37(3):641–668. Boston.

2006        Nine-Tenths of the Law: Title, Possession, and Sacred Obligations. *Connecticut Law Review* 38(2):605–629. Hartford, Conn.

Sioui, Georges
1992        For an Amerindian Autohistory. Montreal: McGill-Queen's University Press.

Sirois, John E., Margaret T. Gordon, and Andrew C. Gordon
2001        Native American Access to Technology Program: Progress Report. A Report to the Bill & Melinda Gates Foundation, December 2001. Seattle: University of Washington, Daniel J. Evans School of Public Affairs.

Skibine, Alex Tallchief
2001        High Level Nuclear Waste on Indian Reservations: Pushing the Tribal Sovereignty Envelope to the Edge? *Journal of Land Resources and Environmental Law* 21(2A):287–316. Salt Lake City.

2003        The Dialogic of Federalism in Federal Indian Law and the Rehnquist Court: The Need for Coherence and Integration. *Texas Forum on Civil Liberties and Civil Rights* 8(1):1–49. [Austin, Tex.]

2003a       Integrating the Indian Trust Doctrine into the Constitution. *Tulsa Law Review* 39(2):247–270. Tulsa, Okla.

Skidegate Repatriation and Cultural Committee
2004        What We Do. Skidegate, B.C.: Skidegate Repatriation and Cultural Committee, Haida Gwaii Museum. (Webpage: http://www.repatriation.ca/what_we_do.htm [6 August 2006].)

Skinner, Alanson B.
1923        A Further Note on the Origin of the Dream Dance of the Central Algonkian and Southern Siouan Indians. *American Anthropologist*, n.s. 25(3):427–428.

1925        Final Observations on the Central Algonkian Dream Dance. *American Anthropologist*, n.s. 27(2):340–343.

Skinner, Linda
1999        Teaching Through Traditions: Incorporating Languages and Culture into Curricula. Pp. 107–134 in Next Steps: Research and Practice to Advance Indian Education. Karen Gayton Swisher and John W. Tippeconnic, III, eds. Charleston, W.Va.: ERIC Clearinghouse on Rural Education and Small Schools.

Skopek, Tracy A., Rich Engstrom, and Kenneth Hansen
2005        All That Glitters: The Rise of American Indian Tribes in State Political Behavior. American Indian Culture and Research Journal 29(4):45–58. Los Angeles.

Slattery, Brian
1979        The Land Rights of Indigenous Canadian Peoples, As Affected by the Crown's Acquisition of Their Territories. Saskatoon, Sask.: University of Saskatchewan Native Law Centre.

1987      Understanding Aboriginal Rights. *The Canadian Bar Review* 66:727–783. Toronto.

2000      Making Sense of Aboriginal and Treaty Rights. *The Canadian Bar Review* 79:196–224. Toronto.

2006      The Metamorphosis of Aboriginal Title. *The Canadian Bar Review* 85:255–286. Toronto.

2007      What Are Aboriginal Rights? In: Let It Be Done: *Calder*, Aboriginal Title and the Future of Indigenous Rights. Hamar Foster, Heather Raven, and Jeremy Webber, eds. Vancouver: UBC Press.

Slattery, Brian, and Sheila Stelck, comps. and eds.
1980–1991      *see* Native Law Centre 1980–1991

Slobodin, Richard
1981      *see* Handbook Vol. 6 (1981:361–371)

Slotkin, James Sydney
1952      Menomini Peyotism: A Study of Individual Variation in a Primary Group With a Homogeneous Culture. *Transactions of the American Philosophical Society* 42(4):565–700. Philadelphia.

1956      The Peyote Religion: A Study in Indian-White Relations. Glencoe, Ill.: Free Press.

Slotkin, Richard S.
1973      Regeneration Through Violence: The Mythology of the American Frontier, 1600–1860. Middletown, Conn.: Wesleyan University Press.

Smet, Pierre-Jean de
1905      Life, Letters, and Travels of Father Pierre-Jean De Smet, S.J. 1801–1873. Hiram Martin Crittenden and Alfred Talbot Richardson, eds. 4 vols. New York: Francis P. Harper. (Reprinted: Arno Press, New York, 1969.)

Smith, Chadwick "Corntassel"
2006      Where the Casino Money Goes. *Cherokee Phoenix* 30(3):15–18. Tahlequah, Okla.

2007      "Smith: Cherokees Vote for Indian Blood." *Indian Country Today*, March 9, 2007. Canastota, N.Y. (Webpage: http://www.indiancountry.com)

Smith, David E., ed.
1992      Building a Province: A History of Saskatchewan in Documents. Saskatoon, Sask.: Fifth House Publishers.

Smith, Dean Howard
1994      The Issue of Compatibility Between Cultural Integrity and Economic Development Among Native American Tribes. *American Indian Culture and Research Journal* 18(2):177–205. Los Angeles.

2000      Modern Tribal Development: Paths to Self-Sufficiency and Cultural Integrity in Indian Country. Walnut Creek, Calif.: Rowman and Littlefield Publishers.

Smith, Derek G.
1993      The Emergence of "Eskimo Status": An Examination of the Eskimo Disk List System and Its Social Consequences, 1925–1970. Pp. 41–74 in Anthropology, Public Policy, and Native Peoples in Canada. Noel Dyck and James B. Waldram, eds. Montreal: McGill-Queen's University Press.

Smith, Huston, ed.
2006      A Seat at the Table: Huston Smith in Conversation with Native Americans on Religious Freedom. Edited and with a Preface by Phil Cousineau. Berkeley: University of California Press.

Smith, Huston, and Reuben Snake, comps. and eds.
1996      "One Nation Under God": The Triumph of the Native American Church. Foreword by Senator Daniel K. Inouye. Sante Fe: Clear Light Books.

Smith, Lincoln B.
1906      Indians. In: Corpus Juris Cyc., Vol. 22. London and New York: The American Law Book Company. (Reprinted, with new cases, in: Indian Affairs: Laws and Treaties, Volume 3: Laws. Charles J. Kappler, comp. and ed. Washington: U.S. Government Printing Office, 1913.)

Smith, Linda Tuhiwai
1999      Decolonizing Methodologies: Research and Indigenous Peoples. New York: Zed Books.

Smith, Paul Chaat
1990      American Indian Movement. Pp. 22–23 in Encyclopedia of the American Left. Mari Jo Buhle, Paul Buhle, and Dan Georgakas, eds. New York: Garland Publishing.

Smith, Paul Chaat, and Robert Allen Warrior
1996      Like A Hurricane: The Indian Movement from Alcatraz to Wounded Knee. New York: The New Press.

Smith, Sherry Lynn
2001      Francis LaFlesche and the World of Letters. *American Indian Quarterly* 25(4):579–603. Lincoln, Nebr.

Smithsonian Institution. National Museum of Natural History (NMNH)
2006      Table of Completed Repatriations as of May 31, 2006. Washington: Smithsonian Institution. National Museum of Natural History. (Webpage: http://www.nmnh.si.edu/anthro/repatriation/pdf/Repatriationstable.pdf [6 August 2006].)

2006a      Repatriation of Anthropology Collection. Washington: Smithsonian Institution. National Museum of Natural History. (Webpage: http://www.nmnh.si.edu/anthro/repatriation/collections/anthrocollections.htm [6 August 2006].)

Smithsonian Institution. National Museum of the American Indian (NMAI)
2000      *see* Ames, Michael, ed. 2000

2004      Celebrating the Grand Opening of the National Museum of the American Indian: Native Nations Procession, Opening Ceremony, First Americans Festival—September 21–26, 2004. Washington: Smithsonian Institution. National Museum of the American Indian.

2006      Repatriation. Washington: Smithsonian Institution. National Museum of the American Indian. (Webpage: http:www.nmai.si.edu/subpage.cfm?subpage=collaboration&second=repatriation [6 August 2006].)

Smythe, Charles W.
1995      Assessment of the Six Nations Iroquois Confederacy: Request to the National Museum of Natural History to Repatriate Two Wampum Items. Washington: Smithsonian Institution, National Museum of Natural History, Repatriation Office.

1999      Assessment of Request for the Repatriation of Seven Wooden Masks from Prince William Sound by the Chugach Alaska Corporation. Washington: Smithsonian Institution, National Museum of Natural History, Repatriation Office.

1999a      Assessment of a Request for the Repatriation of a Kiowa War Shield (Big Bow's Shield) from the National Museum of Natural History. Washington: Smithsonian Institution, National Museum of Natural History, Repatriation Office.

2000    Assessment of Request for the Repatriation of the Ontonagon Boulder by the Keweenaw Bay Indian Community. Washington: Smithsonian Institution, National Museum of Natural History, Repatriation Office.

2000a    Assessment of a Request for the Repatriation of a Scalp from the Gros Ventre Flat Pipe by the White Clay Society. Washington: Smithsonian Institution, National Museum of Natural History, Repatriation Office.

Smythe, Charles W., and Priya Helweg
1996    Summary of Ethnological Objects in the National Museum of Natural History Associated with the Creek Culture. Washington: Smithsonian Institution, National Museum of Natural history, Repatriation Office.

Snake, Reuben
1996    Your Humble Serpent: Reuben Snake, Indian Visionary and Activist. Jay C. Fikes, ed. Santa Fe, N.Mex.: Clear Lights Publishers.

Snipp, C. Matthew
1986    Who Are American Indians? Some Observations About the Perils and Pitfalls of Data for Race and Ethnicity. *Population Research and Policy Review* 5:247–252. Amsterdam: Springer Netherlands.

1989    American Indians: The First of This Land. New York: Russell Sage Foundation Press.

1996    The Size and Distribution of the American Indian Population: Fertility, Mortality, Migration, and Residence. Pp. 17–52 in Changing Numbers, Changing Needs: American Indian Demography and Public Health. Gary D. Sandefur, Ronald R. Rindfuss, and Barney R. Cohen, eds. Washington: National Academy Press. (Reprinted in: *Population Research and Policy Review* 16(1–2):61–93. Amsterdam: Springer Netherlands, 1997.)

1996a    Urban Indians. Pp. 653–654 in Encyclopedia of North American Indians. Frederick E. Hoxie, ed. Boston, New York: Houghton Mifflin Company.

2006    *see* Handbook Vol. 3 (2006:702–711)

Snyder, Peter Z.
1973    Social Interaction Patterns and Relative Urban Success: The Denver Navajo. *Urban Anthropology* 2(1):1–24. [New York, etc.]

Sockbeson, Henry J.
1994    The Larsen Bay Repatriation Case and Common Errors of Anthropologists. Pp. 158–162 in Reckoning with the Dead: The Larsen Bay Repatriation and the Smithsonian Institution. Tamara L. Bray and Thomas W. Killion, eds. Washington: Smithsonian Institution Press.

Solomon, Shirley
1995    Tribal/County Cooperation: Making It Work at the Local Level. *Cultural Survival Quarterly* 19(3):56–60. Cambridge, Mass.

Sorkin, Alan L.
1971    American Indians and Federal Aid. Washington: Brookings Institution.

1978    The Urban Indian. Lexington, Mass.: Lexington Books.

Sotheby's
2006    [American Indian Art Auction, May 8, 2006. Catalog.] New York: Sotheby's.

Spaeth, Nicholas J., ed.
1993    American Indian Law Deskbook. Conference of Western Attorneys General. Nicholas J. Spaeth, Chair, Editing Committee; Julie Wrend and Clay Smith, Chief Editors. Niwot, Colo.: University Press of Colorado.

Speaker, Stuart
1993    Report on [Hawaiian] Funeray Objects and Artifacts Made of Human Remains in the NMNH Anthropology Collections. Washington: Smithsonian Institution, National Museum of Natural History, Repatriation Office.

1999    The Human Remains of Ishi, a Yahi-Yana Indian, in the National Museum of Natural History, Smithsonian Institution. Washington: Smithsonian Institution, National Museum of Natural History, Repatriation Office.

Speaker, Stuart, Erica Jones, and Karen Mudar
1995    Inventory and Assessment of Human Remains and Associated Funerary Objects from Anaktuvuk Pass, Alaska, in the National Museum of Natural History. Washington: Smithsonian Institution, National Museum of Natural History, Repatriation Office.

Speaker, Stuart, Thomas W. Killion, and John W. Verano
1993    Arapaho Repatriation: The Human Remains. Washington: Smithsonian Institution, National Museum of Natural History, Repatriation Office.

Speaker, Stuart, Deanna Kingston, and Karen M. Mudar
1996    Inventory and Assessment of Human Remains and Associated Funerary Objects from Nunivak Island, Alaska, in the National Museum of Natural History. Washington: Smithsonian Institution, National Museum of Natural History, Repatriation Office.

Speaker, Stuart, Javier Urcid, and Beverly Byrd
1995    Inventory and Assessment of Human Remains and Associated Funerary Objects from the Cook Inlet Region Incorporated, Alaska, in the National Museum of Natural History. Washington: Smithsonian Institution, National Museum of Natural History, Repatriation Office.

Speaker, Stuart, et al.
1994    Inventory and Assessment of Human Remains Potentially Related to the Apache and Yavapai Tribes in the National Museum of Natural History. Washington: Smithsonian Institution, National Museum of Natural History, Repatriation Office.

_____, et al.
1994a    Inventory and Assessment of Human Remains Potentially Related to the Kiowa Tribe in the National Museum of Natural History. Washington: Smithsonian Institution, National Museum of Natural History, Repatriation Office.

Spears, Jack
1971    Hollywood: The Golden Era. New York: A.S. Barnes.

Special Joint Committee of the Senate and House of Commons (SJC)
1947, 1948    *see* Canada. Special Joint Committee of the Senate and House of Commons (SJC) 1947, 1948

Speck, Frank G., and Leonard Broom
1983    Cherokee Dance and Drama. Norman: University of Oklahoma Press.

Spicer, Edward H.
1962    Cycles of Conquest: The Impact of Spain, Mexico, and the United States on the Indians of the Southwest, 1533–1960. Tucson: University of Arizona Press.

1977 [Letter from Edward H. Spicer, University of Arizona, to Senator James Abourezk, September 21, 1977.] In: Hearing Before the United States Senate Select Committee on Indian Affairs on S.1633, To Provide for Extension of Certain Federal Benefits, Services and Assistance to the Pascula [sic] Yaqui Indians of Arizona, September 27, 1977. Washington: U.S. Government Printing Office.

Spilde, Katherine Ann
1998 Acts of Sovereignty, Acts of Identity: Negotiating Interdependence Through Tribal Government Gaming on the White Earth Indian Reservation. (Ph.D. Dissertation in Anthropology, University of California, Santa Cruz.)

2004 Creating a Political Space for American Indian Economic Development: Indian Gaming and American Indian Activism. Pp. 71–88 in Local Actions: Cultural Activism, Power and Public Life in America. Melissa Checker and Maggie Fishman, eds. New York: Columbia University Press.

Spivak, Gayatri C.
1994 Can the Subaltern Speak. Pp. 66–111 in Colonial Discourse and Post-Colonial Theory: A Reader. Patrick Williams and Laura Chrisman, eds. New York: Columbia University Press.

Spivey, Michael
2005 Review of: Patrick Minges, ed. *Black Indian Slave Narratives* (2004). *American Indian Quarterly* 29(3–4):718–720. Lincoln, Nebr.

Spotted Elk, Clara
1989 Skeletons in the Attic. *The New York Times*, March 8, 1989. New York.

Sprague, Douglas N.
1995 The New Math of the New Indian Act: 6(2)+6(2)=6(1). *Native Studies Review* 10(1):47–95. Saskatoon, Sask.

Sprague, Douglas N., and R.P. Frye
1983 The Genealogy of the First Métis Nation: The Development and Dispersal of the Red River Settlement, 1820–1900. Winnipeg, Man.: Pemmican Publications.

Sprague, Roderick
1974 American Indians and American Archaeology. *American Antiquity* 39(1):1–2.

Spring, Joel
1996 The Cultural Transformation of a Native American Family and Its Tribe, 1763–1995. *Sociocultural, Political, and Historical Studies in Education.* Mahwah, N.J., and London: Lawrence Erlbaum Associates, Publishers.

Spruce, Duane Blue, ed.
2005 Spirit of a Native Place: Building the National Museum of the American Indian. Duane Blue Spruce, ed. Washington: National Nuseum of the American Indian, Smithsonian Institution. Washington: National Nuseum of the American Indian, Smithsonian Institution.

Spry, Irene, and Bennett McCardle
1993 The Records of the Department of the Interior and Research Concerning Western Canada's Frontier of Settlement. Regina, Sask.: Canadian Plains Research Centre, University of Regina.

St. Germain, Jill
2001 Indian Treaty-Making Policy in the United States and Canada, 1867–1877. Lincoln and London: University of Nebraska Press.

Stabler, Hollis D.
2005 No One Ever Asked Me: The World War II Memoirs of an Omaha Indian Soldier. Edited by Victoria Smith. *American Indian Lives.* Lincoln: University of Nebraska Press.

Stabler, Jack C., and Eric C. Howe
1990 Native Participation in Northern Development: The Impending Crisis in the NWT. *Canadian Public Policy* 16(3):262–283. Toronto.

Stagg, Jack
1981 Anglo-Indian Relations in North America to 1763 and an Analysis of the Royal Proclamation of 7 October 1763. Ottawa: Research Branch, Indian and Northern Affairs Canada.

Standing Bear, Luther
1933 Land of the Spotted Eagle. Boston: Houghton, Mifflin. (Reprinted: see Standing Bear 1978, 2006.)

1978 Land of the Spotted Eagle. Foreword by Richard N. Ellis. Introduction by Melvin R. Gilmore. Lincoln: University of Nebraska Press.

2006 Land of the Spotted Eagle. New Edition. Introduction by Joseph Marshall, III. Lincoln: University of Nebraska Press.

Standing Bear, and Zug G.
1994 To Guard Against Invading Indians: Struggling for Native Community in the Southeast. Pp. 254–301 in Special Edition: Alcatraz Revisited: The 25th Anniversary of the Occupation, 1969–1971. Joane Nagel and Troy Johnson, eds. *American Indian Culture and Research Journal* 18(4). Los Angeles.

Stanley, George F.G., gen. ed.
1985 The Collected Writings of Louis Riel. Text in English and French. Edmonton, Alta.: University of Alberta Press.

1992 The Birth of Western Canada: A History of the Riel Rebellions. New Introduction by Thomas Flanagan; Maps by C.C.J. Bond. Toronto: University of Toronto Press.

Stapp, Darby C., and Michael S. Burney
2002 Tribal Cultural Resource Management: The Full Circle To Stewarship. Lanham, Md.:AltaMira Press.

State of Connecticut
2003 *see* Connecticut, State of

Statistics Canada *see* Canada. Statistics Canada

Stauss, Joseph (Jay) H., and Bruce A. Chadwick
1979 Urban Indian Adjustment. *American Indian Culture and Research Journal* 3(2):23–38. Los Angeles.

Stauss, Joseph (Jay) H., Mary Jo Tippeconnic Fox, and Shelly Lowe
2002 American Indian Studies at the Universtiy of Arizona. Pp. 83–96 in Native American Studies in Higher Education: Models for Collaboration Between Universities and Indigenous Nations. Duane Champagne and Jay Stauss, eds. Walnut Creek, Calif.: AltaMira Press.

Stauss, Joseph (Jay) H., et al.
1979 An Experimental Outreach Legal Aid Program for an Urban Native American Population Utilizing Legal Paraprofessionals. *Human Organization* 38(4):386–394. Washington.

Stavenhagen, Rodolfo
2004 Report of the Special Rapporteur on the Situation of Human Rights and Fundamental Freedoms, Rodolfo Stavenhagen. Addendum: Mission to Canada. *United Nations Commission on Human Rights*; Report No. E/CN.4/2005/88/Add.3. Geneva, Switzerland.

Stearn, E. Wagner, and Allen E. Stearn
1945        The Effect of Smallpox in the Destiny of the Amerindian. Boston: Bruce Humphries.

Stefon, Frederick J.
1978        The Irony of Termination: 1943–1958. *The Indian Historian* 11(3):3–14. San Francisco.

Stein, Wayne J.
1992        Tribally Controlled Colleges: Making Good Medicine. *American Indian Studies* 3. New York: Peter Lang Publishing.

1997        American Indians and Gambling: Economic and Social Impacts. Pp. 145–166 in American Indian Studies: An Interdisciplinary Approach to Contemporary Issues. Dane Anthony Morrison, ed. New York: Peter Lang.

1998        Gaming: The Apex of a Long Struggle. *Wicazo Sa Review* 13(1):73–91. Minneapolis.

1999        Tribal Colleges: 1968–1998. Pp. 259–270 in Next Steps: Research and Practice to Advance Indian Education. Karen Gayton Swisher and John W. Tippeconnic, III, eds. Charleston, W.Va.: ERIC Clearinghouse on Rural Education and Small Schools.

2003        Developmental Action for Implementing an Indigenous College: Philosophical Foundations and Pragmatic Steps. Pp. 25–60 in The Renaissance of American Indian Higher Education: Capturing the Dream. Maenette Kape'ahiokalani Padeken Ah Nee-Benham and Wayne J. Stein, eds. Mahwah, N.J., and London: Lawrence Erlbaum Associates, Publishers.

2006        Tribal Colleges and Universities: A Major Pillar of Self-Determination in Indian Country. (Typescript, Department of Native American Studies, Montana State University, Bozeman, Mont.)

Stein, Wayne J., James Shanley, and Timothy Sanchez
2003        The Effect of the Native American Higher Education Initiative on Strengthening Tribal Colleges and Universities: Focus on Governance and Finance. Pp. 75–98 in The Renaissance of American Indian Higher Education: Capturing the Dream. Maenette Kape'ahiokalani Padeken Ah Nee-Benham and Wayne J. Stein, eds. Mahwah, N.J., and London: Lawrence Erlbaum Associates, Publishers.

Steiner, Stan
1968        The New Indians. New York: Dell Publishing Company.

Steinmetz, Paul B.
1990        Pipe, Bible, and Peyote Among the Oglala Lakota. Knoxville: University of Tennessee Press.

Stepney, Philip H.R., ed.
1990        The Scriver Blackfoot collection: Repatriation of Canada's Heritage. Edmonton, Alta.: Provincial Museum of Alberta.

Stern, Kenneth S.
1994        Loud Hawk: The United States Versus the American Indian Movement. Norman, Okla.: University of Oklahoma Press.

Stern, Theodore
1961–1962   Klamath Livelihood, Tribe, and Reservation. Pp. 172–180 in American Indians and Their Economic Development. Fred Voget, ed. *Human Organization*, Special Issue 20(4). Washington.

1965        The Klamath Tribe: A People and Their Reservation. Seattle: University of Washington Press.

Stevenson, Mark L.
2002        Section 91(24) and Canada's Legislative Jurisdiction With Respect to the Métis. *Indigenous Law Journal at the University of Toronto, Faculty Law* 1:237–262. Toronto.

2004        Métis Aboriginal Rights and the "Core of Indianness". *Saskatchewan Law Review* 67(1):301–313. Saskatoon, Sask.

Stewart, D.
1993        A Critique of the Winnipeg Core Initiative: A Case Study in Urban Revitalization. *Canadian Journal of Urban Research* 2(1):150–166. Winnipeg, Man.

Stewart, Omer C.
1974        Origin of the Peyote Religion in the United States. *Plains Anthropologist* 19(65):211–223. Lincoln, Nebr.

1978        *see* Handbook Vol. 8 (1978:705–712)

1987        Peyote Religion: A History. Norman: University of Oklahoma Press.

Stoffle, Richard W., and Michael J. Evans
1990        Holistic Conservation and Cultural Triage: American Indian Perspectives on Cultural Resources. *Human Organization* 49(2):91–99. Washington.

Stone, That Man
[1900]      [Photography of Quanah Parker's Dance Troop, Chickasha, OK.] (National Anthropological Archives, Photograph 55, 604, Smithsonian Institution, Washington.)

Stonechild, Blair, William Asikinack, and David R. Miller
2002        The Department of Indian Studies at the Saskatchewan Indian Federated College. Pp. 165–182 in Native American Studies in Higher Education: Models for Collaboration Between Universities and Indigenous Nations. Duane Champagne and Jay Stauss, eds. Walnut Creek, Calif.: AltaMira Press.

Storm, Hyemeyohsts
1972        Seven Arrows. New York: Ballantine Books.

1981        The Song of Heyoehkah. San Francisco: Harper and Row.

Strange, Carolyn, and Tina Loo
2001        Holding the Rock: The "Indianization" of Alcatraz Island, 1969–1999. *The Public Historian* 23(1):55–74. Santa Barbara, Calif.

Strauss, Terry
1990        Indians of the Chicago Area. 2d ed. *1981 Conference on Problems and Issues Concerning Chicago Urban Indians*. Chicago: NAES College Press.

Strickland, Rennard
1974        Fire and the Spirits: Cherokee Law from Clan to Court. Norman: University of Oklahoma Press.

1977        Tonto's Revenge: Reflections on American Indian Culture and Policy. Albuquerque: University of New Mexico Press.

_____, editor-in-chief
1982        *see* Cohen, Felix S. 1982

1989        Coyote Goes Hollywood. 2 Parts. *Native Peoples: The Arts and Lifeway* 2(3):46–52; 3(1):38–46. Phoenix, Ariz.

1993        John Rollin Ridge: California's First American Indian Lawyer. *Tulsa Law Journal* 29:193. Tulsa, Okla.

Stripes, James
1999    A Strategy of Resistance: The "Actorvism" of Russell Means from Plymouth Rock to the Disney Studios. *Wicazo Sa Review* 14(1):87–101. Minneapolis.

Stromberg, Ernest
2006    American Indian Rhetorics of Survivance: Word Medicine, Word Magic. Pittsburgh, Pa.: University of Pittsburgh Press.

Stuart, Paul
1987    Nations Within a Nation: Historical Statistics of American Indians. Westport, Conn.: Greenwood Press.

Stull, Donald
1973    Modernization and Symptoms of Stress: Attitudes, Accidents and Alcohol Use Among Urban Papago Indians. (Ph.D. Dissertation in Anthropology, University of Colorado, Boulder.)

———
1977    New Data on Accident Victim Rates Among Papago Indians: The Urban Case. *Human Organization* 36(4):395–398. Washington.

Sturm, Circe
2000    Review of: In Whose Honor? American Indian Mascots in Sports. Film by Jay Rosenstein, New Day Films, Ho-Ho-Kus, N.J., 1995. *American Anthropologist* 102(2):352–353.

———
2002    Blood Politics: Race, Culture, and Identity in the Cherokee Nation of Oklahoma. Berkeley: University of California Press.

Sturtevant, William C.
1971    Creek into Seminole. Pp. 92–128 in North American Indians in Historical Perspective. Eleanor Burke Leacock and Nancy Oestreich Lurie, eds. New York: Random House. (Reprinted: Waveland Press, Prospect Heights, Ill. 1988. Also in: A Seminole Source Book. Edited with an Introduction by William C. Sturtevant, Garland Publishing, Inc., New York and London, 1987.)

———
1986    The Meaning of Native American Art. Pp. 23–44 in The Arts of the North American Indian: Native Traditions in Evolution. Edwin L. Wade, ed. New York: Hudson Hills Press.

Suagee, Dean B.
1982    American Indian Religious Freedom and Cultural Resources Management: Protecting Mother Earth's Caretakers. *American Indian Law Review* 10(1):1–58. Norman, Okla.

Sullivan, Martin
1992    Return of the Sacred Wampum Belts of the Iroquois. *The History Teacher* 26(1):7–14. Long Beach, Calif.

Supreme Court of Canada *see* Canada. Supreme Court of Canada

Surtees, Robert J.
1988    *see* Handbook Vol. 4 (1988:202–210)

Sutton, Imre, ed.
1985    Irredeemable America: The Indians' Estate and Land Claims. Albuquerque: University of New Mexico Press.

———
2001    Tribes and States: A Political Geography of Indian Environmental Jurisdiction. Pp. 239–263 in Trusteeship in Change: Toward Tribal Autonomy in Resource Management. Richmond L. Clow and Imre Sutton, eds. Boulder, Colo.: University Press of Colorado.

Swan, Daniel C.
1990    West Moon-East Moon: An Ethnohistory of the Peyote Religion Among the Osage Indians, 1898–1930. (Ph.D. Dissertation in Anthropology, University of Oklahoma, Norman.)

———
1996–1998    [Field and Interview Notes.] (*Peyoteros* of South Texas and Correspondence Files. Texas Department of Public Safety. In Daniel C. Swan's possession.)

———
1998    [Symbols of Faith and Belief: The Art of the Native American Church.] (Field Notes: Traveling Exhibition Venue Research; in Daniel C. Swan's possession.)

———
1999    Peyote Religious Art: Symbols of Faith and Belief. Jackson, Miss.: University Press of Mississippi.

———
2005–2006    [Interview Notes and Correspondence, Native American Church Administrative History.] (In Daniel C. Swan's possession.)

Swann, Brian, ed.
1983    Smoothing the Ground: Essays on Native American Oral History. Berkeley: University of California Press.

———, ed.
2004    Voices from Four Directions: Contemporary Translations of the Native Literatures of North America. Lincoln, Nebr., and London: University of Nebraska Press.

Swann, Brian, and Arnold Krupat, eds.
1987    Recovering the Word: Essays on Native American Literature. Berkeley: University of California Press.

Swanton, John R.
1952    The Indian Tribes of North America. *Bureau of American Ethnology Bulletin* 145. Washington: Smithsonian Institution; U.S. Government Printing Office. (Reprinted: Several reprintes, incl.: 1969, 1971, 1984, 1995.)

Swepston, Lee
1990    The Adoption of the Indigenous and Tribal Peoples Convention, 1989 (No. 169). *Law and Anthropology* 5(196):221–235. Vienna, Austria.

Swidler, Nina, et al., eds.
1997    Native Americans and Archaeologists: Stepping Stones to Common Ground. Walnut Creek, Calif.: AltaMira Press, and Society for American Archaeology.

Swinton, Katherine, and Carol Rogerson, eds.
1988    Competing Constitutional Visions: The Meech Lake Accord. Toronto: Carswell.

Swisher, Kara
1989    Smithsonian To Surrender Indian Bones, Accord Sets Stage for New Museum. *Washington Post*, September 12, 1989: A1. Washington.

Szasz, Margaret Connell
1977    Education and the American Indian: The Road to Self-Determination Since 1928. Albuquerque: University of New Mexico Press.

Szasz, Margaret Connell, and Carmelita Ryan
1988    *see* Handbook Vol. 4 (1988:284–300)

Takaki, Ronald
1993    A Different Mirror: A History of Multicultural America. Boston: Little, Brown and Co.

Talbot, Steve
1981    Roots of Oppression: The American Indian Question. New York: International Publishers.

———
1994    Indian Students and Reminiscences of Alcatraz. Pp. 93–102 in Special Edition: Alcatraz Revisited: The 25th Anniversary of the Occupation, 1969–1971. Joane Nagel and Troy

Johnson, eds. *American Indian Culture and Research Journal* 18(4). Los Angeles.

Tallmadge, Alice
2002    Cow Creek Tribe Flourishes Despite a Rocky Past. *The Portland Oregonian*, April 28, 2002. Portland, Oreg. (Reprinted, Cow Creek Umpqua Tribe Webpage: http://www.cowcreek.com/media/s01_history/a95-art29.html)

Tanner, Adrian
1979    Bringing Home Animals: Religious Ideology and Mode of Production of the Mistassini Cree Hunters. St. John's, N.L.: Institute of Social and Economic Research, Memorial University of Newfoundland.

———, ed.
1983    The Politics of Indianness: Case Studies and Ethnopolitics in Canada. St. John's, N.L.: Institute of Social and Economic Research, Memorial University of Newfoundland.

1999    Culture, Social Change, and Cree Opposition to the James Bay Hydroelectric Development. Pp. 121–140 in Social and Environmental Impacts of the James Bay Hydroelectric Project. James F. Hornig, ed. Montreal: McGill-Queen's University Press.

Tanner, Helen H.
1986    Atlas of Great Lakes Indian History. Norman: University of Oklahoma Press.

1991    Erminie Wheeler-Voegelin (1903–1988), Founder of the American Society for Ethnohistory. *Ethnohistory* 38(1): 65–68.

Tanner, L.
2006    Pima Indian Study: Early Diabetes Augurs Early Death. *Arizona Daily Star*, July 26, 2006. Tucson.

Tarpy, Cliff, and Ira Block
2000    Pueblo Ancestors Return Home. Photography by Ira Block. *National Geographic* 198(5):118–125. Washington. (See also: Block, Ira 2000.)

Task Force. Assembly of First Nations and the Canadian Museums Association
1992    Turning the Page: Forging New Partnerships Between Museums and First Peoples. Ottawa: Assembly of First Nations and the Canadian Museums Association.

1992a   Task Force Report on Museums and First Peoples. *Museum Anthropology* 16(2):12–20. Tempe, Ariz.

Tatshenshini-Alsek Park
1996    Park Management Agreement, April 29, 1996, Authorized by Order-in-Council under the Environment and Land Use Act. [British Columbia: Tatshenshini-Alsek Park.]

Taukchiray, Wesley, and Kasakoff, Alice
1992    Contemporary Native Americans in South Carolina. Pp. 72–101 in Indians of the Southeastern United States in the Late Twentieth Century. James Anthony Paredes, ed. Tuscaloosa and London: The University of Alabama Press.

Tax, Sol
1978    The Impact of Urbanization on American Indians. Pp. 121–136 in American Indians Today. J. Milton Yinger and George Eaton Simpson, eds. *The Annals of the American Academy of Political and Social Science* 436(March). Philadelphia.

Taylor, Colin F.
1988    *see* Handbook Vol. 4 (1988:562–569)

1990    Reading Plains Indians Artefacts: Their Symbolism as Cultural and Historical Documents. (Ph.D. Dissertation, Department of Literature, University of Essex, Colchester, U.K.)

Taylor, Drew Haden
1996    Alive and Well: Native Theatre in Canada. *Journal of Canadian Studies* 31(3):29–38. Peterborough, Ont.

1997    Storytelling to Stage: The Growth of Native Theatre in Canada. *TDR: The Drama Review* 41(3):140–152. Cambridge, Mass.

Taylor, Jonathan B.
2005    Counting the Benefit$: How a Harvard Research Study Has Begun To Track Increasing Native American Prosperity. *Tribal Government Gaming* [no issue]:28–29.

Taylor, Jonathan B., and Joseph P. Kalt
2005    American Indians on Reservations: A Datebook of Socioeconomic Change Between the 1990 and 2000 Censuses. Cambridge, Mass.: The Harvard Project on American Indian Economic Development, Harvard University.

Taylor, Theodore W.
1972    The States and Their Indian Citizens. Washington: U.S. Government Printing Office.

1984    The Bureau of Indian Affairs. Boulder, Colo.: Westview Press.

Taylor, William B., and Franklin Pease G.Y., eds.
1994    Violence, Resistance, and Survival in the Americas: Native Americans and the Legacy of Conquest. Washington and London: Smithsonian Institution Press.

Tedlock, Dennis, trans.
1972    Finding the Center: Narrative Poetry of the Zuni Indians. New York: Dial Press. (Reprinted: see Tedlock 1978, 1999.)

———, trans.
1978    Finding the Center: The Art of the Zuni Storyteller; From Live Performances in Zuni by Andrew Peynetsa and Walter Sanchez. Lincoln: University of Nebraska Press. (Reprinted in 1999.)

Tedlock, Dennis, and Jerome Rothenberg, eds.
1970–1980   *Alcheringa*. [Published by the editors.]

Teillet, Jean
1999    *see* Métis National Council (MNC) 1999

Telford, Rhonda
1996    'The Sound of the Rustling of Gold Is Under My Feet Where I Stand; We Have a Rich Country': A History of Aboriginal Mineral Resources in Ontario. (Ph.D. Dissertation in History, University of Toronto, Toronto.)

Tennant, Paul, et al.
1984    The Report of the House of Commons Special Committee on Indian Self-Government. Three Comments: "Indian Self-Government: Progress or Stalemate?", by Paul Tennant; "A Commentary on the Penner Report", by Sally M. Weaver; "The Paradoxical Nature of the Penner Report", by Roger Gibbins and J. Rick Ponting. *Canadian Public Policy* 10(2):211–224. Toronto.

1990    Aboriginal Peoples and Politics: The Indian Land Question in British Columbia, 1849–1889. Vancouver: University of British Columbia Press.

The Crees of Quebec, Le Gouvernement de Québec *see* Crees of Québec, The, and Le Gouvernement de Québec

*The Gazette*
2006      Cree Plan Huge Wind Farm: 1100 Windmills; Power Project May Spark Confrontation with Quebec. *The Gazette*, April 5, 2006:A1. Montreal.

Theisz, Ronnie
1974      The Contemporary "Traditional Style" of the Lakota. *American Indian Crafts and Culture* 8(6):2–7. Tulsa, Okla.

Theriault, Bruce, and Felice Tilin
2004      Commentary: Native Radio: At the Heart of Public Radio's Mission. *Current*, May 11, 2004. New York. (Webpage: http://www.current.org)

Thomas, David Hurst
2000      Skull Wars: Kennewick Man, Archaeology, and the Battle for Native American Identity. Foreword by Vine Deloria, Jr. New York: Basic Books.

Thomas, Monica E.
1986      The Alaska Native Claims Settlement Act: Conflict and Controversy. *Polar Record* 23(142):27–36. Cambridge, England.

——— 1988      The Alaska Native Claims Settlement Act: An Update. *Polar Record* 24(151):328–329. Cambridge, England.

Thomas, Robert K.
1961      The Redbird Smith Movement. Pp. 159–166 in Symposium on Cherokee and Iroquois Culture. William N. Fenton and John Gulick, eds. *Bureau of American Ethnology Bulletin* 180(16). Washington: Smithsonian Institution; U.S. Government Printing Office.

——— 1966–1967      Colonialism: Internal and Classic. *New University Thought* 6:37–44. [Detroit, etc.]

——— 1966–1967a   Powerless Politics. *New University Thought* 6:44–53. [Detroit, etc.]

——— 1968      Pan-Indianism. Pp. 77–86 in The American Indian Today. Stuart Levine and Nancy O. Lurie, eds. Deland, Fla.: Everett/Edwards, Inc. (Reprinted: Pelican Books, New York, 1970.)

Thompson, Morris
1976      [BIA Letter Concerning Tribal College Funding.] [Washington: U.S. Department of the Interior, Bureau of Indian Affairs.]

Thorleifsen, Daniel
2006      Repatriation of Greenland Cultural Heritage from Denmark to Greenland. (Paper presented at the United Nations Permanent Forum Workshop on Partnership Visions for the Second International Decade of the World's Indigenous Peoples; Nuuk, Greenland, February 13–17, 2006.)

Thornberry, Patrick
2002      Indigenous Peoples and Human Rights. Manchester, U.K.: Manchester University Press.

Thornton, Russell
1978      American Indian Studies as an Academic Discipline. *American Indian Culture and Research Journal* 2(3):10–19. Los Angeles.

——— 1987      American Indian Holocaust and Survival: A Population History Since 1492. Norman: University of Oklahoma Press.

——— 1990      The Cherokees: A Population History. Lincoln: University of Nebraska Press.

——— 1995      The Mortality Crossover at the Older Ages: Native American and White and African-American Age-Specific Mortality Rates, circa 1995. (Unpublished paper, Department of Anthropology, University of California, Los Angeles.)

——— 1997      Tribal Membership Requirements and the Demography of 'Old' and 'New' Native Americans. *Population Research and Policy Review* 16(1–2):33–42. Amsterdam: Springer Netherlands.

——— 1998      Institutional and Intellectual Histories of Native American Studies. Pp. 79–107 in Studying Native America: Problems and Prospects. Russell Thornton, ed. Madison, Wis.: University of Wisconsin Press.

——— 1998a      Studying Native America: Problems and Prospects. Madison, Wis.: University of Wisconsin Press.

——— 2000      Population History of Native North Americans. Pp. 9–50 in A Population History of North America. Michael R. Haines and Richard H. Steckel, eds. New York: Cambridge University Press.

——— 2002      Repatriation As Healing the Wounds of the Trauma of History: Cases of Native Americans in the United States of America. Pp. 17–24 in The Dead and Their Possessions: Repatriation in Principle, Policy and Practice. Cressida Fforde, Jane Hubert, and Paul Turnbull, eds. *One World Archaeology* 43. New York and London: Routledge.

——— 2004      The Navajo-U.S. Population Mortality Crossover Since the Mid-20th Century. *Population Research and Policy Review* 23(3):291–308. Amsterdam: Springer Netherlands

——— 2004a      Historical Demography. Pp. 24–48 in A Companion to the Anthropology of North American Indians. Thomas Biolsi, ed. Malden, Mass.: Blackwell Publishers.

Thornton, Russell, and Joan Marsh-Thornton
1981      Estimating Prehistoric American Indian Population Size for United States Area: Implications for the Nineteenth Century Population Decline and Nadir. *American Journal of Physical Anthropology* 55(1):47–53.

Thornton, Russell, Gary D. Sandefur, and Harold G. Grasmick
1982      The Urbanization of American Indians: A Critical Bibliography. Bloomington, Ind.: Indiana University Press; Published for The Newberry Library, Chicago.

Thornton, Russell, Gary D. Sandefur, and C. Matthew Snipp
1991      American Indian Fertility Patterns: 1910 and 1940 to 1980. *American Indian Quarterly* 15(3):359–367. Lincoln, Nebr.

Thorson, John, Sarah Britton, and Bonnie G. Colby, eds.
2006      Tribal Water Rights: Essays in Contemporary Law, Policy, and Economics. Tucson: University of Arizona Press.

Tibbles, Thomas Henry
1972      The Ponca Chiefs: An Account of the Trial of Standing Bear. Lincoln: University of Nebraska Press.

Tiger, Georgianna
1995      Testimony to Ralph Regula, Chairman of the Subcommittee on Appropriations for Interior Related Agencies, March, 1995. Washington: U.S. House of Representatives.

Tiller, Veronica E. Velarde, comp. and ed.
2005      Tiller's Guide to Indian Country: Economic Profiles of American Indian Reservations. Albuquerque: BowArrow Publishing Company.

Tippeconnic, John W., III
1999        Tribal Control of American Indian Education: Observations
            Since the 1960s with Implications for the Future. Pp. 33–52
            in Next Steps: Research and Practice to Advance Indian Edu-
            cation. Karen Gayton Swisher and John W. Tippeconnic, III,
            eds. Charleston, W.Va.: ERIC Clearinghouse on Rural Edu-
            cation and Small Schools.

Tirado, Michelle
2005        Native American Stations Inform, Educate and Preserve
            Cultures. *American Indian Report*, July 2005:1215. Fairfax,
            Va.: Falmouth Institute.

Titla, Mary Kim
2006        A Message from the Publisher. *Native Youth Magazine: The
            Online Magazine for Native Youth*, August 22, 2006. Phoenix,
            Ariz. (Webpage: http://www.nativeyouthmagazine.com)

2006a       Native Youth Magazine: The Story. *Native Youth Magazine:
            The Online Magazine for Native Youth*, March 10, 2006.
            Phoenix, Ariz. (Webpage: http://www.nativeyouthmagazine
            .com)

Titley, Brian
1986        A Narrow Vision: Duncan Campbell Scott and the Adminis-
            tration of Indian Affairs. Vancouver: University of British
            Columbia Press.

1997        Unsteady Debut: J.A.N. Provencher and the Beginnings of
            Native Administration in Manitoba. *Prairie Forum* 22(1):
            21–46: Regina, Sask.

Tobias, John L.
1983        Protection, Civilization, Assimilation: An Outline History of
            Canada's Indian Policy. Pp. 30–55 in As Long As the Sun
            Shines and Water Flows: A Reader in Canadian Native Stud-
            ies. Ian A.L. Getty and Antoine S. Lussier, eds. Vancouver:
            University of British Columbia Press.

Toelken, Barre
1998        The Yellowman Tapes: 1966–1997. *Journal of American
            Folklore* 111(422):381–391. [Boston, New York, etc.]

Tolley, Sara-Larus
2006        Quest for Tribal Acknowledgment: California's Honey Lake
            Maidus. Foreword by Greg Sarris. Norman: University of
            Oklahoma Press.

Tough, Frank J.
2004        The Forgotten Constitution: The *Natural Resources Transfer
            Agreements* and Indian Livelihood Rights, ca. 1925–1933.
            *Alberta Law Review* 41(4):999–1048. Edmonton, Alta.

Townsend, Kenneth William
2000        World War II and the American Indian. Albuquerque: Uni-
            versity of New Mexico Press.

Trachtenberg, Alan
2004        Shades of Hiawatha: Staging Indians, Making Americans,
            1880–1930. New York: Hill and Wang.

Trafzer, Clifford E., and Diane Weiner, eds.
2001        Medicine Ways: Disease, Health, and Survival Among
            Native Americans. Blue Ridge Summit, Pa.: AltaMira Press.

Trahant, Mark N.
1995        Pictures of Our Nobler Selves: A History of Native American
            Contributions to News Media. Nashville, Tenn.: The Free-
            dom Forum First Amendment Center.

2000        Native American Newspapers. *Media Studies Journal* 14(2):
            106–113. New York.

2005        Broadcast News: The Absence of Native Storytellers.
            *Nieman Reports* 59(3):30–31. Cambridge, Mass.

Treasury Board of Canada Secretariat *see* Canada. Treasury Board of
Canada Secretariat.

Treaty 7 Elders and Tribal Council, et al.
1996        The True Spirit and Original Intent of Treaty 7. Montreal:
            McGill-Queen's University Press.

Trennert, Robert A.
1974        A Grand Failure: The Centennial Indian Exhibition of 1876.
            *Prologue: The Journal of the National Archives* 6(2):118–
            129. Washington.

1988        The Phoenix Indian School: Forced Assimilation in Arizona,
            1891–1935. Norman: University of Oklahoma Press.

Treuer, David
1995        Little. St. Paul, Minn.: Greywolf Press. (Reprinted: Picador,
            New York, 1996.)

1999        The Hiawatha. New York: Picador.

2006        The Translation of Dr. Apelles: A Love Story. St. Paul,
            Minn.: Greywolf Press.

Trigger, Bruce G.
1980        Archaeology and the Image of the American Indian. *Amer-
            ican Antiquity* 45(4):662–676.

Trope, Jack F., and Walter Echo-Hawk
1992        The Native American Graves Protection and Repatriation
            Act: Background and Legislative History. *Arizona State Law
            Journal* 24(1):35–77. Tempe, Ariz.

Trosper, Ronald L.
1974        The Economic Impact of the Allotment Policy on the Flat-
            head Indian Reservation. (Ph.D. Dissertation in Economics,
            Harvard University, Cambridge, Mass.)

1976        Native American Boundary Maintenance: The Flathead
            Indian Reservation, Montana, 1860–1970. *Ethnicity* 3(3):
            256–274.

1999        Traditional American Indian Economic Policy. Pp. 139–144
            in Contemporary Native American Political Issues. Troy
            Johnson, ed. Walnut Creek, Calif.: AltaMira Press.

2001        Applied Indigenous Studies at Northern Arizona University.
            *Indigenous Nations Studies Journal* 2(1):97–102. Lawrence,
            Kans.

Trujillo, M.H.
2000        One Prescription for Eliminating Health Disparity Legisla-
            tion. [Manuscript.] Rockville, Md.: Department of Health
            and Human Services, Public Health Service, Indian Health
            Service.

Truman, Harry S. (President)
1946        [Statement by the President Upon Signing Bill Creating the
            Indian Claims Commission, August 13, 1946.] In: Public
            Papers of Harry S. Truman. Washington: U.S. Government
            Printing Office, 1962.

1989        Where the Buck Stops: The Personal and Private Writings of
            Harry S. Truman. New York: Warner Books.

Truman's Committee on Civil Rights
1947        *see* Lawson, Steven F., ed. 2004

Tsuk, Dalia
2007 Architect of Justice: Felix S. Cohen and the Founding of American Legal Pluralism. Ithaca, N.Y.: Cornell University Press.

*Tundra Times*
1991 Alaska Native Claims Settlement Act: A Scrapbook History. Introduction by Julie Kitka, President, Alaska Federation of Natives. Fairbanks, Alaska: *Tundra Times.*

Tuska, Jon
1970–1971 In Retrospect: Tim McCoy. *Views and Reviews* 2(1):10–27, (2):12–29, (3):22–40, (4):12–41.

———
1985 The American West in Film: Critical Approaches to the Western. Westport, Conn.: Greenwood Press.

Tweedie, Ann M.
2002 Drawing Back Culture: The Makah Struggle for Repatriation. Seattle: University of Washington Press.

Twist, Kade L.
2004 Twenty-First Century Rez: Media and Telecommunications in Indian Country. New York: Ford Foundation.

———
2006 Changing the World One Digital File at a Time. *Native Peoples*, September–October. Phoenix, Ariz.: Media Concepts Group, Inc.

Tyler, S. Lyman
1964 Indian Affairs: A Work Paper on Termination with an Attempt To Show Its Antecedents. Provo, Utah: Institute of American Studies.

———
1973 A History of Indian Policy. Washington: U.S. Department of the Interior, Bureau of Indian Affairs; U.S. Government Printing Office.

———
1975 The Recent Urbanization of the American Indian. In: Essays on the American West, 1973–1974. Thomas G. Alexander, ed. Provo, Utah: Brigham Young University Press.

U.S. Bureau of the Census *see* U.S. Census Bureau

U.S. Census Bureau
1915 Indian Population in the United States and Alaska, 1910. 13th Census. Washington: U.S. Department of Commerce; U.S. Government Printing Office.

———
1937 The Indian Population of the United States and Alaska, 1930. Washington: U.S. Government Printing Office.

———
1972 Census of Population: 1970. General Population Characteristics. *Final Report* PC (1)-B1. Washington: U.S. Government Printing Office.

———
1973 1970 Census of Population, Subject Reports PC(2)-1F: American Indians. Washington: U.S. Department of Commerce, Social and Economic Statistics Administration, Bureau of the Census; U.S. Government Printing Office.

———
1974 Statistical Abstract of the United States, 1974. Washington: U.S Government Printing Office.

———
1984 1980 Census of Population, Supplementary Report. American Indian Areas and Alaska Villages: 1980. Edna Paisano, et al. comps. Washington: Racial Statistics Branch, Population Division, Bureau of the Census; U.S. Government Printing Office.

———
1986 1980 Census of Population. Subject Reports PC80-2-1D: American Indians, Eskimos, and Aleuts on Identified Reservations and in the Historic Areas of Oklahoma (Excluding Urbanized Areas). 2 Pts. Washington: U.S. Department of Commerce, Bureau of the Census; U.S. Government Printing Office.

———
1990 Census of Population: Summary of Social and Economic Characteristics in the United States. Table 8: Summary of Social and Economic Characteristics for American Indians, Eskimo or Aleut Persons and for Household and Families with an American Indian, Eskimo, or Aleut Householder. Washington: U.S. Department of Commerce, Bureau of the Census.

———
1991 American Indian and Alaska Native Areas: 1990. Edna Paisano, et al. comps. Washington: Racial Statistics Branch, Population Division, Bureau of the Census; U.S. Government Printing Office.

———
2000 Census 2000 Summary File 1. In: The American Indian and Alaska Native Population: 2000. *Census 2000 Brief, C2KBR/01-15*. Washington: U.S. Census.

———
2002 Census 2000 Brief: The American Indian and Alaska Native Population. Washington: U.S. Department of Commerce, U.S. Census Bureau.

———
2002a Census 2000: Table 1. United States—Race and Hispanic Origin: 1790 to 1990. (Washington: Internet release, Sept. 13, 2002.)

———
2003 American Indian and Alaska Native Heritage Month: November 2003. (Webpage: http://www.census.gov/press-release/www/releases/archives/facts_for_features/001492.html [20 Oct. 2003])

———
2006 We the People: American Indians and Alaska Natives in the United States. Census 2000 Special Report. Issued February 2006. Washington: U.S. Department of Commerce, Economics and Statistics Administration; U.S. Census Bureau.

U.S. Code of Federal Regulations
1975 Indian Self-Determination and Education Assistance Act. *U.S. Code of Federal Regulations*, Vol. 25, Section 450. Washington: U.S. Government Printing Office.

———
1976 Indian Health Care Improvement Act of 1976. *U.S. Code of Federal Regulations*, Vol. 25, Section 1601. Washington: U.S. Government Printing Office.

———
1996 Traditional Indian Use of Peyote. *U.S. Code. Title* 42, *Chapter* 21, *Subchapter* I, *Section* 1996a:1–3. Washington: U.S. Government Printing Office.

U.S. Commission on Civil Rights
1981 Indian Tribes, a Continuing Quest for Survival: A Report of the United States Commission on Civil Rights. Washington: U.S. Government Printing Office.

———
2003 A Quiet Crisis: Federal Funding and Unmet Needs in Indian Country. Washington: Office of Civil Rights.

———
2004 Broken Promises: Evaluating the Native American Health Care System. Washington: Office of Civil Rights.

U.S. Commission on Organization of the Executive Branch of the Government
1949 Report of the Commission on Organization of the Executive Branch of the Government. Washington: U.S. Commission

on Organization of the Executive Branch of the Government; Government Printing Office.

U.S. Commissioner of Indian Affairs
1972    [Commissioner of Indian Affairs, Letter to Director, Minneapolis Area Office, Bureau of Indian Affairs, dated September 7, 1972.] (Office of Federal Acknowledgment Files, September 7, 1972, Bureau of Indian Affairs, Washington.)

1975    [Memorandum to Area Office Director, Bureau of Indian Affairs, Sacramento, dated June 25, 1975. Subject: California Rancheria Termination Act, 72 U.S. Stat. 619, as Amended, 78 U.S. Stat. 390.] (Office of Federal Acknowledgment, California Special Project Files, June 25, 1975, Bureau of Indian Affairs, Washington.)

1977    [Commissioner of Indian Affairs to Legislative Council; dated February 25, 1977.) (Office of Federal Acknowledgment, California Special Project Files, February 25, 1977, Bureau of Indian Affairs, Washington.)

U.S. Comptroller General of the United States
1958    Report to the Congress of the United States: Administration of Withdrawal Activities by the Bureau of Indian Affairs, Department of the Interior, March 1958. Washington: U.S. Comptroller General of the United States; Government Printing Office.

U.S. Congress. House of Representatives
1952    Report with Respect to the House Resolution Authorizing the Committee on Interior and Insular Affairs to Conduct an Investigation of the Bureau of Indian Affairs. *82d Congress. 2d Session. House Report* 2503. Washington: U.S. Government Printing Office.

1953    Report with Respect to the House Resolution Authorizing the Committee on Interior and Insular Affairs To Conduct an Investigation of the Bureau of Indian Affairs. *82d Congress. 2d Session. House Report No.* 2503. (Serial No. 11582). Washington: U.S. Government Printing Office.

1955    Interior Department and Related Agencies Appropriations for 1956: Hearings Before the Subcommittee of the Committee on Appropriations. *84th Congress. 1st Session. Appropriations for 1956.* Washington: U.S. Government Printing Office.

1964    Information on Removal of Restrictions on American Indians: A Memorandum and Accompanying Information from the Chairman of the Committee on Interior and Insular Affairs, House of Representatives, To Members of the Committee. *88th Congress. 2d Session, November 2, 1964. Committe Print* 38. Washington: U.S. Government Printing Office.

1965    Federal Opinion on the Need for an Indian Treaty Study. *U.S. Congress. House Report* 1044; *Union Calendar* 449. Washington: U.S. Government Printing Office.

1983    Report on Restoration of Federal Recognition to the Confederated Tribes of the Grand Ronde Community in Oregon, and for Other Purposes. *U.S. Congress. House Report* 98-164. Washington: U.S. Governmment Printing Office.

1986    Report Providing for the Restoration of the Federal Trust Relationship with, and Federal Services and Assistance to, the Klamath Tribe of Indians; June 11, 1986. *U.S. Congress. House Report* 99-630. Washington: U.S. Government Printing Office.

1989    Native American Graves Protection and Repatriation Act. *U.S. Congress. House Report* 5237. Washington: U.S. Government Printing Office.

1994    Testimony of Donald Trump Before the Subcommittee on Native American Affairs of the Committee on Natural Resources: Implementation of Indian Gaming Regulatory Act. *103d Congress. 1st Session, 5 October 1993. Serial No.* 103-17, Part 5. Washington: U.S. Government Printing Office.

1994a   Committee on Natural Resources, Report Together with Dissenting Views on Little Traverse Bay Bands of Odawa Indians and the Little River Band of Ottawa Indians Act: S. 1357. *103d Congress. 2d Session, July 25, 1994.* Washington: U.S. Government Printing Office.

2005    Oversight Hearing Before the House Committee on Resources. *109th Congress. House Report* 109-2, February 16, 2005. Washington: U.S. Government Printing Office.

U.S. Congress. House of Representatives. Committee on Interior and Insular Affairs
1964    Information on Removal of Restrictions on American Indians: A Memorandum and Accompanying Information from the Chairman of the Committee on Interior and Insular Affairs, House of Representatives, to Members of The Committee. *88th Congress. 2d Session. Committee Print* No. 38. Washington: U.S. Government Printing Office.

U.S. Congress. House of Representatives. Committee on Public Lands. Subcommittee on Indian Affairs
1947    Emancipation of Indians. *80th Congress. 1st Session. Hearings on H.R. 2958, H.R. 2165, and H.R. 1113.* Washington: U.S. Government Printing Office.

U.S. Congress, Office of Technology Assessment
1986    Indian Health Care, OTA-H-290. Washington: U.S. Government Printing Office.

U.S. Congress. Senate
1943    Survey of the Conditions Among the Indians of the United States. *78th Congress. 2nd Session. Partial Report No.* 310. Washington: U.S. Government Printing Office.

1954    Transferring the Maintenance and Operation of Hospital and Health Facilities for Indians to the Public Health Service. *83d Congress. 2d Session. Senate Report* 1530. Washington: U.S. Government Printing Office.

1980    Establishment of a Siletz Reservation. Hearing Before the Select Committee on Indian Affairs. *96th Congress. 1st Session.* Washington: U.S. Government Printing Office.

1980a   Establishment of a Reservation for the Confederated Tribes of Siletz Indians of Oregon. *96th Congress. 2d Session. Senate Report* 96-626. Washington: U.S. Government Printing Office.

1986    Native American Cultural Preservation Act. *U.S. Congress. Senate. S.R.* 2952, October 18, 1986. Washington: U.S. Government Printing Office.

1987    Native American Indian Museum Act. *U.S. Congress. Senate. S.R.* 1722, September 25, 1987. Washington: U.S. Government Printing Office.

1988    National American Indian Museum and Memorial Act. *U.S. Congress. Senate Report* 100-494, August 25, 1988. Washington: U.S. Government Printing Office.

1988a     Joint Hearing Before the Select Committee on Indian Affairs and the Committee on Rules and Administration on S.1722 and S.1723. *U.S. Congress. Senate Hearing* 100-547, Part 1, November 12, 1987. Washington: U.S. Government Printing Office.

1988b     Joint Hearing Before the Select Committee on Indian Affairs and the Committee on Rules and Administration on S.1722 and S.1723. *U.S. Congress. Senate Hearing* 100-547, Part 2, November 18, 1988. Washington: U.S. Government Printing Office.

1989     National Museum of the American Indian Act. *U.S. Congress. Senate. S.R.* 101-143:2, September 27, 1989. Washington: U.S. Government Printing Office.

1989a     Native American Graves Protection and Repatriation Act. Washington: U.S. Government Printing Office.

U.S. Congress. Senate Select Committee on Indian Affairs
1977     Hearing on Grants to Indian Postsecondary Educational Institutions and the Navajo Community College Act, July, 1977. Washington: U.S. Government Printing Office.

U.S. Congress. Senate Subcommittee on Governmental Affairs
1991     Efforts to Combat Fraud and Abuse in the Insurance Industry: Hearing Before the Permanent Subcommitte on Investigations of the Committee on Governmental Affairs. *102d Congress. 1st Session* (19 July 1991), No. 112, Pt. 3. Washington.

U.S. *Congressional Quarterly Almanac*
1948     *Congressional Quarterly Almanac*, Vol. 3 (1947). Washington: U.S. Government Printing Office.

U.S. *Congressional Record*
1951     *82d Congress. 1st Session.* Washington: U.S. Government Printing Office.

1951a     *82d Congress. 2d Session.* Washington: U.S. Government Printing Office.

1952     *83d Congress. 1st Session.* Washington: U.S. Government Printing Office.

1953     *83d Congress. 2d Session.* Washington: U.S. Government Printing Office.

1957     *85th Congress. 1st Session. Volume* 103, *Pt. 22*:A6949-6950. Washington: U.S. Government Printing Office.

1989     [Senator John McCain, October 3, 1989, S.12397.] Washington: U.S. Government Printing Office.

1990     [Morris Udall, October 22, 1990; Extension of Remarks, October 27, 1990.] Washington: U.S. Government Printing Office.

U.S. Continental Congress
1774–1789     Journals of the Continental Congress, 1774–1789. Edited from the Original Records in the Library of Congress. 34 vols. Vols. 1–15: 1774–1779, edited by Worthington Chauncey Ford; Vols. 16–27: 1780–1784, edited by Gaillard Hunt; Vols. 28–31: 1785–1786, edited by John C. Fitzpatrick; Vols. 32–34: 1787–1789, edited by Roscoe R. Hill. Washington: U.S. Government Printing Office, 1904–1937.

U.S. Department of Commerce
1974     Federal and State Indian Reservations and Indian Trust Areas. Washington: U.S Government Printing Office.

2001     Overview of Race and Hispanic Origin: Census 2000 Brief. Washington: U.S. Department of Commerce, Census Bureau, Economics and Statistics Administration.

2002     The American Indian and Alaskan Native Population: Census 2000 Brief. Washington: U.S. Department of Commerce, Census Bureau, Economics and Statistics Administration.

2006     Statistical Abstract of the United States: 2004–2005. Washington: U.S. Department of Commerce, Census Bureau.

U.S. Department of Defense
2006     [DefenseLINK; Mil.museum; Native American Medal of Honor Winners.] (Webpages: http://www.defenselink.mil/specials/nativeamerican1/wwii.html [19 July 2006]; http://wpafb.af.mil.museum/pa/haihm1.htm [31 July 2006]; http://www.history.navy.mil/gaq61-3.htm [19 July 2006].)

U.S. Department of Education
1993     Trends in Higher Education by Racial/Ethnic Involvement. Washington: National Center for Educational Statistics.

U.S. Department of Health and Human Services. Public Health Service. Indian Health Service (IHS)
1997     Life Tables for the American Indian and Alaskan Native IHS Service Population by IHS Area and Sex, 1991–1993; With Comparable Data for the U.S. All Races, White and Black Populations, 1992. Rockville, Md.: U.S. Department of Health and Human Services, Public Health Service, Indian Health Service.

1997a     Trends in Indian Health, 1997. Rockville, Md.: U.S. Department of Health and Human Services, Public Health Service, Indian Health Service.

2001     Trends in Indian Health 1998–1999. Rockville, Md.: U.S. Department of Health and Human Services, Public Health Service, Indian Health Service.

2004     Trends in Indian Health, 2001–2002. Rockville, Md.: U.S. Department of Health and Human Services, Public Health Service, Indian Health Service.

2006     Year 2006 Profile, Fact Sheet. Rockville, Md.: U.S. Department of Health and Human Services, Public Health Service, Indian Health Service.

2007     Year 2007 Profile, Fact Sheet. Rockville, Md.: U.S. Department of Health and Human Services, Public Health Service, Indian Health Service.

U.S. Department of the Interior
1894     Report on Indians Taxed and Indians Not Tasked in the United States (Except Alaska) at the Eleventh Census: 1890. (Census Office. House of Representatives Misc. Doc. 340, Part 15. 52nd Congress, First Session.)

1942–1944     Secretary of the Interior Annual Report: Bureau of Indian Affairs. Washington: U.S. Department of the Interior; Government Printing Office.

1947     *see* Haas, Theodore H. 1947

1953     Secretary of the Interior Annual Report: Bureau of Indian Affairs. Washington: U.S. Department of the Interior; Government Printing Office.

1954 Secretary of the Interior Annual Report: Bureau of Indian Affairs. Washington: U.S. Department of the Interior; Government Printing Office.

1967 [Acting Associate Solicitor, Indian Affairs, to Commissioner of Indian Affairs, dated November 16, 1967.] (Solicitor's Opinion M-36799, November 16, 1967, Office of Federal Acknowledgment Files, Bureau of Indian Affairs, Washington.)

1978 Code of Federal Regulations: 25, Indians. Procedures for Establishing That an American Indian Group Exists As an American Indian Tribe. *Federal Register*, September 5, 1978, Vol. 43, No. 172:39361–39364. Washington: U.S. Government Printing Office.

1994 Code of Federal Regulations: 25, Indians. Procedures for Establishing That an American Indian Group Exists As an American Indian Tribe.Procedures for Establishing That an American Indian Group Exists as an Indian Tribe; Final Rule. *Federal Register*, February 25, 1994, Vol. 59, No. 38:9280-9300. Washington: U.S. Government Printing Office.

1995 Supplementary Testimony on S. 479. Pp. 60–69 in Hearing Before the Committee on Indian Affairs, United States Senate on S. 479, To Provide for Administrative Procedures to Extend Federal Recognition to Certain Indian Groups, July 13, 1995. *104th Congress. 1st Session.* Washington: U.S. Government Printing Office.

1999 Indian Labor Force Report: 1999. Washington: Bureau of Indian Affairs, Office of Tribal Services.

2001 Indian Labor Force Report: 2001. Washington: Bureau of Indian Affairs, Office of Tribal Services.

2001–2004 Strengthening the Circle: Interior Indian Affairs Highlights, 2001–2004. Washington: U.S. Department of the Interior.

2002 Indian Entities Recognized and Eligible to Receive Services from the United States Bureau of Indian Affairs. *Federal Register* 67, No. 134, July 12, 2002:46328–46333. Washington: U.S. Government Printing Office.

2003 Indian Entities Recognized and Eligible to Receive Services from the United States Bureau of Indian Affairs. *Federal Register* 68, No. 234, December 5, 2003:68180–68184. Washington: U.S. Government Printing Office.

2005 Indian Entities Recognized and Eligible to Receive Services from the United States Bureau of Indian Affairs. *Federal Register* 70, No. 226, November 25, 2005:71194–71198. Washington: U.S. Government Printing Office.

U.S. Department of the Interior. Assistant Secretary of Indian Affairs (ASIA)

1979 [Recommendation and Summary of Evidence for Proposed Finding for Federal Acknowledgment of the Grand Traverse Band of Ottawa and Chippewa Indians, Peshawbestown, Michigan; dated October 3, 1979.] (Office of Federal Acknowledgment, Legislative Counsel Files, October 3, 1979, Bureau of Indian Affairs, Washington.)

1984 [Recommendation of Summary of Evidence for Proposed Findings Against Federal Acknowledgment of the Principal Creek Indian Nation East of the Mississippi of Alabama, Pursuant to 25 CFR 83, dated June 8, 1984.] (Office of Federal Acknowledgment, Legislative Counsel Files, June 8, 1984, Bureau of Indian Affairs, Washington.)

1985 [Evidence for Proposed Findings Against Federal Acknowledgment of the Tchinouk Indians of Oregon, dated May 5, 1985.] (Office of Federal Acknowledgment, Legislative Counsel Files, May 5, 1985, Bureau of Indian Affairs, Washington.)

1987 [Recommendation for Final Determination That the Wampanoag Tribal Council of Gay Head, Inc., Exists as an Indian Tribe Pursuant to 25 CFR 83, dated January 27, 1987.] (Office of Federal Acknowledgment, Legislative Counsel Files, January 27, 1987, Bureau of Indian Affairs, Washington.)

1987a [Summary Under the Criteria and Evidence for Proposed Findings Against Federal Acknowledgment of the MaChis Lower Alabama Creek Indian Tribe, Inc., dated August 27, 1987.] (Office of Federal Acknowledgment, Legislative Counsel Files, August 27, 1987, Bureau of Indian Affairs, Washington.)

1990 [Summary Under the Criteria and Evidence for Final Determination for Federal Acknowledgment of the San Juan Southern Paiute Tribe, dated December 20, 1990.] (Office of Federal Acknowledgment, Legislative Counsel Files, December 20, 1990, Bureau of Indian Affairs, Washington.)

1992 [Summary Under the Criteria and Evidence for Final Determination Against Federal Acknowledgment of the Miami Nation of Indians of the State of Indiana, Inc., dated June 9, 1992.] (Office of Federal Acknowledgment, Legislative Counsel Files, June 9, 1992, Bureau of Indian Affairs, Washington.)

1994 [Summary Under the Criteria and Evidence for Final Determination for Federal Acknowledgment of the Mohegan Tribe of Indians of the State of Connecticut, dated March 7, 1994.] (Office of Federal Acknowledgment, Legislative Counsel Files, March 7, 1994, Bureau of Indian Affairs, Washington.)

1995 [Final Determination to Acknowledge the Samish Tribal Organization as a Tribe, dated November 8, 1995.] (Office of Federal Acknowledgment, Legislative Counsel Files, November 8, 1995, Bureau of Indian Affairs, Washington.)

1996 [Summary Under the Criteria and Evidence for Final Determination Against Federal Acknowledgment of the Ramapough Mountain Indians, Inc., dated January 16, 1996.] (Office of Federal Acknowledgment, Legislative Counsel Files, January 16, 1996, Bureau of Indian Affairs, Washington.)

1997 [Summary Under the Criteria and Evidence for Final Determination Against Federal Acknowledgment of the Mobile—Washington County Band of Choctaw Indians of South Alabama, dated December 19, 1997.] (Office of Federal Acknowledgment, Legislative Counsel Files, December 19, 1997, Bureau of Indian Affairs, Washington.)

1999 [Summary Under the Criteria and Evidence for Final Determination Against Federal Acknowledgment of the Snoqualmie Tribal Organization, dated August 22, 1999.] (Office of Federal Acknowledgment, Legislative Counsel Files, August 22, 1999, Bureau of Indian Affairs, Washington.)

1999a [Summary Under the Criteria and Evidence for Final Determination Against Federal Acknowledgment of the Yuchi Tribal Organization, dated December 15, 1999.] (Office of

Federal Acknowledgment, Legislative Counsel Files, December 15, 1999, Bureau of Indian Affairs, Washington.)

2000     [Summary Under the Criteria and Evidence for Proposed Finding, Steilacoom Tribe of Indians, dated January 21, 2000.] (Office of Federal Acknowledgment, Legislative Counsel Files, January 21, 2000, Bureau of Indian Affairs, Washington.)

2002     [Summary Under the Criteria and Evidence for Final Determination in Regard to Federal Acknowledgment of the Eastern Pequot Indians of Connecticut as a Portion of the Historical Eastern Pequot Tribe, dated June 24, 2002.] (Office of Federal Acknowledgment, Legislative Counsel Files, June 24, 2002, Bureau of Indian Affairs, Washington.)

2002a     [Summary Under the Criteria and Evidence for Final Determination Against the Federal Acknowledgment of the Muwekma Ohlone Tribe, dated September 6, 2002.] (Office of Federal Acknowledgment, Legislative Counsel Files, September 6, 2002, Bureau of Indian Affairs, Washington.)

2002b     [Reconsideration on Referral by the Secreary and Summary Under the Criteria and Evidence of the Reconsidered Final Determination Against Federal Acknowledgment of the Chinook Indian Tribe/Chinook Nation, dated Juny 5, 2002.] (Office of Federal Acknowledgment, Legislative Counsel Files, July 5, 2002, Bureau of Indian Affairs, Washington.)

2004     [Summary Under the Criteria and Evidence for Proposed Finding Against Acknowledgment of the Burt Lake Band of Ottawa and Chippewa Indians, Inc., dated March 15, 2004.] (Office of Federal Acknowledgment, Legislative Counsel Files, March 15, 2004, Bureau of Indian Affairs, Washington.)

2004a     [Summary Under the Criteria and Evidence for Final Determination Against Federal Acknowledgment of the Golden Hill Paugussett Tribe, dated June 14, 2004.] (Office of Federal Acknowledgment, Legislative Counsel Files, June 14, 2004, Bureau of Indian Affairs, Washington.)

2004b     [Summary Under the Criteria for Final Determination Against Federal Acknowledgment of the Snohomish Tribe of Indians, dated December 1, 2004.] (Office of Federal Acknowledgment, Legislative Counsel Files, December 1, 2004, Bureau of Indian Affairs, Washington.)

2005     [Summary of the Evaluation Under the Criteria and of the Evidence for Reconsidered Final Determination Denying Federal Acknowledgment of the Eastern Pequot Indians of Connecticut and the Paucatuck Eastern Pequot Indians of Connecticut, dated October 11, 2005.] (Office of Federal Acknowledgment, Legislative Counsel Files, October 11, 2005, Bureau of Indian Affairs, Washington.)

2005a     [Summary Under the Criteria and Evidence: Reconsidered Final Determination Denying Federal Acknowledgment of the Petitioner Schaghticoke Tribal Nation, dated October 11, 2005.] (Office of Federal Acknowledgment, Legislative Counsel Files, October 11, 2005, Bureau of Indian Affairs, Washington.)

2005b     [Proposed Finding to Against Federal Acknowledgment of the St. Francis/Sokoki Band of Abenakis of Vermont, dated November 9, 2005: Summary Under the Criteria.] (Office of Federal Acknowledgment, Legislative Counsel Files, November 9, 2005, Bureau of Indian Affairs, Washington.)

2006     Cason Issues Proposed Finding to Acknowledge Mashpee Wampanoag Indian Tribal Council, Incorporated, as an Indian Tribes. *U.S. Department of the Interior. News*, March 31, 2006:1–2. Washington.

2006a     [Summary Under the Criteria for the Proposed Findings on the Mashpee Wampanoag Indian Tribal Council, Inc., dated March 31, 2006.] (Office of Federal Acknowledgment, Legislative Counsel Files, March 31, 2006, Bureau of Indian Affairs, Washington.)

2007     [Summary Under the Criteria and Evidence for Final Determination Against Federal Acknowlegment of the St. Francis/Sokoki Band of Abenakis of Vermont, June 22, 2007.] (Office of Federal Acknowledgment, Legislative Counsel Files, June 22, 2007, Bureau of Indian Affairs, Washington.)

U.S. Department of the Interior. Bureau of Indian Affairs (BIA)
1945     Indians in the War: Burial of a Brave. Chicago: U.S. Department of the Interior, Bureau of Indian Affairs.

1988     [Overview of the Federal Acknowledgment Process.] Written Testimony in: Hearing Before the Select Committee on Indian Affairs on Oversight of the Federal Acknowledgment Process. *100th Congress. 2d Session. Senate Hearing* 100-823. Washington: U.S. Government Printing Office.

1996     Final Decision to Retract 1979 Decision of the Deputy Commissioner of Indian Affairs Regarding the Delaware Tribe of Indians. *61 Federal Register* 50, 862. Washington.

U.S. Department of the Interior. Bureau of Indian Affairs (BIA). Office of Federal Acknowledgment (OFA)
2007     List of Petitioners by State as of February 3, 2007. Washington: Bureau of Indian Affairs, Office of Federal Acknowledgment.

2007a     Status Summary of Acknowledgment Cases, February 3, 2007. Washington: Bureau of Indian Affairs, Office of Federal Acknowledgment.

U.S. Department of the Interior. Interior Board of Indian Appeals (IBIA)
2005     [In Re: Federal Acknowledgment of the Schaghticoke Tribal Nation, dated May 12, 2005.] (Order Vacating and Remanding Final Determination: 41 IBIA 30-42, May 12, 2005; Office of Federal Acknowledgment, Bureau of Indian Affairs, Washington.)

2005a     [In Re: Federal Acknowledgment of the Eastern Pequot Indians of Connecticut and the Paucatuck Eastern Pequot Indians of Connecticut, dated May 12, 2005.] (Order Vacating and Remanding Final Determination: 41 IBIA 1–29, May 12, 2005; Office of Federal Acknowledgment, Bureau of Indian Affairs, Washington.)

U.S. Department of Transportation, Federal Highway Administration
2003     Meeting Minutes: Joint Federal/State Motor Fuel Tax Compliance Project, 23rd Annual Steering Committee Meeting, March 24, 2003 (Webpage: http://www.fhwa.dot.gov/policy/23scmin1.htm [27 September 2006].)

U.S. Environmental Protection Agency
2007     American Indian Tribal Portal. Washington: U.S. Environmental Protection Agency. (Webpage: http://www.epa.gov/tribalportal/)

U.S. *Federal Register*
1976     Code of Federal Regulations: 25, Indians. Revised as of April 1, 1976. Washington: U.S. Government Printing Office.

1978    *see* U.S. Department of the Interior 1978

1994    *see* U.S. Department of the Interior 1994

1994a    Notice of Intent to Repatriate Cultural Items in the Possession of the Denver Art Museum. *Federal Register*, Vol. 59, No. 138: 37052–37053. Washington: U.S. Government Printing Office.

1996    Notice of Intent to Repatriate a Cultural Item in the Possession of the Cheney Cowels Museum, Spokane, WA. *Federal Register*, Vol. 61, No. 38:7122. Washington: U.S. Government Printing Office.

1996a    Notice of Intent to Repatriate Cultural Items in the Possession of the Peabody Museum of Archaeology and Ethnology, Harvard University, Cambridge, MA. *Federal Register*, Vol. 61, No. 92:21486–21487. Washington: U.S. Government Printing Office.

1997    Notice of Intent to Repatriate Cultural Items in the Possession of the Heard Museum, Phoenix, Arizona. *Federal Register*, Vol. 62, No. 19:4328–4329. Washington: U.S. Government Printing Office.

2000    Notice of Intent to Repatriate Cultural Items in the Possession of the Denver Art Museum. *Federal Register*, Vol. 65, No. 41:11075–11076. Washington: U.S. Government Printing Office.

2000a    Notice of Intent to Repatriate Cultural Items in the Possession of the Denver Art Museum. *Federal Register*, Vol. 65, No. 82:24712–24714. Washington: U.S. Government Printing Office.

U.S. General Accounting Office (GAO) [now Government Accountability Office]
2000    Report to Congressional Requesters: Indian Issues. Improvements Needed in Tribal Recognition Process. Washington: General Accounting Office.

2000    Report to Congressional Requesters. Indian Issues: Improvements Needed in Tribal Recognition Process (November 2000). Washington: U.S. General Accounting Office.

2001    Report to Congressional Requesters. Indian Issues: Improvements Needed in Tribal Recognition Process (November 2001). Washington: U.S. General Accounting Office.

2005    Indian Health Service: Health Care Services Are Not Always Available to Native Americans. GAO-05-789. Washington: General Accounting Office.

U.S. Indian Claims Commission
1980    Final Report. Washington: U.S. Government Printing Office.

U.S. National Park Service
2004    Repatriation and Reburial of Ancestors. Washington: U.S. National Park Service. (Webpage: http://www.nps.gov/partnerships/repatriation_pecos.htm [6 August 2006].)

2006    National NAGPRA FY06 Midyear Report for the Period October 1, 2005–March 31, 2006. Electronic File. Washington: U.S. National Park Service. (Webpage: http://www.cr.nps.gov/nagpra/DOCUMENTS/NNReport%20FY2006%20final.pdf [6 August 2006].)

2007    Culturally Unidentifiable Native American Inventories Pilot Database. Electronic File. Washington. U.S. National Park Service. (Webpage: http://www.cr.nps.gov/64.241.25.6/CUI/index.cfm [28 April 2007].)

2007a    Notice of Inventory Completion Database. Electronic File. Washington: U.S. National Park Service. (Webpage: http://www.cr.nps.gov.nagpra/fed_notices/nagpradir/index.htm [28 April 2007].)

Ubelaker, Douglas H.
1976    The Sources and Methodology for Mooney's Estimates of North American Indian Populations. Pp. 243–288 in The Native Population of the Americas in 1492. William M. Denevan, ed. Madison, Wis.: University of Wisconsin Press.

1988    North American Indian Population Size, A.D. 1500 to 1985. *American Journal of Physical Anthropology* 77(3):289–294.

2006    *see* Handbook Vol. 3 (2006:694–701)

Udall, Morris
1990    *see* U.S. Congressional Record 1990

Uhlmann, Julie M.
1972    The Impact of Modernization on Papago Indian Fertility. *Human Organization* 31(2):149–162. Washington.

Underhill, Ruth Murray
1965    Red Man's Religion: Beliefs and Practices of the Indians North of Mexico. Chicago: University of Chicago Press

Unger, Steven, ed.
1978    The Destruction of American Indian Families. New York: Association on American Indian Affairs.

Union of Ontario Indians (UOI)
2005    Maintain, Preserve and Enhance: A Discussion Paper on Casino Rama. North Bay, Ont.: Union of Ontario Indians. (Webpage: http://www.anishinabek.ca/uoi/pdf/FINAL-Casino%20Rama.pdf.)

United Nations Education, Scientific, and Cultural Organization (UNESCO)
1970    Convention on the Means of Prohibiting and Preventing the Illicit Import, Export, and Transfer of Cultural Property. New York and Geneva, Switzerland: UNESCO.

United Nations Human Rights Council (UNHRC)
2006    Resolution 2006/2. (Working Group of the Commission on Human Rights to Elaborate a Draft Declaration in Accordance with Paragraph 5 of the General Assembly Resolution 49/214 of 23 December 1994. New York and Geneva, Switzerland.)

United Nations Permanent Forum for Indigenous Issues (UNPFII)
2007    About UNPFII/History (Webpage: http://www.un.org/esa/socdev/unpfii/en/history.html [30 May 2007])

United Nations Working Group on Indigenous Populations (UNWGIP)
2003    Report of the Working Group on Indigenous Populations on Its 21st Session. (Unpublished report: United Nations Document No. E/CN. 4/Sub.2/2003/22, New York.)

University of Oklahoma Law Center and National Indian Law Library
2005    Native American Constitution and Law Digitization Project. Updated 25 April 2005. (Webpage: http://www.thorpe.ou.edu/ [25 March 2006].)

University of Saskatchewan Native Law Centre
1979–, 1980–1991 *see* Native Law Centre 1979–, 1980–1991

Upstate Citizens for Equality
2006    [Upstate Citizens for Equality, based in Verona, N.Y.: Website.] (Webpage: http://www.upstate-citizens.org/[27 September 2006].)

Useem, Ruth Hill, and Carl K. Eicher
1970      Rosebud Reservation Economy. Pp. 3–34 in The Modern Sioux: Social Systems and Reservation Culture. Ethel Nurge, ed. Lincoln: University of Nebraska Press.

Usher, Peter J.
2003      Environment, Race and Nation Reconsidered: Reflections on Aboriginal Land Claims in Canada. *The Canadian Geographer* 47(4):365–382. Toronto.

2003a    Caribou Crisis or Administrative Crisis? Pp. 179–199 in Wildlife and Aboriginal Policies on the Barren Grounds of Canada, 1947–1960. David G. Anderson and Mark Nuttall, eds. Oxford: Berghahn Books.

Usner, Daniel H., Jr.
2001      The American Indian Program at Cornell University. *Indigenous Nations Studies Journal* 2(1):35–42. Lawrence, Kans.

Utter, Jack
1993      American Indians: Answers to Today's Questions. Lake Ann, Mich.: National Woodlands Publishing Co. (Reprinted: see Utter 2001.)

2001      American Indians: Answers to Today's Questions. 2d ed., rev. and enlarged. Norman: University of Oklahoma Press.

Valentino, Erin
1997      Coyote's Ransom: Jaune Quick-to See Smith and the Language of Appropriation. *Third Text* 38:25–37.

Vance, John T.
1969      The Congressional Mandate and the Indian Claims Commission. *North Dakota Law Review* 45(2):325–336. Grand Forks, N.Dak.

Vander Wall, Jim
1992      A Warrior Caged: The Continuing Struggle of Leonard Peltier. Pp. 291–310 in The State of Native America: Genocide, Colonization and Resistance. M. Annette Jaimes, ed. Boston: South End Press.

Vardac, A. Nicholas
1949      Stage to Screen: Theatrical Method from Garrick to Griffith. Cambridge, Mass.: Harvard University Press. (Reprinted: Da Capo Press, New York, 1987.)

Vassallo, James
2005      Decades-Long Quest for Closure Now at an End. *The Prince Rupert Daily News*, June 23, 2005. Prince Rupert, B.C.

Vecsey, Christopher, and William S. Starna
1988      Iroquois Land Claims. Syracuse, N.Y.: Syracuse University Press.

Velie, Alan R., ed.
1979      American Indian Literature: An Anthology. Norman: University of Oklahoma Press.

1982      Four American Indian Literary Masters: N. Scott Momaday, James Welch, Leslie Marmon Silko, Gerald Vizenor. Norman: University of Oklahoma Press.

Venne, Sharon
1997      Understanding Treaty 6: An Indigenous Perspective. Pp. 173–207 in Aboriginal and Treaty Rights in Canada: Essays on Law, Equality, and Respect for Difference. Michael Asch, ed. Vancouver: UBC Press.

Vennum, Thomas
1982      The Ojibwa Dance Drum: Its History and Construction. Washington: Smithsonian Institution Press.

1994      American Indian Lacrosse: Little Brother of War. Washington: Smithsonian Institution Press.

Verrill, Hyatt A.
1954      The Real Americans. New York: G.P. Putnam's and Sons.

Vestal, Stanley
1942      The Plains Indian and the War. *Saturday Review of Literature* 25(20):9–10. New York.

Veterans Administration
1979      Estimated Number of American Indian Veterans by State of Residence. Veterans Administration, Washington D.C.

Victoria: Government Printer
1875      *see* British Columbia 1875

Villard, Oswald Garrison
1944      Wardship and the Indian. *The Christian Century* 61(13):397–398. Chicago.

Vincent, Sylvie, and Garry Bowers, eds.
1988      James Bay and Northern Quebec—Ten Years After. Montreal: Recherches amérindiennes au Québec.

Vinje, David L.
1996      Native American Economic Development on Selected Reservations: A Comparative Analysis. *The American Journal of Economics and Sociology* 55(4):427–443. New York.

Viola, Herman J.
1978      American Indian Cultural Resources Training Program at the Smithsonian Institution. *American Archivist* 41(2):143–145. Chicago.

Viola, Herman J., and Carolyn Margolis
1991      Seeds of Change: Five Hundred Years Since Columbus. Washington: Smithsonian Institution Press.

Vizenor, Gerald
1978      Darkness in Saint Louis Bearheart. St. Paul, Minn.: Truck Press.

1981      Earthdivers: Tribal Narratives on Mixed Descent. Minneapolis: University of Minnesota Press.

1987      Griever: An American Monkey King in China. Minneapolis: University of Minnesota Press.

1988      The Trickster of Liberty. Minneapolis: University of Minnesota Press.

———, ed.
1989      Narrative Chance: Postmodern Discourse on Native American Indian Literatures. Albuquerque: University of New Mexico Press.

1990      Crossbloods: Bone Courts, Bingo, and Other Reports. Minneapolis: University of Minnesota Press.

1991      The Heirs of Columbus. Middletown, Conn.: Wesleyan Press.

1992      Dead Voices: Natural Agonies in the New World. Norman: University of Oklahoma Press.

1993      Casino Crops. *Wicazo Sa Review* 9(2):80–84. Minneapolis.

1999      Manifest Manners: Narratives on Postindian Survivance. Lincoln: University of Nebraska Press.

Vogel, Virgil J.
1970        American Indian Medicine. Norman: University of Okla-
            homa Press.

_____
1974        This Country Was Ours: A Documentary History of the
            American Indian. New York: Harper and Row. (Originally
            publ. in 1972.)

Vollman, Tim
1979        A Survey of Eastern Indian Land Claims: 1970–1979. *Maine
            Law Review* 31(1): 5–16. Portland, Maine.

Voorhees, Richard
2003        Characteristics of Tribal College and University Faculty.
            Littleton, Colo.: Voorhees Group.

Waddell, Jack O.
1975        For Individual Power and Social Credit: The Use of Alcohol
            among Tucson Papagos. *Human Organization* 34(1):9–15.
            Washington.

Waddell, Jack O., and O. Michael Watson, eds.
1971        The American Indian in Urban Society. Boston: Little,
            Brown.

Wade, Edwin L., ed.
1986        The Arts of the North American Indian: Native Traditions in
            Evolution. New York: Hudson Hills Press.

Wade, Edwin L., and Rennard Strickland
1981        Magic Images: Contemporary Native American Art. Nor-
            man: University of Oklahoma Press.

Wade, Mason
1988        *see* Handbook Vol. 4 (1988:20–28)

Wagner, Angie
2006        For American Indians, It's More Than Health Care: At Least
            Half of the Unique Clinics Would Be Closed Under Bush's
            '07 Budget Plan. *Houston Chronicle*, March 25, 2006. Hous-
            ton, Tex. (Webpage: http://www.chron.com/index.html)

Wagner, James R., and Richard Corrigan
1970        BIA Brings Indians into Cities But Has Few Urban Services.
            *National Journal* 2(28):1493–1502.

Wagner, Roland M.
1975        Pattern and Process in Ritual Syncretism: The Case of
            Peyotism Among the Navajo. *Journal of Anthropological
            Research* 31(2):162–181. Albuquerque.

Waldram, James B.
1984        Hydro-Electric Development and the Process of Negotiation
            in Northern Manitoba, 1960–1977. *Canadian Journal of
            Native Studies* 4(2):205–240. Brandon, Man.

_____
1990        Access to Traditional Medicine in a Western Canadian City.
            *Medical Anthropology* 12(3):325–348.

_____
1990a       Physician Utilization and Urban Native People in Saskatoon,
            Canada. *Social Science and Medicine* 30(5):579–589.

_____
1993        Aboriginal Sprituality: Symbolic Healing in Canadian Pris-
            ons. *Culture, Medicine and Psychiatry* 17:345–362.

_____
1997        The Way of the Pipe: Aboriginal Spirituality and Symbolic
            Healing in Canadian Prisons. Peterborough, Ont.: Broadview
            Press.

_____
2004        Revenge of the Windigo: The Construction of the Mind and
            Mental Health of North American Aboriginal Peoples.
            Toronto: University of Toronto Press.

Waldram, James B., D. Ann Herring, and T. Kue Young
1995        Aboriginal Health in Canada: Historical, Cultural, and Epi-
            demiological Perspectives. Toronto: University of Toronto
            Press. (Reprinted in 1999; see also 2006.)

_____
2006        Aboriginal Health in Canada: Historical, Cultural, and Epi-
            demiological Perspectives. 2d ed. Toronto: University of
            Toronto Press.

Walke, Roger
1991        Federal Assistance to Native Americans: A Report Prepared
            for the Senate Select Committee on Indian Affairs of the U.S.
            Senate. Washington: Government Printing Office.

_____
2003        Federal Recognition of Indian Tribes by Congress. Washing-
            ton: Library of Congress, Congressional Research Service.
            (Copy in Office of Federal Acknowledgment, Bureau of
            Indian Affairs, Washington.)

Walkem, Ardith
2003        Measuring a Work in Progress: Twenty Years of Section 35.
            In: Box of Treasures or Empty Box: Twenty Years of Section
            35. Ardith Walkem and Halie Bruce, eds. Penticton, B.C.:
            Theytus Books.

Walkem, Ardith, and Halie Bruce, eds.
2003        Box of Treasures or Empty Box: Twenty Years of Section
            35. Penticton, B.C.: Theytus Books.

Walker, Deward E., Jr.
1968        Conflict and Schism in Nez Percé Acculturation: A Study of
            Religion and Politics. Pullman, Wash.: Washington State
            University Press.

_____
1994        Anthropologists and Native Americans. Pp. 41–43 in Native
            America in the Twentieth Century: An Encyclopedia. Mary
            B. Davis, ed. New York and London: Garland Publishing.

_____, vol. ed.
1998        *see* Handbook Vol. 12 (1998)

WalkingStick, Kay
1992        Native American Art in the Postmodern Era. *Art Journal*
            51(3):15–17.

Wallace, Anthony F.
1969        The Death and Rebirth of the Seneca. New York: Vintage.

Walters, Mark D.
1999        The "Golden Thread" of Continuity: Aboriginal Customs at
            Common Law and Under the *Constitution Act, 1982*. *McGill
            Law Journal* 44(3):711–752. Montreal.

_____
2006        The Morality of Aboriginal Law. *Queen's Law Journal*
            31(2):470–520. Kingston, Ont.

Ward, Carol J.
2005        Native Americans in the School System: Family, Commu-
            nity, and Academic Achievement. Blue Ridge Summit, Pa.:
            AltaMira Press.

Ward, Steven
1972        [Interview with Muriel Waukazoo, 13 July 1972.] (Tape 853,
            13–14, South Dakota Oral History Center, University of
            South Dakota, Vermillion, S.Dak.)

Warner, Linda Sue
1999        Education and the Law: Implications for American Indian/
            Alaska Native Students. Pp. 53–82 in Next Steps: Research
            and Practice to Advance Indian Education. Karen Gayton
            Swisher and John W. Tippeconnic, III, eds. Charleston,
            W.Va.: ERIC Clearinghouse on Rural Education and Small
            Schools.

Warren, Dave
1984        Why Tribal Archives? Foreword in Native American Archives:
            An Introduction. John A. Fleckner. Chicago: The Society of
            American Archivists.

Warrior, Robert A.
1994        Tribal Secrets: Recovering American Indian Intellectual
            Traditions. Minneapolis, Minn.: University of Minnesota
            Press.

_____
1999        The Native American Scholar: Toward a New Intellectual
            Agenda. *Wicazo Sa Review* 14(2):46–54. Minneapolis.

Warrior, Robert A., and Beverly R. Singer
2001        Wiping the War Paint Off the Lens: Native American Film
            and Video. Minneapolis: University of Minnesota Press.

Wasacase, Ida
1979        The Saskatchewan Federated College. *Saskatchewan Indian*
            9(5):34–35. Prince Albert, Sask.

Washburn, Frances
2007        Storytelling: The Heart of American Indian Scholarship.
            *American Indian Culture and Research Journal* 31(1):109–
            119. Los Angeles.

Washburn, Kevin K.
2001        Recurring Problems in Indian Gaming. *Wyoming Law
            Review* 1(1):427–444. Laramie, Wyo.

_____
2003–2004   Federal Law, State Policy, and Indian Gaming. *Nevada Law
            Journal* 4(2):285–300. Las Vegas.

Washburn, Wilcomb E.
1971        Red Man's Land/White Man's Law: A Study of the Past and
            Present Status of the American Indian. New York: Charles
            Scribner's Sons.

_____ [, comp. and ed.]
1973        The American Indian and The United States: A Documentary
            History. 4 vols. New York: Random House.

_____
1975        American Indian Studies: A Status Report. *American Quar-
            terly* 27(3):263–274.

_____, vol. ed.
1988        *see* Handbook Vol. 4 (1988)

Washington, Sylvia Hood, ed.
2006        Echoes from the Poisoned Well: Global Memories and Envi-
            ronmental Injustice. Lanham, Md.: Lexington Books.

Watahomigie, Lucille, et al.
1982        Hualapai Reference Grammar. Los Angeles: UCLA Amer-
            ican Indian Studies Center.

Watkins, Arthur V.
1954        Termination of Federal Supervision Over Certain Tribes of
            Indians: Joint Hearings Before Subcommittees of the Com-
            mittee on Interior and Insular Affairs. *83d Congress. 2d Ses-
            sion. Hearings on S. 2749 and H.R. 7322, Part 5.* Washing-
            ton: U.S. Government Printing Office.

_____
1957        Termination of Federal Supervision: The Removal of
            Restrictions Over Indian Property and Person. Pp. 47–55 in
            American Indians and American Life. George E. Simpson
            and J. Milton Yinger, eds. *Annals of the American Academy
            of Political and Social Science* 311(May). Philadelphia.

Watkins, Joe
2000        Indigenous Archaeology: American Indian Values and Sci-
            entific Practice. Walnut Creek, Calif.: AltaMira Press.

_____
2002        Artefactual Awareness: Spiro Mounds, Grave Goods and
            Politics. Pp. 149–159 in The Dead and Their Possessions:
            Repatriation in Principle, Policy and Practice. Cressida
            Fforde, Jane Hubert, and Paul Turnbull, eds. *One World
            Archaeology* 43. New York and London: Routledge.

Watkins, Mel
1977        Dene Nation: The Colony Within. Toronto: University of
            Toronto Press.

Watson, Bruce
1993        Navajo Code Talkers: A Few Good Men. *Smithsonian Mag-
            azine* 24(5):34–40, 42–43. Washington.

Watt, Lisa
[2002]      [Notes from approximately 24 months' fieldwork visiting
            some 70 Tribal Museums and Cultural Centers nationwide.]
            (Notes in L.Watt's possession.)

WCC *see* World Council of Churches (WCC)

Wearne, Phillip
1996        Return of the Indian: Conquest and Revival in the Amer-
            icas. Foreword by Rigoberta Menchu. Philadelphia: Temple
            University.

Weatherford, Elizabeth
1992        Starting Fire With Gunpowder. *Film Comment* 28(3):64–67.
            New York.

_____
1995        To End and Begin Again: The Work of Victor Masayesva,
            Jr.-Video Artist. *Art Journal* 54(4):48–52. New York.

Weatherford, Elizabeth, and Emelia Seubert, eds.
1981        Native Americans on Film and Video. [Volume 1.] New
            York: Museum of the American Indian/Heye Foundation.
_____, eds.
1988        Native Americans on Film and Video, Volume II. New York:
            Museum of the American Indian/Heye Foundation.

Weatherford, Jack
1988        Indian Givers: How the Indians of the Americas Transformed
            the World. New York: Fawcett Columbine.

Weaver, Jace, ed.
1996        Defending Mother Earth: Native American Perspectives on
            Environmental Justice. Maryknoll, N.Y.: Orbis Books.

_____
1997        That the People Might Live: Native American Literatures
            and Native American Community. New York: Oxford Uni-
            verstiy Press.

_____
2007        More Light Than Heat: The Current State of Native Amer-
            ican Studies. *American Indian Quarterly* 31(2):233–255.
            Lincoln, Nebr.

Weaver, Sally M.
1972        Medicine and Politics among the Grand River Iroquois: A
            Study of the Non-Conservatives. Ottawa: National Museum
            of Canada.

_____
1981        Making Canadian Indian Policy: The Hidden Agenda, 1968–
            70. Toronto: University of Toronto Press.

_____
1990        A New Paradigm in Canadian Indian Policy for the 1990s.
            *Canadian Ethnic Studies* 22(3):8–18. Calgary, Alta.

Webber, George
2006        People of the Blood. A Decade-Long Photographic Journey
            on a Canadian Reserve. Calgary, Alta.: Fifth House.

Weber, Gloria V., and Rennard Strickland
1996    Observations on the Evolution of Indian Law in the Law Schools. *University of New Mexico Law Review* 26:153.

Weibel, Joan C.
1978    Native Americans in Los Angeles: A Cross-Cultural Comparison of Assistance Patterns in an Urban Environment. *Anthropology UCLA* 9(1–2):81–98. Los Angeles.

Weibel-Orlando, Joan
1988    Indians, Ethnicity as a Resource, and Aging: You Can Go Home Again. *The Journal of Cross-Cultural Gerontology* 3(4):323–348.

——
1999    Indian Country, L.A.: Maintaining Ethnic Community in Complex Society. Urbana and Chicago: University of Illinois Press.

——
2003    Introduction. Pp. 491–504 in Keeping the Campfires Going: Urban American Indian Women's Activism. Susan Applegate Krouse and Heather Howard-Bobiwash, eds. *American Indian Quarterly*, Special Issue 27(3–4). Lincoln, Nebr.

Weist, Katherine M.
1973    Giving Away: The Ceremonial Distribution of Goods Among the Northern Cheyenne of Southeastern Montana. *Plains Anthropologist* 18(60):97–103. Lincoln, Nebr.

Welch, James
1971    Riding the Earthboy 40. San Francisco: World Publishing; London, [etc.]: Penguin Books. (Reprinted in 1976, 1990; see also Welch 2004.)

——
1974    Winter in the Blood. New York: Harper and Row.

——
1979    The Death of Jim Loney. New York: Harper and Row.

——
1986    Fools Crow. New York: Viking.

——
1990    The Indian Lawyer. New York: Norton.

——
2000    The Heartsong of Charging Elk. New York: Doubleday.

——
2004    Riding the Earthboy 40. Introduction by James Tate. New York, London, [etc.]: Penguin Books.

Welch, James, and Paul Jeffrey Stekler
1994    Killing Custer: The Battle of the Little Bighorn and the Fate of the Plains Indians. New York: Norton.

Wells, John Bauchop
1999/2000    Building Partnership for the New Millennium. *Saskatchewan Indian* 30(1). Prince Albert, Sask.

Welsman, Paul
1976    Education of Native Peoples in the Northwest Territories: A Northern Model. Pp. 31–47 in The North in Transition. Nils Orvik and Kirk R. Patterson, eds. Kingston, Ont.: Centre for International Relations.

Wenz, Michael
2006    Casino Gambling and Economic Development. (Ph.D. Dissertation in Economics, University of Illinois, Chicago.)

Weppner, Robert S.
1971    Urban Economic Opportunities: The Example of Denver. Pp. 245–273 in The American Indian in Urban Society. Jack O. Waddell and O. Michael Watson, eds. Boston: Little, Brown.

——
1972    Socioeconomic Barriers to Assimilation of Navajo Migrants. *Human Organization* 31(3):303–314. Washington.

West, W. Richard, Jr.
2000    The Changing Presentation of the American Indian: Museums and Native Cultures. Washington and Seattle: National Museum of the American Indian, and University of Washington Press.

Western Economic Diversification Canada
2005    Urban Reserves in Saskatchewan. (Webpage: http://www.wd.gc.ca/rpts/research/urban_reserve/urban_reserves_e.pdf)

Weston, Mary Ann
1996    Native Americans in the News: Images of Indians in the Twentieth Century Press. Westport, Conn.: Greenwood Press.

Westra, Laura
2004    Ecoviolence and the Law: Supernational Foundations of Ecocrime. Ardsley, N.Y.: Transnational Publishers.

Westra, Laura, and Bill E. Lawson, eds.
2001    Faces of Environmental Racism: Confronting Issues of Global Justice. 2d ed. Lanham, Md.: Rowman and Littlefield.

Westra, Laura, and Patricia H. Werhane, eds.
1998    The Business of Consumption: Environmental Ethics and the Global Economy. Lanham, Md.: Rowman and Littlefield.

Wetsit, Deborah
1999    Effective Counseling with American Indian Students. Pp. 179–200 in Next Steps: Research and Practice to Advance Indian Education. Karen Gayton Swisher and John W. Tippeconnic, III, eds. Charleston, W.Va.: ERIC Clearinghouse on Rural Education and Small Schools.

Weyler, Rex
1982    Blood of the Land: The U.S. Government and Corporate War Against the American Indian Movement. New York: Everest House Publishers.

Whaley, Rick, and Walter Bresette
1994    Walleye Warriors: The Chippewa Treaty Rights Story. Philadelphia: New Society Publisher.

Wheaton, Cathy
1999    The Role of Treaties in the History of Saskatchewan Indian Politics, 1910 to 1992. *Journal of Indigenous Thought* 2(2). Saskatoon, Sask.

Wherrett, George Jasper
1965    Tuberculosis in Canada. Ottawa: Royal Commission on Health Services; Queen's Printer.

Wherrett, Jill
2002    Indian Status and Band Membership Issues. Ottawa: Parliamentary Research Branch, Library of Parliament.

White, John R.
1978    Barmecide Revisited: The Gratuitous Offset in Indian Claims Cases. *Ethnohistory* 25(2):179–192.

White, Mark
1997    Oscar Howe and the Transformation of Native American Art. *American Indian Art Magazine* 23(1):36–43. Scottsdale, Ariz.

White Paper on Indian Policy
1969    *see* Canada 1969

White, Phillip M.
2000    Peyotism and the Native American Church: An Annotated Bibliography. *Bibliographies and Indexes in American History* 45. Westport, Conn.: Greenwood Press.

White, Robert H.
1990    Tribal Assets: The Rebirth of Native America. New York: Henry Holt and Company, Inc.

White Wolf, Shawn
2003    Sale of Scriver Collection Leaves Void in Tribe. *Helena Independent*, August 25, 2003. Helena, Mont.

Whittaker, Gordon
1996    Conversational Sauk: A Practical Guide to the Language of Black Hawk. Written by Gordon Whittaker in collaboration with The Working Group on Sauk Language and Culture. Stroud, Okla.: The Sac and Fox National Public Library.

Wicken, William C.
2002    Mi'kmaq Treaties on Trial: History, Land and Donald Marshall Junior. Toronto: University of Toronto Press.

Wideman, John Edgar
1995    Russell Means: The Profound and Outspoken Activist Shares Some of His Most Ardent Convictions. *Modern Maturity* 38(5):68–79. Lakewood, Calif.

Wiebe, Rudy, and Yvonne Johnson
1998    Stolen Life: The Journey of a Cree Woman. Toronto: Alfred A. Knopf.

Wiedman, Dennis
1985    Staff, Fan Rattle, and Drum: Spiritual and Artistic Expressions of Oklahoma Peyotists. *American Indian Art Magazine* 10(3):38–45. Scottsdale, Ariz.

Wiget, Andrew
1985    Native American Literature. Boston, Mass.: Twayne.

_____, ed.
1994    Dictionary of Native American Literature. New York: Garland.

Wilke, Emma, and Pat Gailfus
1987    [Interview concerning Turtle Mountain Community College, March 2, 1987.] (Conducted by Wayne J. Stein, Belcourt, N. Dak.; Text of interview in Department of Native American Studies, Montana State University, Bozeman, Mont.)

Wilkins, David E.
1997    American Indian Sovereignty and the U.S. Supreme Court: The Masking of Justice. Austin, Tex.: The University of Texas Press.

_____
2006    American Indian Politics and the American Political System. 2d ed., rev. *Spectrum Series: Race and Ethnicity in National and Global Politics*. Lahman, Md.: Rowman and Littlefield Publishers.

_____, ed.
2007    *see* Cohen, Felix S. 2007

Wilkins, David E., and Vine Deloria, Jr.
2000    Tribes, Trials, and Constitutional Tribulations. Austin, Tex.: The University of Texas Press.

Wilkins, David E., and K. Tsianina Lomawaima
2001    Uneven Ground: American Indian Sovereignty and Federal Law. Norman: University of Oklahoma Press.

Wilkins, Kerry
1999    Of Provinces and Section 35 Rights. *Dalhousie Law Journal* 22(1):185–235. Halifax, N.S.

_____
2000    Still Crazy After All These Years: Section 88 of the Indian Act of Fifty. *Alberta Law Review* 38(2):458–503. Edmonton, Alta.

_____
2002    Negative Capability: Of Provinces and Lands Reserved for the Indians. *Indigenous Law Journal at the University of Toronto, Faculty Law* 1:57–111. Toronto.

_____, ed.
2004    Advancing Aboriginal Claims: Visions/Strategies/Directions. Saskatoon, Sask.: Purich Publishing.

Wilkinson, Charles F.
1987    American Indians, Time, and the Law: Native Societies in a Modern Constitutional Democracy. New Haven, Conn.: Yale University Press.

_____
1988a   The Idea of Sovereignty: Native Peoples, Their Lands, and Their Dreams. *NARF Legal Review* 13(4):1–11. Boulder, Colo.

_____
2005    Blood Struggle: The Rise of Modern Indian Nations. New York: Norton.

Wilkinson, Charles F., and Eric R. Biggs
1977    The Evolution of the Termination Policy. *American Indian Law Review* 5(1):135–184. Norman, Okla.

Wilkinson, Glen A.
1966    Indian Tribal Claims Before the Court of Claims. *Georgetown Law Journal* 55(4):511–528. Washington.

Willacy, Aubrey B.
1968    Contract Approval: Attorneys and Indians. *Howard Law Journal* 15(1):149–163. Washington.

Williams, John L.
2005    Paving the Way for the Future: Potential Structures for Tribal Economic Development. *Indigenous Peoples' Journal of Law, Culture & Resistance* 2(1):59–101. Los Angeles.

Williams, Robert A., Jr.
1983    The Medieval and Renaissance Origins of the Status of American Indians in Western Legal Thought. *Southern California Law Review* 57(1):1–99. Los Angeles.

_____
1990    The American Indian in Western Legal Thought: The Discourses of Conquest. Oxford: Oxford University Press.

_____
1999    Linking Arms Together: American Indian Treaty Visions of Law and Peace, 1600–1800. New York: Routledge.

_____
2005    Like a Loaded Weapon: The Rehnquist Court, Indian Rights, and the Legal History of Racism in America. Minneapolis: University of Minnesota Press.

Williams, Stephanie
2002    American Indians Leave Uptown Behind. *The Chicago Reporter*, July/August 2002. (Webpage: http://www.chicago reporter.com/2002/7-2002/indian/indian.htm)

Willis, William S.
1963    Divide and Rule: Red, White, and Black in the Southeast. *Journal of Negro History* 48(3):157–176.

Wilmer, Franke
1997    Indian Gaming: Players and Stakes. *Wicazo Sa Review* 12(1): 89–114. Minneapolis.

Wilmsen, Edwin N., ed.
1989    We Are Here: Politics of Aboriginal Land Tenure. Berkeley: University of California Press.

Wilson, Jake, and John Graham
2005    Relationships Between First Nations and the Forest Industry: The Legal and Policy Context. A Report for the

National Aboriginal Forestry Association (NAFA), the Forest Products Association of Canada (FPAC) and the First Nations Forestry Program (FNFP). Ottawa: Institute on Governance.

Wilson, Terry P.
1979      Custer Never Would Have Believed It: Native American Studies in Academia. *American Indian Quarterly* 5(3):207–227. Lincoln, Nebr.

1985      The Underground Reservation: Osage Oil. Lincoln: University of Nebraska Press.

1992      Blood Quantum: Native American Mixed Bloods. Pp. 108–125 in Racially Mixed People in America. Maria P. Root, ed. Newbury Park, Calif.: Sage.

Wilson, Waziyatawin Angela
2005      Remember This! Dakota Decolonization and the Eli Taylor Narratives. Wahpetunwin Carolynn Schommer, trans. Lincoln: University of Nebraska Press.

Wilson, William H., and Kauanoe Kamana
2001      Mai Loko Mai O Ka ʔiʔini: Proceeding from a Dream—The ʼaha Punana Leo Connection in Hawaiian Language Revitalization. Pp. 147–178 in The Green Book of Language Revitalization in Practice. Leanne Hinton and Kenneth Hale, eds.: San Diego, Calif.: Academic Press.

Wilson, Zandra L., ed.
1979–      *see* Native Law Centre 1979–

Winfrey, Robert Hill, Jr.
1986      Civil Rights and the American Indian: Through the 1960s. (Ph.D. Dissertation in History, University of Oklahoma, Norman.)

Winiata, Te Rua
1999      I Asked Myself: What Does Being Indigenous Mean? Echoes: The Earth As Mother. World Council of Churches. (Webpage: http://www.wcc-coe.org/wcc/what/jpc/echoes-16-06.html [3 August 2006].)

Winnemucca, Sarah Hopkins *see* Hopkins, Sarah Winnemucca

Wishart, David J.
1990      Compensation for Dispossession: Payments to the Indians for Their Lands on the Central and Northern Great Plains in the19th Century. *National Geographic Research* 6(1):94–109. Washington.

Wishart, David J., and Oliver Froehling
1996      Land Ownership, Population, and Jurisdiction: The Case of the *Devils Lake Sioux Tribe v. North Dakota Public Service Commission. American Indian Culture and Research Journal* 20(2):33–58. Los Angeles.

Wissler, Clark
1916      General Discussion of Shamanistic and Dancing Societies. *Anthropological Papers of the American Museum of Natural History* 11(Pt. 12):853–876. New York.

Wolfram, Walt, and Clare Dannenberg
1999      Dialect Identity in a Tri-ethnic Context: The Case of Lumbee American Indian English. *English World-Wide* 20(2):179–216. University of Regensberg, Bavaria, Germany.

Womack, Craig S.
1997      Howling at the Moon: The Queer but True Story of My Life as a Hank Williams Song. Pp. 28–49 in As We Are Now: Mixblood Essays on Race and Identity. William S. Penn, ed. Berkeley and Los Angeles: University of California Press.

1999      Red on Red: Native American Literary Separatism. Minneapolis: University of Minnesota Press.

2001      Drowning in Fire. Tucson: University of Arizona Press.

Wong, Hertha Dawn
1992      Sending My Heart Back Across the Years: Tradition and Innovation in Native American Autobiography. New York: Oxford University Press.

Wood, Mary Christina
1995      Protecting the Attributes of Native Sovereignty: A New Trust Paradigm for Federal Actions Affecting Tribal Land and Resources. *Utah Law Review* 1:109–237.

Woodcock, George
2003      Gabriel Dumont. Edited by J.R. Miller. Peterborough, Ont.: Broadview Press. (Originally publ. in 1975.)

Worl, Rosita
1990      *see* Handbook Vol. 7 (1990:149–158)

1994      Alaska Natives' Changing Relationship to Their Environment. (Keynote Address presented to the Opening General Session of the Society of American Foresters and Canadian Institute of Forestry Convention, September 18, 1994.)

2001      Reconstructing Sovereignty in Alaska. *Cultural Survival Quarterly* 25(3):72–77. Cambridge, Mass.

2003      Models of Sovereignty and Survival in Alaska. *Cultural Survival Quarterly* 27(3):14–19. Cambridge, Mass.

World Council of Churches (WCC)
2000      Justice, Peace and Creation Concerns: Indigenous Peoples' Programme (IPP). (Webpage: http://www.wcc-coe.org/wcc/what/jpc/indig.html [3 August 2006].)

2004      What Do We Do? International Affairs, Peace and Human Security; WCC United Nations Liaison Office: Work on Indigenous Peoples. (Webpage: http://www.wcc-coe.org/wcc/what/international/unliaison-indigenous.html [3 August 2006].)

World Health Organization (WHO)
2001      Legal Status of Traditional Medicine and Complementary/Alternative Medicine: A Worldwide Review. Geneva, Switzerland: World Health Organization.

Wright, James Leitch, Jr.
1981      The Only Land They Knew: The Tragic Story of the American Indians in the Old South. New York: The Free Press. (Reprinted: see 1999.)

1999      The Only Land They Knew: The Tragic Story of the American Indians in the Old South. New Introduction by James H. Merrell. Lincoln and London: University of Nebraska Press.

Wright, Ronald
1992      Stolen Continents: The New World Through Indian Eyes Since 1492. New York: Viking Penguin.

Wright, Victoria C., et al.
2000        Building the Future: Stories of Successful Indian Enterprises. Washington: National Congress of American Indians.

Wunder, John R.
1996        Native American Sovereignty. New York: Garland Press.

Yazzie, Rhiana
2006        The Art of Translation: Native American Theatre in the Global Community. *Native Peoples Magazine* (Webpage: http://www.nativepeoples.com/articles/201/1/The-Art-of-Translation-Native-American-Theatre-in-the-Global-Community/Page1.html.)

Yazzie, Tarajean
1999        Culturally Appropriate Curriculum: A Research-Based Rationale. Pp. 83–106 in Next Steps: Research and Practice To Advance Indian Education. Karen Gayton Swisher and John W. Tippeconnic, III, eds. Charleston, W.Va.: ERIC Clearinghouse on Rural Education and Small Schools.

Yellow Bird (John Rollin Ridge) *see* Ridge, John Rollin (Yellow Bird)

Yellow Robe, William S., Jr.
2000        Where the Pavement Ends: Five Native American Plays. *American Indian Lietrature and Critical Studies Series*. Norman: University of Oklahoma Press.

Yinger, J. Milton Yinger, and George Eaton Simpson, eds.
1978        American Indians Today. *The Annals of the American Academy of Political and Social Science* 436(March). Philadelphia.

York, Geoffrey
1990        The Dispossessed: Life and Death in Native Canada. London, Ont.: Vintage.

York, Geoffrey, and Loreen Pindera
1992        People of the Pines: The Warriors and the Legacy of Oka. Toronto: Little Brown and Company.

Young Bear, Ray A.
1992        Black Eagle Child: The Facepaint Narratives. New York: Grove Press.

_____
1996        Remnants of the First Earth. New York: Grove Press.

Young Bear, Severt, and R.D. Theisz
1994        Standing in the Light: A Lakota Way of Seeing. Lincoln: University of Nebraska Press.

Young, David E., ed.
1988        Health Care Issues in the Canadian North. Edmonton, Alta.: Boreal Institute for Northern Studies.

Young, David E., and L.L. Smith
1992        The Involvement of Canadian Native Communities in Their Health Care Programs: A Review of the Literature Since the 1970s. Edmonton, Alta.: University of Alberta, Canadian Circumpolar Institute and Center for the Cross-Cultural Study of Health and Healing.

Young, David E., Grant Ingram, and Lise Swartz
1989        Cry of the Eagle: Encounters with a Cree Healer. Toronto: University of Toronto Press.

Young, Phyllis
1996        Beyond the Water Line. Pp. 85–98 in Defending Mother Earth: Native American Perspectives on Environmental Justice. Jace Weaver, ed. Maryknoll, N.Y.: Orbis Books.

Young, Robert W.
1961        The Navajo Yearbook: 1951–1961, A Decade of Progress. Window Rock, Ariz.: Bureau of Indian Affairs.

Young, T. Kue
1984        Indian Health Services in Canada: A Sociohistorical Perspective. *Social Science and Medicine* 18(3):257–264. New York.

_____
1988        Health Care and Cultural Change: The Indian Experience in the Central Sub-Arctic. Toronto: University of Toronto Press.

_____
1994        The Health of Native Americans: Towards a Biocultural Epidemiology. New York: Oxford University Press.

Young, T. Kue, and R.I. Casson
1988        The Decline and Persistence of Tuberculosis in a Canadian Indian Population: Implications for Control. *Canadian Journal of Public Health* 79(5):302–306. Ottawa.

Young, T. Kue, and N.W. Choi
1985        Cancer Risks Among Residents of Manitoba Indian Reserves, 1970–1979. *Canadian Medical Association Journal* 132(11): 1269–1272. Ottawa.

Young, T. Kue, and John W. Frank
1983        Cancer Surveillance in a Remote Indian Population in Northwestern Ontario. *American Journal of Public Health* 73(5): 515–520. Washington.

Young, T. Kue, et al.
1985        Epidemiologic Features of Diabetes Mellitus Among Indians in Northwestern Ontario and Northeastern Manitoba. *Canadian Medical Association Journal* 132(7):793–797. Ottawa.

_____, et al.
1990        Geographical Distribution of Diabetes Among the Native Population of Canada: A National Survey. *Social Science and Medicine* 31(2):129–139. New York.

Zaferatos, Nicholas Christos
2004        Planner's Notebook: Tribal Nations, Local Governments, and Regional Pluralism in Washington State: The Swinomish Approach in the Skagit Valley. *Journal of the American Planning Association* 70(1):81–96. Washington.

Zeinert, Karen, ed.
1995        Captured by Indians: The Life of Mary Jemison, by James E. Seaver. North Haven, Conn.: Linnet Books.

Zelio, Judy
2006        States and Tribes: Building New Traditions, Piecing Together the State-Tribal Tax Puzzle. (National Conference of State Legislatures. Webpage: http://www.ncsl.org/bookstore/product detail.htm?prodid=0194030008&catsel=xtrb%3BState%2DTribal%20Relations [7 October 2006].)

Zimmerman, Bill
1976        Airlift to Wounded Knee. Chicago: The Swallow Press, Inc.

Zimmerman, Larry J.
2002        A Decade After the Vermillion Accord: What Has Changed and What Has Not? Pp. 91–98 in The Dead and Their Possessions: Repatriation in Principle, Policy and Practice. Cressida Fforde, Jane Hubert, and Paul Turnbull, eds. *One World Archaeology* 43. New York and London: Routledge.

Ziontz, Alvin J.
1994        Civil Rights. Pp. 117–120 in Native America in the Twenti-
              eth Century: An Encyclopedia. Mary B. Davis, ed. New York
              and London: Garland Publishing.

Zitkala-Ša (Gertrude Bonnin)
1901        Old Indian Legends, Retold by Zitkala-Sa; with Illustrations
              by Angel De Cora Hinook-Mahiwi-Kilinaka. Boston, Lon-
              don: Ginn and Company.

———
1921        American Indian Stories. Washington: Hayworth Publishing
              House.

Zuckerman, Stephen, et al.
2004        Health Service Access, Use and Insurance Coverage Among
              American Indians/Alaska Natives and Whites: What Role
              Does the Indian Health Service Play? *American Journal of
              Public Health* 94(1):53–59. Washington.

# Index

*Italic numbers indicate material in a figure; roman numbers, material in the text. Specific reservations and reserves are at* reservations *and* reserves.

*All variant names of groups are indexed, with the occurrences under* synonymy *discussing the equivalences. Variants of group names that differ from those cited only in their capitalization, hyphenation, or accentuation have generally been omitted; variants that differ only in the presence of absence of one [noninitial] letter or compound element have been collapsed into a single entry with the letter or element in parentheses.*

*The entry* Indian words *indexes, by language, all words appearing in the standard orthographies and some others.*

disease; alcoholism: 83, 97, 103, 222, 229,
230, 262, 309, 312. cancer: 97, 103, 223,
224, 230. cardiovascular disease: 223, 230.
in children: 103. diabetes: 83, 97, 103, 104,
223, *224*. ear infections: 228. epidemics: 97.
gastroenteritis: 223. gastrointestinal
infections: 99–100. heart disease: 83, 103,
104, 223. hepatitis: 250–251. HIV/AIDS:
222, 223, 229. hypertension: 223. impetigo:
223. infectious: 222, 223, 229, 250–251.
influenza: 24, 103, 104, 269. liver disease:
224. measles: 24, 223, 285. mumps: 223.
obesity: 223. observation of: 225.
pneumonia: 24, 103, 222. poliomyelitis:
223. psychosocial: 103. research on:
103–105. respiratory disease and infection:
228, 251. scabies: 223. smallpox: 97, 98,
261, 285. substance abuse: 222, 223, 224,
229, 230, 263. trachoma: 99, *99*.
tuberculosis: 24, 97, 99, *99*, 104, 209, 222,
223, 224, 250–251
Distribution of Judgment Funds Act
(1973): 35
Ditchburn, W.E.: 204
*Doe* v. *Mann* (9th Cir. 2005): 73
Dogrib; political activism: *195*
Dogrib language; number of speakers: 292
dogs: *207*. disease: 247. as food: 330
Doherty, Robert: 394
Dominion Lands Act (1879): 295, 296, 298,
301
Doney, Troy: *371*
Doolan, Robert: 262
Dorris, Michael: 399
Douglas, James: 188, 203, 264
Douglas, Leonard: *265*
Douglas, Tommy C.: 190
Douma, Casey: *422*
Downs, Derek: *132*
Downs, Michael: *371*
Doyon regional corporation: *92, 141*
Dozier, Edward: 415
D-Q University: 404, 405
Dreaver, Joseph: 190, *209*
Dresser, Jordan: *371*
drums. *See* musical instruments
DRUMS (Determination of Rights and Unity
for Menominee Stockholders): 107
D'Souza, Dinesh: 417
Duhlelap; synonymy: 70. *See also* Tulalip
Dumont, Gabriel: 299, *299*
Dumont, W. Yvon: *297*
Duncan, William: 262
*Duncan* v. *Andrus* (U.S.D.C., N.D. Calif.
1977): 109, 110
Durham, Douglass: 46
Durham, Jimmie: 47–48, 54
*Duro* v. *Reina* (1990): 61, 63, 80
Dussault, René: 219
Duwamish; membership: 117. recognition:
117, 123, 127

**E**
Earling, Debra: 400
Eastern Band Free Press Act (Eastern Band of
Cherokee Indians, 2006): 366
Eastern Cherokee Defense League: 151

Eastern Shoshone; education: 404. history: 15.
removal: 90. Wind River: 15, 90, *92–93*,
368, 404
Eastman, Charles A. (Ohiyesa): 38, 394, 413
Eastman, Viola: *14*
Eastwood, Clint: 384, 390
Echo Hawk, Walter: *423*
economy; Aboriginal capital corporations:
237, 239. Aboriginal government and: 194,
207, 233, 237, 239. activism for: 231.
approaches to: 232. Community
Development Entities: 138. cooperatives:
242–243. and culture: 131, 139, 231,
232–233, 235, 237, 239. disparities in:
231–232, 233. federal programs and
incentives: 24, 88, 136–138. gaming
industry and: 131, 132–133, 148–149, 151,
236, 244–245. and health: 224. human
resources for: 231–232. institutions needed
for: 236–237. joint ventures and
partnerships: 243. keys to success: 231,
237, 239. and land claims settlements:
240–242. legal and judicial support:
133–134, 139. legislation: 64. loan and
grant programs: 234, 235, 249. nation
building approach to: 139, 239. native
development organizations: 129, 131–133,
236–237. native museums and: 339, 342,
350. and natural resources: 238–239, 240.
in northern Canada: 236. obstacles to: 236,
238, 241. research on: 239. reservation and
reserve: 42, 210, 220, 403–404. self-
determination and: 231, 232, 234–235.
termination and: 106. theories of: 139.
training and education: 231, 233, 234, 235,
237–238. tribal competitive advantages:
134–139. tribal financing of: 138–139.
tribal government and: 129, 133–134, 139.
urban reserves and: 242. variation by group:
231. *See also* Alaska Native corporations;
business; employment; income; trade
education; and activism: 443–444. adult: 84,
87, *206*. arts: 374, 388. and assimilation: 24.
BIA programs: 86, 87–88. bilingual:
353–354, 355, 356, 359. boarding schools:
99, 174, 213, 218, 249, 250, 252, 253, 356,
363, 393, 394, 395, 443. in Canada: 6, 174,
190, 201, *206*, 209, 213, 218, 224, 231, 233,
234, 235, 237–238, 238, 244, 249, 250, 252,
253, 404, 410. community colleges:
405–406. cultural education programs: 8.
disparities in: 224, 234. and economic
development: 231, 233, 234, 235, 237–238.
federal obligation to provide: 86. funding:
73, 363, 402, 405, 406, 409–410. Indian
language: *344*, 352–354, 355, 356–361.
Indian law: 422, 424, 425–426. journalism
and media: 369, 370, 371–372. legislation:
64, 142. museology: 347, 350. museum
outreach programs: 348. native control of: 6,
8. native museums and: 338. native scholars:
9. pan-nativism and: 8. postgraduate: 393.
postsecondary: 87–88, 238. public schools:
24, 84, 123, 209, 357. reservation and
reserve schools: 84, 190, 201. scholarships
and loans: 86, 87–88, 100, 146, 147, 303,
370, 413. self-determination: 9, 314,

402–403, 406, 408, 410, 412. state denial of
services: 73. state regulation of: 68.
termination and: 24, 106. tribal
administration of: 83–84. tribal law: 9, 314.
trust relationship and: 10. urban programs:
314. U.S. policy: 363. vocational: 26, 87,
218, 403, 408, 413, 414. *See also* colleges
and universities; Native American studies
programs
Edward VII, king of the United Kingdom: 188
Eisenhower, Dwight D.: 22–23, *23*, 69
elderly; care for: 83, *84*. cultural role: 83, 97.
demographics: 290. health care: 228
elections; in Canada: *186*, 190, 207, 246, 253.
Freedmen and: 279. referendums: 257, 259.
tribal: 305, 337
Eli, George: *265*
Elizabeth II, queen of United Kingdom: *214*
*Elk* v. *Wilkins* (1884): 113
Elliot, Charlie: *265*
Elsen, Bill: *371*
Emmons, Glenn L.: 22, 23–24, 25, 310
employment; agriculture: 233, 234. Alaska
Native corporations: 146–147, *147*.
archeologists: *413*. attorneys: *423*. business
and management: 131. in Canada: 231–232.
cannery workers: 190. construction and
repair: 253. cooperatives and: 243. dancing
exhibitions: 330. disparities in: 224, 233.
education: 131. ethnographers: 413.
factories, mills, and manufacturing: 233,
234, 263. federal programs and incentives:
24. fishing: 190, 236, 239. gaming: 151,
242, 245. as goal of economic development:
139. government: 263. guides: 253.
handicrafts: 234. health care: *226*, 227–228.
Indian hiring preferences: 87, 135, 146, 243,
304, 305. journalists: 370. labor unions: 190.
mining: 253. native museums: 339.
powwows: 333. railroad: 309. rates: 224.
relocation programs and: 25–26. reservation:
138, 316. resource industries: 263. social
services: 131, 310. steelworkers: 309.
theater: 379. timber and forest products:
238, 253. in tribal businesses: 132.
unemployment: 256, 263, 309–310, *310*. and
urban residence: 234, 308, 309–311, 314,
316. World War II and: 15. youth summer
programs: *80*. *See also* business
*Employment Division of Oregon* v. *Smith*
(1990): 323
Enfranchisement Act (Canada, 1869): 200
England. *See* history, British period
En'owkin Center: 404
E-numbers: 209, 214
environment; activism: 44, 51–52, *52*, 341.
exemptions from environmental law: 306.
impact assessment requirements: 257, 258.
management in Canada: 179, 181, 182, 240,
256, 258–259. mining damage: 130, 263.
pollution and: 256. relationship to: 44, 81,
98. reservation: 27. respect for: 46. treaty
requirements for: 266. tribal administration
of U.S. environmental laws: 62. tribal laws
and programs: 70, 71, 81–82. *See also*
natural resources
epidemics. *See* disease

in Mexico: 338. mission of: 338, 342–343, 350. native museum associations: 347–348. number of: 338. and repatriation: 427–430, 430–437. repatriation and: 428. toxic preservatives used in: 345, 436. training programs: 347, 350. in United States: 155, 338, *339,* 339–400, *341,* 348, *349*

music; adaptation of: 418. Métis: 300. peyote songs: 321, *325,* 325–326. powwow songs: 328, *332,* 333, 336. prizes and awards: *315*

musical instruments; drums: 321, 322, 324, 325–326, 330, 333. rattles: 321, 324, 325–326. whistles: 321, 334, 428

Muskogee. *See* Creek

*Muskrat* v. *United States* (1911): 29

Muwekma Ohlone; membership: 117. recognition: 117, 123, 124

Myer, Dillon: 22, 25

mythology; peyote origin: 319. Peyote Spirit: 319. Peyote Woman: 319. tricksters: 398. *See also* oral traditions; supernatural beings

## N

Nader, Ralph: 51

Nakai, Raymond: 402

Nakoda; casinos: 244. education: 404

Nakota; synonymy: 360. *See also* Assiniboine

Nambe Pueblo; territory: *31–32*

N.A.N.A. regional corporation: *92–93, 141,* 142

Napoleon, Val: 184

NARF. *See* Native American Rights Fund

Narragansett; history: 122. litigation: 73–74. membership: 117. recognition: 70, 115, 117. sovereignty: 73–74

*Narragansett Indian Tribe* v. *Rhode Island* (1st Cir. 2006): 73–74

Nash, Philleo: 22

Nash, Ruth Adair: *278*

Naskapi; synonymy: 231. *See also* Montagnais

National Aboriginal Achievement Foundation: 227

National Aboriginal Capital Corporation of America: 237

National Aboriginal Health Organization: 228

National Coalition on Racism in Sports and the Media: *50*

National Collection of Contemporary Indian Arts: 347

National Collegiate Athletic Association: 50, 51

National Committee on Indian Rights and Treaties: 211

National Conference of State Legislators: 74

National Congress of American Indians; activism: 27, 39, 50, 414, 438. establishment of: 5, 38, 414. gaming and: 153. health care and: 25, 103. leadership: *53.* media and: 370. policies: 74

National Council of Urban Indian Health: 103

National Day of Action: *195*

National Environmental Policy Act: 94

National Gaming Impact Study Commission: 155

National Indian Brotherhood; activism: 161–162, 193, 211, 212–213, 235, 238. founding: 5, 160, 192. internal conflicts: 162, 195. leadership: *192. See also* Assembly of First Nations

National Indian Council: 5, 192, 211

National Indian Gaming Association: 148, 153

National Indian Gaming Commission: 63, 149, 150, 153

National Indian Health Board: 103

National Indian Law Library: 423

National Indian Youth Council: 3, 5, 39, 192, 314, 414

National Labor Relations Act: 135

*National Labor Relations Board* v. *the Pueblo of San Juan* (2002): 135

National Museum of American History (Washington, DC): 347, *433*

National Museum of the American Indian: 348, *349.* Community Service Department: 347. directors: 426. educational outreach programs: 348. facilities: 348, *349.* film festival: 388. Fourth Museum program: 348. legislation creating: 340, 348, 430, 432, 433. mission of: 348. Native American studies programs and: 420. Native Radio program: 369. in New York: 388, 426. opening: *349,* 370. and repatriation: 345, 428, 430, 432, 434, 435, 436. support for native museums: 345. training programs: 347. in Washington, DC: 345, 347, 348, *349,* 369, 370, 420, 428, 430, 432, 435, 436

National Museum of Denmark: 429

National Museum of Natural History (Washington, DC): 338, 346, 347, 376, 432, *433,* 434, *436*

National Museum of the American Indian Act (1989): 340, 348, 430, 432, 433

National Native American Bar Association: 425

National Native News: 368–369

Native American Business Development, Trade Promotion, and Tourism Act (2000): 136–138

Native American Center for the Living Arts: 339

Native American Church; activism: 45, 322–324. beliefs: 324–325. establishment of: 322–323. growth of: 323, 326. membership: 317, 323. Native American Church of Navajoland: 323. peyote conservation efforts: 319. resurgence of: 8. social dimensions: 326. symbolism: *324,* 324–325, *325. See also* Peyote religion

*Native American Church* v. *Navajo Tribal Council* (1959): 305–306

Native American Cultural Preservation Act: 430

Native American Education Improvement Act (2001): 64

Native American Export and Trade Promotion Program: 138

Native American Graves Protection and Repatriation Act (1990): 9, 64, 83, 303, 340, 343–344, 431, 432–433, 434, 435, 436

Native American Higher Education Initiative Project: 403

Native American Housing Assistance and Self-Determination Act (1996): 64, 96

Native American Journalists Association: 51, 365, *367,* 370, *370*

Native American Languages Act (1990): 64, 340, 363

Native American Languages Act (1992): 363

Native American Law Students Association: 425

Native American Natural Resources Development Federation: 130

Native American Press Association: 365

Native American Producers Alliance: 387–388

Native American Public Broadcasting Consortium: 370

Native American Public Telecommunications: 369–370, 387–388, 390

Native American Rights Fund: 108, 121, 153, 422–424, *423,* 432, 438

Native American studies programs: 412–420. funding: 415. ideological premises: 418. impact of: 416–417. methodology: 418. Native identity issues: 418–420. origins: 412–414. programs: 414–416. research: 417. status as discipline: 412, 417–418. at tribal colleges and universities: 415

Native American Television: 370

Native American Theater Ensemble: 374, 377

Native Brotherhood of British Columbia: 190, 191, *209*

Native Council of Canada; activism: 161, 162, 163, 193, 296, 297. funding: 164. leadership: *297. See also* Congress of Aboriginal Peoples

Native Film and Video Festival: 388

Native Museum of Mashteuiatsh: 340–341

*Native Peoples* magazine: 372

*Native Studies Review:* 415–416

Native Tribe of Koyukuk; membership requirements: 302

Native Voice One (NV1): 369

Native Women's Association of Canada: 162, 164

*Native Women's Association* v. *Canada* (S.C.R., 1994): 164

NativeYouthMagazine.com: 370

natural disasters; mudslides: 345. volcanic eruptions: 261

natural resources; commercial extraction of: 444. development of: 130–131. and economic development: 238–239, 240. gold and diamonds: 260. legislation: 130–131. mineral reserves: 108, 130, 202. oil and gas: 130, 141, *206,* 236, 238–239, 246. pollution and: 256. provincial jurisdiction over: 254. revenue sharing plans: 240, 246, 258, 259. rights to: 3, 6, 141, 142, 170–171, 179, 180–181, 183, 202, 236, 241, 266. termination and: 20. *See also* animal resources

Natural Resources Transfer Agreements (Canada): 167, 241

NATV Online: 370

Nault, Robert: 196

Navajo; activism: 414. business: 135, 149. ceremonies: 322, 327, 397. clothing and adornment: *315.* economy: 25. education: 355, 356, 357, 358, 360, *371,* 376, 402–403, 404, 405, 407, 415. employment: 370, *370, 423.* and gaming: 148. health care: *99,* 103, 104, *104.* history: 2, 15, 18. literary depictions of: 384. literature: 122, 355, 397, 400. litigation: 63, 89. media: 366, 368.

Quebec Boundaries Extension Act (Canada, 1912): 255
Quechan; territory: *31–32*
Queen Victoria Treaty Protective Association: *209*
Quetawki, Arlen: *339*
Quidgeon, William, Jr.: *77*
Quileute; history: 15. territory: *31–32*
Quinault; and recognition process: 119. territory: *31–32*
Quinn, Anthony: 383
Quinney, Norman: *369*
Quintasket, Christine (Mourning Dove): 395

**R**

Rama Mnjikaning; gaming: 244–245. history: 202. litigation: 245. territory: 202
Ramapough Mountain Indians, Inc.; membership: 117. recognition: 117, 123, 124
rancherias. *See* reservations and reserves
Rand, Kathryn: 153
Rankokus; state recognition: 96
Ratt, Walter: *237*
rattles. *See* musical instruments
*Re; Eskimo* (S.C.R., 1939): 214
Reagan, Ronald W.: 149
recognition: 113–128. benefits of: 305–306. claimed previous recognition: 124. congressional: 121, 124, 125–127. cost of: 155. criteria for: 113–114, 116–121, 125, 306–307. division of recognized tribes: 127–128. exploitation of: 306–307. funding of: 121. and gaming industry: 121, 126, 127. groups seeking: 113, 121–124, 273. and land claims: 115. legislation: 125. litigation: 115–116, 124–125. Métis: 7, 295, 296, 301. motivations for: 121. obstacles to: 306. opposition to: 119, 120, 155. as prerequisite for BIA services: 86–87. process: 116–121, 120, 306. recognized tribes: 7, 114–115, 117, 272–273. significance of: 113, 114. and state authority over Indians: 70. by state governments: 96. and treaty rights: 6, 115–116
Red Bird, Stanley: 405
Red Clay Intertribal Band; membership: 117. recognition: 117, 123
Red Crow Community College: 404, 410
Red Earth Performing Arts Company: 376
Redford, Robert: 387, 388, 389
Red Paper. *See Citizens Plus*
Red Pheasant: 189
Rehnquist, William H.: 59
Reid, Ambrose: 190
Reifel, Benjamin: 38
Reisling, David, Jr.: 405
religion; and activism: 43–44, 45, 46–47, 49, 52, 320, 322–324. American Indian Church Brotherhood Association: 322. Azee' Bee Nahagha of Diné Nation: 323. Drum religion: 317. First Born Church of Christ: 322. Ghost Dance: 317, 325. Indian Shaker Church: 322. Kiowa United American Church: 322. Mescal Bean Eaters: 322. Peyote Society: 322. protective legislation: 64. right to traditional ceremonies: 10–11, 229–230, 303. suppression of: 157.

traditional, decline of: 317, 320. Union Church: 322. *See also* ceremonies; Christianity; Native American Church; Peyote religion
Religious Freedom Restoration Act (1993): 323
relocation: 25–27. in Canada: 180, 231. destinations: 311–312. goals of: 19, 25, 236. impact on individuals: 26–27, 312. number relocated: 26. recruitment for: 26. results of: 26–27. return rate: 26, 310. success of program: 26–27, 310. and urban residence: 309–311. women and: 315–316
removal: 90. health effects: 100. politics of: 67–68. recognition and: 124, 125. slavery and: 276. Trail of Tears: 276, 365. treaties and: 56
Removal Act: 90
Rendon, Marcie: 377, 378
Reno, Janet: 426
Reno Indian Colony; territory: 91
repatriation: 427–437. ceremonies: *433, 434,* 436. cultural property: 9, 64, 83, 183, 303, 340, 342, 343–345, 348, 427–430, 431, 434–435, 436, *436.* defined: 213. definition of cultural property: 427. and future of archeology: 435–436. grave protection: 430, 431. human remains: 9, 64, 83, 303, 340, 343–345, 348, 428, 429, 430–431, 432–434, 435–436, 436. impact of: 436–437. legislation: 430–431, 434. and toxic preservatives: 345, 436
*Re Paulette* (D.L.R. 1973): 174
*Report of the Special Committee on Native Self Government. See* Penner Report
Republican Party; restoration and: 107
research; and informed consent: 103–105, 444
reservations and reserves; in 2007: *92–93.* Aboriginal land rights: 215. Acoma: *92–93.* acreage: 177, 197, 200, 201, 203, 204, 205. activism: 190. Adams Lake: 358. adding to: 241–242. administration of: 200. Alabama-Coushatta: *92–93.* Alamo Navajo: *92–93.* in Alaska: 142. Alexander Valley Rancheria: 110. Allegany: 39, *39, 92–93.* Alturas: *92–93.* Annette Island: 36–37, 90, *92–93,* 140, 142. L'Anse: *92–93.* Aqua Caliente: *92–93.* Auburn Rancheria: *92–93,* 110. Augustine: *92–93.* Bad River: *92–93.* Barona: *92–93.* Bay Mills: *92–93,* 114. Becancour: 199. Benton Paiute: *92–93.* Berry Creek: *92–93.* Big Bend: *92–93.* Big Cypress: *92–93.* Big Lagoon: *92–93.* Big Pine: *92–93.* Big Sand: *92–93.* Big Sandy Rancheria: 110. Big Valley Rancheria: *92–93,* 110. Bishop: *92–93.* Blackfeet: *53, 92–93.* Blood: 196, 197, *209,* 410. Blue Lake Rancheria: *92–93,* 110. Bois Forte: *92–93.* Bridgeport: *92–93.* Brighton: *92–93.* Brochet: *207.* Buena Vista Rancheria: 110. Burney Tract: *92–93.* Burns Paiute Colony: *92–93.* business: *132,* 366. Cabazon: *92–93.* Cache Creek Rancheria: 110. Cahuilla: *92–93.* Calista: 273. Campe Verde: *92–93.* Campo: *92–93.* Capital Grande: *92–93.* Carry the Kettle: 190. Carson Colony: *92–93.* Catawba: *92–93.* Cattaraugus: *92–93.* Cedarville: *92–93.* checkerboarding

in: 81, 90. Chehalis: *92–93.* Chemehuevi: *92–93.* Cherokee: *92–93,* 273. Cheyenne-Arapaho: 273. Cheyenne River: *92–93.* Chickasaw: 273. Chicken Ranch Rancheria: *92–93,* 110. Chico Rancheria: 110. Chitimacha: *92–93.* Choctaw: 273. Citizen Potawatomi Nation-Absentee Shawnee: 273. Cloverdale Rancheria: 110. Cochiti: *92–93.* Coconut Creek: *92–93.* Cocopah: *92–93.* Coeur D'Alene: *92–93.* Cold Springs Rancheria: *92–93,* 110. Colfax Rancheria: 110. Colorado River: *92–93.* Colusa: *92–93.* Colville: *92–93.* Comanche, Kiowa, and Apache: 319. Cononcito Navajo: *92–93.* Cook Inlet: 273. Coos, Lower Umpqua, and Siuslaw: *92–93.* Coquille: *92–93.* Cortina: *92–93.* Coushatta: *92–93.* Cow Creek of Umpqua: *92–93.* Cowessess: 189. Coyote Valley: *92–93.* creation of: 167, 177, 200, 201–205, 262, 264, 313. Creek: 273. Crow: 90, *92–93.* Crow Creek: *92–93.* Cuyapaipe: *92–93.* Death Valley Timbi-Sha Shoshone: *92–93.* definition of: 197. demographics: 289, *290,* 291, 292. distribution of: *198.* Dresslerville: *92–93.* Dry Creek: *92–93.* Duck Valley: *92–93,* 368. Duckwater: *92–93.* Eagle Pass Kickapoo: 2. Eastern Pequot Mohegan: *92–93.* economy: 24, 210, 220, 403–404. efforts to eliminate: 205. Elk Valley Rancheria: *92–93,* 110. Ely Colony: *92–93.* employment on: 316. Enterprise: *92–93.* Fallon: *92–93.* Flandreau: *92–93.* Flathead: 23, *92–93,* 357. Fond du Lac: *92–93.* Fort Apache: *92–93,* 273. Fort Belknap: *92–93.* Fort Berthold: 90, *92–93.* Fort Bidwell: *92–93.* Fort Hall: *92–93.* Fort Independence: *92–93.* Fort McDermitt: *92–93.* Fort McDowell: *92–93.* Fort Mojave: *92–93.* Fort Peck: *92–93,* 368. Fort Pierce: *92–93.* Fort Yuma: *92–93.* Gila Bend: *92–93.* Gila River: *92–93,* 273. Golden Hill: *92–93.* Goshute: *92–93.* Grand Portage: *92–93.* Grand River: *429,* 430. Grand Ronde: *92–93,* 107, 109, 111. Grand Traverse: *92–93.* Graton Rancheria: 106, 109, 110, 111. Greenville Rancheria: *92–93,* 110. Grindstone: *92–93.* Guidiville Rancheria: 110. Hannahville: *92–93.* Hassanamisco: *92–93.* Havasupai: *92–93.* Ho-Chunk: *92–93, 133.* Hoh: *92–93.* Hollywood: *92–93.* Hoopa Valley: 71–72, *92–93,* 127. Hopi: *92–93,* 384. Hopland Rancheria: *92–93,* 110. housing: *203,* 205, *207,* 224. Hualapai: *92–93.* Huron Potawatomi: *92–93.* Immokalee: *92–93.* Inaja and Cosmit: *92–93.* Indian Ranch Colony Rancheria: 110. infrastructure: 24, 220. Innu: 200. Inuit: 200. Iowa: *92–93.* Isabella: *80, 92–93.* Jackson: *92–93.* Jamestown S'Klallam: *92–93.* Jamul: *92–93.* Jemez: *92–93.* Jicarilla Apache: *92–93.* Kahnawake: 49, 199. Kahnesatake: *49.* Kaibab: *92–93.* Kalispel: *92–93.* Karuk: *92–93.* Kashia Indian: 15. Kickapoo: 2, *92–93.* Kiowa-Comanche-Apache-Fort Sill Apache: 273. Klamath: *92–93,* 108. Lac Courte Oreilles: *92–93,* 366, 404. Lac du

569